METHODOLOGY, MONEY AND THE FIRM
VOLUME II

ECONOMISTS OF THE TWENTIETH CENTURY

General Editors: Mark Perlman, *University Professor of Economics, Emeritus, University of Pittsburgh* and Mark Blaug, *Professor Emeritus, University of London; Professor Emeritus, University of Buckingham; and Visiting Professor, University of Exeter*

This innovative series comprises specially invited collections of articles and papers by economists whose work has made an important contribution to economics in the late twentieth century.

The proliferation of new journals and the ever-increasing number of new articles make it difficult for even the most assiduous economist to keep track of all the important recent advances. By focusing on those economists whose work is generally recognized to be at the forefront of the discipline, the series will be an essential reference point for the different specialisms included.

A list of published and future titles in this series is printed at the end of this volume.

Methodology, Money and the Firm

The Collected Essays of D.P. O'Brien

Volume II

D.P. O'Brien

Professor of Economics
University of Durham, UK

ECONOMISTS OF THE TWENTIETH CENTURY

Edward Elgar

Published by
Edward Elgar Publishing Limited
Gower House
Croft Road
Aldershot
Hants GU11 3HR
England

Edward Elgar Publishing Company
Old Post Road
Brookfield
Vermont 05036
USA

British Library Cataloguing in Publication Data
O'Brien, D.P.
Methodology, Money and the Firm:
Collected Essays of D.P. O'Brien. –
(Economists of the Twentieth Century
Series)
I. Title II. Series
338.5

Library of Congress Cataloguing in Publication Data
O'Brien, D.P. (Denis Patrick), 1939–
Methodology, money and the firm ; the collected essays of D.P. O'Brien
p. cm. — (Economists of the twentieth century)
Includes index.
1. Economics. 2. Industrial organization (Economic theory)
3. Economic history. I. Title. II. Series.
HB171.027 1994
330—dc20 94–3920
CIP

ISBN 1 85278 966 2 (2 volume set)

Printed and Bound in Great Britain by
Hartnolls Limited, Bodmin, Cornwall.

Contents

Acknowledgements

The publishers wish to thank the following who have kindly given permission for the use of copyright material.

Cambridge University Press for chapter: 'Marshall's Work in Relation to Classical Economics', pp. 127–63 in J.K. Whitaker (ed.), *Centenary Essays on Alfred Marshall*, Cambridge: CUP, 1990.

Duke University Press for articles: 'Customs Unions: Trade Creation and Trade Diversion in Historical Perspective', *History of Political Economy*, **8**, No. 4 (1976), pp. 540–63; 'Torrens, McCulloch, and the "Digression on Sismondi": Whose Digression?' (with A.C. Darnell), *History of Political Economy*, **12**, No. 3 (1980), pp. 383–95; 'Lionel Robbins and the Austrian Connection', *History of Political Economy*, **22** (1990), pp. 155–84.

Economica for articles: 'The Transition in Torrens' Monetary Thought', *Economica*, **XXXII** (August 1965), pp. 269–301; 'Torrens on Wages and Emigration', *Economica*, **XXXIII** (August 1966), pp. 336–40.

The Economic Journal for article: 'Lionel Charles Robbins, 1898–1984', *Economic Journal*, **98**, No. 389 (March 1988), pp. 104–25.

Kluwer Academic Publishers for chapter: 'Classical Reassessments', pp. 179–220 in William O. Thweatt (ed.), *Classical Political Economy*, Boston: Kluwer, 1988.

The Macmillan Press Ltd for: 'Competition and Credit Control', from *The New Palgrave Dictionary of Money and Finance*, London: Macmillan, 1992; 'Ravenstone, Piercy', in J. Eatwell *et al.*, *The New Palgrave*, Vol. IV, p. 124, London: Macmillan, 1987; 'J.R. McCulloch', Vol. III, pp. 262–3 in J. Eatwell, M. Milgate and P. Newman (eds), *The New Palgrave*, London: Macmillan, 1987; 'A. Marshall, 1842–1924', pp. 36–71 in D.P. O'Brien and J.R. Presley (eds), *Pioneers of Modern Economics in Britain*, London: Macmillan, 1981.

Oxford University Press for article: 'Ricardian Economics and the Economics of David Ricardo', *Oxford Economic Papers*, **33**, No. 3 (November 1981), pp. 352–86.

Routledge, Chapman & Hall Ltd for chapters: 'Classical Economics', pp. 110–12 in A. Kuper and J. Kuper (eds), *The Social Science Encyclopaedia*, London: Routledge, 1985; 'Hayek as an Intellectual Historian', in J. Birner and R.v. Zijp (eds), *Hayek, Coordination and Evolution; F.A. Hayek's Legacy in Philosophy, Politics, Economics and the History of Ideas*, London: Routledge, 1994.

The Scottish Economic Society for articles: 'Torrens, McCulloch and Disraeli', *Scottish Journal of Political Economy*, **24**, No. 1 (February 1977), pp. 1–18; 'J.R. McCulloch and the Theory of Value', *Scottish Journal of Political Economy*, **13** (November 1966), pp. 332–51.

Verlagsgruppe Handelsblatt for: 'Petty's *Political Arithmetick*', first published in German translation in T. Aspromourgos, A.W. Coats, D.P. O'Brien and B. Schefold, 'Sir William Petty und seine "Political Arithmetick" – Vademecum zu einem Klassiker der angewandten Nationalökonomie', Klassiker der Nationalökonomie, Verlag Wirtschaft und Finanzen GmbH, Düsseldorf, 1992.

PART I

CLASSICAL MACROECONOMICS AND TRADE

[1]

The Transition in Torrens' Monetary Thought[1]

By D. P. O'Brien

I. Introduction

Lord Robbins, in his important and authoritative study of Torrens[2] wrote: "There is a discontinuity in Torrens' development which seems to defy explanation. In his main contribution in this field [i.e. that of money and banking]. . . Torrens was essentially a Classical economist. The core of the Currency Theory may be regarded as an application in the sphere of banking of the leading implications of the Ricardian propositions regarding the distribution of the precious metals. The main idea of the practical proposals of this school is already to be found in embryo in Ricardo's *Plan for the Establishment of the National Bank;* and in this connection certainly, Torrens may truly claim to be a descendant of the master. But, in his earlier works on the subject, we find him adopting an entirely different, indeed a totally opposite, attitude . . .: the future opponent of the Banking School held views which were much more extreme than any ever held by Tooke or Fullarton." "But for his complete *volte-face* on matters relating to the theory of money and banking, it seems impossible to find any explanation."[3] It is certainly true that there is a strong contrast between the Torrens of the 1812 *Essay*[4] and the Torrens who was such a staunch defender of the 1844 Act that he wrote to Overstone: ". . . as regards the Examination of the Lord's Report[5] my sole object from the first has been to conform to your Lordship's suggestions. I am equally willing to insert it as part of a volume, to publish it as a separate tract, or to throw it aside altogether, as may be deemed most desirable in relation to the advancement of the good cause."[6]

[1] My very great thanks are due to the owners of the letters quoted in this article and to the owner of the Torrens paper printed in the Appendix to this article; and to Professor R. D. C. Black and Lord Robbins for their help and encouragement in the presentation of this article, and also to Lord Robbins for waiving his claims as the foremost authority on Torrens, to publish the paper. His published work was, of course, an invaluable guide to the study of Torrens' thought.

[2] Lionel Robbins, *Robert Torrens and the Evolution of Classical Economics*, 1958.

[3] *Op. cit.*, pp. 73–4.

[4] R. Torrens, *An Essay on Money and Paper Currency*, 1812.

[5] *Report from the Secret Committee of the House of Lords Appointed to Inquire into the Causes of the Distress which has for some Time prevailed among the Commercial Classes, and how far it has been affected by the Laws for regulating the Issue of Bank Notes Payable on Demand.* Parl. Papers 1847–8, vol. VIII, Pt. III. Reprinted in Parl. Papers 1857, Sess. I, vol. II. Torrens' Examination was published in the third edition of his *Principles and Practical Operation of Sir Robert Peel's Act of 1844, Explained and Defended*, 1858; also published separately as *Critical Examination of the Report of the Lords' Committee upon National Distress*, 1857.

[6] Letter of May 20, 1857. This letter is one of the letters of Torrens in the Overstone papers which I was able to examine by the kind permission of their owner, Mr. C. Loyd. The papers are of such interest that I hope to publish some work directly connected with them.

In another letter he wrote: " To the American crisis I shall of course refer, as affording a triumphant verification of the true faith."[1]

This attitude represented a very substantial change from Torrens' earlier views on monetary matters. He was well aware of this, and appears to have been afraid of the effects of some of his earlier writings recoiling on him. For instance he wrote to Overstone, sending a copy of Wilson's book[2]: " The tract to which it refers[3] has been out of print for thirty years, and I did not know until recently, that any copies of it were extant. But as my original sin is still remembered against me, is it not right that I should acknowledge my iniquity and express my contrition ? "[4] However, he seems to have had second thoughts, on Overstone's advice which he had asked for in his letter; for four days later he wrote: " Last evening I dispatched my concluding sheet, with the insertion of the improvements you suggested, and with the omission of the final note. Wilson's reference to my early heresy is contained in his volume "Capital, Currency, and Banking" and as this volume appears to be little more than a reprint of the leading articles of the Economist, it may be so little read that what he says of my forgotten Essay may escape attention. In this event it would not be wise in me to call attention to it. It will be time enough to explain should any further and more conspicuous reference be made to my original sin ".[5] So there is no question, since we have Torrens' own agreement, that his views had changed very considerably since his early writings on money and banking. It will be the contention of this article that we are now in a much better position to trace the course of this change.

This is because of the recent discovery of a hitherto unknown and unpublished paper by Torrens. This paper, written apparently in 1826, has the title " On the Means of establishing a cheap, secure, and uniform Currency; and of placing in the Treasury, for the public service, the sum of £25,000,000 "; and it supplies an important missing link in the chain of development of Torrens' thought.[6] It is preserved amongst the Wilmot Horton papers located in 1962 by R. N. Ghosh.[7] In examining these papers while searching for material relating to J. R. McCulloch, I was struck by the Torrens paper which seemed to me to contain some very important matter from the point of view of

[1] Letter of October 20, 1857. Overstone papers.

[2] *Capital, Currency, and Banking*, 1847.

[3] Wilson had written: " It is an opinion which many of the ablest writers on currency have held, that inconvertible paper notes might be issued to any extent that legitimate transactions required them, provided such issues were confined to the discount of good bills of exchange, and to loans for short periods, without any risk of depreciation, because a larger quantity could never be so issued than was again shortly returnable to the bank in payment of such loans. The most able reasoning with which we have met in favour of this proposition, is in a very clever work by Colonel Torrens published in 1812." *Capital, Currency, and Banking*, p. 42.

[4] Letter of January 24, 1848. Overstone papers.

[5] Letter of January 28, 1848. Overstone papers.

[6] This paper is published as Appendix below, pp. 286–301.

[7] R. N. Ghosh, " Malthus on Emigration and Colonization: Letters to Wilmot Horton," *Economica*, vol. xxx (1963), p. 62.

the history of the theory of money and banking. It was marked as being by Torrens, and although not in Torrens' handwriting, was identified as his work by a letter in the same folder. In the letter he wrote[1]: " Understanding at your office that you will not be in Town until the 13th, I forward to you the currency plan which I alluded to in one of my late conversations. As the questions which it involves are, at this particular juncture, of great national importance, I have also sent a copy of the M.S. to Lord Liverpool."

2. Torrens' Hopes of Preferment

One explanation for the change in Torrens' views might be that he changed his position in the hope of obtaining office. This possibility has been touched on by Lord Robbins who feels that Torrens could have had no hope of office at the time of his speech on Attwood's motion.[2] However, there is substantial evidence that Torrens was a seeker after office somewhat earlier. This is in itself not conclusive. To establish that Torrens actually changed his views in order to gain office, one would have to establish firstly that Torrens sought office, and secondly that this caused him to change his views on a particular question.This the available evidence does not permit us to do. But it does throw considerable light on Torrens' hopes at that time, and one piece of evidence does so directly in relation to his plan of 1826.

The plan itself was part of Torrens' campaign to draw attention to himself in the hope of gaining office. We have already seen that he sent a copy of his plan to Lord Liverpool, which would seem to indicate that his views were not merely, or perhaps even primarily, for the benefit of his fellow economists. But there is considerable evidence of Torrens having sought office.

The diary of Francis Place is the first piece of evidence, apart from Torrens' letter to Wilmot Horton which we will deal with below, which throws light on Torrens' attitude. In his diary for the very month in which Torrens sent his plan to Horton, Place wrote: "Torrens, it is evident is playing a game in which he may not, and I hope will not, be a gainer. He admitted that he did not mean to take a manly, decided part . . . but to act cautiously, that is, to feel his way to some place or office ".[3] Again on December 5, Place writes: " . . . he [Torrens] is a poor creature, and will make no figure as an opponent of Ministers in what is bad, and will not be worth their purchasing ".[4]

From Torrens' letters to Wilmot Horton it is clear that he not only sought office, but that he quite definitely expected to get it. Thus in a letter of July 4, 1827 he wrote to Horton: " Recent events have very much increased my desire for Parliamentary and official employment. . . ." In a document entitled " Memoranda " of five days later, after mentioning his support of Canning, and the hostility of the

[1] November 7, 1826. Letter in Wilmot Horton papers. [2] Robbins, *op. cit.*, p. 88.

[3] Francis Place, diary for November 21, 1826, quoted in G. Wallas, *The Life of Francis Place*, p. 179.

[4] *Ibid.*

Treasury, he wrote: "On Mr. Canning's becoming Prime Minister I wrote to Mr. Huskisson, expressing my desire for official and Parliamentary employment; and offering the Globe as a powerful political organ in support of the Government . . ."; and he asks, in view of the reply he received: "Was it possible for me not to form the most confident expectations that, on the completion of the ministerial arrangements, I should obtain Parliamentary or official employment? I considered the result not as probable but as certain." A fragment of a letter of the following day deals with the same subject.

Next, on August 14, 1827 we find Torrens writing in some consternation to Horton: "You will do me the justice to believe that in applying for a junior situation at the Board of Trade I had no intention of asking for the Privy Council. I did not advert to, indeed I was unacquainted with the political rank attached to the Vice Presidentship. The step I took was prompted by a conviction, I trust not a presumptuous one, that I possessed in some degree the qualifications requisite to enable me to discharge the duties of that office, with credit to the government, and with advantage to the country. . . ." Torrens elaborates on the theme of his fitness for office, and then stresses the necessity of having an economist at the Board of Trade: "it partakes of the nature of a professional appointment, requiring a peculiar course of study, and knowledge of an almost technical nature." Moreover, those at the Board of Trade must possess the power of defending their measures or lose face; and for this an economist is necessary. After holding forth on the importance of the new science he says: "Though the time may not have actually arrived, yet it is rapidly approaching, when it will be deemed as necessary to select the members of the Board of Trade from the Economists, as it is to take the Bishops from the Church, or the Law Officers from the Bar." Clearly Torrens felt himself well suited to the office he desired. This is further confirmed by the fact that his currency plan was, he felt, one of three measures necessary for the country. For in his letter to Horton accompanying the plan he wrote: "It appears to me, that three things are necessary to remove our difficulties, and render the country more flourishing than it ever yet has been—A reduction of poors [*sic*] rate by an extensive plan of Emigration. A modification of tythes, such as would prevent their operating as a Tax upon tillage. And a modification of the pressure of the debt by means of a cheap and abundant yet secure and uniform currency."[1]

But for all his sense of mission, Torrens clearly felt that he had overstepped the mark in the summer of 1827; for at the end of his letter referred to above,[2] he returns to his opening subject. "I trust you will pardon this long letter, dictated by an anxiety to remove any suspicion of my having entertained the preposterous design or wish, to become a member of the Privy Council." "As I am exceedingly anxious that

[1] Letter of November 7, 1826. Wilmot Horton papers.
[2] I.e., that of August 14, 1827.

my conduct and motives should not appear in an unfavourable light to Lord Goderich, I shall feel greatly obliged to you if you will have the goodness to take some favourable opportunity of communicating to his Lordship the substance of this letter. . . ."

However, he returns to the subject of office in his next letter.[1] " When I last had the pleasure of seeing you, you made an observation in which I cannot acquiesce. It was that in consequence of the death of Mr. Canning, the treatment I received from the late Treasury is a string which can be no longer touched. Now in my view of the matter this is a string not only to be touched, but to be incessantly harped upon, until it returns a note in harmony with justice."[2] Torrens must have been bitterly disappointed because later the same year he wrote to Horton referring to " my own extraordinary case".[3]

Early in the next year he returned to the charge. But this time he is not concerned with the Board of Trade but with an appointment related to the colonies, and emigration. Eighteen months previously Horton had assented to Torrens' request to be placed on any body which might be formed to be concerned with emigration. " Having entertained the most perfect conviction that I should be included in any arrangement embracing the subject of Emigration, I heard with extreme surprise and disappointment your announcement of yesterday that the proposed Colonial Board was to comprise only Colonel Cockburn and Major Moodie."[4] Torrens asks Horton to press Huskisson to appoint Torrens to the Colonial Board, which, Torrens feels certain, must be concerned with Emigration. Moreover, Torrens is so anxious to be appointed that he wishes to be so " salaried or unsalaried ".[5] Later the same month he again pressed his claims and referred to his treatment by the Treasury.[6]

Three years later he was still pressing his claims. He wrote to Horton: " I have written to Lord Goderich repeating my request to be placed on the Commission. Pray on all convenient opportunities urge and authorise this application."[7] Torrens must have been using every possible contact which might yield fruit in the form of office, because he is here asking for help from Horton who was by this time no longer in favour with the Ministry. The flattering reference to the Duke of Wellington at the beginning of *The Crisis and the Remedies* may perhaps be some indication of the lengths to which Torrens was prepared to go in order to gain office, since the good Duke would be unlikely to appeal to someone who, like Torrens, regarded himself as a liberal. Then, at the end of 1831, Mallet's diary has the following entry. " He [Malthus] . . . told me that the whole

[1] August 21, 1827. Wilmot Horton papers.
[2] See the " Memoranda " of July 9, 1827, referred to above.
[3] Letter of December 19, 1827. Wilmot Horton papers.
[4] Letter of February 8, 1828. Wilmot Horton papers.
[5] *Ibid.*
[6] Letter of February 28, 1828. Wilmot Horton papers.
[7] Letter of February 24, 1831. Wilmot Horton papers.

evening was occupied in discussing Torrens' proposed Motion in the House of Commons for the substitution of a Property Tax for the Taxes affecting Industry. This sounds very well; but it is the merest two-penny trash that can be conceived, and if Torrens was not a seeker of office and popularity, he is too sensible a man to entertain such views of Taxation."[1]

So Torrens was judged to be an office seeker, and his own letters confirm this. The question has then to be faced of whether there was any ulterior motive for his change of view. Now there can be no question that Torrens was well aware of the dangers of too radical a view of currency matters. This is strikingly illustrated in his letter to Horton already referred to.[2] Having referred to Ricardo's belief in a paper currency, and also that of Mr. Henry Drummond, he then goes on to say: " The plans of these very eminent economists however are liable to great objection: in as much as they go to supersede, and to sweep away, not only the Bank of England, but all the provincial Banks of circulation. My arrangements on the contrary, interfere with no vested interest, or existing establishment, while by a very simple machinery, they give to the currency complete security and an almost uniform value." But none of this points conclusively to any fundamental insincerity in Torrens' thinking. It may well be that Torrens had no wish to be bracketed with Attwood, and this may have influenced his attitude in the House. But the fact is that the position which he came to adopt in 1833 *was likely to be associated with just that position the unpopularity of which he had stressed in his letter quoted above*. So that although Torrens was unquestionably in search of office, this is unlikely to have influenced the position which he took up in 1833, a position quite close to his final one, and unquestionably Ricardian in its fundamental analysis. A much more likely motivating force behind Torrens' evolution is his respect for Ricardo. For, if Torrens himself is any guide, he had a great respect for the great minds of economics. Thus, for instance, he wrote of J. S. Mill to Overstone: " Hitherto I have been in the habit of deferring to him as one of the most original thinkers, and accurate reasoners of our day; and of suspecting some lurking fallacy in my own conclusions when not coinciding with his. But that is past. My self confidence cannot now be shaken, because it is sustained by a ' mightier name [i.e. Overstone] by far than he '."[3] So, what is much more likely is that Torrens' thought on monetary questions evolved under the posthumous influence of Ricardo. This proposition of evolution is now tenable given the contents of the 1826 paper which makes the existence of an evolutionary course much clearer. To trace this evolution is the object of the remainder of this article, and it is perhaps best to start with a short summary of the contents of the 1826 paper.

[1] Political Economy Club, *Centenary Volume*, p. 228.
[2] Letter of November 7, 1826. Wilmot Horton papers.
[3] Letter of January 30, 1848. Overstone papers.

3. The Torrens Plan

The basic problem which Torrens sees is the wide fluctuations to which a mixed currency of metal and convertible paper is liable. It is in the interest of the issuing banks to keep as much of their paper as possible in circulation, and this gives a constant tendency towards excess. Torrens explains how an unfavourable balance of payments arises through the resultant excess causing inflation with its well known effects on the prices of exports and imports. Merchants find it profitable to export gold, and there is a run on the banks to convert paper into gold. This causes the banks to contract violently their issues to stop the run and to enable them to replenish their coffers. This itself will lead to a strong deflation. Hence the fluctuations occur. Of course, other causes than excess can produce an unfavourable balance of payments, and hence, via the mixed currency, a powerful deflation. The deflationary effect is intensified because the banks of circulation will contract their issues further than necessary to stop the run, so as to put their currency at a premium and hence to replenish their reserves on favourable terms. There is in any case nothing which would tell the directors of a bank the precise point at which they could stop contracting issues; so they are liable to overshoot that point and cause a bigger contraction than necessary. The more paper and the less metal there is in a currency, the greater any absolute amount of gold lost will tend to be as a proportion of the total reserve of metal, and the more violent will be the subsequent contraction.

Repeal of the law limiting the number of partners in banks, security for the amount of paper issued by provincial banks, and suppression of small notes, are all dismissed as futile measures on their own which do not attack the central core of the problem, and have their own special difficulties. A simple metallic currency would be a tempting solution, but would have the enormous defect that it would increase tremendously the demand for gold, thus causing a severe deflation which would have disastrous consequences for all those who have to meet fixed money obligations. Ricardo's plan,[1] however, attracts Torrens much more. This has the great advantage of limiting convertibility, although inequitably.[2] But the fact that there is no gold coin in circulation means that the banks feel pressure immediately, and a sudden contraction of issues, with its resultant shock to the monetary system, will follow.

Any satisfactory plan for currency must have means of giving early warning of over-issue, and checking it; it must keep a steady value for the currency; and where contraction is required it should not be a violent process. In addition, any economies in the use of metal should be secured to the Treasury.

[1] D. Ricardo, *Proposals for an Economical and Secure Currency*, in *Works*, ed. Sraffa, vol. IV, pp. 43–141.

[2] Since convertibility is limited to those with £233 to exchange.

The plan proposed is designed to meet these criteria. Gold coin is to be the standard of the currency, and it is to be charged with a 6 per cent. seignorage to remove the temptation to melt it into bullion, at least until there has been a 6 per cent. inflation. Secondly, Bank of England and all other bank notes are to be payable *three months after demand* in bullion, less 1 per cent. seignorage. Without this time lag, Torrens considers that 100 per cent. gold backing of note issue is necessary if convertibility is not to mean periodic breaking of the banks. Given the 1 per cent. seignorage, this is the maximum by which bullion and paper can diverge, before the paper is presented for payment, so that over-issue will be checked quickly. Thirdly, the provincial banks will have to pledge securities to the Mint for the amount of their paper issue so that depositors in these banks have a safeguard in the event of the latter's failure. Finally, unconvertible Mint paper is to be substituted for all gold coin above the value of ten shillings each, which would save £25m. worth of metal. The sum of £25m. of paper curency is to be an absolutely fixed amount.

Under this plan, then, there would not be conversion of coin into bullion, but almost immediate warning to the over-issuing banks once the paper was presented for payment in bullion. Being rational, they would use the intervening three months to put the situation to rights and remove the difference between paper and bullion so that they would not lose in buying bullion to meet the demand.

4. The Antecedents of this Plan

The origins of this plan must surely be found in Ricardo's *Proposals for an Economical and Secure Currency.*[1] Torrens, indeed, claims the support of Ricardo in his letter to Wilmot Horton,[2] although oddly enough, in the letter, in contrast with the paper itself, he refers to Ricardo's *Plan for the Establishment of a National Bank*,[3] which is much less emphatic about the advantages of a paper currency. " The principle of issuing a paper currency upon the credit of the state is supported by the authority of Mr. Ricardo, and of Mr. Henry Drummond. The former in his posthumous work upon the establishing of a National Bank, and the latter in his pamphlet on the elementary principles of currency, have contended for the expediency of a government paper."

In Ricardo's *Proposals for an Economical and Secure Currency* the advantages of a paper currency are put strongly. " A well regulated paper currency is so great an improvement in commerce, that I should greatly regret, if prejudice should induce us to return to a system of less utility."[4] A paper currency, in Ricardo's view, is cheap and flexible. This attitude provides an immediate connection between the plan of 1826 and that of Ricardo ten years earlier. But Torrens had seen the

[1] *Works*, vol. IV, pp. 43–141.
[2] Letter of November 7, 1826 Wilmot Horton papers.
[3] *Works*, vol. IV, pp. 271–97. [4] *Op. cit.*, p. 65.

advantages of a paper currency in his earlier publications, and Ricardo is not breaking new ground for Torrens here. The lead comes from another part of the plan; the limitation of convertibility to amounts of 60 oz. of gold. For it is this which had appealed to Torrens when he came to discuss Ricardo's plan in his 1826 paper. Here was a plan which made the currency fluctuate in accord with movements in the exchanges, albeit somewhat sharply, and yet, by limiting convertibility, made some step towards limiting panics and runs on the banks.

At this stage Torrens still felt that something could be done to cushion the effect of panics, and hence he felt the need to modify Ricardo's plan. Later Torrens was to abandon the belief that a currency plan should make provision to offset the effect of panics.[1] But in 1826, it seems fair to say, he felt that something should be done. Ricardo had felt that his bullion convertibility system would work well under normal circumstances; but he says about panics: "Against such panics, Banks have no security, *on any system*[2]; from their very nature they are subject to them as at no time can there be in a bank, or in a country, so much specie or bullion as the monied individuals of such country have a right to demand."[3] While Torrens accepted, by now, much of what Ricardo contended, he seems to have felt that on this point there were unexplored possibilities. He accepted Ricardo's insistence on the need for a currency to have a standard; in fact he does not even argue this, he takes it for granted,[4] and then tells his reader that gold coin is to be the standard. He was no longer happy about the standardless currency of the Bank Restriction era. Nor does he question the need to make the currency fluctuate in accord with any external pressures. But he does implicitly question the inevitability of the effects of a panic making themselves felt. His answer to the problem is very simple; it is to limit convertibility by inserting a lag in the operation of a plan which has otherwise much in common with a point of view which he had not accepted in his earlier writings. In doing so he achieved a position which was intermediate between the two contrasting ones noticed at the beginning of this article. The following section will attempt to place his plan of 1826 in the context of his thought before and after this date.

5. Torrens' Known Thought in Relation to the Plan of 1826.

The 1812 *Essay*[5] had been Torrens' first contribution to the field of monetary theory. In this he had taken a position some way distant from that of the 1826 paper. Whereas in 1826 we are led to understand that a stable value of the currency is desirable, in 1812 inflation is treated as a process with many desirable characteristics. In chapter III Torrens writes of the effects of an increase in the quantity of money,

[1] See below, p. 282 and p. 284. [2] Italics in original. [3] *Op. cit.*, p. 68.

[4] Except that in the section discussing the operation of his plan, towards the end of his paper, he dismisses the idea of a general price level and the measurement of the relationship of the currency to that, rather as Ricardo had done: *op. cit.*, p. 59.

[5] *An Essay on Money and Paper Currency*, 1812.

causing a rise in prices: " The number of persons who hold annuities and fixed incomes, bears so small a proportion to the whole community, that any inconvenience they may suffer, from a fall in the value of money, sinks into insignificance, nay entirely vanishes, when compared with the universal opulence, the general diffusion of happiness arising from augmented trade, and the rise in the wages of labour, which the increased quantity of money is instrumental in producing. Besides, the annuitants or persons of fixed income, finding their places in society perpetually sinking, will be prompted to some species of exertion in order to avert the evil; and thus the number of idle individuals, who add nothing to the general stock of the society, will be diminished, and industry will receive a two-fold stimulus."[1] It is true that in 1826 (and later[2]) Torrens was to insist on the undesirability of deflation, as he does in chapter IV of his *Essay*. But in this early *Essay* this is associated with a stress on the benefits of inflation : " . . . that poverty and distress follow a diminution of the circulating medium, and that affluence accompanies its increase, are lessons so uniformly and forcibly impressed by experience, that princes and legislators have ever been sufficiently solicitous to retain the precious metals in their countries."[3] This joint emphasis is not to be found in the paper of 1826. The contrast with this latter work is marked also by the reasons which Torrens gave in 1812 for suggesting a paper currency. It is true that in both 1812 and 1826 Torrens emphasizes the economy of a paper currency. But on the earlier occasion this is associated with an emphasis on the elasticity of a paper currency. " From what has here been urged, it follows, that a well regulated paper currency confers a two-fold benefit; it not only saves the expence of maintaining, in the precious metals, an instrument of commerce of similar amount—but it bestows, upon the circulating medium, an elastic power, which fills up, instantaneously, the vacuities that extending demand occasions."[4] This view is not to be found in 1826. Moreover, by 1826 Torrens seems to have abandoned another argument that he had used in 1812 in favour of a paper currency, namely that " where a paper currency is established, every class, in the community, has the strongest interest in supporting the government against the shocks of internal commotion and foreign violence ".[5]

Although convertibility is seen as a possible safeguard against any dangers which may be associated with a paper currency, Torrens is very clear, as he was to be fourteen years later, that convertibility could be profoundly inconvenient. However, "it will be found, that limiting the issues of bank paper, to the discounting of solid mercantile bills, payable at a fixed and moderate rate, is an effectual means of returning all superfluous paper upon the bank that issued it, and of bringing the supply of circulating medium within the measure of demand."[6]

[1] *Ibid.*, pp. 40–1.
[2] See, for instance, *The Crisis and the Remedies*, 1830; published as Letter VI of *The Budget, A Series of Letters on Financial, Commercial and Colonial Business*, 1841.
[3] *An Essay . . . , op. cit.*, p. 49. [4] *Ibid.*, p. 89. [5] *Ibid.*, p. 97. [6] *Ibid.*, p. 125.

So the " real-bills " doctrine is set forth. This was certainly not Torrens' answer to the problem of convertibility by 1826.

The contrast with the later work is still further marked by chapter VIII on " Apparent Depreciation ". In some cases of pressure against the foreign exchanges, the remedy, Torrens argues, is not to adjust the currency but, for instance, to " diminish the expence of supporting fleets and armies abroad ".[1] This kind of suggestion is not given in the paper of 1826, although the possibility of pressure on the exchange arising from forces other than an excess issue of currency[2] was still recognised by Torrens then as indeed it was later.

By the time that Torrens came to write his letters in 1816 to the *Sun* newspaper, ostensibly to the Earl of Lauderdale, he had moved slightly towards a more modified position. It is true that he maintains his distinction between real and apparent depreciation[3]; and for the discernment of this he erects an ingenious measure—the price of goods which do not enter into international trade[4]—although he was to reject, in 1826, all measurements of movements of the price level by changes in the price of goods. It is also true that he argues that the best way of keeping the currency to its customary value in relation to these coarse goods is to restrict the issues of the bank to those made in discounting short term bills[5]; and he is still not happy about the idea of a return to cash payments.[6] But there is perhaps not the same inflationary emphasis as four years earlier. Some of the arguments against the return to cash payments relate to the need to avoid sudden shocks, which Torrens was to be concerned with in his later writings, although of course shocks would be seen by him later to arise from rather different causes. But even when he came to make his speech on Attwood's motion in 1833, he did attack the deflationary aspect of the resumption, blaming it however on the choice of gold instead of silver this time, although he had by then taken up in a large measure the position of his later years on questions of currency.

But that at this time Torrens still had a long way to go towards his final position is shown by the contents of his *Comparative Estimate*[7] of 1819; for although the general tone is more moderate, there is still a very distinct inflationary bias in the work. The moderation is apparent in the treatment of the bullionists. " The error of the bullionists consists, not in their assuming false principles but in their failing to give due consideration to the limitations and exceptions to which just principles are occasionally liable."[8] Moreover, in regard to the bullionists' and the anti-bullionists' differences, "When these opposite theories are examined upon the principles above unfolded, it will be

[1] *Ibid.*, p. 179. [2] Not using the term " excess " in Ricardo's sense.

[3] April 19, 1816. [4] April 20, 1816. [5] April 20, 1816. [6] April 20, 1816.

[7] *A Comparative Estimate of the Effects which a Continuance and a Removal of the Restriction upon Cash Payments are respectively calculated to Produce: with Strictures on Mr. Ricardo's Proposal for Obtaining a Secure and Economical Currency*, 1819.

[8] *Ibid.*, p. 30.

found that each contains something which is correct, combined with something which is erroneous, and that truth lies at middle point between them ".[1] But, even with this attention paid to the bullionist view, the inflationary bias remains. Any fall in real wages resulting from inflation would be " only of short duration, and would be counteracted by the other effects of an increased circulation ".[2] Wages, despite the Combination Laws, should soon rise again to their former real level. Inflation will redistribute wealth " in favour of the productive classes, and tend to encourage industry, and to increase the demand for labour ".[3] The fall in wages would also raise profits temporarily, and the rise in prices would raise confidence and stimulate industry. A reduction in the income of annuitants and civil servants would be in reality a diversion of wealth into more productive channels. Finally, the inflation would lower the burden of debt. Deflation is " beyond all comparison more injurious ".[4]

All this has a marked continuity with Torrens' previous thought, and much less in common with that of 1826. The reproduction of material from the *Sun*, the distinction between real and apparent depreciation, the emphasis on the greater benefit of inflation than deflation—all these mark the continuity. Fundamental to the position of 1819 is the use made of the concept of apparent depreciation and the implication that when this is operative the currency should not be contracted; this attitude contrasts with that of 1826. At the same time there are links between the two works. The emphasis on the desirability of preventing the currency from rising to the extraordinary heights attained by gold has something in common with the desire of 1826 to keep the currency in line with the modal value of gold, as well as with the emphasis in the speech of 1833 on the ill-effects of choosing gold as a standard. Torrens' last point in favour of inflation, that is, the easing of the burden of fixed debt, is in tune, if not explicitly with the paper of seven years later, at least with Torrens' letter to Horton accompanying the paper, in which he spoke of the need for a currency plan to lighten the burden of debt. However, this may have referred to the avoidance of deflation; on the inconveniences of this the paper of 1826 and the *Estimate* are very much at one.

When we come to Torrens' next work, the *Essay on the Production of Wealth* of 1821, we find little change. The continuity of thought is marked by the reproduction of passages, in the Section of chapter VI devoted to " Money and Paper Currency ",[5] both from the *Essay* of 1812, and the *Estimate* of 1819, the former dealing with the advantages of a paper currency, the latter with the benefits of inflation and the evils of deflation. The work does little to advance our knowledge of Torrens' thought.

The paper of 1826 reveals a substantial swing away from Torrens' earlier thought, yet there is still some continuity with his earlier writings,

[1] *Ibid.*, pp. 27–8. [2] *Ibid.*, p. 55. [3] *Ibid.*, p. 56. [4] *Ibid.*, p. 68.
[5] *Essay on the Production of Wealth*, 1821, p. 290.

and noticeable differences from his later position. Although Torrens has now changed his objection to Ricardo's plan that it would cause undesirable fluctuations by allowing bullion convertibility, he still has strong objections to this plan because of the speed and sharpness of its operation. The possible inflationary link with his earlier thought has already been mentioned.[1] His dislike of a strong appreciation is marked in his discussion of the idea of a metallic currency, and he still has marked objections to this plan. He wants the currency to fluctuate as a metallic currency would do, but not exactly to parallel the hypothetical metallic fluctuations. To achieve this compromise he inserts, as we have seen, a lag in the mechanism, to keep the currency close to the *modal* value of gold. This would seem to be an important half-way house between 1819 and 1833. Significantly, he still favours the use of inconvertible paper (for part of the currency) and semi-convertible paper. Yet, at the same time, his division of the currency into two parts can be seen as a parallel with the division of the currency under the 1844 Act, the Mint paper in 1826 corresponding to the fiduciary issue of 1844; and the fluctuation envisaged for the convertible part of the currency may be seen as signifying the recognition by Torrens of the inadequacy of the " real-bills " doctrine, which he had formerly supported, and a step towards the idea of complete bullion convertibility.

In the light of all this, his speech on Attwood's motion,[2] in April 1833 comes as much less of a surprise.[3] Torrens had now moved a stage further in his development and had now reached an almost completely Ricardian position. In 1827 he had disassociated himself from the Ricardians, referring in a letter to Horton to " the ultra-liberals of the Ricardo school, who push general principles to their extremes",[4] a criticism rather reminiscent of that he had made of the bullionists in 1819. But now, in 1833, he advocated a plan similar to that of Ricardo, and made it quite clear that he was doing so, referring to "This arrangement which has been suggested on the soundest principles of political economy by Mr. Ricardo ".[5] But not all is Ricardian in detail. In his speech Torrens still clings to the idea of a silver standard, which he had propounded in the *Comparative Estimate*, and which Ricardo himself had suggested in his *Economical and Secure Currency* but later abandoned. Torrens also, in accord with his earlier thought, stresses the unpleasantness of appreciation, as has already been mentioned. The limited convertibility measure may be viewed as

[1] Among the necessary measures for the good of the country is " a modification of the pressure of the debt by means of a cheap and abundant yet secure and uniform currency ". Letter of November 7, 1826, to Horton.

[2] See *Hansard*, 3rd Series, vol. XVII, cols. 540–8; and *The Mirror of Parliament*, vol. II, 1833, pp. 1414–5.

[3] In fact, the passages in the speech on the fluctuations associated with a mixed currency are lifted almost without modification from the first few pages of the 1826 paper.

[4] Letter of August 14, 1827, Wilmot Horton papers.

[5] *Mirror of Parliament*, vol. II, 1833, p. 1415.

a simple acceptance of Ricardo's views on this; but it could be viewed as a logical development from his plan of 1826. He now saw the need for pressure on the exchanges to make their effects on the currency felt more quickly. But this limited convertibility measure would still protect the banks of circulation; it " would secure the banks of circulation from political passions, and from runs having for object the embarrassment of the government ".[1]

Torrens still felt the need for protection against extraordinary panics. This position was abandoned by him later[2]; and there was no minimum convertible amount of this sort provided for in the Act of 1844.[3] Torrens was also to abandon his belief in the desirability of £1 notes; but he considered in 1833 that " the abolition of 1l. notes was another evil inflicted on the country by the ignorance of Parliament ".[4] His speech also, by reproducing the passages from his 1826 paper on pressure on the exchanges caused by factors such as " foreign expenditure—foreign loans—deficient harvest ",[5] virtually maintained his distinction between real and apparent depreciation, although by accepting the basic Ricardian thesis he had abandoned the policy implications of the distinction. The distinction itself he did not fully abandon for another fourteen years until, in his pamphlet on the 1844 Act and commercial credit,[6] he used the term " redundancy " in the Ricardian sense.[7]

By the time we come to Torrens' *Letter to Lord Melbourne*[8] with its accompanying *Supplement*, Torrens' thought had moved further towards its final position. For in these two publications Torrens becomes completely and explicitly committed to the principle that the circulation should behave exactly as if it were purely metallic. The indictment of the conduct of the directors is on the grounds that they have failed to make this happen. Instead of expanding and contracting their currency with movements in the exchanges, they have expanded and contracted their deposits which, because the deposits are a multiple of the currency, has given smaller fluctuations in currency than necessary: " . . . the recent disturbance in the money market

[1] *Hansard, loc. cit.*, col. 547.

[2] See the discussion below of Torrens' reply to John Stuart Mill's *Westminster Review* article. By the time he came to write his *Edinburgh Review* article, Torrens had this to say of panics: " a sudden and unforeseen calamity affecting large masses of the community must be encountered on the instant by the government of the day. . . . No pre-enactment can prescribe an appropriate remedy for an unknown contingency. Each successive emergency may differ from those which pre-ceeded it. . . . Exceptional cases cannot be brought under general rules ". *Edinburgh Review*, vol. 107 (1858), p. 278.

[3] Subsequently supporters of the Act were to feel that artificial pressures had been brought to bear to engender panic.

[4] *Mirror of Parliament, loc. cit.*, p. 1415.

[5] *Mirror of Parliament, loc. cit.*

[6] *On the Operation of the Bank Charter Act of 1844 as it Affects Commercial Credit*, 1847.

[7] i.e., in the sense of any amount of currency over and above that which is necessary to keep the exchanges at par. See Robbins, *op. cit.*, p. 330.

[8] *A Letter to the Right Honourable Viscount Melbourne on the Cause of the Recent Derangement in the Money Market and on Bank Reform*, 1837.

was occasioned by the error committed by the directors of the Bank of England, in departing from the principle, of leaving the currency to contract or expand under the action of the foreign exchanges: . . . this error originated in the failure of the Bank directors to distinguish between effects produced upon the general medium of exchange, by a diminution of their circulation and by a diminution of their deposits."[1]

In common with all his previous views, and in disagreement with those of Ricardo, Torrens does not propose to take away the power of the Bank of England.[2] Ricardo had been strongly opposed to the Bank of England in his posthumously published *Plan for the Establishment of a National Bank*. Torrens' disagreement on this point, however, does not signify any fundamental disagreement with the basic Ricardian analysis.

The thought of the *Letter* of 1837 shows the course of Torrens' development clearly. He had now moved some way from his position of 1826 by his *complete* commitment to a fluctuating currency; and his discussion of deposits is particularly interesting since the subject was ignored in the paper of 1826.

The *Supplement* to the *Letter* marks the course of Torrens' transition even more firmly. Perhaps the most significant feature of the plan contained in it is that there is no provision for limiting convertibility. Indeed, it is proposed to make " it compulsory on the banks of issue, not only to give gold in exchange for their paper, but also to give their paper in exchange for gold ".[3] This is, of course, a marked change from his position of 1833, and still more that of 1826. Clearly his thought was now evolving away from his former position on panics; and the abandonment of the proposal to limit convertibility was a marked swing away from the more or less Ricardian position, on this issue, of 1833.

The plan itself has little in common with that of 1826. The most important positive difference is the plan for the backing of the note issue. Apart from the initial note issue, which was to have a 25 per cent. gold backing, any further issue was to have 100 per cent. backing. This Torrens did not advocate eleven years earlier, quite clearly, since the banks were to be allowed to use the three months' notice of conversion, in the plan of 1826, to recall notes and to buy bullion. Another difference is the idea of treating all the banks of issue on the same footing as regards limitation of their issues. Eleven years earlier the provincial banks had been singled out as being required to pledge securities to the Mint for the issue of their paper.[4]

[1] *Ibid.*, pp. 61–2.

[2] On p. 8 of the *Supplement*, Torrens implies that this view is due to the need for prescriptions to be practical. This agrees with the view expressed in his letter to Horton quoted above.

[3] *Supplement*, p. 13.

[4] A measure to which Torrens had advanced objections in the first part of his paper which he made no attempt to answer in making his recommendations.

Having taken up his position on the need for the currency to fluctuate, Torrens maintained it. He takes it as his basis for the *Letter to Thomas Tooke*[1] of three years later. He asks Tooke: " Are you prepared to deny that paper money should be so regulated as to maintain the currency in the same state with respect to amount and to value, in which it would exist, were it exclusively metallic ? "[2] There would seem to have been little change in Torrens' thought in the intervening three years, and he reproduces the plan from his *Supplement*.

Continuity with the thought of these last two publications is apparent in the *Inquiry* of 1844.[3] The attitude of the 1837 *Letter* and *Supplement*, the differences of which from the plan of 1826 have already been discussed, is further elaborated and refined. Not that there are no changes from the detail of the two earlier publications. Here, as Lord Robbins has pointed out,[4] Torrens maintains, in contrast with the *Letter*, that the Bank of England is powerless to offset the effects of mismanagement by the provincial banks. But the main thread of thought here is quite consistent with his immediately preceding publications, and there is no evidence of a further swing away from the thought of 1826.

Torrens' reply to John Stuart Mill's *Westminster Review* article[5] not only continues along the path on which Torrens had set himself in 1837, but makes explicit some of the contrasts with his earlier position. For it is now abundantly clear that he has completely abandoned his position on panics. The object of the plan, Torrens considers, is only to remove those fluctuations which have their origin in a currency's failing to be affected directly by movements in the exchanges. " The Westminster Reviewer objects to the Government measure on the grounds that it will not have the effect of preventing the recurrence of those commercial revulsions to which the country would be liable were the currency exclusively metallic. The proper answer to this objection is, that the object of the proposed measure is to prevent the recurrence of those revulsions only which have had their origin in a currency fluctuating alternately above and below the level to which a purely metallic currency would conform."[6] It is nothing more ambitious than that. But this position is only one indication of how far Torrens had moved from his position of 1826. For the arguments which Torrens now used might have applied against his own former position. He wrote: " No advocate of the metallic principle ever contended that the power of issuing convertible paper can give to the

[1] *A Letter to Thomas Tooke Esq., in Reply to his Objections Against the Separation of the Business of the Bank into a Department of Issue, and a Department of Deposit and Discount: with a Plan of Bank Reform*, 1840.

[2] *Ibid.*, pp. 6–7.

[3] *An Inquiry into the Practical Working of the Proposed Arrangements for the Renewal of the Charter of the Bank of England and the Regulation of the Currency with a Refutation of the Fallacies Advanced by Mr. Tooke*, 1844.

[4] Robbins, *op. cit.*, p. 325.

[5] *Reply to the Objections of the Westminster Review to the Government Plan for the Regulation of Currency*, 1844.

[6] *Ibid.*, pp. 35–6.

currency a *permanent* expansion greater than that which it would possess were it purely metallic. What they contend for is, that when the Bank fails to keep its issues upon securities at a uniform amount, it produces a *temporary* excess in the circulation, requiring that bullion should be withdrawn from its coffers for exportation ".[1] Surely Torrens could have argued against his plan of 1826 that there was plenty of opportunity, given the three months convertibility, for a temporary excess of currency. It is also interesting, in view of his plan of 1826 to keep the currency to the modal value of gold, that he regards as a " very startling " proposition the idea that " a purely metallic currency is more liable to abrupt fluctuations than a convertible paper currency ".[2]

From the pamphlet of 1847[3] and even more from the first edition of his *Principles*[4] Torrens was concerned with the defence of the Act of 1844, and his thought, though fascinating in itself, becomes of less interest from the point of view of the half-way house of the 1826 paper. But it is hoped that enough has been said to put this previously unpublished paper in perspective.

6. Conclusion

In the paper of 1826 Torrens' thought was in an intermediate position between its early and final forms. He was still extremely clear about the dangers of convertibility; at the same time he now accepted the need to make the currency fluctuate in response to external pressures as a metallic currency would do, and to provide a better safeguard against over-issue than that provided by the "real-bills" doctrine. But he did not want a complete parallel between the fluctuations of the paper currency and those of a theoretical metallic one, hence his desire to link the paper to the modal value of gold. Moreover, he still felt that a currency plan should have safeguards against panics, and do more than merely avoid those fluctuations to which a less well-designed scheme of currency would be liable.

The 1826 plan would have been an important link in the development of this powerful and original thinker even if it had been short lived. But there is a strong possibility that it stayed with him for some time. For J. L. Mallet wrote in his diary for July 6, 1832: " Torrens had also a scheme [of currency], too absurd to be noticed here, and which I only mention to shew the extreme mischief of leaving such questions constantly afloat, and artificial systems of currency and credit to be concocted by Committees of the House of Commons."[5]

[1] *Ibid.*, p.7.
[2] *Ibid.*, pp. 22–3.
[3] *On the Operation of the Bank Charter Act of 1844, as it Affects Commercial Credit.*
[4] *The Principles and Practical Operation of Sir Robert Peel's Bill of 1844 Explained and Defended Against the Objections of Tooke, Fullarton and Wilson*, 1848.
[5] Political Economy Club, *Centenary Volume*, p. 241.

This scheme was certainly one to which Torrens devoted considerable care and thought, and it is an interesting link in the development of an important economist. Those who read his paper will find Torrens, the anti-bullionist, and Torrens, the ardent defender of the " true faith " of the Act of 1844, put in a new light.

Queen's University, Belfast.

APPENDIX

On the Means of establishing a cheap, secure and uniform Currency; and of Placing in the Treasury, for the Public service, the sum of £25,000,000.

Extensive and calamatous experience has now established the fact, that a currency consisting of the precious metals, and of paper convertible into these metals on demand, is liable to sudden and very considerable fluctuations. Upon the causes which produce these fluctuations it may be proper to make some preliminary[1] remarks.

It is the interest of the Banks which issue paper, to keep in circulation as large an amount of their notes as possible. This occasions a constant tendency towards excess. As the supply of paper is increased, the value of the currency falls, and general prices rise, whether they are estimated in paper, or in the coin which continues to circulate in common with it. The rise in the money prices of commodities checks the exportation of domestic articles, and encourages the importation of foreign ones; and thus occasions an unfavourable balance of payments. The premium upon foreign Bills soon exceeds the cost of transmitting the precious metals; and the bullion merchant can realise a profit by exporting the coin to meet the bills which he sells to those who have foreign payments to effect. But as paper cannot be employed in these profitable transactions, it is taken to the Bank to be exchanged for gold, and the Directors, in order to stop the run, and replenish their coffers, are compelled suddenly to contract their issues until the value of the currency is so raised, and general prices so reduced, that the balance of foreign payments is turned in our favour, and it becomes profitable to export merchandise in exchange for gold. Thus it is, that a Currency composed of coin, and of paper convertible upon demand, must be in a constant state of fluctuation between the extremes of excess and of deficiency.

Though no excess should ever be created, yet deficiency will occasionally occur. Redundant currency, and the general rise of prices which it occasions, are not the only, perhaps not the principle, causes of an unfavourable balance of foreign payments. Foreign expenditure, foreign loans, deficient harvests, excessive and mistaken speculations, may severally or conjointly create an amount of foreign debt beyond what the ordinary amount of foreign credits can liquidate; and thus cause the demand for foreign bills to exceed the supply. In this state of things, foreign bills will bear a premium; and the bullion merchant will obtain a profit by consigning the precious metals to his correspondents abroad, drawing for the amount, and disposing of his bills in the market. Banks of circulation will, as before, have their notes

[1] Inserted in original.

returned in exchange for gold; and, to avert a dangerous run upon their coffers, will be compelled to contract their issues until the value of the currency is so increased, that the exportation of the coin no longer yields a profit.

When paper issued in excess, or an unfavourable balance arising from other causes, has occasioned a run upon the Banks of circulation, it becomes the interest of those Establishments to contract their issues, not merely in the degree necessary to stop the run, and to restore the currency to its standard value; but in that greater degree which may be required in order to raise the currency above its standard value, and to enable the Directors upon favourable terms to replenish the exhausted coffers of the Banks. Let us suppose for example, that the Bank of England deems it necessary to keep in its coffers a treasure of £5,000,000; and that a run has reduced this treasure to £2,000,000; and that the Directors after having contracted their issues so as to prevent any farther drain, are desirous of replacing the £3,000,000 of treasure which they have lost. In this case, it is evident, that by a farther contraction of the paper issues, raising the value of the currency still higher, and causing the market price of gold to fall 2 per cent below the mint price, the Bank, in purchasing the £3,000,000 of Standard bullion which it required, would make a profit of £60,000.

When a run has taken place upon the banks which issue paper, the directors of these establishments cannot ascertain with any precision, the degree in which their issues ought to be contracted, in order to effect the two-fold object of arresting the drain upon their treasure, and of replenishing their coffers upon favourable terms. The necessity of contraction they will see; but possessing no indications of the precise point at which it might safely and advantageously stop, they will often carry it considerably beyond what the actual circumstances of the case require. Hence, after every recurrence of excess or of an unfavourable foreign balance, a mixed currency composed of coin and of paper convertible in (*sic*) demand, will suffer a much more considerable contraction, and acquire a higher value, than a currency purely metallic.

The fluctuations in the value of such mixed currency, when occasioned by an unfavourable foreign balance, become more considerable as the proportion which the paper bears to the gold is increased. Should the currency amount to £60,000,000, and should it be purely metallic, then an unfavourable balance of foreign payment requiring an export of coin to the amount of £5,000,000 would cause a contraction of one-twelfth. Should the currency consist of £40,000,000 of paper convertible on demand, and £20,000,000 of coin; then, the unfavourable balance requiring £5,000,000 of the coin for the foreign payments, would in addition to the contraction of one-twelfth as before, create a drain upon the banks, and cause them to withdraw a portion of their paper, in order to save their remaining treasure, and to replenish their coffers upon advantageous terms. Had the currency consisted of £50,000,000 of convertible paper; and of £10,000,000 of coin;—then, the exportation of £5,000,000 of this coin, besides reducing the currency one-twelfth, would produce a more decided pressure upon the banks of circulation, draining them of one-half, instead of one-fourth, of their gold; and requiring in order to arrest the run and to restore the treasure it had withdrawn, a very sudden and considerable diminution in the customary amount of paper.

Again:—a mixed currency, composed of coin and of paper convertible into coin on demand, is constantly exposed to still more sudden and violent diminutions in amount in consequence of the stoppage of the banks by which the paper is circulated. If we suppose, what is probably the case in this country at present, that a convertible paper currency amounting to £40,000,000 has for its basis a metallic currency of £25,000,000—then, from the physical impossibility of paying £40,000,000 of paper with £25,000,000 of coin, a panic may at any time render the Banks insolvent, discredit the whole paper system, and cause the circulating medium to be contracted to little more than one-third of its ordinary amount.

From all these considerations it appears, that a mixed currency, consisting of coin, and of paper convertible on demand, is the very worst species of circulating medium which it is possible for an extensively mercantile country to adopt. The crisis of 1797, and the panic of 1825–6, are far from being extreme or aggravated instances of the evils inherent in this vicious monetary system. It is on all hands acknowledged, that if, during the late alarm, we had been threatened with danger from abroad, or visited with a scarcity of corn at home, the crash would have been beyond all comparison more extensive and appalling. Under such circumstances the failure of the London and Country Banks would have been followed by the stoppage of the Bank of England. As it was, that establishment had the greatest difficulty in providing gold to meet the extraordinary demand upon its coffers; and all the powers of the Mint, called into the utmost activity, could scarcely convert bullion into coin with sufficient rapidity for the occasion. Unless our present system of currency be amended by the timely interference of the Legislature, it will go on to occasion periodical and aggravated distress until in a National Bankruptcy it finds its Euthanasia.

Measures which have been proposed for giving greater uniformity and Security to our Mixed Currency.

1. Repeal of the Law limiting the number of partners in banks

Measures have been from time to time proposed for correcting or mitigating the evils experienced under our existing monetary system. One of these measures has been, the repeal of the law which limited the number of partners in Banking Establishments to six persons. Though this law was absurd and pernicious, yet the repeal of it cannot operate as a remedy for the evils inherent in a currency composed of coin, and of paper convertible on demand. Increasing the number and respectability of partners in Provincial Banks, can have no tendency to check the issue of paper; but on the contrary may, by inspiring in the first instance greater confidence in the Banking establishments, have a directly opposite effect. Neither can an increase in the number of partners have any influence in preventing the recurrence of an unfavourable balance of foreign payments not connected with the currency. But when there is excessive issue; or when, without any excess, there is an unfavourable foreign balance, then there must of necessity be a sudden contraction of a currency consisting in any considerable proportion, of paper convertible on demand. But farther:—When an excessive issue of paper or an unfavourable foreign balance, has caused the metals to disappear, it is palpably impossible to convert paper into coin on demand, and therefore in periods of discredit and panic, the Provincial Banking Companies, whether consisting of Six, or of Six thousand partners, must of necessity suspend their payments.

2. *Security for the amount of Paper issued*

It has been proposed, in order to give stability to the Country Banks, that security shall be required for the payment of the paper they may issue. This measure is, like the former, an extremely proper one; but it is not, any more than the former, an appropriate remedy for the peculiar evils growing out of our system of mixed currency. It possesses no efficacy whatever in preventing either an unfavourable foreign balance, or an over-issue of paper. If property worth £50,000 be pledged as security for paper issued to a similar amount, that paper may be employed to purchase other property, and this other property be pledged as the security for a farther issue; and so on, till excess is created, and a recoil and collapse brought on. Chartered Companies, extended partnerships, and the deposit of securities equivalent to the amount of paper issued;—these are the specific remedies against the local evils sometimes experienced in consequence of adventurers without adequate capital entering into the Banking business and issuing their notes to the public. Measures of this character, therefore, though they would be proper accompaniments and auxiliaries of an improved system, yet do not of themselves go to the length of touching the causes of the extensive mischief which our existing plan of currency creates.

3. *Suppression of Small Notes*

Another measure for giving greater stability and uniformity to the Currency is the suppression of all notes under the value of Five Pounds. This would increase the proportion of the coin to the paper, and would therefore in the manner which has been already explained, prevent an unfavourable Foreign balance from occasioning so great a contraction of the currency as would occur if the coin bore a less proportion to the paper.

It is abundantly evident, however, that the suppression of notes under the value of £5 cannot prove an adequate remedy against the evils inherent in a currency composed of coin and of paper convertible on demand. Such a measure could neither take away the liability to over-issue, nor contract those operations by which an unfavourable foreign balance is occasionally created. These causes alone, when there were no small notes in circulation to aggravate their effects, produced the greatest run for gold ever known; and brought on a pecuniary crisis so alarming, that it was deemed necessary to protect the Bank of England by the suspension of Cash payments. Thus then, suppressing small notes convertible on demand, and supplying their place with coin, would cause an unfavourable foreign balance of any given amount, to produce a less contraction of the circulating medium than if the small notes had been left in circulation to increase the proportion in which the paper part of the currency exceeds the metallic part. This mitigation, however, of the evil would be accompanied by more than counter-balancing disadvantages. The increase in the metallic part of the currency, while it rendered an unfavourable foreign balance less injurious, would allow excessive issue and depreciation to go on for a longer period before they were arrested by a rise in the price of bullion. It would, besides, occasion an increased demand for gold, and a rise in the value of currency; and would thus be accompanied by a pressure and embarrassment, the nature of which will be explained below.

4. *A simple Metallic Currency*

Struck with the magnitude of the evils inherent in our present system, some intelligent writers have proposed to withdraw paper as much as possible from circulation, and to substitute a metallic currency in its stead. This would be no better than avoiding Scylla by running on Charybdis. On Mr. Mushet's plan of limiting the issue of paper to notes of Fifty pounds each, there would arise in the commercial world, a demand for gold greater, it is probable, by £50,000,000 than that which would exist were this country to conduct her internal transactions by a currency consisting principally of paper. This vast addition to the demand for gold would occasion a corresponding increase in the value of that metal; and this great rise in the value of the currency would show itself in a proportionate fall in the prices of commodities and of property. The public debt, and the pressure of taxation, would be increased in a fearful degree. Land would cease to be worth the charges upon it; and the soil, by one sweeping operation, would be transferred from the present proprietors to the moneyed Capitalist. The obligation to pay in gold sums borrowed in paper, would occasion a revolution in property more sudden and extensive than has hitherto been experienced in any country. Even after the metallic currency had been fully established, and after the value of gold has been raised in proportion to the increased demand, still an unfavourable foreign balance would occasionally occur, and, by diminishing the supply of the precious metals, would give to the currency a temporary rise in value even above the new and elevated level which it had attained. Hence, those who had escaped the pressure occasioned by the rise of the currency to the new and elevated level, would have to encounter other and more trying revulsions. With our existing debt and establishments, the introduction of a purely metallic currency is manifestly impossible. We cannot withdraw from circulation the paper of the National and Provincial Banks, and continue to pay an amount of taxation sufficient to enable us to preserve faith with the public Creditor. For the evils of our present monetary systems some other remedy must be sought.

5. *Mr. Ricardo's Plan for an economical and secure currency*

The plan of Mr. Ricardo, adopted by the Legislature as a temporary measure in 1819, consisted in making Bank Notes payable on demand, not in coin, but in Standard Gold bullion, at the Mint price of £3.17.10½ per oz :—60 ounces of such bullion being the smallest quantity which a Bank could be called upon to exchange for its paper at this price.

That which is most worthy of remark in this plan is, that it recognises, and in part adopts, the principle of making Bank paper not convertible on demand into the precious metals which it purports to represent. This principle, however, is applied in a manner not strictly equitable and impartial. When, in consequence of over-issue, or of an unfavourable foreign balance, an advantage arises from coverting paper into bullion, this advantage is confined to those persons who can command at one time 60 ounces of gold or £233, and is denied to the far more numerous class by which a sum so considerable is unattainable.

In periods of alarm and panic, the less opulent members of society would be exposed, under Mr. Ricardo's plan, to peculiar and extraordinary embarrassments. The holder of Bank paper to any amount under £233 could neither convert his notes into gold, nor offer them as a legal tender in discharge of his engagements. During any serious convulsion, bringing the ability of the Bank into real jeopardy, the rich might secure themselves by converting their paper into gold; while persons in moderate circumstances, legally deprived of such a resource, might be involved in ruin. As a check upon the tendency to an over-issue of paper, Mr. Ricardo's plan possesses some advantages over the existing system. While the currency is composed of coin, and of paper convertible on demand, any over-issue by the Banks depreciates both the paper and the coin; and as the bullion value of the latter becomes greater than its current value, it is melted or exported. Thus, for a considerable period, the metallic portion of the currency is displaced, as the paper portion is extended; and the excess of paper does not manifest itself until after the gold has disappeared and the Banks are called on to replace it. Under Mr. Ricardo's plan, on the contrary, there would be no coin in circulation, leaving space by its displacement for an over-issue of paper; and therefore such issue would immediately increase the amount of the circulating medium, and raise general prices. As the market price of bullion rose above the Mint price, the Banks would be called upon to pay it in exchange for their notes at the Mint price; and thus, before it could be carried to any very considerable extent, the excess of paper would be returned.

But if the plan of Mr. Ricardo would be more efficacious than the present, in promptly arresting over-issue, this advantage would be counter balanced, and perhaps more than counter-balanced by its greater tendency to produce a sudden contraction of the currency whenever over-issue, or an unfavourable foreign balance, occasioned an increased demand for the precious metals. The nature, nay, the express object, of Mr. Ricardo's plan is to establish an economical currency, by supporting a very large superstructure of convertible paper, upon a very small metallic base. This, as has been already stated, is the most precarious and dangerous position in which the currency of a country can be placed. Let us suppose, that in addition to the paper currency, there are £15,000,000 of gold coin in the channels of circulation, and £5,000,000 in the coffers of the Bank; and that the dealers in foreign bills require £2,000,000 for exportation. It is abundantly obvious, that this demand for exportation, supplied as it would be in a considerable degree from the general channels of circulation, would occasion a less drain upon the coffers of the Bank, that (*sic*) that which would occur were there no gold coins in circulation, and were the bullion-merchants in consequence to apply to the Bank for the £2,000,000 which they required. In the latter case, the Bank, to check the drain, and to recover its treasure, would be compelled to contract its issues more suddenly and more considerably than would be necessary in the former case.

Though not calculated without considerable modifications, and several additional provisions, for practical operation, Mr. Ricardo's plan is highly ingenious and original. It does not in its present form afford a remedy for the evils of a currency composed of coin and of paper convertible on demand; but inasmuch as it goes the length of partially limiting that convertibility, it must be regarded as an important approximation towards a better system.

STATEMENT of a PLAN for giving security and uniformity to a paper currency

Experience has established the fact, that a mixed currency, composed of coins, and of paper convertible on demand, exposes the trade of the country to ruinous revulsions. The establishment of a purely metallic currency is impracticable, unless accompanied by measures which would be equivalent to a declaration of national bankruptcy. Hence the all-important problem which the practical Statesman has to solve is how to impart security, steadiness, and uniformity to a pure paper currency.

In order to accomplish this most desirable object, it is necessary that three things should be done.

1. That means should be provided for indicating and checking excessive issue, at a more early stage of its progress than at present.
2. That redundancy, when it occasionally occurs, should be reduced, not by a sudden and unexpected contraction of the currency, and by extensive failures among the Banks of circulation; but by a safe and gradual process, foreseen and provided for.
3. That the currency, instead of being reduced in amount, and raised in value, as often as an unfavourable foreign balance causes an exportation of gold, should be so regulated, as to represent not the accidental maximum value, but the ordinary level value of the standard metal.

It will also be highly expedient, that in addition to these essential requisites, any plan for establishing a safe and uniform Paper Currency should secure to the public treasury the advantage arising from the issue of that portion of the paper which would supply the place of the metallic currency.

The following Plan is submitted as calculated to affect these important purposes.

1. It is proposed in the first place, that gold coin, charged with the same seignorage which is now charged upon the Silver coin, shall be the standard of the currency, and that any person taking to the Mint, gold bullion of standard fineness, shall receive upon demand the same weight of metal, less the seignorage, in the form of coin.

This seignorage is charged for the purpose of keeping in the channels of circulation an equable supply of metallic currency, by preventing the melting and exporting of the coin. Under this arrangement, either the value of paper currency must fall, or else that of bullion must rise upwards of 6 per Cent before a profit could be obtained by melting the coin, or by consigning it to balance an unfavourable foreign account.

In the proposed plan the seignorage is taken at $6\frac{14}{31}$ per cent, because that is the extent to which it is carried by the present regulations of the Mint, with respect to the silver coinage; and because it is desirable not to deviate unnecessarily from the established usage. Should it be deemed expedient to alter the existing seignorage, the principle upon which the alteration should proceed, is that of raising the seignorage until it approaches, without attaining, the limits at which the profits upon illicit coinage would be sufficient to cover the risks attending it.

A seignorage less than that which would afford a sufficient temptation to counterfeit the coin, could have no effect in lowering the value of the metallic currency, so long as this currency was not issued to excess. But while the Royal Mint possesses, as it always should, the exclusive privilege of manufacturing the Standard Coin, no over-issue would take place. Government would have an obvious interest in duly limiting the supply of coin; because by such limitation the Treasury realises a profit equal to the difference between the seignorage and the expence of coinage; while, by permitting an over-issue of the metallic currency, this profit would be lost. No person would carry bullion to the mint, if the coin which he obtained in return was not worth in the market at least the same quantity of metal which he had given for it; and if government purchased bullion upon its own account, and converted it into coin, the profit upon the transaction would be at its maximum, when the supply of coin was so adjusted, that the value of metal in the form of coin exceeded, by the exact amount of the seignorage, the value of metal in the form of bullion.

Government, indeed, by unduly limiting the supply, and raising the value of coin, might obtain a higher profit upon the purchase of bullion, were it not for the important and essential regulation permitting individuals to take bullion to the Mint, and to receive in coin the same weight of metal, less the seignorage.

2. Another provision in the proposed plan is, to render the Notes of the Bank of England, and of all the other Banks of circulation throughout the Kingdom payable *three months after demand*, in Standard bullion at the Mint price; which bullion shall be assayed and stamped at the Mint, and charged with a Seignorage of One per Cent.

It is impossible from the very nature of the Banking business, that Banks of circulation should be able to pay their promissory notes on demand. To enable them to do so, it would be necessary that they should retain in their coffers a Pound Sterling in the Standard metal for every Pound Sterling in the paper which they put into circulation. But, by this arrangement, the Interest lost upon the treasure retained, would equal the interest acquired upon the currency advanced; so that the banks of circulation, instead of being gainers would be losers, by all the expenses incident upon the issuing of their paper. The circulation of paper cannot be attended with a profit, unless the amount of it which is issued, exceed in a very considerable degree, that of the treasure which is reserved; and it is self-evident that a small sum in coin cannot pay on demand, a larger one in paper.

Bank paper payable upon demand carries a falsehood upon its face, and it might become a question how far the uttering of it involves a participation in that species of fraud of which a man is guilty, when he enters into engagements with the foreknowledge that he cannot make them good. It is not a little singular that Bank paper should have been so long permitted to form the main portion of our currency, without some method having been devised for giving it a greater degree of stability and uniformity than that which it can derive from being issued under an impossible and therefore an absurd and deceptive condition.

That Banks of circulation are extensively called upon to convert their paper into gold at those periods only, when an excess of currency, or an unfavourable foreign balance has caused gold to disappear. Enacting that Bank Notes shall be paid in Gold upon demand is the same thing as decreeing a periodical breaking of the Banks and destruction of that portion of the currency [which] consists of their paper. It is for the purpose of obviating these ruinous results, and of affording at the same time a sufficient check upon over-issue, that it is proposed to make Bank Notes payable in Gold *three months after demand*. In practice, this measure will be found to accomplish both these objects:—It will secure the Banks of circulation against those ruinous runs and panics which, from the very nature of their business, it would be otherwise impossible for them to support, and it will provide a more early and effectual check upon over-issue than that of convertibility into gold on demand.

The seignorage of One per Cent upon the ingots stamped at the Mint is imposed in order to replace the expence of manufacturing them, and to operate as a check upon a merely speculative demand for them. This seignorage will prevent the holders of paper from presenting it for acceptance payable in gold, so long as the currency retains its standard value; while it will render One per Cent the maximum, beyond which the difference between the value of paper and of gold cannot permanently extend.

3. In order to complete the plan, and to give to the circulating medium of the country the utmost possible security of which it is susceptible, it is farther proposed,—That the Provincial Banks shall pledge to the Mint securities for the amount of paper which they issue; and that the Provincial Paper, thus secured shall be payable at the Mint in the event of a stoppage of the Bank which issued it; The Mint indemnifying itself by the disposal of the pledged securities.

This part of the plan takes away the possibility of any future distress or inconvenience being experienced by the public in consequence of failures occurring among the Country Banks. The only objection which can be urged against requiring a deposit of securities from the Country Banks is, the impropriety of infringing on the freedom of trade by any interference on the part of the State in the disposal of the capital of persons conducting their own individual concerns. The answer to this objection is decisive. Uttering a portion of the circulating medium of the Country, is not a branch of trade, or an individual and a private concern:—it is essentially a branch of the Sovereign prerogative. Now, when this Sovereign prerogative is delegated to Bankers, nothing can be more reasonable and equitable,—nay, nothing can be more imperative upon the legislature, than that the permission to issue currency should be granted only under such regulations and pledges of property, as may be sufficient completely to secure the public against the risk of employing the paper of the Banks as a substitute for an indestructible medium provided by the state.

4 The last arrangement is, to substitute a Mint or Government paper, in the place of the Gold Coin required under the existing system. To effect this it is proposed that in future no gold coins shall be issued from the Mint above the value of Ten shillings each;—that, instead of the Sovereigns, or Twenty shilling pieces, now in circulation, the Mint shall utter notes of the denomination of One Pound and upwards, to the fixed amount of £25,000,000;—That these Mint Notes shall be a legal Tender;—and that they shall not be convertible into coin.

These regulations have a twofold object—Circulation and Revenue. They are intended to maintain a fixed and uniform amount of currency, always available for the purposes of internal trade;—to save to the Country the outlay of capital, and the annual expence required in maintaining a metallic medium;—and, to place in the Treasury, for the public service, the £25,000,000 issued by the Mint in lieu of Coin.

These very important advantages would be obtained without interfering with any existing interests. The currency of the United Kingdom amounts to from £65,000,000 to £70,000,000,—the metallic part being reckoned at £25,000,000. It is quite obvious that with-drawing the gold coin, and throwing into the channels of circulation an equal and fixed amount of Mint paper, would neither occasion an excess of currency, nor interfere with the present business of the Bank of England and Provincial Banks. Thus the substitution of Mint Notes for gold would be an unmixed good. It would put an end to those fluctuations in the supply of currency which are occasioned by the melting and exporting of the coin;—it would disengage for productive employment no inconsiderable amount of national capital,—it would save to the Country the annual expence estimated at above half a million, of maintaining the metallic currency;—and it would place £25,000,000 in the Treasury without interfering with the existing establishments, and without operating to the injury of any vested interest.

It cannot be denied, and it ought not to[1] be disguised, that there exists in the public mind a prejudice against the issuing of paper by the State. But this prejudice rests upon misconception; and cannot fail to disappear, as soon as the question is correctly stated.

If the state were to put out a paper currency it would possess the power of issuing to excess; and, on any financial emergency, might avail itself of this power, to depreciate the circulating medium to almost any extent. This is the objection;—let us see how it applies.

The State has at all times uttered the metallic Currency; it possesses the power of lowering the Standard; and it may on any emergency, avail itself of this power: and thus lower in an unlimited degree the value of the Pound Sterling.

These two cases are analogous, if not identical. The objection to a paper currency uttered by the State, applies in its full force to a metallic currency. In the former case it is possible that the value of the circulating medium may be lowered by excessive issue;—in the latter, it is equally possible that the same effect may be produced by lowering the standard. In either case, the State possesses the same power, and is under the same temptation to commit the fraud; and in the one, as well as in the other, would be withheld from committing it by the same commanding motives.

The value of a metallic currency is maintained by fixing the Standard;—the value of a paper currency, by limiting its quantity;—and an Act of the Legislature, fixing the amount of paper, is just as efficacious as an Act fixing the weight of the Coins.

In this Country, where the principles which regulate the value of Currency have been so well ascertained, no Minister would be so rash as to require, and no parliament would venture to authorise such an extension of the paper issued by The State, as would occasion depreciation, and be tantamount to lowering the value of money. If the amount of Mint Paper were limited by Law, we should have exactly the same security against its extension, which we now possess against the debasing of the Coin.

It is obvious, that The Treasury should have no power, either directly or indirectly, to cause under any circumstances an extension of Government paper beyond the fixed amount prescribed by the Legislature. The issuing of this paper therefore might be placed under the exclusive control of a Board of sworn Commissioners holding their appointments for life, and subject to removal by Parliament only in the event of misconduct being proved against them. This arrangement for disconnecting the Treasury with the issue of a Government Paper, is similar to that recommended by Mr. Ricardo.

[1] Inserted in original.

THE MANNER in which the Proposed Plan will operate

The first operation of the Plan which has been above detailed, would be that of giving the Banks of circulation, in the first beginning of excess, immediate and unequivocal warning to contract their issues.

When the Currency consists of coin, and of Bank paper convertible upon demand, an over-issue of paper, and a consequent depreciation of the Currency, may go on for a considerable period without being indicated by a rise in the market price of bullion. As the paper falls in value the gold which circulates with it falls in value also; and is worth more as bullion than as coin. The Coin is therefore converted into bullion, and as the supply of bullion in the home market is thus unusually increased, its value falls. Now, as an excess and depreciation of the currency have, under the existing system, the effect of lowering the value, not only of the coin, but of bullion, it is plain that loss of value or depreciation suffered by the currency cannot be shown to its full extent, by the increased price of bullion.

The low value of bullion in the home market will now cause it to be exported; and this, by diminishing the supply, will cause its value to re-ascend. But even when this process has taken place, the loss of value suffered by the currency will not appear in the price of bullion; because the Bill Brokers and Merchants, who can now obtain a profit by the exportation of the metals, will not pay a high market price for them, so long as they can obtain them in exchange for Bank paper at the Mint price. Hence the first notice of an excess of currency which the Banks of circulation receive, is by a run upon their coffers.

The greater the proportion which the Coin bore to the paper, the longer the excess and depreciation would go on, before the run upon the Banks commenced; because the more coin there was to be displaced, the larger would be the supply of bullion in the home market, and the more considerable might be the exportation of it, before recourse was had to the coffers of the Banks. It is probable, however, that the evil, by being thus postponed, would be increased. If the public had been accustomed to see only a small amount of coin in circulation, the abstraction would excite little anxiety; while, if the metals were employed to a considerable extent in the ordinary transactions of trade, their disappearance might create alarm, and convert a partial run upon the Banks into a general panic in the money market.

Under the regulations which have been proposed, very different consequences would ensue. An excessive issue of paper, and consequent fall in the value of currency, would immediately show themselves in the advancing price of bullion. As there would be little coin in circulation, and as that little would be charged with a seignorage of $6\frac{14}{31}$ per Cent, it would not be displaced and melted so as to increase the supply and lower the value of bullion in the home market, and thus prevent the rise in its price from corresponding with the fall in the value of the currency. Neither would a rise in the market price of bullion be prevented by the power of obtaining Gold upon demand at the Mint Price. By the proposed System this power is not given. As Paper was uttered in excess the rise in the Market price of bullion would be in exact proportion to the fall in the value of currency and the Banks and the public would have timely and ample warning not only of the existence but of the extent of the evil.

Another advantage of the proposed arrangements is that they would limit both the degree and the duration of excess. This indeed is the natural and necessary consequence of the early and unequivocal intimation of its existence which they would convey. Under the existing system it is difficult to determine to what extent or for what period over issue and depreciation may go on. During the process by which Coin is displaced and the value of Bullion in the home Market depressed a rise in the price not of bullion but of other commodities in general is the only symptom of redundant currency which is exhibited. But a rise in the price of commodities in general cannot always be ascertained;—the extent of such rise never. Amid the fluctuations of demand and supply which are constantly occurring in the Market some articles rise and some fall while others remain stationary. If those which have risen in price are referred to as proving that the currency has fallen in value those which have fallen may be sighted to shew that it has risen, while those which remain stationary in price may be brought forward to establish the fact that the value of the currency has not varied. Amid such equivocal and contradictory appearances while all the Banks of circulation have an obvious interest in keeping out as much paper as possible; and while none of them can have any accurate knowledge as to the amount of currency which the demands of commerce can permanently retain in circulation it is impossible to ascertain how far and how long during a period of high confidence excessive issue and depreciation may go on. Their ultimate limits are attained only when gold has disappeared from the Channels of Circulation and when confidence begins to be changed into panic.

Very different would be the effects of the proposed System. The rise in the Market price of Bullion would immediately announce to the Banks that they had begun to issue to excess; and the extent of this rise would demonstrate the degree of depreciation. If notwithstanding this warning the excess went on until the market price of gold exceeded the Mint price by more than One per Cent (the amount of the Seignorage on the Mint bars) then the paper of the Banks would be presented in order to be accepted as payable in Gold and thus these Establishments would be distinctly informed that if they did not within three Months contract their issues they would be exposed to inevitable loss. Thus forewarned the Banks for their own security would withdraw a portion of their paper and thereby enhance the value of the Currency until the difference between the Mint and the Market price of gold did not exceed the charge of One per Cent for Seignorage.

This part of the subject is so important that it may be allowed to shew by an example the practical working of the proposed arrangements in arresting the progress of excessive issue. Let it be supposed that the Banks of Circulation inattentive to the indications of excess go on extending their issues until the Market price of gold exceeds the Mint price by Two per Cent. In this Case the Mint ingots notwithstanding the deduction of One per Cent for the Seignorage would be more valuable in the Market by One per Cent than Bank paper. The holders of Bank paper therefore in the expectation of realising this One per Cent would present their Notes for acceptance payable in ingots. Under these circumstances the Banks would have the alternative either of buying Bullion at the Market Price and exchanging it for their Notes at the Mint Price whereby they would lose Two per Cent every three Months upon all the paper they put into circulation; or of contracting their issues until the Market price of Bullion fell to the Mint price by which means they would pay without loss whatever Notes were presented.

It is impossible to suppose that the Banks of Circulation would hesitate to adopt the latter course. By pursuing the former they would render the issuing of paper a decidedly losing concern. Advancing their Notes in discounts at the rate of 5 per Cent per Annum and having them returned with a loss of 2 per Cent every three months or 8 per Cent per Annum, the Banks of Circulation on balancing these transactions would suffer a loss of 3 per Cent per Annum upon the whole amount of paper which they kept in circulation.

To maintain that business would be managed in this way, is to affirm that the Banks of Circulation are conducted by persons labouring under the influence of Insanity. There exists the highest degree of moral certainty that under the arrangement proposed the currency could not even for the short period of three months suffer a depreciation amounting to Two Per Cent.

A third advantage of this System is that it would keep the currency near to the ordinary level of gold and prevent it from participating in those extraordinary and occasional elevations of its value to which that metal, as an Article of Commerce and an object of speculation is liable.—Where our debts to foreign Countries exceed our credits upon them in such a proportion that the premium paid for a Foreign bill exceeds the expence of transmitting gold then an increased demand for the metal is created while its exportation diminishes the supply. This imparts to gold an extraordinary value which must necessarily be communicated to a paper Currency convertible upon demand into bullion of Standard weight. Nay the extraordinary rise in the value of an immediately convertible currency will exceed the extraordinary rise in the value of gold; because Bank Directors cannot ascertain the precise degree in which their issues should be contracted in order to arrest the run upon their Coffers and because they have an obvious interest in limiting the supply and enhancing the value of Currency until the Market price of gold falling below the Mint price, enables them to replace upon advantageous terms the treasure they may have lost.

This extraordinary enhancement in the value of Currency is effectually prevented by making Bank Notes payable Three months after demand in Stamped Bullion from which a Seignorage of One per Cent is deducted. In the first place the deduction of the Seignorage would prevent the Mint ingots from being demanded in exchange for Bank paper until the premium upon foreign bills exceeded the expence of transmitting gold by more than One per Cent. But during the period that the Exchange was falling from par to this point, the increasing premium upon foreign Bills would operate as a Bounty upon export and as a duty upon import and would thus go on liquidating the unfavourable foreign balance before any drain upon the Banks or contraction of the Currency could commence.

In the second place if the encouragement to export and the Check upon import during the period that the premium upon foreign Bills was rising from par to more than one per Cent above the cost of transmitting gold was insufficient to liquidate the unfavourable foreign balance and if in consequence Bank Paper were sent in to be accepted payable in Mint ingots a period of three Months must still elapse before the drain upon the Banks for gold could actually commence. During the whole of this period a more than ordinary export and a less than ordinary import would operate in balancing the unfavourable account. Except upon some very extraordinary occasion the exchanges would be restored in this way, and· before the gold for which the Banks had accepted could be withdrawn from their Coffers.

After their Notes began to come for Acceptance the Banks would as a necessary precaution diminish the supply of paper; and this would have the effect of raising its value. The rise in the value of currency, however, would be considerably less than the rise in the value of Gold. It is obvious that an ingot issued by the Mint for an hundred ounces of gold, would, in consequence of the Seignorage deducted from its weight be worth less by One per Cent than 100 Oz: of equal fineness. It is equally obvious that under an unfavourable foreign balance Bank Paper payable in Mint ingots Three Months after demand would be of less value than such Ingots. These ingots are in demand because the exchanges are so unfavourable that the premium on a foreign Bill exceeds by more than One per Cent the cost of transmitting the metal; and thus enables the Bullion Merchant to obtain a profit from receiving 99 Oz of gold at the Mint price of 100 Oz and consigning it to his Foreign Correspondent in order to draw against it. By the possession of ingots he is able to realise this profit on the instant;—by the possession of Bank Paper payable three Months after demand, he could not realise it before the expiration of that period. Inasmuch therefore as an immediate and certain profit is preferable to a profit deferred for three Months and contingent on the exchanges remaining unfavourable the rise in the value of the ingots would be greater than the rise in the value of the Currency.

From all these considerations it must be abundantly apparent that were Bank Paper made payable three Months after demand in ingots lowered by a Seignorage of One per Cent an unfavourable foreign balance and course of Exchange could have only a very trifling effect in raising the value of the Currency above the ordinary level of the Standard Metal. The rise in the value of the currency, which rendered this inconsiderable would be brought about not in the sudden way in which it would occur were Bank Paper payable on demand in metal of Standard weight but by a process the most gradual and easy;—the Directors of the Banks of circulation being under no immediate alarm for the safety of their treasure and proceeding cautiously and without precipitation to contract their issues so as just to avert the drain which would otherwise occur when their acceptances payable in gold became due.

A rise in the Market price of bullion may as we have seen be occasioned either by over issue lowering the value of the currency or by an unfavourable foreign Balance raising the value of the metals. If the effect were produced by a fall in the value of money there would be a rise in the prices of commodities in general; if it were produced by a rise in the value of the metals, then, as the currency would, in a moderate degree partake in this rise the high market price of Bullion would be accompanied with some decline in the prices of other things.

But from whichever cause the rise in the market price of gold might proceed, the Banks when the rise exceeded One per Cent would be equally called upon to contract their issues. In either case, too, the contraction would be effected in a manner so cautious and gradual as would prevent reaction and recoil. Not being under the necessity of protecting their establishments by instantaneously arresting an unexpected run, the Directors of Banks would no longer be impelled to withdraw their paper to a greater extent than the occasion required and thus to enhance the currency until by a sudden transition the Market price of bullion fell below the Mint price.

Though it might be the interest of Banks to contract their issues beyond what the occasion required in order to reduce the Market price of Bullion below the Mint price and to replace upon favourable terms any portion of their treasure which might have been withdrawn during a period of excess or of unfavourable foreign balance, yet they could not accomplish this object so long as the Mint adhered to the regulation of issuing the Coinage on demand. For as soon as the supply of currency was so reduced that the Market price of bullion fell below the Mint price, the amount of coin which the Mint gave for any quantity of bullion, would be worth more than that bullion and individuals would have an interest in carrying Bullion to the Mint in exchange for coin until the supply if [*sic*] currency was so increased that the Market price of the Metals rose to their Mint price.

Thus then it appears after the fullest examination that the arrangements which have been proposed in this paper would be followed by consequences most important and beneficial. They would act so as instantaneously to reduce excess and supply deficiency. Under their operation, the fluctuations in the value of the currency would be limited to a range of from One per Cent below, to One per Cent above the ordinary level of gold.

Besides securing an almost uniform supply of currency and keeping it nearly at par with the ordinary level value of gold, the proposed arrangement would in all future times secure the Country against a recurrence of the calamaties incident upon the stoppage of the Provincial Banks of circulation. The utmost inconvenience to which the failure of a Country Bank would expose the holders of its Promissory Notes would be the very trifling one of sending them up to the Mint for payment.

To these great and permanent advantages of the proposed plan are to be added the incidental but in the present circumstances of the Country highly important benefits of disengaging for productive occupation a dormant Capital of £25,000,000,—of saving to the country the expence (amounting annually as it is estimated, to above half a Million) of maintaining the present Metallic Currency;—and of placing at the immediate disposal of The Treasury the Sum of Twenty five Millions.*

In considering the above plan it should not be lost sight of that the issuing of a Government paper in lieu of the gold coin is to be regarded as a measure of finance rather than as an essential part of the regulations for giving uniformity and security to the circulation. These two parts of the proposed plan are altogether distinct from and independent of each other. Imposing a seignorage upon the Standard Coin;—rendering paper payable in Bullion three Months after demand;—and requiring adequate pledges of property from the Provincial Banks,—are measures which would of themselves impart to the circulating medium all the steadiness and stability of which it is susceptible. These essential arrangements might be adopted though the incidental provision for issuing a Government Paper should be rejected. The only thing insisted upon is that the uniformity and security of the currency would be in no way endangered by the issue of paper to a fixed amount under the authority of Parliament which [*sic*] at the present juncture such issue would be productive of important advantages.

* On the expiration of the Charter of the Bank of England the State might issue paper to an amount sufficient not only to occupy the Channels from which Coin would be displaced but also to supply as the Bank now does the currency of the Metropolis. The fixed amount of Mint Paper might then be raised to £45,000,000 or £50,000,000, and a large additional sum would thus be placed at the disposal of the Treasury.

. . . .

P.S.—It may be allowable to make one additional remark. It is a well authenticated fact that since the commencement of the struggle for independence, the annual supply of the precious metals from the Mines of South America has been very considerably diminished.—If further experience should prove that this diminution is the effect not of temporary but of permanent causes there will be a gradual enhancement of the value of money throughout the Commercial World; and policy and equity may both require particularly in Countries which have accumulated a considerable debt that the Standard of Currency should be readjusted.

[2]

6. The Macroeconomics of Thomas Joplin*

Denis O'Brien

INTRODUCTION

Thomas Joplin was born probably about 1790 in Newcastle – although this belief is based upon the age claimed by Joplin in late life; an extensive search of the records in both Durham and Newcastle has failed to reveal any record of his birth.[1] The family were timber merchants, hailing originally from a village called Satley, 15 miles south-west of Newcastle upon Tyne. Perhaps because the timber in the area of Satley was becoming exhausted, the Joplins seem to have transferred their business to Newcastle where both Thomas Joplin and his father were timber merchants.[2] A call upon him to act as a guarantor for a bank in financial difficulties turned his attention to the subject of banking, and the result was his essay 'On the General Principles and Present Practice of Banking' which first appeared in 1822. This work, which went through many subsequent editions, acted as the flagship for Joplin's campaign to break the monopoly of joint-stock banking enjoyed by the Bank of England, so as to permit the establishment of such banks in England and Wales. (The Scots already enjoyed the advantages of this form of banking organization, and Joplin repeatedly extolled the virtues of their system.)

Joplin's attention having become fully engaged by the question of banking, it was natural that he should have broadened his enquiry to more general economic matters, and especially to the regulation of the money supply. The initial outcome of this was his *Outlines of a System of Political Economy* which appeared in 1823. It was at this very early stage, several years before the idea became general, that Joplin put forward the basic principle that a mixed currency of metal and paper should fluctuate in amount exactly as an identically circumstanced fully metallic currency would have done. This idea was to become the cornerstone of the Currency School position in the 1830s.[3] However Joplin – throughout his life very much an outsider – was to find himself in sharp disagreement with the Currency School. For whereas the Currency School believed that the Bank of England note issue was central to the money supply and the country banks merely a disequilibrating force, Joplin developed a macroeconomic model designed to show how disequilibrium would occur constantly if the national money supply had *two* unco-ordinated sources, as he believed it had.

The remainder of Joplin's career involved battling on both these fronts. On the one hand he fought long and hard, and ultimately successfully, to establish joint-stock banking. The British commercial bank system that exists today is, to a quite extraordinary extent, the legacy of his efforts.[4] Secondly, he put forward a plan for reform of the British monetary system so as to make it *unicentral*, so that the principle of 'metallic fluctuation' could safely be applied to the regulation of the *national* money supply. In this latter effort he was largely unsuccessful. The Currency School recommendations framed the Bank Charter Act of 1844, which focused almost entirely upon the note issue of the Bank of England, and did nothing to regulate the issues of the country banks beyond placing an overall ceiling on the issues of each bank and aiming at the ultimate extinction of those issues. In the short term such an approach, as Joplin correctly foresaw, could produce only financial crisis.[5]

In the course of his efforts to establish joint-stock banks, Joplin succeeded in establishing not one but two important banks, and was involved with a number of minor ones. In 1824 he established the Provincial Bank of Ireland, a joint-stock bank operating with branches; and in 1833, after prolonged efforts, and with the help of his cousin George Fife Angas, the pioneer of South Australia, he established the National Provincial Bank of England.[6]

But Joplin seems to have been incapable of sustaining a working relationship for any length of time. He was, it is evident from his writings, an extremely abrasive individual. In addition to this he was, as a North-Easterner, very much an outsider in the City of London circles. For reasons that are not entirely clear, he left the Provincial Bank of Ireland, of which he was the Secretary, within two years of its foundation; and, after a prolonged – and exceedingly public – row over the question of whether branches should have local shareholders, he left the National Provincial Bank of England, again within two years of foundation.

Possibly as a result of these conflicts, his health broke down and he seems to have been a sick man from at least the mid-1830s until his death in 1847. Moreover his prolonged conflicts with banks with which he was associated, including the London and County Bank, resulted in his being driven from these organizations with little or no financial compensation. He was in fact, especially after various unsuccessful business ventures in the late 1830s, living in some poverty in Gravesend in Kent. None the less, apparently undaunted by life's rebuffs, he continued to write on macroeconomics, fiercely resisting the proposals which became the Bank Act of 1844, and he also engaged in a campaign to attack the organization of prostitution, seeking as an ally in this the somewhat unlikely figure of Henry Brougham.[7]

It is clear from a rather pathetic appeal for money which appeared in the *Banker's Magazine* of 1846,[8] that Joplin was in considerable financial and personal difficulties and felt, not unreasonably, that the joint-stock banks, by now prosperous organizations, owed him some recognition. This he did not receive – indeed they seem to have been determined to forget about Joplin as quickly as possible, for there is no mention of him at all in the six volumes of Gilbart's works. This is highly significant given Gilbart's position both as a leading joint-stock banker (and one-time associate of Joplin's in the Irish enterprise) and as a leading writer on banking. Joplin died while making a second attempt to secure a remedy for his health problems at a continental spa in April 1847.[9]

Joplin's work has received extraordinarily little attention, which is all the more surprising given the sheer quantity which he wrote and also the intellectual vigour of his contribution. In the limited space available here, all that can be done is to attempt to outline the macroeconomic model to which Joplin adhered consistently, and which turns out to be, at least in some respects, significantly superior to what was on offer from the famous names in the Currency and Banking Schools.

OUTPUT AND EXPENDITURE

The starting-point for Joplin's approach to macroeconomic problems was the annual income of a country. The equality of expenditure with income was the basic equilibrium condition which Joplin called the 'Fulcrum of the Argument'.[10] This equilibrium condition is indeed a key factor in understanding Joplin's macroeconomics. In terms of later classifications, the approach which he based upon this is closer to Keynes than to Wicksell.

Income received from productive activity was expended on consumption and investment or (a quantitatively insignificant possibility) it was hoarded. Demand for loans included not only investment in productive capacity and in stocks but also consumption borrowing. If the capital market were allowed to clear through variation in the rate of interest, consumption borrowing plus investment borrowing should equal savings.[11]

In an open economy expenditure equalled output plus net imports. A balance of payments surplus resulted in aggregate demand being greater than aggregate supply at the existing price level. This excess aggregate demand raised producer incomes, output and the price level.[12]

A balance of payments surplus raised aggregate demand by raising the money supply. The level of aggregate demand depended upon the money supply and its velocity. Velocity of circulation was not, however, fixed. The demand for money could vary. It was a function of the level of income and of the rate of interest. Joplin viewed the demand for balances as being negatively related to the rate of interest. He calculated that the interest elasticity of demand for consumption balances was slightly greater than minus one. He gives no calculation for the interest elasticity of financial balances but is clear that a fall in the rate of interest, and the concomitant rise in property values, would involve the holding of greater balances for transactions in property.

At equilibrium levels of income the demand for balances was proportional to the level of income. However, out of equilibrium it was possible for balances to fall, and velocity to rise, with an upsurge in activity.[13]

JOPLIN'S MACROECONOMIC MODEL

Joplin's macroeconomic model is framed in terms of the concept of a circular flow of income around the system. It thus rests upon the 'Fulcrum of the Argument':

> The demand for labour in money determines the amount of money which the labouring class have to give for corn, and what they have to give the farmer gets. It moves in a circle, consumption is promoted at the price which the corn produces, and the corn produces the price at which its consumption is promoted. (Joplin 1828: 76)

It is upon this basis that Joplin was to explore the way in which monetary arrangements could dislocate the circular flow, resulting in a fall in national income and the emergence of unemployment.

Aggregate demand depends upon the money supply.[14] Changes in the level of aggregate demand, produced by changes in the money supply, will have multiple effects on the level of income. Joplin provided possibly the earliest clear statement of the existence of a multiplier:

> Income, however, once generated, will multiply itself in its progress, and pass through many hands before it is finally expended in a demand for that produce which gave it birth. (Joplin 1828: 71)

The price level depended upon the demand for tradeables – what Joplin called the 'consumptive circulation' in contrast to the 'abstract circulation' which was employed in financial transactions. An increase in the money supply increased aggregate demand. Merchants would then increase the size of their stocks, and the transmission of this demand to producers would increase employment. Increased employment would result in increased consumption. Since supply was less than perfectly elastic, increased output implied increased prices. (There are clear similarities here with the work of Hawtrey, and with some of that of Keynes.) Thus a rise in money income involved a rise in real income *and* a rise in prices.[15]

The money supply, and thus aggregate demand, were necessarily linked to the balance of payments. There was an equilibrium level of national prices at which payments would balance. A rise in the price level above that national equilibrium level would lower exports, and increase imports, with the resulting balance of payments deficit lowering the money supply again.[16]

While a rise in the money supply produced a rise in money income, a contraction in the money supply would result in a movement in the opposite direction. Wages and working hours would fall, labour income and profits would decline, and the consequent reduction in the desired level of merchants' stocks would feed back to producers as reduced demand for output, resulting in the emergence of unemployment. Reductions in the money supply, if accompanied by a rise in the rate of interest, also raised the cost of stock holding, thus further reducing the desired level of stocks. Stocks were thus an extremely important part of the mechanism by which monetary disturbance was transmitted.[17]

Even more important, however, was the role of the labour market. An increase in the demand for labour increased the demand for commodities, especially food, with a consequent rise in prices. In Joplin's view expenditure *on* labour was itself the determinant of the expenditure *by* labour which in turn determined the price of foodstuffs.[18]

The direct conclusion from this model – in strong contrast to most classical writing – was that if depression existed this was due to a lack of aggregate demand. In the early 1820s Joplin pointed both to monetary causes and to reductions in government expenditure as responsible for the reduction in aggregate demand which produced unemployment and depression. He was not talking about aggregate demand failure of the capital-stock adjustment kind associated with Lauderdale and Malthus, but with aggregate demand failure which was a result of monetary, and to some extent fiscal, mismanagement.[19]

If aggregate demand fell, the first output market to be affected was that of agriculture. Agricultural prices fell. Since farmers faced fixed charges this resulted in, at best, depression of agricultural profits and, at worst, bankruptcy. Joplin laid particular stress upon the importance of fixed charges in agriculture and was a life-long defender of the Corn Laws, considering that a 60-shilling price of corn was a desirable target, given the level of agricultural fixed charges.[20]

In all this it is striking to note that Joplin considered the possibility that the circular flow of income and expenditure could be equilibrated at various levels. In other words, monetary contraction could result in an income level which was stable but with unemployment existing. To move from a lower to a higher level, 'pump priming' was necessary. Changes in aggregate demand altered not only the price level, but also national income and employment. It was also true that changes in national income affected the balance of payments; a fall in national income, with a rise in unemployment, would reduce expenditure and thus the demand for imports. However it was possible for the lower level of national income to be an equilibrium one in relation to the balance of payments, because a reduction in British imports would affect the foreign level of money income and thus the demand for British exports.[21]

A model of this kind clearly involves a positively sloped aggregate supply schedule. This seems to have been exactly what Joplin envisaged. An increase in aggregate demand would initially result in an increase in employment at the old wage rate. However the expenditure of the extra wages thus earned would lead to a rise in prices, which would lead in turn to increased agricultural output, profits and investment. Wages were sticky, and would move upwards after the rise in food prices.[22]

Thus an increase in aggregate demand, as a result of an increase in the money supply, would produce an expansion of aggregate supply. Joplin expected that this would occur not only because of a higher participation rate but also because of an increased supply of labour from the existing labour force. (Joplin refers to few other economists, and those mostly in a negative way, but in this context he acknowledged the work of Hume.[23])

However, the effects of an increase in the money supply in increasing aggregate demand were lagged. Joplin believed that the lag between an increase in the money supply and an increase in aggregate demand was as much as twelve months. But through its effects on aggregate demand, a change in the money supply affected stocks, employment, imports and exports, the exchange rate and the price level.[24]

In all this, perhaps the most striking thing is the extent to which Joplin emphasized the importance of unemployment. Amongst his contemporaries, perhaps only Thomas Attwood paid so much attention to this. The essential point which Joplin emphasized was that a defective paper currency, leading either directly or through a balance of payments deficit to monetary contraction, would result in unemployment.[25]

PROBLEMS OF A PAPER CURRENCY

Such monetary changes would arise if a currency which was wholly, or partly, a paper currency did not behave as an identically circumstanced metallic currency would have done. But this general principle extended far beyond the familiar Currency School prescription that it should do so in relation to the balance of payments. Joplin's view was much more comprehensive. He argued that, while a metallic currency would maintain the circular flow which was necessary for macroeconomic equilibrium, the creation and destruction of paper money broke the circular flow. Most critically, a paper currency allowed a banker to lend money which had not first been saved, thus breaking the link between savings and investment.[26] As Joplin put it:

> [I]t may easily be conceived, that without the aid of a proper currency, to assist in keeping the income and expenditure upon a par with each other, the expenditure must at all times have a tendency either to exceed or fall short of the income. (1844a: 27)

Because of the fundamentally faulty mechanisms governing the supply of paper currency (which will be explored further below) the country experienced constant monetary disequilibrium. The changes in the money supply, both directly and through their effect upon flows across the exchanges, resulted in constant changes in aggregate demand and thus in real income.[27]

Joplin's concerns over the mechanisms for varying the supply of money involved several considerations. First, there was the fundamental problem that there were two sources for the money supply, that these were unco-ordinated, and that the most important source (the country banks) was largely unresponsive to the balance of payments. Secondly, there was the problem that what links there were between the country money supply and the London money supply were actually disequilibrating. Thirdly, the nature of the market for loanable funds in the country produced random changes in the money supply.

However, before turning to these problems it is necessary to address one very fundamental distinction concerning the nature of the money supply which Joplin made. This distinction was between the 'abstract circulation' and the 'consumptive circulation', which has been touched on already. The abstract circulation was employed in the exchange of property and financial assets. Such exchange took place, for the most part, in London, and employed the very large denomination Bank of England notes as well as bank deposits. Joplin estimated that half of Bank of England notes were used in this way.

The 'consumptive circulation' was that money employed for expenditure upon consumption goods – principally tradeables. Joplin identified this with the country bank-notes, nine tenths of which were for denominations of less than £20. Although the *total* of Bank of England notes was approximately the same as that of country bank-notes, their velocity was, he estimated, only a quarter of that of the country bank-notes, and so aggregate demand, and hence the national price level, were mainly dependent upon the country bank-note supply. The country bank-note issue was thus the key to monetary equilibrium.[28]

Joplin supported this line of argument not only by reference to population distribution, roughly adjusted for higher consumption per head in London (and Lancashire) – this was the basis of his velocity estimate – but also on the basis of price series for wheat (as representing the general price level) and changes in the supply of bank-notes from London and the country.[29]

Such an approach is in dramatic contrast to the main nineteenth-century monetary writings which placed the issues of the Bank of England at centre stage. For Joplin it was the country banks and their notes which mattered. But if, in turn, there were problems over the determination of the supply of these notes, this had serious implications for the national money supply.

COUNTRY BANKS AND THEIR NOTES

While Joplin recognized that the issues of country bank-notes could be constrained both by relative inter-regional prices and by reserve losses, he concentrated his attention upon the effects of variations in the demand for, and supply of, loanable funds on these issues. The argument was this. The country banks, operating under a paper currency issued at will by bankers, could not know what the equilibrium rate of interest was. In such a state of ignorance, the country banks found it necessary to hold their minimum lending rate at around 5 per cent and to allow the loan market to clear by varying the supply of bank-notes rather than by allowing the rate of interest to clear it. An increased demand for loans would result in the country in an increase in lending. It was the money supply, rather than the rate of interest, which fluctuated in order to clear the market for loanable funds.[30]

What Joplin had in mind is shown in Figure 6.1. In this particular case a shift in the demand for loanable funds, with a given supply of savings, produces a change in the money supply; but equally, a shift in the savings function with a given demand for loans would have a similar effect.[31]

The basic problem, as already indicated, was that without a metallic currency, *or* a paper currency which exactly simulated a metallic currency, there was no way that the country banks could know the equilibrium rate of interest and so, from considerations of safety, they kept their lending rate at the maximum of 5 per cent allowed by the Usury Laws.[32]

> But with a paper currency, issued at pleasure by a great many bankers, all ignorant of the amount of each others issues, the savings of income can never be distinguished. . . . a banker can never know whether his own notes on hand, represent income which has been saved or not; he, consequently, can never know the real value of capital [the market clearing rate of interest], and is compelled to deal with his customers at one fixed rate of interest. (1826: 38–9)

Figure 6.1

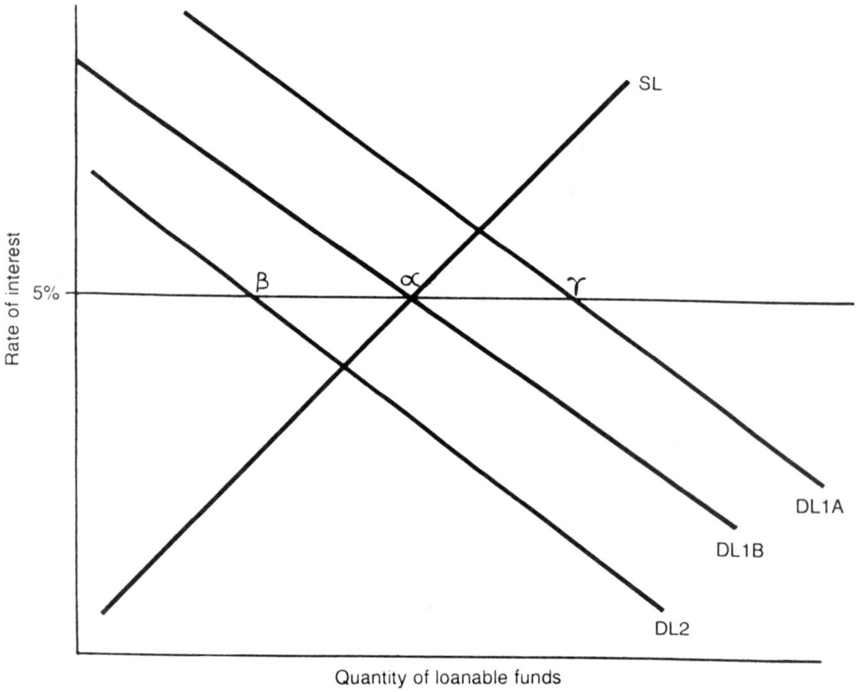

Suppose that, at α, the 5 per cent maximum interest allowed under the Usury Laws clears the loan market at the intersection of SL and DL1B. A shift of DL to DL2, with the rate of interest *fixed* at 5 per cent will result in net money destruction of $\alpha - \beta$, the amount by which money saved at 5 per cent exceeds money invested. If the initial demand for loans had been DL1A, there would have been net money creation per period of $\gamma - \alpha$. A shift from DL1A to DL2 would thus involve a switch from monetary expansion to monetary contraction.

The contrast with a metallic currency was fundamental.

> With a metallic currency, on the contrary, the Banker would always know the state of the market. In the first place, he could not lend money until it had been saved and placed in his hands, and he would have a particular amount to lend. On the other hand, he would have more or fewer persons wanting to borrow, and in proportion as the demand would exceed, or fall short of the amount he had to lend, he would raise or lower his terms. (1832: 109)

It was true that, *within* the domestic banking system, over-issue by an individual bank, or even by banks in a region acting together, would encounter clearing pressures in the form of a demand for bills on London. But if there were expansion by *all* the country banks – which could easily happen if the country as a whole experienced similar variations in the demand for funds – then significant changes in the money supply and aggregate demand would take place, and any correction resulting from an adverse balance of payments (or from a balance of payments surplus if there had been monetary contraction) would be long delayed.[33]

The reason for the delay was two-fold. First, there was a significant lag between expansion of the money supply and a change in the national level of prices and output – Joplin put this at about 12 months. Secondly and most fundamentally, Joplin held that the country bank-note issue would in any case fail to respond in the way in which it ought to have done (if equilibrium were to be achieved) to monetary flows over the balance of payments. He was quite clear that the data showed that the country bank-note supply did not move in the same direction as metallic flows across the exchanges. Rather, it acted independently and not infrequently moved in the opposite direction. In particular he pointed out that exportation of gold in 1824–5 was accompanied by an increase in the supply of country bank-notes, which he attributed to increased demand for loans. Conversely, the assets of the country banks in London increased by more than £10 million in 1818 to 1822 (which, as we shall see, indicated that there had been a significant gold inflow); yet over the same period the country bank-note issue *fell* by £10 million.[34]

To some extent, this perverse behaviour was inbuilt. Thus, when harvest failure led to corn imports and a balance of payments deficit, the money supply should have contracted. But because of increased demand for bank lending *resulting from* the harvest failure, the money supply increased instead.[35]

Although Joplin was, as we shall see, prepared to afford considerable importance to the role of deposits in the *London* money market, the focus of his attention in the country was on notes rather than deposits. The reasoning here was that the prices of commodities were influenced by the expenditure of notes rather than by that of deposits subject to cheque. But in the London money market things were different.[36]

THE LONDON MONEY MARKET

In contrast to the loan market in which the country banks operated, the rate of interest in London fluctuated with alterations in the supply of, and demand for, loans, and thus cleared the market. Even the Bank of England, as the sole supplier of paper currency in London, effectively varied its rate of interest, through altering the terms on which it would buy exchequer bills, even though it appeared to be holding Bank Rate fixed.[37]

But this market was disturbed by the fact that it bore the brunt of all flows across the exchanges initiated by changes in the money supply produced by the behaviour of the country banks. In Joplin's view, the London money market, as essentially a market for savings, should not be affected by flows across the exchanges which related to national income rather than to capital transactions. But the existing monetary system diverted flows of national income across the exchanges to flow through the London money market.[38]

The source of the problem was essentially that international balances were settled in precious metals but that, within the domestic monetary system, there were parallel, and competing, sources of metal substitutes.

There were three aspects to this. First, there was the problem that all imported gold ended up in London. Secondly, there was the related fact that the country bank reserves were held in London. Thirdly – and for Joplin this was the most crucial matter of all – one importation of gold produced a *double* effect upon the money supply, adding an equal amount of country bank-notes and of money in London.

The gold ultimately ended in London because a country banker would buy it with his own notes and then send it to London either for purchasing gilt-edged securities or as a deposit at call. Alternatively, a merchant receiving gold would dispose of the gold in London, receiving in exchange a bill on the London agent which would be sold to the country banks in exchange for their notes. In strong contrast to the case of a metallic currency which would simply pass through London, the gold was detained there.[39]

The practice of the country banks in holding reserves as interest-bearing deposits in London, rather than holding gold, was central to this argument. It in turn led to the process by which a gold inflow not only affected the country bank-note supply, in the ways already seen, but also increased the availability of funds in London. This was the 'doubling' argument. Joplin put forward this line of reasoning from the 1820s. As the debates leading to the Bank Act of 1844 intensified, Joplin restated the argument with increased emphasis:[40]

> In short, on an importation and exportation of the precious metals, a double issue and double contraction takes place: one in the country and one in London; and the issue and contraction in London being illegitimate and unnatural, and such as would not take place with a metallic currency, produces those evils under which we have so long suffered. (1841: 13)

Three years later, as the Act loomed, Joplin wrote:

> The bullion received from abroad, being purchased up by the country bankers, is not only put into circulation in London where it has no business to be at all, but this is done by its being lent out at interest, as if it were money saved out of income. (1844a: 35)

It is important to appreciate that Joplin's argument here did not rely upon deposit multiplication within the London money market. He was simply arguing that an inflow of funds produced, in that market, extra deposits directly. This was buttressed by the idea that a London bank holding the country bank reserves would present the gold to the Bank of England which would issue notes, thus producing extra liquidity in the London market. But at a late stage in the argument Joplin added – probably under the influence of Torrens's supplement to his *Letter to Lord Melbourne* – an explanation of the mechanism of the deposit multiplier. He presented, in fact, what is now the standard explanation in textbooks (probably derived by Torrens himself from Pennington) of the geometric series resulting from the practice of lending on the basis of a fractional reserve system, and estimated that the deposit multiplier was around 6·7.[41]

But this was an important further development because Joplin was quite clear that most transactions in London were by cheque so that 'a transferable deposit and a bank note are equally money' (1844a: 39) – indeed cheques on deposits were 'the chief mode of payment in commercial transactions' (1841: 10).

But the fact that London transactions were conducted to a considerable extent by cheque meant that the Bank of England notes in the 'abstract circulation' were, in truth, the till money of the London banks and, unless they had excess precautionary reserves, could not be drawn down without causing severe difficulties in the London money market. Contraction in fact produced 'sudden and violent' panics (1844b: 40). These were the inevitable outcome of the existing monetary system and occurred in London whenever an outflow of gold was accompanied by a reduction in Bank of England notes, as recommended by the Bank's Currency School critics.[42]

For two reasons Joplin held that the correct response of the Bank to such a panic was to *increase* its note issue, by providing extra financial accommodation to the London money market. First, the circulation of the Bank of England was largely irrelevant to the national price level, and thus to the balance of payments, since it was mainly employed in the 'abstract circulation'. Secondly, the demand for money depended not only on the volume of transactions and the rate of interest, but also on a precautionary motive. In panic, the precautionary demand for funds increased dramatically, and the Bank could safely lend extra funds without the money lent getting into circulation. Notes issued to meet such a precautionary demand would automatically return to the Bank after the panic was over.[43]

Joplin in fact urged this course of action on the Bank in a newspaper article published on a fateful evening in 1825 and later claimed, repeatedly and with some considerable justification, to have stopped the panic of that year.[44]

THE DEMAND FOR AND SUPPLY OF LOANABLE FUNDS

Joplin was not concerned with hoarding, which he regarded as quantitatively insignificant.[45] Nor was he concerned with the kind of capital-stock adjustment problem which seems to have been at the centre of the argument of Lauderdale and Malthus.[46] His concern about savings related directly to its impact, through the market for loanable funds, upon the money supply.

The supply of savings was interest-elastic although the function itself would shift around with variations in the level of income. The demand for funds was also interest-elastic. It represented a demand for borrowing for productive expenditure, to finance losses in trade and commerce, for consumption expenditure and for government expenditure. Just as the savings function could shift with changes in the level of income so the loan demand function could also shift with changes in the general level of prosperity. However, Joplin also stressed the possibility that there might be *exogenous* shifts in the demand for funds. The two he stressed were, first, borrowing by government – sharply reduced after 1815 – and, secondly, harvest failure which increased the demand for loans from the agricultural sector.[47]

With a rigid interest rate, an inequality between savings and investment would produce a change in the money supply along the lines already indicated.[48] (Additionally, such an inequality could produce a change in the velocity of the money supply and thus alter aggregate demand in that way as well.[49]) An excess of borrowing over savings could, by placing command over resources in the hands of borrowers, impose forced saving upon the earners of income at the previous price level.[50]

In his writings in the 1820s Joplin laid particular stress upon changes in government expenditure as producing such inequalities. The majority of his attention, in dealing with government expenditure, is thus concentrated upon the monetary implications – with a fall in government expenditure, savings would be greater than the demand for borrowing, leading to a contraction of the money supply. It was this contraction of the money supply which he blamed for the agricultural depression of the early 1820s.[51] The reason that Joplin concentrated mainly upon the monetary effects is that he regarded government as having the power to crowd out private expenditure to a considerable extent.[52] Private borrowers could not pay more than the maximum of 5 per cent permitted by the Usury Laws, but the price of gilt-edged showed that government pushed the rate of interest higher than this. However, Joplin was prepared to concede that the private sector had recourse to trade credit at such times, trade credit being available when aggregate demand was at a high level because of government expenditure and the economy was buoyant. Government could thus, to some extent, make a net addition to the level of aggregate demand; and reductions in government expenditure, correspondingly, could produce a reduction in the level of aggregate demand quite apart from the effect of such a reduction upon the money supply.[53] Joplin did not think that reform of government expenditure was necessarily going to be of benefit to those sensitive to the level of aggregate demand:

> Now the abolition of sinecures, the reduction of salaries, and the consequent repeal of taxes, are, in themselves, most desirable, more especially to those by whom the taxes are paid; but they can hardly be beneficial to the working and productive classes, the demand for whose labour and industry may be increased by extravagance, but can hardly be so by economy. (1823: 6)

MONETARY CONTROL AND THE BANK OF ENGLAND

But it was the monetary problem which remained paramount for Joplin. In the light of this it is hardly surprising that he directed both his considerable powers of analysis and his considerable powers of invective at the Bank of England and its monetary management.[54] His basic position was that the Bank had managed to apply bad management to a defective monetary system. First, it had, even after the crisis of 1825, failed to learn to distinguish between internal and external sources of pressure upon its resources, and was thus forever in danger of causing panic.[55] Secondly, it was, in the 1830s, moving towards a system of matching gold outflows with note reductions which, because of the 'doubling' effect, could be disastrous if carried through. It was following this policy because it believed that it was able to control the exchanges, the general price level and the inflows and outflows of gold. Joplin was entirely convinced that this was not the case; from that point of view the critical part of the money supply derived from the country banks and these were almost entirely outside the control of the Bank of England. He cited data to show that the country bank-notes and the Bank of England notes moved in *opposite* directions. Thus a contraction by the Bank of England did not affect the amount of those notes which controlled aggregate demand and the price level.[56]

But in any case, even if the Bank had been in such a position, it would have had very limited freedom of manoeuvre. This was partly because it was the government's bank and in this position might – and Joplin pointed to an episode in 1824 when this had very nearly happened – find itself in the position of having to create extra money because of a shortfall in government borrowing.[57] But the main problem was simply that an attempt by the Bank to contract its note issue was likely to precipitate the collapse of the London money market. Indeed, given the irrelevance of the Bank of England note issue to the balance of payments, Joplin believed that the correct course for the Bank was to attempt to *neutralize* the effects of precious-metal flows across the exchanges. It could do this by failing to cancel notes which it received in exchange for gold, using those notes to buy gilt-edged securities and thus returning the notes to the market. Conversely, it could dampen the effect of a gold inflow by selling gilt-edged securities to mop up the extra notes which it issued in exchange for gold.[58] Although the Bank's room for manoeuvre here was limited (partly by its own belief about its power to influence the exchanges and partly by a reluctance to part with gilt-edged securities when gold flowed in, reducing the average yield on the asset side of its balance sheet) Joplin believed such neutralization was extremely important if financial crises were to be avoided. For the Bank was in a very difficult position. In Joplin's view, based upon the experience of 20 years, the maximum reduction in its notes that could be made without causing financial collapse was only of the order of £1.5–2 million even though gold flows could be of the order of £10 million.[59]

But if the Bank did neutralize the effects of monetary flows in this way, the side effects of doing so would be serious. For while it would protect the London money market, and thus the trade of that part of the country which was affected by the London money market, notably Lancashire, it would at the same time *prevent* correction of disequilibrating changes in the money supply, originating in the country banks, by flows across the exchanges. There was thus the prospect of perpetual disequilibria and a continuing threat hanging over the London money market.[60]

The difficulties of the Bank were also considerably increased by the activities of its critics who, under the influence of the Bullion Committee of 1810 and the Ricardian Definition of Excess, impressed upon the Bank the idea that it was necessary to match gold inflows and outflows exactly with changes in the Bank of England note issue, believing this to be the monetary base which controlled aggregate monetary demand for the economy as a whole. If the Bank ignored this opinion it appeared to be ignoring the best professional opinion; but if it followed it, it was in danger of producing financial collapse.[61]

Its most serious attempt to follow it was the so-called Palmer Rule, under which, starting from a position just before the onset of a balance of payments deficit, it aimed to have bullion equal to one-third of its combined liabilities of notes and deposits. The Bank then matched gold flows against note and deposit variations on a one-for-one basis. Joplin found this to be peculiarly inept. Given the fragile state of the London money market, the appropriate reserve against deposits was not bullion at all, but notes. The Palmer Rule not only confused London with England – like the Bank's critics – but confused note circulation with deposits. Moreover, with a given gold reserve, accidental variations in deposits would constrain the Bank to make unnecessary variations in the note issue in order to follow its balance sheet rule.[62]

JOPLIN'S PLAN

The remedy for all these difficulties was clearly to abolish competing and unco-ordinated centres of money supply, and to replace these with a single *national* money supply which would vary exactly as an identically circumstanced metallic currency would have done.[63] It was not necessary to have either a metallic currency, or a 100 per cent reserve which would in any case not cover commercial payments in London, which were made by cheque.[64] A currency organized in this way, because it would behave exactly like a metallic currency, would also have the advantage of allowing the loan market to clear since the bankers would now know the state of that market.[65] A change in conditions in the loan market would change the rate of interest, not the money supply.

Joplin originally proposed a plan which would involve allocating the national equilibrium note issue, to be estimated from past data, between newly established joint-stock banks.[66] Government would guarantee the note issue and the banks would pay government a seignorage for this privilege. Bullion dealings would be in the hands of a Board of Commissioners – Joplin's proposals predate Ricardo's here. Incoming bullion would be purchased by the Commissioners who would issue bullion receipts. Such bullion receipts could be presented at any of the participating banks, and the bank would be obliged to purchase it for *new* notes. The bank would then return the receipt to the Commissioners, acquiring a credit with the Commissioners as a result. In the case of a gold outflow the banks would buy back their own notes by drafts drawn against their balances with the Commission, *cancelling those notes*, and such drafts could then be used to obtain bullion for export. Such flows could also take place between different regions of the country, with drafts on the Bullion Commissioners being used in place of bullion. However, to avoid unnecessary use of such drafts, the Commissioners would charge an amount equal to the cost of transmitting bullion between regions, thus encouraging the use of commercial bills to settle inter-regional balances. Such a system would have the advantage not only of producing a unitary national money supply, linked directly to the balance of payments; it would also ensure that that national money supply was distributed between regions in the correct proportions.

With a unified money supply, a scarcity of funds in London could be matched by flows from the country; the London money market would no longer have a special disruptive role, and there would be no panics.[67]

Perhaps most importantly of all, changes in aggregate demand would be very limited. It would be possible for the country to maintain macroeconomic equilibrium. No longer would the stickiness of wages, and to a lesser extent prices, be reflected in the emergence of unemployment in the train of rapidly fluctuating levels of aggregate demand.[68]

With this in mind, Joplin made the daring proposal that in the event of a significant exogenous change – principally a harvest failure – the country should *temporarily abandon convertibility*. The exchange rate would be allowed to float freely until such time as, first, corn imports had met the immediate emergency and, secondly, harvests had resumed their normal level.[69]

Hardly surprisingly, such a suggestion was anathema to both the Currency and Banking Schools – convertibility was not an issue between them. Once again, Joplin emerges as the outsider. He was in fact a considerable distance intellectually from both groups. A firm belief in the idea that causality ran from the money supply to the price level excluded him from the Banking School. But he was an almost equal distance from the Currency School, with which he has sometimes been associated in the secondary literature, because he believed that to adopt metallic fluctuation for Bank of England notes alone would be disastrous, and that the proposal for the Separation of Departments which was designed to achieve this would achieve nothing but a repetition of crises like that of 1825[70] – a belief which was vindicated by the crises of 1847 and 1857, occurring after Joplin's death.

Joplin made a number of changes in his plan over the years in an attempt to placate the Bank of England and the private banks. By 1839 he was prepared to include the private banks in his scheme as note issuers, alongside the joint-stock banks which by then had been established; and he was even prepared to hand over the management of the currency to the Bank of England, leaving the Commissioners in a supervisory role, which included the possibility of suspending convertibility envisaged above.[71] But the basic plan remained firmly grounded upon the necessity of having a national money supply under firm control, to produce macroeconomic stability and full employment.

CONCLUSION

Joplin presented a macroeconomic model in which an open economy, with two competing sources of money supply, suffered from fluctuations in aggregate demand, unemployment and depression. He showed how changes in savings, investment and government expenditure with a fixed rate of interest would destabilize the level of economic activity. He then used this analysis to show that the Bank of England, under a mistaken belief that it was in a position to control the money supply and to rectify the balance of payments, was responsible, through its mismanagement, for repeated distress and recurrent panics.

Joplin's performance, despite the rough-hewn nature of much that he wrote because of the pressures upon him, deserves to be ranked with, and in some respects above, the well-known contributions from the members of the Currency and Banking Schools. But Joplin, partly through circumstances, and partly through unfortunate personal characteristics, was, and remained throughout his life, an outsider. Had the programme which he first put forward in 1823 been adopted, it is likely that the monetary history of the 1840s and 1850s would have been a good deal less turbulent.

NOTES

* The author is engaged on a full-length study of Joplin.

1. I am grateful to Patricia O'Doherty of Gravesend Public Library for a copy of the 1841 Census Return. See also Crick and Wadsworth 1936.
2. Phillips 1894: 104.
3. O'Brien 1971: 70–144.
4. Gregory 1926.
5. For a Bank of England's eye view of the crises of 1847 and 1857, see Clapham 1944: II. 199–211, 226–38.
6. Hodder 1891: 85–9; Withers 1933: 29–43; Gregory 1936: 16–17, 335–53, 360.
7. Letters of 9 March 1843, 26 February 1844, Brougham MSS, University College, London. See also Phillips 1894: 107.
8. [Joplin] 1846.
9. Crick and Wadsworth 1936: 325–6: *Gentleman's Magazine*, XXIX (March 1848), 320–1.
10. Joplin 1823: 32–3.
11. Ibid.: 44–5; 1825: 24–5; 1839: 14; 1844a: 2–3.
12. Joplin 1823: 171.
13. Ibid.: 176–8, 226; 1825: 46–51, 65, 70–1; 1832: 56–7.
14. Joplin 1825: 60; 1828: 242; 1831a: 6; 1844a: 6, 14, 76.
15. Joplin 1823: xiii, 174, 186, 226; 1833: 97; 1833–4: 26–8; 1838: 107.
16. Joplin 1823: 19, 171–3; 1825: 30–3; 1826: 34–5; 1844a: 13–16.
17. Joplin 1823: 195; 1832: 116, 167–8; 1833–4: 27; 1839: 43; 1841: 12.
18. Joplin 1832: 86, 91; 1844b: 73.
19. Joplin 1823: xv; 1825: xx.
20. Joplin 1825: 60; 1844a: 1, 7, 14–15.
21. Joplin 1825: 60; 1844a: 6; 1844b: 73–9.
22. Joplin 1825: xxi; 1828: 66.
23. Joplin 1832: 142–5, 224–7 (dating from 1825).

24. Joplin 1828: 175–6; 1832: 224–7.
25. Joplin 1825: 60; 1826: 79; 1828: 7, 41, 51, 66, 94–5, 239–41; 1831a: 6–7; 1832: 162; 1833: 97; 1838: 2–5; 1844a: 1, 4, 35–6, 45, 85–7; 1844b: 1.
26. Joplin 1826: 15–16, 34, 38, 54–7; 1832: 101, 107–9; 1844a: 19, 24–5, 27, 29–30, 77–8.
27. Joplin 1823: 192; 1825: 11, 12, 37; 1826: 54; 1844a: 18–19.
28. Joplin 1823: 156–7; 1825: xxv, 23–6; 1826: 48; 1828: 28–32; 1831b: 8; 1832: 89–98.
29. Joplin 1825: 48; 1826: 48–52; 1827: xiii; 1831b: 8; 1832: 87–9, 113–14.
30. Joplin 1822: 572; 1825: 4, 11–12, 25, 53; 1826: 35–6; 1827: 193, 195; 1828: 34, 163–4.
31. It was a pleasure to discover Tom Wilson's priority here (1948: 11).
32. Joplin 1825: 37–8; 1826: 38–9; 1828: 161–2; 1831b: 8–9; 1832: 109, 111; 1839: 15; 1841: 70–1; 1844a: 25, 33.
33. Joplin 1823: 201–14; 1825: 12, 35–7; 1826: 44–5; 1828: 155–8; 1839: 20–1; 1841: 76–7; 1844a: 20.
34. Joplin 1825: 35–8, 40, 82–3; 1826: 41–3; 1828: 139–41, 148–50, 163–6; 1832: 224–7; 1833: 55–6; 1833–4: 25, 28–31; 1841: 14–15; 1844a: 23–4, 28–30, 57; 1844b: 9–10.
35. Joplin 1825: 43–4.
36. Joplin 1828: 187; 1832: 276–7; 1841: 18, 70–1.
37. Joplin 1828: 150–3; 1832: 111–13.
38. Joplin 1839: 38–41; 1844a: 19, 21, 31.
39. Joplin 1823: 211–13; 1825: 84–6; 1833: 90–1; 1844a: 19–20, 35, 46; 1844b: 33; 1845b: 7.
40. Joplin 1823: 206–9; 1825: xxix–xxx, 38, 83–6; 1826: 42, 67–8; 1828: 142–5, 148–54, 159; 1832: 162–8, 273–4; 1841: 13, 23–52; 1844a: 19–20, 34–6, 57; 1844b: 33–5; 1845a (suppt): 7.
41. Joplin 1841: 32–4; 1844a: 41, 43, 49, 53; 1844b: 36–8.
42. Joplin 1839: 36–7; 1841: 9–10, 29–30, 48; 1844b: 35–8.
43. Joplin 1828: 175–6; 1832: 219–20, 227–32; 1833: 55–62; 1833–4: 21–2, 27–8; 1841: 42–5, 51–2; 1844b: 56–7.
44. Joplin 1832: 219, 227–30; 1833–4: 21–2.
45. Joplin 1823: 58; 1826: 15–16; 1828: 52–3; 1832: 102; 1839: 17; 1844a: 2.
46. Joplin 1823: 38. But see 1832: 126, and 1841: 47.
47. Joplin 1823: 57–8, 61–2, 251; 1828: 165; 1832: 105–6.
48. Joplin 1828: 158–64; 1832: 101, 108, 113, 120–1; 1839: 14–15; 1844a: 25–7, 77.
49. Joplin 1823: 64; 1845a (suppt): 7.
50. Joplin 1825: 28; 1826: 35–6; 1828: 146–7.
51. Joplin 1823: xv, 65, 224; 1825: 53; 1831a: 6.
52. Joplin 1823: 66–8; 1825: xix–xx.
53. Joplin 1823: 65; 1828: 165.
54. Joplin 1832: 324–30; 1833: 87–96; 1833–4: 40–4; 1838: 107.
55. Joplin 1833–4: 3–26; 1837: 113–22; 1841: 37–8, 60–1; 1844b: 20–4.
56. Joplin 1823: 259; 1825: xxvi–xxviii, 6–7, 45; 1826: 46–8; 1828: 28–32; 1832: 119–20, 217–19.
57. Joplin 1833: 47–55.
58. Joplin 1825: 86–7; 1832: 168–72; 1839: 45–6; 1841: 13–14, 37–8; 1844a: 46–9, 55; 1844b: 4–5.
59. Joplin 1841: 60–1; 1844a: 50–1; 1844b: 18–24.
60. Joplin 1832: 170–1; 1841: 14.
61. Joplin 1833: 90–100, 112–18; 1844a: 47.
62. Joplin 1828: 148; 1833: 37–47, 76; 1838: 12–13.
63. Joplin 1837: 57–8; 1838: 17–18; 1839: 2, 18–23; 1844b: 50–1, 86; 1845a (suppt): 3–4.
64. Joplin 1841: 28–9.
65. Joplin 1825: 15–16; 1839: 15, 23; 1841: 74.
66. Joplin 1823: 262–77; 1825: 16–17; 1826: 63–70, 78; 1832: 152–6, 172–3; 1839: 22–3, 54–5; 1840; 1841: 74.
67. Joplin 1839: 36, 47–50; 1841: 7, 10, 17–18, 42–4, 50; 1844: 55–6; 1844b: 24, 42–3; 1845b: 9.
68. Joplin 1832: 156–7.
69. Joplin 1826: 76–7; 1828: 243–4.
70. Joplin 1841: 20–1, 56; 1844b: 6–7.
71. Joplin 1839: 56–7; 1841: 15–20, 41–2, 52, 72–6; 1844a: 62–7; 1844b: 44–52.

References

Clapham, Sir J. (1944), *The Bank of England: a history*, 2 vols, Cambridge: Cambridge University Press.
Crick, W. F. and Wadsworth, J. E. (1936), 'Some New Light on Thomas Joplin', *Economica*, NS 3: 323–6.
Gregory, Sir T. E., (1926), 'One Hundred Years of Joint Stock Banking, *Banker*, (April/May): 336–345.
—— (1936), *The Westminster Bank Through a Century*, 2 vols, London: Oxford University Press/Milford.
Hodder, E. (1891), *George Fife Angas*, London: Hodder & Stoughton.
Joplin, T. (1822), 'On the General Principles and Present Practice of Banking, in England and Scotland', *The Pamphleteer*, **24** (48): 529–79.
—— (1823a), *Outlines of a System of Political Economy*, London: Baldwin, Cradock and Joy.
—— (1823b), *An Essay on the General Principles and Present Practice of Banking, in England and Scotland*, 4th edn, privately printed, Newcastle-upon-Tyne.
—— (1825), *An Illustration of Mr. Joplin's Views on Currency, and Plan for Its Improvement*, London: Baldwin, Cradock and Joy.
—— (1826), *Views on the Subject of Corn and Currency*, London: Baldwin, Cradock and Joy, and T. Ridgway.
—— (1827), *An Essay on the General Principles and Present Practice of Banking*, 6th edn, London: Baldwin, Cradock and Joy.
—— (1828), *Views on the Corn Bill of 1827*, London: Ridgway, and Baldwin, Cradock and Joy.
—— (1831a), *An Examination of the Principles of an Improved System of Banking*, 2nd edn, London: Ruffy.
—— (1831b), *The Plan of a National Establishment for Country Banking, and the Principles by which it is Recommended*, London: Ruffy.
—— (1832), *An Analysis and History of the Currency Question*, London: Ridgway.
—— (1833), *A Digest of the Evidence on the Bank Charter taken before the Committee of 1832*, London: Ridgway.
—— (1833–4), *Cases for Parliamentary Inquiry, into the Circumstances of the Panic: in a Letter to Thomas Gisbourne, Esq., M.P.*, London: Ridgway.
—— (1837), *An Examination of the Report of the Joint Stock Bank Committee*, 4th edn, London: Ridgway.
—— (1838), *Articles on Banking and Currency From 'The Economist' Newspaper*, London: Ridgway.
—— (1839), *On Our Monetary System*, London: Ridgway.
—— (1840), *Prospectus of an Association to Promote the Establishment of a Uniform Currency under One General Head*, London: Ridgway.
—— (1841), *The Cause and Cure of Our Commercial Embarrassments*, London: Ridgway.
—— (1844a), *Currency Reform: Improvement not Depreciation*, London: Richardson.
—— (1844b), *An Examination of Sir Robert Peel's Currency Bill of 1844*, London: Richardson.
—— (1845a), *An Examination of Sir Robert Peel's Currency Bill, Second Edition With Supplementary Observations*, London: Richardson.

—— (1845b), *Mr. Joplin's Circular to the Directors and Managers of the Joint Stock Banks*, London: Richardson.

—— (1846), 'Memoir of Mr. Thomas Joplin', Bankers Magazine, **6**: 70–80.

O'Brien, D. P. (1971), *The Correspondence of Lord Overstone*, 3 vols, Cambridge: Cambridge University Press.

Phillips, M. (1984), *A History of Banks, Bankers, and Banking in Northumberland, Durham and North Yorkshire*, London: Effingham Wilson.

Wilson, T. (1948), *Fluctuations in Income and Employment*, London: Pitman.

Withers, H. (1933), *National Provincial Bank: 1833 to 1933*, London: National Provincial Bank.

[3]

Scottish Journal of Political Economy, Vol. 24, No. 1, February 1977

TORRENS, McCULLOCH AND DISRAELI

D. P. O'BRIEN

"Reciprocity is, no doubt, the return of the Protection cry, in a disguised form."
—Lord Overstone. (O'Brien 1971 III p. 1458).

I

One aspect of the work of Robert Torrens and of J. R. McCulloch that has so far gone unrecorded and unrecognised, even in Lord Robbins' masterly *Robert Torrens* (Robbins 1958) and in the present author's *J. R. McCulloch*, (O'Brien 1970) has been their role as advisers to Benjamin Disraeli. Examination of their association with Disraeli reveals, in the case of McCulloch, a significant degree of involvement in the Budget of 1852; and also an attitude towards reciprocity in trade negotiations with France which McCulloch would have found extremely embarrassing had it become publicly known in 1860, at the time of the Cobden–Chevalier treaty. But the case of Torrens is perhaps the most acutely interesting. For here we find nothing less than an attempt entirely to re-orientate the Tory party's protectionism on to lines which had been laid down in Torrens' great Letters II, III, IX (Postscript), and X of *The Budget* (Torrens 1844) this involving, once Disraeli had begun to take the bait, a full and superb statement of Torrens' theory of commercial policy, and a spirited defence of the *re-introduction* of a duty on Corn imports which goes far further than anything in Torrens' published writings.[1]

It is not only economists who have failed to recognise all this. Torrens is not mentioned at all in either the great Monypenny and Buckle biography of Disraeli (Moneypenny and Buckle 1910–20) or in the recent (and widely acclaimed) work by Lord Blake (Blake 1966); while McCulloch appears in the former work really only in connection with the Sinking Fund[2] and in the latter in connection with possible patronage.[3]

II

McCulloch and Disraeli

McCulloch's involvement with Disraeli sheds new light on his political allegiance. Elsewhere I have attempted to show that McCulloch was not a Whig (as he had previously been classified by a number of writers) but a political eclectic (O'Brien 1970 pp. 100–103); and his dealings with Disraeli provide striking confirmation of this. For though McCulloch recognised

[1] There is a very full analysis of the argument in *The Budget* in Robbins (1958, chapter 7 and pp. 310–322). Lord Robbins's superb book must always be the starting point for any discussion of Torrens's thought.

[2] Monypenny and Buckle (1910–20), vol. 3, p. 220.

[3] Blake (1966), p. 323. Disraeli suggested McCulloch as successor to G. R. Porter at the Board of Trade should his first choice, Sir Emmerson Tennent, decline the position.

1 1

that there were differences between himself and Disraeli, and retained his independence,[4] he did in fact place himself at Disraeli's disposal as an economic consultant;[5] and he sided with the latter when he was the subject of a highly abusive *Edinburgh Review* article.[6] He sent Disraeli his publications[7] which, the Hughenden Library copies show, Disraeli did read when looking for political material.

In turn he used Disraeli to protect the Stationery Office against attack in Parliament;[8] and he obtained public praise in the House of Commons for his professional achievements.[9] In addition to this he asked his contact to obtain for him statistical material—something for which he had often used his political and parliamentary associates before.[10]

His advice to Disraeli covered two main aspects of policy; taxation, and trade policy. Firstly, McCulloch was a source of advice on tax matters especially when Disraeli, hampered by an almost total lack of financial

[4] Thus in sending Disraeli a new edition of his version of the *Wealth of Nations*, McCulloch recognised that Disraeli would not approve of some of the notes (McCulloch to Disraeli, 14 Feb. 1850, Hughenden papers B/XXI/M/12); in and thanking Disraeli for a flattering reference to him in Parliament he expressed regret at having to differ from so many of Disraeli's views (McCulloch to Disraeli, 15 Feb. 1851, Hughenden papers B/XXI/M/14). All subsequent references to correspondence are to the Hughenden Papers which I was enabled to work at through the kindness of the staff of the National Trust which now occupies Hughenden Manor.

[5] McCulloch to Disraeli, 24 Dec. 1851, B/XXI/M/20; 25 Feb. 1852, B/XXI/M/21; 2 Oct. 1852, B/XXI/M/25; 14 Oct. 1852, B/XXI/M/26.

[6] [Abraham Hayward] *Edinburgh Review*, vol. xcvii (1853) pp. 420–461. The article asked "How did a gentleman of Jewish extraction, whose previous career was inextricably associated with reminiscences very little calculated to inspire esteem or confidence, manage to become finance minister of the greatest commercial country, and official leader of the greatest, wisest, and most important representative assembly, in the world?" (p. 442). Eight pages later this answer was proferred: "Our own solution of his many Protean transformations is, that he never had any political principles or fixed convictions whatever" (p. 430). McCulloch's disgust at this is expressed in a letter of 17 Apr. 1853, B/XXI/M/27.

[7] McCulloch to Disraeli, 14 Mar. 1848, B/XXI/M/9, sending his *Succession to Property*; 14 Feb. 1850, B/XXI/M/12, sending his *Wealth of Nations*; 26 Mar. 1850, B/XXI/M/13, sending *Commercial Dictionary Supplement*; 15 Feb. and 16 May 1851, B/XXI/M/14, 15, sending the two volumes of the *Geographical Dictionary*; 31 Jan. 1851, B/XXI/M/28, *Commercial Dictionary*; 19 Dec. 1859, B/XXI/M/29 *ibid.*; 6 Feb. 1860, B/XXI/M/30, article on Taxation (1st edn.), written for eighth edition of *Encyclopaedia Britannica*; 31 Mar. 1863, sending third edition of *Treatise on Taxation*. The last letter mentions that McCulloch had marked some passages in the book to draw them to Disraeli's attention. Unfortunately, the Hughenden Library contains the first two editions (with marking, apparently by Disraeli) but not the third.

[8] Mowatt, the M.P. for Penryn and Falmouth attempted to obtain an inquiry into the Stationery Office. The circumstances, which related to the allocation of printing contracts, are set out in *Parliamentary Papers*, 1851, vol. xxxi (127) pp. 461–470. McCulloch asked for help to block this on several occasions—McCulloch to Disraeli 2 June, 4 June and 20 July 1851, B/XXI/M/17, 18, 19. Mowatt did not obtain his inquiry.

[9] *Hansard*, 8 Mar. 1849, vol. 103, cols. 424–453 Disraeli's speech—"Local Taxation—Burdens on Land" (ref. to McCulloch at 447); 11 Feb. 1851, vol. 114, cols. 398–400 (Disraeli quoted the first edition of McCulloch *Treatise* on the need for a measure of agricultural protection to offset the effect of tithes); 14 June 1852, vol. 122, col. 692 (Disraeli referred to McCulloch, Torrens and J. S. Mill as supporting a fixed duty on corn). McCulloch was suitably grateful—McCulloch to Disraeli 9 Mar. 1849, 15 Feb. 1851, 15 June 1852, B/XXI/M/11, 14, 22.

[10] McCulloch to Disraeli, 12 Aug. 1852, B/XXI/M/23, requesting an account of the gold and silver coined at the Mint 1815–51. On McCulloch's use of his associates in such matters see O'Brien (1970), pp. 91–96.

expertise, was preparing his ill-fated Budget of 1852. He particularly encouraged Disraeli to increase the house tax, first of all suggesting a lower limit of ten pounds per annum[11] but later pressing upon him a lower limit of seven pounds ten shillings or "better £5".[12] This was advice which Disraeli took, proposing in his Budget speech to lower the limit of exemption from twenty pounds per annum to ten pounds (while doubling the rates), a proposal which was a major factor in the fall of the Derby government thirteen days later. McCulloch also suggested removing half the Malt duty and half the Hop duty and reducing income tax on occupiers of land, advice with which Disraeli was in agreement.[13] What he was in fact advising was a shift in the tax burden from the countryside to the towns, following the repeal of the Corn Laws; Disraeli took the advice, and the government fell.

At the same time it should be stressed that not all of McCulloch's advice was accepted. He protested unsuccessfully against Disraeli's intention to distinguish between "earned" and "unearned" incomes with respect to their lower exemption limits,[14] and his advice to equalise the duty on foreign and colonial timber was ignored, as was his suggestion for an increase in seignorage on gold coin and the introduction of large scale tax farming—the latter he estimated would save £1 m[15]—together with a shift in the burden of the poor rate.[16]

McCulloch also offered advice on the general question of direct and indirect taxation and expressed the hope that Disraeli would not fail to use the favourable opportunity afforded by the Committee on Income Tax[17] to establish the superiority of indirect over direct taxation. Indeed he offered himself as a witness in support of the view that the house tax was the only tolerable direct tax—resort to other direct taxes on a large scale was evidence of barbarism[18]—and that the customs and excise, at moderate levels, were the best form of tax, the former not interfering with freedom of trade.[19] But the offer was not taken up.[20] Disraeli, in his speeches, seems to have been unwilling to commit himself to anything more definite than the proposition that direct taxes should be as broadly based as indirect taxes.[21]

[11] McCulloch to Disraeli, 25 Feb. 1852, B/XXI/M/21.

[12] Memorandum from McCulloch amongst papers concerning the Budget of 1852, B/IV/D/35.

[13] Another memorandum, B/IV/36/a, together with a long letter from McCulloch (in his own hand—usually they were written by H. G. Reid) dated 6 Dec. 1852—this however three days after Disraeli's proposals had been made public—and McCulloch to Disraeli, 15 Jan. 1852, B/XXI/M/22.

[14] In the letter of Dec. 1852 referred to in the previous note.

[15] *Ibid.* On the question of tax farming he advised "Don't take council from Commissioners, who are mere slaves of routine—A million probably might be saved here."

[16] McCulloch to Disraeli, 15 June 1852, B/XXI/M/32.

[17] Select Committee on Income and Property Tax, *Parliamentary Papers*, 1851 (563), vol. x, p. 339; *ibid.* 1852 (354, 510), vol. ix, pp. 1, 463. McCulloch to Disraeli, 24 May 1851, B/XXI/M/16.

[18] McCulloch usually had Turkey in mind when making assertions of this sort.

[19] "It is the merest twaddle to suppose that moderate customs duties affect the freedom of trade". McCulloch to Disraeli, 20 July 1851, B/XXI/M/19.

[20] Babbage and J. S. Mill were, however, called to give evidence.

[21] See especially Disraeli's budget speech, 3 Dec. 1852, *Hansard*, vol. 123, cols. 836–907, col. 887.

The agricultural interest was, of course, the main basis of Disraeli's support; and on the question of the tax burden on this sector he seems to have been able to find some support in McCulloch's *Treatise on Taxation*, as McCulloch himself pointed out in relation to tithes.[22]

The most interesting part of McCulloch's treatment of trade policy relates to the question of reciprocity. The majority of economists in the 1840's and 1850's certainly favoured unilateral remission of duties—there is no doubt that Peel was following an overwhelming majority of professional opinion in the policy he pursued. McCulloch was in general agreement with this view,[23] which was, after all, that of Adam Smith.[24] But there was also another part of Smith's treatment which McCulloch echoed: the view that reciprocal policy in trade was a satisfactory course if it could be expected to be successful in achieving foreign reductions of duty.[25] Now in McCulloch's published writings this never received any great emphasis; and he was thus able to appear extremely hostile to the 1860 Cobden–Chevalier commercial treaty with France (which pursued duty reduction on the basis of reciprocity) without running the risk of being accused of inconsistency.[26] But amongst Disraeli's papers we now find evidence that McCulloch was prepared to go a great deal further in this direction than his published writings indicate: and had these papers been publicly available in 1860 McCulloch might have felt distinctly uncomfortable.

Disraeli, who hoped for a commercial treaty with France,[27] approached McCulloch about this. The latter replied that Disraeli should send a private and confidential agent to Paris, and avoid dealing with the Board of Trade.

> "The Board of Trade is crammed with partisans hostile to you, and the less you have to do with them the better— . . . I have destroyed your epistle—These matters . . . should be wrapt in the deepest mystery—"[28]

He thought that the silk duty was a good one to bargain with. A reduction in the duty from fifteen to ten per cent would be a godsend to the French so that this duty was a useful bargaining weapon. He did not believe that reduction of the French duty on coal would warrant any British duty changes; but it would be different if France proposed reducing her heavy duties on iron, cotton, or linen. In exchange for a reduction of one or all of these duties, which were near prohibitory, expecially that on linen yarn, it would be satisfactory to reduce the brandy duty from fifteen shillings to twelve shillings

[22] McCulloch to Disraeli, 24 Dec. 1851, B/XXI/M/20. See also note 9 above; O'Brien (1970), pp. 234–235; and McCulloch (1852), pp. 185–186.

[23] O'Brien (1970), pp. 217–223, especially pp. 222–223.

[24] Smith (1904), vol. i, pp. 421–422, vol. ii, pp. 46–51.

[25] Smith (1904), vol. i, pp. 431–433; McCulloch (1849), pp. 162–163.

[26] I have analysed the grounds of his objections in O'Brien (1976). Though his objections were, at bottom, more concerned with the tax implications of the treaty, he did manage to convey the impression of severe hostility to reciprocity as such—an impression which would not have been false—see note 23 above.

[27] See *Hansard*, vol. 124, 18 Feb. 1852, cols. 246–281, Disraeli's speech on relations with France; and Monypenny and Buckle (1910–20), vol. iii, p. 425.

[28] McCulloch to Disraeli, 12 Aug. 1852, Letter marked "Most Confidential and Secret", and Memorandum B/XXI/M/23, 23a.

a gallon, and the silk duty from fifteen per cent to ten per cent. He did, it is true, express the view that perhaps it would be desirable to reduce the duties anyway if negotiations failed: but reciprocity would work in dealing with France.[29]

There were other areas in which McCulloch gave Disraeli economic counsel: he pressed upon him his views on inheritance;[30] he put forward a view of the Corn Laws which shows that his fear of revolution, strong in the 1830s, was still very much with him in 1848;[31] and, as the only heavyweight opponent of Wakefield, he put his views on the sale of colonial land to Disraeli.[32] These were, however, relatively minor matters: it is the taxation and the trade policy advice which is significant in the general context of his thought. But a good deal more interesting still was Torrens' involvement with Disraeli to which we now come.

III

Torrens and Disraeli

Torrens' attempt to re-orientate the Tory party seems to be completely unknown. But, disenchanted with the patronage of the Whigs (who had accepted his resignation from the South Australia commission and been tardy about a compensatory pension, and who were later to tamper with his printing contracts)[33] he explicitly lined himself up with the Tories. Having written a paper on recent commercial policy he declined to publish it until he knew what the party line was to be.[34] Torrens, who as a flatterer was no amateur,[35] loaded flattery on Disraeli in an attempt to persuade him

[29] *Ibid.* On the coal duty question see also McCulloch (1852), pp. 207–208.

[30] McCulloch to Disraeli, 14 Mar. and 2 May 1848, B/XXI/M/9, 10. Disraeli referred him to Thornton (1848) but McCulloch refused to be persuaded either by this or by the works of S. Laing (1842) or H. P. Passy (1842), "I am firmly convinced that a country divided among peasant proprietors must in the end become a mere pauper warren; and that it can have no regal government, no aristocratical or rich class, and consequently nothing worthy of the name of literature, art, or civilisation—".

[31] McCulloch to Disraeli, 14 Mar. 1848, B/XXI/M/9, "Though firmly opposed to the sliding scale and the corn-law, I never supposed that their modification or repeal would be productive of the effects proclaimed by the agitators on the one hand and feared by the landlords on the other . . . . But . . . I cannot help thinking that the repeal of the corn-law has been most fortunate—Had they existed at this moment they would have been a powerful weapon in the hands of the abettors of revolution; who I take it regret their repeal—". On McCulloch's fear of revolution see O'Brien (1970), p. 101. He later told Disraeli it would be suicidal to hint at a corn duty—letter of 25 Feb. 1852, B/XXI/M/21.

[32] McCulloch to Disraeli 9 Mar. 1849, B/XXI/M/11. On McCulloch's opposition to Wakefield see O'Brien (1970), pp. 242–244.

[33] On Torrens's resignation see Lord Robbins (1958), p. 199 n. On Torrens's later difficulties with the Whigs, and specifically on the matter of his printing contracts see O'Brien (1971), vol. i, pp. 423–428, 433–435, 436–442, vol. ii, pp. 482, 512, 867–877, 920–923.

[34] Torrens to Disraeli, 5 Jan. and 10 Jan. 1850, B/XXI/T/129, 130.

[35] See e.g. Torrens to Overstone (O'Brien, 1971, vol. i, pp. 395–396, 400, 401, 410, 412, 418–419, vol. ii, pp. 483–484, 810 and n.).

that reciprocity was the cause which the party should adopt as a substitute for the lost cause of protectionism.

> "I cannot longer withhold the expression of my sincere congratulations on Your admirable speech upon the address, and on the commanding position You have achieved. For the rarely combined elements of excellence —compass, brilliancy, and Science—Your speech—I say it in all the simplicity of truth—was the most perfect I ever read. If I might venture to draw an inference from the effects it produced upon myself, I would predict that it will place You at the head of a great and ultimately triumphant movement. Could I strike off twenty years from my age, I would return to Parliament and enlist under Your banner. As it is, accept all that I can give—my sincere wishes for your success.
>
> "If You can prevail upon the country party to abandon the narrow defile of protection, and to give battle on the open plain of reciprocity, the victory will be theirs. If not—not. In politics as in war, numbers, however great, and courage however high, must ultimately surrender at discretion unless armed with the weapons of modern science.[36] While the country party fought under the banner of protection, every individual who had acquired the slightest reputation for political science, was against them, and therefore they fell. But if the country party will now hoist the flag of reciprocity, the most advanced section of the cultivators of political science will fight in their ranks, and they will therefore succeed . . .
>
> '. . . While saying all this, I do not overlook the difficulties of Your position. You move with the advanced guard of Science, while the main body of Your army halts with the rear Guard of ignorance. How is the junction essential to victory to be formed? The attraction of Genius will effect it. It is a law of mind as well as of matter, that lesser orbs bend their course around the Greater. Inscribe upon Your banners 'Secure to British labour the rewards due to its superior efficacy':—'rescue the Chivalry of England from the vulgar rule of the Factory Moblisse'. Your cries, like Nelson's signal, will electrify. The kindling spirits of the land will gather around You. What a glorious strife! I may not live to witness the ultimate result, but 'I see your triumph from afar, and seize it with my eye' ".[37]

Torrens assured Disraeli that the literary organs of his party made a mistake in treating political economy as an enemy;[38] and he quite dishonestly told Disraeli that reciprocity was endorsed by the majority of economists.

> "Political Economists, as a class, are opposed to protection; but it would be a great mistake to infer that as a class they are in favour of the Manchester free trade School. With scarcely an exception, the more advanced Economists, from Ricardo downwards, were directly opposed to that School.

[36] It should not be forgotten that Torrens had at one time been a professional soldier—and a good one. See F. W. Fetter (1962).

[37] Torrens to Disraeli, 13 Feb. 1849, B/XXI/T/131A. Cf. Torrens to Overstone, 30 Jan. 1848 (O'Brien, 1971, vol. i, pp. 418–419) especially the quotation at the end of the letter. The reference at the end of the letter to not living to see the outcome is an allusion to Torrens's age. He was born in 1780.

[38] Torrens to Disraeli, 1 June 1850, B/XXI/T/132.

Ricardo's chapter on foreign trade, and his pamphlet on protection to British agriculture put Cobden out of court. John Mill—perhaps the most eminent thinker of the age—has demonstrated that when hostile tariffs are not met by countervailing import duties, the value of the produce of British labour is lowered, in relation to the produce of foreign labour. McCulloch, the most learned of our modern Economists, would, with Ricardo, not only impose upon foreign Corn a duty equivalent to the peculiar burthens on domestic agriculture, but grant a bounty upon exportation also equivalent to these burthens. Coulson, the eminent Lawyer recently appointed to prepare the drafts of the Government Bills, and one of the most profound thinkers of the day, advocated the reciprocal laws of international exchange in the Parliamentary Review as far back as 1827. Pennington, who understands Ricardo better than any other member of the Political Economy Club, but who is himself not sufficiently known, has advocated the same principles in a letter addressed to Kirkman Finlay; as has George Norman—second only to S. J. Loyd on monetary science —in a pamphlet on the currency published in 1840. The last, but not the least, upon the list of Economists who advocate perfect as opposed to one-sided freedom of trade, is Dr Longfield, formerly professor of Political Economy in the University of Dublin.[39]

"And who are the distinguished Economists who support the doctrines of the Manchester School? I know of not one, with the exception of Senior; and he possesses in an unusual degree of perfection the faculty of self-refutation.[40] His very valuable lectures on the cost of obtaining the precious metals must be recanted before he can consistently oppose reciprocity. This he feels, and shrinks from again approaching the question. In his article in the October number of the Edinburgh Review upon Mill's Treatise on Political Economy, he declined to grapple with the chapter on international exchange, although, under the actual circumstances of the country, the most interesting and immediately important portion of Mill's great book."[41]

The opponents of reciprocity were, he asserted, simply behind the march of science.

"If Senior may be regarded as hors de combat, there will not remain a recognised authority upon the principles of international exchange opposed to your views. This is a great advantage. When all the philosophers were against the country party, the great mass of the public who take their

[39] It would be disproportionate to document at length the extent of Torrens's attempted misrepresentation of the views of his fellow economists. But, by way of illustration, it may be mentioned that George Warde Norman was in fact the author of the best attempt at refutation of Torrens's Cuba case—see Robbins (1958), pp. 225–226 n.; O'Brien (1971), vol. i, pp. 335, 345–346, vol. ii, pp. 897–898, 899–900, 901; O'Brien (1975), ch. 7.

[40] Cf. Letter X of Torrens (1844) (to Senior), p. 334, "I beg to call your attention to one of the most perfect specimens of self-refutation which the curiosities of literature contain".

[41] Torrens to Disraeli, 13 Feb. 1849, B/XXI/T/131A. The assertion about Senior's review is at least true—Senior (1848), p. 323. The exchanges between Senior and Torrens are analysed in Lord Robbins (1958), pp. 211–225 and in M. E. A. Bowley (1937, pp. 225–234), as well as in O'Brien (1975, ch. 7).

scientific opinions upon trust, regarded the country party as behind the knowledge of the age, and its influence consequently declined. But now when the leading philosophers are with the leaders of the country party, the process will be reversed, the public, who derive their opinions from authority, will begin to believe that the leaders of the country party are in advance of the knowledge of the age, and the Manchester School behind it; and the necessary consequence will be, that the influence of the latter will decline, and that of the former revive. The change may not be very rapid at first, but it will proceed in an accelerating ratio."[42]

In his attempts it does seem that Torrens had some success. There is internal evidence that the writing of at least one of Disraeli's speeches was influenced by Torrens.[43] But this left him in the position (which of course he may have wanted) of having to defend Disraeli when the inevitable attacks came from those who were "behind the knowledge of the age". The first of these defences, written in response to criticisms in the *Economist* is lost.[44]

[42] Hughenden Papers, *loc. cit.* See also Torrens to Disraeli, 22 May and 1 June 1850, B/XXI/T/131, 132. This was also a theme he was to advance in his reply to the *Economist* which is discussed below.

[43] The speech in question was that delivered by Disraeli on the Address in Answer to the Speech, 1 Feb. 1849 (*Hansard*, vol. 102, cols. 89–117). Now there is a curious episode which occurred later in Disraeli's career when, apparently unconsciously, he engaged in a fairly lengthy piece of plagiarism. Having, as Leader of the House of Commons (in 1852) to eulogise the recently deceased Duke of Wellington he used, for part of his speech, material from an obituary by Theirs of Marshall St Cyr which had appeared in English four years earlier. This really does seem to have been an unconscious trick of memory—see Blake (1966), pp. 335–337. But we cannot put the material in the speech on the Address down to such a cause unless we accept that Disraeli was capable of doing this with material which he did not even really understand. Some extracts from the speech will help to illustrate the point.

"Men who have deeply considered the subject of commercial interchange without any of our passions, men not connected with the parties of the State, . . . have always taught us that if you attempt to fight hostile tariffs with free imports, . . . such a policy would have a dangerous effect on the distribution of the precious metals—an effect dangerous to all countries, but more particularly to a country like England, with her fixed debt and great fixed payments" (col. 96). "You may glut markets . . . but the only effect of your systems, of your attempting to struggle against these hostile tariffs by opening your ports is, that you exchange more of your own labour every year and every month for a less quantity of foreign labour, that you render British labour or native industry less efficient, that you degrade British labour, necessarily diminish profits, and therefore must lower wages; while philosophical inquirers have shown that you will finally effect a change in the distribution of the precious metals that must be pernicious, and may be fatal to this country" (cols. 97–98). "But observe how the principle of reciprocity would enable you to reconstruct your commercial system in a manner beneficial to the mother country, and advantageous to the colonies. By extending the tariff of the metropolis to the colonies, you would either secure to them a legitimate advantage in the home market; or, on the other hand, their participation in an interchange of mutual benefit with foreign countries. Reciprocity, indeed, is the only principle on which a large and expansive system of commerce can be founded. Reciprocity is indeed a great principle. It is at once cosmopolitan and national. The system you [the Whigs] are pursuing is one quite contrary: you go on fighting hostile tariffs with free imports, and the consequence is, that you are following a course most injurious to the commerce of the country" (col. 98).

[44] Torrens to Disraeli, 20 and 25 Feb. 1849, B/XXI/T/126, 127. The criticism was occasioned by Disraeli's speech quoted in the previous note. Of course, if the Torrens papers, for which many have already searched, are ever found, there may be a copy there: but I have been unable to find one either amongst the Disraeli papers or in the issues of the *Economist*.

But the second, written in response to another attack in the same newspaper (an attack in all probability written by its founder, the celebrated James Wilson) is amongst Disraeli's papers.

Disraeli had argued in his speech that free trade should be achieved by reciprocity only and that we should not permit free imports from any country which met us with duties. There was, he believed at least partial incidence of import duties on foreign suppliers.[45] The *Economist* (1850), then took this up at length—not surprisingly since it was founded as an anti-Corn-law journal and Disraeli, having assumed the mantle of the protectionist leadership, had become the target for continued abuse in its columns. According to the paper on this occasion, Disraeli had repudiated "protection" in the sense that the word was used by the agricultural interest. He now seemed to be asking for a duty on foreign wheat not on their behalf, but on behalf of the manufacturing interest—agricultural protection was apparently required only so long as manufacturing exports encountered tariffs. In the view of the paper, duties on imports fell on the home consumer and did not affect the terms of trade.[46]

Torrens then rushed to Disraeli's assistance.[47] His reply is summarised in Appendix I. No short summary here can do justice to the sweep and ingenuity of the argument. But what he did essentially was to take the apparatus developed in his writings (1833) and (1844) and use it to show that unilateral duty reductions were equivalent, in their effect on a country's international purchasing power, to falls in productivity. He had done this before; but never anywhere in his published writings with such skill, punch, and panache. (The argument involves some technical assumptions about elasticity; and these are sketched in Appendix II.)

The argument then broadens out to a defence of agricultural protection: and here we find something fairly startling. In the correspondence of Lord Overstone there is a reference to a lost publication by Torrens. Overstone writes to George Warde Norman:

> "I wish much that you were at my elbow. I have brought down with me a proof copy of a proposed Publication by Torrens—The drapery of Scientific Principle thrown over Protectionist doctrine—You will know his ingenuity and acuteness—the low price at which *Serf grown* Corn may be continually poured into this country—The destruction of Agricultural Capital and destitution of Agricultural labourers which *must* be the result of the *sudden* repeal of the Corn Laws after the long encouragement given to the investment of Capital in Agriculture—the inevitable decay of this country which must result from our total repeal of Import duties without Reciprocity on the part of other Nations—England thus surrendering the

[45] *Hansard*, vol. cxi, 14 May 1850, cols. 82–88.

[46] This last point was devastatingly dealt with by Torrens in his reply.

[47] Torrens to Disraeli, 9 June 1850, B/XXI/T/133, 134. Like the work of the previous year this was never published by the *Economist*, if indeed it was sent to that paper. But it was hardly likely that Wilson, who was diammetrically opposed to Torrens on both monetary *and* trade policy, would have given him space.

advantage she ought to derive from the superior efficacy of her labour—The consequent disturbance in the distribution of the precious Metals augmenting fearfully the pressure of our debt—the dismemberment of the Empire which must ensue unless the Colonies be conciliated by discriminating duties in their favour—all these doctrines reconciled—or at least the attempt to reconcile them—with existing phenomena—this done with great ingenuity and craftiness—".[48]

At the time of editing the *Correspondence* I surmised that this referred to Torrens' *Tracts for Electors on Finance and Trade*. It is true that these contain a lot of the arguments referred to here. However, I have not been able to find in them the argument about Serf-grown Corn. But it is in this document which Torrens sent to Disraeli. Moreover we now have here a bald advocacy of the *re*-introduction of agricultural protection—in 1850—which is not to be found anywhere else in Torrens' published writings. The reader will find details of the argument in Appendix I. But all this, taken together with Torrens' attempt to switch the points on the Tory party, explains the quotation at the head of this paper: and it explains too the touchiness displayed by other orthodox economists towards the Cobden–Chevalier treaty.

There were other matters on which Torrens attempted to influence Disraeli. In connection with trade policy he was still pushing the idea of an Imperial Zollwerein[49]—and Disraeli did in fact take this up. Moreover, he stressed what I have called elsewhere "transitional welfare problems"[50] as an argument against the dismantling of protection especially in agriculture.[51] He also attempted to persuade Disraeli to interest himself in emigration from Ireland —and here the weapon of flattery was again in evidence.[52]

But these are matters which are not startling in the general context of what is known about Torrens: while the attempt on the Tory party and the bald advocacy of a return to agricultural protection are much more remarkable.

IV

Conclusion

The roles of Torrens and McCulloch as advisers to Disraeli have so far gone unrecorded and unrecognised. Examination of the involvement of them both (neither may have been aware of the other's, since McCulloch took

[48] Overstone to G. W. Norman, 3 Apr. 1850 (O'Brien 1971, vol. ii, p. 487). The Torrens work is mentioned in Torrens to Disraeli 5 and 10 Jan. 1850, B/XXI/T/129, 130.

[49] Torrens to Disraeli, 25 Feb. 1849, B/XXI/T/127. This idea reappeared in Torrens's (1852).

[50] O'Brien (1970), pp. 201, 221 n.

[51] This is in evidence in the Memorandum in App. I below.

[52] Torrens to Disraeli, 19 Mar. 1847, B/XXI/T/125 "Might not this question be worthy of the consideration of a leader of unrivalled powers?" See also Torrens to Disraeli, 3 Apr. 1849, B/XXI/T/128.

pains to conceal his association with Disraeli[53] even though contemporaries may have suspected it,[54] and Torrens became something of a recluse in his old age) reveals some highly interesting elements which help to fill out the picture of their work given in previous studies.

University of Durham

Appendix I

"Reciprocity considered in reference to the objections urged by the Editor of the Economist against the Scientific Principles of Commercial Policy propounded by Mr. Disraeli in his speech on 14 May 1850".

According to Torrens the *Economist* has failed to understand the basic principles of international trade. The advantage of international trade lies in increased production resulting from international division of labour. Distribution of the gains from trade is determined by reciprocal demand. Productivity in the export industries together with the level of import duties determines reciprocal demand. If productivity in export industries increases then, because of the reduction in their price, demand for British goods will rise; and on Torrens' assumptions the diminution in price will be less than the reduction in their cost. He assumes that price will not fall in proportion to the increase in productivity because of the elasticity of *aggregate* demand. The increase in exports will only be in proportion to the fall in price (if elasticity of *market* demand is equal to one) and not in proportion to the increase in productivity. Supposing, however, that elasticity of foreign *market* demand is equal to one then, even without a change in the balance of payments, we would be obtaining given imports for less labour than before, and thus the single factoral terms of trade will be turned in our favour.[55]

If the balance of payments is actually turned in our favour there will be a correspondingly greater gain. The terms of trade would turn in our favour because there would have to be increased foreign exports (sold at lower prices) to Britain to redress the balance.

A fall in productivity in the export industries would have a directly opposite effect.

"Now an increase or a diminution in the relative amount of the duties which different countries impose upon the productions of each other, alter the terms of International Exchange in a way precisely analogous to that in which they are altered by an increase or diminution in the comparative efficacy of industry" (pp. 7–8). Assume that all foreign countries abolish their import duties on British goods. This would reduce the prices of British

[53] McCulloch to Disraeli, 2 Oct. 1852, "When you do me the favour to send me a note do not put D on the outside—You don't know how even these trifles are noticed."

[54] See G. C. Lewis (1853), p. 249 where the house tax proposal (*supra*) is linked with McCulloch (1852), p. 67 (which had recommended lowering the exemption limit to £10).

[55] This is all a little tricky to make clear without modern apparatus which is used in App. II. Torrens is assuming elasticity of *aggregate* demand greater than one but elasticity of *market* demand equal to one.

goods in foreign markets, yet the fall in prices would be less than the duty reduction because increased consumption of British goods would result from the increased demand for them and there would be a rise in the prices obtained by the producers. The benefit resulting from the remission of the duties would be divided between the foreign consumer and the British producer, the proportion being determined by the comparative force of reciprocal demand. But the price of British goods would be lower to the foreign consumer and higher to the British producer.

But the extension of foreign markets and consequent increase of employment and rise in profits and/or wages in the manufacturing districts would not be the only advantage to England from the abolition of foreign tariffs. The value of all foreign products, including the precious metals, would fall in the British market. Before the abolition of foreign tariffs, the quantity of goods which the foreign exporter sent to England paid for the quantity of British goods which he imported. After the duty abolition the foreign importer buys a greater quantity of British goods at enhanced prices.[56] The additional debt thus incurred must be discharged by sending more exports to England, or sending money. If more goods are sent then their increased supply in the British market would reduce their prices: should metal be sent the value of money will fall in Britain and rise in the foreign market, i.e. British prices will rise and foreign prices will fall. In either case the terms of trade are turned in our favour—the produce of a given quantity of British labour would command the produce of a greater quantity of foreign labour than before. A decrease in the amount of foreign tariffs has the same effects as an increase in the efficacy of British industry. "A reduction of 10 per cent in the duties levied upon British goods in foreign markets would be, in so far as relates to the division of the wealth derived from foreign trade, as beneficial to England as the diminution of 10 per cent in the cost of producing goods for foreign markets" (p. 10).

An increase of foreign duties on British goods, or a decrease of British duties on foreign goods would be, in relation to the division of the gains from trade, as injurious to England as a fall in the efficiency of British industry. In either case, the value of the produce of British labour would be depreciated in relation to the value of foreign labour.

The importance of the subject and the misconceptions about it require that the effects of a duty remission on the value of domestic labour and its products should be traced.

When countries engaged in foreign trade impose equal duties then no alteration in the relative value of their respective products occurs. The same relative quantities of one country's goods exchange for the same relative quantities of the other's. Equal duties of 20 per cent or even 100 per cent would not alter the terms of trade.[57] But imposition of unequal duties would disturb this equilibrium. Suppose England repeals import duties and foreign

[56] That is, prices as received by the British producers, as at the end of the preceding paragraph.

[57] Assuming equal elasticity of the two aggregate demand curves throughout their entire lengths.

countries levy a 20 per cent duty on British goods. The terms of trade will then move against England. The increased consumption of foreign commodities in the British market after duty repeal would increase demand for these commodities and raise their prices in the countries of their production, while the diminished demand for British goods in foreign markets consequent on the imposition of the foreign duties would compel the British producer to submit to lower prices.

The injury then inflicted on the domestic producer would be redressed were England to re-impose a countervailing duty of 20 per cent. The price of British imports would rise and their quantity fall and the amount of British exports necessary to pay for them would diminish, which in turn would raise the prices of British exports in the foreign market until the terms of trade were restored to their previous level.

The principles propounded in Disraeli's speech[58] are in strict conformity with the laws of international exchange as set forth by Ricardo and J. S. Mill. When the hon. member stated that "protection to native industry required that free imports should not be received from any foreign country which by hostile tariffs refused the offer of an equally free interchange"[59] (p. 13) he advanced a principle which is scientifically correct and of the highest practical importance. The objections of the editor of the *Economist* to the principle of reciprocity advanced by Disraeli "betray an extraordinary unacquaintance with the more advanced doctrines of Political Economy, and a total misapprehension of the purport and objects of the Scientific policy which he ventures to assail" (p. 14).

The *Economist* asserts that Disraeli was advocating duties on raw materials and foodstuffs. But in fact Disraeli was not advocating duties on such commodities, because duties upon them would increase the cost of producing exportables and thus defeat the very object which reciprocal imposts are intended to secure.[60] If England put a duty on raw cotton, then the demand for raw cotton would fall here, causing its price in the American market to decline. Some portion of the duty would then be paid by the American grower; but the fall in price of raw cotton would benefit other countries' cotton manufacturers. Britain would then be undersold in third markets, and thus the terms of trade would turn against us.[61]

The *Economist* cannot deny that increased demand for British goods if foreign duties were reduced would raise their prices and that the advanced price obtained by the British manufacturer would be paid by the foreign purchaser. Similarly, the *Economist* cannot deny that British duty reductions have raised the price received by foreign exporters to Britain—prices have not fallen by the full extent of the duties repealed.

Disraeli has affirmed that hostile tariffs, when unopposed, make British industry tributary to foreign states. To this, which has already been shown

[58] See footnote 45.

[59] The quotation is a paraphrase of a passage at the foot of col. 84 of the speech.

[60] Contrast this however with Torrens's advocacy, later in the paper, of a duty on corn.

[61] That is, for our payments to come into balance after being undersold in third markets in this way, it would be necessary for the terms of trade to turn against us.

by Ricardo, J. S. Mill, "and others" (p. 18) the *Economist* objects that British exporters receive the same price from every country to which they export despite a very wide range of duties in different countries. Torrens replies that hostile tariffs diminish the demand for British goods in the foreign market; this diminished demand lowers their value in the Manchester market; and the fall of prices in the Manchester market causes a corresponding and general fall in the prices of British goods throughout all the markets, domestic and foreign, in which these goods are sold. So the argument of the *Economist* amounts to saying that the fall of price in the home market proves that there has been no fall of price at all.[62]

Disraeli does not, as the *Economist* depicts him doing, say we cannot have revenue duties on the productions of countries which admit our goods duty free. They are different from countervailing duties which are explicitly discriminatory against various countries, whereas the revenue duties do not discriminate by source. Protective duties are designed to interfere with the international division of labour but, according to Torrens, revenue and countervailing duties do not.

The imposition of *new*, *protective*, duties has no justification. But when they have been long established so that the division of labour and the internal allocation of resources is in accordance with them, the mischief cannot always be repaired and may be worsened by their abolition. When a long established system of protection has forced large masses of the labour and capital of a country into channels other than those into which they would have gone naturally, the suspension of employment and destruction of capital resulting from the removal of protection might cause a diminution of wealth greater than that which a better division of international employment could supply. "In all such cases, the continuance of an established system of protection is scientifically correct" (pp. 22–23).

The *Economist* says that Disraeli's vote in favour of a recent motion on agricultural protection means that he is at variance with other protectionists and with himself, for after advocating reciprocity he voted for a motion that wholly discarded it and professed only to take the Corn Laws into consideration. But, according to Torrens, Disraeli's vote was in accordance with reciprocal policy which does not involve the abandonment of protection to agriculture—indeed he gave the only rational and scientific grounds on which protection to agriculture could be defended and enforced.

Because of the way in which agriculture is operated in Europe and America, and because of the artificial state into which it has been forced in the United Kingdom, a fixed duty on foreign Corn would operate at one and the same time as a revenue duty, as a countervailing duty, and as a protecting duty. It would be a revenue duty paid by the foreign producer. When agriculture is conducted on capitalist lines as in England, the money price of its produce cannot fall below the cost of production without putting factors out of work. But when production is by peasants as in France or by serfs as in Eastern Europe[63] the supply of Corn is not determined by a money cost of cultivation

[62] See footnote 46 and the text to which this relates.

[63] See footnote 48 and the text to which this relates.

and the producer sells his disposable surplus for whatever he can get. "An increase or diminution of demand in the British market is followed almost instantaneously by a corresponding rise or fall of prices in the peasant and serf cultivated markets which grow for exportation. The surplus produce of almost costless tillage will continue, under a diminution of demand, to be sold at any price which may be sufficient to replace with ordinary profit the expense of carriage" (p. 24). A fixed revenue duty levied on foreign Corn in the British ports would lower its price in the shipping ports by the full amount of the duty; so the incidence would be on the foreign producer.

A fixed duty on foreign Corn would also be a countervailing duty because the countries which are the largest suppliers of Corn for the British market are the countries which levy the heaviest imposts upon British goods. These tariffs lower the value of British goods in relation to foreign agricultural produce and thus require a countervailing duty.

A fixed duty on foreign Corn would also be a protecting duty. In average years it would have little or no perceptible effect upon the price in the British market, because its incidence was on the foreign producer: in years of more than average abundance it would stop a ruinous depression of prices and destruction of agricultural capital. In 1832–34 harvests were abundant and British prices low despite the existence of the sliding scale Corn duty. How much worse would things be now without any duty?[64] The import requirements of the countries of Northern Europe will lead them to make large Corn exports, regardless of the price.[65]

The *Economist* is very ignorant of the Laws of International Exchange in arguing that the commercial policy advocated by Disraeli will harm the manufacturing interests. While countervailing duties upon foreign manufactures would maintain the productions of native industry at their natural value, a fixed duty on foreign Corn would operate as a protection to every branch of domestic manufacture in which foreign raw materials are employed. The imposition of duties on foreign manufactures would act as a bounty upon the importation of raw materials.[66]

Appendix II

This is not a formal taxonomy or proof of the conditions necessary for Torrens' result to hold. Rather it is a sketch of what Torrens meant by his elasticity (outlay) assumptions since this is not at first sight immediately obvious.

[64] Torrens was thus ignoring the fact that if a sliding scale duty which had effectively excluded foreign corn in years of good harvest, had done little to hold up British corn prices, a fixed duty would have a negligible effect.

[65] At this point in the paper Torrens, neglectful of the terms of trade argument for a moment, went on to argue that if the European states were unable to export corn they would send specie which would alter relative prices and thus make corn export possible again. Torrens was thus asking, at this point, for protection to *prevent* the terms of trade moving in our favour—clearly something of an aberration in an otherwise well-argued document.

[66] That is turning the terms of trade in our favour would make imported raw materials cheaper.

Torrens assumes throughout his paper that the market demand curves for imports in the trading countries have a price elasticity equal to one, viz. constant outlay at varying prices. Thus, he assumes that price changes in the foreign market would leave foreign outlay on British goods unchanged. He also assumes that the elasticity of each country's aggregate demand (offer) curve is greater than one. Coupling these two assumptions together he then introduces a fall in the cost of production of British exports. The aggregate demand elasticity assumption is taken to ensure that price in the foreign market will fall by less than the reduction in costs; the market demand elasticity assumption is taken to ensure constant foreign outlay; and thus this outlay will be obtained, because price has fallen by less than cost in return for a smaller quantity of British inputs (labour) than before.

Now, there seems no *prima facie* reason why elasticity of the two curves should not differ. A market demand function contains a wide range of arguments, including the price of all other products and income. The aggregate demand curve, on the other hand, is derived from the production possibility curve and the community indifference map, the latter being derived not from the demand function but from the utility function, and consisting of a set of iso-function curves.

Accepting that the two elasticities can differ, we then have to see the relationship between the cost change supposed and the consequent price change. We can treat a technical improvement of the Classical type as an outward shift in the constant cost transformation curve from *sc* to *sc′* (Fig. 1). Such a shift produces in the aggregate demand curve a movement from OE^1 to OE^2 (Fig. 2). (The shift in the straight part of the offer curve is explainable in terms of the technological improvement; the path followed by the remainder will not be so simply determined but it seems reasonable to assume a shift of the type shown.) *os′* is the quantity of sugar that would have been

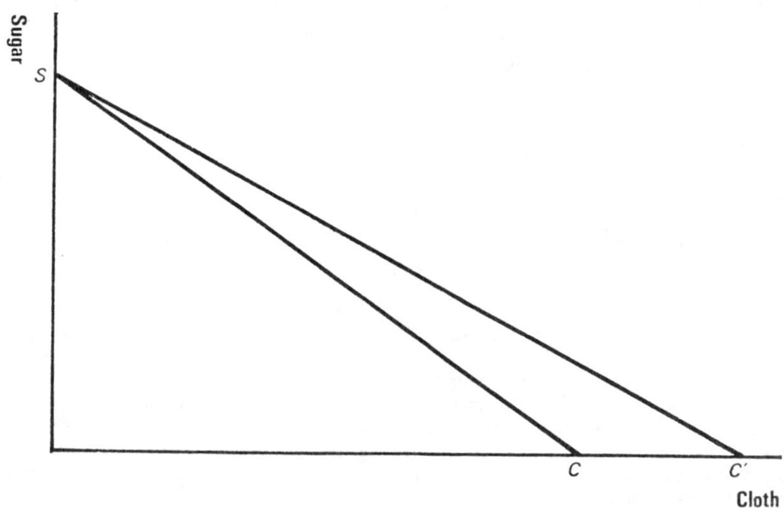

Figure 1.

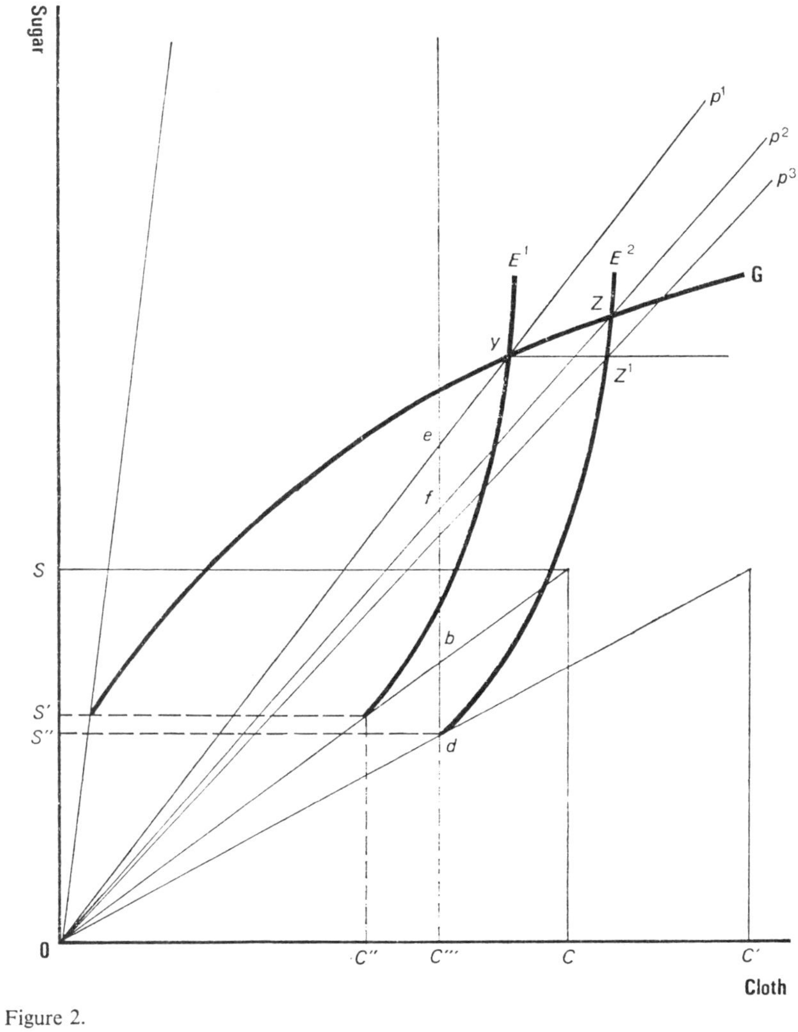

Figure 2.

produced and consumed domestically in the absence of trade, giving up *oc″* of cloth (through moving resources out of cloth production) before the technological improvement: *os″* and *oc‴* are the corresponding quantities after the improvement.

Now if the elasticity of the foreign country's aggregate demand curve is greater than one over the relevant range it will follow a path like OG in Figure 2, where *yz* is the critical range: and the change in the terms of trade from OP^1 to OP^2 will (given that the other offer curve is also well-behaved) be less than the initial change in costs.

We can see this if we erect a perpendicular at *c‴*. This will give us the slope of the original transformation curve as *bc‴/oc‴* and the new slope is *dc‴/oc‴*. The original terms of trade were *ec‴/oc‴*. The new terms of trade are given by *fc‴/oc‴*.

What Torrens requires is that

$$\frac{bc'''/oc'''}{dc'''/oc'''} > \frac{ec'''/oc'''}{fc'''/oc'''}$$

i.e. that

$$\frac{bc'''}{dc'''} > \frac{ec'''}{fc'''}$$

This will normally happen if the slope of the offer curves is as depicted—and it is clear from inspection that it has happened in this case. If, however, the OG offer curve had elasticity equal to one over the relevant range—following a path such as yz' rather than yz—then the change in price to OP^3 would be approximately as great as the fall in costs—*exactly* what happens depending on the slope of the OE offer curve.

References

Blake, R. (1966). *Disraeli.* London: Eyre and Spottiswoode.

Bowley, M. E. A. (1937). *Nassau Senior and Classical Economics.* London: Allen and Unwin.

Economist (1850). Mr Disraeli's new Faith. Protection in a new garb. 18 May, pp. 534–535.

Fetter, F. W. (1962). Robert Torrens: Colonel of Marines and political economist. *Economica*, N.S. vol. 29, pp. 152–165.

Laing, S. (The Elder). (1842). *Notes of a Traveller.* London: Longman.

Lewis, G. C. (1853). The fall of the Derby ministry. *Edinburgh Review*, vol. 97, pp. 240–267.

McCulloch, J. R. (1849). *Principles of Political Economy.* 4th edn., London.

McCulloch, J. R. (1852). *A Treatise on Taxation and the Funding System.* 2nd edn.

Monypenny, W. F. and Buckle, G. E. (1910–20). *The Life of Benjamin Disraeli.* 6 vols. Edinburgh: John Murray.

O'Brien, D. P. (1970). *J. R. McCulloch. A Study in Classical Economics.* London: Allen and Unwin.

O'Brien, D. P. (1971). *The Correspondence of Lord Overstone.* 3 vols. London: Cambridge University Press.

O'Brien, D. P. (1975). *The Classical Economists.* Oxford: Clarendon Press.

O'Brien, D. P. (1976). Customs unions: Trade creation and trade diversion in historical perspective. *History of Political Economy*, vol. 8.

Passy, P. H. (1842). Des changements survenus dans la situation agricole du Département de l'Eure depuis l'année 1800. *Journal des Economistes*, vol. i, pp. 44–66.

Lord Robbins. (1958). *Robert Torrens and the Evolution of Classical Economics.* Macmillan.

Senior, N. W. (1848). J. S. Mill on political economy. *Edinburgh Review*, vol. 88, pp. 293–338.

Smith, Adam. (1904). *An Inquiry into the Nature and Causes of the Wealth of Nations*, ed. E. Cannan, 2 vols., London.

Thornton, W. T. (1848). *A Plea for Peasant Proprietors; with the Outlines of a Plan for their Establishment in Ireland.* Edinburgh: Murray.

Torrens, R. (1833). *Letters on Commercial Policy*, reprinted LSE, 1958.

Torrens, R. (1844). *The Budget. On Commercial and Colonial Policy*, reprinted A. M. Kelley, New York, 1970.

Torrens, R. (1852). *Tracts for Electors on Finance and Trade Submitted to the Consideration of the Constituencies of the United Kingdom, No. II.* London: Chapman and Hall.

[4]

Customs unions: trade creation and trade diversion in historical perspecti

Denis O'Brien

Introduction

Since 1950 there has been a great growth of literature dealing with customs unions—sufficient indeed to warrant two major surveys of the subject.[1] With virtually no exceptions[2] this literature ignores the treatment of the subject, and in particular of the key concepts of trade creation and trade diversion, which existed before the publication in 1950 of Jacob Viner's *The Customs Union Issue*.[3] To those not involved in teaching international economics this historical myopia may not have hitherto been apparent; but it is certainly there.[4]

It would however be surprising if there was not a body of literature dealing with these issues in existence before 1950. Sixteen customs unions were formed between 1818 and 1924[5] and the problems were extensively discussed—the bibliography of Viner's book occupies one third of its entire length. More importantly, commercial treaties, in the analysis of which the trade creation and trade diversion concepts are of key importance, were a matter of passionate

DENIS O'BRIEN *is Professor of Economics at The University of Durham.*

1. R. G. Lipsey, "The Theory of Customs Unions: A General Survey," *Economic Journal* 70 (1960): 496–513, reprinted in A.E.A. *Readings in International Economics*, ed. R. E. Caves and H. G. Johnson (London, 1968), pp. 261–78; M. B. Krauss, "Recent Developments in Customs Union Theory: An Interpretative Survey," *Journal of Economic Literature* 10 (1972): 413–36.

2. The only one that I have found is B. Balassa, *The Theory of Economic Integration* (London, 1962), who though he considers the theory to be of recent origin (p. 21) nevertheless does mention a far wider range of (relatively recent) literature than other commentators.

3. See Jacob Viner, *The Customs Union Issue* (New York, 1950), esp. chap. 4.

4. E.g., "customs union theory can be said to date from the publication of Viner's pioneering work." C. A. Cooper and B. F. Massell, "A New Look at Customs Union Theory," *Economic Journal* 75 (1965): 742–47, at p. 742; see also Lipsey, p. 262; Krauss, p. 413. There are a wealth of other references which could be cited to support the view that Viner's 1950 book is credited with being the *fons et origo* of customs union theory. Reference to three excellent texts will however suffice: C. E. Staley, *International Economics* (Englewood Cliffs, N.J., 1970), p. 135; A. M. Freeman, *International Trade* (New York, 1971), p. 174; B. Södersten, *International Economics* (London, 1970), pp. 430–31.

5. *Customs Unions: A League of Nations Contribution to the Study of Customs Union Problems* (Lake Success, 1947), p. 1. See also ibid. pp. 21 ff. for a number of other abortive attempts.

controversy in the nineteenth century and were in fact the normal way in which tariff adjustments were made.[6] Moreover, by 1950 Viner himself had been writing on the theory of preferential tariffs for more than thirty years.[7]

It seems then unlikely that the historical background is so insignificant that it can be ignored.[8] However, it is true that the early-twentieth-century literature is disappointing. Perusal of the works of J. S. Nicholson,[9] Pigou,[10] S. Culbertson,[11] or G. R. Parkin[12] reveals virtually nothing of interest. Bastable generally has little to say either,[13] although in an article on the concept of an Imperial Zollverein he does distinguish the free trade and protective effects of a customs union.[14] There are even a *few* writers whose work accords with the now generally accepted belief that before 1950 economists simply regarded customs unions as a step on the road to free trade—Haberler,[15] Weststrate,[16] and Sir T. E. Gregory are in this

6. For evidence of their importance see David MacPherson, *Annals of Commerce*, 4 vols. (London, 1805).

7. Viner was one of the authors who assisted with *Reciprocity and Commercial Treaties*, U.S. Tariff Commission (Washington, 1919). This was followed by his article "The Most-Favored-Nation Clause in American Commercial Treaties," *Journal of Political Economy* 32 (1924): 101–29.

8. Or summarized as the belief that customs unions are a step on the way to free trade and therefore improve world welfare, as is alleged by Lipsey, p. 262, an allegation which is then repeated in the secondary literature.

9. J. Sheild Nicholson, *Principles of Political Economy*, 2d ed. (London, 1902). See 1: 204, 2: 236, 242, 246, and 3: 360, 365, 367, 419. See also his article "Commercial Treaties" in R. H. Palgrave, *Dictionary of Political Economy*, new ed., ed. H. Higgs (London, 1925), 1: 354–55; his *The Tariff Question, with Special Reference to Wages and Unemployment* (London, 1903); his introduction to F. List, *The National System of Political Economy*, trans. Sampson S. Lloyd, new ed. (London, 1904); and his *Tariffs and International Commerce* (Edinburgh, 1892), which is noncommittal, even ambiguous.

10. A. C. Pigou, *Protective and Preferential Import Duties* (1906; reprinted, London, 1935).

11. W. S. Culbertson, *International Economic Policies* (London, 1925).

12. G. R. Parkin, "Federation, Commercial," in Palgrave, 2: 45–48.

13. See C. F. Bastable, *The Theory of International Trade with Some of Its Applications to Economic Policy*, 4th ed. (1903; reprinted, London, 1929); and his *The Commerce of Nations*, 9th ed., rev. T. E. Gregory (London, 1923; first published 1891), pp. 56–57, 90–91, and esp. p. 188.

14. C. F. Bastable, "An Imperial Zollverein with Preferential Tariffs," *Economic Journal* 12 (1902): 507–13, at pp. 507, 508–9, 512.

15. G. von Haberler, *The Theory of International Trade*, trans. A. W. Stonier and F. Benham (London, 1936), p. 390. G. Haberler, "The Political Economy of Regional or Continental Blocs," in *Postwar Economic Problems*, ed. Seymour Harris (New York, 1943), pp. 325–44, at p. 331. See also ibid., p. 330 for a view which would fit the Lipsey description noted above. However, Haberler's conclusion in this discussion is that there is no economic case for a customs union which is not an even better case for free trade.

16. C. Weststrate, "The Economic and Political Implications of a Customs Union," *Quarterly Journal of Economics* 62 (1947–48): 362–80.

category (though the latter has a long and thoughtful discussion of customs unions).[17]

But there is a great deal of earlier literature which is deeply interesting. Examination of this will show that the Viner analysis grew out of the theory of preferential tariffs; that this theory was part of the Classical discussion of commercial treaties; that the underlying theory was essentially the Classical mechanism of international trade; and that the essence of Viner's analysis was in fact developed long before 1950, growing out of the Classical discussion and using its tools. We shall also see that before 1950 a neo-Classical analysis of customs unions had already begun to emerge and that this has been almost entirely neglected—Meade's 1954 lectures being taken, incorrectly, as the starting date for this kind of literature.[18] Finally we may note that there is a third branch of modern customs union theory—that associated in particular with the work of Cooper and Massell—which has 19th-century roots in the writings of List (this time anti-Classical roots) and that this lineage is also ignored by its modern successors.

The Classical model

The main subject of interest is the origin of Viner's analysis. Classical trade theory contains the following: constant costs (though with occasional allowance for learning and scale economies in the Long Run); prices determined by reciprocal demand; welfare effects implied by production effects; and a growth orientation; and Viner uses this basic model. It is true that he does not make explicit reference to the determination of prices through reciprocal demand; but this has been a standard omission and one which was carried over into the later work by Gehrels and by Lipsey in their now classic articles on customs unions in the 1950's.[19] Nor is there much explicit reference to growth in this context; and this is interesting because growth also received relatively little emphasis in the Classical treatment of preferential tariffs.

But what is most significant is that this mode differs from a neo-Classical model in two important respects. Firstly, there are no demand curves. This was a conscious decision on Viner's part. He seems indeed to have had reservations about the Long Run normal

17. T. E. Gregory, *Tariffs: A Study in Method* (London, 1921), pp. 12–28, 441–82. The U.N. study (n.5 above) might also come into this category (pp. 75–84), although it does recognize that trade diversion may be involved in a customs union (pp. 81–82).

18. J. E. Meade, *The Theory of Customs Unions* (Amsterdam, 1955).

19. On this see J. Melvin, "Comments on the Theory of Customs Unions," *Manchester School* 36 (1969): 161–68.

demand function as such.[20] But more importantly he had already objected, in his great *Studies in the Theory of International Trade*, to the use of what were effectively partial equilibrium curves in an international trade context, an objection which was repeated in the 1950 book.[21] He had also objected to the use of community indifference curves in an international trade context, on the now familiar (but in 1937 far from familiar) grounds that the curves were not independent of income distribution, which might be altered by changes in trade patterns.[22] This should be noted, not only because it helps to explain Viner's use of a model identical with that of the Classical economists but also because Viner had effectively anticipated and dealt with some of the criticisms which were later to be leveled at his work, by Meade in particular. Viner was not assuming anything so unusual as fixed consumption ratios.[23] Rather, because he was not really dealing with general equilibrium, but making a logical distinction between trade creation and trade diversion, he felt free to assume that welfare effects were in the same direction as production effects and that therefore his production analysis implied the relevant consumption effects. This is not speculation; in an unpublished letter to Corden, Viner argued just this.[24] But, as is now recognized, this wholly Classical analysis runs into difficulties because it fails to take account of consumption changes resulting from changes in the *internal* price ratio in the opposite direction from changes in the terms of trade —which was precisely the Gehrels-Lipsey argument. In addition it is now argued (by such writers as Krauss, and Harry Johnson)[25] that it is meaningless to distinguish trade creation and trade diversion on the basis of production effects alone, because there are consumption effects of the Gehrels-Lipsey type. This is true; but it does not affect the point that Viner was being wholly Classical in his approach.

The absence of demand curves is an important characteristic of the analysis. The second important characteristic which distinguishes it from neo-Classical analysis is the assumption of infinite elasticity of supply—an assumption not used by those pre-1950 neo-Classical

20. Jacob Viner, *The Long View and the Short* (Glencoe, Ill., 1958), p. 357.

21. J. Viner, *Studies in the Theory of International Trade* (London, 1937; reprinted, 1964), pp. 589–91; *Customs Union Issue*, p. 53. I have not been able to trace any review by Viner of Meade's book (n.18 above); but the same objections would apply to Meade's treatment also.

22. Viner, *Studies*, pp. 520–24.

23. Lipsey, op. cit.

24. The letter is quoted in Krauss, p. 414 n.1.

25. Krauss, pp. 416–17; H. G. Johnson, "The Economic Theory of Customs Union," in *Money, Trade and Economic Growth* (London, 1962), pp. 46–73.

writers to which I have already briefly alluded, and an assumption taken by Meade as a basis for the remainder of his criticisms of Viner.

The mercantilist background to the Classical analysis

So Viner was using the Classical model. This model has a long history of application to trade preferences and to commercial treaties. Indeed, when the Classical writers found themselves having to address these problems, they had to deal with a significant body of mercantilist literature on the subject, which preceded them. The mercantilist writers had in general the one ultimate criterion for judging a commercial treaty, viz., the likely outcome for the balance of payments.[26] Thus the 1703 Methuen Treaty, which admitted Portuguese wines into Great Britain on preferential terms in return for the removal of a prohibition on British woolen exports to Portugal, was judged to be a success in respect of the trade balance; and in a publication called the *British Merchant* it was asserted that a statue of Mr. Methuen should be erected in every town.[27] But the 1713 Treaty of Utrecht and the 1786 Pitt-Eden Treaty were a different matter in mercantilist eyes. The mercantilist writers feared that these would lead to an adverse balance of trade and a loss of metal. One mercantilist writer, Joseph Richardson, set out to demonstrate the following proposition: "that in the proportion as the trade between England and France has been open or shut, have the interests of English commerce flourished or declined."[28] The argument was that expenditure on imports of luxuries from France had drained the country of specie via an unfavorable balance of payments. There was also a mercantilist writer called Dennis O'Bryen who argued that there were natural impediments to achieving a favorable balance with a country so generously endowed by nature with the means of production as France.[29] He also argued[30] that British imports of French goods reduced British imports from other countries "and this by the natural course of things decreased the consumption of our commodities in

26. Thus when Defoe sought to defend the Treaty of Utrecht he found it necessary to argue in these terms: see his *An Essay on the Treaty of Commerce with France: with Necessary Expositions* (London, 1713).

27. See J. R. McCulloch, *On Commerce: A Treatise on the Principles, Practice, and History of Commerce* (London, 1833), p. 82; *The British Merchant; or Commerce Preserv'd: in Answer to the Mercator, or Commerce Retriev'd*: Published every Tuesday and Friday (London, 1713).

28. [Joseph Richardson], *A Complete Investigation of Mr. Eden's Treaty, as it May affect the Commerce, the Revenue, or the General Policy of Great Britain* (London, 1787), p. 3

29. [Dennis O'Bryen], *A View of the Treaty of Commerce with France: Signed at Versailles, September 20, 1786, by Mr. Eden* (London, 1787), pp. 1–8.

30. Ibid., pp. 4–5.

those countries" so that the British *overall* balance was worsened by the shift to a competitively strong trading partner. Manufacturing excellence, he argued, rather like Harry Johnson in his 1968 Wicksell Lectures, was a transitional thing, so that Britain could not rely on superiority in particular lines of manufactures to redress the balance. He believed, as David Hume was also later to argue, that manufacturing would migrate to where labor costs were cheapest—in this case, he believed, to France, which was very able to absorb new technology. France could thus compete with British manufactures, while Britain by contrast did not have the resource endowment to compete with the French staple industries.[31] War with France was inevitable; and when this broke out again the British would, having already lost their markets in other countries through trading with France, lose the French market in turn.[32]

The Classical treatment

This kind of attitude to commercial treaties almost[33] disappeared completely under the Classical onslaught. Classical trade theory was directly opposed to mercantilism, particularly on the score of the balance of payments. So it is hardly surprising that the Classical writers should have been strong in their condemnation of the *trade diversion*—Viner's term is used quite deliberately as accurately representative of their argument—of the Methuen Treaty. Hume, who began the attack on mercantilism, also led the attack against the Methuen Treaty:

> But what have we gained by the bargain? We lost the French market for our woollen manufactures, and transferred the commerce of wine to Spain and Portugal, where we buy worse liquor at a higher price.[34]

Smith too condemned the Methuen Treaty, pointing to its mercantilist basis in the search for a favorable balance of precious metals.[35] The

31. Ibid., pp. 8–18, 19–44, esp. p. 43; cf. H. G. Johnson, *Comparative Cost and Commercial Policy Theory for a Developing World Economy* (Stockholm, 1968).

32. O'Bryen, pp. 117–18.

33. In the Goldsmith Library, University of London, there is an election pamphlet of 1881, with no indication of its source, entitled *Our Trade with France under the Cobden Treaty* which opposes renewal of the 1860 treaty on mercantilist (balance of trade) grounds.

34. D. Hume, *Economic Writings*, ed. E. Rotwein (Edinburgh, 1955), pp. 66–67; McCulloch, *The Literature of Political Economy* (London 1845; reprinted, 1938), p. 141.

35. A. Smith, *An Inquiry into the Nature and Causes of the Wealth of Nations*, ed. E. Cannan (London, 1904; reprinted, 1950), 2: 47.

treaty, it was true, contained elements of trade creation (through the removal of the prohibition of British woolens), but more strongly of trade diversion—through the wine duty preference. Trade diversion was harmful to the country which granted such preferences:

> When a nation binds itself by treaty either to permit the entry of certain goods from one foreign country which it prohibits from all others, or to exempt the goods of one country from duties to which it subjects those of all others, the country, or at least the merchants and manufacturers of the country so favoured, [we may note here a welfare distinction which disappeared, to be rediscovered by Krauss in 1972[36]] must necessarily derive great advantage from the treaty. . . . Such Treaties, however, though they may be advantageous to the merchants and manufacturers of the favoured, are necessarily disadvantageous to those of the favouring country. A monopoly is thus granted against them to a foreign nation; and they must frequently buy the foreign goods they have occasion for, dearer than if the free competition of other nations was admitted.[37]

This point was in turn recognized by Ricardo;[38] but it was given very much more prominence by McCulloch, who laid great stress on what he saw as overwhelming evidence of trade diversion in the Methuen Treaty. His love of claret added extra fire to his condemnation —claret as a French product being by the treaty subject to a higher duty than port, so that he had to drink what he regarded as inferior wine at a higher price.[39] He was also incensed by the adulteration which resulted and was fond of quoting a passage from Addison about this.[40] However, apart from his human concern about one of his favorite articles of consumption, he was opposed to the whole philosophy of distorting trade flows by treaty; and he argued, like Smith, that we injured ourselves if we gave a preference which the market would not have given, and that we were likely to be forced to give such a distorting preference in return for any which we were able to obtain for ourselves by commercial treaty.[41]

36. Krauss, p. 421.
37. Smith, 2: 46.
38. Ricardo, *Works*, ed. Sraffa (Cambridge, 1951), 1: 340–42.
39. McCulloch, "Restrictions on Foreign Commerce," *Edinburgh Review* 33 (1820): 331–51, at p. 344; see also *Literature of Political Economy*, p. 141.
40. McCulloch, "Duties on Wine—Restrictions on the Wine Trade," *Edinburgh Review* 40 (1824): 414–27, at pp. 419–20.
41. See also McCulloch's article "Trade with France—Reduction of the Duties on French Wine," *Scotsman*, 27 Dec. 1823, p. 825; and his *Dictionary of Commerce*

In fact he developed what became the standard Classical objections to such treaties, objections which the authors of later contrivances of this sort realized had to be met.[42] He accepted that commercial treaties historically had been valuable as means of creating trade during the emergence from the Middle Ages, when they succeeded in removing the risk of an arbitrary exercise of feudal power.[43] But they had been perverted into futile attempts to secure national advantage by trade diversion.[44]

McCulloch's—and indeed the Classical—attitude is well summarized in the following passage:

> If foreign powers be all treated alike, none of them has just grounds of complaint; and it can rarely be for the interest of any people to show preferences to one over another. Those, for example, by whom *we* may be most advantageously supplied with foreign products, require no preferences; and if we exclude them, or give a preference to others, we incontestably injure ourselves; and yet 19 out of 20 of the regulations as to duties in commercial treaties have been founded on this preposterous principle. They have been employed to divert trade into channels where it would not naturally flow; that is to render it less secure and less profitable than it would otherwise have been.[45]

By diverting trade a commercial treaty also succeeded in limiting its amount. The Methuen Treaty reduced British trade with France, both through weakening the French ability to purchase British exports and through provoking retaliation on the part of the French; and British trade was switched away from the rich French market to the poor Iberian one.[46]

(London, 1832), p. 1057. The theme continued through successive editions of the *Dictionary*; see the 1869 (posthumous) edition, p. 1406.

42. See e.g. H. Reeve, "Commercial Relations of France and England," *Edinburgh Review* 111 (1860): 277–31. See also the discussion of the 1860 Treaty below.

43. *Dictionary of Commerce* (1832), p. 1055; ibid. (1859), p. 1320; ibid. (1869), p. 1404; *On Commerce*, p. 81; *Literature of Political Economy*, pp. 130–40; Note XIV to McCulloch's 1863 edition of the *Wealth of Nations*.

44. Ibid. (1863 ed.), pp. 545–46. See also ibid. (1828 ed.), 4: 412; and *Dictionary of Commerce* (1832), p. 1056; ibid. (1859), p. 1320; ibid. (1869), p. 1405; *On Commerce*, p. 81.

45. *Wealth of Nations* (1863), p. 546; see also ibid. (1828), 4: 413; *On Commerce*, p. 81; *Dictionary of Commerce* (1832), p. 1057; (1859), p. 1321; (1869), p. 1405.

46. *Literature of Political Economy*, p. 141; *On Commerce*, p. 82; *Wealth of Nations* (1863 ed.), pp. 546–47; "Trade with France—Reduction of the Duties on French Wine," p. 825.

The important thing about freedom of trade for McCulloch, and for the Classical economists in general, was not that there should be no import duties levied for revenue purposes, but that these should be nondiscriminatory.[47]

J. B. Say too was opposed to commercial treaties. In his primer of policy, the *Cours complet*, a work directed at guiding the operations of government, Say informed his readers that treaties of commerce were based on the erroneous theory that freedom of trade was harmful to the economic system, whereas in fact liberalization of imports was conducive to exporting.[48]

The 1860 treaty and Classical analysis

Both Cobden and Gladstone, when considering, in September 1859, the possibility of a commercial treaty, were alive to the standard Classical objections to commercial treaties and to the arguments in favor of unilateral remission of duties. Cobden, indeed, explained to Louis-Napoleon that England could not grant preferences;[49] and the treaty was constructed on the basis that duty reductions made by England applied to a range of products (which were admittedly mainly those of France) from *whatever* source they came. The instigators and defenders of the treaty were opposed to *differential* duties themselves, precisely because of their trade-diverting effects; and both Cobden and Cliffe Leslie supported commercial treaties of the 1860 variety, which contained no such duties, as an approach to free trade.[50] Writing to Bright, Cobden insisted that there was no preference and hence no trade diversion in the 1860 treaty.[51] Of course, as was implied by some of the criticisms, there was discrimination *by commodity*: and given intercommodity substitution, there was still some distortion. But what was given away on the part of France was *prohibition*, and so there was likely to be some genuine trade creation. Thus defenders of the 1860 treaty, such as Sir Thomas Farrer and Sir Louis Mallet, were able to argue that it was nondiversionary; and this later became the standard defense of the Cobden-Chevalier Treaty. (What they were arguing was in fact largely true, although

47. McCulloch, *Principles of Political Economy* (London, 1864), p. 112.

48. J. B. Say, *Cours complet d'économie politique pratique* (Brussels, 1832), 2: 360–65.

49. J. Morley, *The Life of Richard Cobden* (new ed., London, 1883), pp. 452–53, 457.

50. See T. C. Leslie, "Financial Reform," *Cobden Club Essays*, 2d ser. 1871–72 (London, 1872), pp. 185–259.

51. Morley, p. 517.

with some reservations about the wine and carrying trade.)[52] Thus Mallet wrote of the treaty:

> If these reforms had been made exclusively in each other's favour, they might justly have been called unsound, but they were made equally for all the countries of the world; on the side of England at once, on the side of France prospectively; and thus, instead of reverting to a system of monopoly, the differential policy of France was forever destroyed, and the equal system of England maintained and consolidated.[53]

A key point in their defense and one which ensured that tariff reductions were made on a uniform basis was the existence, in this treaty and in subsequent ones, of the most-favored-nation clause, which ensured that any tariff reductions had to be made available to a wide range of countries. Of course insofar as the most-favored-nation clause was of the American or conditional type, it was virtually inoperative and could not be relied on to prevent distortion, as Viner himself pointed out at length in 1924.[54] However, it does seem to be the case that it was only the United States which interpreted such conditional clauses at all literally, and after 1860 they became distinctly unfashionable.

It was then with some amazement that the architects of the 1860 treaty, having taken great care to meet the standard Classical objections to such treaties, found themselves under attack from writers like McCulloch and Overstone who disapproved of the treaty. They responded with some fury. Sir Robert Morier, a self-proclaimed disciple of Cobden, wrote of McCulloch, "who with his dying breath in the

52. For reservations on this matter see Sir Stafford Northcote in *Hansard*, vol. 156, cols. 1527–28.

53. Sir L. Mallet, *Free Exchange*, ed. B. Mallet (London, 1891), pp. 80–81. See also B. Mallet, *Sir Louis Mallet: A Record of Public Service and Political Ideals* (London, 1905), chap. 2, "Commercial Treaty Policy," pp. 56–102; and T. H. Farrer, *Free Trade versus Fair Trade* (Cobden Club, London, 1882), esp. pp. 61, 63, 76, 130. This was also the argument used in Parliament. See *Hansard* 3d ser. vol. 156, cols. 1121–22 (Duke of Argyll); vol. 157, col. 560 (Earl of Cork)—"what we give to France by this Treaty she is perfectly aware we give to every other nation"; vol. 199, cols. 882–83 (Gladstone). The same position was taken by other adherents of the Cobden Club both at home and abroad, including the German free-trader Julius Faucher (see his contribution to *Cobden Club Essays*, 2d ser. (n.50 above), pp. 272, 292. The Cobdenites felt that a continuous process of freeing trade through treaties linked by the most-favored-nation clause was taking place—see the introduction by Sir Louis Mallet to *Free Trade and the European Treaties of Commerce* (Cobden Club, London, 1875) p. 6. See also Cobden Club, *Commercial Policy of France and the Treaty with England of 1860*. There was a great deal of truth in what they were arguing—see the U.S. Tariff Commission report of 1919 cited above, pp. 18, 43, 394–95, 413, 464.

54. *Journal of Political Economy*, 1924, loc. cit.

last edition of his dictionary raved against the French treaty in the style of a papal encyclical,''[55] and then denounced the way that

> the soi-disant economist Do-nothings, spellbound by the word *treaty*, have transferred the legitimate horror they have of the *old-fashioned treaty of commerce*, of which the Methuen treaty is the type, to the *modern treaty* of commerce, of which Cobden's treaty is the type, which is very much like confounding black with white, or light with darkness. The essential characteristic of the old treaty of commerce was to establish commercial monopolies between the contracting parties against the rest of the world. The essential characteristic of the modern treaty of commerce is to remove restrictions on trade for the benefit of all, and by the most favoured nation clause, which is the key-stone of the modern treaty, to cut through the vital nerve of commercial monopoly.[56]
>
> [But] *though there are treaties of commerce incompatible with free trade, there are others not only not incompatible with free trade, but of the essence of free trade and its only true and definite expression*. . . . The Alpha and Omega of the modern treaty of commerce is the setting up of an international barrier against the raising of Custom duties, and, by the action of the most favoured nation clause, the securing that every tariff reduction made by one state shall be shared by the great commercial confederacy, bound together by the network of treaties which owe their origin to the Anglo-French Treaty of 1860 and to the great heresiarch Richard Cobden.[57]

In fact the dispute was, on one side at least, based upon a misunderstanding. A viable most-favored-nation clause was a key point in the Classical discussion: and it was on this ground that McCulloch approved the abortive Treaty of Utrecht of 1713, which contained a most-favored-nation clause and which was thrown out by a mercantilist parliament fearing an adverse balance of trade.[58] McCulloch did not, then, attack the 1860 treaty on trade diversion grounds; and he

55. See R. Wemyss, *Memoirs and Letters of the Right Hon. Sir Robert Morier G.C.B.*, 2 vols. (London, 1911), 2: 134.

56. Ibid., pp. 136–37. See also Morley, p. 519.

57. [R. Morier], *Commercial Treaties: Free Trade and Internationalism: Four Letters, Reprinted from the "Manchester Examiner and Times" by a Disciple of Richard Cobden* (Cobden Club, London, 1870), pp. 14, 16, 19–20.

58. See McCulloch, *Literature of Political Economy*, p. 142, and the Schomberg work cited therein.

conceded that it had given a powerful stimulus to trade.[59] His objections were on revenue grounds, as we shall see below.[60] In this context a most-favored-nation clause simply worsened the revenue situation.[61]

But what is interesting about these exchanges—apart from their intrinsic historical interest—is their relevance to the development of our subject. *For what was clearly at issue in the discussions was the relative amount of trade creation and trade diversion involved in the treaty*. The Classical reasoning on this was accepted by both sides.

Because of the history of commercial treaties the Classical writers tended to be suspicious of them and to look in them for elements of trade diversion. At the same time they were prepared to concede the possibility that a commercial treaty, even if it contained substantial trade-diverting elements, might act as a wedge on behalf of the large cause of free trade; and it was on these grounds that McCulloch approved of arrangements made with France in 1786 and 1825.[62] Commercial treaties could be valuable teaching devices in instructing consumers abroad on the benefits of free trade; on this they were in agreement with the defenders of the 1860 treaty.[63]

But their overall appraisal of such an arrangement depended upon the relative amounts of trade creation and diversion which could be expected from it in the long run. Thus a customs union could be beneficial *if* it had a low common external tariff. At first the Zollverein was regarded with great suspicion in England—one writer even

59. *Principles* (1864 ed.), p. 108.

60. See *Supplement to the edition of Mr. McCulloch's Commercial Dictionary Published in 1859; comprising the late Treaty of Commerce with France, the New Tariff for the United Kingdom, the New Indian Tariff with a great variety of Miscellaneous Information in Regard to Commercial Subjects* (Longman's, London, 1860), cited below as CD 1860 Supplement; J. R. McCulloch, *An Article, Practical and Theoretical, on Taxation Written for the Eighth Edition of the Encyclopaedia Britannica* (Edinburgh, A. and C. Black 1860, 2d ed.), subtitled "Comprising Remarks on Some of the Measures Embodied in the Budget of 1860," cited below as EB 8 Taxation. Both these works are very rare—the present writer knows of only one copy of each; hence the full reference to avoid confusion with other publications by McCulloch.

61. CD 1860 Supplement, p. 10.

62. *Scotsman*, 4 Feb. 1826, p. 77; *Literature of Political Economy*, p. 143 (though McCulloch added the rider, p. 144, "At the same time, however we are far from thinking that the treaty of 1786 should be taken for a model. The negotiators were too much influenced by old notions, and the treaty is encumbered with too many conditions"); *On Commerce* pp. 83–84; see however McCulloch's *Wealth of Nations*, 1863 ed., p. 547: "whatever benefit the treaty was fitted to confer either on us or on the French might have been realized without its intervention."

63. Reeve, op. cit.; a *Times* editorial 12 March 1860 (8b), argued that duty reductions under the treaty would teach the French consumer to ask for more of such reductions.

thought it was all a *Russian* plot.[64] McCulloch himself was suspicious at an early stage in its development, arguing that Prussian commercial policy was aiming at self-sufficiency as far as possible, and that the basis of Prussian policy was really protectionism at the behest of manufacturing pressure groups. This distorted the allocation of resources, thereby reducing welfare. He objected in particular to the prospect of the trade diversion involved in a high common external tariff and to the imposition of this high tariff on the smaller German states. The trade diversion itself would be largely for the benefit of Prussia.[65]

Nevertheless, although McCulloch remained suspicious of such unions, and quoted with approval the resolution of Switzerland not to enter into a customs union,[66] he, together with a number of other British writers, later argued that the Zollverein had adopted a sufficiently low common external tariff to make it overwhelmingly trade-creating in character. These writers included Sir John Bowring, whose investigations were undertaken on behalf of the British Government.[67] This favorable view was buttressed in McCulloch's case by the idea that income effects within a customs union could give rise to increasing imports; the creation of trade between the constituent German states in this case having increased income in Germany as a whole, the rise in income had the normal positive effects on the level of imports.[68]

The Classical analysis in perspective

There is, then, both trade creation and trade diversion in the Classical analysis of commercial treaties and customs unions, with the latter effect expected to predominate. Herein in fact is the foundation

64. W. Cargill, *An Examination of the Origin, Progress, and Tendency of the Commercial and Political Confederation against England and France, called the "Prussian League"* (Newcastle, 1840).

65. J. R. McCulloch, "Prussian Commercial Policy," *Foreign Quarterly Review* 9 (May 1832): 455–70, esp. pp. 463, 467. On the development of the union see A. H. Price, *Evolution of the Zollverein* (Univ. of Michigan Press, 1949), esp. chap. 8.

66. McCulloch, "Commerce and Manufactures of Switzerland," *Edinburgh Review* 64 (1836): 168–76, at p. 173. See also p. 176.

67. McCulloch, *A Statistical Account of the British Empire*, 2d ed. (London, 1839), 2: 11; *Dictionary of Commerce* (1856), pp. 1068–69; ibid. (1859), pp. 1068–71; Sir John Bowring, *Report on the Prussian Commercial Union addressed to the Right Hon. Lord Viscount Palmerston, Her Majesty's Secretary of State for Foreign Affairs* (London, 1840), esp. pp. 12–13, 39–40, 52–53; John MacGregor, *The Germanic Union of Customs: the Commercial Treaties and Tariffs; the Agriculture, Manufactures, Commerce and Navigation of Prussia and the Other States of Germany* (London, 1842), esp. pp. 7, 65.

68. McCulloch, *Statistical Account* (1839), 2: 11; ibid. (1854), pp. 14–15; *A Dictionary, Geographical, Statistical and Historical* (1854 ed.), 2: 554.

of Viner's analysis. It would however be quite wrong to give the impression either that this was all that there was to the Classical analysis or that these concepts were consistently and impeccably used.

In fact, the Classical objections to commercial treaties, especially that of 1860, covered a far wider range than, and indeed helped to conceal, the trade-creation and trade-diversion elements. There was the argument that Great Britain's example in adopting unilateral freedom of trade would persuade other countries to follow suit. The benefits which the British received from this action would clearly indicate to other countries the course they should follow.[69] *Per contra*, a treaty set a bad example: it was an apparent admission that the unilateral adoption of free trade in 1846 had been wrong.[70] Then there was the view that because of the achievement of an automatic equilibrium in the balance of payments through the operation of the price-specie-flow mechanism, it was perfectly reasonable to pursue a unilateral policy. This line stems from Hume and shows clearly how the Classical attitude sprang from the antimercantilist movement.[71] The opposition to commercial treaties of Robert Lowe, opposition which embarrassed the government in which he was Chancellor of the Exchequer, was on these grounds.[72] There was, too, it was argued, immediate benefit in a policy of this sort which gave home consumers access to a lower-cost source of supply.

Of course such an argument neglected the terms of trade; but it seems likely that writers like Morier did not understand the latter. For Morier wrote a denial of the process of automatic generation of exports, in order to establish the need for commercial treaties to assist such exports; and in the course of this he thought he had refuted the Classical position, which depends upon the price-specie-flow mechanism, on the basis of a model which contained no money.

69. Say, *Cours complet*, 2: 360–3; McCulloch, *Statistical Account* (1839), 2: 15; CD 1860 Supplement, p. 8; *The Correspondence of Lord Overstone*, ed. D. P. O'Brien (Cambridge, 1971), 1: 67–70, 2: 910, 3: 1232.

70. Henry George Grey, 3d Earl Grey, *Free Trade with France: Letters to "The Times" with an Introduction* (London, 1881), p. 22.

71. Hume, *Economic Writings*, ed. Rotwein, p. 67. See also Smith, *Wealth of Nations*, 2: 49–50 (which has somewhat similar arguments, but not a fully articulated price-specie-flow mechanism); Say, pp. 360, 363; McCulloch, in *Edinburgh Review*, 1824, loc. cit. pp. 422–23; ibid., 1820, loc. cit. pp. 347–48; ibid., 59 (1834): 182–96; "Trade with France," at pp. 195–96; *Wealth of Nations* (1863 ed.), p. 547; *Scotsman*, 27 Dec. 1823, p. 825. On the question of the automatic balance see D. P. O'Brien, *J. R. McCulloch: A Study in Classical Economics* (London, 1970), pp. 204–8.

72. For Lowe's opposition see *Hansard* 3d ser., vol. 117 (17 March 1865), cols. 1861–65; for the embarrassment his attitude caused see ibid. vol. 199 (25 Feb. 1870), cols. 806–7.

He could, he believed, for the purposes of his analysis, "eliminate the phenomenon of money, which we all know does not touch the vitals of the question of exchange."[73] But in the Classical model, money is absolutely essential to the whole mechanism. Morier was probably trying to raise the effect on the terms of trade of a unilateral policy of duty remission;[74] but as an amateur he was insufficiently familiar with the analysis, even that of Torrens, which would have supplied what he required.[75] (However one of his supporters, Cliffe Leslie, who certainly was familiar with the analysis, still managed to assert that a treaty would necessarily improve the terms of trade).[76]

In addition to the arguments about example and automatic balance, there was the view that negotiation of commercial treaties produced international tension and suspicion, and the belief that reciprocity had proved a failure, historically, as a means of freeing world trade.[77] It was also held that entering into a treaty restricted a country's freedom of action on fiscal matters. It was argued that for a country to bind itself by treaty removed its freedom of action to follow whatever trade and fiscal policy was thought best.[78] This is one aspect of the commercial treaty of 1860 which bothered McCulloch and Overstone a good deal. In addition there were special problems connected with this treaty. It involved, through its duty reductions, a very significant sacrifice of revenue on the part of England, necessitating the prolongation of the income tax. The regressive nature of the remaining duties was unjust, and it would in turn lead to a demand for their repeal, and thus a greater reliance on direct taxation, which, since the lowest incomes were excluded from such direct taxation, was progressive. McCulloch was strongly

73. *Memoirs*, p. 135.

74. See his *Commercial Treaties: Free Trade and Internationalism*, pp. 38–39.

75. Robert Torrens, *The Budget: On Commercial and Colonial Policy* (reprinted New York, 1970), Letter IX Postscript (dated 22d April 1843), "On the Injurious Effects which would result from a Reduction of Duties upon Foreign Productions, unaccompanied by a corresponding mitigation of the Duties imposed by Foreign Countries upon British Goods." It is an interesting puzzle for historians of economics that this publication, which caused such a furore when it first appeared, should not have figured in the debates over commercial treaties.

76. Leslie, pp. 258–59.

77. Grey, pp. 17, 21–22; McCulloch, CD 1860 Supplement, p. 9; *Speech Delivered by Lord Overstone in the House of Lords 15 March 1860 on the Address on the Treaty of Commerce with France; with an Appendix* (London, 1860), p. 9; Sir Henry Parnell, *Coup-d'oeil sur les avantages des relations commerciales entre la France et l'Angleterre, basées sur les vrais principes de l'économie politique; par un Membre du Parlement d'Angleterre* (Paris, 1832,) pp. 1–2.

78. Overstone, *Speech*, p. 6; Parnell, op. cit.; Overstone, *Correspondence*, 1: 67–70; McCulloch, CD 1860 Supplement, pp. 8–9; *Wealth of Nations* (1863 ed.), p. 546; Earl Grey, *Hansard*, 3d ser., vol. 165 (1860), cols. 1116–21.

opposed to direct taxation and also to progressive taxation; Cobden on the other hand believed a shift to direct taxation to be desirable. But McCulloch and Overstone as enthusiasts for indirect taxation believed that there should be a 10 to 15 percent minimum duty on anything except raw materials.[79] In addition there was a Club-of-Rome-like obsession with the possibility of the exhaustion of Britain's coal reserves, leading to an end to economic growth. For this reason the critics were very much opposed to the undertaking in the treaty of 1860 not to impose any export duty on coal.[80]

Some Classical writers, though not concerned with the effects on the terms of trade of a unilateral remission of duty, were concerned with the effects on the terms of trade of commercial treaties. Thus we find Adam Smith arguing:

> That part of its own produce with which such a nation purchases foreign goods, must consequently be sold cheaper, because when two things are exchanged for one another, the cheapness of the one is a necessary consequence, or rather is the same thing with the dearness of the other. The exchangeable value of its annual produce, therefore, is likely to be diminished by every such treaty.[81]

In fact it is not necessarily true that a commercial treaty, or even a customs union, will necessarily turn the terms of trade against the contracting parties. Indeed according to one modern critic the possibility of an improvement in the terms of trade is the only valid argument *for* a customs union on Classical lines.[82] Moreover one Classical writer—Robert Torrens—actually argued in favor of an Imperial Zollverein in order to prevent foreign governments' damaging us by turning the terms of trade against us.[83] But this was hardly typical of the Classical writers in general.

79. See J. R. McCulloch, *A Treatise on Taxation*, ed. D. P. O'Brien (Edinburgh, 1975), and editor's introduction; McCulloch, CD 1860 Supplement, pp. 13–14; EB 8 Taxation, p. 27. Overstone, *Speech*, pp. 7–9, 12, 15, 17; on Cobden's tax reform aims see Leslie, pp. 185, 187.

80. See Overstone, *Correspondence*, I: 67–70; EB 8 Taxation, pp. 26–27.

81. Smith, 2: 46.

82. H. G. Johnson, "An economic Theory of Protectionism, Tariff Bargaining and the Formation of Customs Unions," *Journal of Political Economy* 63 (1965): 256–82. For a summary of the modern discussion of the terms of trade effects see Krauss, pp. 421–23. Johnson has argued that a trade diversion production effect tends to improve the terms of trade and that such an improvement will reduce the amount of loss from trade diversion itself.

83. See Lord Robbins, *Robert Torrens and the Evolution of Classical Economics* (London, 1958), pp. 187, 228, 256, 313.

There is also another element which appears in the Classical literature. This was an emphasis on the monopoly power given to producers in a country with which another country concluded a commercial treaty, when the producers in the first country were able to supply only a small part of the market requirements of the second country. (This may be called the "Hawaii effect" on the grounds that the case of Hawaiian sugar is the classic one which was given much prominence by Viner's teacher Taussig and also by Viner himself,[84] although it has been neglected in the subequent rush to credit Viner with the trade-creation and trade-diversion distinction.) This point is to be found in Classical discussions of the Methuen Treaty; and in this Classical literature the further point is made that, unless there is a barrier to entry, producers in the privileged country will not enjoy supernormal profits in the long run, although excessive amounts of resources would be attracted into the export industries supplying the commercial treaty partner.[85]

But despite all these other elements in the analysis, trade creation and trade diversion were there, and the Classical economists would not have argued, as for instance Haberler did in his classic text on international trade, that preferential tariff reduction was better than no tariff reduction at all.

Viner's continuation of the Classical tradition

Viner was exceptionally well-read in the Classical economists, as indeed was his teacher Taussig. It is then not surprising to find that Viner's earlier writings actually continue the Classical tradition. In particular there is an article in a Swedish journal *Index*.[86] In this article, "The Most Favored Nation Clause," Viner, in discussing preferential duties, used the concept of trade diversion to show that such duties were not trade creating, and that *some* duty reduction was *not* necessarily better than *no* duty reduction. In this article he explained that, on economic grounds, a number of objections apply to discriminatory tariffs which do not apply to uniform tariffs at a high level. Indeed the essence of the 1950 analysis is here:

> A tariff that is high, but uniform in its treatment of imports regardless of their origin, may divert trade from the channels which

84. F. Taussig, "Reciprocity," *Quarterly Journal of Economics* 7 (1892): 26–39, reprinted in *Free Trade, the Tariff, and Reciprocity* (New York, 1920), chap. 6; *Some Aspects of the Tariff Question* (Cambridge, Mass., 1931), pp. 59–60; Viner, *Index*, loc. cit., pp. 6–7; see also the 1919 U.S. Tariff Commission Report cited above, pp. 24–26. Taussig was Chairman of the Commission and Viner assisted with the report.

85. McCulloch, *Wealth of Nations* (1863 ed.), p. 243 n.2, and see also Smith's text itself at this point; *Edinburgh Review*, 1824, loc. cit., p. 425.

86. *Index* vol. 6, no. 61 (Jan. 1931): 2–17.

> it would follow if allowed freely to choose its own path much less than would a more moderate tariff which applies different treatment to imports according to their country of origin. Suppose that under free trade country A would find it to its advantage to import a particular commodity from country B, and that even with a high duty it is still not possible to produce the commodity at home at a profit to its producers, so that it continues to be imported from B. While the tariff reduces the volume of trade, it does so only as a revenue measure, and still permits the commodity to be produced there where it can be produced most cheaply. Suppose, now, that the duty is reduced by half on imports from a third country, C, and that by virtue of this preferential treatment C can undersell B and capture A's trade. The result of the discrimination in favor of C is that the commodity which could be most cheaply produced in B, and would be produced there even if A had a high tariff, provided it was nondiscriminatory, is now produced in C, where the conditions for its production are comparatively unfavorable. The reduction in duty, because it is discriminatory and not uniformly extended to all, operates as a deterrent instead of a stimulus to the optimum allocation of the world's resources in production.[87]

All that was required, in order to produce the 1950 analysis, was the assumption that A was also a producer of the commodity—which Viner explicitly did not make (but which Haberler did later make in criticism of him, ironically enough). Indeed the passage quoted is quite startlingly reminiscent of the material in chapter 4 of the 1950 book. This article is in fact a vital link between the Classical literature and the book—for here Viner himself has a discussion of discriminatory tariffs which not only contains the essentials of the later analysis but is also wholly a Classical one, containing a number of the other usual Classical points about discrimination, such as the danger of retaliation and the "Hawaii effect." Moreover Viner goes some way towards applying this idea of trade diversion to a customs union.[88]

It is strange that commentators have ignored what was virtually a lifetime of writing by Viner on trade policy, of which the 1950 work was simply a part, in accord with the general stream of that writing. I think they may have been misled by the absence of any discussion of these matters in Viner's great *Studies*. But even in a 1924 article on the Most Favored Nation Clause he argued that this clause, in its unconditional form, was necessary to avoid the trade diversion usu-

87. Ibid., p. 5.
88. Ibid., p. 11.

ally associated with commercial treaties, thus echoing the discussion of the 1860's:

> Most tariff discriminations are not wanton, but arise out of reciprocity agreements. It was precisely to bring about equality of treatment and to eliminate the economic disadvantages, the ill-feeling, and the diplomatic bickering resulting from such discriminations that the use of the most-favored-nation clause became common. . . . To the world as a whole, also, reciprocity treaties, even on free-trade grounds, are ordinarily not an amelioration, but on the contrary are an intensification of the evils of customs tariffs. They not only do not counteract the tendency of protective import duties to divert international trade from the channels which it would follow under free trade, but they may cause an even wider departure of trade from its "natural" channels than would result from a regime of uniform protective tariffs at the levels prevalent prior to the grant of partial reductions of duties through reciprocity arrangements. Imports which come in over a uniform tariff barrier are still being produced where the conditions are economically most advantageous for their production. If the tariff is not uniform, however, the production of the commodities affected may be diverted from the foreign country best fitted to produce them to another foreign country not so well situated for their production, but able to compete on a price basis because of the tariff differential which has been given to it.[89]

Here we have in fact Viner continuing and restating the Classical view of commercial treaties out of which grew his *Customs Union Issue*. Indeed the only significant points made explicit in his later study were the introduction of a common external tariff, and the assumption noted earlier that both countries in the union were producers of the good in question. But these hardly serve to cut the discussion off from what had gone before as was (no doubt unintentionally) emphasized by Lipsey when defining the theory of customs unions as "that branch of tariff theory which deals with the effects of geographically discriminatory changes in trade barriers"[90]—which could well cover commercial treaties.

Hawtrey and Robbins and the Classical tradition

Viner was not the only writer to continue in this line of enquiry. There are at least two others, both of whom were themselves deeply

89. Viner, *Journal of Political Economy*, 1924, loc. cit., pp. 107–8.
90. Lipsey, p. 261.

versed in Classical literature. There was Hawtrey, who, concentrating on the trade diversion aspects of customs unions, emphasized this to the exclusion of the possibility of trade creation. The breakup of the Austro-Hungarian Empire resulted in the creation of new frontiers, and the new tariff barriers obstructed trade between the new states. "But if the import duties had remained at the same level as before, the markets which the succession States lost in one another would have been more accessible than before to outside producers."[91] The reasoning is clear: if A and B are both "succession States" and C is an outside country, the breakup of the Empire results in C now competing on equal terms in A's market with B, instead of the products of B being duty-free. It may be, indeed it is, true that this analysis neglects trade creation. But it certainly does not fit the received picture of pre-1950 customs unions theory as "customs unions are a step on the road to free trade." And it does not fit it because Hawtrey was writing in the Classical tradition.

Perhaps the most striking case of all is the treatment of the problem by Lord Robbins. In a book published in 1937 he wrote:

> the gain from regional regrouping or wider units of any kind is not a gain of greater self-sufficiency, but a gain of the abolition of so much self-sufficiency on the part of the areas which are thus amalgamated. . . . It is not the possible self-sufficiency of the area as a whole, but the absence of self-sufficiency on the part of the constituent states, which is the advantage of the Union.
>
> It follows, too, that any gain in productive efficiency which is secured by the abolition of "internal" obstacles is a gain which has its cost if it is secured only by the erection of obstacles around the area. From the international point of view, the tariff union is not an advantage in itself. It is an advantage only in so far as, on balance, it conduces to more extensive division of labor. It is to be justified only by arguments which would justify still more its extension to all areas capable of entering into trade relationships. The only possible vindication of the retention of old restrictions or the erection of new ones is the argument that, in their absence, the tendency to restrict would be still more rampageous. No doubt if we could coax the rest of the world into free trade by a high tariff union against the produce of the Eskimos that would be, on balance, an international gain. But it would be inferior to an arrangement whereby the Eskimos were

91. R. G. Hawtrey, *Economic Destiny* (London, 1944), pp. 135–36.

> included. The only completely innocuous tariff union would be directed against the inaccessible produce of the moon.[92]

Now this, from a writer deeply learned in the writings of the Classical economists, is entirely in their tradition and an important link in the chain of development from Adam Smith and Hume to Viner's 1950 book. Like McCulloch, Lord Robbins concluded that the Zollverein had a low common external tariff and was not trade-diverting in character.[93]

Looked at coldly, all that Viner did was to start from the position of the Classical economists, and of Hawtrey and Lord Robbins, and then simply add to this the logical possibility of some trade creation, depending on the relative height of the pre-union tariff and the common external tariff, and on the possibility that both countries in the union were producers of the good in question.

Nevertheless these were short discussions in the context of rather wider issues: it was Viner who successfully focused attention on trade creation and trade diversion, thus ensuring the maintenance of the main Classical tradition.

The new theories of protectionism

The new alternative to this tradition, embodied particularly in the work of Professors Cooper and Massell, has, by implication, grasped this point exactly. For they have argued that in terms of the Viner (i.e. Classical) model there is no reason for preferring a customs union to complete free trade. In this they are correct; and in espousing the idea of nationalism as a public good (and in developing the idea of maximum welfare in terms of public and private goods, where industrialization is a public good, as Harry Johnson has done) these writers are in fact returning to another line of development which has all along been distinct from the Classical one which Viner maintained. They have argued that an economic theory of protection is required, one which would allow comparison of nonpreferential and preferential tariff policy as alternative welfare-yielding protectionist policies rather than as mechanisms for the removal of trade barriers.[94] But the Zollverein, even though it ultimately passed through the Classical

92. Lord Robbins, *Economic Planning and International Order* (London, 1937), pp. 121–22. Both Hawtrey and Robbins are mentioned (the latter is quoted) by Viner.

93. Robbins, pp. 122–23.

94. Cooper and Massell, *Economic Journal*, 1965, loc. cit.; and "Towards a General Theory of Customs Unions for Developing Countries," *Journal of Political Economy* 73 (1965): 461–76; H. G. Johnson, *Journal of Political Economy*, 1965, loc. cit., esp. pp. 279–80. See also Krauss, p. 417.

tests, owed its origins in part to visions of this sort.[95] List saw customs unions as protective devices and thought the Zollverein a particularly successful example—one which he wished to extend to include Austria; and he believed protection to be a highly necessary element in economic development if countries were to emerge from the primary-producer stage.[96] All of this is remarkably anticipatory of the work of Cooper and Massell, and of Harry Johnson. The only *vital* difference that I can find between their work and that of List is that they do not rely upon the eventual emergence of increasing returns to justify protection.[97] But it is still easy to see that there is continuity; yet suprisingly List is not mentioned in either of the two surveys to which I referred at the beginning, or even in Balassa's superb *Theory of Economic Integration*.

The neo-Classical treatment

To the historian of economic thought it is fascinating to see how these two streams of thought still continue. But now there is a third stream in the form of the neo-Classical analysis. This, as we have already noted, is generally thought to date from the work of Meade. Meade's criticisms are based on Viner's neglect of a demand curve (which we have seen was conscious and deliberate) and also on various other possible forms of trade diversion arising from removing the assumption of infinite elasticity of supply.[98] Thus, increased imports from the customs union partner B could release factors and increase the elasticity of supply of production of industries in which A competes with imports from C.[99] It is also possible that where A's exports to B rise because of a reduction in import duty, not only will B's imports from C fall (which is Vinerian trade diversion) but there will also be a reduction in A's exports to C if supply elasticity is less than infinite.[100] Moreover these possible repercussions which Meade has raised may not be the end of the matter, as he points out, because, after their operation, balance-of-payments difficulties may be in evidence and so further adjustments required.[101] There is also the possi-

95. See Bowring's 1840 report, cited above, pp. 1, 53–54.

96. F. List, *The National System of Political Economy*, trans. S. Lloyd (London, 1885), pp. 323–24, 398, 434.

97. Cooper and Massell, *Economic Journal*, 1965, loc. cit., p. 742; *Journal of Political Economy*, 1965, loc. cit., p. 463; Johnson, ibid., loc. cit., p. 261.

98. Meade, p. 77.

99. Ibid., pp. 71–72.

100. Ibid., p. 76.

101. Ibid., p. 83.

bility (which has also been raised by Spraos but neglected by Viner because of his Classical model) that prices may diverge from opportunity costs, thus making the whole analysis inapplicable.[102] Harry Johnson, who has also contributed to this analysis, has argued that if supply is not perfectly elastic, trade diversion has two further consequences. Firstly, the terms of trade with country C will be improved if any trade survives the customs union; secondly, inelasticity of supply reduces the amount of trade diversion. A favorable movement of the terms of trade helps to offset the loss from trade diversion. There is also the problem that if some particular foreign goods are complementary to imports from B, trade creation will produce further trade creation; and conversely there may be losses of this type. A great deal comes to depend in this analysis on the values of elasticity of supply.[103]

This is all perfectly valid analysis of its type and developed with all the acuteness and virtuosity which we associate with the works of Professors Meade and Johnson. But I would like to suggest that most, if not all, of it could have been developed out of the work of two writers who receive virtually no credit in the literature whatever. As Balassa alone has pointed out, another writer published an analysis of customs unions in 1950. But it appeared in French, and it was not translated into English until 1953; and therefore in the consciousness of Anglo-Saxon economists it did not exist until that date![104] This writer was Byé; and indeed it seems to me that Balassa's book owes more to Byé than to Viner. Not only did he distinguish trade creation and trade diversion but he dealt with the case of less than infinite elasticity of supply, the role of elasticity of demand, the distribution of benefits, and the mobility of factors. Earlier still there was De Beers, who, publishing in 1941, used a Marshallian partial equilibrium analysis and distinguished trade creation and trade diversion clearly.[105] He then built up an analysis of cases where the original tariff was revenue or protective in intent; he compared the free trade pattern with the customs union trade pattern; he dealt with cases of both constant *and* increasing costs; he explicitly introduced the level of the common external tariff as of critical importance; he took some

102. Ibid., pp. 91–92; J. Spraos, "The Condition for a Trade-Creating Customs Union," *Economic Journal* 74 (1964): 101–8, at pp. 101–2.

103. H. G. Johnson, *Money, Trade and Economic Growth*, 2d ed. (London, 1964), pp. 56–57.

104. Balassa, p. 22; M. Byé, "Customs Unions and National Interests," *Economie Appliquée*, 1950, reprinted in *International Economic Papers*, 1953, pp. 208–34.

105. J. S. De Beers, "Tariff Aspects of a Federal Union," *Quarterly Journal of Economics* 56 (1941–42): 49–92, at p. 62.

account of the public good benefit arising from the expenditure of tariff revenues and related this to the benefit of consumers from the lower cost of consuming the good;[106] and he introduced consumption effects on Marshallian lines very similar to those later used by Harry Johnson. He also considered the effect on the terms of trade of a sharply rising export supply curve in country C—the argument is similar to Johnson's later one—and he included the repercussions of income changes on imports.

The analysis was, it is true, incomplete. There was only one good, and thus there were none of the general equilibrium considerations introduced by Gehrels and by Lipsey. But this hardly justifies the total absence of De Beers' name from survey articles. De Beers did have the benefit of Viner's earlier article and of discussion with Viner. But he went a good deal further than Viner's later analysis, and in doing so he clearly laid the foundations for the modern neo-Classical analysis of customs unions.

Conclusion

It seems clear that the Viner analysis grew out of the theory of preferential tariffs; that this theory was part of the Classical discussion of commercial treaties; that the underlying theory was essentially the Classical mechanism of international trade; and that the essence of Viner's analysis was in fact developed long before 1950, growing out of the Classical discussion and using its tools. In addition, both of the other two streams of current customs union theory have roots which go back much further than is recognized—in the case of the Cooper-Massell analysis right back to early-19th-century German protectionism.[107]

This is a shortened version of a paper delivered at the History of Economic Thought Conference held in London, September 1974. I am grateful to an anonymous referee for helpful comments.

106. Cf. also Cooper and Massell, *Economic Journal*, 1965, loc. cit., p. 746.

107. A striking instance of the poor communications which have hampered appreciation of the historical perspective is provided by Krauss, who points out (p. 415) that Melvin and Bhagwati published virtually identical analyses two years apart; moreover they were in recognized academic journals, both published in English in the same country.

[5]

Competition and credit control

This monetary regime, which takes its name from a document issued by the Bank of England, was introduced in May 1971, failed comprehensively, and was abandoned in December 1973. In essence it sought to replace quantitative controls over bank lending by operations designed to influence the structure of interest rates. Credit rationing was thus to be replaced by an approach in which the market for credit was allowed to clear at a price which the monetary authorities hoped to be able to control. With this aim it was announced that they would no longer freely buy gilt-edged securities of more than one year to maturity and that all banks would henceforth be required to keep a liquid assets ratio of 12.5 per cent. Gilts sales induced by the liquidity requirement would thus raise interest rates.

The background to this involved three elements. Firstly, there was broad agreement that the imposition of ceilings on bank lending had harmful effects. These included distortion of competition within the financial sector, and 'disintermediation' whereby the banks engaged in off-balance sheet activities and lending also bypassed the controlled sector of the banking system completely. The latter not only penalized the banks but also distorted the data available to the monetary authorities. Secondly, there was a desire to introduce some competition into the banking sector itself and, in particular, to persuade the clearing banks to abandon their interest-rate cartel. Thirdly, there was a belief that research, *including* research within the Bank of England, had identified stable single-equation estimates of money demand functions, and it was reasoned that if demand for money was a stable function of the rate of interest, and if the money supply was determined by demand for money, it would be possible to control the money supply by the rate of interest.

In the words of the best account of this experiment, 'The competition and credit control era, 1971–3, was a disaster' (Gowland, p. 13). Over two years (1972 and 1973) bank lending increased by 100 per cent while real underlying growth in the economy continued, as usual, at low single digit levels. The money supply, as measured by M_3, rose by 60 per cent in a little over two years, price inflation (after the standard monetarist lag) rose to nearly 30 per cent, and both the residential and commercial property markets underwent astonishing speculative booms.

The reasons for the failure of the new policy are numerous. There was no clear view at all of the way in which the Bank would seek to control rates and in the event it failed to do so. Indeed, its own document had recognized the possibility that willingness to buy gilts of a maturity of up to a year, but not longer dated stock, would affect the portfolio composition of the financial sector and *increase* liquidity: but this insight was, rather remarkably, not pursued. (While the policy was actually in operation the links between the rate at which the Bank would lend and those at which the banks would lend was further weakened by the replacement of Bank Rate by Minimum Lending Rate, thus removing one important, if conventional, link.) The hopes that the banks could be induced to sell gilt-edged proved delusory; when the banks required more reserves they simply narrowed their margins by raising the interest they were prepared to pay on deposits while not increasing proportionately their lending rates. This was perfectly normal oligopolistic behaviour; the banks, as oligopolists, were concerned about their market share. But it seems to have caught the Bank by surprise, despite the consideration which it had apparently given to the structure of competition within the financial sector.

Had the Bank succeeded in controlling interest rates, to the extent that was originally envisaged, it is still highly doubtful whether this would in turn have produced the desired effect on aggregate demand since the impact of interest rates on borrowing is both uncertain and, to an unpredictable extent, perverse, because of distress borrowing by companies. The monetary authorities however approached matters in this way because, as already noted, they believed that there was a stable demand function for money and that this could be used to control money demand and, consequently in the Bank's view, money supply.

The reasoning was a strange inversion of a normal monetarist approach. The latter seeks to identify a stable demand for money on the basis that if the money *supply* is then controlled, and the money market clears, this will stabilize the level of national money income. The 1971–73 policy however sought to identify a stable demand for money as a *means* of controlling the money supply.

This approach implied the necessity of using interest rates freely. Such an approach however was flatly contrary to the whole history of Bank of England policy which had attached high priority to an 'orderly' gilts market. Subsequently, Bank insiders have placed the blame for the fact that interest rates were not used with much vigour, at least for a long time, upon politicians: yet this is unlikely to be the whole story, particularly as the Bank had traded freely between cash and gilts in the 1960s while ostensibly operating under the aegis of the Radcliffe Report in which control of 'liquidity' through the 'structure of interest rates' was of key importance. The unwillingness of the Bank to use interest rates freely may also have been concealed by the fact that subsequent accounts of this era have been couched in terms of *nominal* interest rates even though these were often extremely low in real terms and became zero or even negative at times.

Finally, the belief that controlling the price of borrowing and its quantity were exactly equivalent, and that controlling supply could be achieved directly through controlling demand, depended clearly upon the idea of money markets clearing instantaneously, a belief which has been attacked persuasively both by those who believe that the money market adjusts only slowly to equilibrium and by those who stress the 'buffer-stock' role of money.

References

Artis, M.J. and Lewis, M.K. (1976), 'The Demand for Money in the United Kingdom: 1963–1973', *Manchester School*, **44**, pp. 147–81.

Bank of England (1971), *Competition and Credit Control.*

Goodhart, C.A.E. (1984), *Monetary Theory and Practice*, London: Macmillan.

Gowland, D. (1982), *Controlling the Money Supply*, 2nd ed., London: Croom Helm.

Pepper, G. (1990), *Money, Credit and Inflation*, London: Institute of Economic Affairs.

PART II

ENGLISH ECONOMICS 1660–1860

[6]

Petty's *Political Arithmetick**

Introduction – Biographia

Petty was born on 26th May 1623 at Romsey, Hampshire where his father was engaged, on a small scale, in the clothing trade. He was educated in Romsey but in 1637 went to sea as a cabin boy. After ten months he was put ashore at Caen in Normandy with a broken leg. Showing great resource, he obtained treatment for the leg and secured, on the basis of a request in Latin, admittance to the Jesuit college there. This would no doubt have provided a quality of education very significantly superior to anything he had experienced before. He returned to England about 1639 and between 1640 and 1643 he served in the Navy, a period about which he maintained total silence for the rest of his life (Strauss, 1954, p. 25). In 1643, perhaps moved by a desire to distance himself from the Civil War, he went to the Netherlands where he studied medicine. By 1645 he was in Paris with the philosopher Thomas Hobbes, who employed him as a research assistant. In 1646 he returned to England, and apparently attempted to revive the business of his father, who had died in 1644. He also pursued an aptitude for inventions. Indeed, Petty remained a prolific inventor throughout his life though only one of his inventions, the twin-hulled boat, seems to have survived. In 1647 he moved to London where he mixed with the moving spirits in the new burgeoning endeavour to develop science on an empirical base. In 1648 he moved to Oxford; and by 1650 he was Professor of Anatomy and a Fellow of Brasenose, becoming Vice Principal of the College.

Petty's meteoric rise was not solely due to his extraordinary qualities. The Parliamentarians were bent on reorganizing Royalist Oxford, and Petty was undoubtedly one of their men.

While in his Oxford position, Petty was for ever in need of medical specimens. In the course of his search for such specimens he received the body of a young woman who had been hanged for 'child murder' – in truth, for concealing a miscarriage. However Petty perceived that, despite strenuous attempts to kill her, the woman was still alive and he achieved, in conjunction with a colleague, her resuscitation.

But Petty was of too restless a cast of mind to pursue a medical career for long. While remaining Vice Principal of Brasenose, he was also made Reader in Music at Gresham College in London; and early in 1651, shortly after his inaugural lecture at Oxford as Professor of Anatomy, he obtained two years leave of absence from Oxford. The following year he became physician to the Cromwellian army in Ireland.

* This appeared in German as an introduction to a facsimile reprint of Petty's book (Düsseldorf, Verlagsgruppe Handelsblatt, 1992).

Petty remained in Ireland until 1659. During his time there he completed the astonishing 'Down Survey' of the forfeited lands in Ireland, which were to be distributed amongst the soldiers and those who had financed the Cromwellian expedition (Matsukawa, 1955, pp. 67–71). Showing remarkable administrative ability, Petty completed this survey between February 1655 and March 1656. In July 1656 he became one of the Commissioners to distribute the forfeited lands amongst the soldiers, and was the Commissioner who undertook the bulk of the work which was completed by February 1657.

The dealings in which he engaged in the course of this distribution led to Petty acquiring a huge Irish estate. He spent much of the rest of his life defending it against attacks both legal and physical. He never succeeded in obtaining preferment under Charles II – though he was not deprived of his (probably ill-gotten) gains at the Restoration of the Monarchy in 1660 (indeed he was knighted in 1661) – and the remainder of his life was spent, when not concerned with the problems his Irish estates had brought him, with the affairs of the scientific community in London and his writings on economics and statistics.

Of these, the most important is undoubtedly his *Treatise of Taxes* of 1662. But other important items include *The Political Anatomy of Ireland* possibly written about 1672 and the *Political Arithmetick* completed around 1676, although neither of these was published until after Petty's death. Another work, which was to find favour with later generations, was his *Quantulumcunque Concerning Money* of 1682.

Petty died on 16th December 1687. In a sense he was a victim of his own success in appropriating lands in Ireland; for his struggles, not only over his title to these, and the physical defence of them, but also over tax farming in Ireland, proved a great drain upon the resources of even this ever-resourceful individual. But perhaps Petty's very restlessness and fertility of mind were bound to result in failure to achieve anything substantial in any one field, as Letwin (1956) has argued; Petty simply could not concentrate his attention for long enough on any one of his myriad interests to achieve what his powers had the potential to produce. Nonetheless it is this restlessness, and fertility, which have made his economic writings a subject of interest throughout the centuries since his death.

The *Political Arithmetick*

Petty's work was fortunate to receive, from the American scholar Charles Henry Hull, a quality of editing that was about 50 years ahead of its time (Hull, 1899). Hull's work was set against the background of a sustained 19th-century interest in Petty – indeed the economist J.R. McCulloch regretted in the 1840s the absence of a complete edition of Petty's works. However, because Petty received very high quality editing at an early date, he is now beginning to suffer from that degree of over-interpretation which (to a far greater degree) also afflicts Ricardo; and we have both Keynesian and Marx–Sraffa interpretations. It is therefore fortunate that in the present volume readers have the opportunity to decide for themselves what Petty wrote.

Petty seems to have been the inventor of the phrase 'Political Arithmetick', in around 1671 or 1672 (Hull, 1899, pp. 239–40n; Matsukawa, 1977, p. 34). The slogan of this form of exercise is provided by Petty in the preface where he speaks of '*Number, Weight, or Measure*', a phrase which has been traced to biblical origins (Strauss, 1954, p. 185). The political arithmetic in this volume is only one of a number of exercises bearing this general title which Petty produced, and which are included in the volumes edited by Hull (1899), although it is much the most important. (See also Hull, 1900.) The work was probably composed between 1671 and 1676 while Petty was back in Ireland, though this seems rather a long period of composition for such a rapid worker as Petty, who habitually dictated his text. It was published posthumously; the political turmoil of the 1670s and 1680s had the effect of discouraging many authors from having their work printed.

The *Political Arithmetick* had a very clear policy aim, however, and may have been written originally to exercise influence at Court, rather than with publication in view. Essentially Petty was attempting to show that England was not in an especially weak condition compared with France and that, more generally, a small country could be equivalent in wealth and strength to a much larger one (Chapter One). While such a message may have been extremely acceptable at Court, it was more than a little misleading concerning the relative strengths of England and France, and Petty was to incur the censure of Charles Davenant after his death.

> The King was well pleased to be lulled asleep by a flattering council, which suggested, that the power of France was not so formidable, and could never be prejudicial to this kingdom; ... But if such as meddled with computations at that time, had truly compared the strength of both kingdoms, and if the ministers themselves had duly weighed the encreasing wealth, trade, naval force and growing greatness of that nation, it might perhaps have awakened both the King and parliament, from that lethargy which has since proved so fatal and expensive to us (1771, pp. 130–31).

Petty was writing against a background of the fears expressed by writers like Child and Coke of English decline, and he makes this clear in the preface of this book. While conceding that there are real problems facing the country, the succeeding chapters of the book are designed to show that in truth England is very strong. A small country may be as strong as a large one (Chapter One), taxation may actually increase national wealth (Chapter Two), natural impediments limit French sea power (Chapter Three), the population *and* overseas territories of England are not significantly less than those of France (Chapter Four), the difficulties England faces are not inherent but remediable (Chapter Five), England has increased in economic strength in the last 40 years (Chapter Six), ten per cent of GNP is sufficient to maintain powerful land and naval forces (Chapter Seven), there is untapped employment and output potential (Chapter Eight), England has sufficient money (Chapter Nine), and England has a capital stock sufficient even to finance world trade (Chapter Ten).

Throughout this discussion, Petty employs numerical argument in line with his 'number, weight, measure' slogan. Undoubtedly this is in part – a very significant part – a rhetorical device; and although the attention of modern economists has been drawn to rhetoric by McCloskey (1985), this was an aspect of Petty's work which was much appreciated by his contemporaries – as Letwin has shown it was satirized with deadly effect by Swift (Letwin, 1963, pp. 138–40). The use of numbers was not Petty's sole rhetorical device; inevitably, a penchant for anatomical analogies came naturally to him. But his main device was the sweeping use of numbers, of which a splendid example is to be found in the *Political Arithmetick* where he explores the gain to national income, and national wealth, of transplanting the population of Ireland, and of the highlands of Scotland, to England and lowland Scotland (Chapter Four).

In the course of such exercises, Petty displayed not only a cavalier way with numbers, as Hull was able to show (1899, p. lxviii), but also a tendency to report existing data inaccurately (ibid., pp. 252, 297). Nonetheless, what Petty was able to achieve with the existing data was remarkable. In this work his main sources seem to have been Chamberlayne (1672) and Fortrey (1674). But there was really very little data available, and some of Petty's guesses seem to have been inspired – notably the estimate of the population of England and Wales, Scotland and Ireland together as being 9.5 million, which conforms well with later detailed research, even though the figure which he elsewhere estimated for Ireland, and on which he should have been best informed (Matsukawa, 1955 pp. 71–2), was only 50 per cent of the true figure, it now appears (*Pol. Arith.*, p. 75; Hull, 1899, pp. 141–2; Mitchell, 1962, p. 5).

But the essential point to grasp about the use which Petty was making of these numbers is that he was not concerned with precise accuracy. Rather the argument proceeds along the following lines. For the purposes of an argument the relationship between two economic magnitudes is stated as an inequality. Petty, in accordance with the Baconian spirit, then seeks to move from what is essentially a qualitative statement towards a more quantitative formulation. He follows his 'number, weight or measure' injunction to try to make these magnitudes more precise, so as to see (a) what needs to be argued to ensure that the inequality holds, and (b) what is the sensitivity of the stated inequality to the likely degree of error in the estimation of the numbers. Although what he was doing bears some similarity to the Baconian revolution in natural science in which qualitative argument was replaced by quantitative argument, both the subject matter and the nature of the statistical sources meant that Petty could not proceed so far along the path of quantification and he was thus limited to dealing with inequalities in the way described. A nice example is provided by the material in Chapter One about the comparison between France and Holland. Petty sets out to show that though the land area of Holland is only 1/80 of that of France, the wealth and income of Holland bear a much higher ratio to that of France. Thus on the basis of yields per acre the Dutch agricultural net income is £10m per annum, whereas that of France is £15m, but Petty is prepared to settle for a ratio of 7:1 rather than 3:2, as this is enough for his argument that ratios of land area will be greater than ratios of national income. With respect to relative wealth, the same line of argument is followed. Though France has 13 times the population of Holland, its housing stock is worth only five times that of Holland; and the Dutch have nine times the shipping of the French, showing Dutch wealth to be much greater in relation to Holland's large neighbour than mere comparisons of size would have implied. All the way through, it is not the *absolute* value of the figures which bears the weight of the argument; it is the plausible *relative* values which Petty employs.

There is no doubt that the appearance of mathematical expertise had considerable rhetorical power – even though, in fact, Petty makes a number of errors. Although logarithms had been available from the beginning of the 17th century, Petty makes no use of them in calculations. He thus calculates present values simply by multiplying an annual flow by a number of years' 'purchase' without discounting, and he believed that if population increased from 10 million to 20 million in 200 years it would have increased in 40 years by one-fifth of 10 million (*Pol. Arith.*, p. 97). (In fact, the implied annual rate of increase is 0.35 per cent and after 40 years the increase would have been less than 1.5 million.) But the sweeping use of ratios enabled Petty to go with a flourish from one estimate to another; armed with his (remarkable) estimate of population, and a commonsense observation of income per head, he multiplied the two to produce an estimate of GNP and then multiplied this by a number of years' 'purchase' to produce a present value figure.

Petty's main use of numerical data is thus to provide, however shakily, the 'number, weight or measure' to buttress his arguments concerning the magnitudes central to national economic and diplomatic policies. However, as is well known, Petty also took an interest in (and possibly had a hand in) the important work of Graunt on vital statistics – the 'bills of mortality' – and compiled data of his own for Dublin (Hull, 1899, pp. 479–98). As Hull pointed out (1899, p. lxxv) there is a clear distinction to be made between political arithmetic and statistics, especially vital statistics (though see Matsukawa, 1955), in the development of which Petty also played an important part. But both the political arithmetic and the vital statistics work combined to present a case for improved statistics, a case which Petty advanced (see Hull, 1899, p. lxvi for citations).

Economics and policy

The content of the *Political Arithmetick* allows the reader to glimpse other aspects of Petty's work and personality. Underlying it all is, not surprisingly in view of Petty's connections with Hobbes as well as his own career, a Hobbesian ruthlessness and a Hobbesian willingness to use the power of the State in sweeping ways. Examples of this include not only the proposal to transport Irish people to England, so that they would bear the same proportion to the population there as they did in the two countries combined (pp. 92–5) but the proposal that, in order to offset the effects of a backward bending supply curve of labour, the State should appropriate abundant harvests to stop the price of grain falling, because such a fall would raise real incomes and reduce the supply of labour (p. 45).

In matters economic, Petty was a genuine mercantilist. We can find the identification of wealth with precious metals (pp. 18–19, 35–6, 38, 116) and a concern with the balance of trade (pp. 44, 50–51, 82, 89) in the *Political Arithmetick*, as well as that mercantilist commonplace, the backward bending supply curve of labour (p. 45; cf. Bowley, 1973, pp. 179–80). But it is in his *étatism* that Petty, the Hobbesian, is most mercantilist of all. Though there may be room for argument about the extent of his concern with the balance of trade (Hull, 1899, p. lxix), there is none about his willingness to use the power of the State against the individual in what he perceived to be the national interest (Hull, 1900, p. 340).

Nonetheless Petty's analysis of many issues is still interesting. We find in this work a cash balance approach to velocity of circulation of money with the required balances determined by the frequency of different kinds of payments (pp. 110–11). and we find an analysis in which the supply of bank deposits, through increasing velocity, effectively provides the increased money which trade requires (pp. 28–30, 113–14). In contrast to those, like Child, who believed that prosperity was *caused* by a low rate of interest, Petty believed a low rate of interest to result from prosperity (pp. 22, 99).

Petty had a lifelong interest in taxation (Johnson, 1937), and in this work we find two of his particular themes: the idea that taxes could redistribute wealth to the productive classes (pp. 35–9) and the idea that the best form of tax is that on expenditure (p. 40).

We also find the idea that saving and investment ('superlucration') raises national wealth, and the associated argument that the economy had the latent capacity to raise savings and investment and thus to strengthen the nation-State (pp. 73, 77, 106–7).

Petty has been credited – perhaps generously – with founding the study of national income (Endres, 1985, p. 254). While he had precursors in the national income field, and while he was more interested in employing global numbers for the purposes of exploring the strength of his inequality propositions than in simply making estimates, it is nonetheless true that he was interested in national wealth as such; indeed he set about capitalizing the value of the labour force as part of national wealth (pp. 31–3) and suggested State employment of the idle to maintain that labour force (p. 37) since losses from it were losses of national wealth. But this is not surprising; in comparing the relative strength of nations (in inequality form) it was necessary to make some estimates of absolute values on which to base the argument.

Other concerns of Petty are also evident. His naval interests, on which he remained so silent as a matter of biography, are displayed at length in this essay (pp. 51–61); and his Dissenter connections make their appearance in his stress upon the economic benefit of liberty of conscience, coupled with the generalization that the trade of a country (crucially important to a mercantilist) is generally managed by 'the Heterodox party' (pp. 21–2, 25–7).

Petty and the later generations

There is no doubt that the work of Petty enjoyed considerable prestige in the centuries after his death, and that he had considerable influence not least in Germany through the work of Süssmilch (Matsukawa, 1955, p. 63). In France, Cantillon was influenced by, and indeed acknowledged, Petty, and although Smith avoids mentioning him some influences are clear – not least in Smith's formulation of equality in taxation.

Because Marx also wrote approvingly about Petty, economists of a Marxist persuasion have also been drawn to approve of Petty. But it is perhaps worth stressing that recognition of the importance of Petty is certainly *not*, as has been implied, due to Marx (Roncaglia, 1985, pp. 16–17). For Petty had certainly not been forgotten before Marx eulogized him.

His daughter married into a powerful family which has taken a prolonged and active interest in his work (e.g. Fitzmaurice, 1895; Lansdowne, 1927). Even a cursory glance at the catalogue of the British (Museum) Library or the National Union Catalogue reveals a mass of entries, showing his works to have been frequently reprinted – indeed the NUC entries extend over six pages. McCulloch, the most learned of the classical economists, not only referred to Petty in his *Historical Sketch* but noted that the present work, the *Political Arithmetick*, was 'too well known to require any particular notice in this place' (McCulloch, 1826, pp. 29–31). McCulloch also appended material on Petty to his editions of the *Wealth of Nations* and wrote about Petty at length in his *Literature of Political Economy* (McCulloch, 1845, pp. 155, 210, 211–12, 318). He also reprinted one of Petty's works (McCulloch, 1856) and called for a complete edition of his writings. Nor was recognition confined to Britain. In Germany, Roscher recognized the importance of Petty (Hull, 1900, p. 339).

Conclusion

Petty was a complex figure. He was highly intelligent, opportunist, indiscreet, and perhaps rather unprincipled in financial matters, though not unusually for his era. Of all his works the *Political Arithmetick* gives, within a short compass, a remarkably condensed picture of the strengths and weaknesses of this remarkable man and his methods. It is probably true to say that Petty was the outstanding economist of his era (Hutchison, 1988, p. 40). There is much more to his work than the *Political Arithmetick*, but there is no better place to start reading it.

References

Bowley, M.E.A. (1973), *Studies in the History of Economic Theory before 1870*, London: Macmillan.

Chamberlayne, E. (1672), *Angliae Notitia; or the Present State of England*, 6th ed., London; T.N. for J. Martyn.

Davenant, C. (1771), *The Political and Commercial Works*, ed. C. Whitworth, London: Horsefield and others, repr. Farnborough: Gregg, 1967.

Endres, A.M. (1985), 'The Functions of Numerical Data in the Writings of Graunt, Petty, and Davenant', *History of Political Economy*, **17**, pp. 245–64.

Fitzmaurice, E. (1895), *The Life of Sir William Petty*, London: Murray.

Fortrey, S. (1674), *England's Interest and Improvement*, London: Nathaniel Brook, reprinted in J.R. McCulloch (ed.), *Select Tracts on Commerce*, London: for the Political Economy Club, 1856.

Hull, C.H. (ed.) (1899), *The Economic Writings of Sir William Petty*, 2 vols, Cambridge: Cambridge University Press.

Hull, C.H. (1900), 'Petty's Place in the History of Economic Theory', *Quarterly Journal of Economics*, **14**, pp. 307–40.

Hutchison, T.W. (1988), *Before Adam Smith*, Oxford: Blackwell.

Johnson, E.A.J. (1937), *Predecessors of Adam Smith*, London: P.S. King.

Lansdowne, H.W. (1927), *The Petty Papers*, 2 vols, London: Constable.

Letwin, W.L. (1956), Review of E. Strauss *Sir William Petty*, *Journal of Political Economy*, **64**, pp. 180–81.

Letwin, W.L. (1963), *The Origins of Scientific Economics*, London: Methuen.

McCloskey, D. (1985), *The Rhetoric of Economics*, Madison: University of Wisconsin Press.

McCulloch, J.R. (1826), *Historical Sketch of the Rise and Progress of the Science of Political Economy*, Edinburgh: Balfour.

McCulloch, J.R. (1845), *The Literature of Political Economy*, London: Longman.

Matsukawa, S. (1955), 'Origin and Significance of Political Arithmetic,' *Annals of the Hitotsubashi Academy*, **6**, pp. 53–79.

Matsukawa, S. (1977), 'Sir William Petty: An Unpublished Manuscript', *Hitotsubashi Journal of Economics*, **17**, pp. 33–50.

Mitchell, B.R. (1962), *Abstract of British Historical Statistics*, (with P. Deane), Cambridge: Cambridge University Press.
Roncaglia, A. (1985), *Petty*, Cardiff: University College.
Strauss, E. (1954), *Sir William Petty*, London: Bodley Head.
Vickers, D. (1960), *Studies in the Theory of Money 1690–1776*, London: Peter Owen.

[7]

Ravenstone, Piercy

Attention was drawn to a book bearing this author's name because it is mentioned in the Ricardo–Malthus–Mill correspondence. The true identity of the author is not known for certain, although Sraffa, on the basis of two separate identifications in libraries, suggests it was Richard Puller (fl. 1789–1831); on the basis of internal evidence, Dorfman had previously suggested that the author was an Anglican clergyman, Edward Edwards.

The author has been classified (by Seligman and by Halevy) as a Socialist; as a Tory Democrat (by Beer); and as an Institutionalist (by W.C. Mitchell). The content of the work discussed by Ricardo is however essentially Physiocratic; there is no understanding of division of labour, productivity or exchange; tradesmen add no value but simply pass wealth through their hands; and a large sterile class enjoys revenue generated by a productive class employed in agriculture. Property is perfectly justifiable where it originates in labour, but it has developed into an institution enabling the sterile class to live on the productivity of the productive class. This abstraction takes place through both rent and profits – capital is an imaginary concept designed to justify the revenue enjoyed as profit. Poverty is not caused by Malthusian population pressures – with remarkable self-confidence in the employment of arithmetical ratios, the author satisfied himself that the rate of population increase was everywhere constant – but to the abstraction of revenue for the sterile classes. Since debt service taxes were also used to this end, public debt was undesirable.

References

Ravenstone, P. (1821), *A Few Doubts as to the correctness of some opinions generally entertained on the subjects of Population and Political Economy*, London: J. Andrews, reprinted with an introduction by J. Dorfman, New York: A.M. Kelley, 1966.

Ravenstone, P. (1824), *Thoughts on the Funding System and Its Effects*, London: J. Andrews.

Sraffa, P. (ed.) (1952, 1973), *The Works and Correspondence of David Ricardo*, vols. IX, XI, Cambridge: Cambridge University Press for the Royal Economic Society.

[8]

Classical economics

The term Classical Economics, although sometimes given the rather broader meaning of any economics which is not Keynesian, is generally taken to refer to the body of economic ideas stemming from the work of David Hume, whose most important work was published in 1752, and Adam Smith whose great *Wealth of Nations* was published in 1776. These ideas came to dominate economics particularly but far from exclusively in Britain throughout the last quarter of the 18th and the first three-quarters of the 19th century.

Hume's contribution principally concerned money and the balance of payments But Smith's work is a virtual compendium of economics, focusing on the key question of economic growth, and covering division of labour, distribution, capital accumulation, trade and colonial policy, and public finance. Amongst their successors was T.R. Malthus; though chiefly famous for his writings on population, he covered the whole field of economic enquiry. A major impetus to the development of Classical economics was provided by David Ricardo. He read Smith's work critically and from it constructed a 'model' which, unlike Smith's work, produced fairly clear and definite predictions. Ricardo succeeded initially in attracting disciples, notably J. Mill and – though he later drifted away from Ricardo's influence – J.R. McCulloch, as well as Thomas De Quincey. But his influence waned after his death and the work of J. Mill's son, J.S. Mill, is much closer to Smith in range, reliance upon empirical material, and the avoidance of precise predictions.

Classical economics covered the whole field of economic enquiry, but with an emphasis on questions dealing with large aggregates – economic growth, international trade, monetary economics, public finance – rather than with the analysis of the behaviour of the maximizing individual which came to be of dominant interest after 1870. (In the field of value theory, in particular, the Classical economists generally made do with various costs of production theories emphasizing, in varying degrees, the importance of labour cost in total cost.) At the same time a fundamental premise lying behind the analysis of aggregates, and stemming from Smith, was that individuals were motivated by the pursuit of self-interest, and that their pursuit had to be limited by a framework of law, religion and custom, to ensure coincidence of private and social interest. This in turn meant that in the field of economic policy Classical economics, while predisposed against government interference (partly because of the way in which such interference could be used for purely sectional interest, and partly because of a belief that decentralized individual knowledge was superior to State knowledge), was pragmatic – the necessary legislative framework could only be learnt by experience and enquiry.

At the heart of the Classical vision is the idea of economic growth occurring through the interaction of capital accumulation and division of labour. Capital accumulation made it possible to postpone the sale of output, permitting the development of specialization and division of labour. Division of labour in turn increased total output permitting further capital accumulation. Economic growth would be increased by allowing capital to flow to where it was most productive; thus, other things being equal, it was desirable to remove restraints on the free allocation of resources. Division of labour itself was limited by the extent of the market. The extent of the home market depended on population and income per head. As capital was accumulated, the available labour supply found itself in greater demand and wages rose above the necessary minimum – 'subsistence' which could be either psychological or physiological. Population responded to the rise in wages by increasing; this in turn increased the labour supply which pushed wages back towards subsistence, though if subsistence was a psychological variable – as it was with many Classical writers – population growth might well stop before wages had fallen to the old level of subsistence. As wages rose, profits fell; this might check capital accumulation, but as long as profits were above a necessary minimum, capital accumulation would continue. Output, population and capital thus all grew together. However, a brake on growth was provided by the shortage of a third input, land. With the progress of economic growth, food became more and more expensive to produce, while landlords enjoyed the benefit of an unearned rent arising from ownership of this scarce but vital resource – this aspect was particularly stressed by Malthus and Ricardo. The rising cost of food also meant that the floor below which subsistence could not fall – the minimum wage necessary to procure basic physical necessities of life – rose; and Ricardo in particular emphasized that such a rise would depress profits and might eventually stop capital accumulation and growth altogether. (Smith had believed that growth would only stop when investment opportunities were exhausted.) He then argued that repeal of the Corn Laws (restricting food imports) was urgent, since subsistence could be obtained more cheaply abroad. (Later Classical economists such as McCulloch and J.S. Mill were, however, optimistic about technical progress in agriculture which could postpone any slowdown in economic growth by lowering the cost of agricultural output.)

The argument for repeal of the Corn Laws provided one part of a general Classical case for freedom of trade; the desire to widen the market to maximize possible division of labour provided another. However, a more general and sophisticated argument for freedom of trade was provided by R. Torrens and Ricardo, in the form of the theory of comparative costs (later refined and developed by J.S. Mill) which showed that a country could gain from importing even those commodities in which it had a competitive advantage if it had an even greater competitive advantage in the production of other commodities – it should concentrate its scarce resources on the latter.

Balance of payments equilibrium was ensured by a mechanism which was due to David Hume, and which was also basic to Classical monetary theory, the price-specie-flow mechanism. A balance of payments deficit would, through gold outflow, reduce the money supply, and thus the price level, making exports competitive and imports less attractive, and this equilibrating mechanism would continue until the gold outflow stopped and payments came into balance. The price level was thus dependent on the money supply: and the predominant Classical view from Ricardo to Lord Overstone was that the note issue, as part of the money supply, should be contracted if gold was flowing out, since the outflow was a symptom of a price level which was too high. Monetary control was also necessary to dampen the effects of an endogenous trade cycle, an element introduced into Classical economics, chiefly by Overstone, from the late 1830s. (A minority of Classical economists however viewed the money supply as demand-determined.)

Classical economics represented a major intellectual achievement. The foundations which it laid in the fields of monetary and trade theory, in particular, are still with economics today. Eventually however it lost some of its momentum; it was always policy-orientated, and as the policy questions were settled – usually along the lines indicated by the Classical analyses – and as economists came to take continuing economic growth for granted, they turned their attention to different questions requiring different techniques of analysis.

D.P. O'Brien
University of Durham

Further reading

Blaug, M. (1958), *Ricardian Economics*, New Haven.
O'Brien, D.P. (1975), *The Classical Economists*, Oxford.

[9]

RICARDIAN ECONOMICS AND THE ECONOMICS OF DAVID RICARDO

By D. P. O'BRIEN

THE interpretation of Ricardo's work is not easy. Some of the best minds in the economics profession have bent their attention to it. A picture of some internal consistency, which showed Ricardo to be a very powerful theorist, had eventually emerged. But now an enormous book by Professor S. Hollander *The Economics of David Ricardo*,[1] which challenges this picture, has appeared. There should be no misunderstanding about the magnitude of the challenge which Professor Hollander is making; he suggests that almost every recent commentator on Ricardo, however eminent, has misinterpreted Ricardo's work so that the book is nothing less than a full scale frontal attack on the existing body of Ricardo scholarship.

There is no new evidence: virtually everything to which Hollander refers in Ricardo's work is in the Sraffa volumes. Hollander has had, however, the benefit of working with the magnificent Sraffa Index which was not published until 1973.

It is undoubtedly a very difficult book to read; but the reasons for this are hard to isolate at first.[2] For the book is baffling. This means that there is a very real danger of doing less than justice to it. It would be easy to say that the trouble is that Hollander uses only words and no algebra; and it would also be satisfyingly modish. I am not, however, sure that the matter is that simple. Words can serve very well. One has only to turn to the work of Popper, or, to take a recent example, Kolakowski, to see how well words can be used. But they do not seem to do very well for Ricardo—at least not here. Yet this is a serious matter for Hollander. The algebraic models of Ricardo are, if I understand the book correctly, comprehensively rejected; but the words representing what is apparently the true interpretation, seem difficult to follow.

The difficulties are compounded by the fact that at times the very subject of the argument becomes obscure. For instance the account of Torrens' Capital Theory of Value (pp. 208–18, and 257) is extremely laborious and does not really make clear the issues involved. Around page 320 the thread again disappears. We start off with waiting as the origin of the agio, and then find that the discussion is about the supply conditions of capital—which is certainly related but not the same thing. The discussion of Ricardo on machinery also seems to be extremely long drawn out (pp. 339 ff) after an earlier foray into the matter (pp. 298–9).

[1] Hollander (1979).

[2] For an account of similar difficulties with Hollander's earlier book on Smith see Corry (1974).

Yet another problem lies in the quite exceptionally free use of italics. As a matter of habit Hollander italicises those words in each quotation which support his particular interpretation of the passage. A few examples will suffice. On p. 613 the words "in time" are italicised in a discussion of the prospect of the stationary state. The words are not however italicised by Ricardo, and in context they merely meant 'not immediately'. As italicised, however, they give the impression of a long run perspective which is not in the original passage—at least I do not read it that way. On p. 619 the words "I am by no means ready to admit that we may not have a more limited measure of prosperity not withstanding the continued operation of our Corn Laws, and the continued existence of our debt" are italicised, giving them far more prominence than they had in the original passage. Hollander is perfectly honest about his addition of 'emphasis'; but the end result is rather confusing and increases the difficulty of interpretation. Hollander does not confine himself to italicising Ricardo. At the end of a confused (or at least confusing) section on profits we find italics used for the conclusion that:

> "*Nevertheless, it appears that there is nothing in the main body of Ricardian analysis which precludes the notion of interest as a reward for abstaining from present consumption*". (p. 326).

The use of italics here seems to me to imply a much stronger conclusion—that Ricardo held such a theory, at least incipiently—than the words (or the preceding text) would justify.

The content of the volume seems to me—perhaps not surprisingly—to be highly contentious. While it is not difficult to agree that the equation of Ricardo with the work stemming from Sraffa's *Production of Commodities* (Sraffa, 1960) is mistaken, it seems to me that, in a number of respects, Hollander's text, which has as its aim to establish that not only the post-Sraffian but indeed almost all other interpretations of Ricardo are wholly or partly mistaken, is equally unpersuasive.

In two rather special senses of the word this could be said to be a reactionary book: on the one hand its interpretation of Ricardo is rather in the spirit of J. H. Hollander; and, on the other, it is reacting against the extraordinarily garbled version of the history of economic thought which has emerged from Cambridge (England), particularly following *Production of Commodities.* I sympathise with Hollander's recoil from the latter—including such propositions as the one that Ricardo saw profit as an exploitation income. But so do authors as diverse as Terence Hutchison and Mark Blaug, both of whom have published on this matter; and both these authors (together with almost everyone else who has written on Ricardo) come in for criticism in the book, essentially for failing to react as far as Hollander. But this reaction has taken him so far that the picture of Ricardo which he produces is not one which most people will find easy to accept.

Hollander's thesis

Despite these difficulties, however, I think that a thesis—or rather a series of theses—can be detected in the book. My interpretation of what Hollander is trying to argue is that it involves the following propositions.

1. Ricardo's work was in the centre of the Classical mainstream and not a Ricardian detour.
2. Ricardo's method was identical with that of Adam Smith.
3. Ricardo's profit theory did not originate in concern over the Corn Laws.
4. The origin of Ricardo's treatment of profits and wages lies in his criticism of Adam Smith's view that a rise in wages increased prices except in agriculture where lower rents resulted.
5. Ricardo made free use of special assumptions which should not be taken to represent a model.
6. The use of models in interpreting Ricardo is not helpful.
7. The corn-input–corn-output model was not used by Ricardo.
8. Ricardo relied on rising *money* wages from 1814, not the corn model, to produce falling profits.
9. The corn model of the *Essay on Profits* was merely a 'strong case'.
10. Ricardo did not regard the Invariable Measure as important.
11. Ricardo had a value theory which was essentially the same as that of Alfred Marshall.
12. In particular Ricardo had a developed theory of demand.
13. This theory of demand was essentially Marshallian.
14. Ricardo's work involved a number of general equilibrium considerations and has links with that of Walras.
15. In particular distribution and pricing are interdependent and not sequential.
16. Wages were not viewed as being at subsistence nor were they fixed in commodity terms.
17. Ricardo relied on marriage rate variation as the control mechanism for population.
18. Ricardo did not think in terms of a pre-accummulated wage fund.
19. The notion of a fixed corn wage was not part of Ricardo's argument.
20. Ricardo's monetary theory was derived from (and close to) that of Adam Smith.
21. Ricardo's monetary theory was not a simple rigid Bullionist position but highly complex and sophisticated in a way not previously recognised.
22. Ricardo was not a quantity theorist in the conventional sense.
23. Ricardo laid emphasis on such matters as variations in velocity of circulation, and the short term transitory effects of changes in the money supply, and allowed for the possibility of temporary excess demand for money.

24. Ricardo believed that the same traded good could sell at different retail prices in different national markets.
25. Ricardo's analysis of the transfer problem is far more subtle than previously recognised.
26. Ricardo gave great weight to the transitional effects which might be associated with abolishing the Poor Law.
27. Ricardo did not forsee a rising rental share.
28. Ricardo did not take the prospect of a stationary state seriously.
29. The Corn Laws did not pose serious problems, in Ricardo's view, for the general level of profit. He merely exaggerated the problem in the House of Commons.
30. Ricardo was primarily concerned about the Corn Laws because of the associated price fluctuations and allocative loss.
31. Ricardo did not attach weight to the possibility of class conflict.
32. The Dissenters from Ricardo merely failed to recognise the full range of his theory—their dissent was unnecessary.

Interpretation

Hollander rejects the Stigler position on textual exegesis—that we reconcile problems of interpretation by seeing how many of the author's main theoretical conclusions can be deduced from any one interpretation. If I understand him correctly, this is on the grounds that we cannot be sure what the main theoretical conclusions *are* until we have solved the problem of exegesis. This is all of a part with throwing away the explicit Ricardian model on the grounds that it is a strong case. But in fact Hollander has gone beyond this to develop his own (very individual) view of Ricardo's work; and in his evaluation of conflicting evidence he seems to me to have adopted precisely 'Stigler's Rule' though taking his 'Ricardo' and not Stigler's. At the same time he seems to have allowed himself to indulge in flights of what might be called 'negative imagination'—because Ricardo did not actually say anything which Hollander regards as inconsistent with (e.g.) marginal productivity theory, it is possible that he (Ricardo) may have had it at the back of his mind, even though there is not actually any textual evidence for this.

Hollander also attaches great weight, in arriving at his 'Ricardo', to the qualifications conceded by Ricardo to his basic view of economic relationships. In fact, because he ostensibly rejects Stigler's position, he is free to attach whatever weight he desires, to particular statements by Ricardo. This freedom Hollander uses. In particular, a good deal of weight is attached by Hollander to his interpretation of correspondence. Thus he concedes that, although in correspondence Ricardo "allowed explicitly for variations in money wages due to productivity increases in manufacturing" he did not "formally" do so in the *Essay on Profits*, but denies that this meant that agricultural profits were given a determining role (pp. 145–6). Thus he is relying on correspondence after the *Essay* was published. This raises a problem because once Ricardo stepped outside his model his predictions did not always follow. That is why it is important for Hollander to attempt to show that Ricardo did not attach much weight to his model. Indeed there was a sort of guerilla warfare in which every time Malthus succeeded in drawing Ricardo from the stronghold of his model he inflicted casualties. Once we step outside the corn model then, arguably, the Ricardian system begins to collapse. As Hollander notes:

> "There obviously exists a one-to-one relationship between the share of labour in the *value* of output and the share of labour in *physical* output in the case where only one product exists. But with a variety of products the one-to-one relationship is not self-evident and Ricardo merely leaves us with an assertion that it holds good. An 'act of faith' was required to accept the proposition that an increase in the labour embodied in wages must necessarily entail an increase in the share of *every* commodity which is devoted by each employer to wage payments. This act of faith is apparent in the ...response to Malthus's critique of his procedures". (p. 252).

Again Hollander agrees that:

> "Ricardo jumped to the conclusion that because in the one-product case an increase in labour input in wage payments implies both an increase in labour's share in *value* and in physical product, the same must be true in the multi-product case as well." (p. 253).

However, Hollander continues:

> "That Ricardo was obliged to revert to the one-commodity case when the analytical difficulties of the more complex model became too great, *must not, however, be interpreted as disinterest in the complex case.*" (p. 253, italics in original).

Hollander clearly believes that Ricardo only used the model on an *ad hoc* basis without taking it very seriously. This leads to the disturbing conclusion that Ricardo's use of the corn model in connection with improvements (I, pp. 79–82)[3] is, despite the attention which it has attracted subsequently, and despite the conclusions which Ricardo himself drew from it, just another piece of *ad hoc* theorising.

More generally, without a corn model, Ricardo's inverse relationship between wages and profits is much more difficult to establish—hence the ambiguity of J. S. Mill's treatment. But this inverse relationship is virtually all that is left after Hollander has thrown out everything else. Of course if that *is* all that is left, it is easier to dismiss Ricardo's critics (a point to which I shall return below) and argue that his work leads directly to that of

[3] References of this form indicate passages in Sraffa (1951–73), where the Roman numeral is the volume number.

Marshall. But such a position can only be maintained at the cost of a picture of Ricardo which I, for one, find hard to recognise.

Nonetheless Hollander feels that Ricardo was often more consistent than he appears. Thus (pp. 248–50) we have an account of what appear to me to be quite significant vacillations in Ricardo's views. For Ricardo had originally accepted that taxes could raise prices (Hollander p. 108). But in 1817 he applied the quantity theory to show than an increase in wages could not affect general prices without an increase in the money supply. Then in 1821, by assuming, in contrast to his normal assumption of zero price elasticity, a price elasticity of demand for corn equal to unity, Ricardo was able to show that a tax on corn could raise prices. But this kind of *ad hoc* theorising does not bother Hollander because he does not see it as a departure from a limited model; rather the modelling apparent in Ricardo's work was itself *ad hoc*.

Thus we can see that Hollander starts from a different position from most of those with whom he disagrees. He is not looking for a consistent model, in the sense in which this term is normally used in relation to Ricardo, and he is not impressed by interpretations which are consistent with a particular model.

Ricardo and Smith

A major theme in Hollander's work is the methodological identity of Smith and Ricardo. Indeed Hollander virtually refuses to accept that there is *any* distinction between the two methodologies. (See especially p. 654). The equation of the two seems to me one of the most questionable premises on which the book rests; and it has come about at least partly because Hollander persistently gives more weight to the qualifications which Ricardo made to his basic vision of economic relationships, especially in Parliamentary speaking, than to the vision itself.[4] Ricardo was not well thought of in Parliament—as is well-known Brougham said that he spoke "as if he had dropped from another planet" (V pp. 56, 85)—and it seems to me that Ricardo had every incentive to play down his analytical conclusions for a Parliamentary audience. But Hollander attaches great weight to the Parliamentary material.

Essentially Hollander is arguing that the role which Ricardo afforded to models was no greater than that afforded by Adam Smith; that the models are occasional strong cases and that we have to look to the main body of the argument, as with Smith. But this is very difficult to agree with. I can recall only one example in Smith of the kind of reasoning to which Ricardo resorted habitually—the case of the passing on of a tax on wages. I suspect

[4] Henceforth I shall refer to this vision as Ricardo's model.

that the fact that Hollander has got this particular piece of Smith out of perspective lies at the root of the version of the history of economic thought which he presents. For he is then able to build upon this and present Ricardo as correcting that part of Adam Smith, while offering the rest uncorrected.

In fact, the methodological identity of Smith and Ricardo seems to me difficult to accept. Smith used short chains of reasoning in the Scottish tradition, while Ricardo essentially used 'as if' methodology but with the status of verification somewhat unclear. Smith had continuous resort to factual material while Ricardo's 1815 *Essay* and 1817 *Principles* contain no facts at all. There is a clear contrast between Ricardo's treatment of taxation and that of Smith. It does not seem helpful to blur over issues of this sort in order to establish the separate point that Ricardo would have had no use for the methodology of Sraffa's *Production of Commodities.*

In part Hollander's view of methodological identity is based upon a simple misunderstanding—that there ever *could* be a wholly inductive methodology. Once he finds that Smith ruled out a *wholly* inductive methodology he feels able to conclude that Smith's methodology was the same as that of Ricardo. Smith is presented as an abstractionist; and this view is supported by a ragbag of quotations from around 1800 concerning contemporary views of Smith's methodology which seem to prove nothing. (Pp. 27–40). But anyone who believes that Smith and Ricardo had an identical methodology should ask themselves the simple question whether Smith could ever have written the *Essay on Profits.*

Hollander is of course anxious to reject the charge, stemming from Schumpeter, of the existence of a Ricardian Vice in methodology; but it is strange that in this encyclopaedic treatment there was not room for a discussion of Ricardo on tithes and taxes on raw produce which in fact show the mechanical nature of his analysis very well.

The supposed identity of Smith and Ricardo in methodological terms enables Hollander to reach two other rather surprising conclusions. The first is that Ricardo and Malthus were really very close—a conclusion which can only be reached not only by equating Ricardo with Smith but also by throwing away Ricardo's models. (Pp. 666–7). Secondly, and more seriously, it enables him to defend Ricardo against the charge of having made predictions that failed—by arguing that Ricardo did not make predictions.

> "I do not believe that Ricardian theory should be interpreted in terms of specific predictions regarding the actual course of events, for Ricardo was thoroughly aware that all depends upon the satisfaction of the *ceteris paribus* conditions...upon which the formal model is constructed." (p. 639).

This leads (p. 640) to a defence of Ricardo which is either tautological or involves admitting that his predictions were falsified. Ricardo was only trying to say what would happen if certain conditions were fulfilled, in Hollander's view. Now either (i) it did not happen because other things (not fully specified *ex ante*) were not equal—which is really tautology; or (ii) it did not happen even though the main '*if*'—the continued existence of the Corn Laws—was satisfied. Then we have falsification. Hollander's main defence however must rest upon the proposition that, because Smith and Ricardo are methodologically identical, Ricardo, like Smith, had two (or *n*) way causation rather than the one-way models with which he is normally associated. Hollander's position (pp. 660, 647, 656) appears to be that Ricardo did not adopt his model because it had predictive content; rather, its form was dictated by the desire to combat Smith's investment-opportunity-exhaustion model—Ricardo being, according to Hollander as we shall see, an extreme optimist about economic growth—and/or by '*dissatisfaction on purely logical grounds*' (p. 647 Hollander's italics) not only with this notion but also with the idea of a dependence of the price level upon profits and wages. But in any case, if there is no specific model there are no specific predictions.

I found Hollander's account of Smith's own work rather odd. I cannot recognise the account of the key features of the Smithian system given by Hollander and which appears to be based on an interpretation of some passages in the Digression on the Price of Silver which do not seem able to bear the interpretative weight placed upon them. All that I read in the Digression is what it purports to be: a digression on the price of silver which cannot avoid the question of its international distribution but does so rather shakily and without the key material on price-specie-flow—even though we know from Smith's lectures that he understood it.

Moreover Hollander attaches far too much importance to Smith's material on the effect of a tax on wages on prices. This was just a particular theory of incidence which occupies no great space in the *Wealth of Nations*. Hollander also commits himself to the view that "the corn-export bounty [is] the issue which...provides the key to any evaluation of the status of Smithian economics in the early 1800s" (p. 31). The emphasis upon the corn price and the general price level in Hollander's account of Smith makes it possible to represent Ricardo as continuing the work of Smith but correcting the mistaken analysis. This allows the rest of Smith's work to be smuggled in largely by implication. It is however upon this last that Hollander bases his 'Walrasian' claims for Ricardo's analysis.

Ricardo's profit theory

It is Hollander's contention that Ricardo's theory of profit developed before the debate on agricultural protection and concern with the Corn

Laws. There seem to be two grounds for this argument. Firstly, the view that the Corn Laws did not become a major issue until 1814; secondly, some speculation, originating in part of an article by Tucker, about the Malthus-Ricardo correspondence in 1813.

Neither of these seems to me persuasive. Firstly, although Corn Laws were not particularly contentious until the latter part of the Napoleonic Wars, this was only because corn prices were so high that even the quite stiff level of protection introduced in 1804 was ineffective. Corn prices were continuously high from about 1795 onwards and the effect was particularly marked from 1808. From 1810 to 1813 the corn price level was nearly double the 18th century level and public concern was reflected in petitions and in the setting up of the Select Committee of 1813. There had been a record price in 1795 and great suffering. Riots followed. It is from this time that the Speenhamland system dates. There was a deficient harvest in 1799 and food riots at the end of the year. By July 1800 the price of corn was about two and a half times the 18th century level and by March 1801 it was three times that level. There were food riots again in 1804. The problem of high corn prices was then one which was present throughout most of the Napoleonic Wars and the extension of domestic cultivation a matter of some interest.

In an interesting article in 1954 Professor G. S. L. Tucker suggested a number of possible origins of Ricardo's theory of profits (Tucker, 1954); one of these was the possibility that it originated in a suggestion by Malthus (not recorded, and Tucker had to rely on material in Malthus' *Principles* of 1820) in which Malthus, following Smith, argued that foreign trade, by widening the market, increased profits. Tucker himself, however, also pointed out that *prior to* the August 1813 letters on which this speculation is based, there had been a debate in the House of Commons (15th June 1813) on the general question of agricultural protection. Hollander nonetheless feels that Tucker's suggestion about foreign trade is sufficiently convincing to provide an explanation of the origin of Ricardo's theory of profit *independent of* corn prices and agricultural protection. However, the scraps of correspondence, related tenuously to material not appearing until 1820, do not seem to me to provide any convincing evidence for Hollander's thesis. Indeed, both the letters of Ricardo which he quotes reject an increase in foreign trade as *evidence* that profits had increased—which is a different matter from *causing* profits to increase. So we have several reasons for being chary about accepting Hollander's view; corn prices had been an issue for 18 years by the date of the correspondence; the correspondence does not support the conclusions which are drawn from it; and the Corn Laws were already an issue in Parliament before the date of the correspondence.

Of course it is highly likely that Ricardo decided that wages and profits moved inversely at quite an early stage. But this hardly amounted to a new theory of profit. The obvious Bullionist objection (that either the money supply or velocity must rise if cost increases are to raise the price level) to Smith's cost-push view of inflation hardly amounts to laying the foundation of Ricardo's later models. Because Ricardo was a Bullionist he would, in his typically single-minded way, have rejected all explanations for price rises that did not involve increases in the money supply.

But in any case, whether Ricardo's theory of profit developed from considerations apart from the high price of corn—and this seems to me highly debatable—the fact is that the full Ricardian system, however far it stretched back (which is one thing) and however free in origins from the influence of the high price of corn (which is quite another) undoubtedly related to a high corn price and the potential role of the Corn Laws in achieving this.

Profit determination

Commentators have seen in Ricardo's work a number of different explanations of the way in which profits in agriculture affect those in the rest of the economy. These include a rise in the price of the manufacturing input—capital in the form of agricultural wage goods—as the corn price rises and agricultural profits fall; a rise in the price of the manufacturing labour input because of a rising price of subsistence; capital moving out of agriculture into manufacturing following a fall in agricultural profits; and a rise in the price of wheat in terms of the invariable measure depressing the relative prices of manufactures and manufacturing profits. The textual support for these interpretations is variable; the second and fourth are clearly to be found, and the third does appear in the *Essay* of 1815. The first explanation is that associated with the Sraffa-Dobb introduction to Ricardo's *Principles*; and Hollander takes very strong exception to it. He is satisfied that the causality works solely through rising money wages.

Such a view encounters two difficulties. The first is that it raises problems of valuation some of which the corn-input corn-output model avoids. Indeed Hollander is forced to conclude

> "that Ricardo did not intend by his formal statement to maintain that the profit rate in agriculture literally determines the rate elsewhere, but rather that agricultural productivity alone influences profits generally in the event that corn alone enters the wage basket; and, secondly, that it does so by way of the effect of the price of corn upon money wages. According to this view, in the event that the wage basket contains manufactured goods, an alteration in the prices of manufactures also may alter the general profit rate by way of precisely the same mechanism." (p. 145).

Such an interpretation of the role of agricultural productivity has to contend with a rather serious problem. It is that Ricardo apparently took the firm view, at least in the *Essay*, that agricultural profits *determined* the general rate of profit:

> "Nothing is more common than to hear it asserted, that profits on agriculture no more regulate the profits of commerce, than the profits of commerce regulate the profits on agriculture. It is contended, that they alternately take the lead; and, if the profits of commerce rise, which it is said they do, when new markets are discovered, the profits of agriculture will also rise; for it is admitted that if they did not do so, capital would be withdrawn from the land to be employed in the more profitable trade. But if the principles respecting the progress of rent be correct, it is evident, that with the same population and capital, whilst none of the agricultural capital is withdrawn from the cultivation of the land, agricultural profits cannot rise, nor can rent fall: either then it must be contended, which is at variance with all the principles of political economy, that the profits on commerical capital will rise considerably, whilst the profits on agricultural capital suffer no alteration, or, that under such circumstances, the profits on commerce will not rise."
>
> (IV, pp. 23–4).

Moreover we have (I, pp. 119–20) the argument that manufacturing innovation will be offset by a capital inflow from other sectors of manufacturing so that profits are lowered again. Even when Ricardo concedes that a fall in the prices of non-agricultural wage goods will lower wages and that this will raise profits, agriculture is again the agency.

> "If by foreign commerce, or the discovery of machinery, the commodities consumed by the labourer should become much cheaper, wages would fall; and this, as we have before observed, would raise the profits of the farmer, and therefore all other profits."
>
> (IV. p. 26n).

The second difficulty is that it is not clear to me that Ricardo would have been very happy about reliance on money wages. I have in mind in particular the statement that

> "Profits, it cannot be too often repeated, depend on wages; not on nominal, but real wages; not on the number of pounds that may be annually paid to the labourer, but on the number of days' work, necessary to obtain those pounds."
>
> (I, p. 143).

Of course this last quotation occurs in the context of a discussion of international trade and it is not conclusive in relation to the particular problem under discussion here. But it certainly raises a question mark in my mind, particularly as Hollander uses material from this same chapter on foreign trade in an attempt to explain Ricardo's belief that a rise in profits outside agriculture could not raise profits generally (pp. 145, 297–8).

Value theory

The picture of Ricardian value theory which Hollander presents is one which will surprise many readers. The first point to note is that, in his view, Ricardo did not attach very much importance to the Invariable Measure. Now there is no doubt that Ricardo's discussion of the Invariable Measure was confused as Hollander (pp. 197–201) is able to demonstrate. His discussion is not exhaustive; and I am far from clear that he has noted that the measure of value has to change as the composition of total output changes, if it is to remain a commodity produced with the average capital/labour ratio. (See pp. 218, 223–7; Hollander deals with factor substitution but (apparently) with a basket of goods in fixed proportion.) But all this does not mean that the Invariable Measure was unimportant to Ricardo. Failure to solve a theoretical problem does not mean that the problem is automatically regarded as unimportant. It is particularly noteworthy that Hollander devotes little attention to the posthumous paper on Absolute and Exchangeable Value in which the Invariable Measure is given a central role. It is perfectly clear (see especially IV, pp. 358–9) that the measure of value was of great concern to Ricardo. Yet Hollander does not seem to me to afford it much weight in his overall picture of Ricardo. It is in the posthumous paper that Ricardo makes the explicit assumption (IV pp. 405–6) that corn and gold have the same period of production—an assumption which Hollander admits (p. 214) is also implied in the *Principles* although at a later stage (p. 256 f) he appears to object to others seeing this implication.

But if the negligible role afforded by Hollander to the Invariable Measure will surprise some readers they are likely to be even more surprised to learn that "Ricardo's treatment of demand turns out to be particularly sophisticated" and that previous formulations which have not attached much weight to this have been mistaken (p. 273). To regard the material upon which Hollander bases this assertion as either important or sophisticated—especially when compared with Senior, let alone Longfield—seems to me highly questionable. From a few scattered remarks he attempts to credit Ricardo with a sophisticated understanding of elasticity, when all that Ricardo had was a commerical man's intuition. Hollander's only support for his view appears to be a quotation (I p. 241) which merely says that the response of individuals to a rise in price is not uniform, one quotation from a speech of 1822 which indicates that total expenditure at first increases then diminishes as price falls, and some other even more fragmentary material. Yet Hollander even goes so far as to claim (p. 277n) that "Ricardo must be considered as one of the 'originators' of the elasticity concept".

But he goes further. For in a subsequent section (pp. 285–93) he seems to be crediting Ricardo with an essentially Marshallian analysis of demand. Yet in this discussion he refers only once (and that only in relation to a special case) to Ricardo's *Principles* chapter 30 which contains some rather key statements in relation to Hollander's thesis. Ricardo wrote:

> "It is the cost of production which must ultimately regulate the price of commodities, and not, as has been often said, the proportion between the supply and demand: the proportion between supply and demand may, indeed, for a time, affect the market value of a commodity, until it is supplied in greater or less abundance, according as the demand may have increased or diminished; but this effect will be only of temporary duration."
>
> (I, p. 382).
>
> "The opinion that the price of commodities depends solely on the proportion of supply to demand, or demand to supply, has become almost an axiom in political economy, and has been the source of much error in that science." (*ibid.*)

Of course, in agriculture the cost of production was variable—this could not be denied—and demand had a role in selecting the marginal unit. But demand was of zero *price* elasticity; and Ricardo's analysis really does not go beyond this. (See especially I, p. 385). Yet Hollander refers (p. 679) to "Ricardo's sophisticated appreciation of demand–supply technique."

Satisfied that Ricardo had a sophisticated understanding of demand theory, Hollander then employs this to defend Ricardo against the charge that his analysis of agricultural improvements left him with two profit rates in the industry. Now it is unfortunate that there is no systematic discussion of such improvements in Hollander's book. He uses no formal analysis in his discussion of this particular issue and this makes it difficult to be sure exactly what he has in mind. For Ricardo there were three kinds of improvement—labour saving, capital saving, and land saving. In the case of an improvement which saved capital and labour in fixed combination together, Hollander's argument is that the displaced demand would re-employ these factors elsewhere at the same rates as before. But suppose that the capital/labour ratio is variable, and that capital is saved, or that there has been a land saving invention. Then profit rates in agriculture should have risen because of the improvement so that even if some displaced factors are employed elsewhere there are still two profit rates. Now I *think* that Hollander is relying upon the idea that profits do not rise because farmers are subject to competition and they will bid up rents. But this is far from clear. The Stigler diagram (Stigler 1941 pp. 90-ln) in which the argument originated, does have increased factor rewards in agriculture. In this case, price will not fall in proportion to the factors released and thus the demand transfer which Hollander apparently envisages (pp. 294–5)—*and* believes that Ricardo envisaged—will not be sufficient to re-employ the factors even at their old rates of return let alone at the new increased rates of return. Hollander, it later turns out (p. 301), believes that profits will *not* rise in the agricultural sector. But I am not clear *how* this is supposed to happen; and it would have been helpful to have the matter treated analytically.

It is by imputing to Ricardo a 'sophisticated understanding of demand' that Hollander is enabled to interpret him in quasi-Walrasian terms. Indeed, on the basis of the material in his chapter 6, he feels able to imply (pp. 679–83) either that Ricardo had a general equilibrium system in mind or that he could have got his results from a general equilibrium system. While I am not sure whether he *could* have really done this, the fact that he *did not* do so seems to me indisputable as a matter of history of economic thought. Indeed this 'Walrasian' view of Ricardo fits ill with Ricardo's remarkable tendency to carve the economy up into one giant farm and one giant firm for the purposes of the corn model.

I feel that the explanation for all this must be over-reaction. To proceed from rejecting Sraffa's new system (and work associated with it) as truly Ricardian to asserting that "Ricardo's model involves the use of something akin to the equilibrium conception of marginalist theory in the context of distribution" (p. 688) seems to me going much too far.

Wages

1. *Subsistence*

Hollander firmly rejects the idea (p. 309) that Ricardo thought of wages as typically at a subsistence level. His view is flatly contradictory to the more or less unanimous view of the secondary literature, including that of St. Clair (1957, p. 120) whose book is still an excellent guide to what Ricardo actually said.

Although Hollander is dissenting from the vast majority of present-day opinion on Ricardo's wage analysis it is nonetheless true that Marshall also believed that wages would not be forced down to subsistence in Ricardian analysis. The argument about this has been going on, as Hollander notes, since Ashley's attack on Marshall (Ashley, 1891). The logic of the argument seems to me to be undoubtedly with the majority, unless we accept that the dubious marriage rate explanation of population control, discussed below, is either valid or important in the context of Ricardo's works as a whole.

In fact the material referred to in Hollander's own discussion of poor relief (pp. 559–66) suggests, to me at least, that Ricardo did indeed believe that wages were at subsistence though, in this context, he blamed the Poor Law for this. In turn, Ricardo approved of harshness in the administration of the Poor Law to stop population increasing too fast, and he was clearly in favour of the abolition of the Poor Law (pp. 563–5). His objections carried over even into private philanthropy. (Hollander seems to attempt to write-off Ricardo's hard line attitude on the Poor Law, on the grounds that prudence would miraculously develop once the Poor Law was abolished (pp. 569–70)).

Hollander commits himself to the view (p. 567–89) that Ricardo did not expect population to increase faster than subsistence, thus equating him with Senior. Yet, as Marian Bowley made clear in her classic study, Senior really had something to attack (Bowley 1937 pp. 311–12). Hollander bases a great deal of his interpretation on the observation in the *Principles* that subsistence may be variable and conventional. Yet it seems to me that one has to see Ricardo as a whole: and if one does then the usual conclusion seems to be valid, particularly as Hollander later concedes (p. 574) that it was Ricardo's opinion that wages 'tended' to be "depressed to the minimum subsistence requirements of the single labourer". For *why* did population increase in this way if the real limit was conventional subsistence? The married labourer was still at minimum subsistence; he had physical subsistence for himself plus the parish provision of physical subsistence (and surely Hollander is not implying that the parish supplied more than physical subsistence) for his family. Moreover Hollander quotes later, and in a different discussion (p. 584), a passage which seems to me to indicate clearly that Ricardo had subsistence wages in mind. "I limited my proposition to the case when wages were too low to afford him [the labourer] any surplus beyond absolute necessaries".

2. *Taxes on wages*

One of the difficulties with which Hollander's view that wages in the Ricardian system were not at subsistence has to cope is discovery of the mechanism by which taxes on wages are passed on. It has normally been assumed that taxes on wages were passed on via population variation because wages were at subsistence. It seems (Hollander pp. 378 ff) that Hollander starts by envisaging that there were variations in infant mortality assumed in Smith's work even when wages were not at subsistence. This is rather puzzling. Hollander then decides (p. 380) that the answer must lie in the postponement of marriage. Yet looking back over Hollander's references, I can find none which would support this interpretation of Smith. There is a short unreferenced quotation on page 377 but Hollander himself concedes that Smith did not lay much emphasis on this—and when one tracks the quotation down and finds it in context (*Wealth of Nations*, Cannan edition I, p. 88) it turns out that the opposite is true and that poverty is not significantly unfavourable to marriage and child-bearing though it is to infant survival.

Starting from a picture of Smith which does not seem to me to accord with the text, or with the later history of economic thought (for it was Senior who substituted 'fear of deficiency' for actual deficiency although Malthus from his second edition onward had paid attention to this point) Hollander then sets about crediting Ricardo with the same mechanism. On p. 381 he gives a quotation from Ricardo which seems clearly to involve physical subsistence. But then Ricardo is held, on the basis of his view that subsistence rates varied between countries, to have "placed somewhat more emphasis than did Smith upon the marriage rate in defining the relation between earnings and population growth" (p. 382). Since Adam Smith placed virtually no 'emphasis' on this matter, and since Ricardo did not appear to have mentioned the marriage rate in the material quoted here, I was not sure what meaning could be attached to Hollander's conclusion.

But Hollander does give four other references and on checking these do turn out to yield statements about variations in marriage rate as wages rise above subsistence. But this is not enough for Hollander's purposes. For he needs to establish that the prospect of variations in the marriage rate produce *changing expectations* and these are what produce the passing on of taxes on wages.

Now Ricardo himself seems clearly to envisage that a tax on wages will be passed on via the subsistence mechanism (I, p. 159). Indeed, he is so satisfied of the effectiveness of this mechanism that he feels that, because such a tax must then fall on profits, this makes it superior to an income tax, for taxing wages thus enables profits to be taxed without any form of enquiry (I, pp. 159–61).[5] It seems to me that some of the material, including some of that quoted by Hollander, indicates clearly that Ricardo was not arguing that a wage tax would be passed on if wages were not already at subsistence (e.g. Hollander p. 384; and I p. 118).

However, (pp. 386–9) Hollander sets out to demonstrate that the wage tax theorems do not depend upon the subsistence wage but upon marriage rate variation. But we very soon encounter a key problem. Hollander quotes Ricardo as saying: "Labour will, therefore, rise, because the demand continues and it is only by raising the price that the supply is not checked when wages are taxed (p. 387)." But the question is *how* does this come about. The answer must surely—though Hollander does not appear to appreciate the problem because he has rejected the view of Ricardo as a simpliste model builder—lie in Ricardo's habitual practice of telescoping the long run and the short run. For it can hardly be argued, even if we accept Hollander's view that Ricardo relied on the marriage rate variation to control population, that employers will raise wages simply because they *fear* a fall in the marriage rate or increased infant mortality. Yet this is what Hollander's argument seems to require.

[5] Hollander himself quotes one such passage on p. 404.

Hollander, it seems to me, fails to show that Ricardo's argument does not depend upon subsistence (whether physical, or conventional as affecting the marriage rate) let alone show that it does not all depend upon telescoping the long and short run. Of course it is possible to find a quotation in which Ricardo slightly qualifies his naive belief in the passing on of taxes on wages (Hollander p. 389); but, as noted above, he was also so happy about such taxes that he thought them superior to an income tax.

Finally (pp. 389–90) Hollander concedes that the 'telescope' exists and then tries to use, in Ricardo's defence, one of Ricardo's own naive pieces of modelling whereby the government demands labour with the proceeds of a tax on wages. The defects in this procedure were pointed out to Ricardo by his contemporaries. At last (p. 393) Hollander concedes: "The precise mechanism he [Ricardo] envisaged in the market remains difficult to grasp". However, he recognises the need for an expectations induced adjustment, for he goes on: "but it would appear that Ricardo allowed for a *forecast* by employers of the consequences of permitting real wages to decline—namely a reduced growth rate of labour supply—and their consequential decision to pay higher money wages unilaterally and thus short-circuit the otherwise lengthy process of adjustment." But the basis for Hollander's belief turns out to be one rather desperate concession by Ricardo when cornered by McCulloch (VIII, p. 196) over his 'government demanding labour with the proceeds of the wage tax' argument.

3. *The wage fund*

Hollander also argues that Ricardo did not use the concept of a pre-accumulated wage fund. Actually Hollander may be right here; but since the evidence which he produces (pp. 334–5) seems to me to show that Ricardo did not think the matter through, and since the wage fund was a straightforward deduction by McCulloch from the implications of Ricardo's reasoning, I am not at all sure how fair it is to blame the model builders for making the same deduction as Ricardo's contemporary.

4. *Fixed commodity wages*

Hollander also finds fault with the model builders for their attribution to Ricardo of a fixed commodity wage. Indeed, according to one of Hollander's italicised assertions:

> "*It is crystal clear that the fundamental prediction of rising money wages upon which so much depends in the Ricardian vision of expansion—particularly the fall in the profit rate—is made despite the decline in commodity wages which is assumed to occur.*"
>
> (p. 398 Hollander's italics).

To this reader, at least, the matter seems less then crystal clear however. Indeed Hollander has to concede in his next sentence that:

> "It is unfortunate that Ricardo chose, in the very next paragraph, to give the famous numerical illustration relating the money-wage rate to rising corn prices which seems, on a casual view, to be based on the assumption that the actual wage basket remains constant."

Having explained this to his satisfaction on the grounds that

> "the illustration was intended to demonstrate the particular proposition that a rise in money wages is not necessarily productive of comforts to the labourer" (p. 399),

Hollander then has to concede that

> "It is true that in the strategic chapter 'On Profits' Ricardo also used these same illustrative data (in his demonstration that the money-wage share out of a product of given value divided between wages and profits will rise secularly)."

For this Hollander has to offer the

> "probable explanation...that he used a set of figures conveniently at hand, taking for granted that little damage was done since he believed that money wages will rise even though real wages decline." (p. 399).

He then gives a quotation from Ricardo which he believes to confirm this 'probable explanation'. I can only say that to me it seems not to do so.

5. *Conclusion on wages*

Hollander is clearly convinced of the validity of his interpretation; and since it is not one which has been arrived at by any superficial study this is something that one must take seriously. But I must say that I found much of the argument concerned with wages unconvincing. This was particularly the case when I learned that Hollander concluded that Ricardo must have made a mistake (p. 404) when he advanced an argument which was clearly at variance with Hollander's 'potential marriage rate variation' interpretation. Hollander believes that some of the quotations to which he refers (p. 403, footnote 265)[6] indicate that Ricardo was assuming constant population growth. If this were true it would be indeed puzzling. But having checked all the references I am not able to draw from them the conclusions which Hollander is able to. All that I can find is that occasionally we have population increasing faster than capital. But this is always what is happening during the down swing of the looped course of market wages in Baumol's well-known diagrammatic treatment. Since Hollander has dismissed the Baumol interpretation he is then forced to interpret some passages from Ricardo as assuming constant population growth and is thus forced to 'correct' Ricardo.

[6] I also checked some other references (VI 303–4, 147) given by Hollander in n263.

There seems to me at times to be an element of special pleading in Hollander's account of Ricardo on wages. Indeed, in a supplementary note on poor relief Hollander, faced with the fact that Ricardo undoubtedly recommended the abolition of the Poor Law, attempts to argue, on the basis, it seems to me, of no real evidence at all, that

> "It cannot, therefore, be excluded that in the event of some *alternative* form of relief for the able-bodied, without these defects, he [Ricardo] might have been prepared to reconsider the issue" (p. 723 Hollander's italics).

Monetary thought

My severest reservations about Hollander's treatment concern his discussion of monetary thought. The first problem relates to Ricardo's use of a cost of production theory of monetary value. This was typical, as it has always seemed to me, of Ricardo as a model builder and user, but it receives very little emphasis in Hollander's treatment, consistently with his general minimisation of this aspect of Ricardo and in particular his playing down of the importance of the Invariable Measure. (pp. 177, 203, 244). Ricardo himself thought that his model applied without commodity money—even with paper; but as Hollander notes (p. 245), this involved "an extraordinary degree of wishful thinking". Nevertheless Hollander defends Ricardo on the grounds (pp. 246–7) that the inverse relationship could work under a paper currency via a diminution in the purchasing power of profits, basing himself on *Principles* pp. 126–7.

I am particularly concerned, however, about Hollander's attempt to establish that Ricardo's monetary theory was somehow Smithian. This involves playing down the importance of David Hume in the history of monetary thought to the point where he virtually disappears. Thus the so-called 'Smithian' (pp. 105–6) position that the rate of interest is not affected by increases in the money supply is not only Hume's (and thus derived from the same place as the rest of Ricardo's monetary thought) but also available in the work of Massie. By inflating the role of Adam Smith vis-a-vis classical monetary theory Hollander is able to give the impression of a continuity between Smith and Ricardo which otherwise does not exist. The account of pre-Bullion-Report monetary theory I found strange. It leaves out Hume (apart from a few oblique references to Hume-type mechanisms) placing Adam Smith in the forefront of pre-Ricardian monetary theory (where he certainly does not belong) and considerably overrating Ricardo's own importance as a monetary theorist vis-a-vis Thornton and others.

Smith's monetary theory was of course close to that of the anti-Bullionists—indeed he offered the Real Bills doctrine. Thus it was that Torrens, in his anti-Bullionist phase, put forward the Smithian argument about a rise in corn prices raising wages and thus general prices which Ricardo, as leader of the strict Bullionists, rejected.

At times the account is startling. On p. 476 we have apparently the attribution to Ricardo of the (anti-Bullionist) position that causality runs from the price level to the money supply. This will seem so surprising to some readers that quotation is necessary here. Hollander begins by quoting Schumpeter who, in his definition of the quantity theory, wrote (not unreasonably) that it included the proposition that "the quantity of money is an independent variable—in particular that it varies independently of prices and of physical volume of transactions". Hollander then asserts "The first proposition is certainly *not* attributable to Ricardo in the case of an open economy. Where a fully operative gold standard is presumed the equilibrium (domestic) level of prices is frequently taken as given and the question posed relates to the corresponding money supply required to assure such a level." It turns out that this attribution is based upon an exchange before the Lords Committee on Resumption of 1819 which, one finds from inspecting the context, was concerned with an exposition of the price-specie-flow doctrine—causality does not run from the price level (as with the anti-Bullionists) but from a money supply dependent on the *world* value of gold.

Hollander also, by laying stress on variations in velocity (which were, in truth, mainly due to institutional factors, so that Ricardo was really a quantity theorist in Schumpeter's sense—a matter I should have thought which was never seriously in doubt) manages to imply (p. 479) that Ricardo had the sort of comprehensive view of variations in velocity that Thornton possessed.

A passage in which Ricardo had actually been trying to argue that an increase in the money supply had only a transitory effect on the rate of interest is used (pp. 480–1) to illustrate Hollander's proposition that Ricardo really attached importance to these transitory effects. But a look at the context clearly indicates that he was trying to minimise them (*High Price of Bullion* in III, pp. 91–2; see also V p. 445). Here as elsewhere, by presenting Ricardo's qualifications as the main argument[7] and the main argument as the qualifications, Hollander manages to achieve a picture which is a complete reversal of the normal—and, it seems to me, correct—view of Ricardo.

Similarly, Ricardo's recognition of the harmful effects of contraction, and his willingness to allow flexibility to the monetary authorities, is greatly overplayed (pp. 488–500, 523–35) by concentrating on the question of

[7] See especially 482 where Hollander, having presented what seems to me a highly misleading picture, concedes

"It should at the same time be recognised that Ricardo frequently played down his allowances for the monetary influence on the interest rate."

Resumption. The attitude displayed by Ricardo in his 1823 ***Plan for a National Bank***—which sought to impose completely automatic control on the monetary authorities—is relegated to a footnote.

The section (pp. 484–7) dealing with forced saving fails to make clear the very restricted nature of Ricardo's insights compared with those of his contemporaries, and implies (incorrectly) that there were no inflationists among the latter. It also appears to me (pp. 483–4) to fail to distinguish metallic (Hume) and paper inflation.

Finally, while Hollander seems to me to recognise that Ricardo was far more rigid in his application of 'Say's Law' than was Say, he still attempts to insist that Ricardo

> "adhered to that version of the law of markets labelled 'Say's Equality', which allows for temporary deviations between the money values of commodities supplied and demanded, that is, for temporary excess demand for money."
>
> (p. 513).

This belief is however based upon two quotations which only show that, given inelastic expectations, prices can be sticky downwards, and they do not seem, to me at least, to support at all the position which Hollander is endeavouring to maintain. But in this connection the next two of Hollander's sentences are revealing. For he writes:

> "We are not, however, yet out of the woods. For as we shall now see, in his analysis of the post-war depression Ricardo failed to recognise the relevance of temporary excess money demand."
>
> (p. 513)

It seems to me that Hollander, in his charitable zeal to do the best by Ricardo, is determined to drag Ricardo right out of the woods, even if this means demolishing a lot of the timber in the process.

This impression is further accentuated by something which is very apparent throughout the discussion but particularly in the section on the post-war depression. For, by confining himself to the Ricardo-Malthus correspondence, the notes on Malthus, and the published volumes generally, the wider debate is almost totally omitted. This must explain the curious reference to William Blake as an opponent of the Bullionists (p. 421n) a reference which neglects his earlier (Bullionist) work.

International Trade

Despite its length, the book contains very little about trade theory. Yet there are two matters which seem to call for comment. Firstly, Hollander apparently believes that Ricardo held that wine could sell permanently in two national markets at different prices, despite the absence of tariff and transport costs. Hollander's explanation is in terms of different profit rates with the retail price differing but not the wholesale (pp. 465–6)—although Ricardo does not actually discuss this matter. The contrast with the standard interpretation is clear enough; and it seems to me straining common sense to believe other than that the latter is correct.

The section (pp. 442–57) dealing with the transfer problem seems to me to muddle the issues rather badly. I was not even clear that Hollander accepts the existence of the Ricardian definition of excess. In relation to Ricardo's rejection of harvest failure as an explanation for a depressed exchange Hollander asserts that:

> "In these passages Ricardo recognised clearly that the import of corn *may* be paid for in gold rather than commodities."
>
> (p. 446).

If Ricardo had really recognised such a possibility he could no longer have remained the strict Bullionist he was, applying the Ricardian definition of excess in the way he did. But Hollander seems to me to be offering a very strange interpretation of the quotations on p. 445 which come from III pp. 59–61 (*High Price of Bullion*) and are part of Ricardo's *attack* on Thornton for suggesting exactly what Hollander is crediting Ricardo with saying.

Hollander does throw in (pp. 450–1) an ingenious suggestion about adjustment to the internal price structure following harvest failure—as the price of corn rises, other prices fall and thus exports are stimulated. But I cannot see any support in Ricardo's own writings for this. It really is not good enough to say (p. 451):

> "It cannot therefore be precluded that the altered price structure (and a reduction in the prices of exportables) was taken for granted throughout Ricardo's discussion of the transfer problem even when he does not make explicit reference thereto."

Policy effects and outlook

1. *Transitional effects*

It was noted above that Hollander's account of Ricardo's monetary thought gives far greater weight to transitional effects than the original material would seem to warrant. However this tendency to stress Ricardo's qualifications is not confined to Hollander's discussion of the monetary material or, to take another instance already noted, the neglect of Ricardo's habit of telescoping the long run and the short run in dealing with wage taxation. It is also particularly evident in Hollander's account of Ricardo's views on the desirability of abolishing the Poor Law. Hollander argues that Ricardo waited for the return of prosperity in the manufacturing sector in 1821 before pressing for repeal: I think it is true that Ricardo said on several occasions that abolition should be gradual. (Hollander cites some rather inconclusive references but there is a clear reference in I, pp. 106–7).

Moreover I agree with Hollander's characterisation of Inglis's work (1971) as "a totally distorted picture of Ricardo's position which has recently been presented in a popularisation of the classical view on social policy." (p. 574). But I remain unconvinced that Ricardo deserves much credit in this respect because he, of all the classical economists, seems to me the one who used his 'telescope' to ignore transitional effects. I certainly agree that Ricardo did not, anticipating that wages would fall below subsistence at least for the married pauper, with the abolition of the Poor Law, decide to grit his teeth and put up with suffering to the last pauper—which is what I feel Inglis's picture amounts to. But he was a good deal less prepared to make special arrangements to accommodate the transitional period before wages rose to the level which would restore physical subsistence (the usual interpretation) or the marriage rate (Hollander's interpretation) than Hollander implies. Moreover there is a clear distinction between Ricardo and Malthus—who were undeniably at one extreme of the debate on the Poor Law—and the rest of the classical economists from Senior to McCulloch. This distinction is lost sight of. Here as elsewhere, by giving undue prominence to the reservations and qualifications which Ricardo expressed in correspondence, a rather misleading picture is presented—misleading at least to anyone not already familiar with the wider literature of the period.

2. *The longer run*

(i) *Secular shares*

The conventional view—from Cannan to Blaug—is that Ricardo thought he had demonstrated a rising rental share in total product but had failed to do so. Hollander's position (p. 407) is that "Ricardo denied ever having maintained that the rental share in output rises secularly". This is apparently based on II, pp. 193, 197. This matter has already been dealt with by Barkai (1966) who saw the denial as a device adopted by Ricardo when faced by Malthus with the fact that rental share was actually declining—even though, if followed through, his new defensive position would have led to the abandonment of his model. Barkai's case seems very reasonable in view of the wealth of other evidence in Ricardo's work for the rising rental share, especially in the *Essay on Profits*. What Ricardo actually denied (in II, p. 193) was that rent was rising as a share of *gross* output. However rent as a share of *net* output rises in the *Essay* from 7.3% to 60.4%. As a share of gross output (net output plus cost of production, interpreting capital in the table (IV, p. 17) as cost of production) rent rises from 2.3% to 13%. Rent also rises as a percentage of capital, which was probably the figure which Ricardo meant to indicate the course of rent as a share of gross output. So there are three things which Ricardo could have meant: rent per cent, rent as a proportion of gross produce, and rent as a proportion of net produce. The denial—which only seems to be supported by one passage—relates only to gross produce, which is the least interesting prediction. However Hollander insists, on the basis of this passage, that Ricardo only meant something far less interesting—a rising rental share of gross produce on intra-marginal land. Yet in the end, despite his apparent disagreement with the conventional view, he seems to be forced to conclude that Ricardo's intentions are at best unclear. At the same time he commits himself to the view that "the entire matter was of little significance" (p. 410) a conclusion which I find very hard to swallow—and one which I think Hollander would have found hard to swallow himself had he not neglected Ricardo's treatment of improvements and the conflict of interest between landlords and the rest of the community.

(ii) *The ends of economic activity*

Hollander asserts (p. 550) that a major theme of Ricardo's chapter on Value and Riches was to show how capital accumulation can be financed, without reducing present consumption, by technical progress. Frankly I cannot see the basis for such a view. The theme, both of the chapter and of the quotation which Hollander gives from it, is that the labour of a given number of men, however productive, still has the same total value. This, incidentally, is how Bailey saw it—as illustrating what Ricardo thought he meant by total value.

(iii) *The outlook for economic growth*

Fundamental to Hollander's interpretation of Ricardo is the view that Ricardo was extremely optimistic about the prospects for economic growth. This view results in a chapter (pp. 599–642) on the Corn Law issue which seems to me the most difficult to accept of all the chapters. Schumpeter wrote of Ricardo's pessimism:

> "The most interesting thing to observe is the complete lack of imagination which that vision reveals. Those writers [Ricardo, Malthus, West and James Mill] lived at the threshold of the most spectacular economic development ever witnessed. Vast possibilities matured into realities under their very eyes. Nevertheless they saw nothing but cramped economies, struggling with ever decreasing success for their daily bread."
>
> (quoted in Hollander p. 600).

This is no doubt an over-drawn view—especially as regards Malthus. But Hollander's view seems to me even more extreme in an opposite direction. Quite apart from the correctness of Hollander's interpretation of Ricardo as optimistic—and it seems to me incorrect (indeed, were it correct, Ricardo's theoretical work, even in the attenuated version presented here, would have been pointless)—the interesting point from the history-of-economic-theory standpoint is not so much whether Ricardo really believed his model—and it seems to me that Ricardo believed in simple models more unreservedly than almost any economist in the nineteenth century—but what the model predicted.

Of course, as noted earlier in this discussion, Hollander does not accept that Ricardo's theory 'predicted'. If we agree with this we must then examine Hollander's evidence for the optimism in isolation from the model. Even so the evidence seems to me extremely unpersuasive.

On page 604 we have the assertion, italicised as is Hollander's wont, that:

> "*the case made [by Ricardo] against agricultural protection was not based upon the secular downward trend in the rate of return on capital.*"

I find this about the most difficult thing to swallow in the entire book; and even Hollander apparently realises that this is untenable, because he adds a footnote both qualifying and attempting to justify the assertion.

Hollander appears to be arguing (pp. 606–8) that Ricardo did not detect any depression of the growth rate of capital and was not even clear about the rate of return on capital. Yet it is clear from the 1815 *Essay* that Ricardo not only assumed, for the purposes of his model, which exhibited declining profit, that there were no agricultural improvements which could offset this decline, but did so on the grounds that diminishing returns always got the better of whatever improvements there were. Hollander's view is that when we turn from the 'pure theory' we find there is great optimism. This seems to me a serious misreading of the 1815 pamphlet. The passage in the *Essay* on which Hollander relies is one in which Ricardo concedes to Malthus that technical improvement has great scope in British agriculture. But the balance of the *Essay* is surely concerned with the inevitable depression of profits resulting from Corn Laws. Ricardo wrote:

> "I think it may be most satisfactorily proved, that in every society advancing in wealth and population, independently of the effect produced by liberal or scanty wages, general profits must fall, unless there be improvements in agriculture, or corn can be imported at a cheaper price."
>
> (IV, p. 23).

Again, Ricardo's analysis (at the time) of the commerical distress in 1819 was not that it was due to monetary causes—the 1819 Resumption Act "was totally inadequate to produce such an effect, and therefore the evil must be traced to other sources" (V, pp. 37–41, at p. 37). Rather, distress was due to capital shortage which resulted from low profits due to Corn Laws, and to the weight of the National Debt and taxation. The latter are perhaps emphasised even more; but the role of the Corn Laws does not seem to be in doubt. Ricardo is reported in *Hansard* as saying that

> "He conceived that the distress was chiefly to be ascribed to the inadequacy of the capital of the nation to carry on the operations of trade, manufacture, and commerce.....Now, he thought they had greatly aggravated this evil [of capital export] by bad legislation, and he had formerly mentioned instances. He had referred to the Corn-Laws as one example; and however unpopular the doctrine might be with some gentlemen, he would state his opinion freely that he believed Corn-Laws to have materially increased the evil. These laws had tended to raise the price of sustenance, and that had raised the price of labour, which of course diminished the profit on capital."
>
> (V, p. 38).

This surely contrasts with Hollander's view.

Interestingly enough, the attribution to Ricardo of optimism may link with Hollander's failure to discuss at all properly the question of improvements. I find it surprising that a question about Ricardo debated at length by authors like J. S. Mill, Marshall, and Cannan did not command Hollander's attention. Indeed I find Hollander's view (p. 611) that Ricardo was optimistic about improvements very unconvincing. On checking the references, I find only material which bears the normal interpretation, giving rise to what has been previously understood to be the standard Ricardian thesis of profit decline.[8]

Hollander himself recognises that Ricardo wrote:

> "No point in political economy can be better established, than that a rich country is prevented from increasing in population, in the same ratio as a poor country, by the progressive difficulty of providing food. That difficulty must necessarily raise the relative price of food, and give encouragement to its importation."
>
> (I, p. 373).

Hollander dismisses this as a strong statement because Ricardo is using his model to counter an argument of Smith's. But the subsequent material (I, pp. 373–4) seems to me to contradict the interpretation by Hollander of p. 126 which he uses in support of his belief in 'optimism'.

> "However extensive a country may be where the land is of a poor quality, and where the importation of food is prohibited, the most moderate accumulations of capital will be attended with great reductions in the rate of profit, and a rapid rise in rent; and on the contrary a small but fertile country, particularly if it freely permits the importation of food, may accumulate a large stock of capital without

[8] See in particular I, 126, 120. The reference to improvements on p. 120 seems, to me at least, a parenthetical qualification, perhaps intended to explain why diminishing returns had not already manifested themselves strongly, and a qualification to a straightforward statement of what is normally regarded as the standard Ricardian position:

> "The very low rate of profits will have arrested all accumulation, and almost the whole produce of the country, after paying the labourers, will be the property of the owners of land and the receivers of tithes and taxes."
>
> (I, pp. 120–21).

any great diminution in the rate of profits, or any great increase in the rent of land".

(I, p. 126)

Hollander feels that the 'small but fertile country' is "an obvious reference to Britain" and takes this to mean that "there is little emphasis on a falling rate of return." (p. 611). But in I, pp. 373–4 Ricardo makes it clear that Corn Laws are only called for where they are going to have perceptible effect to benefit landlords:

> "It is only in rich countries, where corn is dear, that landholders induce the legislature to prohibit the importation of corn. Whoever heard of a law to prevent the importation of raw produce in America or Poland?"
>
> (I, pp. 373–4).

The contrast of these countries with Britain is clear enough.

Of course Ricardo not infrequently tried to have his cake and eat it, notably in his Notes on Malthus: but there seems to me to be no stress on improvements in the third edition of his *Principles.* It is true, as Hollander points out (p. 612), that Ricardo did say (IV, p. 179, I, pp. 108–9) that the richest country in Europe was still far from the stationary state. But the dimension is not clear; it is not clear whether he is referring to distance in time, or population increase, or capital stock, and the phrase is merely a qualification in the general argument that the stationary state is a *very* real possibility. Many of the qualifications to Ricardo's view come in correspondence and relate to discussions with others in which Ricardo fell back on the economist's time-honoured device of appealing to the Long-Run but, as with Hollander's account of the monetary theory, it seems to me wrong to lay so much stress on the qualifications as to make them appear the substance of the argument.

Indeed (p. 614), Hollander concedes that it was Ricardo's objective to persuade Parliament to repeal the Corn Laws. He thus has to explain how it was, and on what Ricardo's case was based. He is also faced with the problem of explaining why Ricardo should adopt a position which reduced the fundamental importance of his model—even in Hollander's formulation of it, the rising level of wages associated with diminishing returns is critical.

Now it seems to me that Ricardo was not particularly optimistic in his speech of 7th March, 1821 (V, pp. 81–91) which Hollander (pp. 615 ff) regards as important evidence for Ricardo's optimism—the optimistic material came right at the end of the speech and was only a device (when seen in context) to be used against those who said that the flood of corn imports would intensify depression. But Hollander's interpretation derives in a substantial measure from correspondence between Ricardo and McCulloch following this speech. Ricardo as quoted (and italicised) by Hollander apparently gives much more weight to 'optimism' than in the quoted letter

(VIII, p. 355–60) when one reads it as a whole. Indeed, in this letter Ricardo had also written (VIII, pp. 357–8):

> "My opinion is this—if we were allowed to get corn as cheap as we could get it, by importation, profits would be very considerably higher than they now are"[9]

Faced with the undeniable fact that Ricardo was frequently not 'optimistic' in Parliament, Hollander's judgement (p. 621) is that in the House of Commons Ricardo had an incentive to exaggerate the prospect of doom and that, accordingly, much weight should be attached to any passages in which he qualified his pessimism. My own judgement is precisely the opposite of this. Ricardo was not highly regarded in the House and he had every incentive to adopt a more moderate tone, in order not to alienate an audience who already regarded him as a visionary out of touch with reality.[10] Moreover this would explain the contrast between concessions that the stationary state might be more distant, and the quotations which Hollander introduces late in the chapter (the chapter starts at p. 598 and these quotations begin at p. 621) in which Hollander very fairly admits that

> "There exist, however, a number of speeches which emphasise low profits and loss of capital abroad in consequences of protection as phenomena *actually responsible for the contemporary depression.*"
>
> (p. 621, Hollander's italics).

Now this material could not be clearer, and Hollander fairly summarises it. He quotes from speeches of 16th December 1819, 24th December 1819, 30th May, 1820 and (in a footnote) 12th May, 1820. He also has to explain (pp. 625–6) the 1822 pamphlet *Protection to Agriculture* in which Ricardo clearly believed that the Corn Laws were depressing the profit rate. In addition he has to explain (p. 626) several pessimistic 'Parliamentary interventions' during the Spring of 1822. The material is simply dismissed (p. 627) as "uncharacteristic of Ricardo's general position". With respect, this is precisely what needs to be proved. To me, on the contrary, it seems wholly characteristic.

Indeed the pessimistic material seems to me to provide a good deal of very clear material to set against the one letter to McCulloch following one speech of 7th March 1821—even if I accepted that that had been interpreted in context, which I do not—and the scraps of correspondence quoted on pp. 610–611. The case for 'optimism' seems to me to rest largely on a construction of a portion of the material, which admits of rather different

[9] The exchange is not helped because McCulloch, with whom the correspondence was exchanged, was using a factor mobility, absolute advantage, model while Ricardo was using a comparative advantage, factor immobility, one.

[10] See especially Ricardo to McCulloch 13th June 1820 (VIII, 197) and Ricardo to Wilmot Horton 19th January 1823 (XI, xv).

(and, to me at least, more obvious) interpretations. However, faced with the evidence which flatly contradicts his own position, Hollander simply asserts that these "interventions" "were *atypical*" of Ricardo's position. (p. 624, Hollander's italics).

The issue is confused by Hollander's implied insistence that the only alternative to the Corn Laws as an explanation for the depression was 'friction' and misallocation of resources. In fact, however, Ricardo blamed the depression in part upon the Bank of England which he believed to have completely mishandled Resumption. Indeed the Bank was an institution to which Ricardo was extremely hostile—hence the *Plan for the Establishment of a National Bank*, a pamphlet which Hollander hardly mentions—(in fact I found only one reference (pp. 492–3n)). Earlier Ricardo had written to Malthus (9 July 1821):

> "I very much regret that in the great change we have made, from an unregulated currency, to one regulated by a fixed standard, we had not more able men to manage it than the present Bank Directors. If their object had been to make the revulsion as oppressive as possible, they could not have pursued measures more calculated to make it so than those which they have actually pursued. Almost the whole of the pressure has arisen from the increased value which their operations have given to the standard itself. They are indeed a very ignorant set."
>
> (IX, p. 15).

I do not myself feel that there is any doubt that, although Ricardo had believed in 1819 that commercial distress was not due to monetary causes, by 1821 he had come to attribute some blame to the Bank.

(iv) *Agricultural price fluctuations*

Hollander's view, in direct contrast with the received one, is that Ricardo was primarily worried about the Corn Laws not because of their effect on profits and economic growth, but because they produced price fluctuations. Hollander's judgement is based largely on the relative weight of material in *Protection to Agriculture* which, he claims, lays more emphasis on price fluctuations than profit depression. This seems to me unconvincing for two reasons. Firstly, the bulk of Ricardo's publications referring to the Corn Laws, prior to 1822, had dealt with the profit issue, starting with the *Essay on Profits* of 1815, so that a concern with price instability was then added to his established concern with profits—an issue which, as Hollander notes, is also dealt with in *Protection to Agriculture*. Indeed the vast bulk of the references which Hollander cites concerning prices dates from 1822 onwards when agricultural prices were depressed to a point which Ricardo could not ignore despite a model which predicted high prices. He was therefore *forced* to add price fluctuations to his concern. Secondly, the price fluctuation argument had already been developed by others before Ricardo's 1822 pamphlet—and I find it surprising that in this section (pp. 629–32) neither Tooke nor McCulloch are mentioned as analysing price fluctuations (despite the fact that Tooke had dealt with price fluctuations before the 1821 Agriculture Committee and his evidence is referred to in Ricardo's pamphlet) and Torrens and Malthus are not referred to at all.

In any case I do not read the balance of *Protection to Agriculture* as Hollander does. The pamphlet occupies pp. 209–266 of Volume IV. Of this only pp. 240–43 are primarily concerned with price fluctuations although there are a few scattered references in other contexts. In other words, the price fluctuations were secondary to the main Ricardian thesis but, as elsewhere, Hollander has emphasised the secondary at the expense of the primary—and thus altered the picture.

(v) *The corn laws and allocative loss*

Hollander also believes that Ricardo attached much weight to the allocative loss resulting from Corn Laws. (pp. 632–7). Now such a loss would be obvious to anyone who had read Adam Smith, let alone been privy to the development of the theory of comparative advantage. But it was hardly in the forefront of Ricardo's picture; and if it had been it would diminish his independent standing as an *original* thinker. But in fact Hollander is not able to muster any substantial collection of references in support of his view that "Ricardo allowed a very conspicuous role indeed for the allocative disadvantages flowing from agricultural protection."

(p. 632).

Coverage

1. *Topics*

This must surely be the biggest book on Ricardo ever written. There is no doubt that it is a product of enormous effort. It is however only fair to warn the reader that on a number of issues its coverage is seriously incomplete. The reader will search in vain for much discussion of what Ricardo had to say on the National Debt—a matter which concerned him—and I did not find at all Ricardo's extraordinary argument that tax finance in war imposed no heavier burden than debt because tax payers capitalised the future value of their income stream in the debt case. Similarly I did not find the argument that people could easily borrow to pay heavy war taxes, or the argument that if taxes fell solely on the property earning classes this would be counter-balanced by adjustment of the rate of entry into the professions. Ricardo's scheme for a levy to pay off the National Debt I found mentioned only briefly and unilluminatingly in another context (pp. 593, 625). The Sinking Fund is mentioned only once (p. 70) and this in connection with

Lauderdale and not Ricardo. The argument over whether government should borrow at 3% or 5% does not appear to be discussed and, as already noted, the plan for a National Bank is only mentioned once and the Ingot Plan only obliquely. The truck system does not appear to be mentioned, and Ricardo's views on emigration are mentioned only briefly in a footnote. Nor did I find the argument about the terms of trade effect of colonial protection. Colonies appear only once in the index; this turns out to be a reference to Bentham, and Ricardo's entire chapter in the *Principles* appears to be ignored by Hollander. The problem of the hierarchy of wages, which involves serious problems for Ricardo's use of labour measures, receives insufficient discussion; Hollander simply attempts to justify it (pp. 193–4) on the grounds that Ricardo was only interested in *changes* in relative values—yet it is precisely because an unfixed hierarchy could produce changes in relative values that the matter is of considerable importance. It is perfectly clear that Ricardo had simply assumed away this problem which also arises in the context of passing-on of taxes on wages—a mechanism which would only apply to the lowest grade of labourer. But Hollander refuses to concede this (p. 386); instead he argues that the concept of what constitutes subsistence must be viewed as varying from group to group in the labour force. This is really only another version of Ricardo's implied assumption that the hierarchy is fixed.

Perhaps the most surprising omission is a failure—or rather a refusal—to recognise the importance of class conflict in Ricardo. It is very surprising that in the section (pp. 586–93) 'Ricardo as a Radical' his attitude towards improvements is not mentioned. Indeed I find it puzzling that Hollander can quote (pp. 590–1) a statement in the Notes on Malthus, that Malthus is not justified in calling Ricardo an enemy of the landlords, while failing to mention pp. 79–82 of the *Principles* in which Ricardo sought to show that the landlord must lose in the short-term by improvements. After all, Ricardo had stated in his 1815 *Essay*:

> "It follows then, that the interest of the landlord is always opposed to the interest of every other class in the community. His situation is never so prosperous, as when food is scarce and dear: whereas, all other persons are greatly benefitted by procuring food cheap."
>
> (IV, p. 21).

Ricardo concluded the same pamphlet with the words:

> "I shall greatly regret that considerations for any particular class, are allowed to check the progress of the wealth and population of the country. If the interests of the landlord be of sufficient consequence, to determine us not to avail ourselves of all the benefits which would follow from importing corn at a cheap price, they should also influence us in rejecting all improvements in agriculture, and in the implements of husbandry; for it is as certain that corn is rendered cheap, rents are

> lowered, and the ability of the landlord to pay taxes is for a time, at least, as much impaired by such improvements, as by the importation of corn. To be consistent then, let us by the same act arrest improvement, and prohibit importation."
>
> (IV, p. 41).

In his *Principles*, Ricardo wrote:

> "a relatively high price of corn is at all times greatly beneficial to the landlord; for first, it gives him a greater quantity of corn for rent; and secondly, for every equal measure of corn he will have a command, not only over a greater quantity of money, but over a greater quantity of every commodity which money can purchase."
>
> (I, p. 337).

Since Ricardo did not admit that high corn prices were in the interests of the community the implication of this is quite clear enough. In 1821, if *Hansard* is to be believed, Ricardo stated in Parliament that "he would say, as he had said before, that the interest of the landholders must necessarily be opposed to that of the consumers in the present [agricultural] case."

(V, p. 87).[11]

2. *Contemporaries of Ricardo*

Perhaps even more serious is the cursory and unsympathetic treatment given to those who differed from Ricardo. On p. 663 Bailey is dismissed as "outrageous" on the grounds that he criticised Ricardo for failing to appreciate the relative nature of value. This seems to me quite unjustified. For Bailey saw perfectly well what Ricardo was seeking to achieve in his discussions of value—and saw equally well that Ricardo's aim was impossible. Bailey knew very well that value was being used in two senses—hence the acid exchanges with James Mill from which it is clear that Bailey realised this particular point rather earlier than Mill. It also seems to me that Hollander misrepresents the force of Whewell's criticism of Ricardo (p. 248n), and that he blurs the distinction between Ricardo and West (p. 332n75); and I am quite unable to accept what Hollander believes to be the reasonable interpretation of a passage in Barton (p. 351).

The main problem however is simply that the unsatisfactory treatment of the dissenters from Ricardo is possible only because of the particular loose and generalised version of Ricardo which Hollander has presented. It seems to me that Hollander is basing himself on a version of Ricardo which Ricardo's 19th century critics would have recognised no better than I can. As a result, Hollander is able to accuse them of a lack of insight. Having

[11] It should however be added that the newspaper account which Ricardo believed to have reported him best merely reported him as saying that "When he heard that all the interests of the country were equally consulted, he could not help saying, because he felt it, that the interests of landlords were chiefly considered."

(V, p. 81).

recently re-read both Bailey and the *Westminister Review* attack on him, together with Bailey's reply, I find Hollander's endorsement of James Mill's attack very strange. Again, on p. 665 he asserts that "the fact is that in the *Principles* Ricardo had shown a thorough awareness that differential rent is but a special case of a more general phenomenon." But on re-reading Ricardo's rent chapter I found no support for this sweeping assertion. Yet this is quite important because, if Hollander's assertion were true, it would rob Bailey and Senior of credit for generalising the rent concept to which they are surely—and generally held to be—entitled.

Longfield's striking analysis of intensity of demand is hardly mentioned and is brushed aside (p. 671) as of no importance. At times the chapter dealing with Ricardo's critics can give rise to some wry amusement. Thus on p. 670 we learn that "we cannot rule out the possibility" that Ricardo had a marginal productivity theory of distribution at the back of his mind. Similarly on pp. 671–2, Hollander, instead of discussing the McCulloch-Ricardo disagreement on the origin of the interest or profit premium, tells us that "it is by no means certain that he [Ricardo] would have objected to the investigation of the time preference notion which the so-called 'dissenters' insisted upon."

Hollander's attempt to explain away the possibility of taxes falling on wages via *anticipated* reductions in labour supply is then taken for granted and used as a basis for criticising Longfield. Another writer who receives little credit is James Anderson. In an appendix Hollander deals with Anderson on increasing returns but fails to quote and discuss the vital material on diminishing returns which McCulloch believed meant that Anderson should be credited with inventing rent theory; and although this material is mentioned earlier (pp. 41ff) it is only introduced rather grudgingly and as criticism of Adam Smith.

The material on Barton seems to me greatly to underplay Barton's contribution. Indeed at times Hollander seems to be trying to imply that all that Ricardo obtained from Barton was the idea that the capital/labour ratio might not be fixed. He overstresses Ricardo's qualifications to his machinery case and at one point seems to me to get involved in a flat contradiction between the textual evidence (given in a footnote—n100 p. 342) and an assertion in the text that the displacement of employment by machinery was not Ricardo's primary concern. The matter is too complicated to be explored at length here but, as in other cases, I feel that Hollander has read too much into Ricardo's qualifications and hints in correspondence.

Conclusion

This is a beautifully produced book with footnotes at the foot of the page so that the argument, with qualifications and quotations, can be followed.

No reader can fail to have admiration for Hollander's moral courage. I agree that many of the interpretations of Ricardo to which he objects are extreme. But having said that, it seems to me that one must have severe reservations about this book. Surely there is a via media between neo-Marxian interpretations on the one hand, and a return to J. H. Hollander on the other. I think there is a very real danger of throwing out a great deal of material which has been painstakingly built up, simply because of a disagreement with Cambridge. Hollander clearly does not like the kind of economics which, claiming Ricardian ancestry, has been built up in Cambridge since Sraffa's *Production of Commodities.* But neither, so far as I can judge, do many of the people on whom Hollander is so hard in this book. But Hollander feels constrained to throw out all the work that has been done to make sense of Ricardo, and instead to reinterpret Ricardo in a kind of loose general equilibrium framework. Now one of the key features of general equilibrium—which renders it vitually useless—is that it results in a model of complete generality in which virtually anything can happen, and which is almost completely devoid of predictions that can be subject to empirical testing. And this is more or less true of the end-product of Hollander's re-interpretation of Ricardo. The Hollander version goes something like this. 'Wages will no longer be necessarily at subsistence. They may or they may not be. Rental share may or may not increase. It is not clear what Ricardo thought about this. Profits can decline it is true. But this is not an immediate problem'. Almost all the predictive element (and all the rigour) of Ricardo's own thinking have gone. The Ricardian Vice therefore never existed. Ricardo did not really even build models.

In summary then, while admiring the energy and tenacity which went into this beautiful piece of book production, I find Hollander's frontal assault upon the accumulated body of Ricardo scholarship unconvincing, and believe that a more selective approach might have yielded greater benefits. But the assault is a serious one and I hope that I have indicated that it requires serious consideration fully to appreciate what is involved.

Durham University.

REFERENCES

ASHLEY, W. J. (1891) 'The Rehabilitation of Ricardo' *Economic Journal* I, 474–89.

BARKAI, H. (1966) 'Ricardo's Second Thoughts on Rent as a Relative Share' *Southern Economic Journal* XXXII, 285–93.

BOWLEY, MARIAN (1937) *Nassau Senior and Classical Economics* (London: Allen & Unwin).

CORRY, B. (1974) review of S. Hollander *The Economics of Adam Smith, History of Economic Thought Newsletter* No. 12, Spring 1974, 22–4.

HOLLANDER, S. (1979) *The Economics of David Ricardo* (Toronto: University of Toronto Press) pp. xiv + 759.

INGLIS, B. (1971) *Poverty and the Industrial Revolution* (London: Hodder & Stoughton).
ST. CLAIR, O. (1959) *A Key to Ricardo* (London: Routledge).
SRAFFA, P. (1951–73) ed. *The Works and Correspondence of David Ricardo* (Cambridge: C.U.P.).
SRAFFA, P. (1960) *Production of Commodities by Means of Commodities* (Cambridge: C.U.P.).
STIGLER, G. J. (1941) *Production and Distribution Theories* (New York: Macmillan).
TUCKER, G. S. L. (1954) 'The Origin of Ricardo's Theory of Profit' *Economica* XXI, 320–33.

[10]

6 CLASSICAL REASSESSMENTS

Denis P. O'Brien

In this chapter a group of six economists—Longfield, James Mill, Senior, Bailey, Torrens, and Say—is discussed. These are all writers who have frequently been treated as living in the fearful shadow of Ricardo (or Smith and Ricardo) and as being lacking in the intellectual strength to do more than question the Ricardian analysis. They have been treated as being mere regurgitators or, at best, as mosquitoes around the Ricardian giant.

The process of questioning this approach was due in particular to two people, Schumpeter and Robbins, although Mark Blaug's *Ricardian Economics*, despite its title, was also important in the reappraisal. Schumpeter's great *History*, for all its irritating features, contained an appraisal of the great figures of classical economics which was on a much broader canvas than had previously been conventional, while Robbins' *Theory of Economic Policy* (and perhaps above all his *Robert Torrens* as well as his earlier encouragement of Marian Bowley's *Senior*) helped to show how misleading the neglect of writers other than Ricardo had been. Building on the work of these writers, the literature discussed in this chapter has resulted in an appraisal of the six writers discussed here, and of others not included, which makes clear that the picture of classical economics as Ricardo and water is entirely misleading. The writers discussed here were men of independent mind and independent spirit. While they could hardly fail to be affected by Ricardo in some way, they looked for solutions to economic problems without being unduly trammelled by the question of whether or not they were keeping within some kind of Ricardian orthodoxy—indeed one of them (Mill) helped to *create* it.

The work of these economists has been subject to considerable discussion and reappraisal. An account and some evaluation of the critical literature will be given here, together with an indication of further research requirements. The order in which these writers are discussed follows that given by Schumpeter. Thus we begin with Longfield.

Mountifort Longfield (1802–1884)

Despite the limited scope of his economic writings [Black, 1971], in a career which was almost entirely that of a professional lawyer—he occupied the Chair of Political Economy at Trinity College, Dublin, as its first encumbent, for only four years from 1832–1836 [Black, 1971; Smith, 1935, p. 22; see also O'Brien 1975, pp. 9–11]—there seems little doubt about the very high intellectual standing as an economist accorded to Samuel Mountifort Longfield[1] since his belated recognition, starting with a few references by that great scholar Edwin Cannan [1903], at the end of last century, and his subsequent classification by Seligman [1903] in his justly celebrated article as a "Neglected British Economist."

Rather, the questions raised about Longfield concern such issues as the nature of his distribution theory, his importance as a trade theorist and as a monetary theorist, his alleged role as an apologist for capitalism, the claim that he was in some sense a "Ricardian," and the more general issue of the extent to which he was a forerunner of neo-classical economics.

Value

Longfield's background was in mathematics and natural science [Black, 1980; pp. 3–4; McKinley, 1968; Moss, 1974, pp. 183–184; Tait, 1982]. Given the familiarity with calculus that this implies, it is hardly surprising that Longfield should have adopted an incremental rather than an average approach to the theory of value. Despite some Ricardian elements in his discussion of value [Black, 1945, p. 142; 1971, p. 12; O'Brien, 1975, p. 103]—he accepted that labor was the best measure of value, he appeared to agree that utility was only a preliminary condition of value, he accepted the distinction between natural and market value, he at times appeared to offer a labor theory of value and/or a cost of production theory of value, and he "got rid of rent" in the normal classical manner—Longfield has usually been classified as a subjective value theorist [Black, 1945; Bowley, 1937; O'Brien, 1975, p. 103; Schumpeter, 1954; Seligman, 1903][2].

The Ricardian elements will be discussed further below; consideration of Longfield's *Lectures* as a whole seems to leave no reasonable doubt that he was a subjective value theorist indeed, and one of very considerable creative theoretical insight. We find value dependent on demand and supply, cost of production regulating supply, utility lying behind demand, utility varying with places and with persons and with varying wants of the same individual, and, related to this, a concept of "intensity of demand" (similar to Dupuit's maximum sacrifice), from which is derived a downward sloping demand curve for both the individual and the market [Black, 1971, p. 14; Black, 1982, pp. 17–18; Bowley, 1973, pp. 151–152; O'Brien, 1975, p. 103; Seligman, 1903, p. 527]. The only real question, which has been a matter of some dispute, concerns the precise role of utility in his analysis. It is clear that he did not relate utility *directly* to price. Some writers have gone even further and questioned whether he really formulated the principle of diminishing marginal utility [Bowley, 1972, p. 20; Stigler, 1965, p. 79], and it has also been suggested that he was confused over the relationship between marginal utility, price, total, and intramarginal utility [Bowley, 1972, pp. 20–21, 26–28]. But all concede that Longfield did use a utility analysis and that this lies behind his demand analysis. With the exception of the minority view that Longfield had merely a supply-and-demand analysis, the general consensus seems to be that Longfield was, at the very least, moving in the same direction as the post-1870 writers [Black, 1980, 1983; Bowley, 1973; see, however, Moss, 1974, 1976]. It seems clear, indeed, that Longfield had not thought through the connection between demand and utility completely; it is rather more clear from the material in his lectures that he had it lying behind the masterly treatment of demand and that only determination to ignore this can conceal the point.

Distribution

Longfield's distribution theory has generally been classified as foreshadowing the marginal revolution. Schumpeter described it as a "reasonably complete and reasonably correct theory of distribution based upon the marginal productivity principle" [1954, p. 465; see also Seligman, 1903, pp. 528–529]. Indeed Schumpeter rated Longfield's marginal productivity approach, as he understood it, highly [1954, pp. 656, 658, 664, 674, 677, 682, 915, 939, 941, 1033]. There seems even less doubt here, than there is concerning the value theory, of the neo-classical character of the approach.

As Moss has said, there is "something approximating a complete non-Ricardian theory of income distribution and not simply a series of modifications to the Ricardian analysis" [1976, p. 97; see also 1973, pp. 325–330].

It is certainly true that the theory is in general character marginalist, and that the "order" of distribution runs from prices to factor rewards, not the other way around as in classical theory. It is also true that Longfield dispensed with discrete economics and regarded labor as being paid out of current sales. And yet, oddly, his treatment of the return to labor is actually the least neo-classical and forward-looking part of his distribution theory, for although wages are governed by the supply of labor and the demand for labor, and the demand for labor depends upon the value of labor's product, and although this is a discounted product, commentators generally agree that Longfield talks about the productivity of individual laborers rather than marginal productivity, and has something which is in the nature of a "product less deductions" theory, as Cannan classified it in his original discussion, rather than a proper marginal productivity theory [Black 1971, pp. 14–15; Black, 1980, p. 18; Blaug, 1958a, pp. 127–128; Cannan, 1903, p. 267; Moss, 1976, p. 85; O'Brien, 1975, p. 117; Viner, 1933]. Nonetheless, the analysis is much more typical of post-1870 than of pre-1870 wage theory and, as Seligman emphasized in his original discussion, the standard of living in this analysis is *a result of*, not a determinant of, the level of wages [Seligman, 1903, p. 530; see also Blaug, 1958a, p. 127].

Longfield's theory of profit is both the most marginalist and the most thoroughly neo-classical part of the distribution analysis. Capital has a falling marginal product due to changing capital/labor ratios, relative over-production of capital-intensive goods, and the non-homogeneity of the co-operating labor input; the return on capital is determined by the marginal product of capital, as demand for capital, interacting with a limited supply of saving. The time preference limitations on saving are not very clearly worked out, and Longfield seems to reason in terms of physical rather than value productivity; but the end result still has a distinctly post-1870 look to it [Black, 1980, p. 18; Moss, 1976, pp. 65–83; O'Brien, 1975, p. 121; Seligman, 1903, p. 528].

Longfield's treatment of rent reflects the result of applying this basically marginalist analysis to the standard classical theory. The emphasis is upon scarcity rent rather than differential rent, and the end result is a substantially modified classical theory of rent which has an elegance and generality superior to that of Ricardo and of most other classical writers. We shall also note below that Longfield was unable to accept Ricardo's conclusion concerning the trend of rental share [Black, 1980, p. 18; Bowley, 1937, p. 127; Moss, 1976, pp. 50–64; O'Brien, 1970, p. 397; 1975, p. 125].

Trade Theory

It was not until the 1930s that the importance of Longfield's analysis of trade began to be recognized by, in particular, Viner and Ohlin [Black, 1971, pp. 16–19; Moss, 1976, pp. 127–150; Viner, 1933; 1937, pp. 297–298, 303–4, 316, 321, 446, 454–456, 494, 503]. Longfield applied himself to the question of trade with *n* commodities and investigated the question of which commodities on the scale of comparative advantage would be exported and which would be imported [Schumpeter, 1954, p. 613; Viner, 1937, pp. 454–456]. He decided that relative wages in two countries, dependent in turn on relative labor productivities, would determine which commodities would be traded. This was a distinct advance upon the Ricardian analysis—as Viner pointed out, Longfield showed that trade will depend on wage costs, not just labor quantities [Viner, 1937, p. 494]. But because Longfield stopped short at average productivities of labor across all commodities, including nontraded goods, he was not able to push the analysis through [O'Brien, 1975, p. 180].

It is particularly clear that Longfield paid more attention to the sources of comparative advantage than his contemporaries, and some of his discussion will bear a Heckscher-Ohlin interpretation [O'Brien, 1975, p. 181]; but the range of considerations is much wider than that of the modern theory, with particular reference to the quality of the work force, capital, land, natural resources, soil, and climate.

Another aspect of his work on trade to attract belated attention was his analysis of the transfer problem—he not only seems to have recognized the income effect of transfers, but raised the question of the terms of trade effects and was apparently the first writer to do so [Black, 1960, pp. 77, 80; O'Brien, 1970, p. 216; 1975, p. 200; Viner, 1937, pp. 303–304]. His treatment of the role of demand in international trade was distinctly superior to that of Ricardo and even Senior [Viner, 1937, p. 446], though his performance here was indisputably inferior to that of Torrens and Mill.

Money

Longfield's monetary theory is less significant. He has been categorized by Viner [1933] as a supporter of the Banking School position; and it is true that he recognized the monetary significance of deposits, arguing that notes were only important because of their higher velocity of circulation. But in many respects, as Black has argued, Longfield's position has more in common with the Currency School, with his emphasis upon overissue by the country banks, the necessity of concentrating note issue in a single concern, and the fallacy of the "Real Bills" doctrine [Black, 1971, pp. 19–21]. It is only because Longfield endorsed the Palmer Rule, which failed to give primary importance to notes and to ensure that these matched gold movements and thus the balance of payments position, that he cannot be classified as a full member of the Currency School whose members (especially Overstone and Torrens) were extremely critical of the Palmer Rule [see also O'Brien 1970, p. 172; Viner, 1937, pp. 242–243].

A Capitalist Apologist?

The charge that Longfield developed his analytical novelties as some form of apology for capitalism stems not from the work of Marx—who was unaware of Longfield—but from subsequent Marxist writings. As T.W. Hutchinson has put it:

> However, for making so bold as to criticize the preposterous abstractions of Ricardo, it has been the lot of these authors [including Longfield] to be dismissed as "hired prize fighters" and "apologists for capitalism" by apologists for Stalin following the original denunciations by Marx [Hutchison, 1977, p. 22; see also Black 1983, p. 132].

Such an accusation against Longfield is itself essentially propagandist; and since it is, in another guise, a version of the *ad hominem* logical fallacy, it need not detain us very long.[3]

The fact is that Longfield—whose appointment was opposed on the grounds of his radical tendencies [Murphy, 1983]—was concerned both with income distribution and with poor relief in a form which was far from "apologetic" and which included support for old age pensions, poor relief, and public hospitals. The poor had a natural right to relief [Black, 1960, pp. 49, 68, 81, 238; 1971, pp. 8, 21ff., 24–25; 1983, pp. 132–133; Bowley, 1972, p. 283; Moss, 1976, pp. 153–182; O'Brien, 1975, pp. 282, 287]. Against this background, a few scattered remarks about the necessity of profit as a reward and the futility of exaggerated hopes of trade union activity hardly amount to "apologetics."[4]

Longfield and Ricardo

However, the apologetics categorization is associated with a broader argument that there were two traditions in classical economics, the one comprising Ricardo and leading to Marx and to Sraffa, the other being bourgeois economics concerned to defend the status quo. This view, while it blurs a number of very fundamental distinctions, made in the earlier "two-traditions" analysis of Marian Bowley, between the subjectivist classical economists and the others, does at least see a clear division between Ricardo and Longfield.[5] In fact, the vast majority of commentators, whether they accept any version of the "two-traditions" picture, or none, have seen a clear distinction between the analysis offered by Longfield, and that offered by Ricardo. And yet, strangely, we find it being argued more recently that Longfield was a Ricardian—indeed that Longfield accepted Ricardo's analysis, that Ricardo had a detailed treatment of market value as well as of the labor-based approach to value with which readers of his *Principles* will be familiar, and that Longfield was merely clarifying Ricardo's treatment of market value [Hollander, 1977, pp. 232–236; 1979; 1980; see Black, 1980, pp. 18–19; 1983 for other references].

But it is clear, firstly, that Longfield's sources were not Ricardo's. While Longfield does not make acknowledgments, the influence of both Malthus and of Say on his work on value has been widely recognised [Black, 1945, p.141; 1980, p. 4; Bowley, 1972, p. 19; Moss, 1976, ch. 2; O'Brien, 1975, p. 103]. Say—and possibly Sir Edward West—seems to have been the source for the distribution theory [Bowley, 1972, p. 19; 1973, p. 216; O'Brien, 1975, p. 117]. When we come to the matter of trade, the problem is more complicated. On the one hand, Longfield started from the theory of comparative costs; on the other, as Thweatt has pointed out [1976], this was unnecessary for, and irrelevant to, the main Ricardian system;[6] and we might note further that it had no value as capitalist apologetics.

But we have to recognize also that there is an apparent puzzle in Longfield's lectures which was referred to above and which has been noted by a number of commentators. But while it may be puzzling to nonacademics, it is rather surprising that to academics, inconsistencies in, and developments within, an unrevised course of lectures (written by somebody in the first year of teaching moreover, and separated in the middle by the long summer vacation) should be even remarkable, let alone the basis for detailed textual exegesis. It seems perfectly clear that the Ricardian elements in the lectures were borrowed before Longfield got properly into his stride—and when he did so, it was so the basis of other sources [Black, 1945, p. 142; 1971, pp. 11–12; 1980, p. 19; O'Brien, 1970, p. 144; Tait, 1982].

Nevertheless we have to recognize that Longfield did not engage in a direct critique of the labor theory of value—Schumpeter's comment that "his argument against the labor theory of value is one of the best ever penned" [1954, p. 465] has baffled commentors from Blaug onward.

There clearly are labor-standard elements in the first part of the lectures [Black, 1945, p. 142], although, as Black has pointed out, the labor measure has a purpose in Ricardo's system which it does not have in Longfield's [1980, p. 16]. It is certainly clear that Longfield's analytical capabilities placed him in that exceedingly small and select group who actually understood what Ricardo was trying to say [Black, 1983, pp. 127–128; Blaug, 1958a, pp. 161, 222n; O'Brien, 1970 p. 293].[7] It may even be possible to detect some elements of compromise with Ricardo.[8] But the fundamental fact is that Longfield rejected that cornerstone of the whole Ricardian system, the determination of general profitability by agricultural profits [Black, 1980, pp. 19–20; 1983, pp. 127–129; Blaug, 1958a, p. 161; Seligman, 1903, p. 526]. For Longfield, profits declined because of capital accumulation. He also, consistently with his rejection of the idea that subsistence needs determined wages, rejected that other pivot of the Ricardian model, the Malthusian population theory [1971, pp. 202–203]. He rejected the pessimism that almost all later commentators have seen in the work of Ricardo [1971, pp. 16, 229–235; 1980, pp. 19–20; Blaug, 1958a, p. 162; Bowley, 1973, p. 215; Moss, 1973, pp. 323–325]. A society with low profits (and this is perhaps not irrelevant to the "apologist" accusation) would possess many advantages as a result of this. Longfield did not even expect the price of corn to be borne relentlessly upward [Blaug, 1958a, p. 162]—agricultural improvements spread imperceptibly, not reducing prices but preventing prices rises [Black, 1971, pp. 137–138; O'Brien, 1970, p. 404]. Longfield also rejected the idea of a necessarily rising rental share [Moss, 1976, pp. 58–63; Tait, 1982, p. 24].

Only if one accepts the unusual interpretation of Ricardo—the optimistic noncorn model, incipient General Equilibrium, Ricardo [Hollander, 1979]—can there be any ground for regarding Longfield as a Ricardian. Most other commentators, from Seligman onward [Seligman, 1903, p. 527], observing Longfield's analysis of marginal demand, marginal cost, marginal productivity theory of interest, and productivity theory of wages with the standard of living a result and not a cause of the level of wages, leading to conclusions about social progress very different from those of Ricardo, have concluded the opposite.

A Neo-Classical Forerunner

It seems reasonable to take the view that, unless we pick on what is unimportant in Longfield and neglect what is important, we cannot say that Longfield was Ricardian.[9] Indeed we can quite clearly say that he was not

Ricardian. But can we go further and say that he was a forerunner of neo-classical economics? This is certainly the overall evaluation of the commentators. As Schumpeter said: "He overhauled the whole of economic theory and produced a system that would have stood up well in 1890" [Schumpeter, 1954, p. 465]. A similar evaluation was shared by Blaug, Black, McKinley, and Bowley [Black, 1971, pp. 11, 16; Blaug, 1958a, p. 223; Bowley, 1973, p. 217; McKinley, 1968]. In view of the features of his analysis already discussed, there seems to be no ground for disputing this verdict;[10] and only if one believes that Ricardo was also a forerunner of neo-classical analysis can one see any parallel between the two writers. But if this distinction between Longfield and Ricardo is correct, why was Longfield's influence so limited? As nearly every commentator has pointed out, it was, in England, virtually nonexistent [Black, 1971, p. 5; 1980, p. 2; Blaug, 1958a, pp. 127–128, 159, 227; Moss, 1976, pp. 22, 120–126; O'Brien, 1970, p. 143; Schumpeter, 1954, p. 648; Seligman, 1903, pp. 531–532; Tait, 1982, p. 25].[11] Indeed there is the strange puzzle that although Senior and Longfield were apparently known to each other and were the mutual friends of Whately, there seems to have been no interaction between them [Bowley, 1937, pp. 94, 109, 185]. Several writers have pointed to Longfield's unaggressive presentation of his ideas as an explanation for his neglect [Blaug, 1958a, p. 159; 1985, p. 307; Tait, 1982]. Mention has also been made of the temporary tenure imposed by the conditions of the Dublin chair [Black, 1945, pp. 140–141; Bowley, 1937, p. 156; Tait, 1982]—although Longfield's interest in economics continued after 1836 [Black, 1971, p. 8].

It seems clear that the explanation must lie in the intellectual relations between England and Ireland. For in Ireland Longfield's unusual approach to economics was recognized as such by his successors, and his work enjoyed both prestige and influence [Black, 1945, Moss, 1976, ch. 3; Viner, 1937, p. 303]. It is clear that despite some more detailed examination of the record [Moss, 1976, ch. 2], the picture drawn by Black in 1945 is essentially correct, and that Longfield did in fact to some extend succeed in founding a school of followers.[12]

Conclusion

Although the position of Longfield's work has been the subject of a good deal of discussion and commentary in recent years, the picture presented by Seligman in 1903 still seems to be intact. The revisions seem not to have succeeded in altering the picture convincingly: and the recent full-length study of Longfield by Moss [1974], while downplaying (in the opinion of this writer, mistakenly) the utility elements, has not fundamentally altered the picture presented originally by Seligman.

James Mill (1773–1836)

The conventional picture of James Mill that emerges from the literature in the history of economic thought is well known; and much of the detail of this picture, relating to Mill's theoretical reasoning on various issues, is still valid. But at vital points in the story, questions both of priority, and indeed of who was a disciple of whom, have been increasingly raised. Some of the points had been recognized in the earlier accounts; but they have recently been seen to have greater importance.

The Conventional View

The conventional picture of Mill as the dedicated disciple of Bentham and Ricardo, the radical journalist and propagandist, is well known. In particular he is seen as a dedicated follower of Ricardo who, despite his best efforts, was unable either to understand Ricardo or to help him in the development of his analytical vision [Blaug, 1958a, p. 123; Halevy, 1928, p. 356; Hollander, 1979; Schumpeter, 1954, pp. 470, 476, 478, 559, 592, 595, 637, 657, 676; Winch, 1966, pp. 181, 188].[13] Indeed he had retired from economics by the time he began to work with Ricardo [Blaug, 1958a, p. 62; Winch, 1966, p. 182]. He was thoroughly confused over value, believing that Torrens' capital (indirect labor) theory of value was the same as a theory that counted direct and indirect labor [O'Brien, 1970, pp. 129, 131, 137; 1975, pp. 92, 96–97], he struggled with the notion of profit [Blaug, 1958a, pp. 50–52], and he bowdlerized Ricardo's value theory by omitting the invariable measure, while failing to understand the significance of the inverse relationship of wages and profits which he converted into a truism [Blaug, 1958a, pp. 60, 221–222]. An incompetent theorist, he produced a crude textbook (the *Elements*) [Winch, 1966, p. 189] in which he made the silly mistake of according to both parties to trade *all* the gains from trade until this obvious mistake was pointed out by his son and friends [O'Brien, 1975, p. 182; Viner, 1937, pp. 444–446; Winch, 1966, pp. 119, 272–273, 301]. Although he put forward the Law of Markets, he obtained this (with acknowledgment) from Say [Blaug, 1958a, p. 64; O'Brien, 1975, pp. 159–160; Winch, 1966, p. 34] whose priority was, as Schumpeter said, "beyond the possibility of doubt" [1954, p. 491n].[14] He obtained the concept of comparative cost—which is not present in his *Commerce Defended* of 1808—from Ricardo [Viner, 1937, p. 440; Winch, 1966, p. 32].

Much of his treatment of policy issues, in particular of taxation, followed Ricardo as well. He generally imitated Ricardo in telescoping the long run and short run together in dealing with taxes on wages, arguing that such a tax, with wages at physical subsistence, would be passed on via the Malthusian population mechanism and reduce profits [O'Brien, 1975, p. 247; Winch, 1966, pp. 344, 347–348]. More generally, his treatment of taxation was particularly arid and largely irrelevant; the only real taxes with which he and Ricardo dealt were the corn duty and the poor rate, while they addressed themselves not to the British land tax but to problems of a fixed tax per acre and the idea of a general ad valorem tax, adopting an a priori methodology rather than taking notice of the facts of the situation [O'Brien, 1975, pp. 244, 251; Shoup, 1960, chs. 7, 15; Winch, 1966, pp. 352–355, 358–360]. In the matter of land taxation, however, Mill went far beyond what Ricardo considered prudent, especially in the case of India. He believed in making rent the basis of taxation, advocated land nationalization (with auctioning of ground rents) under some circumstances, and proposed taxing increments of rental value [Blaug, 1958a, p. 277n; O'Brien, 1975, pp. 240, 250; Winch, 1966, pp. 197–202, 338, 391–395; see also Hutchison, 1978; Winch, 1965, pp. 159–1965].

The narrowness of his analytical outlook was such that he was unable to contemplate any suggestion that inflation might affect the level of activity in the economy [O'Brien, 1975, p. 165; Winch, 1966, pp. 294–295]. In matters of wages and population he followed Malthus, though putting forward a peculiar version in which wages necessarily outran *capital* accumulation [Blaug, 1958a, p. 105; Winch, 1966, pp. 33, 193–197]—this was important because Mill used a particularly crude version of the wage fund theory—making him a (for his time) outspoken advocate of contraception [Blaug, 1958a, pp. 106, 107, 109; O'Brien, 1975, p. 114; Winch, 1966, pp. 193–197].

To complete this unattractive picture, Mill was an intolerant propagandist, responsible for a violent attack upon Samuel Bailey and personally unpleasant to a remarkable degree [O'Brien, 1970, p. 14; O'Brien and Darnell, 1982, ch. 6; Rauner, 1961, pp. 149–157; Winch, 1966, pp. 190–192]. His education of his hapless son J.S. Mill has occasioned particular censure [Schumpeter, 1954, pp. 527–528].

While not denying that there is very much truth in many of these charges (the present author freely admits to being among those cited in the previous references), there is another side to the discussion of Mill that requires attention.

The Unconventional View

Some qualifications to this picture have long been recognized. Thus Mark Blaug had shown that Mill was not a slavish follower of Ricardo [1958a, p. 46], and noted that Sraffa had indicated that Mill wrote part of Ricardo's *Principles* [Blaug, 1985, p. 117], while the idea of Mill and McCulloch as Ricardo's two close disciples are not helped by the evidence that they were in conflict on matters of theory and policy [O'Brien, 1970, pp. 113–115; Winch, 1966, pp. 197–202].

Increasingly it has come to be recognized that Mill had a reputation prior to his dealings with Ricardo [Blaug, 1958a, p. 40; Winch, 1966, pp. 23,25], and that when he wrote to Ricardo about having become an amateur in economics a vital part of the quotation was omitted by Sraffa and others—the qualification that his contact with Ricardo rekindled his interest [Thweatt, 1977c, p. 119]. It has become increasingly clear, as indeed some writers have always maintained, that Mill has very strong claims indeed to be the originator of the Law of Markets, whatever the analytical niceities of interpretation which his treatment affords [Blaug, 1958a, p. 94; 1985, pp. 154–155; Sowell, 1972; Thweatt, 1977a]. It is indeed clear that this was a matter on which Ricardo was Mill's follower [Hutchison, 1978, pp. 31–32; Winch, 1966, p. 190]—while Say was much less rigid in his own version of the idea.

But the reappraisal of Mill has now gone much further. Firstly, the work of Donald Winch drew attention to the importance of Mill's early economic writings [Winch, 1966]. Consideration of these raises interesting questions. In particular, if Mill was so muddled over profits later on (and there seems little doubt that he was), how did he manage to handle the matter perfectly well by advancing a productivity theory of profit in controversy with Spence [Winch, 1966, p. 32]?

Secondly, his priority concerning the Law of Markets has been much more firmly established and is now widely recognized [Chipman, 1965b, p. 709n; Hutchison, 1978, p. 147, Sowell, 1972, p. 23; Thweatt, 1977a, p. 19; 1977c, p. 122 n3; 1979a; 1980b].[15] Thirdly, it is now clear that much of what Mill contributed came from Smith, *including* the Law of Markets [Sowell, 1972, p. 21; 1974; Thweatt, 1977a, pp. 8–9; 1977b; 1979b; Winch, 1966, pp. 33–34]. However, as Thweatt has noted, in typical Millian fashion, he omitted the important qualifications [1980b, p. 467]. Mill also obtained from Smith a theory of the dependence of wages and prices upon the price of corn, long before any association with Ricardo [Blaug, 1958a, p. 206; Thweatt, 1977b, p. 8]; and he made corn the center of his analytical system well before any such connection [Hutchison, 1978, p. 30; Thweatt, 1977b, pp. 8–9, 1977c, p. 20]. It is clear, indeed, that he did understand the corn model; while most commentators have recognized this for some time, the newer view emphasises that Mill had a corn model of his own which influenced Ricardo, one which is based upon Smith's chapter on bounties [Thweatt, 1977b, pp. 7–8; 1979b, pp. 8–10].[16] Indeed, as early as 1804, he had, as Terence Hutchison has pointed out, three vital building blocks in place:

> (1) the simplified concept of "corn" as a shorthand for worker's subsistence, a unique commodity in that it is a raw material for all productions; (2) an extremely drastic, hard-line version of the Malthusian proposition regarding the relations between population changes and wages; and (3) the idea that adjustments take place so rapidly and completely that lags, or 'disequilibria' can be left out of the argument [Hutchison, 1978, p. 31].

Fourthly, it is also clear that the material from Smith was passed through the peculiar filter of Mill's method, emerging stripped of all its qualifications at the other end. Though Mill was, at first, a strenuous propagandist for, and defender of, Smith [Winch, 1966, pp. 27–28], there is a very strong contrast between Mill's methodology and Smith's [Hutchison, 1978, p. 56]. This is exemplified by the extraordinary approach to India which Mill adopted, being totally blinkered by his a priori preconceptions [Barber, 1969, 1975; Hutchison, 1953, 1978, pp. 37–39].[17] Indeed a highly plausible case has been argued for the view that the "Ricardian Vice" was actually Mill's, and that Mill relentlessly pushed Ricardo into his analytical approach [Hutchison, 1978, pp. 26–57; see also Rima, 1975 and Winch, 1966, p. 369]. This influence upon Ricardo can be detected at an early stage, in the scornful attitude of the *Reply to Bosanquet* toward the man of facts as compared to the man of theory.

It was not only material from Smith which was altered in character by Mill's methodological preconceptions—the same is true of his borrowing from Malthus, as Halevy pointed out long ago [1928, pp. 358–359].

Thus Mill influenced Ricardo, not only over the choice of a corn model, and in methodological questions, but also over the question of the landlords and the conflict between their interests and those of the rest of the community [Thweatt, 1979b, p. 9]. Indeed, his radicalism, it is clear on closer inspection, was a middle-class kind—he was antilandlord, but he was not an enthusiast for the elevation of the proletariat [Hutchison, 1978, pp. 40–41].

Perhaps the most fundamental questions about the influence of Mill *on* Ricardo (rather than being merely his befuddled disciple) have been raised by Thweatt, concerning comparative cost—so long regarded as Ricardo's crowning achievement. While conceding that Torrens had priority in the development of comparative cost, he suggests that Torrens' 1815 *External Corn Trade* was the source for Mill's understanding of comparative advantage while his motive in supplying it to Ricardo was a desire to provide Ricardo with all the available arguments for freedom of trade—the propagandist in Mill coming out again. This would certainly explain why Ricardo never used the concept again while his acuteness of mind made him see its intellectual content immediately. This is particularly important because there are very curious questions about the whole matter of Ricardo and comparative cost, to which Thweatt has drawn attention. In particular, Ricardo was advocating free trade in corn, not free trade generally. His statement of comparative advantage is brief, poorly worded, unrealistic, and irrelevant to his central concern about the import of corn to raise profits and permit economic growth to continue. There are only three paragraphs in Sraffa's 10 volumes; Ricardo was not interested in free trade in anything but wage goods, and he had no need of comparative cost for his basic model [Thweatt, 1976, 1977b, pp. 23–24; 1979b; pp. 14–15].

Conclusion

There is much in this new reading of Mill which is persuasive. But doubts are still permissible. First, his monetary theory seems to have been rather muddled—along Smithian Real Bills lines—until his dealings with Ricardo [Winch, 1966, pp. 37–38]. Second, there is no gainsaying the fact that all the old value theory confusions remain [O'Brien, 1970, p. 131; 1975, p. 92]. Third, although he may enjoy substantial priority in the matter of the Law of Markets, there was undoubtedly some influence exercised on him by Say—it is even evident in the arrangement of the *Elements* [Winch, 1966, p. 190n]. Finally, on the question of comparative cost, there is no evidence that Mill wrote the three crucial paragraphs; he made a vital mistake in the first two editions of his *Elements* concerning comparative cost; and it was Ricardo, not Mill, who integrated comparative advantage with price-specie-flow theory so as to make the vital step by which it became a theory of *prices* on the basis of which trade would actually take place. However, having said that, it must be conceded, first, that Mill did make contributions to trade theory elsewhere and that Thweatt has supplied a convincing source, sequence, and motive for Mill to supply Ricardo's paragraphs. Moreover, whatever the ultimate decision about his influence upon Ricardo and comparative cost, Mill's own claims to be treated seriously in his own right, and not merely as a muddled, arrogant, and unpleasant disciple of Ricardo,[18] have been considerably increased by work on him, all of which has been published since Schumpeter's treatment was written.

Nassau Senior (1790–1864)

While the interpretations of the work of James Mill which have been advanced over the last three decades have together produced substantial changes of focus, the work of Nassau Senior has not been subject to the same degree of reappraisal. As a result of work done in the 1930s, however, the facile classification of Senior as a Ricardian, which was never very secure, is now hard to defend [Bowley, 1934, 1937, 1968]. But since it is not so much Senior's relative priority which has been a matter for discussion as the importance of the intellectual positions which he held on a number of different topics in classical economics, it seems best to approach this writer on a topic-by-topic basis.

Methodology

Senior's methodological position has been subject to varying emphases; ambiguities and some changes of emphasis in Senior's own work have perhaps invited this. But, essentially, Senior's approach is axiomatic [Bowley, 1937, pp. 47–48; O'Brien, 1975, pp. 70–71]: we have the famous four postulates (individual wealth maximization coupled with minimum sacrifice; a modified Malthusian mechanism in which population may be limited by *fear* of of deficiency; the productivity of increased roundaboutness; and diminishing returns in agriculture with fixed technology) leading Schumpeter to claim that; "As a venture in pure theory, his performance is clearly superior to that of Ricardo" [1954, p. 576]. The deductive nature of Senior's work was stressed by Bowley in her famous study [1937, pp. 27–65], and by the present author [O'Brien, 1975, p. 66; see also Hutchison, 1978, pp. 8, 294]; at the same time both Bowley and Schumpeter [1954, p. 576] have pointed to the "empirical" elements in Senior's work, notably his "introspection" as a source of premises, and his "verification"—the latter meaning not the testing of theories, but testing whether they are suitable for a particular factual situation [Blaug, 1980, p. 81]. Whether introspection is really empiricism in any serious sense is probably a futile debate; but Senior was concerned with data, though his main use of data was in what he classified as the "art" of economics, something which he distinguished clearly from the science of economics. Indeed some of his contemporaries, notably McCulloch, saw a clear contrast between his axiomatic, "pure" approach and their own [O'Brien, 1975, p. 60]. In sum, it seems fair to say that Senior was essentially on the deductive side of the fence (though not, as Blaug has pointed out [1980, p. 92; see also Bowley, 1937, pp. 64–65], an a priorist in the Austrian sense) and that uncertainties in the secondary interpretations reflect ambiguities in Senior's position and in classical methodology more generally.

Value

On the question of value, Senior's position has been subject to some varying interpretations; but the bulk of the opinion is clearly that while his value theory was not Ricardian, it was more classical than modern. In Bowley's original and extremely valuable study of Senior, his use of marginal utility was stressed rather heavily [Bowley, 1937, ch. 2] and, Bowley new feels, too heavily [1972; see, however, 1968], in that it suggested that Senior was an advocate of subjective value theory. In fact, it seems clear that Senior correctly formulated the principle of diminishing marginal utility, but that he did not relate this to the demand curve or to price, and that the bulk of his discussion concerned conditions under which, because supply is less than perfectly elastic, a simple cost of production approach will not do [Blaug, 1985, p. 304; O'Brien, 1975, pp. 99–102]. As Blaug has pointed out, this owes not a little to Bailey's *Critical Dissertation* of 1825 [1958a, pp. 58, 157]. Nonetheless it is clear that Senior's value theory was, as Schumpeter argued, a promising but ultimately incomplete performance resulting, in Bowley's later words, in a "revolution that wasn't" [Bowley, 1972].[19]

Capital Theory

On the question of capital and profit it seems clear that Senior substantially anticipated Böhm-Bawerk, and that his work was nonetheless incomplete and required further development by J.S. Mill [Blaug, 1958a, pp. 153–159; Bowley, 1937, ch. 4]. Senior's third postulate states, "That the power of Labour, and of the other instruments of production which produce wealth, may be indefinitely increased by using their Products as the means of further Production" [Bowley, 1937, p. 48]. Although this requires the additional idea of diminishing returns to extensions of the production period, before we can regard the analysis as being similar to Böhm-Bawerk's, the link with the latter's approach via periods of production is clear enough. In this way, Senior was able to explain the existence of a demand for capital; and his abstinence theory, involving time-preference, provided a limitation on supply. Thus there were conditions for the emergence of a positive price—interest [Blaug, 1985, pp. 194–195; O'Brien, 1975, p. 120]. The approach involved the assumption of constant disutility of saving, and was incapable, as formulated by Senor, of dealing with questions of inherited funds—he classified the return on the latter as rent—although J.S. Mill managed to solve this through the use of marginal supply price. What is especially significant about Senior's treatment is that it fills a noticeable gap in classical analysis: in particular, neither Smith nor Ricardo had been able to do much more than treat saving as a social phenomenon which was, in Ricardo's case, responsive to the rate of interest.

The idea has been floated that this was some kind of bourgeois apologetics [Dobb, 1973, pp. 104–105; Teilhac, 1934; cf. Hutchison, 1978, p. 241]; but apart from the ad hominem logical fallacy implied in such an approach (the validity of the ideas should, of course, be assessed independently of the motives of those advancing them), only those convinced of the notion of profit originating in surplus value (which followed Senior a good few years later) would look for such an explanation.

In connection with Senior's capital theory, mention should be made of the "last hour" [Johnson, 1969]. As Mark Blaug has pointed out, this has been kept alive by Marxist criticism, but Senior's calculations actually only show a fall in the profit rate and the issue is essentially a red herring [Blaug, 1985, p. 270].

Rent

It is clear—and was stressed by Marian Bowley in her study—that Senior generalized the rent concept, seeing rent of land as a "species of an extensive genus." It is also clear that he hinted at the concept of quasi-rent [Bowley, 1937, pp. 126–136; see also O'Brien 1975, pp. 59–61]. But it is also apparent that the source for this was Bailey [Blaug, 1958a, p. 58], and that Senior's own independent contribution was probably small. Moreover, like other classical writers—*including* Bailey—Senior persisted in "getting rid of" rent as a cost, thus neglecting transfer earnings [O'Brien, 1975, p. 91, n26].

International and Monetary Economics

Senior's most important contributions were to classical trade theory. In particular there were the Lectures on the Transmission of the Precious Metals, and the Lectures on the Cost of Obtaining Money. Though

Senior's contribution was recognized by Angell [1926, pp. 72–75], it is perhaps particularly due to the persistent efforts of Robbins that the value of Senior's contribution has been brought out in our own century, though it was clear enough to Senior's contemporaries [Bowley, 1937, ch. 6; Robbins, 1958a, p. 26; 1976, p. 155]. For Senior, building on Hume, and advancing analysis much superior to Ricardo's, managed to show how the price level was determined by the productivity of labor in the export industries. But of course relative wages and prices affected the terms of trade and thus which industries were sufficiently competitive to be export industries. A difficulty was therefore left unresolved. J.S. Mill solved this difficulty unforgettably with his analysis of reciprocal demand.

Senior's reputation in this particular field was probably clouded because of his controversy with Torrens over the Cuba Case; Robbins, in his superb account of Torrens, made clear the points on which Senior was wrong in trying to make prices depend on costs in international trade, a position at variance with his own *Lectures*, and in trying to use an argument about the *cost* of producing metal at the margin as a counter to an argument about the *distribution* of precious metal throughout the world [O'Brien, 1975, p. 195]. But he *was* correct to stress that average product would fall with the loss of specialization following distortions introduced by tariffs, and thus lead to a loss of gold, especially in a multicommodity case. He was also correct to emphasize that the tariffs might simply cause a switch to other exports by the country whose products were met by duties but which had a lower wage and price level, a move which would reduce that country's loss of gold.

Senior's contributions to international trade theory, and their monetary aspects, have been widely noted. However, Senior also discussed money in a narrower sense, and his work here has received very much less attention.[20] But it has been established that he left us with the earliest version of a clear and detailed analysis of the demand for money in terms of cash balances, explaining the relationship between M, V, and k (in the historically later notation) and was Marshall's most important predecessor in this regard [Eshag, 1963, pp. 14–15; see also Bowley, 1937, pp. 213–221].

Policy

A major part of Bowley's book was devoted to policy [Bowley, 1937, pp. 237–334], and this aspect of Senior's work has attracted a good deal of attention since that study appeared. His hostile attitude to socialism has been illuminatingly discussed [Robbins, 1952, pp. 134–141], with attention drawn to his expectation of jobbing, and adverse effects on capital accumulation and work. At the same time, the view of Senior as inflexibly opposed to government intervention has been corrected [Robbins, 1952, pp. 45, 47, 60]. It is apparent that he approached policy as both lawyer and economist[21] and that he was (cautiously) willing to use the legal framework to increase welfare [Robbins, 1952, pp. 95–98; Samuels, 1966, pp. 138, 140–141, 191, 192, 198, 217–219]. He took—though late in life—a particular interest in education, which he perceived as having consumption benefits and investment benefits (via a stable work force) [Miller, 1966, pp. 298–299; Samuels, 1966, p. 95; Tu, 1969, p. 701], arguing that its provision was a case of market failure and that government should make it compulsory and (almost) free [Blaug, 1975, pp. 581, 586–587, 589; Miller, 1966, pp. 302–303; West, 1964a, p. 123; 1964b, p. 134]. Less reassuringly, it appears that he was responsible—rather in the role of lawyer presenting a case—for distortion in the selection of evidence which led to the 1834 Poor Law [Blaug, 1963, p. 177; 1964, p. 231], and that although other economists may also have been opposed initially to factory legislation in which they later acquiesced [Blaug, 1958b], he remained a strong opponent [O'Brien, 1975, pp. 277–279].

Conclusion

The outcome of the secondary literature in Senior's case seems clear; he was classical but not Ricardian. Indeed, as Blaug has said, "Senior was amongst the most original of the classical economists" [1980, p. 59]. Though there has been some general agreement that Bowley's classic study [1937] overstates the extent of Senior's independence from mainstream classical economics (and this is now the author's own view),[22] the comment of Schumpeter, whose appraisal of Senior is much in accord with that outlined here, that he had few significant differences with Bowley's book [Schumpeter,1954, p. 484n], reflects the tone of the secondary literature.

Samuel Bailey (1791–1870)

The Established Picture

Samuel Bailey is well known in the literature of the history of economic thought as the author of the brilliant, if negative, *Critical Dissertation on the Nature, Measure and Causes of Value* of 1825—and for little else. Thus

Schumpeter praises this work highly; but it is the only one of Bailey's works (apart from a polemical *Reply*) which he mentions at all [Schumpeter, 1954, pp. 478, 486, 487, 599, 679, 935]. Although Mixter had published earlier on Bailey [Mixter, 1898], it was really Seligman who drew attention to Bailey's *Dissertation* [1903, pp. 352–355]. Noting Bailey's critiques of Ricardo's verbal muddle, of the concept of absolute value, of the use of the cost of production theory of value, of the equation of cost of production with labor cost, of the idea of homogeneity of labor input, and of the Ricardian inverse relationship of wages and profits without reference to labor productivity, as well as Bailey's introduction of time preference, and his generalization of the rent concept, Seligman really set the tone for most of the later discussions. But an important subsequent influence in bringing Bailey's work before economists was Robbins; not only did he refer to the *Critical Dissertation* in his highly influential *Essay on the Nature and Significance of Economic Science* [1932, pp. 56, 60–62] but he supervised the doctoral theses of Marian Bowley [1937] and Robert Rauner [1956], the first of which, on Senior, paid a good deal of attention to Bailey while the second was a study of Bailey himself.[23] Mention should also be made of Blaug's *Ricardian Economics* [1958a] which contains excellent material on Bailey. A detailed discussion of Bailey's value theory was provided by the publication of part of Rauner's thesis in book form [1961].

As a result of the work of these writers, a number of elements of Bailey's work have become well known. They include his excellent understanding of Ricardo (by no means a common achievement), his sustained criticism of the invariable measure, and his discussion of Ricardo's inverse relationship of wages and profits. On the more positive side he is generally credited (correctly in the opinion of this writer) with generalization of the rent concept,[24] and with pointing out that degrees of fertility are not necessary for the emergence of rent while, on the other hand, and in practice, nonhomogeneity characterized labor as well as land [Blaug, 1958a, p. 70; Rauner, 1956, pp. 229n; Schumpeter, 1954, pp. 679, 935]. He is also credited with establishing (by introspection—a point to which we shall return below) the existence of positive time preference.

Although his *Critical Dissertation* was the occasion of a violent attack in the *Westminster Review* (which, it is now fairly well established, was by James Mill) [O'Brien and Darnell, 1982, ch. 6; Rauner, 1961, pp. 149–157] it seems quite clear that he did have a limited, but important, influence. In particular his influence on Senior has been noted by Blaug [1958a, pp. 58, 157] and by Bowley both in her original work [1937, pp. 94, 193], and in her return to the subject nearly 40 years later [1973, pp. 163–164]. It is also clear that he influenced J.S. Mill in a number of areas, including the treatment of rent, the abstinence theory of profit, the inverse relationship of wages and profits, the hierarchy of wages as affecting exchangeable value, and the rejection of the invariable measure—this despite Mill's failure to credit Bailey [Blaug, 1958a, pp. 167, 173; 1985, p. 220; Bowley, 1973, p. 167; Rauner, 1961, pp. 135–140]. But these were probably the only important influences; the influence claimed on his behalf on Cotterill and Read [Seligman, 1903, p. 355] seems to be unimportant [Rauner, 1961, pp. 127–129], and neither counts as a major writer.

Although Bowley contended, in her 1937 book, that Bailey was part of a separate tradition of economic thought, contemporary with mainstream classical economics, it now seems clear that Bailey was in the main classical tradition insofar as his positive value theory was concerned and that he did not provide material either for a separate tradition or for a revolution in value theory. This view is shared by, among others, Blaug [1958a, p. 227], and Bowley in her later writings [1972, 1973]. Indeed it seems clear that Bailey's main emphasis is on inelasticity of supply, in the more positive aspects of his writings, and that he had no proper demand theory [Bowley, 1973, pp. 108, 161–163].

More recently there has been some discussion of Bailey's possible authorship of an anonymous pamphlet *Observations on Certain Verbal Disputes* of 1821. In particular Sowell has argued persuasively that the work was by Bailey [Sowell, 1970, 1974, pp. 107–108, 140, 143]. However, this opinion had already been considered, and rejected, by Rauner both in his thesis [1956, p. 277] and in his book [1961, p. 89], and Kenneth Dennis finally found fairly conclusive proof that the work was not by Bailey [1973]. This has been confirmed in subsequent study [O'Brien and Darnell, 1982, ch. 5]. But authorship of this pamphlet itself would not have added a great deal to our knowledge of Bailey, and certainly not in those areas where further published discussion is required.

New Lights

It is perhaps ironic that the major study of Bailey was not Rauner's book, but his thesis [1956] which remains unpublished. Unfortunately the book did not point readers in the direction of the thesis which seems to have remained largely unconsulted. This thesis explained the philosophical basis from which Bailey started. In particular it showed that the 1821 *Essay on the Formation and Publication of Public Opinions*, which set out the Utilitarian need for free critical discussion, provided the basis for the 1825 critique. (It is also the success of this work, which was taken up with enthusiasm by philosophical radicals including James Mill, J.S. Mill—

whose *Liberty* was influenced by it—Place, and Brougham, which may explain James Mill's later fury at the appearance of the 1825 critique.) Although Rauner's book explains that the subjective nature of value, as discussed by Bailey in 1825, was grounded in his philosophy [1961, p. 5], it is the thesis which contains a really extensive discussion of Bailey's philosophical position and makes an understanding of the significance of his work very much easier [Rauner 1956, pp. 496–682]. It becomes clear that Bailey placed the rationale of economic activity in mental phenomena [Rauner 1956, p. iii], that he rejected the physical material conceptions of classical economics, and that his use of introspection as empiricism was entirely consistent with this [Rauner 1956, pp. 504–506]. Indeed Rauner's thesis emphasizes that Bailey saw economics as a science of mind [1956, pp. 496–526]—it was not concerned with technology. His basic philosophical position is extraordinarily "Austrian" and is much more post-1870 than the recently received interpretation would suggest, in this respect at least. It is no wonder that it was attractive to Robbins; both in the subjectivism and in the Utilitarianism there are striking parallels with Robbins' 1932 *Essay*.

However, the thesis sheds little light on Bailey's macroeconomics. Rauner's discussion of money [1956, pp. 385–445], and of the Currency and Banking controversy [1956, pp. 446–495], is unsatisfactory, although the thesis does contain some details of Bailey's Banking School position and of his statement of the Principle of Reflux eight years prior to Fullarton. Rauner makes no reference to a pamphlet *An Inquiry into Those Principles Respecting the Nature of Demand and the Necessity of Consumption, lately advocated by Mr. Malthus* of 1821 which, it now seems likely, was indeed written by Bailey—in contrast to the *Observations* which was probably written by Brougham [O'Brien and Darnell, 1982, ch. 5]. As Sowell has pointed out [1972, pp. 133, 224, 235], this pamphlet had a number of merits. It made clear that it was the *marginal* efficiency of capital which was crucial; it employed marginal and schedule concepts for saving, investment, and labor supply; and it analyzed the weaknesses of both sides in the general glut controversy with acuteness. It analyzed the possibility of effective demand failure and argued that the problem was not of market clearing but of profitable sale [Sowell, 1972, p. 132]. The fact that there was a long-run solution to this problem, through the withdrawal of investment, did not prove that there was not depression in the short run [Sowell, 1974, p. 46]. This argument couples nicely with one which Rauner had found in other work of Bailey—the idea that fresh monetary demand could activate *unemployed* resources [1956, p. 411]. At the same time it is clear that the *Inquiry* did not accept the Malthusian analysis; it challenged the Law of Markets, at least in its Millian form, without accepting the dissenting doctrine [Sowell, 1972, pp. 131–135, 139].

Conclusion

It is possible that some further work remains to be done on Bailey, bringing together the analysis of the *Inquiry* (unless some indication emerges that this is not, after all, by Bailey) with that contained in his known work on money. It is also arguable that, except perhaps in Rauner's thesis, Bailey's *Questions on Political Economy* is a work which has received too little attention in the literature. But what is clear is that the evaluation of Bailey is now much broader and more fully grounded than that which rested solely on his 1825 masterpiece.

Robert Torrens (1780–1864)

Introduction

In his famous article of 1903 on neglected British economists, E.R.A. Seligman drew attention to the work of Torrens [1903, pp. 341–347]. He noted Torrens' contributions on the questions of diminishing returns and rent, wages, profit, and, in particular, comparative cost. Seligman was challenged on the matter of comparative cost by J.H. Hollander [1911; Seligman, 1911], but the latter's argument rested on several confusions including one in rudimentary mathematics [Chipman, 1965a, pp. 480–481]. Nonetheless although Seligman had succeeded in establishing a claim for Torrens, the matter rested very largely there for a long time; the 1934 *Encyclopaedia of the Social Sciences* article [Fraser, 1934] added little to what Seligman had already said, and it was only writers on money and trade who, incidentally and without attempting any overall assessment of Torrens' position, drew attention to his contributions in a number of fields [Mints, 1945; Morgan, 1943; Viner, 1937; Wood, 1939]. Nor did Torrens attract sustained attention in Schumpeter's great *History* [Schumpeter, 1954]. While Schumpeter appreciated Torrens' powers of abstraction and found him appealing, he regarded him as a careless writer. But most significantly he said that Torrens needed the kind of interpretative work which Ricardo had enjoyed [Schumpeter, 1954, pp. 489–490].

The process of this interpretative work was begun by S.A.Meenai, under the supervisions of Lord Robbins [Meenai, 1953, 1956, 1955–56,

1959–60]. But it was Robbins himself who, in one of the major studies in the literature of the history of economic thought [1958a], produced what Schumpeter had said was needed. He had been commissioned to write an introduction to Torrens' *Budget*: but he relates that, "Reluctantly, but not without a certain surreptitious enjoyment, I came to recognise that what I was writing was going to be not an introduction but a book" [1958a, p. vii]. The result was a major work of scholarship. Robbins deliberately did not attempt to oversell Torrens' merits as an economist [1958a, pp. 2–3, 258]—and he was taken at his word by some reviewers [Fetter, 1958, 1962, p. 152; Hutchison, 1958, p. 316]. Yet the figure that emerges from the book is clearly not a minor figure, and it has become increasingly clear since 1958 that Torrens had analytical ability on a par with the very best in classical economics. Seligman had not made this clear, but Robbins' analytical mind with its own delight in abstraction immediately appreciated the acute analytical subtlety of Torrens. In particular, after the 1958 book and Robbins' introduction of the same year to Torrens' *Letters on Commercial Policy* [1958b] it was difficult to ignore the importance of Torrens' contributions to monetary, trade, and colonization theory. This is clear from the tone of post-Robbins discussions of Torrens [e.g., Corry, 1962, 1968; Fetter, 1965]. Moreover Robbins' book stimulated subsequent work on Torrens, some of it helping to fill gaps in his account which he (with quite unnecessary modesty) insisted on regarding as an interim report [Robbins, 1958a, p. viii].

Biographia

Although a complete biography is still lacking,[25] the years since Robbins' book have produced an accumulation of material concerning particular episodes in Torrens' life. Some details were already known, including a somewhat distant, if respectful, interest in religion[26] and the matter (still not fully cleared up) of his divorce and remarriage [Meenai, 1956, p. 55; Pike, 1957, *passim*; Samuels, 1966, p. 40]. In addition, shortly before the appearance of Robbins' book, Torrens had been denigrated in a book on South Australia [Pike, 1957].[27] But since 1958 we have had a detailed and definitive study of his military career [Fetter, 1962], evidence of his seeking office in the 1820s [O'Brien, 1965, pp. 271–274], and a fair amount of detailed information on his (ultimately successful) attempts to obtain a pension [Fetter, 1965, p. 182; O'Brien, 1971, pp. 426–428, 442, 512]. We also know about a rather nasty episode in which he was deprived of a lucrative printing contract, apparently at the instigation of one of his adversaries in the Currency and Banking controversy [O'Brien, 1971, pp. 867–877, 885, 920–922]. We now also know that he claimed to have been *the* originator of the Political Economy Club [O'Brien, 1971, p. 506]. We know, too, of an attempt by Torrens to reorient the Tory Party under Disraeli's leadership in accordance with Torrens' own particular views on protection [O'Brien, 1977]. Moreover, we now have detailed correspondence between Torrens and Overstone [O'Brien, 1971], something of which Robbins had noted the lack in his study [1958a, p. viii]. This makes clear the closeness of the collaboration between Overstone and Torrens in defense of the Bank Charter Act of 1844. It also suggests, however, that Overstone really did not trust Torrens very far. The correspondence reveals his hostility over the Cuba case [O'Brien, 1971, pp. 27, 335, 336, 345, 346, 347], his fury over a proposed publication by Torrens advocating a corn duty [O'Brien, 1971, p. 487], and his unwillingness to intervene with Lord John Russell on behalf of Torrens, an unwillingness which stopped only just short of an outright snub [O'Brien, 1971, pp. 434–435]. But a well-researched and balanced biography is an important need.

Trade Theory

Torrens' priority in the formulation of the theory of comparative costs now seems to be generally accepted [Chipman, 1965a, p. 482; Corry, 1962, p. 122; 1968; Hollander, 1979, p. 461; Robbins, 1958a, pp. 18–21, 31–35; 1958b, p. vi; Schumpeter, 1954, pp. 474n, 489–490, 607; Seligman, 1903, pp. 344–345; Viner, 1937, pp. 440–444]. Yet although his original formulation is arguably superior to Ricardo's, the general view that it was Ricardo (albeit through the agency of J.S. Mill) rather than Torrens who succeeded in getting the concept established [Chipman, 1965a, pp. 482n; Schumpeter, 1954, p. 607; Viner, 1937, p. 442] seems to be correct. Oddly enough, the reason appears to be that, whereas Ricardo paid little attention to trade theory after his initial statement, Torrens returned to the matter on a number of occasions, and his insistence upon using a comparative cost approach seems to have been rather variable [O'Brien, 1975, pp. 174–175; Viner, 1937, pp. 442, 447–448; see, however, Robbins, 1958a, pp. 31–35]. Yet he was undoubtedly an important and creative trade theorist and, in the development of a solution to the unsolved problem of the terms of trade under comparative costs, his formulation of "reciprocal demand" (his own phrase) [Viner, 1937, p. 536] must rank as a major contribution even though it was J.S. Mill's exposition that was the influential one [O'Brien, 1975, pp. 182–183; Robbins, 1958a, pp. 25–30;

1958b, p. vii; Schumpeter, 1954, p. 608; Viner, 1937, pp. 446–447]. His use of this analysis in the famous "Cuba case" has received detailed discussion [O'Brien, 1975, pp. 191–197; Robbins, 1958a, pp. 187–225; Viner, 1937, pp. 298–299, 322, 463–464]. But it is still worth emphasizing that Torrens himself laid less stress upon the barter formulation of the argument than upon the form in which the analysis led to the conclusion that unilateral tariff reductions would produce monetary deflation, which was a life-long preoccupation of Torrens. The Cuba case thus provided an argument for lowering tariffs on a bilateral basis. This led in turn to an argument for a customs union. Torrens' interest in colonialism, possibly combined with his military background,[28] led naturally to the selection of the Britain Empire as the desirable union area—the case for an Imperial Zollverein [Robbins, 1958a, pp. 225–231]. But this leaves the question of where Torrens stood on free trade rather open—as indeed his contemporaries were aware. On the one hand he argued for many years for a free trade in corn [Blaug, 1958a, pp. 203, 211; Robbins, 1958a, pp. 183–187]; on the other, although it is true that as late as 1844, the year of the Cuba case, he was still arguing consistently against duties on raw produce [Robbins, 1958a, p. 186], it is clear that subsequently, both in private communication with Disraeli and in a proposed publication, he was arguing for the *reintroduction* of the duty on corn abolished in 1846 [O'Brien, 1971, p. 487; 1977].

Monetary Theory

Although Torrens is famous as one of the great defenders of the Bank Charter Act of 1844, his earlier phase as an Anti-Bullionist has now been documented and explored [Robbins, 1958a, pp. 74–80; Viner, 1937, pp. 148–149]. It is clear that he was among the better of the Anti-Bullionists [Mints, 1945, pp. 49–50; O'Brien, 1975, p. 152]. From this time dates his obsession with the avoidance of monetary deflation which was later to resurface in his arguments against unilateral reduction of tariffs [Fetter, 1965, p. 140; O'Brien, 1975, p. 278; Robbins, 1958a, pp. 81–86; Viner, 1937, p. 207]. But the detailed and very valuable critical discussion has noticed a discontinuity in Torrens' monetary thought between this earlier Anti-Bullionist phase and his later Currency School position [Meenai, 1956, p. 59; Robbins, 1958a, pp. 73–74, 142; see also O'Brien, 1971, pp. 413–414]. It is, however, now clear that the discontinuity was less sharp than previously thought, and there is certainly no evidence that his change of position was caused by the search for office [Fetter, 1965, p. 161; O'Brien 1965]. His post-1830 monetary thought involved the proposal for the separation of the departments of the Bank of England,[29] leading to a major role in the Currency and Banking controversy [Robbins, 1958a, pp. 86–143]. Yet there were differences in his approach from that of Overstone and Norman. He ultimately conceded Overstone's view that the country banks could produce monetary disequilibrium [Morgan, 1943, p. 134; Robbins, 1958a, pp. 101–105; Viner, 1937, pp. 235–236], but he returned—sometimes to Overstone's alarm—to the question of deposits to which he accorded very much more importance than Overstone [Fetter, 1965, pp. 168–169; Mints, 1945, pp. 80–83; O'Brien, 1971, pp. 80, 112, 713–717; 1975, p. 143; Robbins, 1958a, pp. 105–116; Viner, 1937, pp. 232, 250]. Indeed, after Pennington, he is the author of the concept of the deposit multiplier [O'Brien, 1971, pp. 94n; 1975, p. 156; Viner, 1937, p. 243]. He believed that the credit super-structure could be controlled through control of the high-powered money base—as long as reserve ratios were fixed [Mints, 1945, p. 81; Wood, 1939, p. 54].

Economic Progress

Although Torrens' major contributions are undoubtedly in the field of trade and money, his restless and fertile mind was active on other topics. His importance in relation to the concepts of diminishing returns and rent—he published simultaneously with Malthus, West, and Ricardo—is now recognized [Blaug, 1958a, p. 6; 1985, p. 77; O'Brien, 1975, p. 125; Robbins, 1958a, pp. 41–42]. It is also acknowledged that he led the revolt against Malthus and believed that family size declined with per capita wealth—which is broadly true and a very considerable advance on Ricardo's *simpliste* position [Blaug, 1958a, pp. 113, 116–117, 233]. But he had previously been a supporter of colonization on population grounds. After changing his mind on population, he came to support colonization as an outlet for capital where investment opportunities were less than available saving [Blaug, 1958a, p. 99; O'Brien, 1975, pp. 291–292; Robbins, 1958a, p. 179]. Indeed he became Wakefield's most important (and analytical) supporter, having earlier supported Wilmot Horton [Robbins, 1958a, pp. 141–181; 1958b, pp. viii–ix; Winch, 1965, pp. 72, 73, 81, 88, 99–100, 130].[30]

But this raises the question of Torrens' attitude to the Law of Markets. On this there are differences of view. In summary, the majority view would seem to be that Torrens accepted the equality, but certainly not the identity, version of this law, envisaging both the possibility of general overproduction and of excess demand for money [Blaug, 1958a, pp. 43, 91–93, 99; Corry, 1962, pp. 8, 100; Hutchison, 1958, p. 318; Robbins, 1958a, pp. 176–178]. But since one of the key references is of disputed authorship [De Vivo, 1985 O'Brien and Darnell, 1980a, 1980b, 1982; Robbins, 1958a, p. 187; Thweatt, 1974, 1980a] and another contains varying positions within its covers [O'Brien and Darnell, 1980b, p. 415], this its issue is never likely to be resolved fully.

Torrens' analysis of wages, although not intrinsically interesting in any particular way, has received a fair amount of discussion, starting with Seligman [Fetter, 1958, pp. 345–346; O'Brien, 1966, 1975, pp. 114–117 and references; Robbins, 1958a, pp. 48–51; Seligman, 1903, pp. 342–343]; and his plan for unemployment relief for those displaced by technological progress has been noted by a number of writers [e.g., O'Brien, 1975, p. 279]. The latter is not surprising, given his very qualified attitude toward Laissez Faire and his belief—possibly due to a military background [Fetter, 1962, pp. 164–165]—in the efficacy of government action to solve social problems [Blaug, 1958a, p. 194; Corry, 1962, pp. 157–158]. But this is a useful counter to the stereotype of the older literature of Torrens as the last-ditch opponent of factory legislation—his opposition here turns out, again, to be linked to a fear of monetary deflation resulting from an adverse balance of payments produced by uncompetitive exports [O'Brien, 1975, p. 278].

Conclusion

Although Torrens' methodological position [Blaug, 1958a, pp. 163–164, 188; Meenai, 1953; O'Brien, 1975, p. 66] and his (circular) capital theory of value [Blaug, 1958a, p. 47; O'Brien, 1970, p. 129; 1975, pp. 91–93; Robbins, 1958a, pp. 60–72; 1958b, p. vi] have received discussion in the literature, they are not elements of his thought which greatly enhance his reputation. But, in the light of his work on trade and on money, and (to a lesser extent) on colonies, it seems clear that he was among the very best of the classical theorists.[31] The mental vitality which enabled him to produce, in his late seventies, a major *Edinburgh Review* article on currency and the third edition of his *Principles*, despite, as is clear from his correspondence with Overstone, persistent ill health, has very few rivals indeed. His grasp of theory, both his own and other people's, was outstanding. As a controversialist he was, it seems clear, the most formidable adversary in nineteenth century English economics [Fetter, 1958, p. 345; 1965, pp. 167–168, 187, 193; Robbins, 1958a, pp. 207–225].[32] Yet at the end of the day his direct influence was limited [Robbins, 1958a, p. 234]. Why that should have been is not entirely clear. Perhaps his readers—like Overstone—did not entirely trust him. While Ricardo's discussions have every appearance of candour (though, in fact, he hardly ever altered his position), Torrens' discussions are redolent of a Marine assault in which no quarter is given or asked.

J.B. Say (1767–1832)

Origins

Ever since the early nineteenth century there has been a tendency to regard Say as merely the popularizer (even the vulgarizer) of Adam Smith, for the benefit of a French audience.[33] It is tempting to regard this as a purely Anglo-centric phenomenon; it is, however, the case that some of the strongest statements of this view of Say are to be found among French writers [Leduc, 1968; Molinier, 1958; Teilhac, 1934]. Such a view is not difficult to sustain because there are undoubtedly significant influences of Smith upon Say, and a number of outright borrowings [O'Brien, 1975, pp. 240, 270; Spengler, 1945, Thweatt, 1979a, pp. 86–87]. However, even to the most ardent Anglo-centric, it must be apparent that Say's analysis was significantly different from that of Smith's other successors, in the British Isles; and one reason for this difference is undoubtedly that, as more scholarly work has revealed, French sources were important to Say, both directly and also, to some extent, through their influence on Smith. This was emphasized by Bowley in 1937 [Bowley, 1937, pp. 74, 76, 112; see also 1972, p. 12], and Schumpeter made it the centerpiece of his appraisal of Say [1954, pp. 234, 302, 491, 828, 1010n]. Schumpeter's appraisal was a major corrective of the traditional view, in his emphasis upon the independent achievement of Say in matters of subject organization, value theory, distribution, the role of the entrepreneur, and, especially, aggregate demand [1954, pp. 491, 710–711n]. Later writers have contributed significantly to our understanding of the French, especially Physiocratic, sources of Say's thought [Lambert, 1956, pp. 8, 14; O'Brien, 1975, p. 160; Skinner, 1967, p. 154; Sowell, 1972, pp. 7, 8; Spengler, 1945, pp. 161, 194].[34] These are important even where Say was reacting against some elements in Physiocratic thought [Baumol, 1977, p. 149; Sowell, 1974, pp. 35–38; Spengler, 1945, p. 190].

Utility

A major difficulty with the idea of Say as a mere popularizer of Smith is that Say adopted a diametrically opposed attitude to value and distribution, working in the long utility tradition in France [Blaug, 1985, p. 34; Kauder,

1953], assigning a key role to utility in value theory, and in production [Bowley, 1937, p. 77; 1973, p. 143; O'Brien, 1975, pp. 98–99], leading him, in turn, to reject Smith's distinction between productive and unproductive labor [Bowley, 1937, p. 76; O'Brien, 1975, pp. 233–234; Schumpeter, 1954, p. 626]. Such an approach led to a theory of distribution with the value of factor services determined by the value (utility) of the final product [Bowley, 1937, p. 77; O'Brien, 1975, pp. 98–99]. With increasing recognition of this has come also the recognition that it was really only the absence of the marginal concept, and the consequent failure to distinguish total and marginal utility and total and marginal product, that impeded Say's further progress in this direction [Bowley, 1972, pp. 16–18; 1973, pp. 146–147; Houghton, 1958; O'Brien, 1975, pp. 98–99; Stigler, 1965, p. 77]. But his analysis nonetheless marked a significant departure from that of Smith, as did an analysis of tax incidence based upon the elasticity of supply of inputs and the elasticity of demand for the output [O'Brien, 1975, pp. 240–258].

Methodology

Bowley's work, which drew attention to the importance of Say's utility analysis, also paid attention to his methodology. Her work, and subsequent commentary, have helped to bring out the essentially anti-Ricardian attitude of Say on methodological issues, his emphasis upon the importance of empirical premises and of what he believed to be induction, and his desire to make economics similar to physics [Bowley, 1937, p. 35; O'Brien, 1975, p. 66; Schumpeter, 1954, p. 576; Sowell, 1974, pp. 116–117]. At the same time we have, rather paradoxically, the attitude on his part that statistical material was merely descriptive (and a bureaucratic indulgence) and his opposition to mathematical economics [Ménard, 1980, Sowell, 1974, pp. 116–117]. While this may seem to us to amount to an odd methodological stance, it has helped to bring out the fact that Say took seriously the methodological basis of economics and devoted time and care to establishing his own methodological position.

Entrepreneurship

Although Smith enjoyed the company of Scottish merchants, he devotes surprisingly little attention to the role of the entrepreneur. Say, however, probably starting from the work of Cantillon and some Physiocratic writers [Blaug, 1985, p. 460; James, 1977; Koolman, 1971, pp. 278, 282–284; Schumpeter, 1954, pp. 491, 555, 645], then filled this gap by developing an analysis of the role of the entrepreneur, something for which he was particularly fitted, having been an entrepreneur himself for seven years in the cotton business [Koolman, 1971, p. 286; Leduc, 1968; Schumpeter, 1954, p. 491; see also Schoorl, 1979]. The entrepreneur in his analysis is the person who bears risk, brings knowledge and means together, observes and profits from opportunities, and provides industrial leadership and innovation [Koolman, 1971, pp. 271–280]. While economists have discussed this, work by historians and political scientists has helped to place the analysis in perspective. It is now clear that Say's writings in this area were bound up with the events of the French Revolution and constituted an argument for a new industrial order, raising the status of industry [James, 1977]. Moreover he was working in a tradition in this field, embodied in the writings of Roederer, and his work here is essentially anti-Physiocratic. Say was a member of "*Les Ideologues*" who stressed the importance (for both economic growth and social order after the Revolution) of allowing industry to flourish. Not only does this give critical importance to labor (as against land) but the dependency relationship between different sectors of society, as envisaged by the Physiocrats (and to some extent by Smith), is replaced by a mutual interdependence [Kaiser, 1980]. With the placing of Say's work on entrepreneurship in context, the perspective has been corrected in another way. For a number of writers had previously lamented the lack of influence of his ideas on this topic [Blaug, 1958a, pp. 153–154; Bowley, 1973, p. 40; Koolman, 1971, pp. 284–285; Schumpeter, 1954, p. 557]; but it is now clear that he had very considerable influence in France, especially on St. Simon and his followers [James, 1977, pp. 472–473; Kaiser, 1980, p. 160].

Say's Law

While Keynes is a secondary (though, outside the context of literature on the history of economic thought, probably a primary) source of distortion on this important aspect of Say's work, the primary source of the distortion is undoubtedly an identification of Say's position with Ricardo.[35] Ricardo's version of the Law of Markets, supplied by James Mill, involved a rigid identity between output and demand, making effective demand failure impossible by definition, in order to establish that profits could not fall due to overproduction but only due to diminishing returns in agriculture [Hollander, 1979, p. 506; Stigler, 1965, pp. 314, 317; Thweatt, 1979a, pp. 88,

90, 92]. In truth, then, he was thus highly critical of Say who did believe that profits could decline over time, because of the complementarity of output and leisure, which could lead to an exhaustion of (marginal) investment opportunities [Blaug, 1958a, p. 90; Hollander, 1979, pp. 93, 509, 520; O'Brien, 1975, p. 124; Schumpeter, 1954, p. 654; Sowell, 1972, p. 12]. Historians of economic thought, at least, recognized this conflict between Say and Ricardo fairly clearly. Although Say undoubtedly took refuge in tautology (including, at a later stage in his work, the embarrassing tautology that output which could not be sold at cost covering prices was not output) [Baumol, 1977, p. 159; Blaug, 1958a, p. 64; Sowell, 1972, pp. 19–20, 121, 140–141; 1974, pp. 52, 141–142], it is recognized that he did not adhere to an identity version of Say's Law and that he was critical of Ricardo for using one. He was undoubtedly much more subtle and flexible than Ricardo in his treatment of aggregate demand. The whole basis of his analysis lay not in the needs of Ricardo's model, but in an analysis of economic growth, springing in turn from his concern with industrialization [Baumol, 1977, pp. 152, 160; Blaug, 1958a, pp. 64, 75; Hollander, 1979, p. 83; O'Brien, 1975, p. 44; Skinner, 1967, pp. 157–158; Sowell, 1972, p. 13]. It was thus not necessary for him to argue that effective demand failure could not occur in the short term. The causes of excess demand failure included, as has been recognized at least since Blaug's work [1958a, p. 89], not only miscalculations on the part of producers but also excess demand for money, possibly because of political mistrust, and supply-side barriers to mobility. Government interference could not only produce market failure but sectional advantage—Say has recently been credited with anticipating the modern theory of "rent seeking" [Euzent and Martin, 1984]. Taxation could reduce demand (an argument which Ricardo opposed by using *his* version of Say's law [O'Brien, 1975, pp. 243, 260] and savings could be greater than investment [Blaug, 1958a, p. 89; Thweatt, 1979a, p. 92], a matter on which Say was critical of Ricardo—he was not an advocate of the "Treasury View." Indeed it may be argued that he gradually moved toward the idea of an equilibrium income with injections equal to leakages only at this level [Sowell, 1972; cf. Vatter, 1959]. In addition, there could be excess demand for money [Hollander, 1979, p. 93; Schumpeter, 1954, pp. 710–711; Sowell, 1963, p. 201; 1972, pp. 98–99; 1974, pp. 56, 61, 65] in depression, and the wrong mix of commodities might be produced for the given composition of demand [Baumol, 1977, p. 154; Sowell, 1972, pp. 19–20; Thweatt, 1979a]—although, as Schumpeter emphasized, this was the wrong mix of commodities at the same stage of production, not the mix of consumption goods and investment goods [1954, p. 739].

There are considerable differences of opinion about how far Say's argument developed between editions of his *Traité*, although the majority view is quite clearly that there was some development [Baumol, 1977, pp. 147, 157–159; Skinner, 1967, p. 166; Sowell, 1972, pp. 17–18, 77, 140–141, 238; 1974, pp. 47–48; see Hollander, 1979, for a contrary view]. The case seems fairly clear that the 1803 version contained the proposition that products demand products, and that for completion the argument also required some demonstration that available purchasing power would necessarily be used. It seems evident that the latter was supplied in Say's second edition, although Thweatt has argued convincingly [1980b] that the missing material had already been supplied by Mill and that Say was doing nothing more than following Mill's later exposition. On the other hand, if this is true, Say was still far more flexible and less dogmatic than Mill.

This leads us to the vexed question of priority. There has been considerable debate about this in the literature. On the one hand Schumpeter, Lambert, Spengler and others attribute priority in the formulation of Say's law to Say [Lambert, 1956; Schumpeter, 1954, pp. 491, 621; Spengler, 1945, p. 191]. On the other hand, a number of equally important writers—J. H. and S. Hollander, Gregory, Chipman, Stigler, Sowell, and, most recently, Thweatt, give James Mill priority [Chipman, 1965b, p. 709n; Hollander, 1979, p. 96; Sowell, 1963, p. 198; 1972, pp. 17–18, 21, 32–33; Stigler, 1965, pp. 313–314; 1976, p. 64; Thweatt, 1979a, 1980b]. The debate has certainly not been valueless; it has made clear the important role of James Mill in the development of 'Ricardian economics', and helped to bring out the important fact that he was a great deal more than Ricardo's popularizer and mentor. But this is ultimately beside the point. Say clearly has priority for the economic growth argument, while Mill equally clearly has priority for the "1814" version from which Say then retreated.

Influence

Some mention has already been made of the influence (or lack of it) of Say's ideas on entrepreneurship. It is, however, a useful corrective to the Anglo-centric view of the history of economic thought to note that Say had considerable influence on Bailey, Lauderdale, Butt, Banfield, [Bowley, 1937, pp. 91–93, 109–110], and (especially) Senior [Bowley, 1937, pp. 16, 42, 51n, 94, 100, 105, 111, 113, 137, 181]. It also seems highly likely that he had an influence on Longfield's whole approach [Bowley, 1972, p. 19; 1973, pp. 150, 216], although this must remain an open question. He was also influential in Germany [Bowley, 1937, pp. 112, 133, 135]. This influence has been referred to extensively by Bowley, and there is no need to pursue the matter here. It is, however, a useful corrective to the idea of Say as merely the popularizer of Adam Smith.

Conclusion

It seems to this writer that historians of economic thought, at least in this century, have little to be ashamed of in their treatment of Say. It is perfectly true that a better perspective has been gained through the involvement of writers with both a wider knowledge of history and of political thought, and that a much greater understanding of Say has been gained by a closer study of other writers such as James Mill and Sismondi. Clearly there are areas in which further research could proceed. There are apparently extensive Say papers;[36] and his monetary theory still remains little explored [Schumpeter, 1954, pp. 710–711n]. But the record of historians of economic thought in dealing with Say is not at all bad. The real divide is between the historians of economic thought who have read Say and the writers on macroeconomics who, taking their lead from Keynes, have produced an unrecognizable caricature.

Conclusion

It should be clear that any account of classical economics which treats the writers considered here[37] as offering only minor variations on Ricardo and/or Smith is highly misleading and that many of the classical economists apart from Ricardo and Smith were men of outstanding capabilities who solved problems left unsolved by more famous names. In particular it is now clear to most economists (or rather, to most historians of economic thought) that the idea of classical economics as the pale reflection of Ricardo is a gross distortion. In fact, despite the grandiose English and the patronizing tone, Schumpeter's judgment seems frequently to have been vindicated, and the process of reappraisal which he helped to initiate has resulted in a fundamental change of perspective on classical economics.

Notes

1. See, for instance, Schumpeter's own view [1954, p. 484; see also Bowley, 1937, p. 91]. As O'Brien [1970, p. 405; 1978, p. 7] indicates, this is certainly the present writer's view.

2. See, however, Moss [1974, 1976].

3. Moss' book, while in many ways excellent, and while not advancing the "apologist" thesis, has an unfortunate tendency occasionally to attribute both sources and motives to Longfield, without evidence. On the ad hominem fallacy, see also the discussion of Senior below.

4. Both Black and Moss agree on the essential consistency of Longfield's position on the State and welfare. Hollander [1980, pp. 404–405] points out that Longfield insisted that the question of desirable distribution was very much in the domain of the economist. Indeed Hollander concedes that the range of legitimate government intervention envisaged by Longfield extended far beyond anything conceived by Ricardo—including tax-financed redistribution schemes.

5. References can be found in Black [1980, p. 13; 1983] and Hollander [1977, p. 222].

6. See the section of this chapter dealing with James Mill.

7. Longfield's *Lectures* [Black, 1971, pp. 175–177] correctly pointed out that the inverse relationship of wages and profits requires the invariable measure.

8. "Longfield's *Lectures*...affords yet another example of that tendency to compromise with Ricardian economics which we have seen at work in Senior's *Political Economy*" [Blaug, 1958a, p. 159].

9. As Black says in his (unfortunately) unpublished 1980 paper, "The attempt to make Longfield in to a Ricardian seems to me to involve playing up minor features of his *Lectures* and playing down major ones; and the outcome can only be unfortunate distortion of the historical record" [p. 21].

10. Despite its aggressive tone, Moss's study [1976] does not actually present a different picture from that of Black and Bowley except in the downplaying of the utility material in Longfield.

11. See, however, Viner [1937, p. 457]. Tantalisingly there was, Black points out, a brief meeting with Jevons [Black, 1971, p. 26].

12. See also Black's later discussion [1947–1948] and Schumpeter's endorsement [1954, p. 464].

13. It is surprising that Schumpeter managed to maintain both that Mill and McCulloch were Ricardo's only two disciples and that Ricardian economics had run its course by 1831, while being aware that McCulloch flourished *as an economic writer* until his death in 1864.

14. See also, Schumpeter [1954, p. 668]; see, however, the same reference [p. 621].

15. The best examination of Say's individual discussion is in Baumol [1977].

16. Thweatt [1977c] establishes a striking parallel between Mill's 1804 "Corn Bounty" and Ricardo's general approach, including the vital role of corn prices, the use of Malthusian mechanism, and Mill's analytical conclusion that the Corn Laws hurt England and benefited only the landlord.

17. Barber's book [1975] documents Mill's methodological approach and his extraordinary influence; Miller's review of this book [1976] brings out clearly that Mill's mental blinkers prevented him from appreciating the difficulties of his rent-tax approach in a situation where rents greater than the competitive level could be extracted.

18. Even on the (analytically unimportant) matter of Mill's unpleasant character, we may note that he was genuinely affected by Ricardo's death [Bain, 1882, p. 211], and the correspondence with Ricardo shows the best side of him [Winch, 1966, p. 186]. For some questioning of his influence on Ricardo see Stigler [1953, pp. 590–591].

19. However, there is a remarkable degree of continuity between Bowley's article of 1934, her book of 1937, and her article of 1968.

20. It is remarkable that he is not mentioned in Wood's great text [Wood, 1939] nor in

Mints' seminal work [1945] and that he appears only once (and briefly) in Fetter's important book [1965, p. 141].

21. He was a practicing lawyer—see Bowley [1968, p. 170].

22. Bowley [1972]; but see note 19 above.

23. Robbins was presumably also instrumental in securing the LSE reprint of the *Critical Dissertation*.

24. Bailey's originality is denied by S. Hollander [1979, pp. 662–664].

25. Peter L. Moore of the Archives of Business and Labour, Australian National University, is at work on a biography of Torrens.

26. "...though I have no pretensions to be righteous overmuch, yet I infinitely prefer a man who prays too much to one who swears too much and prays too little" [Torrens, quoted in Pike [1957, p. 271].

27. Pike unfortunately also confuses Torrens with another soldier of the same name at one point [Pike, 1957, p. 92; cf. Fetter, 1962, pp. 161–163].

28. This at least is Fetter's suggestion [1962, pp. 161–163].

29. But having advocated this, Torrens' restless mind led him to another plan [Morgan, 1943, p. 137].

30. Torrens' wage analysis, which appeared in print in five different forms, originated in a private paper sent to Wilmot Horton [O'Brien, 1966]. However, the colonization material did not make its appearance as early as 1808, as Robbins had believed, but in 1817 [Thweatt, 1981].

31. See the appendix to O'Brien [1977] where use of the now standard technical apparatus shows the full subtlety of the analysis which Torrens managed to deploy, without access to that apparatus. See also O'Brien [1971, p. 85; 1975, p. 6] and Robbins [1958a, pp. 241–242, 245].

32. Of Torrens' reception of Senior's attack on *The Budget*, Robbins wrote: "One can almost hear the old Colonel of Marines snort with pleasure as he perused its contents, perceived its weaknesses, reached for that formidable pen, and began *Letter X* of *The Budget*, the famous *Letter to Nassau Senior*. The result is a debating triumph of the first order" [1958a, p. 219]. "The demonstration is so crushing that one instinctively seeks to discover some way out for his opponent" [p. 223].

33. Koolman [1971, p. 269] documents the slighting treatment of Say and the continuation of the tradition of treating him as a popularizer of Adam Smith.

34. However, it is *not* true that commentators prior to the 1970s were misled because of a reliance on the Prinsep translation of the fourth edition of Say's *Traité*. Among others, Bowley [1937] and Spengler [1945] both used the French sixth edition.

35. Whose version however did *not* capture English economics; see Gordon [1965].

36. *History of Economic Thought Newsletter* No. 11, Autumn 1973, p. 12.

37. J.R. McCulloch (1789–1864) is not discussed here mainly for reasons of space but also because he has not attracted the varied secondary literature which has arisen around the work of the six writers discussed.

References

Angell, J.W. (1926). *The Theory of International Prices*. Cambridge MA: Harvard University Press.

Bain, A. (1882). *James Mill. A Biography*, reprinted. (1961) New York: A.M. Kelley.

Barber, W.J. (1969). "James Mill and the Theory of Economic Policy in India." *History of Political Economy* 1:101–122.

————. (1975). *British Economic Thought and India 1600–1858*. Oxford: Clarendon Press.

Baumol, W.J. (1977). "Say's (at least) eight laws, or what Say and James Mill may really have meant." *Economica* 44:145–162.

Black, R.D. Collison. (1945). "Trinity College, Dublin, and the Theory of Value, 1832–1863" *Economica* N.S. 12:140–148.

————. (1947–1948). "Economic Studies at Trinity College, Dublin," parts I & II. *Hermathena* 70:65–80; 71:51–63.

————. (1960). *Economic Thought and the Irish Question 1817–1870*. Cambridge: Cambridge University Press.

————. (1971). Introduction to *The Economic Writings of Mountifort Longfield*. New York: A.M. Kelley.

————. (1980). "A Review of the Work of Irish Economists in the Nineteenth Century." (mimeo).

————. (1982). "Political Economy and the Irish." *History of Economics Society Bulletin* 4 pp. 33–47.

————. (1983). "The Irish Dissenters and Nineteenth Century Political Economy." *Hermathena* 135:120–137.

Blaug, M. (1958a). *Ricardian Economics*. New Haven: Yale University Press.

————. (1958b). "The Classical Economists and the Factory Acts—A Re-examination." *Quarterly Journal of Economics* 72:211–226.

————. (1963). "The Myth of the Old Poor Law and the MaKing of the New" *Journal of Economic History* 23:151–184.

————. (1964). "The Poor Law Report Re-examined." *Journal of Economic History* 24:229–245.

————. (1975). "The Economics of Education in English Classical Political Economy: A Re-examination." In A.S. Skinner and T. Wilson (eds.), *Essays on Adam Smith*. Oxford: Clarendon Press, pp. 568–599.

————. (1980). *The Methodology of Economics*, reprinted (1982). Cambridge: Cambridge University Press.

————. (1985). *Economic Theory in Retrospect*, 4th ed. Cambridge: Cambridge University Press.

Bowley, Marian. (1934). "Senior, Nassau William." In E.R.A. Seligman *Encyclopaedia of the Social Sciences*, vol. 13. New York: Macmillan, pp. 662–663.

————. (1937). *Nassau Senior and Classical Economics*. London: Allen & Unwin.

————. (1968). "Senior, Nassau William." In D. Sills (ed.), *International Encyclopaedia of the Social Sciences*, vol. 14. New York: Macmillan, pp. 169–172.

————. (1972). "The Predecessors of Jevons—The Revolution That Wasn't." *Manchester School* 40:9–29.

————. (1973). *Studies in the History of Economic Theory Before 1870*. London: Macmillan.

Cannan, E. (1903). *A History of the Theories of Production and Distribution in*

English Political Economy from 1776 to 1848, 2nd ed. London: P.S. King.
Chipman, J.S. (1965a). "A Survey of the Theory of International Trade: Part 1, the Classical Theory." *Econometrica* 33:477–519.
———. (1965b). "A Survey of the Theory of International Trade: Part 2, the Neo-Classical Theory." *Econometrica* 33:685–760.
Corry, B.A. (1962). *Money, Saving and Investment in English Economics 1800–1850*. London: Macmillan.
———. (1968). "Torrens, Robert." In D. Sills (ed.), *International Encyclopaedia of the Social Sciences*, vol. 16, New York: Macmillan.
Dennis, K. (1973). "The Bailey Notebooks and Authorship of 'Verbal Disputes'." *History of Economic Thought Newsletter* No. 11:17–18.
De Vivo, G. (1985). "The Author of the Article on Owen in the October 1819 *Edinburgh Review*: Some Neglected Evidence." *History of Political Economy* 17:199–201.
Dobb, M. (1973). *Theories of Value and Distribution Since Adam Smith*. Cambridge: Cambridge University Press.
Eshag, E. (1963). *From Marshall to Keynes. An Essay on the Monetary Theory of the Cambridge School*, reprinted (1964). Oxford: Basil Blackwell.
Euzent, P.J., and Martin, T.L. (1984). "Classical Roots of the Emerging Theory of Rent Seeking: The Contribution of Jean-Baptiste Say." *History of Political Economy* 16:255–262.
Fetter, F.W. (1958). "Robbins on Torrens." *Economica* N.S. 25:345–348.
———. (1962). "Robert Torrens: Colonel of Marines and Political Economist." *Economica* N.S. 29:152–165.
———. (1965). *The Development of British Monetary Orthodoxy*. Cambridge, MA: Harvard University Press.
Fraser, L.M. (1934). "Torrens, Robert." In E. R.A. Seligman (ed.), *Encyclopaedia of the Social Sciences*, vol. 14. New York: Macmillan, p. 352.
Gordon, B.J. (1965). "Say's Law, Effective Demand, and the Contemporary British Periodicals, 1820–1850." *Economica* 32:438–446.
Halevy, E. (1928). *The Growth of Philosophic Radicalism*, trans. Morris. London: Faber & Gwyer.
Hollander, J.H. (1911). "Ricardo and Torrens." *Economic Journal* 21:455–468.
Hollander, S. (1977). "The Reception of Ricardian Economics." *Oxford Economic Papers* 29:221–257.
———. (1979). *The Economics of David Ricardo*. Toronto: University of Toronto Press.
———. (1980). "The Post-Ricardian Dissension: A Case-Study in Economics and Ideology." *Oxford Economic Papers* 32:372–410.
Houghton, R.W. (1958). "A Note on the Early History of Consumer's Surplus." *Economica* 25:49–57.
Hutchison, T.W. (1952). "Some Questions About Ricardo." *Economica* 19:415–432.
———. (1953). "James Mill and the Political Education of Ricardo." *Cambridge Journal* 7:81–100.

———. (1958). "Robert Torrens and Classical Economics." *Economic History Review II* 11:316–321.

———. (1977). Review of *Mountifort Longfield* by L.S. Moss. *History of Economic Thought Newsletter* 18:22–23.

———. (1978). *On Revolutions and Progress in Economic Knowledge*. Cambridge: Cambridge University Press.

James, M. (1977). "Pierre-Louis Roederer, Jean-Baptiste Say, and the Concept of Industrie." *History of Political Economy* 9:455–475.

Johnson, O. (1969). "The "Last Hour" of Senior and Marx." *History of Political Economy* 1:359–369.

Kaiser, T.E. (1980). "Politics and Political Economy in the Thought of the Ideologues." *History of Political Economy* 12:141–160.

Kauder, E. (1953). "Genesis of the Marginal Utility Theory from Aristotle to the End of the Eighteenth Century." *Economic Journal* 63:638–650.

Koolman, G. (1971). "Say's Conception of the Role of the Entrepreneur." *Economica* 38:269–286.

Lambert, P. (1956). "The Law of Markets Prior to J.-B. Say and the Say-Malthus Debate." *International Economic Papers* 6:7–22.

Leduc, G. (1968). "Say, Jean Baptiste." In D. Sills (ed.), *International Encyclopaedia of the Social Sciences*, vol. 11. New York: Macmillan, pp. 23–25.

McKinley, E. (1968). "Longfield, Samuel Mountifort." In D. Sills (ed.), *International Encyclopaedia of the Social Sciences*, vol. 9. New York: Macmillan, p. 473.

Meenai, S.A. (1953). "Robert Torrens and Classical Methodology." *Pakistan Economic Journal* 3:16–26.

———. (1956). "Robert Torrens—1780–1864." *Economica* N.S. 23:49–61.

———. (1955–56). "Robert Torrens and Classical Economics: A Study in the Development of Orthodox Economic Theory." *Federal Economic Review* 2: 155–200; 3:18–40.

———. (1959–60). "Robert Torrens and Classical Economists. A Study in the Development of Orthodox Economic Theory." *Federal Economic Review* 6/7: 86–123.

Ménard, C. (1980). "Three Forms of Resistance to Statistics: Say, Cournot, Walras." *History of Political Economy* 12:524–541.

Miller, W.L. (1966). "The Economics of Education in English Classical Economics." *Southern Economic Journal* 32:294–309.

———. (1976). Review of *British Economic Thought and the India* by W.J. Barber. *History of Political Economy* 8:305–309.

Mints, L.W. (1945). *A History of Banking Theory*. Chicago: University of Chicago Press.

Mixter, C.W. (1898). "Samuel Bailey on Appreciation." *Quarterly Journal of Economics* 12:43–48.

Molinier, J. (1958). *Les Metamorphoses d'une théorie economique*. Paris: Armand Colin.

Morgan, E.V. (1943). *The Theory and Practice of Central Banking 1797–1913*.

Cambridge: Cambridge University Press, reprinted London: Cass (1965).

Moss, L.S. (1973). "Isaac Butt and the Early Development of the Marginal Utility Theory of Imputation." *History of Political Economy* 5:317–338.

———. (1974). "Mountifort Longfield's Supply-and-Demand Theory of Price and its Place in the Development of British Economic Theory." *History of Political Economy* 6:405–434.

———. (1976). *Mountifort Longfield: Ireland's First Professor of Political Economy*. Ottawa, IL: Green Hill Publishers.

Murphy, A.E. (1983). "Mountifort Longfield's Appointment to the Chair of Political Economy in Trinity College, Dublin, 1832." *Hermathena* 135:13–24.

O'Brien, D.P. (1965). "The Transition in Torrens' Monetary Thought." *Economica* N.S. 32:269–301.

———. (1966). "Torrens on Wages and Emmigration." *Economica* N.S. 33:336–340.

———. (1970). *J.R. McCulloch. A Study in Classical Economics*. London: Allen & Unwin.

———. (1971). *The Correspondence of Lord Overstone*, 3 vols. Cambridge: Cambridge University Press.

———. (1975) *The Classical Economists*. Oxford: Clarendon Press.

———. (1977). "Torrens, McCulloch and Disraeli." *Scottish Journal of Political Economy* 24:1–18.

O'Brien, D.P., and Darnell, A.C. (1980a). "Torrens, McCulloch and the Digression on Sismondi: Whose Digression?" *History of Political Economy* 12:383–395.

———. (1980b). "A Rejoinder." *History of Political Economy* 12:411–419.

———. (1982). *Authorship Puzzles in the History of Economics*. London: Macmillan.

Pike, D. (1957) *Paradise of Dissent. South Australia 1829–1857*. London: Longmans.

Rauner, R.M. (1956). *Samuel Bailey and Classical Economics*, Ph.D. thesis, University of London.

———. (1961). *Samuel Bailey and the Classical Theory of Value*. London: G. Bell.

Rima, I.H. (1975). "James Mill and Classical Economics: A Reappraisal." *Eastern Economic Journal* 2:113–118.

Robbins, Lord. (1932). *An Essay on the Nature and Significance of Economic Science*, 3rd ed. (1984). London: Macmillan.

———. (1952). *The Theory of Economic Policy in English Classical Political Economy*. London: Macmillan.

———. (1958a). *Robert Torrens and the Evolution of Classical Economics*. London: Macmillan.

———. (1958b). Introduction to R. Torrens. *Letters on Commercial Policy*. London: London School of Economics.

———. (1976). *Political Economy: Past and Present*. London: Macmillan.

Samuels, W. J. (1966). *The Classical Theory of Economic Policy*. Cleveland: World Publishing.

Schoorl, E. (1979). "J.B. Say in the Midlands, 1814." *History of Economic Thought Newsletter* 23:11.

Schumpeter, J. A. (1954). *History of Economic Analysis*. London: Allen & Unwin.

Seligman, E. R. A. (1903). "On Some Neglected British Economists." *Economic Journal* 13:335–363, 511–535.

———. (1911). "Ricardo and Torrens." *Economic Journal* 21:448–455.

Shoup, C. S. (1960). *Ricardo on Taxation*. New York: Columbia University Press.

Skinner, A. S. (1967). "Say's Law: Origins and Content." *Economica* 34:153–166.

Smith, J. G. (1935). "Some Nineteenth Century Irish Economists." *Economica* N.S. 2:20–32.

Sowell, T. (1963). "The General Glut Controversy Reconsidered." *Oxford Economic Papers* 15:193–203.

———. (1970). "Samuel Bailey revisited." *Economica* N.S. 37:402–408.

———. (1972). *Say's Law. An Historical Analysis*. Princeton: Princeton University Press.

———. (1974). *Classical Economics Reconsidered*. Princeton: Princeton University Press.

Spengler, J. (1945). "The Physiocrats and Say's Law of Markets." Reprinted (1960) in J. J. Spengler and W. R. Allan (eds.), *Essays in Economic Thought*. Chicago: Rand McNally, pp. 161–214.

Stigler, G. J. (1950). "The Development of Utility Theory. I" *Journal of Political Economy* 58:307–327.

———. (1953). "Sraffa's Ricardo. "*American Economic Review* 43:586–599.

———. (1965). *Essays in the History of Economics*. Chicago: University of Chicago Press.

———. (1976). "The Scientific Uses of Scientific Biography, with Special Reference to J. S. Mill." In J. M. Robson and M. Laine (ed.), *James and John Stuart Mill*. Toronto: University of Toronto Press, pp. 55–66.

Tait, A. C. (1982). "Mountfort Longfield, 1802–84; Economist and Lawyer." *Hermathena* 133:15–28.

Teilhac, E. (1934). "Say, Jean-Baptiste." In E. R. A. Seligman (ed.), *Encyclopaedia of the Social Sciences*, vol. 13. New York: Macmillan, p. 559.

Thweatt, W. O. (1974). "The Digression on Sismondi: by Torrens or McCulloch?" *History of Political Economy* 6:435–453.

———. (1976). "James Mill and the Early Development of Comparative Advantage." *History of Political Economy* 8:207–234.

———. (1977a). "The Law of Markets: Say's, Mill's or...?" (Mimeo).

———. (1977b). "Mr. Smith and the Classics." (Mimeo).

———. (1977c). "Mr. Mill and the Classics." *Journal of Economics* 3:119–122.

———. (1979a). "Early Formulators of Say's Law." *Quarterly Review of Economics and Business* 19:79–96.

————. (1979b). "Adam Smith, James Mill and Ricardian Economics" *Mid-south Journal of Economics* 3:7–19.

————. (1980a). "Torrens, McCulloch and the "Digression on Sismondi: Whose Digression? A Reply." *History of Political Economy* 12:396–411.

————. (1980b). "Baumol and James Mill on "Say's" Law of Markets." *Economica* 47:467–469.

————. (1981). "Lord Robbins on Robert Torrens' The Economists Refuted." *History of Economics Society Bulletin* 3:45–48.

————. (1985). "De Vivo's Neglected Evidence: A Reply." *History of Political Economy* 17:201–202.

Tu, P.N.V. (1969). "The Classical Economists and Education." *Kyklos* 22:691–718.

Vatter, H.G. (1959). "The Malthusian Model of Income Determination and its Contemporary Relevance." *Canadian Journal of Economics* 25:60–64.

Viner, J. (1933). "Longfield, Samuel Mountifort." In E.R.A. Seligman (ed.), *Encyclopaedia of the Social Sciences*, vol. 9. New York: Macmillan, pp. 605–606.

————. (1937). *Studies in the Theory of International Trade*. London: Allen & Unwin.

West, E.G. (1964a). "The Classical Economists on Education." *British Journal of Educational Studies*, reprinted (1970) in *Education and the State*. London: Institute of Economic Affairs, pp. 111–125.

————. (1964b). "Private Versus Public Education, a Classical Dispute." *Journal of Political Economy* reprinted (1971) in A.W. Coats (ed.), *The Classical Economists and Economic Policy*. London: Methuen, pp. 123–143.

Winch, D. (1966). Introduction to *Selected Economic Writings of J. Mill*. Edinburgh: Oliver & Boyd for the Scottish Economic Society.

————. (1965). *Classical Political Economy and Colonies*. London: G. Bell.

Wood, E. (1939). *English Theories of Central Banking Control 1819–1858*. Cambridge, MA: Harvard University Press.

[11]

J. R. McCULLOCH AND THE THEORY OF VALUE*

D. P. O'BRIEN

THERE are several reasons for attempting this study of McCulloch's theory of value.[1] Firstly, the idea seems to have become accepted in some quarters that McCulloch was 'more Ricardian than Ricardo himself'.[2] That this view was at least not entirely correct was made clear by the publication of Mr. Sraffa's great edition of Ricardo.[3] It will be argued here that in fact, as far as the theory of value is concerned, McCulloch was not only not propounding the same theory as Ricardo; he was not even concerned with the same central question.

Secondly, and following from this, the view of McCulloch which has become common, has been a very simplified one although his emphasis on popularity of exposition is partly to blame for this. It has not hitherto been realised that McCulloch's views on the theory of value changed and developed extensively; and a most important change between the 1825 and 1830 edition of his *Principles* has been more or less completely ignored, as have the changes between the first (1828) and second (1838) editions of his notes to the *Wealth of Nations*.

Thirdly, McCulloch was one of the most successful popular economists of his day, and one of the first academic economists.[4] It is surely important to discover what his views were, views propagated in lectures, articles, and books of all kinds including the immensely successful *Commercial Dictionary* and a textbook (his *Principles*) which was probably the standard textbook before the advent of J. S. Mill's *Principles.*

II. THE DEVELOPMENT OF THE THEORY

The development of McCulloch's theory of value has been obscured by his retention of a popular theory of value which made no concessions to analytical refinement, while his 'scientific' theory developed

* I am deeply indebted to Professor R. D. C. Black and Professor M. E. A. Bowley for their helpful comments on this paper.

[1] The author is at present engaged in a comprehensive study of McCulloch.

[2] E. Halevy, *The Growth of Philosophical Radicalism,* trans. Morris, London 1928, p. 343. See also J. H. Hollander, 'The Work and Influence of Ricardo', *American Economic Review Suppt.,* April, 1911, p. 76.

[3] *The Works and Correspondence of David Ricardo,* Cambridge 1951, cited below as *Works.* See Professor Stigler's remarks on this point when reviewing the above work, *American Economic Review,* Sept., 1953, pp. 586-99.

[4] See S. G. Checkland, 'The Advent of Academic Economics in England', *Manchester School,* Vol. 19, Jan., 1951, pp. 43-70. I have examined McCulloch's academic career in detail in work at present unpublished.

continuously. The simple popular theory was a straightforward labour quantity theory of value. But alongside this McCulloch developed a cost of production theory of value in which he recognised and was at pains to solve the problem of capital. The contrast between the two theories is shown in the following exchange between McCulloch and Ricardo. After reading some of the lectures which McCulloch had prepared Ricardo wrote ' You go a little farther than I go in estimating the value of commodities by the quantity of labour required to produce them: you appear to admit of no exception or qualification whatever, whereas I am always willing to allow that some of the variations in the relative value of commodities may be referred to causes distinct from the quantity of labour necessary to produce them '.[5] To this McCulloch replied: ' In order to give any chance of making the subject popular I must pass slightly over some of the more difficult parts '.[6] McCulloch is clear that he is simplifying, and his reason for doing so is most instructive. As a pioneer of popular exposition, he wanted a simplified version of the theory. By assuming away the problem of capital he was able to provide a simplified version. This version[7] he tended to retain while his scientific theory developed. The main concern of this article is to trace the development of the ' scientific ' theory; but it should constantly be borne in mind that McCulloch continued to point to the simplified version as suitable for the ' non-scientific ' reader,[8] and it is this which has led to his being referred to as more Ricardian than Ricardo. In tracing the scientific theory this article will attempt to establish that this charge was less than fair. But it is true that for McCulloch as for Ricardo labour was 93 per cent. of the value of commodities. When examining the economic system as a whole as for instance in the *Principles*, an operation designed as in any textbook to disseminate a particular view of the economic system, it was natural to stress the primacy of labour. The problem of capital could largely be relegated to a limbo for ' scientific ' readers. However, when pressed for a definition of ' price ' taken in isolation, McCulloch clearly felt obliged to be comprehensive and to mention the problem of capital; and in his definitional work in the *Commercial Dictionary* and in his contributions to *Brande's Dictionary*[9] he used a definition of price which included both labour and capital.

[5] Letter of 19th March, 1822, *Works*, Vol. IX, p. 178.

[6] Letter of 17th April, 1822, ibid., p. 185.

[7] It seems fair to date the appearance of this version from McCulloch's *Scotsman* review of Ricardo (3rd May, 1817). See below, p. 334.

[8] As late as 1849 McCulloch still wrote of the chapter 'Effect of the Employment of Capital in Production and of Variations in the Rate of Wages and Profits on Value'; 'Being principally . . . intended for the use of the scientific reader, it may, without impropriety, be passed over by others'. *Principles*, 4th edition, Edinburgh and London 1849, p. 352.

[9] See below, p. 349.

McCulloch's theory of value received three general statements. The first is to be found in the article 'Political Economy' in the Supplement to the 4-6th editions of *Encyclopaedia Britannica*,[10] the second is in the 1825 edition of McCulloch's *Principles*,[11] and the third is in the 1830 edition of that work. Finally in the second (1838) edition of his version of Smith's *Wealth of Nations* McCulloch produced his most satisfactory statement. All of these expositions contain as a first approximation the popular theory; and together with it the qualifications to produce the 'scientific' one. Each will be dealt with separately for, as will be shown, none contains quite the same analysis. But before examining each of them we must briefly examine the debates which led to them.

(i) THE DEBATE TO 1823

The Encyclopaedia statement was the result of six years' discussion and writing. McCulloch's first contribution to the subject had been in a review of Ricardo's *Principles* in the *Scotsman*.[12] In this, not only did he appear to misunderstand Ricardo, but he seemed to believe that Ricardo held a pain cost theory of value.[13] The question of capital was ignored although McCulloch was no doubt aware of the problem and when he defended Ricardo against the strictures of the *British Review*[14] he made it clear that he accepted that employment of capitals of differing degrees of durability would cause changes in relative value following a wage rise,[15] thus accepting that something other than a change in relative labour content could alter values.

Two things should be noted at this stage. Firstly, McCulloch has nowhere mentioned the invariable measure. Despite the central im-

[10] Usually dated 1824 as appearing in the Supplement to the 4-6th editions of *Encyclopaedia Britannica* but first appearing as an article in the Supplement to the 4-5th editions and dated April, 1823. The article is stated by McCulloch to have been written in January, 1823 (*Encyclopaedia*, p. 356).

[11] The first edition. The later editions were in 1830, 1843, 1848, and 1864.

[12] *Scotsman*, 3rd May, 1817, pp. 119-120; 'Literature, On the Principles of Political Economy and Taxation by David Ricardo, Esq.'

[13] '. . . Mr. Ricardo has set out from the same premises with Dr. Smith. "The real price of everything" says that great writer "[. . .] is the toil and trouble of acquiring it. What everything is really worth to the man who has acquired it, and who wants to dispose of it, or exchange it for something else, is the toil and trouble which it can save himself, and which it can impose upon other people".' Ibid.

[14] *Scotsman*, 15th November, 1817, p. 343, 'Mr. Ricardo and the British Review'.

[15] Henceforth referred to as 'the wage/durability of capital theorem'. McCulloch's acceptance of this point was consistent and continuous. In the interests of brevity therefore it is not specifically mentioned in the consideration of each of McCulloch's discussions of value, being taken as datum.

portance of this to Ricardo,[16] it did not concern McCulloch who was solely interested in the far more obvious and immediate problem of the simple determinants of exchangeable value, not the discovery of the origins of changes in that value. To avoid misunderstanding it should perhaps be said that it is not asserted here that Ricardo's *sole* interest in the theory of value was in relation to the invariable measure. All that is contended is that the peculiar character of Ricardo's theory of distribution made the invariable measure his main preoccupation in value analysis; and in this he can fairly be contrasted with McCulloch who was not at all interested in the invariable measure. Secondly, despite McCulloch's later verbal gymnastics, the importance of capital is clearly recognised.

But in his *Edinburgh* review[17] of Ricardo's *Principles* he put forward a version of Ricardo's theory of long run exchangeable value which presented it as a simple modification of Smith's position. The invariable measure is not mentioned. 'Demand and Supply' effects are banished to the short run and neither profit nor rent is price determining. Profit, as distinct from an amortisation charge, is recognised[18] but, because time is dismissed as without influence on value,[19] profit does not affect value, merely varying inversely with wages. Such a position, it need hardly be added, was inconsistent with his recognition[20] of the wage/durability of capital theorem.

The basic constituents of value as envisaged by McCulloch were then payments to direct and indirect labour (wages and amortisation) *added together*. This is important because McCulloch became thoroughly confused over this point in his public debate arranged[21] with Robert Torrens. The confusion has been dissected with great clarity elsewhere[22] and nothing needs to be added; McCulloch simply

[16] See Mr. Sraffa's masterly introduction to volume I of his edition of Ricardo and chapter 2 of Dr. Blaug's important study *Ricardian Economics* (New Haven, 1958). See also Professor Knight's famous article, 'The Ricardian Theory of Production and Distribution', *Canadian Journal of Economics and Political Science*, Vol. I, February and May 1935, pp. 3-25 and 171-96, especially pp. 176-7n. See also J. M. Cassells, 'A Re-interpretation of Ricardo on Value', *Quarterly Journal of Economics*, May, 1935, pp. 518-32.

[17] 'Ricardo's *Political Economy*', *Edinburgh Review*, Vol. XXX, September 1818, pp. 59-87.

[18] Even distinguished critics have accused McCulloch of confusing profits and amortisation (see e.g. O. St. Clair, *A Key to Ricardo*, London 1957, p. 27). Although his later writings may have led to this view he in fact described profit here as 'remuneration for the use of capital' (loc. cit., p. 66) which was different from payments to the labour embodied in the capital (ibid.).

[19] He reduced the two days' 'rude' labour to one hour's skilled, ignoring the question of the time (two days instead of one hour) required to bring the product to market. He was following Smith's mistake here.

[20] Both in this review (pp. 68-70) and in the *Scotsman*.

[21] See Ricardo's *Works*, Vol. VII, pp. 313 ff.

[22] L. Robbins, *Robert Torrens and the Evolution of Classical Economics* (London 1958), pp. 60-67 and pp. 277-8.

failed to see that Torrens counted only accumulated labour[23] and that this gave a different result from his own position.[24] What does not seem to have been pointed out by commentators on McCulloch is that he remained confused over this for some years.[25]

Though he continued to correspond with Ricardo[26] he took no part in Ricardo's debate with Malthus over the invariable measure. But in the course of the correspondence he put forward what has become known as McCulloch's position over the question of profit and the increase in value resulting from the maturing of wine.[27] His solution which seems to have become known as the 'labour [embodied in capital] -goes-on-working' explanation was simply to call natural processes such as fermentation which had to be 'set in motion' by the application of (accumulated) labour, 'labour' themselves. McCulloch refers to 'the mistaken hypothesis that it is required in your [Ricardo's] theory that labour should be applied by the instrumentality of workmen; while it is altogether immaterial, provided the quantities be the same, whether it is by human hands, by machines for making beef, or by the action of natural juices such as fermentation'.[28] This was not a solution with which McCulloch was entirely happy; and it was based on a confusion the nature of which will be examined below. It was interred prior to the Encyclopaedia article but was exhumed again for the 1825 *Principles.*

The debate continued. McCulloch's review of Malthus' *Principles*[29] added nothing new; nor did his review of Say's *Traité*.[30] The problem

[23] Torrens' position was that as rates of profit could be assumed to be equal the products of equal capitals were of equal value—he propounded a 'Capital theory of value' and thus took account only of accumulated labour.

[24] He also declared that Ricardo had not put forward the wage/durability of capital theorem. But see above and note 20.

[25] It is noteworthy that James Mill was also confused on this point. In the first edition of his *Elements* (1821) he ignored the problem of the maturing of wine and indeed produced a theory which was effectively the same as Torrens' (although he failed to stipulate in this connection that profits were equal and that the residue of capital had to be taken into account). It is interesting that Mill seems to have taken virtually no part in the debate round Ricardo on value. Professor Stigler ('Sraffa's Ricardo', *American Economic Review,* Vol. 43, 1953, pp. 586-99, pp. 590-1) has raised some pertinent doubts about the usual role afforded to Mill.

[26] See, for instance, *Works,* Vol. VII, pp. 351 ff., especially p. 354. From this it is clear that he still did not appreciate Torrens' position. Ricardo corrected him over his acceptance of the wage/durability of capital theorem. See *Works,* Vol. VII, p. 337.

[27] *Works,* Vol. VIII, p. 137. This letter also shows him to have remained confused over Torrens.

[28] Ibid. It is worth emphasising that the date of this letter is December, 1819, in view of the statement by no less an authority than Dr. Blaug (op. cit., p. 49) that McCulloch did not put forward this solution until 1823, in the *Encyclopaedia* article (in which in fact it did not appear).

[29] *Scotsman,* 29th April, 1820, p. 143.

[30] Prinsep's translation, *Scotsman,* 21st April, 1821, p. 126.

of capital both Ricardo and McCulloch had in common[31]; but Ricardo was as confused over this as McCulloch, and although he considered the influence of time on value important, he failed to give any reason for this. That was unfortunate because the resulting discussion between Ricardo and McCulloch seems to have been based on a confusion between necessary and sufficient conditions.

In the simple model with which they were concerned, two conditions were necessary for profit as a rate of interest (which is largely how it was treated in the discussion) to emerge. Firstly ' waiting ' had to involve a real cost for which compensation had to be paid—Ricardo saw this point clearly enough but seemed to think that it was not only a necessary but a sufficient condition.[32] McCulloch on the other hand saw that no premium could or would be paid unless waiting was productive; but he thought that productivity was both a necessary and a sufficient condition for such a premium.[33] This problem was to continue to dog McCulloch's value theory.

McCulloch's other confusion, over the meaning of Torrens' position was again revealed when in 1821 Torrens published his *Essay on the Production of Wealth.*[34] When McCulloch reviewed the work in the *Scotsman*[35] he appeared to accept Torrens' position. ' The quantity of capital which set these agents [mason's labour and wine fermentation] in motion was in both cases exactly the same; and consequently both products were brought into existence by the same quantity of labour.'[36] This seems to be nothing more than Torrens' capital theory of value.[37] Yet, as will be seen, he had not renounced his former posi-

[31] E.g. *Works,* letter 368. Ricardo was also still concerned with the measure, (e.g. letter 362) which McCulloch (despite letter 372) ignored.

[32] ' Profits again cease to have anything to do with the productive power of capital ', Cannan aptly remarked. *A History of the Theories of Production and Distribution in English Political Economy from 1776 to 1848,* second edition, London, 1903, p. 206.

[33] It must be emphasised that this argument about necessary and sufficient conditions is intended to apply only to the model under discussion between McCulloch and Ricardo. It is recognised that Fisher's ' Impatience ' may by itself produce a premium, where it is possible for an individual to modify his income stream by way of consumption loans. But Ricardo and McCulloch were in their discussions envisaging the case of modifying the income stream through productive investment. In this case ' Impatience ' and ' Investment opportunity ' have to work together to produce a premium. G. Arvidsson's view that Bohm-Bawerk's third ground is sufficient to produce a premium, seems to rest on a misunderstanding of what ' Impatience ' embraces. (See ' On the Reasons for a Rate of Interest ', *Economisk Tidskrift,* March, 1953, reprinted in *International Economic Papers,* No. 6, 1956.)

[34] *An Essay on the Production of Wealth with an Appendix in which the Principles of Political Economy are applied to the Actual Circumstances of this Country.* London, 1821.

[35] 22nd December, 1821, pp. 406-7.

[36] *Scotsman,* loc. cit.

[37] Subject to the problem of the residue of capital and the equality of profits where he was as unsatisfactory as James Mill (see above note 25).

tion of *adding* direct and indirect labour. He was now in the unhappy position of holding two theories of value at once.

But McCulloch now to some extent clarified his main theory. He contributed two articles to the *Scotsman*[38] entitled ' Cost of Production the regulating Principle of Price '. In these he made it clear that by cost of production he meant that of the marginal unit[39] produced at either the extensive or the intensive margin; for he referred to price falling to ' such a sum as would just yield the average rate of profit to the cultivators of the worst soils, or the improver of the best '.[40] The discussion was primarily agricultural[41] but McCulloch finally generalised his position: ' the ever-acting *principle of competition*[42] will, wherever industry is free and unshackled, always ensure a supply of articles, whose quantity can be indefinitely increased by the expenditure of additional capital and labour, at the very lowest price that will suffice to cover the expense necessary to produce the quantity required '.[43] He seems moreover to have appreciated that the role of demand (in selecting *which* was to be the marginal unit) could not be ignored and that the assumption of constant costs (the only possible way of ignoring demand) would hardly be consistent with the Ricardian view of agricultural progress. In saying *' no variation of demand, if it be unaccompanied by a variation in the cost of production, can have any lasting influence on prices '*[44] and saying that rent was paid ' because the demand is such that it cannot be supplied without cultivating soils of a diminished degree of fertility, as com-

[38] 8th June, 1822, p. 182, and 27th June, 1822, p. 207.

[39] Perhaps one should be careful about this particular point. It is perfectly true as pointed out by a succession of critics that Ricardo and those associated with him talked of Diminishing Returns in its proportionate form, relating to average product, rather than its incremental form relating to marginal product. But Professor Stigler has shown (*Production and Distribution Theories,* New York, 1941, pp. 112 ff.) that it was not until Edgeworth that the difference was made clear. Certainly McCulloch's words, in the articles referred to, imply the cost of the last *unit* produced.

[40] *Scotsman,* 8th June, 1822. Ricardo also took this position—see *Works,* Vol. I, p. 73. See also O. St. Clair, op. cit., pp. 54-5.

[41] Because of the dispute which had occasioned it—see *Works,* Vol. IX, p. 206, n. 1.

[42] McCulloch's italics.

[43] *Scotsman,* loc. cit.

[44] *Scotsman,* 8th June, 1822, McCulloch's italics. See also his article ' Political Economy ' in the supplement to the 4-6th editions of *Encyclopaedia Britannica,* p. 257.

pared with the best '[45] he made it clear that he recognised the role of demand in selecting the marginal unit.[46]

(ii) THE ENCYCLOPAEDIA

Despite the clarification the treatment of value in the *Encyclopaedia* is far from satisfactory. McCulloch purported to show in the tradition of Locke and Hobbes, to both of whom he referred, that labour was the only scarce factor and hence the only source of wealth. By labour he seems not to mean simply hours of labour but actual disutility involved,[47] a position which would follow from his original interpretation of Ricardo in 1817. Once this is understood the reason for his attempts to generalise the term ' labour '[48] becomes clear. He was trying to produce a Real Cost theory of value.

The explanation of value in the section *Distribution* in the article then follows from this, and McCulloch is concerned to explain the determination of exchange value by relative labour cost. The treatment is fairly predictable up to a point. The capital-less early stage of society is passed through, and demand and supply dismissed as short-run phenomena. Cost of production is then the main concern in an advanced society and this has to be reduced to labour. Rent is dismissed as price determined not price determining[49] and this leaves

[45] *Scotsman*, 27th June, 1822.

[46] It seems clear that the role of demand was widely recognised amongst the Classical economists. On this see V. E. Smith 'The Classicists' Use of Demand '. *Journal of Political Economy*, Vol. 59, 1951, pp. 242-57. Lord Robbins and Professor Viner in their reviews of Schumpeter's *History of Economic Analysis* (*Quarterly Journal of Economics*, Vol. 69, 1955, pp. 13-14 and *American Economic Review*, Vol. 44, 1954, p. 905) have drawn attention to Ricardo's recognition of demand and Professor Viner has made the telling point that: ". . . it was semantically unfortunate that it later on became common to use the same term " demand " (and correspondingly for " supply ") both for *the* quantity that would *actually* be taken in a given historical market at a given *actual* price in a given *actual* moment of time and for " that highly abstract creation of the observer's mind " the long run normal demand function '. (loc. cit. p. 905).

[47] For instance he quotes a passage referring to value being created by ' the ploughman's pains, the reaper's and the thresher's toil, and the baker's sweat ' (p. 236).

[48] As distinct from his *ignoring* the problem of capital altogether in his simplified theory.

[49] Professor Samuelson has attempted to show (' A Modern Treatment of the Ricardian Economy I. The pricing of goods and of labour and land services '. *Quarterly Journal of Economics*, Vol. 73, February, 1959, pp. 1-35) that it is illegitimate to eliminate rent as a cost by going to the margin. However, this is only true once one allows for commodity substitution so that transfer earnings of land enter into price as a determinant; as pointed out by Dr. Pasinetti (' A Mathematical Formulation of the Ricardian System '. *Review of Economic Studies*, Vol. 27, 1960, p. 90, n. 1) the Ricardian model did not allow for commodity substitution—the workers' ' corn ' was a basket of goods in fixed proportion. The point at issue was in fact made clear in a number of previous publications—see especially D. H. Buchanan ' The Historical Approach to Rent and Price Theory ', *Economica*, 1929, pp. 123 ff.

only the question of capital. Its amortisation presented no problem since it was viewed as accumulated labour. But the problem of profits McCulloch entirely failed to solve on this occasion, referring to them as the 'wages of accumulated labour',[50] as if confusing them with amortisation. He did not even introduce his 'Labour goes on working' argument here,[51] although he again made clear that, popular exposition apart, he accepted the wage/durability of capital theorem[52] and hence that capital was a problem which had to be solved. But it is made clear to the reader that for general purposes this was not an important problem.[53]

To produce a real cost theory of value might or might not have required the reduction of all cost to labour cost. But it certainly did require that labour cost should be equated with pain cost or disutility of labour. To follow a point made by Professor Viner in his review of Cannan's *Review of Economic Theory*[54] relative quantities of labour in different commodities can only mean to the classical economists relative quantities of wages since this was the only method of reducing skilled labour to its 'rude' equivalent.

Yet in McCulloch's system wages are largely not determined by disutility schedules. They are determined in the short run by market forces (the wage fund theory) and in the long run by the minimum level of subsistence, whether physical or psychological (natural wages). The long run would (in view of the nature of the dismissal of demand and supply) seem to be the main concern,[55] and the difference between a natural wage theory and a disutility theory is obvious.[56] But not all reflection of disutilities in wages is ruled out. The analysis did allow for disutilities to make themselves felt in determining relative wages (through the equalisation of net advantages).[57] But the payment for labour which was the major cost constituent was that which satisfied the needs of a labour force working a fixed number of hours. To summarise the argument, if two commodities in McCulloch's system have different values, the payments will represent different amounts of

[50] *Encyclopaedia*, p. 263.

[51] This is important to note because the equation of the *Encyclopaedia* article and the *Principles* by some of the best known commentators (e.g. Blaug, op. cit., p. 49) has obscured the evolution which was in progress.

[52] *Encyclopaedia*, pp. 264-7.

[53] See the quotation from Ricardo, ibid., p. 267.

[54] Reprinted in *The Long View and the Short*. Glencoe, Illinois, 1958, p. 400.

[55] See the *Encyclopaedia*, p. 269.

[56] See Marshall's *Principles* (8th edition) p. 339, n. 1 and G. J. Stigler *Production and Distribution Theories*, pp. 64-5.

[57] A further (unexplored) possibility might have been to find some tenuous connection between a psychological subsistence level and wage payments for disutility.

labour kept alive by subsistence wages, not different numbers of man hours worked by men lured from leisure by high wages.[58]

McCulloch's attempt cannot be saved by asserting that if commodities exchange for each other in relation to the amount of labour time embodied in them, they are exchanging in relation to the amount of 'real cost' embodied in them. For this is to use 'real cost' synonymously with hours of labour. This is not permissible without assuming a great deal more than McCulloch did. We should have to assume identical disutility schedules, and, to avoid difficulties over the relative worth of commodities made in the first and last hour of work, constant disutility of labour. Moreover, McCulloch was to arrive at a proper cost of production theory of value. He did not believe, finally, except for purposes of popular exposition, that commodities exchanged simply in relation to relative quantities of labour. Once a cost of production theory replaces a labour quantity theory, the labour content *has* to be represented by total wage payments. But it has already been emphasised that wage payments do not, in McCulloch's scheme, represent real costs.

McCulloch had failed to explain profits, and he had failed to make cost *real* cost, although what remained still approximated to a cost of production theory of value. But McCulloch also failed to rid himself of the confusion over Torrens' analysis; and having accepted Torrens' position[59] he then accused the latter of differing by doing what he himself had done earlier in adding direct and indirect labour. Further debate was bound to follow.

(iii) THE BREAK WITH RICARDO AND BAILEY'S ATTACK

McCulloch added nothing to the Ricardo-Malthus measure dispute[60] but in May 1823 he visited London and the debates took place which have been immortalised by Mrs. Grote's letter.[61] It is clear from this that McCulloch's mind was far from made up.[62] Yet much of the verbal debate must have been at cross-purposes; for Ricardo at least believed that he, McCulloch and Malthus were *all* seeking an invariable measure.[63] He must then have been somewhat

[58] Possibly this was a result of the Classical Economists' general tendency not to envisage relationships in the sort of functional form to which we have become accustomed—cf. the quotation from Viner, note 46.

[59] *Encyclopaedia*, p. 268.

[60] *Works*, Vol. IX, pp. 280, 289 and 297.

[61] Reprinted in George Grote's *Posthumous Papers*, ed. Mrs. Grote (London, 1874), p. 25, and quoted in Ricardo's *Works*, ed. Sraffa, pp. 301-2n.

[62] After an hour and a half's discussion the meeting is reported to have been closed by McCulloch with the words: 'Wall, I think the *quastion* must be *soobjacted* to a more *sevear anallasis* before we shall arrive at a definitive conclusion'. Ibid.

[63] *Works*, Vol. IX, pp. 303 ff. See also pp. 311 ff. especially p. 312.

shaken by McCulloch's letter of 11th August.[64] Having dealt with the problem of the increase in value of a growing oak tree which Ricardo had raised once again[65] in terms of his argument that natural processes should be called labour, he turned to the invariable measure. His rejection was complete and explicit. 'There is a radical and essential difference' he wrote, 'between the circumstances which determine the exchangeable value of commodities, and a measure of that value, which I am afraid is not always kept sufficiently in view. . . . It is evident I think that there neither is nor can be any real and invariable standard of value; and if so it must be very idle to seek for that which can never be found. The real inquiry is to ascertain what are the circumstances which determine the exchangeable value of commodities at any given period—and these I think are all clearly reducible to one—the comparative quantities of labour bestowed on their production. If we establish this proposition we shall make the subject as plain as it ever can be made, and will at once put to rest the objections of Malthus, Torrens, and so forth; but if we fail in this the subject will always be encumbered with difficulties.'[66] This surely is a plain enough declaration of McCulloch's sole interest in exchangeable value, to which he was still trying to make labour the key.

He had still to solve the problem of profit; but at least there was substance in his objection to Ricardo's argument that profit was a payment for time: that time without productivity was valueless.[67] His verbal expedient did not satisfy Ricardo[68] who kept returning to the problem of a measure which McCulloch *again* explicitly rejected. '. . . this is no part of my object—I am only endeavouring to ascertain the circumstances which determine the comparative values of the commodities in the same market—The question agitated between you and Malthus is totally different—it is, what are the circumstances necessary to give invariability of value to any commodity—This is a question which I believe is quite insoluble, but at any rate it does not come within the scope of my enquiries.'[69] The grounds for believing that McCulloch misunderstood Ricardo do not seem strong.

Moreover, he maintained his own position over profits. 'Now I think that profit is not a compensation for time, but a positive additional

[64] Ibid., pp. 342 ff.

[65] Ibid., pp. 330 ff.

[66] *Works,* Vol. IX, pp. 344-5. McCulloch used very similar words when rejecting the Measure just as unequivocally in the *Scotsman* article of 21st February, 1824, cited below.

[67] Ibid.

[68] Ibid., pp. 353 ff. and pp. 358 ff.

[69] *Works,* Vol. IX, p. 369.

value; and I think so for the reason that if I keep a cask of wine a twelvemonth in which an effect is to be produced I shall get a profit; whereas were I to keep a cask which had already arrived at maturity . . . for a hundred years I should get no profit whatever.'[70]

It is quite possible that he never saw the paper on Absolute and Exchangeable Value for although he knew of the existence of MSS. of Ricardo's[71] he was assured by Mill that they were of no interest.[72] But had he seen it it would probably not have altered his position. Firstly he was already clear about the differences between himself and Ricardo;[73] secondly he was quite happy to use Ricardo's name as an endorsement for his 'popular' simplified theory. For in his second[74] *Scotsman* obituary of Ricardo he used the latter's name as an endorsement for a simple labour theory of exchange value, an endorsement which he repeated the same year in the *Edinburgh Annual Register.*[75] It is difficult to accept, in the light of the original appearance of this so shortly after the disagreement with Ricardo, that any misunderstanding was involved. McCulloch went so far as to write 'The fundamental principle maintained by Mr. Ricardo in his great work [the *Principles*], is, that the exchangeable value or relative worth of commodities, as compared with each other, depends exclusively on the *quantity of labour necessarily expended in their production*'[76] He is here baldly asserting that a simple labour cost theory of value is Ricardo's *main* thesis. This, in the light of the correspondence referred to above (especially the letter of 24th August, 1823)[77] it is doubtful whether he believed; and he is also asserting that Ricardo held a *simple* labour cost theory of exchange value. This he knew perfectly well was not true.[78] But for an exposition such as this, intended to make a popular impact, the weight of Ricardo's name was clearly invaluable.

[70] Ibid., p. 367.

[71] See *Scotsman,* 6th December, 1823, p. 777. See also *Works,* Vol. IV, p. 358 n. 1.

[72] Letter in University of London Library, M.S.A.L. 187, 10th January, 1824.

[73] See *Works,* Vol. IV, pp. 410-12, for Ricardo's view of these differences in the paper referred to.

[74] 'Works and Character of Mr. Ricardo', *Scotsman,* 6th December, 1823, p. 777. The first and relatively well known one, *Mr. Ricardo,* 17th September, 1823, was reprinted in the *Morning Chronicle,* 23rd September, 1823.

[75] *Edinburgh Annual Register,* 1823, p. 398. See Ricardo's *Works,* ed. McCulloch, London, 1846, pp. XXIII-XXIV, for a very similar wording and McCulloch's *Catalogue* (1862 edition), p. 289.

[76] *Edinburgh Annual Register,* 1823, p. 398. Italics in original.

[77] *Works,* Vol. IX, p. 369.

[78] See the letter of 19th March, 1822, in *Works,* Vol. IX, p. 178, referred to above.

Neither Malthus nor De Quincey nor Mill[79] added much to the debate at this stage. But then in 1825 Samuel Bailey published his *Dissertation.*[80] This famous onslaught might have been expected to have a significant impact on McCulloch. But for a number of reasons it did not. Firstly, his main fire was directed against the invariable measure; McCulloch was with him here.[81] Then again much of his analysis was devoted to working out the implications of a completely different set of assumptions.[82] He devoted much of his criticism to Ricardo's verbal inexactness,[83] and he accepted that relative costs of production determined value.[84] He had no demand theory proper and he solved the 'diamonds and water' paradox by simply *ignoring* value in use.

Finally John Craig[85] and the author of the pamphlet *Observations on Certain Verbal Disputes*[86] had made many similar criticisms already, and McCulloch knew of and disagreed with most if not all of these views.[87] That Bailey made little impact on McCulloch is clear from the continuity between an article which McCulloch published in the *Scotsman*[88] in 1824 on exchangeable value, and the position which he took in the first edition of his *Principles.* In the *Scotsman* he expressed explicit disagreement with Ricardo over the effect of time, a disagreement based on the confusion which has already been examined, and again solved the problem of profit by calling processes such as fermentation 'labour' on the grounds already noted. It is interesting that he believed himself to have produced a

[79] Malthus in his review of the *Encyclopaedia* article misunderstood McCulloch—see *Occasional Papers of T. R. Malthus,* ed. B. Semmel, New York, 1963, pp. 171-208. De Quincey, for instance, not only rejected the invariable measure but credited Ricardo with doing the same—*Dialogues of Three Templars* in *Works,* ed. Masson, Vol. IX, pp. 92-4. Mill followed McCulloch into his version of the confusion between necessary and sufficient conditions, in the second edition of his *Elements.*

[80] *A Critical Dissertation on the Nature, Measure and Causes of Value; Chiefly in Reference to the Writings of Mr. Ricardo and his followers.* London, L.S.E. reprint, 1931.

[81] See McCulloch's *Principles* (1st edition), p. 214, and corresponding passages in all the four subsequent editions.

[82] It is a little difficult to accept entirely Dr. Rauner's position over this in his important study *Samuel Bailey and the Classical Theory of Value,* London, 1961, e.g. pp. 93-5.

[83] See K. Marx *Theories of Surplus Value,* ed. Kautsky, trans. Bonner and Burns, London, 1951, p. 210.

[84] Bailey, op. cit., pp. 183 ff. especially p. 205.

[85] *Remarks on Some Fundamental Doctrines in Political Economy Illustrated by a Brief Inquiry into the Commercial State of Britain since the year 1815.* Edinburgh, 1821.

[86] *Observations on Certain Verbal Disputes in Political Economy particularly relating to Value and to Demand and Supply.*

[87] He may not have known of the *Observations,* particularly since he credited Bailey with destroying the Invariable Measure.

[88] 1st February, 1824. 'Principles which determine the Exchangeable Value of Commodities and the Rate of Profit'.

theory of value superior to Ricardo's.[89] Certainly he did not believe that their theories were the same; and once again he rejected the measure of value as the philosopher's stone.

(iv) THE 1825 *Principles*

In the *Principles* the key role is again given to labour and again there is the failure to realise that pain cost is not reflected in remuneration. The chapter following the historical sketch is identical[90] with the corresponding section in the *Encyclopaedia*[91] and Locke is again cited as giving a statement of the primacy of labour which is even possibly superior to Smith's.[92] Part III the *Distribution of Wealth* contains a more elaborate treatment than before. As previously it is explained that Cost of Production is the regulating principle of price[93] and much of the argument reduces to the now familiar proposition that given freedom of entry, supernormal profits could not be earned in the long run, a proposition which hardly amounted to a theory of value. But there is a much greater stress than before on the distinction between Real and Exchangeable Value.[94] It was not a simple carry-over from Ricardo's distinction between absolute and exchangeable value; this, being related to the invariable measure problem, did not interest McCulloch. The intention of the analysis seems to have been to demonstrate that commodities' exchangeable value tended to reflect their cost or real value which in turn reflected the labour, i.e. disutility, involved in the appropriation. He explicitly rejected the idea of an invariable measure, citing Bailey's critique in support,[95] and propagated a simple cost theory of value; but the cost was meant to be real cost. Demand was a necessary pre-requisite before a commodity would have toil and trouble expended on its production; but from then on it was the quantity 'as Dr. Smith has termed it, of *toil and trouble*'[96] that mattered. 'But however the same quantity of labour may be laid out, and whatever may be the amount of its produce, its performance must unavoidably occasion

[89] 'In so far as the law of profits is concerned this theory is in its *result* quite the same as that of Mr. Ricardo; but the method of investigation we have pursued has led us to this result in a much more simple and direct manner, and without engaging us in the enquiry respecting the effects of that rise of wages which is caused by the increased value acquired by raw produce in the progress of society.' Ibid.

[90] Except for the removal of one paragraph (*Encyclopaedia*, p. 235, col. 2).

[91] *Encyclopaedia*, pp. 234-7.

[92] Ibid., p. 236 n. *Principles*, p. 69 n.

[93] *Encyclopaedia*, pp. 255-8, *Principles*, pp. 248-61.

[94] *Principles*, pp. 211-27.

[95] *Principles*, pp. 213-14.

[96] Ibid., p. 215. McCulloch's italics.

the *same sacrifice*[97] to those by whom it is performed; and hence it is plain, that the products of equal quantities of labour, or of toil and trouble, must, however much they may differ in magnitude, always be of precisely the same real value.'[98] Such a proposition his theory of wages would not, as already seen, permit him to establish. This meant in turn that his theory could only be treated as a simple cost of production theory of value. But, given his continued recognition of the wage/durability of capital theorem[99] there remained the problem of reducing all cost to labour cost, and of the role of demand. Enough has already been said about the latter. His treatment of the former problem is important, and different from that in the Encyclopaedia. For he now made fully public[100] his disagreement with Ricardo over the question of time and profits, and in contrast with the *Encyclopaedia* article he reverted to his position of calling natural processes 'labour' on the ground already discussed.[101] He was still not free of his confusion over Torrens[102] but most of the discussion was concerned with his verbal expedient over profits (in referring to the activity of natural agents as labour) which, however, did not save his theory. For it still did not explain why the activity of natural agents, under any name, should result in increased value; and indeed in an earlier part of his work, in the chapter explaining that labour was the only source of value, McCulloch had accepted the view that natural agents were not productive of value.[103] But at least he could no longer be charged with confusing profits and amortisation; and he went on to speak of the 'common and ordinary rate of profit . . . exclusive of a sum to replace the wear and tear of the machines'.[104] He had now achieved a cost of production theory of value and it was the deficiencies in this which remained to be removed.

[97] McCulloch's italics.

[98] Ibid., p. 217. It should be noted that he is not using 'real value' in Smith's sense which Dr. Blaug has aptly named 'esteem value' (*Economic Theory in Retrospect*, London, 1961, p. 49), but in his own sense of the cost underlying exchangeable value.

[99] Ibid., pp. 298-312.

[100] The circulation of the *Scotsman* in which this disagreement had first been aired was almost entirely confined to Edinburgh and the article was anonymous.

[101] It should perhaps be emphasised, since a distinguished authority (Blaug, op. cit., p. 49) has stated that this was McCulloch's final solution, that there was much change to come.

[102] *Principles*, p. 316; contrast with ibid., pp. 288-9 where direct and indirect labour are added. He later (p. 319) tried to reconcile the two by calling a man 'capital'.

[103] If something 'is the free gift of nature, it is impossible it can be possessed of the smallest value'. Ibid., pp. 69-70.

[104] Ibid., p. 319.

(V) NEW ATTACKS, AND THE *Wealth of Nations*

The only significant[105] attack came from Malthus in his *Definitions.*[106] While he failed to correct McCulloch's confusion between necessary and sufficient conditions, and to grasp the latter's point about the necessity of productivity, he did draw attention to McCulloch's mutually contradictory treatment of natural agents.[107] McCulloch reviewed the work in the *Scotsman*[108] in a manner which must confirm the view that he was a very poor controversialist.[109] This was not important. But when he published the first edition of his *Wealth of Nations* in 1828, some improvement was apparent. For although he dismissed time as unproductive, citing the case of wine which was already mature, Malthus had so far forced him to modify his position that he now attributed the increase in value following e.g. fermentation not to natural agents but to the 'amount of capital wasted' (amortisation) during the process.[110] He was now subject to attack from another quarter, that of Samuel Reed,[111] but since his old enemy disavowed Bailey and claimed to be returning to Smith, his work may not have seemed very important to McCulloch. But his complaint about the lack of definition of profit[112] may have been responsible for McCulloch's care over this in the second edition of his *Principles.*[113]

(vi) MCCULLOCH'S *volte-face*

But the main importance of the second edition of the *Principles* is that it contains a complete *volte-face* (in relation to the first edition) over the question of the origin of profits. It appears to have gone unnoticed; indeed McCulloch told the non-scientific reader that he might pass over the chapter (iv) containing it.[114] Yet it provides

[105] J. Mill (*Elements*, 3rd edition, pp. 102-3) supported McCulloch and Senior (Appendix to Whately's *Elements of Logic*, London, 1826) attacked him, neither very significantly.

[106] *Definitions in Political Economy*, London, 1827, reprinted New York, 1954.

[107] Ibid., p. 105.

[108] 10th March, 1827, p. 153.

[109] Since he admitted that wind was of no commercial value his view that a windmill laboured was difficult to reconcile with a view of labour as the source of value. But he believed his review to be a 'complete demolition' (*Catalogue*, 1862).

[110] Vol. IV, pp. 78-9.

[111] *Political Economy. An Inquiry into the Natural Grounds of Right to Vendible Property or Wealth.* Edinburgh, 1829.

[112] Which, incidentally, was unfounded, since Tooke had already done this in his *State of the Currency*, second edition, London, 1826, p. 12.

[113] Although he does not appear to have owned the book.

[114] *Principles*, 2nd edition, p. 332.

McCulloch with an almost complete cost of production theory, even if the cost is not real cost.[115] The first edition dissent from Ricardo over the question of time has received a good deal of critical comment as has the idea of calling natural agents 'labour'. But its complete replacement by the following appears to have gone unnoticed.

> 'In thus endeavouring,' McCulloch wrote, 'to trace the real value of all descriptions of non-monopolised commodities to the quantity of labour required for their production, it is not meant to deny that a very large portion of the useful or desirable qualities of such commodities may be the result of the action or labour of natural agents. But it is, as I formerly stated, the peculiar and distinguishing feature of natural agents, or powers, that they render their services gratuitously. . . . And hence, though their assistance and co-operation be necessary to the production of every species of useful and desirable articles, they add nothing to its value. . . . It may be thought, perhaps, that this principle is at variance with what is observed to take place in the production of certain descriptions of commodities. Thus, if a cask of new wine be kept for a definite period, or till it arrives at maturity, it will acquire a higher value: now as the change produced on the wine is entirely brought about by the operation of natural agents, and as, without the change, wine would have no higher value, it has been contended that this is a case in which the labour of natural agents is plainly productive of an increased value. But it is easy to see that this is a mistake. The cask of wine is a capital . . . [and] . . . it is necessary, in order to give time for the processes of fermentation, decomposition, &c. to effect the desired changes in the wine, that it should be laid aside until they are completed. The producer of wine would not, however, employ his capital in this way, unless it were to yield him the same return that is derived from the capital employed in other businesses. And hence it follows, that though the processes carried on by nature render the wine more desirable, or bestow on it a greater degree of utility, they add nothing to its value; the additional value which it acquires being a consequence of the profit accruing on the capital required to enable the processes to be carried on'.[116]

McCulloch neglects to mention that it was he who suggested the view in which it is now, five years later, easy to see the fallacy. But

[115] There are also a number of detailed changes which it would be tiresome to enumerate.
[116] *Principles*, 2nd edition, pp. 352-4.

since additional value no longer results from the labour of natural agents but from the accrual of profit on capital,[117] this is a *volte-face.* Unfortunately he had now apparently adopted Ricardo's version of the confusion between necessary and sufficient conditions although he had now also become more obviously aware of the role of capital in value and in his discussion of capital[118] he recognised both productivity and abstinence. Moreover he now shed, though he did not correct, his confusion over Torrens.[119] The analysis presented here remained substantially unchanged in the three final editions of the *Principles,*[120] despite many detailed changes, notably the frequent substitution of 'cost' for 'real value'. He had by now arrived at a (marginal) cost of production theory and the presentation in his 'practical' works followed the 1830 *Principles.* In the various editions of the Commercial Dictionary he included an article 'Price' which contained a long run cost of production theory. Both labour *and* capital (including profit on that capital) are *explicitly* included in costs of production and there is no attempt to reduce capital to accumulated labour, and more prominence is given to demand and supply.[121] The same statement appeared in the various editions of Brande's Dictionary[122] (where, it is worth noting, profit is defined as 'a premium on accumulation').[123] The statements in the seventh and eighth editions of the *Encyclopaedia* were also substantially the same as in the 1830 *Principles.*

But when the 1838 edition of McCulloch's version of the *Wealth of Nations* appeared, there were some important changes from that of 1828. These mainly brought it into uniformity with the 1830 position though making this more explicit—instead of dismissing time as unproductive he allowed for the fact that time was required for the completion of productive change; and this had to result in added value because of waste (amortisation) of capital and locking up of capital (profit). But there was an important improvement over the 1830 *Principles.* McCulloch now removed the apparent confusion between necessary and sufficient conditions. Both waiting *and* produc-

[117] Identified (ibid., pp. 506 ff.) with interest, wages of management, and compensation for non-insurable risk.

[118] Chapter II.

[119] It is worth noting that it was not until now that it was removed.

[120] In the fifth edition there were a number of changes such as the introduction of the rejection of natural agents into a chapter heading.

[121] *A Dictionary of Commerce and Commercial Navigation,* 1840 edition, p. 946. The same statement appeared in all the editions.

[122] *A Dictionary of Science, Literature and Art,* ed. W. T. Brande, e.g. 1853 edition.

[123] Ibid., p. 986.

tivity are now recognised as necessary conditions.[124] This left his cost of production approach in a much more satisfactory position; at least he was much less confused than he has generally been thought to be. Yet misunderstanding his position was even here perfectly natural. For all these developments are contained in a short note defining Labour[125] and the subsequent note on Value[126] proceeds on the basis of the popular theory with only a note[127] referring to the earlier section on labour to indicate that he is not using the term in its lexicographical sense.

III. Conclusion

Ricardo's theory of value, it is generally and reasonably argued, developed as a result of his interest in the debate over the Corn Laws. His aim was to discover changes, in the felicitous phrase of Dr. Mark Blaug, 'in the terms of trade between agriculture and manufacture'.[128] The invariable measure was central to Ricardo's system. It never interested McCulloch at all: it was to him a mere chimera and he wrote of the search for it as had Torrens and Lauderdale[129] as 'entitled to no more respect, and, we believe, will be crowned with no better success, than the search after the philosopher's stone.[130] Like Torrens he had a deep respect for the great minds of economics; and there was no denying the quality of Ricardo's mind. But although Ricardo greatly influenced McCulloch's tone and phraseology, he never even succeeded in interesting the latter in the same problem of value. Though McCulloch paid a great deal of lip-service to Ricardo, he never accepted his position; hence his acknowledgment of Bailey's comments on the invariable measure.[131] Moreover, as we have seen, there is evidence that McCulloch was perfectly aware that he was adopting a different position from Ricardo; the suggestion by Dr.

[124] See particularly p. 436, col. 2, para. 3. He also made the fact that by real value he meant the cost of production much more explicit (compare Vol. IV, p. 93 and 2nd para., p. 94 of 1828 edition with p. 441 and 2nd para., p. 442 of 1838 edition).

[125] 'Note I. Definition of Labour', pp. 435-7.

[126] 'Note II. Definition, Sources, and Regulating Principles of Value', pp. 437-44.

[127] p. 438. 'It is, perhaps, unnecessary to remark that the word labour means here, and in all discussions respecting value, unless the contrary be distinctly mentioned, the immediate labour of man, or the labour of the capital produced by man, or both; *as explained in the note on Labour*' [my italics].

[128] *Ricardian Economics*, p. 21.

[129] See L. Robbins, *Robert Torrens and the Evolution of Classical Economics*, London, 1958, p. 69.

[130] *Scotsman*, 21st February, 1824, p. 114. 'Principles which determine the Exchangeable Value of Commodities and the Rate of Profit.'

[131] See McCulloch's *Principles* (1825 edition), pp. 213-14 (and corresponding passages in the four later editions).

Blaug[132] that McCulloch misunderstood Ricardo may perhaps be a little misleading. McCulloch in fact attempted to produce a real cost theory of value, and, having no satisfactory micro-economic theory of wages, he failed; but produced a cost of production theory of value which was far more complete than he has generally been given credit for. The course by which he arrived at his final theory of value owes almost as much to Smith and Locke as to Ricardo. Although at times incomplete and unsatisfactory, and although suffering during much of the course of its development from a confusion (of which Ricardo was also guilty though in a different way) between necessary and sufficient conditions, it was not an absurd theory although it was misunderstood by no less a person than Nassau Senior,[133] and has been much misunderstood since. For this McCulloch was however largely to blame for his retention of a popular approach to the problem of value while he continued to wrestle with the problem of capital.

The Queen's University of Belfast

[132] Op. cit., p. 34.

[133] Senior understood McCulloch to argue that in the event of a rain of golden aeroliths, their value would depend on the amount of labour required to pick them up (see Senior's *Outline*, pp. 23-4). Yet this interpretation McCulloch explicitly rejected (see his *Principles*, 3rd edition, pp. 70-1). There is unfortunately not space to deal with the reasons why Senior, Longfield, Lloyd, Whately, Cotterill and Scrope, had little effect on McCulloch.

[12]

Torrens on Wages and Emigration[1]

By D. P. O'Brien

Lord Robbins in his definitive study of Torrens has drawn attention to a most interesting analysis of the determination of wages which Torrens first published in an Appendix to the 1829 edition of his *Essay on the External Corn Trade*.[2] As Lord Robbins points out,[3] this Appendix eventually found its way, more or less complete, into four other publications.

The original appearance of this analysis in print was in association with an argument for freedom of trade in corn.[4] The next was as a virtual reprint of the first,[5] the third was concerned with wages and combinations,[6] the fourth with Poor Laws in Ireland,[7] and the last with wages and hours.[8]

Yet this analysis does not seem to have originated with any of these particular problems, but in connection with emigration.[9] Torrens was very closely associated with Wilmot Horton, and a very considerable discussion of the theory and practice of emigration seems to have taken place between the two men.[10] Both Torrens' fluency and his analytical ability must have been useful to Horton who sent him a number of objections raised by others to his (Horton's) emigration project.[11] Torrens replied as follows:

> Having been long convinced that an extensive system of emigration affords the most immediate and effectual means for lowering the Poor

[1] I am most grateful to Mr. D. N. Neilson for permission to quote from the Torrens letters referred to herein, which I came across while working on my study of J. R. McCulloch, and to Professor R. D. C. Black for his helpful comments.

[2] *Robert Torrens and the Evolution of Classical Economics*, 1956, pp. 49–50 and p. 273.

[3] *Ibid.*, p. 273.

[4] *I.e.* the *Essay on the External Corn Trade*.

[5] *Colonel Torrens on the Wages of Labour and on the Means of Improving the Condition of the Labouring Classes*, 1832.

[6] *Wages and Combinations*, 1834 (cited as *Wages*).

[7] *A Letter to the Right Honourable Lord John Russell, on the Ministerial Measure for Establishing Poor Laws in Ireland, and on the Auxiliary Means which it will be necessary to employ in Carrying that Measure into Effect*, 1837; cited as *Russell*.

[8] *A letter to Lord Ashley, on the Principles which Regulate Wages and on the Manner and Degree in which Wages would be reduced, by the Passing of a Ten Hours Bill*, 1844, cited as *Ashley*.

[9] It is true that the Letter to Lord John Russell contains material on emigration; but this was not the original appearance of the analysis.

[10] See R. N. Gosh "The Colonisation Controversy: R. J. Wilmot-Horton and the Classical Economists", *Economica*, vol. xxxi (1964).

[11] Horton proposed to reprint Torrens' article from the *Pamphleteer* (No. XX, 1817); see letter of 26th March, 1826, Wilmot Horton papers. Torrens also sent an article to the *Globe* espousing Horton's point of view, and proposed further articles (letter of 29th August 1826, Wilmot Horton papers). D. N. Winch (*Classical Political Economy and Colonies*, 1965, p. 68) makes the point that co-operation between Torrens and Horton continued until 1831. Dr. Winch here refers to the letter to Horton discussed below, but does not seem to recognise its significance.

> rate in England, and for relieving distress in Ireland, I dissent in toto from the objections to your emigration project[1] contained in the correspondence with the perusal of which you have favoured me. These objections, as it appears to me, all originate in a misconception of the circumstances which regulate the wages of labour. A correct exposition of the doctrine of wages would answer these and all similar objections *en masse*. Such an exposition I will therefore attempt.[2]

The wage analysis then follows. Torrens begins with a section entitled "*The Minimum of Wages*" which is largely identical with the same section in the 1829 Appendix.[3] This is followed by "*The Maximum of Wages*" which corresponds with the similarly titled section of the Appendix.[4] As elsewhere, there are slight differences of phrasing, but the argument (and the numerical example) are the same,[5] although the Manuscript does not contain the material attacking the Corn Laws which is in the Appendix.[6] Torrens then moves on to "*The Circumstances which determine Actual Wages*",[7] and again the argument and the figures are the same as in the 1829 Appendix.[8] This is followed by a section entitled "*Beyond a Certain Point the Proportion between Capital and Labour ceases to have any influence upon Wages*"[9] in which Torrens rejects a *simple* Wage-Fund analysis,[10] arguing that although labour and capital may remain in the same relative proportion, their increase will force resort to inferior soils. This will, in Torrens' analysis, lower the maximum of wages by reducing the productivity of labour.[11]

The Manuscript continues, like the 1829 Appendix,[12] with material headed "*The means by which wages may be increased*"; but here the

[1] Ins. in Ms.

[2] Letter of 23rd March 1826, Wilmot Horton papers. The letter is in fact a 32 page Ms. setting forth Torrens' analysis of the problem.

[3] Pp. 460–1. Since Lord Robbins has already established the correspondence between the five published versions, page references will be confined to the 1829 Appendix.

[4] Pp. 456-8. The Minimum of Wages is in the conventional minimum level of subsistence and the Maximum of Wages is total product minus replacement of non-wage capital and a reasonable rate of profit.

[5] "Maximum" for instance is qualified by "Moral" in the Appendix.

[6] Pp. 459-60.

[7] Actual wages depending on the ratio of the number of labourers to the amount of capital.

[8] Although the Ms., unlike the Appendix (p. 463), contains no separate heading "How the proportion between Capital and Labour regulates actual Wages", the argument is the same. In both Torrens argues that, assuming full employment and a fixed labour supply, every new accumulation of capital will result only in increased wages, being entirely shared out amongst labour. In both he saves this apparently untenable argument by adding the extra assumptions of fixed factor proportions and (implicitly) a perfectly elastic supply of co-operating factors. Some of the 1829 material does not appear in the Ms., but the missing material is again largely concerned with the effects of the Corn Laws.

[9] 1829 Appendix, pp. 467-9.

[10] He later made it clear that it was Mill he was attacking here (*Wages*, p. 21).

[11] It was in this section that Torrens was to introduce a small but significant modification of his statement of the wage fund. In later versions, instead of speaking of the ratio of labour to capital, he spoke of the ratio of labour to that part of capital destined for the support of labour. Compare 1829 Appendix para. 1 p. 468 with *Wages* para. 1 p. 21, *Russell* para. 2 p. 21 and *Ashley* para. 3 p. 11.

[12] Pp. 469–73.

difference in purpose between the Manuscript and the Appendix becomes clear. Free importation of corn rather than reduction of population is given as the first remedy for resort to inferior soils, in the Appendix; it is not mentioned in the Manuscript. It is from this point that the two expositions part company. The 1826 Manuscript, while omitting some matter later included in the Appendix, contains new material.

Firstly, Torrens wrote a section to complete the statement of the argument in terms of the need for emigration:

> By only regulating population in relation to the extent and fertility of the soil, we may enlarge the range of maximum wages; and by only regulating the number of labourers in relation to the amount of capital employed, we may cause wages to ascend to their ultimate maximum.
>
> The proportions between numbers and the extent of fertile land, and between numbers and the amount of capital, may be regulated either by prudential precautions for limiting the frequency of births, or by an extensive system of emigration.
>
> The adoption of prudential precautions for limiting the number of births must be remote; nor can it be strictly necessary, until the command to replenish the earth has been previously obeyed. Emigration upon an extended scale would afford instantaneous relief; and while it[1] extended the British name and the British race, with the blessings of civilisation and of rational liberty, throughout the vast regions of Canada, Southern Africa, and Australia, it would give the enlightened and energetic government which might adopt it, a claim to the gratitude of the world throughout succeeding generations.

So far, then, we have traced Torrens' presentation of his analysis of wages, in its original form in connection with an argument in favour of emigration, and the passage just quoted would appear to be all that is finally required. But the Manuscript contained a second additional section which is particularly interesting. For Lord Robbins has drawn attention[2] to the fact that Torrens did not, in his published writings, make the obvious answer (from a Classical point of view) to James Mill's objections to Emigration schemes. Mill's position was that to get rid of paupers through emigration used up as much capital as would have employed them at home. Emigration reduced population and capital *pari passu*. As Lord Robbins says:

> Now, for a Classical Economist the obvious answer to this kind of argument would have been to invoke the law of diminishing returns. If the emigrant were transferred from a margin of low to a margin of high productivity, then certainly someone would gain at both ends; and if, as would seem to follow from the Classical theory of Value and Distribution, the immediate gain was to the capitalists, then it was arguable that further accumulation would take place and the funds destined for the maintenance of labour at each end of the transfer would be greater than they

[1] In Ms. followed by another "it" deleted.
[2] *Op. cit.*, pp. 175-6.

> otherwise would have been. . . . But, in fact, although this kind of argument is immanent in much of Torrens' analysis, his overt reply to the case . . . takes other and more ambitious lines.[1]

Torrens in fact later argued that, firstly, experience contradicted Mill's position, and secondly, that a glut of capital was possible, and that increased capital did not necessarily mean either increased wages, or employment. But here, in the Manuscript, we find Torrens making the explicit Classical answer to Mill which appears nowhere in his published writings. For he wrote:

> *Objections answered*
>
> After bestowing upon this important subject all the attention of which I am capable, I can anticipate but one objection to a plan of emigration upon an extended scale. This objection is, that sending out unemployed paupers might require such an expenditure of the national capital that the demand for labour would be reduced in the same or perhaps in a greater proportion than the supply, and that though maximum or possible wages might be enlarged, yet actual wages might be still further reduced.
>
> To this objection I reply in the first place, that even on the supposition that a system of emigration, in its immediate operations, should reduce capital in as great or even in a greater proportion than it reduced population, still, such a system, in its ultimate operation, would be highly beneficial. Emigration upon an extended scale, by rendering it less necessary to cultivate inferior lands, would enlarge the maximum of wages. Now if the operation which extended maximum wages, should, as is contemplated in the objection, leave actual wages stationary, or even depress them then, the rate of profit would necessarily advance. The advanced rate of profit would give a stimulus to industry throughout all its branches, and would cause capital to accumulate more rapidly than before. This more rapid accumulation of capital would speedily replace that which had in the first instance been expended in forming new settlements; and thus occasion such a ratio between capital and labour as would elevate actual wages above the level to which they had fallen when a redundant population rendered it necessary to resort to more inferior soils.

A clearer statement of the missing argument can hardly be imagined. Having delivered himself of this, Torrens adds another answer to Mill's objection:

> In the second place, I deny in toto that a system of emigration on an extended scale would be attended with any loss or waste of the national capital. When we take into consideration the astonishingly high reproductive power to which industry attains when the skilled labour of an old country is applied to the unexhausted and first rate soils of a new one, we must be fully convinced that in fact settlements regulated according to[2] the sound principles of Political Economy might speedily be made, not only to replace the expenditure incurred at their first establishment, but to yield, should it be required, a permanent revenue to the mother country.

[1] Robbins, *loc. cit.* See, e.g., the 1829 Appendix, pp. 471-2.

[2] Ins. in Ms.

Torrens' interesting analysis of wages first appeared then, not as previously appeared to be the case, in connection with his attacks on the Corn Laws, but as an important part of his arguments in support of Emigration. Moreover, in the Manuscript of 1826 referred to, he used the obvious Classical argument against the position of those who opposed emigration, an argument which he used nowhere else, and the absence of which from his published writings has been somewhat puzzling. At least it is now clear that he was aware of it, though he only used it on one occasion.

The Queen's University of Belfast.

[13]

History of Political Economy 12:3

Torrens, McCulloch, and the "Digression on Sismondi": whose digression?

D. P. O'Brien and A. C. Darnell, University of Durham

I. *The Literary Evidence*

In October 1819 there appeared in the *Edinburgh Review* an article entitled "Mr. Owen's Plans for Relieving the National Distress."[1] The authorship of this article has been a matter of dispute for some time and we hope to be able to make some contribution to the discussion in the present study.

The article draws heavily upon a speech by Robert Torrens which was reported in the *Scotsman*, 21 August 1819.[2] The first ten pages of the article draw upon and paraphrase it in places[3] and the next five reproduce material directly from it, as does the last page. However in between the two sections which reproduce the speech directly, there is a critical section dealing with Sismondi—the "Digression on Sismondi"—and it is this which has been the bone of contention.[4]

It has normally been assumed that the article was entirely by Torrens himself. The authorities who have taken this view include such illustrious names in economic scholarship as Lord Robbins, Mr. P. Sraffa, and Professor F. W. Fetter.[5] Recent authors who have supported the view include Professors J. S. Chipman[6] and T. Sowell.[7] Ricardo (and we shall have occasion to return to this below) was convinced that the article was by Torrens;[8] and there are also compelling internal reasons for thinking that the article came from his hand. In general those who believe that this is the case rely upon the inclusion of Torrens' speech; the reply by Torrens in his *Essay on the Produc-*

1. *Edinburgh Review* 32 (Oct. 1819): 453–77.
2. *Scotsman*, 21 Aug. 1819, pp. 265–66 "On Mr. Owen's Plan, and the Causes of the Present Distress."
3. Especially *Edinburgh Review*, loc. cit., pp. 455 and 459.
4. The critical disputed section is p. 469 (lower half) to p. 475 (upper half) of the article.
5. Detailed references will be found in W. O. Thweatt, "The Digression on Sismondi: By Torrens or McCulloch?" *History of Political Economy* 6 (1974): 435–53, at pp. 438–9 n.18.
6. J. S. Chipman, "A Survey of the Theory of International Trade: Part 2," *Econometrica* 33 (1965): 710-12.
7. T. Sowell, *Say's Law* (Princeton, 1972), pp. 11–12.
8. Ricardo, *Works*, ed. P. Sraffa (Cambridge, 1951), 8: 159.

tion of Wealth to an attack by Malthus on the article;[9] Ricardo's belief in the authorship at a time when he was intimate with Torrens; the acceptance by Malthus that the author was Torrens;[10] the use of numerical examples; the reproduction of arguments used in the article in the *Essay*; and one or two less persuasive factors.

There are, however, two weighty exponents of a different view. The late Jacob Viner, in his *Studies*, attributed the authorship to J. R. McCulloch;[11] and in a recent issue of *HOPE* Professor W. O. Thweatt has sided with this view.[12] Viner gave no reasons for his attribution in his book; but, through the courtesy of Professor Donald Winch, we have learnt that in correspondence with Sraffa, Viner relied on five main grounds.[13] These were (i) a reference in the article to a previous *Edinburgh Review* article which is known to be by McCulloch,[14] (ii) McCulloch's claim to a monopoly of economic articles in the *Edinburgh Review* for twelve years covering the period 1819-29, (iii) Sismondi's belief that McCulloch was the author, (iv) praise of Mrs. Marcet in the article, which Viner attributed to a request from Leonard Horner to McCulloch to praise Mrs. Marcet, and (v) laudatory references to the Say-Mill law of markets and citations from French economists. There are a number of fairly important objections to these grounds—as Sraffa made clear to Viner—but it will be convenient to deal with them after summarising Professor Thweatt's important and scholarly contribution to the debate.

Thweatt's argument is based upon the following considerations. Firstly, he argues, the material in the *Essay* replying to Malthus is based upon arguments in Ricardo's *Notes on Malthus* which were transmitted to Torrens via their incorporation by McCulloch in a subsequent article in the *Edinburgh Review*.[15] Secondly, he believes that McCulloch was unwilling to claim authorship of the article when Ricardo attributed it to Torrens because of the amount of Torrens' material which was contained in it.[16] Thirdly, he believes that the omission from the article of material in the speech about colonisation as a remedy for economic distress is significant, in that he believes

9. R. Torrens, *An Essay on the Production of Wealth* (London, 1821): 378–89.

10. Ricardo, *Works*, 8: 376.

11. J. Viner, *Studies in the Theory of International Trade* (New York, 1937), p. 194 n., 621.

12. See note 5 above.

13. The Viner papers are not available for public inspection and we are very grateful to Professor Winch for making this information available to us privately.

14. The reference is at p. 473 of the disputed article.

15. Thweatt, "Digression," pp. 440–43. The reference is to "Effects of Machinery and Accumulation," *Edinburgh Review* 35 (March 1821): 102–23.

16. Thweatt, "Digression," pp. 443–44, 452.

Torrens to have been an enthusiast for colonisation and McCulloch not to have been one. Fourthly, he points to opposition elsewhere in Torrens' work to the Say-Mill law of markets;[17] fifthly, he believes that Torrens never mentions Sismondi elsewhere in his work;[18] and finally he points to the reference to the earlier *Edinburgh Review* article which Viner had also lighted on.

None of the arguments seems to us, despite their scholarly presentation, completely convincing, and some of them seem open to serious objection. We are unconvinced by the argument that Torrens was relying on McCulloch's version of the *Notes on Malthus*, and anyone aware of Torrens' mental vitality and flair for controversy would find this hard to accept, unless the internal evidence were overwhelming, which, in our view, it is not. In any case, whatever the *origin* of the ideas, Torrens undertook the refutation of Malthus' attack and it is *this* which has been held to be acknowledgement of authorship of the original article. Secondly, the correspondence between Ricardo and McCulloch over this article could hardly be more unambiguous. Ricardo in a letter of 28 February 1820 says quite plainly that Torrens is the author of the article; and McCulloch, in a letter of 19 March which explicitly replies to that of 28 February, lays no claim to the authorship of the article, but instead refers to a different *Edinburgh Review* article, which is undoubtedly his, for Ricardo's approbation.[19] Thirdly, McCulloch was indeed an advocate of colonisation and emigration from his earliest days and an enthusiastic supporter of the colonisation schemes of Wilmot-Horton. The omission of the colonisation material has absolutely no significance in relation to differences of opinion between McCulloch and Torrens.[20] Fourthly, although it is true that Torrens was an opponent of the Say-Mill law of markets his position was not entirely consistent on this as can be seen from the *Essay*.[21] The fact that Torrens did not mention Sismondi elsewhere seems to us relatively unimportant; and the form of the reference to a previous *Edinburgh Review* article, in a journal in which everything was published anonymously, looks to us like a straightforward exercise of the editor's hand.

In addition there are other factors which we find persuasive of

17. Ibid., pp. 448–49.

18. Ibid. p. 450.

19. Ricardo, *Works*, 8: 159, 165. See also ibid. pp. 82, 227, 376. The article was "Taxation and the Corn Laws," *Edinburgh Review* 33 (Jan. 1820): 155–87.

20. "Throughout all McCulloch's changes of attitude to population problems and to the Poor Law one factor remained fairly constant—his advocacy of emigration." D. P. O'Brien, *J. R. McCulloch: A Study in Classical Economics* (London, 1970), p. 331.

21. Evidence of Torrens' varying attitude towards Say's Law may be found in his *Essay*, pp. 371–83 and 381–430.

Torrens' authorship. Firstly, McCulloch was not a plagiarist (as distinct from a *self*-plagiarist).[22] In any case Torrens, who was a very touchy character, would not have allowed plagiarism of his speech on this scale. Secondly, there seems to us to be close correspondence between the disputed six pages of the article and the section of Torrens' *Essay*.[23] Thirdly, there is *not* any very obvious correspondence between the Edinburgh article and three other pieces by McCulloch referring to Sismondi where his penchant for self-plagiarism might have led one to expect such correspondence.[24] Fourthly, the article was not listed as being by McCulloch in the list of his articles compiled by his confidential clerk and son-in-law H. G. Reid, who had access to McCulloch's own list. Nor is it in McCulloch's own bound volumes of his *Edinburgh* articles at Reading. Fifthly, the florid style is redolent of Torrens, not McCulloch. Sixthly, there is a reference to an article by McCulloch in the disputed article which would have amounted to self-advertisement of a kind which the editor, Jeffrey, would have been unlikely to allow.[25] Seventhly, the Wellesley index cites the Copinger list as well as the letter by Ricardo as authority for the attribution to Torrens; and this list is believed to have been based upon a record of the *Edinburgh*'s publishers, Longmans.[26] Eighthly, McCulloch never had the monopoly of the *Edinburgh*'s economic articles which he claimed.[27]

These seem to us persuasive objections. But debates on literary and historical evidence of this sort must inevitably result in an inconclusive deadlock, especially when one faces a case as scholarly as that presented by Professor Thweatt. In view of this we decided to apply a statistical test of authorship to the disputed section of the *Edinburgh* article.

22. Chipman, op. cit., asserts, without evidence, that McCulloch was "a notorious plagiariser." This is simply not true. The only person who ever, to our knowledge, accused McCulloch of plagiarism, was Samuel Read; and he was mistaken. McCulloch was a self-plagiarist; but that is a different matter. We cannot recall any instance in his writings where he failed to use quotation marks when transcribing material; and it is noteworthy that he reproduced Torrens' speech, in quotes, *as* Torrens' work, in the *Scotsman*. But in any case the last person to steal from would have been the formidable Marines officer and controversialist Robert Torrens.

23. Especially between pp. 371–83 of the *Essay* and 471–73 of the *Review*. This had earlier been indicated by Lord Robbins (*Robert Torrens and the Evolution of Classical Economics*, London, 1958, p. 177).

24. The three references are the *Edinburgh* article "Effects of Machinery and Accumulation" (note 15 above), McCulloch's review of Sismondi's *Nouveaux Principes*, *Scotsman*, 24 April 1819, and the section in McCulloch's *Principles of Political Economy*, 1st ed. (Edinburgh 1825), pp. 165–92.

25. On Jeffrey's control of McCulloch see O'Brien, p. 35.

26. W. E. Houghton, ed. *The Wellesley Index to Victorian Periodicals* (Toronto, 1966), 1: 426–27, 460.

27. See O'Brien, p. 34.

II. *The Statistical Evidence*

The statistical analysis of authorship has quite a long history. It certainly predates the availability of computers by many years. What the computer enables us to do however is to select, by use of a special programme, the characteristic 'fingerprints' of a given author, such as the use of particular words, and to count their frequency without laborious hand calculation.[28] Early work in this area concentrated on sentence length (which worked well in distinguishing Greek authors, but not English ones) and on uncommon words. Perhaps the most impressive example of the latter is the dogged piece of work by H. A. Ellegard on the authorship of the *Junius* letters.[29] Having established that sentence length worked poorly with English prose, he used the frequency of unusual words. This enabled him to test for authorship using a normal probability distribution. Unfortunately such a method involves very large samples—around 100,000 words—for it to be reliable; and it is also extremely laborious, even with the aid of a computer, because texts have to be read two or three times to find the characteristic unusual words.

The pioneering work on which we have built, however, was done by W. C. Wake, who showed "that what is most characteristic of an author is not his few personal idiosyncrasies but the rates at which he performs the operations which he shares with all his colleagues."[30] This has been built upon by the Reverend A. Morton and his co-workers, who have turned attention from low-frequency vocabulary to high-frequency vocabulary and to the study of the position in sentences of the high-frequency words. They have found that this has proved a powerful method of discriminating between authors writing in English. They have also emphasised the use of chi-squared (of which more will be said below) thus enabling relatively small samples of text to be used.[31]

The fundamental principle employed in the statistical analysis of

28. For the analysis of the texts discussed in this article we used the programme COCOA (Count and Concordance generation on Atlas) by G. L. M. Berry-Rogghe and T. D. Crawford. We are grateful to the staff of the computer facilities shared between Durham and Newcastle for assistance with the use of this programme, especially Camilla Boldyreff.

29. H. A. Ellegard, *Who Was Junius*? (Stockholm, 1962), and *A Statistical Method for Determining Authorship: The Junius Letters 1769–1772* (Gothenburg, 1962).

30. S. M. Michaelson and A. Q. Morton, "Positional Stylometry," in A. J. Aitken, R. W. Bailey, and N. Hamilton-Smith, eds., *The Computer and Literary Studies* (Edinburgh, 1973), pp. 69–83, at p. 70.

31. We are very grateful to the Rev. A. Q. Morton for a preliminary analysis of the problem which is the subject of this article, and for drawing to our attention his work on Sir Walter Scott, which provided valuable suggestions on the collocations to be used.

authorship used here is, then, to identify habits of style which are consistently and frequently exhibited by the individual authors under consideration, but which differ markedly from one author to another. We are thus able to use these tests to compare statistical results obtained from an anonymous text with the work of known authors.

The problem of the authorship of the "Digression on Sismondi" is relatively simple in that we have only two candidates for its authorship—McCulloch and Torrens. Of course we cannot *prove* that either was the author; but we can establish, with a very high degree of probability, that one was the author and that the other was not the author. Since this technique has not hitherto been used in the study of the history of economic thought our results may be of particular interest.

The October 1819 *Edinburgh Review* article is our disputed text, and, as indicated above, it may be divided into three component parts. These are a paraphrase of Torrens' London speech, direct quotation from the same speech, and the disputed section known as the "Digression." The first stage was to examine the whole of the anonymous text for internal consistency, i.e., to test whether it was all by the same hand. We also examined the work of Torrens and McCulloch for internal consistency. For Torrens we used a substantial portion of the *Essay on the Production of Wealth* and the full reprint of his London speech. McCulloch was represented by the section from his *Principles* dealing with the same subject as the disputed article and by another *Edinburgh Review* article which is indisputably by McCulloch, "The Effects of Machinery and Accumulation."[32] Once the work of each of the authors had been subjected to a test of consistency, it was examined for consistency or otherwise with both the "Digression" on its own and the whole of the anonymous article.

We settled on two broad classes of literary characteristics. One is the usage of a particular word as the first word of a sentence. The other is the usage of particular 'collocations.' A collocation is, for our purposes, an ordered pair of words such as "WILL BE" and "IN THE," the former being a collocation of "BE" and the latter a collocation of "THE." First word usage may be used to illustrate how a test of consistency was carried out statistically.[33] An analysis of the disputed article produced the figures shown in Table 1.

32. See notes 2, 9, 15, and 24 above. The text of the 5th (1864) edition of McCulloch's *Principles* was used.

33. In the interests of brevity we have confined ourselves in this article to summarising the results of our chi-squared tests. However it seemed to us important that the detailed tables from which these results are derived should be available on request; and, accordingly, we have incorporated them into a Discussion Paper which is available on request, from the Department of Economics, University of Durham.

Table 1. First words from the disputed text

First word	Section of the disputed text			
	Paraphrase	*Direct speech*	*"Digression"*	Total
BUT	12	6	4	22
IN	12	3	6	21
THE/IF	15	9	10	34
WE/IT, AND/THIS	12	13	4	29
Other first words	48	27	26	101
Total	99	58	50	207

The entries show us that, for example, of the 99 sentences in the Paraphrase section, 15 begin with either "THE" or "IF," and taking the article as a whole, 34 of its 207 sentences begin in this way. Notice that one of the rows represents two first words and one of the rows represents four. This amalgamation was necessary in order to avoid low expected cell entries which pose a threat to the validity of the test statistic. This amalgamation may be justified in that it yields consistency within the acknowledged work of Torrens and McCulloch and also discriminates most clearly between these two writers.

The hypotheses appropriate to this table are as follows:

> H_0: the source of text and first word classification are independent.
> H_1: the source and first-word classification are not independent.

Acceptance of H_0 is equivalent to an acceptance of consistency, and rejection is equivalent to an acceptance of inconsistency. Under H_0 we compute expected frequencies according to the rule:

$$E_{ij} = \frac{(\text{total of row } i) \times (\text{total of column } j)}{\text{grand total}},$$

where E_{ij} is the expected frequency of the cell in the ith row and jth column.

Thus, corresponding to our observed frequency of 15 THE/IF in the Paraphrase, we have an expected frequency of

$$E_{31} = \frac{34 \times 99}{207} = 16.26$$

Defining O_{ij} as the observed frequency in cell (i,j) we then compute the test statistic as:

$$X^2 = \sum \frac{(O_{ij} - E_{ij})^2}{E_{ij}}$$

Under H_0, X^2 has a chi-squared distribution with $(r-1)(c-1)$ degrees of freedom, where r is the number of rows (6), and c the number of columns (3), i.e., with 10 degrees of freedom.

If H_0 is true we would clearly expect close correspondence between E_{ij} and O_{ij} for all cells, and hence we would expect a 'low' computed X^2. Correspondingly, if H_0 is false we would expect to calculate a relatively 'large' X^2. A decision rule is formulated by reference to the tabulated values of the χ^2 distribution and the probability statement

$$\text{Prob}\ (X^2 > \chi^2_{.95}) = .05,$$

where $\chi^2_{.95}$ is the value of the χ^2 (for a particular number of degrees of freedom) which will be exceeded with a probability of .05. If the computed value exceeds this critical value, this may be explained in one of two ways: either H_0 is true and we have been unfortunate in observing an atypical sample; or H_0 is false. The implausibility of the first interpretation allows us to accept the second, but we cannot be certain that the former explanation is not the true one. What we can say in this situation is that if H_0 is true, there is only a 5 percent probability that we are making a mistake in rejecting it.

In our example the computed $X^2 = 7.65$ while the tabulated 95 percent critical value is 18.31. We therefore accept H_0, i.e., accept consistency in the anonymous article in the usage of first words according to our classification. This technique is an example of the χ^2 test of interdependence.[34]

We used the frequency of occurrence of "BUT," "IN," "THE" or "IF," "WE" or "IT," "AND" or "THIS," and "all other first words" as our classification of first words for the anonymous article. This also proved perfectly satisfactory in dealing with the work of Torrens. Examination of the specimens of McCulloch's work we used showed that in addition to the frequent use of the above as first words, McCulloch also uses "SUPPOSE," "WERE," and "THERE" regularly and consistently. Thus, to establish McCulloch's consistency we employ a classification of seven. The results are to be found in Table 2 from which the following conclusions may be drawn.

34. For further details see, for example, W. W. Daniel and J. C. Terrell, *Business Statistics* (Boston, 1975) ch. 11, §§ 1, 2, and 4.

Table 2. First-word usage

Texts analysed	X^2	d.f.	$\chi^2_{.95}$	Conclusion
Paraphrase vs Direct speech vs "Digression"	7.65	8	15.51	Accept the consistency of the disputed article.
Torrens' *Speech* vs *Essay*	2.36	4	9.49	Accept the consistency of Torrens' works.
McCulloch's "Employment" vs *Principles*	3.40	6	12.59	Accept the consistency of McCulloch's works.
Torrens' works vs McCulloch's works	20.30	6	12.59	Reject the consistency between Torrens' and McCulloch's works.
Torrens' works vs "Digression"	3.60	4	9.49	Accept the consistency between Torrens' works and the "Digression."
McCulloch's works vs "Digression"	13.22	5	11.07	Reject the consistency between McCulloch's works and the "Digression."
Torrens' works vs "Mr. Owen's Plans"	1.78	5	11.07	Accept the consistency between Torren's works and the disputed article.
McCulloch's works vs. "Mr. Owen's Plans"	25.89	6	12.59	Reject the consistency between McCulloch's works and the disputed article.

NOTE: Because of low cell expected frequencies it was judged desirable to amalgamate some cells to obtain the X^2 figures in rows 1, 2, 5, and 6 of the table. See W. G. Cochran, "Some Methods for Strengthening the Common χ^2 Tests," *Biometrics* 10 (1954): 417–51.

(i) The disputed text and the two Torrens pieces used are each internally consistent in first-word usage using identical classifications, while McCulloch's two articles are internally consistent using the slightly extended classification system. McCulloch's work is, of course, internally consistent using the smaller classification set, but this is an inefficient test of consistency because it ignores valuable information on his use of three extra words.

(ii) Torrens' works and McCulloch's works show a marked contrast in first-word usage, with a calculated chi-squared of 20.30, which is very much greater than the 95 percent critical value of 12.59.

(iii) Torrens' first-word usage is entirely compatible both with the "Digression" and with the whole of the disputed article.

(iv) McCulloch's usage is not compatible with either the "Digression" or the whole of the disputed piece. Probabilities of our being mistaken in these two conclusions are less than 5 percent and 0.5 percent respectively.[35]

(v) It is also interesting to note that using the crude measure of average sentence length, which is normally not very sensitive to differences between English authors, we find an average sentence length of 50 words in each of the three sections of the disputed piece. The average length for the section of Torrens' *Essay* used is 48. The average sentence lengths for the two pieces by McCulloch used are 39 and 37 words.

Turning from the pattern of first words to the use of particular collocations, we analysed the relative frequency of "THE" preceded by "AND" or "WHICH," "OF" or "IN," "TO" or "THAT," "FOR" or "FROM" or "WITH," "ON" or "BY," and "all other preceding words." These collocations prove capable of showing internal consistency within the acknowledged work of one author while distinguishing sharply between different authors. Examining Table 3 we may draw the following conclusions.

(i) The anonymous text, Torrens' two works, and McCulloch's two works all exhibit internal consistency.

(ii) Torrens and McCulloch show marked differences in their use of words preceding "THE."

(iii) Torrens' habits are entirely consistent with those to be found in the "Digression" and in the whole of the disputed text.

(iv) McCulloch's habits are not consistent with either the "Digression" or with the whole of the disputed text. The probabilities of our being mistaken in these two statements are less than 6 percent and 0.5 percent respectively.

The last literary characteristic we examined was the use of the word "BE." "BE" is used preceded by "WILL," "CAN," "MUST," "SHALL," "WOULD," "COULD," "MAY," "MIGHT," "SHOULD," "TO," or a noun or pronoun. The first four words in this list express positive statements, while the next five express conditional or normative statements. We grouped the positive statements together and the conditional statements together; this provided us with two groups of collocations. The remaining two items on the list provided us with two more collocations. The results of the statistical tests upon the frequency of these collocations are given in Table 4. From this we conclude the following.

35. 0.5 percent probability values for χ_2 are given in Daniel and Terrell, at p. 630.

Table 3. Collocations with "THE"

Texts analysed	X^2	d.f.	$\chi^2_{.95}$	Conclusion
Paraphrase vs Direct speech vs "Digression"	6.57	10	18.31	Accept the consistency of the disputed article.
Torrens' *Speech* vs *Essay*	2.74	5	11.07	Accept the consistency of Torrens' works.
McCulloch's "Employment" vs *Principles*	2.99	5	11.07	Accept the consistency of McCulloch's works.
Torrens' works vs McCulloch's works	32.79	5	11.07	Reject the consistency between Torrens' and McCulloch's works.
Torrens' works vs "Digression"	7.37	5	11.07	Accept the consistency between Torrens' works and the "Digression."
McCulloch's works vs "Digression"	10.74	5	10.70[a]	Reject the consistency between McCulloch's works and the "Digression."
Torrens' works vs "Mr. Owen's Plans"	6.38	5	11.07	Accept the consistency between Torrens' works and the disputed article.
McCulloch's works vs "Mr. Owen's Plans"	21.50	5	11.07	Reject the consistency between McCulloch's works and the disputed article.

[a] 10.70 is the $\chi^2_{.94}$ value.

(i) The disputed text, pieces by Torrens which we used, and pieces by McCulloch which we used all exhibit internal consistency on this set of tests.

(ii) Torrens' work is markedly different from that of McCulloch.

(iii) Torrens' work is not distinguishable with regard to the use of these collocations from either the "Digression" or the whole of the disputed text.

(iv) McCulloch's use of these collocations in his other work is wholly incompatible with the use of them in the "Digression" and the whole of the disputed text. The probabilities of our being mistaken in this are each less than 0.5 percent.

Analysis of collocations with "BE" is most illuminating because it is entirely consistent with differences between the approaches to economic problems used by the two candidates for authorship of the disputed piece. In 46 percent of the occurrences of the word "BE" in

Table 4. Collocations with "BE"

Texts analysed	X^2	d.f.	$\chi^2_{.95}$	Conclusion
Paraphrase vs Direct speech vs "Digression"	6.91	4	9.49	Accept the consistency of the disputed article.
Torrens' *Speech* vs *Essay*	1.38	2	5.99	Accept the consistency of Torrens' works.
McCulloch's "Employment" vs *Principles*	6.64	3	7.82	Accept the consistency of McCulloch's works.
Torrens' works vs McCulloch's works	34.22	3	7.82	Reject the consistency between Torrens' and McCulloch's works.
Torrens' works vs "Digression"	1.83	2	5.99	Accept the consistency between Torrens' works and the "Digression."
McCulloch's works vs "Digression"	13.22	2	5.99	Reject the consistency between McCulloch's works and the "Digression."
Torrens' works vs "Mr. Owen's Plans"	1.60	3	7.82	Accept the consistency between Torrens' works and the disputed article.
McCulloch's works vs "Mr. Owen's Plans"	34.00	3	7.82	Reject the consistency between McCulloch's works and the disputed article.

NOTE: See note *a* to Table 2 above. Amalgamations of cells were judged desirable in obtaining the figures in rows 1, 2, 5, and 6 of Table 4.

that part of his output which we have used, Torrens precedes it by one of our positive words. McCulloch, by contrast, used such words in only 21 percent of the occurrences. Torrens used one of our conditional words preceding "BE" on only 29 percent of the occasions on which he employs "BE," while the corresponding figure for McCulloch is 59 percent. Within the crucial section of the disputed text, the "Digression," we find "BE" preceded by one of our positive words on 52 percent of occasions and preceded by one of our conditional words on only 32 percent of occasions.

This is rather striking because it is entirely consistent with the differences between Torrens and McCulloch as classical economists. Torrens used a Ricardian model, or his own variants of it, which led directly to definite conclusions; McCulloch used a Smithian approach in which there were usually several possible outcomes from any given set of economic circumstances though with one outcome more likely than others.[36]

III. *Conclusion*

We have reviewed the literary evidence on the authorship of the "Digression" and of the disputed *Edinburgh Review* article; and for the first time so far as we know in the study of the history of economic thought, we have supplemented this by statistical tests. The cumulative weight of the statistical results in Tables 2, 3, and 4 seems to us to indicate that the "Digression," and indeed the whole article, are much more likely to be the work of Torrens than that of McCulloch. The probability of our having accepted this hypothesis when the alternative one is true would seem to be of the order of less than 1/8 of 1 percent, given independence of the tests.

We are grateful to the Rev. A. Q. Morton for answering our preliminary enquiries which preceded this work, and to an anonymous referee for helpful comments.

36. For the Smithian basis of McCulloch's work see O'Brien, op. cit., passim; for the Ricardian nature of Torrens' work see Lord Robbins, op. cit., passim.

[14]

J.R. McCulloch

John Ramsay McCulloch, 1789–1864, was born 1st March 1789 in Galloway, Scotland. After education at Edinburgh University, he secured employment as a lawyer's clerk. In 1816 he began his contributions to economics with two essays on the National Debt. He was editor of the *Scotsman* 1817–21 and a contributor to that paper until 1827. In 1818 he began writing for the *Edinburgh Review* and this he continued until 1837, contributing nearly 80 articles. He also contributed to *Encyclopaedia Britannica*, and was a prolific author, his works including editions of the *Wealth of Nations*, a *Commercial Dictionary*, a *Geographical Dictionary*, *Principles of Political Economy*, a *Statistical Account of the British Empire* and a *Treatise on Taxation*. He was a noted bibliophile, and after his death his library was purchased by his friend Lord Overstone and ultimately presented to Reading University.

It was not only as an author that McCulloch was influential; he was also called as an expert witness before the Select Committee on machinery of 1824 and that on Ireland of 1825. He was also one of the first public teachers of economics. He began lecturing in Edinburgh in 1820; and although attempts to establish a Chair at Edinburgh University on his behalf in 1825 fell through, he had been selected in 1824 to give the Ricardo Memorial lectures in London and in 1828 he was appointed, largely through the agency of James Mill, as the first professor of political economy at London University. He remained professor until 1837, though largely supporting himself by his pen; but in 1838 he was appointed Comptroller of the Stationery Office, a post which he occupied until his death in 1864. This did not, however, prevent him from continuing his literary activities and he remained active as an author, producing new editions of his works, and some completely new ones especially the *Treatise on Taxation* (1945, 1852, 1863) and the *Geographical Dictionary* (1841–2, 1845–6, 1849, 1852, 1854).

As an economist McCulloch came, at one stage, very much under the influence of Ricardo but the influence was, in the long run, largely transient. His treatment of value shows clear traces of the influence of Ricardo. He put forward a simple labour theory of value under the influence of Ricardo, while aware that this was a simplified version, assuming away the problem of capital, for popular exposition. But though the emphasis is on labour quantity, and undoubtedly derived from Ricardo, it was a theory of relative (exchangeable) value, and McCulloch's analysis never borrowed from Ricardo the fundamental (to Ricardo) concept of the invariable measure. Indeed, McCulloch rejected the concept emphatically.

The vicissitudes of McCulloch's exposition over the years included, without doubt, a number of erroneous positions and a strange solution to the origin of profits as being in stored labour continuing to work. He also attempted to make labour cost a real (disutility) cost. But in the second edition (1830) of his *Principles* he advanced an almost complete cost of production theory, where cost was, as in an earlier *Scotsman* article, marginal cost. Labour cost, amortization, and profit were now recognized as costs as they had been with Smith; the influence of Ricardo was now largely apparent in treating rent, not as a cost but as a price-determined surplus, thus ignoring transfer earnings. Finally, in the 1838 edition of McCulloch's notes to the *Wealth of Nations*, he clarified the nature of the profit reward with both waiting (as stressed by Ricardo) and productivity (as stressed by McCulloch) combining to produce a positive return.

McCulloch's treatment of money and banking derived from Smith, Hume and Thornton, though he for long followed Ricardo in advancing the idea that the value of commodity money was determined by its cost of production, an idea he finally abandoned in the 8th edition of *Encyclopaedia Britannia.* He accepted Hume's theory of the distribution of the precious metals, drawing also on Smith and especially Thornton, though he did accept, at least in relation to external losses of metal, the Ricardian definition of excess. In considering the internal level of activity in relation to money, he accepted Say's identity as an equilibrium proposition, but he also recognized the possibility that excess demand for money in disequilibrium might cause economic dislocation thus magnifying fluctuations originating in the real side of the economy, such as over-investment. He also recognized, and approved, in contrast to Ricardo, the effects of mild inflation in producing forced saving and economic growth. On the issue of banking control he at first accepted Ricardo's view that convertibility was its own safeguard, but he came to recognize the problems of over-issue of notes much earlier than many writers – he was firmly opposed to *laissez-faire* in banking – and was one of the earliest writers to put forward the principle that a note issue should fluctuate in amount in response to the balance of payments exactly as an identically circumstanced metallic money would do, though he saw this as providing only a partial solution to monetary control.

McCulloch's analysis of international trade followed Smith rather than Ricardo, in basing trade on absolute advantage assuming international factor mobility. McCulloch may have done this because he saw that the possibility of trade advantage, as explained in comparative cost theory, was incomplete until this was translated into relative costs and prices. At all events he considered Ricardo's treatment of international trade to be faulty. In his view there was a complete parallel between international and inter-regional trade. McCulloch's treatment went well beyond that of Smith in some respects; and in particular, his analysis of the transfer problem, based on the work of Parnell, was an important precursor of modern developments. He discussed not only the effects of a transfer in the form of specie, or of commodities, but also a demand transfer of the kind made famous by Ohlin in his controversy with Keynes after the First World War. On matters of trade policy McCulloch has had the image of a crude free trader, but in fact, though he recognized the harm that protection could do, freedom of trade could, in his view, involve the imposition of substantial import duties – even as high as 25 per cent – as long as these were balanced by home excise duties so as to avoid distortion of choice.

McCulloch's treatment of public finance used the Smithian framework; the analysis inevitably acquired a number of Ricardian accretions, but many of these were ultimately discarded. Moreover, McCulloch drew on a wide range of earlier writers on taxation and was particularly indebted to Hume and to Robert Hamilton. He presented a broad synthetic treatment which did much to give tax theory practicality after the Ricardian detour into the corn model. His main focus of attention was the use of fiscal policy in such a way as to ensure the maintenance of growth. Heavy taxation could interfere with growth, but if taxation were sensibly used it could be a stimulus to growth, increasing the supply of both effort and savings. A widely-based regime of moderate indirect taxes, extending even to postage, was what McCulloch favoured, on ability-to-pay grounds, despite the distortions of the price system and the regressive elements. He opposed Gladstone's tax policy, not only because of the narrow base, but also because of the reliance upon income tax which McCulloch believed to interfere with growth, failing to stimulate effort and, where not proportional, subverting economic motivation.

The basic process of economic development was seen largely in terms of Smith's apparatus involving the accumulation of capital (but including human capital) and division of labour. It also involved the institutional requirements of security of property, internal freedom of trade, and a substantial role for government including education, control of public utilities, and employer liability for accidents. On to this Smithian basis McCulloch grafted specific Ricardian features, notably the Ricardian explanation for the declining rate of profit. However, he finally rejected the idea of inevitably diminishing returns in agriculture, as well as the inverse movement of wages and profits, and the Ricardian stagnation thesis. Writing later than Smith, McCulloch's treatment of development shows a much heavier emphasis on technology. Indeed this was the basis of a fundamental disagreement with Ricardo over the role of machinery, and led him also to reject the primacy which Smith had afforded to agriculture – he attached key importance to the manufacturing sector though he was worried about the distributional consequences.

On agriculture itself however he wrote a good deal. He believed in large-scale capitalist farming (and supported primogeniture though not entails), and came, after a long period of believing in the (at least ultimate) inevitability of diminishing returns, to the view that under such a system improvements might continuously offset the diminution of returns. Thus his attack on the Corn Laws did not emphasize the Ricardian concept of stagnation but other matters, notably the idea that they encouraged price fluctuation. In this context he employed not only arguments about elasticity of demand and supply but also an agricultural cobweb. On this basis he argued, in contrast to Ricardo, that all classes, including the landlords, lost by the Corn Laws (though he followed Ricardo's argument for a measure of agricultural protection) and he also came to reject Ricardo's argument that improvements were against the interest of the landlords.

Classical economics, unlike modern economics, contained, as an integral part, a theory of population, which served in turn as the basis for various theorems about wages and welfare. McCulloch's population theory initially followed the first two editions of Malthus's celebrated *Essay*. But, probably under the influence of Nassau Senior, he became opposed to the Malthusian argument, believing prudential restraints to predominate. Indeed, amongst mainstream Classical economists he was probably the most extreme anti-Malthusian, a development which harmonized with his move away from Ricardo's influence. Having sided with Malthus and Ricardo in opposing the Poor Law, he changed his mind quite openly after 1826 and became a supporter of the old Poor Law, believing that it did not undermine prudential restraint and that it preserved social stability. He opposed the 1834 Poor Law as harsh and over-centralized. As a measure to raise wages generally he supported emigration and colonization, though he did not favour retention of control of colonies, and objected, in particular, to Wakefield's schemes for 'scientific' colonization.

All this raises directly McCulloch's concept of the operation of the labour market. McCulloch is particularly associated with the idea of the wage fund, because of his *Essay on Wages* (1826) and, with a given wage fund, reducing supply will raise wages, as implied in McCulloch's treatment of emigration. His analysis of demand for labour thus equated capital with demand for labour, though in his more careful treatments he distinguished total and wage capital (and total population and labour supply). But this only provided half the analysis; on the supply side McCulloch employed four different labour supply functions, including a rising supply schedule as normal, two negatively inclined short-run schedules, the first when wages rose after excessive hours had been required to survive at the previous level of wages, the second where women and children enter the labour force as wages fell, to maintain family income. Fourthly, there was a secular population function. McCulloch favoured high wages, and his writings in defence of trades unions were important in the successful struggle to secure repeal of the Combination Laws.

As an economist, McCulloch was a fairly representative Classical writer in that his work involved a synthesis of elements deriving from Smith and Ricardo. Yet McCulloch's case is particularly interesting because his own evolution over the very long period (48 years) of his writings, mirrors the development of Classical economics itself. Starting from a basis of Smith and Malthus, he fell under the influence of Ricardo's magnetic personality and remarkable powers of abstraction, but he gradually passed through this phase, the Smithian elements of his work resuming their predominance and leading in turn to an emphasis on empirical work and a methodological position foreign to the tenor of Ricardo's work.

References

McCulloch, J.R. (1825), *The Principles of Political Economy: with some inquiries respecting their application, and a sketch of the rise and progress of the science*, 3rd. ed., Edinburgh: W. Tait, 1843.

McCulloch, J.R. (1832), *A Dictionary Practical, Theoretical, and Historical, of Commerce and Commercial Navigation*, 10th ed., London: Longmans, 1859.

McCulloch, J.R. (1845), *A Treatise on the Principles and Practical Influence of Taxation and the Funding System*, ed. D.P. O'Brien, Edinburgh: Scottish Academic Press for The Scottish Economic Society, 1975.

O'Brien, D.P. (1970), *J.R. McCulloch. A Study in Classical Economics*, London: Allen & Unwin.

[15]

INTRODUCTION

I. J. R. McCULLOCH

John Ramsay McCulloch, the author of the work on taxation which is reprinted in this volume, was born on 1 March 1789 at Whithorn, Wigtownshire, in the South-West of Scotland and died 11 November 1864 in London. He was educated at Edinburgh University which he left (without graduating) in 1811 having studied mathematics, agriculture, and ethics. His first published works on economics were two essays on deflation and the National Debt[1] published in 1816. He was editor of the *Scotsman* 1817–21, during its stormy early years, and he published seventy-eight articles in the *Edinburgh Review* in the years 1818–37.

McCulloch contributed also to the 6th, 7th and 8th editions of *Encyclopaedia Britannica*, and was the author of a successful textbook, the *Principles of Political Economy*, the first edition of which appeared in 1825 and the final (5th) edition of which appeared in the year of McCulloch's death.[2] After pioneering public lecturing on economics in Edinburgh and delivering the Ricardo Memorial Lectures in London he became, in 1828, the first Professor of Political Economy at London University. He held this position until 1837. In 1838 he became Comptroller of the Stationery Office, an appointment he still occupied at the time of his death in 1864.

He was a prolific writer on economics, and until his appointment to the Stationery Office he lived largely by his pen. Apart from his

[1] *An Essay on a Reduction of the Interest of the National Debt, proving that this is the only possible Means of Relieving the Distress of the Commercial and Agricultural Interests; and Establishing the Justice of that Measure on the Surest Principles of Political Economy*, Edinburgh, 1816; *An Essay on the Question of Reducing the Interest of the National Debt, in which the Justice and Expediency of that Measure are fully established*, Edinburgh, 1816. Cited as 'First 1816 Essay' and 'Second 1816 Essay' respectively.

[2] *The Principles of Political Economy with a sketch of the Rise and Progress of the Science*, Edinburgh and London, 1825, 1830, 1843, 1849, 1864. (Cited as *Principles* followed by date of edition.)

economic writings he also produced three vast statistical compilations, the *Commercial Dictionary*, the *Statistical Account of the British Empire*, and the *Geographical Dictionary*[3] which were highly successful.

McCulloch was essentially a writer in the Scottish tradition, intertwining fact and theory and testing the one against the other. He came, however, under the influence of Ricardo's personality, and attempted to incorporate the latter's ideas into a basically Smithian framework. But in the fullness of time he almost entirely discarded the Ricardian elements from his work. The present editor has completed a full study of McCulloch's thought,[4] and the reader requiring a detailed treatment is referred to that work, which also contains further biographical material.

The *Treatise on Taxation* which is reprinted here is a work of McCulloch's mature years, the first edition appearing in 1845 with subsequent editions in 1852 and 1863. This particular work will now be considered in detail.

II. THE *TREATISE ON TAXATION*

(i) *The objectives of the book and contemporary reaction*

The *Treatise on Taxation* first appeared in 1845 and it can well claim to be the first really full length and systematic work in English in the field of public finance.[1] There had of course been a fairly substantial amount of writings on public finance topics preceding this. But these had really fallen into three main classes. Firstly there were the theoretical treatments of particular problems which had appeared as part of general

[3] *A Dictionary, Practical, Theoretical, and Historical, of Commerce and Commercial Navigation*, London, 1832, 1834–9, 1840, 1844, 1846, 1847, 1852, 1854, 1856, 1859 (cited as CD followed by date of edition); *A Statistical Account of the British Empire, exhibiting its extent, physical capacities, population, industry, and civil and religious institutions*, London, 1837, 1839, 1847, 1854 (cited as *Statistical Account* followed by date of edition); *A Dictionary, Geographical, Statistical, and Historical, of the Various Countries, Places, and Principal Natural Objects in the World*, London, 1841–2, 1845–6, 1849, 1852, 1854.

[4] D. P. O'Brien, *J. R. McCulloch, A Study in Classical Economics*, London, 1970.

[1] Many of the earlier writers can be found in McCulloch's *Literature of Political Economy*, London, 1845, ch. xix, 'Revenue and Finance', pp. 318-49 and in the bibliography appended to E. R. A. Seligman, *Progressive Taxation in Theory and Practice*, 2nd edition, Princeton, 1908, pp. 325-31.

works on economics. These included the works of Smith and Ricardo; and in the former case the theoretical material was interwoven with institutional considerations in a similar manner to McCulloch's. Secondly there were works which had dealt – sometimes very well – with specific problems, such as the national debt or the idea of a property tax. The works of such authors as Hume, Hamilton and Price all stand out here. Thirdly there were works of a 'statistical' nature of which the outstanding example was perhaps Parnell's *On Financial Reform*.[2] Now McCulloch had been a contributor to all three fields; his *Principles* had included material on taxation[3]; he had written extensively in the *Scotsman*, *Edinburgh Review* and *Encyclopaedia Britannica* on the theoretical and practical problems of taxation[4] (and not a little of the material in the *Treatise* first saw the light of day in one of these three publications); and in his statistical works, especially the *Statistical Account of the British Empire*,[5] he had provided information on the actual flows of revenue. But he clearly felt the need for a systematic treatise.

This was partly because of a certain dissatisfaction with the work of his predecessors. Ricardo's 'investigations' he thought 'too abstract to be of much practical utility'.[6] Smith's work dated from 1776, and by 1845 was distinctly outdated in the institutional and factual background; and Parnell's work was hardly comprehensive.[7] Hence the need for a systematic treatise – 'the influence of taxation over public prosperity . . . cannot be advantageously treated of in parts. To be properly understood and appreciated, it should be considered as a whole, and in a general point of view'.[8]

The work first appeared in 1845. It is clear that McCulloch was given strong support in his project by Monteagle who, as Spring Rice, had been Chancellor of the Exchequer 1835–9.

> Science, and that which is more important still, its practical application, owes you many debts for essential services, but the

[2] London, 1830; see also J. Marshall, *A Digest of all the Accounts relating to the population, productions, revenues, financial operations, manufactures, shipping, colonies, commerce . . . of the United Kingdom of Great Britain and Ireland*, London, 1833.

[3] E.g. *Principles*, 1830, pp. 114, 116, 475, 493–5, 501, 503.

[4] See the bibliography in O'Brien *op. cit.*, especially pp. 411–25.

[5] E.g. *Statistical Account*, 1847, vol. II, Part V, ch. ii, pp. 392–437; CD1840, pp. 584–91 (art. 'Funds') and 982–4 (art. 'Revenue and Expenditure').

[6] See below, p. 8. [7] *Ibid.* [8] *Ibid.*

> question of the Incidence of Taxation is I think more important than anything you have lately discussed.[9]

Nevertheless, despite Monteagle's anxiety, expressed to McCulloch, that the work should appear before the meeting of Parliament, it was definitely intended as an objective study rather than as a controversial work on economic policy. As McCulloch wrote to his patron Peel:

> There are things in it of which I am afraid you will not approve – I have however endeavoured, as well as I could, to treat the subject in a philosophical point of view, and with reference only to the well-being of the community; and I am not conscious that it has anything about it of a party or partisan taint – Had it been otherwise I certainly should not have presumed to send it to you – But being (in intention at least) a philosophical treatise I venture to submit it to your superior judgment".[10]

Although the work ran to three editions (1845, 1852, 1863) it is difficult to be certain just how successful it was. Longman's Impression Books are incomplete in their details of this work.[11] It is possible that McCulloch hindered its sales by his attempt to cut down on the allowance to the trade on the book, although Longman's argued strongly against the adoption of such a course.[12] But in general the book was well received. Merivale, reviewing it in the *Edinburgh Review*, said that it was a 'work with which not only every Statesman and Legislator, but every reflecting member of the community, ought to make himself acquainted', and added that 'Mr. M'Culloch has, by the thought and labour he has devoted to its composition, added another strong claim to those he had before established on the gratitude of his countrymen'.[13] He had begun his review with the words:

> This work embraces one of the most extensive, and pre-eminently the most practical department of the all-important science

[9] Monteagle to McCulloch, 2 Oct. 1844, Ms. AL 187 in University of London Library. He also wrote that it was 'impossible to estimate too highly' the importance of McCulloch's work on the book.

[10] McCulloch to Peel, 11 Jan. 1845, Add. Mss. 40557, f. 344.

[11] The only entry found in Longman's records is a record of 500 copies of the 2nd edition.

[12] 'We should strongly dissuade you from making less than the customary allowance to the trade. If published at 16s/ the price to the trade will be 11/4 in cloth. If at 15s/ – 10/9 in cloth.' Thomas Longman to McCulloch, 6 Jan. 1845, Ms. AL 187 in University of London Library.

[13] 'M'Culloch on Taxation and Funding', *Edinburgh Review*, vol. 82 (Oct. 1845), pp. 369–80, p. 380.

> to which it belongs; and it comes to us recommended by the authorship of one of the most distinguished cultivators of that science. He has here, in addition to his other great services, presented the Public with what is, strictly speaking, new in economical science; namely, a systematic and comprehensive survey of the whole field of Taxation.[14]

The Times too waxed enthusiastic.

> We congratulate the public upon the appearance of this excellent treatise from the pen of Mr. McCulloch. It is, we believe, the first publication, of any authority at least, that exclusively deals with the subject of taxation. Particular parts of our fiscal system, it is true, have been at different times, and for different purposes, elaborately considered, but the whole has never been at one time passed under review, nor subjected to a general and scathing interpretation.[15]

Not that particular points in the book were entirely without critics; Merivale in particular had some (very gently expressed) criticisms to offer, notably of McCulloch's very rigorous requirements if an income tax was to be deemed satisfactory as contrasted with his much less rigorous treatment of indirect taxes. *The Times* too, devoting a great deal of space to the work,[16] had some points to make; in particular the anonymous reviewer thought it dangerous to rely on the stimulating effects of taxation, doubted whether Holland really *had* declined at all, and offered a very dubious criticism of the mechanism of population adjustment to taxes affecting wage earners.[17] Another anonymous reviewer, this time in the *Westminster Review*,[18] had objections, notably to the idea of dutying corn,[19] and to the idea that the supply of effort and saving increased with the need for it.[20] However, his fundamental differences with McCulloch arose because the reviewer was a benefit theorist[21] whereas McCulloch was an ability to pay

[14] *Ibid.*, p. 367. [15] *The Times*, 27 Sep. 1845 (8a–c).

[16] In addition to the very lengthy review referred to above *The Times* also carried another two and a half of its enormous columns devoted to this work in the issue of 7 Oct. (7a–c).

[17] The argument was that the labouring classes did not have their remuneration in their own hands because one man alone could not affect the supply of labour by his own prudence; and it *was* used by McCulloch himself in the 1st and 2nd editions – see below, *Treatise on Taxation*, Part I, ch. 3, note 15.

[18] 'Principles of Taxation', *Westminster Review*, vol. XLVI (Oct. 1846), pp. 1–28. The review is signed 'F' and the author has not been identified.

[19] *Ibid.*, p. 1. [20] *Ibid.*, p. 4. [21] Cf. *ibid.*, especially pp. 5–6.

writer; and the former, in contrast to McCulloch, had a strong preference for direct taxes.[22] Nevertheless even this reviewer wrote:

> While, in this article, we have found so much to dissent from in Mr. M'Culloch's work, we must not withhold our testimony to the great industry and research which it displays, to the large number of interesting facts it contains, and to the irrefragable proofs it affords of the folly and mischievousness of, at least, high taxes on consumption.[23]

There is evidence too that later editions were well received; of the third edition McCulloch's old paper the *Scotsman*, although it had some criticisms to offer in defence of Gladstone's financial policy,[24] wrote:

> a work so full of wise remark and well-compacted information would require not one but a series of notices. We can only add that one charm of the book is the thorough command everywhere shown of the literature of the subject; and another not less potent is its excellent English style – clear, full, vigorous, often axiomatic, always masculine, and never rhetorical.[25]

(ii) *The contents of the book*

(*a*) *The Introduction*

The coverage of the book is designedly that of a general survey. After the Introduction the work is divided into three parts. Part I deals with direct taxes, Part II with indirect taxes, and Part III with public debt. Each of these divisions will be examined in turn.

The Introduction 'General Observations on Taxation' contains a number of important elements of McCulloch's thought on problems of public finance. After a brief discussion of the meaning of terms[26] McCulloch launches himself into a bald statement of the need for taxation, and for the assessment of that taxation on an ability-to-pay basis: 'all the subjects of a state should contribute according to their respective abilities, to the sums required, for its defence against hostile aggression, the preservation of internal tranquillity, and the protection

[22] See *ibid.*, especially pp. 19–25. The reviewer also objected to McCulloch's approval of taxing postage.

[23] *Ibid.*, p. 25.

[24] The reviewer argued that a secure base for taxation was better than a broad base. He also objected to McCulloch's tax-stimulation argument, asserting that this was inconsistent with free trade.

[25] *Scotsman*, 26 May 1863.

[26] Below, p. 15.

of the citizens in the undisturbed enjoyment of their property and rights'.[27] The state's wants are to be taken as given[28] – it was not the economist's role to enquire into governmental effectiveness[29] – and the enquiry to be made was into the manner in which the necessary amount of revenue could be raised with the least interference with growth. It is true that McCulloch sometimes made statements that will bear a benefit interpretation[30] but his adherance to an ability-to-pay approach was quite specific[31] and his position was recognised by his contemporaries and critics.[32] It was an ability-to-pay approach in the most simple and direct sense[33] with none of J. S. Mill's equal welfare sacrifice subtleties.[34] Government had no direct concern with the relative wealth of taxpayers, except in so far as this affected their ability to pay;[35] and the benefit approach was inoperable.[36] It is important to be clear about all this; McCulloch has been classed as a benefit theorist by Seligman and Myrdal[37] but he was no such thing. He did indeed refer to Thiers' 'insurance' concept of taxation. But he rejected it quite explicitly[38]; and as he remarks in this introduction: 'The best tax may not be that which is most nearly proportioned to the means of

[27] Below, p. 16.

[28] See R. A. Musgrave, *The Theory of Public Finance*, New York, 1959, p. 90, for a discussion of the distinguishing characteristics of the ability-to-pay approach. See also McCulloch's article 'Taxation' in the Supplement to the 4th–6th editions of *Encyclopaedia Britannica* (cited as EB6 Taxation; the articles in the 7th edition will be cited as EB7 Taxation), pp. 608–9, and first 1816 Essay, pp. 34–7.

[29] Below, p. 16.

[30] Thus he sometimes wrote as Smith had done about taxation in proportion to revenue enjoyed under the state – EB7 Taxation, p. 108; article 'Taxation' in the 8th edition of *Encyclopaedia Britannica*, reprinted as *An Article Practical and Theoretical on Taxation*, Edinburgh, 1860 (cited as EB8 Taxation), p. 3.

[31] E.g. EB6 Taxation, *loc. cit.*; EB8 Taxation, *loc. cit.*

[32] See especially *Westminster Review*, Oct. 1846, *loc. cit.*, pp. 4–6.

[33] See below, pp. 30, 136 'It is of trifling consequence whether a tax be theoretically good or bad'.

[34] See R. A. Musgrave *op. cit.*, *loc. cit.*, for an examination of various forms of the ability to pay concept.

[35] Below, p. 32.

[36] This had for long been McCulloch's position – see 'Commutation of Taxes – Proposed Tax on Property and Income', *Edinburgh Review*, vol. LVII, Apr. 1833, pp. 143–68.

[37] E. R. A. Seligman, *Progressive Taxation in Theory and Practice*, Princeton, 1909, p. 166; G. Myrdal, *The Political Element in the Development of Economic Theory*, trans. P. Streeten, London, 1953, p. 164.

[38] Below, p. 30; EB8 Taxation, pp. 6–8.

individuals, but it is that which is most easily assessed and collected, and is, at the same time, most conducive, or at least opposed, all things considered, to the public interest.'[39]

The level of government expenditure which had to be taken as given for ability-to-pay purposes might be quite high; and although McCulloch had been prepared on occasion to criticise military expenditure[40] and call for minimum necessary resource use by government,[41] this is not truly representative of his position. He was strongly opposed to cramping needlessly the role of government by surveying its expenditure too closely[42]; and he explicitly rejected the idea that it was merely the role of government to hold the ring.[43] The role he afforded to government was fairly considerable; and he was quite outspoken in his attack on Laisser-Faire extremists.[44] But whatever the *level* of the government's expenditure this was, from the public finance point of view, to be taken as given.[45]

McCulloch's treatment of Smith's four great maxims of taxation – benefit, certainty, convenience and economy – follows from this. The first he rejected[46]; but the other three provided the basic value judgments of McCulloch's system.[47] The taxes of Eastern countries failed the second requirement[48] (and here we may note the contempt, almost hatred, which McCulloch, so typically of a Victorian liberal, felt for

[39] Below, p. 30.

[40] E.g. second 1816 Essay, pp. 177–9; 'British Finances', *Scotsman*, 20 Jan. 1821, p. 17; 'Taxation and the Corn Laws', *Edinburgh Review*, vol. XXXIII, Jan. 1820, pp. 155-87, p. 185. But McCulloch was strongly opposed to impressment – see especially his Note on the subject in his editions of the *Wealth of Nations*, e.g. WN1863, pp. 542–4.

[41] EB6 Taxation, p. 611; 'General Principles of Taxation – No. II', *Scotsman*, 1 Feb. 1823, p. 73; below, p. 27. McCulloch was fond of quoting Say's dictum that 'Le meilleur de tous les plans de finance est de dépenser peu, et le meilleur de tous les impôts est le plus petit', e.g. *Scotsman*, 14 Nov. 1818, p. 361, 'British Finances'. He included it in the *Treatise on Taxation*, 1852, p. 18, but omitted it from the 1863 edition (below pp. 26–27).

[42] McCulloch to Wilmot Horton, 2 Jan. 1827, Catton Hall Papers.

[43] *Principles*, 1830, pp. 249–50.

[44] McCulloch to Napier, 23 Dec. 1830, Add. Mss. 34614 f. 469. On McCulloch's views on the role of government see O'Brien, *op. cit.*, pp. 285–91.

[45] See below, p. 319, 'The public exigencies require that a sum of seventy millions a year should be raised, one way or other'.

[46] Below, pp. 28–30. Smith's first canon actually encompassed both benefit and ability to pay principles.

[47] Below, pp. 28-31.

[48] Below, p. 34.

Turkey[49]). The need for the third maxim brought from him a spirited defence of the warehousing system[50]; and he was insistent on the fulfilment of the fourth (economy in collection) maxim (a matter with which Sir Henry Parnell had dealt at some length).[51]

Another important element in this introductory section is the notion that taxation may have an important effect in stimulating and increasing the supply of effort and ingenuity.[52] This idea, of which McCulloch made perhaps more use than any other writer,[53] derived, so far as McCulloch was concerned, from David Hume.[54] It has been much criticised by other writers[55] although McCulloch's important use of it is acknowledged by them. He even used the idea as the basis for an argument that taxation could actually increase the national wealth through over-reaction to its imposition[56]; and he also argued at one stage that if taxation were imposed then removed this would leave the supply of effort and ingenuity at the higher (stimulated) level.[57] Together with this McCulloch advanced the more obvious idea, also found in Ricardo, that the supply of saving will be maintained in the face of additional taxation, through a reduction in consumption.[58] The tax stimulation and 'resilient-savings' arguments taken together led McCulloch to argue that these two in combination could stimulate growth thus enabling the community to bear taxation – he

[49] Below, pp. 35–6.

[50] Below, pp. 36–8.

[51] Below, pp. 38–9; Sir Henry Parnell, *On Financial Reform*, London, 1830, chap. ix, 'Collection of the Revenue'.

[52] Below, pp. 19–24.

[53] 'General Principles of Taxation – No. I', *Scotsman*, 25 Jan. 1823, p. 58; 'Funding System – British Finances', *Edinburgh Review*, vol. XXXIX, Oct. 1823, pp. 1–43, pp. 7–9, 17, 30; 'Taxation – Retrenchment – Reduction of the Public Debt', *ibid.*, vol. XLVI, Oct. 1827, pp. 390–414, pp. 413–14; 'Progress of the National Debt – Best Method of Funding', *ibid.*, vol. XLVII, Jan. 1828, pp. 59–86, p. 82; *ibid.*, Jan. 1833, *loc. cit.*, pp. 329–30; EB6 Taxation, p. 610.

[54] D. Hume, 'Essay on Taxes', in *Essays and Treatises on Various Subjects*, new edition, Edinburgh, 1809, vol. I, p. 363. The essence of Hume's position was that the effect depended on *gradual* increases in taxation; and this McCulloch adopted.

[55] E.g. P. Leroy-Beaulieu, 'On Taxation in General' reprinted in R. A. Musgrave and A. T. Peacock, *Classics in the Theory of Public Finance*, London, 1958, pp. 151–64, pp. 159–61.

[56] *Principles*, 1849, pp. 115–18.

[57] *Treatise on Taxation*, 1845, pp. 14, 385; however, he later abandoned this – *ibid.*, 1852, p. 157; WN1863, p. 618.

[58] *Scotsman*, 1823, *loc. cit.*; *Edinburgh Review*, Oct. 1823, Oct. 1827 and Jan. 1828, *loc. cit.*

was even critical of Smith and Hume for neglecting this,[59] despite his intellectual debt to the latter on this very score.

But, like Hume, McCulloch recognised that this was not an unlimited resource. Firstly, as he points out here,[60] any savage or punitive increase in taxation could give a shock to economic activity and harm it.[61] Moreover he recognised that taxation could have harmful effects in causing capital export – this was consistent with his factor mobility model of international trade discussed elsewhere – and he cited the supposed decline of Holland as an example of this.[62] However, there are changes of emphasis compared with his earlier work. His concern in the early post-war period about the effects of heavy taxation on growth[63] had abated[64] and in the end he had come to view Britain as a lightly taxed country.[65] Nevertheless he continued to recognise that heavy taxation could interfere with growth and he continually emphasised, as he does here,[66] that if taxation was sufficiently heavy to affect either new saving or the existing capital stock its effects would be serious because it was reducing the means of future production

McCulloch was not then, either in this book or in his other writings, a complete apologist for taxation whatever the level; he was perfectly well aware that it could interfere with economic growth, which was the overriding consideration.[67] But more important than the absolute amount of taxation was the way it was raised; on how far this conformed with Smith's last three requirements depended its weight as interfering

[59] *Scotsman*, 1823, *loc. cit.*; *ibid.*, 26 Feb. 1823, p. 130, 'Financial Situation of the Country – Reduction of Taxes'; *Edinburgh Review*, Oct. 1823, *loc. cit.*, p. 18; *ibid.*, Jan. 1828, *loc. cit.*, pp. 66–7; WN1850, p. 629.

[60] Below, p. 23.

[61] *Scotsman*, Jan. 1823, *loc. cit.*; EB6 Taxation, p. 610.

[62] *Edinburgh Review*, Jul. 1830, *loc. cit.* (Decline of Holland), pp. 434–6; EB6 Taxation, p. 610; *Principles*, 1830, pp. 493-4. See also *Edinburgh Review*, Jan. 1828, *loc. cit.*, pp. 66–7. On McCulloch's trade model see O'Brien, *op. cit.*, ch. x.

[63] First 1816 Essay, p. 37; *Scotsman*, 15 Feb. 1817, p. 30; 'Taxation and the Corn Laws', *Edinburgh Review*, vol. XXXIII, Jan. 1820, pp. 155-87, p. 155. Many of McCulloch's articles in the *Scotsman* during the years 1817–20 show this concern.

[64] *Edinburgh Review*, Oct. 1827, *loc. cit.*, pp. 404–6; *ibid.*, Jan. 1828, *loc. cit.*, p. 67.

[65] *Statistical Account*, 1847, vol. II, p. 393.

[66] Below, pp. 19, 23.

[67] E.g. *Treatise on Taxation*, 1852, pp. 101-2 (see below Part I, ch. 3, note 21); *Edinburgh Review*, Oct. 1827, *loc. cit.*, p. 392. This was recognised by J. S. Mill – see his *Principles of Political Economy*, ed. W. J. Ashley, London, 1915, p. 747.

with economic processes.[68] Nevertheless he did lay great stress on its stimulating effects as the reader of his introductory section will find; and he was quick to knock down some of the sillier arguments used by those who bewailed taxation. Thus in this section we find him arguing[69] that the weight of taxation is to be estimated by the single factoral terms of trade between taxpayer and government, not the gross barter terms.[70] But here also he argues (following Hamilton closely) that the effects of taxation were not removed by spending its receipts[71]; the spending of tax receipts did not create an additional market but merely one which, accepting Say's equality as an equilibrium proposition, would already have existed.

A number of additional points emerge in this introduction. Firstly, we find[72] McCulloch's reservations about democracy being made clear enough. He was not alone in this of course.[73] McCulloch belonged strictly speaking to no political party. The anti-Tory *Scotsman* which he had edited was not a Whig paper – yet it had a marked distaste for radicalism. The same could be said of McCulloch. Rather he attached himself to those politicians (especially Peel) who pursued the economic policies he thought desirable. But he had a very real fear of excessive political liberalism; he hated and feared the radicals. He seems genuinely to have anticipated revolution at one stage.[74] But this was not due to any dislike of the 'lower orders'. Indeed, as will be seen below, he was very concerned about their position in an inequitable society.[75] But he believed that universal suffrage would be subversive of that security

[68] Below, pp. 24-5, 32-8; see also 'Expense of Collecting the Revenue – Custom-House Establishment – Smuggling', *Scotsman*, 11 Oct. 1823, pp. 649-50; EB6 Taxation, p. 612.

[69] Below, p. 18.

[70] *Scotsman*, 25 Jan. 1823, p. 58; EB6 Taxation, p. 609.

[71] Below, pp. 12-14; Second 1816 Essay, p. 178; *Scotsman*, Jan. 1823, p. 58; R. Hamilton, *An Inquiry concerning the Rise, Progress, Redemption, Present State, and Management, of the National Debt of Great Britain and Ireland*, reprinted in McCulloch (ed.) *A Select Collection of Scarce and Valuable Tracts and other Publications on the National Debt and the Sinking Fund, from the originals of Harley, Gould, Pulteney, Walpole, Hume, Price, Hamilton, and others*, 1857, pp. 421-688, pp. 452-3.

[72] Below, pp. 39-40.

[73] See W. D. Grampp, 'The Politics of the Classical Economists', *Quarterly Journal of Economics*, vol. 62 (1948), pp. 714-47.

[74] McCulloch to Napier, 28 Feb. 1831, Add. Mss. 34615, f. 48.

[75] See below, pp. 106-7 and n 21. See the *Treatise on Taxation*, 1845, pp. 110 and 394-5.

of property which, as noted elsewhere, he regarded as the great *sine qua non* of economic growth.[76]

Secondly there is the discovery, surprising because he was here (as elsewhere) much impressed by what Arthur Young had written of the pre-revolutionary tax system in France,[77] that McCulloch was not opposed to tax-farming in principle.[78] This was not Smith's attitude; but McCulloch here believed that the system could be economical and was acceptable if it did not involve investigation into the taxpayers' means.[79]

Thirdly there is a lengthy section[80] on corvée and impressment. McCulloch opposed the former mainly on the grounds that it was uneconomical as Turgot had established; but his opposition to impressment, even though it might be an economical means of manning the services, was moral, and very outspoken.[81]

Fourthly we may note McCulloch's adoption[82] of the principle, so strongly espoused by his friend Overstone in the latter's attack on Gladstone's tax changes, that changes in taxation were *per se* undesirable, and caused, *of themselves*, a loss of welfare. It was not, however, an idea of which McCulloch made great use.

Fifthly there is the appearance here of McCulloch's concept of sacrifice. This was very different from the modern concept and a good deal more tangible. It related not to welfare but to income – it was in fact a concept of 'income-sacrifice'. If a consumer's demand for a commodity was totally inelastic, he sacrificed income automatically as that commodity was taxed. If the consumer's demand was elastic he was to some degree able to reduce his purchases; and in so far as he did this he was viewed by McCulloch as avoiding the tax and hence reducing his income-sacrifice. It was this which enabled McCulloch to argue[83] that payment of consumption taxes was voluntary. The very fact that the reduction in consumption was in part an income effect of reduced purchasing power resulting from a tax-induced price rise, did

[76] See D. P. O'Brien, *J. R. McCulloch*, p. 278. [77] Below, pp. 33–4.

[78] Below, pp. 43–4. [79] See also EB6 Taxation, p. 615.

[80] Below, pp. 44–50. [81] See below, pp. 49–50.

[82] Below, pp. 40–1 and notes 36–38. The material was introduced in the 3rd edition.

[83] Below, p. 31. This of course despite the fact, which McCulloch could hardly be expected to appreciate, that where elasticity of demand was positive but less than one a rise in price would increase total outlay even though consumption diminished.

not cause him to alter his view.[84] Nor, of course did he consider the problem that the consumer was being pushed to a less preferred position on his welfare surface even if he did avoid the tax.[85] But it is important to understand McCulloch's particular concept of sacrifice in order to understand his writings on taxation.

Finally there are in this introductory section three points which will be referred to in greater detail below but which will be noted at this stage. The first is McCulloch's insistence[86] that progressive taxation is subversive of the motives which achieve economic growth. The second is his preference for indirect taxes on ability-to-pay grounds. The third is McCulloch's dislike, shared by Overstone, of any sacrifice of revenue not strictly necessary, coupled with his opposition to Ricardo's ideas on war finance.[87] All these points will be returned to at later stages in this (editorial) introduction.

In dealing with McCulloch's Introduction there is one point which, since it underlies much of what McCulloch has to say, should be raised here. This is his requirement of *inter-sectoral* justice. *Interpersonal* equality did not concern him very greatly; we have already noted that he believed the means of taxpayers were not the concern of tax-raising government. But, for reasons obviously connected with achieving optimal and balanced growth, intersectoral equality of treatment was important. It was something on which he laid particular stress in dealing with the agricultural sector[88]; but it is to be found fairly frequently in his writings on taxation.

(*b*) *Part I of the* Treatise: *Direct Taxes*

Part I which follows the Introduction is concerned with Direct Taxes, and covers taxes on rent, profits, wages, and property and income. The treatment of these originated in a series of articles in the *Scotsman*, although the analysis here is by no means identical.

[84] For criticism, see J. S. Mill, *Principles of Political Economy*, ed. W. Ashley, London, 1909, p. 866.

[85] However, he did recognise that a welfare loss arose when a producer was forced by the market mechanism to leave an industry – see below, pp. 80–1, and WN1863, p. 612.

[86] Below, p. 32.

[87] Below, pp. 41–3.

[88] This was a continuing theme in his writings – see 'Effects of a Reduction in the Price of Corn on the Pressure of Taxation', *Scotsman*, 17 Feb. 1827, p. 105; EB7 Taxation, pp. 114–15.

McCulloch dealt first with taxes on the rent of land,[89] and followed this by a discussion of taxes on the rent of houses. His treatment of the problem of taxes on rent started with the distinction between gross rent and pure economic rent. Having asserted that Smith was in error in believing that taxes on rent fall wholly on the landlord, he made it clear that the error is only in relation to gross rent. Rent which originated in the varying fertility of the soil[90] could be totally abstracted from the landlord without affecting any other class. A tax on *gross* rents would, in so far as it affected profit on capital invested in improvement, cause price to rise. But this was not the case with a tax on pure rent.

Obviously all this was not very satisfactory. As Ricardo had pointed out[91] the return on capital invested in the soil was also rent if the capital could not be extracted. Nor was the argument very happy that a tax on gross rent would fall on the two constituent parts of rent exactly in proportion as they formed the whole.[92] As, however, McCulloch was to make a similar mistake in relation to the rent of houses, consideration of this will be deferred for the moment. But, by the time this book first appeared, McCulloch had come to disapprove of taxes on rent in any case as difficult of operation and discouraging of improvements[93] as well as violating intersectoral justice by taxing one kind of property only.[94]

In this chapter on taxes on rent we find too that McCulloch rejected James Mill's suggestion that in new countries where there was no established ownership of the land the state should hold it and auction the ground rents, this rejection being on the grounds that private property in land was necessary to encourage investment in improvements. Private property indeed was 'the grand source of civilisation.'[95]

[89] See Part I, ch. i and compare 'Inquiry into the Incidence and Effect of Taxes on Rent', *Scotsman*, 18 Oct. 1823, p. 665.

[90] McCulloch's rent theory was more complicated than this implies – he recognised that the return to co-operating factors would be equalised on the intensive and extensive margins – *Principles*, 1825, p. 273. But the treatment here is very much as in the *Scotsman* article cited in the previous note.

[91] D. Ricardo, *On the Principles of Political Economy and Taxation*, vol. I of *The Works and Correspondence of David Ricardo*, ed. P. Sraffa, Cambridge, 1951–5, pp. 261–2n. Other references will be given as 'Ricardo's *Works*' followed by the volume.

[92] Below, pp. 54–5; see also 'Inquiry into the Incidence and Effect of Taxes on Rent', *Scotsman*, 18 Oct. 1823, p. 665; EB6 Taxation, p. 617; WN1828, vol. IV, p. 537.

[93] Below, pp. 55–6.

[94] See also WN1838, pp. 604–5; *Literature of Political Economy*, p. 346.

[95] Below, p. 58.

McCulloch had not always taken such an attitude to Mill's proposal[96]; but the one expressed here represents no sudden and dramatic change of mind.[97]

A fairly routine attack on the Physiocrats (and on the Physiocratic elements in Smith) – on the lines that land is not a unique source of wealth and that natural powers assist other activities than agriculture – was followed by the observation that total government expenditure in the United Kingdom was in any case greater than total gross rental, and the majority of the latter, it is asserted, consists of return on capital. The remainder of the material dealing with taxes on the rent of land is confined to tracing their history and illustrating the harmful effects of such taxes, especially when variable – the existing land tax was supportable precisely because it was fixed.

McCulloch then passed in the second part of the chapter to taxes on the rent of houses. He distinguished building rent and ground rent, and argued that, because of the peculiarly inelastic supply of housing in the short run, a tax on house rent would fall on the builder. But after there had been sufficient time for adjustment the burden would fall on the occupiers and ground landlords in the proportion that building and ground rent were of total rent.[98] This was in fact incorrect although it passed J. S. Mill's inspection sufficiently well for him to borrow the idea from McCulloch.[99] As Edgeworth pointed out, this would only be true where total tax equalled total rent and the landlord was prepared to accept some reduction of rent rather than face the effects of a reduction in house building where houses and land were in fixed proportions. Normally the division of the burden would be indeterminate, although where elasticity of demand for houses was zero the occupier would probably bear the whole tax.[100]

Oddly enough McCulloch was, later in the volume,[101] quite happy with taxes on houses which were proportioned to the rent. He believed

[96] *Scotsman*, Oct. 1823, *loc. cit.*; 'Abolition of the Corn Laws', *Edinburgh Review*, vol. XLIV, Sep. 1826, pp. 319–59, p. 351.

[97] See EB7 Taxation, p. 102, and compare with EB6 Taxation, p. 617; see below, pp. 57–9. However, he had not at any stage approved of Mill's suggestion of taxing increments of rental value – see EB6 Taxation, pp. 616–17.

[98] Below, pp. 71–2; see also EB6 Taxation, p. 618.

[99] J. S. Mill, *Principles of Political Economy*, ed. W. J. Ashley, London, 1909, pp. 832–4.

[100] F. Y. Edgeworth, *Papers Relating to Political Economy*, London, 1925, vol. II, pp. 82–5.

[101] Below, p. 75–6.

(in Chapter 1 of Part I) that part of such a tax would fall on ground rent; and earlier in the same chapter, as already noted, he condemned taxes on the landlord's rent as unjust.[102] It is interesting too, that although he was strong on the difficulties of separating the different elements in gross rent of agricultural land, he still felt able to recommend a house tax which included a tax on shop rents (to be charged at different rates depending on how much of the building was used for business purposes) without apparently being concerned about how much of the rent was due to investment in a fine building suitable for a good shop.[103]

In this chapter we find McCulloch a spirited defender of house taxes as not interfering with the allocation of resources (which would only be true if elasticity of demand for them were zero) and as requiring very little of the 'inquisatorial proceedings' he associated with the income and property taxes.[104] He opposed lower limit exemptions from the tax on the grounds of his comprehensive opposition to progressivity, although for the very cheapest houses he was prepared to accept that the tax should be collected from the owner.[105] He recognised that there were practical difficulties – Wood had encountered some as Chancellor in 1852.[106] Organisation was not easy and there was the added difficulty that 'baronial halls' which were owner-occupied would command a negative rent.[107] He had earlier avoided this problem[108] but now faced it squarely and suggested assessment by building cost of such abodes. But, despite the difficulties, he thought the house tax a good tax, whereas he dismissed the windows tax as unrelated to value and bad for health.[109]

The introduction of these 'assessed taxes' (ostensibly dealt with later in the work under the heading of indirect taxes) into the discussion of taxes on rent is illustrative of two aspects of McCulloch's writing. On the one hand he had, like Smith, a tendency to digress severely

[102] Below, pp. 55–7. See also WN1838, pp. 604–5, and EB7 Taxation, p. 101.

[103] Below, pp. 72–3.

[104] Below, pp. 73–4; see also 'Inexpediency of the Farther Reduction or Repeal of the Assessed Taxes', *Scotsman*, 19 Feb. 1825, p. 113; *Edinburgh Review*, Apr. 1833, *loc. cit.*, p. 166; 'Complaints and Proposals regarding Taxation', *Edinburgh Review*, vol. LVI, Jul. 1833, pp. 434–48, p. 435.

[105] Below, p. 74.

[106] Below, pp. 75–6.

[107] Below, pp. 75–6.

[108] *Edinburgh Review*, Apr. 1833, *loc. cit.*, pp. 166–7.

[109] Below, p. 76.

from the main analytical problem facing him; on the other, he was, by and large, incapable of discussing theoretical problems purely on their merits and divorced from a social and institutional framework. The methodological approach of this chapter could hardly be in stronger contrast to Ricardo's chapter.[110]

Following the discussion of taxes on rent, McCulloch turned his attention to taxes on profits in a discussion which again stems from his original *Scotsman* article.[111] But, again, relatively little of the chapter is concerned with the purely theoretical issues involved. McCulloch's position on this subject, which he consistently held to, was that if a tax on profits was universal it would depress profits and interfere with accumulation; if partial it would alter relative prices as capital was re-allocated through the usual profit equalisation mechanism.[112] However, by 1863 he had come to make four qualifications to this piece of pure Ricardian treatment. Firstly he had decided that the idea of a universal profits tax was a purely theoretical curiosity – and therefore of no interest to McCulloch.[113] Secondly he decided that whether a partial profits tax raised prices depended on the response of producers to it – the tax-stimulation effect might wholly or partially offset it.[114] Thirdly he came to stress the imperfect mobility of capital in relation to the profit equalisation mechanism.[115] Fourthly he pointed out, in criticism of Ricardo, that if there were free import of the goods in question the scope for the prices of those articles whose profits were taxed, to rise, was limited.[116] Fifthly McCulloch points out that Ricardo's conclusion that a tax on agricultural profits would increase rent also depends upon the assumption that demand for corn is completely inelastic.[117] But that again is the limit of the purely theoretical considerations which the chapter contains.

The remainder of the chapter is concerned with more institutional material, covering the French *taille* and *contribution foncière*, and largely borrowed from Smith, Hume and Arthur Young. Again, as in the previous chapter, it is apparent that McCulloch cannot for long shake

[110] Ricardo's *Works*, vol. I, pp. 173–5.

[111] 'Inquiry into the Incidence and Effect of Taxes on Profits', *Scotsman*, 8 Nov. 1823, p. 713.

[112] Below, pp. 78–81; see also *Scotsman, loc. cit.*; EB6 Taxation, pp. 618–19; WN1828 vol. IV, p. 540.

[113] Below, p. 79; see also EB7 Taxation, p. 102; WN1863, p. 612.

[114] Below, p. 80; see also WN1863, p. 612.

[115] Below, pp. 80–1.

[116] Below, pp. 81–2; see also EB7 Taxation, p. 103.

[117] *Ibid.*

himself free from institutional considerations; and he is prone to digress. For these were only very partially taxes on profits at all. In fairness to McCulloch it should be said that these taxes were *intended* to be profits taxes, but became, in effect, property taxes because of the difficulties of assessment – McCulloch was much concerned with the operational characteristics of various taxes. Nevertheless he allows the discussion to spill over into a consideration of the desirable mode of operation of a land tax, and progresses from this to some of the conditions for agricultural progress.[118]

Following the chapter on taxes on profits comes one on taxes on wages. This has a strong claim to be the most muddled chapter in the book, although such a muddle was by no means confined to McCulloch. Throughout this chapter (which again derived from the *Scotsman*[119]), and indeed all McCulloch's writings on this particular problem, there is no clear attempt to distinguish between a tax on wages and a tax on wage goods. After distinguishing long run (psychological subsistence) from market wages (in which not all of his later modifications to the Malthusian analysis appear, partly because the text follows the *Scotsman* article fairly closely[120]) he went on to separate time-rate receivers and piece-rate receivers, further separating the former into domestic servants and those providing their own accommodation. Taxes on the wages of piece-rate earners would be counteracted by an increased supply of effort on their part – McCulloch's attitude to piece-rates was much more favourable than Smith's.[121] Taxes on domestic servants' *wage goods* (note the switch) would fall wholly on their employers. McCulloch admitted that this might be counteracted to some extent by a reduction in the demand for domestic servants – but failed to spot the point which Merivale was later to make about this argument[122] viz. that if the effect of the tax falling on employers was

[118] Below, pp. 83–93.

[119] 'Inquiry into the Incidence and Effect of Taxes on Wages', *Scotsman*, 27 Sep. 1823, p. 617; see also EB6 Taxation, p. 260; WN1828, vol. IV, p. 542.

[120] Nevertheless there are significant modifications as compared with the *Scotsman* article, and one particularly uncompromising statement of the Malthusian death control which appeared there is omitted. But fifteen paragraphs and substantial parts of two others are from the *Scotsman*. See O'Brien, *op. cit.*, pp. 314–19, on the evolution of McCulloch's views on population.

[121] Adam Smith, *An Inquiry into the Nature and Causes of the Wealth of Nations*, ed. E. Cannan, London, 1904, vol. I, Book I, ch. viii, pp. 83–4.

[122] *Edinburgh Review*, Oct. 1845, *loc. cit.*, p. 370.

to make domestic servants better off than other wage earners this would increase competition for servant jobs and depress wages.

The other time-rate earners would bear a tax on *wage goods* in the short run, and their real incomes would be depressed, although in the long run population would adjust and wages would rise. (In the population adjustment McCulloch used the Malthusian death mechanism which was inconsistent with his concept of *psychological* subsistence.) Now it is important to note this analysis. Neither Smith nor Ricardo had believed that a tax on wage earners *or* their consumption goods would actually fall on them. But McCulloch explicitly rejected such a view.[123] Here he argues that because the psychological subsistence level is *not* fixed but following behind the market rate,[124] and because population adjusted very slowly to any change in wages, taxation would certainly fall on such wage-earners in the short run. In addition, if this resulted in any downward movement of the psychological subsistence level, they might bear the tax in the long run too.[125]

Yet in the end he seems to expect population adjustment to shift the burden of the tax – and he rejects[126] the argument which he himself had used in the previous two editions[127] (and which curiously had been used *against* him by *The Times*[128]) that population would not adjust because one man would see that his prudence alone would have no significant effect on the general level of population. He now recognises that each man's individual self-interest should be enough to produce prudence.

Reverting then to a tax on *wages* he uses the *simpliste* Ricardian argument that because such a tax would not affect employers' demand for labour while enabling government to demand labour also, it would raise wages by the amount of the tax.[129] But then he raises his own criticism of this argument – that the wage tax receipts might not be spent on hiring labour[130] in which case any adjustment had to be via population. (If spent on increasing the salaries of existing employees the tax receipts would not affect wages because demand for commodities was not demand for labour.)[131]

[123] Below, pp. 98-100; Ricardo's *Works*, vol. I, p. 159; Ricardo to McCulloch, 29 Mar. 1820, *Works*, vol. VIII, pp. 168-73; Smith, *op. cit.*, vol. II, Book V, ch. ii, pp. 348-9.

[124] Below, pp. 99-100.

[125] Below, p. 101.

[126] Below, pp. 101-3.

[127] See below, Part I, ch. 3, note 12.

[128] *Loc. cit.*

[129] Below, p. 105.

[130] Below, pp. 105-6.

[131] See also J. S. Mill, *op. cit.*, pp. 827-8 for a similar view.

Because of all this, McCulloch considered a tax on wages undesirable.[132] Even if wages *did* rise, it might be difficult to convince wage-earners of this; and if wages were going to adjust immediately it was better to tax employers directly. Yet having advanced this view he still feels able to argue that the real harm of wage taxes lies in their effect on accumulation[133] – which would only be true if they were certainly passed on to the employer. He concludes the chapter by dismissing poll taxes as unjust, and assessment of taxation by social class as impossible.

The way in which McCulloch swings from one view to another and from one emphasis to another all the way through this chapter reflects the continual conflict in his mind over the effect of taxes both on wages and on wage goods. For although he was intellectually impressed by arguments that wages adjusted to take account of these, it was a matter of observation that they did not.[134] Apart from the fact that the simpliste Ricardian argument assumed a frictionless and lagless world, it conflicted with what McCulloch saw. Hence his proneness to stress the difficulties of population adjustment and to doubt its efficacy.[135] There were also the complications of child labour and immigration to keep wages depressed.[136] In particular he often stressed the danger that the psychological subsistence level would move rather than population adjust.[137] He was, in short, concerned that the analysis should be relevant, and not conflict with observation; and this does him credit even if his attempts to reconcile his observations with his analysis were not really successful.

After the problem of wage taxation McCulloch turns in Chapter 4

[132] Below, p. 106. [133] Below, p. 107.

[134] *Scotsman*, 29 Aug. 1818, p. 277; 'Expediency and Practicability of Mr. Ricardo's plan for Paying Off the National Debt', *ibid.*, 8 Jan. 1820, pp. 9–10; *Edinburgh Review*, Jan. 1820, *loc. cit.*, pp. 156–60.

[135] E.g. *Edinburgh Review*, Jan. 1820, *loc. cit.*, pp. 160–1; EB6 Taxation, pp. 620–1; EB7 Taxation, p. 105; below, pp. 99-100; EB6 Taxation, p. 14.

[136] *Edinburgh Review*, Jan. 1820, *loc. cit.*, pp. 168–9; *Treatise on Taxation*, 1845, p. 109; *ibid.*, 1852, pp. 102-43; below Part I, ch. 3, note 21.

[137] This was first fully developed by McCulloch in the *Treatise on Taxation*, 1845, pp. 109–12 and 106–7; but it appears partly in earlier works, e.g. *Edinburgh Review*, Jan. 1820, *loc. cit.*, pp. 160–2; EB7 Taxation, pp. 105–6. But McCulloch ultimately took the view that the worker 'avoided' the effect of such taxes, at least in part, by extra effort and adjustment of his purchases – EB8 Taxation, p. 14, below pp. 100-104 – although the state should not even take the risk of depression of subsistence occurring (below, p. 106).

to the major problem of property and income taxation. It is perhaps unfortunate that this chapter should come before McCulloch's discussion of the advantages and disadvantages of direct and indirect taxation in general because his strong preference for the latter underlies much of what he has to say. But it is noteworthy that McCulloch devoted a fair amount of attention to property and income taxes which had been almost completely neglected by Ricardo.[138] McCulloch was concerned with actualities.

McCulloch begins the chapter with a long critique of property taxation,[139] mainly on the grounds of difficulty of valuation. To this is added different productivity of property of nominally the same value (why this does not adjust their values is not made clear), inducements to concealment, fraud and evasion, and disincentives to investment. Some of these problems McCulloch admits would be alleviated if property engaged in industrial undertakings was excluded, but the advantages would be more than offset by the violation of the requirement of inter-sectoral justice, while the taxing of that kind of property (landed) to which the manufacturing classes aspired would interfere with their accumulation.

McCulloch was not here adopting a new attitude. He had for long opposed property taxation. He agreed that its distorting effects were not marked and that it did not cause smuggling.[140] But there was not, he was inclined to argue, any limit to which such a tax could be carried; and it excluded many of the wealthy who did not *own* property, such as bishops. It would possibly involve capital and liquidation where the yield on property was low, and it was likely to cause capital emigration.[141]

He was little more enthusiastic about income tax. In this work, as in his previous writings on the subject, he recognised that this tax had certain advantages. It did not automatically involve regression as did taxes on consumption, and it did not affect relative prices and the distribution of resources.[142] He had long recognised that such a tax might be economical to collect, did not encourage adulteration or

[138] See C. Shoup, *Ricardo on Taxation*, New York, 1960, pp. 219-20.

[139] Below, pp. 109-118.

[140] *Edinburgh Review*, Apr. 1833, *loc. cit.*, p. 144.

[141] *Edinburgh Review*, Apr. 1833, *loc. cit.*, p. 151; EB8 Taxation, pp. 20-1; see also below, pp. 109-118, though the arguments are not so fully developed here.

[142] Below, p. 119.

smuggling, and did not distort the choice between goods[143] (it distorted the choice between income and leisure but this he ignored). Indeed for a long time he seems to have considered these advantages sufficient to justify an income tax.[144] But his final conclusion, as exhibited in this work, was that such a tax was unsatisfactory.

The first group of his objections came under the general head of difficulties involved in discovering incomes.[145] Evasion was a problem on which he had for long laid great stress.[146] An income tax either involved taxing honesty, or giving wholly undesirable powers to the tax officers. One aspect of this was the problem of amortisation, especially that of capital invested by the professional classes in their training. He had for long recognised that to make official allowances for amortisation would lead to fraud[147] – but he also knew that payers of schedule D income tax made themselves unofficial allowances.[148]

A second group of objections to income tax raised by McCulloch related to the difficulty of taxing incomes justly even where their actual amounts were known. Now McCulloch here argued that professional (i.e. non-permanent) incomes should not be taxed at the same rate as perpetual ones.[149] This had not always been his position, in a controversy which continued throughout the nineteenth century.[150] He had originally argued that all incomes, of varying expected durations, should not be charged at the same rate.[151] He had then changed his position and come to argue that it did not matter whether professional incomes were taxed at the same rate as other incomes or not – entry into or exit from the professions would ensure that the relative advantages of professional incomes were the same as those of other incomes. (He had even applied this argument to a temporary war-time

[143] For earlier recognition of this see *Scotsman*, 26 Jan. 1822, pp. 26-7; 'Inexpediency of the Farther Reduction or Repeal of the Assessed Taxes', *ibid.*, 19 Feb. 1825, p. 113; *Edinburgh Review*, Apr. 1833, *loc. cit.*, pp. 144, 153.

[144] In particular see *Edinburgh Review*, Oct. 1823, *loc. cit.*, pp. 15-16; EB6 Taxation, p. 628.

[145] Below, pp. 120-126.

[146] 'Inquiry into the Incidence and Effect of Taxes on Income', *Scotsman*, 29 Nov. 1823, pp. 761-2, EB6 Taxation, p. 625; *Statistical Account*, 1837, vol. II, pp. 515-16.

[147] *Edinburgh Review*, Apr. 1833, *loc. cit.*, pp. 157-8; EB7 Taxation, p. 108. See below, pp. 120-126 and 135-6.

[148] Below, pp. 123-126, 139-40.

[149] Below, pp. 127-8.

[150] On this see F. Shehab, *Progressive Taxation, A Study in the Development of the Progressive Principle in the British Income Tax*, Oxford, 1953.

[151] *Scotsman*, 26 Jan. 1822, pp. 26-7; 'Finances of Great Britain – No. I – Principles of the Funding System', *ibid.*, 5 Apr. 1823, pp. 217–18.

income tax, on the grounds that wars occurred fairly regularly.[152]) It was an argument consistent with his concept of sacrifice which did not extend to welfare losses involved in adjustments; but it obviously neglected the implied distortion of resources. (It was McCulloch's own argument in relation to the income tax but it was rather similar to one that Ricardo had used in relation to his plan of war finance.[153]) However, McCulloch abandoned this position. He changed his mind, and adopted the position (held in this book) that all incomes should be reduced to a perpetual value according to the age of the recipient.[154] He noted and rejected his former argument on frictional grounds.

Having adopted this position he for long based it on the requirements of justice but he later added to this Mill's ground that those with temporary incomes should be allowed to build up capital.[155] Having adopted Mill's argument he was able to use it to counter those who replied to the 'justice' argument, that temporary incomes paid tax temporarily and permanent incomes paid permanently[156] – although he did regard the allowance of insurance premiums as a deduction from taxable income as too narrow a method of making provision.[157]

McCulloch's new requirement of the income tax encountered the difficulty that different life-tables and differing rates of discount produced different tax rates.[158] (Allowances should also be made for differences in health as well as differences in age.[159]) All the difficulties arising from McCulloch's new position which were involved in operating the tax satisfactorily, were in addition to the difficulties already noted of allowing for amortisation of capital invested in training. But professional men could not be exempted from income-tax because this would violate the requirement of inter-sectoral justice.[160]

[152] *Scotsman*, 29 Nov. 1823, pp. 761-2; *Edinburgh Review*, Oct. 1823, *loc. cit.*, pp. 13-15; EB6 Taxation, pp. 623-4.

[153] Ricardo's *Works*, vol. IV, pp. 188-9, art. 'Funding System'; Ricardo to McCulloch, 15 Sep. 1820, *Works*, vol. VIII, pp. 237-40, p. 238.

[154] Below, p. 127; see also EB7 Taxation, pp. 106-9 (and compare EB6 Taxation, pp. 623-6); *Edinburgh Review*, Apr. 1833, *loc. cit.*

[155] *Treatise on Taxation*, 1852, pp. 125-6 (see below, Part I, ch. 4, note 21); J. S. Mill, *op. cit.*, pp. 813-14.

[156] Taxation, 1852, *loc. cit.*

[157] Below, pp. 129-30.

[158] Below, p. 128; see also *Edinburgh Review*, Apr. 1833, *loc. cit.*, p. 156; EB7 Taxation, p. 107.

[159] Below, p. 129.

[160] Below, pp. 134-5.

Moreover, if professional incomes *were* excluded, it had to be recognised that similar difficulties arose in relation to manufacturing incomes. The treatment of the latter was further complicated because a part of entrepreneurial income was permanent (after depreciation had been allowed for) and another part temporary; once this division had (somehow or other) been accomplished the temporary part of the income had to be reduced to its present value.[161] The amortisation problem also applied[162] to income from the rent of improved land. The very *existence* of the amortisation problem meant that the introduction of an income tax would violate the inter-sectoral justice requirement: some income receivers were in a position to deduct unofficial 'allowances' while others (notably civil servants, including no doubt the Comptroller of the Stationery Office) were not.[163]

Because of all these difficulties, to which were added a number of subsidiary objections which McCulloch made to the tax – the precariousness of professional income (a point of which Smith had made much),[164] its 'inquisatorial' nature, its ability to encourage capital emigration, its disincentive effects, his reservations about its historical operation[165] – it was necessary to reserve the tax for war-time (emergency) use, or when faced with the sort of difficulties with which Peel had been faced in 1842.[166]

If, however, an income tax was introduced, whether for these or for less sufficient reasons, it was a prime requirement that it should be proportional. Such a view really had very little to do with benefit. There were two main grounds on which McCulloch opposed progression, and both are to be found in this chapter. One was that proportionality was the only *rule* that could be followed – once it was abandoned 'you are at sea without rudder or compass, and there is no amount of injustice and folly you may not commit'.[167] He was particularly worried about the 'injustice and folly' likely to occur in a democratic society.[168] The other, on which McCulloch was, in general,

161 Below, pp. 135-8. 162 Below, pp. 137. 163 Below, pp. 139-40.

164 Below, p. 139; Smith, *op. cit.*, vol. I, Book I, ch. x, pp. 107-9.

165 Below, pp. 131-4; see also *Scotsman*, 19 Feb. 1825, p. 113; *Edinburgh Review*, Apr. 1833, *loc. cit.*, pp. 158-60, 163; EB6 Taxation, pp. 619-20, 623; *Statistical Account*, 1847, vol. II, pp. 400-1. However, in *Edinburgh Review*, Oct. 1827, *loc. cit.*, pp. 409-10, he did seem to approve of its wartime operation.

166 Below, pp. 140-1; see also *Edinburgh Review*, Jan. 1828, *loc. cit.*, p. 84; *ibid.*, Apr. 1833, *loc. cit.*, p. 164.

167 Below, p. 147. 168 Below, p. 147.

inclined to lay more emphasis, was that redistribution was not legitimately a part of the role of government.[169] This of course implied that the system of distribution produced by the price system was an optimal one. Now McCulloch seems to have believed that it was indeed optimal. It was morally correct.[170] Now at first sight such a judgment lies outside the sphere of the economist. McCulloch by leaving the matter as he does in this chapter is open to misunderstanding and criticism. But in fact a study of his other writings shows that what McCulloch was getting at was this: any attempt by government to re-distribute income received under the price system would be subversive of all the incentives of that system[171] – and it would then interfere with growth. This was what was 'morally wrong' with progression.

But in adopting such a firm opposition to progression McCulloch involved himself in some inconsistencies, though in fewer, it should be added, than J. S. Mill. He was firm in advocating proportionality in legacy duties while Mill, as Myrdal has pointed out, advocated proportionality in taxation of income, yet also advocated severe legacy duties.[172] However, McCulloch, like Mill, was prepared to adopt a lower limit of income for tax purposes, which obviously involved a degree of progression; and although this was consistent with his opposition to a wage tax, McCulloch wanted it applied to all low incomes, whatever their source.[173] More importantly, McCulloch wrote as if the distribution of income produced by the price system was 'morally right': yet he sometimes showed deep concern about the *social* effects of that distribution. He had stated this at some length in the first edition of the *Treatise on Taxation* and also expressed concern in the second edition, although the material was omitted from the third edition. As, however, it is of some significance it is perhaps worth quoting here:

> It is impossible at this moment to cast the horoscope of this [the manufacturing] system, to foresee its revolutions, or to estimate its future influence over society. We confess, however, that our

[169] Below, p. 145–6. [170] Below, p. 145.

[171] See especially *Edinburgh Review*, Apr. 1833, *loc. cit.*, p. 163; *Scotsman*, 29 Nov. 1823, pp. 761–2; EB6 Taxation, pp. 624–5.

[172] J. S. Mill, *op. cit.*, pp. 808–9; Myrdal, *op. cit.*, pp. 170–1.

[173] Below, pp. 141–3. However, he was uneasy about this and used this as an argument against having an income tax at all – see below, p. 168. See also *Statistical Account*, 1847, vol. II, p. 401 where McCulloch seems to have had doubt about such a provision.

> anticipations are not of the most agreeable kind. It appears to be, of its essence, that most sorts of employments should be conducted on a large and continually increasing scale, in great establishments, with the assistance of highly improved and expensive machinery; providing, in this way, for the exaltation of a few individuals by the irremediable helotism of the great majority. And this conclusion would seem to be consistent not only with the nature of manufacturing industry, but with the fact, that though there has been a vast increase of production, and of wealth and comforts among the upper classes engaged in business during the last twenty or thirty years, and a considerable diminution of taxation, the condition of the workpeople during that period has certainly not been in any degree improved, but has rather, we incline to think, been sensibly deteriorated.[174]

Nevertheless McCulloch did not allow such considerations to deter him from his opposition to progression.

(*c*) *Part II of the* Treatise: *Indirect Taxes*

The chapter on income and property taxation is followed by three of the most important in the whole volume in relation to understanding McCulloch's thought on taxation. For we now pass to the second Part of the volume, which deals with indirect taxes, and here McCulloch begins by a discussion of the relative merits of direct and indirect taxation.[175] The discussion spills over into Chapters 2 and 3 of this part of the book, covering Taxes on Necessaries and Luxuries, and the Ad Valorem Taxes, and it will be convenient to deal with the ideas in the three chapters together.

Basically McCulloch's belief became, after some uncertainty,[176] that a broadly based system of indirect taxes was the most practical. That is to say he believed that indirect taxes, levied on both home produced goods *and* imports, had the ability to produce revenue with the least disruption of the growth process.[177] This was the important requirement; McCulloch was very conscious of the harm which an ill-designed tax system could do to growth. Direct taxes had the *prima facie* disadvantage that the pain of paying was very marked compared with indirect taxes while the benefits of government, though very real

[174] *Treatise on Taxation*, 1845, p. 110 (and see *ibid.*, pp. 394–5 and *Treatise on Taxation*, 1852, p. 105. See below, pp. 106–7.

[175] Below, pp. 155–72.

[176] Typified in EB6 Taxation, p. 623.

[177] Below, pp. 170–1; see also *Edinburgh Review*, Jul. 1833, *loc. cit.*, p. 448; *Statistical Account*, 1837, vol. II, pp. 505–8.

were less immediately apparent.[178] Anything which caused discomfort to the taxpayer was likely to interfere with growth, especially if it led to capital emigration. The discomfort of direct taxes was further increased because they were designedly inescapable, while indirect taxes were to some extent 'voluntary'. Of course misused indirect taxes could be just as harmful; in particular they could be too high and divert economic activity from normal channels into smuggling.[179]

But, in strong contrast to property and income taxation, indirect taxes did not, except where smuggling was involved, require investigation[180]; and this greatly reduced the discomfort which they caused and the level of interference with normal economic processes. Moreover they were, as Hume had argued, extremely 'convenient' (in Smith's sense); and they combined effective revenue raising with a sumptuary role[181] – McCulloch, who suggested a sumptuary tax on servants later in this book[182] had few qualms about interfering with preferences if this was likely to increase rather than diminish economic growth.

He believed too, as we see in this chapter, that the 'voluntary' nature of indirect taxes would increase accumulation and growth in so far as these taxes were avoided by reducing consumption[183]; and this in turn increased the demand for labour.[184] Obviously such a view is open to attack,[185] not least on the grounds that the scope for avoidance of such taxes is inequitably distributed; moreover elasticity of demand varies and may reach very low values on taxed commodities, a large proportion of the consumer's income may be affected

178 Below, p. 155.

179 This was an extremely recurrent topic in McCulloch's writings, see e.g. 'Spirit Trade', *Scotsman*, 2 Aug. 1826, p. 485; 'Duties on Wine – Restrictions on the Wine Trade', *Edinburgh Review*, vol. XL, Jul. 1824, pp. 414-27.

180 *Taxation*, 1852, pp. 130-1.

181 Below, pp. 178-80; 337-40, 364-7; CD1832, pp. 985-8; CD1859, pp. 1222-7; *Statistical Account*, 1837, p. 508.

182 Below, pp. 275-6.

183 The implication is that the reduction in consumption which increased accumulation was separate from any reduction in consumption simply because of the income effect of the tax. One way of looking at this would be to view the argument as implying a demand curve of greater than unit elasticity: the income effect could then be seen in terms of a curve of unit elasticity. The higher elasticity value would then have to be seen as due to a substitution effect, not between different goods for present consumption, but between present and future goods.

184 Below, p. 165; see also WN1863, p. 618.

185 See especially J. S. Mill, *op. cit.*, p. 866.

(e.g. by a tax on foodstuffs) in which case income effects cannot be ignored, and anyway all price changes involve income effects of some magnitude. Indeed McCulloch himself recognised in Chapter 2 of this part of the book that such taxes could have marked income effects,[186] although his uncertainty about the incidence of taxes on wages clouded the issue; in the same chapter as he recognises these effects he contrives to argue that such taxes are passed on.[187]

Nevertheless McCulloch's argument accords perfectly well with his concept of 'income sacrifice' already noted; and if the distinction between 'voluntary' and direct taxes exists in the consumer's mind, it becomes analytically significant.

In addition to all this, indirect taxes had the very great advantage from a growth point of view that the tax stimulation effect, which McCulloch regards here[188] as *necessary* for growth, increased exertion, ingenuity and saving, while direct taxes stimulated only the last of these.[189]

However, indirect taxes had their disadvantages too; there was, he recognised here, no such thing as a perfect tax.[190] He admitted that they distorted the allocation of resources; and, as already noted, there was always the danger of smuggling.[191] This last point was one on which he laid considerable emphasis, stressing that the more easily a good was smuggled, the more moderate had the tax on it to be.[192] McCulloch recognised too that indirect taxes were regressive,[193] that they increased the price of the final product by the interest required by producers advancing the amount of the tax,[194] and that they created opportunities for fraud when drawbacks were allowed, as they should be, on exports.[195]

These admissions are, however, less obvious in the chapter under

[186] See below, pp. 173, 177–8. [187] Below, pp. 173–4, 174–5.

[188] Below, pp. 166–7.

[189] Below, pp. 158–61; see also WN1863, p. 616 and compare EB7 Taxation, pp. 110–11 and EB8 Taxation, pp. 21–2. McCulloch had originally believed that moderate taxes of either kind could produce both effects – EB6 Taxation, p. 627.

[190] Below, p. 161.

[191] Below, pp. 161–4; see also EB6 Taxation, pp. 627–8; EB8 Taxation, pp. 110–11.

[192] If the difference between the pre- and post-tax price was greater than the return to smuggling discounted for risk, smuggling would occur.

[193] Below, p. 165; see also EB6 Taxation, pp. 625, 628; CD1832, pp. 722–3.

[194] Below, pp. 162–3; see also EB7 Taxation, pp. 110–11.

[195] *Edinburgh Review*, Apr. 1833, *loc. cit.*, p. 144.

discussion than in some of McCulloch's other writings. There is indeed no doubt that McCulloch came to lay less emphasis on them as time passed.[196] As in this volume he came to argue that the distortion involved in such taxes was only an impact effect (thus confusing the distortions with the frictions associated with adjustment to them),[197] that the stimulus to effort and ingenuity might offset the tax, and that any price increase would be confined to the home market (because of the drawbacks on exportation).[198] He came to argue that smuggling served a socially useful function in showing when duties were too high; and that this potentiality was actually a significant advantage which indirect taxation had to offer over direct taxation.[199] He defended too the regression involved[200]; redistribution was not the state's duty.[201] Indeed he argued in this chapter[202] that indirect taxes were definitely preferable to direct taxes which were bound to become *pro*gressive – and progression was subversive of the motives to growth[203] – as well as causing fraud, evasion, and capital emigration, and reducing the demand for labour.[204]

Yet criticisms parallel to these could be made of indirect taxes: and there is, as Merivale pointed out,[205] a strong contrast between the exacting tests that McCulloch was wont to apply to direct taxes and his rough and ready treatment of any defects in indirect taxation. The truth of the matter is that McCulloch made the fundamental judgment that direct taxes were more likely to interfere with growth and accumulation than indirect ones: and it was growth which was, in his view, the overriding consideration. Indirect taxes he judged to be the means of providing the government which he recognised as necessary for growth, while interfering as little as possible with that growth. Hence the critical attitude adopted both in Chapter 2 of this section,[206]

[196] Compare, e.g., EB6 Taxation, pp. 627–8 with EB7 Taxation, pp. 110–11.

[197] Below, p. 161.

[198] Below, pp. 161–2; see also EB8 Taxation, pp. 21–2; WN1863, p. 616. After a certain amount of vacillation McCulloch rejected the view of James Mill and Ricardo that indirect taxes affected the price level through increasing the velocity of circulation – see especially *Treatise on Taxation*, 1845, pp. 170–1.

[199] Below, p. 164; see also WN1863, p. 617.

[200] Below, p. 165.

[201] *Treatise on Taxation*, 1852, pp. 159–60; below, p. 168; EB8 Taxation, p. 7.

[202] Below, pp. 167–8.

[203] *Ibid.*

[204] Below, pp. 169–70.

[205] Merivale, *op. cit.*, pp. 377–8.

[206] See especially, pp. 175–7.

and indeed throughout the book, towards what McCulloch considered the needless repeal of indirect taxes – having always at the back of his mind that any deficiency of revenue was likely to involve the prolongation of the income tax.

Two other points in connection with McCulloch's preference for indirect taxation should be noted in dealing with these three chapters. One, which he deals with in the third of them, is that *ad valorem* taxes were, in his view, not really an operational proposition even in selected areas – he had for long recognised that a universal *ad valorem* tax was of purely theoretical significance,[207] (although in treating of such a concept he had pointed out that it would alter relative values according to the relative proportions of fixed and circulating capital[208]). Such taxes had then to be at arbitrary rates.

The other point which strangely hardly appears during this discussion is that McCulloch always stressed the need for imposing indirect taxes on widely consumed commodities – the tax-revenue producing capacity of luxury goods was severely limited[209] – and the taxable capacity of a good depended not only on how easily it was smuggled, but on how far it was a commodity 'in general request'.[210]

Having examined these three chapters which contain the essence of McCulloch's thought on indirect taxation, we can now pass to his treatment of two issues, both of considerable interest, which he dealt with in connection with indirect taxation. The first, dealt with in the following chapter (Chapter 4), though it sits ill in a section on indirect taxation, is his treatment of tithes. This involves a most interesting aspect of the development of his thought. At first he had, in his writings on tithes, advanced the Ricardian argument that tithes fell wholly on the consumer of corn in the form of price increases. This was on the grounds that tithes fell on all land, including that which paid no rent; and as the farmer had to earn his normal profits, the price of corn had to increase by the amount of the tithe. He had thus rejected Smith's view that tithes fell on the landlord in the form of a diminution

[207] WN1828, vol. IV, p. 558; EB7 Taxation, p. 111; WN1863, p. 623.

[208] See below, pp. 181–3; see also WN1828, vol. IV, pp. 554–6. The reasoning was pure Ricardo in its style, and it fits nowhere into McCulloch's general discussion.

[209] Below, p. 180; see also 'Effects of High and Low Taxes', *Scotsman*, 1 Dec. 1821, p. 377; 'Comparative Productiveness of High and Low Taxes', *Edinburgh Review*, vol. XXXVI, Feb. 1822, pp. 516–36, p. 518.

[210] *Treatise on Taxation*, 1845, pp. 316–28; below, Part II, ch. 9; EB6 Taxation, p. 636; *Statistical Account*, 1837, vol. II, p. 509.

of rent.[211] Then McCulloch changed his mind and rejected Ricardo's argument.[212] He pointed out that, given the usual Classical assumption of a rising supply schedule in agriculture, this assumed zero elasticity of demand for corn, all land to be tithed, and no imports. In the absence of the first assumption price would rise by less than the full amount of the tithe as production was reduced, and rent would fall. Free imports also would not permit price to rise by the full amount of the tithe (making the usual assumptions about the level of the corn import point). Most importantly, if not all land were tithed, cultivation would be extended on the untithed land and reduced on the tithed land so that price would not be raised by the full amount of the tithe. Unfortunately McCulloch for long did not get this part of the analysis quite right.[213] While accepting the Ricardian view he had argued that the marginal cost of cultivation on tithed land, plus the tithe, determined price.[214] When he came to denounce 'Ricardo's theory with regard to the effect of tythes on the price of produce as one of the most rash speculations of that writer'[215] he adopted the position that price was determined by marginal cost on *un*tithed land – which would only be true if the extension of cultivation on untithed land did not result in any increase in its marginal cost. However, he finally got the argument right in the *Treatise on Taxation*,[216] where he showed that price would rise, but not by the full amount of the tithe, as the extensive margins on the tithed and untithed land were re-equated.[217]

However, he disapproved of tithes. In the case of normal capitalist farming they would he believed, following Smith and others, adversely affect the supply of effort and agricultural investment[218]; and where

[211] 'On the Incidence and Effect of Tithes', *Scotsman*, 27 Aug. 1823, p. 546; 'Tithes', *Edinburgh Review*, vol. XXXIV, Aug. 1820, pp. 61-79, especially pp. 65-9: EB6 Taxation, pp. 629-30.

[212] 'Abolition of the Corn Laws', *Edinburgh Review*, vol. XLIV, Sep. 1826, pp. 353-4; 'On the Nature and Operation of Tithe', *Scotsman*, 1 Nov. 1826, p. 689; EB7 Taxation, pp. 112-14.

[213] *Scotsman*, 1826, *loc. cit.*; *Edinburgh Review*, 1826, *loc. cit.*

[214] This was not correct given the existence, which he recognised, of untithed land.

[215] Political Economy Club, *Centenary Volume*, p. 254.

[216] *Treatise on Taxation*, 1845, pp. 176-7; *ibid.*, 1852, pp. 180-1. See also below, p. 187 n. 6.

[217] This of course neglects, however, the intensive margins.

[218] *Treatise on Taxation*, 1852, pp. 180-4; below, pp. 187-92; WN1828, vol. IV, p. 551.

normal capitalist conditions did not prevail because the tenant farmers had no capital (the mobility of which was necessary to the price adjustment) they were strongly to be condemned.[219]

The whole process of the evolution of McCulloch's thought on the question of tithes is illustrated in this Chapter 4. Firstly there is a rehearsal of the Ricardian argument[220] followed by an apparent rejection of the Smithian view on strictly Ricardian lines[221] – all of which uses old material which had originally appeared in the *Scotsman.*[222] But then McCulloch goes on to point out that this rejection is dependent on the assumptions already noted (although his argument here is very much abbreviated as compared with former editions of the *Treatise*[223]). He then goes on to deal with the damaging effect of tithes through their interference with effort and investment[224] and is particularly critical of Irish tithes.[225] He next passes to a lengthy defence of the provisions for the commutation of tithes in England and Wales and in Scotland[226] (though here again there are important changes from former editions[227]). Finally he returns to his old argument that there should be a fixed duty on corn on account of agriculture's special burdens – though this too is substantially modified compared with his previous statements.[228]

The chapter on tithes is followed by Chapter 5 dealing with import duties. Here it becomes apparent that the image of McCulloch as a crude free-trader will not bear examination. He believed import duties to fall on the home consumer (which implicitly requires the assumption of infinite elasticity of foreign supply, as McCulloch seems to have recognised perfectly well[229]); but despite this, and despite reiteration of the advantages which he saw in freedom of trade[230] he was still an advocate of import duties. This is not to say that he was in any sense a protectionist – it would be absurd to take such a

[219] He was particularly opposed to Irish tithes – see, e.g., 'Church Establishment of Ireland – Tithes not Property', *Scotsman*, 27 June 1822, p. 199; see also 'Plan for Commutation of Tithes', *Edinburgh Review*, vol. XXXIV, Aug. 1820, pp. 61-79, pp. 73-6.

[220] Below, p. 185.

[221] Below, pp. 186-7.

[222] *Scotsman*, 1 Nov. 1826, p. 689.

[223] See note 6 to this chapter of the text.

[224] Below, pp. 187-9.

[225] Below, pp. 190-1.

[226] Below, pp. 191-6.

[227] See notes 16 and 17 to this chapter of the text.

[228] Below, pp. 196-9. See note 22 to this chapter of the text.

[229] *Treatise on Taxation*, 1852, pp. 208-9; see below, p. 206 n. 12.

[230] Below, pp. 206-7. On McCulloch's views on free trade and protection see O'Brien, *op. cit.*, pp. 217-26.

position, for if any part of the *Wealth of Nations* had completely convinced all the classical economists (with the possible exception of Torrens) it was that which argued for the general desirability of freedom of trade. Sure enough we find McCulloch arguing, on the basis of his doctrine of the automatic balance of trade, that trade only affected the direction of employment of labour not its total amount and that it increased national income at the cost of mere frictional adjustments. The pursuit of self-interest optimised resource allocation. Specialisation according to absolute advantage was the proper course[231]; but in addition to the direct benefits of this there was too the dynamic stimulus of trade and the multiplication of motives which resulted from it.

Nevertheless McCulloch recognised that there were great advatages in imposing import duties *for revenue purposes*. They combined ease and cheapness of collection[232] with a minimum of investigation, they were 'convenient', and they involved little price-increasing locking-up of the importer's capital if the bonded warehouse system was employed.[233] They should be at a fairly moderate level – but this permitted duties of 12-15% and even 25%.[234] However, they should avoid raw materials[235]; and they should be as broadly based as possible. In stressing this McCulloch launched a powerful attack on Gladstone's financial policy.[236] The attack was not confined to the third edition of the *Treatise*[237]; but it is perhaps as well developed here as anywhere else in his writings. Peel's tidying up of duties, eliminating many that were not productive, had, McCulloch believed, been beneficial.[238] But Gladstone had gone too far. Instead of dutying forty items, it would be preferable to spread the load over four hundred.[239] McCulloch's

[231] Below, pp. 206-10. On McCulloch's theory of the automatic balance of trade, see O'Brien, *op. cit.*, pp. 204-8. [232] Below, p. 240. [233] Below, p. 206.

[234] CD1832, p. 355; *Principles*, 1849, p. 168; CD1860, Supplement, pp. 13, 22-3; below pp. 206, 223-4; *Treatise on Taxation*, 1852, p. 228 (not included in *Treatise on Taxation*, 1863; see below p. 222 n. 40).

[235] Below, pp. 217-21. [236] Below, pp. 224-9.

[237] See also CD1860, Supplement, pp. 12-13; *Principles*, 1864, p. 108. There is also a rare *second* edition of McCulloch's *Article on Taxation* for the 8th edition of *Encyclopaedia Britannica* (the only copy known to the present writer is in the Goldsmith Library) and this contains strong attacks on Gladstone, especially pp. 20-2, 25-8, 39, 40-1. [238] Below, p. 234.

[239] Below, pp. 224-5. See, however, S. Buxton, *Finance and Politics; An Historical Study*, London, 1888, vol. I, p. 201 for examples of duties abolished by Gladstone which were hardly productive of revenue.

objection rested on several grounds. Firstly, there was the needless sacrifice of revenue involved.[240] (This was coupled with the belief, not explicit here, but to which both McCulloch and Overstone, to whom he refers,[241] subscribed, that but for Gladstone's sacrifice of indirect taxation, the income tax could be abolished. McCulloch's opposition to the latter has already been noted.) Secondly there was the savage regression involved in concentrating duties, at much higher levels than would be necessary with a broadly based system, on a very few items of mass-consumption.[242] Thirdly, and following from this, there was the danger of agitation and social discontent[243] – McCulloch's fear of upheaval was never very far away. Fourthly there was the argument that a strong revenue was a fruitful deterrent to potential aggressors – unlike Ricardo,[244] who thought that the aggressive tendencies of home politicians necessitated keeping tax revenue as low as possible, McCulloch at least had faith in the peacefulness of his own politicians, and argued for revenue surplus to deter 'foreigners' i.e. the French.[245] Fifthly there was the argument used by Arthur Young after surveying the French system, that the broader the base the less the whole weight was felt – the welfare loss from taxation then increased with the concentration of that taxation.[246] Sixthly, while moderate broad-based duties were not inconsistent with freedom of trade, the significant distortions involved in a narrowly based system definitely were.[247]

McCulloch was then fully in approval of revenue duties and to aid them he was prepared to support such measures as the prohibition of home-grown tobacco[248] (a drug of which he had a particular dislike) and even, in the first edition of the *Treatise*,[249] the destruction of home-grown chicory mills.

But he was strongly opposed to the imposition of duties for *protective* purposes.[250] All his arguments about the advantages of freedom of trade were employed against them; and he was caustic about American protectionism. Now at first sight such a position is not quite satisfactory. Any duty must have some protective effect

[240] Below, pp. 224-7.
[241] See Appendix III to the *Treatise on Taxation*.
[242] Below, pp. 224-6.
[243] Below, pp. 226-7.
[244] Ricardo's *Works*, vol. IV, pp. 197-8.
[245] Below, p. 226.
[246] Below, pp. 227-8.
[247] Below, pp. 228-9.
[248] Below, p. 231.
[249] See below, p. 231 n. 54.
[250] Below, pp. 207-15.

where there is home production of the tariffed article; and even where there is no directly competing home production, other home produced goods will benefit from a protective effect as the consumer re-arranges his purchases to take account of the increased price of imports, all goods being to some extent substitutes. But if we make this criticism of McCulloch we have to recognise two points. Firstly, he does seem to have grasped, as the *Treatise* shows, that the revenue and protective effects of a duty were maximised at different levels[251] – and the distinction between revenue and protective tariffs is thus meaningful. Secondly, he did argue strongly for the complementarity of the excise and customs duties. Repeal of all customs duties would necessitate the repeal of all excise duties.[252] It follows from this that the protective effect of customs duties can be counterbalanced by equalising excise duties – and this does seem to be what he had in mind.[253] This in turn led to another argument for the imposition of import duties, viz. to counteract sectorally disproportionate taxation at home.[254]

However, McCulloch was not very happy about the use of tariffs as a weapon of foreign policy[255]; they were as expensive as military weapons of foreign policy and damaged the user's economy by distorting the allocation of resources. This in turn created vested interests which made the removal of such tariffs difficult. Yet at times, although not in this volume, McCulloch does seem to have been prepared to accept the idea of some strategic duties.[256]

It was not only import duties for revenue purposes of which McCulloch approved. He was also strongly in favour of export duties which he believed to fall entirely on the foreign consumer[257] – and this provided further grounds for his opposition to the commercial treaty

[251] See below, pp. 208, 223-4.

[252] Below, pp. 233-4. This was a point which contemporaries sometimes found it difficult to grasp. It was mentioned by McCulloch prior to this 3rd edition in a letter to Lord Stanhope who replied: 'why do you say that "the abolition of the Customs *necessarily* involves that of the Excise Duties'? It will require some proof to show that these could never be disjoined', letter of 13 Feb. 1863, Ms. AL 187 in University of London Library.

[253] See especially below, p. 217 for an explicit statement to this effect.

[254] Below, p. 217; see also *Principles of Commerce*, pp. 47-8; *Statements*, 1841, pp. 12-13.

[255] Below, pp. 216-7.

[256] At first he was opposed to such an idea – see, e.g., *Principles of Commerce*, pp. 58-9; see, however, *Principles*, 1864, pp. 110-11 and contrast, *Principles*, 1849, p. 164.

[257] Below, pp. 199-200.

of 1860 with France.[258] This had not always been the case, and his attitude towards export duties had vacillated considerably.[259] But he now saw considerable advantages in them,[260] partly as a means of enabling Britain to retain her absolute advantage in manufacturing,[261] although he did not believe that such duties would be great revenue raisers.[262]

From all this it should be clear that the image of McCulloch as a crude free-trader is, to put it mildly, misleading. Import duties were examined by him, like other actual or potential sources of revenue, on ability-to-pay grounds, but with a due regard to possible distortions; and, having found them very satisfactory as revenue raisers and as involving little distortion when broadly based, McCulloch strongly endorsed them.

From import duties McCulloch then turned his attention, in Chapter 6, to their complement, excise duties. The amount of general analysis of these taxes which he presents is very limited, and there is little added to the analysis of indirect taxation which had already been dealt with. We do find here the argument that excise duties fall wholly on the consumer – which of course is only true given infinite elasticity of supply. McCulloch did generally make this assumption in relation to agriculture. However, he unfortunately makes the same assertion about the malt duty,[263] which clearly involved an agricultural product.

There is little else that requires comment from an analytical standpoint. But taking together Chapters 6–8 as containing the main discussion of 'inland duties' the reader is struck by the remarkably few duties which McCulloch regarded as satisfactory. He states the general proposition that they are, as a type, unobjectionable if simple[264], and quotes Arthur Young to the effect that they are fair and to some extent voluntary[265] (a proposition already discussed). Yet in the light of his insistence on the general superiority of indirect taxation, his arguments in favour of a balance between import duties and excise duties, and his belief in the need for a broadly based structure of indirect taxation, it really is rather surprising that he should have disapproved of quite so many taxes.

[258] Below, pp. 204–5.

[259] Compare *Edinburgh Review*, May 1820, *loc. cit.*, p. 348, EB6 Taxation, p. 633, EB7 Taxation, pp. 115–16, and below, pp. 204–6.

[260] Below, pp. 200–206.

[261] Below, pp. 203–4

[262] Below, p. 206.

[263] Below, p. 248.

[264] Below, pp. 243–4.

[265] Below, p. 244.

Thus he approved of the repeal of the beer duty,[266] agreed that the imposition of a hop duty involved insoluble difficulties,[267] approved of the repeal of the salt duty,[268] and objected to the glass duties[269] (although a good deal of his opposition seems to have stemmed from the level at which historically they had been imposed). He asserted that leather as a raw material should not be taxed,[270] and that the candles tax was bad (because of the enforcement difficulties encountered,)[271] regarded the brick duty as unsatisfactory because stone buildings avoided it[272] (this would have been more reasonable had he not, at an earlier date, condemned the duty on stone[273]) and thought the hair powder tax useless because unproductive of revenue.[274] Finally he condemned, as on many previous occasions,[275] the coal duty.[276] As his own Appendix IV showed, this left relatively few of the existing duties unscathed.

Some of his condemnations arose because the duties concerned interfered markedly with the overriding requirement of growth. Thus he had *earlier* taken a hostile view of duties on insurance (as tending to interfere with the preservation of accumulation),[277] on coal (as slowing industrialisation as well as being inter-sectorally unjust),[278] on auctions (as interfering with the free market),[279] on law (following Bentham his objection rested mainly, however, on the idea that they acted as taxes on distress)[280] and on paper[281] (as interfering with the spread of

[266] Below, p. 250.
[267] Below, pp. 254–6.
[268] Below, p. 261.
[269] Below, pp. 265–7.
[270] Below, pp. 267–9.
[271] Below, p. 269.
[272] Below, pp. 269–70.
[273] 'Duty on Slate and Stone carried Coastwise', *Edinburgh Review*, vol. XXXVIII, Feb. 1823, pp. 235–40.
[274] Below, p. 276.
[275] *Edinburgh Review*, Apr. 1830, *loc. cit.*; see also two pamphlets springing from the article: *Observations on the Duty on Sea-Borne Coal* and *Remarks on the Coal Trade*.
[276] Below, pp. 280–2.
[277] 'Taxes on Policies of Insurance', *Edinburgh Review*, vol. LV, Jul. 1832, pp. 527–30.
[278] See *supra*, note 275.
[279] *Treatise on Taxation*, 1845, pp. 240–1; below, pp. 262–3.
[280] 'Law Taxes', *Scotsman*, 21 Nov. 1818, p. 369.
[281] 'Taxes on Literature', *Edinburgh Review*, vol. LIII, Jun. 1831, pp. 427–37, especially p. 428; CD1832, pp. 811–12; *Observations Illustrative of the Practical Operation and Real Effect of the Duties on Paper, showing the Expediency of their Reduction or Repeal*, London, 1836.

knowledge as well as being unjust to authors). But these considerations are not all present in this third edition of the *Treatise*. Indeed when we look to see what duties McCulloch was prepared to countenance we now find among them some which he had previously condemned on growth grounds. Those which did pass muster were the malt duty[282] (although here he was inconsistent with his previous analysis in condemning a countervailing import duty as impracticable), the *paper* duty[283] – indeed he was strong in his condemnation of the way its repeal had been forced through the House of Lords – and the soap duty (which he believed should have been extended to Ireland, not repealed).[284]

But these, apart from the duty on cards and dice,[285] were virtually the only excise duties of which McCulloch showed full approval; and when we look to other 'inland duties' we find again that few of these pass muster, while some of those that do McCulloch had earlier condemned. Thus he here regarded auction duties as unobjectionable[286]; but he also thought low duties on fire and marine insurance acceptable,[287] in contrast with his earlier objection on growth grounds. He approved of the duty on carriages including rail carriages, which he believed to fall wholly on the passenger[288] (although these were open to objection on growth grounds since McCulloch, like Smith, thought communications important to growth) and he does not condemn the 'Parliamentary Trains' (which arguably interfered with rationally undertaken railway investment).[289] He approves of the house tax[290] (although his earlier analysis had shown that some of this fell on rent, and he had also condemned taxes on rent) and he approved too of a horse tax (including agricultural horses,[291] although this arguably interfered with agriculture). A duty on private carriages (although unlikely to be productive of much revenue) he approved,[292] and also those on dogs and servants,[293] although these would seem to be open to his *a priori* objection to taxes on luxuries as poor revenue raisers. The same objection could be made to the duty on plate which he

[282] Below, pp. 249–50.
[283] Below, pp. 251–3.
[284] Below, pp. 253–4.
[285] Below, p. 290.
[286] Below, pp. 262–5.
[287] Below, pp. 288–90.
[288] Below, pp. 270–2.
[289] Below, pp. 271–2.
[290] Below, pp. 273.
[291] Below, pp. 274–5.
[292] Below, p. 275.
[293] He also approved of the levying of a duty on (male) shop assistants where their job could be done by women (below, pp. 275–6).

accepted.[294] Despite his approval of the duties on carriages he insisted that tolls and port-dues must only be used to cover the costs concerned not as sources of general revenue – indeed they should be supplemented out of general revenue.[295] There were other inland duties which he found satisfactory; but they could hardly be regarded as balancing import duties as the *a priori* argument suggested they should. Thus stamp duties were (he now thought) satisfactory if *ad valorem* and proportional[296] (he rejected the Say–Ricardo argument of interference with the market here[297]). He had now decided, after a series of changes of mind, that the newspaper duty was legitimate[298]; and he approved of duties on cheques.[299] He disagreed with Ricardo that legacy and succession duties fell on capital, arguing that legators would adjust their effort so as to leave a net sum[300], and he strongly approved of the tax. Duties on probate and letters of administration were 'sound in principle' though ill-operated because regressive (which he opposed here as much as progression) and because the latter were arbitrarily subject to a heavier duty. There was also the objection that they applied in full only to personal property and hardly touched real property. But the answer was to extend them not repeal them, though McCulloch did not accept the argument (J. S. Mill is not mentioned by name) for more severe inheritance duties.[301]

All this does not add up to a very satisfactory picture. McCulloch had offered very few approved excise duties to balance his import duties; and he had approved other sources of revenue, some of which he had earlier recognised as interfering with his overriding consideration, growth. In addition, most writers would have put a duty on postage in this latter category; and McCulloch should have done so in view of his position on road charges. Yet, precisely reversing the modern judgments, he adhered to his view on roads yet consistently argued that postage was a fit source of taxation; and here he bitterly attacked the Penny Post for needlessly sacrificing revenue.[302]

Yet there were other duties, more eligible some might judge,

[294] Below, pp. 277-8. [295] Below, pp. 278-82. [296] Below, pp. 282-6.

[297] See, e.g., Ricardo's *Works*, vol. I, pp. 153-5 (which also quotes Say), 204.

[298] Below, pp. 286-7. For the different phases of McCulloch's thought on this matter see 'Advertisement Duty', *Scotsman*, 22 Jan. 1825, p. 49; *Edinburgh Review*, Jun. 1831, *loc. cit.*, p. 436; *Treatise on Taxation*, 1845, p. 285; *ibid.*, 1852, p. 291.

[299] Below, p. 290. [300] Below, pp. 292-3. [301] Below, pp. 292-301.

[302] See below Chapter VII of the text, pp. 310-23, and see also pp. 279-80; see also *Statistical Account*, 1847, vol. II, pp. 406-8; CD1859, p. 1041; EB8 Taxation, pp. 29-30.

which he condemned. He approved of the house tax but condemned the window tax (though his grounds were not entirely unreasonable),[303] he approved stamp duty yet objected to taxes on contracts and law taxes,[304] he approved newspaper duty but condemned advertisement duty (because it did not relate proportionately to the value of the property advertised),[305] he attacked the existing duty on fire insurance (though in fairness it must be said it was the level of this that he mainly attacked),[306] and he condemned licence duties as not related to the size of business.[307] He also condemned lotteries as a source of revenue[308] though this was understandable enough,[309] not only because of their effects on the populace but also on the grounds of McCulloch's apparent belief that their revenue was offset by a loss of excise revenue and an increase in poor relief.[310]

Now it is possible to produce a defence for each of these preferences taken individually. Whether it is possible to produce a consistent overall defence is much more doubtful. The fact of the matter does seem to be that although McCulloch recognised *a priori* the need for a balance between customs and excise, the actual tax system which he desired to have operated (and it is to his credit that, unlike Ricardo, he did address himself to such a concrete problem) seems to have involved a balance between 'assessed taxes' and customs duties, supplemented by very few excise duties. It is noticeable too that when we come to Chapter 9 on smuggling and Chapter 10 on the comparative productiveness of high and low taxes[311] we find that the *actual* taxes with which McCulloch concerns himself are nearly all import duties. They include the duties on tobacco,[312] tea,[313] coffee,[314] imported

[303] Below, pp. 273-4. He had for long approved of *both* the house and window taxes; see, e.g., 'Reduction of the Duties on Coffee', *Edinburgh Review*, vol. XLI, Jan. 1825, pp. 488-97, p. 489; *ibid.*, Apr. 1833, *loc. cit.*, pp. 165-6; *Statistical Account*, 1837, vol. II, pp. 512-13.

[304] Below, p. 285.

[305] Below, pp. 287-8; see also *Scotsman*, Jan. 1825, *loc. cit.*

[306] Below, pp. 288-9.

[307] Below, pp. 301-10.

[308] Below, pp. 323-6.

[309] Before public lotteries were banned the *Scotsman*, in common with many other papers, had carried some outrageous lottery advertisements.

[310] Below, p. 324.

[311] The main *a priori* considerations adduced in these chapters have already been discussed above.

[312] Below, p. 338.

[313] Below, pp. 341-9.

[314] Below, pp. 749-50.

spirits,[315] and wine.[316] The only excise duty to which he devotes any real attention is that on home produced spirits.[317]

This completes the analysis of the actual tax system as McCulloch envisages it *ought* to work. If the tone of the above discussion has been at times critical, it is not intended to imply that McCulloch was foolish; merely that in addressing himself to a problem that his classical contemporaries largely ignored, he failed to avoid some inconsistencies – but this is hardly a unique occurrence of the failing amongst economists writing in this context.

Part II of the *Treatise*, however, has more to offer; for it concludes with two chapters (11 and 12), on the influence of variations in the value of money on taxation, and on international comparisons of taxation.

Chapter 11 represents an important strand in McCulloch's monetary theory. It contains his analysis of forced saving and inflation, applied to the operation of taxation. The core of the analysis is contained in the first five paragraphs. Here McCulloch makes it clear that, in marked contrast to Ricardo and James Mill,[318] he accepted the essence of Hume's doctrine of the effects of changes in the money supply on the level of activity. This is particularly significant because it implies the possibility of an inequality between planned saving and planned investment. As elsewhere in his writings McCulloch modifies the argument slightly. Hume had believed that an increase in the money supply stimulated the level of activity by coming into the hands of capitalists; whereas McCulloch advanced the argument that the mode of stimulation was through the increased money supply which raised profit margins as prices rose while fixed burdens, stated in money terms, remained static in amount and fell in real terms. The increased profits which resulted stimulated the level of activity. The analysis is not quite as fully developed here as elsewhere in his writings. For instance the idea that inflation increased accumulation by forcing saving on the fixed income receivers to the benefit of the capitalist (accumulating, class is not fully spelt out as it is elsewhere.[319] But the essence is here; and we also find the argument that inflation redistributes capital

[315] Below, pp. 361-4. [316] Below, pp. 364-7. [317] Below, pp. 350-61.

[318] D. Ricardo, *High Price of Bullion* in *Works*, vol. III, pp. 120-2; *Essay on Profits*, *ibid.*, vol. IV, pp. 36-7; J. Mill, *Elements of Political Economy* in *Selected Economic Writings*, ed. D. Winch, pp. 294-5.

[319] *Principles*, 1849, pp. 556-62; *Principles*, 1864, pp. 475-81.

between different occupations when taxation is fixed in money terms.[320] The idea is not indisputable – indeed it arguably involves a temporary adoption by McCulloch of the Ricardian vice[321] – but it is interesting.

McCulloch's recognition of the effects of changes in the quantity of money on the level of activity appears frequently in his work from the second 1816 *Essay* on the National Debt which contains the essential borrowing from Hume.[322] Thereafter it re-appears with a fair degree of regularity.[323] Inflation could have positively beneficial effects, while deflation was extremely harmful through its effect in increasing the weight of fixed burdens and narrowing profit margins.

This is not to say that McCulloch was an out and out inflationist. He was not, and he very little sympathy with Attwood. So we find him pointing here to the unjust effects of inflation[324] and the danger it raised of a capital flight.[325] He was here explicitly endorsing Smith's cautionary attitude. We find him inveighing against proposals for 'tampering' with the standard in his discussion of the effects of Resumption[326] and stressing that such activities did not fall legitimately within the field of government.[327]

Now these were points that McCulloch almost always made.[328] But having said that, it should be recognised that he was nowhere near as much a 'hard money' man as Ricardo or Overstone: and in the Political Economy Club he defended the inflationary mechanism very strongly, even against Tooke, apparently going so far as to reject considerations of justice and endorse inflation wholeheartedly in the cause of economic growth.[329] Paper inflation was of no long-run benefit because of the deflation which must necessarily succeed it.

[320] Below, pp. 380–1; *Treatise on Taxation*, 1852, p. 386; the argument derived from Ricardo's *Works*, vol. I, p. 208.

[321] See J. A. Schumpeter, *History of Economic Analysis*, London, 1954, pp. 472–3.

[322] Second 1816 Essay, p. 23; Hume, *Essay on Money* in *op. cit.*, vol. I, pp. 303, 305.

[323] E.g., 'Effects of Fluctuations in the Value of Money on the Condition of Different Classes of Society', *Scotsman*, 27 Jan. 1827, p. 57; 'Pernicious Effects of Degrading the Standard of Money', *Edinburgh Review*, vol. XXXV, Jul. 1821, pp. 468–88, pp. 478–9; *Principles*, 1830, pp. 500–4; CD1840, p. 808; *Principles*, 1849, pp. 135–6.

[324] Below, pp. 375–6.

[325] Below, p. 376.

[326] Below, pp. 378–9.

[327] Below, pp. 381–2.

[328] Second 1816 Essay, pp. 187–9; 'The Proposed Reduction of the Standard of the Currency considered as a means of relieving the public distresses', *Scotsman*, 14 Apr. 1821, p. 113; EB6 Money, p. 526; *Principles*, 1830, p. 503; *Principles*, 1849, pp. 559–60.

[329] Political Economy Club, *Centenary Volume*, p. 219.

But McCulloch did become, for a while, extremely optimistic about the possibilities of metallic inflation through an increase in the world's gold supplies[330]; and it is only in this third edition of the *Treatise* that he finally decided that his optimism about the size of future supplies had been misplaced.[331]

This monetary analysis, combined with the recognition (which appears more strongly in his other writings[332]) of the harmful effects of deflation, led McCulloch naturally (though slightly away from the central issue of taxation) to the problem of the 1819 Resumption, to which he here devotes several pages. It was a subject to which he had constantly referred, and his view of the matter in this third edition of the *Treatise* represents his final and considered one. Like Tooke he attributed the post-Resumption depression to real rather than monetary factors,[335] arguing that the true deflation had occurred during the destruction of country bank paper in 1814–16.[334] Although when writing prior to Resumption he had argued that it should be carefully phased,[335] he had never believed that the Bank of England's conduct after 1819 had much to do with what had occurred.[336] He now argued that devaluation in 1815–16 was never a real possibility although up to 1852 he had, somewhat erratically, maintained the position that such a course would have been desirable.[337]

The final chapter in Part II, Chapter 12, which is concerned with estimating the weight of taxation, reaches nothing like the same level

[330] CD1854, pp. 1055–[1056]; CD1859, pp. [1047-1049], [1052] and [1055]-[1056]; EB8 Money, pp. 429, 466; article 'Precious Metals', in 8th edition, *Encyclopaedia Britannica*, pp. 464, 475-6; *Treatise on Taxation*, 1852, p. 385.

[331] Below, pp. 379-80.

[332] EB6 Money, pp. 522-3; *Scotsman*, 27 Jan. 1827, *loc. cit.*; *Edinburgh Review*, Jul. 1821, *loc. cit.*, pp. 478-9; *Principles*, 1849, pp. 135-6.

[333] 'Supply and Consumption of the Precious Metals', *Edinburgh Review*, vol. LV, Apr. 1832, pp. 43-61, pp. 57-9; WN1838, p. 498; *Statistical Account*, 1847, p. 35; T. Tooke, *A History of Prices and of the State of the Circulation from 1793*, London, 1838-57, vol. II, London, 1838, p. 353.

[334] Below, pp. 377-8; see also Second 1816 Essay, pp. 53-6; 'Notice of Mr. Peel's Bill – Reasons for Maintaining it Inviolate', *Scotsman*, 2 Feb. 1822, p. 33; *Statistical Account*, 1847, vol. II, p. 34.

[335] E.g. *Scotsman*, 10 Apr. 1819, p. 117.

[336] See especially his *Historical Sketch of the Bank of England with an Examination of the Question as to the Prolongation of the Exclusive Privileges of that Establishment*, London, 1831, pp. 25-6; and contrast Ricardo's *Works*, vol. V, pp. 311-12.

[337] *Treatise on Taxation*, 1852, p. 381 (and contrast below, p. 378).

of interest as the preceding chapter, and it would be easy to dismiss it as an incoherent rag bag. Yet there are points of interest. The main burden of the chapter is that it is impossible to estimate the weight of taxation; even if the actual amount is arrived at by counting civil service salaries only net of tax, it still had to be compared with taxable capacity to estimate its 'burden', and there was no conceptually satisfactory method of estimating capacity. Population was rejected out of hand (citing the case of Ireland), and capital was rejected because of the difficulties of measurement and because of international differences in its average and marginal product.[338] Average income per head was too difficult to learn and had to be deflated to real values. In addition heavier taxation might stimulate the taxpayers to a higher income[339] (a constant thread in his writings already noted). Finally there was the central importance of the way in which a given amount of taxation was raised – France being an instance of how harmful could be a tax burden which was relatively small by any absolute measurement.[340]

This is the burden of the chapter but there are other points in it of interest; for here McCulloch returns to some of his central themes. That of the stimulating effect of taxation appears on two occasions,[341] and here we find the view that the effect may be sufficient to cause whatever was taken by government to be replaced by an equivalent increase in private sector investment.[342] We also find the idea that capital is completely mobile internationally, which as has already been noted, was basic to McCulloch's international trade theory; and it was spelt out and forcefully reiterated, although with the usual qualification that French political instability and American untrustworthiness were the only barriers to complete mobility – '*coeteris paribus*, it is quite as natural that capital should leave a country where profits are low to seek employment in one where they are high, as that water should flow from a high to a low level'.[343]

This led to a reiteration of McCulloch's view that direct taxes cause discontent and capital emigration even if they are not objectively very high[344]; and this in turn led to the argument that it was heavy

[338] Below, p. 385.

[339] Below, pp. 386–7.

[340] Below, pp. 388–9.

[341] Below, pp. 386–7, 391.

[342] Below, p. 391. See also WN1850, p. 620.

[343] Below, pp. 389–91 especially p. 391; Second 1816 Essay, pp. 156–7, 159–60, 192; *Edinburgh Review*, Oct. 1823, *loc. cit.*, p. 17; *ibid.*, Oct. 1827, *loc. cit.*, pp. 392–4.

[344] Below, p. 392.

taxation which brought about the decline of Holland, inducing capital emigration.[345] It is interesting in this latter connection that McCulloch did not mention his non-Ricardian view expressed elsewhere, that profits fell in Holland because of capital accumulation[346]; nor did he refer to his view expressed earlier in the book[347] that England and Holland were better off with heavy indirect taxation than were other continental countries with lighter direct taxation.

Finally, and in a sense rounding off this part of the book, McCulloch returned to the idea that high although British taxation might be, it was no longer high enough to be a cause for concern. It *was* large in aggregate but its weight had been greatly reduced and was greatly exaggerated.[348] Returning to a point on which he had digressed earlier[349] he argued that there was little further benefit to be expected for the working classes from the repeal of taxation unless it had been possible to repeal the tea and sugar duties; which it was not because of the repeal of the paper duty and of the duties on silk and other luxuries.[350] This was another attack on Gladstone's financial policy: and McCulloch concludes the chapter by stressing that there is, in his view, very little scope for further reductions in expenditure and that the hope for the working class lay in a reform of their habits.[351] All this is in striking contrast to the concern about the level of taxation that McCulloch had expressed in his earlier years[352] and which had abated with the passage of time.[353]

(*d*) *Part III of the* Treatise: *Debt Policy*

The remainder of the *Treatise* is devoted to three chapters on debt creation and policy. This was a subject to which McCulloch turned continually throughout his writings. It was the burden of his first publications, the two 1816 *Essays* on the National Debt interest; and he was still concerned about it in this 1863 edition of the *Treatise on Taxation* which comes not much more than a year before his death.

Four main threads recur in McCulloch's treatment of debt creation

345 Below, pp. 392–4.

346 *Edinburgh Review*, Jul. 1830, *loc. cit.*, p. 436; see also EB8 Interest, p. 425 on shortage of investment opportunities in Holland, and compare with EB6, Pol. Econ., p. 271.

347 Below, p. 103.

348 Below, pp. 394–5.

349 Below, pp. 387–8.

350 Below, pp. 396–8.

351 Below, pp. 398–400.

352 E.g. *Edinburgh Review*, Jan. 1820, *loc. cit.*, p. 155.

353 E.g. *Statistical Account*, 1847, vol. II, p. 393.

and policy. The first is a recognition of the need for, and the inevitability of, the creation of debt; and this is usually combined with the second thread, the emphasis on the burden of such debt. These two points are the essence of Chapter 1 of this Part III. Thirdly, McCulloch devoted a great deal of attention to whether the correct method of borrowing involved variation of interest or principal, and it is to this that Chapter 2 of Part III is devoted. Finally, McCulloch considered two methods of debt redemption: Archibald Hutcheson's capital levy scheme; and sinking funds. Chapter 3 of Part III is concerned with this.

McCulloch was never very happy about debt creation.[354] However there were two main qualifications to this, both of which appear in Chapter 1. Firstly, war required debt creation.[355] McCulloch had not always taken this position and had, for a while, supported Ricardo's view of the need to finance wars by taxation.[356] (He then rejected Hume's view of the desirability of pre-war surpluses because he believed these interfered with growth and thus a country would enter a war unnecessarily weak.[357]) But he came to recognise that taxation could not be considered an exclusive source of war finance; and in this chapter he argues that some balance between taxation and debt was what was required.[358]

He had recognised, when accepting Ricardo's view, that there were dangers in reliance on tax finance[359]; and he came in the end to regard these as of real substance. Thus we find him in this chapter arguing that although it was possible for individuals to fund through the market to meet a large tax bill, as Ricardo had argued, the latter had pushed the argument too far: the individual borrower would get worse terms than the state thus increasing the total interest charge.[360] Moreover (and this was perhaps the key objection in McCulloch's view) while taxation at a level to service the debt might have the effect of stimulating effort and saving, taxation at a high enough level for

[354] E.g. WN1828, vol. IV, pp. 560–1.

[355] Below, pp. 401–2.

[356] 'Finances of Great Britain – No. I – Principles of the Funding System', *Scotsman*, 5 Apr. 1823, pp. 217–18; *Edinburgh Review*, Oct. 1823, *loc. cit.*, pp. 21–2; *ibid.*, Jan. 1828, *loc. cit.*, pp. 60–2.

[357] See below, pp. 401–2; see also WN1828, vol. IV, p. 561.

[358] Below, pp. 402–3.

[359] E.g. *Scotsman*, 5 Apr. 1823, *loc. cit.*

[360] Below, pp.410–11; see also *Edinburgh Review*, Oct. 1823, *loc. cit.*, pp. 11–12, in which McCulloch, when supporting Ricardo, had reversed this supposition.

complete war finance would probably pass beyond this to deliver a damaging shock to economic activity.[361] This was not certain; taxation and debt had each to be examined on their merits in any given war situation. But it was likely; and it was important to safeguard the tax-stimulation effect because as long as it operated it could counteract much of any harm involved in debt creation. At least this was McCulloch's view, and he was critical of Hume and Smith for their neglect of this point.[362]

The second valid reason for government borrowing was governmental instability; McCulloch recognises in this chapter that the government had had no option but to borrow after the Revolution of 1688.[363]

But government was nevertheless bound to keep a balance between borrowing and taxation and McCulloch was far from satisfied that historically this had been done correctly.[364] There was, he argued,[365] greater scope for tax finance than had been used, between 1797 and 1815. Had it been relied on to a greater degree, the remaining loans would have been on more favourable terms. However, in developing this argument[366] McCulloch, using material taken over from Sir Henry Parnell, got himself into rather serious difficulties. By taking the interest charge at 1797 and adding it to the current account charges for each year and comparing this with the annual revenue he made an estimate of the annual surplus or deficit. Having shown that the total deficits were £151,327,007 he left this figure hanging in the air and proceeded to calculate the value of government deficits for the period at 5% compound, finding that the final figure was less than the total of government borrowing for the period. The difference, he said represented the net additional cost of debt finance. In fact it did nothing of the sort. It represented the difference between the 5% maximum allowed under the usury laws and the (higher) rate which the government had had to pay by selling below par. The alternative of tax finance would, on McCulloch's earlier reasoning, have resulted in an even greater discrepancy because individuals could only borrow at higher rates than government. In addition to this error, McCulloch made what can only be described as a blunder which confused the argument completely. His calculation of the accumulation of the

[361] Below, pp. 411-12. [362] Below, p. 413.

[363] Below, pp. 419-20. McCulloch was fervently anti-Jacobite.

[364] Below, pp. 420-2. [365] Below, pp. 424-8. [366] Below, pp. 426-8.

deficits at compound interest was stated[367] to be a calculation of the gain to the public of leaving sums in their hands to be invested, and hence to accumulate, instead of divesting the public of them by taxation. This involved two errors. Firstly, the net transfer of resource command from the private to the public sector was the same in both the tax and the debt case. In the former the sum was tax principal plus private sector profits foregone less tax not raised to service the debt; and these last two items cancelled out since McCulloch calculated them both at 5%. In the latter it was payment by the purchaser of gilt-edged to the state plus tax to service this gilt-edged, less interest received by the gilt-edged holder, these last two items cancelling out again. Secondly McCulloch's use of a 5% interest and profit rate was quite arbitrary; indeed it assumes a correspondence between the maximum allowed under the Usury Laws and the marginal efficiency of capital which in other contexts he hotly denied.[368] However, if the two were not equilibrated at 5% they would, unless the Usury Laws were effective, be equilibrated at some other (probably higher) rate, so that the holder of gilt-edged would receive the same rate as the deprived investor turned taxpayer would have foregone. If, however, there *was* a disequilibrium lack of correspondence between the real and monetary rates, perhaps because of effective Usury Laws, the foregone profit and the interest received would not cancel out. In the tax case the private sector profits foregone would be greater than the tax not raised to pay interest while in the debt case the retained profits would be greater than the tax raised. The private sector would then retain a greater resource command in the debt case, if the problem is viewed, as it was in this example of McCulloch's, purely in terms of income flows. (Whether it is legitimate to treat private sector profits in a case of this sort purely as an income flow, is of course another matter.) McCulloch does not face this problem; but by assuming arbitrary correspondence, *at* 5%, between real and money rates of interest, he finds a non-existent fault in borrowing.

However, this unfortunate episode aside, McCulloch had advanced a fairly useful analysis of the role of debt finance, and presented a respectable case against total reliance on tax finance.

[367] Below, p. 427.

[368] *Scotsman*, 10 May 1817, p. 125; *ibid.*, 4 Apr. 1818, p. 105, 'On the Principles of the Usury Laws'; *Principles of Commerce*, pp. 76–7; EB7 Interest, p. 321; EB8 Interest, pp. 426–7.

But we have already noted his opposition to debt creation at the beginning of Chapter 1 of this part, and his reluctance to rely solely on debt finance. This implies that debt constitutes a burden; and it is this which is the second thread of the chapter. We find McCulloch here not only rejecting the argument that debt constituted a source of wealth but following Hume in his attack on Melon's argument (endorsed by Ricardo[369]) that debt was of no importance because it was merely what was 'owed by the left hand to the right hand'.[370] This was partly because, in his view, the creation of the debt would involve either capital consumption or the transfer of what would otherwise have been invested productively in the future, to government which spent it. It was also partly because payment of debt interest involved a burden on future generations.[371] This was not of the kind envisaged in Professor Buchanan's brilliant work[372]; rather the problem lay in the fact that there was involved a stealthy increase in taxation to service the debt, an increase which continued until the taxation became oppressive. Capital emigration then resulted from the consequent depression of profits.[373] It was true, McCulloch agreed,[374] that the existence of a public debt provided an easily transferred asset, helped saving (this would presumably help to offset the capital-consumption or investment-deflection effect of debt noted above), and was most important in the operation of banking and insurance. But the disadvantages already noted were, in his view, strong; and the very facility of raising funds disguised the increase in the supply of effort and saving which a war made necessary.[375]

At first sight this is an inconsistent argument with the one noted earlier that taxes to service a debt would be at a level to stimulate the supply of effort and saving while taxes large enough to avoid debt would probably pass beyond stimulation to shock.[376] But this is really a problem of presentation. What McCulloch was essentially arguing was that tax finance was preferable so long as it did not pass beyond stimulation. Total reliance on tax finance would certainly pass this point. Debt finance should be used to prevent this happening; taxation

369 Ricardo's *Works*, vol. I, p. 240. Nevertheless Ricardo was not in favour of debt creation.

70 Below, pp. 403-5.

371 *Edinburgh Review*, Oct. 1823, *loc. cit.*, p. 8.

72 J. M. Buchanan, *Public Principles of Public Debt*, Homewood, Illinois, 1958.

73 Below, pp. 405-6, 413-4.

374 Below, p. 405.

75 Below, pp. 406-10.

376 Below, pp. 405, 411-12.

to service debt would not for a long time pass the stimulation point, and the stimulation itself might help to replace some of the capital consumed or not invested through its impetus to growth.[377]

Nevertheless, the very ease of debt finance made it dangerous – it could go on increasing almost without check. Tax finance should then be pushed as far as possible but stopping short of shock; and in McCulloch's view it had often not been pushed far enough.[378] A number of countries had rather bad histories of borrowing, especially France, and the U.S. after the start of the Civil War.[379] If the increase in debt did result in capital emigration (and there was scope to work against this by peacetime funding of the debt although Gladstone – not mentioned by name – had made a poor job of recent British conversions[380]) this emigration would reduce the ability of the economy to bear service taxes, at the same time as it increased foreign competition.[381]

Strangely this is all that McCulloch has to say at this point about what he conceived to be the burden of debt. It is strange, because a major consideration in McCulloch's mind in relation to debt was the problem of the effect of fixed interest charges in deflation, on the lines of the analysis, already discussed, in Chapter 11 of Part II. This was the burden of his 1816 *Essays*[382]; and it was not until Mushet's calculations finally convinced McCulloch that the gilt-edged holders had not gained by the post-war deflation, that he stopped recommending a unilateral reduction of the debt interest.[383]

The second chapter of Part III is concerned with the third major element in McCulloch's writings on debt creation and policy; the correct method of borrowing, and the varying of either interest or principal to pay the market rate of interest. Ricardo had considered variation of one or the other as equivalent, but McCulloch firmly rejected such a view on the grounds that it completely disregarded the problem of debt redemption.[384] His argument, which followed closely

377 Below, p. 413.

378 Below, pp. 413-4.

379 Below, pp. 414-8.

380 Below, pp. 422-4.

381 Below, pp. 429-30.

382 See in particular First 1816 Essay, pp. 38-44; Second 1816 Essay, pp. 193-4.

383 R. Mushet, *A Series of Tables, exhibiting the Gain and Loss to the Fund-Holder, arising from the Fluctuations in the Value of the Currency, from 1800 to 1821*, 2nd edition corrected, London, 1821; McCulloch, 'Sir James Graham's Pamphlet – Tax on the Funds', *Scotsman*, 8 Jul. 1826, p. 425; *Statistical Account*, 1837, vol. II, p. 536.

384 *Edinburgh Review*, Jan. 1828, *loc. cit.*, pp. 74-5; below, pp. 437-9.

that of another Scot, Robert Hamilton, was essentially as follows. If government borrowed by issuing low interest stock below par during wartime, it found itself having to repay sums it had never received, if it wished to repay debt. On the one hand, he asserted, if government raised interest instead of varying principal it would have to do so less than proportionately; and, on the other, if interest rather than principal were raised, it could be reduced by conversion operations once the war had passed.

McCulloch had been advancing this argument since 1837[385] and it had already encountered some criticism.[386] But here he maintained his position. After a brief discussion and condemnation of annuities[387] the major part of the chapter[388] (indeed the remainder apart from a tailpiece on the desirability of borrowing abroad if cheaper[389]) is devoted to the Hamiltonian argument.

At times it does not look very happy. Thus McCulloch admitted that it was easier to raise money at 3% than 5% and borrowing at the latter rate involved offering proportionately *more* principal. The five per cent's did not sell well because purchasers knew that their interest would be reduced in peacetime.[390] He argued that a small *certain* increase in interest would be sufficient to offset the *uncertain* capital gain which made the three per cents attractive; but apparently fails to recognise that this increase in interest would have to be on top of the addition to interest necessary to balance the reduction in principal in moving from three per cents to five per cents, thus implying in *total* a greater interest payment in the five per cent case. So McCulloch's position was not very happy; and indeed it was precisely the difficulty of placing five per cents which had led Ricardo to disagree with Hamilton's view.[391] Newmarch too had argued, in criticism of McCulloch, that Pitt would have encountered great difficulties in trying to borrow at par, and indeed that the 5% legal maximum would not have been high enough to achieve this.[392]

Nevertheless there was some sense in McCulloch's argument[393]

[385] *Statistical Account*, 1837, vol. II, p. 533; WN1838, p. 616.

[386] W. Newmarch, *On the Loans raised by Mr. Pitt during the First French War, 1793–1801; with some statements in defence of the Methods of Funding employed*, London, 1855.

[387] Below, pp. 430–6.

[388] Below, pp. 436–43.

[389] This is consistent with McCulloch's analysis of the transfer problem – see O'Brien, *op. cit.*, pp. 208–17.

[390] Below, pp. 437–8.

[391] Ricardo's *Works*, vol. IV, p. 185.

[392] Newmarch, *op. cit.*

[393] Below, pp. 439–40.

that if the state borrowed at 3% and then attempted to redeem debt this would bring the three per cents to par, increasing the sum the state would have to redeem. It was possible to reduce the interest on five per cents in peacetime because they were normally at or above par except in wartime, and government could threaten to pay off at par value if conversion was refused.

On the basis mainly of this principle, McCulloch proceeded to a critique of British debt policy.[394] Of course the analysis was incomplete: for both he and his critics were ignoring the problem that the terms which a very large borrower like the state could obtain were not independent of what it was prepared, or was believed to be prepared, to offer. But the treatment is not without interest for all that.

The final chapter, Chapter 3 of Part III, is concerned with the problem of debt redemption. Now McCulloch's views on this particular topic had gone through a number of changes. At first, after Mushet's calculations had caused him to abandon his scheme for unilateral reductions of debt interest (as distinct from conversion operations) he had advocated the scheme propounded by Ricardo (though as McCulloch pointed out it was originally Archibald Hutcheson's) for a capital levy to pay off the debt.[395] He did once describe this as a last resort[396]; but for a long time his attitude was generally that it was a practical course of proceedings. He believed that it could be used, and that to do so would permit £29mn. of taxes to service the debt to be repealed. This in turn would remove a significant stimulus to capital emigration.[397]

Now this was not really satisfactory. Firstly, governments invariably had wars and invariably borrowed. This created a long-run prospect of a series of capital levies. Secondly there was Hume's criticism of Hutcheson[398] that, because the professional classes passed unscathed, the scheme would violate inter-sectoral justice. To this McCulloch

394 Below, pp. 440–3.

395 'Expediency and Practicability of Mr. Ricardo's Plan for Paying Off the National Debt', *Scotsman*, 8 Jan. 1820, p. 9; see also 'Sadler on Ireland', *Edinburgh Review*, vol. XLIX, Jun. 1829, pp. 300–17, pp. 316–17 where the plan is attributed to Hutcheson without mention of Ricardo.

396 *Edinburgh Review*, Jan. 1820, *loc. cit.*, p. 180.

397 *Scotsman*, Jan. 1820, *loc. cit.*; *ibid.*, 10 May 1823, p. 297, 'Finances of Great Britain, No. III – Operation of the Sinking Fund since the Peace. – Present State of Revenue and Expenditure'; *Edinburgh Review*, Oct. 1827, *loc. cit.*, pp. 407–14.

398 Hume, *op. cit.*, pp. 381–2.

had originally answered, on Ricardian lines, that competition would adjust their earnings proportionately. But by the time of the first edition of this *Treatise* he had come to accept Hume's view[399]; and in this chapter he is critical of the capital levy scheme.[400]

But the alternative to a capital levy, accepting that the debt was a burden, was a sinking fund. Now for a long time McCulloch seems to have disapproved of such an idea, despite Smith's approval,[401] and to have carried Ricardo with him.[402] He seems, during this period, to have believed that such an institution would needlessly encourage government spending and so pressed for repeal of taxes as superior to surplus budgeting.[403]

But by 1863 McCulloch had changed his mind and was arguing for budget surpluses and their use in debt reduction.[404] He was not optimistic about the possibility of *continual* realisation and employment of such surpluses to pay off debt, and so was still opposed to a formal sinking fund which would necessitate borrowing in deficit years.[405] The main hope for reducing the burden of debt must always lie in pursuing policies of economic growth; but if surpluses could be achieved so much the better. If the achievement of surpluses necessitated widening the tax base from the one which Gladstonian financial policy had produced by 1863, then this was all to the good.[406] He now rejected Ricardo's idea that budget surpluses made governments warlike; instead he argued, with Overstone and others opposed to Gladstone's financial policy, that budget surpluses would impress foreigners with British strength and discourage their warlike tendencies.[407]

But the bulk of the chapter[408] is taken up with criticism of Pitt's Sinking Fund and of Price's calculations which provided the intellectual basis for it. As McCulloch points out, following Robert Hamilton very closely, any debt reduction must come from taxation. Compound

[399] *Treatise on Taxation*, 1845, pp. 463-4; *Literature of Political Economy*, p. 319.

[400] Below, pp. 461-3.

[401] Smith, *op. cit.*, vol. II, Book V, ch. iii, p. 423.

[402] McCulloch to Ricardo, 19 Nov. 1816, Ricardo to McCulloch, 4 Dec. 1816, Ricardo's *Works*, vol. VII, pp. 93-4, 102-6; Ricardo's speech of 9 Jun. 1819, *Works*, vol. V, pp. 20-1.

[403] *Scotsman*, 26 Feb. 1823, p. 130; 'Agricultural Distress – Causes – Remedies', *Edinburgh Review*, vol. XXXVI, Feb. 1822, pp. 452-82; *ibid.*, Oct. 1827, *loc. cit.*, p. 407; *Treatise on Taxation*, 1845, pp. 462-3.

[404] Below, pp. 40-3, 461, 463.

[405] Below, pp. 453, 459, 460.

[406] Below, p. 463.

[407] Below, pp. 40-3.

[408] Below, pp. 450-61.

interest calculations are completely delusive unless the capital is invested in something productive – which was not the case with a sinking fund.[409] As it was, the existence of the fund, founded on delusive reasoning, had necessitated government borrowing more than it would otherwise have required in deficit years, simply in order to maintain the annual payment into the fund.[410] As Hamilton had shown, the fund's existence had led to a net increase in debt.[411] This in turn had worsened the terms on which government had been able to borrow; it was already overloading the market with gilt-edged and the additional borrowing for the sinking fund had made this worse.[412] This was not a position that McCulloch adopted late in life; he consistently agreed with Hamilton on this matter.[413]

(e) *The Appendices*

The remainder of the *Treatise* consists of McCulloch's appendices. Those appended to the third edition are included because they give some flavour of McCulloch's 'statistical' work which was a significant part of his total output, as well as helping to underline the way in which his approach to economic problems never lost touch with the basic factual material. Another point of interest is Appendix III containing the portion of Overstone's speech on the commercial treaty with France of 1860. For it harmonises exactly with the anti-Gladstonian spirit which pervades much of this third edition, and also helps to emphasise the closeness of McCulloch and Overstone, a point borne out by the latter's correspondence.[414]

(iii) *Conclusion*

McCulloch's work on taxation, as exemplified in this book, was of a much more comprehensive nature than that of any of the writers who preceded him. Here we have, really for the first time, a comprehensive work on the theory and policy of public finance, with a fairly well-integrated coverage of general tax theory, direct and indirect taxation, and debt policy. Obviously it is not wholly satisfactory.

409 Below, pp. 452–4.

410 Below, pp. 454–5.

411 Below, pp. 455–7.

412 Below, pp. 458–9.

413 See, e.g., 'Finances of Great Britain No. II – Progress and Present Amount of the Public Debt – Sinking Fund', *Scotsman*, 26 Apr. 1823, p. 265.

414 See D. P. O'Brien (ed.), *The Correspondence of Lord Overstone*, 3 vols., Cambridge, 1971, especially vol. II.

But as an example of the kind of writing in which McCulloch excelled and which was typical of the Scottish tradition, intertwining fact and theory, not reasoning in terms of the corn model but keeping both feet firmly on the ground, it was a good production. Essentially it was Scottish; for apart from the obvious debts to Hume and Hamilton, there is, underlying the whole thing, the Smithian growth analysis. It is against this that taxation is tested, and largely by its test different forms of taxation stand or fall. Apart from the requirement that taxation must not be too heavy because even good taxes, if too severely imposed, could interfere with economic growth, the growth requirement led to a fairly definite preference for indirect taxes. Direct taxes had overwhelming administrative defects, and suffered from the severe failing that they stimulated only saving, not saving and effort as did indirect taxes. Moreover there was the danger that an income tax might be allowed to depart from strict proportionality; and this would subvert the motives so essential to growth. Direct taxes too were especially likely to encourage capital export. Property taxes were no better than income taxes; apart from considerable difficulty of operation which they shared with income taxes, they interfered with investment and even encouraged capital consumption in the case of property which yielded no return.

On the other hand indirect taxes at moderate levels on a wide base were a largely satisfactory system. Used in such a way their disadvantages, which McCulloch recognised – principally distortion of the price system and regression – were minimised; and they had the advantage, which appealed to McCulloch's basic ability-to-pay approach, that they were productive of revenue. If indirect taxes were used at a *high* level on a *narrow* base they were much less acceptable; and it was this which, in a large measure, led to McCulloch's strong opposition to Gladstone's financial policy. Gladstone's policy involved substantial effects on the prices and/or consumption of a few basic goods; and because McCulloch recognised, unlike Ricardo, that the adjustment of wages to taxes on wage goods was extremely imperfect, this involved not only distortion and injustice but also the social unrest of which McCulloch was continuously afraid. Moreover Gladstone was not exploiting the ability of indirect taxes, used as McCulloch prescribed, to produce revenue; and so he had to rely on the income tax which McCulloch believed so unsatisfactory.

The concern with Gladstone's policy is typical of the book and of

McCulloch's approach: but the attack was couched in terms of general principles and their infringement by Gladstone. Such an approach is typical of the Scottish tradition; and it is in the light of this tradition that McCulloch's work must be viewed and, it is to be hoped, appreciated.

PART III

ENGLISH AND AUSTRIAN ECONOMICS AFTER 1870

[16]

2 A. Marshall, 1842–1924

D. P. O'BRIEN

Introduction – biographia

The main facts of Marshall's life are well-known, and are set out in the very fine account given by Keynes who worked from material supplied by Mrs Marshall.[1] Alfred Marshall was born on 26 July 1842. Rebelling against a parental preference for classics and the Church, he went to St. John's College, Cambridge, read mathematics, and graduated as Second Wrangler in 1865. A period spent as a Fellow of St John's led him to economics and to marriage with Mary Paley, one of the pioneer women undergraduates at Cambridge. The years 1877–82 were spent at Bristol University College, chiefly as its principal. After a short spell at Oxford, Marshall was elected to the Chair of Political Economy at Cambridge, taking up the post in January 1885 and holding it until his retirement in 1908 when he was followed by his chosen successor A. C. Pigou. Greatly revered as the leading economist in the Anglo-Saxon world he died on 13 July 1924.

Marshall pursued a lifetime of literary labour. His first book, written jointly with his wife, appeared in 1879 as the *Economics of Industry*. Although Marshall disliked the book it had sold over 15,000 copies by his death and since then has sold about another 23,000. It was followed in 1890 by his *Principles of Economics* which ran through eight editions up to 1920, had sold 37,000 copies at the time of his death, and has since sold another 95,000. The book was intended to be the first volume of a large work, and Marshall's ambition was partially realised with the publication in 1919 of *Industry and Trade* of which 12,000 had been sold by his death, with a further 4,000 sold subsequently, and by the publication in 1923 of his *Money, Credit and Commerce* of which 7,000 were printed prior to his death, with another 2,000 subsequently.[2] Yet even that was not intended to be the end; in extreme old age he was contemplating a fourth major work.[3]

His marriage, though childless, was happy. The impression which emerges from the accounts of contemporaries is of a shy, rather timid man, devoid of a sense of humour.[4] Yet, with the aid of a legacy of £250, he set off for a trip to the United States in 1875 and was bold enough to visit – and report on – the Wild West.[5] Moreover he engaged in a certain amount of newspaper controversy (a fact which has not been fully appreciated because the Keynes bibliography is incomplete) although he had the bitterest distaste for controversy. He also engaged in controversies within the University of Cambridge, vigorously opposing degrees for women. But he was essentially a thinker and a writer, not an administrator or man of affairs; and it is, for the most part, the extraordinarily diverse tapestry of his writing on economics which makes him chiefly interesting.

Sources and methods

(i) *Sources*

Marshall owed a clear debt to his classical predecessors and it was one which he was anxious to acknowledge. He defended the classical economists vigorously against their latter-day critics especially Jevons and Böhm-Bawerk.[6] His most important debt was undoubtedly to J. S. Mill who influenced not only Marshall's theoretical apparatus, which developed from the application of mathematics to Mill, but also his policy attitudes. His first book is indeed avowedly *an introduction to* J. S. Mill. But a wide range of classical writers influenced Marshall, including Smith, Ricardo, Overstone and McCulloch. Of course Marshall was also influenced by a number of continental writers, especially Cournot, and Von Thünen, and also by Dupuit and the German Historical school.[7] But his attitude to Jevons, to whom he owed his utility analysis, was, for a long time, hostile, and it was only relatively late that Marshall mellowed.[8]

Marshall's general approach, with its emphasis upon continuity, was significantly influenced by the philosopher Hegel and also by Spencer. Of course it is true that Schumpeter has claimed that these influences were so much excess baggage which could be ignored.[9] But it is not easy to sustain this view without taking a narrowly neoclassical view of Marshall's work – which would leave one holding the tautological position that what we choose to ignore is unimportant.

The same point may be made about the influence of Darwin, which led Marshall to look towards biology as providing the way forward in economic methodology and to emphasise the evolving nature of economic phenomena.

(ii) *Methodology*

The influence of Darwin was shown in the first of Marshall's two methodological mottos '*Natura non facit saltum*' (Nature does not make jumps).[10] But perhaps even more important was Marshall's other motto 'The many in the one, and the one in the many'.[11] By this Marshall meant that there are many different forces and causes acting to produce one economic phenomenon which we observe; while these forces and causes are not unique to each case but reappear in different guises throughout the world of economic phenomena. This led him to the conclusion that there must be continuous study of the real world, with the aim of finding a few fundamental principles; but it also led him to lay great emphasis upon the importance of factual material and the particular details of each case, for only in this way could the relative importance of the multiplicity of causes be judged. This was associated with Marshall's emphasis upon the importance of observation; he believed that good methodology followed the eighteenth-century procedure of an inextricable intertwining of induction and deduction. The deduction should only involve short chains of reasoning and there should be a constant return to the facts for verification.[12]

Yet there is something of a puzzle in all this. For Marshall followed his own methodological pronouncements somewhat incompletely. There is an important statement in an article by Marshall of 1885[13] in which he wrote out the following expression:

$$\frac{\mathrm{d}U}{\mathrm{d}t} = \frac{\mathrm{d}U}{\mathrm{d}X} \cdot \frac{\mathrm{d}X}{\mathrm{d}t} + \frac{\mathrm{d}U}{\mathrm{d}Y} \cdot \frac{\mathrm{d}Y}{\mathrm{d}t} + \frac{\mathrm{d}U}{\mathrm{d}Z} \cdot \frac{\mathrm{d}Z}{\mathrm{d}t}$$

(where the derivatives on the right-hand side are partial)

and then explained that time series observations supplied

$\frac{\mathrm{d}X}{\mathrm{d}t}, \frac{\mathrm{d}Y}{\mathrm{d}t}, \ldots,$ while theory supplied $\frac{\mathrm{d}U}{\mathrm{d}X}, \frac{\mathrm{d}U}{\mathrm{d}Y}, \ldots.$

Such a statement would seem to point the way towards development of the eighteenth-century chain of reasoning in conjunction with modern collection of statistics and modern statistical and mathematical methods. Yet Marshall did not follow this road. Despite his view that the nineteenth century had completed the main qualitative tasks in economics, and that the need was now for quantitative analysis, he did not himself do empirical work except through the collection of descriptive material as in *Industry and Trade*. Although he looked forward to such things as the development of empirical studies of demand, and although he collected a great deal of factual information, he did little empirical work of the kind which he said was required, although he used statistical evidence before the Indian Currency Commission and although he constructed a book of time series with a common time axis for his private use.[14]

His methodological ideals led him to adopt a rather deprecatory attitude towards pure theory.[15] He roundly condemned the claims of pure theory to be economics proper; and even his attitude towards mathematics was ambivalent. He was originally trained as a mathematician and was probably, at one time, a good one, although there are differing views on this. He seems to have regarded mathematical training as valuable but to have doubted the usefulness of mathematics in economics. As is well known, he believed that if the results of mathematical economics could not be translated into English they should be burned. The question was not whether it was possible to use mathematics in economics; it was whether it was useful to do so. But there is no doubt that Marshall himself became rather rusty as a mathematician even though his work in the 1870s shows that his early development as an economist owed a great deal to his mathematical training. None the less, the view that he constructed an entire mathematical skeleton for the *Principles*, and then simply clothed it with factual material, is surely no longer tenable.[16]

There were, in any case, characteristics of his whole approach which would have predisposed him against the kind of simple models to which mathematics led. These included the importance of time, his concern with *movements to* equilibrium, and, perhaps most fundamental, his insistence that the whole subject matter of economics involved evolutionary phenomena.

(iii) *Economics as a science*

All this did not prevent Marshall viewing economics as a science – and one for which he was prepared, if necessary, to make very large claims. It should aspire to the same status as the physical sciences even though it was hampered by an inability to experiment.[17] It is arguable that his emphasis on this waned with time; the early *Economics of Industry* is full of 'Laws', some of them very dubious. But though the emphasis may have become less, Marshall did not abandon this position.

To advance the science of economics it was perfectly proper to use such devices as static analysis – though this must not be pushed too far – and partial equilibrium. In the latter connection Marshall was responsible for making explicit the device of *coeteris paribus* which had frequently been implied in classical discussions but not often made explicit. Partial analysis was significantly advanced by Marshall.[18] Nevertheless he was well aware that general equilibrium considerations were sometimes unavoidable, especially in the context of distribution. But he was concerned about the almost total lack of useable content in general equilibrium analysis.[19]

Economic laws would, subject to *coeteris paribus*, produce, 'normal' results. By 'normal' Marshall meant competitive, although the realisation that competition had to be conducted within a framework of some sort seems to have led him to a change of mind which was more apparent than real, in that he came to stress the limitations – of law and custom – on competition under which normality could be achieved.[20]

Marshall drew very wide boundaries for the science of economics, including most things which were subject to the measuring rod of money, and a number that were not.[21] He distinguished, like Senior, between the science of economics and the art of economics, the latter drawing on the results of science but requiring a substantial measure of common sense as well.[22] He also distinguished between normative and positive economics. Yet he systematically ignored these distinctions in his own work, which is full of ethical considerations. These include not only Marshall's pet aversions – alcohol, gambling and lavish personal expenditure – as well as his reverence for motherhood, but also his interests in social reform. He was interested in the limits and benefits of state intervention, of cooperation, and of redistribution, because of the evils resulting from 'excessive' freedom and competition without sufficient regulation, and because of the conflicts which arose between public and private interests.[23] He was, however, in the last resort an individualist; and he was very concerned about the dangers of collectivism and corruption.[24] But all these considerations appear in the broad tapestry of his economic writings.

Demand theory

Perhaps the most important single point about Marshall's demand analysis is that it starts with the prior existence of the negatively-sloped market demand curve. This is initially explained by reference to income distribution. Given the curve, it was natural to explore its properties and this led to Marshall's (subjective) invention, and development, of elasticity, together with an analysis of its determinants. Because the curve was a partial one, and because other things could not be expected to remain equal over time, Marshall concentrated his analysis on the short run.[25]

Marshall's utility analysis, which involved the theory of the maximising consumer, clearly comes after the demand curve and owes a good deal to Jevons. We start from an analysis of wants and the idea that utility is the basis of consumption. We then have a statement of eventually diminishing marginal utility (as the utility of the marginal purchase rather than as the derivative of the utility function) leading to the derivation of the demand curve from diminishing marginal utility. This provided us with the demand curve for the individual.[26] For each individual taken in isolation, price paid is a measure of his marginal utility, though Marshall continually emphasised that a shilling had a different marginal utility for a poor man and for a rich man. The now familiar equilibrium of the consumer is obtained and this is extended to inter-temporal maximisation without discounting of future benefits both for futurity and uncertainty. Intra-temporal and inter-temporal maximisation are then combined.[27] However, for this Marshall used an additive utility function which possesses all the properties and limitations which have been explored at great length in the secondary literature; and, as we shall see, he treated the marginal utility of money as a quasi-constant. Despite awareness of the problems involved, he was, in general, quite prepared to sum the demand curves of individuals to produce a market demand curve and to suggest that, although individual purchases might be discontinuous, in the aggregate they produced a smooth curve.[28]

The utility analysis was linked with his initially high hopes for the development of consumer surplus. As is now well-known, the failure of this concept to prove sufficiently robust for his purposes was one of the great disappointments of his life.[29] So aware was he of the difficulties associated with it that on only one occasion did he throw caution to the wind and estimate consumer surplus.[30] It was defined by Marshall as the now familiar area underneath the demand curve and above the prevailing price.[31] The difficulties with it were formidable. The consumer surplus obtained from one commodity was not independent of the supply of another – Marshall illustrated this with the example of being deprived of both tea and coffee. Secondly, there was the problem of treating this area, which had a money value, as measuring utility – which relied upon a constant marginal utility of money. Thirdly, there was a danger of double counting. Because of these problems it was difficult to aggregate over one individual's consumption of a wide range of commodities while aggregation over the community – moving the apostrophe so that consumer's surplus becomes consumers' – posed even more serious problems. For the integral concerned cannot be a utility (as distinct from a money) measure in the presence of differences in the marginal utility of money income – the existence of which Marshall had recognised publicly since the 1879 *Economics of Industry*. Moreover there are insoluble general equilibrium limitations on using consumer surplus, derived from partial analysis, as a community welfare tool.[32]

The problem which has attracted most attention in the literature however is that of the assumption of constant marginal utility of money. In fact Marshall made this only for convenience; and in other contexts he was prepared to say that it was not justified, or even to make a completely different assumption – Bernoulli's hypothesis that equal percentage increases in income produced equal absolute increases in utility – in order to analyse the particular problem of gambling.[33] Nevertheless, though Marshall's careful and selective use of this particular assumption of constancy was sensible, there are so many different difficulties associated with the concept of consumer surplus, especially in the context of the broad canvas on which Marshall painted, involving, as it did, changing tastes, to make its use as an operational tool highly questionable. In view of these difficulties it is hardly surprising that Marshall lost heart. He had originally hoped that the qualifications applied less strongly to what are now known as the 'Marshallian Triangles' relating to small price and quantity changes, and that the concept might be operationally useful in that kind of context.[34] Yet, although he apparently lost heart, he continued to reproduce, in successive editions of the *Principles*, material, dating from the 1870s, which relied for its validity upon these problems having been solved. Of course he warned his readers against taking the analysis too literally; and he was worried about the implications drawn from it by Pigou.[35] But this was one development over which he ultimately became discouraged.

None the less there is no doubt that Marshall significantly influenced the development of demand analysis. But the main thrust of his contribution to microeconomics concerned problems of supply.

Supply

To Marshall we owe the universal use of the supply curve. This is built up from the supply prices of the services of factors, including gross earnings of management, in a Representative Firm rather than a Marginal Firm.[36] The costs incurred are divided into fixed and variable costs – Marshall led the profession into following accountancy practice – and are money costs, although there is some (imprecise) relation between money and real (i.e. disutility) costs. However there are rents *below* the supply curve, as well as between it and the prevailing price, because of differential efficiencies – Marshall embodied this notion in a concept called the Particular Expenses Curve.[37]

Marshall extensively analysed the supply conditions affecting each of the factors of production, which he classified as land, labour, capital, and organisation.[38] Supply of labour is affected by the growth of population, its health and strength, industrial training and labour mobility which leads, somewhat imperfectly, to equalisation of net advantage.[39] Supply of capital depends on the strength of sources of accumulation and of the motives to save. There is positive time preference in the aggregate and the cost of this 'waiting' has to be covered as part of the normal cost of production.[40]

Marshall's discussion of land is characterised by a wholly classical emphasis on diminishing returns – which might be offset by technical progress – and a tendency to confuse these with decreasing returns to scale and to contrast them with increasing returns. This was despite the fact that he ultimately conceded that they were not the same, and despite the fact also that he generalised the concept of diminishing returns to all factors.[41] It was central to the search for optimal factor combinations by the entrepreneur – dependent upon relative factor prices and productivities – which Marshall called the Principle of Substitution.[42] Two particular points about this are of interest; first, Marshall's discussion did not involve a fixed and unique production function;[43] secondly, he managed to perpetuate the curious classical error that rent did not enter into supply price, despite recognising the existence of transfer earnings.[44]

The fourth factor of production was entrepreneurship or organisation. Marshall attached very great importance to the role of the specialised entrepreneur who was a man with organisational ability in command of capital and who was also the risk bearer. Risk was part of supply price.[45]

It is however important to understand that, for Marshall, supply price is *not* governed by marginal cost as ordinarily understood – though the idea that it is, is commonplace in the secondary literature. For marginal cost is of a different nature from the mathematical concept now familiar. It is the marginal cost of a process and not of a product. Price is determined with respect to large discrete changes in output not (in Marshall's phrase) 'each separate small parcel'. Moreover there are *no* unique costs associated with particular products in a multi product firm.[46]

Central to Marshall's treatment of the firm itself was his concept of the Representative Firm. Marshall envisaged that there was a range of firms from the very powerful to the marginal, and used the Representative Firm, one in the middle of the spectrum, as a device for analysing the response of the industry to a change in conditions facing it. Firms experience a life cycle, and during the course of this they pass through the stage at which they are representative of the industry – the trees of the forest simile.[47] Increase in demand facing the industry will then increase the growth of the rising firms and slow the decay of the falling firms, resulting in an increase in total production.

Competition is important; but it is *not* perfect. Each firm was envisaged as selling in the general market and also to particular customers with whom it had a special relationship.[48] Marshall provided the elements for the construction of the theory of imperfect competition.[49] He examined many of the factors which have become prominent in later discussions of market power such as product-differentiation, advertising, barriers to entry, limit pricing, loss leaders and tying clauses.[50] He envisaged significant oligopolistic inter-dependence between firms, especially where there was a high ratio of fixed to variable costs.[51] He also analysed monopoly at length, and provided a theoretical treatment from which it is only a small, and mathematically trivial, step to reach the analysis of the 1930s. However he also emphasised the conditional nature of monopoly and the limits to maximising behaviour by monopolists, as well as price discrimination and the allocation of overheads according to elasticity and the possibilities of regulation – though not nationalisation.[52] His attitude to cartels was somewhat ambivalent, because he saw a conflict between the advantages of cooperation and the dangers of market power.[53] He was also concerned about the dangers of bureaucracy in large firms, especially joint stock companies, and exercised about the threat to small companies whom he regarded as important in relation to innovation.[54]

The large capitals of joint stock companies afforded them access to economies of scale which gave them particular advantages. Marshall's discussion of these, and their division into internal and external economies is well known, and constitutes a major contribution. External economies, available to all firms, did not represent a threat to competition; but internal economies did so and Marshall eventually relied upon marketing difficulties, managerial diseconomies, the life cycle of the firm, and the mortality of entrepreneurship, as explanations for what he *observed* to be the case – that monopoly had not become the main industrial form.[55]

An important aspect of Marshall's analysis relates to time. Although it is well known that Marshall regarded the length of time in which supply had to adjust to a change in demand as critical, it has not often been recognised that the long run supply curve, as envisaged by Marshall, had a time dimension as well as a quantity one, and that progress along it involved both these variables. Such a device permitted Marshall to include technical change in a downward sloping curve; but it involved the cost that he had to view the supply curve as irreversible, which may partly explain his reluctance to use elasticity of supply as a concept parallel with that of elasticity of demand.[56]

Value theory

In the preceding two sections the elements which Marshall used to construct the blades of his famous scissors were discussed. It should be clear however that these blades were complex constructions; Marshall would not have countenanced the idea that they could be fitted simply together and used to cut, without difficulty, through any value problem:

> changes in the volume of production, in its methods, and in its cost are ever mutually modifying one another; they are always affecting and being affected by the character and the extent of demand. Further all these mutual influences take time to work themselves out, and, as a rule, no two influences move at equal pace. In this world therefore every plain and simple doctrine as to the relations between cost of production, demand and value is necessarily false.[57]

Nevertheless Marshall devoted some attention to the interaction of demand and supply. His treatment starts, as so often with Marshall, from J. S. Mill. Value is defined as relative price at a particular time and place, and it depends upon both demand and supply – hence the scissors. The emphasis is upon mutual determination – following Cournot – and Marshall made clear that he believed the demand-oriented approach of Jevons to be even more faulty than the supply-oriented approach of Ricardo. A market is defined as an area of price uniformity; and the extent of the market depends upon such matters as uniformity and portability of the commodity, information, and the existence of an extensive demand.[58]

Adjustment to equilibrium within the market takes time. This was an early obsession of Marshall – although it really only required the further development of the distinction between the market and the long period in classical economics – and it ultimately led to a treatment which has found its way into all the textbooks. However, Marshall's detailed exploration of market clearing in the case of a commodity, such as corn, with a fixed supply has received a good deal less attention than it really deserves. Closely linked to his discussion of this is the question of stability. As is well known, Marshall relied upon quantity adjustment to achieve equilibrium of normal demand and supply. Marshall's industrial wanderings were perhaps responsible for his possessing a much greater awareness than some of his contemporaries, especially Walras, of the problems associated with equilibrium and, in particular, of the possibilities of multiple equilibria and the difficulties introduced by the recognition that neither long run demand nor supply were truly reversible. At the same time, as D. G. Davis has pointed out, it is not true that Marshall relied solely upon a quantity adjustment model; in his analysis of the corn market he used a price adjustment model. But Marshall's use of quantity adjustment surely makes better sense in terms of the maximising producer than Walras' rather simple *tâtonnement* based, as it probably was, on a country market at Evreux.[59]

The achievement of equilibrium in the market would result in 'normal' value. There were two kinds of normal value; a short run normal value and a long run normal value – a concept derived from Adam Smith – which would only be achieved in the unlikely circumstances of stationary conditions existing over a long period. 'Normal' values for Marshall meant values achieved by competitive forces within the constraints of law and custom – though he came to believe that his increased emphasis on the latter constituted a change of mind.[60]

Marshall also dealt with other problems affecting value. He noted the influence of expectations on value; and he dealt at great length with problems of joint demand and joint supply. His concern with this problem, and much of his treatment of it, stemmed from J. S. Mill; and it would probably be true to say that Marshall left the matter in a somewhat unsatisfactory state. His analysis has been strongly criticised by Stigler; but it would be fair to say that he did not make strong claims for it and that he was aware that there were serious problems with the exposition as it stood.[61]

The main thrust of Marshall's value theory was, then, an attempt to explore the achievement of equilibrium in different time periods through the integration of the supply analysis which he had developed with the demand theory which owed much to the influence of Jevons and, to a lesser extent, Menger. This was a substantial achievement; it significantly affected the development of mainstream value theory and all subsequent expositions owe something to Marshall, though they have tended increasingly to side-step the really interesting problems concerning adjustment which he raised. His own use of the tools in a practical context was limited[62] – at least outside his advanced lectures – but he had achieved, to a considerable extent, his main aim of forging the tools for his successors.

Distribution

Marshall's distribution theory started from the work of J. S. Mill but was worked out fully only in the 1880s and owed a good deal to Von Thünen and F. A. Walker. It took him some time to free himself of the wage fund analysis, but his basic approach came to be to treat the demand for factors as determined by their marginal products in all the different possible employments. Marshall actually used *discounted* marginal *revenue* product although the mathematical basis of the approach remained largely concealed. He did not however regard marginal productivity analysis as more than a part of the theory of distribution; this was partly due to the problem of estimating net marginal product, but mainly because the supply side was of equal (or more than equal) interest. Moreover, he never formally endorsed Euler's theorem and showed considerable reluctance to accept the idea of product exhaustion according to marginal productivity – the latter is in a marginal note to the *Principles* but not in the text.[63]

(i) *Factor supply*

Labour was defined by Marshall as 'any exertion of mind or body undergone partly or wholly with a view to some good other than the pleasure derived directly from the work'. The discussion of labour supply conditions was a curious blend of classical and marginalist considerations. On the one hand, Marshall reproduced the disutility analysis of Jevons (though without always mentioning Jevons), insisting that free human beings have a choice about the supply of factor services and that thus a cost of production approach is inappropriate to the analysis of factor supply. On the other, a great deal of the discussion is of a predominantly classical nature and is concerned with the long run supply conditions of labour including such matters as the growth of population, the health and strength of the population and the costs of investment in education. There is also a discussion of labour mobility, which operated through the ability of each grade of labour to move into the next grade, though it was limited by the existence of non-competing groups. The discussion of the supply of skilled labour was dominated by the question of investment in education and the speed with which supply could adjust to changing demand patterns for different kinds of skills. The supply of unskilled labour was determined primarily by the population mechanism and the conventional level of subsistence. Those fit only for unskilled labour were diminishing relatively in number but their wages had not risen much because the demand for them had been reduced through mechanisation.[64]

Marshall's discussion of labour income is notable for the emphasis on the interaction between poverty and low wages, the one affecting the supply of labour and perpetuating the other, and on the disadvantage of labour in bargaining compared with the employer: 'a man who employs a thousand others, is in himself an absolutely rigid combination'. Marshall was a firm believer in the economies of high wages.[65] However he was cautious about advocating remedies for low wages. He looked rather to technical advance and the rapid growth of capital, together with family limitation amongst the unskilled; his attitude towards minimum wage legislation was uncertain, and his attitude towards trade unions, despite a sometimes naive view of such activities as picketing, was extremely ambiguous. He was sceptical about their role, and opposed to their seeking sectional gains at the expense of other workers; and he ultimately came to view them as destructive of economic growth and even (privately) to be prepared to consider their complete destruction. But his instinctive reaction towards them was warm and friendly – on a par with his romantic attitude towards the cooperative movement. He was also concerned about working hours and the problem of working women.[66]

Capital was viewed by Marshall as a store of things, the result of human efforts and sacrifices, devoted mainly to securing benefits in the future rather than in the present. Profit itself derived partly from interest, which was the supply price of this capital, partly from earnings of management (which could include rent of ability), and partly from compensation for risk and the reward of innovation. Risks were of two kinds; trade risks and the risk of default on the part of an entrepreneur working with borrowed capital.[67]

Marshall regarded the entrepreneur as a vital figure in economic development and believed that total entrepreneurial remuneration was less than government would have 'wasted without good to anybody' under state enterprise. Entrepreneurial earnings were, like other factor rewards, subject to the marginal productivity analysis and the equalisation of task earnings, though they were affected by barriers to entry, and they were higher, the greater the ratio of circulating to fixed capital in an enterprise.[68]

Net interest, after deduction of risk allowance, depended on the demand for and supply of liquid capital – the return to fixed capital was in the nature of a rent ('quasi-rent'). The demand for capital depended upon its expected marginal productivity together with borrowing for consumption purposes. The supply of capital was controlled by the need for 'waiting' – a term which Marshall borrowed from McVane to replace 'abstinence' because of the existence *in the aggregate* of positive time preference, despite exceptions such as the Sargent effect. The sources of accummulation were profits, rent and labour incomes, the latter being directly invested in education and the health of children.[69]

Capital was supplied to the production process in combination with entrepreneurship even though many entrepreneurs worked with borrowed capital. The mobility of entrepreneurs ensured that profits were equalised, in the classical manner, between different employments of capital. In the short run they were, however, subject to wide variations because the first brunt of industrial fluctuations fell upon them.[70]

Marshall's analysis of the income accruing to land formally corresponded with that of the return to other factors. Rents depended upon demand and supply. The demand for land depended upon its marginal productivity (with a small additional demand because of the social distinction of land ownership) while the supply of land was taken to be fixed as in the classical analysis. Rent was then net produce, or the area under the marginal product curve less the return to cooperating factors.[71]

Marshall's discussion of land is surprisingly full of the main classical preconceptions. Rent is due to the existence of diminishing returns, and Marshall has a Ricardo-like emphasis upon variable fertility. Nevertheless he did not accept Ricardo's argument about the conflict of interest between landlords and the community over agricultural improvements. Despite his classical preconceptions – which extended to blurring the role of transfer earnings and avoiding distinguishing rent from an individual and social point of view – he managed to advance the discussion by showing the key role of elasticity of supply in the earning of rent, and was thus able to generalise the rent concept and introduce the important notion of rent of ability.[72]

(ii) *Redistribution*

Marshall viewed the long run trend of distribution as being away from rent and profit and towards wages. Capital accumulation lowered profits and transport lowered the value of agricultural land, while rising labour efficiency raised wages.

Wages had risen over time and middle incomes were increasing faster than those of the rich, because of education, prudence and opportunities for the investment of small capitals. Nevertheless Marshall was very concerned with the poverty which he observed, and with its degrading and self-perpetuating effect in particular. While he believed that many schemes of income redistribution were reckless he did not believe that redistribution would reduce growth. It would merely divert investment to the health of children. He was concerned not only at the skewed nature of the existing distribution of wealth – leading to ostentatious forms of expenditure which offended his puritanism – but, more particularly, with the existence of a 'residuum' of low paid and unskilled people, and the problem of the unemployable. As we shall see later he looked mainly to progressive taxation as a remedy.[73]

Economic growth

Marshall's treatment of economics is permeated by a concern over growth. The post-Walrasian view of Marshall is totally misleading because it fails to appreciate that, for Marshall, economic phenomena were observed not at rest but in the course of growth. Marshall's simile of the man packing parcels on the rack of a moving train 'for although all the things are moving they are relatively at rest' is instructive here. He was impressed by England's industrial leadership, and, after more than a century of growth, was concerned for the maintenance of both that growth and of England's premier position; and in this he was wholly classical. He saw both material and non-material wealth increasing with economic growth which followed three stages and produced rising living standards with expanding wants. This last was itself an important part of Marshall's view of the process of economic growth, for he saw wants expanding with activities and the development of the human character.[74]

Marshall approached the analysis of economic growth in two different, but complementary, ways. One the one hand there was a pioneering (and until recently unpublished) system of growth equations for the size of the working population, the standard of living, the efficiency of the worker, the capital stock, total output, net annual product, the task wage, the time wage and the rate of interest. There is, unfortunately, not space to reproduce that here; but modern readers are much in the debt of Professor Whitaker for disentangling all this from Marshall's unpublished manuscripts.[75] At the same time it is arguable that Marshall showed good sense in suppressing what was simply a mathematical translation of J. S. Mill because, like all mathematical growth models, it really said nothing about the genuinely interesting questions affecting economic growth, and the conscientious Marshall would have been acutely aware of this.

(i) *Factor supply in growth*

Marshall's published treatment of growth, however, was a broad classical discussion, firmly grounded in economic history, with detailed consideration (as distinct from the facile assumption of suitably signed partial derivatives) of the conditions for a process of growth. He paid particular attention to factor supply.

Marshall discussed the growth of population – the chief means of production – and coupled consideration of its size and increase, advancing a sort of weak Malthusian mechanism, with eugenic and natural selection preoccupations (under Darwin's influence). This was a recurrent concern of Marshall and one which should never be left out of account in evaluating his work. It naturally related to the health and strength of the population, which affected the efficiency of the labour force.[76] In this connection he devoted considerable attention to human capital and investment in education. He was particularly concerned about industrial training and scientific education, and he had a very forward-looking concern with the development of business education.[77]

Capital was vital to growth because it provided the essential means without which increasing division of labour could not proceed. It was necessary for the realisation of internal economies made possible by technical progress and assisted by standardisation. External economies were also important in growth, particularly in relation to the labour force and transport and their origin lay largely in localisation of industry.[78] Accummulation of capital depended upon the size of the net product and the motives to saving including foresight, security, family affection and the rate of interest. Marshall ultimately looked forward, in the standard classical manner, to a 'secular' decline in the rate of profit – although if he took the idea of a stationary state seriously this was probably due more to Jevons's prediction of the exhaustion of coal reserves.[79]

Associated with capital was Marshall's fourth factor of production, organisation, which also had a vital role to play in economic growth because it brought capital and labour together and achieved the division of labour and the use of specialised machinery.[80]

Marshall regarded the English system of cultivation as harsh but effective in using land in economic growth. It produced an excellent technology and diffused this. Despite a lingering affection for smallholdings and peasant proprietorship Marshall clearly considered that the English pattern of farming was the suitable one for growth purposes.[81]

(ii) *The framework for growth*

The analysis of the process of economic growth was combined with a discussion of the institutional framework in which it could take place, and it was strongly influenced by the classical literature, from Smith onwards, in its emphasis on security of property and property rights, climate, natural resources, human character and human freedom – which Marshall associated with free enterprise though not in an unbridled form.[82]

The growth of financial institutions was also important, as was the rise of joint stock companies (despite the continuingly important role of the entrepreneur) and the development of communications.[83] However Marshall was not, on balance, enthusiastic about the direct involvement of government in the process of production, through government enterprise. He was convinced that the involvement of government was inimical to efficient management and, above all, to the innovation which was vital to growth. His pet hate in the sphere of government enterprise was the postal monopoly. Government certainly had a vital role to play in the sort of areas – health, welfare, defence and, perhaps above all, education – which had found favour with the classical economists; and Marshall was also a strong advocate of steeply progressive taxation. This was partly because of his concern about the National Debt – Marshall subscribed to the classical view that it was a burden rather than to the comfortable Mercantilist and Keynesian view that it was what the right hand owed to the left – but mainly because he believed that increased activities which the State would have to undertake should be financed more than proportionately by the rich.[84]

(iii) *Growth, welfare and poverty*

The desirability of growth was very much linked in Marshall's mind with the question of welfare. In particular he was genuinely and intensely anxious to find remedies for poverty. As already noted, he was very concerned about the vicious circle of poverty leading to poor health and education, leading in turn to low productivity and thus perpetuating low wages; and he was also very anxious about the problem of urban deprivation which was a recurrent theme in his writings. He was very exercised about overcrowding and the lack of fresh air in towns, and he advocated such remedies as a Fresh Air Rate and the removal of large parts of the population and industry of the cities to the country.[85] One fancies that Marshall approved of the Garden Cities and would even have welcomed the New Towns.

For the relief of those in need Marshall favoured a combination of public and private provision. His attitude towards the 1834 Act was not unfavourable and he was, like his predecessors, very hostile to the Speenhamland system and indeed to outdoor relief in general – though he was not prepared to argue for its total abolition. He offered only limited approval of public works as a supplement to poor relief and believed that the latter should be confined to deserving cases – he took a strong interest in the work of the Charity Organisations Society.[86] Although he was genuinely concerned with the alleviation of poverty, Marshall did not believe that socialism had much to offer in this connection. He respected the hearts of socialists; but not their heads. Indeed he came to believe that socialism represented a considerable threat to economic progress and to liberty; 'I think it more important to dwell on the truths in Mill's *Liberty* than on those in his *Essays on Socialism*'.[87]

Ultimately he looked towards economic growth, and the softening of economic conditions through the development of economic chivalry, to alleviate poverty.[88]

International trade

Marshall's trade theory was one of the earliest parts of his work to be developed. A manuscript which Professor Whitaker dates at 1872–4 includes offer curves, multiple equilibria, exploration of the effects of tariffs and a variety of other material. Moreover Marshall wrote, and never published, a book on international trade which was largely completed by 1877. It is in his international trade theory that Marshall's development as an economist through the mathematisation of J. S. Mill is most strikingly apparent.[89]

(i) *Theoretical apparatus*

The most famous part of Marshall's apparatus is the aggregate demand curve which he related to the downward sloping demand curves in the home market. He used these curves to explore the implications of the elasticity concept and the question of stability of equilibrium in international trade, developing – though only fleetingly – the well-known 'Marshall–Lerner condition'.[90] The main use to which he put the apparatus was to analyse the effects on the terms of trade of shifts in the curves, particularly in relation to the imposition of duties. The discussion is very classical with its emphasis upon specie flows; and it is unfortunate that Marshall does not appear to have taken much account of the work of Torrens. He was quite clear that elasticity was in part dependent upon the range of *potential* exportables within a country; and that, outside a two-country model, the scope for turning the terms of trade in a country's favour was extremely limited.[91] He also used his apparatus to show the gains from trade in the form of a surplus.[92] His treatment gave rise to two celebrated controversies in both of which he was ultimately vindicated. The first was the claim by F. D. Graham that there was no link between the offer curves and the underlying production conditions. The second arose from criticism by Graham of Marshall's results concerning the effect on the net barter terms of trade of an increase in demand. The first criticism was unfair even in terms of what Marshall himself had published, although Professor Meade has shown the full implications of the analysis; the second criticism hinges upon an ambiguity in the term 'increase in demand'.[93]

(ii) *The development and effects of trade*

Much of what Marshall had to say under this heading is available in writings which were, until recently, unpublished. Foreign trade developed, in Marshall's view, from supplying the luxuries of the rich, to supplying basic foodstuffs. It was of benefit to all countries, including backward ones, despite the scale economies enjoyed by the developed ones. It limited the freedom of an individual industry with regard to prices, including the prices paid to inputs; but its effect on capital and labour was discussed primarily in the context of migration opportunities which produced a tendency towards factor price equalisation. It facilitated technical advance and increased division of labour, but it also led to increased use of fixed capital, a separation of the employers and the employed, and the development of money and capital markets which increased fluctuations. However the widening of markets and improvement of communications steadied demand and Marshall concluded that, on balance, trade had steadied employment in England – though there was always a risk of over-specialisation.[94]

The most immediate benefit of trade lay in the principle of comparative advantage which Marshall, stressing the usual classical distinction between intra-country factor mobility and inter-country factor immobility, expressed in opportunity cost form. Even if capital and labour were mobile, trade would still take place on the basis of comparative advantage because land was immobile and there would also be trade arising from technological superiority and important natural resources. Marshall provided a 'range of comparative advantage' table leading to the kind now common in international trade textbooks, indicating how the selection of exports from the possible range would be affected under various assumptions. His publication postdated Edgeworth's more sophisticated treatment; but it is quite possible that Marshall had subjective priority.[95]

(iii) *Free trade and protection*

Marshall was not only a free-trader by conviction, but a unilateral free-trader. Free trade was essential for England, though not for America, in the interests of the stimulation to economic progress which was required. A broad system of protective duties would deprive Britain of financial strength, confer sectional benefits at the cost of much greater injury to the public at large, make it harder to reduce the National Debt, and reduce total trade, depriving the country of scale benefits while yielding little revenue and causing much friction. There were more urgent tasks for government than the imposition of protection. Taxes on imported raw materials were particularly harmful; and the only justification for protection to agriculture was strategic.[96]

There is no doubt of the strength of Marshall's condemnation of protection. Taxes on foreign trade would help to turn the terms of trade in favour of the dutying country but only to a very limited extent and at the cost of a dead-weight loss, a distortion of consumer choice, the substitution of high cost for low cost sources of supply, and regressive effects.[97]

It is clear, then, that Marshall believed that duties fell in part on the consumer. He analysed their incidence with the aid of his aggregate demand apparatus and concluded that the burden would fall largely on the foreign exporter where home demand was elastic and foreign demand was inelastic. The price of imports *appeared* to rise by the full amount of the tariff but this failed to take account of the redistribution of the precious metals following the imposition of the tariff. But the scope for this was very limited because exports would be diverted to non-tariffed markets outside a two country model. After the tariff controversy of 1903 Marshall seems to have come to the conclusion that the incidence of import duties was largely on the consumer in the home country, whatever the theoretical niceties. Apart from the effects on the exchange rate and on the consumer, import duties also had collection effects which hampered production and trade.[98]

Marshall's analysis really amounted to working out, on the basis of what had been supplied by J. S. Mill, results which had already been obtained by Torrens, Senior and G. W. Norman. Nevertheless it is only with Marshall's apparatus that we can see clearly what the earlier authors meant.

Marshall was also opposed to the levying of import duties because of the danger of political corruption – and on this ground he believed in free trade for the United States. Marshall believed that tariff lobbyists had strategic political advantages compared with the vast inarticulate mass of consumers. He was quite unmoved by the protagonists of an Imperial Zollverein which would, in his view, be largely trade-diverting, in contrast to the original German model.[99]

He was no more enthusiastic about export duties. They required a lack of competitive alternatives to be successful and their importance was largely a short-run one. With the possible exception of coal we were not in a position to levy export duties.[100]

Nor would duties help the British export performance which should be assisted by more direct intervention. This was even true of the case of infant industries which Marshall did regard as one of the legitimate grounds for protection, althought he believed that such protection was likely to be retained long after it was necessary and that in any case the argument was not applicable to Britain. The only other duties which he regarded as defensible were non-differential (revenue) duties on luxuries, and special export duties if some export indispensable to foreigners were found – a prospect which he regarded as unlikely.[101]

Money

(i) *The quantity theory*

Marshall's monetary theory was undoubtedly derived almost entirely from classical writings, especially those of J. S. Mill; though he drew upon the work of Giffen, the latter possessed no insights not available to the classical writers.[102] But Marshall was an important bridge between the classical writers and twentieth-century theorists like Keynes.

Money was defined in a classical way so as to exclude deposits; and Marshall identified the usual classical functions of money as a medium of exchange, store of value, and standard for deferred payments, with particular emphasis on its role in transactions. He used the quantity theory as his main theoretical framework though he was aware that it was reconcilable with the cost of production theory of the value of money,[103] and although he was aware also of the danger of tautology. This latter point led him to spell out what other things were assumed to be equal for the relationship between money and the price level to be straightforward. They included population, transactions per person, the percentage of business effected directly by money, and the velocity of circulation of both goods and money. He was clear that the latter was variable; and Marshall followed the Bullion Report in stressing fluctuations in commerical confidence and activity as well as the growth of credit and changes in transport and production. Like Thornton he recognised that the velocity of circulation of paper money was intimately linked to the confidence which people felt in it, which was likely to vary inversely with quantity. Because he did not regard bank deposits as money he treated banks as institutions which affected velocity, though he advanced the concept of a deposit multiplier. His source for this was Giffen rather than the classical writers who had worked it out, notably Torrens.[104]

His treatment of the quantity theory was, however, distinctive in that a primary place was given to the demand for cash balances. This was determined by equating the marginal utility of cash holdings with alternative uses for funds. Such an approach came relatively late in his writings after he had come under the influence of Jevons and the latter's work on marginal utility; but it provided an important bridge between the classical analysis, especially that of Thornton, and the Keynesian analysis of liquidity preference.[105]

As the inheritor of the classical analysis, Marshall clearly understood the mechanism of specie flows and the achievement of equilibrium in the balance of payments and in the distribution of the precious metals. He has been credited by Keynes with anticipation of Cassel's 'restatement' of Purchasing Power Parity. This is perhaps a little unfortunate; the classical economists showed good sense in not advancing Purchasing Power Parity as a theory, for it is only very roughly true, due to the importance of non-traded goods and of capital movements. But it is true that Marshall did advance a position very close to Cassel's, only occasionally referring to the problem of non-traded goods, though he may have been relying upon factor mobility to produce the relationship between the prices of traded and non-traded goods. But he recognised the power of interest rates to affect exchange rates; and it is noticeable that he does not mention Cassel in his 1923 *Money, Credit and Commerce*.[106]

Although Marshall inherited the classical analysis there were different strands in this and he, like J. S. Mill, exhibited certain Banking School influences. In particular he advocated the plan, which Tooke had put forward, of a large gold reserve which could be allowed to fall some way before contraction of the note issue was initiated, an increased fiduciary issue, a formal power to suspend the 1844 Act at times of crisis, and an issue of £1 notes to reduce the sensitivity of the money supply to metal flows. Serious objections had been advanced by participants in the Currency and Banking controversy to these suggestions, and it is rather surprising that Marshall did not feel it necessary to take much account of the problems.[107]

He did however attempt to clarify the nature of the transmission mechanism. He argued that changes in the supply of precious metals affected the money supply partly through the effect on 'hoards' of changes in expectations generated by the discoveries, but mainly through the inflation of credit. The main effect of an inflow of metal was to increase banking reserves and bring about a lowering of the rate of interest. This in turn caused an increased demand for loans and an upward speculative movement which was itself fuelled by expectations of rising prices consequent upon the arrival of the gold. As prices rose the demand for loans increased because of the higher price level, and some of the extra money was absorbed into cash balances in order to retain their real value. The extra demand for loans following the lowering of the rate of interest was brought about through a discrepancy between the money and the real rate, the latter being determined by investment and consumption demand on the one hand and the supply of free capital (income minus consumption plus non-specialised circulating capital) on the other. Marshall tended to identify it with the average profitability of business. A money rate below this would cause a demand for loans and a speculative upward movement, with equilibrium occurring only when the rates were equated. The analysis was borrowed from Thornton; and Marshall deserves credit, together with Wicksell, for reintroducing it. It explained the positive correlation observed between rising prices and the rate of interest; as Fisher had pointed out, once prices started rising there was greater eagerness to borrow and interest rates had to rise again in order to check the demand for loans.[108]

Marshall was well aware of the theory of the inflationary mechanism which had been present in classical economics since David Hume; but he was not an enthusiast for price inflation. The effect on wages and prices was regressive, rising prices were not of much assistance to employment, and falling prices caused beneficial caution in consumption and managerial behaviour. He was also unhappy about the benefit to debtors in inflation.[109]

(ii) *The analysis of fluctuations*

Marshall accepted the validity of 'Say's Law', as expressed by J. S. Mill, regarding the idea of general overproduction as a 'monstrous fallacy' but qualified this view by insisting on the possibility of a *short-run* failure of aggregate demand, for 'though men have the power to purchase they may not choose to use it'. A failure of economic confidence could, as indeed Mill had envisaged, bring about a short-run failure of effective demand, resulting in disorganisation of credit, production and (especially) consumption.[110]

Fashion also caused a problem for it induced demand fluctuations resulting, where elasticity of supply was low, in considerable price fluctuations. There was also a short-run cycle of commercial confidence – Marshall derived this from Overstone. Associated with this was a theory of regular shocks to the economic system produced by wars and harvest failure, and a credit cycle. Credit expansion followed a good harvest which would also encourage demand for other commodities because food prices were low. This strengthened entrepreneurial optimism and encouraged speculation. The banks would have difficulty in contracting their loans, but once they refused to renew them a cumulative failure of speculators would follow. In all this the capital goods industries were hardest hit. The cycle was intensified by the problem of moral hazard – entrepreneurs continued trading when they should have closed down because, having lost all their own capital, they had only that of lenders to lost thereafter, and it was intensified also by stock exchange and other forms of speculation which Marshall was anxious to discourage, as well as by changes in expectations.[111]

Price fluctuations in the cycle produced uncertainty, altered the distribution of income in favour of fixed income receivers, and produced changes in profit margins which magnified both the upswing and the downswing, while wages, being rigid, helped to intensify these profit fluctuations.[112] Despite the occasional assumption, for theoretical convenience, of full employment, and a belief that the inconstancy of employment in modern industry had been exaggerated, Marshall was concerned about unemployment and discussed a number of possible remedies of a rather cautious kind. These included an improvement in market knowledge, avoidance of fashion changes, discouragement of fraud, gambling and speculation, the use of a tabular standard of value, an increased fiduciary issue, and a reduction in trade secrecy. He also believed that the interest rate was a suitable policy variable to check expansion, and that stocks, which otherwise moved cyclically, were interest-elastic. But it is quite clear that he did not see government expenditure as a desirable remedy for unemployment because it would harm incentives and induce corruption.[113]

Marshall also envisaged a variety of real-balance effects, some of them counter-cyclical (the desire to maintain the real value of cash balances) but others of a pro-cyclical nature, particularly the inducement to substitute commodities for cash in a period of rising prices. It would be misleading to give the impression that Marshall neglected these matters altogether, though it would be equally misleading to suggest that he was aware of all the considerations to which Patinkin has drawn attention.[114]

(iii) *The debate over the standard*

During the period when Marshall's monetary views were largely formed bimetallism was a subject of frequent and vigorous public debate. Marshall did not believe that bimetallism would reduce price fluctuations because it was not necessarily true that gold and silver output fluctuations would offset each other. The comparative steadiness of silver prices in recent years had been caused by an increase in silver output paralleling an increase in commodity output. But in any case Gresham's Law would be bound to operate and bimetallism would degenerate into monometallism.[115]

Marshall was particularly concerned to counter the argument that bimetallism would encourage Indian exports. He was correct to oppose the argument in that bimetallism was irrelevant to it – a fall in the price of Indian exports expressed in silver would still encourage Indian exports even if Britain were on a gold standard – but he did so in a way which was wrong because, by telescoping the long- and short-run together, he denied that there could be any significant effect of this sort.[116] His own preference was for a plan, stemming from Ricardo, for symetallism, involving two bars of different metal, in exchange for a fixed amount of paper. Anyone who wanted silver or gold alone could obtain it through the market. The attractiveness of the scheme was that it could not degenerate into monometallism. The gain from selling one of the metals which had risen in price would be mirrored by the loss from selling the other metal which could not be used as currency because we would be on a paper standard. But Marshall did not press this case very strongly; rather his aim was to show what was required for true bimetallism, with the subsidiary possibility of paving the way for an international currency.[117]

He was much more enthusiastic about a plan which he put forward for a tabular standard of value which would become the standard for deferred payments, especially contracts, and which would, because it was not subject to the hazards of mining, help to reduce price instability. It would discourage speculation by those hoping to benefit as debtors in inflation; indeed he believed that the lack of a proper standard of this sort explained the persistence of the fallacy of the possibility of over-production. Marshall acknowledged that the plan was not his but derived from Lowe, Scrope, and above all Jevons. He put forward the plan seriously, and it was attacked; but he failed to recognise that, over a long period, the precious metals might very well adjust to changing weights in the commodity basket better than a price index.[118]

Conclusion

Most of the literature on Marshall's economic writings concentrates upon minutiae. This is perfectly understandable for two reasons. First, Marshall was an extremely powerful theorist, especially in his youth, and it is worth taking the trouble to try to tease out the meaning from some of his apparently obscure theoretical positions. Secondly, much of the literature has been written by people who were more or less weaned on Marshall and for whom it constituted the major source book in their economic education. But this is certainly not true for the bulk of the present generation of economists and it seems necessary to try to get some overall view of an economist who, whatever his theoretical powers, was very concerned to produce a balanced overall picture of the economic system with due weight given to historical and institutional factors and with due acknowledgement of the insights of earlier writers to whom he, and his contemporaries, were deeply indebted. In many ways what Marshall wrote, in a private letter to L. L. Price, about Adam Smith could apply very well to him.

> It was his balance, his sense of proportion, his power of seeing the many in the one and the one in the many, his skill in using analysis to interpret history and history to correct analysis (especially as regards the causes that govern human nature, but also in other matters), that seemed to mark him out as unique.[119]

NOTES

1. J. M. Keynes, 'Alfred Marshall, 1842–1924', in A. C. Pigou (ed.), *Memorials of Alfred Marshall* (London: Macmillan, 1925) [hereafter cited as *Mems.*] pp. 1–65. Reprinted with minor alterations in J. M. Keynes, *Essays in Biography* (London: Macmillan, 1933), repr. as vol. X of *The Collected Writings of John Maynard Keynes* (London: Macmillan for the Royal Economic Society, 1972). Further biographical material is to be found in J. K. Whitaker (ed.), *The Early Economic Writings of Alfred Marshall, 1867–1890*, vol. I (New York: Free Press, 1975) [hereafter the two volumes of this work will be cited as *Wh.*I and *Wh.*II], and in journal articles by Professor Whitaker cited therein.
2. I am grateful to Macmillan Press for these sales figures.
3. A. Marshall, *Money, Credit and Commerce* (London: Macmillan, 1923) [hereafter cited as *MC&C*] pp. 210, 245.
4. *Mems.*, pp. 74–80; C. W. Guillebaud, 'Some Personal Reminiscences of Alfred Marshall', *History of Political Economy* [hereafter cited as *HOPE*], III (1971) 1–8; B. Webb, *My Apprenticeship* (London: Longmans, 1926) p. 314.
5. *Wh.* I, pp. 53–5.
6. See, in particular, his unusually caustic comment about Böhm-Bawerk in a letter to Wicksell, reproduced in T. Garlund, *The Life of Knut Wicksell*, trans. N. Adler (Stockholm: Almqvist & Wiksell, 1958) pp. 342–3, and his defence of J. S. Mill in *Mems.*, pp. 119–33.
7. A. Marshall, *Principles of Economics*, 1890, 9th (variorum) edn, ed. C. W. Guillebaud (London: Macmillan, 1961) vol. I, pp. ix–x, 522–3, 723–34; vol. II, pp. 617, 764, 782 [hereafter the two volumes will be cited as *G.*I and *G.*II]; *Wh.*I, pp. 39–40, 48, 69 and *passim*; *Wh.*II, pp. 178–204, 240–52, 302–5 and *passim* (the two Whitaker volumes contain much excellent material on Marshall's sources); *Mems.*, p. 165.
8. *Mems.*, pp. 93–100, 163, 371.
9. J. A. Schumpeter, *History of Economic Analysis* (London: Allen & Unwin, 1955) p. 780.
10. *G.*I, title page and pp. xiii, 249.
11. A. Marshall, *Industry and Trade* (London: Macmillan, 1919; repr. New York: A. M. Kelley, 1970) [hereafter cited as *I&T*] pp. v, 5, 6; *Mems.*, p. 423; *Wh.*I, p. 110.
12. *G.*I, pp. v–vi, 29–31, 771–4, 781–2; *Mems.*, p. 153.
13. *Mems.*, p. 181.
14. *Mems.*, pp. 175–87, 301, 324, 358–9, 422, 429, 438–9, 474–5; J. M. Keynes (ed.), *Alfred Marshall Official Papers* (London: Macmillan for the Royal Economic Society, 1926) [hereafter cited as *OP*] pp. 284–8.
15. *G.*II, pp. 72, 534–6; *Mems.*, p. 437; *I&T*, pp. 449–50n; see also *Wh.*II, pp. 118, 129; R. H. Coase, 'Marshall on Method', *Journal of Law and Economics*, XVIII (1975) 25–32; A. W. Coats, 'Alfred

Marshall and the Early Development of the London School of Economics: Some Unpublished Letters', *Economica*, n.s., 34 (1967) 408–417, at pp. 410, 413.

16. *Mems.*, pp. 313, 382, 422, 427–8; *Wh.*I, p. 38; *Wh.*II, pp. 265–8. On the question of Marshall's mathematical competence contrast Keynes in *Mems.*, at pp. 24–5 and Whitaker in *Wh.*I, pp. 4–5.
17. *G.*I, pp. 26, 30–1, 43–4; *G.*II, pp. 161–81.
18. *G.*I, pp. 366, 379–80, 460–1; *G.*II, p. 49; *Mems.*, pp. 312, 314–15.
19. *Mems.*, p. 417. Those who have quoted this passage have usually failed to note that Marshall was concerned to give note XXI of his Mathematical Appendix '*realistic form*' (italics supplied). On Marshall's relations with Walras, see *Wh.*I, pp. 103–7.
20. *G.*I, pp. 32–6; *G.*II, pp. 155–6.
21. *G.*I, pp. 1–3, 14–17, 22–3, 40–3, 770–1, 780; *G.*II, pp. 762–70; *Mems.*, pp. 158–64 *passim*.
22. *Mems.*, pp. 164–5; A. Marshall and M. P. Marshall, *The Economics of Industry* (London: Macmillan, 1879; 2nd edn, 1881) [hereafter cited as *EI*] pp. 3–4; R. Harrsion, 'Two Early Articles by Alfred Marshall', *Economic Journal* [hereafter cited as *EJ*], LXXIII (1963) 422–30.
23. *G.*I, pp. 2–4, 35–6, 41–3, 750–2; *Mems.*, pp. 172, 174, 326.
24. *G.*I, pp. 5–10, 46–8, 712–14, 721–2; *Mems.*, pp. 282–3, 333–7; *I&T*, pp. 43–4.
25. *G.*I, pp. 99, 100, 103, 106n, 108, 109–10, 839–40; *EI*, pp. 69, 71; *I&T*, pp. 403–4; *Wh.*I, p. 42; for Marshall's (subjective) invention of elasticity (Whewell can objectively claim priority) see Keynes' *Essays* (n 1 above) p. 240.
26. *G.*I, pp. 64, 86–91, 93–4, 95–6.
27. *G.*I, pp. 92–3, 94–5, 100, 117–23, 230–4, 838–9, 841, 845–6; *G.*II, pp. 236–8, 245; *EI*, pp. 69–70, 71.
28. *G.*I, pp. 98–9, 104–5; *G.*II, p. 244.
29. *HOPE*, p. 6.
30. *The Times*, 12 April 1891, p. 13 (b–c).
31. *G.*I, pp. 124–5, 841–2.
32. *G.*I, pp. 96, 128–9, 130–1, 131–2n, 133n, 134, 842; *G.*II, p. 241; *EI*, p. 70; *Mems.*, p. 162.
33. *G.*I, pp. 717, 842, 843.
34. *G.*I, p. 133. Marshall was aware that it was unlikely, in any case, that the entire demand curve could be estimated with any accuracy.
35. *G.*I, pp. 467–75, 489–93, 811; see also *Wh.*II, pp. 72, 285–302; K. Bharadwaj, 'Marshall on Pigou's *Wealth and Welfare*', *Economica*, XXXIX (1972) 32–46.
36. *G.*I, pp. 317, 338–9, 342–3, 344 (and Fig. 18), 459–61, 808–9n; *EI*, pp. 72–3, 74, 76, 77.
37. *G.*I, pp. 140–1, 339, 359–60, 419–20, 811; *EI*, pp. 74, 96–7.
38. *G.*I, pp. 138–9.
39. *G.*I, pp. 173–219, 312, 661; *G.*II, pp. 303–4.
40. *G.*I, pp. 229–36, 353, 618–20.
41. *G.*I, pp. 150–2, 153, 157, 163, 166, 169–72, 319n, 355, 407–9;

*G.*II, p. 358. See also C. J. Bullock, 'The Variation of Productive Forces', *Quarterly Journal of Economics* [hereafter cited as *QJE*], XVI (1901–2) 473–513.

42. *G.*I, pp. xvi, 169–72, 341, 351–4, 404–6, 418–21, 434–37, 662–3, 665–6. Strangely, G. J. Stigler asserts that Marshall does not use the concept of opportunity cost explicitly – *Production and Distribution Theories* (New York: Macmillan, 1941) [hereafter cited as *P&D*] p. 66. However it is to be found in *G.*I, p. 626.
43. *G.*I, p. 355.
44. For example, *G.*I, pp. 427–8. See also *G.*II, p. 439. For implicit recognition of the existence of transfer earnings, see *G.*I, pp. 499–500; see also *EI*, p. 74.
45. *G.*I, pp. 138–40, 291–313, 357–9, 398–400, 612–13; *EI*, pp. 114–18; *I&T*, pp. 350–94, 645–6; *Mems.*, pp. 281–4; *MC&C*, pp. 290–4.
46. *G.*I, pp. xvi, 361–2, 376 (the quoted phrase is from here), 394–402, 501–2, 850; *G.*II, p. 529; *I&T*, pp. 181–96, 269–71, 424; *EI*, pp. 79–80.
47. *G.*I, pp. 285–6, 315–17, 323, 342–3, 378, 457–9; *G.*II, pp. 69–70. See also R. Frisch, 'Alfred Marshall's Theory of Value', *QJE*, LXIV (1950) 495–524 at pp. 512–13.
48. *G.*I, pp. 5–12, 374, 458, 500–1, 540–1, 849–50; *G.*II, pp. 75, 411–12, 569, 573–4; *I&T*, p. 182. See also G. J. Stigler, 'Perfect Competition, Historically Contemplated', *Journal of Political Economy* [hereafter cited as *JPE*], LXV (1957) 1–17 at pp. 9–10; ibid., 'Marshall's *Principles* after Guillebaud', *JPE*, LXX (1962) 282–6 at p. 282.
49. *G.*I, pp. 341–2, 412, 425–6; *I&T*, p. 397. See also S. Stykolt, 'A Curious Case of Neglect: Marshall on the Tangency Solution', *Canadian Journal of Economics* [hereafter cited as *CJE*], XXII (1956) who cites *G.*I, p. 616 n. 3; G. Gerbier, *Alfred Marshall. Théoricien de l'action efficace et critique radical de l'économie pure* (Doctoral thesis, Grenoble, 1976) p. 409. (I am indebted to Professor A. W. Coats who kindly lent me this excellent thesis.) S. Peterson, 'Anti-trust and the Classic Model', *American Economic Review*, XLVII (1957) 60–87; E. H. Chamberlin, 'Origin and Early Development of Monopolistic Competition Theory', *QJE*, LXXV (1961) 515–43.
50. *I&T*, pp. 270–1, 300–2, 304, 396–7, 398, 458n, 524, 597.
51. *G.*I, pp. 360, 373–5, 458–9, 497–8; *EI*, p. 18; see also R. Frisch, op. cit. (n 47 above).
52. *G.*I, pp. 478–9, 486–9, 493–5, 663, 856–8; *G.*II, pp. 534–6; *EI*, p. 181; *I&T*, pp. 395–672, esp. 397–8, 403–6, 414–22, 440–4, 449–50n, 467–71, 481–2, 492–7, 520–2, 596–7; *Mems.*, pp. 274–7.
53. *G.*I, pp. 375n, 686n; see also *G.*I, pp. xiv, 282–3, 304–5, 417n, 477; *G.*II, pp. 47, 57, 390–1, 504n; *I&T*, pp. 179, 507–26, 533, 544–65, 576, 600, 604, 620–35; *EI*, pp. 182–4; *Mems.*, pp. 272–4, 277–81; 'How far do Remediable Causes Influence Prejudicially (a) the

Continuity of Employment, (b) the Rates of Wages?', *Industrial Remuneration Conference: The Report of the Proceedings and Papers ... under ... Sir Charles W. Dilke* (London: Cassell, 1885) [hereafter cited as *Ind. Rem.*] pp. 173–99 at p. 179.

54. *G*.I, pp. 298–304; *G*.II, pp. 659–60; *EI*, pp. 139–42; *I&T*, pp. 171–4, 308–28, 667; *Mems*., pp. 279–81, 307, 332–3; see however *Mems*., p. 308.
55. *G*.I, pp. 250–66, 278–90, 457–9, 471–8, 500–1; *G*.II, pp. 69n, 333, 334, 521, 523–9; *I&T*, pp. 214–34, 424–5; *Mems*., p. 407; *Wh*.II, pp. 194–8; Stigler, *JPE*, loc. cit., 1962.
56. *G*.I, pp. 455–7, 807–10; *I&T*, pp. 107–8n; *Mems*., pp. 439–41; *Wh*.II, pp. 184–5, 190, 193; see also P. Newman, 'The Erosion of Marshall's Theory of Value', *QJE*, LXXIV (1960) 587–601 at pp. 589–90.
57. *G*.I, p. 368.
58. *G*.I, pp. 61, 84, 85, 90, 324–30, 348–9, 813–21; *EI*, pp. 67, 68, 91–3, 147, 148, 165.
59. *G*.I, pp. 330–6, 345, 348, 369–72, 378–80, 805–9; *G*.II, pp. 361–3; *EI*, pp. vii, 158; *Wh*.I, pp. 119–64, esp. pp. 132, 143–4; P. Newman op. cit.; D. G. Davies, 'A Note on Marshallian versus Walrasian Stability Conditions', *CJE*, XXIX (1963) 535–40.
60. *G*.I, pp. 32–6, 337–50, 363, 366–9, 372; *G*.II, pp. 155–6, 380; *EI*, pp. vi–vii, 65–6, 77–8, 146–9; see also *Mems*., pp. 285–9, 342–6; C. W. Guillebaud, 'Marshall's Principles of Economics in the Light of Contemporary Economic Thought', *Economica*, n.s., XIX (1952) 111–30 at p. 122.
61. *G*.I, pp. 337, 381–93, 852–6; *G*.II, p. 400; *Wh*.I, pp. 160–4; J. S. Mill, *Principles of Political Economy, with Some of their Applications to Social Philosophy*, (ed.) J. M. Robson (Toronto: University of Toronto Press, 1965) [hereafter cited as JSM] Book III, ch. XVI, pp. 582–6; Stigler, *P&D*, pp. 83–7.
62. He applied the tools he had created to urban rents and to taxation – *G*.I, pp. 440–54.
63. The marginal note is at *G*.I, p. 536. For material relating to the rest of the paragraph see *G*.I, pp. 138, 140–1n, 357, 385, 387, 406, 407, 409n, 410–11, 447–9, 514–18, 521–3, 525–9, 532, 580–3, 598–600, 660–1, 670–1n, 678–9, 704–6, 822–9, 846–54; *G*.II, pp. 39–41, 232–3, 580–1, 598–614, 818–19, 822–7; *EI*, pp. 13–20, 22–3, 72–3, 95–6, 119–27, 131, 133–4, 142–3, 146–9, 199–213; *Ind. Rem.*, pp. 186, 194; *Mems*., pp. 161, 405, 412–14; *Wh*.I, pp. 43, 70, 73–6, 81, 96, 120, 129, 178–204; *Wh*.II, pp. 322–33; Lecture 2 (pp. 191–200) of 'Three Lectures on Progress and Poverty by Alfred Marshall' (ed. G. J. Stigler and R. Coase), *JPE*, LVIII (1950) 181–226 [hereafter cited as *P&P*]; Stigler, *P&D*, pp. 344–56 *passim*; J. K. Whitaker, 'The Marshallian System in 1881: Distribution and Growth', *EJ*, LXXXIV (1974) 1–17 at pp. 3–4, 5, 15–16.
64. The quotation in the paragraph is from *G*.I, p. 65. For other references relating to this paragraph see *G*.I, pp. 67–70, 80, 138–43,

173–203, 217–19, 331, 504–5, 525–30, 556–8, 567–74, 660–2, 716–19, 721–2, 843; *G*.II, pp. 670–5; *EI*, pp. 101–13, 128–34, 147, 173–5; *Wh*.II, pp. 385–93; Whitaker, *EJ* (1974) op. cit., p. 7; Stigler, *P&D*, pp. 63–6.

65. The quotation is from *G*.I, p. 568. See also *G*.I, pp. 509–10, 529–33, 546–50, 559–63; *EI*, p. 173; *Wh*.I, pp. 79–80.

66. *G*.I, pp. 5–10, 684–5, 693–700, 702–8, 714–15; *I&T*, pp. 289–307, 577–98, 854–6; *EI*, pp. 102, 128–9, 175–7, 187, 228; *Wh*.II, pp. 112, 126–7, 345–52; *Mems*., pp. 113–14, 227–53, 384–6, 396–9, 402–3; *Ind. Rem*., p. 182; Lecture 3 of *P&P*, pp. 200–10; Preface to L. L. F. R. Price, *Industrial Peace: Its Advantages, Methods, and Difficulties: A Report of an Inquiry made for the Toynbee Trustees* (London: Macmillan, 1887) pp. xi–xiii, xviii, xxii, xxv; Whitaker, *EJ*, op. cit.; ibid., 'Alfred Marshall: The Years 1877 to 1885', *HOPE*, IV (1972) 1–61, App. D, pp. 49–61; A. Petridis, 'Alfred Marshall's Attitudes to the Economic Analysis of Trade Unions: A Case of Anomalies in the Competitive System', *HOPE*, V (1973) 165–98.

67. *G*.I, pp. 71–82, 138–43, 313, 505–10, 589–92, 598, 612–15, 618–20, 635–6, 719, 785–90; *G*.II, pp. 670–5; *EI*, pp. 13–20, 75, 78–9, 135; *MC&C*, pp. 285–90; *Wh*.I, pp. 204–24.

68. *G*.I, pp. 605–15, 622–4, 657–75; *G*.II, pp. 661–2; *EI*, pp. 74–5, 135–45, 177–8; *Ind. Rem*., p. 174 (the quotation is from here); *Wh*.I pp. 211–12.

69. *G*.I, pp. 21, 73, 74, 81–2, 122, 220–36, 362n, 377, 411–12, 419–20, 518–21, 533–5; *G*.II, pp. 358, 374, 461–83, 495; *EI*, pp. 41–2, 119–27, 146–9; *MC&C*, pp. 289–90; *Wh*.II, pp. 181–236.

70. *G*.I, pp. 596–8, 602–8, 620–4; *G*.II, pp. 648–9, 670–5; *EI*, pp. 135–45, 147.

71. *G*.I, pp. 155, 422–4, 534–6; *EI*, pp. 81–7, 169; *Wh*.I, p. 231; *Wh*.II, pp. 319–22.

72. *G*.I, pp. 149–70, 418–31, 436–9, 450, 499–500, 577–9, 622–4, 629–36; *G*.II, pp. 431, 439, 441–61, 492–512, 516–17, 540–1, 670–5; *EI*, pp. 21–6, 82, 84–6, 88–90, 110, 179; *Wh*.I, pp. 244–60.

73. *G*.I, pp. 229–30, 248, 625–8, 678–88, 712–15, 717–18, 843–4; *EI*, pp. 48, 113, 132, 145; *Mems*., pp. 162, 228–9, 324–5, 347–50, 366, 443, 462–3; preface to Price (n 66 above) p. ix; *The Times*, 18 January 1887; *OP*, pp. 249–50; A. Marshall, 'National Taxation after the War' in W. H. Dawson (ed.), *After-war Problems* (London: Allen & Unwin, 1917) pp. 313–45 [hereafter cited as *NT*] at pp. 317–29.

74. The quotation is from *Mems*., p. 312. For references relating to the rest of the paragraph, see *G*.I, pp. 49, 56–7, 59, 80–1, 220–39, 587, 675–8, 689–93, 749–52; *EI*, pp. 6, 13; *I&T*, p. 697; *P&P*, Lecture I, pp. 184–91; *OP*, pp. 402–12; *Wh*.II, p. 112; T. Parsons, 'Wants and Activities in Marshall', *QJE*, XLVI (1932) 101–40; T. Parsons, 'Economics and Sociology: Marshall in relation to the Thought of his Time', *QJE*, XLVI (1932) 316–47; J. K. Whitaker, 'Some Neglected Aspects of Alfred Marshall's Economic and Social Thought', *HOPE*, IX (1977) 161–97.

75. *Wh*.I, p. 97; *Wh*.II, pp. 305–16; Whitaker, *EJ* (1974) op. cit., at pp. 11–15.
76. *G*.I, pp. 173–203, 219, 243–8, 739–42; *G*.II, pp. 303–4; *Ind. Rem*., p. 198; *EI*, pp. 9, 27–37; J. J. Spengler, 'Marshall on the Population Question', *Population Studies*, VIII, IX (1955) 264–87, 56–66.
77. *G*.I, pp. 204–19, 229–30, 236, 560–6, 571, 619, 622, 660–1, 670–5, 681–4, 858; *EI*, p. 39 (see also pp. 10–11, 32); *I&T*, pp. 121–39, 356–7; *Mems*., pp. 117–18, 173; *The Times*, 3 March 1905 (15a–b), 29 November 1905 (4c), 18 December 1905 (13d), 29 December 1905 (5d). See also R. Blandy, 'Marshall on Human Capital: A Note', *JPE*, LXXV (1967) 874–5.
78. *G*.I, pp. 221, 240–1, 250–90; *EI*, pp. 43, 46–7, 49–59; *I&T*, pp. 106, 140–62, 214–34, 281–2, 698–9; *MC&C*, pp. 77–80, 244–5.
79. *G*.I, pp. 223–30, 236, 680–1; *EI*, pp. 25–6, 36–9, 41–2, 48, 127, 146.
80. *G*.I, pp. 240–77, 291–313; *I&T*, pp. 350–94.
81. *G*.I, pp. 645–51, 653–6, 744–7, 833–7; *EI*, pp. 23–4, 57–61; JSM; Book II, ch. vi–vii, pp. 252–96.
82. *G*.I, pp. 528, 691, 726–33, 740–2, 750–2, 798–800; *EI*, pp. 10, 36–8, 64; *I&T*, p. 106.
83. *G*.I, pp. 222, 273–4, 301–4, 678–9, 744–7; *EI*, p. 55; *I&T*, pp. 106, 171–4; *MC&C*, pp. 68–97.
84. *G*.I, p. 304; *EI*, p. 113; *I&T*, pp. 486, 494–7, 666–72; *Ind.Rem*., p. 174; *Mems*., p. 118; *NT*, pp. 313–14, 317–22, 325–9, 345; *The Times*, 24 March 1891 (11e), 6 April 1891 (13b–c), 16 November 1909 (10c); *The Economist*, 30 December 1916, p. 1228.
85. *G*.I, pp. 199–200, 202–3, 320–1, 350, 718, 803–4; *OP*, pp. 197–262, 361–3; *Ind. Rem*., pp. 183–4; *Mems*., pp. 142–51; *EI*, p. 26; A. Marshall, 'Where to House the London Poor', *Contemporary Review*, March 1884; and 'Is London Healthy?', *Pall Mall Gazette*, 13 April 1887; *The Times*, 25 June 1885 (3e); 16 November 1909 (10c).
86. *OP*, pp. 199, 201, 211–25; *EI*, pp. 32–4; *Ind. Rem*., pp. 187–8; *Mems*., pp. 345, 373, 403; *The Times*, 2 February 1885 (3e), 15 February 1886 (13b).
87. The quotation is from *Mems*., p. 444. See also *Ind. Rem*., p. 173; *Mems*., pp. 155–6, 173, 283–4, 291, 327–9, 462; *G*.I, pp. 712–14, 722; *The Times*, 24 March 1891 (11e), 16 November 1909 (10c).
88. *Mems*., pp. 323–46.
89. *Wh*.I, pp. 260–89; *Wh*.II, pp. 3–181; *Mems*., p. 451.
90. *MC&C*, pp. 158–65, 167–76, 330–60; *Wh*.II, pp. 117–81; J. Bhagwati and H. G. Johnson, 'Notes on Some Controversies in the Theory of International Trade', *EJ*, LXX (1960) 74–93; A. Amano, 'Stability Conditions in the Pure Theory of International Trade: A Rehabilitation of the Marshallian Approach', *QJE*, LXXXII (1968) 326–39.
91. *MC&C*, pp. 177–89. On Torrens, see D. P. O'Brien, *The Classical Economists* (Oxford: Clarendon Press, 1975) [hereafter cited as O'Brien] pp. 189–97 and references therein.

92. *MC&C*, pp. 338–40; *Wh*.I, pp. 279–81; see also Bhagwati and Johnson, op. cit., and J. Viner, *Studies in the Theory of International Trade* (London: Allen & Unwin, 1964) [hereafter cited as *Studies*] pp. 570–5.
93. A. Marshall, *The Pure Theory of Foreign Trade* (repr., London: London School of Economics, 1930) [hereafter cited as *PT*] pp. 5–6, 13, 26–7 164–5; *MC&C*, pp. 338–40; *Wh*.II pp. 140, 164–5; to abbreviate secondary references, see the following and references therein: Viner, *Studies*, pp. 536–46 and 548–55; Bhagwati and Johnson, op. cit.; J. E. Meade, *A Geometry of International Trade* (London: Allen & Unwin, 1952) chs i–iv.
94. *G*.I, pp. 672–7; *Wh*.II, pp. 14–23, 33–61; *EI*, pp. 18–19.
95. *MC&C*, pp. 1–11, 102–6, 109–12, 156–7, 321–9; *I&T*, pp. 16, 22; *Wh*.II, pp. 31–3; Viner, *Studies*, pp. 458–62 (and Edgeworth references therein). Mangoldt really has priority over both Marshall and Edgeworth.
96. *MC&C*, pp. 213–17; *OP*, pp. 395–9, 408–12; *Wh*.II, pp. 89–91, 106–8; *Mems*., pp. 258–65, 471–4; *I&T*, pp. 760–2; *NT*, pp. 330–41, 345; 'Discussion on Mr Schuster's Paper', *Journal of the Institute of Bankers*, XXV (1904) 94–8 [hereafter cited as *DS*] at p. 95; *The Times*, 23 November 1903 (10e); H. W. McCready, 'Alfred Marshall and the Tariff Reform, 1903: Some Unpublished Letters', *JPE*, LXIII (1955) 259–67.
97. *Wh*.II, pp. 62–89.
98. *MC&C*, pp. 193–8; *OP*, pp. 365–420; *Wh*.II, pp. 80–88; *Mems*., pp. 449–50.
99. *MC&C*, pp. 219, 265; *OP*, pp. 389–90, 394, 399, 415–20; *NT*, pp. 329–30, 341–5; *DS*, p. 97.
100. *MC&C*, p. 204; *Mems*., pp. 320–2; *The Times*, 10 November 1898 (10c), 2 December 1898 (8a); *NT*, pp. 330–2, 336–8; *Wh*.II, pp. 88–9.
101. *G*.I, pp. 464–5; *I&T*, p. 762; *Wh*.II, pp. 56–61, 100–102; *MC&C*, pp. 218–24; *OP*, pp. 387–92; *DS*, p. 97; *NT*, pp. 329–33; *Mems*., pp. 258–65, 320–2; *The Times*, 22 April 1901.
102. *OP*, p. 37; *Wh*.I, p. 164; E. Eshag, *From Marshall to Keynes: An Essay on the Monetary Theory of the Cambridge School* (Oxford: Blackwell, 1963) [hereafter cited as Eshag] pp. xiii, 16–18.
103. *OP*, pp. 35–8, 139–40, 323; *Wh*.I, pp. 164, 171–2; *MC&C*, pp. 12–20, 38, 49; *The Times*, 25 January 1889 (13f).
104. *OP*, pp. 5–6, 22, 24–7, 34–5, 37, 40, 115ff., 267–8; *MC&C*, pp. 42–3, 46–8, 282–4; H. Thornton in F. A. Hayek (ed.), *An Enquiry into the Nature and Effects of the Paper Credit of Great Britain (1802)* (London: Allen & Unwin, 1939) [hereafter cited as Thornton] pp. 96–100, 197n; Lord Robbins, *Robert Torrens and the Evolution of Classical Economics* (London: Macmillan, 1958) pp. 109–11.
105. *MC&C*, pp. 38–9, 43–5; *OP*, pp. 177, 267–8 (see also pp. 36, 44); *Wh*.I, p. 164–77; Thornton, pp. 232–3.

106. *OP*, pp. 66, 144–7, 150, 170–4, 177–80, 188, 191, 293, 296–7 (see also pp. 189, 193–5, 312); *Mems.*, pp. 30–1; *MC&C*, pp. 147–9, 152–4, 179, 225–33, 315–20.
107. *OP*, pp. 25, 26, 29, 30, 54, 110–12, 124, 162–4, 282–4; *MC&C*, p. 66; *Ind. Rem.*, p. 179; O'Brien, pp. 153–9.
108. *OP*, pp. 10, 22–3, 38, 40–1, 51–2, 124, 126–8, 130–1, 158, 272, 274; *MC&C*, pp. 45, 73–6, 131, 255–8, 270, 272; *Mems.*, p. 190; see also Eshag, p. 13 n 55 and p. 57 n 51.
109. *OP*, pp. 19–20, 58, 75, 91–3, 168–9, 193, 285 (see also ibid., pp. 7, 9, 97–8, 100, 270–2, 284–7, 300–3, 317, 322–3); *G.*I, pp. 593–5; *Mems.*, p. 191; *MC&C*, pp. 18–19, 74; *EI*, pp. 155–7, 165–6.
110. The first quotation is from *Mems.*, p. 192; the second is from *G.*I, p. 710. For references relating to this paragraph see *G.*I, pp. 709–11; *OP*, p. 91; *PT*, p. 34; *EI*, pp. 154, 161, 191–2; *Mems.*, pp. 130, 463; JSM, pp. 557–61.
111. *EI*, pp. 150–3, 161–4; *G.*I, pp. 709–11; *MC&C*, pp. 18–19, 75, 89–97, 238ff, 246, 249, 257, 287; *Ind. Rem.*, p. 178; *Mems.*, pp. 190–4; *OP*, pp. 6, 9–10, 209, 451; Marshall had a marked personal copy of Overstone's *Tracts* – Eshag, p. 95.
112. *G.*II, pp. 709–11; *OP*, pp. 9–10; *MC&C*, pp. 18, 261; *Mems.*, p. 191; *EI*, pp. 155–6.
113. *G.*I, pp. 594–5, 687–8; *OP*, pp. 9–11, 92, 94–7, 168; *Mems.*, pp. 191, 205 n 2, 365 (see also p. 206 n 2); *MC&C*, pp. 18, 176–81, 246–8, 251–3, 258–9, 260–3; *Ind. Rem.*, pp. 174–9; see also *EI*, p. 155n.
114. D. Patinkin, *Money, Interest and Prices* (New York: Harper & Row, 1965) pp. 186–8, 603–10; *MC&C*, pp. 18, 43, 256; *OP*, pp. 5–6, 22, 52; see, however, *EI*, pp. 155–6 for neglect of the real balance effect.
115. *MC&C*, pp. 60–4, 67; *OP*, pp. 24–7, 30–1, 55, 292 (see also pp. 13, 26); *Mems.*, pp. 188, 193, 195–6, 199–203, 206, 207 n (see also p. 477); *The Times*, 25 January 1889 (13f), 6 October 1897 (9c).
116. *OP*, pp. 21, 65–7, 75, 82, 115, 173, 192–3, 275–7, 288, 317; *MC&C*, pp. 315–20; *The Times*, 25 January 1889 (13f), 30 January 1889 (13c).
117. *OP*, pp. 14, 28–31, 101–4, 135; *Mems.*, pp. 204–6, 476–7; *MC&C*, p. 65.
118. *Mems.*, pp. 191–9, 207–11, 476–7; *Ind. Rem.*, pp. 178–9, 185–6; *OP*, pp. 10, 31; *MC&C*, pp. 36–7, 52–4, 64–7; *The Economist*, 5 March 1887, pp. 303–4; 12 March 1887, p. 339.
119. *Mems.*, p. 379.

[17]

6

Marshall's Work in Relation to Classical Economics

DENIS P. O'BRIEN

I Introduction

The question of Marshall's classical inheritance is a complex one, made more complex by both the extent and the peculiar nature of Marshall's claims in this respect. Following the introduction, the second section of this chapter will examine these claims – Marshall's own version of the achievements of Classical economics and thus, by implication, his claims about the differences between his own work and that of the Classical writers. Marshall made remarkable claims, both for the continuity of economics as a subject and for the prescience (indeed at times almost for the omniscience) of the Classical economists. Section III examines Marshall's own work, as distinct from his claims, in relation to Classical economics, and identifies what seems to be indisputably Classical at least in origin. Section IV shows that much of what is regarded as characteristically Marshallian is certainly not Classical. The conclusion which emerges is that Marshall's own acknowledgements, in their generosity of spirit towards his Classical predecessors, significantly distort the true distribution of the weight of his Classical inheritance. On the one hand, in those areas in which he was prone to make the most startling claims for Classical economics, he owed the least to the great Classical writers – the areas of value and distribution. On the other hand, in the areas of monetary and trade theory, and in his general habit of underpinning the analysis with a moving equilibrium of economic

I am extremely grateful to Professor John Creedy, Bob Black, John Whitaker and Roger Backhouse for constructive comments on an earlier draft of this paper.

growth, Marshall really did do what he claimed to have done in the areas of value and distribution, that is, he worked out the implications of the Classical analysis, restating it in terms which were more precise, and which, in the case of trade and economic growth theory, contained a basic mathematical skeleton (though not all of this was published).

We thus begin with an examination of Marshall's claims.

II Marshall's Claims

Marshall warned repeatedly of the dangers of misunderstanding Classical economics.[1] The Classical economists frequently failed to spell out their assumptions and to make clear what they were doing, in order to avoid unnecessary controversy. Because of their shortcomings in this respect, they were easily misrepresented. Care was required to distinguish Classical economics from popular renderings of Classical ideas.[2] The Classical economists themselves were not dogmatic: "[T]he dogmatism which seemed to pervade the chief English economic writings of the first half of the nineteenth century was apparent, rather than real" (*IT*, pp. 758–9). Adam Smith and Ricardo had developed the "main outline" of long run value theory,[3] the old wage theories were working towards the modern one (*Principles*, p. 543, marginal note), and Smith's distribution theory was grounded in an appreciation of demand for, and supply of, factor services.[4] Ricardo was "well aware" of the marginal character of rent analysis "though he did not emphasise it enough" (*Principles*, p. 154), and he even, Marshall claimed at one stage (though he later withdrew from such an exposed position), appreciated that keystone of Marshallian analysis, the "principle of (factor) substitution".[5] Ricardo's inverse relationship between wages and profits was interpreted by Marshall in purely proportionate terms[6] while Ricardo

1. *Principles*, pp. 37, 84, 97 n., 101 n., 763 n.; *Variorum*, p. 599; 1879*a*, p. 167.
2. *Principles*, p. 379; *Variorum*, p. 396; *IT*, p. 764. See also note 1.
3. *Variorum*, p. 407. See also 1879*a*, pp. 77–9.
4. Smith "goes a good way towards explaining how they [wages and profits] are determined by the ever fluctuating conditions of demand and supply" (Marshall, *Principles*, p. 507).
5. *Variorum*, pp. 592, 593. Ricardo and his followers "were familiar with the action of the law of substitution, but they laid insufficient stress on the side of [factor] demand" (ibid., p. 593). Groenewegen correctly notes that the claim for Ricardo made in the first edition of the *Principles* was significantly reduced in the *text* of the third. However, the words quoted above come not from the first edition but from a *marginal note* to the third. Marshall, it would seem, was reluctant to recant.
6. *Principles*, p. 550 n. This turns it into a truism empty of its peculiarly Ricardian, and indeed of all, content.

and Smith were both held to have understood all the essentials of modern capital theory.[7]

Understanding of the essential modernity of the Classical position was hampered by carelessness in formulation of the wage-fund idea (*Principles*, p. 823; see also *Variorum*, p. 821) which, in its vulgar form, was actually inconsistent with Ricardo's and Smith's reasonings (*Variorum*, p. 817), while Mill's famous fourth proposition on capital (demand for commodities is not demand for labour) was held to express his meaning badly.[8] Indeed, the errors of the Classical economists on wages "when traced back to their origin are little more than careless modes of expression" (*Principles*, p. 763 n.).

Smith, Ricardo, and J. S. Mill

Three particular Classical economists attracted Marshall's attention and admiration, Smith, Ricardo, and J. S. Mill. Marshall appreciated Smith's "philosophic thoroughness" and "practical knowledge" (*Principles*, p. 240) and held that there was "scarcely any economic truth now known of which he did not get some glimpse" (*Principles*, p. 757). Where Ricardo was critical of Smith, Marshall, despite his intense admiration for Ricardo, was for the most part inclined to defend Smith.[9]

His expressed admiration for Ricardo's powers of analysis, however, was almost unlimited.

> Ricardo's power of threading his way without slip through intricate paths to new and unexpected results has never been surpassed. (*Principles*, p. 761)

> Ricardo himself had no mathematical training. But his instincts were unique; and very few trained mathematicians could tread as safely as he over the most perilous courses of reasoning. Even the acute logical mind of Mill was unequal to the task. (*Principles*, p. 836)

However, there was a real danger of misunderstanding Ricardo. His unfortunate literary style omitted many things which "statesmen and businessmen", as readers, "would regard as obvious".

7. *Principles*, p. 583. This claim was aimed at Böhm-Bawerk – see Gårdlund, 1958, pp. 339–43.
8. *Principles*, p. 828. See also 1879*a*, p. 16, on Mill's first proposition ("Industry is limited by capital").
9. See, for example, *Principles*, pp. 167 n., 439. See, however, *IT*, p. 734, where Marshall endorses Ricardo's rather than Smith's position on the colonial trade.

> If then we seek to understand him rightly, we must interpret him generously, more generously than he himself interpreted Adam Smith. (*Principles*, p. 813)

> Unfortunately however he delighted in short phrases, and he thought that his readers would always supply for themselves the explanations of which he had given them a hint.
> (*Principles*, p. 816; see also *Variorum*, pp. 279, 396)

But we were getting to understand Ricardo better:

> [R]ecent progress has developed Ricardo's work; and has pruned away only the dogmas deduced from it by followers of a different stamp of mind from his. (*Variorum*, p. 493, dating from 1893)

Ricardo's value theory did not need reconstructing (*Variorum*, p. 813), while his obsession with an Invariable Measure could be dismissed as concern with an index number problem (*MCC*, p. 22).

Particularly startling are Marshall's claims concerning Ricardo's "awareness" of demand. He and his associates were "aware that the conditions of demand played as important a part as those of supply in determining value, yet they did not express their meaning with sufficient clearness, and they have been misunderstood by all but the most careful readers" (*Principles*, p. 84; see also p. 503). Indeed, Mill and Ricardo "regarded the natural laws of variation of utility as too obvious to require detailed explanation" (*Principles*, p. 817; see also pp. 818–20). Ricardo was perfectly well aware that costs affect value only in relation to supply at the margin where it equals demand (*MCC*, p. 321; see also *IT*, p. 396).

Marshall's attitude to Ricardo led him, especially from 1890 onwards, to give insufficient credit to Mill, a point which will be discussed further below. If Mill presumed to criticise Ricardo's treatment, Marshall immediately came to the latter's defence (*Principles*, p. 510 n.). In the field of trade, Marshall, in discussing reciprocal demand, freely attributed the work of Torrens and Mill to Ricardo (*MCC*, Book III, Chapter 8). Marshall seems literally, in his later work, to have been unable to believe that Mill said anything on international trade which had not already been said (even if not fully explained) by Ricardo (*MCC*, pp. 225, 351; *OP*, pp. 170, 372).

His willingness to credit Ricardo with particular ideas can be disconcerting at times. At one point he even claims that Ricardo's "celebrated" chapter on sudden changes in the channels of trade "is in effect an argument that even a bad system of taxation should seldom be violently changed".[10] As Hutchison has remarked:

> There is, perhaps, something rather questionable in the sort of intellectual generosity which assumes that Ricardo's interests and purposes, rightly understood, must certainly have been the same as one's own, when, after all, Ricardo was as explicit as he could have been that they were distinctly different.
>
> (1952, p. 423; see also 1978, Chapter 8, especially pp. 234–6)

The somewhat embarrassing truth is that Marshall's treatment of Ricardo verges on what might be known in another context as "apologetics". This may stem in part from J. S. Mill, who hid his own brilliant originality behind reverential references to Ricardo just as Marshall, in the *Economics of Industry* (discussed below), hid the origins of his distribution theory and much else. Starting from the position that Ricardo had not written a formal treatise (he quotes Roscher with approval in support of this untenable opinion),[11] Marshall felt free to interpret Ricardo in a most imaginative way. Phrases such as "Assumptions such as these are made quietly by Ricardo: he took for granted that his readers would supply them" (*MCC*, p. 323 n.) do not inspire confidence.

When one considers the achievements of Classical economics in general, and of J. S. Mill in particular,[12] Jevons's excited claims to originality, and his denigrations of Ricardo (who shunted economics onto the wrong track)[13] and of Mill (whose authority exercised a noxious influence),[14] could hardly fail to produce a reaction, especially in someone like Marshall, who had already learned so very much from working at Mill before Jevons's claims appeared. But from the perspective of a later generation, and of later scholarship, the effects of Marshall's claims are unfortunate. He can be found attributing to Ricardo, for instance, a passage from the

10. *MCC*, p. 195; "in effect" is certainly a very necessary qualification because the issue referred to by Marshall is only a very subsidiary part of the argument of Ricardo's chapter which is mainly concerned with distinguishing economic dislocation from a state of stagnation.
11. *Principles*, pp. 163, 503; *Variorum*, p. 279. See also Groenewegen (pp. 10–12 and p. 36, n. 7), who points out that Sraffa decisively refuted such a claim.
12. "In terms of identifiable theories, he was one of the most original economists in the history of the science" (Stigler, 1955, p. 7).
13. "That able but wrong-headed man, David Ricardo, shunted the car of economic science on to a wrong line – a line, however, on which it was further urged towards confusion by his equally able and wrong-headed admirer, John Stuart Mill" (Jevons, 1879, p. 72).
14. "If, instead of welcoming inquiry and criticism, the admirers of a great author accept his writings as authoritative, both in their excellences and in their defects, the most serious injury is done to truth" (Jevons, 1879, p. 260).

Bullion Report, one almost certainly written by Thornton, which stressed variable velocity of circulation in a way Ricardo certainly did not (*MCC*, pp. 41–2). Moreover, while he was prepared to acknowledge the work of J. H. Hollander in showing that Ricardo's monetary theory was essentially unoriginal, Marshall still insists that "his masterly genius, like that of Adam Smith, was largely occupied with the supreme task of building up a number of fragmentary truths into coherent doctrine. Such a doctrine has constructive force, because it is an organic whole" (*MCC*, p. 41 n.). Perhaps most strikingly of all, when John Stuart Mill applied his theory of reciprocal demand in international trade to explain relative price levels, without any reference to Ricardo, Marshall promptly attributed the work to Ricardo (*MCC*, p. 231; Mill, 1848–71, p. 620).

As various commentators have noted, Marshall's attitude to Mill (who was, in truth, the starting point for virtually everything in Marshall's economics which could be called Classical) underwent something of a transformation (Whitaker, 1975, p. 50 n.; Groenewegen, pp. 7–8). In the 1870s, when his debt to Mill was most recent, he defended Mill. Many of the attacks on Mill were "due to their [his critics] not having perceived the full power, which is latent, if not patent, in Mill's work" (1876, p. 119). Mill's value theory was basically sound (1876, p. 121). There was little in Mill's treatment of value and distribution which was not true when properly interpreted.[15] Marshall's *Economics of Industry* of 1879 was presented to the public as simply an exercise in bringing Mill up to date in the light of recent writings while at the same time providing an introduction to Mill. In fact the "updating" went much further than acknowledged. It included the introduction, based on Jevons's work, of diminishing marginal utility, a demand curve, and the equality of price with marginal utility (1879*a*, Book II, Chapter 1, pp. 65–71). The only acknowledged departure from Mill was in the treatment of distribution. Mill had separated distribution from exchange whereas Marshall integrated the two treatments while implying quite clearly that he was merely bringing out what was "latent" in Mill's work (1879*a*, p. v). However, Marshall's symmetrical treatment of the earnings of skilled and unskilled labour, capital, and management, through (on the demand side) a discounted product approach, goes far beyond Mill (1879*a*, Book II, Chapters 6–12). Only the fact that the margin itself appeared intermittently and at times indistinctly prevents this treatment from being linked directly to Marshall's later work,[16] despite his

15. 1879*a*, p. v. See also 1898, p. 41, for strong claims about Mill's treatment of distribution.
16. For instances of marginal analysis see 1879*a*, pp. 122, 133, 142. See also 1898, p. 58, for a claim that "The general notion of distribution in the *Economics of Industry* . . . is the same as in my *Principles*."

claims to the contrary. Whitaker judges that in the book Marshall had broken free of the wage fund (as indeed he had) so that the misleadingly similar "earnings and interest fund" could easily be developed into a proper marginal productivity theory. But, as Whitaker correctly notes (1975, 1, pp. 77, 81), Marshall did not attempt this (cf. Marshall, 1879*a*, pp. 96, 203–5).

In this connection two points are of particular interest. First, Marshall gives only belated credit to other writers whose work pointed at least partially in the same direction (though he was later to acknowledge Thünen), while at the same time implying that the analysis is actually J. S. Mill's.[17] Second, it is apparent from Whitaker's researches in Marshall's papers that Marshall was still using a wage fund approach in the years 1870–74.[18] This leads inevitably to the conclusion that Marshall claimed J. S. Mill had a more modern theory only after he (Marshall) had abandoned what he clearly believed in the years 1870–4 to be both J. S. Mill's, and a correct, theory.

In defending Mill in 1876 he attributed to him a real cost theory of price, from which it was easy to attribute to him also a utility approach (1876, pp. 122–6). At the same time he argued that Mill regarded cost of production as variable with output, and thus dependent upon demand (1876, pp. 126–9).

It was not only Mill who benefited from such generosity of interpretation. Some of Marshall's defences go beyond what might politely be called "strained" interpretation to statements which it is hard to regard as anything but fiction. The most flagrant example is Marshall's repeated statement that Senior became a keen supporter of the Factory Acts.[19]

Critics of Classical Economics

Even after Marshall's ardour in defence of Mill had cooled somewhat, he still assailed the critics of the Classical economists along the lines already established. Thus, in the *Principles* he argued, just as he had done in the *Economics of Industry*, that demand and supply mutually determined value, and that, simply because the Classical economists had laid insufficient stress upon demand, there had been a reaction to an opposite extreme (*Principles*, pp. 85, 525, 817; 1879*a*, pp. 146–9). Jevons was no less misleading and one-sided than Ricardo. In fact, Marshall informed

17. 1879*a*, p. 205. On Marshall's acknowledgement of priorities see Whitaker, 1975, 1, pp. 39, 69.
18. Whitaker, 1975, 1, pp. 43, 48, 69. Marshall's early discussion of wages is in *EEW*, 1, pp. 184–201.
19. *Principles*, p. 763 n. (dating from the 5th edition); *IT*, pp. 763–4. See also Blaug, 1958*a*, p. 119; Bowley, 1937, pp. 256–7, 269–72.

his readers, Jevons's success was aided by his faults in misunderstanding and misrepresenting Ricardo:

> [H]e led many to think he was correcting great errors; whereas he was really only adding very important explanations.
>
> (*Principles*, p. 101)

Marshall felt similarly strongly about Böhm-Bawerk, despite apparently cordial personal relations with the Austrian economist.[20] His public comments were restrained, but he wrote to Wicksell:

> While he was still at school, I learnt from the men whom he reviles everything which he has vaunted as a great discovery: and especially in America, he has been taken at his own valuation by people *who have never studied the great men* on whose burial places he dances his war dance.[21]

But Jevons, like Böhm-Bawerk, in intellectual terms a self-proclaimed revolutionary, undoubtedly influenced Marshall, who borrowed from his work in "updating" Mill. Cairnes, by contrast a follower of Mill, had, in Marshall's opinion, done more harm, through his failure to interpret Mill "correctly", than the self-proclaimed intellectual revolutionaries (1876, p. 120; *Principles*, pp. 97, 218, 339 n.; *Variorum*, p. 796). This is not an entirely surprising attitude; Marshall, in seeking to stress both the intellectual coherence and the theoretical comprehensiveness of Mill, and the compatibility of his work with that of people like Jevons, could hardly accept as correct the writings of one (Cairnes) who sought to expound Mill while admitting to complete bafflement with regard to the work of Jevons (Cairnes, 1875, pp. vi–vii).

From 1890 onwards, as Marshall came to allot almost transcendental importance to the work of Ricardo, there was a corresponding down-playing of Mill's importance.[22] He claimed that work at the India Office must have lowered the quality of Mill's economics and compared Mill's analytical powers unfavourably with Ricardo's (*Principles*, pp. 252 n., 836).

It was not only Mill who suffered in this way. While continuing to maintain his curious version of Senior's views on the Factory Acts, Marshall showed a strange reluctance to recognise Senior's generalisa-

20. M. P. Marshall, 1947, p. 48. Mrs. Marshall relates that she had feared some friction if the subject of the rate of interest arose, as "he [Böhm-Bawerk] and Alfred had recently been corresponding warmly upon it" (ibid.).
21. Gårdlund, 1958, p. 342. See also *Memorials*, p. 417. For public comment on Böhm-Bawerk, see Marshall, *Principles*, pp. 235, 528 n., 532–3 n., 583–4 n., 790 n., 821; *Variorum*, pp. 215 n., 247, 368 n., 462 n., 552 n., 628 n., 631 n., 638 n., 643 n., 644 n., 783 n., 785. Some of these, though relatively restrained, are nonetheless distinctly tart by Marshall's self-denying standards.
22. On this see especially Groenewegen, pp. 7–9 and Whitaker, 1975, 1, p. 50 n.

tion of the rent concept, though he himself, in describing rent of land as the "leading species of a large genus" was almost echoing Senior's words.[23] Torrens also suffered to some extent. Though Marshall cites him only once, it is clear that he was familiar at first hand with some of Torrens's work,[24] which may have been more important to Marshall than he acknowledged.

These omissions are as unfortunate as the exaggerated claims. There seems no doubt that Mill's work was the origin of the basis of Marshall's economics, as Marshall's earlier accounts of his own development reveal clearly. This is particularly true when we look at the material on international trade and on growth found in his early papers.[25] Marshall also borrowed from Mill the latter's own particular version of the Law of Markets (*Principles*, pp. 710–12; 1879*a*, pp. 154–5; *IT*, p. 640). He even adopted Mill's ambiguity in this matter, both with respect to the likelihood of the arrival of the stationary state in the near future, and with respect to the reasons for a decline in profits. Endorsing Mill's statement of the Law of Markets, he also drew on Mill's use (in the context of Wakefield and colonisation) of Smithian ideas of possible exhaustion of investment opportunities (1879*a*, pp. 126–7). He followed Mill to some extent in matters of methodology (*Principles*, pp. 50, 771; 1879*a*, p. 211), of capital theory (*Principles*, p. 75; 1898, p. 56; see also Whitaker, 1975, 1, p. 220), on the equalisation of net advantage (1879*a*, pp. 103, 131, 139), and on noncompeting groups (1879*a*, p. 107). He was directed by Mill not only to matters of trade theory,[26] but also to problems like the valuation of joint products (*EEW*, 1, pp. 156–8; *Principles*, pp. 435–6 n.). His attitudes to such things as low wages (*Principles*, p. 509) and even investment in education[27] were influenced by Mill.

Of course Marshall drew on other Classical authors as well. He attrib-

23. *Principles*, p. 432; *Variorum*, p. 463. For land rent as "the leading species of a large genus" see *Principles*, pp. viii, 412, 421, 629; *Variorum*, pp. 51, 59, 495. For Senior see his Appendix to Whately, 1826. On his generalisation of the rent concept see O'Brien, 1975, p. 131, and Bowley, 1937, pp. 126–36.
24. *MCC*, p. 161. Although J. S. Mill refers to Torrens, none of his citations refers to the point on which Marshall refers to Torrens, viz. reciprocal demand. Marshall was already 22 when Torrens died, so his knowledge of a writer whose work rapidly disappeared into obscurity after his death in 1864 is less surprising than it might at first seem.
25. See Whitaker, 1975, 1, pp. 37–8, 260; 2, pp. 306–9; 1974; Marshall, *EEW*, 2, pp. 309–16; *MCC*, pp. 157, 160–1, 163, 168–9, 177; *Variorum*, pp. 8–9; *Memorials*, p. 412. See also Groenewegen, pp. 7–8.
26. *MCC*, pp. 157, 160–1, 163, 168–9, 177; *EEW*, 1, pp. 261–79, 280–9; 2, pp. 3–186; Whitaker, 1975, 1, pp. 260–1, 279–80.
27. 1879*a*, pp. 11, 105–7. See, however, note 49. In addition, the text for Marshall's Bristol lectures of 1879–80 on taxation was Book V of Mill (1848–71). See Whitaker, 1975, 2, p. 378.

uted his concept of long run normal value to Smith (*Principles*, p. 347), he acknowledged his debt to Overstone on the trade cycle (1879*a*, p. 153), and his "Symmetalism" proposal was explicitly derived from Ricardo's *Economical and Secure Currency* (*MCC*, pp. 65–7; *Memorials*, pp. 14, 28, 30, 102–3, 143–4, 165). (Indeed, one commentator has argued that this is Marshall's only clear and unambiguous borrowing from Ricardo; Groenewegen, p. 28). It is apparent from the Whitaker volumes that Marshall's early lecture notes dealt with particular problems in Smith and Ricardo (rent, corn duties, bounties on production, and demand and supply) – and here, in contrast to his later apologetics, he is sometimes critical of Ricardo (*EEW*, 2, pp. 257–61). Moreover, he had other sources than the English classics, especially Cournot and von Thünen.[28] But again and again when one looks at Marshall's work, especially in its formative years, the influence of Mill is writ large.

The balance of Marshall's indebtedness will be explored in much more detail in the following two sections, but even at this stage it should be clear that there is something wrong with Marshall's own account. He made astonishing claims for continuity, and he persisted in these claims in the face of contemporary criticism, despite his acute personal sensitivity to criticism.[29] In so far as the aim was rhetorical, he seems to have had some success – even Shove not only took Marshall at his word when conflating Mill and Ricardo but also very largely accepted his claims concerning continuity.[30] Moreover, it was the continuity of "truth" which he claimed; to be referred to as a synthesiser irritated him intensely

28. *Variorum*, pp. 242–8, 250–2; Whitaker, 1975, 2, pp. 240–1, 248–50. There are also numerous citations of both writers in the *Principles*. Both Hutchison, 1956, pp. 64–6 n. and Whitaker, 1975, 1, p. 45 n. express surprise that Marshall makes no reference to Whewell as a predecessor. In terms of the evidence now available about Whewell that is perfectly reasonable, but it would appear from Marshall's papers that he did not know of Whewell's work except in connection with the publication of Richard Jones's writings. Although Whewell undoubtedly developed a price elasticity concept it seems clear that Marshall arrived at his own elasticity concept independently, and some considerable time after his study of economics had developed. Mrs. Marshall dates it at 1881 (1947, p. 28). Had he known of Whewell's work he would hardly have spent time on the matter himself. But it is certainly puzzling that he did not know of it, particularly as it would appear, from a discovery by Professor Whitaker, that Marshall did know of the work of Tozer which was published in the same journal as that of Whewell; see Collard, 1968, p. xxi.
29. Ashley, 1891, correctly pointed out several misinterpretations of Ricardo by Marshall in the *Principles*, including the nature of Ricardo's value theory and a quotation, out of context, about a supposedly upwardly movable psychological subsistence level. See also Marshall, 1898, p. 44, on the broader question of continuity.
30. Shove, 1942, p. 295. This is all the more remarkable because, despite a small published output, Shove was an extremely able economist to whose lectures Joan Robinson (1933) is apparently indebted. For a defence of Marshall's style of "personal exegesis", see S. Hollander, 1979, pp. 643–4 and for comment on this position see Groenewegen, pp. 13, 29.

(*Memorials*, p. 418). As we shall see, however, his own acknowledgements give a somewhat unbalanced picture – his claims in the fields of analysis of value and distribution are hard to accept, while his acknowledgements in the macroeconomic fields of money and trade, while less insistent (perhaps because more obviously correct), are actually much more consistent.

III Marshall's Classical Inheritance

Marshall certainly owed a clear debt to his Classical predecessors. In this section we will examine that debt, and in the following the picture will be qualified by indicating those aspects of Marshall's work which cannot be called Classical. Undoubtedly, the most important debt was to J. S. Mill. Marshall's initial forays into economics involved mathematisation of Mill, his policy attitudes were influenced by Mill, and his first book, *The Economics of Industry*, is both an introduction to, and an updating of, Mill.

Value and Distribution

From classical economics, Marshall took the concept of "normal" values for economic variables as being competitive equilibrium values within a framework which limited the operation of competition.[31] These economic variables could be analysed by the economist as scientist. To go beyond this to policy and to particular situations it was necessary to move outside the science of economics. The influence of Senior and of Mill is apparent here.[32]

The whole economic system existed within a framework of continuing economic growth, for Marshall as for the Classical economists, and in such a framework a good deal of judgement was necessary to supplement analysis before arriving at practical conclusions.

Such an outlook influenced Marshall throughout his writings. In dealing with the supply of goods, he analysed the supply conditions affecting the goods-producing factors of land, labour, and capital (to which he added the fourth factor of "organisation") (*Principles*, pp. 138–9, 240–3). In dealing with the supply of labour he discussed the growth of population, its health and strength, industrial training and labour mobil-

31. *Principles*, pp. 34–6; 1879*a*, pp. vi–vii. On the operation of competition within a framework see Samuels, 1966, O'Brien, 1975, and above all Robbins, 1952.
32. 1879*a*, pp. 3–4, 211; 1874, pp. 423–30; *Memorials*, pp. 164–5; *Principles*, pp. 771, 774. On Senior see Bowley, 1937, Chapter 1. However, Marshall was arguing that practical decisions involved considerations from outside economics. He did not envisage capturing them within an "art" of economics (*Variorum*, p. 154).

ity, as well as that central classical labour market concept, equalisation of net advantage (*Principles,* pp. 173–219, 547, 557, 661; see also *Variorum,* pp. 303–4). The discussion of the supply of capital reflects the work of Mill in particular. It is held to depend on the size of the possible sources of accumulation, and on the strength of the motives to save. Positive time preference exists in the aggregate, so that meeting the cost of this "waiting" is a necessary cost of production.[33]

Marshall's consideration of land naturally involves a very classical emphasis on diminishing returns (and an equally classical recognition that these might be offset by technical progress). It also exhibits a tendency – widespread in the classical literature because of the historical origins of the so-called "Ricardian" rent theory but perhaps surprising in a writer as clear headed as Marshall – to confuse diminishing returns with decreasing returns to scale and to relate these to increasing returns to scale.[34] As will be seen in the next section, Marshall did not stop there, but the Classical starting points are clear enough.

His demand theory really owed nothing to Classical origins, despite his claims. His discussion of adjustments to equilibrium value, however, though it went far beyond the classical analysis, betrays the initial influence of Smith (whom, as already noted, Marshall greatly admired)[35] in its initial concentration on market and "normal" (that is, long run) values, with price adjustment in the first case and quantity adjustment in the second.[36] Moreover his reading of Mill, as already indicated, directed him to some other value problems, especially those of joint demand and supply.[37] Though not the most distinguished part of his discussion of value (Stigler, 1941, pp. 83–7) it is clearly classical in origin.

Not surprisingly, given his emphasis on conditions of factor supply, his work on distribution exhibits classical elements. His discussion of labour supply, while bowing in the direction of Jevons's disutility analysis, is predominantly concerned with Classical issues such as population size, and population quality – health, strength, and investment in education.

33. *Principles,* pp. 229–36, 353, 618–20; J. S. Mill, 1848–71, I, pp. 160–72, 400–15; II, pp. 733–46. Marshall was quite clear that his treatment of capital owed most to Classical economics and to Turgot. It is this which lies behind his comment to Wicksell on Böhm-Bawerk (note 21). Interestingly enough it may well have been Jevons who, on this issue at least, was closer to Ricardo; see Black, 1981, pp. 8–9.
34. *Principles,* pp. 149–70, 418–31, 436–9, 450, 499–500, 629–36; *Variorum,* pp. 492–512; 1879*a*, pp. 21–6, 82–7.
35. See *Memorials,* p. 379, for a particular tribute by Marshall to Smith.
36. 1879*a*, pp. vii, 146–9, 158–67; *EEW,* 1, pp. 125–64; see also Whitaker, 1975, 1, pp. 119–25, 160; Davies, 1963; Newman, 1960.
37. J. S. Mill, 1848–71, Book III, Chapter 16, pp. 582–6; Marshall, *Principles,* pp. 381–93, 852–6; *Variorum,* p. 400; *EEW,* 1, pp. 160–64. See also Whitaker, 1975, 1, p. 160.

His discussion of noncompeting groups as a constraint on labour mobility[38] also shows the influence of Mill and Cairnes.

Like the classical economists, he was concerned with poverty and the interaction between poverty and low wages, though with more emphasis on labour *productivity* than on the problems associated with labour force increase in a situation in which a low "psychological subsistence" level is the key factor. Like Mill, he looked to education, family limitation, and capital accumulation, together with technical advance (and not to trades unions or socialism),[39] as the remedies for poverty.

His analysis of profit contained classical elements. Gross profit was a combination of interest and wages of management (as it had been for Smith) and of compensation for risk (as stressed by Tooke and McCulloch).[40] He went further than the classical analysis, however: in particular, earnings of management included rent of ability.[41]

Marshall's discussion of rent itself started from a Classical base, though it ultimately proceeded to a much higher level of generality. In dealing with land, Marshall attributed rent to the existence of diminishing returns (or decreasing returns to scale) and exhibited a Ricardo-like emphasis upon variable fertility. Moreover he managed to blur the role of transfer earnings and to avoid distinguishing rent from an individual and a social point of view, leaving a puzzle for twentieth century interpreters.[42] Indeed, he offered the Delphic remark, in rebuking Jevons, that it was "inexpedient to say that the rent of land does not enter into . . . price. But it is worse than inexpedient to say that the rent of land does enter into . . . price: that is false" (*Variorum*, p. 460; see also p. 439, and *Principles*, pp. 436–7 n.). Nonetheless he succeeded in developing rent analysis further. He made rent ultimately depend on the marginal productivity of land – it was the area under the marginal product curve after payments to cooperating factors – which was implicit in the Classical writers but not explicit. In

38. *Principles*, pp. 65, 138–43, 173–203, 217–19, 331, 525–30, 556–58, 567–74, 660–2, 716–19, 721, 843; 1879*a*, pp. 101–13, 173–5; *EEW*, 2, pp. 387–93; Whitaker, 1974, p. 7; Whitaker, 1975, 2, pp. 385–7. See also the discussion in Stigler, 1941, pp. 63–6. On the question of investment in education see also note 49.
39. *Principles*, pp. 509–10, 529–33, 559–63, 568, 684–5, 693–6, 702–8, 714–15; 1879*a*, pp. 102, 187–213; *Memorials*, pp. 227–53, 384–6, 396–9, 402–3; 1885*a*, p. 182; 1883, pp. 200–10; 1887*a*, pp. xi–xiii, xxv–xxvi; Whitaker, 1972, especially pp. 49–61; 1975, 1, pp. 79–80; Petridis, 1973.
40. Smith, 1776, 1, pp. 105–15, especially p. 113. For references to Tooke and McCulloch on this matter see O'Brien, 1970, p. 310.
41. *Principles*, pp. 71–82, 313, 505–10, 589–92, 598, 612–15, 618–20; *Variorum*, pp. 670–5 (from 1887*b*); 1879*a*, pp. 119–27, 135–45; *MCC*, pp. 285–94; *EEW*, 1, pp. 206–12; Whitaker, 1975, 1, pp. 204–6.
42. See Buchanan, 1929, and Robbins, 1930, pp. 209–11. See also Worcester, 1946, who, oddly, makes no reference to either Buchanan or Robbins. See also Stigler, 1941, pp. 92–4.

generalising the rent concept (as Senior and Bailey had done before him)[43] he was able to show the importance of the elasticity of factor supply in rent and, as noted, to introduce the concept of rent of ability.[44]

Economic Growth

The emphasis on the classical elements in the analysis of factor supply was an inevitable part of Marshall's treatment because his whole work is based entirely upon the concept of a moving economic system – a growing economy in which static equilibrium theorems (now particularly associated with Marshall) could only be explained in terms of all elements moving forward together at the same speed. Marshall explained this in terms of an analogy with a man packing parcels on the rack of a moving train; an equilibrium could be attained as long as everything was moving at the same relative speed, but it was likely to be disrupted if the onward motion was checked (*Memorials*, p. 312; see also 1898, p. 38). Understanding of economic growth was thus very important. Like Mill, Marshall was impressed by the premier position which England had attained through economic growth and was concerned with its preservation. Like Mill, he looked to economic growth to increase both material and nonmaterial wealth *and* aspirations so that wants increased with output.[45]

His formal analysis of growth – never published in his lifetime – was a differential equation version of J. S. Mill, with equations for the size of the working population, the standard of living, the efficiency of labour, the capital stock, total output, net annual product, piece wages, time wages, and the rate of interest.[46] But in his published work Marshall dealt with the growth of the economic system as a whole in more distinctly Classical terms, without recourse to such formality. Labour force increase in both quantity and (especially) quality was necessary for economic growth. In dealing with population he coupled a weak version of Malthus with eu-

43. For references see Bowley, 1937, pp. 126–36; O'Brien, 1975, pp. 130–1; Blaug, 1958*b*, pp. 55, 58, 155, 157, 158, 167, 171, 223.
44. *Principles*, pp. 149–70, 418–32, 436–9, 450, 499–500, 534–6, 577–9, 622–4, 629–36; *Variorum*, pp. 440–512, 670–8; 1879a, pp. 81–90, 110, 179; *EEW*, 1, pp. 239–60; 2, pp. 321–2; Whitaker, 1975, 2, pp. 319–21.
45. *Principles*, pp. 49, 56–7, 59, 80–1, 220–39, 675–8, 689–93, 749–52; 1879*a*, p. 6; *IT*, p. 697; 1883, pp. 184–91; *OP*, pp. 402–12. See also Parsons, 1931 and 1932; Whitaker, 1977. On the growth context of Marshall's work see also Walker, 1983. On the concept of endogenous tastes in Marshall's work see also Loasby, 1978, who correctly distinguishes this idea from the Galbraithian conception. On Parsons's critique, which economists may have cited a little too uncritically, see Wearne, 1981, and Chasse, 1984.
46. *EEW*, 2, p. 309–16. See also Whitaker, 1974, pp. 11–15; 1975, 2, pp. 305–9.

genic considerations[47] and maintained the Classical interest in investment in education,[48] extending this to the question of business education.[49]

Increase in the supply of capital was also necessary because it was required, as Smith had argued, to support increased division of labour. Marshall extended the meaning of "division of labour" enormously. His discussion of internal and external economies is the great source for all subsequent economists. Following Mill, accumulation depended on the size of the net product and the motives to save, including foresight, security, family affection, and the rate of interest (*Principles*, pp. 220–36, 353; Mill, 1848–73, 1, pp. 160–72, 400–15; 2, pp. 733–46). In the standard classical manner Marshall looked forward, in the *Economics of Industry*, to a "secular" (a corruption of the Latin *saecula*) decline in the rate of profit, as already noted.[50]

Government

Economic progress required, as Smith had recognised, a suitable institutional framework (Robbins, 1952; Samuels, 1956). Like the classical writers, Marshall emphasised security of property, human freedom, and the development of communications and financial institutions.[51] He was a little, but not very much, more enthusiastic about government involvement than the classical writers: Government involvement in enterprise was harmful to both managerial and innovative efficiency. He does, however, seem to have seen the role of government expanding in the areas of health, welfare, defence, and education. His concern with the link between poverty and low wages extended to the problem of urban overcrowding, and the lack of fresh air in towns, problems he proposed to

47. *Principles*, pp. 173–203, 219, 243–8, 740–5; *Variorum*, pp. 303–5; 1885*a*, p. 198; 1879*a*, pp. 27–37. See also Spengler, 1955.
48. For references to the Classical literature in this area, see O'Brien, 1975, pp. 282–5 and notes.
49. *Principles*, pp. 204–19, 229–30, 236, 560–6, 570–1, 619, 622, 660–1, 681–4, 858; 1879*a*, p. 39 (see also ibid., pp. 10–11, 32); *IT*, pp. 129–34, 356–7; *Memorials*, pp. 117–18; 1905*b*; 1905*c*; 1905*d*. See also 1905*a* and Blandy, 1967. It is both interesting and puzzling in the context of this chapter to note that Marshall apparently believed that he was going beyond the Classical economists in this respect. "The older economists took too little account of the fact that the human faculties are as important a means of production as any other kind of capital; and we may conclude, in opposition to them, that any change in the distribution of wealth which gives more to the wage receivers and less to the capitalists is likely, other things being equal, to hasten the increase of material production, and that it will not perceptibly retard the storing-up of material wealth" (*Principles*, pp. 229–30).
50. See *Principles*, p. 379 for "secular". For profit decline see 1879*a*, pp. 126–7.
51. *Principles*, pp. 197–8, 273–4, 301–4, 528, 678–9, 691, 726–33, 740–2, 744–7, 750–2; *IT*, pp. 32–85, 700–18; *MCC*, pp. 68–97.

tackle not only through taxation but also through a removal of some of the urban population to the country.

Much of this can be regarded for the most part as a development of the classical position with Sidgwickian overtones.[52] The only significant departure is that Marshall favoured increased *income* (and capital) taxation, with progression, to finance these excursions into welfare activities. He certainly did not favour government expansion financed by debt (1917, pp. 313–14, 317–22, 325–9, 345; *OP*, pp. 361–3). In the area of poor relief he showed no great hostility to the 1834 Poor Law – although, like Senior, condemning the Speenhamland system in particular, and widespread (though not small scale) "outdoor" relief in general – despite a very genuine concern with the alleviation of poverty and a strong interest in the work of the Charity Organisations Society.[53] Ultimately he believed, like Mill, that economic growth (together with the development of what he quaintly called "economic chivalry")[54] was the answer to poverty.

Whether in all this there are Utilitarian, as distinct from straightforward Classical, influences is a moot point. Marshall was probably not a wholehearted Utilitarian though not completely free of Utilitarian traits, many of them absorbed through J. S. Mill, others through Sidgwick. Utilitarianism influenced his economic psychology – thus he was able to absorb Jevons's Utilitarian-based approach to consumer maximisation – much more than his general stance on policy matters.[55] His aversion to ostentation and the influence of fashion more probably stemmed from his Calvinistic upbringing[56] – and possibly from the Classical distinction be-

52. *Principles*, pp. 199–200, 202–3, 304, 718, 803–4; 1879*a*, p. 113; *IT*, pp. 486, 494–7, 666–72; *Memorials*, pp. 118, 142–51; 1917, pp. 325–9, 345; 1885*b*; 1891*a*; 1891*b*; 1909; 1916; *OP*, pp. 197–262; 1885*a*, pp. 183–4; 1884; 1887*c*.
53. *OP*, pp. 199–262 especially pp. 199, 201, 211–25; 1879*a*, pp. 32–4; 1885*a*, pp. 187–8; *Memorials*, pp. 345, 373, 403; 1886; 1892*a*; 1892*b*. Marshall was tolerant, however, of localised and limited outdoor relief and did not favour its complete abolition.
54. *Memorials*, pp. 323–46 (from 1907). On the significance of economic chivalry, and the related question of Utilitarianism, see Birch, 1985.
55. See Birch, 1985; see also the contrary view in Jensen, 1985, which juxtaposes two misreferenced and very widely separated quotations from Marshall. Despite Jensen's contentions, Marshall's renunciation of a thoroughgoing Utilitarianism is clear enough (*Principles*, p. 17 n.), as was observed long ago by Schumpeter (1954, pp. 1056–7; Schumpeter also noted the point about Jevons made in the text of this chapter). Moreover, it is of interest that when Marshall transferred the chapter which originally included this note (*Principles*, p. 17 n.) to Appendix C in the 5th (1907) edition of the *Principles*, he retained the note itself in a prominent place in the main text of the book.
56. On this upbringing see Coase, 1984. On fashion and ostentation see, for example, Marshall, *Principles*, pp. 88 n., 288, 688, 720–1; *Memorials*, pp. 324–5, 443.

tween productive and unproductive labour – than from explicit adherence to Utilitarian ideals.[57]

Trade Theory and Policy

In the areas of trade and money, Marshall's classical inheritance is so clear as almost to require no comment. The treatment of international trade theory is undoubtedly the highest point of J. S. Mill's majestic *Principles;* and it seems to have been this area which, together with the material on economic growth (resulting in the equation system referred to above), first attracted Marshall's attention. A manuscript which Professor Whitaker dates at 1872–4 includes the now familiar offer curves, an investigation of the effects of tariffs, and an exploration of multiple equilibria (also explored by Mill). Indeed Marshall wrote (but did not publish) a book on international trade which was essentially complete by 1877 – and examination of this shows it to have been building almost completely on Mill (the other – unacknowledged – source is Torrens).[58] It is true that when Marshall used his famous apparatus – first published (with errors, some fairly obvious) by Sidgwick in 1879 on Marshall's behalf[59] – the discussion lacked the hallmarks of the Classical discussions, with their emphasis on balance of payments equilibrium being adjusted through specie flows, and the effects of these flows on relative income and price levels. But these considerations, it is apparent from *Money Credit and Commerce,* were present in the larger manuscript from which Sidgwick had extracted the Pure Theory (*MCC*, pp. 177–89, 338–40; Whitaker, 1975, 2, p. 6).

It should be emphasised that this was no mere regurgitation. The work was that of a properly trained mathematician; and Marshall, it is apparent from later work, considered many of the difficulties raised by the analysis while (as was his unfortunate habit) avoiding any indication to the reader that a number of difficult possible cases had been reviewed before the final version was presented (Chipman, 1965, pp. 689, 704, 722–4, 733, 734, 738, 739; Whitaker, 1975, 2, p. 115).

Beyond the formal technical discussion, Marshall followed the stan-

57. See also Chasse, 1984, for an informative discussion. The suggestion about productive and unproductive labour comes from this source (p. 393). The matter clearly requires further exploration.
58. *Principles*, pp. 261–79; *Variorum*, pp. 11–61, 63–89, 94–111, 116–81. See also Whitaker, 1975, 1, pp. 260–1; 2, pp. 3–11, 62–3, 89–94, 111–16. On Torrens see O'Brien, 1975, pp. 189–97 and O'Brien, 1977.
59. *EEW*, 2, p. 4 (Marshall to Seligman, April 1900). See also Whitaker, 1975, 1, pp. 20–1. Happily the errors have been corrected in the Whitaker edition of the material though they were preserved in the 1930 LSE reprint of the material; see Whitaker, 1975, 2, p. 7 n.

dard Smithian and Millian paths, with foreign trade originating in the supply of luxuries and then moving to more basic commodities. In this it benefitted all parties to trade. Trade facilitated technical advance and increased division of labour. It also enhanced the development of financial institutions in the form of money and capital markets. Perhaps Marshall was less optimistic than some of his predecessors; he also argued that the very process of expansion (and the increased capitalisation involved) separated employers and employees, and that the widening of financial markets increased fluctuations, though these could be offset by the demand-steadying effects of wider goods markets and better communications (*Principles*, pp. 672–5; *EEW*, 2, pp. 14–20, 33–61).

It was not just the trade analysis which was classical: it was the attitudes. Marshall's commitment to unilateral free trade as a concept had a fervour recalling the heated classical rejection of Torrens's *The Budget*.[60] Free trade was necessary, in Marshall's view, not only as a stimulus but also to avoid the conferring of sectional benefits at the cost of larger injury to the wider community. Protection not only distorted the distribution of income but reduced its level by interfering with the full realisation of scale economies.[61]

Marshall recognised that taxes on foreign trade could turn the terms of trade in favour of the country levying the duties, as Torrens had argued (though Marshall does not refer to him in this context) but he did not approve of such duties. They were limited in their effectiveness, in a many-country world, they involved a deadweight loss, product and factor market distortions, and regressive effects, as well as political corruption.[62]

Money

When we turn from the trade theory to the monetary theory, the roots in the Classical literature are clear enough. As Marshall himself said, the Classical economists "left very little to be added as regards fundamentals by their successors" (*MCC*, p. 41).

In context this statement refers to the work of the Bullionists and it reflects Marshall's habit, especially in later life, of neglecting the importance for his own thought of what he had derived from J. S. Mill. Mar-

60. *OP*, 365–420; *MCC*, pp. 193–8; *EEW*, 2, pp. 80–9, 94–111; *Memorials*, pp. 449–50. See also Whitaker, 1975, 2, pp. 89–94. On the controversy over Torrens's *The Budget* see Robbins, 1958, Chapter 7, and O'Brien, 1975, pp. 189–97.
61. *MCC*, pp. 213–17; *OP*, pp. 395–9, 408–12; *EEW*, 2, pp. 106–8; *Memorials*, pp. 258–65, 471–4; *IT*, pp. 760–2; 1917, pp. 330–45; 1904, pp. 94–8. See also 1903; McCready, 1955; Wood, 1982; and Whitaker, 1975, 2, pp. 89–91.
62. *EEW*, 2, pp. 63–89; *MCC*, pp. 219, 265; *OP*, pp. 389–90, 394, 399, 415–20; 1917, pp. 329–30, 341–5; 1904, p. 97.

shall's monetary thought was in fact derived very largely from Mill, though supplemented by other writers including Ricardo and (especially) Thornton. It represented a continuation of the Classical tradition, particularly in its special Millian version, incorporating elements of both Currency and Banking Schools in the literature which developed both before and after the Bank Charter Act of 1844.[63] Marshall also drew on the work of Giffen, particularly in relation to the bank deposit multiplier (*OP*, pp. 27, 37; *MCC*, p. 60n.; Eshag, 1963, pp. xiii, 16–18), but this does not alter the truth of the statement above because Giffen's work is essentially classical and, in any case, the deposit multiplier had been put forward much earlier by Torrens on the basis of work by Pennington.[64]

Marshall's main theoretical approach was thus via the quantity theory, but with a recognition of the variability of velocity of circulation, and of the importance of commercial confidence. Like Thornton, he recognised the existence of links between velocity and confidence. Thus, accepting that velocity could vary if commercial confidence altered or if paper currency was increased in amount and its status undermined, Marshall could not accept the full rigour of the Currency School position that the amount of paper currency could only be equal to the metallic currency it had displaced. Nonetheless his whole emphasis was, as in the classical writings, on currency rather than bank deposits. He regarded the latter as devices for increasing velocity rather than as money themselves.[65]

Approaching monetary theory from this direction, Marshall showed clear appreciation of the operation of precious metal flows and their interaction with the balance of payments, and of the concept of the equilibrium distribution of the precious metals.[66] His discussion of the transmission mechanism emphasised the "indirect" mechanism, just as Thornton's had done; it is ironic that textbooks should treat this, indisputably inherited by Keynes from Marshall,[67] as some kind of particularly Keynesian innovation.[68] An inflow of precious metals increased

63. On the Currency and Banking controversy background see O'Brien, 1975, pp. 153–9. Marshall's monetary theory is in *OP*, pp. 1–195, 263–326, and *MCC*, pp. 12–97, 225–72, 282–4; see also *EEW*, 1, pp. 164–77; 2, pp. 277–8.
64. On Torrens and Pennington see Robbins, 1958, pp. 109–11; Pennington, 1826–40, and O'Brien, 1984, pp. 15–16.
65. *OP*, pp. 5–6, 22, 24–7, 34–40, 118, 267–8; 1923, pp. 42–50, 81–8, 246–63, 282–4; Thornton, 1802, pp. 96–100, 197 n.
66. *OP*, pp. 65–7, 115–26, 144–7, 150, 170–4, 177–80, 188, 191–5, 293, 296–7; see also Keynes in *Memorials*, pp. 30–1; *MCC*, pp. 38–67. On the Classical background see O'Brien, 1975, Chapter 6.
67. On this Keynes, 1911, is instructive. On the more general question of Marshall and Keynes see Jensen, 1983; Birch, 1985; and Loasby, 1978.
68. The idea is also central to the work of Wicksell, 1898, and of Mises, 1912, and Keynes certainly knew of Wicksell's work. But it has roots that go back far beyond those writers and Marshall – see Angell, 1926, p. 120, and O'Brien, 1984, pp. 30–1.

banking reserves, leading to a lowering of the rate of interest below the marginal profitability of investment, producing an increased demand for loans. Price rises resulted. These were further enhanced by expectations of inflation following the inflow of gold. Rising price levels in turn increased the demand for working balances.[69]

Marshall used this analysis, and showed his appreciation of the issues involved, to very considerable advantage, in the debate over the metallic standard. His exposition is contained in his answers to enquiries on trade depression (1886), gold and silver (1887), and Indian currency (1899) (*OP*, pp. 1–16, 17–195, 265–326). He was able to show the irrelevance of bimetallic proposals both to the question of price level stability and to that of India's exports; and he put forward a plan, deriving from Ricardo's *Economical and Secure Currency* for "Symmetallism", proposing that paper could only be exchanged for metal on the basis of receiving two bars of two different metals (*OP*, pp. 14, 28, 30, 165; Ricardo, 1816, especially pp. 65–73). Gresham's Law would thus not be able to produce monometallism, because the gain from selling one of the metals would be mirrored by the loss on the other, while the latter could not be used as currency since currency requirements would be met by paper.[70]

The scheme was a neat one, but it involved no great jump from the proposals of the 1810s and 1820s. On the other hand, his enthusiasm for indexed contracts (a "tabular standard of value") did involve a significant advance beyond the classical position. Though index numbers have a very long history (Maunder, 1970), they played virtually no part in the classical literature. Even the great *History of Prices* by Tooke and Newmarch did not use them, although Arthur Young had done so (Young, 1812). Marshall's starting point was, unsurprisingly, Jevons.[71]

Acceptance of the classical macroeconomic apparatus did not, it should hardly now need emphasizing, involve an unwillingness to recognise problems of aggregate demand fluctuations. While Marshall accepted J. S. Mill's version of the Law of Markets as the long run proposition which Mill meant (that is, economic growth should not result in general overproduction because purchasing power would rise with output), Marshall also recognised (again like Mill) the possibility of excess

69. *OP*, pp. 10, 22–3, 38, 40–1, 51–2, 124, 126–8, 130–1, 158, 272–4; *MCC*, pp. 73–6, 255–8; *Memorials*, p. 190. See also Eshag, pp. 13 n. 55, 57 n. 51.
70. *OP*, pp. 14, 28–31, 101–4; *Memorials*, pp. 204–6 (see, however, ibid., pp. 476–7); *MCC*, pp. 64–7.
71. Marshall notes (*Memorials*, p. 197) also the work of Joseph Lowe and of Scrope. Marshall did work on index numbers himself (for example, *Memorials*, pp. 207–11); he is credited by Keynes (in ibid., p. 31) with developing the "chain" method of index numbers. See also Edgeworth, 1925, Vol. 1, p. 213, where Marshall is acknowledged as arriving independently at a formulation used by Edgeworth.

demand for money as a disequilibrium problem which could arise, in particular, if there were a loss of economic confidence.[72]

Marshall also borrowed from Overstone the theory of an *endogenous* cycle of commercial confidence which could (as Overstone himself had argued) be amplified by banking accommodation of entrepreneurial demands for loans in the upswing.[73] In the course of the cycle, profits varied while wages remained fairly rigid. The labour market adjusted through quantity variation and thus exhibited unemployment. Marshall's cautious discussion of the remedies for this – improved market knowledge, discouragement of fraud, of speculation, and of fashion changes, reduced trade secrecy, an increased fiduciary issue (this a Banking School element) and the use of a tabular standard of value[74] – would not, with the exception of the last, have seemed at all unusual to the Classical economists.

It is then undeniable that Marshall had a very substantial Classical inheritance, that he began his economics by working at the Classical writers, and that their influence persisted throughout his life as a writer on economics. But there is very much more to the picture than this, and to leave the story at this juncture would be to overstate greatly the degree of continuity between Marshall's thought and that of the Classical economists.

IV The Nonclassical Material

It is important to examine closely the Nonclassical elements in Marshall's work because of his tendency to overstress the continuity of his own work with that of his predecessors. It might almost be said that his famous motto about continuity in economic phenomena (*natura non facit saltum*) extended to the subject matter of economics itself – *economica* as well as *natura*. When we look at Marshall's microeconomic work, however, both the extent of his departures from his predecessors and the degree of his own achievement become rather clearer.

72. *Principles*, pp. 709–11; *OP*, pp. 91–4; 1879*b*, p. 34; 1879*a*, pp. 154–5; *Memorials*, pp. 130, 192, 463; J. S. Mill, 1848–71, II, pp. 570–6.
73. 1879*a*, pp. 150–5; see also ibid., pp. 161–4; *Principles*, pp. 594–5, 709–11; *MCC*, p. 246. See also ibid., pp. 18–19, 75, 238–45, 249–53, 257; 1885*a*, p. 178; *Memorials*, pp. 190–4; *OP*, pp. 9–10. According to Eshag, 1963, p. 95, Marshall had a marked personal copy of Overstone, 1837–48.
74. *Principles*, pp. 555–6, 594–5, 687–8, 710–11; *Variorum*, p. 180; *OP*, pp. 9–11, 92–7; *Memorials*, pp. 191, 205 n. 2 (see also p. 206 n. 2); *MCC*, pp. 18, 244, 258–63; 1885*a*, pp. 174–9.

Markets

His development of partial equilibrium analysis, with *ceteris paribus* made explicit, was a significant development.[75] One has only to look at the use Marshall made of it compared with *any* of his predecessors, let alone the classical writers whose discussion of individual markets was of a much more generalised nature, to see the extent of Marshall's contribution. His detailed exploration of market clearing, and of stability, encompassing both quantity adjustment and price adjustment models, goes far beyond anything in the classical literature and thus altered the whole *balance* of the treatment, in its emphasis upon the detailed microeconomic underpinnings.[76]

Demand

Although demand curves predate Marshall – as a concept in Say, as a function in Cournot, and as a graphical device in Fleeming Jenkin – demand itself received very little analysis in the main body of classical literature (despite Marshall's startling claims noted earlier in this discussion) except for J. S. Mill's great discussion of *aggregate* demand in the context of international trade. Nor did classical analysis, with a few limited exceptions (Say, Longfield, and, to some extent, Senior) make much use of utility. Ricardo, despite Marshall's claims, satisfied himself that utility had no influence on price.[77] Marshall himself, however, used utility analysis extensively and the major source is clearly Jevons. Marshall's analysis makes utility the basis of consumption, with the individual demand curve derived from the premise of diminishing marginal utility.[78] This enabled Marshall to make sense of Say's dictum, rejected by Ricardo, that price measured utility (Say, 1803, p. 62). Price, in Marshall's analysis, measured the *marginal* utility for a *given* individual though, as Marshall repeatedly emphasized, a shilling had a different marginal utility for a rich man and a poor man. He extended the analysis to intertemporal maximisation and combined intertemporal and in-

75. See in particular *Principles*, pp. 366, 379–80, 460–1; *Variorum*, p. 49; *Memorials*, pp. 312, 314–15; 1898, p. 49 and *passim*.
76. *Principles*, pp. 330–6, 345, 348, 369–72, 378–80, 805–9; *Variorum*, pp. 361–3; 1879*a*, pp. vii, 158; *EEW*, 1, pp. 119–59, especially pp. 132, 143–4; Newman, 1960, pp. 587–93; Davies, 1963.
77. Ricardo, 1817–21, p. 281. The idea of a (functional) relationship between price and quantity goes back to long before Say. See Creedy, 1986.
78. *Principles*, pp. 64, 86–91, 93–4, 95–6. Marshall also seems to have drawn on Jevons's discussion of the King-Davenant law; see Creedy, 1986, pp. 195, 202.

tratemporal equilibrium.[79] Of course the analysis, with its additive utility function and quasi-constant marginal utility of money, has limitations which have been endlessly discussed since Marshall's time, but it clearly represents such a major departure from the classical literature that the gap between Marshall and later demand theory (Slutsky and Hicks) is incomparably smaller than the gap between Marshall and the classics, not only in the analysis itself but in the very choice of topic on which to concentrate. This is particularly apparent in the concentration of the analysis on the individual demand curve, making the transition to a market curve by a somewhat imprecisely defined process of aggregation. (*Principles*, pp. 98–9, 104–5; *Variorum*, p. 244).

Consumer Surplus

Linked with the demand analysis is the discussion of consumer surplus, a concept which could hardly have originated with classical economics, with its very limited treatment of demand. Marshall did have forerunners in the French engineering school, particularly Dupuit,[80] but his own analysis was probably developed independently of them.[81] In view of the insoluble aggregation problems and the partial equilibrium limitations, almost all well known to Marshall,[82] the classical economists may have had good sense in not pursuing this path. But the truth is that it was never on their agenda. Marshall, by contrast, was deeply concerned about this tool, and was very disappointed that its problems proved insoluble[83] – even though it was never really likely that a partial equilibrium tool could be used for general equilibrium problems of community welfare.[84] Yet his concern demonstrates how far his own analysis had gone beyond that of the classical economists, in both distance and direction. Even on the question

79. *Principles*, pp. 92–7, 100, 117–23, 230–4, 838–9, 841, 845–6; *Variorum*, pp. 236–45; 1879*a*, pp. 69–71. On the nature of Marshall's demand analysis see the excellent article by Loasby, 1978.
80. For references to Dupuit see Marshall, *Principles*, pp. 101 n., 476 n.; *Variorum*, p. 263 n. For general discussion see Hébert and Ekelund, 1984, pp. 55–60; Ekelund and Hébert, 1985.
81. *EEW*, 1, p. 39 (Marshall to Seligman, October 1896). Whitaker's view that Marshall did not know of Dupuit's work when developing consumer surplus seems indisputable, 1975, 2, p. 281.
82. Marshall discusses a number of these problems in *Principles*, pp. 124–37; see also ibid., pp. 96, 842; *Variorum*, p. 241; *Memorials*, p. 162. On Marshall's awareness of the problems with consumer surplus see also Dooley, 1983.
83. However, he continued to reproduce material dating from his original work on the concept, in successive editions of his *Principles*. See pp. 467–75, 489–93, 811; *EEW*, 2, pp. 72, 279–302. See also Bharadwaj, 1972. On his disappointment with the concept, see Guillebaud, 1971, p. 6.
84. See, however, Ekelund and Hébert, 1985, for a discussion of the reasons why the concept refuses to fade away.

of the precise nature of the marginal utility of money income, where not assumed constant, Marshall drew not on classical analysis (for which the problem had not arisen) but on the analysis of gambling by the eighteenth century mathematician Bernoulli (*Principles*, pp. 135, 842–3).

Supply and the Firm

When we come to the supply blade of Marshall's partial equilibrium "scissors" we find much the same picture. To Marshall economics owes the widespread use of the supply curve. It was, for him, a very much more complex concept than it has become: cost curves had a time dimension[85] (making them nonreversible) while rents lay below the supply curve as well as above because of differential cost advantages enjoyed by different firms ("particular expenses") (*Principles*, pp. 810–11 n.; see also *Variorum*, pp. 811–12). Knowledge of the supply response of an industry was obtained by examination of a Representative Firm (*Principles*, pp. 317–18, 342–3, 367–8, 377, 396, 459–61, 497, 805).

While the emphasis on a time dimension betrays classical roots, the whole emphasis on an industrial supply curve goes far beyond what is to be found in classical literature. Even where, in discussing the factor supplies which underlay cost curves, Marshall betrayed classical starting points most clearly, he still went beyond them. Despite ambiguities inherited from the classical analysis over increasing returns, diminishing returns, and decreasing returns to scale, he ultimately conceded the necessary distinctions, and generalised the concept of diminishing returns in the form of diminishing marginal product to all factors (*Principles*, pp. 150–9, 169–72, 319 n., 403–9).

To the analysis of the firm itself, Marshall made contributions of lasting influence. On the one hand he stressed entrepreneurship in a way that no one except Say (for rather special historical reasons) had done before him.[86] On the other, he placed the entrepreneur at the centre of the marginal adjustments leading to optimal factor combinations where relative factor prices and productivities were given – the "principle of substitution" (*Principles*, pp. xvi, 169–72, 341, 351–9, 404–6, 662–3, 665–6; see also pp. 418–21, 434–7). Despite Marshall's eccentric attempt in the first edition of the *Principles* to credit Ricardo with this, there is nothing like it in the classical literature.

Marshall's discussion of the firm itself has no parallels anywhere in the

85. *Principles*, pp. 455–7, 807–10; *IT*, pp. 187–8 n.; *Memorials*, pp. 439–41; *EEW*, 2, p. 193; see also Whitaker, 1975, 2, pp. 184–5; Newman, 1960, pp. 589–90.
86. See Hébert and Link, 1982, especially pp. 29–35; Koolman, 1971; James, 1977; Kaiser, 1980.

classical literature. Though Mill and Babbage had certainly discussed industrial organisation, Marshall's treatment is his own. Pricing is explored in terms of a (long run) marginal cost approach (though with a very different concept of marginal cost from that in modern textbooks since Marshall thought in terms of large finite changes and also recognised the problem of cost allocation in a multiproduct firm) and the firm is placed in the context of the industry via the Representative Firm.[87] We have the famous analogy of the trees of the forest, with demand changes affecting the relative rates of growth and decay of constituent firms in the industry.[88]

Within the industry, the discussion of competition – emphatically *not* perfect[89] – encompasses many of the issues present in later discussions of market power.[90] In particular, Marshall discussed product differentiation, advertising, barriers to entry, limit pricing, loss leaders, and tying clauses.[91] He also considered oligopolistic interdependence (including the question of the effect of high fixed costs – he led the profession into

87. *Principles*, pp. xvi, 361–2, 376, 394–402, 500–2; *Variorum*, p. 529; 1898, pp. 50–1; *IT*, pp. 181–96, 269–71, 424; see also 1879*a*, pp. 79–80. Cost "is to be estimated with regard to a whole process of production rather than a particular locomotive or a particular parcel of goods" – *Principles*, pp. 361–2. On the Mill–Marshall links on business organisation see also Phillips, 1979, and Rainelli, 1983.
88. *Principles*, pp. 285–6, 315–17, 323, 342–3, 378, 457–9; *Variorum*, pp. 69–70. See also Frisch, 1950, pp. 512–13. Cf. Levine, 1980, 1983, who believes that the biological elements in Marshall's work are irrelevant to the question of increasing returns and competition. But see Phillips, 1979.
89. *Principles*, pp. 5–12, 374, 458, 500–1, 540–1, 849–50; *Variorum*, pp. 411–12, 569, 573–4; *IT*, p. 182; see also Stigler, 1957, pp. 9–10; 1962, p. 282; Peterson, 1957, pp. 63, 65. On the question of the relation between increasing returns and competition see also Levine, 1980, 1983, and (especially) Loasby, 1978. See also Gee, 1983. Gee argues convincingly that Marshall saw only a limited use for statics and that he avoided a hard and fast distinction between the long run and the short run in the matter of fixed costs.
90. In particular he pointed the way towards "Monopolistic Competition". See *Principles*, pp. 341–2; *IT*, p. 397; see also Stykolt, 1956, citing *Principles*, p. 616 n. 3; Gerbier, 1976, p. 409, citing *Principles*, pp. 846–52; Peterson, 1957, pp. 73–4. Chamberlin has testified that his work was not part of the attacks on Marshall, and indeed that he obtained "marginal value product" from Note XIV of Marshall's Mathematical Appendix – 1961, pp. 516, 524, 532–43. The account by Blitch, stressing the Marshallian origins of the thought of Allyn Young, Chamberlin's supervisor, in this area, strengthens the connection between the later analysis and Marshall's work – see Blitch, 1985, p. 397. See, however, Loasby, 1978, pp. 6, 10–11, for a contrary view.
91. *IT*, pp. 234, 270–1, 300–2, 304–7, 396–8, 439, 524, 536–7, 597. The influence of American literature on Marshall's *IT* is important, but more important still was his study of the details of industrial organisation and practices. His *IT*, originally planned as (part of) Volume 2 of his *Principles* (see Whitaker, 1975, 1, p. 93, and *IT*, p. vi) reflects the continuation of his work beyond the *Principles* and it is unfortunate that its influence, despite good sales, was limited (Liebhafsky, 1955; Stykolt, 1956; Andreano, 1965).

adopting the accounting practice of distinguishing fixed and variable costs) and monopoly.[92]

It should hardly need emphasising that none of this has any parallel in the Classical literature which was concerned with macro distribution and growth, not the microeconomics of markets. Marshall's achievement was remarkable. On the one hand it is a small, and mathematically trivial, step from his analysis of monopoly to the marginal cost and marginal revenue analysis which apparently gave economists so much trouble in the 1930s[93] (Chamberlin himself used the *average* cost and revenue curves of Marshall for most of his analysis). On the other hand, Marshall not only explored price discrimination and the allocation of overheads according to elasticity, but at the same time emphasized something which tended to be forgotten in the 1930s literature – the *conditional* nature of monopoly, and the limitations on the maximising behaviour of monopolists.[94]

In all this discussion of the firm, there is very little indeed which is Classical. Marshall's concern about bureaucracy in large firms, and his belief in the need for small, innovative, firms, may bear some relation to Mill and even Babbage (Mill, 1848–71, Book 1, Chapter 9; Babbage, 1832; see note 87 above). But what Marshall has to say goes far beyond these authors, as does his path-breaking discussion of economies of scale under the headings of internal and external economies.[95]

92. *Principles*, pp. 285–7, 359–62, 373–5, 397, 415–17, 454, 458–9, 477–95, 497–8, 502, 805, 856–8; *IT*, pp. 397–9, 403–22; 425, 450 n., 515–20, 824–9, 835; see also Peterson, 1957, pp. 72, 76.
93. On the intellectual difficulties apparently posed at that time by the first derivative of the revenue function see Robinson, 1933, p. vi. Marshall's profit (π) maximisation condition is simply that average revenue (p) minus average cost (c), multiplied by output, is at a maximum, that is, $\pi = (p - c)q$ is maximised. The first order maximum condition obtained from this is, of course,

$$p + q\frac{dp}{dq} = c + q\frac{dc}{dq}$$

or marginal revenue equals marginal cost.

In relation to note 90 above, if $p = c$ *by definition* (because only normal profits are being earned) then, trivially, the slope of the average revenue curve (dp/dq) and the slope of the average cost curve (dc/dq) will be equal at precisely the value at which average revenue equals average cost. As Schumpeter remarked, "the formal part of the marginal principle would be as familiar [to Marshall] as would be his breakfast bacon" (1954, p. 838). However, Marshall's economics are much more complicated than his mathematics, explicit or implied, and there are difficulties over his concept of marginal cost which cannot be explored here. They certainly helped to confuse his successors. But he himself clearly warned about the limitations of mathematics (*Principles*, p. 850).
94. *Principles*, pp. 493–5, 663, 693 (and see also pp. 486–9, 856–8); 1879*a*, p. 181; *IT*, pp. 395–672, especially pp. 397–8, 403–6, 414–22, 440–4, 449–50 n.
95. *Principles*, pp. 250–66, 278–90, 457–9, 500–1; *Variorum*, pp. 69, 521, 523–9; *IT*, pp. 214–49; *Memorials*, p. 407; *EEW*, 2, pp. 194–8.

Thus it is hardly surprising that his treatment of value, symmetrically placed after the discussion of the demand and supply "scissor blades" in Book V of the *Principles*, is significantly different in virtually every important respect from the classical cost of production theories, let alone the very special Ricardian theory. We do not have the classical emphasis (to the point of exclusion of other considerations) on cost of production, nor the particular approach of Menger and, to a lesser extent, Jevons, in which everything is viewed from the perspective of demand. Above all, Marshall emphasised, in obvious contrast to Mill's unfortunate dictum that value theory was settled, that "every plain and simple doctrine as to the relations between cost of production, demand and value is necessarily false."[96]

Thus, though Marshall started from J. S. Mill in value matters, he finished at a destination which was the other side of a watershed in the history of economics from Mill's work. He explored, in the context of different time periods of adjustment, the achievement of equilibrium through the interaction of the supply analysis that he had developed himself with the demand theory which he had made his own on the foundations of Cournot, Jenkin, and Jevons. The end result was a treatment of value which had such influence that it is difficult to imagine the history of economics without it.

Distribution

When we come to the matter of distribution, though the classical roots are more visible the end result would still have been unrecognisable to the Classical economists. Marshall started from the work of J. S. Mill, whose influence is particularly apparent in the *Economics of Industry*, but the source on which he ultimately drew more was von Thünen, developing a theory which treated the demand for factors in terms of marginal product.

It was marginal product equalised across different employments; and the marginal product was *net* (effectively *discounted*) marginal *revenue* product. Moreover the analysis was extended from the triad of land, labour, and capital to include entrepreneurship, the factor on which Marshall laid such stress.[97] Entrepreneurial earnings depended on demand for

96. *Principles*, p. 368. For Mill's unfortunate dictum see 1848–71, 2, p. 456. "Happily, there is nothing in the laws of Value which remains for the present or any future writer to clear up; the theory of the subject is complete". See also *Principles*, pp. 84–5, 90, 324–30, 348–9, 813–21; 1879*a*, pp. 91–3, 147–8, 165–7. On the distinction to be made in this context between Jevons and the Austrians see Black, 1981, p. 10.

97. *Principles*, pp. 409–10, 515–23, 536–40, 596–608, 620–4, 660–7, 846–52; *Variorum*, pp. 580–8, 670–5; 1879*a*, pp. 128–45 [Marshall explains (p. 133) that "net" marginal product takes account of implicit discounting]. Thünen's influence is stressed

the services of entrepreneurs which depended on their marginal productivity in different occupations, though equalisation of the rewards at the margin could be impeded by barriers to entry, and the rewards were higher if there was less routine management (allowing more scope for genuine entrepreneurship) as indicated by a relatively high ratio of circulating to fixed capital.[98]

Marshall's marginal productivity theory was not in as complete a form as that associated with Wicksteed and Euler's theorem[99] (Marshall never formally endorsed the latter), and the idea of product exhaustion is a little oblique in the *text* of the *Principles* though it *is* clear in a marginal note.[100]

It is true that when we look at Marshall's treatment of distribution as a whole, we see that the supply of factors was analysed very largely in Classical terms, with only a subsidiary emphasis on disutility in factor supply. The Classical elements noted in the previous section undoubtedly predominated. But by unifying these with the marginal-productivity factor-demand analysis, Marshall managed to provide a completeness of distribution theory which both his predecessors *and successors* (who neglected supply) lacked. In particular, he was able to draw on the classical analysis of capital supply through "abstinence", substituting McVane's term "waiting", and to combine this with his marginal productivity theory of demand for capital, thus using the most "modern" part of the classical analysis of factor supply and linking the two analytical streams further.[101]

This produced an analysis which his Classical predecessors would scarcely have recognised. The most advanced Classical analysis, that of

by H. M. Robertson, 1970, and by Marshall, who expressly denied any indebtedness to Walker. (Marshall to J. B. Clark, 2 July 1900, and 24 March 1908, in *Memorials*, pp. 412–13, 416–18). See also Marshall, 1898, p. 58. On Marshall's acknowledgement of priorities see Whitaker, 1975, 1, pp. 39, 69. Walker's distribution theory in his (1876) and even in his (1887) fell a good way short of Marshall, 1879*a*, both in analytical development and in clarity of exposition. See Walker, 1876, pp. 128–73 especially pp. 128–30 and 1887, *passim*, and cf. Marshall, 1887*b*. Essentially Walker made the Classical theory of rent the basis of his determination of rent and profit, leaving wages *as a residual*. See especially Walker, 1887, pp. 281–2, 287–8. See also Solow, 1987. Marshall's characteristically clear-headed reply (1887*b*) courteously identified a number of points at which Walker's analysis was inferior to that in Marshall, 1879*a*, notably in the treatment of the *supply* of entrepreneurship.

98. *Principles*, pp. 605–24; *Variorum*, pp. 661–2; 1879*a*, pp. 74–5, 135–45, 177–8; see also 1885*a*, p. 174; *EEW*, 1, pp. 206–12.
99. For a comprehensive discussion of this see Stigler, 1941, Chapter 12.
100. *Principles*, p. 536; see also ibid., p. 830, and Whitaker's comment, 1975, 2, p. 326.
101. The reference to McVane is in *Principles*, p. 233 n. On the return to capital more generally see *Principles*, pp. 21, 73–4, 81–2, 122, 220–36, 362, 377, 411–12, 419–20, 518–21, 533–4; *Variorum*, pp. 374, 461–92, 495; 1879*a*, pp. 41–2, 119–27, 146; *MCC*, pp. 285–94.

Cairnes, went no further than treating distribution as the result of the demand for each other's output by noncompeting groups (except within the groups themselves, where normal Classical analysis applied).[102]

Macroeconomics

The Classical inheritance is much more dominant outside the microeconomic core of Marshall's work. But this is hardly surprising. Of the three subjects, economic growth, international trade, and money, the last two are those in which developments and refinements of the classical analysis are still the basic part of modern theory. Marshall's Classical continuity was greatest in precisely those areas where modern continuity with the Classical analysis is greatest. Even with Marshall there are differences of emphasis. Apart from the differential equation approach to economic growth noted above, Marshall's work is also characterised by an emphasis on the role of entrepreneurship in economic growth (*Principles*, pp. 240–77, 291–313; *IT*, pp. 350–94) and by the idea that increased state activities would have to be financed by increased (and progressive) taxation of incomes.[103] The idea of progression in relation to income tax was anathema to the chief Classical writers on public finance, McCulloch and J. S. Mill (see O'Brien, 1975, pp. 245–6, 251–2, 255, for references). The departures from the Classical analysis in the treatment of economic growth are few, however, and they are even fewer in the trade material. Even Marshall's comparative advantage table (anticipated in any case, in superior form, by Edgeworth) was only working out the implications of what Senior and (unknown to Marshall) Longfield had been driving at (see O'Brien, 1975, pp. 180–1 for references).

In the field of monetary economics Marshall's treatment is distinct from what went before in only two respects. First, he spelt out what had to remain fixed in the "pound" of *ceteris paribus* for there to be a straightforward relationship between money and the price level (*OP*, pp. 5–6, 21–2, 24–7, 34–5, 37, 40, 267–9; *MCC*, pp. 42–8). Second and more important, his theory, in harmony with his individualistic and nonclassical emphasis on microeconomic underpinnings, laid stress on the demand for cash balances and interpreted this in a marginal, maximising, manner

102. Cairnes, 1874, pp. 149–294. According to Cairnes "wages and profits, regarded as relative phenomena, are governed by Cost of Production, where the producers are in effective competition with one another, and, where they are not, by Reciprocal Demand" (1874, p. 149).

103. *OP*, pp. 337, 362; 1909; 1916; 1917, pp. 317–22, 325–28. For consideration of the role of the State more generally see *Principles*, p. 304; 1879*a*, p. 113; *IT*, pp. 486, 494–7, 666–72; 1885*a*, p. 174; *Memorials*, p. 118; 1917, pp. 313–14, 345; 1891*a*; 1891*b*.

with the marginal utility of cash balances equated with the marginal utility of alternative uses of the funds. He was thus enabled to explore tentatively a variety of real balance effects.[104] Marshall provided a direct link between the classical analysis and the Keynesian treatment of liquidity preference (which, not surprisingly, has been linked by twentieth century writers with Thornton's work on which Marshall also drew).[105]

V Conclusion

Marshall was certainly not "just" a Classical economist. The whole history of economics would have been very different without Marshall's writings, which one cannot say, for instance, of such later nineteenth century economists as Fawcett or even Sidgwick. But neither can one say that his work would even have existed, let alone taken the form it did, without his Classical inheritance. The essential point is that Marshall, more aware than any of the leading economists of his time of the achievements of Classical economics, made the marginal revolution "work" by plugging it into the general circuit of the existing body of economic literature in England. This not only helped others to grasp the nature of the new forms of analysis and to see their potential, it also enabled the new forms of analysis to develop enormously, not least in Marshall's own hands, so that their achievements distracted attention from the Classical inheritance and ultimately produced a Gestalt switch for economists. Marginalism, once Marshall had shown its role, was recognised as (to use the terminology of the philosophy of science) much more than a progressive scientific research programme: and for this perception, the work of Marshall is to a very considerable extent responsible. Unfortunately, in the very process of "plugging in" the new forms of analysis, Marshall was led to make claims about the nature of classical analysis – notably in the Appendices to the *Principles* – which are difficult to interpret as anything other than an exaggerated "pietas" with rhetorical undertones. To many this is probably a great deal less objectionable than the posture adopted by any self-proclaimed intellectual revolutionary striving to attract public attention and caring little for elementary accuracy, let alone scholarship, in his references to his predecessors. Viewed from the perspective of a century later the effect is nonetheless unfortunate.

104. *MCC*, pp. 18, 256; *OP*, pp. 5–6, 22, 52. See, however, 1879*a*, pp. 155–6 where a possible real balance effect is ignored; see also Patinkin, 1965, pp. 186–8, 603–10.
105. *MCC*, pp. 38–9, 43–5; *OP*, pp. 177, 267–8 (and see also pp. 36, 44); *EEW*, 1, pp. 165–77; Whitaker, 1975, 1, pp. 164–5; Thornton, 1802, pp. 232–3; Hicks, 1967, pp. 174–88.

When Marshall had done his work, the change of focus thus produced so affected economists that they came to interpret Marshall himself in purely static, *post-Marshallian,* terms thus *mis*-interpreting and, not infrequently, maligning him. This in turn led other commentators to react by making unsustainable claims about the "Ricardian" nature of Marshall's analysis.[106]

The essential truth is clear enough: Marshall started economics by reading J. S. Mill, and, while still an able mathematician in the 1870s, followed a "research programme" of mathematising parts of Mill.[107] In the course of his research he read more extensively in classical literature and reacted strongly against the claims of those like Jevons who sought to neglect the classical inheritance. He was influenced by Jevons, however, by the Austrians, and by Walker, as well as by Cournot and Thünen, and he had the breadth of vision to appreciate the necessity of connecting their work with the classical apparatus in which his own beginnings as an economist lay. His life's work then involved reconciling these two streams, developing the more recent one in its own right, but always restraining it by appeals to factual information, economic history, and his own highly developed sense of economic reality. The result was a synthesis which, at least as far as English economics went, made the marginal revolution work. Without Marshall, the message of the bewildered Cairnes on reading Jevons might have become the theme of many economists of a later generation.

> So far as I can see, economic truths are not discoverable through the instrumentality of Mathematics. If this view be unsound, there is at hand an easy means of refutation – the production of an economic truth, not before known, which has been thus arrived at; but I am not aware that up to the present any such evidence has been furnished of the efficacy of the mathematical method.[108]

By the time Marshall died the younger generation were in no doubt, as a result of his powers of analysis, synthesis, and exposition, as to what

106. See note 30 above.
107. See also Hicks, 1976, p. 368. In correcting Keynes's account of the development of Marshall's ideas, Hicks wrote, "It is now quite clear that that is all wrong. Marshall began, as one would expect, from Mill. He does not stress the filiation to Mill, since he was conscious of moving on from Mill, and wished to call attention to his differences from Mill. Yet Mill is the basis from which he starts".
108. Cairnes, 1875, pp. vi–vii. Schabas, 1985, has pointed out that nonetheless Cairnes (and J. S. Mill) had more in common with the general methodological position of the post-1870 marginalists than with the Historical School; see also Black, 1960. But, as Schabas argued, a gulf existed between the Mill–Cairnes continuation of the Classical thinking and the post-1870 developments, concerning mathematical (and mathematically inspired) theorising. Marshall was effectively able, without ever overplaying the role of mathematics, to bridge that gulf.

these truths were. Economics as a subject looked very different from that which Cairnes knew.

References

Andreano, R. L. (1965). "Alfred Marshall's *Industry and Trade:* A Neglected Classic in Economic History". In Andreano (ed.), *New Views on American Economic Development.* Cambridge, Mass.: Shenkman.

Angell, J. W. (1926). *The Theory of International Prices.* Cambridge, Mass.: Harvard University Press.

Ashley, W. J. (1891). "The Rehabilitation of Ricardo", *Economic Journal* 1:474–89.

Babbage, C. (1832). *On the Economy of Machinery and Manufactures.* London: Knight.

Bharadwaj, K. (1972). "Marshall on Pigou's *Wealth and Welfare*", *Economica* N.S. 39:32–46.

Birch, T. D. (1985). "Marshall and Keynes Revisited", *Journal of Economic Issues* 19:194–200.

Black, R. D. C. (1960). "Jevons and Cairnes", *Economica* N.S. 27:214–32.

(1981). "W. S. Jevons, 1835–82". In D. P. O'Brien and J. R. Presley (eds.), *Pioneers of Modern Economics in Britain.* London: Macmillan.

Blandy, R. (1967). "Marshall on Human Capital: A Note", *Journal of Political Economy* 75:874–5.

Blaug, M. (1958a). "The Classical Economists and the Factory Acts – A Reexamination". Reprinted in A. W. Coats (ed.), *The Classical Economists and Economic Policy.* London: Methuen, 1971.

(1958b). *Ricardian Economics.* New Haven: Yale University Press.

Blitch, C. P. (1985). "The Genesis of Chamberlinian Monopolistic Competition Theory: Addendum", *History of Political Economy* 17:395–402.

Bowley, M. E. A. (1937). *Nassau Senior and Classical Economics.* London: Allen and Unwin.

Buchanan, D. H. (1929). "The Historical Approach to Rent and Price Theory", *Economica* 9:123–55.

Cairnes, J. E. (1874). *Some Leading Principles of Political Economy Newly Expounded.* London: Macmillan.

(1875). *The Character and Logical Method of Political Economy.* London: Macmillan.

Chamberlin, E. H. (1961). "Origin and Early Development of Monopolistic Competition Theory", *Quarterly Journal of Economics* 75:515–43.

Chasse, J. D. (1984). "Marshall, the Human Agent and Economic Growth", *History of Political Economy* 16:381–404.

Chipman, J. S. (1965). "A Survey of the Theory of International Trade: Part 2, the Neo-Classical Theory", *Econometrica* 33:685–760.

Coase, R. H. (1984). "Alfred Marshall's Mother and Father", *History of Political Economy* 16:519–27.

Collard, D. (1968). Introduction and editorial material in J. E. Tozer, *Mathematical Investigation of the Effect of Machinery (1838)*. Reprinted, New York: Kelley.

Creedy, J. (1986). "On the King-Davenant 'Law' of Demand", *Scottish Journal of Political Economy* 33:193–212.

Davies, D. G. (1963). "A Note on Marshallian versus Walrasian Stability Conditions", *Canadian Journal of Economics* 29:535–40.

Dooley, P. C. (1983). "Consumer's Surplus: Marshall and his Critics", *Canadian Journal of Economics* 16:26–38.

Edgeworth, F. Y. (1925). *Papers Relating to Political Economy*. 3 vols. London: Macmillan.

Ekelund, R. B., and Hébert R. F. (1985). "Consumer Surplus: the First Hundred Years", *History of Political Economy* 17:419–54.

Eshag, E. (1963). *From Marshall to Keynes*. Oxford: Blackwell.

Frisch, R. (1950). "Alfred Marshall's Theory of Value", *Quarterly Journal of Economics* 64:495–524.

Gårdlund, T. (1958). *The Life of Knut Wicksell*. Stockholm: Almqvist and Wiksell.

Gee, J. M. A. (1983). "Marshall's Views on 'Short Period' Value Formation", *History of Political Economy* 15:181–205.

Gerbier, G. (1976). *Alfred Marshall. Théoricien de l'Action Efficace et Critique Radical de l'Economie Pure*. Doctoral thesis, Grenoble.

Groenewegen, P. (nd). "Marshall on Ricardo" (mimeo).

Guillebaud, C. W. (1971). "Some Personal Reminiscences of Alfred Marshall", *History of Political Economy* 3:1–8.

Harrison, R. (1963). "Two Early Articles by Alfred Marshall", *Economic Journal* 73:422–30.

Hébert, R. F., and Link, A. N. (1982). *The Entrepreneur*. New York: Praeger.

Hébert, R. F., and Ekelund, R. B. (1984). "Welfare Economics". In J. Greedy and D. P. O'Brien (eds.), *Economic Analysis in Historical Perspective*. London: Butterworths.

Hicks, J. R. (1967). *Critical Essays in Monetary Theory*. Oxford: Clarendon.

(1976). Review of *EEW*. *Economic Journal* 86:367–9.

Hollander, S. (1979). *The Economics of David Ricardo*. Toronto: University of Toronto Press.

Hutchison, T. W. (1952). "Some Questions about Ricardo", *Economica* N.S. 19:415–32.

(1956). *A Review of Economic Doctrines 1870–1929*. Oxford: Clarendon.

(1978). *On Revolutions and Progress in Economic Knowledge*. Cambridge: Cambridge University Press.

James, M. (1977). "Pierre-Louis Roderer, Jean-Baptiste Say, and the Concept of *Industrie*", *History of Political Economy* 9:455–75.

Jensen, H. E. (1983). "J. M. Keynes as a Marshallian", *Journal of Economic Issues* 17:67–94.

(1985). "Marshall Revisited: A Reply", *Journal of Economic Issues* 19:967–74.

Jevons, W. S. (1879). *The Theory of Political Economy.* 2d ed. London: Macmillan. Reprinted, ed. R. D. C. Black. London: Penguin, 1970.

Kaiser, T. E. (1980). "Politics and Political Economy in the Thought of the Ideologues", *History of Political Economy* 12:141–60.

Keynes, J. M. (1911). Review of I. Fisher, *The Purchasing Power of Money. Economic Journal* 21:393–8.

Koolman, G. (1971). "Say's Conception of the Role of the Entrepreneur", *Economica* N.S. 38:269–86.

Levine, A. L. (1980). "Increasing Returns, the Competitive Model and the Enigma that was Alfred Marshall", *Scottish Journal of Political Economy* 27:260–75.

(1983). "Marshall's *Principles* and the 'Biological Viewpoint': A Reconsideration", *Manchester School* 51:276–93.

Liebhafsky, H. H. (1955). "A Curious Case of Neglect: Marshall's *Industry and Trade*", *Canadian Journal of Economics and Political Science* 21:339–53.

Loasby, B. J. (1978). "Whatever Happened to Marshall's Theory of Value?", *Scottish Journal of Political Economy* 25:1–12.

McCready, H. W. (1955). "Alfred Marshall and Tariff Reform, 1903. Some Unpublished Letters", *Journal of Political Economy* 63:259–67.

Marshall, A. (1874). See Harrison, R. (1963).

(1876). "Mr. Mill's Theory of Value", *Fortnightly Review*, April. Reprinted in *Memorials* 119–33.

(1879*b*). *The Pure Theory of (Domestic) Values.* Reprinted London: London School of Economics, 1930, 3d impression 1949. Also in *EEW*, 2, pp. 186–236.

(1883). Published as "Alfred Marshall's Lectures on Progress and Poverty", ed. G. J. Stigler and R. H. Coase, *Journal of Law and Economics* 12(1969):181–226.

(1884), "Where to House the London Poor", *Contemporary Review*, February: 224–331. Reprinted in *Memorials*, pp. 142–51.

(1885*a*). Contributions (pp. 76–9, 82, 173–99, 213–14, 505) to *Industrial Remuneration Conference. Report of the Proceedings and Papers . . . under the Presidency of Sir Charles W. Dilke*. London: Cassel.

(1885*b*). "Present Position of Political Economy", *The Times*, 2 June (11e).

(1886). "Political Economy and Outdoor Relief", *The Times*, 15 February (13b).

(1887*a*). Preface to L. L. F. R. Price, *Industrial Peace: Its Advantages, Methods and Difficulties*. London: Macmillan. Substantially reproduced in *Memorials:* 212–26.

(1887*b*). "The Theory of Business Profits", *Quarterly Journal of Economics* 1:477–81.

(1887*c*). "Is London Healthy?", *Pall Mall Gazette*, 13 April: 3.

(1891*a*). "The Post Office and Private Enterprise", *The Times*, 24 March (11e).

(1891*b*). "The Post Office and Private Enterprise", *The Times*, 6 April (13b–c).

(1892*a*). "The Poor Law in Relation to State-Aided Pensions", *Economic Journal* 2:186–91.

(1892*b*). "Poor-Law Reform", *Economic Journal* 2:371–9.

(1893). "On Rent", *Economic Journal* 3:74–90. Reprinted in *Variorum*, pp. 492–512.

(1898). "Distribution and Exchange", *Economic Journal* 8:37–59. Partly reprinted in *Memorials*, pp. 312–18; *Variorum*, pp. 62–75, 229–33.

(1903). Letter to F. Manners-Sutton, secretary of the Unionist Free Food League. Published in *The Times*, 23 November (10e).

(1904). "Discussion of Mr. Schuster's Paper", *Journal of the Institute of Bankers* 25:94–8.

(1905*a*). "Education and the Classics", *The Times*, 3 March (15a-b).

(1905*b*). "Education for Business Men", *The Times*, 23 November (4c).

(1905*c*). "Education for Business Men", *The Times*, 18 December (13d).

(1905*d*). "University Education for Business Men", *The Times*, 29 December (5d).

(1907). "The Social Possibilities of Economic Chivalry", *Economic Journal* 17:7–29. Reprinted, with alterations, in *Memorials*, pp. 323–46.

(1909). "Rates and Taxes on Land Values", *The Times*, 16 November (10c).

(1916). "The Need for More Taxation", *Economist*, 30 December: 1228.

(1917). "National Taxation after the War". In W. H. Dawson (ed.), *After-war Problems*. London: Allen and Unwin.

Marshall, A., and Marshall, M. P. (1879*a*). *The Economics of Industry*. London: Macmillan.

Marshall, M. P. (1947). *What I Remember*. Cambridge: Cambridge University Press.

Maunder, W. F. (1970). *Bibliography of Index Numbers*. London: Athlone Press.

Mill, J. S. (1848–71). *Principles of Political Economy*. 7 eds., 1848–71. Ed., J. M. Robson, 2 vols. Toronto: University of Toronto Press, 1965.

Mises, L. von (1912). *The Theory of Money and Credit*. Trans. H. E. Batson. London: Cape.

Newman, P. (1960). "The Erosion of Marshall's Theory of Value", *Quarterly Journal of Economics* 74:587–601.

O'Brien, D. P. (1970). *J. R. McCulloch. A Study in Classical Economics*. London: Allen and Unwin.

(1975). *The Classical Economists*. Oxford: Clarendon.

(1977). "Torrens, McCulloch and Disraeli", *Scottish Journal of Political Economy* 24:1–18.

(1984). "Monetary Economics". In J. Creedy and D. P. O'Brien (eds.), *Economic Analysis in Historical Perspective*. London: Butterworths.

Overstone, Lord (1837–48). *Tracts and Other Publications on Metallic and Paper Currency*. London: privately printed, 1857.

Parsons, T. (1931). "Wants and Activities in Marshall", *Quarterly Journal of Economics* 46:101–40.

(1932). "Economics and Sociology: Marshall in Relation to the Thought of his Time", *Quarterly Journal of Economics* 46:316–47.

Patinkin, D. (1965). *Money, Interest and Prices*, 2d ed. New York: Harper and Row.

Pennington, J. (1826–40). *Economic Writings*. Ed. R. S. Sayers. London: London School of Economics, 1968.

Peterson, S. (1957). "Antitrust and the Classic Model", *American Economic Review* 47:60–78.

Petridis, A. (1973). "Alfred Marshall's Attitudes to the Economic Analysis of Trade Unions: A Case of Anomalies in the Competitive System", *History of Political Economy* 5:165–98.

Phillips, J. D. (1979). "The Theory of Small Enterprise: Smith, Mill, Marshall, and Marx", *Explorations in Economic History* 16:331–40.

Rainelli, M. (1983). "Entrepreneur et Profits dans les 'Principes' de John Stuart Mill et d'Alfred Marshall", *Revue Economique* 34:794–810.

Ricardo, D. (1816). *Proposal for an Economical and Secure Currency*. In P. Sraffa (ed.), *Works and Correspondence of David Ricardo*, Vol. 4. Cambridge: Cambridge University Press, 1951.

(1817–21). *On the Principles of Political Economy and Taxation*. In P. Sraffa (ed.), *Works and Correspondence of David Ricardo*, Vol. 1. Cambridge: Cambridge University Press, 1951.

Robbins, L. (1930). "On a Certain Ambiguity in the Conception of Stationary Equilibrium", *Economic Journal* 40:194–214.

(1952). *The Theory of Economic Policy in English Classical Political Economy*. London: Macmillan.

(1958). *Robert Torrens and the Evolution of Classical Economics*. London: Macmillan.

Robertson, H. M. (1970). "Alfred Marshall's Aims and Methods Illustrated from his Treatment of Distribution", *History of Political Economy* 2:1–65.

Robinson, J. V. (1933). *The Economics of Imperfect Competition*. London: Macmillan.

Samuels, W. J. (1966). *The Classical Theory of Economic Policy*. Cleveland, Oh.: World Publishing.

Say, J. B. (1803). *A Treatise on Political Economy*. 4th ed., 1819. Trans. C. R. Prinsep. Reprinted New York: Kelley, 1971.

Schabas, M. (1985). "Some Reactions to Jevons' Mathematical Program: The Case of Mill and Cairnes", *History of Political Economy* 17:337–53.

Schumpeter, J. A. (1954). *History of Economic Analysis*. London: Allen and Unwin.

Senior, N. W. (1826). Appendix to Whately (1826).

Shove, G. F. (1942). "The Place of Marshall's *Principles* in the Development of Economic Theory", *Economic Journal* 52:294–329.

Smith, A. (1776). *An Inquiry into the Nature and Causes of the Wealth of Nations*. Ed. R. H. Campbell, A. S. Skinner, and W. B. Todd. 2 vols. Oxford: Clarendon.

Solow, R. M. (1987). "What Do We Know That Francis Amasa Walker Didn't?", *History of Political Economy* 19:183–9.

Spengler, J. J. (1955). "Marshall on the Population Question", *Population Studies* 8:264–87; 9: 56–66.

Stigler, G. J. (1941). *Production and Distribution Theories.* New York: Macmillan.

(1955). "The Nature and Role of Originality in Scientific Progress". Reprinted in *Essays in the History of Economics.* Chicago: University of Chicago Press, 1965.

(1957). "Perfect Competition Historically Contemplated", *Journal of Political Economy* 65:1–17.

(1962). "Marshall's *Principles* after Guillebaud", *Journal of Political Economy* 70:282–6.

Stykolt, S. (1956). "A Curious Case of Neglect: Marshall on the Tangency Solution", *Canadian Journal of Economics and Political Science* 22:251.

Thornton, H. (1802). *An Enquiry into the Nature and Effects of the Paper Credit of Great Britain.* Reprint, ed. F. A. von Hayek. London: Allen and Unwin, 1939.

Walker, F. A. (1876). *The Wages Question.* London: Macmillan.

(1887). "The Source of Business Profits", *Quarterly Journal of Economics* 1:265–88.

Walker, L. W. (1983). "A Comment on 'Marshall and the Classical Tradition' ", *Journal of Post Keynesian Economics* 5:664–6.

Wearne, B. C. (1981). "Talcott Parsons's Appraisal and Critique of Alfred Marshall", *Social Research* 48:816–51.

Whately, R. (1826). *Elements of Logic.* London: Mawman.

Whitaker, J. K. (1972). "Alfred Marshall: the Years 1877 to 1885", *History of Political Economy* 4:1–61.

(1974). "The Marshallian System in 1881: Distribution and Growth", *Economic Journal* 84:1–17.

(1975). Introductory and editorial material in *EEW.*

(1977). "Some Neglected Aspects of Alfred Marshall's Economic and Social Thought", *History of Political Economy* 9:161–97.

Wicksell, K. (1898). *Interest and Prices.* Trans. R. F. Kahn. London: Macmillan, 1936.

Wood, J. C. (1982). "Alfred Marshall and the Origins of his 'Memorandum on the Fiscal Policy of International Trade', (1903): Some Unpublished Correspondence", *Australian Economic Papers* 21:261–9.

Worcester, D. A. (1946). "A Reconsideration of the Theory of Rent", *American Economic Review* 36:258–77.

Young, A. (1812). *An Enquiry into the Progressive Value of Money in England as Marked by the Price of Agricultural Products.* London: McMillan.

The Economic Journal, **98** (*March* 1988), 104–125
Printed in Great Britain

LIONEL CHARLES ROBBINS, 1898–1984*

D. P. O'Brien

Lionel Robbins was a leading figure in what Harry Johnson (1972, p. 835) has called 'the second golden age of British economics', a leading British academic, a prolific writer on economics, and a majestic public figure whose fame extended far beyond the narrow academic community. All this makes it difficult to write about Lionel Robbins – an outsize figure – within a small compass.[1] The approach adopted here is to intertwine the academic output with the biographical framework so as to produce a form of literary biography. The discussion begins with an account of Robbin's origins, covering the years up to 1920. The account of the following two decades provides some picture of the rising academic and the pugnacious controversialist. A brief account of his war service, 1940–5, is followed by a discussion of his rise to more general public prominence in the post-war years and then by an account of his last two decades as a leader not only of the community of British academic economists but also of the wider academic community, following the publication of the Robbins Report.

I. ORIGINS[2]

Robbins came of country origins. The family was nonconformist by religion, but at quite an early age Robbins lost his religious faith, as a result of the successive deaths of the mother and of a younger sister. He became a life-long agnostic, although not bigotedly anti-religious. Perhaps partly because of the loss of his mother he became very close to his father. Although, after Robbins's return from World War I, there was a period of partial estrangement, this was only temporary; and the influence of the father on the son is evident from a study of Robbins's writings in the 1930s, not only in such matters as agricultural cartels, and production, but also in other, more personal, ways. Robbins's splendid rolling literary style, which graces not only his *Autobiography* but all his writings, has marked similarities to that of his father, who made a number of public utterances in connection with his duties in the National Farmers' Union; and the elder Robbins's pugnacious controversial style was to find reflection in Robbins's own contributions to debates in the 1930s.

Robbins was educated, as a result of a deliberate decision not to send him to a public school, at Southall County School in Middlesex. From there he went briefly to University College London and then into World War I. He eventually saw active service, and was wounded; he bore some marks of this to the end of his days. He gained early administrative experience in the process

* I am extremely grateful to John Creedy for his comments on an earlier draft of this paper.
[1] A full length study is to be published by Macmillan.
[2] See Robbins's splendid *Autobiography* (1971*a*) for more details of his early life.

of demobilisation and then went through a socialist phase. But he quickly became disillusioned by the 'fun revolutionaries'. As he recounts in his *Autobiography*, he attempted, as a former army officer, to explain to some of them that without the army on your side a revolution was not likely to succeed;

> To this, as I thought, very cogent and simple argument, a young woman, very plain with an underslung jaw and fingers like raw carrots, exclaimed with deep seriousness: 'but we should give ourselves to the officers for the sake of the revolution.' At this point something happened in my head analogous to what happens in the head when, after a stuffy cold, one succeeds in clearing one's nose. How could I take these people seriously? What was I doing in such a set? (1971*a*, p. 65).

But he had nowhere to turn. Disenchanted with socialism, he did not know what course to pursue. But with funds provided by his then partially-estranged father, following an amazingly coincidental meeting in a tea shop when Robbins was on his way to accept a job with a stockbroker, Robbins went to LSE (1971*a*, pp. 69–71).

II. 1920–1940

(i) *Development of an Academic Career*

Robbins's three years as a student at LSE came to him both as a revelation and as a liberation. The teachers who had the greatest influence upon him, in the three years up to his graduation with First Class Honours in 1923, were Cannan, Dalton, Wallas, and Gregory. Intellectually, the most important input came from Cannan.

Cannan had a very sharp mind, a wide-ranging knowledge of economic (especially Classical) literature, and an impatience with elaborate theoretical structures. He wielded Occam's Razor with enthusiasm; and it says much for his teaching that Robbins, a man whose mind delighted in abstraction, should have found him so very stimulating.[3]

Graham Wallas is particularly important, not so much perhaps for his advice to Robbins to memorise his lectures and practise delivery in front of a mirror – Robbins tried this only once – as for having turned Robbins into a Benthamite.[4] (Sir) T. E. Gregory, to whose teaching Robbins was to pay tribute many years later (Robbins, 1971*b*), must have contributed to Robbins's detailed appreciation of the issues involved in the Currency and Banking controversy.[5]

The association with Dalton was to prove of fundamental importance for Robbins's career; but it was by no means intellectually negligible, for Dalton was an accomplished economist, and one of Robbins's most famous early articles stems from a passage in Dalton's *Public Finance*[6]. Robbins, through the intervention of Dalton, obtained on graduation a job as a research assistant to

[3] Robbins (1935, p. 394); see also Robbins (1971*a*, pp. 83–6).

[4] Robbins (1971*a*, pp. 86–9, 104); Robbins (1965).

[5] See in particular Gregory (1928).

[6] Robbins (1930*a*); Dalton (1929, p. 106). The article is discussed further below.

Beveridge. This was particularly fortunate on a personal level since, shortly after graduating, Robbins had become engaged to Iris Gardner, sister of an old friend, the artist Cliver Gardner. They were married in the summer of 1924; and though it may seem impertinent for an outsider to speculate, it is difficult to resist the thought that Robbins's strong attachment to marriage as an institution, which was to appear at a number of points in his economic writings, especially those on taxation, owed a great deal to his own marriage.

The year of working for Beveridge was followed by a Lectureship at New College, Oxford in 1924, a Lectureship at LSE in 1925–7, a Fellowship and Lectureship at New College, 1927–9, and appointment to the LSE chair in 1929. At quite an early stage, Robbins began publishing. The first publication I have traced was a review which appeared in 1925 (Robbins, 1925) – and interestingly, in the light of subsequent events, it contained an attack (quite unprovoked it would seem) on Keynes for wishing to have monetary policy influenced by popular sentiment. This was followed by a book, *Wages* (Robbins, 1925/6), and a series of articles including a review, in 1927, of a book by Hawtrey (Robbins, 1927). This review is significant in that it was to be partly incorporated five years later in Robbins's celebrated *Essay on the Nature and Significance of Economic Science*. In this review he attacked the idea that economics and ethics were necessarily intertwined, arguing that it was fundamentally necessary to separate the two.

Despite intimations at Oxford that premature publication might be seen as exhibitionist (Robbins, 1980*a*, p. 66), Robbins continued to publish and to establish a name for himself, particularly with the celebrated article on the elasticity of demand for income in terms of effort, using a concept from the partial equilibrium analysis of which he was later to fight shy, to counter Frank Knight's contention that the individual labour supply function was necessarily of negative slope.[7]

Robbins's argument, developed before the work of Hicks and Allen on income and substitution effects, was that the sign of the labour supply response to a change in net remuneration was indeterminate – it depended on the elasticity of demand for income in terms of effort. To develop this ingenious employment of the Marshallian elasticity tool Robbins, with some help from Hicks, posited a demand curve for income in terms of effort (thus producing an outlay rectangle of 'effort') and an associated total outlay (of effort) curve. He argued, in amplification of Dalton's original position on the issue, that there was no *a priori* theoretical reasoning which would indicate the necessary size of the elasticity involved.

Robbins's association with Dalton had continued while at Oxford. Dalton, however, lured Robbins back from Oxford to LSE and to the chair – or rather to a chair since the one left vacant by the death of Allyn Young was never filled. Dalton undoubtedly had to fight for this. He noted in his diary:

> Great jealousy of Lionel in the Ghetto, but I think I shall succeed in getting him back.[8]

[7] Knight (1921, p. 117); Robbins (1930*a*).
[8] Dalton (1986*a*, p. 53); see also Robbins (1971*a*, p. 122).

Laski, with whom Robbins had already developed a somewhat troubled relationship during his third year as an undergraduate, opposed the appointment.[9]

Dalton showed considerable disinterestedness in securing this appointment – something to which Robbins, who felt it must have been clear to Dalton that he did not sympathise with the latter's political position, paid tribute in an obituary article (Robbins, 1962). But the truth is that Dalton was disappointed with the very unsocialist turn which the LSE Department of Economics took under Robbins's direction,[10] even though he remained Robbins's mentor and intervened on his behalf during the dispute with Keynes over tariffs which is referred to below.[11]

The appointment to the LSE Chair had been, to a considerable extent, on the basis of promise rather than proven performance, and the publications which raised Robbins to prominence mostly appeared after his return to LSE in 1929. Dalton was at first pleased with his protégé's progress (Dalton, 1986*a*, pp. 67–8). But as Robbins's own work developed, his thinking became increasingly dominated by the work of Austrian writers, especially Mayer, Mises, and Hayek, and by that of Wicksteed. This not only moved him in an unsocialist direction; it had two important intellectual effects of a more general nature. Firstly, it directed him increasingly away from partial equilibrium analysis towards an emphasis upon Austrian general equilibrium. Secondly, it moved him in a subjectivist direction.[12]

Two particular outcomes of these developments in his thought were an article on the nature of equilibrium in this JOURNAL in 1930 and an article on costs in the JOURNAL in 1934. In the first of these Robbins argued that many of the disputes about the nature of factor rewards stemmed from an ambiguity over the nature of equilibrium. In a completely general framework, all factor supplies had to be treated as variable, by allowing for alternative uses (including own-consumption), so that factor rewards were necessary rewards in the particular uses to which factors were put (Robbins, 1930*b*).

In the second article Robbins took Wicksteed's opportunity cost approach as the basis for an argument that, costs having no meaning except in terms of the valuation of output foregone by employing factors in one way rather than another, the (then recent) cost controversies (involving Sraffa, D. H. Robertson and others) were completely beside the point. For the cost of expanding output could not be considered in *partial* equilibrium: it was necessary to approach the matter from a general equilibrium point of view and to consider demand as well. In particular, if increased output were a response to increased demand, demand for some other product must have been reduced and thus resources must have been freed to enable output of the now-favoured industry to expand without incurring increased factor costs. But if output were expanded without

[9] On Robbins's troubled relations with Laski see Robbins (1971*a*, pp. 80–3, 94–5, 124).

[10] Pimlott (1985, pp. 160–2, 215); Dalton (1986*a*, p. 165).

[11] Pimlott (1985, p. 162); Dalton (1986*a*, pp. 122–4).

[12] There are ambiguities over the precise nature of this subjectivism. See the important article by Wiseman (1985).

such a demand adjustment, factor costs, representing preferred alternative outputs, would be higher at higher levels of output.[13]

(ii) *The Nature and Significance of Economic Science*

The subjectivist and general equilibrium influences also combined with his dissatisfaction at Cannan's materialist definition of economics to result in Robbins's most famous single work, the *Essay on the Nature and Significance of Economic Science*, the first edition of which appeared in 1932. In this book Robbins also sought to separate economics and ethics, and to distinguish value judgements from those parts of economics which were 'scientific'. This led in turn to the exclusion from scientific discourse of all forms of interpersonal comparison – a frontal attack upon the kind of welfare economics associated with Pigou, which was the then dominant orthodoxy. Robbins was not arguing, it should be emphasised, that economists should not enter into policy debates; rather he was arguing that they should make clear the conclusions which were arrived at as a result of the use of the tools of 'scientific' economics, and distinguish these clearly from the imposition of value judgements about the desirability of different outcomes.

Robbins himself, of course, entered freely and with vigour into policy debates, and it is surprising that some critics (Fraser, 1932; 1937) should have seen him as attempting to deprive economists of their role in influencing policy. Robbins in fact wrote extensively on matters of economic welfare, covering such issues as equality, State intervention, redistribution, taxation, socialism, competition and economic growth. He did so from an explicitly Utilitarian standpoint – the Greatest Happiness principle seemed to him 'better, more sensible, more humane, more agreeable to the moral conscience' than any other (Robbins, 1965, p. 12; 1970*a*, p. 80). It was a salutary test for legislators and administrators. But he wished to introduce a demarcation criterion between science and non-science: and the value judgements necessary for policy conclusions, including the conventional but scientifically unsustainable interpersonal comparisons, definitely fell into the latter category. Predictions derived from economic models were scientific; choice between different economic policies, the different outcomes of which could be predicted by economic models, involved extra-scientific value judgements.

The sources for this methodological position were, unsurprisingly, David Hume, Max Weber, the Austrians and Wicksteed. Yet Robbins succeeded in welding the sources together in a way which produced an *Essay* the influence of which is still felt today.

The distinction between positive ('wertfrei') and normative economics did not, however, carry Robbins to the position of the post-Friedman 'positive economics'. For that, which is in turn post-Popper, involves an emphasis on falsification which Robbins did not accept. Despite some ambiguities in his

[13] Robbins (1934*a*). Elsewhere Robbins was blunt about what he regarded as intellectual confusion: 'until the propositions which Wicksteed stressed...are incorporated into the general body of cost analysis, the whole controversy will continue to present an appearance of paradox and unreality – an intellectual backwater, full no doubt of strange fish and queer animalculae, but lacking that relation to the main stream of general equilibrium theory which alone can give it real significance'. Robbins (1933, p. xv).

treatment of such issues, and an apparent unwillingness to resolve these, his position essentially was this. Economic models were (as with Cairnes) necessarily true if they were arrived at logically from plausible assumptions; empirical work was essentially concerned not with *falsification*, but with *verification* – with testing whether the underlying conditions assumed in constructing the model itself did in fact hold in the particular case under consideration.[14]

Nevertheless, the ambiguities remained: and his *Economic Causes of War* of 1939 involved testing, and falsifying, the quasi-Marxist concept of war as the product of capitalist class interests.

The *Essay* was undoubtedly of fundamental importance and one of the two major methodological statements of this century (the other being Friedman's). Although it naturally attracted a great deal of comment, much of it critical, Robbins made relatively few concessions to his critics in his second edition of 1935, other than stressing that he had no intention of excluding economists from policy debates.

(iii) *National and International Liberalism*

Other high points of his published output during the 1930s were *Economic Planning and International Order* of 1937, and the *Economic Basis of Class Conflict* and the *Economic Causes of War* both of 1939. The message of the 1937 book is that the way forward to a better world order lies not in nationalism, authoritarianism, and the regulation of trade but in international liberalism. But just as national internal freedom of trade required a strong superstructure of a State, so *international* liberalism required a *supra*-national authority. Thus Robbins was an advocate of Federalism, with the devolution to a federal authority of crucial national powers so as to ensure freedom of trade and of factor movements.

The emphasis upon the global aspect is important: Robbins deliberately and explicitly adopted, like J. S. Mill, the standpoint in his book that the overriding concern was *world* and not *national* welfare.[15] But from a national as well as a global standpoint planning was, in Robbins's view, a recipe for disaster. It led necessarily to socialism; and socialism was an inherently faulty concept of economic organisation. As Robbins argued in his *The Great Depression* of 1934, following Mises's famous critique in *Gemeinwirtschaft*, it lacked a resource allocation system. Resources had to be allocated so as to equalise marginal returns, and this could not be achieved by a *political* process. It was necessary to *know* not only prices which consumers *would be* prepared to pay, but also the opportunity costs of factors in different occupations, in order to equalise marginal revenue products in different factor employments. This raised insoluble computational problems. In a competitive system the problem is solved by comparing costs and prices. But costs embody competitive factor market information about opportunity costs, which is not available under socialism. 'Playing at competition' does not work because resources – including

[14] See Blaug (1980, ch. 3) for a discussion of 'verification'.

[15] See Robbins (1937, pp. 9, 41n, 55, 60, 309–27); (1971*a*, pp. 159–62).

entire firms – have to be free to move in and out of industries. This could not be allowed to happen under socialism, a system which lost sight of the fundamental distinction between the *technical*, involving the satisfaction of one end, and the *economic* which involved the allocation of resources so as to balance the satisfaction of many competing ends.[16]

The fundamental message of the 1939 books was that the Marxist concept of class was completely misleading. Conflict occurred not between *horizontal* strata in society but between *vertically*-constituted groups each seeking special privileges for their particular industry or other interest. Protectionism was a manifestation of the activities of these vertically-constituted groups.

The *Economic Basis of Class Conflict* also marked a cautious shift in the direction of approval of counter-cyclical public expenditure, even though the discussion emphasised – correctly – many of the difficulties involved in the monetary and open-economy aspects (Robbins, 1939*a*, pp. 217–27, 256–77).

The *Economic Causes of War* reviewed, and found wanting, the standard themes in the Marxist literature in this area – under-consumption and lack of investment outlets as causes of war. Having found this theoretical structure falsified by the evidence, Robbins, consistently with the position in *Economic Planning and International Order*, advanced the argument that national sovereignty itself was the cause of war. The answer to war then lay in his plan for international Federalism.[17]

(iv) *The 'feud' with Keynes*

But dominating the whole decade 1930–40 was Robbins's long-running controversy with Keynes, which related to a significant extent to Robbins's opposition to protection. This was, however, by no means the whole of the story.

Mention has already been made of Robbins's attack on Keynes in his first publication. It is then not the case that the tensions originated in the Economic Advisory Council, although they certainly developed to a very considerable extent in that context because it was there that the first real clash over tariffs occurred. Both Dalton (1986*a*, pp. 122–4) and Robbins (1971*a*, pp. 150–2) have written their accounts of this episode, and it has also been the subject of scholarly outside study (Howson and Winch, 1977, pp. 57–63). But it does rather seem as if Robbins became a little dominated by this dispute – indeed it was Dalton's view that 'he over-cultivates his feud with Keynes' (Dalton, 1986*a*, p. 165). Be that as it may, the rift was genuine enough. Partly it related to the question of free trade. Throughout the 1930s Robbins constantly reiterated the case against protectionism, determined, it would seem, to run every argument down and expose it as fallacious.[18]

On this Robbins remained unrepentant in later years. He was outraged at Keynes's endorsement of protection, and in one publication even went so far

[16] Robbins (1934*b*, pp. 148–56); see also (1934*c*).

[17] (1939*b*) especially ch. IV.

[18] See in particular Robbins (1931*a*) as an example of this.

as to refer derisively to a 'funk hole' in a way which hints at personal scorn for Keynes as a quasi-conscientious objector.[19]

But the second leg of the disagreement related to macroeconomic policy. Here Robbins put forward a position, most notably in his 1934 book *The Great Depression*, derived from the work of Mises and of Wicksell and, more remotely, from the Currency School. Robbins held that the cause of depression was previous monetary expansion which had altered the relative price levels of consumption and investment goods in such a way as to bring about over-investment. This in turn meant that the only way out of depression was to endure the hangover while resources were freed again from the investment goods industries and a new equilibrium restored.

Monetary expansion made available extra funds to investing entrepreneurs who, faced with newly profitable investment opportunities at the margin because of the fall in the rate of interest, bid resources away from consumption goods industries to investment goods industries. As consumption goods supply curves shifted to the left, their prices rose, and resources were thus freed through the imposition of forced saving. But the bidding for resources by the investment goods industries raised wages: and as the new purchasing power worked its way through the system, this raised the demand for and the prices of consumer goods, restoring their profitability relative to that of investment goods – relative (equilibrium) profitability having been upset by the initial monetary expansion and lowering of the rate of interest. The rise in labour costs thus upset the marginal profitability calculations of the expanding entrepreneurs in the investment goods industries. Initially they sought more credit – this is a crucial weakness of the argument since the whole basis of the model involves a *positive* relationship between demand for credit and profitability – and this produced a new phase of disequilibrium. However, banking prudence eventually called a halt to credit expansion, and half-completed investment schemes were abandoned while, because of various labour market rigidities, re-absorption of the labour thus freed would take a long time.

Monetary expansion was then no cure for unemployment: rather it reactivated the disequilibrium which produced the unemployment in the first place.[20]

Robbins engaged in 'verification' both in an article on the trade cycle and in *The Great Depression*[21] –this has 36 pages of statistical appendices – and was satisfied that the facts assumed by the theory were correct and that it was thus, in terms of his methodology, an appropriate theoretical structure to use in explaining the depression of the 1930s.

Hardly surprisingly, this view was not shared by Keynes and his associates. It is true that Keynes's own position at this time, as expressed in his *Treatise* of 1930, was some considerable distance from that which was finally developed in 1936, and it had, whether acknowledged or not, remarkable Wicksellian

[19] Robbins (1931*b*, p. 100); on Keynes as conscientious objector see Moggridge (1976, pp. 17–9, 168 n7), and Skidelsky (1983, pp. 315–27).

[20] Robbins (1932*b*; 1934*b*, especially pp. 33–40).

[21] Robbins (1932*b*, especially pp. 424–8; 1934*b*).

similarities if not roots. But Keynes's position moved quickly away from this following the publication of his *Treatise* and an acrimonious controversy between London, Vienna and Cambridge ensued. Hayek was brought in as an ally and a Viennese representative, and joined the staff of LSE. Controversy raged in the *Economist*, in *Lloyds Bank Review*, and in the *Banker*,[22] as well as in other publications, with Robbins urging monetary restraint, free trade, a return to the gold standard, and even wage cuts.[23]

In post-war years Robbins was to express bitter contrition for his macroeconomic views of the 1930s.[24] Yet this was both somewhat unnecessary and rather misleading. It was unnecessary in the sense that *The Great Depression* was a far from negligible performance intellectually; and it was misleading in the sense that detailed analysis of Robbins's post-war macroeconomic writing shows that, while he had abandoned the explicitly Austrian elements, the basic analytical framework remained very much intact.

III. 1940–1945

Robbins spent the war years in, and for 1941–5, as Director of, the Economic Section of the Offices of the War Cabinet, an episode to which he devotes an entire chapter in his *Autobiography* (1971*a* ch. VIII). The chapter itself is allusive and somewhat frustrating: but there is no doubt that he was highly effective in his role in government. On the one hand, he organised his fellow economists into a kind of seminar. On the other, Robbins kept open his lines of communication with the powerful politicians and civil servants – in particular he remained on good terms with Dalton and developed, as Meade has indicated, a good working relationship with Sir John Anderson.[25]

As Meade (1984) has put it:

> The Economic Section was in reality a seminar of young academic economists chaired by their Professor, Lionel Robbins. Their day-to-day duty was to prepare essays . . . on the basic economic aspects of the wide range of problems which came up from the various departments for co-ordination at the Cabinet level . . . How easy it would have been for a small academic group to have been totally ineffective with such an assignment. Lionel showed the greatest wisdom and diplomatic skill in confining the work of the Section within manageable bounds and in establishing good relations between the Section and the other departments in Whitehall . . . In very large measure it is to Lionel Robbins, backed by John Anderson, the Minister in charge, and Edward Bridges, the Secretary of the Cabinet, that the country owes the firm establishment of organised professional economic advice in our machinery of government. (pp. 5–6)

Apart from his provision of leadership, Robbins as an economist working in

[22] Robbins made particular use of *Lloyds Bank Review* as a platform for his views.
[23] See Robbins (1934*b*, pp. 69–71, 82–4, 115–7, 160–9, 176–8, 185–9).
[24] (1971*a*, pp. 152–5); (1979*a*, p. 14) (House of Lords speech).
[25] (1971*a*, pp. 173–5); Dalton (1986*b*, pp. 404, 520, 522, 525, 538, 618, 631).

government, contributed in perhaps three particular ways. Firstly, through the application of Austrian general equilibrium analysis (with the emphasis on general rather than equilibrium) he explored the logic of the allocation of raw materials in a war-time economy. The particular lessons which he drew from this, and which he imparted to others, are contained in two post-war publications, *The Economic Problem in Peace and War* (1947) and in an appendix to his *The Economist in the Twentieth Century* (1954). But they may be summarised in the propositions that no industry, or other economic grouping, can be looked at in isolation, and that in allocating resources it is *marginal* valuations which are significant. The economist, as he had emphasised in his pre-war writings, has to be aware of the difference between economics and technology. Whereas technology is concerned with the meeting of one particular end, the economist has to look at a variety of competing ends with their different claims upon resources and to balance these at the margin. Robbins's war-time experiences left him with a clear reinforcement of his view – at a time when many British intellectuals still admired Stalin – that there was no substitute for the price system as an allocation mechanism which would meet these marginalist criteria. He expounded this view, with at times some tongue-in-cheek humour, to a no doubt not entirely appreciative audience at the 1947 Marshall Lectures in Cambridge (Robbins, 1947).

Secondly, he used his position in government service to provide strong support for those like G. C. Allen, also in temporary government service, who were attempting both to resist the efforts of industrialists (in association with some civil servants) to use war allocation as a means to cartelisation, and to lay the basis for the development of a post-war competition policy. Robbins is reticent about this in his *Autobiography*, but the researches of Denys Gribbin have helped to throw some light on the matter. There seems no doubt that Robbins was a powerful and effective force, in association with Hugh Dalton, in pressing for a framework of competition policy and that the post-war developments in this field have their origins in the work of the war-time temporary civil servants (Gribbin, 1977*a*,*b*; 1985). Some of the sharpest remarks in *The Great Depression* are directed at cartels in general, and officially sponsored cartels (especially those associated with the NRA in the United States) in particular (Robbins, 1934*b*, ch. VII). Moreover Robbins held that cartels led to planning and planning led, necessarily, to socialism, an organisational concept which, in his view, led only to economic disaster (Robbins, 1934*b*, pp. 144–59).

Thirdly, Robbins was a skilled and powerful negotiator working with Keynes, their emnity buried, in the dealings with the Americans over the negotiations for the post-war world. These negotiations led to the Bretton Woods system and the IMF and GATT. There is no doubt that Robbins's contribution here was important, and Harrod (1951) has paid tribute to it in his biography of Keynes (pp. 554–5). But the views which Robbins formed at this time, themselves building upon much of his pre-war thinking, were to play a major part in the development of his writings on economic policy in the years after the war.

IV. POST-WAR DEVELOPMENTS

(i) *Rebuilding*

Robbins seems to have had little difficulty in deciding not to remain a civil servant. But the return to academic life was not completely straightforward. Robbins had to undertake what he later (1947, p. 1) described as 'a painful effort at re-education'. But contemporaneously with, and subsequent to, this effort, his work in the post-war world developed along three main lines.

First, and by no means insignificantly, he began rebuilding the department at LSE, in the development of which he had played such a major part in the inter-war years. But it was in the post-war period, rather than the inter-war years, that his love affair with economics, begun in the course of his discovery of the subject after his abandonment of socialism, transmuted into a love of LSE as an institution. This love not only helped to sustain Robbins; it helped to sustain LSE itself during the difficult years of the late 1960s and early 1970s when his strength of mind and firmness of purpose were to be essential in the handling of the student disturbances.

His feelings on his return to LSE in 1946 are beautifully put in his *Autobiography*.

> Returning to L.S.E. after all these ardours and endurances was returning home again. There was the same freedom, the same atmosphere of friendship, the same serious pursuit of high excellence, the same wide international contacts, the same sense of special function which always made me feel that, if I was to be academic, I would rather be there than in any other university institution in the world. (1971*a*, p. 213).

(ii) *History of Economic Thought*

Secondly, Robbins made the greatest individual contribution to the revival of the study of the history of economic thought in Britain. He had naturally, as a Cannan pupil, not only an excellent grounding in the subject but also an early love for it. Moreover he was a close friend and admirer, throughout his professional life, of Jacob Viner, whose all-round excellence as an economist included an expertise in the history of economic thought which has had few if any rivals.[26] Robbins himself was extraordinarily widely read, not only in contemporary literature ('in the main language areas' as he once put it) but in the historical literature of his subject.

The two high points of his work in the history of economic thought are undoubtedly *The Theory of Economic Policy in English Classical Political Economy* of 1952 and *Robert Torrens and the Evolution of Classical Economics* of 1958. The first book, originating in LSE lectures, was aimed at combatting those who sought to advance their own standing by caricaturing the Classical economists. In this, it was undoubtedly highly successful. It is not possible to discuss the attitudes of the Classical economists to policy matters without reference to this book.

The 1958 work is one of the most important studies – possibly *the* most

[26] Robbins (1971*a*, pp. 132, 163, 217, 219–20; 1966*d*; 1970*b*; 1980*b*). Robbins's greatest work in the history of economic thought, *Robert Torrens* (1958*a*), is dedicated to Jacob and Frances Viner.

important study – of a single economist ever written. It started as an introduction to Torrens's *Letters on Commercial Policy* but, as Robbins related, 'Reluctantly, but not without a certain surreptitious enjoyment, I came to recognise that what I was writing was going to be not an introduction but a book.' (1958*a*, p. vii.) In its broad but incisive discussions of the Classical analysis, and of Torrens's place within that, it really has no rival[27] – this despite the fact that its remarkable bibliographical appendix has produced virtually no imitators. Although the book discusses value and distribution theory and colonisation, its main themes are money and banking theory and the theory of trade and commercial policy. The discussions of these provide one of the highest points in the voluminous critical literature on these aspects of Classical economics, a survey to which the reader can turn again and again for enlightenment and stimulus.

(iii) *Macroeconomics*

Thirdly, there was a return to writing on macroeconomics and the open economy. In his work in this area there are some interesting contrasts with Robbins's pre-war work. In the first place, he abandoned the precise Mises–Hayek version of the macro model which he had used in *The Great Depression*. Secondly he did not, despite the elaborate contrition of his *Autobiography* and the frequent (though not unqualified) expressions of regard for Keynes, become a Keynesian.

It is perhaps worth amplifying this point. Robbins sometimes gave the impression that he had wholeheartedly surrendered to Keynes and to Keynesianism, both because of tributes to Keynes's intellect and personality and, perhaps more particularly, because of expressions of penitence over his opposition to fiscal expansion in the 1930s and over the various positions advanced in *The Great Depression* including advocacy of wage cuts.[28] But these did not constitute a surrender. In 1951, at a time when his wartime association with Keynes was still a recent memory, he wrote:

> the status of the *General Theory*, where his concern was with the widest type of generalisation and where his claims to far-reaching innovation were emphatic, is still a matter of some dispute. It must be admitted, I think, that a case, which is not intellectually negligible, can be made for the view that his claims in this respect were overstated; that some of what he thought to be novel was in fact in line with developments of the past, and some of what was truly novel was one-sided in its emphasis.[29]

Robbins then went on to concede that the impact of the book was still formidable – indeed unique. But it is clear that he had reservations about the content, and in his *Autobiography* which appeared twenty years later, and which certainly contains penitent remarks about his pre-war opposition to Keynes over macroeconomic policy, he also wrote:

[27] As Spengler said when reviewing the book: 'Robbins' mode of presentation might well serve as an exemplar to economists doing books on a single economics author' – Spengler (1959).

[28] E.g. Robbins (1971*a*, pp. 152–5, 224; 1979*a*. p. 14).

[29] *The Times*, 26 January 1951, p. 7 reprinted in Robbins (1970*a*, p. 244).

> It would not be true to say that then [during planning for the post-war era], or at any subsequent period, I had become a Keynesian in the sense of accepting *au pied de la lettre* all the analytical propositions of the *General Theory*. Although I had greatly benefited by the intellectual shake-up involved in studying them, I found many that were confused and even wrong-headed in their formulation and much that was cogent in the arguments of some of their critics – Dennis Robertson for instance. (1971 *a*, p. 188).

In the third place he returned instead to the Classical and Wicksellian foundations on which Mises and Hayek – both exemplary scholarly economists in a style congenial to Robbins – had built. In the strange post-war era of passive monetary policy, Robbins lamented that 'the shades of Tooke and Newmarch reign in Great George Street' (1951, pp. 17–8) and when he came to give evidence to the Radcliffe Committee he referred in evidence to Wicksell.[30]

The Radcliffe episode is an important one. Robbins, who had been involved in providing advice on macroeconomic policy at an earlier stage, put to the Committee, both in a Memorandum and in evidence, the idea that monetary and fiscal policy were *both* necessary – he had been feeling his way towards an acceptance of the importance of fiscal policy in the late 1930s, some while before his war-time association with Keynes.[31] He did feel that in the post-war world there had been an excessive emphasis on fiscal policy which had been expected to bear too great a burden. As he described the reliance on fiscal policy, without recourse to complementary monetary policy, in the post-war years:

> we have been attempting to drive our car through this difficult post-war country with the steering gear out of action, the wheels lashed rigidly in one direction, our only means of equilibration an occasional stop, every few months, for the wheels to be unlashed and turned at another angle – while ministers stand on the roof and deliver salutary exhortations.[32]

But he did not believe that fiscal policy should be entirely replaced by monetary policy. He then felt very sore when the Committee appeared both to misunderstand and indeed (through the line of questioning) to misrepresent him (Robbins, 1963, p. 213) and he was very disappointed with the report of the Committee, which took the line that money did not matter and/or could not be measured and/or could not be defined and/or could not be controlled and that what mattered was 'liquidity'. Robbins published – *three* times – a lengthy and closely-reasoned critique, arguing that at the root of the Radcliffe Committee's belief lay a fallacy of composition.[33] In his view, the liquidity of the economy, the realisability of securities, depended *in the aggregate*, not so much on the nature of the securities as on the availability of monetary means

[30] (1958*b*, q. 10219.) However Robbins held that, because in the real world there was a complex structure of rates rather than the single interest rate of the Wicksellian model, it was better to concentrate monetary control on the money supply itself rather than on its price.

[31] (1958*b*, q. 10205; 1958*c*, pp. 217–9; 1939*a*, pp. 224–30, 256–7; 1941, pp. 24–5.)

[32] 1951, p. 21; see also 1954, pp. 73–4.

[33] (1960; 1963, pp. 197–226; 1971*c*, pp. 90–119.)

of payment to enable liquidation *plans* to be *realised*. He rejected the apparent belief of the committee that there was no upper limit to velocity of circulation, so control of the money supply was crucial – and distinctly preferable to attempting to control a multitude of interest rates.

With the monetarist counter-revolution, and the changes in the opinions of British economists during and after the Heath–Barber years, Robbins may be said to have had the last laugh.[34]

In another connection his views on macroeconomic policies, unpopular at the time of delivery, have found later favour. For in the 1960s, during the era of fashionable belief in incomes policies, Robbins maintained that such policies were of use only as secondary shock-absorbers in a situation in which a decision had been taken to restrict the growth of monetary aggregate demand but in which expectations in the labour market had been adjusted to previous inflations of expenditure.[35] He was contemptuous of the Heath government's attempts to maintain an incomes policy while allowing extremely rapid growth in the money supply.[36] It was not that he approved of inflation itself – far from it. Indeed he attacked those economists who believed that it was a process which could be held at a steady, sustainable, level, who believed they could 'determine by mathematics optimal rates of robbing the widows, orphans and other owners of fixed interest securities.' (1966*a*, p. 31.) Inflation was an inherently destructive, subverting, and unstable process which could ultimately destroy a free society itself.[37] But it was pointless trying to tackle it with an incomes policy.

(*iv*) *The Open Economy*

In the field of open-economy economics, Robbins abandoned the position which he had maintained until the Second World War, that the Gold Standard should be restored. He now thought that although, so far, paper standards had performed worse than any commodity money, we *should* be able to design a paper system that was better than gold. As one of the participants in the Bretton Woods conference, he supported the rigid paper exchange rate system involved in IMF arrangements, and opposed strongly the idea of floating exchange rates.

Although he had, in his pre-war writings, poured scorn on Keynes's advocacy of moveable paper exchange rates (Robbins, 1937, pp. 290–9), he supported the Keynes plan at Bretton Woods. When this was rejected by the conference, he was disappointed, but he later became a strong supporter of the IMF system and accepted that Keynes's plan would have been inflationary (*Hansard*, 29 March 1961, vols. 79–82) But he was happy with the high degree of rigidity of exchange rates involved in the IMF system; he opposed

[34] For a rather striking example of this see Little (1974).

[35] (1971 *c*, p. 6.) Both in his *Autobiography* (1971 *a*, p. 234) and in a speech in the House of Lords (*Hansard* vol. 291, 10 April 1968, col. 399) Robbins referred to an unpleasant episode in this connection. The reference was removed when Robbins reprinted the speech (1979*a*, pp. 20–5).

[36] See especially 1979a, pp. xi, 9, 18–9, 32–3, 37–8, 45, 50, 62–5, 68–9, 71, 75, 105–7. See also 1954, pp. 67, 71; 1958*d*, p. 24; 1971 *a*, p. 231; 1971 *c*, p. 3; 1972, pp. 138–40; 1974*a*, pp. 104–5; 1974*b*, pp. 23–5; 1976, pp. 94–6.

[37] See especially (1979*a* p. 85).

devaluation in 1958 and in 1964–6.[38] His concept of that IMF keystone 'fundamental disequilibrium' involved the idea that disequilibrium had to be very fundamental indeed before a change in exchange rates was justified. In the 1960s he for long took the view that with unemployment at only 2 %, a balance of payments problem did not require a change in the exchange rate, it required a reduction in the level of aggregate demand.[39]

This in turn reflected the fact that Robbins, steeped in the analytical apparatus of Classical economics, approached the problem in terms of the Ricardian definition of excess on which he had himself written so illuminatingly in *Robert Torrens*. With a *given* exchange rate, a balance of payments problem indicated that there was, *by definition*, excess monetary aggregate demand. The correct response therefore was not to change the exchange rate but to reduce the level of aggregate demand – unless this resulted in too high a level of excess capacity in the economy.[40]

But although Robbins had a strongly developed preference for a high degree of rigidity in exchange rates he was a first-class economist: and he did not, like so many economists in the 1950s (even some first-class ones) fall for the myth of the prospect of an everlasting dollar shortage. He saw that the problem was simply one of the relative prices of different currencies: though he strongly favoured fixed exchange rates, he did not become a prisoner of the fixed exchange rate mentality.[41]

Free exchange rates, however were unsatisfactory. They were the antithesis of a liberal economic arrangement. They interfered with trade. Moreover, if they were to be successful in producing equilibrium, they required money illusion. They produced cost changes which fed through into more general inflation – Robbins was an early proponent of the 'vicious circle' hypothesis (Robbins, 1963, pp. 124–8). They undermined monetary discipline and would ultimately cause traders to have resort to some stable outside currency rather than to their own unstable national currency, a development which, because it undermined national monetary autonomy, would lead to exchange control. Once the world adopted free exchange rates the outcome would, he believed, be a series of currency blocs with limited flexibility in their exchange arrangements, as the disadvantages of free exchange rates became apparent to all.[42]

This brings us back to the question of economic unification and of Federalism. Faced with the prospects of European unification after World War II Robbins, revolted by the antics and attitudes of the French Left, moved away from his pre-war Federalist dream.[43] He favoured Atlantic rather than

[38] (1958*d*, p. 10; 1971*c*, p. 19; 1979*a*, pp. xi, 5, 13).

[39] (1971*c*, pp. 133–6; 1975, p. 23; 1958*d*, p. 10; 1979*a*, pp. 5, 13–4; 1968, pp. 674–7).

[40] (1951, p. 17; 1971*c*, pp. 14–7, 153–9); cf. (1958*a*, pp. 97–100).

[41] (1958*e*; 1953*a*, pp. 2–7, 14; 1963, pp. 159–65; 1971*b*, pp. 17, 144–62); Yeager (1976, pp. 589–94).

[42] (1971*c*, pp. 23, 143; 1975, p. 20; 1979*a*, pp. xi, 24; 1967, p. 12; 1968, pp. 669–71; 1973, p. 9).

[43] As he was later to relate:

'Readers of Madame de Beauvoir's not very distinguished but immensely informative novel, *The Mandarins* – a palpable description of the group in which she and her great friend, Jean-Paul Sartre, moved – will remember the state of mind depicted. Of all the main characters, only one – Camus in disguise, I suppose – did not feel that there was little to choose between Stalin's Russia and

European union, and initially opposed the Common Market. This was not inappropriate – Robbins, like Viner, was in some important senses a Classical economist, and long before Viner's 1951 lectures Robbins had appreciated the trade-diverting nature of a customs union.[44]

But Robbins gradually came to terms with the EEC, though a wider federation, involving North America, undoubtedly remained his long term aim.[45]

V. THE ROBBINS REPORT AND AFTER

(i) *The Public Figure*

By 1963 Robbins was already a public figure, known to a much wider world than that of academic economists. He was a respected figure in the art world, something for which his family background (and especially his marriage) had given him some preparation. He was a Trustee of the National Gallery from 1952, a position which he retained until 1974, and of the Tate Gallery from 1953, and a Director of the Royal Opera House from 1955. Moreover he had been raised to the peerage, taking (very appropriately, in view of his love of LSE) the title of Baron Robbins of Clare Market, in 1959.

It was made clear at the time of Robbin's ennoblement that this was a non-political conferment (*The Times*, 23 January 1959), and Robbins took his seat on the cross benches. He participated vigorously in debates, was frequently reported in *The Times*, and thus gained much increased recognition by the wider public.

In 1961 he became Chairman of the *Financial Times*, a position which he retained until 1970. He clearly enjoyed his role in business, as was apparent to any visitor to Bracken House, but Robbins had to pay a price for this; it was his enforced resignation from his chair at LSE even though his colleagues at the School were prepared to let him retain it. This was a reverse which deeply upset Robbins (Corry, 1986). His *Politics and Economics* of 1963 is dedicated to his friends at LSE who had rallied to support in this time of crisis; and even ten years later, when Robbins's *Autobiography* appeared, it was apparent that he still felt very deeply about the matter (Robbins, 1971*a*, pp. 269–70, 283). It was not a matter of wounded vanity: it was that the activities of (as he felt) one individual had threatened to separate him from his beloved LSE (1963, p. vii).

(ii) *The Robbins Report*

But it was the Robbins Report – although Robbins disliked this term for the Report of the Committee on Higher Education (Robbins, 1966*b*, p. xiii) – which very greatly increased his public profile. As some of his collaborators on

contemporary America, only one did not feel that to reveal the truth about Russian concentration camps and ideological murder was betraying the last best hopes of humanity. I asked myself, what had I in common with men and women capable of such attitudes.' (1971*a*, p. 237.)

[44] (1937, pp. 121–2); see also O'Brien (1976).

[45] (1963, p. 153; 1971*c*, pp. 36–8; 1973, pp. 18–21; 1975, pp. 20–1; see also 1954, pp. 183–9, 1968, pp. 676–7).

the report were later to note, by 1969 the only official reports with greater sales had been Beveridge on social insurance and Denning on Christine Keeler (Layard *et al.*, 1969, p. 26). Robbins spent a good deal of the year or more after publication of the report, speaking and writing on the subject both at home and abroad. The literary outcome of this was his *The University in the Modern World* of 1966. The volume ranges through the issues raised by the Robbins Report, the effects of university expansion on admission standards, and the appropriate machinery of government to deal with the expanded university sector, the state of Oxford University (Robbins gave unwilling evidence on this to the Franks Commission (Robbins, 1966*b*, pp. xi–xii)), problems of higher education in arts, technology and business, and, finally, the creation of the 'binary system' in higher education. This last, involving the development of a sector of higher education in parallel with, rather than integrated with, the universities, contained some of Robbins's most forceful writing on education as he attacked 'the abracadabra of this precious Binary system' (1966*b*, p. 149).

In Robbins's own involvement in the Robbins Report itself – and to anyone reading the minutes of evidence, the central involvement of the chairman is very much apparent – two factors were of overriding importance. The first was his natural egalitarianism, and his opposition to privilege, especially in education. It may well have been this which led to a certain suspicion of Oxbridge, which is reflected in the report itself as well as in utterances of Robbins's own.[46] The second was a certain romanticism about the role of education and the good which it could do in the world. The emphasis upon allocative efficiency which characterised his writings on wartime public administration is not greatly in evidence in Robbins's own writings on education, or indeed in the Report itself, despite the important researches which the Committee undertook. To the latter, it is true, Robbins attached great importance. He regarded the committee as having established that there was a pool of ability which was capable of taking advantage of higher education but which was as yet untapped. Indeed of all the results of the committee this seems to have been the one of which he was most proud[47] even though, as the student troubles developed in the late 1960s, he came to stress that the report had indicated that *ability* to undertake study must be coupled with *willingness* to make good use of the facilities offered by higher education.[48] The emphasis on places for all well-qualified and motivated applicants may in part have sprung from Robbins's own reservations about manpower planning.[49] But it did enable the Report to pass rather lightly by some of the resource allocation issues.[50]

But in the end higher educational developments did not really follow the lines suggested by the Robbins Report. Robbins himself was very conscious of this. Yet it did have a very substantial impact upon higher education as a whole, and as Robbins himself concluded:

[46] (1966*b*), pp. 44–5 (a reference to 'talk over nuts and wine'), pp. 57–100; see also the Robbins Report (Cmnd 2154, 1963) pp. 177–8 and Coats (1982, p. 20).

[47] (1971*a*, pp. 275, 278; 1966*b*, pp. 2–3, 40–1, 138; 1980*a*, p. 25.)

[48] (1966*c*, p. 4; 1976, pp. 125–7; 1980*a*, pp. 39–40.)

[49] (1966*b*, pp. 19–20, 29–30; 1980*a*, pp. 28–9).

[50] On this see Blaug (1967).

> In a world in which the labours of this sort of enquiry are so frequently ignored and their recommendations quietly shelved, we certainly had little cause for dissatisfaction, either with the notice attracted by our report or with the degree to which its suggestions were accepted. (1971*a*, pp. 282–3.)

The report itself raised Robbins much higher in public perception, and gave him a continuing involvement in the discussions of higher education development to which he was to devote one of his last publications, the volume *Higher Education Revisited* of 1980.

One of the topics to which he paid some attention in this book was that of student 'militancy' and there is no doubt that Robbins had had his fill of experience in this matter. As Chairman of the LSE Governors, a position he held in the critical years 1968–74, he resisted the rebels. Despite attempts by a faction of the LSE staff to undermine his position,[51] he met the rebels more or less head on; and he won.[52] The personal strain must have been enormous: indeed his *Autobiography* was written as a distraction from the troubles. Reading today the newspaper accounts of what was happening at LSE at the time produces the traumatic quality of a re-lived nightmare. But Robbins remained firm and (and this was what really mattered most to him) saved his beloved LSE.

For, as already noted, one of the things in Robbins's evolution which is so striking is that his love of economics at least partly transmuted itself into a love of LSE as an institution. There was in Robbins's character a deeply romantic and emotional strain: Sir Claus Moser has recorded him as weeping in front of a Rembrandt (Moser, 1984, p. 14). There was indeed an odd juxtaposition of elements in his make-up: the 'country bred commonsense' (Robbins, 1971*a*, p. 56) to which he himself referred was joined with a Gallic transparency of mind and a sometimes deep emotionalism. In the context of his career, this was most noticeable in his general dealings with the arts (in which the allocation conditions carefully developed during war-time were largely disregarded) and education. This helps to explain the very personal disappointment which Robbins, it would seem, came to feel at the failure of higher education to develop as he had hoped.[53]

(iii) *The Public Economist*

But the economist was still very much to the fore in many of Robbins's public utterances. As a member of the House of Lords he took part vigorously in debate. Although he published, in 1979, a volume of his speeches (with some excisions), these do not really give anything like an adequate picture of his contributions, which can be gained only from studying *Hansard*. The volume of speeches, *Against Inflation*, together with the two remarkable speeches 'Expansion and the Machinery of Government' and 'Expansion and the

[51] Robbins, 1971*a*, p. 296. See *The Times*, 12 May 1969 (10a), 5 December 1969 (1d), 27 June 1970 (2a), 23 October 1971 (12d).

[52] See Norman (1986).

[53] See, e.g. *The Times*, 3 July 1981 (4e), 24 July 1981 (7a), 16 Oct. 1981 (2g), *Times Higher Education Supplement* 16 Oct. 1981 (13a), *Times Educational Supplement* 7 May 1982 (5c).

Binary System' which he reprinted in *The University in the Modern World*, give only a limited picture of his participation although they are in themselves full of interest. While Robbins, consistently with his view of the duties of a university teacher, took his seat on the cross benches, avoided party political points, and adopted a thoroughly independent line, he contributed vigorously and effectively to debates in the Lords.

Robbins's academic career enjoyed a quite extraordinary finale – almost an apotheosis – when in 1980, at the age of nearly 82, he addressed the AEA meeting at Denver. During the post-war years he had maintained his interest in methodological questions, although he had not really shifted his position very much – his ambiguity over the precise nature of 'verification' certainly did not take him into the 'falsificationist' camp, as some would have liked to believe. In the post-war years until his appearance at Denver, his two main methodological statements had been a review of Dennis Robertson's *Utility and All That* in 1953 and a lecture on 'The Present Position of Economics' published in an Italian journal in 1959 and subsequently in a volume assembled by other editors.[54] It is interesting that, although Robbins reprinted many of his lectures and reviews, he included neither of these items in any of his compilations in the post-war period. But in Denver in 1980 he made a wide-ranging and powerful restatement of his methodological position, demonstrating little substantial shift from that in his classic *Essay* of nearly fifty years earlier. It was a personal triumph of a remarkable magnitude. As the then President of the American Economic Association has testified:

> There, in a Denver ballroom, 2,000 assembled economists, made sleepy by the dinner they were digesting, sated by a full day of talks, colloquia and debates, ready to go off to their evening parties, rose to cheer Lionel as I have never seen a group of academics do. For they knew that they had that night seen and heard to what true civilization and scholarship aspire.[55]

VI. CONCLUSION

Within a brief compass I have attempted to give some account of the outsize figure that was Lionel Robbins. It is apparent that Robbins was not, as Keynes was, a great builder of new tools, a creative architect in his subject. Rather, he was a brilliant economic essayist who took the tools, made sure that he knew the range of what was available (thus, unlike others, avoiding 'subjective originality' to borrow Schumpeter's phrase) and applied them to economic problems. In these applications, and in his efforts to bring home to his professional colleagues the range and strength of the tools already available through centuries of economic writings, he experienced both successes and failures. He was not successful in moving economists in the direction of Austrian general equilibrium, or its associated cost theory, an outcome which is hardly surprising since this achievement would be destructive of much of mainstream

[54] Robbins (1953*b*, 1959). See also Robbins (1979*b*).

[55] Baumol (1984) p. 11. Robbins's address is Robbins (1981).

economics and of the technocratic pretensions which go with it. But he did have some considerable success with other aspects of his methodological writings, and methodological discussion can certainly never be the same after the publication of the *Essay*. In macroeconomics, having been, in his own judgement, on the wrong side, in the pre-war era, he came ultimately, without any really fundamental change in his analytical approach, very much into his own in the post-war era. This is not true of his writings on international economic matters, however. Federalism is still a very distant vision, while free exchange rates have been general since 1973 without the disastrous consequences he anticipated. As a teacher he was, by all accounts, unforgettable, although it is perhaps ironic that his success in reviving history of economic thought in Britain has been largely confined to the area of research rather than of taught courses.

But even where Robbins failed, he still had an influence. He was a great economist with an open mind and a passionate commitment to liberty, and an inspiring leader. Though his own strength and firmness of character and personality were very different from those of J. S. Mill, in his values and influences he invites comparison – and with such a comparison he would have been delighted.

University of Durham
Date of receipt of final typescript: July 1987

References

Baumol, W. (1984). In *Tributes in Memory of Lord Robbins*, pp. 10–1. London: LSE.
Blaug, M. (1967). 'Approaches to educational planning.' ECONOMIC JOURNAL vol. 77, pp. 262–87.
—— (1980). *The Methodology of Economics*. Cambridge: Cambridge University Press.
Coats, A. W. (1982). 'The distinctive LSE ethos in the inter-war years.' *Atlantic Economic Journal* vol. 10, pp. 18–30.
Corry, B. (1986). 'Robbins, Lionel.' In *The New Palgrave*, vol. 4. London: Macmillan.
Dalton, H. (1929). *Principles of Public Finance* (revised edn.). London: Routledge.
—— (1986*a*). *The Political Diary of Hugh Dalton 1918–40, 1945–60* (ed. B. Pimlott). London: Cape.
—— (1986*b*). *The Second World War Diary of Hugh Dalton 1940–1945* (ed. B. Pimlott). London: Cape.
Fraser, L. (1932). 'How do we want economists to behave?' ECONOMIC JOURNAL vol. 42, pp. 555–70.
—— (1937). *Economic Thought and Language*. London: Macmillan.
Gregory, T. E. (1928). Introduction to Tooke and Newmarch, *History of Prices*. London: P. S. King.
Gribbin, J. D. (1977*a*). 'The postwar revival of competition as industrial policy' (mimeo).
—— (1977*b*). 'The development of United Kingdom competition policies from the war until 1948' (mimeo).
—— (1985). 'The wartime contribution of G. C. Allen to the development of U.K. competition policy' (mimeo).
Harrod, R. (1951). *The Life of John Maynard Keynes*. London: Macmillan.
Howson, S. and Winch, D. (1977). *The Economic Advisory Council, 1930–1939*. Cambridge: Cambridge University Press.
Johnson, H. G. (1972). Review of Robbins (1971*a*). *Journal of Political Economy* vol. 80, pp. 835–6.
Keynes, J. M. (1930). *A Treatise on Money*. London: Macmillan.
Knight, F. (1921). *Risk, Uncertainty and Profit*, repr. London: LSE, 1933.
Layard, R., King, J. and Moser, C. (1969). *The Impact of Robbins*. London: Penguin.
Little, I. (1974). 'The right shape for a budget.' *The Times*, 6 February (15e).
Meade, J. (1984). In *Tributes in Memory of Lord Robbins*, pp. 5–7. London: LSE.
Moggridge, D. (1976). *Keynes*. London: Fontana.
Moser, C. (1984). In *Tributes in Memory of Lord Robbins*, pp. 12–5. London: LSE.
Norman, M. (1986). 'The rebels who lost.' *Daily Telegraph*, 8 May.
O'Brien, D. (1976). 'Customs unions: trade creation and trade diversion in historical perspective.' *History of Political Economy* vol. 8, pp. 540–63.

Pimlott, B. (1985). *Hugh Dalton*. London: Cape.

Robbins, L. (1925). Review of T. E. Gregory, 'The present position of banking in America', *Economica*, vol. 5, pp. 358–9.

—— (1925/6). *Wages. An Introductory Analysis of the Wage System under Modern Capitalism*. London: Jarrolds. The work is undated: Nat. U. Cat. gives [1925], B.M. Cat. gives [1926].

—— (1927). 'Mr Hawtrey on the scope of economics.' *Economica* vol. 7, pp. 172–8.

—— (1930*a*) 'On the elasticity of demand for income in terms of effort.' *Economica* vol. 10, pp. 123–9.

—— (1930*b*) 'On a certain ambiguity in the conception of stationary equilibrium.' ECONOMIC JOURNAL vol. 40, pp. 194–214.

—— (1931*a*) 'Economic notes on some arguments for protection.' *Economica* vol. 11, pp. 45–62.

—— (1931*b*). 'A reply to Mr. Keynes.' *New Statesman and Nation* vol. 14, March, pp. 98–100.

—— (1932*a*). *An Essay on the Nature and Significance of Economic Science*. London: Macmillan, 2nd ed., 1935.

—— (1932*b*). 'Consumption and the trade cycle.' *Economica* vol. 12, pp. 413–30.

—— (1933). 'Introduction.' In Philip H. Wicksteed, *The Commonsense of Political Economy* (1910), repr. London: Routledge.

—— (1934*a*). 'Remarks upon certain aspects of the theory of costs.' ECONOMIC JOURNAL vol. 44, pp. 1–18.

—— (1934*b*) *The Great Depression*. London: Macmillan.

—— (1934*c*) 'Production.' *Encyclopaedia of the Social Sciences*, vol. 12, (ed. E. R. A. Seligman), pp. 462–7. New York: Macmillan.

—— (1935). 'A student's recollections of Edwin Cannan.' ECONOMIC JOURNAL vol. 45, pp. 393–8.

—— (1937). *Economic Planning and International Order*. London: Macmillan.

—— (1939*a*). *The Economic Basis of Class Conflict*. London: Macmillan.

—— (1939*b*). *The Economic Causes of War*. London: Cape.

—— (1941). *Economic Aspects of Federation*. London: Macmillan for the Federal Union Research Institute.

—— (1947). *The Economic Problem in Peace and War*. London: Macmillan.

—— (1951). *The Balance of Payments*. Stamp Memorial Lecture. London: Athlone Press.

—— (1953*a*). 'The international economic problem.' *Lloyds Bank Review* vol. 17, January, pp. 1–24.

—— (1953). 'Robertson on utility and scope.' *Economica* NS vol. 20, pp. 99–111.

—— (1954). *The Economist in the Twentieth Century and Other Lectures in Political Economy*. London: Macmillan.

—— (1958*a*). *Robert Torrens and the Evolution of Classical Economics*. London: Macmillan.

—— (1958*b*). Evidence to the Committee on the Working of the Monetary System (Radcliffe Committee) 24 July 1958, pp. 673–8, qq. 10190–254. London: HMSO, 1960.

—— (1958*c*). *The Aims of Monetary Policy and the Means of Achieving Them*. Memorandum to the Committee on the Working of the Monetary System (Radcliffe Committee), pp. 211–9. London: HMSO, 1960.

—— (1958*d*). 'Thoughts on the crisis.' *Lloyds Bank Review* vol. 48, April, pp. 1–26.

—— (1958*e*). 'MacDougall on the dollar problem.' *Crossbow*, January, pp. 43–4.

—— (1959). 'The present position of economics.' *Rivista di Politica Economica*, reprinted in *Guest Lectures in Economics* (ed. E. Henderson and L. Spaventa), pp. 31–46. Milan: Giuffré, 1962.

—— (1960). 'Monetary theory and the Radcliffe Report' reprinted in *Guest Lectures in Economics* ed. E. Henderson and L. Spaventa pp. 87–109. Milan: Giuffré, 1962.

—— (1962). 'Lord Dalton. An outstanding teacher.' *The Times*, 20 February (15b).

—— (1963). *Politics and Economics*. London: Macmillan.

—— (1965). *Bentham in the Twentieth Century*. London: Athlone Press.

—— (1966*a*). 'An economist looks at business.' In *Economics, Business and Government*, pp. 25–31. London: IEA.

—— (1966*b*). *The University in the Modern World*. London: Macmillan.

—— (1966*c*). *On Academic Freedom*. An Inaugural Lecture under the 'Thank-Offering to Britain Fund'. London: OUP for the British Academy.

—— (1966*d*). Review of J. Rae, *Life of Adam Smith*, with introduction by Jacob Viner. *Economica* NS vol. 33, pp. 348–9.

—— (1967). 'Issues and alternatives,' pp. 7–25 and 'Concluding observations', pp. 143–50. In *Monetary Reform and the Price of Gold* (ed. R. Hinshaw). Baltimore: Johns Hopkins University Press.

—— (1968). 'The international monetary problem.' *Journal of Political Economy* vol. 76, pp. 664–77.

—— (1970*a*). *The Evolution of Modern Economic Theory*. London: Macmillan.

—— (1970*b*). *Jacob Viner. A Tribute*. Princeton: Princeton University Press.

—— (1971*a*). *Autobiography of an Economist*. London: Macmillan.

—— (1971*b*). 'Sir T. Gregory. Gifted teacher.' *The Times*, 23 February (14g).

—— (1971*c*). *Money, Trade and International Relations*. London: Macmillan.

—— (1972). 'Inflation: an international problem', pp. 10–25 and 'Concluding observations', pp. 128–46. In *Inflation as a Global Problem* (ed. R. Hinshaw). Baltimore: Johns Hopkins University Press.

—— (1973). *The International Monetary Problem.* Second Keynes Lecture in Economics. London: OUP for the British Academy.

—— (1974*a*). 'Causes, effects, developments', pp. 1–9 and 'Summing up', pp. 104–5, In *Inflation: Causes, Consequences, Cures.* London: IEA.

—— (1974*b*). *Aspects of Post-War Economic Policy* (5th Wincott Memorial Lecture). London: IEA.

—— (1975). 'Issues and choices', pp. 11–27 and 'Concluding reflections', pp. 145–57. In *Key Issues in International Monetary Reform* (ed. R. Hinshaw). New York: Marcel Dekker.

—— (1976). *Political Economy: Past and Present.* London: Macmillan.

—— (1979*a*). *Against Inflation.* London: Macmillan.

—— (1979*b*). 'On Latsis's 'Method and appraisal in economics': a review essay.' *Journal of Economic Literature* vol. 17, pp. 996–1004.

—— (1980*a*) *Higher Education Revisited.* London: Macmillan.

—— (1980*b*). Review of J. Viner (op. posth.) 'Religious thought and economic society'. *Economica* NS vol. 47, pp. 489–90.

—— (1981). 'Economics and Political Economy.' Richard T. Ely Lecture. *American Economic Review* vol. 71 (May Supplement), pp. 1–10.

Skidelsky, R. (1983). *John Maynard Keynes*, Vol. 1. *Hopes Betrayed. 1883–1920.* London: Macmillan.

Spengler, J. (1959), Review of Robbins (1958*a*). *American Economic Review* vol. 49, pp. 722–4.

Viner, J. (1950). *The Customs Union Issue.* New York: Carnegie Endowment for International Peace.

Wiseman, J. (1985). 'Lionel Robbins, the Austrian School, and the LSE tradition.' *Research in the History of Economic Thought and Methodology* vol. 3, pp. 147–59.

Yeager, L. B. (1976). *International Monetary Relations*, 2nd ed. New York: Harper and Row.

[19]

Lionel Robbins and the Austrian connection

D. P. O'Brien

I. *Introduction*

Lionel Robbins was a major figure in English economics for more than fifty years and a prominent figure in public controversy, particularly during the 1930s. During the controversies of the 1930s it was widely held that the basis of positions advanced by the critics of Cambridge, including Robbins, lay in Austrian economics. (Indeed, in the macroeconomic controversies, the Cambridge side seems to have regarded the London School of Economics as "a suburb of Vienna.") But Robbins lived for a very long time; and he was active as a writer on economics long after the controversies of the 1930s had receded into the middle distance (O'Brien 1988a, 1988b). As they so receded, the question of the extent of the Austrian base for Robbins's thought also receded, although it was revived at the end of his life in connection with his important writings on methodology (Addleson 1984).

This paper attempts to evaluate the strength of Robbins's Austrian connection and to indicate how far he can honestly be called an Austrian economist. As will become clear, the task of disentangling the roots of his *micro*economic views can never be completely solved, because in this area his primary source was undoubtedly Wicksteed's *Common sense,* while he drew from the Austrians precisely those elements which coincided most directly with what he had drawn from Wicksteed. The task in dealing with his *macro*economics is more straightforward, both because he rejected much of aggregated macroeconomics on straightforwardly Austrian grounds (there could, he held, be no useful concept of production in the aggregate) and because his adoption of the Mises-Hayek theory of economic fluctuations was explicit and clear-cut, at least in the 1930s. However, even here we shall find that, partly because of the very roots of the work of Mises and Hayek themselves, the filiation is not absolutely straightforward.

This is not really surprising. Robbins was an eclectic, seeking to assemble the common strands in a wide range of different sources in economics so as to weld together, to present to the public, and to use in controversy, a common body of developed, received, and professionally attested economic theory. This in itself was connected with his pride in the intellectual content of a subject which had proved a revelation to him when he first became an undergraduate.[1] Seeing the compatibility of the analyses originating in different countries, from the pens of different writers, at different historical times, he felt considerable satisfaction at the progress which economics had made. Indeed students and contemporaries of Robbins have stressed the almost messianic quality of his lectures on economic theory. The message was made very clear. This stuff was important. A corpus of theory had emerged and it had to be grappled with, absorbed, and used.[2]

Robbins's drive to "open up" British economics must be seen in this light. He was not motivated merely by a desire to weaken what he saw as the predominance—at times amounting almost to an intellectual monopoly—possessed by Cambridge, although this was undoubtedly a motive, especially during the 1930s. Rather, he was concerned to draw together the different threads of what he regarded as being not only a valid body of theory but also an outstanding intellectual achievement. This in turn reinforced the authority possessed by the subject and the persuasive strength of its conclusions.

It was not that he was blind to the differences in the work of different authors. But drawing on what Wicksteed had made of Jevons's approach (especially the replacement by Wicksteed in his *Common sense* of utility by ranking) and on the material in the Austrian writers, he pulled together what he felt to be the corpus of *modern* economic theory (circa 1930) and was then critical of those developments—partial equilibrium analysis of costs, for instance—which were at variance with this corpus of analysis (1934c, 465; 1933a, xv n.; 1934a, 6–11). In particular, he criticized Marshall's Representative Firm from the (somewhat irrelevant) standpoint of Austrian general equilibrium (Robbins 1928).

This concern with authority also led Robbins to read into earlier, and indubitably great, authors, a rather Austrian view of the world. In particular, he was prone in the 1930s to view *The wealth of nations* more in terms of general equilibrium than as an essay in economic development (1935a, 50, 68–69).

In drawing together this corpus of modern theory, the two most important sources, at least in the initial stages of Robbins's development as an economist, after his graduation, were Wicksteed and Wicksell. He

1. "For me, at least, this was an entry to a new world. Here was really first-rate intellect. Here was free discussion of the great problems of man in society. Here, without abatement of personal convictions, was integrity and a search after truth" (1971a, 74–75).

2. On Robbins's delight in economics see 1930a, 194; 1930b, 16, 24; 1934a, 1; 1935a, 2–3. See also Hutchison 1979 and (on Robbins as a young lecturer at Oxford) Meade 1984. Various people who were students of Robbins in the postwar years have also confirmed this picture. On this, as on many other aspects of Robbins's personality, Phelps Brown (1988) is a valuable source.

was thus initially exposed to Austrian economics at one remove; Wicksteed essentially reinterpreted his Jevonian origins in a way which *mirrored* Austrian economics (though the *stimulus* for this seems to have come, ironically, from Lausanne rather than Vienna, through the influence of Pareto), while Wicksell ranks as the most important expositor and developer of Austrian economics outside the ranks of the Austrians. Having, so to speak, imbibed this initial message, Robbins then explored the Austrian literature; and he strengthened his assimilation of principles which he had derived from Wicksteed and Wicksell to the point where he felt able to contrast favorably the composite tradition which he had absorbed with that of Cambridge.

As will become particularly clear when we turn attention to the macroeconomic aspects of Robbins's work, he regarded Wicksell as a very important economist (1935b; 1970, 223–28; 1958c, q. 10219). Indeed Wicksell's work had the advantage that it incorporated (and indisputably improved) not only much Austrian theory but also much that was valuable in the classical treatment of capital (1935b, xiii–xiv), thus yet again enabling Robbins to point with pride to the achievements of economists in producing a coherent body of theory over a long period.

Nonetheless, despite these complications it should prove possible to give some indication of the weight to be attached to Austrian sources for Robbins's thought. There is no doubt that he regarded Austrian economics as a whole as being of very considerable importance, as is shown by the links which he established with Vienna in the 1930s (1934a, 1; 1971a, 127, 132, 143). Moreover, while he suggested that the study of economics could begin with Wicksteed's *Common sense,* followed by Wicksell's *Lectures* in the second year of study (1935b, xi n., xviii, xix), the London School of Economics was prominent in making Austrian works available to a wider audience—in particular there were translations of two of Mises's major works, *Money* and *Socialism* (Mises 1934, 1936), and a reprint of the works of Menger (1933–36).

II. *Microeconomics*

1. *Analytical structure: content*

Robbins sought a microeconomics which was capable of including both nonmaterial aims and activities and also destructive (rather than constructive) activities, such as war, which nonetheless used resources, as well as the more obvious categories of economic activity (1971a, 146; 1935a, 129; 1929b, 249). He also sought a system which would allow him to separate economics and ethics (1927a; 1935a, 91, 147–48, 151; see also Weber 1949, 11). He was anxious to place outside the domain of "scientific" economics both value judgments and the scientific pretensions of Pigovian welfare economics.[3] He thus wanted a demarcation criterion to exclude such forms of analysis from scientific economics proper. Value judgments were indispensable for the application of analysis to particular policy situations; but they did not themselves enjoy scientific status (1938a).

Robbins found what he was looking for in the distinction between positive and normative economics.[4] Only the former was economics proper; the latter required extrascientific value judgments. Positive economics involved the employment of a maximization model (though without perfect consistency of rankings).[5] Thus economics was essentially to be about choice models. Rational behavior, which amounted to acting consistently in accordance with the ranking of different possibilities, lay behind demand, which was the ultimate force in economics.[6] The supply curve was merely the sellers' own demand curve (1933a, xx; Wicksteed 1910, 510, 785). In the perfect form of this model the chooser has, in effect, perfect information. Factor allocation thus falls into place as the reflection of the communal rankings of the outcome of the employment of factor services, expressed through the market (1934c; 1935a, 32–38, 65; Wicksteed 1910, 358–98). *All* ends, which involved scarce resources, and which were thus subject to choice, came within the purview of this analysis—there was no special category of economic ends (1935a, 24–32; 1971a, 147).

We thus have microeconomic analysis as essentially an a priori analysis of the implications of choice for the allocation of scarce resources. The focus of the analysis was upon equilibrium—*general* and not *partial* equilibrium.[7] This led in turn to an approach to cost theory which was in terms of opportunity cost—which could *only* be analyzed in a general equilibrium framework (1934a). Throughout, the emphasis is upon a high degree of subjectivism. This enabled Robbins to adopt an extremely agnostic attitude towards index numbers. In particular he was able to cite in his support the argument put forward by Haberler in his book on index numbers that it was impossible to say which of two incomes was the larger, on any objective basis. Such a question could only be answered by each individual income recipient (1935a, 63; Haberler 1927, 83).[8]

3. See in particular 1938c, 635–38; 1934c, 464–65; 1971a, 147–48; 1935a, 87; 1939a, 164; 1959, 45; 1932c, 173–74; 1953, 107–8.

4. 1935a, 88–90, 106; 1981, xviii; 1963, 6–7, 19; 1938c, 639; 1927a; 1971a, 147–48; 1964, 18–19; see also Weber 1949, 52; Menger 1963, 46; Kirzner 1976, 137.

5. Robbins 1932a, 92–94. Such a view is to be found alike in Mises (1949, 103) and Wicksteed (1910, 32–34).

6. 1935a, 7, 12, 14, 16, 30, 87–88, 152–53; 1930b, 24; 1954, 201–25; 1934c, 465; 1971a, 147. See also Menger 1871, 52–53; 1950, 94–95.

7. 1935a, 55, 67–68; 1933a, xvi; 1934a, 11, 14–15; 1934c, 465; 1930. See also Wicksteed 1910, 212–400.

8. He was still stressing this point in his postwar lectures at LSE.

Building upon premises which were either obviously true empirically or derived from introspection (1935a, 73–75, 78, 104–6; 1938a, 347–49; 1971a, 149), the individual subjective maximization model resulted in theorems which were necessarily true. Quantification work was not required to test them. "*Verification,*" however—checking whether the assumed initial conditions were actually fulfilled—was a proper form of quantitative analysis.[9] But the emphasis throughout Robbins's work is upon a very substantial degree of apriorism.

2. *Analytical structure: sources*

This approach was founded upon a fusion of English- and German-language sources. The German-language sources were entirely Austrian, with the exception of Weber. The general methodology came from strands in English classical economics, especially the work of J. S. Mill and Cairnes, but the most important English source by far was Wicksteed. From Weber came the distinction between positive and normative economics and the idea of the necessity of a *Wertfrei* character for economics (1935a, xii, 90, 148; see also Weber 1949, 1–47, 52; Hutchison 1979). But Wicksteed and the Austrians—and Robbins typically couples these two sources together in acknowledgment—provided the vast majority of the intellectual apparatus. From Wicksteed came the emphasis upon equilibrium, upon ranking, upon the primacy of demand, even upon the lack of perfect consistency in ranking (1910, 32–34). Though ranking is to be found throughout the work of the Austrians and is clearly involved in Menger's work (Hayek 1934, xiv–xv), it is Wicksteed's *Common sense* which provides Robbins's main source.

But here we encounter a major problem in the intellectual history we are considering. Wicksteed's treatment of ranking seems to derive from the influence upon his own Jevonian thought of his reading of Pareto (Steadman 1987). It is difficult to find Wicksteed drawing *directly* from the Austrians, even though Robbins, time and time again, while recognizing the significance of Pareto (1933a, xix), makes a direct connection between Wicksteed and the Austrians and indeed refers to Wicksteed as illustrating Wieser's "Law of Cost" brilliantly (1933a, xviii)—even though Wicksteed makes no reference to Wieser at all and even though the very phrase "Law of Cost" comes not from Wieser himself but from Pantaleoni (1898, 183–84, 250–51; Robbins 1934a, 2).

The influence of Pantaleoni, whose book dated from 1889 (and from 1898 in English), on Robbins seems to have been peripheral. He stated clearly the proposition that the marginal utility of a productive instrument will be determined by the marginal utility of the least significant

9. 1935a, 116–19; 1937a; 1934c, 465; 1971b, 188–89; 1938a, 352; 1938b, 161; O'Brien 1988a, 34–39; 1988b. The best discussion of "verification" is in Blaug 1980.

final product that it produces, and that its services will be spread across products to equalize the marginal utility of these services in producing different products. But the whole approach, based very firmly on marginal utility, not mere ranking, went much further than Robbins in the direction of cardinalism. In the treatment of this issue, indeed, it is Robbins's eclecticism which is most apparent. In introducing Wicksteed he refers to Wicksteed's exposition of the work of one economist (Wieser) using a term which he had got from another (or others—apart from Pantaleoni it is also in Mayer 1925, 638), although in the Wicksteedian exposition, which uses ranking rather than marginal utility for the most part, there is no reference to these other sources.

A number of Austrian economists writing in the 1920s have attracted relatively little attention from later commentators. But in this story they may be important. The particular form in which they couched their analysis made it easy for Robbins to couple Wicksteed's name with a general reference to the Austrians. Having come across the work of Schönfeld (1924)—possibly through Hayek ([1925] 1984)—Robbins was then enabled to cite Schönfeld and couple his name with that of Wicksteed in a most illuminating way.

> It does not require much knowledge of modern economic analysis to realise that the foundation of the theory of value is the assumption that the different things that the individual wants to do have a different importance to him, and can be arranged therefore in a certain order. This notion can be expressed in various ways and with varying degrees of precision from the simple wants system of Menger and the early Austrians to the more refined scales of relative valuations of Wicksteed and Schönfeld and the indifference systems of Pareto and Messrs. Hicks and Allen. (1935a, 75, replacing 75–76 of 1932a)

So we have the presentation of a corpus of theory now extending from Menger to Hicks and Allen, an extension which is facilitated by the replacement of material referring to *marginal utility* in the first edition of Robbins's *Essay* with this material from the second edition centered around *ranking*.

There seems no doubt that the microeconomic work of Austrian writers in the 1920s enabled Robbins to come to appreciate, progressively and over quite a long period, that Wicksteed's work involved ranking and was not dependent upon cardinalism. This enabled Robbins to continue to utilize his assimilations from Wicksteed, to whose work he attached particular importance—"A failure to sit through the *Common Sense* is a pretty sure sign of intellectual smallness," he informed his readers (1933a, xiv).

Nonetheless it should be emphasized that there are significant points of difference between Robbins's own approach and that of Wicksteed at various junctures; again, Robbins's eclecticism in building up a corpus of theory is in evidence. Although Robbins was slow to shed the residues of the marginal utility treatment which Wicksteed had carried over from his *Alphabet* to his *Common sense* (1910, 412), residues which are in evidence in Wicksteed's 1914 *Economic Journal* article (1910, 772–96), he quickly shed most of the elements of cardinalism (1910, 457) and he certainly did not make the exalted claims which Wicksteed made for marginalist ranking as the development of a general psychological principle to be used in explaining all human action (1910, 403–4, 776, 780, 800, 816). Indeed Wicksteed's emphasis on the psychological—and his denial of the existence of economic laws (1910, 780)—went far beyond Robbins's own position, while his references to psychological literature, and his interpretation of Pareto as providing psychological interpretation of human action, are much stronger than anything to be found in Robbins's own work (1934b).

In other respects too Wicksteed's work was not entirely satisfactory from what one can see was Robbins's own point of view. On the one hand there was his lack of acknowledgments of the work of others, whether he was drawing upon them or criticizing them;[10] on the other, the discussions of macroeconomics and trade in the *Common sense* are distinctly weak,[11] and Robbins would have had to look elsewhere in building up a body of accepted theory.

But much else in Wicksteed clearly struck a deep responsive chord in Robbins. The impossibility of having simultaneously valid partial equilibrium curves (1910, 528, 536, 545), the refusal to accept the commonly drawn supply curve on the same diagram as a demand curve, the classification of the supply curve itself as not a cost curve (which is what Wicksteed meant by the common variety) but as the sellers' own demand curve (499–500, 542, 785–87), the emphasis upon competing valuations for productive resources as dictating both their valuation and their allocation (517, 545, 788), the all-pervasive emphasis on choice (772–96), the sweeping dismantling of English classical rent theory to

10. See Wicksteed 1910, 479, where Marshall's "tea and coffee" example in discussing interdependence in consumer surplus is used without acknowledgment; see also the (Giffen) case (490) and the criticism of (Marshall's) conflation of increasing and diminishing returns (528).

11. Wicksteed 1910, 664–66, 670–71, 701. The discussion of trade is particularly weak, presenting a conception based upon specialization on the basis of absolute advantage—indeed at one point Wicksteed commits himself to the statement that "there is, properly speaking, no economic theory of foreign trade as distinct from home trade" (666). The discussion of tariffs displays no inkling of the "Cuba case" and is much inferior to Marshall.

show that the choice of which factor to hold fixed was arbitrary (552, 562, 574, 788–89; Robbins 1933a, x–xi; O'Brien 1988a, 209–11)—an achievement which Robbins would have found satisfyingly destructive of the Shove–Joan Robinson "exploitation" approach to distribution (1910, 571, 792): all these clearly appealed to Robbins and underlay his work.

But these elements were fused with what Robbins obtained elsewhere in building up a corpus of theory.

He read German fluently (1932a, 119; 1935a, 108; see also 1927b, 1931c, 1936c, 1937d), and he read the works of a wide range of German-language writers, in particular those of Mises and of Mayer (1934a, 1932a, 1935a). In reading these works he found a close coincidence between the intellectual apparatus which he had already gathered from Wicksteed himself and the content of the Austrians. His reception of the Austrian works as an additional source may have been assisted by the fact that after embracing economics as preferable to socialism, he would have had little sympathy for Wicksteed's own Fabian associations and found the more neutral attitude of the Austrians more immediately acceptable. But in this connection it is important to make the point that no simple ideological lesson can be learned here. As Hutchinson has observed (1981, 207), Wieser, an Austrian economist of whom Robbins was particularly fond, was highly critical of free market institutions. Robbins did not accept this line of criticism any more than he accepted Wicksteed's Fabianism, so that any attempt to see his Austrian borrowings as purely ideological—"political economy"—is bound to be misleading (O'Brien 1989).

Despite Robbins's fondness for referring to Wieser, it was, in the microeconomics sphere, Mises and Mayer who among the Austrians seem to have had the greatest influence on Robbins. The influence of Mises is particularly important in the first edition of Robbins's *Essay on the nature and significance of economic science,* for several of the citations disappear in the second edition. Robbins in fact acknowledged a particular debt to Mises, with whom he had personal contact (1935a, 16, 18, 39, 54, 77, 78, 83, 89; 1971a, 107, 143). The apriorism of Mises would also have appealed to Robbins, preconditioned as he was by the work of Cairnes, Mill, and Wicksteed. The rejection of interpersonal comparisons, by Jevons and Wicksteed, was in turn echoed by Mises in his emphasis upon the idea that we could only scale (i.e., rank) preferences (1932, 93; Robbins 1932a, 56; 1935a, 93; 1953, 102–4).

Robbins's methodological position on a number of issues, whether in his famous *Essay* or in lesser-known publications (1938b), was very much in tune with the Austrian position, especially as put forward by Hayek. Hayek not only regarded introspection as a valid source of information (1933, 27–38, 232; Robbins 1935a, 105) but also held—in contrast to Menger himself—that there was not a parallel between natural and social science (Hutchison 1981, 213–14). Moreover, Hayek was critical of the extensive use of statistical material, holding that this had only the limited role of "verification" noted above (1931a, 133). Indeed in this he was a great deal more purist than Robbins himself was in practice (at least in his *Great Depression*) if not in precept (in his *Essay*).

Mayer seems to have been most important to Robbins in his interpretation of Wieser. For Mayer's work (1925) set Wieser's concept of opportunity cost clearly in the concept of general equilibrium, precisely as Wicksteed had done. As already noted, Wicksteed's own general equilibrium approach, like his replacement of marginal utility by ranking, seems to have had Lausanne sources. But the way in which Mayer spelled out the implications of Wieser's analysis enabled Robbins to interpret Wicksteed in Austrian terms and indeed to classify him together with the Austrians (Robbins 1933a, 1934a, 1935a).

Mayer's account of Wieser's work is remarkable. He shows, with far greater clarity than Wieser himself, the way in which Wieser's theoretical contributions can be used to illuminate the unity of economic phenomena, building on Menger's initial insights. For Mayer, it was Wieser who really built up Austrian economics. It seems clear that this view influenced Robbins greatly; not only did this perception of the unity of economic phenomena form a key element in Robbins's own view of the evolved body of economic theory to which he attached such importance, but it also significantly affected his view of the relative importance of different Austrian economists. Indeed it seems clear that Mayer, Strigl, Hayek, and Mises greatly influenced Robbins, not only with respect to their ideas but also with respect to his perception of the nature of the Austrian School and the contribution of the earlier Austrian economists.

These later writers made very clear, in the 1920s and early 1930s, a general equilibrium view of the economic system. Such a view was to form a fundamental part of Robbins's approach to economics and to be employed by him in both a micro and a macro context. Precisely how far this was genuinely Austrian in origin is, however, a question which is insoluble because of the influence of Wicksteed. The Austrians essentially sharpened Robbins's appreciation of the general equilibrium elements in Wicksteed. Perhaps this is most of all true of Hayek, who until 1937 was very much a general equilibrium theorist (Hutchison 1981, 210–19; McCloughry 1984; Caldwell 1988) and whose elegant expositions would have strengthened Robbins in his search for, and his utilization of, the body of evolved and established theory.

3. The basic micro model applied

It is thus clear that while Wicksteed and the Austrians together constituted, for Robbins in the 1930s, the *modern* representation of a long, evolving corpus of valid microeconomic theory, disentangling the precise Austrian input is a matter of some difficulty. However, if we examine the uses to which Robbins put the basic model which he had assimilated, the issue becomes a little clearer if not wholly clear.

Allocation. Robbins considered allocation in two particular contexts: wartime and the problems of a socialist economy. Coupling together the general equilibrium framework of choice and the ends/means distinction, Robbins was able to analyze the operation of a wartime economy. Although wartime conditions ultimately meant that all other ends had to be subordinated to that of victory, there were still problems of the allocation of resources to achieve subgoals which themselves were conducive to victory. Here Robbins employed the marginal analysis so as to produce optimal allocation at the margin of different factors which could be substituted within and between uses. As far as possible this allocation should be achieved by the market, since the capacity of the state to allocate resources efficiently was extremely limited—primarily because state knowledge was extremely limited (1947, 5, 7, 8, 22, 41–42, 44–46, 50, 53–54; 1954, 201–25; 1935a, 16; 1971a, 146).

This question of knowledge arises again in Robbins's treatment of the problems of allocation within a socialist economy, and it is particularly interesting because otherwise his basic approach, as already indicated, neglected the problem of the generation of knowledge, in its concentration on choice. It is also interesting because where Robbins recognizes the problem of knowledge, as in dealing with wartime and socialist allocation, the source is unambiguously Austrian: the work of Mises.

Socialism involved both allocative and adaptive failures. Because consumer preferences could not be known and because there were no objective engineering data on costs, there was no possibility of efficient allocation, in accordance with consumer rankings, without a market system to register those rankings. Adaptive failure arose both because of the bureaucratic nature of socialism and also because of the lack of knowledge not only of changes in preferences but also of changes in technological opportunities.[12]

All this was based squarely upon Mises's classic critique (1932, 86–138)—and it contrasts both with Robbins's own tendency to neglect

12. Mises 1932, 86–138. See Robbins 1934d, 146–56; 1935a, 17–18; 1935c, 92; 1937b, 130–34, 141–54, 194–218; 1939a, 27–28, 85–87, 189, 192, 194–202; 1940, 95–96; 1947, 22–23, 77–80; 1963, 38, 40, 104; 1966, 28–29; 1971a, 55–56, 61–62, 64, 67, 191–92; 1976, 29–31, 142–50.

knowledge-generation elsewhere and to focus on choice, and also with Wicksteed's own Fabian sympathies (though these were not entirely without recognition of some of the problems of socialism). It is, however, interesting that with some weakening of the Austrian influence on Robbins, after World War II, there was also some distancing from the Austrian position on the role of the state in allocation. Robbins certainly did not completely dissociate himself from the analysis. Indeed he reaffirmed its importance in his *Autobiography* of 1971. But he did seem to distance himself from Hayek's position (though without mentioning Hayek by name) as set out in *The road to serfdom,* in which Hayek had viewed nationalization as the thin end of a totalitarian wedge (Robbins 1976, 137–38). It is evident too in Robbins's treatment of education during the 1960s and in his treatment of state patronage of the arts, in both of which the careful general equilibrium analysis of the wartime years played little if any part (Robbins 1963, 53–72; O'Brien 1988b, ch. 6).

Costs and markets. Three key elements derived from the basic model provided, for Robbins, a unified and internally consistent treatment of costs and markets. The first was the insistence upon the general equilibrium context of any market problem. Coupled with this was an emphasis upon the importance of asking *general* equilibrium questions about the "sensitivity" of partial equilibrium conclusions to general equilibrium considerations (1933a, xv n.; 1934a, 10). The second, derived from the general equilibrium approach, was the insistence that cost meant *opportunity* cost, so that it was impossible to have given and fixed cost schedules (1933a, x; 1934a, 2–3; Wieser 1889, 171–73, 176; Wicksteed 1910, book 1, ch. 9 and p. 732). Thirdly, factor supplies, having alternative uses, *including* own consumption, could never be taken as fixed (1930a, 208; 1934a, 3; Wicksteed 1910, book 1, ch. 9; O'Brien 1988b, ch. 7). The analysis of costs and markets, therefore, started from the concept of general equilibrium and analyzed adjustments in terms of disturbances from, and returns to, equilibrium, with the focus of attention upon the equilibrium points themselves rather than upon the intermediate process of adjustment and the knowledge-generation thereby involved (1928, 395–97; 1930, 194; cf. Addleson 1984, 508).

The approach was thus opposed both to aggregation—there was no sense in talking about production in the aggregate, and the study of production was essentially a study of factor allocation (1934c)—and to partial equilibrium analysis which neglected the wider complications (1934a, 8–9; 1933a, xv n.). Robbins criticized Marshall's fishing industry example, a partial equilibrium paradigm, both because it neglected the source of the demand shift (and the implied effect on cost curves if resources were freed from elsewhere) and also—more surprisingly—

for its neglect of expectations (1934a, 16). It was the former criticism which, however, seems to have carried most weight with him. Increasing and diminishing returns to scale could not be discussed in a partial equilibrium context; he insisted that the cost controversies of the 1930s were simply working along the wrong lines (1933a, xv n.). Factor supply variations reflected demand changes. Factor valuation reflected the valuation of the next most highly valued alternative use of the services of any factor (1934a, 6; 1930a, 207–8).

In insisting on a general equilibrium, opportunity cost approach to costs, Robbins made the most of his insistence on the existence of a generally received corpus of sophisticated theory coalescing from a variety of eras and sources. In an article on costs he cited Wieser, Wicksteed, Davenport, Knight, Henderson, Pantaleoni, Wicksell, and Mayer (Robbins 1934a). The work of these authors was all held to lead to the analysis which Robbins was expounding, with costs determined by the *values* of the "goods of first order" displaced.

In the context of costs Robbins placed particular emphasis on Mayer's interpretation of Wieser. This is important because, in contrast to Robbins's writings on socialism, we have in this analysis a fixed range of opportunities between which consumers choose without having to search for information. There clearly *is* an Austrian input here; ultimately, though, it is impossible to separate the message which Robbins took from Wieser (as interpreted by Mayer) from the influence of Wicksteed. For Wicksteed had variable factor supplies seen as a result of demand changes within a given technical environment; Wicksteed drew a parallel between factor allocation and the optimization of personal expenditure, with balancing and substitution at the margin and factor costs determined by the anticipated value of the product (1910, 370–98, 506, 540, 545); Wicksteed was himself quoted by Robbins as showing the true nature of the supply curve (i.e., the sellers' own demand curve), thus demonstrating the irrelevance of the cost controversy around 1930 (1933a, xv); and Wicksteed it was who emphasized the all-pervasive importance of choice.

Nonetheless it does seem reasonable to argue, particularly given the rather prolix nature of Wicksteed's exposition and his fondness for what Hutchison has nicely called "wayside sermons" (1953, 99), that as Robbins found the parallels with Wicksteed's work in that of Austrian writers, the Austrian sources sharpened and deepened Robbins's own perception and influenced him in the discussion of those particular aspects of Wicksteed's treatment of costs upon which he chose to lay key emphasis.

Production. As already indicated, Robbins considered production—most notably in an encyclopaedia article of 1934—to be merely one aspect of allocation theory. He treated it in explicitly Austrian terms. Production was activity, involving goods of higher order, directed to increasing the number of scarce economic goods of the first order. The business of the theory of production was not the summation of technologies but the study of the system of relations within the price system (1934c). Approached in this way, the Austrian approach fundamentally undermined what Robbins regarded as a persistent tendency among economists to confuse the technical and the economic.[13] It also fundamentally undermined, as already noted, the idea of production in the aggregate; and Robbins, in the encyclopaedia article referred to, rejected this concept completely. Production could not be measured in the aggregate without valuations; but the valuations, if not arbitrary, must change with the very composition of output (1934c, 464–65; 1935a, 67–68).

Distribution. Robbins's distribution theory illustrates some interesting aspects of his intellectual capital. At the highest level of generality, the approach was Austrian, based upon Austrian capital theory received via Wicksell, although received by a mind already preconditioned by exposure to the classical wage fund approach, a mind moreover which was able to find important points of contact between the Austrian and wage fund elements. But a key role was given to variations in factor supplies, so that (to use Wicksteed's phrase) they had a "reserve price." Indeed on this basis Robbins was able to oppose one particular branch of the Austrian tradition, albeit a heterodox one: that embodied in the work of Schumpeter (Robbins 1930a).

The treatment of capital was thus along these lines. Because capital was demanded and was limited in supply by time preference, its services enjoyed a price. Interest was a necessary reward—a fundamental tenet of Austrian economics. But given the point about own-consumption of factors and their services, Robbins went further. The very existence of a stock of capital required people to be prepared not to consume that capital, by failing to provide for depreciation. Thus it was necessary, even in a stationary state in which the capital stock did not grow, that capital should receive a reward. (This also reflected an argument of John Stuart Mill; see Robbins 1930a, 211–14; see also O'Brien 1975, 120.)

But as we move away from capital, the treatment becomes much more English and much less Austrian. The treatment of rent bears classical scars, although it was undoubtedly affected by Wicksteed's discussion which stressed the parallel between rent and other factor rewards. It thus avoided the standard pitfall of neglecting transfer earnings. But

13. 1934c; 1935a, 35. See also Weber 1947, 147, 201, 207; 1949, 34–35. Cf. Kirzner 1976, 127, 131.

there was nothing uniquely Austrian about this, and Robbins's own treatment seems to have stemmed from an attempt to work out the puzzles which he experienced on reading Marshall's careful, but ultimately rather ambiguous, treatment (1930a, 209–11).

The discussion of labor, in which Robbins did some of his most distinguished microeconomic work in the 1930s, is neither English classical nor Wicksteedian, nor Austrian—it is Marshallian. He used the elasticity of demand for labor as a key concept on the demand side, when examining the effects of variations in labor hours (1929a); and in examining labor supply he used his famous concept (borrowed from Dalton) of the elasticity of demand for income in terms of effort (1930c).

In fact it seems that Robbins, in his detailed treatment of distribution, tended to depart from the highest level of generality as espoused by Menger, Wieser, and Wicksteed and move towards the tripartite English classical division of factors into land, labor, and capital. There was nothing that was particularly Austrian in this. He accepted the high-level generalizations of Wicksteed and the Austrians. But in applying the theory the eclecticism of his approach allowed him to draw on much more traditional analyses. Faced with particular problems, indeed, he frequently seemed to owe more to Marshall than to either the Austrians or Wicksteed, although the point should be made that much of his distribution theory was written before he had come as completely under the influence of Austrian economics as he was to show himself in his 1934 "production" article.

III. *Macroeconomics*

1. *Prewar macroeconomics: content*

Robbins's prewar writings on macroeconomics are to be found chiefly in an article on the trade cycle (1932b) and in *The Great Depression* (1934d), a book which enjoyed considerable success in its time, together with more miscellaneous writings including articles in *Lloyds Bank Review* (1935d, 1937c, 1938d; see also 1936a, 1936b).

Robbins approached macroeconomic fluctuation from the direction of trade cycle theory. Such an approach was in accordance with his general desire, noted already, to perceive the existence of a long-accumulated and well-established body of theory. However, he concentrated on a monetary approach to the trade cycle rather than a "real" approach, whether of the "overinvestment" or other kind. This in itself is interesting in relation to the origins of his thought. In contrast to English classical economics—or at least to the currency school (O'Brien 1971, 63)—Robbins did not start from the idea that there was an endogenous trade cycle which could be magnified or damped by inappropriate or appropriate monetary policy. Rather, he treated the trade cycle as being *in itself* a monetary phenomenon. Thus the origins of his theory, at least in the form in which, finally evolved, he presented it to the world, lie outside English classical roots.

The basic model worked liked this. An exogenous increase in the money supply resulted in a lowering of the rate of interest. This caused investment to increase because marginal investment was now more profitable. This in turn raised demand for investment goods. The relative price of investment goods increased—relative prices of consumption and investment goods are important in this analysis—and resources were bid away from consumption goods industries. Forced saving ensued. The supply curves in the consumption goods industries shifted to the left, resulting in higher prices for consumption goods, reduced consumption of these goods, and the freeing of resources for the investment goods industries. This is critical, because the essence of a monetarily induced boom in this vision is increased investment without increased *voluntary* saving—and this mismatch between voluntary saving and investment is disequilibrating.

As resources, principally labor, are bid away into the investment goods industries, they receive higher wages. The spending of these higher wages shifts the demand schedules for consumption goods. Consumption goods outputs recover their old level. Consumption goods price levels are now higher than before the disturbance, as output has expanded along the new higher supply schedule. Consumption goods are thus able to compete for resources. Wages rise throughout the economy. The *relative* prices of consumption goods and investment goods have been restored to the old ratio, although at a new higher general price level. Forced saving has, for the moment, ceased. In order to continue with investment projects to which they are committed, entrepreneurs seek yet more credit in order to capture resources. This involves bidding up resource prices further and reimposes forced saving. However, this has the effect of raising the rate of interest as the entrepreneurs compete for credit, and thus the boom is choked off (1932b, 424–29; 1934d, 30–37).

The key propositions in all this are, firstly, that monetary expansion, through a lowering of the rate of interest, is the key to the trade cycle; secondly, that investment is very sensitive to the rate of interest. The latter was an argument which Keynes used in his Wicksellian *Treatise*, although his particular employment of it was very effectively criticized by Hawtrey (Davis 1981).

Monetarily induced booms were always faulty. By contrast, a non-monetary boom could occur as a result of an upward shift in the demand for investment goods, accompanied by a leftward shift in the *demand* curve for consumption goods. This involved more *voluntary* saving, and the relative price of consumption goods and investment goods would really represent people's preferences. It is highly significant that Robbins, like Mises and Hayek but unlike the long line of overinvestment theorists (some of whose work was criticized in Robbins's 1932 trade cycle article), believed that there was no harm in this kind of general *equilibrium* adjustment. By contrast, a monetarily induced boom involved a leftward shift in the *supply curve* for consumption goods, so that there was *forced* saving rather than an increase in voluntary saving. The change in the relative price of consumption goods and investment goods did not, in the forced saving case, represent people's true preferences, and thus a *disequilibrium* was created.

Unemployment was, in a sense, incidental to the whole theory. As investment goods industries shrank again, after the rise in the rate of interest, unemployment emerged as essentially an adjustment problem in an economy which tended to a general equilibrium set of relative prices, appropriate to full employment in the long run. Sticky wages might prolong labor market disequilibrium—hence Robbins's approval of wage cuts (an approval of which he was later so very ashamed) and his reservations about trade unions and unemployment insurance (1931a, 51–52; 1931b, 100; 1932b, 429–30; 1934d, 69–71, 82–83, 107, 117–18, 185–89).

Thus it was essential to "sweat out" the unemployment produced by the monetary disequilibrium—monetary expansion to counter unemployment merely reproduced the problem which had caused unemployment in the first place. Arguments that the price level should be raised by monetary expansion, as put forward in particular by the *Economist*, were in Robbins's view wholly mistaken—indeed there were conclusive reasons within Austrian macroeconomic theory for allowing the price level to *fall* if the trend of productivity was upwards. For as we shall see, in Wicksell's model the price level could be *stabilized* by allowing an increase in the money supply in line with productivity increases; but in the Mises-Hayek development of Wicksell's work, the distortion in *relative* prices caused by even this degree of monetary expansion was fundamentally disequilibrating and thus undesirable (1932b, 418; 1932d, 1932e, 1932f, 1932g; 1934d, 73–75).

As a model this has a number of fairly obvious drawbacks. It is not really clear why entrepreneurs should seek further funds when their expansion of investments is initially checked (1934d, 39); the implication is that unless they can obtain further funds they will lose all that they have already invested, because the project will be incomplete. This is not spelled out, although there are scattered references to incomplete investment projects in Central Europe. Moreover, Robbins argued that *proportionately more* funds would be required at the second round of borrowing—again this is not explained, although the implication is that it is due to the need to outweigh the newly enhanced flow of consumption good demand following the initial expansion (cf. Hayek 1931b, 132–35). But the model as a whole is weak on the secondary phases of the cycle, and it does not spell out exactly what it is in the monetary regime that stops banks from creating yet more credit—an issue which indeed Wicksell had explored in his concept of the pure credit economy, although treading, as Hicks has noted, on the borderline between stability and hyperinflation (Hicks 1939, 251–54; 1982; cf. Robbins 1934d, 38–41; Hayek 1931b).

The question of what happens to the *general* price level, given an increase in the money supply, also involves a significant ambiguity in the Austrian model. The Austrians were critical of Fisher for envisaging a general proportionate rise in prices; and Hayek insisted that the key issue was *relative* prices. He emphasized this element in the work of Mises and contrasted it with the attention which Wicksell had focused on the general price level (Hayek 1933, 16, 103–4, 118–19). Yet in fact the general price level *must* change in this model. Firstly we have a rise in the relative price of investment goods caused by an increase in the demand for investment goods; then we have an upward shift in the supply curves for consumption goods; then we have an upwards shift in the demand curves for consumption goods to restore parity of relative prices at a higher general price level. Robbins himself was vague on this issue, although chapter 3 of *The Great Depression* does envisage general price level variations. He rejected the quantity theory in its most direct form, but he avoided the issue of effects on the general price level produced by successive changes in relative prices (1932b, 424). On the one hand it is difficult to argue that he anticipated the neoclassical synthesis, at least in the form in which this involves an exogenous price level; on the other hand his ambiguity over the question of the general price level enabled him to revert to the Wicksellian framework after World War II.

Nonetheless, despite these problems the model satisfied Robbins's desire for continuity in economic thought and for a body of analysis which could be presented as embodying accumulated economic wisdom—indeed, quite apart from the main sources for this approach, to be discussed below, there are also points of contact with Marshall's discussion of monetary transmission in *Official papers* and with Keynes's Wicksell-like model in his *Treatise*.

The approach had the attraction that it could be couched in terms of the disaggregated general equilibrium to which both the Austrians and Robbins attached such importance at that date. In terms of that general equilibrium approach the role of the rate of interest in checking excessive investment, in the absence of monetary disturbance, could be clearly spelled out. Hayek in particular explained the general "intertemporal" equilibrium concept involved. Changes in the money supply then violated this intertemporal general equilibrium by producing demand changes for which there were not corresponding initial supply changes, thus disequilibrating savings and investment (1933, 74–75, 93, 102). Robbins was able to draw upon this general equilibrium framework in criticizing J. A. Hobson and arguing that the price and cost information, and the rate of interest, facing entrepreneurs would prevent the overinvestment envisaged by Hobson. A rise in *voluntary* saving was a general equilibrium adjustment and simply reflected a change in society's preference for present and future goods (1932b, 420–27).

All this was strongly influenced by, in particular, Hayek (1931a, 150; [1928] 1984); and it is perhaps ironic that Hayek should have changed his mind so firmly, in 1937, over the fundamental importance of employing a general equilibrium framework (Hutchison 1981, 210–19; McCloughry 1984; Caldwell 1988).

This whole approach to macroeconomic problems came under very considerable attack. Robbins, in its defense, produced *The Great Depression* with a mass of statistical material to buttress his contention that, in the world of the 1920s and 1930s, this model had significant explanatory power. He argued, as Hayek had done (1984, 124–25), that the United States had provided the motor of world monetary expansion (1934d, 22–29, 44–54). What was needed to counter this kind of thing was a tight gold standard regime, not the bogus post-1925 gold standard in which domestic monetary expansion and contraction had not followed gold movements. A "managed money supply" of which Keynes was an advocate (and attacked over this, though rather obliquely, by Robbins in 1925 in his very first publication) was exactly what was *not* required (Robbins 1925; see also 1929c, 412).

As already indicated, monetary expansion in the face of unemployment was another dose of what, in this model, had already created the unemployment in the first place. (This fundamental belief was also coupled with a fear, stemming in particular from the 1923 German hyperinflation, of inflation itself as a socially destructive force which was to produce the rise of the Nazis in Germany; see Robbins 1936b, 415; cf. 1937a; 1939a, 272–74; 1972, 20.)

There is a bit more to Robbins's prewar macroeconomics than all this. By 1939 he had retreated a little from the position of *The Great Depression*, in which he had held that public expenditure diverted voluntary saving, which was required for investment, and thus aggravated disequilibrium. In the model of this book, a shortage of voluntary saving is of central importance. At the time of its writing Robbins was very critical of the National Recovery Administration's policies in the United States and hostile towards the idea of government as the pacemaker of the economy.[14] But by 1939, in his *Economic basis of class conflict,* he recognized that in the presence of unemployed resources a vital part of the model was no longer relevant. It was no longer true that resources were captured from consumer goods industries, which previously employed them, by expanding investment goods industries. Since Robbins was methodologically a "verificationist," to whom the appropriateness of assumptions was of key importance, the change of position in the face of *sustained* unemployment was perfectly understandable. (The approach in his earlier writings had been that the unemployment then being experienced was a temporary disequilibrium phenomenon which would not last, given correct monetary policies, and which would not have existed in the first place but for ill-advised monetary expansion.) In the late 1930s he repudiated the "Treasury view" of crowding out, and he explored—in *Lloyds Bank Review* of 1938—the conditions for successful deficit finance (1937c, 239–41, 1939a, 217–22, 224–25, 256–57; see also 1941, 24–25; 1976, 26).

Nonetheless Robbins hedged all this around with qualifications, and it is only slightly misleading to represent his prewar macroeconomic thought by the kind of model already described (1937c, 239–41; 1939a, 217–30, 256–77).

2. *Prewar macroeconomics: sources*

In essence, the origins of this model lie in three sources. From English classical economics Robbins took a concern with the money supply and the basic presupposition that causality ran from the money supply to the price level. From Wicksell he took a concern with the implications of changes in that money supply for the rate of interest and the subsequent effect on demand in the economy. From Mises and Hayek he took a concern with the *way* the rate of interest affected aggregate demand and, in particular, the way it altered *relative* prices so as to impose forced saving on the community. The result was classified by Haberler as Austrian trade-cycle theory (1937, 30, 31, 44n., 54n., 56, 57n., 76), and there is no doubt that in fitting Robbins into this group Haberler was doing no violence to the evidence. Despite the other authors referred to, Robbins's principal sources seem to have been the second edition of Mises's *Money* ([1924] 1934) and his 1928 book on monetary stabilization and economic policy; Hayek's essays on intertemporal equilibrium

14. 1934d, 58, 63–64, 91–92, 125, 130–31, 135–36, 141, 144, 190, 192–94, 197; 1937b, 261–62; see also Hutchison 1978, 185.

([1928] 1984) and the paradox of saving (1931a) and his *Monetary theory and the trade cycle* ([1929] 1933); and an article by Strigl on the effects of monetary expansion (1928). To these should be added Hayek's lectures at the London School of Economics, which were published as *Prices and production* (1931b). All the items apart from this were read by Robbins in the original German; indeed neither Mises's 1928 book nor the article by Strigl have ever appeared in English, and Hayek's piece on intertemporal equilibrium only appeared in English in the year of Robbins's death, 1984.

There are undoubtedly some points at which the Austrian affiliation is less than complete. In particular Robbins's treatment of the rate of interest poses something of a problem. Robbins had imbibed Austrian capital theory both directly from Austrian authors and also indirectly from Cassel, Fetter, and Wicksell (1932b, 422, 427; cf. Cassel 1923, 2:537–47; Haberler 1937, 68–70). But he never clearly spelled out the concept of a period of production, unlike Hayek, for whom this was a central concept in the inner mechanics of the trade cycle model ([1927] 1984; 1931b, ch. 2).

But Robbins's analysis was Austrian for all that. Indeed he was writing his 1932 article on the trade cycle at about the time that Hayek was actually lecturing at the London School of Economics, expounding the theory which was to appear in *Prices and production*. Moreover, the latter part of Robbins's trade cycle article is a straightforward exposition of Hayek's theory, with Strigl cited in support. The work of the Austrians would in any case have particular appeal for Robbins, with his desire to obtain a corpus of accepted theory, because their approach was scholarly and involved extensive citation from the work of predecessors. Thus Mises referred to the work of the currency school; and while he did not accept their concept of an endogenous cycle, there was considerable agreement over the fundamentally fallacious nature of the banking (passive money supply) principle, which Mises emphatically rejected in his 1928 book (58, 63–66). Mises too was very conscious of the value of Wicksell's work; and he forms the essential bridge between the work of the Swedish economist and that of Hayek, who was indeed in the habit of referring to the Wicksell-Mises theory (1933, 47, 111, 116–19).

Hayek's work built on that of Mises, as Hayek himself acknowledged, but laid particular emphasis on three factors. Firstly, there was the importance of forced saving (1933, 93, 214–26; 1931b, 54–60). This became central to Robbins's own approach (1932b, 423–27). Secondly, Hayek paid some attention to the structure of interest rates (1933, 200–202, 226–30)—this, as Wesley Mitchell was to note in reviewing *The Great Depression*, seems to have made rather less impression on Robbins (Mitchell 1935). Thirdly, Hayek emphasized expectations ([1928] 1984). This particular message was very firmly accepted by Robbins (1935a, 62), who stressed in his 1934 book that a recovery of business confidence was vital if the economy was to come out of depression (160–61; cf. 1939a, 242–44).

Of all Hayek's works the volume *Geldtheorie und Konjunkturtheorie* of 1928, which appeared in English in 1933 as *Monetary theory and the trade cycle,* was undoubtedly the most influential on Robbins. In introducing the English translation Robbins wrote:

> The criteria of scientific validity take no account of origins, and the economist who refused to avail himself of a particular set of propositions because they were foreign would be acting no less unscientifically than the chemist or physicist who acted on similar principles. It has been well said that there are only two kinds of Economics—good Economics and bad Economics. All other classifications are misleading.
>
> Unfortunately, the economist, far more than the practitioner of the natural sciences, is victim to the curse of Babel. The chemist and the physicist . . . can converse in what to all intents and purposes is an international language. . . . In Economics this is not so. The complicated social relationships which are its chief preoccupation lend themselves much less to merely symbolic analysis. . . . Small wonder too that, in consequence of these conditions, there is probably more overlapping and wasteful duplication of effort in Economics than in any other branch of scientific knowledge. I know of no natural science in which it would be possible for a man to devote years to the discovery of propositions which are already commonplace in language areas other than his own. It is notorious that in Economics this frequently happens. (1933b, 5–7)

To put the matter crudely: here was a well-developed and refined body of macroeconomic thought which people in Cambridge had been rediscovering with a futile waste of effort. They should read Hayek's work.

But in one important respect Robbins was closer to Mises than to Hayek. Robbins typically treated monetary disturbances as exogenous—the result of foolish behavior by central bankers. This was also Mises's position. But Hayek argued that increases in the money supply were endogenous (1933, 150–79), resulting from the operation of the deposit multiplier in the commercial banking system, and that the initiating cause need not even be monetary at all (182).

However, Robbins and Hayek were very much in agreement with the idea that credit expansion would simply make macroeconomic problems worse. Robbins's opposition to such expansion has already been noted. Hayek argued that counter-cyclical monetary policy, even if directed towards consumption goods, would raise the price of production goods in a search for means to increase output of consumption goods (1933, 18–19; 1931a, 150).

Hayek was also one of the sources for Robbins's view that depression in Austria itself had been accompanied by capital shortage (1932b, 430; 1934d, 91), a finding which was exactly as predicted by the Austrian model, in which forced saving plays a transient role in providing extra resources for investment and is ultimately overcome. Hayek had argued that the problem lay partly in public investment, which exacerbated the problems facing firms in a disequilibrium situation by crowding out the available funds (1931c). Another source cited by Robbins was Morgenstern, who argued that the whole capital base of Austrian industry had become eroded through the disequilibrium resulting from monetary expansion (1931, 255). The case of Kaldor, who was also cited by Robbins, is particularly interesting in this context. Kaldor's basic thesis was that rising costs were making business unprofitable but that Austrian firms were investing more. He explained this by the institutional fact of banks' equity participation in firms in Austria. They were thus reluctant to close down firms which they at least partly owned, while they kept receiving savings which they could invest in the firms as long as confidence in the banks remained (1932, 27–29). But in the last part of the article Kaldor retreated from this institutional explanation and for the first time related the argument to forced saving and disproportionality along Austrian trade cycle theory lines (34–35).

One important matter, which had exercised economists since Wicksell's day, concerned the correct monetary policy to be pursued in an economy with secularly rising productivity. As had emerged from an earlier controversy—of which the Austrians themselves apparently remained long unaware (Hayek 1932, 115)—it was necessary to keep the money rate of interest below the real rate of interest in order to achieve a stable price level, because the secularly rising level of output would require an increasing money supply for price stability (see also Hayek 1933, 119–20). But the purity of the Austrian position required that such increases in the money supply should not occur, because they would distort *relative* prices in the economy and thus cause disequilibrium along the lines of the Austrian trade cycle theory. The logical conclusion of this position was that secularly rising productivity should be accompanied by a secularly falling price level. This conclusion was in fact explored and defended as a position by Haberler in 1927 (112–17) and by Mises in 1928 (30–34). It was possible to argue, in terms of the Austrian apparatus, that there was an asymmetry between monetary deflation (which increased the weight of fixed burdens) and a price fall due to rising productivity. This reflected costs *falling* for producers, while fixed income receivers would share in the generally increased prosperity. This was also the position taken by Hayek in his 1929 book ([1929] 1933, 111–16) and the position defended by Robbins in his trade cycle article (1932b, 418). Robbins was able to call in his aid, in a passage which in its reference to "sadistic deflationists" reflected wounded sensitivity, Marshall, Edgeworth, Pigou, Robertson, and Taussig. But the source for his position was Austrian, at least primarily.

In fact there are extra problems here—the celebrated "machinery question" raised by Barton and Ricardo is involved. Both Haberler (1927, 114–15) and Hayek (1931a, 150) explored this aspect of the problem, but Robbins avoided it.

Nonetheless there is no doubt that he had read, digested, and thought a great deal about the Austrian writings. They were certainly the immediate sources for the microeconomic positions which he expounded in the early 1930s. They also had the advantage that they fitted in as *further developments* of the general corpus of evolved theory, to the existence of which Robbins attached such importance in all aspects of economics, whether macroeconomics or microeconomics. Such a corpus of theory could, so to speak, be brandished at Cambridge to show the Cambridge crowd the error of their ways and the subjective nature of their own originality. Robbins attached great importance to "the authority of competent economists," and this was not merely, though it certainly was also, a polemical device. It reflected his "conversion" to economics from socialism.

3. *Postwar macroeconomics*

Robbins went out of his way, at least in his later postwar writings, to stress his repudiation of the precise Mises-Hayek model and its implications for policy. As he wrote in his *Autobiography:* "I had become the slave of theoretical constructions which, if not intrinsically invalid as regards logical consistency, were inappropriate to the total situation which had then developed and which therefore misled my judgement" (1971a, 117).

Robbins now accepted that government should act counter-cyclically (1971a, 188–89). But he had not become a Keynesian; and the underlying model which informed his judgment on macroeconomic matters was not all that different from what had gone before. He certainly did not accept the whole of the analytical apparatus in *The general theory.* As he was later to write: "It would not be true to say that then [during war service], or at any subsequent period, I had become a Keynesian in the sense of accepting au pied de la lettre all the analytical propositions of the *General Theory*" (1971a, 188). He was publicly skeptical about the fundamental importance of *The general theory* when he reviewed Harrod's biography of Keynes (Robbins 1951; 1970, 244), and he was some considerable distance both from Beveridge, with the latter's concept of permanent excess demand in the labor market (Robbins 1954, 18–40; 1978, 10), and from what Keynes's associates in the so-called Circus believed to be macroeconomic truth.

The Radcliffe Report attracted Robbins's particular criticism, and he published, no fewer than three times, a closely reasoned critique in which he argued that in replacing the money supply with liquidity the committee had been guilty of a fallacy of composition—the money supply determined how far liquidity could be *realized*. He also thought the committee's view that there was no upper limit to velocity of circulation "highly implausible." He certainly did not accept—and here we go back to the currency and banking controversy—that the money supply depended on the price level, as the later self-styled Keynesians tended to believe (1963, 204–10; 1971a, 235; 1971b, 7–9; 1979, ix).

Robbins's position in the postwar world was basically this. He held that macroeconomic disturbances originated in excess monetary aggregate demand. In this view changes in the money supply were critical. The money supply could be controlled either through the use of interest rates or through operation directly on monetary aggregates (1971a, 233). In practice he believed it was better to control the money supply directly than to operate on the rate of interest (though bank rate was a valuable supplementary weapon), and the monetary aggregate that he had in mind was sterling M_3.[15] Control of aggregate demand was important, both because of the economically destructive and disruptive effects of inflation and because of its social injustice.

But there are two fundamental characteristics of this later work which mean that it is, for the most part at least, no longer Austrian. Firstly, the whole emphasis on *relative* prices of consumption and investment goods, and the importance of forced saving and of the dislocation produced by monetary expansion, is played down. Although Robbins approached the matter primarily from the monetary side, he did so essentially in terms of the Keynesian aggregates, for the most part. (His prewar opposition to the concept of aggregation as a whole had disappeared; but in any case the Mises-Hayek model itself implied a significant degree of at least sectoral aggregation in practice, so this change may not be important.) Robbins's attention had now switched from relative prices to the general price level as a whole, something strongly

15. 1949, 21; 1954, 76–80; 1958a, 12–14; 1958b, 217–19; 1963, 210–21; 1971b, 9; 1976, 98; 1979, 19, 36–37, 58, 66, 76, 96.

opposed by Hayek in *Monetary theory and the trade cycle* (1933, 111–12). Secondly, the approach was no longer *exclusively* monetary. Robbins now held that fiscal policy had a fundamental role to play in controlling aggregate demand. It had to operate in conjunction with monetary policy, but it could not be ignored: "I do not believe in tying one arm behind my back when coping either with inflation or deflation" (1979, 80).

So what were the Austrian residues in Robbins's postwar macroeconomics? Firstly, there are traces—but only traces—of an Austrian general equilibrium approach to the economy in some of his writings. Secondly, Wicksell, on whose work Mises and Hayek had built, still clearly exercised an influence on Robbins, an influence which could all the more easily be exercised now that Robbins had switched his attention from relative prices to the general price level. Indeed Robbins referred to Wicksell in his dealings with the Radcliffe Committee (1958c, q. 10219). He thus still attached importance to the expansion of bank credit. Thirdly, some of the discussions of the harmful effects of inflation have an Austrian ring—especially the argument that inflation produces a cumulative shortage of working capital, which was one that had been put forward by Hayek in *Prices and production* (1931b, 151–52). Fourthly, although it does not occupy the central position which it had enjoyed in Robbins's prewar writings, the forced saving argument pops up from time to time, particularly in the 1970s, when he expressed concern about credit creation unmatched by saving, a rate of interest lower than the going rate of profit, and the operation of adaptive expectations in preventing forced saving from filling the gap between voluntary saving and investment demand (1958a, 24; 1958b, 21; 1958c, q. 10190; 1971b, 12–14; 1979, 28–29).

IV. *Conclusion*

The Austrian connection in Robbins's work is thus important, but it is not exclusive of other influences or completely overwhelming. Separating the influence of the Austrians from that of Wicksteed in Robbins's microeconomic writings is virtually impossible, partly because Wicksteed gave so very few clues as to the nature of the development of his own thought. But if it is in fact true that Wicksteed relied little on the Austrians and evolved his own body of thought by developing the work of Jevons and then coming into contact with the work of Pareto, then the influence of the Austrians on Robbins in the area of microeconomics is limited. But if limited, it is nonetheless important. Quite clearly it significantly affected Robbins's own view of *writers other than the Austrians*. It was an Austrian perspective which he adopted in synthesizing, in the interwar period, that corpus of economic theory to which he attached such importance. As he read the Austrians' works, he found in them not only elements which coincided with what he had already learned from Wicksteed but also insights which enabled him to see what was essential to Wicksteed and what could be dispensed with in the building up of an authoritative treatment of microeconomics.

In the area of macroeconomics, on the other hand, the story is very much clearer. Beginning from a base in English classical economics and in the work of Wicksell, Robbins became an articulate and influential expositor of the monetary trade cycle theory developed on a Wicksellian base, but in the light of the English classical monetary literature, by Mises and Hayek. At the height of the influence of Mises and Hayek in the 1930s, not only on Robbins but on economics generally, Robbins could be classified without difficulty as, in macroeconomic matters, a disciple of the Austrian economists. But the last part of the 1930s saw some fairly subtle shifts of position on his part; and in the postwar years, after wartime association with Keynes and, perhaps more importantly, with "Keynesians," Robbins no longer put forward the Mises-Hayek model. Nonetheless he certainly did not become a Keynesian; and many of the concerns of the Mises-Hayek approach continued to influence his attitude towards macroeconomic theory and policy, even though he now recognized the value of fiscal policy and accorded it significant weight in macroeconomic management.

But throughout all the shifts of emphasis, and even of position, one thing stands out very clearly. Without the literature of Austrian economics, and Robbins's own capacity to read it in the original German, the positions on theory and policy adopted by one of the most influential British economists of the twentieth century would have been significantly different.

I am most grateful to Bob Black, John Creedy, Sir Henry Phelps Brown, and Jack Wiseman for comments.

References

Addleson, M. 1984. Robbins's essay in retrospect: on subjectivism and on "economics of choice." *Rivista internazionale di scienze economiche e commerciali* 31:506–23.
Blaug, M. 1980. *The methodology of economics*. Cambridge.
Caldwell, B. 1988. Hayek's transformation. *HOPE* 20:513–41.
Cassel, G. 1923. *The theory of social economy*. Translated by J. McCabe. London.
Davis, E. G. 1981. R. G. Hawtrey, 1879–1975. In *Pioneers of modern economics in Britain*, edited by D. P. O'Brien and J. R. Presley, 203–33. London.
Haberler, G. von. 1927. *Der Sinn der Indexzahlen*. Tübingen.
———. 1937. *Prosperity and depression*. Geneva.

Hawtrey, R. 1938. *A century of bank rate*. London.
Hayek, F. von. [1925] 1984. Review of L. Schönfeld, *Grenznutzen und Wirtschaftsrechnung*. Reprinted in *Money, capital and fluctuations*. London.
———. [1927] 1984. On the problem of the theory of interest. Reprinted in *Money, capital and fluctuations*. London.
———. [1928] 1984. Intertemporal price equilibrium and movements in the value of money. Reprinted in *Money, capital and fluctuations*. London.
———. [1929] 1933. *Monetary theory and the trade cycle*. Translated by N. Kaldor and H. Croome. London.
———. 1931a. The "paradox" of saving. Translated by N. Kaldor and G. Tugendhat. *Economica* 11:125–69.
———. 1931b. *Prices and production*. London.
———. 1931c. Wirkungen des Mietzinsbeschrankügen. *Schriften des Vereins für Sozialpolitik* 182:253–70.
———. [1932] 1984. The fate of the gold standard. Reprinted in *Money, capital and fluctuations*. London.
———. 1934. Carl Menger. In Menger 1933–36, v–xxxviii.
Hicks, J. 1939. *Value and capital*. 2d ed. 1946. Oxford.
———. 1982. LSE and the Robbins Circle. In *Collected essays in economic theory*, vol. 3, *Money, interest and wages*. Oxford.
Hutchison, T. W. 1953. *A review of economic doctrines 1870–1929*. Oxford.
———. 1964. *Positive economics and policy objectives*. London.
———. 1978. *On revolutions and progress in economic knowledge*. Cambridge.
———. 1979. Robbins, Lionel. *International encyclopaedia of the social sciences*, edited by D. L. Sills, vol. 18, *Biographical supplement:* 660–63. New York.
———. 1981. *The politics and philosophy of economics*. Oxford.
Kaldor, N. 1932. The economic situation of Austria. *Harvard Business Review* 11:23–34.
Kirzner, I. 1976. *The economic point of view*. 2d ed. Kansas City.
McCloughry, R. 1984. Introduction to Hayek, *Money, capital and fluctuations*. London.
Mayer, H. 1925. Friedrich Wieser zum Gedächtnis' *Zeitschrift für Volkswirtschaft und Sozialpolitik*, n.s. 5:633–45.
Meade, J. E. 1984. In *Tributes in memory of Lord Robbins*, 5–7. London (LSE).
Menger, C. 1871. *Grundsätze der Volkswirthschaftslehre*. Vienna.
———. [1871] 1950. *Principles of economics*. Translated by J. Dingwall and B. Hoselitz. Glencoe, Ill.
———. [1883] 1963. *Problems of economics and sociology*. Translated by F. J. Nock. Urbana, Ill.
———. 1933–36. *Collected works*. With an introduction by F. von Hayek. Reprints of Scarce Tracts in Economic and Political Science, nos. 17–20 (LSE). London.
Mill, J. S. 1844. *Essays on some unsettled questions of political economy*. Reprinted in *Essays on economics and society*, edited by J. M. Robson. Toronto, 1967.
Mises, L. von. [1924] 1934. *The theory of money and credit*. 2d (1924) ed. translated by H. E. Batson. London.
———. 1928. *Geldwertstabilisierung und Konjunkturpolitik*. Jena.
———. 1932. *Die Gemeinwirtschaft*. 2d ed. Jena.
———. [1932] 1936. *Socialism*. 2d (1932) ed. translated by J. Kahane. London.
———. 1949. *Human action*. 3d ed. Chicago, 1966.

Mitchell, W. C. 1935. Review of L. Robbins, *The Great Depression*. *Quarterly Journal of Economics* 49:503–7.
Morgenstern, O. 1931. Kapital—und Kurswertänderungen der an der Wiener Börse notierten österreichischen Aktiengesellschaften 1913 bis 1930. *Zeitschrift für Nationalökonomie* 3.2 (December): 251–55.
O'Brien, D. P. 1971. *The correspondence of Lord Overstone*. Cambridge.
———. 1975. *The classical economists*. Oxford.
———. 1988a. Lionel Charles Robbins, 1898–1984. *Economic Journal* 98:104–25.
———. 1988b. *Lionel Robbins*. London.
———. 1989. Robbins as a political economist. *Economic Journal* 99:479–80.
Pantaleoni, M. [1889] 1898. *Pure economics*. Translated by T. Bruce. Reprinted. New York, 1957.
Phelps Brown, H. 1988. Lionel Charles Robbins, 1898–1984. *Proceedings of the British Academy* 1987 [publ. 1988] 73:601–29.
Robbins, L. 1925. Review of T. E. Gregory, *The present position of banking in America*. *Economica* 5:358–59.
———. 1927a. Mr. Hawtrey on the scope of economics. *Economica* 7:172–78.
———. 1927b. Review of M. J. Bonn, *Das Schicksal des Deutschen Kapitalismus*. *Economic Journal* 37:613–16.
———. 1928. The representative firm. *Economic Journal* 38:387–404.
———. 1929a. The economic effects of variations of hours of labour. *Economic Journal* 39:25–40.
———. 1929b. Review of Sir J. Stamp, *Some economic factors in modern life*. *Economic Journal* 39:248–50.
———. 1929c. Review of E. Cannan, *A review of economic theory*. *Economic Journal* 39:409–14.
———. 1930a. On a certain ambiguity in the conception of stationary equilibrium. *Economic Journal* 40:194–214.
———. 1930b. The present position of economic science. *Economica* 10:14–24.
———. 1930c. On the elasticity of demand for income in terms of effort. *Economica* 10:123–29.
———. 1931a. Economic notes on some arguments for protection. *Economica* 11:45–62.
———. 1931b. A reply to Mr. Keynes. *New Statesman and Nation*, 14 March, 98–100.
———. 1931c. Review of M. S. Braun, *Theorie der Staatlichen Wirtschaftspolitik*. *Economica* 11:469–72.
———. 1931d. Review of F. Machlup, *Borsenkredit, Industriekredit und Kapitalbildung*. *Economica* 11:472–75.
———. 1932a. *An essay on the nature and significance of economic science*. London.
———. 1932b. Consumption and the trade cycle. *Economica* 12:413–30.
———. 1932c. Tariffs for revenue. In *Tariffs: the case examined*, edited by Sir W. Beveridge et al., 170–84. London.
———. 1932d. Letter to the *Economist*, 14 May, 1081.
———. 1932e. Letter to the *Economist*, 28 May, 1118–19.
———. 1932f. Letter to the *Economist*, 11 June, 1295.
———. 1932. The Ottawa resolutions on finance and the future of monetary policy. *Lloyds Bank Review*, n.s. 3, no. 32 (October): 422–38.
———. 1933a. Introduction. In *Philip H. Wicksteed: the common sense of political economy* [1910]. London.

———. 1933b. Introduction to F. von Hayek, *Monetary theory and the trade cycle*. London.
———. 1934b. Remarks upon certain aspects of the theory of costs. *Economic Journal* 44:1–18.
———. 1934b. Remarks on the relationship between economics and psychology. *Manchester School* 5:89–101.
———. 1934c. Production. *Encyclopaedia of the social sciences*, edited by E. R. A. Seligman, 12:462–67. New York.
———. 1934d. *The Great Depression*. London.
———. 1934e. Introduction. In Mises, *The theory of money and credit*. 2d ed., translated by H. E. Batson, 11–13. London.
———. 1935a. *An essay on the nature and significance of economic science*. 2d ed. London.
———. 1935b. Introduction. In K. Wicksell, *Lectures on political economy*, translated by E. Classen. London.
———. 1935c. The planning of British agriculture—a rejoinder. *Lloyds Bank Review*, n.s. 6:89–92.
———. 1935d. The problem of stabilisation. *Lloyds Bank Review*, n.s. 6:207–18.
———. 1936a. The consequences of economic nationalism. *Lloyds Bank Review*, n.s. 7:226–39.
———. 1936b. Economic nationalism and monetary policy. *Banker* 38:192–97.
———. 1936c. Review of R. Nurkse, *Internationale Kapitalbewegungen*. *Economica*, n.s. 3:108–9.
———. 1937a. Foreword. In C. Bresciani-Turroni, *The economics of inflation* [1931], translated by M. E. Sayers. London.
———. 1937b. *Economic planning and international order*. London.
———. 1937c. How to mitigate the next slump. *Lloyds Bank Review*, n.s. 8:234–44.
———. 1937d. Review of G. Haberler, *Der internationale Handel* and of *The theory of international trade*, translated by A. Stonier and F. Benham. *Economica*, n.s. 4:102–5.
———. 1938a. Live and dead issues in the methodology of economics. *Economica*, n.s. 5:342–52.
———. 1938b. Les méthodes d'observation économique et les problèmes de la prévision en matière économique [delivered 1934]. In L. Robbins et al., *Cinq conferences sur la méthode dans les recherches économiques*. Paris. Translated in O'Brien 1988b.
———. 1938c. Interpersonal comparisons of utility: a comment. *Economic Journal* 48:635–41.
———. 1938d. The long-term budget problem. *Lloyds Bank Review*, n.s. 9:158–67.
———. 1939a. *The economic basis of class conflict*. London.
———. 1939b. The export problem. *Lloyds Bank Review*, n.s. 10:214–27.
———. 1940. Review of B. Souvarine, *Stalin: a critical survey of Bolshevism*. *Economica*, n.s. 7:94–96.
———. 1941. *Economic aspects of federation*. London.
———. 1947. *The economic problem in peace and war*. London.
———. 1949. The sterling problem. *Lloyds Bank Review* 14 (October): 1–31.
———. 1951. Review of R. F. Harrod, *The life of John Maynard Keynes*. *The Times*, 26 January, 7f–g. Reprinted in Robbins 1970.
———. 1953. Robertson on utility and scope. *Economica*, n.s. 20:99–111.

———. 1954. *The economist in the twentieth century and other lectures in political economy.* London.
———. 1958a. Thoughts on the crisis. *Lloyds Bank Review,* 48 (April): 1–26.
———. 1958b. *The aims of monetary policy and the means of achieving them.* Memorandum to the Committee on the Working of the Monetary System (Radcliffe Committee). London, 1960.
———. 1958c. Evidence to the Committee on the Working of the Monetary System (Radcliffe Committee), 24 July, pp. 673–78, qq. 10190–254. London: HMSO, 1960.
———. 1959. The present position of economics. *Rivista di politica economica.* Reprinted in *Guest lectures in economics,* edited by E. Henderson and L. Spaventa, 31–46. Milan, 1962.
———. 1963. *Politics and economics.* London.
———. 1966. An economist looks at business. In Institute of Economic Affairs, *Economics, business and government,* 25–31. London.
———. 1970. *The evolution of modern economic theory.* London.
———. 1971a. *Autobiography of an economist.* London.
———. 1971b. *Money, trade and international relations.* London.
———. 1972. Inflation: an international problem. Concluding observations. Both in *Inflation as a global problem,* edited by R. Hinshaw. Baltimore.
———. 1976. *Political economy past and present.* London.
———. 1978. Economists and trade unions, 1776–1977. In Institute of Economic Affairs, *Trade unions: public goods or public "bads"?* 5–16, 19–20. London.
———. 1979. *Against inflation.* London.
———. 1981. Economics and political economy. *American Economic Review* 71 (May suppl.): 1–10. Reprinted in *An essay on the nature and significance of economic science,* 3d ed., xi–xxxiii. London, 1984.
Schönfeld-Illy, L. 1924. *Grenznutzen und Wirtschaftsrechnung.* Reprinted. Vienna: International Carl Menger Library, 1982.
Steadman, I. 1987. Wicksteed, Philip Henry. *The new Palgrave,* edited by J. Eatwell, M. Milgate, and P. Newman, 4:915–19. London.
Strigl, R. 1928. Die Produktion unter dem Einflus einer Kreditexpansion. *Schriften des Vereins für Sozialpolitik* 173.2:185–211.
Weber, M. 1947. *The theory of social and economic organisation* [part 1 of *Wirtschaft und Gesellschaft*]. Translated by A. R. Henderson and T. Parsons. London.
———. 1949. *The methodology of the social sciences.* Translated by E. Shils and H. Finch. Glencoe, Ill.
Wicksteed, P. H. 1910. *The common sense of political economy and selected papers and reviews on economic theory.* Edited by L. Robbins. London, 1933.
Wieser, F. von. 1889. *Natural value.* Translated by C. A. Malloch. London.

[20]

Hayek as an intellectual historian

Introduction

The basic problem encountered by anyone trying to write about Hayek as an intellectual historian is this. His actual 'history of ideas' output is quite modest, while his total output is huge (even allowing for double counting) and the corpus as a whole contains much that is relevant for Hayek's treatment of the history of ideas. Moreover, Hayek's work extends well beyond economics; he was at least as much a philosopher with a good knowledge of economics (although the only system of which he was 'master' was the Menger–Wieser–Mises line) as an economist who wrote on philosophical subjects. All of his huge output is from the same mould as the intellectual history material, in citing similar sources and stressing similar themes. This is not intended as a criticism; Hayek was neither propagandist nor polemicist. But it does make it necessary to try to take a view of his whole output.

Studying Hayek as an intellectual historian is in fact quite a good way of holding up a mirror to Hayek – a signal of the elements in economics, law and politics which he considered to be important. Indeed, in teaching the history of economic thought he told the students what he had learnt from other writers, not what those writers themselves would have regarded as their most important contributions (1978, p. 52). Thus in his view the decisive contributions of Hume and Smith lay in demonstrating the emergence of the rule of law and of spontaneous order (1978, pp. 124–5).

Of course all intellectual history is written within a particular intellectual framework. But the intellectual historian has an overriding duty to ask continuously whether the account of the history of the subject given would appear coherent to the unconverted. Most Marxist, and indeed much Keynesian, history of ideas fails this test. In a few instances the same is true of Hayek, as we shall see.

For Hayek, it was necessary that the historian should have commitment. His heroes in this context – de Tocqueville, Burke and above all Acton for whom his admiration was intense – showed the way (1949, pp. 4, 23; 1960; 1992, pp. 209–18, 232–3, 247). The historian must have a moral standpoint (1992, pp. 201–15). Relativism was not enough. The future historian who displayed a relativist attitude towards Hitler would end up by glorifying him (1992, p. 208). For Hayek – an agnostic in religious matters – the moral standard was freedom, a position he held passionately while the overwhelming majority of his academic colleagues adopted an attitude of judicious agnosticism and relativism towards the horrors of the Stalinist and other Marxist regimes. He believed that history teaching which failed to stress freedom could do, and indeed had done, great harm; in Germany it had been responsible for the spread of anti-liberal sentiments (1992, p. 243).

Hayek and the history of ideas

Hayek's original training, based on Menger, Wieser and Böhm-Bawerk, was distinctly narrow.[1] But he set about remedying this narrowness with great vigour. Apart from his association with Mises, which was undoubtedly decisive in the development of his macroeconomics, he made (with help from Schumpeter, who wrote him letters of introduction) a trip to the United States in the early 1920s to study American economics (1992, pp. 19–41). He participated actively in the intellectual life of Vienna, and there are some signs in his work of an interest in the history of mathematics and natural science (1941, I, pp. 9–10, 17). Throughout his life he seems to have read endlessly.[2] He was a book collector (1934a, pp. 396, 419; 1992, p. 167) – indeed, he was a major collector of economic literature – and, if my own experience is anything to go by, he was very generous with his books.[3] It is thus not surprising that his great *Law, Legislation and Liberty* (1973–9) should reveal staggering erudition.[4] Indeed, about 25 per cent of the text was devoted to footnotes covering a huge range of literature from several centuries.[5] Whatever his standing as a political philosopher, there can be little doubt about his standing as a scholar (Hicks, 1940; Clapham, 1941; Fetter, 1940; Machlup, 1976, pp. 25, 42; 1979, p. 280), least of all as a scholar in the history of economics, though one whose range extended much further than that.

His erudition enabled him to be widely read in a number of different languages. It is true that he did not read Swedish (1933c, p. 115n); it is not clear whether in fact he could read Dutch (1991, p. 344) and his Greek citations, despite evident classical knowledge, are mainly from Loeb (parallel text) editions (1960, p. 419; 1978, pp. 92, 122, 225–6; 1988, pp. 38–47). But apart from an encyclopaedic knowledge of literature in German and English, he also read Italian (1978, p. 71), and displayed a detailed knowledge of the Latin texts of the later Schoolmen (1978, pp. 5, 28, 123, 253–5; 1992, pp. 43–4). He took a pleasure in nice linguistic points; *Geistgewissenschaft* was, he pointed out, introduced into German by the translator of J.S. Mill so there was not a lot of point in borrowing it in English (1942–4, I, p. 277n). He read extensively in French, and displayed a remarkable knowledge of French intellectual history and of the history of the Enlightenment (1941).

To some extent this multilingual background causes problems for the reader. The great series of articles on Science and Scientism (1941, 1942–4) read as if they are beautifully translated from the German, and the text is very dense.[6] Of course some of Hayek's work did appear first in German (1978, pp. 3, 31n7), but the problem seems to lie with texts which originally appeared in English. However it is a problem which is much less significant in Hayek's later output – from about 1946 onwards – and indeed his later cool, elegant, incisive prose contrasts very favourably with much of the critical material written about him contained in the volumes edited by Wood and Woods (1991).

Hayek attached enormous importance to the history of ideas. He viewed the development of ideas as part of that seamless evolutionary development which was at the heart of his view of the world. The influence of ideas – whether disastrous as in 'scientism' and French positivism, or benign as in the doctrine of unintended consequences from Mandeville, Smith and Hume to Menger – was enormous. Individuals, seized of particular ideas, could do enormous harm – there was nothing 'historically inevitable' about what Bismarck had done to Germany, paving the way for the rise of Hitler (1992, pp. 201–15; 223–36). It was necessary to understand the motivating ideas involved in particular events. Hayek agreed with Keynes's view, expressed in the famous quotation about 'Madmen in authority' (1949, p. 108; 1967, pp. 182, 347; Keynes 1936, pp. 383–4) and he was very much aware of the importance of historical myths – especially myths about the Industrial Revolution, the history of which had been largely written by socialists in his view (1954; 1991, pp. 56–72). (Whether Thorold Rogers, Ashley, or Archdeacon Cunningham could be described as socialists is of course very doubtful, but there are plenty of other individuals to support Hayek's general contention.)

Although Hayek ranged far and wide in dealing with intellectual history, he was certainly a significant writer on the history of economics, of which he described himself as a student (1992, p. 19). He lectured for more than four decades on the history of economic thought 'and enjoyed so doing' (1978, pp. 52n, 267). Indeed, the history of economic thought could be regarded as integral with Austrian economics (1968b, pp. 25–6) – as in the first volume of Böhm-Bawerk's *Capital* (1884–9). Menger himself lectured on the subject. Austrian scholarship thus helped to alleviate the narrowness of Hayek's original training. When Hayek himself turned to monetary theory, he approached it through the history of monetary thought (1984, p. 3; 1991, p. 127n), an exercise which in itself seems to have contributed significantly to the broadening of his knowledge. He developed a remarkable knowledge of French and Italian monetary literature (1991, pp. 155–76); while Jacob Viner had a perhaps more profound knowledge of the English language literature (though even here Hayek's grasp (1991, pp. 127–54, 177–244; 295–344) is certainly not negligible), Hayek's work ranged over the literature of four languages with assurance. Even within the English literature he showed remarkable knowledge; amongst his achievements here was the demonstration that the doctrine of forced saving originally owed something to Bentham. Others published earlier, but Bentham's work circulated in manuscript. From this source Hayek traced the development of the idea through to Walras and Wicksell (1932b; 1935, pp. 18–24). The concept ultimately became a key part of the monetary theory of Mises (1935, p. 25), from which Hayek's own monetary theory was derived.

Ironically, it was only the monetary history part of the work which survived; the larger project of a book on money had to be abandoned because of the rise of the Nazis (1984, pp. 3, 113n).

Hayek's intellectual inspirations

With the exception of David Hume, the three authors to whom Hayek refers most are Adam Smith, Adam Ferguson and Edmund Burke (1949, pp. 4, 7; 1960; 1973–9; 1978, p. 264; 1988, pp. 3, 34–5, 145; 1991, p. 106). It is on the work of these authors that Hayek grounded his ideas of spontaneous order, selective evolution, and the fundamental importance of unintended consequences of individual human actions taken on the basis of limited knowledge. Indeed, his treatment of Adam Smith is an interpretation so strongly in these terms that the more narrow aspects of Smith's analysis with which readers of the *Wealth of Nations* are familiar are obscured (1942–4, III, p. 28; 1978, pp. 124–5; 1988, pp. 34–5). It is perhaps because of this that Hayek confessed that, despite recognizing Smith's greatness, he found the history of economic thought lectures on Smith the hardest to give (1978, p. 267). But Smith, undoubtedly aware of the work of Mandeville (1978, p. 252), not only provided the intellectual basis for a critique of socialism, but also (in his *History of Astronomy*) for a critique of the simple-minded application of natural science ideas to complex economic phenomena (1942–4, I, p. 267). In attacking the 'man of system' Smith was, Hayek believed, attacking that 'constructivism' which was at the basis of socialism and social planning (1978, p. 269; 1988, p. 86). Even Smith's discussion of division of labour is interpreted as an example of the operation of unintended consequences (1978, p. 268).

Hayek also makes reference to Montesquieu and to Kant. Needless to say, Kant's separation of science and morals, his emphasis on the idea that morality consists in treating persons as ends and not as means, his insistence that rules of just conduct were independent of wider social goals, and his view that the State should provide general law, designed to protect individual freedoms, rather than detailed legislative interference, all appealed to Hayek. Yet, to this reader at least, it is doubtful how much Hayek derived ideas, as distinct from support, from the works of Kant. His overwhelming admiration was for David Hume, and Hume is much the most important single source for Hayek's general position. Hume was 'perhaps the greatest of all modern students of mind and society' (1978, p. 264).

It was Hume who had, through his critical rationalism, replaced constructivism with an explanation of the evolutionary nature of social and economic institutions where that evolution was governed by utility. It was Hume who, before Smith, had explained the end-independent nature of rules of just conduct. It was Hume who had explained the role of law, the importance of general laws rather than government by interests, and the emergence of spontaneous order within the framework provided by law. It was Hume who had explained how the market made it possible for individuals to perform services for others of whom they had no knowledge, through unintended consequences of their actions (1949, p. 4; 1960; 1967, pp. 106–21; 1973–9; 1978, pp. 71–2, 77n, 124, 264; 1988, pp. 13, 32–3, 86, 145; 1991, pp. 101–18).

Hume is thus very important for Hayek. Indeed, a glance at the citations in his *Constitution of Liberty*, one of his major statements, demonstrates this. At times, perhaps, he claimed too much for Hume; it really is not correct to say (1991, p. 153) that Hume anticipated most of classical international trade theory. But he was scrupulous in bringing out the strong possibility that Hume was familiar with Cantillon's *Essai* before its publication and thus owed it a debt (1935, p. 9; 1991, pp. 151, 287–8).

Amongst the Austrians, it is undoubtedly true that Mises had a significant influence on Hayek. Hayek admired Mises very greatly, and was associated with him in his private seminar in Vienna. It was Mises who secured for Hayek his first job. Before coming in contact with Mises Hayek had been, by his own account, a Fabian-type socialist, but after reading Mises's *Gemeinwirtschaft* (1922) he abandoned socialism (1942–4, I, p. 281n; 1992, pp. 4, 53, 131). He was particularly impressed by Mises's insistence that things such as a commodity, an economic good, or even money could not be defined in physical terms but only in terms of views that people held about them. A thoroughgoing subjectivist approach to economics was required. Needless to say, this ruled out physical planning. Mises's book on money (1912) was also an important influence on Hayek; indeed it was the entire source for Hayek's monetary theory since it was through this book that the influence of Wicksell reached Hayek.

But the evolutionism on which Hayek laid such stress does not come from Mises.[7] It comes from what was undoubtedly the most fundamental Austrian influence on Hayek – Menger himself. Though Menger's influence on economics generally was limited and to a considerable extent indirect, the *Grundsätze* was effective in transmitting its main message (1978, pp. 274–81; 1988, p. 97). But it is not this book which exercised the key influence upon Hayek.

The key work was Menger's 1883 *Untersuchungen*. Again and again in Hayek's interpretation of other writers, it is the evolutionary themes, the treatment of law, and the emphasis upon unintended consequences in that book which Hayek picks up in the earlier writers (1942–4, III, pp. 27–30; 1960; 1973–9, II, pp. 184–5; 1978, pp. 3–22, 249–66; 1988; 1992, pp. 28, 50, 77–8n; Menger 1883, pp. 139–59, 223–34). In his attack on 'scientism', in his attacks upon constructs such as 'the nation' and 'society', and in his opposition to constructivism, it is the individualism of this book and the emphasis upon the evolution of law, language, the State, money and markets which Hayek starts from. It is undoubtedly the most important influence on his *Constitution of Liberty* (1960, p. v). The earlier writers treating these themes, especially Mandeville, are seen as leading to the definitive statement in Menger. It is this book which explains the importance which Hayek attached to the work of Mandeville and of Hume, and the particular interpretation which he gave to it and to that of Adam Smith. It is thus of considerable importance in understanding Hayek as an historian of ideas. But the emphasis upon evolution, in particular, requires some further examination.

Evolution

Despite the fact that the influence of Menger's 1883 book is the key unifying factor in Hayek's treatment of the history of ideas, and indeed of much else – it is the unifying thread of his *Individualism and Economic Order* (1949) – there is a slight puzzle. For despite the narrowly Austrian nature of Hayek's training, this particular aspect of Menger's work does not seem to have impressed him at first. Hayek's early work in the history of economic thought, dealing with money, is not within the evolutionary mould. Both the history of John Law's schemes, and of the monetary antics of the revolutionary maniacs in the 1790s, provided plenty of material in support of Hayek's thesis about evolution in money and the dangers of 'constructivism' in monetary matters i.e. of the dangers of revolutionary monetary schemes irrespective of accumulated experience. That he made little play with this point suggests that in the late 1920s (1991, pp. 155–76) he had not made evolutionism a key factor either in his thought or in his approach to the history of ideas. Its importance really dates from the late 1930s and his attacks upon 'scientism'.

Later on he was also to stress that the evolution of social forms embodies knowledge (1978, pp. 3–22, 59, 71; 1988, p. 21) and that values are transmitted by the cultural environment (1978, pp. 67–8). These values are socially beneficial.

Individuals, acting within the constraints of these social values, created benefits which were beyond their design. The system which had evolved was designed to compensate for the extremely limited knowledge of each individual. Indeed, Hayek went so far as to argue that cultural evolution led to intelligent behaviour – to the surprise no doubt of those who think in left/right stereotypes, Hayek was firmly in the 'Nurture' corner in the debate between 'Nurture' and 'Nature' (1978, pp. 290–94).

The competitive selection of cultural institutions was linked directly to the key idea of unintended consequences of individual actions under partial information (1978, pp. 11, 73; 1988, p. 71; 1991, p. 26; 1992, p. 2; Menger 1883, p. 146). Social forms evolved so that pursuit of individual goals could produce social good. None of our ancestors could have known that protection of property and contracts would lead to division of labour, specialization, and the operation of markets. But the way in which unintended consequences produced an order, an order which was not designed, was, Hayek held, the key question in economics from the time of Hume and Smith onwards (1942–4, I, pp. 284, 288; III, pp. 27–30, 37; 1949, pp. 15, 77–89; 1973–9, I, pp. xviii–xix; 1978, p. 73).

This evolutionary approach was not, as it had indeed not been with Menger, confined to purely economic phenomena. Religion was also an evolutionary form (1988, pp. 135–40). It was a spontaneous and unplanned development, embodying much of the necessary evolutionary cultural wisdom. A moral code was an evolutionary phenomenon, though this did not preclude the questioning of any single moral value within a given framework (1960, pp. 397–411; 1978, pp. 18–19, 84, 298–9; 1988, p. 52; Menger 1883, pp. 8, 139–59). The same was true of institutions; we had to try to understand them, and there was always the possibility of improvement. But wholesale restructuring of society would simply destroy civilization (1988, p. 6; 1992, pp. 259–60). Our civilization depended on the human cooperation and order associated with the market – or with 'capitalism', a word which, as Hayek pointed out, Sombart (not Marx) had introduced and which he associated with the Nazis (1988, p. 111). The evolved forms, produced without an overall purpose (1978, p. 77n), embodied the painful learning processes of society and were capable of incorporating that multiplicity of objectives which was necessary for freedom (1949, p. 19). It is important to stress in this context that the full range of these objectives could never be known in advance. Indeed the market could not be judged by a hierarchy of known ends (1978, pp. 90–92).

Needless to say, a number of earlier writers were criticized by Hayek for their failure to appreciate this viewpoint. Bentham, as a constructivist (1973–9, II, pp. 45, 155), was contrasted with Hume the non-interventionist. Rousseau was roundly criticized for his substitution of the idea of a popular will for a general *opinion* embodying social learning (1978, p. 99; 1988, p. 13). He had, in Hayek's view, 'made what had been called the savage the virtual hero of progressive intellectuals' (1988, p. 49) because of his rejection of accumulated wisdom.

But it was Hobbes who received the sharpest criticism. It was Hobbes with his social contract myth who was responsible for propagating 'naive design theories of human institutions' (1978, pp. 256–7; 1988, p. 13). The idea of unlimited powers of government intervention, even under democracy, derived from sources like this. The argument that supreme authority must be unlimited was 'a misunderstanding deriving from the totalitarian-positivist conceptions of Francis Bacon and Thomas Hobbes, or the constructionism of Cartesian Rationalism, which fortunately in the Anglo-Saxon world was at least for a long time held back by the deeper understanding of Sir Edward Coke, Matthew Hale, John Locke and the Old Whigs' (1978, p. 158).

Hayek's introduction of the Common Lawyers here is important. Since this impinges upon his treatment of the history of ideas it is necessary to say a little about his legal philosophy.

Law

Hayek's general evolutionary framework gave him a particular interest in legal and constitutional theory and led him to stress the importance of *general* law (1978, p. 134), as distinct from interventionist government of the kind intensely vulnerable to pressure group politics. He contrasted freedom under the law with the use of legislative machinery to interfere with freedom (1949, p. 18). It was general law as stressed, he argued, by Locke, Hume, Smith and Kant which was both the safeguard of individual freedom and the framework within which beneficial evolutionary development could take place.

There is no doubt that this position derives initially from Menger's 1883 book. But, as always, Hayek sought to place it within its context in the history of ideas. He was a great admirer of the Anglo-Saxon system of case law and in particular of the great common lawyers (1991, pp. 77, 102–3; 1992, pp. 257–8; Menger 1883, pp. 9, 11, 223–34). The State undoubtedly had a role to play as a part of the framework for economic activity (1949, pp. 22–3); but the role of general law (as distinct from particular State action) as espoused, Hayek believed, by the constitutional theorists whom he admired, was paramount. Thus it was to the British tradition, rather than to that of Continental liberalism which Hayek looked (1949, pp. 28–9, 110; 1978, pp. 119–20; 1992, pp. 216, 244). He believed that evolutionary concepts predominant in British legal philosophy had protected ancient liberties which had been largely destroyed on the Continent. Indeed, French liberalism had remarkable totalitarian propensities. It had been corrupted by 'aggressive rationalism' and scientism 'which presumed that science was competent to tell us not only what is but also what ought to be' (1992, p. 244). This tradition, which had infected J.S. Mill, was contrary to the true (British) tradition of liberalism.

It is possible to see difficulties in this position. In citing 'the classical theorists of representative government' especially John Locke, in support of the idea that democratic government's law making should be confined to general law making (not specific interference, the latter making government vulnerable to pressure groups) Hayek neglected the fact that even very limited government could be (and at the time of these theorists was) subject to pressure groups – the phenomenon known as mercantilism. Indeed, under the (limited though non-democratic) Cromwellians detailed regulations concerning personal life were laid down. There is a case for arguing that Hayek's view here was part romantic and part rhetorical. But it would be quite untrue to argue, on this basis, that there is no substance whatever in Hayek's position and in his treatment of these constitutional issues and their theorists.

Hayek believed, as we have seen, that Continental liberalism had become corrupted. Let us examine some of the sources of that corruption.

Historism, constructivism, and scientism

History and historism

Hayek attacked the idea that it was possible to develop some kind of scientific history, an attempt which he called 'Historism'. Such an approach involved two difficulties. Firstly, it involved aggregating social phenomena in a way which had no real meaning – Hayek referred to the 'astounding assertion' (1941, III, p. 307) that in dealing with social phenomena the whole is better known than the sum of the parts. Secondly, it involved attempting to find laws governing the development of society when viewed in this holistic way. This Historism was contrasted with genuine history (1941, III, pp. 307–12, 1942–4, II, pp. 50–63). Real historians attempt to understand real unique historical episodes whereas Historism 'attempts to treat historical situations as species of a genus' (1941, III, pp. 311–12). Historism was a product of a misconceived attempt to apply what were believed to be the methods of natural science to history. In fact, as Popper later convinced Hayek, natural scientists did not proceed in this way (1967, p. 8), but the belief that observation could lead to the formulation of historical 'laws' was certainly present in the literature, stretching from Comte to Marx, which Hayek criticized. The latter variant, for extrinsic rather than intrinsic reasons, was particularly important. 'Though merely one among many characteristic nineteenth century products of this kind, Marxism more than any of the others has become the vehicle through which this result of scientism has gained so wide an influence' (1942–4, II, p. 59).

Such an approach, involving 'Objectivism' (in opposition to the subjectivism of social science in general and Austrian economics in particular), Collectivism (in opposition to individualism) and Historism (in opposition to theory) led in turn to Constructivism (1942–4, II, p. 34).

Constructivism

The consequence of Historism and Scientism was a failure to grasp that individual action produces socially coherent unplanned systems. Devotees of such an approach could not understand the evolution of social and economic systems. This led to their belief that if institutions were not designed they could not be satisfactory. From this they proceeded, by a non sequitur, to the belief that we could simply refashion institutions in any way we desired (1942–4, III, pp. 29–30; 1978, pp. 3–22; Menger, 1883, pp. 8–9). As Hayek observed, 'This belief that processes which are consciously directed are necessarily superior to any spontaneous process is an unfounded superstition'(1942–4, III, p. 30).

Constructivism was in fundamental opposition to the individualism, subjectivism, and evolutionism which Hayek had derived from Menger (1941; 1942–4). Thus the origins of socialism lay in Constructivism (1978, p. 15). From his detailed study of the work of Saint Simon and Comte, Hayek was able to conclude that the origins of both positivism and socialism were 'definitely reactionary and authoritarian' (1941, I, p. 31). These writers planned a complete reconstruction of society placing control in the hands of intellectuals. There was to be a dictatorship of the 'scientific' (1941, II, pp. 122–4; 1941, III, p. 315).

In fact, the constructivists suffered from scientific delusions. With a grand sweep, and a very impressive knowledge of the literature of the Enlightenment, Hayek traced – convincingly – the scientific pretensions not merely of those who wished to ape physics but of those who wished to plan society 'scientifically'.[8] These people engaged in 'slavish imitation of the method and language of Science' (1941, I, p. 16; 1942–4, I, p. 169).

Most of those who are guilty of this were themselves either undistinguished in science or not scientists at all (1942–4, I, p. 268; 1991, p. 77) Bacon was one prime example (1991, pp. 75–8); the dilettante picker of scientists' brains, Saint Simon, was another. Nonetheless, Hayek believed that the origins of this view within French intellectual tradition lay with somebody whose mathematical credentials, at least, were not open to question – Descartes (1949, p. 8; 1978, pp. 5, 158, 255; 1988, p. 48).

But the truth was that natural scientific methods did not transfer to the vastly more complicated world of social science (1942–4, I, p. 267). Science attempted to look *behind* man's perceptions to ultimate realities, but social science had to deal with people's *beliefs* because it was upon these that action was based (1942–4, I, pp. 271–81, 286). Most of the objects of human or social action were not objective facts which could be defined in physical terms. Moreover, there was no coherent and consistent body of the knowledge on which people based their actions. 'It only exists in the dispersed, incomplete and inconsistent form in which it appears in many individual minds and this dispersion and imperfection of all knowledge is one of the basic facts from which the social sciences have to start' (1942–4, I, p. 280). The essence of social sciences is subjectivism and methodological individualism, and introspection had a significant part to play in their constructs. Indeed economists, unlike natural scientists, knew about individual elements, and the task of economics was to explain how these individual elements interacted to produce markets and allocation. Scientism, therefore, in attempting to transfer the procedures and priorities of natural science to social science was simply unscientific (1942–4, I, p. 269). Indeed natural science training did not enable one to *discern* order in social phenomena so the scientists wished to *impose* it (1942–4, III, pp. 38–9). Natural science training also led to an extremely primitive attitude towards such complex matters as optimization – the engineering concept of optimization involved no more than a single maximand *viz.* technical efficiency (1942–4, III, pp. 35–6).

Borrowing from the work of Mises and others, Hayek accepted that science had had to struggle to overcome many difficulties placed in its way by established philosophical positions. The struggle, once successful, had led through a so-called 'law of inertia' to an overshooting of the original objective with science claiming expertise in areas for which it was not suitable (1942–4, I, pp. 270, 278). But this was only part of the explanation. Intellectuals in general displayed an infatuation with socialism, safe in the luxury of never having had to live under a regime which attempted the comprehensive planning of society (1967, pp. 178–94; 1988, p. 85). Indeed Hayek was able to illustrate his argument with some particularly silly statements by Albert Einstein about 'production for use' (1988, pp. 58–9), and it is clear that he took a (somewhat sardonic) interest in the writings of scientists and, more particularly, of scientific popularizers, on matters of economics (1988, pp. 55–60). To understand his attitude towards them it is necessary to explore a little further his attitude towards economic methodology.

Science and economics

Hayek had a strong interest in the philosophy of science and seems to have developed a close personal and intellectual relationship with Karl Popper (1967, p. viii; 1991, pp. 6, 9, 42n; Popper in Streissler 1969, p. 190). But although Popper convinced him that natural scientists proceeded from theory to observation, Hayek remained convinced that natural science methods did not transfer to economics. For the theory which economics developed was not suitable, for the most part, for testing with facts. As already noted, facts in economics were not physical attributes but mental perceptions (1949, pp. 61–2). In fact, economic theory offered very few testable predictions (1942–4, I, p. 290; 1978, p. 278). Hayek had no doubt about the importance of systematic testing in *natural* science (1942–4, I, p. 272); but, although one author has seen signs of a definite change in Hayek's position from 1937 onwards (Hutchison, 1981, pp. 210–24), there seems to be little doubt that he remained highly sceptical about both measurement and testing in economics. Indeed, this was to remain a fundamental part of his opposition to Keynesian macroeconomics (1983, p. 46). It is true that in his 1937 article 'Economics and Knowledge' there are passages referring to 'verification', and a reference in a footnote to 'falsification' (1937a, p. 33). But what Hayek was talking about here was the 19th-century concept of 'verification' – testing whether the assumptions necessary for a theory were met. Elsewhere one can find plenty of references *after* 1937 dismissing the importance of prediction[9] (1942–4, I, p. 290; II, pp. 42, 49–50; 1949, p. 73; 1978, p. 180; 1992, p. 148).

The emphasis upon subjectivism can be linked to Hayek's interest in psychology, which dated from his student days (1952; 1978, pp. 38–9; Klein in Hayek 1992, p. 4). It naturally led him to assign a key role to introspection (1942, I, pp. 285–6, 289–90; II, pp. 44–7, 61; 1949, p. 63; 1978, p. 277). This was crucial in separating social science from natural science.

> The physicist who wishes to understand the problems of the social sciences with the help of an analogy from his own field would have to imagine a world in which he knew by direct observation the inside of the atoms and had neither the possibility of making experiments with lumps of matter nor opportunity to observe more than the interactions of a comparatively few atoms during a limited period. From his knowledge of the different kinds of atoms he could build up models of all the various ways in which they could combine into larger units and make these models more and more closely reproduce all the features of the few instances in which he was able to observe more complex phenomena (1942–4, I, pp. 289–90).

Of course introspection involves serious methodological difficulties since we can never be sure that our own introspection represents a uniform reaction, a question never really faced by *a priorists* from Cairnes to Mises. But, for our purposes here, the point is that this viewpoint gave Hayek a clearly defined perspective on intellectual history. He did not allow possible difficulties with introspection to affect his belief in its importance when dealing with the history of ideas. It is therefore hardly surprising that Hayek found the 'social physics' approach of French intellectualism, and especially of Comte, deeply distasteful.

Saint Simon and Comte

In his series of articles 'The Counter Revolution of Science' (1941), Hayek developed a detailed and scholarly critique of the work of Saint Simon and of Comte. In the context of its time, this scholarly and ultimately devastating investigation, published in an institution whose staff contained not only Laski but a great many who felt socialism was 'rational' if not, indeed, chic, must have been deeply unpopular. The pitiless glare of Hayek's spotlight on the bizarre intellectual origins of totalitarianism – for this is indeed what was under discussion – is salutary indeed, not least because of the respectful support enjoyed by Marxist regimes from intellectuals in Western universities who talked glibly of 'the Soviet experiment' and other euphemisms. It is true that Hayek was able to draw upon a background of scholarly German literature for these articles and for the articles 'Scientism and the Study of Society' (1942–4), but for the English-speaking world Hayek provided a significant exposition, while his focus on all the disparate elements was a significant contribution to the study of the origins of collectivist and totalitarian ideas. Hayek's extraordinary learning enabled him to demonstrate the quite remarkable extent of the influence of Saint Simon (1941, III, pp. 281–2, 292) which, as he pointed out, was much greater than normally realized because many who had borrowed his ideas attempted to distance themselves from the ridicule which the originator of those ideas had drawn upon himself by his antics in later years. Hayek showed that the influence spread through Belgium, Italy, Sweden, Russia, Spain and even South America as well as to the obvious countries – Britain and Germany. He was particularly effective in demonstrating the link to Hegelianism and, both directly and indirectly, to Marx (1941, II, pp. 129, 131, 139, 145; III, pp. 287, 289–92; 1942–4, II, p. 45). Indeed, those familiar only with Marx's borrowings from Hegelianism and from classical economics can find Hayek demonstrating how deeply unoriginal Marx was in other respects when account is taken of the French literature. It was from Saint Simon that the idea of only two classes, and these engaged in a class struggle, was borrowed, as was the idea that scientific politics has to discover the necessary laws of political development. Engels also drew from this source and Proudhon was largely Saint Simonian in his socialist doctrines (1941, III, pp. 289–92). Indeed in some respects, the French literature was well in advance of Marx and Engels, Hayek believed; for it broached the matter of the organization of a planned society and the problems of socialist calculation (1941, II, p. 145).

In all this Hayek showed a quite extraordinarily detailed knowledge of the original Saint Simonian literature (1941, II, p. 141) and indeed – though here he relied on work by others – of the character of Saint Simon (1941, I, pp. 19–30) – part spiv, part self-deluding fraud, part 'visionary megalomaniac' (1941, I, p. 29). Saint Simon's chief asset seems to have been an ability to attract followers, some of whom were intellectually his superiors (1941, II, p. 119). His descent into the construction of a new religion, with a new theology, has strong elements of farce (1941, II, pp. 133, 147, 149; III, p. 281). It resulted ultimately in the setting up of a community which was acidly described by Hayek as half monastery half Nazi Führerschule (1941, II, p. 149). But some of his other delusions – especially the idea that production as a whole could be planned (1941, II, pp. 125–6) – proved highly influential.

So also did the idea that liberty in society would impede planning and it must therefore be abolished – not merely economic liberty but even freedom of conscience (1941, II, pp. 127, 130, 137). As Hayek showed – and the modern echoes are recognizable enough – the demands of the Saint Simonians for liberty were, as they acknowledged with 'an amazing frankness, rarely equalled by later socialists', purely to enable them to seize power (1941, II, p. 148).

The most able follower attracted by Saint Simon was Comte. His influence too was extremely widespread even though he was a 'singularly unattractive figure' who attracted few disciples in his lifetime (1941, III, p. 298, 318; 1978, p. 14). It was because the great figure of John Stuart Mill was attracted to him – though not permanently – that Comte was able to exercise an enormous, though indirect, influence.

Unlike Saint Simon, Comte did have a genuine scientific background. But his writings on economics and society are hardly coherent, and Hayek in his treatment showed exemplary patience in attempting to construct a coherent account from the published sources. But the account is not without entertainment; and Hayek reveals that Comte, in the course of abusing economics, of which he knew virtually nothing, originated the phrase 'in the long run we are all dead' associated with another flamboyant figure in intellectual history (1941, III, p. 314).

But the critique is serious and substantial. It revolves around three main issues. The first was Comtean 'wholeism', which, he argued, led to the paradox that we could only study man by rejecting every man and viewing society as a whole (1941, III, pp. 299, 307; 1942–4, II, pp. 41–6; 1988, p. 108). Hayek regarded it as an 'astounding assertion' (1941, III, p. 307) that in dealing with social phenomena the whole was better known than the sum of the parts. It led to the indefensible position that we could treat wholes like 'society' or 'the economy' or 'capitalism' as definitely given objects about which we could discover laws by observing their behaviour. We thus had the paradox of positivists postulating 'metaphysical entities' (1942–4, II, p. 45). Of course this made it possible to talk in terms of conflicts between vague collectives – the class struggle and so on.

Secondly, Comte essayed to construct a 'social physics'. Sociology was to be social physics and Comte was determined to find laws governing the development of society as definite as gravity (1941, III, pp. 303, 309; 1942–4, II, p. 39). Yet, as Hayek pointed out, on the crucial matter (in this context) of what constituted an 'observed fact' Comte was studiously vague (1941, III, pp. 300–301).

The third basis for Hayek's criticism of Comte was the neat paradox that Comte believed that the human mind, which by its weakness had resulted in a society apparently in need of fundamental change, had the unique power to decide on a better plan of society. Even though one individual must act with extremely limited knowledge, within a small sphere, it was apparently possible for a human mind to comprehend the whole of society and to plan accordingly (1941, III, pp. 306, 310; 1942–4, III, pp. 31, 33). But a major part of Hayek's output was taken up with a critique of socialism and this deserves separate consideration.

Socialism

There is some dispute about whether Hayek and Mises considered socialism impossible or merely inefficient. This is not surprising because Hayek was not entirely consistent about this matter (compare 1949, p. 90; 1992, pp. 127, 140), and in any case there is a fine line between impossibility and hopeless inefficiency leading to ultimate breakdown (as ultimately proved to be the case). But the threads of Hayek's criticism stem from his intellectual sources and thus throw some light upon his approach to intellectual history.

Hayek's original position seems to have been grounded upon the Austrian form of general equilibrium, stressing the sheer complexity of an economic society made up of a myriad of different individuals (1984, pp. 159–62). Later on, as McCloughry has pointed out (in Hayek, 1984, p. viii), Hayek changed his emphasis to one laying stress on the problem of knowledge[10] (1937a; 1949, p. 91; Klein in Hayek 1992, p. 2). This problem was serious enough in goods markets, but once factor markets were taken into account it became apparent that the idea of planning was incoherent, since, without a developed market system to register preferences for factor uses, there was simply no way of assigning values to factors (1949, pp. 90, 123, 143, 167–8; 1978, p. 300). Without a developed factor market 'cost' simply had no meaning. Thus in his treatment of the body of ideas encompassed within the labels 'Scientism', 'Historism', and 'Constructivism', Hayek was able to point to a central fallacy of the engineering approach deriving from Saint Simon, Comte, and their associates – the engineer failed to appreciate that it was only a competitive society which provided him with the costs and prices which entered into his calculations. Thus an attempt to engineer *society* would lack such data. But from Saint Simon to Marx and Lenin the fallacy of the idea of running society as a single factory had seduced intellectuals (1942–4, III, pp. 34–7).

From this vantage point Hayek was able to advance not merely a critique of such historical episodes as Bismarckian socialism which, he maintained, had been the direct precursor of National Socialism (1988, p. 114; 1992, pp. 223–36 espec. pp. 228–9), but also to provide, as early as 1936, a prophetic critique of the 1960s vogue of 'indicative planning' (1984, pp. 176–7).

A myth used to exist – surely the position is no longer tenable (Vaughn, 1980) – that Mises, Hayek and Robbins were somehow 'defeated' in the socialist calculation debate by Lange and Taylor employing Lausanne general equilibrium. In fact, Hayek's extraordinarily fair-minded evaluation of the socialist calculation debate (1949, pp. 148–80) made it perfectly clear that all these writers had done was to recognize that the formal (marginalist) principles of economic theory had to apply to a socialist economy – but they had, because of the knowledge problem, totally failed to demonstrate *how* this could be done without markets. But in any case, the perfect competition at the heart of the Lausanne model was completely irrelevant to any real economic system (1949, pp. 92–106) – choice was not only an essential component of welfare (1984, pp. 173–4) but also vital to successful and beneficial economic evolution.

Macroeconomics

Hayek's macroeconomic model

Hayek approached historical macroeconomic literature from an Austrian standpoint. Since Hayek's own macroeconomics have been the subject of extensive critical comment, it is necessary to identify the key elements in order to see what provided the basis for his evaluation of other writers.

The essential model is that derived from Mises. It is a variant of Wicksell's model in which a quantity theory approach is replaced by one in which the prices and outputs of consumer goods and those of producer goods are distinguished and given a key role. Hayek was thus opposed to the degree of aggregation involved in both Keynesian macroeconomics and in a purely quantity theory approach. The basic argument was that monetary expansion, through lowering the lending rate below the marginal rate of profit, altered the relative prices of consumption and investment goods, and in turn distorted factor markets. I have explained the basic model involved elsewhere (O'Brien, 1988, pp. 108–10) and there is no space to go into greater detail here. What it is necessary to emphasize, however, is that the 'period of production' is not only *not* essential to this macroeconomic model but is absent from much of Hayek's macroeconomic writings and his attempts to grapple with the problem eventually brought these writings to a halt (1933c; 1939, pp. 135–56; 1984, pp. 5–32, 55–70, 71–117; Machlup, 1976, p. 30). What *is* essential, however, is the idea that monetary disequilibrium results in an output of consumption goods and producer goods in proportions which are different from those reflected by consumer preferences for consumption goods and savings (1984, pp. 71–117, 142).[11] To avoid such disequilibrium it is not enough, however, to aim for a stable price level; for with secularly rising productivity, a stable price level would require a secularly increasing money supply which in turn would require the lending rate to be below the marginal rate of profit. This was a common idea amongst Austrian economists from the late 1920s, although it was a point originally put forward by the Swedish economist Davidson in controversy with Wicksell (1933c, pp. 113–15; 1984, pp. 122–4, 129).

The absolute worth of such a model need not detain us here. It certainly has a great deal to offer in considering the inflationary world since 1945; and Hayek's employment of it during the 1930s depression was wrongheaded, as he came reluctantly to recognize, because of an absolutely fundamental mistake on a matter of *fact* – a failure to recognize the catastrophic decline in the United States money supply (1984, pp. 118–35 espec. p. 130). What is of concern for our present purposes is that it provided the intellectual basis for Hayek's writings on the history of monetary economics.

Cantillon

Although it was Higgs who did the pioneering work on Cantillon, and who deserves every credit for a great scholarly achievement, Hayek did much to establish the importance of Cantillon (1991, pp. 245–94). Not surprisingly, the feature of Cantillon's analysis which he found most worthy of note was that Cantillon had pointed out the defects in the traditional quantity theory, as expounded by Locke, and had explained the importance of the path followed by an increase in the money supply and the effect on *relative* prices (1935, pp. 1, 8; 1978, p. 216). But Hayek deserves great credit for bringing out what he called the 'subterranean influence' of Cantillon's book. He established that Smith was familiar with it, and demonstrated its influence upon the Physiocratic literature. His account of the recognition of Cantillon by different authors in several languages over the centuries showed a huge knowledge although he was indebted, as he acknowledged, to Cannan. His account of Cantillon, although apparently written as early as 1931, is still an excellent reference and his picture of Mirabeau's attempts to plagiarize Cantillon, and the success of others in so doing, is fascinating. In particular he shows the way in which Postlethwayt incorporated, without acknowledgement, substantial chunks of the *Essai* in his own work (1991, pp. 177n, 245), and, despite his great admiration for David Hume, he insisted on the likelihood that Hume had also had access to the essay before writing his own *Essays*.

Classical monetary economics

Hayek's knowledge of English classical monetary writing was formidable by the late 1920s (1991, pp. 177–244). Although there was a long German language tradition of interest in this literature, and although Mises was widely read in it, the latter's own *Money* does not provide the sort of systematic history of ideas treatment which Hayek wrote, although this was not published until late in life.

His judgement of the balance of the issues involved was, despite his particular stand-point, good. In particular he clearly perceived Ricardo's singular lack of originality on matters of monetary economics as well as his over-simplification (1935, p. 14; 1991, pp. 200–206, 321; Fetter, 1940). He was particularly aware of Ricardo's debt to Thornton, though offering a generous view of Ricardo's lack of acknowledgement of him. Of course, as Hayek pointed out, Ricardo was hardly alone in this; Thornton's work was borrowed by Lord King, J.L. Foster, and the Bullion Report as well. On the other side, he gave some recognition to Joplin at a very early date (1935, pp. 15–16; 1991, pp. 219–20, 319) even though he certainly did not appreciate Joplin's full significance and mistakenly believed that Joplin had borrowed ideas from Thornton which were in fact not only his own but pointed in a direction different from that of Thornton. He provided a beautiful little sketch of the work of George Warde Norman (1933b), at that time a figure little known even in England and recognized the value of Cairnes's work on international monetary transmission (1935, p. 10).

But it is his work on Thornton which is perhaps his major claim to fame as a monetary historian (1935, pp. 11–14, 17; 1991, pp. 295–344). Launched upon the task of producing an edition of Thornton's *Paper Credit* (Thornton, 1802), Hayek drew upon extensive manuscript sources, as well as on historical material relating to the Clapham Sect, to provide not only a rounded picture of the banker and economist who was also a religious activist, but an account of his place as a monetary writer which is still of considerable interest today. He had earlier emphasized the importance of Thornton, whose monetary theory indeed had much in common with that of Mises and Hayek, in his *Prices and Production* and he was able, as a result of his detailed knowledge of classical monetary economics, to show the way in which Thornton's influence extended to Tooke, Horsley Palmer, Senior, and (though watered down) J.S. Mill.

Given Hayek's own macroeconomic approach, it was hardly surprising that he should be both sympathetic and illuminating on the subject of Thornton. It is equally unsurprising that, if not always unilluminating, his attitude to Keynes, both personally and intellectually, was distinctly unsympathetic.

Keynes

Apart from his celebrated controversy with Keynes following his adverse review of the *Treatise* (1931b; 1931c; Keynes, 1931), Hayek wrote about Keynes on a number of occasions. Virtually none of these contributions is innocent of some dig at Keynes (1960, p. 447; 1967, pp. 344–8; 1978, pp. 283–9; 1983), even where he pays tribute to his intellectual powers. Moreover Hayek distrusted Keynes's leanings in favour of significant State influence on the economy – as a German speaker he was aware of the 1936 preface to the German edition of the *General Theory* (1967, p. 346), unlike many in this country.

The controversy between Keynes and Hayek was certainly restrained compared with the celebrated Methödenstreit between Menger and Schmoller (Hayek, 1934a, p. 407). Nonetheless, Hayek deplored both Keynes's lack of scholarship and, quite emphatically, what he considered to be Keynes's lack of knowledge of economics. His view was that Keynes really knew no economics outside Cambridge economics (1967, p. 345). On this topic he was noticeably more frank in an article written for the *Oriental Economist* (1978, pp. 283–9) than in one written for the London *Economist* (1983). In particular Keynes's knowledge of international trade theory and of capital theory was inadequate, Hayek believed, and in the monetary field he knew little of the classical monetary literature (even Thornton) while his inability to read German sufficiently well to understand the argument meant that he was unaware of important contributions by Wicksell and Mises (1978, pp. 218, 230–31). As Hayek put it, perhaps rather sardonically, 'The world might have been saved much if Lord Keynes's German had been a little better' (1992, p. 131).

While Hayek's stand-point is obvious enough, this is not entirely unfair. Certainly it would be difficult to deny that Keynes's Wicksellian *Treatise* would have benefited from a better knowledge (and acknowledgement) of Wicksell.

Hayek, familiar with the literature on under-consumption (1931a), regarded Keynes's *General Theory* as a 'tract for the times' (1978, p. 284). He believed, partly as a result of personal conversations with Keynes, with whom he seems, like Robbins, to have developed amicable personal relations during the war, that on seeing the inflationary effects produced by his disciples Keynes would have produced another tract for the times, had he lived. While he viewed what he regarded as Keynes's monetary nationalism with distinct disfavour, especially during the 1930s (1937b, p. 2; 1984, pp. 118–35), he did not believe that Keynes himself could be blamed personally for the inflation associated with 'Keynesian' policies

(1978, pp. 23, 191–231, 286–7) even though he did draw a parallel between Keynes and John Law (1978, p. 229).

But he was concerned that the dominance of macroeconomics after Keynes had brought about a significant decline in microeconomics – by which, of course, he meant Austrian microeconomics. Moreover, writing in the 1980s, he believed that the defeat of Keynesian economics had left economists bewildered because during the era of Keynesian dominance, economists had 'forgotten much that had been fairly well understood before the "Keynesian revolution"' (1983, p. 45).

Hayek's parallel between Keynes and John Law has just enough truth in it to make it interesting. This is not an accident. Hayek had a detailed knowledge not only of John Law but also of monetary history in France.

John Law

An interest in the work of John Law was well established in the Austrian School. Menger had already recognized Law whom he credited with founding a correct theory of the origin of money. In an essay on French paper money, written in the late 1920s although not published until his old age, Hayek himself exhibited a detailed knowledge of Law's work and correctly identified the fundamental weakness in Law's macroeconomics – the proposition that a demand-determined money supply could do no harm (1991, pp. 155–76). His account of Law is restrained and scholarly – remarkably so since he clearly had a detailed knowledge of Law's schemes and their discreditable collapse.

Law is one of a number of minor figures treated sympathetically and illuminatingly by Hayek. The cases of Cairnes and Norman have also been noted. But there were a number of other writers concerning whom he exhibited particular sympathy and expertise.

Sympathies and expertise

The minor cases

Hayek devoted his considerable scholarly resources to such figures as Bastiat (1991, pp. 347–50) (whom he treated with generosity,[12] noting that writer's intellectual vitality, though concentrating on the matter of unintended consequences and taking the opportunity to have a dig at Keynesian protectionism), and Dupuit (1991, pp. 350–52) to whom he paid tribute as a pioneer of marginal utility analysis and an important influence on Walras. He produced a scholarly treatment of Macleod and his monetary theory (1933a), even though he was evidently irritated by Macleod's subjective originality and a certain feeling (possibly in his mind a Keynesian parallel) that Macleod, unappreciative of his own ignorance of his predecessors, had expected more recognition than he deserved. He wrote an eminently fair-minded obituary of Wesley Mitchell (1948) even though his account of his trip to the United States as a young man (1992, pp. 19–41) showed him to be unimpressed with Mitchell's work. He showed interest in John Rae (1943a), exhibiting meticulous scholarship in matters of detail and being obviously drawn to Rae both by the connection with J.S. Mill and by Rae's pioneering work on capital theory. He wrote illuminatingly about the history of LSE (1946), and his excellent narrative contains a fair and generous account of the activities of Sidney Webb for whom, it is evident, Hayek had considerable regard despite their fundamental differences. (The same could not be said, perhaps understandably, of Beatrice Webb (1967, pp. 341–4).)

Mandeville

His treatment of Mandeville (1978, pp. 249–66) deserves special mention. For Hayek regarded Mandeville as a very important writer. This was not primarily as an economist (despite his discussion of division of labour) or even (a reflection of Hayek's interest) as a psychologist. Rather Mandeville's importance lay in his pioneering statement of the doctrine of unintended consequences leading, so Hayek believed, to Hume and to Menger's 1883 book. Indeed Mandeville had, as Menger was to do later, regarded language itself as an evolutionary phenomenon.

Mandeville's thesis – that what are private vices are often public benefits – had caused considerable outrage in his lifetime, but in Hayek's view it had become increasingly evident that it was simply a special case of the more general principle of unintended consequences. The complex order of society resulting from men's actions was very different from what they had intended and individuals, in pursuing their own ends, whether selfish or altruistic, produced useful results for others which they could not anticipate. Indeed, the whole order of society resulted from the unintended consequences of individuals striving for their own ends, their strivings being channelled by the evolved rules of behaviour (1949, pp. 4, 9; 1978, pp. 252–3, 258–9; 1988, pp. 13, 146).

The next step was for Mandeville to ask how it was that institutions grew up which achieved this result. His answer was the growth of law through an evolutionary process characterized by trial and error (1973–9, III, pp. 153–4; 1978, p. 260; 1988, p. 86; 1991, pp. 79–98). But Mandeville went far beyond the area of law to show that this evolutionary process applied to morality, convention, language and money. It was this which was passed to Hume, Smith, Ferguson, Burke, and ultimately to Menger.

J.S. Mill

Like Lionel Robbins, Hayek showed not only interest in, but considerable affection for, John Stuart Mill (1945; 1951). It was Hayek who did the pioneering work in organizing J.S. Mill's correspondence which was finally edited by F.E. Mineka (1963). He greatly enjoyed the scholarly detective work involved although he was less keen on the editorial work. Indeed he believed that he had had the pleasure (in assembling much of the correspondence) while Mineka had had to do the hard work (Hayek in Mineka, 1963, p. xxiv).

His reluctance to get involved in detailed editorial work stems from his publication (1951) of the correspondence of J.S. Mill and Harriet Taylor.[13] The sympathy and care of his work on this correspondence is remarkable – even in dealing with the highly rationalist and constructivist Mrs. Taylor who, although dedicated to the emancipation of women, somehow neglected to have her daughter educated. Despite his instinctive sympathy for Mill himself, he was not at all blind to the weaknesses of character and personal judgement which the relationship made clear.

But after his work on their correspondence, he came to the conclusion that the choice lay between doing editorial work and doing other work. Editorial work was simply too exhausting and time-consuming, and so he chose the latter.[14]

His work on J.S. Mill showed meticulous scholarship in matters of detail as well as considerable knowledge of 19th-century intellectual history far beyond the bounds of economics. He appreciated Mill's intellectual importance, but on the whole it seems fair to conclude that he did not appreciate the full extent of Mill's originality (Hayek in Mineka, 1963, p. xvi; 1978, p. 270; Stigler, 1955). He was also aware that Mill had ignored important developments during his lifetime (1978, p. 271; 1988, p. 148). But his attitude towards Mill's flirtations with socialism, and the continental brand of liberalism, was judicious and temperate, though necessarily coloured by his own attitude towards socialism and constructivism (1949, pp. 28–9, 110, 270n; 1988, p. 149); and he did not over-play the fact of Mill's ultimate realization that in endorsing (and, given his position, thus spreading the influence of) the work of Comte he had been in the service of a totalitarian cause (1941, II, p. 132). Occasionally, Hayek's interpretations of Mill are idiosyncratic; thus the famous fourth proposition on capital (demand for commodities is not demand for labour) Hayek managed to interpret in terms of Mises–Hayek trade cycle theory (1984, pp. 142, 157n6). But for the most part his interpretations of Mill are illuminating and scholarly.

The Austrian School

Hayek's writings as historian of the Austrian School (1934a; 1934b; 1944; 1968a; 1968b; 1968c; 1992, pp. 19–41, 108–25, 160–65) are naturally of particular interest. His essays on Wieser (1968c; 1992, pp. 108–25) are one of the most informative sources on the second generation of Austrians – much more so than Schumpeter's *History* (1954) in many ways. It is Hayek's humility and respect for individuality – which comes through in his writing on the history of ideas as much as in his methodological individualism – which contrasts so strongly with Schumpeter's bombast, even though Schumpeter was a great scholar and knew the older Austrians at first hand. Indeed Hayek is illuminating about Schumpeter himself (1967, pp. 339–41; 1992, pp. 160–65) as well as about minor figures such as Schams, Strigl (1944), and Mach. He also wrote informatively about Philippovich (1934b) and explained Mises's failure to obtain an academic appointment – it was possible to obtain an academic appointment in Vienna if you were Jewish but only if you were of left-wing sympathies since these were required to obtain the endorsement of the Jewish community there (1992, p. 128n).

Hayek was also able to write illuminatingly about Gossen (1932a), whose priority over the Austrians he acknowledged. As early as 1927 he wrote an introduction to the third edition of Gossen's *Entwicklung* with a complete bibliography of all the earlier writings on Gossen (1991, pp. 352–71; 1992, pp. 42–60). It was true that Menger did not know of Gossen's work before he wrote his *Grundsätze*, but this did not alter the objective fact of priority (1978, p. 273).

On Wieser – whose economics represented, in his opinion, a separate branch of Austrian economics (1968c; 1992, p. 122) – Hayek was also illuminating. As Hayek makes clear it was Wieser who introduced marginal utility, imputation, and indeed much of the apparatus associated with Austrian economics. There is no doubt that in some respects Hayek was over-generous to Wieser (notably in crediting Wieser with introducing marginal utility analysis into monetary economics, followed 'somewhat later in the Anglo Saxon countries' (1992, pp. 118–19)). But his appraisal is still interesting.

Perhaps because he had derived so much from Menger's 1883 book, it is his appraisals of Menger which hold particular interest (1934a; 1968b). Moreover, the first was published at a time when it was still possible to feel, at least at LSE, that Austrian economics was the dominant school (1934a, pp. 408–9). The key contributions which he stressed in his introduction to Menger's *Grundsätze* were the discussions of needs and of means of satisfying them, the distinction between goods of first and higher order, and complementarity (1934a, pp. 399, 414; 1978, pp. 275–6). This showed the importance which the Austrian School attached to 'the technical structure of production' (1934a, p. 399) by which, of course, he meant something very different from that understood by Marshall. He also believed that Menger had given a prominent role to time in his analysis, in contrast to Walras.

In Hayek's view, what made the *Grundsätze* effective was its 'persistent slow approach to its main object' (1978, pp. 274–5) with a steady build up of the subjective basis of the analysis, extending it to factor pricing. Important also was Menger's 'atomistic' method and his reliance upon introspection.

Indeed Hayek sometimes wrote as if the extension of subjectivism, Austrian subjectivism, was coterminal with advances in economics (1942–4, I, pp. 280–83; 1988, p. 97; 1992, p. 55). According to Hayek, 'it is probably no exaggeration to say that every important advance in economic theory during the last hundred years was a further step in the consistent application of subjectivism' (1942–4, I, p. 281). Even if one accepts such a view, for the purposes of argument, there is no doubt that Hayek was prone to overstate the importance of the Austrians within this process of advance. But in any case the approach is not really tenable. When Hayek attempts to illustrate his general thesis with a discussion of rent the problems become clear (1942–4, I, pp. 282–3). For his account of the theory of rent is only just recognizable to anyone familiar with it and with the history of the concept, and his attempt to identify subjective factors in the theory of rent is notably unsuccessful.

Perhaps the biggest single puzzle concerning Hayek's discussion of the Austrian School relates to his treatment of Menger's 1883 *Untersuchungen*. For it is clear that this book was by far the most important one in providing Hayek with his standpoint on intellectual history; yet, as already noted, in dealing with Menger as a writer he emphasizes it relatively lightly (1968a, p. 460; 1968b, pp. 125–6).

Although Hayek is fascinating on Austrian economists, he has relatively little to say about those in Germany. There are exceptions, notably Röpke and Eucken (1992, pp. 195–9). But he seems to have felt a very marked distaste for much of intellectual life in Germany, well before 1933 (1992, p. 188), and there is little to be learned about the German economists from his works.

Antagonisms and questionable judgements

As indicated above, some of Hayek's judgements in the matter of intellectual history are somewhat idiosyncratic. For the sake of completeness there are a few others which should also be mentioned. They include a curious contention that Aristotle, and the traditions stemming from him, were entirely innocent of the idea of evolution (1988, p. 143).[15] At the other end of the historical scale, Beveridge, in a phrase no doubt reflecting a particular episode at LSE, is dismissed as having 'understood no economics whatever' (1978, p. 230; Robbins, 1971, p. 158). In between we find the remarkably over-generous interpretation of Petty who 'deserves to be considered a forerunner of later business cycle theorists' (1991, pp. 136–7), the contention that the labour theory of value caused the breakdown of classical economics (1949, p. 136) (a view easily derived from the emphasis on Austrian subjectivism but somewhat over-simple to put it mildly) and the surprising misconception that 'oligopoly' was invented by the Austrian financier Karl Schlesinger (1992, p. 25). (Schumpeter certainly knew better than this (1954, p. 208).)

The two most serious criticisms to be made, however, relate to Marshall and to Ricardo. On the one hand there is absolutely no doubt that Hayek – perhaps because of an antipathy towards everything Cambridge – seriously underrated Marshall. It is certainly interesting that Marshall seems to have been more deeply read in Menger's work than his *Principles* would indicate – Hayek reported that Marshall's personal copy of the *Gründsatze* in the Marshall Library contained detailed marginal commentary (1968b, p. 124; 1978, p. 279). But to view Marshall, as Hayek seems to do, as merely one of the 'Anglo Saxons' riding on the coat tails of not merely the first but the second generation Austrians, is hardly adequate.

His attitude to Ricardo (Hayek, 1950) was distinctly temperate. Indeed it is a welcome change to anyone not enamoured of the excesses of the Ricardo industry in the recent past, for he believed Ricardo's main contribution to be comparative cost. But in dealing with Ricardo there is a problem. It is the celebrated 'Ricardo Effect' (1939, pp. 3–71; 1949, pp. 220–54).

This effect, which would have been better called the 'Mises Effect' simply involves an increase in the use of less capital intensive methods of production as a result of a fall in real wages. As a proposition it is not particularly surprising to anyone familiar with the standard literature on investment decisions, although Hayek employed considerable ingenuity in some of his presentations (1978, pp. 165–78). But it is not in Ricardo.[16] The two passages which Hayek cited – one from the chapter on value, dealing with the effect of a rise in wages in altering relative values of commodities produced with differing capital/labour ratios, even without factor substitution, and the other from the chapter on machinery (where Ricardo, following Barton, satisfied himself that mechanization could cause unemployment) do not correspond in any serious sense to the point which Hayek was trying to make (Ricardo, 1817, pp. 38–43, 386–97). The question arises as to why Hayek did this. Was it excessive humility, or was it a rhetorical device? There seems to be no clear answer to this. My own suspicion is that it was, at least unconsciously, a desire to highlight what he considered to be a lack in Cambridge of knowledge of the established economic literature.

Conclusion

There is no doubt that Hayek was a very considerable scholar. Indeed there are times when it seems that his own essential message is obscured by his scholarship. In a sense Hayek as an intellectual historian was his own worst enemy. The beautifully crafted but sometimes almost impenetrable prose, the lengths to which the scholarship drew him, the substitution of patient repetition (shades of Menger) for rhetoric and polemic – all these led to a situation in which his work to a significant extent remained unread. Anyone who has, as I have, ploughed through the 'Counter Revolution of Science' and 'Scientism and the Study of Society' will recognize what I am saying – but not many, and certainly not many economists, have done so. The contrast with Robbins's lucid, polemical, beautifully written, and at times impatient *Essay on the Nature and Significance of Economic Science*, which *has* been widely read by economists, is clear. An episode involving Leontief is indeed a grotesque illustration of this. After Hayek (in 1976, following a lifetime of writing about the fallacies of economic planning, which were laid bare for even the most obdurate to see as the Soviet empire collapsed) had criticized *inter alia* Leontief over the advocacy of planning, the latter replied that he knew of no published evidence that Hayek had any right to criticize him. That Hayek wrote that he despaired of rational debate with these people is understandable enough, but the form in which he delivered his message was in part the cause.

Hayek's scholarly care to acknowledge his predecessors has proved a significant disadvantage to him. For not only has it denied him the ability to make what Hicks (1936), in reviewing Keynes's *General Theory*, regarded as Jevons-like claims to originality; it has also caused him to adhere to concepts like Böhm-Bawerk's 'period of production' which his macroeconomic theory did not need (and which neither its Wicksellian and Misean origins nor its later Robbinsian formulation contained) and which Hayek himself later abandoned.

Of course in a sense those who are prepared to plough through Hayek's work will find that, from a scholarly point of view, he commands the high moral ground; for much of the work critical of Hayek certainly does not adhere to comparable scholarly standards. Moreover his patience and tenacity were remarkable. Indeed so patient was he, especially with some of the works in the area of legal philosophy, that he might be regarded as having been patient to a fault. This was certainly Schumpeter's view when he reviewed *The Road to Serfdom* (Hayek, 1967, p. 184n; 1973–9, I, p. 161n). But, as Hayek explained, his patience stemmed from a belief that many of those whose work he thought to be most deeply mistaken were fundamentally well-intentioned.

> It is necessary to realise that the sources of many of the most harmful agents in this world are often not evil men but high-minded idealists, and that in particular the foundations of totalitarian barbarism have been laid by honourable and well-meaning scholars who never recognise the offspring they produce. (1973–9, I, p. 70)

Hayek himself was a major scholar, and it is sad to reflect that he has rarely enjoyed this open-minded tolerance himself.

Notes

1. This becomes very clear on reading the early essays reprinted in Hayek, 1984, especially pp. 33–54.
2. Indeed, at the Adam Smith celebrations in Glasgow in 1976 he carried a holdall full of books.
3. When I began work on J.R. McCulloch he wrote to me, in response to a letter of mine asking for source material which the *Economist* published, offering to lend me his copy of H.G. Reid's sketch of McCulloch's life. The book was extremely rare and he had no personal knowledge of me at all.
4. Thus in 1973–9, I, p. 154 n.48 he even noted a variation in different published versions of Hegel, a philosopher whom, as 'the fountain head of most modern irrationalism and totalitarianism' (ibid., p. 32), Hayek did not venerate.
5. Thus in 1973–9, II, pp. 159–60 n.5 runs from Paley (1785) to Kelsen (1960) and contains quotations in English, French, German and Italian. Yet this was never a parade: Hayek paid his readers the compliment of assuming that they were as well read, and as linguistically versatile, as he was.
6. Consider the following sentence. 'Consistently pursued historism necessarily leads to the view that the human mind is itself variable and that not only are most or all manifestations of the human mind unintelligible to us apart from their historical setting, but that from our knowledge of how the whole situations succeed each other we can learn to recognise the laws according to which the human mind changes, and that it is the knowledge of these laws which alone puts us in a position to understand any particular manifestation of the human mind' (1942–4, II: p. 60).
7. See however Mises, 1969, pp. 42–3.
8. He slipped on one small point: see Stonier, 1943 and Hayek, 1943b.
9. 'All that the theory of the social sciences attempts is to provide a technique of reasoning which assists us in connecting individual facts but which, like logic or mathematics, is not about facts. It can, therefore, … never be verified or falsified by reference to facts' (1949, p. 73).
10. 'Any approach, such as that of much of mathematical economics with its simultaneous equations, which in effect starts from the assumption, that people's *knowledge* corresponds with the objective *facts* of the situation, systematically leaves out what is our main task to explain' (1949, p. 91).
11. Hayek made this very clear in his *Profits, Interest and Investment*. 'The starting point for a fully developed theory of this kind would be (a) the intentions of all the consumers with respect to the way in which they wish to distribute at all the relevant dates all their resources (not merely their "income") between current consumption and provision for further consumption, and (b) the separate and independent decisions of the entrepreneurs with respect to the amounts of consumers' goods which they plan to provide at these various dates. Correspondence between these two groups of decisions would be characteristic of the kind of equilibrium which we now usually describe as a state where savings are equal to investments and with which the idea of an equilibrium rate of interest is connected. A rate of interest below that equilibrium rate would then induce entrepreneurs to devote a smaller share of the available resources to production for current consumption than the share of the income earned by these resources actually spent on consumption' (1939, pp. 153–4). Hayek then glosses this with reference to an 'investment period' but it is clearly not central to the argument.
12. See however Dorn, 1981.
13. It is apparent from Hayek, 1943b that he had contemplated a complete edition of J.S. Mill's correspondence.
14. Sabine (1951, pp. 113–14, 228–9) stresses the evolutionary nature of human society in Aristotle. Hayek's view of Aristotle seems to have come from Ernst May (Hayek, 1988, pp. 148–9).
15. This is a separate question from the analytical validity of the 'Effect' on which see Moss and Vaughn, 1986.
16. The key passages in Sraffa's edition (Hayek cited McCulloch's) are Ricardo, 1817, pp. 40, 395–6.

Bibliography

Böhm-Bawerk, E.v. (1884–9), *Kapital und Kapitalzins*, 2 vols., Innsbruck: Wagner.

Cantillon, R. (*c.* 1730), *Essai sur la Nature du Commerce en Général*, trans. H. Higgs, repr. New York: Kelley, 1964.

Clapham, J.H. (1941), Review of F.A. Hayek (ed.), *An Enquiry into the Nature and Effects of the Paper Credit of Great Britain*, by Henry Thornton, *Economica*, NS, **8** (May), 210–11.

Dorn, J.A. (1981), 'Law and Liberty: a Comparison of Hayek and Bastiat', *Journal of Libertarian Studies*, **5** (Fall), 375–97, repr. in Wood and Woods (1991), vol. 3, pp. 306–30.

Fetter, F.W. (1940), Review of F.A. Hayek (ed.), *An Enquiry into the Nature and Effects of the Paper Credit of Great Britain*, by Henry Thornton, *Journal of Political Economy*, **48** (5), 766–7.
Garrison, R.W. and Kirzner, I.M. (1987), 'Hayek, Friedrich August von', in J. Eatwell *et al.*, *The New Palgrave*, vol. 2, pp. 609–14, London: Macmillan.
Hayek, F.A. (1931a), 'The "Paradox" of Saving', *Economica*, **11** (May), 125–69.
Hayek, F.A. (1931b), 'Reflections on the Pure Theory of Money of Mr. J.M. Keynes', *Economica*, **11** (Aug.), 270–95.
Hayek, F.A. (1931c), 'A Rejoinder to Mr. Keynes', *Economica*, **11** (Nov.), 398–403.
Hayek, F.A. (1932a), 'Gossen, Hermann Heinrich', in E.R.A. Seligman (ed.), *Encyclopaedia of the Social Sciences*, vol. 7, p. 3, New York: Macmillan.
Hayek, F.A. (1932b), 'A Note on the Development of the Doctrine of "Forced Saving"', *Quarterly Journal of Economics*, **47** (Nov.), 123–33.
Hayek, F.A. (1933a), 'Macleod, Henry Dunning (1821–1902)', in E.R.A. Seligman (ed.), *Encyclopaedia of the Social Sciences*, vol. 10, p. 30, New York: Macmillan.
Hayek, F.A. (1933b), 'Norman, George Warde (1793–1882)', in E.R.A. Seligman (ed.), *Encyclopaedia of the Social Sciences*, vol. 11, p. 397, New York: Macmillan.
Hayek, F.A. (1933c), *Monetary Theory and the Trade Cycle*, trans. N. Kaldor and H. Croome, London: Jonathan Cape.
Hayek, F.A. (1934a), 'Carl Menger', *Economica*, NS **1** (Nov.), 393–420 also reprinted as the Introduction to the LSE reprint of Menger's *Grundsätze der Volkswirtschaftslehre*.
Hayek, F.A. (1934b), 'Philippovich Von Philippsberg, Eugen', in E.R.A. Seligman (ed.), *Encyclopaedia of the Social Sciences*, vol. 12, p. 116, New York: Macmillan.
Hayek, F.A. (1935), *Prices and Production*, 2nd ed., London: Routledge.
Hayek, F.A. (1937a), 'Economics and Knowledge', *Economica*, NS **4** (Feb.), 33–54.
Hayek, F.A. (1937b), *Monetary Nationalism and International Stability*, London: Longmans.
Hayek, F.A. (1939), *Profits, Interest and Investment*, London: Routledge.
Hayek, F.A. (1941), 'The Counter Revolution of Science',
Part I *Economica*, NS **8** (Feb), 9–36;
Part II *ibid.* (May), 119–50;
Part III *ibid.* (Aug.), 281–320.
Hayek, F.A. (1942–1944), 'Scientism and the Study of Society',
Part I *Economica*, NS **9** (Aug. 1942), 267–91;
Part II *Economica*, NS **10** (Feb. 1943), 34–63;
Part III *Economica*, NS **11** (Feb. 1944), 27–39.
Hayek, F.A. (1943a), 'John Rae and John Stuart Mill: A Correspondence', *Economica*, NS **10** (Aug.), 253–5.
Hayek, F.A. (1943b), 'Miscellaneous Notes', *Economica*, NS **10** (May), 188–9.
Hayek, F.A. (1944), 'Richard von Strigl', *Economic Journal*, **54** (June–Sept.), 284–6.
Hayek, F.A. (1945), 'Notes on N.W. Senior's *Political Economy* by John Stuart Mill', *Economica*, NS **12** (Aug.), 134–9.
Hayek, F.A. (1946), 'The London School of Economics 1895–1945', *Economica*, NS **13** (Feb.), 1–31.
Hayek, F.A. (1948), 'Wesley Clair Mitchell, 1874–1948', *Journal of the Royal Statistical Society*, **111**(3), 254–5.
Hayek, F.A. (1949), *Individualism and Economic Order*, London: Routledge.
Hayek, F.A. (1950), 'Ricardo, David', in *Chambers Encyclopaedia*, new edition, vol. 11, pp. 680–81, London: George Newnes.
Hayek, F.A. (1951), *John Stuart Mill and Harriet Taylor. Their Correspondence and Subsequent Marriage*, London: Routledge.
Hayek, F.A. (1952), *The Sensory Order. An Inquiry into the Foundations of Theoretical Psychology*, London: Routledge.
Hayek, F.A. (1954), *Capitalism and the Historians*, London: Routledge.
Hayek, F.A. (1960), *The Constitution of Liberty*, London: Routledge.
Hayek, F.A. (1967), *Studies in Philosophy. Politics and Economics*, London: Routledge.
Hayek, F.A. (1968a), 'The Austrian School', in D.L. Sills (ed.), *International Encyclopaedia of the Social Sciences*, vol. 4, pp. 458–62, New York: Macmillan and Free Press.
Hayek, F.A. (1968b), 'Menger, Carl', in D.L. Sills (ed.), *International Encyclopaedia of the Social Sciences*, vol. 10, pp. 124–7, New York: Macmillan and Free Press.
Hayek, F.A. (1968c), 'Wieser, Friedrich von', in D.L. Sills (ed.), *International Encyclopaedia of the Social Sciences*, vol. 16, pp. 549–50, New York: Macmillan and Free Press.
Hayek, F.A. (1973–9), *Law, Legislation and Liberty*,
vol. 1 *Rules and Order* (1973),

vol. 2 *The Mirage of Social Justice* (1976),
vol. 3 *The Political Order of a Free People* (1979),
one volume edition 1982, London: Routledge.

Hayek, F.A. (1978), *New Studies in Philosophy, Politics, Economics and the History of Ideas*, London: Routledge.

Hayek, F.A. (1979), 'Foreword', pp. xix–xxiv in L.v. Mises, *Socialism*, repr. Indianapolis: Liberty Classics.

Hayek, F.A. (1983), 'The Austrian Critique', *Economist,* 11 June, 1983, pp. 45–8.

Hayek, F.A. (1984), *Money, Capital and Fluctuations. Early Essays*, ed. R. McCloughry, London: Routledge.

Hayek, F.A. (1988), *The Fatal Conceit. The Errors of Socialism. The Collected Works of F.A. Hayek,* vol. 1, ed. W.W. Bartley III, London: Routledge.

Hayek, F.A. (1991), *The Trend of Economic Thinking. Essays on Political Economists and Economic History. The Collected Works of F.A. Hayek,* vol. 3, ed. W.W. Bartley III and S. Kresge, London: Routledge.

Hayek, F.A. (1992), *The Fortunes of Liberalism. Essays on Austrian Economics and the Idea of Freedom. The Collected Works of F.A. Hayek,* vol. 4, ed. P.G. Klein, London: Routledge.

Hicks, J.R. (1936), 'Mr. Keynes' Theory of Employment', *Economic Journal,* **46** (June), 238–53.

Hicks, J.R. (1940), 'Review of F.A. Hayek (ed.), *An Enquiry into the Nature and Effects of the Paper Credit of Great Britain* by Henry Thornton', *Economic History Review,* **10** (2), 182.

Hicks, J.R. (1967), *Critical Essay in Monetary Theory*, Oxford: Clarendon, repr. 1979.

Hutchison, T.W. (1981), *The Politics and Philosophy of Economics: Marxians. Keynesians and Austrians*, Oxford: Blackwell.

Keynes, J.M. (1930), *A Treatise on Money*, 2 vols., reprinted London: Macmillan for the Royal Economic Society, 1971.

Keynes, J.M. (1931), 'The Pure Theory of Money. A Reply to Dr. Hayek', *Economica,* **11** (Nov.), 387–97.

Keynes, J.M. (1936), *The General Theory of Employment, Interest and Money,* reprinted London: Macmillan for the Royal Economic Society, 1973.

Machlup, F. (ed.) (1976), *Essays on Hayek*, New York: New York University Press.

Machlup, F. (1979), 'Hayek, Friedrich A. Von', in D.L. Sills (ed.), *International Encyclopaedia of the Social Sciences*, vol. 18, pp. 274–82, New York: Free Press.

Menger, C. (1871), *Grundsätze der Volkswirtschaftslehre*, Wien: Bergmüller, repr. London: LSE 1934.

Menger, C. (1883), *Untersuchung über die Methode der Socialwissenschaften und der Politischen Oekonomie insbesondere*, trans. F.J. Nock, ed. L. Schneider as *Problems of Economics and Sociology*, Urbana: University of Illinois Press, 1963.

Mineka, F. (ed.) (1963), *The Earlier Letters of John Stuart Mill*, Toronto: University of Toronto Press.

Mises, L.v. (1912), *The Theory of Money and Credit*, 2nd ed. 1924, trans. H.E. Batson, London: Cape, 1953.

Mises, L.v. (1922), *Gemeinwirtschaft*, trans. as *Socialism*, by J. Kahane, repr. Indianapolis: Liberty Classics, 1979.

Mises, L.v. (1969), *The Historical Setting of the Austrian School of Economics*, New Rochelle, New York: Arlington House.

Moss, L. and Vaughn, K. (1986), 'Hayek's Ricardo Effect: A Second Look', *History of Political Economy*, **18** (Winter), 545–65, repr. in Wood and Woods (1991), vol. 4, pp. 156–76.

O'Brien, D.P. (1988), *Lionel Robbins*, London: Macmillan.

Ricardo, D. (1817), *On the Principles of Political Economy and Taxation* reprinted as vol. 1 of *The Works and Correspondence of David Ricardo*, ed. P. Sraffa, Cambridge: Cambridge University Press, 1951.

Robbins, L.C. (1932), *An Essay on the Nature and Significance of Economic Science*, 2nd ed., London: Macmillan, 1935.

Robbins, L.C. (1934), *The Great Depression*, London: Macmillan.

Robbins, L.C. (1971), *Autobiography of an Economist*, London: Macmillan.

Sabine, G.H. (1951), *A History of Political Theory*, 3rd. ed., London: Harrap.

Schumpeter, J.A. (1954), *A History of Economic Analysis*, London: Allen and Unwin.

Stigler, G.J. (1955), 'The Nature and Role of Originality in Scientific Progress', reprinted pp. 1–15 in *Essays in the History of Economics*, Chicago: University of Chicago Press, 1965.

Stonier, A.W. (1943), 'Miscellaneous Notes', *Economica*, NS **10** (May), 188.

Streissler, E. (ed.) (1969), *Roads to Freedom. Essays in Honour of Friedrich A. von Hayek*, London: Routledge.

Thornton, H. (1802), *An Enquiry into the Nature and Effects of the Paper Credit of Great Britain*, ed. F.A. Hayek, London: Allen and Unwin, 1939.
Vaughn, K.I. (1980), 'Economic Calculation under Socialism: The Austrian Contribution', *Economic Inquiry*, **18** (Oct.), 535–54, repr. in Wood and Woods (1991), vol. 3, pp. 206–26.
Wood, J.C. and Woods, R.N. (eds) (1991), *Friedrich A. Hayek. Critical Assessments*, 4 vols., London: Routledge.

Name index

Economists of the Twentieth Century

Monetarism and Macroeconomic Policy
Thomas Mayer

Studies in Fiscal Federalism
Wallace E. Oates

The World Economy in Perspective
Essays in International Trade and European Integration
Herbert Giersch

Towards a New Economics
Critical Essays on Ecology, Distribution and Other Themes
Kenneth E. Boulding

Studies in Positive and Normative Economics
Martin J. Bailey

The Collected Essays of Richard E. Quandt (2 volumes)
Richard E. Quandt

International Trade Theory and Policy
Selected Essays of W. Max Corden
W. Max Corden

Organization and Technology in Capitalist Development
William Lazonick

Studies in Human Capital
Collected Essays of Jacob Mincer, Volume 1
Jacob Mincer

Studies in Labor Supply
Collected Essays of Jacob Mincer, Volume 2
Jacob Mincer

Macroeconomics and Economic Policy
The Selected Essays of Assar Lindbeck, Volume I
Assar Lindbeck

The Welfare State
The Selected Essays of Assar Lindbeck, Volume II
Assar Lindbeck

Classical Economics, Public Expenditure and Growth
Walter Eltis

Money, Interest Rates and Inflation
Frederic S. Mishkin

The Public Choice Approach to Politics
Dennis C. Mueller

The Liberal Economic Order
Volume I Essays on International Economics
Volume II Money, Cycles and Related Themes
Gottfried Haberler
Edited by Anthony Y.C. Koo

Economic Growth and Business Cycles
Prices and the Process of Cyclical Development
Paolo Sylos Labini

International Adjustment, Money and Trade
Theory and Measurement for Economic Policy, Volume I
Herbert G. Grubel

International Capital and Service Flows
Theory and Measurement for Economic Policy, Volume II
Herbert G. Grubel

Unintended Effects of Government Policies
Theory and Measurement for Economic Policy, Volume III
Herbert G. Grubel

The Economics of Competitive Enterprise
Selected Essays of P.W.S. Andrews
Edited by Frederic S. Lee and Peter E. Earl

The Repressed Economy
Causes, Consequences, Reform
Deepak Lal

Economic Theory and Market Socialism
Selected Essays of Oskar Lange
Edited by Tadeusz Kowalik

Trade, Development and Political Economy
Selected Essays of Ronald Findlay
Ronald Findlay

General Equilibrium Theory
The Collected Essays of Takashi Negishi, Volume I
Takashi Negishi

The History of Economics
The Collected Essays of Takashi Negishi, Volume II
Takashi Negishi

Studies in Econometric Theory
The Collected Essays of Takeshi Amemiya
Takeshi Amemiya

Exchange Rates and the Monetary System
Selected Essays of Peter B. Kenen
Peter B. Kenen

Econometric Methods and Applications (2 volumes)
G.S. Maddala

National Accounting and Economic Theory
The Collected Papers of Dan Usher, Volume I
Dan Usher

Welfare Economics and Public Finance
The Collected Papers of Dan Usher, Volume II
Dan Usher

Economic Theory and Capitalist Society
The Selected Essays of Shigeto Tsuru, Volume I
Shigeto Tsuru

Methodology, Money and the Firm
The Collected Essays of D.P. O'Brien (2 volumes)
D.P. O'Brien

Economic Theory and Financial Policy
The Selected Essays of Jacques J. Polak (2 volumes)
Jacques J. Polak

Sturdy Econometrics
Edward E. Leamer

METHODOLOGY, MONEY AND THE FIRM
VOLUME I

ECONOMISTS OF THE TWENTIETH CENTURY

General Editors: Mark Perlman, *University Professor of Economics, Emeritus, University of Pittsburgh* and Mark Blaug, *Professor Emeritus, University of London; Professor Emeritus, University of Buckingham; and Visiting Professor, University of Exeter*

This innovative series comprises specially invited collections of articles and papers by economists whose work has made an important contribution to economics in the late twentieth century.

The proliferation of new journals and the ever-increasing number of new articles make it difficult for even the most assiduous economist to keep track of all the important recent advances. By focusing on those economists whose work is generally recognized to be at the forefront of the discipline, the series will be an essential reference point for the different specialisms included.

A list of published and future titles in this series is printed at the end of this volume.

Methodology, Money and the Firm

The Collected Essays of D.P. O'Brien

Volume I

D.P. O'Brien

Professor of Economics
University of Durham, UK

ECONOMISTS OF THE TWENTIETH CENTURY

Edward Elgar

Published by
Edward Elgar Publishing Limited
Gower House
Croft Road
Aldershot
Hants GU11 3HR
England

Edward Elgar Publishing Company
Old Post Road
Brookfield
Vermont 05036
USA

British Library Cataloguing in Publication Data
O'Brien, D.P.
Methodology, Money and the Firm:
Collected Essays of D.P. O'Brien. –
(Economists of the Twentieth Century
Series)
I. Title II. Series
338.5

Library of Congress Cataloguing in Publication Data
O'Brien, D.P. (Denis Patrick), 1939–
Methodology, money and the firm ; the collected essays of D.P. O'Brien
p. cm. — (Economists of the twentieth century)
Includes index.
1. Economics. 2. Industrial organization (Economic theory)
3. Economic history. I. Title. II. Series.
HB171.027 1994
330—dc20 94–3920
CIP

ISBN 1 85278 966 2 (2 volume set)

Printed and Bound in Great Britain by
Hartnolls Limited, Bodmin, Cornwall.

To Julie Bushby
For all those deadlines,
met with promptness, efficiency,
and, above all, a sense of humour.

Contents

PART IV MONEY AND THE CURRENCY PRINCIPLE

Preface

In compiling a collection of the kind represented in these two volumes, an awful lot of acknowledgements are due. Many individuals must take some credit (or blame, according to taste) for what is included here. It is conventional to start with one's undergraduate teachers, and there is no doubt that I learned a great deal from, in particular, George Allen, Marian Bowley and John Spraos at University College London, despite the very deeply unsatisfactory nature of the position of undergraduates at UCL at that time. Subsequently I accumulated a huge debt to Bob Black for the nearly ten years which I spent at Queen's University Belfast where, as supervisor, friend, colleague, mentor (and occasionally even as substitute teacher when I fell ill, which was unfortunately far too often), he shaped my work in ways of which even now I am only partially conscious. Other less directly personal influences were also important – Jacob Viner, from whose work I learned so much and who encouraged my early work on Overstone, Lionel Robbins (who also took a major hand in securing support to enable an edition of Overstone's papers to be produced) and Mark Blaug and Terence Hutchison from whose works I have, over the years, derived enormous insight and stimulus. Of course there have been many others along the way, and I remain grateful to them all, even though in acknowledgements of this sort it seems proper to concentrate on the most powerful influences. But amongst the latter must be mentioned John Creedy, who in twenty years of friendship has proved an endlessly stimulating, informative, and patient friend from whom I have learnt a great deal.

In the preparation of these volumes I have once again had the benefit of his advice and help, for which I am, yet again, grateful. I have also benefited from his incisive and sympathetic comments on my introduction and also from those of Dr Julia Stapleton.

The contents of this volume also represent something else which should be mentioned – deadlines met. In the meeting of such deadlines I have been, over the years, enormously fortunate in the secretarial help I have received. I cannot type. I play the violin and at an age when I might have learnt to type I found that the old manual typewriters deadened my finger ends to such an extent that I could no longer play. But my incapacity as a typist has been entirely remedied by the secretaries who have worked hard, fast, and efficiently, to enable me to meet deadlines all the same. It is to one of these – to one who in the last thirteen years has met more deadlines that I can count – both in her own right and as the representative of all those who have helped in this way, that these two volumes are dedicated.

Acknowledgements

The publishers wish to thank the following who have kindly given permission for the use of copyright material.

Australian Economic Papers for article: 'Marshall, Monopoly and Rectangular Hyperbolas' (with J. Creedy), *Australian Economic Papers*, **29**, No. 55 (December 1990), pp. 141–53.

British Journal of Industrial Relations for article: 'Economists and Data', *British Journal of Industrial Relations*, **30**, No. 2 (June 1992), pp. 253–85.

Federal Legal Publications Inc. for article: 'Competition Policy in Britain: The Silent Revolution', *The Antitrust Bulletin*, **XXVII**, No. 1 (Spring 1982), pp. 217–39.

JAI Press Inc. for chapter: 'Theories of the History of Science: A Test Case', pp. 89–124 in A.W. Coats (ed.), *Methodological Controversy in Economics*, London: JAI Press, 1983.

The Macmillan Press Ltd. for: 'The Evolution of the Theory of the Firm', pp. 25–62 in Frank H. Stephen (ed.), *Firms, Organization and Labour*, London: Macmillan, 1984. (The kind permission of Professor Frank H. Stephen for the use of this item is also gratefully acknowledged.); 'Overstone, Lord', Vol. III, p. 784 in J. Eatwell, M. Milgate and P. Newman, *The New Palgrave*, London: Macmillan, 1987.

MCB University Press Ltd. for article: 'Research Programmes in Competitive Structure', *Journal of Economic Studies*, **10**, No. 4 (1983), pp. 29–51.

The Manchester School for article: 'Information Agreements – A Problem in Search of a Policy' (with D. Swann), *The Manchester School*, **24** (September 1966), pp. 285–306.

Routledge, Chapman & Hall Ltd. for chapter: 'Theory and Empirical Observation', pp. 49–67 in David Greenaway, Michael Bleaney and Ian Stewart (eds), *Companion to Contemporary Economic Thought*, London: Routledge, 1991.

The Royal Economic Society for: '[Overstone's] Monetary Thought', pp. 70–144 in D.P. O'Brien (ed.), *The Correspondence of Lord Overstone*, Vol. I, Cambridge: CUP, 1971.

The Scottish Economic Society for article: 'Marshall's Industrial Analysis', *Scottish Journal of Political Economy*, **37**, No. 1 (February 1990), pp. 61–84.

Simon and Schuster International Group for chapter: 'Divestiture: the Case of AT & T', pp. 166–201 in J. Coyne and M. Wright (eds), *Divestment and Strategic Change*, Deddington, Oxford: Philip Allan, 1986.

Sweet and Maxwell for chapter: 'Patents: An Economist's View', pp. 32–41 in Jeremy Phillips (ed.), *Patents in Perspective*, Oxford: ESC Publishing, 1985.

Every effort has been made to trace all the copyright holders, but if any have been inadvertently overlooked, the publishers will be pleased to make the necessary arrangements at the first opportunity.

Introduction

The papers in this two-volume set cover a fairly wide spread from methodology, and the history and philosophy of science, to statistical techniques for the investigation of disputed authorship. In Volume I, Part I focuses on methodology, and leads into Part II which is concerned with industry, both from the point of view of the practitioner of industrial economics (and especially of competition policy), and from the point of view of the treatment of industry by economists. Part III then leads into the matter of the firm, and the focus here is on the way in which economists have attempted to deal with this large, and in many ways intractable, problem. In Part IV monetary topics are treated both broadly – the first item is an attempt to set monetary literature in its historical perspective – and more narrowly with discussions of the work of the leading member of the Currency School.

Part I of Volume II continues the monetary theme, dealing first with another luminary of the Currency School, Robert Torrens, before moving on to a discussion of Thomas Joplin's macroeconomics. Matters of trade theory and policy are covered in the next two items, and Part I ends with consideration of a recent experiment in monetary control. Since a significant part of my working life has been spent teaching economics, especially the monetary and exchange rate aspects of this, I find the combination of money and trade particularly congenial. Part II consists very largely in straightforward intellectual history – English economics 1660–1860 – though included is a piece on a question of disputed authorship in the literature of economics. Part III deals with the neo-classical era, with two papers relating to the giant (intellectually speaking) figure of Alfred Marshall, and with two more dealing with economists who exercised a widespread personal as well as intellectual influence in the 20th century, Robbins and Hayek. Finally I attempt to draw some lessons from all this.

Volume I

Part I Methodology

Part I is concerned with methodological issues. The opening contribution – my inaugural lecture at Durham – was an attempt to ask what was happening to economics as the mathematical/formalistic tide swept forward, like the broom in the fable of the Sorcerer's Apprentice. It would be comforting to think that some of the things about which I, and many others at that time, were concerned had proved to be unnecessary worries. This is however far from the case. Though some of the wilder claims for general equilibrium have now been abandoned, a whole area in which economists were, at that time, in daily contact with data – industrial economics – has fallen to game theory in which, to put it unkindly, the difficulties of confrontation with real world data are such that practitioners are forced to make up their own data under the guise of 'experimental economics'.

Yet the role of (real world) data is, or should be, of key importance in *any* subject which has claims to real world policy implications and relevance. I have explored this issue in two recent papers – Chapters 3 and 4. Amongst other things I have attempted to show in these that a misplaced conception of what actually goes on in other subjects (and subjects which, like medicine, or physics, are conspicuously more successful in delivering the promised goods than economics) may be behind much that has happened in economics in the recent past – introverted model building, claims about the 'irrelevance' of assumptions, formalism for its own sake, even professional journals which seem increasingly to remain unread by the professionals.

All this raises serious questions not merely about progress in economics but also about the way in which economists choose to attack (or to sidestep) the problems facing them. This matter is explored in Chapter 2. While the bulk of this material dates from the 1970s, the paper focuses on what still seems to me, in the 1990s, the really important contributions to the history and philosophy of science – those of Popper, Kuhn, and Lakatos. Though the 1980s witnessed a huge explosion in the literature of this field, it is difficult to find genuinely original thought in all the welter of material – indeed it is often difficult to find genuinely 'tight' (for want of a better word) thought, where tightness is not to be confused with nit-picking.

Part II The industry

Part II is about industry. Having come from a family background which was business rather than academic, and having begun my career as an industrial economist, I have frequently been appalled by the gap between economic training and the reality of industry, and this has led me to maintain an interest in industry itself and in the way in which economists have looked at it. The first piece which I wrote (not included here, basically because the issues which it covered are now a long-forgotten part of what has become, in the intervening years, business history) was about patents (O'Brien, 1964). It related to the role of patent protection in the development of polyamide (nylon) and polyester fibre manufacture. In the writing of that earlier article, I was much helped by the then editor of the *Journal of Industrial Economics*, P.W.S. Andrews, and by a referee who was, it turned out, Tom Wilson. I have always remained grateful to them for their patience with, and encouragement of, my early effort. (Since tenure in Queen's University Belfast, long before this rule spread to English universities, depended on refereed journal publications during one's period as an Assistant Lecturer – Kingsley Amis's *Lucky Jim* was not *at all* funny for an Assistant Lecturer in Queen's – I also owe them a more mundane debt.)

In that early work the treatment of patents by economists seemed, though I did not stress this, significantly defective. When I came to look at the matter again in the mid-1980s I was even less reassured, and this is one of the themes of the piece on patents which is included here (Chapter 9).

An industrial background, experience of industry, and some concern with the inadequacy of mainstream treatment of competition (as well as an interest in law) led to a natural concern with competition policy. The piece with Dennis Swann which begins Part II attracted some attention at the time (as did our book – O'Brien and Swann 1969), and has been commented on since. But the issues involved in it were both central to the way in which competition works *and* excluded by mainstream

approaches (though Andrews, and George Richardson, were two important dissidents who had interesting things to say about the problems involved).

As competition policy evolved, and as it began to be possible to appreciate its effects (Swann, O'Brien *et al.*, 1974a, b), it became clear that what was really driving the policies was, as G.C. Allen had explained to his undergraduates at University College London (of whom I was one), not the application of some irrelevant model but a vision (which had its origins in Smith's *Wealth of Nations*) of the need to remove constraints imposed on the price system by what are now called 'rent seekers'. It could, thus freed, respond, not only to meet *existing* consumer preferences and production technologies, and resource availabilities, but to meet *changes* in those things. It was then a welcome opportunity, when approached by a BBC producer at the 1976 Glasgow Bicentenary celebration of the *Wealth of Nations* – no doubt he merely had a vacant twenty-minute slot to fill rather than anything more pressing in mind – with a request to provide a talk related to Smith's great book. For it enabled me to make the point that the roots of the policy did indeed lie in Smith's work. The talk is published here (Chapter 6) for the first time.

British policy towards competition evolved slowly, and in some respects is still far behind American policy. But it has moved away from the court-based (and extremely legalistic) approach of the 1956 Restrictive Trade Practices Act to a system involving much more administrative discretion (though the ultimate threat of court involvement remains). This change is documented in Chapter 7. The early development of policy in this country, especially when the fearsome Lord Devlin was President of the Restrictive Practices Court (seven of the first eight cases in which firms defended their restrictions were lost), was probably necessary, both to establish a body of precedent and, perhaps even more importantly, to convince industry (which had comfortably avoided any serious inconvenience at the hands of the – administrative – Monopolies Commission procedures) that government was now serious about restrictive practices. But it cannot be denied that this approach ultimately ran into the sand, and the changes discussed in Chapter 7, though not without their dangers, were inevitable.

But competition policy in this country remains a relatively humble instrument compared with the apparatus developed in the United States. In particular, the power to order divestiture, though theoretically available in the UK, is little used. Some of the lessons to be learned from the US experience with this potentially drastic weapon are explored in Chapter 8.

A constant realization in all the work on competition policy has been, as already indicated, the inadequacy of mainstream economics, especially the so-called 'theory of the firm' (which is, in truth, nothing of the sort) to provide any help. This was a point stressed to his students by G.C. Allen, who himself played such a key role in the development of competition policy, especially in the 1955 Monopolies Commission report on Collective Discrimination (Allen, 1968, pp. 64, 82–3, 107); and it is explored in Chapter 10, as well as in Part III, Chapters 11, 12 and 13.

Part III The firm

One point which emerges clearly, at least in my opinion, is the retrogression that occurred in the 1930s. As I argue in Chapter 10, Marshall's industrial analysis was

extremely wide ranging and well secured, and it would have provided an excellent base on which to have developed further work. But this was not to be the way forward, as I indicate in Chapters 11 and 12. Rather, economists preferred to abandon industrial reality for models – models which now seem very primitive (Shubik has suggested that Joan Robinson's *Imperfect Competition* might look to a future archaeologist like 'an early precursor of Newton' (Shubik, 1970, p. 416)) but models none the less. As Shackle has written 'Clear and definite questions cannot be asked about a vague, richly detailed, fluid and living world. This world must therefore be exchanged for a model'. (Shackle, 1967, p. 47). The problem with this model, as with game theory now, is that the model did *not* help us to 'see our way' in Kenneth Boulding's classic verse.[1] Instead it provided a comprehensive set of blinkers, to fence economists off from the real world of competition, and it enabled them (like modern game theory) to generate a whole series of 'pseudo-solutions to non-problems' (to refer to *Lucky Jim* again). Of course there was a hidden agenda here, for Joan Robinson's *Imperfect Competition* (1933) is really a radical development of Pigou's welfare economics, not a book about the firm, or even one about competition (imperfect or otherwise) at all; and this agenda finally surfaced in Joan Robinson's embracing of Marxism and in Lerner's *Economics of Control* (1944). The majority of economists preferred to avert their eyes from this unseemly enthusiasm for totalitarianism, and continued to treat this kind of work with all seriousness. This is true even of Lerner's 'index of monopoly' though Bauer had pointed out as early as 1941 that this was a better reflection of the ratio of fixed to variable costs than of monopoly power (Bauer, 1941, pp. 197–8).

Marshall's contributions, indeed Marshall's preoccupations, were lost sight of. Even his brave attempt to deal with the problem of the determination of profit-maximizing output, through his device of profit hyperbolas, was scorned. Yet, as John Creedy and I show in Chapter 13, there were very good reasons indeed for Marshall to take this approach, even though it left writers like Joan Robinson so apparently baffled by the concept of the first derivative of a total revenue function that they struggled to arrive at 'this particular Pole' (1933, p. vi). As we show, there were both mathematical reasons (multiple roots) and economic reasons (multiple unstable equilibria in the monopoly context) why Marshall should have taken this approach.

Part IV Money and the currency principle

With Part IV we come to the topics of money and trade. In Chapter 14 I have attempted the extremely difficult task of setting mainstream monetary economics in its historical context. I have tried to show both the failures of scholarship (sometimes very blatant, such as the oft-repeated orthodoxy that Keynes's *General Theory* was the origin of the 'indirect mechanism' of monetary transmission, a claim so blatantly false – by at least 200 years – that one despairs of scholarly standards) and failures of perspective, leading to over-emphasis on small points which were long established.

From that point on the monetary focus in the papers is on the 19th century debates which are still the origins of almost everything useful that economists know about money. A short over-view of Overstone's contributions (Chapter 16) is followed

by a detailed discussion of his monetary thought taken from the three-volume edition of his papers and correspondence which I prepared. Both this discussion, and the following paper on Torrens, were much influenced at the time of writing by a Currency School perspective, though they also reflect the influence of Lionel Robbins, whose great book *Robert Torrens* (Robbins, 1958) was my starting point for the study of the metamorphosis of Torrens into a pillar of the Currency School.

Volume II

Part I Classical macroeconomics and trade

With Volume II the theme of money is continued with a discussion of the work of Robert Torrens and the way in which he evolved from being one of the most ingenious of the Anti-Bullionist writers during the period of the suspension of the convertibility of the note issue into gold (1797–1819) to being the most ingenious theoretical advocate of the Currency School position in the 1830s and beyond. Torrens is an endlessly interesting and challenging economist, with a capacity for intellectual abstraction of a very high order, and the position he eventually reached on monetary theory and control seemed highly persuasive, not only to many of his contemporaries but also to me. But then we come to a piece (Chapter 2) which marks a watershed in my own thinking – 'The Macroeconomics of Thomas Joplin'. As I indicate in this, and as I have explained at length in a full-scale study of Joplin (O'Brien, 1993), I now think that the Currency School, as well as the Banking School, was fundamentally mistaken concerning the evidence on monetary causation. The hypotheses put forward by Thomas Joplin, the founder of joint stock banking in this country but a figure shunned by both the Currency School and the Banking School members, who seem indeed to have gone out of their way to avoid mentioning him, now seem to me to be the ones consistent with the data. Joplin's model – which can be expressed as a rather complicated variant of an open economy neo-Keynesian model, with a fairly elaborate money-supply treatment, and two sectors (O'Brien, 1993, ch. 14) – is also very much more satisfying intellectually than the Hume-based model used by the Currency School, let alone the Banking School's intellectually weak 'endogenous money' model.

From macroeconomic theory we pass, in Chapters 3 and 4 to trade theory. In Chapter 3 a remarkable episode in the development of the theory of protection, and one hitherto unknown, is discussed. It is well known that, in an extremely controversial work entitled *The Budget* (Torrens, 1841/1844), Robert Torrens had used the analysis of reciprocal demand (in the formulation of which he had played a crucial role, though Joplin can claim priority over both Torrens *and* J.S. Mill here – O'Brien, 1993, ch. 12) to argue for trade policy as a strategic tool. Torrens's case was in fact that the terms of trade loss from *unilateral* duty remissions was, via the ensuing balance of payments deficit with a fixed (gold) exchange rate, and with the money supply linked to the balance of payments, the way to monetary deflation and economic depression. This was, as Lionel Robbins pointed out in his book on Torrens, a useful weapon for Torrens in attacking the Whigs (Robbins, 1958, pp. 198–204). But after the split in the Tory Party over the repeal of the Corn Laws, Torrens attempted, as the article reveals, to employ his apparatus to

suggest a case for protection (under the guise of reciprocity in trade negotiations) which the protectionist wing of the Tory Party could support, and even urged the reintroduction of agricultural protection after 1846. It is also interesting to see here that McCulloch – a strong opponent of the argument for reciprocity, in public – was prepared to offer Disraeli some support in private for such a position, as well as offering his advice to the then Chancellor of the Exchequer on more general economic matters, particularly taxation.

Torrens's position in the creation of international trade theory is now more widely recognized since Robbins's great book – the extremely unfortunate habit, stemming from Marshall, of attributing all classical international trade theory to Ricardo (even reciprocal demand theory) has been greatly weakened. But the achievements of classical trade theory were enormous, and it is no coincidence that the two 20th century economists most thoroughly versed in the classical literature were the ones most aware, in the 20th century, of the real nature of customs unions long before these came to the attention of economists in general. This matter is explored in Chapter 4. Robbins had regarded the trade diversion aspect of a common external tariff as so obvious that he dismissed it in one throw-away line about it being harmless to discriminate against 'the inaccessible produce of the moon'.[2] But it was Jacob Viner, in his *The Customs Union Issue* (Viner, 1950), who set up the basic trade creation/trade diversion distinction in a way which was wholly classical. That those who sought to build on Viner's contribution were apparently completely unaware of the roots of the analysis was remarkable, and in Chapter 4 I have attempted to show that the issues involved in customs union theory have not only a long history in economics but a long pedigree of analytical understanding.

Many classical economists – though not all (Ricardo is an obvious exception) – took account of the data relating to economic problems and attempted, with varying degrees of success, to relate the data to their theories. But in considering data they drew on a wide range of sources – this is especially true not only of Tooke but of McCulloch (O'Brien, 1970) – and it is highly unlikely that they would have allowed one single relationship, established within a probabalistic (i.e. regression analysis) context, to exclude not merely analysis but common sense. Yet this is essentially what happened when the Bank of England adopted the policy of controlling the money *supply* through controlling money *demand*, on the grounds that there was ostensibly a simple stable relationship between the rate of interest and money *demand* established by early single equation monetary models. This policy – bizarre in retrospect if not, indeed, at the time – is examined in the short article on 'Competition and Credit Control' which concludes Part I.

Part II English economics 1660–1860

Parts II and III contain a variety of studies, many dealing with particular individuals, which focus exclusively on the history of economic thought. We start, in Chapter 6, with the extraordinary figure of Sir William Petty, whose combination of brilliance, charlatanism, and unscrupulous carpet-baggery has no real parallels in the history of economic thought. Petty is important not only for the quality of what he wrote – his tax analysis certainly seems to have influenced Adam Smith – but for the way in which he made quantitative estimates with an almost unbelievable bravura and,

occasionally, with surprising accuracy. In the last resort it has to be acknowledged that the charlatanism was much in evidence; and since the piece reprinted here is about Petty's *Political Arithmetick*, the issue is faced. His contemporaries were aware of this, and it led in the next century to Swift's brilliant parody *A Modest Proposal* (Letwin, 1963, pp. 138–40). But for all that, Petty is well worth attention. If the 17th century is the start of the era of scientific economics – if indeed there *is* such a thing as scientific economics – then Petty has very strong claims to be regarded as the first scientific economist. (That he was also a brilliant rogue is something that those who contend for the scientific status of economics will have to chew on. My own evaluation of the subject is closer to that of Hicks (1979, p. viii), who said it was an art – or a discipline (Hicks, 1983) – not a science.)

Petty's life and work are well documented, and, despite recent attempts by workers in the Marx–Sraffa industry to make out that Marx rediscovered Petty, his work was well known, and frequently reprinted, in both the 18th and 19th centuries. But even the true identity of the next figure, 'Piercy Ravenstone', is not known for certain, though there are reasonable guesses as to his real name. What is however interesting about this man – and this is something not to be learnt from the secondary commentaries on Ravenstone – is the extent to which Physiocracy had influenced English economic thought. For the basis of Ravenstone's work is clearly the Physiocrats: and the same was to be true a little later of the remarkable Thomas Joplin, whose *Outlines* exhibits clear Physiocratic influences (O'Brien, 1993, pp. 47–8). Yet it seems inconceivable that Joplin could read French, and the manner in which these influences found their way into this country remains mysterious.

The body of classical economics as a whole managed, despite Adam Smith's strictures in Book IV of the *Wealth of Nations*, to absorb some limited Physiocratic influence – indeed the whole circular flow analysis can be seen to derive (though mainly indirectly, via Smith himself and J.B. Say) from that source. But this should not be a matter of surprise if we look at the classical literature as a whole, and realize what a broad church it constituted. I have tried to explain something of this in Chapter 8, and have dealt with the matter at much greater length in Chapter 10, where I have looked at the literature on the so-called minor classical economists. The bad old habit of viewing classical economics as made up of the work of Adam Smith and David Ricardo, and simply treating every other writer as a regurgitating also-ran, is still to be found, not only in undergraduate courses but also in some history of economic thought text books. But the contributions of Longfield, James Mill (for all his – to me – personal repulsiveness), Senior, Bailey, Torrens and Say are all far too important to be downgraded in this way, and in Chapter 10 I have attempted to explore the way in which their significant individual contributions have become more widely appreciated.

But the topic of Ricardo will not go away. Broadly speaking there are three sub-branches of the (by now grossly over-expanded) Ricardo-interpretation industry. Firstly there is that which I find most congenial and which has diverse roots in the work of Jacob Viner, George Stigler, Mark Blaug, and even to some extent Lionel Robbins. This attempts to treat Ricardo's work on its own merits without dressing it up as something else and without finding it necessary to depart – at least too far – from what Ricardo actually wrote in his published work. Next is the Sraffa

industry. This is essentially Marxist in inspiration and origins, and has developed an interpretation of Ricardo in terms of Sraffa's own curious theoretical apparatus (Rip van Winkle economics as Mark Blaug (1974, p. 31) has categorized it) which I personally find so hard to relate to what Ricardo (as distinct from Marx) actually wrote that I can only stand back in admiration when someone like Mark Blaug (1987) or Terence Hutchison (1978, pp. 240–76; 1993) has the patience to take it apart. Thirdly there is the strand represented by the extraordinary individual efforts of Professor Samuel Hollander (1979). Sam Hollander's technique is essentially textual interpretation, of an all-inclusive nature (no half-considered private letter, no reported Parliamentary utterance, is too trivial to be accorded equal weight with the published work) and with a tenacity and intensity previously associated with biblical exegesis, though whether biblical exegesis also involves the free insertion of italics into the original texts I cannot say. The picture which Sam Hollander obtains from this process could perhaps be described – albeit a little unfairly – as Ricardo the post-Walrasian. It is not a picture of Ricardo which I find easy to recognize, though it does not – to me at least – seem to involve the re-engineering which characterizes the Italo-Cambridge Ricardo industry. Even though Hollander can certainly not be accused of lacking imagination in his interpretation of what Ricardo's text will bear, it is at least possible to relate what he says to what Ricardo wrote. But at all events my differences with this last approach are set out in Chapter 9, a contribution which, hardly surprisingly, led to further exchanges with Hollander which I have spared the reader.

Over-concentration on the work of Smith and Ricardo led, as already noted, to a distorted picture not only of the corpus of classical economic literature as a whole but also of the work of individual classical writers, and the remaining items in Part II deal mainly with such economists. Chapter 11 was the first shot in my attempt, culminating in a book (O'Brien, 1970), to draw together a coherent picture of the work of J.R. McCulloch. McCulloch was so often, and so facilely, classed as a slavish follower of Ricardo, that it was not hard (in terms of the available material that is – the work involved was, however, quite a different matter) to show that McCulloch, whose writings as an economist continued for forty years after Ricardo's death, was a far more complex and interesting figure than the sterile stereotype. In a sense, the value theory discussion was the least promising place in McCulloch's whole output to start – and yet even here it turned out that, within a few years of Ricardo's death, McCulloch's treatment of value had undergone a significant change. In fact the value theory is not the most interesting part of McCulloch's work, and I am very glad that the full-length study of McCulloch, which resulted from my work covering the whole range of his output, has recently been reprinted.[3] But at least the item included here gives some flavour of the discussion. I have also, in the short article in Chapter 14, attempted to give some overall view of McCulloch's contribution within the context of which the value discussion may be set.

McCulloch was at his best in blending fact and theory in a way recalling his Scottish predecessors, and especially the master of all classical economists, Adam Smith. Some flavour of this is given in Chapter 15, which reprints the introduction to the edition of McCulloch's *Treatise on Taxation* which the Scottish Economic Society commissioned. McCulloch's book, which went through three editions in his lifetime,

was a major text in public finance in the 19th century, and represents a startling contrast with the work of McCulloch's supposed source Ricardo, whose tax chapters contain not a fact and are simply exercises in working through (what at least the first school of Ricardo interpretation referred to above regard as) Ricardo's model. Ricardo even failed to discuss the income tax, despite the fact that it was a matter of considerable public controversy in his own lifetime.

McCulloch also features in Chapter 13 as one of two possible authors who may have been responsible for the whole (or possibly a part) of an *Edinburgh Review* article. In this joint article we attempted to apply a non-parametric statistical technique to resolution of the problem. I have a long interest in non-parametric techniques in the investigation of industrial data (O'Brien, Howe *et al.*, 1979), and it was particularly gratifying to be able to explore such techniques in the context of the history of ideas. It should however be stressed, as it was indeed stressed in the original article and in the book which subsequently appeared (O'Brien and Darnell, 1982), that such techniques are *no substitute* for proper scholarly research work on the background and content of a piece.

The remaining piece in Part II, Chapter 12, concerns that (to me) endlessly fascinating figure Robert Torrens. Torrens was much involved in the debates over emigration, as Robbins made clear in his book (Robbins, 1958, ch. 6); and it was interesting to discover that Torrens's particularly subtle classical analysis of wage determination (one which took explicit account of productivity) had originated in this concern with emigration.

Part III English and Austrian economics after 1870

Part III is devoted to economics after 1870, beginning with two essays on Marshall, and followed by two on Robbins and one on Hayek. Marshall is a marvellously interesting writer, complex, subtle, occasionally remarkably courageous (as in his pleas, at the height of World War I, for moderation in attitudes towards Germany) but always suggesting new ways forward and maintaining a balance between the role of theory and the factual constraints. The rejection of Marshall, especially in his beloved Cambridge, so soon after his death, resulted in the loss of much of value; at the same time the word 'Marshallian' became debased, passing through inaccuracy (the attribution to Marshall of positions on, for example, the full measurability of utility which he never held) to pejorative status. In Chapter 16 I have attempted to give an accurate overall view of Marshall's analysis, though this is necessarily very compressed – Marshall's output is far wider than the *Principles*, just as the scope of what he wrote covers issues hardly touched upon in that great book. Although attempts (e.g. Liebhafsky, 1955) have been made to remind economists of that neglected classic *Industry and Trade* (Marshall, 1919), they have fallen on deaf ears.

Where Marshall is, I think, open to criticism is in his attitude to the classical literature, a matter explored in Chapter 17. For Marshall committed the opposite sin to that of Jevons and Keynes;[4] rather than claiming excessive originality for his work, he sought to find a continuity in economic thought which was not always there, above all in the fields of value and distribution. Even in money and trade, where his claims have far more substance, he elevated the status of Ricardo far beyond that justified by the content of Ricardo's writings, attributing to him in particular

the trade theory developed by Torrens and J.S. Mill and anticipated by Joplin. Marshall's contemporaries were well aware of this – Ashley's challenging article (Ashley, 1891) is still worth reading. But, because of Marshall's own prestige, and the undeniable merits of his own work, he succeeded in establishing a tradition in this respect which is still well secured today. Though Terence Hutchison raised pertinent questions about Ricardo at the time of the publication of Sraffa's great edition (Hutchison, 1952), these questions are now taken even less seriously than they were then before the gross over-inflation of the Ricardo-interpretation industry.

The influence of Marshall's work declined seriously during the late 1920s and the 1930s. At Cambridge it did not so much languish as succumb to frontal assault, sometimes of a rather personalized nature – there seems really to have been an element of dancing on Marshall's grave – despite the attempts of Dennis Robertson and Gerald Shove to halt the tide. At the same time the Marshallian tradition failed to find succour elsewhere. For in London an alternative school, with roots in two different soils, neither of which were Marshallian, was developing under the influence of Lionel Robbins. Though Robbins's early work owed something to Marshall – the famous article on the elasticity of demand for income in terms of effort (Robbins, 1930) has its roots in Dalton's work which, in turn, was Marshallian – Robbins was the author of a critique of the Representative Firm (Robbins, 1928) which, in the view of one commentator, virtually succeeded in eliminating the concept from economics (Blaug, 1978, p. 445). Though Robbins distanced himself in that article from the denigration of Marshall which he believed (rightly) to be occurring (Robbins, 1928, p. 387n), his thought, already influenced by continental sources, notably Cassel, and owing a fundamental debt to Wicksteed's *Common Sense* (Wicksteed, 1910), took a distinctly Austrian turn. This was especially true of his macroeconomics which, despite roots in English classical economics, came to derive almost entirely from that of Mises, supplemented by the work of Hayek whom Robbins persuaded to join him at LSE. Even in his microeconomics, despite the Wicksteedian roots, there are significant Austrian influences. Here the important influences were not the first generation Austrians – Menger, Böhm-Bawerk, even Wieser – but the interpretation of the work of these founders by writers like Strigl and Mayer. It was from Mayer in particular that Robbins's conviction of the importance of Austrian general equilibrium (or 'total equilibrium' as Mark Blaug prefers) came, and it was this which provided him with the basis for his justly famous critique of the (partial equilibrium) 1930s cost controversy (Robbins, 1934). Wieser had provided opportunity cost: but it was, at least if one looks at the matter from the viewpoint of Robbins's writings, Mayer who elevated opportunity cost into the key to general equilibrium.

I have explored these issues in Chapter 18, which attempts to provide an overview of Robbins's work within the short compass of a journal article (there is a subsequent book – O'Brien, 1988) and in Chapter 19 which deals with the explicitly Austrian links. But Robbins's appreciation of these sources was coupled with a deep appreciation also of the classical literature and a positivist (not to say purist) methodological position (Robbins, 1935). The latter owed not a little to the desire to stigmatize Cambridge (especially Pigovian) welfare economics as 'unscientific' – as involving judgements about interpersonal comparisons which we were all free to make, but which were extra-scientific. Even Robbins's emphasis on the general

equilibrium aspects of economic problems had an element of Cambridge-beating about it – the undesirable provincialism in space, as well as that provincialism in time of which Robbins complained (the latter concerns a lack of knowledge of the classical literature) which apparently circumscribed Cambridge reading could be thus highlighted – especially after Keynes's neo-Wicksellian *Treatise* appeared in 1930 with scant reference to Wicksell.

Hayek, as Robbins's newly arrived Austrian ally at LSE, with a detailed knowledge of the literature which Keynes had apparently made an attempt to recreate in his *Treatise*, reviewed the book (Hayek, 1931a), and a bad-tempered exchange ensued in which – in true Oxbridge style – the young Piero Sraffa was brought in to argue on Keynes's behalf (Keynes, 1931; Hayek, 1931b, 1932; Sraffa, 1932a, b). But Hayek was a formidable intellect and scholar, and in the final essay in this volume I have attempted to say something about Hayek, not merely as an intellectual historian, though that is the ostensible subject of the paper, but about the way in which Hayek's own deeply held convictions, his ranking of not merely good and evil (very evident in his writings on 'Scientism') but of what was of fundamental importance in intellectual matters (and what was not), affected his treatment of intellectual history. Like all great intellectual figures who have ventured into intellectual history, and Hayek did much more than simply venture, Hayek's writings (though in his case deeply scholarly, which is more the exception than the rule for such types) are almost of more interest for the light they shed on Hayek's own priorities than for their account of say Smith or Mandeville.

Conclusion

If there is a theme throughout these diverse papers it is, I suppose, that as economists we need to be careful. The power of economists for good or evil is enormously greater than is realized, and much of the damage inflicted on the British economy since about 1960 has been the result of economists pretending to be able to deliver what they could not.[5] More care in methodological matters might lead to less flamboyance, and more respect for the data, both with respect to the assumptions that are made and with respect to the conclusions that are reached, would certainly help. Care might also help economists to be rather more humble, both about what their own subject can achieve (it is patently *not* physics, but it cannot even achieve the level of the biological sciences and of medicine) and about their own role in putting forward policy prescriptions. It might also lead economists to be more aware of the achievements of their predecessors, to avoid caricature, and to listen to the wisdom of intellectual giants like Marshall. Intellectual history – the history of any intellectual pursuit – does matter. It may be that we learn only from the mistakes of the past – though this seems unlikely. It seems far more likely that we will also learn to avoid not only merely re-inventing the wheel, but re-inventing the wheel-spoke and mistaking it for a whole wheel.

Such care is not, of course, the way to build a flamboyant and successful academic career. But it may be better for *economics* in the long run (even though individual economists may well reflect that, as Keynes said of the proportionate version of the quantity theory, in the long run we are all dead – Keynes, 1923, p. 65) if economists in general thought more, read more, and claimed less.

Notes

1. "Models help us to see our way.
Model-building's here to stay.
But ultimately only God'll
Formulate the perfect model"

Kenneth E. Boulding

2. 'It follows, too, that any gain in productive efficiency which is secured by the abolition of "internal" obstacles is a gain which has its cost if it is secured only by the erection of obstacles around the area. From the international point of view, the tariff union is not an advantage in itself. It is an advantage only in so far as, on balance, it conduces to more extensive division of labour. It is to be justified only by arguments which would justify still more its extension to all areas capable of entering into trade relationships. The only possible vindication of the retention of old restrictions or the erection of new ones is the argument that, in their absence, the tendency to restrict would be still more rampageous. No doubt if we could coax the rest of the world into free trade by a high tariff union against the produce of the Eskimos that would be, on balance, an international gain. But it would be inferior to an arrangement whereby the Eskimos were included. The only completely innocuous tariff union would be directed against the inaccessible produce of the moon.' (Robbins, 1937, pp. 121–2).
3. Aldershot: Gregg Revivals, 1992.
4. 'The reviewer of this book [Keynes's *General Theory*] is beset by two contrary temptations. On the one hand, he can accept directly Mr. Keynes' elaborate disquisitions about his own theory, and its place in the development of economics; praising or blaming the alleged more than Jevonian revolution. Or, on the other hand, he can concentrate upon investigating these disquisitions, and tracing (perhaps) a pleasing degree of continuity and tradition, surviving the revolution from the *ancien regime*.' (Hicks, 1936, p. 238).
5. On the earlier history of this see Hutchison, 1964, 1968.

Bibliography

Allen, G.C. (1968), *Monopoly and Restrictive Practices*, London: Allen & Unwin.
Ashley, W.J. (1891), 'The Rehabilitation of Ricardo', *Economic Journal*, **1**, pp. 474–89.
Bauer, P.T. (1941), 'A Note on Monopoly', *Economica*, NS **8**, pp. 194–202.
Blaug, M. (1974), *The Cambridge Revolution: Success or Failure?*, London: Institute of Economic Affairs.
Blaug, M. (1978), *Economic Theory in Retrospect*, 3rd ed., Cambridge: Cambridge University Press.
Blaug, M. (1987), 'Classical Economics', Vol. 1, pp. 434–45 in J. Eatwell, M. Milgate and P. Newman (eds), *The New Palgrave*, London: Macmillan.
Hayek, F.A.v. (1931a), 'Reflections on the Pure Theory of Money of Mr. J.M. Keynes', *Economica*, **11**, pp. 270–95.
Hayek, F.A.v. (1931b), 'A Rejoinder to Mr. Keynes', *Economica*, **11**, pp. 398–403.
Hayek, F.A.v. (1932), 'Money and Capital: A Reply', *Economic Journal*, **52**, pp. 237–49.
Hicks, J.R. (1936), 'Mr. Keynes' Theory of Employment', *Economic Journal*, **46**, pp. 238–53.
Hicks, J.R. (1979), *Causality in Economics*, Oxford: Blackwell.
Hicks, J.R. (1983), 'A Discipline not a Science', pp. 365–75 in *Classics and Moderns. Collected Essays on Economic Theory*, Vol. 3, Oxford: Blackwell.
Hollander, S. (1979), *The Economics of David Ricardo*, Toronto: University of Toronto Press.
Hutchison, T.W. (1952), 'Some Questions about Ricardo', *Economica*, NS **19**, pp. 415–32.
Hutchison, T.W. (1964), *'Positive' Economics and Policy Objectives*, London: Allen & Unwin.
Hutchison, T.W. (1968), *Economics and Economic Policy in Britain, 1946–1966*, London: Allen & Unwin.
Hutchison, T.W. (1978), *On Revolutions and Progress in Economic Knowledge*, Cambridge: Cambridge University Press.
Hutchison, T.W. (1993), '"Ricardian Politics", Another Version of Ricardian Hagiography', *History of Economics Review*, **19**, pp. 1–17.
Keynes, J.M. (1923), *A Tract on Monetary Reform*, reprinted London: Macmillan for the Royal Economic Society, 1971.
Keynes, J.M. (1930), *A Treatise on Money*, 2 vols, reprinted London: Macmillan for the Royal Economic Society, 1971.

Keynes, J.M. (1931), 'The Pure Theory of Money. A Reply to Dr. Hayek', *Economica*, **11**, pp. 387–97.

Lerner, A.P. (1944), *The Economics of Control*, New York: Macmillan.

Letwin, W. (1963), *The Origins of Scientific Economics*, London: Methuen.

Liebhafsky, H.H. (1955), 'A Curious Case of Neglect: Marshall's *Industry and Trade*', *Canadian Journal of Economics and Political Science*, **21**, pp. 339–53.

Marshall, A. (1919), *Industry and Trade*, London: Macmillan.

O'Brien, D.P. (1964), 'Patent Protection and Competition in Polyamide and Polyester Fibre Manufacture', *Journal of Industrial Economics*, **12**, pp. 224–35.

O'Brien, D.P. (1970), *J.R. McCulloch. A Study in Classical Economics*, London: Allen & Unwin.

O'Brien, D.P. (1988), *Lionel Robbins*, London: Macmillan.

O'Brien, D.P. (1993), *Thomas Joplin and Classical Macroeconomics*, Aldershot: Elgar.

O'Brien, D.P. and Darnell, A.C. (1982), *Authorship Puzzles in the History of Economics*, London: Macmillan.

O'Brien, D.P., Howe, W.S. *et al.* (1979), *Competition Policy, Profitability and Growth*, London: Macmillan.

O'Brien, D.P. and Swann, D. (1969), *Information Agreements, Competition and Efficiency*, London: Macmillan.

Pigou, A.C. (ed.) (1925), *Memorials of Alfred Marshall*, London: Macmillan.

Robbins, L. (1928), 'The Representative Firm', *Economic Journal*, **38**, pp. 387–404.

Robbins, L. (1930), 'On the Elasticity of Demand for Income in Terms of Effort', *Economica*, **10**, pp. 123–9.

Robbins, L. (1934), 'Remarks upon Certain Aspects of the Theory of Costs', *Economic Journal*, **44**, pp. 1–18.

Robbins, L. (1935), *An Essay on the Nature and Significance of Economic Science*, 2nd ed., London: Macmillan.

Robbins, L. (1937), *Economic Planning and International Order*, London: Macmillan.

Robbins, L. (1958), *Robert Torrens and the Evolution of Classical Economics*, London: Macmillan.

Robinson, J. (1933), *The Economics of Imperfect Competition*, London: Macmillan.

Shackle, G.L.S. (1967), *The Years of High Theory*, Cambridge: Cambridge University Press.

Shubik, M. (1970), 'A Curmudgeon's Guide to Microeconomics', *Journal of Economic Literature*, **8**, pp. 405–34.

Sraffa, P. (1932a), 'Dr. Hayek on Money and Capital', *Economic Journal*, **42**, pp. 42–53.

Sraffa, P. (1932b), 'A Rejoinder', *Economic Journal*, **42**, pp. 249–51.

Swann, D., O'Brien, D.P. *et al.* (1974a), *Competition in British Industry*, London: Allen & Unwin.

Swann, D., O'Brien, D.P. *et al.* (1974b), *Competition in British Industry: Case Studies*, Loughborough: Loughborough University.

Torrens, R. (1841/1844), *The Budget. A Series of Letters on Financial, Commercial and Colonial Policy*, London: Smith Elder.

Viner, J. (1950), *The Customs Union Issue*, New York: Carnegie Endowment for Peace.

Wicksteed, P.H. (1910), *The Common Sense of Political Economy and Selected Papers and Reviews on Economic Theory*, ed. L. Robbins, 2 vols, London: Routledge & Kegan Paul, 1933.

PART I

METHODOLOGY

[1]

WHITHER ECONOMICS?

I. The Problem

Economics is a subject which is apparently prospering. In contrast to such subjects as classics it has apparently well maintained its student numbers in the course of university expansion: undergraduate and postgraduate courses multiply, grants for research flow forth abundantly, and eminent economists become stars of screen and radio if not yet of stage. We now have a Nobel Prize for economics; and the demand for economists in industry and government is high—indeed it has reached an all time high in the last decade. The last Governor of the Bank of England has recently claimed that by the time he left the Bank it was 'crawling' (his word) with economists.[1] Some may suspect that there is a Say's Law with Devons' multiplier at work here: that the supply of economics graduates creates a climate of opinion that demands their services in government (supply thus creating its own demand); and that industry in a spirit of emulation matches, or more than matches, government's recruitment of economists (the multiplier as formulated by the late Professor Ely Devons). But such doubts are easily dismissed. The profession possesses an ability to re-write intellectual history so as to place any blame that may be going on the unfortunate politicians. Thus for instance it is now widely claimed that virtually the whole economics profession was in favour of devaluation from 1964 onwards.[2] Palpable falsehoods such as this do seem to serve the profession quite well as a protective device. Critics who doubt the merit and usefulness of the activities of economists are easily dismissed. Those who since the 1920's have tried to argue that economics should be doing something useful have traditionally been met easily by the argument (which apparently satisfies the economics profession) that history is not useful except as mind-training, and the same is true of classics.[3] Why should economists bother themselves about such a sordid matter as practicality? (More recently the trendy reply has involved some allusion to the work of theoretical physicists).

Yet doubts about the activities of economists persist in arising.

They are to be found both inside and outside the profession, amongst commentators, students, and professional economists. When one finds that banking firms are indifferent in seeking economics and metallurgy or chemistry graduates except for certain very specialised tasks, a little unease may be felt; but it is easy to dismiss this as misguided since academic economists make quite a speciality of feeling superior to businessmen. The hostility of economic historians towards economists is perhaps more disturbing to academics however: and this seems to have got worse rather than better over time. Fifty years ago there were comments from economic historians about 'empty economic boxes' and a reference to 'the spells and incantations of economists'—the allusion is to Voltaire's observation that spells and incantations are capable of destroying whole flocks of sheep if accompanied by sufficient quantities of arsenic[4]. More recently a frontal assault was launched by Professor Postan.[5] Personally I think the points he made were almost entirely mistaken: but the attack was important as a symptom, and it aroused an enormous amount of comment elsewhere, some of which the profession should have found deeply disquieting. In addition some of the natural scientists have openly expressed disquiet. Jacob Viner tells a story about a distinguished Princeton atomic scientist who stated that some experiments had revealed that a particular atomic reaction took place only about one billionth as rapidly as calculated by the theoretical physicists and then went on 'this would be a major error even for an economist'.[6] At the same time some of the general public seem to have been pretty aghast at the policy conclusions deduced from patently tautological models and to have echoed Cicero's words (as quoted by Adam Smith) that there is nothing so absurd that it has not been proposed by some philosopher.[7] The public dismay has moreover been enhanced by the fact that several of the most prominent members of the profession seem to have a considerable capacity for making themselves look ridiculous by claiming the supposed authority of their subject in support of their ideological positions on such issues as the effect of the creation of the E.E.C.[8]

The complaints from within the profession are perhaps the most serious however. We can begin with those of the economics

graduates who are now employed in industry since their theme is quite simple. It should also be rather devastating; and that it is not so regarded is itself one of the most disturbing aspects of the whole situation. Their complaint—and it is one that I remember myself very clearly from my own time as a business economist though I have heard it from people in government service also—is that very little indeed of what they learnt in university turned out to explain anything at all—in short to be little more than intellectual gadgetry. Secondly, we have complaints from students of economics in many universities. Their complaints are of two main kinds. Firstly they argue that the corpus of economics lacks relevance. As one American academic put it recently 'Relevance is a word that makes professors of economics wince these days'.[9] Yet it is a complaint which has itself received an echo from one of the best known of the current generation of pure theorists, Professor C. E. Ferguson.[10] Sometimes however the academic response is a good deal less forthright. To claim, as has sometimes been done, that all will come right when we have a Walrasian (i.e. general equilibrium) system which takes account of ecological values and private and social costs divergences[11] seems to me downright silly.

The second complaint relates to the kind of information which would be required to make such a system of any significance beyond that accorded to, for instance, double acrostics. The complaint is that economists simply assume away difficulties of this sort and get on with playing with their models. It is nicely summarised in a story told me by students at my previous place of employment. An economist, an engineer and a chemist were stranded together on a desert island with a large tin of ham but no tin-opener. After various unsuccessful exercises in applied science by the engineer and the chemist aimed at opening the tin, they turned in irritation to the economist who all the while had been wearing a superior smile. 'What would *you* do?', they asked. 'Let us assume we have a tin-opener', came the unruffled reply.

This charge that economists simply assume solved any particularly awkward problems they encountered receives an echo in another story, told this time by a leading economic theorist, although one who is deeply critical of the path which economics

has followed. He relates how a centipede with 99 sore feet asked the owl for advice and was told to walk one inch above the ground for the next two weeks. The centipede was suitably impressed with the logical incisiveness of the owl's mind. Then a thought struck him and he asked the owl how he was to implement this advice. The reply was, 'I have solved your conceptual problems. Do not bother me with technicalities.'[12]

One has only got to look at reviews in the leading journals to see just how disturbed some members of the profession are feeling.

Take the following as an example:

> To be fair [X] himself made all the careful academic qualifications, pointing out that his conclusions were based on assumptions about the nature and stability of relationships . . . which are virtually without foundation and which might well be utterly mistaken. In academia this is sufficient; the cognoscenti all know from these cues that this is another game with the Meccano-sets of our profession and that little operational significance should be attached to the results.[13]

Another reviewer refers to 'the abstract, irrelevant, arid bias that much contemporary writing contains'. And he goes on

> True, one feels at times, when faced with these efforts, like a handloom weaver. But this thought is made easier to bear by the suspicion, . . . that the powerloom weavers are weaving the emperor's clothes.[14]

Now all this might be taken as misguided rumblings at the grass roots—though most of those I have quoted are in fact eminent figures. But the fact is that several of the most important figures in the profession have expressed extreme disquiet at the paths that economics has taken. The Presidential Address by Sir Henry Phelps Brown to the Royal Economic Society in 1971 was entitled 'The Underdevelopment of Economics' and it contained a disturbing analysis of the attempts of the profession to run before its members could walk and of the useless directions in which their efforts had then taken them.[15] The Director of the National Institute of Economic and Social Research in his capacity as President of Section F of the British Association in 1971 asked his hearers 'Is Progress in Economic Science Possible?' and expressed very grave disquiet indeed about the state of the subject.[16] Perhaps most significant of all however were the

charges made by one recognised to be amongst the greatest of all living economists—indeed the recipient of a Nobel Prize for economics. Noting these worries within the profession, with which he obviously sympathised, he went on to point out that even where the profession selected relevant targets it usually failed to hit them. 'The uneasiness of which I spoke before is caused not by the *irrelevance* of the practical problems to which present day economists address their efforts, but rather by the palpable *inadequacy* of the scientific means with which they try to solve them.' He pointed to 'the ephemeral substantive content of the argument behind the formidable front of algebraic signs' and put his finger squarely upon a sort of schizophrenia which assails members of the profession, a number of whom both complain about these developments and continue to push the subject even further in the direction of which they complain.[17] They are in acute danger, it seems to me, of doing themselves injury by trying to ride two horses (bandwagons?) at once.

I do not think then that there can be any doubt, if there ever was, about the state of economics in recent years. What I want to do for the remainder of the time here is to attempt to answer three questions. Firstly, is this a new development? Secondly, if it is *not* new, is there anything special about the mess that we are in now? Thirdly, what way is there out of this mess?

II. The Historical Background

When one studies the history of economic thought over a long period, and in depth, one cannot but be struck by two things. Firstly, that economists have usually had a very bad press—that is that the general public (as distinct from politicians whom they persuaded to implement their nostrums) have almost always been highly suspicious of economists. Secondly, that brief periods of heady optimism apart, economists themselves have usually been pessimistic about their subject. During the periods of pessimism there has been a tendency, sometimes very pronounced, to retreat into tautology. Whether the rest of the population liked it or not economic theories were correct whatever the outcome of events. Thus the Malthusian theory of population became a

tautology: if population was outrunning subsistence then the theory was vindicated; if it was not outrunning subsistence the theory was still right because it had predicted the possible action of a (largely non-observable) moral restraint. Space permitting it would be easy to point to other examples.

The bad press can easily be documented, though I have not time to do so at length, and in any case Jacob Viner and William Grampp have already done this—and superbly.[18] Suffice to note that the economists' craze for measurement received in the seventeenth century the name 'pantometry' while in the nineteenth century the subject of economics as a whole was satirised and attacked by authors as diverse as Charles Dickens, Thomas Carlyle, Thomas Love Peacock, and the poets Coleridge and Wordsworth. That such writers never looked to see if there was a baby under the (admittedly muddy) bathwater is beside the point. They were critics of economics root and branch: and many of their criticisms (suitably Garni à la Marx) have reappeared in the New Left so superbly dissected by Professor Lindbeck.[19]

The phases of optimism and pessimism have not, to my knowledge, been fully documented. The easiest point of departure is the group known as the Economists, or later the Physiocrats, who grouped themselves around the Royal Physician and friend of Madame de Pompadour in the France of the 1760's, Francois Quesnay. For a time they really believed they had unlocked economics as Newton had unlocked nature. Quesnay's invention of the Tableau Economique which showed the circular flow of economic life was hailed by one of his disciples (the Marquis de Mirabeau) as an invention on a par with those of writing and of money.[20]

Adam Smith, who added to his other great qualities a good deal of common sense, did not have such an effect upon his contemporaries. But David Ricardo, whose *Principles* appeared in 1817, really did succeed in attracting around himself a group of men who, *for a short while*, believed the millennium of economic thought was at hand. Thus the Scottish economist J.·R. McCulloch wrote:

> the errors with which Political Economy was formerly infected have now nearly disappeared, and a very few observations will suffice to show that it

really admits of as much certainty in its conclusions as any science founded on *fact and experiment* can possibly do.[21]

According to one of his contemporaries, Robert Torrens:

> With respect to Political Economy the period of controversy is passing away, and that of unanimity rapidly approaching. Twenty years hence there will scarcely exist a doubt respecting any of its fundamental principles.[22]

In the year that this was written the Political Economy Club was founded, rather it would seem to produce discussion to resolve the few remaining difficulties.[23] James Mill's *Elements*, a book written as a result of instructing his son into the mysteries of Ricardo, appeared so as to enable the fundamental discoveries to be conveyed to the weaker minded.[24]

Now none of these men was stupid, bigoted, or even merely unbalanced. If they had been they might not have recovered from this early flush of enthusiasm. But by 1831 we find the same Political Economy Club apparently in general agreement with the contention of Torrens no less 'that all the great principles of Ricardo's work had been successively abandoned, and that his theories of Value, Rent and Profits were now generally acknowledged to have been erroneous.'[25] Later we find McCulloch writing of Mill's *Elements* that the subject was not in such a settled state as was supposed by Mr. Mill.[26] The later Classical economist J. E. Cairnes informed his audience in Dublin in the 1850's that 'it must be admitted that . . . the present condition and prospects of the science are not such as a political economist can contemplate with unmixed satisfaction.'[27]

The Classical economists were as remarkable a body of men to have associated themselves with the subject of economics as the subject has ever known: and they achieved a great deal. I am not questioning their achievements: if we had done as much during a comparable period we could feel well satisfied. But it is difficult to resist the conclusion that there was some loss of nerve, certainly of certainty, as the nineteenth century progressed. It was thus upon a body of economic thought more than a little lacking in self confidence that there burst the work of Jevons and his contemporaries. Jevons was a man trained primarily in natural science, and secondly in mathematics which he had studied under the great mathematician Augustus de Morgan. He was one of

the most lively, intelligent and stimulating men which economics has been fortunate enough to attract. He could have had an excellent career as a natural scientist: but instead he decided to reform economics. The natural scientists had found a small number of fundamental principles: and Jevons was proposing that, through the instrumentality of mathematics, the same should be done for economics. To his sister he wrote:

> does it not strike you that just as in Physical Science there are general & profound principles deducible from a great number of apparent phenomena, so in treating of Man or Society there must also be general principles and laws which underlie all the present discussions & partial arguments? Is it not worth years of labour to dive into these innermost and obscurest principles, and after obtaining some good clue to follow it up with all the intense pleasure of mental success into a multitude of useful conclusions?[28]

There seems no doubt that Jevons felt that he was setting economics on the right road, and that this explains the fulminations in the last few pages of his seminal *Theory of Political Economy*[29] against 'The Noxious Influence of [J. S. Mill's] Authority'.

Others involved in the events which historians of economic thought call the marginal revolution (from its turning of attention towards derivatives and small increments) seem to have been equally confident of what they were doing: Menger's battle against the German Historical School was waged with the authoritative confidence of a Napoleon, and Walras spent his inherited fortune propagating his ideas of general equilibrium and was only bailed out by marrying a well-to-do spinster of 58.[30] But the next generation of marginalists was not possessed of this revolutionary fire. The ever-wise Alfred Marshall stressed the continuity of the economic thought expounded in his great *Principles* with that of his Classical predessors; and he was singularly sensitive to criticism. By the time the marginal revolution had thoroughly permeated academic teaching of economics it seems to have filled mainly the role of what economists call a barrier to entry—in this context a device to prevent competition with the professional economists from the untrained.[31]

The decline in self-confidence from this time was, I think, fairly marked: the tone of Cannan's brilliant but hypercritical

Production and Distribution and his later *Review*[32] are I think fully authentic—and Cannan was a major figure in the establishment of L.S.E. But a new impetus came from the United States. It does not seem to have been particularly influential on this side of the Atlantic. But on the other a craze for correlation coefficients swept American postgraduate students: and amongst them at least there does seem to have been some feeling that correlation was the way to the new scientific economics. As the author of one statistics text book has written:

> In the United States, 'correlation analysis' spread like wildfire among the younger members of the economics profession until no doctoral dissertation was complete without some correlation coefficients.[33]

Less charitably the great Chicago economist Viner wrote of those who 'began correlating furiously and indiscriminately and with an inverse correlation between zeal and discretion which . . . approached . . . perfection. As might have been anticipated in a world full of nonsense correlations, the results were grotesque'.[34] Some of the greatest of the genuine statisticians poked fun at the trend: A. L. Bowley used apparently to inform his students that he had found a perfect relationship between imports of bananas into the United Kingdom and marriages in non-conformist churches;[35] and it is from this era that the well-known correlation between the Swedish birth rate and the number of storks in the country dates.

The sceptics won; but this had in any case been only a small upsurge of confidence—a ripple. But with (and indeed before) the publication of Keynes' *General Theory* in 1936 there was a quite extraordinary uplift in the spirits of economists. The following is an account by the great Joseph Schumpeter of the spirit of expectation which developed in Cambridge (Mass.) as the publication of the *General Theory* approached.

> Glimpses of the new light began to be caught by individuals all over the Empire and in the United States. Students were thrilled. A wave of anticipatory enthusiasm swept the world of economists. When the book came out at last Harvard students felt unable to wait until it would be available at the booksellers: they clubbed together in order to speed up the process and arranged for direct shipment of a first parcel of copies.[36]

Even amongst British postgraduates in London something of the

same fervour seems to have developed.[37] The surge of confidence reached something of a peak in the late 1940's and is epitomised in a book entitled *The New Economics*, the tone of which, partly perhaps because Keynes had recently died, was positively hagiographic. I find the following a particularly nice example.

> Keynes indeed had the Revelation. His disciples are now dividing into groups, each taking sustenance from the Keynesian larder. The struggle for the Apostolic Succession is on.[38]

With the expansion in university education after World War II the number of academic economists rose sharply and with the publication of articles in economic journals having increased secularly at 6·8% per annum in the years since 1885, a growth which it continued after the War,[39] it is tempting to expect that both the frequency and amplitude of these surges of optimism will increase. At all events the next surge occurred around 1960. Under the influence of the Chicago economist Milton Friedman a number of economists began to preach 'Positive Economics': and they did so with such effectiveness that the profession was gathered up in a new wave of enthusiasm. The term 'positive economics' should perhaps be explained. There is in economics, from the time of Nassau Senior's *Introductory Lecture* of 1826 a distinction between the 'science' and the 'art' of economics. The latter refers to the role of the economist in policy, the former to the 'pure' core of economics. Now this distinction emerged, transmuted into another form in one of the great methodological statements of this century Lord Robbins' *Essay on the Nature and Significance of Economic Science*. It became a distinction between positive and normative economics, the former describing the *is* of the economic system, the latter describing what 'ought to be'. But positive economics by the 1960's had come to mean something rather different. It had come to mean quite specifically the formulating of economic theories in mathematical forms which were supposed to be non-tautological—to be capable of being proved wrong. Applied econometric work was to do the testing of right or wrong. Economics would march forth as a science which could look other scientific disciplines in the eye. Anyone who was a professional economist in the early 1960's will remember this episode, the apparent dawning of the new day: and

anyone who doubts this should look at the first year text book by R. G. Lipsey, a leading figure in British economics at that time, which was published in 1963 and was based on lectures delivered in the preceding two years. It reflects, accurately I think, the mood of the profession in the early years of the decade. It was almost as if the profession, nettled by Ely Devons' Essay 'Applied Economics: the application of what?'[41] felt that they could now show Devons (and every other doubter) the way to science.

III. The Present Depression

Now positive economics had, in its new garb, required two things: the formulation of theories in mathematical form, and the testing of these theories. It follows that in order to diagnose our present ill we need firstly to look at the role of mathematics in economics, and secondly to look at the testing procedures used.

The great economist Alfred Marshall, who was by training primarily a mathematician and had intended to follow a career as a theoretical physicist, had a splendid sense of proportion about the usefulness of mathematical formulation in economics. As Dr. G. Hallett has written:

> The great economists of the older Cambridge tradition, such as Marshall and Keynes, were accomplished mathematicians, but they kept mathematics to an appendix and used the conclusions, combined with common sense and a broad factual knowledge, to illuminate the discussion of current problems. What these economists would have kept to an appendix, or simply worked out on the back of an envelope, some of their successors treat as the subject matter of economics. They produce theoretical analyses of great complexity and jump straight to policy conclusions.[42]

This is not just the rationalisation of a later commentator. Marshall himself was quite specific.

> In my view every economic fact whether or not it is of such a nature as to be expressed in numbers, stands in relation as cause and effect to many other facts: and since it never happens that all of them can be expressed in numbers, the application of exact mathematical methods to those which can is nearly always a waste of time, while in the large majority of cases it is positively misleading; and the world would have been farther on its way forward if the work had never been done at all. It is chiefly when the mathematical method is used not for direct construction, but to train sound instinctive habits, (like the practising of scales on the piano), that it seems to me generally helpful.[43]

Now this is a particularly apt parallel. Musicians find the practice of scales and technical exercises—every violinist knows the works of Sevcik—to be of fundamental importance. But musicians have long ago got over the worship of mere technique. Artists who are brilliant technical machines alone have a very short career; and were it not well outside the scope of this lecture I might name some. But such a sense of proportion does not exist amongst economists: indeed it would be truer to say that the reverse is the case. Mathematics indeed has assumed the role of the broom in the fable of the Sorcerer's Apprentice; with the economists cast in the role of the foolish Apprentice. Unfortunately the Sorcerer himself does not show any sign of returning to stop the nonsense. There are three particular aspects to this. Firstly there is the tiresome development of what might be called 'dog Mathematics' rather like the 'dog Latin' of earlier generations. Thus one reviewer referred to a 'ghastly pseudocalculus' in reviewing a recent work;[44] and every economist will know what he meant. Secondly mathematics has assumed the role of barrier to entry, a role, as I noted earlier, which was originally taken up by marginalism. It excludes the intellectually unwashed from the pages of the professional journals. Ironically however, a major effect in this respect has been to encourage the admission into the same pages of those originally trained in natural science disciplines, some of whom have been unable to find employment within those disciplines. Thirdly it has led to a complete obsession with building mathematical models. As Leontief himself has put it:

> The mathematical model-building industry has grown into one of the most prestigious, possibly the most prestigious branch of economics. Construction of a typical theoretical model can be handled now as a routine assembly job. All principal components such as production functions, consumption and utility functions come in several standard types; so does the optional equipment as, for example, 'factor augmentation'—to take care of technological change. . . . any model can be modernised with the help of special attachments.[45]

The results of this have been put very well by Mr. Worswick in his address to the British Association.

> There now exist whole branches of abstract economic theory which have no links with concrete facts and are almost indistinguishable from pure mathematics. Indeed, it might be more correct to say that there have come into

being new branches of mathematics whose distinguishing feature is that some of the axioms and some of the terminology show traces of the ancestry of this particular branch of mathematics, which originated in the distant past in some real economic question.[46]

Now there can be no doubt that mathematics has a vital role to play in the work of the economic theorist: and this is shown in the use that was made of it by Marshall, Wicksell, and Hicks. But there does seem to be reason to believe that, even in its clarifying role, it may have led us badly astray. Consider the following episode. The leading theorist P. A. Samuelson recalls:

> I must confess that my own first reaction to the *General Theory* was not at all like that of Keats on first looking into Chapman's Homer. . . . My rebellion against its pretentions would have been complete except for an uneasy realisation that I did not at all understand what it was about. And I think I am giving away no secrets when I solemnly aver—upon the basis of vivid personal recollection—that no one else in Cambridge, Massachusetts, really knew what it was about for some twelve to eighteen months after its publication. Indeed, until the appearance of the mathematical models of Meade, Lange, Hicks and Harrod there is reason to believe that Keynes himself did not truly understand his own analysis.[47]

I used to think that this was one of the strongest examples of the clarifying (not to say purifying) role of mathematics in economics. But now professors Shackle and Leijonhufvud have, in their different ways, convincingly suggested to us all that the interpretation of Keynes in those models was wrong: in particular the vital role of expectations largely disappeared during the course of mathematisation.[48]

But, even were the interpretations of Hicks and others correct, there does not seem to be any doubt that, feeding on the successes of mathematics in this area, the priorities of the profession have gone badly wrong. The howls of derision and rage when some sociologists were granted nearly £16,000 to study why a publisher decides to accept a book could be heard from a great distance—they even penetrated the letter columns of the *Times*. But economists at least might care to reflect on the fact that a grant of public money was received by the economist who undertook the following piece of research: *and* that the area of research is one of the most admired in the profession.

> Given a set of economic agents and a set of coalitions, a non-empty family of

subsets of the first set closed under the formation of countable unions and complements, an allocation is a countably additive function from the set of coalitions to the closed positive orthant of the commodity space. To describe preferences in this context, one can either introduce a positive, finite real measure defined on the set of coalitions and specify, for each agent, a relation of preference-or-indifference on the closed positive orthant of the commodity space, or specify, for each coalition, a relation of preference—or—indifference on the set of allocations. This article studies the extent to which these two approaches are equivalent.[49]

Now there is no doubt which of the two is more taxing intellectually. But before assuming that that settles the right of the economist to his money for such exercises we in the profession might ask ourselves whether we honestly believe that the results of such an exercise are likely to advance the subject. As one commentator put it:

> the translation of economic theory into mathematical language has now passed the levels of refinement that could be sustained by the concepts embodied in it. As a result of the momentum derived from its successful earlier clarifications, the mathematical treatment of economics has achieved a considerable degree of autonomy, and is no longer dependent for its prestige on the production of genuine insights.[50]

General equilibrium economics seems to have become almost the Olympus for economic theorists: and when taxed with this pre-occupation it is defended on the grounds which I should have thought were quite untenable, either in the light of what Smith actually wrote or given the points made about such an interpretation nearly 30 years ago,[51] that the *Wealth of Nations* is really all about General Equilibrium.[52] Of course the virtuosi in this and similar fields have never taken kindly to criticism; and since they are usually better at scoring debating points than their opponents they emerge from the encounter convinced that their work is untouched by criticism.[53]

Of course some of the criticism has been counter productive. This seems to me to be true both of Marxist criticism and of American institutionalist criticism. The former is apparently claiming to have an alternative set of economic theories to mainstream orthodoxy which contain *the* revealed truth; and this is hardly likely to be persuasive to those who are concerned about the path which economics has taken, particularly as they are well aware that the Marxist claim that all economic theory for the last

hundred years is completely irrelevant cannot be sustained. Marxism after all is hardly radical intellectually; indeed the Marxists above all fit into the category of men who, in Keynes' delightful phrase are the 'slaves of some defunct economist'. In any case the totalitarian associations of Marxism seem to cause some closing of ranks and to mute the criticism by the uncommitted of the opposite (Chicago) extreme. Marxism does however at least claim to possess some sort of logical structure; the same could hardly be said of institutionalism, especially in its American variety; and in the writings of the institutionalists it is often difficult to find any kind of logical chain at all. It thus enhances rather than diminishes the prestige of what it is attacking.

But there has been plenty of criticism from those who are neither Marxist nor institutionalist; and a good deal of it has hit the target. Martin Shubik who certainly falls into neither camp highlighted the difficulty with general equilibrium very well.

> General equilibrium economics is undoubtedly a splendid intellectual achievement. But it is not by any means on the level of Newtonian mechanics. In a world with large complicated corporations, selling thousands of goods and services (and often selling whole systems), the way we stick to our simple models (which at best cover one simple limiting case) is ludicrous. I am reminded of the story of the drunk who had lost his keys at night and spent his time searching for them under a street lamp fifty yards from where he had lost them because that was the only place where he could see anything.[54]

In some ways the preoccupation of the profession with subjects like General Equilibrium is essentially a problem of what K. E. Boulding has called the grants economy—a section of economic activity which is denied feedback from its source of finance. Firms which produce the wrong products get feedback from the market—they lose sales and eventually, if they persist, go out of business. Academics do not, and the remedy for the present state of affairs must lie within the academic profession. As a matter of fact, and although Boulding does not say so, the problem was actually set out perfectly clearly by Adam Smith in the *Wealth of Nations* 198 years ago.[55]

What has really happened is that we have taken the fairly good ground floor of economic theory and built upon it a house of cards, or rather a Tower of Babel. The basic framework of the

ground floor is good. But instead of trying to fill in the framework with bricks, mortar and concrete, we carry on erecting scaffolding above. The Norman builders who built the spire of Chichester Cathedral on top of *one* beam were more careful than economists: and that spire fell through the roof. I think it is apt to call what we have constructed a Tower of Babel because the original Tower of Babel was, I understand, built to make its occupants self-sufficient, perhaps to guard them against a second Flood; and *our* Tower has been built to provide its occupants with protection against getting wet through contact with the world. It is a building which gets narrower as it gets higher; and were there time it would be interesting to illustrate this by some of the developments which have occurred in specific areas of theory, notably international trade theory.[56] The fact that we have constructed this Tower helps to explain why, as Leontief has pointed out, we keep missing the targets. Firing downwards from a high position makes accurate aim notoriously difficult.

So much of the building has been done in the name of 'rigour', apparently neglectful of the fact that such rigour will not help fuzziness in the basic concepts on the ground floor. When reproached the response is typically to rely upon what Thomas Schelling has called a 'fictitious colleague'. This gentleman, who never actually turns up, is the one who is going to make use of the results obtained by general equilibrium and growth theorists; but any possible candidates for the role turn out to be playing with their own toys.[57]

But how did economics get on to this wrong track? My own personal belief is that it starts in the turn which the subject took in Cambridge in the 1930's: specifically with the intervention of Mrs. Joan Robinson into the debate over imperfect competition. Professor G. L. S. Shackle has explained what happened very lucidly.

> there is . . . a sharp and striking difference in style of attack. The authors we have been considering [previously] were Marshallians. They examined the existing world in a spirit of respect, they brought as much of it intact into their discourse as they could, they valued the contours and features of the landscape they beheld and tried to mould their argument upon them rather than cut a path direct to rigorous conclusions. Mrs. Robinson did the opposite. Clear and definite questions cannot be asked about a vague,

> richly detailed, fluid and living world. This world must therefore be exchanged for a *model*, a set of precise assumptions collectively simple enough to allow the play of logic and mathematics . . . the model is a work of art, freely composed within the constraints of a particular art-form, namely the logical binding together of propositions.[58]

Another commentator writes:

> The mathematical apparatus she assembled to do this job was such that von Neumann once remarked that if the archaeologists of some future civilisation were to dig up the remains of ours and find a cache of books, the *Economics of Imperfect Competition* would probably be dated as an early precursor of Newton.[59]

The emphasis was now on model building: and the way was thus clear for a complete departure from the Marshallian methodology which stressed the empirical derivation of the postulates. Words became habitually perverted in a way which would have warmed the heart of Humpty Dumpty. Competition came to be a state in which competition did not exist;[60] while 'efficiency' assumed a meaning so special that the ordinary (and much more important) meaning had to be rediscovered by theorists (it was always known to industrial economists) in the 1960's and christened X-efficiency.[61] A great fillip to this trend was given by the publication of Friedman's *Essays in Positive Economics* which led to what has become known as 'as if' methodology. The basic characteristic of this methodological position is that the realism of postulates is irrelevant so long as testable conclusions are produced. If the model predicts well according to the testing procedure used then the model is satisfactory. As a methodological position it has been subject to sustained and accurate criticism by those who bother themselves about such unfortunate and unfashionable matters as methodology.[62] But it has become *the* methodology of the positive economics which the profession embraced with such enthusiasm around 1960.

Given such preconceptions it was entirely natural that economic history and business studies should be excluded from the inner temple of Babel and pushed out into the darkness as unclean. Such contact with the world was intellectually impure: impure degrees like the B.Com. disappeared, and the attitude of the profession is summed up in the story of the Birmingham lecturer (now Cambridge professor) who in an examination meeting

suddenly burst out with the words 'give him a third; and let him be a business man'.[63]

So the building of the models for testing seems to have gone grievously astray. What about the testing itself? This too is badly wrong—dealing what should have been a fatal blow to 'as if' methodology. For if the testing was no good the case for relying on hypothetical postulates could no longer be sustained. But in truth, as Mr. Worswick has remarked 'the fact is that econometric models are not, as a rule, sharp instruments for discriminating between hypotheses'.[64] The reason that they are not sharp enough is twofold. Firstly, and quite fundamentally, the data was never remotely good enough to support the conclusions which were drawn from it. These matters have been explored (devastatingly) and at length by the Princeton economist Oscar Morgenstern and more recently by Dr. Alan Coddington who has pointed out that even the most reliable figures in the National Income accounts are uncertain to within the region of 3% and for some figures single revisions of the order of 30% are commonplace. Thus, as Coddington points out, National Income is quoted to five digits even though on the *admitted* margin of error only the first two digits are significant.[65]

Undaunted however, builders of models of the economy have persisted in attempting to obtain from government figures which use an even greater number of digits than published, and to do so for some of the most unreliable items in the National Income accounts. Other instances that might be cited are the serious inaccuracy in estimates of economies of scale in steel production which were made by econometricians;[66] and the use of straightforward exchange rate conversions to compare wages and prices in different countries when the basic data to adjust the exchange rate conversions for divergences from purchasing power parity has been lacking.[67] In addition there has apparently been a confusion between statistical relations and causality in some of the work.[68] Finally there was no way to measure some of the things which economists believed to matter and ludicrous 'proxies' were derived. Only a few economists considered it vital to set about trying to obtain the basic data—a long, arduous, unglamorous and professionally unrewarding task. At the end of

all the econometric sound and fury the great Leontief was able to conclude:

> In no other field of empirical enquiry has so massive and sophisticated a statistical machinery been used with such indifferent results.[70]

The second part of the answer as to why econometric testing has proved unsatisfactory is in some ways even more disturbing; for it seems clear that the data *even as available* have not supported the hypotheses which were apparently convincingly vindicated by testing. Two clear-cut examples will suffice. Firstly it should have been clear at a very early stage in the Phillips Curve debate that the data did not support the conclusions which were being drawn from it; and this was in fact pointed out in articles by Routh and (for the United States) by Bhatia.[71] Secondly the econometric techniques which were used to test the effectiveness of incomes policy seem (and here I defer to the opinion of the full time professional) to have been applied distinctly inexpertly.[72] Related to this has been the way in which the theoretical model has sometimes been bent to fit the econometrics; one highly publicised model for instance assumed that there was zero elasticity of demand for imports (that is that import demand was totally unresponsive to changes in price) and to forecast dire consequences for the British exchange rate on this basis. These experiences have led I think to considerable unease among the full blown statisticians about the use which was being made of statistics: and a leading theoretical statistician wrote in a review:

> Anyone reading this book could be excused if he were left with the impression that at last Economics has become a Science. For here are set out first the underlying mathematical techniques, then the mathematical structure of the various econometric models, the techniques of estimation of the parameter values and the properties of the various estimators obtainable. Problems are duly provided at appropriate points in the text, and there are half a dozen or more tables of down-to-earth statistics which form the basis of many further tables illustrating techniques of estimation. One almost has to pinch oneself to keep in mind that it is highly dubious whether the structure of the determination of the variables in the real world approximates the structure of the theoretical models for which this impressive apparatus of thought is designed to provide parameter estimates. However it would be as churlish to blame an author expounding econometrics for the fact that the real world can seldom be fruitfully studied by econometric methods, as it would be to criticise a monarch for taking part in pageantry which has no

immediate practical utility. The fact is that a wide section of American students want qualifications in econometrics, just as a wide section of the British public require pageantry.[73]

But instead of taking the unease seriously the economists rushed to provide their supposed econometric results with full-blown apartments in the Tower of Babel; and the Phillips Curve was duly fitted out with Walrasian accessories.

IV. The Remedies

What then are the remedies for this mess? The first thing to recognise is that any remedies are not going to be slick and easy ones—there can be no grasping of a dramatic new approach which will, in an instant, remedy the situation.

Starting from the premise that economics should be useful—not a series of publicly subsidised intellectual games—we are faced with describing and predicting the work of a decentralised liberal economy. Very few economists—at least outside Cambridge—could be described as enthusiasts for totalitarianism, and in any case the course I am going to propose would have no application to a totalitarian régime since the statistical sources for such régimes typically contain fictitious statistics or are non-existent.[74]

To try to find the workings of such a liberal economy we have to recognise that our findings will, as J. S. Mill emphasised, need modifying to account for institutional details in every country. But allowing for that we can aim at a fair degree of generality.

The method to be used is essentially the eighteenth-century Scottish method of procedure. It involves formulation of premisses on the basis of empiricism, and the derivation of empirical laws: reasoning on the basis of the generalisations thus established, and testing the results obtained against other historical data is the next stage.[75] The testing procedure itself suggests points of departure for further reasoning. So we have a process of empiricism—deduction—verification—empiricism and so on. Now in fact this turns out to be not very different from the Marshallian method which is ably described by J. N. Keynes, the father of Lord Keynes.

> In the first place, observation guides the economist in his original choice of premisses .... In the second place observation enables the economist to determine how nearly his assumptions approximate to the actual facts under given economic conditions .... In the third place the economist has recourse to observation in order to illustrate, test, and confirm his deductive inferences.[76]

Marshall himself, in the preface to the first edition of his *Principles*, indicated a similar line of approach[77] and his correspondence contains a particularly striking example of the importance which he attached to the empirical derivation of premisses.[78]

We must concentrate on the Marshallian method of economics, which essentially involves making tools which help to illuminate particular economic problems without providing universal conclusions. We need to bear in mind David Hume's warning against long chains of reasoning in dealing with economic matters.[79] For it is by the indulgence in long chains of reasoning, which have taken us further and further away from the data, that the present impasse has developed. Marshall thought that he was leaving a programme of applied economics behind him. Pigou was even advised to write a thesis for a Fellowship on 'the Variations in the Prices of Tinned Meat in the Nineteenth Century'.[80] The thesis was successful; but one of today's economists upon receiving such advice would assume that he was being advised, and sarcastically at that, to leave the profession.

Such a restructuring will involve recognition of the proper place of pure theory as a subsidiary one. As Marshall put it:

> If we include in our account merely all the conditions of real life, the problen is too heavy to be handled; if we select a few, then long-drawn-out and subtle reasonings with regard to them become scientific toys rather than engines for practical work.[81]

Economists will have to be prepared to be more critical of pure theorists rather than simply bowing in deference to the luminosity of their minds. Ricardo possessed one of the very best pure theory minds that economics has ever attracted. Yet he produced an entire system of thought which was designed to prove one point only: that the Corn Laws would soon bring economic growth to a premature halt. It was a system which has been characterised (correctly in my view) by the great economist Schumpeter as a detour. In addition, although mathematically gifted individuals

will continue to ply their trade, the onus will be upon them to explain their discoveries.[82] As Marshall put it 'it seems doubtful whether any one spends his time well in reading lengthy translations of economic doctrines into mathematics, that have not been made by himself.'[83]

The majority of the profession would be concerned then with developing the 'ground floor' of the theoretical structure so that in time it might be strong enough to bear some upper floors. This would be a fruitful exercise; at the moment only those who shoot from the ground floor ever seem to hit the target. In preparation for this lecture I read some of the reminiscences of economic advisers: and universally they seemed to have felt that it was the ground floor which was viable.[84] But strong support for such an argument can be gained from reading Professor H. G. Johnson's inaugural lecture at L.S.E. 'The Economic Approach to Social Questions'.[85] For here we find a virtuoso applying the tools of economic theory to social problems: and without exception we find him using only those to be found in the ground floor of the building (even though some of them are recent additions to that floor). A similar reflection is prompted by surveying Mr. Samuel Brittan's new book *Is There an Economic Consensus*.[86] Wherever there is consensus it seems to rely upon the tools of the ground floor.

Now such a programme would involve a major expansion in the acquisition of economic data and a major expansion in *genuinely* empirical research—which does *not* involve simply running regressions on published figures. But such a programme encounters a series of difficulties which must be recognised at the outset. Firstly, there is the difficulty I have already referred to relating to the reliability of economic data. Anyone proposing research in a particular field should read the relevant chapter of Morgenstern's work to brief himself on the pitfalls. Secondly, collecting statistics involves substantial costs to those *from whom* the information is collected. This is often not recognised—especially by academics—although some of the difficulties involved were recently set out in the form of complaints to the *Times*.[87] If industry finds itself too disadvantaged in this way it simply refuses its co-operation. The Ministry of Technology earned itself some

well-merited ridicule at one stage by obtaining questionnaire answers by telephone; but one can see their difficulties. Thirdly, such statistical results as are obtained are in need of constant revision. It took a major study for O.E.C.D. to produce a corrective to the straight exchange rate conversions which I talked about earlier.[88] But such exercises need revisions as economies grow and progress. Fourthly, we have to recognise that there are areas where we just cannot have definite numbers—for instance the valuation of travelling time or of Norman churches—so that instead of trying to present single answers to cost benefit exercises we should always be prepared to provide a set. Fifthly, we have to recognise—and it will not be before time—that not only do some concepts require clarification before they can be measured in numbers but also that there is virtually no correspondence between the figures of for instance rent and what the economist means by rent. Similarly we mean about five different things by the word 'profit'—so that to take profit figures from National Income statistics (always assuming them to represent accurately what the accountant means by profit, and after the vicissitudes of Pergamon Press's reported profits we certainly cannot do that with much confidence yet) and to attempt to use them to prove some grand theory about the relative shares of labour and capital in the economy is simply fatuous.

In addition there is the problem that as people learn of statistical results they modify their conduct accordingly. This has been given the delightful name of the generalised Heisenberg principle by K. E. Boulding who illustrates it as follows. A patient asked about his health replies that he is fine; and the effort kills him.[89] More seriously I believe that learning by trade unions of the supposed existence of the Phillips Curve helped to remove whatever tenuous validity it ever had.

Moreover having established numbers we shall have to guard very carefully against the fallacies which can arise from treating them as definite answers to everything. I will illustrate what I mean by the following episode in the history of economic thought. The Currency school used to argue that both money and near-money including bills of exchange were reduced in

amount at times of Bank of England contraction. Calculation from (admittedly imperfect) stamp duty returns indicated that bills of exchange actually increased in number during contraction. But this result had no meaning until it could be established by further empirical study (which it was not) that there was not a more than compensating fall in their velocity of circulation. But if we take the Scottish methodology seriously we should avoid this kind of trap.

Our collection of data can be extended significantly by a means still rarely used by economists—the questionnaire. Some interesting work on the nature of demand curves was done by this means some time ago; but it seems to have produced little emulation. However a major and extremely interesting study seems to be in progress at the University of Sussex.[90] Of course questionnaires have their limitations; but we really have had enough of permutations based on a few highly restrictive assumptions and some rather casual introspection.

If we take seriously our obligation in this respect we should perhaps avoid getting again into the situation in which economists went on making grand generalisations about the effect of taxation on incentives on the basis of (almost) zero knowledge—it was not until about 1970 that serious study of this began in the U.K. although anyone with shop floor (or W.E.A.) experience could not help but doubt the conventional wisdom that incentive effects were unimportant. It should also help us to avoid slipping back into 'as if' methodology—and this must be avoided. In a science which cannot experiment contact with as much of reality as possible, and at every stage of the process, is vital. We cannot, like Faraday and Davey, be experimenting continuously.

But this in turn will require us to admit descriptive studies as respectable—instead of dismissing them contemptuously as 'contemporary economic history' which I have heard done. In turn we shall have to re-admit economic history to the fold. Instead of thanking God, like the Pharisees, that we are not as other men (economic historians) we shall have to recognise again the importance of an historical sense which has been emphasised in the past by such great figures as Schumpeter and Keynes. That economic history ever got pushed out is I think a sorry com-

mentary on the profession. We shall also have to link up with business studies which have not infrequently been showing interest in exactly the sort of problems which economists have neglected. Finance and marketing are not merely low but actually off the academic scale as viewed by economists. This is particularly true of the latter. Yet they are of vital importance in understanding how a market economy works. A link with business studies should also help us to meet the well-merited criticism that almost all the problems which are of interest to the entrepreneur are simply assumed as solved by the economist—the tin-opener problem in fact.

If we are prepared to return to the Scottish method, and to Marshall, then fruitful results should follow. The work of Chamberlin, P. W. S. Andrews, J. Bain, and H. R. Edwards, are testimony enough to this. But we shall have to be prepared for rebuffs. The authors of one empirical study met the following from a reviewer:

> This book is the product of four researchers, working for six years, studying the pricing decisions of 13 firms. One cannot conclude, on this evidence, that their time was very well spent.[91]

But we should not allow ourselves to be depressed by this. Empirical work of the kind I have mentioned—specifically, painstakingly digging out the basic economic data—was not a task beneath the great A. L. Bowley, whose work on wages and on family expenditure was path-breaking. It should not be beyond us. Even in the field of human capital, one of the most successful areas of economic research precisely because it has maintained contact with its world, the basic data are distinctly thin on the ground as yet.

Having been highly critical throughout this lecture let me try to finish on an optimistic note. Despite the mess into which the subject has got, the fact remains that the ground floor, the system of basic relationships conceived by economists, is valuable, and has proved valuable in the past. As Lord Robbins, at one stage the Director of the Economic Section of the Treasury, wrote:

> The most useful economic principles, when stated in their most general form, seem often mere banalities, almost an anti-climax after the formidable controversies amid which they have evolved. Yet experience seems to show

> that, without systematic training in the application of such platitudes, the most acute minds are liable to go astray; the economist, if he is humble, is heir to perpetual surprises, as he witnesses the incredible muddles which continually emerge from lay discussions of these matters.[92]

One has only to see the ludicrous assertions by natural scientists on matters of economic policy which appear with depressing frequency in the correspondence columns of the *Times* to realise the profound truth of this statement. There is also the highly illuminating (and true) story of the M.P. who wrote to several publications indicating that he could not understand how devaluation could increase both profitability and competitiveness.[93] The success of the basic Keynesian message is I believe yet another illustration of this point. Economics has got beyond the stage of competing assertions. But if we want to strengthen the first, viable, floor instead of crushing it under the weight above, we have I think to pursue the path I have indicated in this lecture.

1 Lord O'Brien addressing the Kircaldy Celebrations of the 250th Anniversary of Smith's birth, 5th June 1973.

2 On this claim see the review by T. W. Hutchison of W. Beckerman (ed.), *The Labour Government's Economic Record 1964–70,* London 1972 in *Economica*, vol. 40 (May 1973).

3 See for instance A. C. Pigou, 'Empty Economic Boxes: A Reply', reprinted in K. E. Boulding and G. J. Stigler (eds.), *Readings in Price Theory*, London, 1953, pp. 131–42.

4 Sir J. Clapham, 'Of Empty Economic Boxes', *Economic Journal*, 1922, reprinted in Boulding and Stigler, pp. 119–30; George Unwin, *Studies in Economic History*, ed. R. H. Tawney, London, 1927, quoted by A. W. Coats, *History of Political Economy*, vol. I (1969), p. 10.

5 M. Postan, 'A Plague of Economists?', *Encounter*, vol. 30, Jan. 1968, pp. 42–7; see also H. G. Johnson's reply in *ibid.*, vol. 30, May 1968, pp. 50–4.

6 J. Viner, 'The Economist in History', *American Economic Review* (Suppt.), vol. 53 (1963), pp. 1–22, p. 16.

7 *Wealth of Nations*, ed. E. Cannan, London, 1904, vol. II, pp. 359–60.

8 See in particular the pronouncements examined in T. W. Hutchison, *Economics and Economic Policy in Britain 1946–66*, London, 1968; see also G. Hallet, 'The Role of Economists as Government Advisers', *Westminster Bank Review*, May 1967, pp. 2–20.

9 R. L. Heilbroner, 'On the limited "relevance" of economics', reprinted in *Readings in Economics '72–'73*, Duskin Publishing Group, Guilford, Connecticut, 1972, p. 2.

10 C. E. Ferguson, 'The Specialisation Gap: Barton, Ricardo, and Hollander', *History of Political Economy*, vol. 5 (1973), p. 11: 'the theoreticians, with *some* notable exceptions, are becoming more and more second-rate mathematicians'.

11 This appears in the otherwise superb monograph by A. Lindbeck, *The Political Economy of the New Left*, London, 1971, p. 15.

12 M. Shubik, 'A Curmudgeon's Guide to Macroeconomics', *Journal of Economic Literature*, vol. 8 (1970), pp. 405–34, p. 422.

13 *Economic Journal*, December 1972, p. 1458 (T. Nulty).

14 *Ibid.*, September 1972, p. 1078 (P. Streeten). There is also the knockabout farce ('*Occam's Razor* . . . slash, slash, another phenomenon more simply explained') contained in Professor P. J. Wiles, 'Cost Inflation and the State of Economic Theory', *ibid.*, vol. 83 (1973), pp. 377–98.

15 *Economic Journal*, vol. 82 (1972), pp. 1–10.

16 *Ibid.*, pp. 73–86.

17 W. Leontief, 'Theoretical Assumptions and Nonobserved Facts', Presidential Address to the American Economic Association published in *American Economic Review* (Suppt.), vol. 61 (1971), pp. 1–7. A specific example of the schizophrenia may be found in F. H. Hahn, 'Some Adjustment Problems', *Econometrica*, vol. 38 (1970), pp. 1–17.

18 Viner, *op. cit.*; W. D. Grampp, 'Classical Economics and Its Moral Critics', *History of Political Economy*, vol. 5 (1973), pp. 359–74.

19 Lindbeck, *op. cit.*

20 Quoted in H. K. Recktenwald, *Political Economy*, London, 1973, p. 1.

21 J. R. McCulloch, *A Discourse on the Rise, Progress, Peculiar Objects, and Importance, of Political Economy*, London, 1824, p. 9.

22 R. Torrens, *An Essay on the Production of Wealth*, London, 1821 (reprinted New York, 1965), p. xiii.

23 Political Economy Club, *Centenary Volume*, London, 1921, pp. xi–xii. As the editor of the volume rightly stresses the mood was not characteristic of the Club in the long run.

24 J. Mill, *Elements of Political Economy*, editions London, 1821, 1823, 1826.

25 *Centenary Volume*, p. 223.

26 *Literature of Political Economy*, London, 1845, p. 18.

27 J. E. Cairnes, *The Character and Logical Method of Political Economy*, 2nd edition, London, 1888, p. 19.

[28] W. S. Jevons to Henrietta Jevons, 30th January 1859 in *Papers and Correspondence of William Stanley Jevons*, vol. II. Correspondence 1850–62, ed. R. D. C. Black, London, 1973, p. 361.
[29] London, 1871.
[30] W. Jaffé, 'Leon Walras', *International Encyclopaedia of the Social Sciences*, vol. 16, pp. 447–53.
[31] See the articles by C. D. Goodwin and G. J. Stigler in R. D. C. Black, *et al.*, ed., *The Marginal Revolution in Economics*, Durham, N. Carolina, 1973.
[32] E. Cannan, *A History of the Theories of Production and Distribution*, second edition, London, 1903; *A Review of Economic Theory*, London, 1929.
[33] K. A. Fox, *Intermediate Economic Statistics*, New York, 1968, pp. 168–9. I am indebted to Mark Blaug for this reference.
[34] J. Viner, *American Economic Review* (Suppt.), 1928, quoted in T. M. Humphrey, 'Empirical Tests of the Quantity Theory of Money', *History of Political Economy*, vol. 5 (1973), p. 307.
[35] *Economist*, 27th December 1958, p. 1172. I am indebted to Mr. M. C. Fleming for this reference.
[36] J. A. Schumpeter, *Ten Great Economists*, London, 1952, p. 280.
[37] See G. L. Shackle's reminiscences in *Expectations, Investment and Income*, 2nd edition, Oxford, 1968, p. xviii.
[38] S. Harris (ed.), *The New Economics*, London, 1948, p. 5.
[39] K. E. Boulding, 'The Misallocation of Intellectual Resources in Economics' in I. L. Horowitz (ed.), *The Use and Abuse of Social Science*, New Brunswick, 1971, p. 40.
[40] N. W. Senior, *Introductory Lecture on Political Economy*, delivered 6th December 1826, published 1827.
[41] Ely Devons, *Essays in Economics*, London, 1961, pp. 13–32.
[42] Hallett, *op. cit.*, p. 12.
[43] Alfred Marshall to A. L. Bowley, reprinted in A. C. Pigou, ed., *Memorials of Alfred Marshall*, London, 1925, p. 422, quoted in L. G. Reynolds, *The Three Worlds of Economics*, New Haven, 1971, pp. 314–5n.
[44] H. G. Johnson reviewing T. Scitovsky, *Money and the Balance of Payments*, London, 1969, *Journal of Political Economy*, vol. 78 (1970), p. 424.
[45] Leontief, *op. cit.*, p. 2.
[46] Worswick, *op. cit.*, pp. 78–9.
[47] Samuelson in Recktenwald, *op. cit.*, p. 408.
[48] G. L. S. Shackle, *The Years of High Theory*, London, 1967; *Expectations, Investment and Income*; *Epistemics and Economics*, London, 1972; Leijonhufvud, *On Keynesian Economics and the Economics of Keynes*, London, 1968.
[49] G. Debreu quoted by P. M. Sweezy in *Readings in Economics*, p. 23.
[50] A. Coddington, 'Are Statistics Vital', *The Listener*, 11th December 1969, p. 823.
[51] See H. Myint, 'The Classical View of the Economic Problem', *Economica*, n.s., vol. 13 (1946), pp. 119–30.
[52] This is apparently the position of Professor F. Hahn, 'The Winter of Our Discontent', *Economica*, n.s., vol. 40 (1973), pp. 322–30.
[53] See the article by Pigou cited above, and the contribution by Solow to *Readings in Economics* as examplesof this.
[54] Shubik, *op. cit.*, p. 415.
[55] *Wealth of Nations*, Book V, vol. II, pp. 449–60; K. E. Boulding, 'Misallocation', p. 36.
[56] Compare Haberler's 1936 textbook with the recent works of Heller and Sodersten; and consider the sad history of the Samuelson-Stolper theorem.
[57] See Reynolds, *Three Worlds*, pp. 7, 13.
[58] *Years of High Theory*, p. 47.
[59] Shubik, *op. cit.*, p. 416.
[60] The late P. W. S. Andrews has stressed this in particular; see also O. Morgenstern, 'Thirteen Critical Points in Contemporary Economic Theory: An Interpretation', *Journal of Economic Literature*, vol. 10 (1972), pp. 1163–89.

[61] On this see H. Townsend, 'Six Studies of Industrial Organisation', *Scottish Journal of Political Economy*, vol. 20 (1973), p. 78.

[62] See in particular the contributions by E. Nagel, H. Simon and P. A. Samuelson to *American Economic Review* (Suppt.), vol. 53 (1963), pp. 205–36; E. Rotwein, 'Mathematical Economics: The Empirical View and an Appeal for Pluralism' in S. R. Krupp (ed.), *The Structure of Economic Science*, Prentice Hall, 1966, pp. 102–13; T. C. Koopmans, *Three Essays on the State of Economic Science*, New York, 1957, pp. 138–40; E. Rotwein, 'On the Methodology of Positive Economics', *Quarterly Journal of Economics*, vol. 73 (1959), pp. 554–75; E. Rotwein, 'Empiricism and Economic Method: Several Views Considered', *Journal of Economic Issues*, vol. 7 (1973), pp. 361–82.

[63] Letter from Professor H. S. Ferns relating this incident, in *Times*, February 1974.

[64] Worswick, *op. cit.*, p. 80.

[65] O. Morgenstern, *On the Accuracy of Economic Observations*, 2nd edition, Princeton, 1963; Coddington, *op. cit.* and 'Economists and Policy', *National Westminster Bank Quarterly Review*, February 1973, pp. 59–68.

[66] See C. K. Rowley, *Steel and Public Policy*, London 1971, chapter 3.

[67] P. A. David, 'Just How Misleading are Official Exchange Rate Conversions?', *Economic Journal*, vol. 82 (1972), pp. 979–90 and 'Interchange' (B. Balassa, P. A. David) on the same subject in *ibid.*, vol. 83 (1973), pp. 1258–76.

[68] On this see P. Davidson and S. Weintraub, 'Money as Cause and Effect', *ibid.*, pp. 1117–32, p. 1117, n. 2. See also Phelps Brown, *op. cit.*, pp. 5–6.

[69] The outstanding example is of course that of Sir Henry Phelps Brown. See in particular his, *A Century of Pay*, London, 1968.

[70] Leontief, *op. cit.*, p. 3.

[71] G. Routh, 'The Relation between Unemployment and the Rate of Change of Money Wage Rates', *Economica*, n.s., vol. 26 (1959), pp. 299–315; R. Bhatia, 'Unemployment and the Rate of Change of Money Earnings in the United States 1900–1958', *Economica*, n.s., vol. 38 (1961), pp. 289–96.

[72] K. Wallis, 'Wages, Prices and Incomes Policies: Some Comments', *Economica*, n.s., vol. 38 (1971), pp. 304–10.

[73] D. G. Champernowne, *Economic Journal*, vol. 82 (1972), pp. 222–3.

[74] On this see V. G. Treml and J. P. Hardt *Soviet Economic Statistics*, Durham, N.C. 1972 (and the review of this by P. Hanson, *Economic Journal*, vol. 82 (1972), pp. 1482–3).

[75] The best starting point for a discussion of this method is A. Skinner's introduction to Sir J. Steuart, *Inquiry into the Principles of Political Economy*, Edinburgh, 1966, pp. lx-lxii.

[76] J. N. Keynes, *Scope and Method of Political Economy*, London, 1891, pp. 215-8.

[77] Marshall, *Principles*, 8th edition, London 1920, pp. v-vi.

[78] Letter to A. W. Flux quoted in M. E. A. Bowley, *Studies in the History of Economic Theory*, London 1973, p. 173.

[79] D. Hume, *Ecomonic Writings*, ed. E. Rotwein, Edinburgh 1955, p. 3.

[80] Recktenwald, p. 358.

[81] *Principles*, pp. 460–1.

[82] See Reynold's, *op. cit.*, p. 315.

[83] *Ibid.*, pp. x-xi.

[84] See especially Sir A. Cairncross, 'On Being an Economic Adviser' *Scottish Journal of Political Ecomony*, vol. 2 (1955), pp. 181-97; 'Economists in Government', *Lloyds Bank Review*, No. 95. (January 1970), pp. 1-18. This was also a consistent theme in the writings of Devons.

[85] *Economica*, vol. 35 (1968), pp. 1-21.

[86] London, 1973.

[87] Letters from Mr. G. Wright and Mr. A. McGlashan, *Times*, 13 February 1974.

[88] Milton Gilbert and Associates, *Comparative National Products and Price Levels*, Paris, O.E.C.D., 1958.

[89] K. E. Boulding, 'Economics as a Moral Science', *American Economic Review*, vol. 59 (1969), pp. 1-12, p. 3.

[90] The pioneering work I referred to was by A. Gabor. For the Sussex work see Pickering, *et al.*, 'Identification and Measurement of Consumer Confidence', *Journal of the Royal Statistical Society*, Series A., vol. 136, Part I (1973), pp. 43–63.

[91] K. Cowling, *Economic Journal*, vol. 82 (1972), p. 1430.

[92] Quoted in Cairncross, *Lloyds Bank Review*, *loc. cit.*, p. 15.

[93] Hallett, *op. cit.*, pp. 11–12.

[2]

THEORIES OF THE HISTORY OF SCIENCE: A TEST CASE

D. P. O'Brien

I. INTRODUCTION

The historical importance of Adam Smith as an economist is without any real parallel in the entire development of economics. When John Maynard Keynes died *The Times* wrote that "To find an economist of comparable influence one would have to go back to Adam Smith" (*Times*, 1946). But Keynes has only been dead for less than 40 years so that, although his influence has been enormously wide throughout a greatly enlarged body of professional economists, it will take historians of the distant future to decide whether he ever attained a sway comparable to that achieved by *The Wealth of Nations*. Smith's legacy remains the standard of comparison.

Smith's huge achievement was to provide the foundation for the whole of classical economics. Of course, he did not build up the body of thought which we now know as classical economics single-handedly; David Ricardo's contribution cannot be disregarded, and indeed one major study of classical economics is actually entitled *Ricardian Economics* (Blaug, 1958). But, in the last resort, classical economics *is* conceivable without Ricardo, whose influence progressively waned from 1830 if not before; it is quite inconceivable without Adam Smith and *The Wealth of*

Nations. This paper will aim to trace the way in which classical economics developed out of *The Wealth of Nations* and how its importance survived well beyond what we think of as the Marginal Revolution. Having traced the pattern, an attempt will be made to see which of the philosophies of the history of science drawn from the works of Popper, of Kuhn, and of Lakatos, as well as of those writers who favor a dialectical approach, will help us to understand the progress of Smith's influence during the development of economics.

II. THE SMITHIAN BASIS OF CLASSICAL ECONOMICS

It seems indisputable that the basic vision of the economic system as a *system* was supplied for the whole of classical economics (and beyond) by Adam Smith. The concept was of an economic system with knowledge and decision–making as an individual responsibility within a framework of law, justice, and security of property provided by government. Partly because of this framework the effects of individual decisions coalesced into a systematic whole affecting society. Within the framework, individuals pursued their self-interest—but it was a self-interest shot through with social values.[1] It is important to appreciate this. Any interpretation of the view of self-interest propounded in *The Wealth of Nations* that does not take account of the "sympathy" theory propounded in *The Theory of Moral Sentiments* (Smith, 1759, Pt. I, Sec. III, Chap. III) will be seriously misleading. This pursuit of self-interest within the framework of law and of social values which permeated both the law and the self-interest produced a resource allocation which was conducive to economic growth, as capital owners sought to take advantage of *new* profit opportunities, products, and techniques. It produced an allocation of resources which, though it may not have been optimal (Smith did not possess the concept of optimality in our sense, which may or may not have been his loss), was relatively *superior* to anything that government allocation of resources could produce instead.

Since it was relatively better (and thus the best that an *imperfect* world could manage) it implied a harmony between social values and self-interest, as defined above.

It is true, as we shall see, that this optimistic view did come into question during the time when Ricardo's influence was at its zenith. For Ricardo believed that there was a real disharmony involved in the system of economic relationships, in that the interests of the landlords conflicted with those of the rest of the community both with respect to the

general progress of diminishing returns in agriculture and, in particular, in relation to the introduction of improvements in agricultural technology. But this view found relatively little support and certainly not long-lasting support. The majority of the classical economists, while conceding, as indeed Smith had done in specific instances, that there was always the possibility of areas of disharmony, preferred to take the view that the landlords had mistaken their real interests. Ricardo's attempts to show that, for instance, it was against the interests of the landlords to introduce improvements were regarded as unsuccessful by his fellows. In general Smith's vision predominated.

It was not, of course, only a general vision which Adam Smith gave to classical economics. In a number of specific areas the analysis provided in his great book was either taken over entirely or used as the basis for more developed treatments by later writers.

Most fundamental of all, Smith's vision of growth was taken over whole and entire by classical economics. It is true that Ricardo gave it a peculiar twist through his particular version of the stagnation thesis. But the idea of growth as the interaction of capital accumulation, division of labor, technical change, and population increase was the fundamental one which classical economics retained. Spanners (or "monkey wrenches", as our American cousins say) could be thrown into these works by, for instance, the premature depression of the rate of profit via the Corn Laws; but the interactions in those works were accepted by all. So, with the exception of Ricardo's tax chapters (and their reproduction by James Mill), was the Smithian treatment of the *finance* of government. J. R. McCulloch's *Treatise* (1845), the great public finance work of classical economics, is wholly Smithian. Only John Stuart Mill really tried to advance the analysis by introducing Utilitarianism into the discussion of tax incidence.

To have provided the whole of the basic vision of classical economics *and* the growth theory for a set of economic ideas which were *fundamentally* concerned with growth would have been an enormous achievement on its own. But Adam Smith would not have expected all that he wrote to be taken over whole and entire. He believed in the evolution of systems of knowledge, not in the arrival at a final and immutable truth.[2] So it was appropriate that elements in his system provided the basis for later developments in classical economics. On the subjects of population and of wages Smith laid the foundations for all the later classical treatments. His book contained a loose version of T. R. Malthus's population mechanism: Malthus made it rigid, but in the hands of his successors—this is particularly true of the work of McCulloch and of N. W. Senior, though it is also applicable to that of J. S. Mill—it became a loose fluid relation-

ship very similar in its essence to that envisaged by Smith. The embryo wage fund in *The Wealth of Nations* (part of Smith's growth model, like his population mechanism) was made more rigid, especially by McCulloch, Ricardo, and Senior, and then partially relaxed again. The analysis of *relative* wages in *The Wealth of Nations* was retained intact throughout virtually all the classical treatments, the only development being the introduction, by J. S. Mill and J. E. Cairnes, of noncompeting groups. The Smithian treatment of rent, both price determined and price determining, without any indication of how these two concepts might be reconciled, provided the basis for the classical rent theory developed by Malthus, E. West, and Ricardo—though, through neglect of transfer earnings, their analysis was in important respects, while clearer, less satisfactory than that from which it sprang.

The Smithian view of profit as interest plus a risk premium provided the basis for the later, more detailed treatments of the components of the profit reward by T. Tooke and McCulloch;[3] and Smith's view of the savings mechanism (with his vagueness as to whether the rate of time preference was zero, positive, or negative) led to the later developments, by J. Rae and J. S. Mill, while the ambiguities in *The Wealth of Nations* about the *origin* of the interest agio made necessary the development of the theory of abstinence by Senior and J. S. Mill.

Smith's value theory was enormously influential. His adoption of a cost of production theory of value gave a stamp to virtually the whole of classical value theory. Even the Ricardian version, which differed from Smith's in important respects (since it recognized labor as the only major input and, being designed as a part of the Corn Law model, was concerned, via the Invariable Measure, with the measurement of progress toward the stationary state), was still a constant-cost, supply-determined price model. Moreover the successors of Ricardo gradually turned his value theory back into a Smithian one, so that when we reach J. S. Mill we find a Smithian value theory (except for the elimination of rent as a price-determined surplus) back in office. Even the subjective value theorists, at least J. B. Say and those influenced by him, took Smith's preservation of the position of S. von Pufendorf and F. Hutcheson in his treatment of market value as the starting point.[4]

In other areas, not surprisingly, developments went far beyond what *The Wealth of Nations* had to offer. Classical international trade theory, it is true, started from the Smithian concept of absolute advantage. The source of supply for a commodity which entered into international trade was, in this view, simply that place where the absolute input requirements were lowest. But R. Torrens and Ricardo were faced with the problem of showing that a country could still gain from trade if it were

superior to other countries with respect to productivity in the supply of all commodities. Their solution to this, in the form of the theory of comparative cost, was a major advance on what Smith had to offer, particularly as Torrens (and later J. S. Mill) developed a theory to explain the division of the gains arising from trade on the basis of comparative advantage, through the theory of reciprocal demand. This was pure theory at its very best; and Ricardo must undoubtedly be given the credit for many of these achievements, for it was he who provided the impetus to pure theorising in this area. Yet even here, for those who were not pure theorists, the Smithian vision of trade on the basis of absolute advantage and the concept of the interaction of trade and growth (as stressed by Smith rather than by Ricardo, whose analysis was essentially static) were probably more important. In particular, there was the so called vent-for-surplus doctrine, which saw countries engaging in international trade so as to rid themselves of surplus commodities in which they had an absolute advantage and which they were producing in ever increasing amounts as economic growth took place. Such surpluses could then be exchanged, through trade, for commodities which were not produced under favorable domestic conditions. In nineteenth century Britain, with its fast-growing manufacturing sector which was in advance of any other country in the world for so long, this must have seemed an intuitively reasonable approach.[5]

Another Smithian concept which must have had an intuitive appeal was the one that trade, by introducing new products, stimulated effort, enterprise, and further trade. Indeed this was a point which Malthus—under Smith's influence—made to Ricardo in discussing the gains from trade (see Viner, 1937, pp. 528–9). These gains could not, then, be assessed solely in terms of the increased productivity of resources in obtaining, indirectly through trade rather than directly through domestic production, a *given* range of commodities.

In the field of monetary theory classical economics also went far beyond what Smith had to offer. The basic concept of the nature and role of money, supplied by Smith (and, inter alia, Joseph Harris) did of course stay with classical economics. The "great wheel of circulation and distribution" (Smith, 1776, Book I, p. 279), the peculiar qualities of the precious metals, the economizing effects of paper money, and the use of banking likened to "wagon ways through the air" which left the road free for pasture (Smith, 1776, Book I, p. 304)—all these stayed with classical economics. But classical monetary theory, as one of the really great achievements of the classical economists, went far beyond this. Starting from David Hume's exposition of the price–specie-flow mechanism (of which Smith knew, of course; see Smith, 1763, p. 197), it went

on to the self-regulating distribution of the precious metals, inflation, the theory of an inconvertible paper currency under a free exchange rate, the theory of a convertible currency under a fractional reserve system, and the credit multiplication of bank deposits (Torrens and J. Pennington being the authors who achieved this last advance). Adam Smith had the perhaps dubious distinction in the two great monetary controversies, the bullion debate and the currency and banking debate, of being the author of the Real Bills Doctrine (later renamed the Doctrine of Reflux), which was quite clearly on the losing side of these debates.

But all this is hardly surprising. Not only did Adam Smith never conceive of a science (including, for this purpose, economics) as having reached, or being likely to reach, the end of its development; but the great steps forward in monetary and international trade theory were stimulated by pressing practical economic problems resulting from a degree of growth and development in the British economy which Smith did not live to see. This may also explain why his view of the complementarity of labor and machinery and his neglect of the problem of aggregate demand failures—Say's Law is, of course, embryonically in *The Wealth of Nations* (Smith, 1776, Book I, p. 359)—both came under some pressure, especially in the second and third decades of the nineteenth century. Yet eventually Smith's view prevailed on both these matters: Despite J. Barton and Ricardo, the majority of the classical economists, while conceding that the installation of machinery could harm labor in the short run (and thus being prepared to advocate cushioning measures to mitigate this short-run harm) were firmly of the opinion that in the *long run* there was no such conflict. Similarly, on the question of aggregate demand, Lord Lauderdale and Malthus found very few supporters for their fears that capital-stock adjustment problems would lead to demand failures in a growing economy.

On matters of policy and the *role* (as distinct from the finance, touched on earlier) of government, new problems, emerging in the century after publication of *The Wealth of Nations,* brought forth new insights and recommendations from the classical economists. Yet Smith's influence proved extremely durable, not only in giving the classical economists the pragmatic approach to intervention which characterized their recommendations (intervention was, at bottom, only a way of producing the correct framework so that individual and social interests coincided as far as possible, and Smith himself had been prepared to recommend intervention in a number of areas) but also on some specific matters. In particular, Smith (1776, Book II, p. 114) viewed colonization as a wasteful development for the benefit of merchants:

> To found a great empire for the sole purpose of raising up a people of customers, . . . is . . . a project altogether unfit for a nation of shopkeepers; but extremely fit for a nation whose government is influenced by shopkeepers. Such statesmen, and such statesmen only, are capable of fancying that they will find some advantage in employing the blood and treasure of their fellow-citizens, to found and maintain such an empire.

This view was for a long time highly influential with the classical economists, although, as D. N. Winch (1965) has shown, it was ultimately largely superseded by the new wave of "scientific colonization"—McCulloch being the only major figure among the classical economists to remain faithful to Smith's original view.

III. THE SMITHIAN VISION BEYOND 1870

In discussing the longevity of Adam Smith's vision we have, of course, to focus in the first instance on classical economics. But to provide a complete picture of the durability of the view of the economic world set forth in *The Wealth of Nations* we have to go well beyond the era of classical economics. While there is no obvious date at which to draw a line (and Smith's influence is still clearly with us in a number of areas), it is I think worth showing how a basically classical approach (and hence a basically Smithian one) continued to be characteristic of mainstream economics works well after 1870 and the beginning of the era that we now think of as the Marginal Revolution.

When we look at a work published as late as the second edition of J. S. Nicholson's *Elements* (1909), we find that there are 55 separate subheadings in the index under "Adam Smith" and 38 under "J. S. Mill," while Alfred Marshall rates 29 page references but no subheadings at all. When we look at the details of the text we find *traces* of the Marginal Revolution, but little more. The distinction between total and marginal utility (Nicholson, 1909, pp. 23–8) is recognizably post-1870, and this has some influence (though actually remarkably little) on the treatment of value later in the book. But the treatment of wages for instance is largely confined to a review of the wage fund and a vague productivity theory. The latter is not *marginal* productivity; and Smith may be said to have had both a wage-fund theory and a vague productivity theory.

H. Sidgwick's discussion in his *Principles* (1887) is also in the classical vein, and remarkably unmarked by the Marginal Revolution, despite the acknowledgments in his preface to such diverse authorities as W. S. Jevons, J. E. Cairnes, A. Marshall, W. E. Hearn, and F. A. Walker. Criticism from F. Y. Edgeworth and P. H. Wicksteed is also acknowl-

edged in the second edition. Yet, despite the statement that Sidgwick believed himself to "owe most to Jevons' *Theory of Political Economy,* the leading ideas of which have been continually in my thoughts" (Sidgwick, 1887, p. v.), we find the treatment of value, of wages, and of interest and capital to be apparently innocent of Jevonian influence. The work as a whole is marked by a broad common sense very reminiscent of Adam Smith.

Another example is the famous work by C. F. Bastable, *Public Finance* (1892). This is, in design and spirit, an updated version of McCulloch's classic *Treatise* (1845), although the treatment is considerably broadened in content by including the expenditure as well as the revenue side of government.

Of course, it is true that, during the period after 1870, among the leaders of the profession both in England and abroad, men like W. S. Jevons, Wicksteed, Edgeworth, Léon Walras, and Carl Menger, and their followers were forging ahead in developing the system of economics which we now associate with that era in the history of economic thought. But if we consider the works which were offered by other men, men in influential academic positions and sometimes (as in the case of Sidgwick) men with a considerable intellectual reputation, we find the hand of Adam Smith still lying heavily upon the pages.

Indeed there seems to be absolutely no doubt that the "Marginal Revolution," as it is now called, was an extremely gradual process. The phrase in fact "relates to a process and not to an event" (Black, 1973, p. 98). Blaug, (1973, p. 8), noting that this revolution, like the Industrial Revolution, "went unrecognised by those who lived through it" observes:

> One is struck in reading the treatises of the 1870s and 1880s by the bewildering variety of attitudes adopted towards the principal tenets of classical economics, such as the labor theory of value, the quantity theory of money, the Ricardian theory of differential rent, et cetera (pp. 12–13).

Indeed, one commentator has remarked that:

> The idea [of marginal utility] penetrated the thinking of economists most slowly, and had to win its victories, one by one, over inertia and, less frequently, over active opposition. . . . The Marginal Utility School emerged at the end of these twenty years [1870–1889], but throughout this period, and for a long time thereafter, the idea of marginal utility stood alongside the older views as a new but minor variant of economic thought (Howey, 1960, pp. vii–viii).

All this is true of those who could be, in any sense, regarded as profes-

sional economists. As T. W. Hutchison (1953, pp. 1–5) has observed, the adherence of the amateurs to classical economics was even more marked; and, except insofar as they were monetary theorists deriving their theoretical approach from a tradition originating with Ricardo's exposition (and many of them were), their adherence to classical economics meant primarily adherence to the economics of Adam Smith.

It is, then, hardly surprising that the work of Jevons made very slow progress. As Hutchison (1953, p. 15) observes:

> Not only Marshall in reviewing the *Theory*, but Bagehot, Sidgwick, and Cairnes were all markedly unenthusiastic. Bagehot complained that the new theory of Jevons and Walras was 'much worse' than the old, in looking 'too unlike life and business.'

The essential point is this. There is abundant evidence that classical economics took a very long time to expire. But classical economics was essentially Smithian. There is no doubt that it lingered on while writers like J. S. Nicholson, W. Bagehot, H. Sidgwick, and the large number of economists who did not hold academic positions continued to adhere to what were largely classical views. Moreover, despite Jevons's attack on J. S. Mill, his relations with Cairnes were excellent—indeed, Jevons regarded Cairnes's work, outside the field of value theory, as admirable and believed that his own work complemented rather than contradicted classical economics (Black, 1960). Moreover, as the leading authority on Jevons has observed: "What is an undeniable fact is that the *Theory of Political Economy* was no more a complete system than a rough-hewn corner stone in a complete building" (Black, 1972, p. 8).

In giving the post-1870 period its characteristic as one of transition rather than of revolution, the role of Alfred Marshall was of crucial importance. Although Marshall was an original thinker, he was very much influenced by the work of his classical predecessors; it was not just "filial piety" and his own modesty which caused him to lay little emphasis on the extent of his contributions. In the development of economics there have been two distinct kinds of economists: there are those who preeminently start with a tabula rasa and work from first principles—Ricardo (despite his reading of Smith), Jevons, and Keynes are perhaps the clearest examples; and there are those who work carefully through the material of their predecessors, criticizing, synthesizing, and developing their own original contributions. J. S. Mill and Marshall—the second owing a great debt to the first—are undoubtedly in this latter category. Marshall acknowledged and defended the contribution of the classical economists on both policy matters and theoretical ones: even when they were at fault, there was a danger of overreacting against them. He de-

fended Smith, Ricardo, and J. S. Mill vigorously and went to great lengths to attempt to distill the truth from their doctrines. Undoubtedly he was too generous to be a reliable guide. Not only was he more critical of Jevons for concentrating on utility than of Ricardo for neglecting it, he even credited Ricardo with part-authorship of the great Bullion Report. Nor was his admiration confined to the English classical economists. He lectured on the inaccuracies of E. V. Böhm-Bawerk's account of A. R. J. Turgot and told K. Wicksell:

> While he [Böhm-Bawerk] was still at school, I learnt from the men whom he reviles everything which he has vaunted as a great discovery: and especially in America, he has been taken at his own valuation by people *who have never studied the great men* on whose burial places he dances his war dance (Gardlund, 1958, pp. 342–3).

The key position of such a man was of very considerable importance. H. S. Foxwell's observation that, as early as 1887, half the chairs in economics in England were occupied by Marshall's pupils is well known (Coats, 1967, p. 707). Yet this is critical for, if we accept that the Marginal Revolution was, for its first two decades, about marginal utility rather than the generalized margin concept, we must also recognize that marginal utility was very far from being central to Marshall's own preoccupations. Indeed in the view of one commentator: "Marshall paid slight heed to marginal utility until after 1889" (Howey, 1960, p. 80). Of course other leaders of the subject—the Austrians, Walras, Wicksell, Edgeworth, V. Pareto, and I. Fisher—were pursuing "modern economics." But the position of Marshall, holding a key position, remains curiously ambiguous. The position of some of Marshall's pupils was even closer to the classical school. This is particularly true of Nicholson. [Coats (1967, pp. 725–6) thinks that Nicholson, like Bastable, "might more accurately be termed a Millian than a Marshallian"], and he was particularly insistent on gradualism and incremental progress in economics (Coats, 1964 p. 99).

The prolonged survival of classical economics is hardly surprising if one remembers the tendency of economics to become more empty as it becomes more rigorous. The importance of topical issues in the journal literature of even the post-1890 period, issues on which the more "modern" and rigorous works could throw little light, ensured that the classical apparatus, uninhibited from dealing with such matters by the need for rigor, continued to survive.

IV. THE WAXING AND WANING OF THE SMITHIAN STAR

The enormous longevity of Adam Smith's influence, and the quite fundamental nature of his contribution to classical economics, can then

hardly be disputed. But it would be misleading to give the impression that Smith's influence was constant throughout the era of classical economics. It was not. It was not only the post-1870 era which saw a decline in Smith's influence.

From the publication of *The Wealth of Nations* in 1776 through to the economic events of the Napoleonic Wars, Smith's great book was clearly the dominant work on economics. But then there arose a new star. Monetary events and the era of inconvertibility raised problems which were not covered in *The Wealth of Nations;* and increasing corn prices, coupled with agricultural protection, raised questions about the future courses of both economic growth and of income distribution. On the first score, the great bullion debate succeeded in developing monetary theory to a pitch far higher than that achieved by Adam Smith; while on the second, Ricardo's system, in the form of his corn model, provided an analysis of the corn question (including, under this head, growth prospects and the macroeconomic distribution of income) which economists, or at least the leaders among them, found highly persuasive. Part of this new wave proved long lasting. The monetary theory not only lasted but was refined and developed further as the century progressed. But then there was nothing in it which was inconsistent with the basic Smithian analytical approach. The corn model, however, suffered a severe decline—there is first-hand testimony to this in a report of the proceedings of the Political Economy Club (1921, pp. 223–4)—a decline so severe indeed that by 1846 even the attack on the Corn Laws themselves probably owed as much to Smith as to Ricardo. In particular McCulloch's analysis of the likely course of corn prices in the absence of protection was made on the basis of an absolute advantage model; and McCulloch was highly influential. Nevertheless a bastard form of the Ricardian corn model lingered on in the publications of the Anti-Corn-Law League and other of the cruder supporters of free trade, who endeavored to persuade the working population that repeal was in their interests, as it would lead to cheap bread, while persuading the manufacturers that repeal was in their interests as it would lead to cheap labor. But as far as the leaders among the classical economists were concerned, the Smithian system—still bearing Ricardian scars, especially in the work of J. S. Mill, but recognizably Smithian for all that—remained in the ascendant for the remainder of the classical era. From 1870 onward there developed of course the phenomenon known as the Marginal Revolution. But this was a slow process, although (unlike the Ricardian ascent) it was not due to be reversed. However, because it was slow, the Smithian view of the world continued to be the stock in trade of economists long after shining new tools had been refined and developed. For the most part these tools remained long unused in dealing with any real economic problem.[6]

Smith's influence then fluctuated and was of varying pervasiveness during (and beyond) the era of classical economics. But there is a large (and growing) body of literature in the history and philosophy of science which purports to provide explanatory frameworks for the rise, ascendancy, and fall of bodies of ideas. It is then interesting to see how these perform as explanations of the vicissitudes of Smith's influence.

V. THEORIES OF THE HISTORY OF SCIENCE

The Popperian Falsificationism

Popperianism as a theory of what scientists actually do (as distinct from what they *ought* to do, which is surely its main purpose) can be dismissed fairly quickly, not necessarily because of any intrinsic lack of merit on its home ground of the natural sciences, but because several critical features of its schema are missing in the history of economics.

The Popperian schema sees scientific progress as taking place through the formulation of hypotheses which are then subject to testing. Falsifiability is the hallmark of true science. A hypothesis will survive so long as it is not falsified by testing or—outside the domain of the naive or dogmatic falsificationists, of whom Popper is not one—until such falsification is accepted as conclusive by the general body of scientists. It is fairly obvious why this approach need not detain us very long in the context of the present discussion. For Smith's ideas were not subjected to a testing program of attempted falsification; indeed, unlike Ricardo, Smith offered very few unambiguous predictions which would invite attempts at falsification. Nor, of course, was there any serious use of statistical apparatus to test Smith's ideas. We cannot, then, explain the longevity of the Smithian vision by reference to a long period of successful testing followed by ultimate failure (while a number of writers, e.g., Nicholson, Sidgwick, and Bastable, persisted in judging that the tests were inconclusive). This would be a pretentious caricature of the history of our subject during the nineteenth century. The Popperian apparatus simply does not help us here. It should hardly be necessary to say that there were none of the "crucial experiments" which Popper sees as occuring in the history of natural science (1959, Sec. 30; 1963, pp. 112–13, 174, 246).

This does, however, raise the very interesting question of the availability and use of statistics during the classical era. There seems no doubt that quite extensive statistical data were available to the classical economists and they were involved in the development of social statistics (Blaug, 1958, p. 41; O'Brien, 1970, pp. 84–98). Moreover, some statisti-

cal techniques were available, although they were not employed in the social science field (Blaug, 1958, p. 49, citing H. M. Walker, 1929, Chap. 2). Some of the classical writers undoubtedly did extensive statistical work. They included not only McCulloch but also P. Colquhoun, Tooke, and W. Newmarch, and even Malthus whose *Essay* became more and more weighted with data in successive editions. (Tooke and Newmarch provide an interesting illustration of the slowness to adopt available techniques since, despite writing a *History of Prices,* they did not use index numbers which had been available since at least 1812.)

In principle, a writer might have wanted to use statistical material for (i) falsification, (ii) verification (both of these relating to his own theoretical position), (iii) illustration, (iv) refutation of an opposing view, and (v) "measurement without theory." This last is largely a myth invented in criticism of Wesley Mitchell and his associates and can be disregarded for our purposes. But a great deal of classical statistical work comes into category iii. This is not really a variant of category ii, as might appear to be the case because there is no implied test of any kind; as with Keynesian national income estimation, we simply say that there are such magnitudes as output, consumption, and so on and then try to measure them.

However, a great deal of the classical work in this category was capable of shading over into category i. Thus McCulloch's work on foreign corn prices probably influenced his position on the Corn Laws and led him to the view that their repeal would not produce any very startling results; and there are other instances in his work of data influencing his theoretical position (see O'Brien, 1970, pp. 97–8). Of course, several of those working under the general heading of classical economics but whose methodology derived from Ricardo were impatient of—indeed, hostile toward—use of statistical data; this is particularly true of J. E. Cairnes. But it would not be true of those who worked under the direct methodological influence of Adam Smith.

Perhaps the key point to recognize in the present context is that whatever use was made of statistical data by the classical economists, it could not be described as a Popperian use. In collecting data for illustrative purposes the classical writers did not regard any particular hypothesis as being at risk except when they were engaged in controversy and anxious to collect data in order to refute an opponent—category iv. Moreover, those working under the influence of Scottish methodology regarded the collection of statistics as a source of hypotheses. Such a view of method is of course rejected by Popper on the grounds that the hypothesis is antecedent to the collection of data, for otherwise there would be no way of choosing the data to be collected. In fact, this may not always be true—vital statistics are an example. But what does seem clear is that classical statistical collection and discussion were not Popperian.

In any case there is a very real problem about "testing" in economics. For repeated testing in economics—and, except for naive falsificationists, replication of results is very important in natural science—merely means more sophisticated statistical tests *on the same set of data* that everyone else has used. In natural science, by contrast, it means replication of an experiment and the obtaining of new data. This is a vital contrast; and it exists not so much because of the problems of data collection in the social sciences, vital though these problems may be, but because the subject matter of economics is a unique historical process, not a replicable laboratory experiment.

There are also other problems associated with testing, linked particularly in the literature with the name of P. Duhem. The most important point is that no hypothesis is ever tested in isolation. Significant though this point may be in natural science, it is of even greater importance in economics, where we do not have laboratory control over conditions in the ceteris paribus clause (Stewart, 1979, pp. 128–32, 145, 163, 195). Because of these difficulties, it is much harder to secure "inter-subjective agreement" (Stewart, 1979, p. 58) in economics than in natural sciences on the status of empirical results.

The Kuhnian Revolutions

The ideas put forward in Kuhn's charming and deeply impressive *The Structure of Scientific Revolutions* (1962) are now well known to economists. We have had the concept of a paradigm introduced and this concept—the view of what science (or sometimes a branch of it) is about and what and how it does its work that is accepted by the "scientific community"—governs all "normal scientific" activity, *including the actual process of testing.* "Normal science" is a puzzle-solving activity; failure to solve the puzzles suggested by a particular paradigm reflects on the scientist not the paradigm, except at a time of crisis when a paradigm is under attack. The process of paradigm replacement, when a new paradigm comes to be accepted by the scientific community, is a "Scientific Revolution."

This is all a much more relativist way of looking at science than that offered by Popper—though it should be said that Kuhn has attempted to deny the charge of relativism.[7] Crucial to this aspect of the argument is the idea that paradigms are incommensurable (so that we cannot speak of *progress*) and that testing (because it involves accepted instruments and techniques developed under the reign of any particular paradigm) is very much paradigm-dominated. Falsification then becomes a paradigm-limited operation.

Described baldly in this way Kuhn's system sounds very much less persuasive than it seems when presented by its author buttressed with numerous examples from the history of several branches of natural science. Yet in many ways it is, *for economists,* a much more illuminating way of looking at their subject than that supplied by Popper. This is for two reasons. First, although the concept of paradigm has come under considerable attack from philosophers—one of Kuhn's supporters handed a great weapon to his opponents by painstakingly passing a period spent in hospital recording 21 different uses of the term by Kuhn in his book (Masterman, 1970)—it is actually a very helpful one. It can be seen to be useful when we consider a paradigm as a pair of spectacles through which we see the world. This is the interpretation suggested by Kuhn's discussion of the concept in connection with Gestalt psychology (1962, pp. 111ff.). Secondly, it is helpful because one of the important things which a paradigm does is to limit our view of what is the proper area of scientific concern. The changes of focus which occurred with the (eventual) triumph of the Marginal Revolution have often been noticed by economists; and here the Kuhnian approach is illuminating (see Coats, 1969). The concept of "normal science" is also valuable in that it is much easier to interpret classical collection of, and use of, statistical data in these terms than in Popperian ones, even though it did not involve any real "puzzle solving." But does all this help us to understand the vicissitudes of Adam Smith's ideas?

It is perfectly possible to regard *The Wealth of Nations* as providing a paradigm—that of self-interest pursuit and decentralized decision taking in a growth context viewed as producing a relatively best state of affairs and relatively efficient allocation of resources. So far, so good. But, if we are to take Kuhn's apparatus seriously within the context of the history of economic thought, we need to address ourselves to two vital sets of questions.

First, did Ricardo's system provide an alternative paradigm—a different way of looking at the world from that provided by the Smithian paradigm? Now it certainly fulfilled one of Kuhn's paradigm functions—that of insulating scientists from important problems; and we can see this exhibited very clearly in Ricardo's discussion of tax matters in which he managed altogether to avoid dealing with the burning tax question of his day, the income tax. But, if Ricardo's system really did offer an alternative paradigm, were the economic events of the Napoleonic wars truly the occasion for a "crisis" which led to its replacing the Smithian paradigm? This seems doubtful, although a case might certainly be made for it. But, supposing that we do accept all this, there seems to be no provision within Kuhn's apparatus for the old paradigm

to come back and replace the new one. Yet, as we have seen, this is effectively what happened in the course of the development of classical economics with the return of Smith's influence to predominance. However, if Ricardo was *not* really offering an alternative paradigm, we are forced to conclude, as we might in any case conclude if we were not satisfied by the evidence for the existence of a "crisis" and of "anomalies," that Kuhn's apparatus, in its interesting form (as distinct from its watered-down form[8]), has nothing of interest to say about the vital developments in economics between 1815 and 1825, the period of Ricardian ascendency, and Ricardo is reduced to the status of a puzzle solver within the Smithian paradigm. Yet such a view is sustainable only by removing the corn model and the invariable measure from a central role in his work.

Moreover, it would be hard to sustain the view that the Ricardian and Smithian paradigms were "incommensurable." This perhaps requires some amplification. In support of his view Kuhn (1962, pp. 100–2) argues that, for instance, the Einsteinian and Newtonian paradigms are incommensurable because terms come to mean different things: *space, time,* and *mass* mean different things, he asserts, in terms of the two different paradigms. But can we say that the terms *wages, subsistence, capital,* or *population* have different meanings in the works of Smith and Ricardo? Only *value* acquired a different meaning. Yet perhaps it should be conceded that there was *an element* of incommensurability; for when McCulloch attempted to introduce Ricardian corn model elements into the Smithian growth model, they failed to graft (O'Brien, 1970, Chap. 12).

The first set of questions about the applicability of Kuhn's apparatus to the history of Smith's economics cannot then be answered entirely in favor of the application of the apparatus. The second set of questions that we have to ask ourselves about the use of Kuhn's theory of the history of science in explaining the history of Smith's bequest, relates to the whole collection of "normal" science "puzzle solving" and "anomalies" that are so important to Kuhn in his view of natural science. It does seem that these questions can be answered even less satisfactorily. What is in question, it should be emphasized, is not their applicability in a natural science context; rather, it is the use of these concepts in a discussion of classical economics. For it does seem clear that very little "puzzle solving" was engaged in by the classical economists. Of course, Ricardo was by inclination a puzzle solver. But if we reduce him to the role of a puzzle solver within the Smithian paradigm we achieve generality at the expense of meaning, for we then have nothing by which to delineate the phenomenon of the Ricardian explosion. The truth seems to be that

the concept of puzzle solving does not transplant from natural to social science any more easily than Popper's "testing" or "falsification" and "crucial experiments." Moreover, it is extremely hard, even today, to envisage a situation in economics when a research failure would reflect on the researcher.

It does seem clear that classical economics was not really a mature science in the Kuhnian sense—even though it probably did have a scientific community (O'Brien, 1975, pp. 11–16).

But what about the post-1870 developments? Here it seems to me that Kuhn's approach does help a little. For the Smithian spectacles *were* gradually replaced. Although, as we have seen, they continued in use past the turn of the century, the economists' switch from the growth context to static optimization is well enough documented; and with this came a change in the range of the subject. Population, for instance, which Smith had given a central role in his vision of the growth process, faded from the economic literature. Even Marshall's attempt to include some discussion of it in his *Principles* seems in retrospect only a Marshallian act of filial piety. Moreover, there was (at least in the British Isles) some sense, if not of crisis, then at least of *decay* in the subject of economics before the publication of Jevons's *Theory of Political Economy* (1871). Another of Kuhn's characteristics of paradigm change is present during this era: that the solutions had all been at least partially anticipated (by Senior, W. F. Lloyd, and M. Longfield). In addition there really does seem to have been a major communication problem between the old and new schools during this era, as Cairnes's total incomprehension of Jevons's work on value makes very clear (Cairnes, 1888, p. iv). Moreover, the Continental dimension to the Marginal Revolution, which has made Kuhn seem less applicable to events after 1870 in the view of some writers, on the grounds that there was no crisis in Continental European economics, is of no importance, because we are talking about the British scientific community in this context.

So Kuhn's apparatus is not valueless; and, by getting rid of Popper's concept of a crucial experiment,[9] Kuhn does offer a philosophy of the history of science which has distinctly more applicability to economics than has Popper's. Nevertheless, Kuhn's apparatus seems to throw little light on some of the most interesting developments, especially those in the early years of the nineteenth century, and boldly transplanting it from the natural sciences seems, to put it mildly, a little premature.

Lakatosian Research Programs

The late Imre Lakatos offered another view of the history of science which has also attracted attention from economists.[10] Here we have the

vital concept of *scientific research programs* (SRPs), which comprise whole sets of related theories, in place of Popper's theories or Kuhn's paradigms.[11] SRPs are always appraised in competition with each other (so that one may replace another without a "crisis") and are of two forms—*progressive* and *degenerating*. Into which box a particular program fits is a matter of judgment for the community of scientists at any particular point in time; and this judgment will dictate which program attracts adherence from scientists.

A program consists of a hard core, a negative heuristic, a positive heuristic, and a belt of auxiliary hypotheses. The hard core is the basic, unchallengeable (and unprovable) set of assumptions, metaphysical in nature, which are at the center of the research program. The negative heuristic protects the hard core from disproof by suggesting how auxiliary hypotheses may be changed to protect the hard core from potentially damaging experimental results. The positive heuristic indicates a plan of procedure for testing and improving the explanatory power of the SRP; and from following this positive heuristic we develop a number of subsidiary theories.

An SRP is progressive if it predicts novel facts and if some of these are confirmed by experimental work. [Note the return to verification in contrast to the Popperian falsification: though Lakatos makes little of this, several commentators have noted the role of verification both as strengthening the defenses of the hard core and as incorporating the fact, which the Popperian approach neglects, that highly corroborated theories have an important role in the applications of science (Maxwell, 1972, p. 141; Remenyi, 1979, p. 38)]. An SRP is degenerating if it fails to predict novel facts, if the facts it does predict are not confirmed, and if further novel facts have to be accommodated into the theory by ad hoc stratagems.

In all this the concept of a "novel fact" is rather critical, and it has passed through several stages of development in Lakatos's work. The version of this concept proposed by Zahar did however seem to meet with Lakatos's approval.[12] Zahar (1973, p. 103) offers the following concept: "A fact will be considered novel with respect to a given hypothesis if it did not belong to the problem-situation which governed the construction of the hypothesis." Facts which were known, then, before the construction of an hypothesis and which were not involved in its formulation, *but which are explained by it,* then come into the category of novel facts.

Lakatos explicitly thought of his apparatus as applicable to social science, and indeed he was instrumental in the convening of a conference at Nafplion in order to test its usefulness in explaining the history of

economics. Moreover, he gives social science examples in his discussions (although he was highly—and explicitly—skeptical about the scientific pretentions of psychology and sociology[13]). Marxism, for instance is viewed by Lakatos as the classic case of a degenerating SRP on the grounds that (1) it has failed to predict any new facts since 1917, (2) the facts it has predicted have not been confirmed, and (3) it has had to adopt a series of ad hoc stratagems to accommodate uncomfortable new facts as they have appeared.

What happens when we apply the Lakatosian vision to Smith's grand progress? There does seem little doubt that, interpreted generously, it provides vastly more illumination than the Popperian or Kuhnian approaches. Let us initially adopt a generous stance. Then, in terms of this apparatus, we can interpret the initial success of the SRP of *The Wealth of Nations,* the challenge from the Ricardian SRP, which was at first apparently successful, the continuation over a fairly lengthy period of the Malthusian SRP, and the final phase of the Smithian SRP as a degenerating one in the hands of Nicholson et al.

The Smithian hard core contained the concept of self-interest pursuit on the basis of individual knowledge, this being superior to governmental knowledge, leading to a relative optimum in a context of growth, through the operation of the division of labor and technical advance combined with capital accumulation. The positive heuristic indicated that free trade should be adopted and that regulations interfering with the liberty to pursue economic activity should be removed. Subsequent observation of what happened to the economy under this sort of regime, as well as the study of economic history to see how other regimes had fared, were also indicated. Economic growth resulted from the progressive adoption of the Smithian prescriptions, and trade increased welfare. However, the program was a little vague in its predictions about the effects on growth and income distribution of restrictions on the imports of basic foodstuffs; and with a rising price of corn, the Ricardian SRP, sharing much of the same hard core but with changes in that hard core on the score of the harmony of individual and social interests, then came into competition with the Smithian one. Class conflict was not part of the Smithian hard core, so there does seem to have been a hard-core change, which is necessary for a change in approach to qualify as a new SRP rather than simply as a *problem shift.* Class conflict was certainly not a "novel fact" in the latest (Zahar's) sense because it was intimately involved in the formation of the theory; and this degree of involvement suggests that a hard-core change had taken place.

The associated positive heuristic then indicated that the Corn Laws should be repealed and that the consequent avoidance of the stationary

state should then be observed. It also predicted (though again this was not truly "novel" in Zahar's sense because it was intimately bound up with the theory's construction) that stagnation would ensue if the Corn Laws were not repealed. When this prediction failed the SRP moved into its degenerating phase and ad hoc strategems were employed, notably by J. S. Mill, in whose *Principles* (1848) the Ricardian predictions became "tendencies" which might or might not be observed depending upon the strength of (nonobservable) countervailing tendencies.

During roughly the same period as the ascendancy of the Ricardian SRP the Malthusian one, derived very directly from Adam Smith, was also in operation, though it had of course a very narrow base of acceptance. The hard core contained a number of the same elements as Smith's, but it also contained (and gave very special weight to) a number of elements which were either not present in Smith's hard core or which were unimportant there. These included fundamental propositions about sexual proclivities and possible agricultural progress, as well as propositions about property distribution. The positive heuristic indicated that population and birth, marriage, and death rates should be studied both at home and in other countries, and that measures (such as denial of poor relief) should be taken to deal with growth of population. Malthus also attacked the problem of corn prices and rising rents. But his population predictions were not confirmed; and his rent theory, tacked on as an auxiliary hypothesis to a hard core very similar to Smith's—in contrast to Ricardo's rent theory, which was an integral part of the entire system—meant that Malthus's SRP failed to attract support or to gain the judgment that it was progressive. This argument seems plausible when one compares Malthus's two essays on the corn question (1814, 1815) and also the publications by McCulloch which were in part based on them (1816a,b) with Ricardo's *Essay on Profits* (1815)—and indeed one can see clearly how McCulloch, as an emergent member of the community of economists at that time, switched his allegiance from the Malthusian to the Ricardian SRP,[14] in turn abandoning that for a return to the Smithian one. Yet we have to be honest in pursuing this line of argument and concede that Malthus offered important predictions about deflation and the burden of the national debt which were, to a considerable extent, borne out by events; and still this success did not save his program.

Once the Smithian SRP was reestablished as the ascendant one, it developed new life; and the concept of the savings function and the nature of the interest reward were developed from Smith's rather than Ricardo's hints by Senior, Rae, and J. S. Mill. Finally, in the era of the Marginal Revolution, more and more economists, especially the younger

ones, came to see the Smithian SRP as a degenerating one. It no longer predicted novel facts, and as some countries moved away from free trade in the last part of the nineteenth century it was necessary to adopt ad hoc stratagems to explain why this did not harm them. Similarly, it was necessary to adopt ad hoc devices to explain a degree of concerted action in the form of cartels (replacing competition) in Germany which went far beyond what was considered part of the Smithian SRP (see Clapham, 1923, pp. 309–22).

The Lakatosian apparatus is also helpful in the understanding of the classical economists' collection and use of statistics. For it has been argued in defence of the classical economists against the charge of ignoring the statistical evidence that:

> it was Ricardo's and Mill's greater concern with 'understanding' (explanation *ex post*) than with predictive accuracy that made them unwilling to abandon their propositions in the face of contrary facts (De Marchi, 1970, p. 275).

This has a rather Lakatosian ring. It implies that these writers were clinging to a degenerating SRP because they believed it was *theoretically* progressive even though it was clearly not empirically progressive. [On the ambiguities involved in the distinction between theoretically and empirically progressive SRPs, see Quinn (1972).] The Lakatosian flavor is reinforced by the same author's quotation from Cairnes, which is redolent of Lakatos's emphasis upon novel facts; Cairnes (1874, p. 20) refers to

> the only test by which a theory is justified, namely, by explaining facts, and, if it be a new theory, by explaining facts not explicable, or not so simply explicable, by received theories.

Yet it all fits *too* well; and there are some disquieting questions left. For one thing there are basic ambiguities about what constitutes the hard core and what constitutes the auxiliary hypotheses, so that Blaug is able to argue, in a brilliant paper (1976, pp. 164–5) that the same hard core was common to the Smithian, Ricardian, and Marginalist developments and that each of these simply involved a progressive problem shift within a given SRP. In contrast, it was argued above that there were separate SRPs involved for the earlier part of the period; and for the later part it seems equally permissible to argue that there was a hard-core change because the maximizing individual of the Smithian hard core, one who is always in search of *new* opportunities, is replaced by the individual who accepts a permanently fixed range of opportunities. But obviously Blaug's interpretation is entirely defensible. There is then considerable

ambiguity in the Lakatosian concepts; and one is left wondering whether the ability of Lakatos's system to internalize so much of intellectual history (which was Lakatos's criterion for a good theory of the history of science) is due to such ambiguities. As Blaug himself remarks, in noting his disagreement with S. Latsis, "two Lakatosians need not agree on how to apply MSRP [the Methodology of SRPs] to a particular case in question" (1976, p. 167, n.62).

There are other disquieting features too. The Marginal Revolution did not really involve the prediction of any novel facts at all—it was hardly a novel idea that demand curves sloped downward. The interaction of demand and supply to determine price was to be found in several classical SRPs—Malthus's in particular. Indeed the whole idea of "novel facts" becomes a little strained when applied to economics; the predictions of the research programs were, with the exception of Ricardo, a good deal too vague and unspecific.

When we look at what happened to the Smithian research program in the Marginal Revolution another ambiguity of the Lakatosian approach manifests itself. We can see what is involved if we consider the Venn diagrams shown in Figures 1 and 2.

Figure 1.

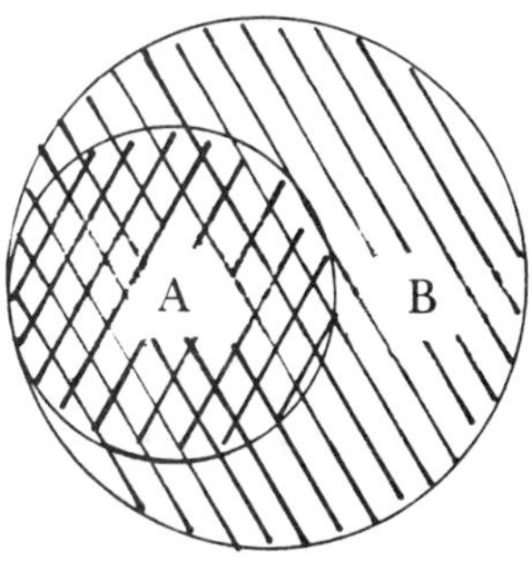

Figure 2.

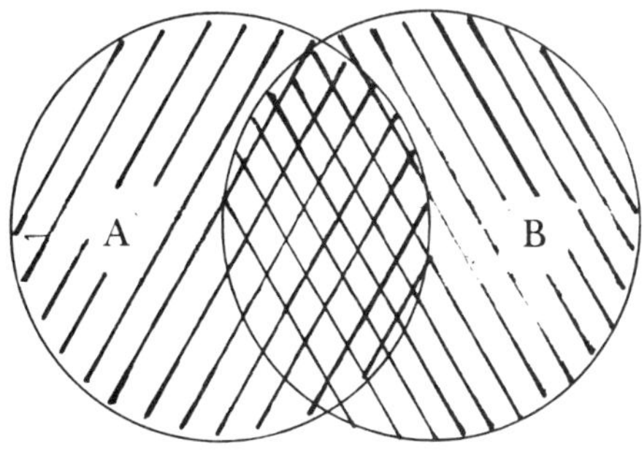

Figure 1 is Popperian. Scientific advance proceeds by accretion. The area of scientific knowledge is continually increasing through the trial (of hypotheses) and error discovery (through falsification) process. Thus it is true that for Popper $A \subset B$, where set B is the set of scientific knowledge after some progress in the trial-and-error process and set A is the set of scientific knowledge before that progress has taken place. For instance, in Popper's view, Newton's results become a special case of Einstein's more general ones.

Figure 2 is Kuhnian. We have only those elements in $A \cap B$ which are

common between paradigms. The elements in A ∩ B are the anomalies which the new paradigm, referring to the range of scientific questions in set B, is able to solve but which the old paradigm, referring to the set of scientific questions in set A, was unable to solve.

Now the difficulty with Lakatos is to know which of these Venn diagrams applies to him. One of his critics[15] has claimed that for a research program to be progressive, not a single old anomaly need be explained. If this is so, the change of focus of economics which occurred with the decline of the Smithian SRP in the last part of the nineteenth century is within Lakatos's system; and, additionally, the fact that the failure of the Smithian SRP to explain economic developments in Germany was not remedied by the arrival of Marginalism, which had the same regard for competition, need not bother us. But Lakatos himself seems to be unclear on this matter, and this is disturbing because we have a real ambiguity on an important aspect of the whole schema.

There are other difficulties which suggest themselves. The standards of judgment used by economists in appraising a research program can only be defined ex post; and hence a progressive SRP can only be distinguished from a degenerating one ex post. One man's degenerating SRP is another man's progressive SRP, as the continued existence of Marxist economists should remind us. There is indeed a danger that the system can be used to explain everything and that the circumstances are not conceivable in which it could be proved wrong. This is precisely the (valid) objection made by both Popper and Lakatos to Freudianism and Marxism.[16] This danger is all the more real because of the lack of a time dimension in Lakatos and because of Lakatos's insistence that we should use a history of science which internalizes most of what has occurred—the more successful this is, the more difficult it becomes to envisage a set of facts it would not fit.

At this point perhaps we should note that Lakatos's distinction between "internal" and "external" history is not, as Kuhn (1971, pp. 140–1) has pointed out, the standard usage. Lakatos's use of "internal" to mean "rational within the Lakatosian history of science approach" differs from the standard use which refers merely to the professional activities of scientists. But there is no reason why Lakatos's terminology should not be used.

However, we do run into difficulties in seeking to "internalize" everything in his sense. For, if the search for internalization over the whole period of a subject's history is completely successful, it becomes so difficult to conceive of circumstances which would not fit the schema employed that the schema itself no longer contains anything of interest. Thus, if we ask the Popperian "ought" questions about Lakatos's "is," we

are bound to come up with some disquieting answers. (They are, as we shall see, however, much less disquieting than the answers we get when we ask the same questions of the "dialectical" approach.)

There are also, however, problems of an opposite kind from internalizing everything in a limited period of a subject's history; and these questions come into particular prominence when we consider an extension of Lakatos's system by Remenyi (1979). The essence of his position is that the protective belt is made up of the separate specialities within a subject and that each speciality has *its own* core, which he calls a *demi-core*. The discussion does valuable service in attempting to list the contents of the hard-core, positive heuristic and negative heuristic in SRPs in economics; and it also demonstrates the problems associated with developing the Lakatosian concepts along Remenyi's lines so as to internalize all *twentieth century* developments in economics. For Remenyi's concept of hard-core–demi-core interaction fits the present state of economics, particularly since World War II, relatively well, especially the profusion of applications of microeconomics stemming in part from the energy and intellectual vitality of the Chicago participants. But it does not fit the nineteenth century history of the subject at all; and in Remenyi's work, in contrast to Lakatos's own contribution, internalization has meant adapting the details of the historical approach to one era so closely that there is a complete loss of generality.

There is also a very real difficulty in applying Lakatos's apparatus when we take into account monetary and trade theory in discussing classical economics. For a great chunk of the Ricardian SRP, in the form of the theory of comparative costs, survived and prospered even when the rest of the program had foundered; and, in an age when the British prided themselves on their superiority over the rest of the world in just about every matter,[17] the prediction of the theory of comparative costs that, in such a situation of superiority, trade would still be beneficial was not irrelevant. Similarly the monetary theory which was taken over by Ricardo prospered after the demise of his program. However, this last is less serious because the theory did not originate with Ricardo but with Hume and the Bullionists like H. Thornton, and it was perfectly compatible with *The Wealth of Nations*.

A further difficulty arises when we consider the overall perspective of the history of science which is produced by Lakatos's methods. Lakatos uses "rational reconstruction." This means in effect, as his critics have pointed out (Kuhn, 1971, pp. 140–3; McMullin, 1970, pp. 31–4), that his treatment of historical facts tends to be a little cavalier, for the facts are interpreted in a way which makes them consistent with the dominance of whichever SRP happens, at the moment of writing, to be lead-

ing. But this is not a new observation; it is a criticism of the history of science in general as being "paradigm-dominated," made by Kuhn in his first edition (1962, pp. 1–2). Nor is it necessarily a very serious matter, because the inevitability of this process enables us to understand why it is that historians of economics rewrite the history of economics in the light of developments in their own subject. Rather, the Lakatosian perception of the importance of competition between SRPs carries with it a warning that the perspective from which the history of a subject is viewed changes over time.

A little nit-picking is probably in order then. But Lakatos's apparatus does seem to help us to understand what happened to Smith's economic program and, the difficulty over novel facts after 1870 notwithstanding, to provide some insight into its rise, its temporary eclipse, its resurgence, and its decline.

Dialectical Interpretations

Dissatisfaction with attempts to transfer Kuhn's work into a social science context has led some writers to look instead to a dialectical interpretation of the development of economics. The difficulties with Kuhn which apparently prompt this include doubts about the strength of his approach even on its home ground, particularly the difficulty of isolating the paradigm concept, the different terrain of the social sciences, and—perhaps above all—the fact that Kuhn developed his ideas in relation to natural science, which deals with an unchanging physical universe, whereas economic theories and concepts relate to relationships within a specific set of institutions that are evolving historically (Kunin and Weaver, 1971, pp. 391–5).

The Hegelian dialectic is regarded as more suitable than the Marxian one. Although the reason for choice is not discussed, it may well be because the Marxian dialectic envisages total changes as the feudal state is replaced by bourgeois capitalism, which is to be replaced in turn by the dictatorship of the proletariat, to be succeeded by the classless society. These are all complete changes, indeed more complete than Kuhn's paradigm changes. They would require a *new* scientific community to "operate" the new science, whereas Kuhn, although he envisages difficulty in the older members of the scientific community transferring their allegiance to a new paradigm, does not push such difficulties beyond reasonable bounds and certainly does not envisage some kind of scientific Gulag for the luminaries of the old regime. The vaguer form of Hegelian dialectic, in which elements of the previous thesis and antithesis appear in the synthesis, is regarded as more suitable; but, as we shall see, this involves rather serious difficulties of its own.

The inbuilt implicit values of the dialectical view naturally result in a rejection of Kuhn's "pure relativism" (Kunin and Weaver, 1971, p. 396) and the adoption of the teleology of the dialectic with each succeeding stage superior to its predecessor, having been born out of the internal contradictions of the latter. Advocates of the dialectical approach to the history of economics seem to shrink from saying this explicitly, and this may be connected with the reluctance of both Marxists and Hegelians to apply their own brand of relativism to their own ideas, as Popper has noted (1963, p. 334); but the implication seems to be there.

The idea of applying evolutionary forms to the history of ideas is not confined to those who wish to draw upon the works of Hegel and his successors. There is also a Darwinian version (Cohen, 1973). But this does not seem so far to have been applied to economics.

The nineteenth century emergence of the historical school of economics provides, for would-be dialecticists, a possible antithesis to classical economics or even the emergent neoclassical economics. This is quite an important point because it is only in recent years that the significance of this historicist movement has received full recognition (Coats, 1954; Koot, 1975, 1980). With the evolution of social conditions and, in particular, the development of urbanization, the historical school emphasized the importance of relating economic ideas to time and place. Indeed, this was the basis of Archdeacon Cunningham's Inaugural Lecture, as well as of his unfair and misconceived attack on Marshall (see Cunningham, 1892a,b). The growth of interest in labor economics, especially trade unions and strikes, afforded a considerable opportunity for the historicists. The same was true of the poverty studies to some extent (Jha, 1973). The historicists were even able to claim a common origin with the mainstream—Cliffe Leslie in particular claimed Smithian ancestry—and thus historicism can be represented as an antithesis to the classical thesis deriving from the same source.

The new recognition of the importance of the historical school helps to place in context Marshall's anxiety to secure the election of A. C. Pigou as his successor. The relationship of this episode to the tariff reform campaign has been noted (Coats, 1968, pp. 227–8) but the issue was wider than this. As Koot (1980, p. 176) has pointed out: "the writings of the English historical school can be characterised as neomercantilist." The same author has pointed out that Foxwell, the chief rival to Pigou for the Chair, was a historicist (p. 175 and ref.). So, as Coase (1972, p. 477) has put it, "The fact is that Marshall's conception of economics and his views on economic teaching were very different from those of Foxwell."

There is then no reasonable doubt that historicism became quite a significant force in the latter part of the nineteenth century so far as English economics is concerned. But it is a long step from this to accepting that it played the role of an antithesis in some kind of Hegelian dialectic. For instead of a synthesis being achieved in which the classical and historical elements were blended—something which indeed Alfred Marshall might have welcomed—economics moved in a more analytical and abstract direction, in the *opposite* direction from the antithesis, with the advent of the Marginal Revolution. Moreover, whatever his sympathies for elements in the historical school's approach, Marshall in 1908, when the chips were down, so to speak, put his weight firmly behind the abstract, analytical Pigou, and opposed the historical school's candidate, Foxwell. Had a synthesis of classical and historical economics emerged, as it would have done if this dialectical approach were correct—something which might have been expected with the growth of urbanization giving new prominence to the forces previously stressed by the historicists—then the dialectical approach would have been on strong ground. But, as the situation is, we are forced to identify not historicism but marginal utility, ex post, as an antithesis; and we have to give it this role despite the fact that as marginal utility was gaining acceptance historicism continued to be a strong force and even grew in strength.

The difficulties which this approach encounters in dealing with post-1870 economics can be seen very well in a paper by Bronfenbrenner (1971). The discussion identifies post-1870 economics with Alfred Marshall, whose work is seen as a synthesis of Ricardian cost theory (which is wrong, because Marshall adopted marginal productivity partly under the influence of F. A. Walker) with marginal utility theory (which is again wrong, because Marshall only tacked marginal utility on to a preexisting demand curve). Then, by misrepresenting Marshallian competition as perfect, it is possible to represent Imperfect Competition theory as an antithesis (Bronfenbrenner, 1971, pp. 144–6). This really produces an account of the history of economics which is very difficult to recognize, not least because Marshall certainly did not mean "perfect competition" when he wrote of competition. It is noteworthy too that Walras and Pareto are not mentioned in the discussion, perhaps because their work did *not* emerge in a form which would permit it to be represented as some kind of synthesis of Ricardo and marginal utility. Other attempts to apply this analysis to the Marginal Revolution also encounter significant difficulties. For instance Kunin and Weaver (1971, pp. 395–6) believe that precursors are ignored because the economic universe has not evolved to the point where their ideas are relevant to what becomes a pressing social problem. Apart from the fact that this offers

no advance upon Kuhn, who also envisages precursors of a new paradigm that are unrecognized (in natural science dealing with an unchanging universe), one is forced to ask in what way did marginal utility suddenly become "socially relevant" in the 1870s?

Other episodes in the history of economics fail even more badly to provide a "dialectical" pattern of evolution. Thus Bronfenbrenner (1971, pp. 141–2) interprets the emergence of classical economics as the synthesis between the mercantilist thesis, i.e., that interests of the merchant class should be fostered, and the Physiocratic thesis, i.e., that the interests of the agricultural class should be fostered—a synthesis in which the classical school argued that the interest of *no* class should be specially fostered. This interpretation depends however upon the *prior* imposition of the Marxian notion that economics is about class interests. It is, in other words, an exercise in petitio principii. In no other way could classical economics be seen as a synthesis of mercantilism and Physiocracy.

If we pay attention to the *analytical* issues involved, the replacement of mercantilism by classicism in England (for Physiocracy never gained the assent of the *British* "scientific community") was a paradigm switch in Kuhn's sense, with a view of the world seen through balance-of-payments spectacles being replaced by a view of the world seen through economic-growth-through-decentralized-decision-taking spectacles—a Gestalt switch, in fact. Moreover, the prior anticipation which Kuhn requires existed in the work of D. North and others. The change is also capable of being interpreted in Lakatosian terms, with a switch from a degenerating SRP (mercantilism, which had been forced into a series of ad hoc expedients, as exemplified in Mun's *England's Treasure,* to cope with the evident wealth-creating effects of exporting treasure) to a progressive SRP which offered new predictions about the benefit to economic growth from free, individual, decentralized decision making, some of these predictions being verified by the upsurge in economic growth in the last quarter of the eighteenth century. We have then an historical experience which will bear either Kuhnian or Lakatosian interpretations, but not a dialectical one.

When we enter the classical era Bronfenbrenner finds it necessary to identify the utility economists as a separate school offering an antithesis to classical economics. Yet, in fact, the subjective value theorists—Senior, Longfield, and Say, in particular, whom he mentions—were clearly adherents of the classical school and only differed slightly from it. Indeed, Say (the author of Say's Law which was central to classical economics) was regarded primarily as the French interpreter of Adam Smith.

Similarly Bronfenbrenner has some difficulty in depicting Keynesian-

ism as an antithesis to neoclassical economics, for it is of course an antithesis to Say's Law as ordinarily understood.

Given the imprecisions undoubtedly present in the work of Kuhn and Lakatos, it is hardly surprising that the dialectical approach also suffers from imprecision. At one point we find a list of "antitheses" to classical economics as follows: (i) objections to free trade; (ii) objections to Ricardo's class conflict view; (iii) objections to the idea of harmony of interest of capitalist and worker in a large wage fund; (iv) objections to neglect of demand; (v) objections to the Ricardian level of abstraction; and (vi) objections to hedonist psychology (Bronfenbrenner, 1971, pp. 142–4). Later on, however, (pp. 145–6), entire programs such as Marxism and historicism are apparently regarded as antitheses. Without more precision about the meaning of both thesis and antithesis—single idea or entire program—the vagueness of this dialectical interpretation deprives it of any usefulness. It would seem that we have here a concept which is even at one point (p. 140) capable of including under one umbrella both Imperfect Competition theory and Cambridge neo-Marxism.

There are, of course, also serious problems with the concept of dialectic itself. Popper has reasonably objected to the idea that the thesis *produces* its antithesis. Moreover, as he points out, the only force which propels the dialectic development is our determination not to accept contradiction (Popper, 1963, pp. 315–7). Popper illustrates clearly the way in which the concept can be imposed on historical—even other—facts (p. 323):

> It is only too easy to force a dialectic interpretation on all sorts of developments and even on quite different things. We find, for instance, a dialectic interpretation which identifies a seed of corn with a thesis, the plant which develops from this seed with the antithesis, and all seeds which develop from this plant with the synthesis. That such an application expands the already too vague meaning of the dialectic triad in a way which dangerously increases its vagueness is obvious; it leads to a point where by describing a development as dialectic we convey no more than by saying it is a development in stages—which is not saying very much.

However, Popper also shows that Hegel's use of dialectics was very special—and very specially untenable—so that the difficulties encountered in using a Marxian dialectic are not avoided by resorting to a Hegelian one instead. In particular there is the identification of events with some kind of inner logic—the attempt to establish, indeed, dialectics as a form of logic itself. Such a view involves, as Popper points out, discarding a fundamental law of logic as normally understood, the Law of Contradiction, which may be briefly summarized as the idea that a proposition and its opposite cannot both be true.

But the fundamental problem with the use of Hegelianism in the context of the history of ideas is well delineated by Popper (1963, p. 333):

> Hegel was one of the inventors of the historical method, a founder of the school of thinkers who believed that in describing a development historically one has causally explained it.

This surely is the *fundamental* problem with the dialectical analysis of the history of economic thought. For Popper, Kuhn, and Lakatos do all, in their different ways, succeed in providing some *explanation* of scientific progress. For Popper it is a process of trial and error, hypothesis formulation and falsification, which produces developments, through a piecemeal accretion, in a body of ideas. For Kuhn it is the accumulation of anomalies, in the course of normal-science activities, which eventually generates a crisis and a scientific revolution. For Lakatos it is the competition between SRPs which leads to a choice of the SRP judged most progressive (or conceivably, at least in economics, least degenerating). But in saying that economic thought progresses dialectically one loses track of causality: the conflict between thesis and antithesis which is presumably supposed to be the causality actually says nothing about causality at all.

VI. CONCLUSION

As we saw at the beginning of the discussion, Adam Smith is, with Lord Keynes, one of the two most influential economists the world has ever known. To explain the longevity of Smith's influence and the power of his system to make a comeback when temporarily eclipsed is not easy. But of all the philosophies of the history of science which deserve to be taken seriously, that of Lakatos seems the most successful in explaining the history of Smith's unparalleled achievement.

It should be stressed however that what we are concerned with is a philosophy of the *history* of science and not with a philosophy of science.[18] Much of the literature in this area is bedeviled by the fact that these two become intermingled and even that "ought" and "is" become confused—which they should not unless we are Hegelians. Now Lakatos (1971b, p. 179) has explicitly rejected the interpretation of his work as providing a choice between methodologies; Popper, on the other hand, is primarily concerned with the criteria of best practice in science.

Yet there is a serious problem here. For it is clear that Popper's methodology has been formulated by his interpretation of the facts of the

history of science; and the implication is certainly present that scientists have actually behaved in an optimal manner—which indeed accords with his piecemeal progression approach. But this is in the last resort a metaphysical proposition, like that of belief in regularity in the universe. Where Kuhn parts company with him is precisely over this: he refuses to accept Popper's teleology.[19]

It would still be open to us to argue that it would be optimal if economists had behaved in a Popperian way but that, as a matter of the history of the subject, it was true that economics has developed suboptimally. This would certainly be a defensible proposition. It is important to bear in mind that much of the literature in both the history and philosophy of science, relating to the *natural* sciences, takes the view that natural science has delivered the goods and that we must try to "internalize" its progress in any explanation of its history both so that we may lay down certain canons of good methodology and because we may in that way obtain a satisfactory philosophy of the history of science. But suppose one took the view that economics has *not* delivered the goods? Then the history of economics becomes a history of error—a view shared by Marxists (for whom absolute truth was revealed between 1868 and 1894) and by the more uncritical of the positive and Samuelsonian economists (some of whom seem to believe that "valid" economics started sometime between 1936 and 1953). In this paper we have not taken the view that the history of economics is a catalog of errors, and thus it has made sense to explore the contributions which the writings of Popper, Kuhn, and Lakatos can make to an understanding of the history of economics.

One final point should be made. Whatever may be the position in the natural sciences, it is undoubtedly the case that there is no uniformity of method in economics. A recent excellent book on methodology distinguishes "Apriorism," the "Analytical School," "Positive Economics," and "Moderate Empiricism" (Stewart, 1979, pp. 118–28). It would be difficult to maintain that any of these approaches has contributed *nothing* to what progress there has been in economics; and it then follows that any one approach to the history of the subject is likely to be less than completely satisfactory, even though both the Kuhnian and Lakatosian approaches are able to handle methodological diversity by classifying the methodologies themselves as paradigms or SRPs.

ACKNOWLEDGMENT

This paper represents a revised and lengthened version of one which appeared in the *Scottish Journal of Political Economy* 23:133–151 (1976).

NOTES

1. Cf. Samuels (1966) and Hirsch (1975).

2. Cf. Thomson (1965, p. 233). See also Smith's own remarkable venture into the history of science (1795), especially the deeply impressive essay on the "History of Astronomy" (*ibid.*, pp. 2–93).

3. See Smith (1776, Book I, p. 109). The myth of a lack of discussion of profits in classical economics has been promoted in particular by those who see Surplus Value as the first (and usually the only) theory of profit. On Tooke and McCulloch, see O'Brien (1970, p. 310; 1975, p. 119).

4. See Smith (1776, Book I, pp. 57–65) and Bowley (1972, pp. 12–13).

5. See Myint (1977) and Bloomfield (1978).

6. In the late 1950s a lecturer in the University of London, committed to giving a course of lectures on applied economics, was told by his professor that whatever applied economics was, it was *not* the application of economic theory. Similarly, the late Professor Ely Devons asked in his *Essays in Economics* (1961), "Applied Economics—The Application of What?" We certainly find a serious gap between "theory" and applied economics as late as the 1950s.

7. The relativism of Kuhn's early work is most marked in Chapter IX of the second edition (1970). See also Kuhn in Lakatos and Musgrave (1970, pp. 11–12). For a distinct retreat on this matter see, however, *ibid.*, p. 264. For a defense of Kuhn on this score see Meiland (1974). Kuhn's relativism is strongly criticized in Shapere (1971).

8. For a discussion of the retreat made by Kuhn from the position advanced in the first edition of his book, see Musgrave (1971) and Shapere (1971).

9. Lakatos has also rejected the Popperian concept of a crucial experiment (see Lakatos and Musgrave, 1970, pp. 120, 154–9; Lakatos, 1973/4). Lakatos's argument is that "crucial experiments" can only be identified ex post, after a long period, when the direction which the science has taken has finally become clear.

10. See in particular the outstanding discussion by Blaug (1976). I am, like a number of others, deeply indebted to this paper for introducing Lakatos's work in the context of economics.

11. The distinction between an SRP and a paradigm is explored by Kulka (1977).

12. According to Zahar (1973, pp. 101–3), Lakatos had a concept of "novel fact" in his 1968 work (pp. 381–7) which was so narrow that it would have given Einstein no credit for explaining Mercury's perihelion because it had been recorded long before General Relativity was proposed. Then, in his 1970 contribution (pp. 155–7), Lakatos modified his opinion, in deference to the opinion of physicists, by saying that in the light of a new theory some known facts could become novel ones. But this extension was so wide as to be fatal to his program, for it permitted a well-known fact to be considered novel if it was merely reinterpreted in terms of concepts (such as mass) which had acquired new connotations.

13. For Lakatos's outspoken attitude see his 1971 paper (1971a, pp. 102, 119) and the reference in Lakatos and Musgrave (1970, p. 176) to "proliferating intellectual garbage" and to "intellectual pollution which may destroy our cultural environment."

14. This assertion is made poker-faced, so to speak, in the text, in order to make as good a case for Lakatos as possible before moving on to examine the defects in that case. However, it has to be said that McCulloch was a very eclectic writer and that even in his essay (1816a) which shows a friendly—indeed deferrential—attitude towards Malthus and which is in marked contrast to his later attitude (see O'Brien, 1970, p. 35 and note; cf. McCulloch (1816a, p. 6), where Malthus is referred to as "the great political economist"). McCulloch's solution to the problem of fixed payments in deflation, raised by Malthus, was a reduction in interest payments on the national debt, while Malthus's solution was agricultural protection. Moreover, although McCulloch's attitude remained friendly in his

second essay (1816b, pp. 133, 198–201), he drew there on a very wide range of authors indeed. But having said that, there is no doubt that the Ricardian SRP had not, at that stage, secured McCulloch's adherence. There are very few references to Ricardo and only one to the vital *essay on profits* (Ricardo, 1815).

15. This and other points are to be found in the critically penetrating essay, by Koertge (1971; the specific criticism referred to in the text is on p. 162).

16. See Popper (1963, pp. 34–5); Lakatos (1970, p. 92).

17. For a striking illustration of this, see J. S. Mill (1848, p. 105n).

18. The logic of a union between the history and philosophy of science is questioned in Giere (1973). See, however, McMullin (1970, 1974) and Burian (1977).

19. For the view that progress itself provides a demarcation criterion see Quay (1974).

REFERENCES

Bastable, C. F. *Public Finance*. London: Macmillan, 1892.

Black, R. D. Collison 'W. S. Jevons and the Foundation of Modern Economics' pp. 98–112 in Black R. D. Collison, Coats A. W., and Goodwin C. D. W., *The Marginal Revolution in Economics* Durham, N. Carolina: Duke University Press, 1973.

Black, R. D. Collison 'Jevons and Cairnes' *Economica* 27 (1960) pp. 214–232.

Black, R. D. Collison 'Jevons, Marginalism and Manchester' *Manchester School* 40 (1972) pp. 2–8.

Blaug, M. 'Was There a Marginal Revolution?' pp. 3–14 in Black R. D. Collison, Coats A. W., and Goodwin C. D. W. *The Margin Revolution in Economics* Durham, N. Carolina: Duke Univ. Press, 1973.

Blaug, M. *Ricardian Economics*. New Haven: Yale University Press, 1958.

Blaug, M. 'Kuhn versus Lakatos or Paradigms versus Research Programmes in the History of Economics' in S. Latsis (ed.) *Method and Appraisal in Economics*. Cambridge: C.U.P. 1976.

Bloomfield, A. 'The Impact of Growth and Technology on Trade in Nineteenth-century British Thought' *History of Political Economy* 10 pp. 608–635, 1978.

Bowley, M. 'The Predecessors of Jevons—the Revolution that Wasn't' *Manchester School* 40 pp. 9–29, 1972.

Bronfenbrenner, M. E. 'The "Structure of Revolutions" in Economic Thought' *History of Political Economy* 3 pp. 136–151, 1971.

Burian, R. M. 'More than a Marriage of Convenience: on the Inextricability of History and Philosophy of Science' *Philosophy of Science* 44 pp. 1–42, 1977.

Cairnes, J. E. *Some Leading Principles of Political Economy Newly Expounded*. London: Macmillan, 1874.

Cairnes, J. E. *The Character and Logical Method of Political Economy*. 2nd ed. reprinted New York: Kelley, 1965, 1888.

Clapham, Sir J. *The Economic Development of France and Germany*. Cambridge: C.U.P., 1923.

Coase, R. H. 'The Appointment of Pigou as Marshall's Successor' *Journal of Law and Economics* 15 (1972) pp. 473–85.

Coats, A. W. 'The Historist Reaction in English Political Economy' *Economica* 21 pp. 143–153, 1954.

Coats, A. W. 'The Role of Authority in the Development of British Economics' *Journal of Law and Economics* 7 (1964) pp. 85–106.

Coats, A. W. 'Sociological Aspects of British Economic Thought (CA. 1880–1930)' *Journal of Political Economy* 75 (1967) pp. 706–729.

Coats, A. W. 'Political Economy and the Tariff Reform Campaign of 1903' *Journal of Law and Economics* 11 (1968) pp. 181–229.

Coats, A. W. 'Is There a 'Structure of Scientific Revolutions' in Economics?' *Kyklos* 22 pp. 289–95, 1969.

Cohen, L. J. 'Is the Progress of Science Evolutionary' *British Journal for the Philosophy of Science* 24 (1973) pp. 41–61.

Cunningham, W. 'The Relativity of Economic Doctrine' Inaugural Lecture, delivered by the Tooke Professor, King's College, London *Economic Journal* 2 (1891a) pp. 1–16.

Cunningham, W. "The Perversion of Economic History' *Economic Journal* 2 (1891b) pp. 491–506.

De Marchi, N. B. 'The Empirical Content and Longevity of Ricardian Economics' *Economica* 37 (1970) pp. 257–275.

Devons, E. 'Applied Economics—The Application of What' in his *Essays in Economics*. London: Allen & Unwin, 1961.

Gårdlund, T. *The Life of Knut Wicksell*. trans. N. Adler Stockholm: Almqvist and Wiksell, 1958.

Giere, R. 'History and Philosophy of Science: Intimate Relationship or Marriage of Convenience' *British Journal for the Philosophy of Science* 24 (1973) pp. 282–297.

Hall, R. J. 'Can we use the History of Science to decide between Competing Methodologies' *Boston Studies* VIII pp. 151–159, 1971.

Hirsch, F. 'The Bagehot Problem' *Warwick Economic Research Papers*. No. 65, 1975.

Howey, R. S. *The Rise of the Marginal Utility School, 1870–1889* Lawrence: Univ. of Kansas Press, 1960.

Hutchison, T. W. *A Review of Economic Doctrines 1870–1929*. Oxford: Clarendon, 1953.

Jevons, W. S. *The Theory of Political Economy*. ed. R. D. C. Black London: Penguin, 1970, 1871.

Jha, N. *The Age of Marshall: Aspects of British Economic Thought*. 2nd ed. London: Cass, 1973.

Koertge, N. 'Inter-Theoretic Criticism and the Growth of Science' pp. 160–73 in R. C. Buck and R. S. Cohen (eds.) *Boston Studies in the Philosophy of Science* VIII Dordrecht: Reidel, 1971.

Koot, G. M. 'T. E. Cliffe Leslie, Irish Social Reform, and the Origins of the English Historical School of Economics' *History of Political Economy* 7 pp. 312–336, 1975.

Koot, G. M. 'English Historical Economics and the Emergence of Economic History in England' *History of Political Economy* 12 pp. 174–205, 1980.

Kuhn, T. S. *The Structure of Scientific Revolutions* 2nd ed. Chicago: Univ. of Chicago Press, 1970, 1962.

Kuhn, T. S. 'Notes on Lakatos' *Boston Studies* VIII pp. 137–146, 1971.

Kulka, T. 'Some Problems Concerning Rational Reconstruction: Comments on Elkana and Lakatos' *British Journal for the Philosophy of Science* 28 (1977) pp. 325–344.

Kunin, L., and Weaver, F. S. 'On the Structure of Scientific Revolutions in Economics' *History of Political Economy* 3 pp. 391–97, 1971.

Lakatos, I. 'Changes in the Problem of Inductive Logic' pp. 315–417 in *The Problem of Inductive Logic*. Amsterdam: North Holland, 1968.

Lakatos, I. 'History of Science and Its Rational Reconstruction' pp. 91–136 in R. C. Buck and R. S. Cohen (eds.) *Boston Studies* VIII, 1971a.

Lakatos, I. 'Replies to Critics' *Boston Studies* VIII pp. 174–182, 1971b.

Lakatos, I. 'The Role of Crucial Experiments in Science' *Studies in the History and Philosophy of Science* 4 pp. 309–325, 1973/4.

Lakatos, I and Musgrave, A. *Criticism and the Growth of Knowledge*. Cambridge: C.U.P., 1970.

McCulloch, J. R. *An Essay on a Reduction of the Interest of the National Debt, Proving that this is the only Possible Means of Relieving the Distress of the Commercial and Agricultural Interests.* London: J. Mawman, 1816a.

McCulloch, J. R. *An Essay on the Question of Reducing the Interest of the National Debt; in which the Justice and Expediency of that Measure are fully Established.* Edinburgh: D. Brown, 1816b.

McCulloch, J. R. *A Treatise on the Principles and Practical Influence of Taxation and the Funding System.* ed. D. P. O'Brien Edinburgh: Scottish Academic Press, 1975, 1845.

McMullin, E. 'The History and Philosophy of Science: A Taxonomy' pp. 12–67 in R. Stuewer, (ed.), *Historical and Philosophical Perspectives in Science* Minnesota Studies in the Philosophy of Science Vol. V Minneapolis: University of Minnesota Press, 1970.

McMullin, E. 'History and Philosophy of Science: A Marriage of Convenience' *Boston Studies* 32 pp. 585–601, 1974.

Malthus, T. R. *Observations on the Effects of the Corn Laws, and of a Rise and Fall in the Price of Corn on the Agricultural and General Wealth of the Country.* London: Murray, 1814.

Malthus, T. R. *The Grounds of an Opinion on the Policy of Restricting the Importation of Foreign Corn.* London: Murray, 1815.

Masterman, M. 'The Nature of a Paradigm', pp. 59–89, in: Lakatos and Musgrave, 1970.

Maxwell, N. 'A Critique of Popper's Views on Scientific Method' *Philosophy of Science* 39 pp. 131–152, 1972.

Meiland, J. W. 'Kuhn, Scheffler, and Objectivity in Science' *Philosophy of Science* 41 pp. 179–87, 1974.

Mill, J. S. *Principles of Political Economy with Some of their Applications to Social Philosophy* ed., W. J. Ashley, London: Longmans, 1929, 1848.

Musgrave, A. E. 'Kuhn's Second Thoughts' *British Journal for the Philosophy of Science* 22 (1971) pp. 287–297.

Myint, H. 'Adam Smith's Theory of International Trade in the Perspective of Economic Development' *Economica* 44 pp. 231–248, 1977.

Nicholson, J. S. *Elements of Political Economy.* London: A. and C. Black, 1909.

O'Brien, D. P. *J. R. McCulloch. A Study in Classical Economics.* London: Allen and Unwin, 1970.

O'Brien, D. P. *The Classical Economists.* Oxford: Clarendon, 1975.

Political Economy Club *Proceedings* Vol. VI Centenary Volume, London: Macmillan, 1921.

Popper, K. R. *The Logic of Scientific Discovery.* London: Hutchinson, 1959.

Popper, K. R. *Conjectures and Refutations. The Growth of Scientific Knowledge.* London: Routledge, 1963.

Quay, P. M. 'Progress as a Demarcation Criterion for the Sciences' *Philosophy of Science* 41 pp. 154–70, 1974.

Quinn, P. 'Methodological Appraisal and Heuristic Advice' *Studies in the History and Philosophy of Science* 3 (1972) pp. 135–149.

Remenyi, J. V. 'Core demi-core interaction: toward a general theory of disciplinary and subdisciplinary growth' *History of Political Economy* 11 pp. 30–63, 1979.

Ricardo, D. *An Essay on the Influence of a Low Price of Corn on the Profits of Stock* (London: J. Murray) reprinted in *The Works and Correspondence of David Ricardo* ed., P. Sraffa, Cambridge: C.U.P., 1951–73, Vol. IV pp. 9–41, 1815.

Samuels, W. *The Classical Theory of Economic Policy.* Cleveland, Ohio: World Publishing, 1966.

Shapere, D. 'The Paradigm Concept' *Science* 172 pp. 706–709, 1971.

Sidgwick, H. *The Principles of Political Economy.* London: Macmillan, 1887.

Smith, A. *The Theory of Moral Sentiments; or, an Essay Towards an Analysis of the Principles by which Men Naturally Judge Concerning the Conduct and Character, First of their Neighbours, and Afterwards of Themselves* New ed., London, 1853; reprinted New York: Kelley, 1966, 1759.

Smith, A. *Lectures on Justice, Police, Revenue and Arms.* ed., E. Cannan Oxford: Clarendon, 1896, 1763.

Smith, A. *An Inquiry into the Nature and Causes of the Wealth of Nations.* ed., E. Cannan London: Methuen, 1961; reprinted Chicago, 1976, 1776.

Smith, A. *Essays on Philosophical Subjects.* London: T. Cadell, 1795.

Stewart, I. M. T. *Reasoning and Method in Economics.* London: McGraw-Hill, 1979.

Thomson, H. F. 'Adam Smith's Philosophy of Science' *Quarterly Journal of Economics* 79 (1965) pp. 212–33.

Times 'Lord Keynes'; obituary 22 April 1946 reprinted in S. E. Harris (ed.) *The New Economics. Keynes' Influence on Theory and Public Policy.* London: Dobson, 1948.

Viner, J. *Studies in the Theory of International Trade.* London: Allen & Unwin; reprinted 1964, 1937.

Walker, H. M. *Studies in the History of Statistical Methods* Baltimore: Williams and Wilkins, 1929.

Winch, D. *Classical Political Economy and Colonies.* London: G. Bell, 1965.

Zahar, E. 'Why did Einstein's Programme Supersede Lorentz's?' *British Journal for the Philosophy of Science* 24 I pp. 95–123, (1973), II pp. 223–262.

4

THEORY AND EMPIRICAL OBSERVATION

DENIS P. O'BRIEN

4.1 INTRODUCTION

The interaction between theory and observation in economics is not a simple matter and it raises a number of complex issues. First, there is a persistent confusion between the 'is' and the 'ought' issues in methodology. The work of Kuhn (1970) and Lakatos (1978), which is of fundamental importance for the history and philosophy of science, has led to a persistent conflation of 'is' and 'ought' questions. The focus here will be on 'ought' questions. Second, there is in the literature of economic methodology what might be called an 'implied scientism'. Sometimes this can involve generalizations about what 'scientists' 'do' by people who themselves (unlike Kuhn and Lakatos) have neither scientific training nor much acquaintance with the literature on methodology written by scientists. But in any case the question of whether natural science, especially physics, is an appropriate model for economics is not one which should be left to emerge by implication, and the matter will be addressed explicitly below.

The focus of this discussion is upon empirical observation. To avoid misunderstanding, however, it is probably best to say at this early stage that theory *must* have primary importance. Data, as will become clear, are only of importance in the matter of *theory choice*. But theory choice is absolutely fundamental if a subject is to make progress rather than to exhibit the sort of self-contained record associated with the history of painting.

If the matter of theory choice does not arise, then the role of data will be much less pronounced. It is important to stress this because there are significant areas of economics, including such crowning achievements as the theory of international trade from Torrens (1815, 1833) and Ricardo (1817) to Meade (1952), which have very little empirical content. But they are not seriously challenged.

None the less, the role of empirical observation is, or should be, of funda-

mental importance in economics taken as a whole. It enters into theory formulation, theory application and theory choice.

4.2 THE POSSIBLE USES OF DATA

Induction?

There are standard philosophical grounds, dating from David Hume in the eighteenth century, for rejecting the idea that data can be used directly to provide us with reliable information. Simply accumulating facts and then looking vaguely for some pattern in them is not a direct source of information (although it can be a source of hypotheses). Although the observation of a particular conjunction of events may condition us *psychologically* to regard such a conjunction as stable, there is no *logical* basis for expecting the relationship to continue.

In any case, the data are not just 'there' to be modelled. We need the world of concepts and ideas in order to construct data at all. This should be apparent to any economist, for it clearly affects the form in which the official statistics, which are so often the raw material for regression analysis, are collected. Yet economists sometimes do not seem to be conscious of this. On the one hand there are those who believe that it is possible to model time series without recourse to theory at all, making reference to a 'data-generation process'; on the other, there are those who are prepared to use official figures, which have virtually no correspondence with the economic concepts, for testing hypotheses about income distribution based upon the theoretical concepts.

But Hume's general problem has particularly serious implications for economists. It is not just a philosophical fine point which may have dubious relevance in practice. Economics, far more than natural science, is vulnerable to 'parameter shift'. An observed pattern can change markedly in the course of a decade – as, for instance, recent monetary history shows.

Even more treacherous are what appear to be causal relationships apparently obtained by direct inspection of the data. While econometrics formally distinguishes between correlation and causation, econometric procedures subtly confuse the two (Black 1982).

Despite these points, there are amongst economists a number of writers who have resisted the idea that induction is impossible. This group contains writers of considerable standing including R. F. Harrod (1956). But, concluding that 'Harrod has not found the answer to Hume', A. J. Ayer wrote: 'I think that the moral to be drawn is that no theory of this logical type is going to be successful' (Ayer 1970: 37). That is the view of a philosopher; however, Hume's basic position, coupled with Popper's point that the probability of an occurrence and its information content are inversely related (Popper 1959:

270), has proved decisive for most economists – but not all. Nevertheless the reader should beware of references to 'inductive logic' which occur in the literature of economic methodology, for it is clear that there can be no such thing – at least, if induction is understood as it is here.

It is important to make this point because Popper's claim to have 'solved' the problem of induction has been widely misrepresented, particularly in the literature of economic methodology. The problem is that, if we cannot have induction, how can we have knowledge? Popper's solution is to solve not the problem of induction, which is insoluble, but the problem of knowledge by using another route – that of conjectures and refutations (Popper 1959: ch. 1). But if we proceed in this way the sources of the conjectures – our hypotheses – become vital.

The sources of hypotheses

To accept the logic of Hume's criticism of the possibility of induction as a source of knowledge is not necessarily to accept it as a criticism of data patterns as a source of hypotheses. If we take the position that virtually any source for the initial hypothesis is valid, it then follows that hunches formed by inspecting the data are a perfectly legitimate source of hypothesis.

Indeed, it is apparent that in the world of natural science 'pattern recognition' is of considerable importance. This is particularly ironic since it was also once considered important in economics, particularly in industrial economics; but, partly through a mistaken belief that Hume's criticism ruled it out, which arose in the 1960s, economists no longer consider it of any value.

In the formation of hypotheses, intuition also has a vital role. We certainly cannot rely entirely upon pattern recognition as a source of hypotheses. Imagination is of fundamental importance in the generation of hypotheses. But this role for the imagination does seem to be much more fruitful when it is associated with an intense curiosity about the real world and when it interacts with, and is constrained by, data from that world. As the great biologist François Jacob has emphasized, it is the constant interaction between imagination and experiment that produces scientific advance (Jacob 1988: 306).

But if we are to construct hypotheses we need to be able to make some assumptions concerning the world about which we are hypothesizing.

Assumptions

Since the publication of Friedman's influential essay in 1953, and particularly since the early 1960s, economists have tended to regard the realism and accuracy of assumptions as irrelevant. The basis for this is a part of Friedman's argument which has become known by Samuelson's name of the 'F-twist'

(Samuelson 1963). Essentially this amounts to the argument that because assumptions are unrealistic, but that what they neglect is of negligible importance, we can 'therefore' conclude not only that the unrealism of all assumptions is not a matter for concern but even that a theory is better the more unrealistic the assumptions.

As we shall see below, this series of *non sequiturs* derived from an initial confusion about what was meant by the unrealism of assumptions. However, it led to a form of instrumentalism – along the lines of 'we do not know why it works but it does'. While this approach seems to have a sort of engaging pragmatism, instrumentalism is, in the last resort, highly unsatisfactory if we are interested in truth. There is, as Popper has noted, a clear distinction between theories and computation rules, and the latter do not enable us to distinguish between true and false theories on their own (Popper 1974: 111–13). Moreover, we are left without resource when the computation rule breaks down. The position is thus essentially anti-rational. Indeed, to put the matter bluntly, a purely instrumentalist position would be unconcerned by the question of whether stock market prices were the results of individuals taking economic decisions or were produced by little green men from Mars, just as long as a computation rule, relating stock market prices to, for instance, changes in the rate of growth of the money supply, could be obtained.

It is perhaps ironic, since so much of this position is based upon what some economists, especially in the 1960s, believed to be the position in natural science, that the truth of the initial assumptions is not considered irrelevant in physics. Indeed, as one physicist has remarked: 'It is all too easy to derive endless strings of interesting-looking but untrue or irrelevant formulae instead of checking the validity of the initial premises' (Ziman 1978: 14).

Of course it is usual to object at this point that assumptions can never be completely accurate. But there are two points to be made here. First, assumptions are in the nature of a map which is accurate in outline while not reflecting every detail of the terrain described. While we clearly do not include every detail, we equally clearly do not want a map of Central London when we are in Northumberland. Second, it is – or should be, and is in natural science – the case that assumptions pre-package much previously learned information. The assumptions of a theory are necessarily based upon previous work by scientists which has stood up to both theoretical criticism and repeated replication. (Since the latter, as we shall see, is largely absent from economics, this may help to explain why economists have neglected this aspect of scientific procedure.)

Of course a degree of conventionalism is still required here; if we state what is in *ceteris paribus*, and regard the content of *ceteris paribus* as testable (Hutchison 1938), we get into a position of infinite regress (McCarthy 1978). But conventionalism – agreement between scientists about what it is reasonable to

accept – has the basis, at least in natural science, that what it is agreed to accept has already been through a testing time of criticism and replication. Since this is so much less true in economics – a difference of kind and not merely of degree – it follows that the conventionalism used is likely to have a much shakier base than in physics and thus it is even more necessary to look at the assumptions which an economist is making.

Of course it is true even in natural science that scientists may *appear* to be neglecting assumptions. As one writer has noted, plant taxonomy is scorned by many modern biologists who prefer to concentrate on the molecular aspects. But 'their research is inevitably parasitic on a whole body of taxonomic knowledge' (Ziman 1978: 46).

Checking the assumptions is even more vital in economics for another reason: if we make statistical inferences from a body of data 'with large and uncontrollable variances' (Ziman 1978: 170), checking the assumptions does at least give us some idea of the possible sources of these variances.

It seems so obvious that the map-like accuracy of assumptions is *not* irrelevant that it is an interesting question how economists got themselves into their present position. The answer to this has been supplied, to some extent, by the philosopher Alan Musgrave (1981), in a dissection of Friedman's original essay. He shows that in the original Friedman paper, 'negligibility', 'domain' and 'heuristic' assumptions were confused. In the first group it is simply assumed that the disregarded factors are unimportant in their effect on the phenomenon under investigation. The assumptions in the second category limit the applicability of a theory to a particular set of circumstances. Those in the third category are made in order to develop a particular line of argument. Musgrave shows that Friedman failed to distinguish between these three categories of assumption and that, by focusing on the first category, he arrived at the F-twist.

In fact, however (as in the case of Central London and Northumberland), the realism of domain assumptions is critical. As Koopmans (1957: 139) pointed out at an early stage, it is necessary that we know to what a theory can be expected to apply.

But this, interestingly enough, leads us back to the concept of 'verification' which was a central concern of economic methodologists in the years before Friedman (Blaug 1980: ch. 3; cf. Robbins 1932), for domain assumptions are critical with regard to both applicability and falsifiablity. Thus we need to verify whether the assumptions which a theory makes are actually met in a case under consideration before we can conclude that the predictions of the theory can be expected to hold. But the problem goes deeper than this, for in order for economic knowledge to have any reliability we need to know the sensitivity of the model to falsity of its assumptions. Again, we necessarily conclude that the assumptions matter.

A standard reason for rejecting testing of a theory by its conclusions is the so-called Duhem–Quine thesis that we never test a single hypothesis but always a cluster of hypotheses and that when a theory fails a test we do not know which hypothesis has been faulted. But if we pay attention to the asumptions we are making we certainly have a better chance of knowing. Moreover, if we test two competing theories, with the same background knowledge for both, we do have some basis on which to make a choice. After all it is not very surprising that it is better not to throw away evidence voluntarily – and evidence about the truth or falsity of our assumptions is still evidence.

Testing

As noted in the previous section, economists nowadays tend to pay scant attention to assumptions. The bulk of their interest now centres upon the results of testing the conclusions of theories against the data. Although the immediate stimulus for this emphasis comes from Friedman, it can be traced back to the work of Popper (1959, 1963) who advanced the following propositions: first, a theory can never be proved but it can always be disproved; second, our scientific knowledge is always conditional and can never be absolute – all theories are permanently at risk of being falsified; third, the testing of hypotheses with the aim of falsification is both the correct way to proceed and, in practice, the way that science works. Popper's work is voluminous, subtle and enormously impressive. But a very simplified version of it, reflecting in part Friedman's absorption of Popper, became the ruling position in economics in the 1960s.

In fact, however, it did not take very long to discover that testing, on its own, was a limited programme. There are a number of standard difficulties, including multicollinearity in the data, the Duhem–Quine problem noted above, and the difficulty of discerning causality by purely statistical means when there is no control available (as is the case in economics), and these have all been rehearsed at length in the last ten years or so. In addition there are problems over what is to be judged to constitute falsification – precisely what degree of disconfirmation constitutes falsification? – and there is thus an important element of conventionalism in what we are prepared to count as evidence. Economists were at first neglectful of these points; indeed, much of the 1960s falsificationism was of an extremely crude kind which not only neglected the problems already mentioned but placed an extraordinary reliance upon published statistics (Coddington 1972: 9).

But the problems have to be recognized. Because of the Duhem–Quine problem there are in economics particular difficulties over *ceteris paribus* in testing theories, especially if investigators adopt the dogmatic position that the truth of assumptions is irrelevant. A particular problem with *ceteris paribus* is

that it can be used to immunize a theory from testing, simply by claiming that a falsified theory must have failed because of some changes in initial conditions which were not allowed for – and which are themselves then not tested (McCarthy 1978: 13–14).

Economists should, but typically do not, deal with this problem by using tests in which there is a much greater prior knowledge about the auxiliary assumptions than about the hypothesis to be tested – this would constitute a 'well-constructed test' (McCarthy 1977: 8, citing Yoshida 1975).

Despite these difficulties, there is a strong case for persevering with testing, using well-constructed tests. In fact, although the difficulties are much less in natural science, physicists also face difficulties in testing hypotheses because the fit between theory and observation is far from perfect (Ziman 1978: 39). However, despite this, research workers 'Under the lash of scholarly competition . . . unconsciously act out the Popper principle of falsification, not only in relation to the theories but even against the objective "facts" claimed by their rivals' (Ziman 1978: 59). This is particularly important since it is replication of results outside the particular group which originally produced them which can be decisive in determining acceptance or rejection of a theory.

Reproducibility

In fact, the reproducibility of scientific results is a key issue to which economists have paid relatively little attention. The recent debate over cold nuclear fusion, aside from the entertainment value for non-scientists, has focused the attention of the wider non-scientific world upon this aspect as laboratories throughout the world have attempted to reproduce the results originally claimed by Pons and Fleischman (Garwin 1989).

But in the production of what Ziman has tellingly called 'reliable knowledge' it is reproducibility – testing – which is the key. Thus, when a research worker (Steele) claimed to have secured the inheritance of acquired characteristics in mice the reaction from his fellow biologists was that 'Clearly, the basic result must be repeated in other laboratories' (Taylor 1980; see also Mitchison 1980). Scientific activity involves the selection of those hypotheses that appear in the journals that will actually stand replication – perhaps as little as 10 per cent of the whole (Ziman 1978: 30–1, 40–1, 130, 143).

This issue of the reproducibility of results, second nature to the natural scientists, has been very largely ignored in social science. Perhaps the most dramatic illustration occurred in anthropology when a researcher (Freeman 1983), adopting an explicitly Popperian approach, treated Margaret Mead's account of Samoa as a series of hypotheses to be tested against the data rather than as received truth. To put it mildly, he found that Mead's results were not supported by the available data. But before economists enjoy the *schaden-*

freude too much, we should remember that assiduous avoidance of contact with data through fieldwork is the rule amongst economists – and what is at issue in the Samoa case relates to the results of fieldwork.

An example from the field of social psychology which springs readily to mind is the case of Sir Cyril Burt. Whether or not he fabricated his results on intelligence – and there is undoubtedly a strong body of opinion which believes that he did – it is indeed remarkable that it was not until after his death that a sustained attempt to check these results was made (Hearnshaw 1979).

Unfortunately every practising economist knows of areas where it is very difficult to reproduce the published results (see also Mayer 1980). There are, it is true, some bright spots in economics. The repeated investigations into the effects of mergers, and into the effects of exchange rate fluctuations on trade, have indeed involved replication of results in all sorts of different ways. But these are exceptional areas. Their exceptional nature derives from two main causes affecting most studies: technical econometric problems and data problems. (The possibility of moral hazard in the career structure – ease of publication of 'impressive' although non-reproducible results – will not be explored here.)

Measurement problems

Economists habitually employ regression as the first, and last, resort in dealing with data. Unfortunately the employment of regression techniques on time series data requires an enormous suspension of disbelief, and it now seems clear that this is not a fruitful suspension. We are employing a technique derived from agricultural experiments: in this, even the standard test of linearity requires a distribution of Y values for each X value, whereas in time series we have only one observation on Y for each value of X so that what passes as regression is in fact closer to the correlation analysis of the 1920s which enjoyed a transient vogue amongst economists. The lack of a distribution of Y for each X, and thus the absence of the possibility of repeated sampling, raises questions about significance levels which economists simply ignore. Randomization is a blatantly false assumption (Leamer 1983). The typical end-product of our suspension of disbelief is an estimated equation showing clear symptoms of multicollinearity in which the estimated parameters are, consequently, unstable. (This instability is a separate issue from instability in the basic economic relationships themselves which is also frequently ignored even though there are standard techniques, involving splitting the data, for testing for it.)

Partly because of the availability of standard computer packages, which are in themselves very desirable since they increase reproducibility, poor proce-

dures are adopted, including routinely correcting for serial correlation without checking first for its existence.

In addition, it is well known that a reported regression equation in a published article, ostensibly significant at 5 per cent, may have been obtained after nineteen (unreported) insignificant equations. Indeed, it has been suggested that it would be desirable if all the regressions run could be reported (Mayer 1980). But, as it is, we have the computer, adept at tedious arithmetic, obligingly performing specification search (which of course invalidates the traditional theory of inference (Leamer 1983: 36)) and, worse, the possibility that economists are prone to adjust the theory to the equation which works (Blaug 1980: 257).

There seems to be even more reluctance to accept that data are frequently of poor quality (Wilber and Harrison 1978: 69; Mayer 1980: 169). We have already noted the problem over government statistics; and in fact access to the worksheets from which these statistics were compiled by no means always provides the research worker with confidence. This would be a problem even if it were true that government statistics correspond to economic concepts – which they rarely do.

A common set of 'dirty data' is then subject to different tests by economists. Natural science researchers do not have to trust other people's numbers; reproducing them is indeed critical for the acceptance of a new result. There is thus a fundamental difference between economics and physics or chemistry. Working from a common data set, we can only perform different statistical tests on the same data, and, as Coase is reported to have remarked, if you torture the data long enough they will confess. The answer to data problems is emphatically not just to use a different mathematical technique, which has, in one sense, become a substitute for more basic empirical work. As Mayer (1980: 176–7) has commented: 'The stress on using advanced mathematical tools allows us to have a good conscience while ignoring some very elementary rules of good research procedure'.

The answer, however, is assuredly *not* to give up hope. That way lies irrationalism. It might indeed be a very good idea to cool the love affair with one particular statistical technique – regression – and to be more modest in our demands upon data which, in truth, may only be suitable for tests which assume ordinal ranking. As has been argued by Mayer, improvements in data and (where not published) in its availability to other parties, and an increased emphasis upon the elementary requirement of replicability, would certainly be a start. In addition, economists should be prepared to construct their own data sets, and in a way which would allow their method of construction, as well as the resultant data, to be open for public inspection. Reid (1987) has suggested a series of rules which should be followed in the use of interviews and questionnaires, and acceptance of such rules would be an important first step.

4.3 THEORY CHOICE

Not all economists agree that we need to choose between theories. Rather, they favour 'methodological pluralism' (Caldwell 1982). If we are to treat economics as simply a self-contained art form, with no relevance to the real world, such a position may be defensible. However, if we are concerned with economic truth it is rather less easy to accept. Quite apart from the view (persuasive because it was formed while witnessing the rise of Nazism in Germany) that an 'anything goes' approach to methodology is likely to end up with mob rule or Stalin (Hutchison 1981: 218), there are persuasive scientific reasons for believing that we should have theory choice. Unless we have choice, we have no competition between theories. But if we have no competition between the theories, we can make no pretence of contributing to knowledge or of testing those theories to see whether there is anything of value in them. Moreover, economic policy, which affects the lives of ordinary people in a far more fundamental way than merely paying taxes for the upkeep of economists, is grounded in, and/or claims the support of, theory. Therefore the position will be taken here that we need to make theory choice.

One view is that conventionalism – the implied votes of the academic community – is the basis of theory choice (Tarascio and Caldwell 1979; Caldwell 1982). It is perhaps ironic that this (anti-Popperian) position has been arrived at by applying what is essentially a Popperian approach to the methodology of methodology. For those who end up at conventionalism have looked at the claims for what is supposed to be economic methodology, tested them against the practice of economists and decided that those claims have been falsified (Boland 1982; Caldwell 1982; McCloskey 1983, 1985, 1987). They thus fall back on the proposition that theory choice is governed by whatever economists agree to do. Yet this is ironic because it amounts to accepting that a confrontation between theory and evidence is a valid way of resolving disputes. In any case, we do not *have* to conclude that because economists do not follow their own rules there is no point in the rules and that we should accept what they do instead. Such a position is essentially circular; conventionalism amounts to saying that theory choice is explained by theory choice.

Clearly, we need to go further than this. One attempt to explain conventionalism is in terms of 'rhetoric'. This is such an important subject, however, that it will be considered below in a separate section.

Conventionalism involves fashion. But fashion on its own, without any attempt to decide what determines fashion, is a very bad guide to theory choice. It is also a bad guide to methodology itself. Philosophical positions which one could not possibly *not* believe ten years ago are now rejected as clearly false – so that we have had a succession of logical positivism, logical

falsificationism and methodological anarchy. Those with slightly more knowledge of philosophy assure those with slightly less that 'real philosophers have given up positivism'. This argument is of course vulnerable to the charge that, if a once strongly held philosophical position is now considered outmoded, the new one may equally well be wrong.

In their drawings on the literature of the philosophy of science, economists of a conventionalist persuasion may have been misled because writers dealing with natural science *take for granted* that theory selection is on the basis of reliability. Because this is taken for granted it is not always brought out very clearly. But in fact 'scientific knowledge *evolves by critical selection*' (Ziman 1978: 131). Even a philosophy of science which appears to involve significant elements of conventionalism, such as that of Kuhn, has a requirement of reliable knowledge as its background. Despite all the material about paradigms and scientific revolutions, experience and experiment are essential for Kuhn.

This is not to deny the importance of intuition and its role in what has become known as 'methodological tenacity' – clinging to a theory which is in trouble – nor is it in any sense to deny the importance of logic which is vital for communication and consensus. But in natural science the empirical check on what can be accepted is always there.

This is very evident from the work of Lakatos. For Lakatos focuses upon competition between Scientific Research *Programmes* rather than between individual *theories* (an approach which has the advantage of getting away from the Duhem–Quine objection to testing individual theories), and in this competition between research programmes the testing of predictions about novel facts is absolutely central. In natural science, conventionalism arises because theories keep delivering results. It is productive of technology. In economics we cannot even produce the equivalent of turning on a light. Therefore conventionalism in economics needs careful examination as a justification of procedure.

Above all, testing is in natural science, and should be in economics, essential in cases of theory conflict. That a particular confrontation between theory and evidence may not be admitted as decisive by everyone is hardly surprising, given both human nature and methodological tenacity, but that such a refusal should be claimed to be destructive of the need for such confrontation is really very surprising. The precise form of confrontation with the data is a separate issue. All procedures, especially in economics where there is no scientific control, clearly face difficulties. But to claim that because it faces difficulties we give up on it seems to be a form of defeatism leading ultimately only to irrationalism. Of course it is true that one can cite all sorts of reasons why economists may believe that demand curves slope downwards, hardly any of which have reference to data (McCloskey 1987: 174), but this does not affect the basic point that, if there were economists who believed that demand curves slope upwards as a general rule, the empirical evidence would be vital.

Essentially, any subject with claims to truth needs empirical discipline. This is of course true in natural science; a striking example is Wegener's hypothesis of continental drift which was long resisted. It was a crucial piece of empirical evidence – rock magnetism – which resolved the controversy. Otherwise, without such discipline, we are left with a position reminiscent of Benjamin Franklin's characterization of theological disputes: 'one Divine says it is so, another Divine says it is not so'.

Rhetoric

It is the role of rhetoric in economics which has been the subject of McCloskey's highly entertaining writings (McCloskey 1983, 1985, 1987). McCloskey's position is that it is 'the aptness of economic metaphors, the relevance of historical precedents, the persuasiveness of introspections, the power of authority, the charm of symmetry, the claims of morality' (McCloskey 1983: 482) which persuade economists. He is notably entertaining about the role of mathematics as rhetoric, particularly in relation to Samuelson's *Foundations*. This is not an entirely new point; as Viner pointed out Swift, Defoe and Mandeville 'discovered early that a fool can be a bigger fool with the aid of mathematics than without' (Viner 1963: 16).[1] Mathematics as a form of rhetoric is related to the role of authority. The implication is that the mathematical expertise conveys a unique authority for the pronouncements, even where these extend to matters not covered by the mathematics.

It is of course perfectly true that rhetoric is not absent from physics. Since economists have typically borrowed most of their mathematics from natural science – possibly the wrong mathematics as we shall see later – it is perhaps worth observing that mathematics without an empirical check is also capable of leading natural scientists astray. The episode of continental drift has been referred to above. As already indicated, it was finally decided by empirical evidence. But, as Ziman has observed: 'The epistemological irony is that the geologists – supreme experts in the observation and interpretation of visual patterns – rejected first-rate evidence from fossils, rocks and landscapes because they thought it was in conflict with quantitative mathematical reasoning [on the strength of tides] which few of them really understood' (Ziman 1978: 94). However, the empirical evidence *did* ultimately prove decisive.

Without it, the danger is, as this physicist and others have pointed out, 'that enormous efforts can be made towards the displaced goal of solving more and more elaborate mathematical puzzles that have less and less relevance to any conceivable reality' (Ziman 1978: 173; Phelps Brown 1980: 6; Berry, in Wolpert and Richards 1988: 47). As Coddington has observed, without testing 'the development of economic theory may consist to an uncomfortable extent of formulating new questions to which the theories we have provide the

answers, rather than creating theories which provide answers to the questions we originally wanted to ask and answer' (Coddington 1975: 541).

Coddington's paper is in fact a devastating dissection of the claims made for the policy relevance of general equilibrium analysis. In the course of his discussion he identifies another rhetorical device – one which has a history which certainly goes back to the Cambridge conflicts of the 1930s. This is the device of taking a theory which does not belong in a particular, e.g. general equilibrium, framework, fitting it into that framework, discarding everything that does not fit the framework and then pronouncing the theory invalid. Rhetorical devices such as these may, none the less, persuade. But ultimately they are deceptive. In the last resort they are of no help in deciding theory conflict – although they may fool people into thinking that they are – and empirical evidence must be crucial.

4.4 PHYSICS AS A MODEL

The influence of natural science, especially physics, upon economics is almost as old as economics. But this involves two problems. First, there is the question of whether physics – by which essentially economists mean nineteenth-century classical physics – is a proper model. Second, there is the question of whether physics, as a whole, is really as economists and methodologists think it is.

It is perfectly clear, for the reasons already indicated – the lack of replication where time series data are concerned and the lack of control – that physics is likely to be, at best, an imperfect model. In fact physicists themselves seem very doubtful about whether their subject provides a good model for economics. This is partly because the logic of empirical statements, as distinct from that of mathematical theory, falls into three categories: 'true', 'false' and 'undecided' (Ziman 1978: 26). The physicist's view here is that 'in the physical sciences, this objection, although a large nail in the coffin of doctrinaire positivism, is not of great practical significance. But when we go beyond biology to the behavioural and social sciences it is devastating' (Ziman 1978: 28).

But in any case the kind of physics which economists take as their model is essentially not modern physics but the physics of Newton. As a theoretical physicist has observed, economists 'have an outmoded paradigm of physics' (Berry, in Wolpert and Richards 1988: 44). This itself involves two issues. First, there is the problem that, since Heisenberg, it is accepted that we cannot simultaneously ascertain both the position and the velocity of a particle so that the objectivity and certainty of classical physics are disturbed. Second, it seems quite likely that the mathematics of smooth continuous twice-differentiable functions is not suitable for many economic problems. The issue of chaos will be examined in the next section, but there is also the question of catastrophe theory. Whether or not this proves, as its advocates claim, to provide an

appropriate form of mathematical modelling for oligopoly (Woodcock and Davis 1978: 126–34), there is no doubt that in trying to model multiple outcomes and discontinuous changes it has recognized that economics is not well served by the mathematics of classical physics (see also Weisskopf 1979).

In matters of observation alone, there are very serious problems for economics compared with physics – the difference between disentangling 'noise' and 'signal' in physics and in economics is one of kind, not of degree (see also Ziman 1978: 67–70).

It is possible that economists might have done better to look at medicine as a model (Kornai 1983). While testing, and the pressures for success, are much stronger and more immediate in medicine, the role of observation in medicine has an important part to play in instructing economists. In the development of the cephalosporin group of antibiotics, hypothesis formation followed the development of a hunch which arose when looking at a sewage outfall into the sea (Florey 1955; Abraham 1962). The chance observation which was ultimately to result in penicillin is also well documented (Wilson 1976).

Moreover, medicine also indicates that a degree of instrumentalism does no harm as long as we do not stop there. The action of certain common substances, e.g. aspirin, is still not really understood; the structure of penicillin itself was only broken down some time after the development of the drug, while that of insulin was not discovered until as late as 1969 (Wolpert and Richards 1988: 69). But in all cases the researchers did not rest with instrumentalism.

Thus in the history of medicine there may well be lessons for economics. But it is physics – and classical physics at that – which has, both explicitly and implicitly, been taken as a model by economists. However, fairly recent mathematical developments indicate that this was probably not a very good choice.

Chaos

Chaos is an important mathematical development of which accounts for the non-specialist are gradually becoming available (Cvitanović 1984; Bai-Lin 1984; Peitgen and Richter 1985; I. Stewart 1989). The basic nature of chaos can be stated as follows:

> The often repeated statement, that given the initial conditions we know what a deterministic system will do far into the future, is false. . . . Given infinitesimally different starting points, we often end up with wildly different outcomes. Even with the simplest conceivable equations of motion, almost any non-linear system will exhibit chaotic behaviour.
>
> (Cvitanović 1984: 3)

A simple deterministic equation of the form $X_{t+1} = F(X_t)$ 'can possess dynami-

cal trajectories which look like some sort of random noise' (May 1976: 466). One of the critical things in chaos is that if the dynamic relation contains non-linear terms this produces fundamental consequences for the behaviour of the whole system. Recognition of the problem goes back to the nineteenth century with the formulation by P. F. Verhulst of a law of population growth containing a growth limitation. The algebraic form which he used for this has found much wider applications in the last twenty years because it turns out to describe certain aspects of turbulent flow.

Scientists themselves are aware of the widespread implications of this: 'Not only in research, but also in the everyday world of politics and economics we would be better off if more people realized that simple nonlinear systems do not necessarily possess simple dynamical properties' (May 1976: 467).

Variations in the non-linearity parameters produce changes in the paths followed by a dynamic system, and *bifurcations* – essentially, multiplication of the paths followed by the system – occur: 'The successive bifurcations take place in smaller and smaller regions of the phase space' (as the value of the non-linear parameters is changed) and ultimately 'practically all memory of the global structure of the original dynamical system is lost' (Cvitanović 1984: 18). As another source puts it: 'Every nonlinear rule leads to branch points, to forkings in the path at which the system may take one branch or another. Decisions are made whose consequences cannot be predicted because each decision has the character of an amplification' (Peitgen and Richter 1985: 61).

But equally important are the tiny differences in initial conditions. Lorenz has coined the term the 'butterfly effect' to indicate the smallness of change in initial conditions in a weather model, produced by the fluttering of a butterfly's wings, which could produce chaos as the system develops: 'A very small imprecision in the initial conditions can grow to an enormous effect in the later motion. Both the expert and the layman are confused to an equal degree by the complexity contained in what were thought to be simple equations' (Peitgen and Richter 1985: 62). Differences in initial conditions can also produce intermittent chaos – a condition which when shown graphically (Cvitanović 1984: 30) looks extraordinarily like the behaviour of some exchange rates. The implications even for classical mechanics are serious since this is no longer fully determinate (Bai-Lin 1984: 13). The implications for both meteorology and economics are absolutely devastating, especially as the problems increase markedly the higher the dimensions of the system.

Mathematicians, notably Mitchel Feigenbaum, have made considerable progress with chaos in recent years, but at low dimensions (Cvitanović 1984: 19, 30). For the moment the critical messages for economists are, it may be suggested, threefold. First, the sort of mathematics which economists have been inclined to think of as being well developed, simple and applicable to economics may well not be appropriate. Second, the fundamental conclusion

of chaos theory that assumptions *do* matter is yet another reason for abandoning the pernicious doctrine that assumptions do *not* matter. Third, the implications for a purely falsificationist approach to economics are disastrous. If the bifurcations produce so many possible outcomes it is clearly impossible to rely solely upon falsification, above all in the area of macroeconomics.

4.5 ECONOMICS AS A SCIENCE?

Throughout the history of economics there has been a perpetual methodological tension between an axiomatic approach and an approach constrained by respect for the data. Simple contemplation of the contrast between Ricardo and Smith, or between Marshall and Edgeworth, is enough to illustrate this point. But none of these doubted that they were, at least in some sense, trying to do something scientific. If we are prepared to be modest in our aims, if we are prepared to respect the facts of a situation – as Smith indeed recognized facts as constraining imagination – if we are prepared to confront the results of our theorizing with data and to seek conscientiously to construct data sets, then there seems no reason why economics should not have a utilitarian, as distinct from a purely artistic, role. It seems virtually certain that economics will never become a 'hard science' (cf. Solow 1986), but it does not then follow that we simply give up on the data.

Economics has substantial achievements to its credit. While, as a physicist observed, if we want to learn about love we do not read a sociology handbook but, for instance, Jane Austen (Ziman 1978: 185), we do not turn to Jane Austen if we want to learn about inflation. If we want to learn about consumer choice we do not do so either (although we might have to concede that we would learn more from a book on marketing than from John Green's classic *Consumer Theory* (Green 1971). But we need to build upon this achievement and not to retreat into models which tell us nothing about the real world. One thing that we can certainly learn from physics is the idea that modelling which has no discernible reference to the real world is pure self-indulgence (Berry, in Wolpert and Richards 1988: 47).

Moreover, economists do have considerable influence and this influence should be exercised responsibly. It may well be true that they are prone to overrate their influence. But hubris is certainly not a monopoly of economists and its existence should not lead us to neglect the influence – for good *or ill* – which economists can have. They should thus be prepared to constrain the wilder flights of their imagination by reference not only to the facts which they assume but also, as far as possible, to the facts which they predict. They will never produce anything analogous to physics in this way, but they will at least avoid claiming the authority of their subject for both theories and prescriptions which have no basis whatever in the economic world.

NOTE

1 I am not of course suggesting that Professor Samuelson is a fool.

APPENDIX: SOME KEY REFERENCES

The literature of economic methodology dealing with the relationship of theory and observation is enormous and in recent years it appears to have grown particularly fast. Three classics are J.N. Keynes (1890), Robbins (1932) and Friedman (1953). By far the best modern books, in the opinion of the present writer, are those of I. M. T. Stewart (1979) and Blaug (1980), two complementary volumes which together provide an admirable basis for further reading. The McCloskey references (McCloskey 1983, 1985, 1987) and also Stigler (1977) should be read for enjoyment, and all of T. W. Hutchison's numerous methodological writings yield both enjoyment and illumination.

REFERENCES

Abraham, E. P. (1962) 'The cephalosporins', *Pharmacological Review* 14: 473–500.

Ayer, A. J. (1970) 'Has Harrod answered Hume?', in W. Eltis, M. Scott and J. Wolfe (eds) *Induction, Growth and Trade*, Oxford: Clarendon Press.

Bai-Lin, H. (1984) *Chaos*, Singapore: World Scientific Publishing.

Black, F. (1982) 'The trouble with econometric models', *Financial Analysts Journal* 38: 29–37.

Blaug, M. (1980) *The Methodology of Economics*, Cambridge: Cambridge University Press, reprinted 1982.

Boland, L. (1982) *The Foundations of Economic Knowledge*, London: Allen & Unwin.

Caldwell, B. (1982) *Beyond Positivism*, London: Allen & Unwin.

Coddington, A. (1972) 'Positive economics', *Canadian Journal of Economics* 5: 1–15.

—— (1975) 'The rationale of general equilibrium theory', *Economic Inquiry* 13: 539–58.

Cvitanović, P. (1984) *Universe in Chaos*, Bristol: Adam Hilger.

Florey, H. (1955) 'Antibiotic products of a versatile fungus', *Annals of Internal Medicine* 43: 480–90.

Freeman, D. (1983) *Margaret Mead and Samoa. The Making and Unmaking of an Anthropological Myth*, Cambridge, MA: Harvard University Press.

Friedman, M. (1953) *Essays in Positive Economics*, Chicago, IL: University of Chicago Press.

Garwin, R. L. (1989) 'Consensus on cold fusion is still elusive', *Nature* 338: 616–17.

Green, H. A. (1971) *Consumer Theory*, London: Penguin.

Harrod, R. F. (1956) *Foundations of Inductive Logic*, London: Macmillan.

Hearnshaw, L. S. (1979) *Cyril Burt, Psychologist*, London: Hodder & Stoughton.

Hutchison, T. W. (1938) *The Significance and Basic Postulates of Economic Theory*, New York: A. M. Kelley, reprinted 1965.

—— (1981) *The Politics and Philosophy of Economics*, Oxford: Basil Blackwell.

Jacob, F. (1988) *The Statue Within*, London: Unwin Hyman.

Keynes, J. N. (1890) *The Scope and Method of Political Economy*, London: Macmillan.

Koopmans, T. C. (1957) *Three Essays on the State of Economic Science*, New York: McGraw-Hill.

Kornai, J. (1983) 'The health of nations: reflections on the analogy between medical sciences and economics', *Kyklos* 36: 191–212.

Kuhn, T.S. (1970) *The Structure of Scientific Revolutions*, 2nd edn, Chicago, IL: University of Chicago Press.

Lakatos, I. (1978) *The Methodology of Scientific Research Programmes*, eds J. Worrall and G. Currie, Cambridge: Cambridge University Press.

Leamer, E. (1983) 'Let's take the con out of econometrics', *American Economic Review* 73: 31–43.

McCarthy, M. (1977) 'The status of the Leontief paradox', University of Kent Studies in Economics 21.

—— (1978) 'On *ceteris paribus*', University of Kent Studies in Economics 28.

McCloskey, D. (1983) 'The rhetoric of economics', *Journal of Economic Literature*, 21: 481–516.

—— (1985) *The Rhetoric of Economics*, Madison, WI: University of Wisconsin Press.

—— (1987) 'Rhetoric', in J. Eatwell, M. Milgate and P. Newman (eds) *The New Palgrave*, vol. 3, pp. 173–4, London: Macmillan.

May, R. M. (1976) 'Simple mathematical models with very complicated dynamics', *Nature* 261: 459–67.

Mayer, T. (1980) 'Economics as a hard science: realistic goal or wishful thinking?', *Economic Inquiry* 18: 165–78.

Meade, J. E. (1952) *A Geometry of International Trade*, London: Allen & Unwin.

Mitchison, N. A. (1980) 'Inheritance: the immunological challenge', *Nature* 288: 306.

Musgrave, A. (1981) '"Unreal assumptions" in economic theory: the F-twist untwisted', *Kyklos* 34: 377–87.

Peitgen, H.-O. and Richter, P. H. (1985) *Schönheit im Chaos*, Bremen: University of Bremen.

Phelps Brown, H. (1980) 'The radical reflections of an applied economist', *Banca Nazionale del Lavoro Quarterly Review* no. 132: 3–14.

Popper, K. R. (1959) *The Logic of Scientific Discovery*, London: Hutchinson, reprinted 1974.

—— (1974) *Conjectures and Refutations*, 5th edn, London: Routledge & Kegan Paul (originally published 1963).

Reid, G. C. (1987) 'Applying field research techniques to the business enterprise', *International Journal of Social Economics* 14: 3–25.

Ricardo, D. (1817) *On the Principles of Political Economy and Taxation*, London: J. Murray.

Robbins, L. (1932) *An Essay on the Nature and Significance of Economic Science*, London: Macmillan; 2nd edn, 1935.

Samuelson, P. A. (1963) 'Discussion', *American Economic Review* (May Supplement) 53: 232.

Solow, R. (1986) 'Economics: is something missing', in W. Parker (ed.) *Economic History and the Modern Economist*, pp. 21–9, Oxford: Basil Blackwell.

Stewart, I. (1989) *Does God Play Dice?*, Oxford: Basil Blackwell.

Stewart, I. M. T. (1979) *Reasoning and Method in Economics*, London: McGraw-Hill.

Stigler, G. J. (1977) 'The conference handbook', *Journal of Political Economy* 85: 441–3.

Tarascio, V. and Caldwell, B. (1979) 'Theory choice in economics: philosophy and practice', *Journal of Economic Issues* 13: 983–1006.

Taylor, R. B. (1980) 'Lamarckist revival in immunology', *Nature* 286: 837–8.

Torrens, R. (1815) *An Essay on the External Corn Trade*, London: Hatchard.

—— (1833) *Letters on Commercial Policy*, London: Longman.

Viner, J. (1963) 'The economist in history', *American Economic Review* (Supplement) 53: 1–22.

Weisskopf, W. (1979) 'The method is the ideology: from a Newtonian to a Heisenbergian paradigm in economics', *Journal of Economic Issues* 13: 869–84.

Wilber, C. and Harrison, R. (1978) 'The methodological basis of institutional economics: pattern mode, storytelling, and holism', *Journal of Economic Issues* 12: 61–89.

Wilson, D. (1976) *Penicillin in Perspective*, London: Faber & Faber.

Wolpert, L. and Richards, A. (1988) *A Passion for Science*, Oxford: Oxford University Press.

Woodcock, A. and Davis, M. (1978) *Catastrophe Theory*, Harmondsworth: Penguin, reprinted 1985.

Yoshida, R. M. (1975) 'Five Duhemian theses', *Philosophy of Science* 42: 29–45.

Ziman, J. (1978) *Reliable Knowledge*, Cambridge: Cambridge University Press.

British Journal of Industrial Relations
30:2 June 1992 0007–1080 $3.00

Economists and Data

*D. P. O'Brien**

Final version accepted 1 October 1991.

Abstract

This paper is concerned with one central question: the choice between theories, and the role played by data in that choice. It deals with the uses economists may make of data and the importance of understanding the institutional basis that gives rise to the data — an area in which labour economists have traditionally been particularly strong — and with the relevance of assumptions. It deals with the ultimate need to choose between competing theories (despite the role of conventionalism) on the basis of data rather than retreating into a comfortable 'methodological pluralism'. It considers the role of test replication, with reference to the practice in natural science (and its role there in checking scientific fraud) and concludes that, despite extensive technical problems of testing, economists have to accept a data check if the rhetoric of mathematical technicality is not to overwhelm the need to explain. Parallels are drawn with experience in physics (and the implications of the development of Chaos and Catastrophe for a naively predictionist view are noted), medicine and history (of which, it is argued, modern economists are far too neglectful).

1. Introduction

This paper is concerned with one central question: the choice between theories, and the role played by data in that choice. It seems incontestable that theory (rather than what Marshall called 'mere crude unanalysed history — Pigou 1925: 437) must have primacy. In a labour market context we cannot investigate the effects on labour supply of tax changes without some explicit, or implicit, theory about the relationship between economic variables. But there is usually no shortage of competing theories, and thus theory *choice* is necessary. For instance, labour economics provides the examples of 'screening' and 'productivity' approaches to investment in education, a wide variety of competing theories of pay structure, and a number of economic models of trade unions. Data help us not only to choose between theories but also to judge the circumstances to which a particular theory may be applied, and can also suggest different theoretical approaches.

* Professor of Economics, University of Durham

2. Data and social science

Direct information

Inspection of data does not *directly* provide reliable information. In the first place, in order to interpret the data we need not merely some system of concepts — Popper's World 3 (Popper 1972) — but at least some explicit hypotheses about possible relationships between those concepts. Secondly, observation of a particular relationship within data provides no *logical* reason for believing in a necessary association in the future. Thirdly, data on their own tell us nothing about causality — hypotheses about causality are external to the data. Fourthly, as Popper has pointed out, the probability of a particular data relationship and its informational content are inversely related (Popper 1959: 270) — it is precisely those things that are not obvious which are interesting.

All these problems pose particular difficulties for economists who wish to obtain information directly from data; for, not only can we not inspect the data without preconceptions, but the very process of *construction* of the data involves prior concepts; anyone who doubts this should have a look at the *National Accounts Statistics: Sources and Methods* produced by HMSO (Maurice 1968). Yet economists routinely ignore the fact that official data may be prepared on a conceptual basis which is different from that of their model. One small but illuminating example is provided by official figures for rent: not only do these not correspond with the economic concept , but rent is lumped together with income from self-employment 'and the imputed charge for the consumption of non-trading capital' in *Economic Trends*.

Of course, the problem that data are not independent of the observer is certainly not confined to economics. The paradox of Schroedinger's cat — which, in a box with a phial of poison, is neither dead nor alive but in a 'super position' state, as described by Schroedinger's wave equations, until observed — is well known to physicists. But the cavalier nature with which published data are employed by many economists (though, emphatically, not all — Henry Phelps Brown is an important exception) would suggest a certain insensitivity to the underlying problem. Certainly, attempts to discover a 'data generation process', by powerful time-series techniques in which 'it is easily possible to generate more test statistics than there are data points in the sample' (Johnson 1991: 55), encounter this problem.

There is also the problem of instability in the data, which has of course implications far wider than mere attempts to learn directly from the raw data. The problem of parameter shift (as distinct from the problem of unstable parameter *estimates* in the presence of multicolinearity) has led, following the apparent breakdown of demand-for-money equations in the years 1971–3, to what is known widely as 'Goodhart's Law' (Goodhart 1984: 96). Whether that particular episode is in fact a good example of such

instability is another matter; but that such instability exists can hardly be doubted, given that economic data are the unique result of an historical process.

That data relationships do not establish causal relationships is so well understood in general philosophical terms that 'post hoc ergo propter hoc' is a phrase in universal use. It is true that economists have been persuaded to employ the word 'causality' in a sense not recognized by the dictionary, namely, that associated with Grainger where, 'if prediction of the current value of *y* is enhanced by using past values of *x*' (Kennedy 1985: 64), there is said to exist causality. But this is not causality in any ordinary sense of the term, but rather association.

Some economists have attempted 'probabilistic induction'. The leading exponent of this was Roy Harrod (1956). (An excellent summary is provided by Phelps Brown 1980a: 28–9; see also Braithwaite 1958.) Harrod believed that to be in general correct, on the basis of experience, was a sufficient justification of induction, whereas, as critics pointed out, what was relevant was the likelihood of being correct on any one occasion — and this could not be established logically without smuggling in what was required to be proved, namely the idea of a uniformity of nature. (Induction in this sense is, of course, to be distinguished from the logical procedure of pure mathematics.)

None the less, economists have continued to hanker after induction. This seems to have been for a variety of reasons. In some cases it has apparently been based on the (usually implicit) belief that this is the *only* way to obtain knowledge. Wesley Mitchell is usually cited in this respect; the charge however was unfair in that particular case (Mitchell 1928: 3; Burns and Mitchell 1946: 9–10), as was the widely quoted charge of 'measurement without theory'. Others appear to have believed that induction is at least *an important* way to obtain knowledge. This is true of such outstanding figures in the field of economic methodology as John Stuart Mill (1868, VI: ch. 5) and J. N. Keynes (1917: ch. 6). Others believe that it is an important check on *a priorism*. While agreeing wholeheartedly that such a check is needed, for reasons to be discussed below, the data *alone* will not provide this.

Indirect information — hypotheses

We cannot obtain information directly from data. But we can obtain knowledge indirectly through the formation of hypotheses. These hypotheses may themselves be suggested by the recognition of patterns within data, even though the patterns themselves do not constitute information. The importance of pattern recognition is acknowledged in natural science (Ziman 1978: 43–56). Indeed, it is something that requires a great deal of specialized practice (p. 54). Historically it has proved to be of critical importance in medicine — epidemiology — in which the link between smoking and lung cancer is the most familiar example. The fact that, as we shall see, such an approach can be abused does not invalidate its

importance if sensible procedural rules are adhered to. Although biologists nowadays all aspire to be reductionists (Wolpert and Richards 1988: 103–4), so that taxonomy has been pushed into the background, it is still an essential foundation.

But the stability of the background pattern for economists is different in kind rather than degree. Thus, economists, dealing with data produced by historical processes, need to be ever alert to *changes* in the underlying pattern. Whereas pattern recognition led ultimately to the theory of continental drift, although only after decades of controversy, the pattern of strike behaviour suggested by 1970s data is likely to be fundamentally different from that exhibited by 1980s data. The same might well be expected of observed patterns in union/non-union differentials. But this mutability does not mean that the patterns can be disregarded: rather, it means that they cannot be pushed too far into the background.

Patterns, Institutions and Data Gathering

Because these patterns occur within an institutional environment, economists need to take account of that institutional structure. The sort of painstaking search for patterns in industrial economic data which characterized American industrial economics even as late as the end of the 1970s cannot be independent of the framework in which the industry operates — including tariffs, competition policy and government procurement. Of course, the patterns thus detected are not immutable. But this did not prevent Marshall, who indeed emphasized the evolutionary nature of economic forms very strongly, from seeking the sort of patterns in industrial life that inform his *Industry and Trade* (A. Marshall 1919). He disciplined himself to read almost entirely factual material, despite his original background in mathematics (Pigou 1925: 439–40; see also pp. 419–30), and he spent his vacations studying industrial conditions (M. Marshall 1947: 42–3). As a result, even today, the careful reader of *Industry and Trade* can learn a lot, despite the huge changes that have taken place in industrial organization. But careful reading of this book is about the last thing that most economists would admit to doing — it would have to be a secret vice.

Yet without some detailed industrial knowledge, which implies some contact with firms, that skill in pattern recognition which is prized in natural science is unlikely to be developed in economics. But not only do most economists not have any first-hand knowledge of firms: they feel that such experience would be a handicap. If economists were once again to concede that questionnaires had a part to play in constructing data bases, this would at least have the advantage of bringing them into contact with firms. (Labour economists, though sometimes enduring derisive references to 'trade union chaplains', seem much less reluctant to come into contact with their subject material.)

The influence of Friedman may be in part responsible for the reluctance to employ questionnaire material, which he described as 'a procedure for

testing economic theories that is about on a par with testing theories of longevity by asking octogenarians how they account for their long life' (1953: 31). As McCloskey has sardonically observed,

> One can literally get an audience of economists to laugh out loud by proposing ironically to send out a questionnaire on some disputed economic point. Economists are so impressed by the confusions that might possibly result from questionnaires that they abandoned them entirely, in favor of the confusions resulting from external observation. (McCloskey 1983: 514).

In a sense, Friedman's influence here is not surprising. He has been a major figure in postwar economics. But it may be unfortunate none the less. Even if there are plenty of grounds for criticism of the way in which questionnaire and interview investigations have been conducted in the past, and even though the Margaret Mead episode to be referred to below should be warning enough of the danger of 'travellers' tales', these are matters to be corrected by the use of a carefully controlled questionnaire methodology rather than by simple dismissal of detailed on-the-spot investigation. Even some investigations that have seemed to later commentators particularly loose, such as the Oxford Studies, which are an easy target because the process of investigation involved inviting prominent industrialists to dine (Lee 1981), have been the source of interesting hypotheses. The kinked demand curve was, it is true, in Joan Robinson's *Imperfect Competition* (1933: 38, 81); but it was ignored until formulated independently by Hall and Hitch on the basis of the Oxford investigations (though they acknowledge the influence of Chamberlin — see Hall and Hitch 1939: 23, 29) as well as by Sweezey (1939) in the USA.[1]

Certainly, the information required by economists goes far beyond what appears in published official statistics. They also need a great deal more than what might be unkindly referred to as 'establishment musings'. The case of the Radcliffe Report is perhaps salutary. As Lionel Robbins was to observe,

> Businessmen appear before government committees, beat their breasts, and swear that the rate of interest doesn't mean a thing to them, but as soon as the rate of interest is raised in some attempt to control the situation, you find them all giving interviews to financial journalists, saying what an unfortunate thing it is and how they hope that cheap money will be restored again. (Robbins 1972: 130–1)

That particular set of 'establishment musings' was in fact subject to sustained attack. But it seems at least more likely that investigations of this sort provide material on which a reasonably accurate picture of the relevant mechanisms can be built than the single-equation estimates of demand for money which preceded Competition and Credit Control, and which are now (rightly) regarded as discredited.

But one of the odd things about economists is their choice of those results which they select to believe. Late 1960s single-equation estimates of the demand for money attracted considerable credence, not to say credulity. Perhaps the two strongest empirical results now available — far stronger

than those demand-for-money equations — concern the indifferent performances of merged firms and the lack of interference with trade resulting from exchange rate fluctuations; and these results, which are derived from a variety of data sources and all sorts of different research strategies, are routinely ignored in discussions of industrial or exchange rate policy. Yet if economists were really to take seriously the need to consider the rich variety and complexity of economic data, there is no doubt about which results deserve greater credence.

The Place of Assumptions

As a result of Friedman's celebrated 1953 essay (Friedman 1953), economists have come to regard the realism of assumptions as completely unimportant. Indeed, as Samuelson (1963) has pointed out, Friedman's position can at least be interpreted as putting forward the view not only that the realism of assumptions is unimportant, but even that it is a positive virtue (the 'F-twist').

The position that assumptions are unimportant involves a series of non-sequiturs:

1. Some assumptions are acknowledged to be unrealistic.
2. But their unrealism is of negligible importance.
3. 'Therefore' the unrealism of *all* assumptions does not matter.
4. 'Therefore' (in the strong version) unrealism is an advantage.

As the philosopher Alan Musgrave (1981) has argued, Friedman's 1953 essay confused 'negligibility', 'domain' and 'heuristic' considerations in discussing assumptions. 'Negligibility' involves assuming that factors ignored are unimportant in their effect on the phenomena to be investigated. 'Domain' assumptions, however, limit the applicability of a theory to a particular situation. 'Heuristic' assumptions are those made to enable the argument to be developed. Friedman however managed to confound 'domain' and 'heuristic' assumptions with negligibility, and this explains some — but not all — of the *non sequiturs*.

At all events, the proposition that assumptions are unimportant proved very popular, especially in the 1960s 'positive economics' era.

It may also have — though Friedman can not be directly blamed for this — a bearing on the later jettisoning of the structure–conduct–performance (S–C–P) approach to industrial economics in favour of game theory, where the assumptions are (to put it mildly) stylized. (The same may be true of the application of game theory to industrial relations.)

The abandonment of the S–C–P approach has subsequently been justified by reference to the relatively poor correspondence between the available *published* data and the economic concepts involved. Yet it does not follow that economists should react to such poor correspondence not by trying to improve the data but by retreating into formal game theory, in which:

> Modelling typically begins with the specification of the *extensive form* of a game: a description of which players move when, the actions and information available at each move, the probabilities of any random events to be chosen by 'nature', and the functions determining each player's pay off . . . It is then assumed that observed behaviour will correspond to a *Nash equilibrium* of the specified game, a situation in which each firm's *strategy* (a list of the moves it will make in all possible situations [sic]) is a best response to the strategies of its rivals. (Schmalensee 1988: 645)

With the aid of this material, economists have introduced social and psychological considerations, with many of the 'results' apparently representing algebraic formalization of what has been casually *assumed* about (or unsystematically borrowed from works about) the sociology/psychology of the participants. There is no doubt about the career enhancement value of such work; but it is extremely hard to reconcile with Friedman's insistence that 'economic theory must be more than a structure of tautologies if it is to be able to predict and not merely describe the consequences of action; it is to be something different from disguised mathematics' (1953: 11–12). Thus, game theorists, in citing Friedman in support of their approach (Aumann 1964), would seem to be going beyond what he himself envisaged.

Friedman's position did however lead in the 1960s to instrumentalism. This was highly unsatisfactory, because if economists had actually been able to achieve satisfactory computational rules they would have had no recourse when the rules eventually broke down — as they must. Computational rules that make deliberately unrealistic basic assumptions provide no way of knowing why an apparent statistical regularity has broken down.

It is perhaps ironic that the most telling, and most oft quoted, example used to justify this kind of approach is Friedman's discussion of the acceleration of a falling body:

> The formula $s = (\frac{1}{2})gt^2$ is valid for bodies falling in a vacuum and can be derived by analysing the behaviour of such bodies. It can therefore be stated: under a wide range of circumstances, bodies that fall in the actual atmosphere behave *as if* they were falling in a vacuum . . . The formula is accepted because it works, not because we live in an approximate vacuum — whatever that means. (Friedman 1953: 18)

It is ironic because physicists *are* concerned — with good reason — with the accuracy of their assumptions. According to an eminent physicist,

> The statement, 'a neutral carbon atom contains *seven* electrons' is precise, unambiguous, consensible, logically self-consistent, etc. — but it happens to be *false*. This seems a trivial remark, but a great deal of scientific nonsense is generated through failure to appreciate its force . . . It is all too easy to derive endless strings of interesting looking but untrue or irrelevant formulae instead of checking the validity of the initial premises. (Ziman 1978: 14)

Assumptions need to be accurate, at least in outline. James Mill has, rightly, been criticized for his attitude towards Hindu society:

> Mill had, of course, never been further East than, let us say, perhaps Southend, and hardly knew a word of any Oriental language. However, as he explains in his Preface, such merely empirical equipment may well be highly misleading for the historian, and is of far less importance than a grasp of 'the laws of society' and what Mill calls 'a masterly use of evidence'. Anyhow, Mill has no hesitation in pronouncing the most severe, definite, and detailed condemnation of every aspect of Hindu civilisation. (Hutchison 1978: 38)

It is however not too difficult to recognize in Mill's stance the claims to generality which many economists consciously or unconsciously make as they ignore the content of assumptions. But assumptions pre-package information. In natural science this means successfully replicated results, as well as taxonomy. Since we have very little in the way of such results, some correspondence with the taxonomy seems all the more important. Yet economists are notoriously reluctant to inspect what has been pre-packaged.

The case of labour economics is particularly illuminating here. The complex institutional structure that exists hardly ever permits the degree of *individual choice* posited in some well articulated brands of labour economics. Specialist labour economists seem well aware of these particular difficulties (e.g. Creedy and Thomas 1982: 5–6); indeed, if one is to judge by a recent book on microeconomic issues in labour economics, labour economists still have their collective feet very firmly on the ground and exhibit a deep respect for the institutional facts of a situation (Drago and Perlman 1989). It is true that the volume contains a critique of models of union behaviour: but it *is* a critique, and one that notes (p. 122) the very large element of *ad hoc*ery in what purport to be general models. Yet this willingness to respect the institutional peculiarities of the particular market under consideration, which labour economists exhibit, is very largely absent from microeconomic discussions as a whole, which rely upon a few stylized assumptions. As a natural scientist has emphasized, however, research is, or should be, parasitic on a whole body of taxonomic knowledge (Ziman 1978: 46), and checking assumptions does at least give some idea of what is *not* under 'control' in statistical investigation.

In fact, earlier generations of economists writing on methodology, up to and including Lionel Robbins (1935), were only too well aware (sometimes to the exclusion of other empirical checks on theory) of the need to check assumptions. In particular, they focused on the 'domain' aspect. In this they were well advised; for the truth of domain assumptions is critical for falsifiability (with which they were not in general concerned), as well as for applicability (with which they certainly were). Indeed, there is something rather preposterous about academics holding forth on matters of policy without considering the applicability of the models on which they base their recommendations.

It is rather startling that matters have reached such a pitch in this respect that the Sraffa model, a purely mathematical model (originating in Ricardian and Marxian preconceptions but with no recognizable correspondence with the world), is deemed to have important policy implications —

though not of a testable variety. This, in methodological terms, represents what might be called the MRS-twist. Without explicitly addressing the issues, but combining the belief that there is no need to inspect assumptions with the difficulties that have been encountered by economists in adopting a falsificationist attitude, the Sraffians end up with the proposition that a self-contained model with, as Mark Blaug put it, its foundations 'planted firmly in mid air' (1988: 34) has important things to tell us about the real economic world.

If however we are to test, a question to be discussed below, the assumptions that we make do matter. One of the difficulties of testing involves the so-called Duhem–Quine problem, in that any one test is in practice a joint test of a series of hypotheses, so that if falsification occurs we have no automatic way of knowing which of the individual hypotheses has been falsified. But if we test theories with the *same* background knowledge — if we ask what the assumptions are — then we have a better chance of knowing what the source of falsification is.

The Need to Test

The following propositions of Popper have proved influential with economists. (Popper was, of course, one of the glories of LSE philosophy; but reception of his message by economists was undoubtedly aided by Friedman's celebrated essay, despite the fact that Friedman does not refer to Popper.)

1. A theory can never be proved, but it can always be disproved.
2. All scientific knowledge is conditional upon the stage reached in the piecemeal accretion of that knowledge — all theories are permanently at risk.
3. The testing of hypotheses is (a), normatively, the *correct* way forward, and (b), positively, the *actual* way forward as scientists add to the body of knowledge. This is the procedure which Ziman says, in his apt phrase, produces 'reliable knowledge' in natural science.

Popper's own work is complex, and subtle, and has shown some development over the years. In particular, after Kuhn's *Structure of Scientific Revolutions* (1962), Popper now acknowledges the importance of 'normal science', in which falsification is not a serious objective (Popper 1970: 51–8). But the combined influence of Popper and Friedman produced what became in effect the ruling position on testing in the 1960s. (One version of what happened to the LSE adherents of this programme has been given by De Marchi, 1988.)

But inevitably, in adopting a falsificationist position, economists encountered difficulties, especially when they proclaimed a naive falsificationist position, which were different in kind rather than degree from those encountered by natural scientists when testing. They included not only the Duhem–Quine problem noted above, but multicolinearity in the data,

which usually came from official statistics compiled for different purposes, and the limited usefulness of what were in effect historical data, especially in situations where causality is posited, and there was no 'control' in a scientific sense. What inevitably happened was that judgements concerning what constituted falsification were highly variable; economists displayed what Lakatos was to call 'methodological tenacity' in their adherence to research programmes; and, because economists, like nature, abhor a vacuum, any theory, however rickety, was preferred to none.

Ultimately, the LSE's Philosophy Department again provided a way forward. In Lakatos's 'Falsification and the Methodology of Scientific Research Programmes' (1970), the naive brand of falsificationism that economists had embraced was replaced by the idea of competition between scientific research programmes. This in turn provided a place for the employment of judgement by the scientific community on the status of a particular theoretical approach, with its introduction of 'methodological tenacity' and its emphasis upon 'sophisticated falsificationism'. There is no doubt that this was a most valuable contribution. In particular, it helped to ensure that the difficulties encountered with falsificationism in the naive version that economists initially espoused did not lead to a retreat from data. But it had its costs. One of these was the acceptance of a high degree of conventionalism — or '*mob psychology*', as Lakatos himself called it in one of his acerbic footnotes to a discussion of Kuhn (Lakatos 1970: 178; italics in original). But this conventionalism had a shaky basis. Because the contents of *ceteris paribus* were not subject to prior inspection, false theories were immunized from rejection by reference to an implied, *ex post*, change in initial conditions. One particularly fertile field of examples is provided by demand-for-money studies in the 1980s, where almost any failure could be explained by some (unspecified) financial innovation.

Of course, economists should have responded to this difficulty by using tests involving a much greater degree of prior knowledge and by specifying their assumptions much more precisely (Yoshida 1975; McCarthy 1977). But even after the initial impetus of Friedman's *Essays* had been lost, economists continued to be averse to regarding assumptions as matters for inspection.

Clearly, economists need to modify this attitude. They are certainly not alone in facing difficulties in testing, but if economics is ever to produce reliable knowledge, the issue of *replication* of the results of tests in which hypotheses have withstood attempted falsification is crucial, and without specification of the assumptions it is not clear how replication can have any meaning.

The Role of Test Replication

The most important single issue in controversy in natural science is whether or not results initially obtained can be replicated. It is attempts at replication that check whether a genuine advance in knowledge has been made or a

genuine puzzle encountered, or whether either mistake or fraud lies behind the results. Four recent examples will suffice.

In March 1989, Stanley Pons and Martin Fleischmann claimed to have achieved nuclear fusion at ordinary room temperature rather than at the very high temperatures and energy uses which physicists believed would be necessary. If this result were valid it would be of enormous importance, indicating a source of cheap energy. The immediate response of scientists was to attempt to replicate the Pons–Fleischmann results. Large budgets were set aside and laboratories around the world attempted to reproduce the results. Most failed to do so. (Of those that did succeed, there is a suggestion of fraud in one case — Science 1990.) The failure to reproduce the Pons–Fleischmann results proved decisive: a year later the results had established no credibility with the scientific world, and although research continues it is on a small scale.

The second case involves a claim to have achieved the inheritance of acquired characteristics, using mice as the experimental subjects. The response from the scientific community was unambiguous; for this result to have any standing, it must be repeated by independent research workers (Mitchison 1980; Taylor 1980). However, it was not successfully repeated.

A third case involves the apparent discovery by scientists at Leningrad University of what would appear to be an entirely new form of magnetism (Economist 1991a). Like cold fusion, standard theory would offer no explanation for this; and attempts to reproduce the results, which emerged in the course of experiments involving organic chemicals derived from benzene, are under way. Given the history of episodes of this sort — one example in the postwar history of physics is the so-called 'polywater' episode (Ziman 1978: 73–5; Science 1990) — it seems hard to be optimistic. However, the crucial point is that the decision of the scientific community concerning these results will depend upon independent replication.

A fourth case — that of Dr Margot O'Toole and a paper on immunology — is interesting as illustrating not only the general point about replication but also the troublesome matter of fraud. This is hardly a new development. Even the great Keppler, it appears, falsified his data (Donahue 1988). But the O'Toole case has attracted widespread publicity. The problem first arose when Dr O'Toole found that she was unable to reproduce results claimed in a published paper. This in itself is not unusual. But Dr O'Toole had access to the notebooks on which the published article was based, and she became convinced that they did not support the data presented in the article. Dr O'Toole shortly afterwards found herself unemployed. It was only as a result of investigations from *outside* the academic community that it emerged that the published paper cited some experiments which its author subsequently admitted had never been carried out. Further investigation revealed that the notebooks themselves had been falsified. Publicization of the O'Toole affair led to other allegations. One scientist claimed that, having encountered a similar problem himself, and 'Being made aware, rather pointedly, that I had the choice of remaining silent or terminating my career without being

able to correct the problem, I chose to remain silent.' His interest having been aroused by this episode, he spent some efforts investigating the matter and came to the conclusion that as many as a quarter of all published papers were tainted in this way — though mostly to a small extent (Cutler 1990).

Of course, replication is not the only way in which fraud may be exposed. When results conflict with the background taxonomy — as in an important case involving the distribution of fossils reported to be found in India's Himalayan region — the matter is likely to be detected in the long term. But the long term may be very long. The Indian researcher who falsified the information about fossils is estimated to have published more than 300 papers before the matter received public attention (Talent 1989).

Scientific controversy may also revolve around the precise specification of the assumptions — the initial conditions of the test — as in a recent controversy over an anti-ulcer drug (Economist 1991b). At the end of the day, however, the single most important issue is replication. Indeed, a distinguished scientist has argued, firstly, that scientific activity concentrates on those journal results which *can* be reproduced and, secondly, that these are perhaps 10 per cent of the whole (Ziman 1978: 30–1, 40–1, 130–1, 143).

With some exceptions — notably concerning anomalous results in the matter of exchange fluctuations and trade — economists pay little attention to the matter of replication. Yet in a social science context generally, an emphasis upon reproducibility can have dramatic results. Perhaps the most remarkable instance of this is provided by the experience of Derek Freeman. Sailing, so to speak, under a Popperian flag, he attempted to 'reproduce' the (to a non-anthropologist at least) rather surprising results obtained by Margaret Mead in her *Coming of Age in Samoa* of 1928. The result (Freeman 1983) was not only completely destructive of Mead's original claims: it also resulted in a fierce controversy (Freeman was described to me, by an anthropologist, as 'out of his tree'), and for the outsider there remains the impression from the controversy that attempted replication is somehow outside the rules of the game for social scientists.

For it is not only anthropologists who are vulnerable on this score. A prominent sociologist has claimed that the results of interviews were 'cooked up' in the researcher's favourite pub (Andresky 1972: 109). The fabrication of results by the social psychologist Sir Cyril Burt — fabrication which seems to have been done with a cavalier disregard for the probability of detection, presumably because it was so low — is well known and seems to be accepted in the scholarly biography of Burt (Hearnshaw 1979).

In economics, the difficulties of reproducing results are notorious (Mayer 1980). There is indeed a persistent 'oral tradition' concerning some particular pieces of empirical work in economics, and anyone who has given undergraduates projects that involve the replication and then the development of published work knows the difficulties which this presents. One has to conclude that economists are really not very interested, for the most part, in the matter of replication. I myself was involved in a research project for which a data base was painstakingly built up from data obtained directly

from companies. The results were published (O'Brien *et al.* 1979), and the data were retained on computer file for fifteen years. During that time nobody asked for access to them. Yet the results of the study had significant policy implications.

Technical Problems of Testing

It is easy, if embarrassing, for an economist to run through a list of the technical problems involved in testing economic theory against published data. Virtually all of these problems are well recognized. They include the use of regression techniques, derived from carefully controlled agricultural experiments, on time-series data in which, because there is no distribution of Y values for each X value, the end result is arguably correlation analysis by another name, though with the assumption concerning the direction of causality made explicit. There is the very common presence of multicolinearity in the explanatory variables, resulting in unstable parameter estimates. There is the careless use of computer packages. This itself has several aspects. It can include correction for serial correlation without testing for its presence (Gotur 1985) and the availability of a battery of test statistics which, according to an eminent econometrician, few are in a position fully to comprehend (Johnson 1991: 52). It involves data transformations which even go as far as adding a constant to the observations to eliminate negative values so that log forms may be employed; reporting the one successful run (significant at 5 per cent) out of twenty; and adjusting the theory to the equation that works. It encounters the presence, through step-wise procedures, of pre-test bias, and it attempts to 'compensate' for poor quality data by the adoption of more and more complex tests, and the employment of 'filters' (or 'beating the data to death', as a colleague of mine put it). It is even possible to find economists inferring causality from co-integration.

The matter of subjecting poor quality data to more and more complicated statistical routines, made simple for the investigator by ever more elaborate computer packages, deserves further attention. Relentlessly recycled data from published sources has, in journal articles, replaced the data that used to be provided in the descriptive type of article that journals once published, which combined economic categorization with historical/judgemental techniques. As Johnson has observed,

> It is thus all too possible for someone to activate an econometric software package, of which he has only a dim understanding, to apply it to data of whose nature and provenance he is ignorant, and then to draw conclusions about an economic situation, whose historical and institutional realities he has, perhaps, not studied in any depth. (Johnson 1991: 52)

For this, the 'publish-or-perish' pressures must take a lot of the blame. As Friedman, with characteristic shrewdness concerning the profession, has observed,

> . . . the easiest way to avoid perishing by not publishing is to access an existing database, download a batch of data to your computer, and put the data through the econometric wringer. (Friedman 1991: 36)

Does this, together with the predominance of purely theoretical work, to which Morgan has referred in his survey of journal articles, imply that there has been some question of market failure? That there has been some kind of failure is certainly possible; huge amounts of human and capital resources have been poured into economics in the last twenty-five years without, it could well be argued, any very great advance in understanding.[2] But if there is a failure, it is not a market failure but a failure in what Boulding (1971, 1973) has called the 'grants economy', which, of course, operates by a different set of rules. None the less, it is difficult to dispute Buchanan's contention that 'the discipline's ultimate *raison d'être* fails to exert positive feedbacks on the structure of inquiry' (1991: 20).

In processing the published data, economists have displayed a relentless adherence to one statistical technique: regression. They have also (rather in contrast to psychologists) displayed a systematic disregard of techniques (non-parametric) designed to cope with poor quality data where differences in numbers may have only ordinal or even categoric significance.

In the face of all these difficulties, it is hardly surprising that published results cannot be reproduced on different data sets. The fact that they cannot be reproduced on what is ostensibly *the same* data sets is of course even more worrying. But the situation is not irremediable. Economists need, first of all, to clean up the data and make sure that they have at least a minimal understanding of what they mean and where they came from. Secondly, despite the fact that as Friedman pointed out (1991: 36), and as I myself can certainly testify, construction of one's own data set is extremely hard work, they need to construct their own data sets *and* to make these available to other researchers. In the processing of these data sets, they need to draw upon a much wider statistical palette and not to demand high quality answers from data that are not sufficiently precise to provide them. Certainly the difficulties that have been encountered do not in any sense provide a case for retreating from the attempt to confront theories with data. For without data — including data on assumptions — we have no basis on which to choose between theories.

3. Data and the choice of theories

The Need for Choice

Ultimately, if economists are to produce 'reliable knowledge' they have to choose theories that perform well. The alternative to accepting this discipline is a massive, self-contained, construction of great irrelevance. Such a construction can hardly justify public funding on the scale enjoyed by

economists. Yet economists seem reluctant to recognize this. Of course, it is true that enthusiasts for totalitarianism do not like theory choice on the basis of empirical testing. But this reluctance is much more widespread and is manifested in conventionalism. The conventionalist argument is essentially this: whatever economists may claim that they do, and in particular whatever their supposed position on falsification, there is in fact a large element of agreeing to agree without making any judgement about the occurrence of falsification. 'Therefore' let us simply settle for conventionalism as the state of the (epistemological) world.

The problem with conventionalism is that, if it is accepted as a satisfactory state of affairs, it offers no way of resolving theory conflict other than 'a conclusion emerging' (to borrow the language of 'committee-speak'). Moreover, it makes economics vulnerable to changes in fashion. This is a long-standing problem in economics (Black 1963), even though in the 1980s, with the huge increase in specialization, the fashions themselves became more specialized and, not infrequently, became fashions of technique rather than of subject matter or ideas. In quantitative matters, co-integration has come to be applied widely and perhaps without discrimination, while in microeconomics, and even in matters of macroeconomic policy, the role of game theory has become so expanded that one distinguished exponent sees the 1980s as the *decade* of game theory (Rubinstein 1990: xi). But fashion — unless it is fashion guided precisely by the aim of producing reliable knowledge, rather than by the aim of employing the latest statistical technology — is a poor guide to the effective use of resources.

In this respect, economics compares badly with natural science. Whereas the conventionalism involved in Kuhn's 'normal science' has at its basis a network of theory which has withstood attempts at falsification — has proved reliable — that involved in economics is not required to have such a backing, according to the conventionalists.

The conventionalists can gain no support for their position from the work of Lakatos. While Lakatos was perfectly happy to see scientific research programmes (SRPs) in competition, testing is central to that competition. SRPs are progressive if they predict novel facts, and if these novel facts feature successfully in a testing programme. But in economics violent shifts in fashion (in adherence to SRPs) do take place without any novel facts (facts which, even if known beforehand, are not involved in the construction of the new theory — Zahar 1973: 103). Game theory has replaced structure–conduct–performance (S–C–P) not only without any novel facts, but with a wholesale withering of the empirical aspect of industrial economics.

As F. M. Fisher (1989) has pointed out, real industries do not have one-shot games, while repeated games simply produce a vast collection of possible equilibria. Theorists do not even appear to be working towards the perfectly sensible goal of producing theory in a form that would enable empirical studies to be done. The game theory approach actually suppresses relevant information. As Fisher says, 'the full rich contextual story of how

multimarket contact affects the ability to get to joint maximisation cannot be told by concentrating on Nash equilibria' (1989: 122). Of course, some of those engaged in game theory believe that the development of 'experimental economics' will provide the empirical material that game theory so conspicuously lacks (Plott 1991; Roth 1991; Schmalensee 1991). This seems unlikely for a number of reasons. On the one hand, experience of questionnaires in other contexts suggests that people react differently in an artificial situation from that in which their own financial welfare is genuinely and significantly affected. Secondly, the use of experiments suppresses a mass of relevant empirical material. To ask whether we would learn more about the nature of innovation from Jewkes, Sawers and Stillerman's classic and careful set of case studies in *The Studies of Invention* (Jewkes *et al.* 1969) or from a highly stylized game about a patent race (Fudenberg *et al.* 1983) is to answer the question.

Of course, it is true that the empirical studies conducted under the S–C–P banner did not, by any means, always test what they purported to be testing. In particular, the profit–sales ratio is not an indicator of market power, although a large empirical literature assumes that it is. The ratio, however, takes no account of differing capital structures and thus of varying depreciation charges — as pointed out by Bauer in 1941 and by Fisher in 1987. Again, some tests of the Schumpeterian hypothesis concerning firm size and innovation have not specified the relevant hypothesis adequately and have arguably tested something different (Fisher and Temin 1973).

But this indicates the need to improve the testing, not to abandon it. For abandonment leads not merely to conventionalism, but to the employment of various institutional devices to ensure that a particular favoured view gains and retains ascendency. Conventionalism may be relatively harmless where there is no serious dispute — as in the case of the generally negative slope of demand curves; but it raises serious problems, culminating in some very ugly spectres indeed, where there are fundamental disputes.

The Need for an Empirical Check

Ultimately, a subject needs empirical discipline. In the natural sciences there seems to be no dispute over this, even in the largest and most speculative areas such as Lovelock's 'Gaia' hypothesis. Indeed, Lovelock (1988) cites one key piece of empirical evidence concerning atmospheric turbulence in support of his thesis. There is really no point in the pages of economic journals aping those of journals in physics and chemistry with regard to their deployment of algebraic symbolism if there is a painful contrast in empirical content between the former and the latter.

The contrast is however much more strong than a count of articles containing empirical data of some sort would suggest (Oswald 1991), because many of the 'empirical' articles contain recycled published data. In Morgan's classification (1988), only 5 per cent of the articles categorized as 'empirical' in the *American Economic Review* (*AER*) involved data

generated by the author's initiative, for the years 1982–6. (This excludes 'experimental' data for reasons already indicated: that would add another 6 per cent.) For the *Economic Journal* (*EJ*) in the same years, considerably less than half the articles (42 per cent) involved empirical analysis, and of these only 2 per cent were accounted for by data generated, with another 2 per cent involving experiments. The comparison with physics and chemistry is dramatic: while the *AER* published 42 per cent of its articles as mathematical ones without any data, with the corresponding figure for the *EJ* being 52 per cent, a sample of physics and chemistry journals produced figures of 12 and 0 per cent, respectively.

The journal material is then, to some extent, 'mock physics'. Of course, this has significant rhetorical aspects, as has been emphasized by Donald McCloskey (1983, 1985, 1987). McCloskey manages to be both entertaining and scholarly, a sufficiently rare achievement perhaps to be in itself worthy of note. Of Samuelson's *Foundations*, he wrote:

> The mathematics is presented in an off hand way, with an assumption that we all can read off partitioned matrices at a glance, inconsistent with the level of mathematics in other passages. The air of easy mathematical mastery was important to the influence of the book, by contrast with the embarrassed modesty with which British writers at the time (Hicks most notably) pushed mathematics off into appendices.
>
> Samuelson's skill at mathematics in the eyes of his readers, an impression nurtured at every turn, is itself an important and persuasive argument. He presents himself as an authority, with good reason. That the mathematics is so often pointless, as here, is beside the point. Being able to do such a difficult thing (so it would have seemed to the typical economist reading in 1947) is warrant of expertise. (McCloskey 1983: 500)

Samuelson's *Foundations* is a genuinely original work, and a significant intellectual achievement within its own terms; but the rhetorical example has had very significant fall-out. Indeed, it has been firmly grasped by those with whom Samuelson has engaged in lengthy controversy — the Cambridge (England) Marx–Sraffa school (Blaugh 1988: 42). But it is certainly far from being confined to them. Contributors to the *EJ* centenary volume, who could not be accused of lacking expertise in mathematics, have pointed to the extent to which mathematical display in the journals is an art form for its own sake (Baumol 1991: 6; Friedman 1991: 36).

Of course, the idea of mathematics as a signalling device to indicate those with intellectual authority is also to be found in natural science. Indeed, it is the case that in one important historical episode — discussions over the continental drift hypothesis — this authority led scientists astray (Ziman 1978: 94; Hallam 1975: 82–5). But ultimately in natural science there is an empirical check, whereas the mathematics of the economics journals have often moved economists further away from data — indeed, it is hard to imagine the possible dimensions of some economic concepts (though this is far from being a new problem). It is also true that related problems arose earlier in the history of natural science — Phlogiston being an example

(Duveen 1956: 38–9). But these episodes have usually been checked by the need for empirical counterparts to concepts; the same cannot be said of economics.

Yet, ultimately, solving elaborate mathematical puzzles, in which economic names have been attached to variables, is a sterile pursuit. Henry Phelps Brown has put this very well:

> Before long he [the economist] is making models in which the components do indeed bear the names of entrepreneurs or holders of money balances, trade unionists or investors; but these are such stereotypes that the patterns they form and the problems they pose seem, like chess problems, to owe their interest to their intellectual difficulty, and not to any identity between the pieces on the board and the flesh and blood of those they nominally represent: nor to any help their solution will give in the world's work. (Phelps Brown 1980b: 6–7)

Lest this be taken as the complaint of someone whose work has been distinguished by the high quality of its empirical foundations, the words of one of the world's leading mathematical economists are salutary:

> I have discussed myself in a separate essay how Japanese mathematics . . . in the Tokugawa period, though it had attained a high level of sophistication, came to a wretched end due to its total absence of interaction with natural science. It turned into a technique for the setting of puzzles, and the . . . scholars were reduced to being the playmates of culture-loving Samurai and members of the newly risen merchant class, just like the masters of the tea ceremony, of flower arrangement and of the *haiku*. At the same time, the mathematics itself regressed. The following words by John von Neumann can be read as a warning against decadence of this kind: 'At a great distance from its empirical source, or after much "abstract" inbreeding, a mathematical subject is in danger of degeneration'. (Morishima 1991: 70)

Towards the end of the same article, he writes:

> I know of course that one section of GET scholars may regard with hostility those who make statements such as I have made above, on the grounds of their loyalty to mathematics. Scholars of this group expend their energies on competing with each other in demonstrations of intellectual and theoretical ability, and regard as their inferiors those who contend the need to observe the real world. This phenomenon is a palpable symptom of scientific degeneration. (Morishima 1991: 74)

None of this should be taken as representing the argument that mathematics has no place in economics. The essential point is that there has to be an empirical check on the castles in the air which we build. Yet the rhetorical temptations to continue along the present lines are powerful indeed. As Alan Coddington (1975) showed to devastating effect in discussing general equilibrium, such an approach can be used to reformulate opposing theoretical approaches in terms of the preferred approach, as a result of which they can be dismissed because they do not answer questions suggested by the preferred theory as well as the preferred theory itself does. (The hapless Dennis Robertson, and other critics of Keynes, found themselves in a somewhat similar position in the 1930s, and indeed,

Robertson at one point wrote plaintively to Keynes *à propos* of Hayek's critique of Keynes's *Treatise*: 'If I *must* try to express myself in two foreign languages at once . . .' (Keynes 1973: 271). The correspondence between Keynes and Hawtrey provides numerous other examples.)

The temptation to persevere with complex theoretical formulations of systems that have apparently no empirical counterpart is strengthened by the fact that, precisely *because* there is no clear relationship between the theory and any set of facts, the theory can be used to rationalize anything that does happen in the real world, so long as the outcomes are carefully boxed in terms of its own classifications. This is particularly true of game theory, which, with its multiple outcomes in repeated games, has enabled industrial economics to part company with industrial data to a degree that would have seemed inconceivable even a dozen years ago. In the process economists get further and further away from informative theorizing — as Popper has pointed out (1963: ch. 1), a theory that can explain everything has no informational content.

4. Natural science as a guide

Physics

Since the seventeenth century, when economics finally cut its links with the great moral questions confronted by Aquinas and his successors, economists have taken inspiration and guidance from natural science, especially physics. Petty, one of the founders of the Royal Society, was a man who sought 'to apply the empirical processes of observation and experiment, in the first instance to the study of the natural world and technology, and then to the study of society, which was Petty's own main interest' (Hutchison 1988: 28). Petty's own statement of his aims is striking:

> The Method I take . . . , is not very usual; for, instead of using only comparative and superlative Words, and intellectual Arguments, I have taken the course (as a Specimen of the Political Arithmetick I have long aimed at) to express my self in Terms of Number, Weight, or Measure; to use only Arguments of Sense, and to consider only such Causes as have visible Foundations in Nature. (Petty 1690: 244)

From that time on it is easy enough to find economists who, as a rhetorical device, refer to the natural sciences. What is of importance for present purposes is, however, whether there is more than rhetoric involved in this and whether, in truth, physics provides a good model for economists.

This seems doubtful for a number of reasons. Firstly, there are simple difficulties of test replication when results depend upon time-series data — which are essentially a unique historical record. Secondly, there is no *controlled* experimental process in economics, despite the development of 'experimental economics' noted above. This involves asking subjects (almost invariably undergraduates) to simulate behaviour in a complex

industrial situation (one which in practice it would take many years to learn about) and reporting the results. Chamberlin attempted this in 1948, but at that time attracted few followers. However, the 1980s have seen a significant increase in this type of activity, not least because it is almost the only way in which many applications of game theory can be given any semblance of contact with reality (Plott 1991).

Perhaps most seriously of all, these two problems interact with a third, which of itself is of small consequence in physics but of considerable consequence for economics. The problem is that the logic of empirical statements falls into three categories: true, false and undecided (Ziman 1978: 26–30). Whereas the last category is of small significance in physics, it is, because of the two problems concerning time-series data and controls already noted, a very large category indeed for economics. In fact, in Ziman's view it is 'devastating' in its implications for social science because it is, in truth, by far the largest single category. It is almost impossible to think of a single uncontested empirical result in economics,[3] and there are only a few (notably those concerning mergers and concerning exchange rate fluctuations and trade referred to above) that would command the assent of the vast majority. It follows from this that attempting to make all social science like physics is, in the words of a physicist, 'merely a specialised and naive form of *scientism*, which holds that all reliable knowledge of the world and its workings should be, or should strive to be, or will eventually be, "scientific" in some ill-defined sense' (Ziman 1978: 30).

But in any case, the vision of physics which economists have is of an obsolete kind of physics. Economists still think in terms of the elegance and determinateness of what is essentially nineteenth-century physics. This is, as a theoretical physicist has observed, 'an outmoded paradigm of physics' (Berry in Wolpert and Richards 1988: 44; see also Weisskopf 1979). As already noted, in alluding to the case of Schroedinger's cat, problems not envisaged by classical physics are recognized since the quantum revolution. Indeed, since Heisenberg, physicists accept that the position and velocity of particles are not simply facts that can be simultaneously discovered. This is hardly the world of certain and objective nineteenth-century physics. This in turn, as Weisskopf has pointed out, has serious implications for a methodology based upon prediction:

> *Heisenberg's principle of uncertainty (or indeterminacy)* implies that — in microphysics — that influence of the observer on the position and velocity of particles makes it impossible to ascertain both their position and velocity, together. Thus, the bases of precise prediction are destroyed. (Weisskopf 1979: 871; italics in original)

Another problem is that, even were this not the case, the difficulties in distinguishing between 'noise' and 'signal' in economics are different in kind, and not in degree, from those in physics (Ziman 1978: 67–70), so it is doubtful whether techniques borrowed from physics for this purpose — Kalman filters — really do more than smooth the data.

All these issues reinforce the views of those economists who, even when they had only classical physics in mind, doubted the suitability of physics as a model for economics. Viner (1963: 14), Hicks (1979: 38–9) and Popper (1957: 143) have all doubted this parallel, notably because of the impossibility of 'control' and because the great constants of physics are never going to have their equivalents in economics; with modern developments in both mathematics and physics, the parallels seem even less well founded.

Catastrophe and Chaos

The challenge to the idea that smooth continuous twice-differentiable functions do not pose problems for economics comes from two new branches of mathematics: catastrophe and chaos.

(a) Catastrophe

Catastrophe theory has attracted the attention of economists for some time, and there are popular expositions, including a moderately technical one aimed directly at economists (George 1988; see also Woodcock and Davis 1978). In the journals there are now treatments of catastrophe theory both in relation to monopoly (Bonanno 1987) and in relation to the more general lessons to be learned by economics from this branch of mathematics (Dodgson 1982). It has long been known that 'The possibility of . . . discontinuous jumps in [monopoly] output, resulting from only a small change in a smooth curve, can easily arise in situations where there are multiple solutions' (Creedy and O'Brien 1990: 148). In the 1980s both Walters (1980) and others (Formby *et al.* 1982) have examined the problem of multiple equilibria under monopoly if marginal revenue increases over a range of output. The idea goes back to Marshall, though he is not mentioned by any of these authors. But the existence of this kind of problem makes reliance upon prediction as a test of theory a weak reed indeed; for a discontinuous series of outcomes of the kind envisaged in catastrophe theory does not provide the means by which the predictive powers of a deterministic theory can easily be assessed.

(b) Chaos

Although the origins of this mathematical development lie in the nineteenth century, it is only the computer age that has allowed mathematicians, physicists, biologists and most recently some economists (Baumol and Benhabib 1989; De Grauwe and Dewachter 1990) to explore the paths that can be taken by apparently simple dynamic systems, given slight variations in initial conditions and the existence of nonlinearity, and to discover that the outcomes have been far from simple — in a word, chaotic.

The problem about nonlinearity can be encapsulated by a simple example given by Stewart (1989: 19–20). Consider the equation

$$X_n = -1 + \beta X_{n-1}^2 \tag{1}$$

With β = 1.4, this equation will go through a complicated cycle of 16 different values. If β is raised to 1.5, the behaviour of the equation becomes chaotic. With increases in β up to 1.74, chaos reigns. However, once β reaches 1.75, it turns out that, after 50 iterations, 'it settles into a cycle of length *three*, with numbers around 0.744 −0.030 −0.998' (Stewart 1989: 20).

An example with origins in the nineteenth century is given by Peitgen and Richter (1985). We start with a growth equation:

$$X_{n+1} = (1 + r)X_n, \tag{2}$$

$$\text{where } r = \frac{X_{n+1} - X_n}{X_n}$$

We then introduce an upper limit X_{max}, and the growth rate r is replaced by

$$g = (r - CX_n), \tag{3}$$

$$\text{where } C = \frac{r}{X_{max}} \tag{4}$$

Thus, as $X_n \rightarrow X^{-}_{max}$, $g \rightarrow 0^{+}$. Substituting (3) into (2) produces the following equation:

$$X_{n+1} = X_n(1 + r) - CX_n^2. \tag{5}$$

As Peitgen and Richter (1985: 67–9) demonstrate, this apparently innocuous formulation can behave very strangely indeed. At $r = 2.57$,

> it jumps around incessantly among an infinite number of values in a way which is actually deterministic *but cannot be predicted over long periods of time* [italics added]. The term *chaotic* has become customary for this behaviour. (Peitgen and Richter 1985: 68)

As the value of nonlinear parameters is changed in a chaotic system, 'bifurcations' (branchings) occur, and the possible paths followed by the system can become so varied that 'practically all memory of the global structure of the original dynamical system is lost' (Cvitanović 1984: 18).

Thus, nonlinear systems may very well not have predictable paths. Yet, as a leading macroeconomic theorist has observed,

> For the most part, formal dynamic analysis is usually carried out for linear systems or by taking linear approximations to more general systems. In important respects linear analysis is highly misleading and it is important to see the further application and development of nonlinear dynamic analysis. (Turnovsky 1991: 146)[4]

However, it is not only nonlinearities that are important. Very small differences in initial conditions also have a significant part to play. In the history of the development of chaos, it seems that this first came to attention in the simulation by Lorenz of weather systems, when, to save time, the

latter part of a simulation was duplicated but with fewer decimal points in the inputs for that later stage of the simulation than the computer had generated by starting at the beginning (Gleick 1988).

A simple example which illustrates the problem nicely is given by Stewart (1989: 19). If equation (1) has a starting value of 0.54322, the resulting pattern, after about fifteen iterations, looks completely different from that resulting if the starting value is 0.54321. As Peitgen and Richter point out, differences in initial conditions can also produce *intermittent* chaos — and the picture produced by graphing intermittent chaos bears an interesting visual resemblance to that of some economic time-series, most notably exchange rates.

All this represents bad news for economists, especially for those economists who believe that theories can be appraised solely by their predictive power. This view is reinforced by the emerging theory, which goes by the name of 'self-organized criticality' and which indicates that systems with many degrees of freedom evolve naturally into a critical state giving rise to chaotic behaviour. Things do not, where there are many degrees of freedom involved, settle naturally into their most stable states.

There is no reason why economists should not grapple with the problem of chaos itself. Methods are being developed to distinguish between genuine randomness and chaos (Brock 1986; Brock and Sayers 1988), even though the two can be found together (noisy chaos). Moreover, mathematicians are making some progress in finding order in chaos, not only with the concept of 'attractors' (Ruelle 1980) — what may be represented visually as stable areas towards which the patterns of chaotic equations gravitate — but also in achieving some understanding of the conditions controlling bifurcations — Feigenbaum's delta (Cvitanović 1984: 19, 30). Indeed, Turnovsky believes that the computational power now available will lead to a revival of interest in nonlinear business cycles (1991: 146).

But from a methodological point of view, the emergence of chaos has disastrous implications for the world of Friedman's *Essays*. We cannot test a theory by its predictions if we have no idea what those predictions are because they are crucially dependent upon small changes in nonlinear parameters and upon changes (which may be of the order of 10^{-3} or less) in initial conditions.[5] The history of the development of chaos, which is recent history, is full of colourful characters, idiosyncratic geniuses and one-liners (Gleick 1988). But economists seem remarkably reluctant to accept its serious implications — implications that are possibly even more devastating for the social sciences, so long as they persist in emphasizing predictability to the exclusion of other considerations, than even for meteorology. For, if the essence of chaotic behaviour is in nonlinearities and in sensitivity to initial conditions, we are in trouble. The importance of the first in economics hardly needs emphasizing. With regard to the initial conditions, these are (perhaps partly under the influence of Friedman) *hardly ever clearly specified anyway*; and even where they are specified, they are subject to measurement errors of a huge magnitude, not least because of

the poor fit between the concepts in the models and the available published data. The consequences, both for the doctrine that assumptions do not matter and for a purely falsificationist approach to economics, are disastrous.

Medicine as a Model?

Petty, one of the founding fathers of economics, was originally a doctor. Indeed, a number of physicians, including Quesnay and Juglar, have interested themselves in economics and made contributions. This suggests the possibility (though perhaps no more than that) that a medical training may be helpful in dealing with economic problems. Moreover, as Kornai has argued,

> We have every reason to look at medical science with due modesty and respect. It has a past of many centuries; ours is only two or three hundred years old. Mankind spends incomparably more intellectual capacity, labour, material means and technical equipment on medical science than it does on economics. (Kornai 1983: 191)

In particular, the role of observation and of pattern formation are of crucial importance in medicine. Of course, sometimes the patterns that appear to exist are not confirmed by more structured research. But the hunches are still worth investigating in many cases. One particular example involved the development of the cephalosporin group of antibiotics where observation of the sea near a sewage outfall led to isolation of an antibiotic-producing organism (Florey 1955: 480). Penicillin itself seems to have started with no more than a chance observation (though accounts differ somewhat — Wilson 1976: 57–87). Both cases have two characteristics: firstly, observation and pattern recognition were a fundamental source of hypothesis formation; secondly, further data were then gathered to test the hypothesis. The latter stage is of course vital: without the amazing work of Florey and Chain and their associates, penicillin would have remained no more than a curiosity.

Medicine also indicates that instrumentalism can have a useful role to play, at least as an intermediate stage. The use of acetylsalicylic acid is said to have been appreciated for centuries; yet the action of such an everyday substance as aspirin is still not really understood. It was long after the miraculous development of penicillin as a drug that its structure was fully explored (Wilson 1976: 263–8), while the distance in time between the work by Banting and Best on insulin and the understanding of its structure extended from 1922, when it was first used to treat patients, until 1969 (Jewkes *et al.* 1969: 260–2; Wolpert and Richards 1988: 69).

Of course, not everything in the world of medical research can be regarded by economists with admiration. The pressure to publish, and the pressures for apparent clinical success, are so strong that highly dubious results are not only published but publicized through press releases. Bizarre

research results are, in particular, obtained from cohort data of a sometimes rather insecurely based kind, and in violation of the rules followed by the best medical researchers, as in Hill's standard works on the subject (1961, 1962). An association should be strong, should be consistent over different studies, should hold over time, should involve a biological gradient (higher intake, higher risk) and, if possible, should be confirmed by experiment. Ignoring these rules in the pressure to publish has undoubtedly resulted in the publication of nonsense. But perhaps economists can learn from the negative aspects of medical research as well as from the positive ones.

5. History

So far this discussion has concentrated on what economists can learn from endeavours in natural science. But there is a major question which has been significantly (though not completely — see Arrow 1985; McCloskey 1976; Solow 1986) neglected by economists: the role of history. This itself represents a significant change in the outlook of economists. Until the Second World War, few economists would have doubted the importance either of economic history as a subject or of some education in economic history for an economist. The change in opinion is dramatically illustrated by the fact that the centenary issue of the *Economic Journal* (January 1991) contained not a single contribution by an economic historian (though a veteran economist, Sir Austin Robinson, did introduce historical material).

Rather than learning from economic history, economists seem more frequently in the postwar years to have conducted raids into the subject, processing historical data, sometimes with scant regard for its meaning, as a means of testing highly simplified models which bear little resemblance to the historical situation that generated the data. In the process, it would seem, they have achieved little more than the sapping of confidence of economic historians (Crafts 1987). There are of course significant exceptions which show that economists (or some economists) can do good work in economic history. Henry Phelps Brown's *Century of Pay* is exemplary not only in this respect but also in its lucid and balanced discussion of the uses to which such enormously detailed and painstaking work can be put (Phelps Brown with Browne 1968: esp. 25–37, 319–46).

It is work of this kind that exemplifies Schumpeter's point that the subject matter of economics is in fact a unique historical process (Schumpeter 1954: 12–13). One aspect of this is that all economic data are the product of specific, and evolving, institutional circumstances. Yet how few economists have learnt the lessons that Sir Henry put forward in his 1971 presidential address to the Royal Economic Society — that history is an essential part of the training of the economist so that economists, with their models, may 'learn from the historians about actual affairs in all their complexity' (Phelps Brown 1972: 8), and that 'Every practical economic problem . . . presents

itself as an historical situation, and our capacity to understand it is our capacity to understand history' (p. 8).

In fact, however, economic history itself has suffered a serious decline. Economic history departments have been closed and chairs in the subject have been abolished. The reasons for this must surely lie, at least in part, in the 'publish-or-perish' pressures alluded to earlier. Economic history is very hard work. Faced with a vast mass of data, to get any grasp of which might take years of study, why not formulate a few highly simplified hypotheses, test them on whatever data, however inappropriate, are to hand, and hope that you will 'pick up' the hypothesized effect? You can then announce that you have — in preliminary form of course, because more work *always* remains to be done — a satisfactory hypothesis reducing all the variables evolving over time, in response to a myriad of influences, to a few simple one-way relationships.

Yet there is so much to be learnt from doing economic history properly. There is no point in trying to use more and more refined statistical techniques to test whether the money supply is exogenous or endogenous if attention to historical circumstances reveals that the authorities have deliberately chosen endogeneity at various times. More generally, the work of Friedman and Schwartz (1963) remains, despite some criticisms which have subsequently been levelled at it (Hendry and Ericsson 1983), enormously impressive. In fact, detailed historical work in the field of monetary economics is often extremely illuminating, not least in the understanding of sustained inflation (Wood 1990: 9).

But the lessons of economic history, and of an approach grounded in historical techniques, go much wider than this. The economics graduate with a knowledge of Chandler's *Strategy and Structure* (1969) and *The Visible Hand* (1977) is more suited to the multi-faceted world of industry (of which most academic economists have no first-hand experience) than an expert in game theory, who might well conscientiously lose sight of all but a few aspects of a problem, and then not be alert to potentially significant losses of information when the importance of various factors changed. It used to be the case that the structure–conduct–performance approach, happily still alive in Scherer's third edition (Scherer and Ross 1990), embodied much that had been learned from economic history; but S–C–P too, alas, has become unfashionable.

Yet, as a recent paper by Lal (1990) on comparative studies shows, there is still so much to be learned by economists who do not despise history. As Lal correctly points out, comparative studies 'are a form of comparative historical analysis which has a distinguished pedigree in social science' (1990: 4). This was discussed by J. S. Mill and by J. N. Keynes, as Lal notes, but in fact it goes back to Hume and the Scottish Historical School as well as to Montesquieu. Lal also rightly stresses the role of judgement in the use of this technique. However, if economists continue to eschew contact with historical and descriptive data, it seems unlikely that they will ever develop this judgement.

Of course, economics is not history. But it has a lot to learn from history, and it has a ready-made link in the work of the economic historians. From historians, economists can learn that the complexities of problems do matter, and that some evaluation of the scale of the influences operating in a particular situation (the sort of thing which Marshall seems to have dealt with in his 'advanced' lectures) is extremely important. It is even possible that economists would be wise to lay more emphasis on what is to be learned from history and less on what can be copied (or parodied) from physics.

6. Conclusion

Economists have always believed that what they were attempting was in some sense 'scientific'. They were not merely describing, or narrating: they were, and are, concerned with causal relationships. Because of the methodological tensions generated by the subject matter of economics, and in particular by attempts to apply 'scientific' procedures to an historical process, there has always been some tension between the axiomatic approach and that which starts with the data. Of course, not all economists have been anxious to claim 'scientific' status — and the doubters include no less a person than Hicks (1979: viii). But the majority of economists — conscious perhaps that, as seekers after funds, their research grants may have an opportunity cost in terms of hospital equipment or other desirables[6] — would take a more utilitarian line. This, it was argued above, rules out a comfortable retreat into 'methodological pluralism'. But if that is ruled out, then economists have to make theory choices; and to make theory choices it will be necessary to recognize that theoretical speculations have to be constrained by the data, and the meaning of those data has to be carefully considered.

The end result will never be 'hard' in the sense that physics is hard — indeed, it will almost certainly never attain the degree of hardness of the biological sciences. But it will be better than either wall-to-wall algebra of the most incestuous kind or journalistic description.

For, in their efforts over the centuries, economists have, despite their many false dawns, achieved much. If it is true that the last place that anyone would turn to learn about human relations is a work on sociology (Ziman 1978: 185), it is not true that we would turn to an American 'best-seller' writer to learn about the air transport industry. But, equally, we would not turn to the wilder shores of the theory of the firm to learn how the firm in a particular industry would be likely to behave. For this, there is really no substitute for knowledge of that industry.

Of course, economists are prone — and have been particularly prone during their periodic bouts of optimism, such as the 1960s — to claim too much for themselves. A sort of scientific conceit is not pretty to observe, especially when it is ill-founded. But this is by no means a monopoly of economists. None the less, the sometimes ridiculous postures that

economists have adopted have made them fair game for the brilliant pen of Terence Hutchison (1964, 1968). A less cavalier attitude towards factual information of all sorts, and a greater humility when faced with the complexities of a particular situation, would make economists less vulnerable — indeed, it might even lead to better economics.

Acknowledgements

I am very grateful to John Creedy for comments on an earlier version of this paper.

Notes

1. Sweezey's formulation was not empirically based.
2. For a more optimistic, and much longer-term, view see Faulhaber and Baumol (1988).
3. Engel's Law is a possible exception to this statement; but this is essentially a statistical regularity.
4. For evidence of nonlinearity in some macroeconomic series, see Brock and Sayers (1988).
5. On predictions and chaos, see Baumol and Quandt (1985).
6. This should not be taken to imply that ranking *within* medical priorities is necessarily optimal.

References

Andresky, S. (1972). *Social Sciences as Sorcery*. London: André Deutsch.

Arrow, K. (1985). 'Economic history: a necessary though not sufficient condition for an economist'. *American Economic Review*, 75: 320–3.

Aumann, R. J. (1964). 'Markets with a continuum of traders'. *Econometrica*, 32: 39–50; reprinted in A. Rubinstein (ed.), *Game Theory in Economics*, Aldershot: Edward Elgar, 1990: 622–33.

Bauer, P. (1941). 'A note on monopoly'. *Economica*, 8: 194–202.

Baumol, W. J. (1991). 'Towards a newer economics: the future lies ahead!'. *Economic Journal*, 101: 1–8.

—— and Benhabib, J. (1989). 'Chaos: significance, mechanism, and economic applications'. *Journal of Economic Perspectives*, 3: 77–105.

—— and Quandt, R. E. (1985). 'Chaos models and their implications for forecasting'. *Eastern Economic Journal*, 11: 3–15.

Black, R. D. C. (1963). *Economic Fashions*. Queen's University of Belfast.

Blaug, M. (1988). *Economics Through the Looking Glass*. Occasional Paper no. 78. London: Institute of Economic Affairs.

Bonanno, G. (1987). 'Monopoly equilibria and catastrophe theory'. *Australian Economic Papers*, 26: 197–215.

Boulding, K. (1971). 'The misallocation of intellectual resources in economics'. In I. L. Horowitz (ed.), *The Use and Abuse of Social Science*. New Brunswick, NJ: Transaction Books.

—— (1973). *The Economy of Love and Fear*. Belmont, Cal.: Wadsworth.

Braithwaite, R. B. (1958). Review of *Foundations of Inductive Logic* by R. Harrod. *Economic Journal*, 68: 146–9.

Brock, W. (1986). 'Distinguishing random and deterministic systems'. *Journal of Economic Theory*, 40: 168–95.

—— and Sayers, C. (1988). 'Is the business cycle characterised by deterministic chaos?' *Journal of Monetary Economics*, 22: 71–90.

Buchanan, J. M. (1991). 'Economics in the post-socialist century'. *Economic Journal*, 101: 15–21.

Burns, A. R. and Mitchell, W. C. (1946). *Measuring Business Cycles*. New York: National Bureau of Economic Research (reprinted 1964).

Chamberlin, E. H. (1948). 'An experimental imperfect market'. *Journal of Political Economy*, 56: 95–108.

Chandler, A. (1969). *Strategy and Structure*. Cambridge, Mass.: MIT Press.

—— (1977). *The Visible Hand*. Cambridge, Mass.: Belknap Press.

Coddington, A. (1975). 'The rationale of general equilibrium theory'. *Economic Inquiry*, 13: 539–58.

Crafts, N. (1987). 'Economic history'. In J. Eatwell, M. Milgate and P. Newman (eds.), *The New Palgrave*, Vol. 2. London: Macmillan.

Creedy, J. and O'Brien, D. P. (1990). 'Marshall, monopoly and rectangular hyperbolas'. *Australian Economic Papers*, 29: 141–53.

—— and Thomas, B. (1982). *The Economics of Labour*. London: Butterworth.

Cutler, A. (1990). 'Fraud in labs'. *The Economist*, 7 July: 6.

Cvitanović, P. (1984). *Universality in Chaos*. Bristol: Adam Hilger.

De Grauwe, P. and Dewachter, H. (1990). *A Chaotic Monetary Model of the Exchange Rate*. London: CEPR Discussion Paper no. 466.

De Marchi, N. (1988). *The Popperian Legacy in Economics*. Cambridge University Press.

Dodgson, J. S. (1982). 'Kinks and catastrophes: a note on the relevance of catastrophe theory for economics'. *Australian Economic Papers*, 21: 407–15.

Donahue, W. H. (1988). 'Kepler's fabricated figures: covering up the mess in the *New Astronomy*'. *Journal for the History of Astronomy*, 19: 217–37.

Drago, R. and Perlman, R. (1989). *Microeconomic Issues in Labour Economics*. Brighton: Harvester Wheatsheaf.

Duveen, D. (1956). 'Lavoisier'; reprinted in O. Gingerich (ed.), *Scientific Genius and Creativity*. New York: W. H. Freeman, 1987.

Economist (1991a). 'New bearings'. *The Economist*, 9 February: 110–13.

—— (1991b). 'Too much acid'. *The Economist*, 30 March: 108–9.

Faulhaber, G. and Baumol, W. J. (1988). 'Economists as innovators: practical products of theoretical research'. *Journal of Economic Literature*, 26: 577–600.

Fisher, F. M. (1987). 'On the misuse of the profits-sales ratio to infer monopoly power'. *Rand Journal of Economics*, 18: 384–96.

—— (1989). 'Games economists play: a noncooperative view'. *Rand Journal of Economics*, 20: 113–24.

—— and Temin, P. (1973). 'Returns to scale in research and development: what does the Schumpeterian hypothesis imply?' *Journal of Political Economy*, 81: 56–70.

Florey, H. (1955). 'Antibiotic products of a versatile fungus'. *Annals of International Medicine*, 43: 480–90.

Formby, J. P. Layson, S. and Smith, J. (1982). 'The Law of Demand, positive sloping marginal revenue and multiple profit equilibria'. *Economic Inquiry*, 20: 303–11.

Freeman, D. (1983). *Margaret Mead and Samoa: The Making and Unmaking of an Anthropological Myth*. Cambridge, Mass.: Harvard University Press.

Friedman, M. (1953). *Essays in Positive Economics*. University of Chicago Press.

—— (1991). 'Old wine in new bottles'. *Economic Journal*, 101: 33–40.

—— and Schwartz, A. (1963). *A Monetary History of the United States, 1867–1960*. Princeton University Press.

Fudenberg, D., Gilbert, R., Stiglitz, J. and Tirole, J. (1983). 'Preemption, leap frogging and competition in patent races'. *European Economic Review*, 22: 3–31.

George, D. (1988). *Mathematical Modelling for Economists*. London: Macmillan.

Gleick, J. (1988). *Chaos*. London: Heinemann.

Goodhart, C. (1984). *Monetary Theory and Practice*. London: Macmillan.

Gotur, P. (1985). 'Effects of Exchange Rate Volatility on Trade: Some Further Evidence'. *IMF Staff Papers*, 32: 475–512.

Hall, R. L. and Hitch, C. J. (1939). 'Price theory and business behaviour', *Oxford Economic Papers*, no. 2: 12–45.

Hallam, A. (1975). 'Alfred Wegener and the hypothesis of continental drift'; reprinted in O. Gingerich (ed.), *Scientific Genius and Creativity*. New York: W. H. Freeman, 1987.

Harrod, R. (1956). *Foundations of Inductive Logic*. London: Macmillan.

Hearnshaw, L. S. (1979). *Cyril Burt, Psychologist*. London: Hodder & Stoughton.

Hendry, D. and Ericsson, N. (1983). 'Assertion with empirical basis: an econometric appraisal of . . . Friedman and . . . Schwartz.' Bank of England Panel of Academic Consultants, Paper no. 22.

Hicks, J. (1979). *Causality in Economics*. Oxford: Basil Blackwell.

Hill, A. B. (1961). *Principles of Medical Statistics*, 7th edn. London: Lancet.

—— (1962). *Statistical Methods in Clinical and Preventive Medicine*. Edinburgh: Livingstone.

Hutchison, T. W. (1964). *'Positive' Economics and Policy Objectives*. London: Allen & Unwin.

—— (1968). *Economics and Economic Policy in Britain, 1946–1966*. London: Allen & Unwin.

—— (1978). *On Revolutions and Progress in Economic Knowledge*. Cambridge University Press.

—— (1988). *Before Adam Smith*. Oxford: Basil Blackwell.

Jewkes, J., Sawers, D. and Stillerman, R. (1969). *The Sources of Invention*, 2nd edn. London: Macmillan.

Johnson, J. (1991). 'Econometrics: Retrospect and Prospect'. *Economic Journal*, 101: 51–6.

Kennedy, P. (1985). *A Guide to Econometrics*, 2nd edn. Oxford: Basil Blackwell.

Keynes, J. M. (1973). *Collected Writings*. Vol. 13. London: Macmillan.

Keynes, J. M.)1917). *The Scope and Method of Political Economy*, 4th edn. London: Macmillan.

Kornai, J. (1983). 'The health of nations: reflections on the analogy between medical science and economics', *Kyklos*, 36: 191–212.

Kuhn, T. S. (1962). *The Structure of Scientific Revolutions*, 2nd edn. University of Chicago Press, 1970.

Lakatos, I. (1970). 'Falsification and the methodology of scientific research programmes'. In I. Lakatos and A. Musgrave, *Criticism and the Growth of Knowledge*. Cambridge University Press.

Lal, D. (1990). *Comparative Studies*. Mimeo, University College London.

Lee, F. S. (1981). 'The Oxford challenge to Marshallian supply and demand: the history of the Oxford economists' Research Group'. *Oxford Economic Papers*, 33: 339–51.

Lovelock, J. (1988). *The Ages of Gaia*. Oxford University Press.

Marshall, A. (1919). *Industry and Trade*, 3rd edn. London: Macmillan, 1920; reprinted 1927.

Marshall, M. P. (1947). *What I Remember*. Cambridge University Press.

Maurice, R. (ed.) (1968). *National Accounts Statistics: Sources and Methods*. London: HMSO.

Mayer, T. (1980). 'Economics as a Hard Science: Realistic Goal or Wishful Thinking?' *Economic Inquiry*, 18: 165–78.

McCarthy, M. (1977). 'The Status of the Leontief Paradox'. University of Kent Studies in Economics, no. 28.

McCloskey, D. (1976). 'Does the past have useful economics?' *Journal of Economic Literature*, 14: 434–61.

—— (1983). 'The rhetoric of economics'. *Journal of Economic Literature*, 21: 481–516.

—— (1985). *The Rhetoric of Economics*. Madison: University of Wisconsin Press.

—— (1987). 'Rhetoric'. In J. Eatwell, M. Milgate and P. Newman (eds.) *The New Palgrave*, vol. 3. London: Macmillan.

Mead, M. (1928). *Coming of Age in Samoa*. New York: Morrow; reprinted Harmondsworth: Penguin, 1965.

Mill, J. S. (1868). *A System of Logic, Ratiocinative and Inductive*, 7th edn. London: Longman.

Mitchell, W. C. (1928). *Business Cycles*. New York: National Bureau of Economic Research.

Mitchison, N. A. (1980). 'Inheritance: the immunological challenge'. *Nature*, no. 288 (20 Nov.): 306.

Morgan, T. (1988). 'Theory versus empiricism in academic economics: update and comparisons'. *Journal of Economic Perspectives*, 2: 159–64.

Morishima, M. (1991). 'General equilibrium theory in the twenty-first century'. *Economic Journal*, 101: 69–74.

Musgrave, A. (1981). '"Unreal assumptions" in economic theory: the F-twist untwisted'. *Kyklos*, 34: 377–87.

O'Brien, D. P., Howe, W. S., Wright, D. M. and O'Brien, R. J. (1979). *Competition Policy, Profitability and Growth*. London: Macmillan.

Oswald, A. J. (1991). 'Progress and microeconomic data'. *Economic Journal*, 101: 75–80.

Peitgen, H.-O. and Richter, P. H. (1985). *Schönheit im Chaos*. University of Bremen Press.

Petty, W. (1690). *Political Arithmetick*, reprinted in C. H. Hall (ed.), *Economic Writings*. Cambridge University Press, 1899.

Phelps Brown, E. H. (1972). 'The underdevelopment of economics'. *Economic Journal*, 82: 1–10.

—— (1980a). 'Sir Roy Harrod: a biographical memoir'. *Economic Journal*, 90: 1–33.
—— (1980b). 'The radical reflections of an applied economist'. *Banca Nazionale del Lavoro Quarterly Review*, no. 132: 3–14.
—— with Browne, M. (1968). *A Century of Pay*. London: Macmillan.
Pigou, A. C. (ed.) (1925). *Memorials of Alfred Marshall*. London: Macmillan.
Plott, C. R. (1991). 'Economics in 2090: the views of an experimentalist'. *Economic Journal*, 101: 88–93.
Popper, K. (1957). *The Poverty of Historicism*. London: Routledge & Kegan Paul.
—— (1959). *The Logic of Scientific Discovery*, reprinted London: Hutchinson, 1974.
—— (1963). *Conjectures and Refutations*, 5th edn. London: Routledge & Kegan Paul, 1974.
—— (1970). 'Normal science and its dangers'. In I. Lakatos and A. Musgrave, *Criticism and the Growth of Knowledge*. Cambridge University Press.
—— (1972). *Objective Knowledge*. Oxford University Press.
Robbins, L. C. (1935). *An Essay on the Nature and Significance of Economic Science*, 2nd edn. London: Macmillan.
—— (1972). 'Concluding observations'. In R. Hinshaw (ed.), *Inflation as a Global Problem*. Baltimore: Johns Hopkins University Press.
Robinson, J. V. (1933). *The Economics of Imperfect Competition*. London: Macmillan.
Roth, A. E. (1991). 'Game theory as a part of empirical economics'. *Economic Journal*, 101: 107–14.
Rubinstein, A. (ed.) (1990). *Game Theory in Economics*. Aldershot: Edward Elgar.
Ruelle, D. (1980). 'Strange attractors'. *Mathematical Intelligence*, 2: 126–37.
Samuelson, P. A. (1963). 'Problems of methodology — discussion'. *American Economic Review*, May supplement, 53: 231–6.
Scherer, F. M. and Ross, D. (1990). *Industrial Market Structure and Economic Performance*, 3rd edn. Boston: Houghton Mifflin.
Schmalensee, R. (1988). 'Industrial economics: an overview'. *Economic Journal*, 98: 643–68.
—— (1991). 'Continuity and change in the economics industry'. *Economic Journal*, 101: 115–21.
Schumpeter, J. A. (1954). *A History of Economic Analysis*, London: Allen & Unwin.
Science (1990). 'Cold fusion conundrum at Texas A&M'. *Science*, no. 4961 (15 June): 1299–1304.
Solow, R. (1986). 'Economics: is something missing'. In W. Parker (ed.), *Economic History and the Modern Economist*, Oxford: Basil Blackwell.
Stewart, I. (1989). *Does God Play Dice?* Oxford: Basil Blackwell.
Sweezey, P. (1939). 'Demand under conditions of oligopoly'. *Journal of Political Economy*, 47: 568–73.
Talent, J. A. (1989). 'The case of the peripatetic fossils'. *Nature*, 338 (20 April): 613–15.
Taylor, R. B. (1980). 'Lamarckist revival in immunology'. *Nature*, 286 (28 August): 837–8.
Turnovsky, S. (1991). 'The next hundred years'. *Economic Journal*, 101: 142–8.
Viner, J. (1963). 'The economist in history'. *American Economic Review*, (supplement), 53: 1–22.

Walters, A. A. (1980). 'A note on monopoly equilibria', *Economic Journal*, 90: 161–2.

Weisskopf, W. (1979). 'The method is the ideology: from a Newtonian to a Heisenbergian paradigm in economics'. *Journal of Economic Issues*, 13: 869–84.

Wilson, D. (1976). *Penicillin in Perspective*. London: Faber & Faber.

Wolpert, L. and Richards, A. (1988). *A Passion for Science*. Oxford University Press.

Wood, G. E. (1990). 'Preface'. In G. Pepper, *Money, Credit and Inflation*. London: Institute of Economic Affairs, pp. 9–10.

Woodcock, A. and Davis, M. (1978). *Catastrophe Theory*; reprinted London: Penguin, 1985.

Yoshida, R. M. (1975). 'Five Duhemian theses'. *Philosophy of Science*, 42: 29–45.

Zahar, E. (1973). 'Why did Einstein's programme supersede Lorentz's?' *British Journal for the Philosophy of Science*, 24(1): 95–123; 24(2): 223–62.

Ziman, J. (1978). *Reliable Knowledge*. Cambridge University Press.

PART II

THE INDUSTRY

[5]

Information Agreements—A Problem in Search of a Policy

Introduction

The Restrictive Trade Practices Act of 1956 was expected to bring about a significant increase in competition, and it is certainly true that a large number of agreements have been abandoned, a result which is satisfactorily consistent with the philosophy underlying the Act. By 30th June 1963, the end of the period covered in the latest report of the Registrar of Restrictive Practices, "the total number of agreements which had been terminated by act of the parties or effluxion of time or from which all registrable restrictions had been removed by virtue of an Order of the Court or by act of the parties was 1,610."[1] It has however been widely observed that the abandonment of these agreements has not resulted in any great increase in competition.[2]

Faced with the necessity or advisability of abandoning an agreement, there are several possibilities open to the firms involved. One such possibility is to reduce the number of firms through mergers. This has the effect of changing the competitive structure of the industry by reducing a large number case to a small number or oligopolistic case, where price leadership may most easily emerge. This has been the path followed to some extent in Lancashire after the Yarn Spinners' agreement was condemned in 1959,[3] and elsewhere. For instance the Registrar has drawn attention to a case in which a price agreement concerning a "major electrical component" was abandoned in 1959 before reference to the Court. Thereafter there was a severe bout of

[1]Registrar of Restrictive Trading Agreements, *Report for the period 1st July, 1961 to 30th June, 1963*, Cmnd. 2246, p. 10.

[2]See for instance J. B. Heath, "Freer Prices—What Progress?" *The Banker*, Vol. 110, 1960, pp. 107–11; J. B. Heath "Restrictive Practices and After," *Manchester School*, Vol. 29, 1961, pp. 173–202; and D. L. MacLachlan and D. Swann, "Next Steps in Monopoly Policy," *Scottish Journal of Political Economy*, Vol. XI, 1965, pp. 136–50.

[3]26th January, 1959, L.R.1 R.P.118. Initially, in this case, the competitive effects which would normally have followed on the judgement were, at least in part, supplanted by the operation of the Government re-organisation scheme. This however can hardly be regarded as a likely general consequence of unfavourable judgements.

price cutting, prices in several companies being said to be below cost. Mergers subsequently took place leaving 11 firms in business. Subsequently one firm raised prices to restore part of the cuts made previously and the rest followed suit.[1] Alternatively, one firm might emerge as price leader without mergers taking place. Another, rather more popular choice has been to formulate an agreement which does not appear to come within the scope of the 1956 Act. These agreements fall into three types ; all of them were mentioned in the White Paper on Monopolies, Mergers and Restrictive Practices[2] of 1964, but none of them was dealt with in the subsequent Act.[3] The first type of agreement is known as a "Bilateral Agreement". In this the Act is circumvented by a trade association entering into a separate agreement with each of its members, only one member accepting a registrable restriction. The Act, covering only agreements in which two or more parties accept restrictions is therefore evaded. There are also agreements which merely reformulate a condemned one but which, for technical reasons, are not "to the like effect" as the former, and can be operated until they in turn come before the Court. These however do not seem to be sufficiently widespread to constitute major evasions of the 1956 Act (although this alone would not justify the absence of legislation respecting them). But the third type of agreement which has generally not been held to come within the scope of the Act and which certainly *does* seem to be a major problem is the Open Price or Information Agreement. In such agreements a number of firms agree to notify each other, through a central secretariat, of prices and conditions of sale and changes therein, and often agree to supply other relevant data such as costs and turnover. It has generally been thought that such systems did not fall within the ambit of the 1956 Act since it would be impossible to prove the existence of an agreement or meeting of minds. Firm A might notify Firm B of its prices but Firm B could not be said to be necessarily influenced by that fact. Even if Firm B adopted Firm A's prices, it could plead that it had independently decided that such a

[1]Registrar of Restrictive Trading Agreements, "Developments under the United Kingdom's Restrictive Trade Practices Act," (Summary of a paper read before the American Bar Association), 1960.

[2]Cmnd. 2299, pp. 5–6.

[3]Monopolies and Mergers Act 1965, Eliz. II, 13 and 14. c.50.

price was commercially justified. Although no precise information is available as to the extent of these agreements[1] there appears to be fairly widespread consciousness of their importance, and the most prominent investigator of the impact of the 1956 Act has gone so far as to say that "it is already clear that by far the most *significant* change [following the 1956 Act] has been the substitution—so far to only a limited extent—of non-registrable agreements to exchange information, principally about prices".[2] The Registrar has also commented on these agreements stating in his second report : "Not infrequently on the ending of a price agreement the parties enter into an information agreement under which they send to their trade association or to a central agency their price lists or the prices at which they have entered into contracts. . . . Information agreements are considered under two heads ; first as arrangements tending to hinder the revival of competition in industries in which there have been price agreements or other restrictive agreements for substantial periods ; secondly as a framework within which, consciously or unconsciously, there may arise understandings about prices, allocation of contracts and so on."[3]

Economic Implications

Such agreements may be divided into two main types ; those in which notification is given *prior* to the change in price and those in which notification is only given *after* the change has taken place. It is possible however to make further distinctions which are highly relevant to an analysis of the impact of such agreements upon market behaviour. Thus information agreements may require the association of firms' names with the data on prices and turnover ; on the other hand such data may be supplied anonymously. Then again data on prices and costs may be specified in the form of actual levels over a period, or merely in the form of an average or range of fluctuation.

[1]See J. B. Heath, *Manchester School loc. cit.* pp. 184–5 on the incidence of these agreements in the sample dealt with there.

[2]J. B. Heath, "Some Economic Consequence [of Restrictive Practices Legislation]," *Economic Journal*, Vol. LXX, 1960, pp. 474–84, p. 474.

[3]Registrar of Restrictive Trading Agreements, *Report for the period 1st January, 1960 to 30th June, 1961*, Cmnd. 1603, pp. 3–4. See also the *Report for the period 1st July, 1961 to 30th June, 1963*, p. 4.

It would seem that the temporal distinction is relevant to the analysis. An agreement which requires notification of price changes before they occur (referred to henceforth as a "pre-notification agreement") gives the most obvious opportunities for pressure to be brought to bear on a price changer *before* he has actually disturbed the market situation. It was presumably this type that the Registrar had chiefly in mind when he wrote that "If a measure of competition considered undesirable by the majority should emerge, the price information agreement provides both the material and the forum for the persuasion of the minority".[1] The second type ("post-notification agreement") reduces a large number to a small number case,[2] by perfecting the flow of information, but does not make the application of pressure so easy. Nevertheless a fear of social obloquy may deter a price changer even in the second case. (It would in our opinion be a great mistake to underrate the importance of this factor. There is clearly in many industries an *esprit de corps* which is built up within the trade association and anyone who disturbs the market situation is bound to feel, or be made to feel, uncomfortable.[3] In the United States there is evidence in the case of open price agreements of members being "put on the carpet" and being subjected to searching questions about their conduct[4]). But although the second type would appear to give more scope to the would-be price changer, it is unfortunately the case that a post-notification agreement is unlikely to remain in that form for long—and in the Galvanised Tank Case to be discussed below, an arrangement which was nominally of the post-notification type was operated as a pre-notification agreement.

There are of course disadvantages to these agreements other than the opportunity for exercising pressure on firms. Most

[1]*Report* (1960–1) p. 4.

[2]That this point is not widely understood is made clear by a recent analysis in which this effect does not appear to be envisaged and in which the distinction between pre- and post-notification agreements also seems to be overlooked—see A. Hunter, *Competition and the Law*, London, 1966, pp. 169–71.

[3]See R. Hall and C. J. Hitch, "Price Theory and Business Behaviour" in T. Wilson and P. W. S. Andrews (Eds.), *Oxford Studies in the Price Mechanism*, Oxford, 1951, p. 118.

[4]See A. D. Neale, *The Antitrust Laws of the U.S.A.*, Cambridge, 1960, p. 45.

obviously perhaps there is the danger of a pre-notification agreement providing a temptation and a forum to move on to explicit (though secret) collusion. Secondly, a form of "gentleman's" agreement may arise, whereby one firm notifies the others, through the secretariat, of an intended price change, in the full expectation that the others will infer from the notification a course of action which will ensure the continued damping of competition. Thirdly, it has been observed that information agreements lead to product standardisation.[1] This last has a number of advantages : it can bring about longer production runs, reduced stockholdings, reduction in design and selling costs, and, by removing product differentiation it increases the elasticity of the firm's average revenue curve, thus reducing its market power. But on the other hand it may not only make the maintenance of uniform prices easier, but also act as a bar to product innovation.

But the opportunities provided by such an agreement for opposing price competition are the most obvious and striking. Any incentive to take advantage of a potentially more favourable cost situation, perhaps arising from a possible method change, will quite conceivably be stifled. If a price cutter can be identified straight away, and if he knows that he will gain nothing from this because his prices will be quickly, possibly immediately, matched by his competitors, then there is no incentive to him to cut prices. "Perfecting of the game" would seem here to have positive disadvantages, since in the absence of perfect information, the price cutter is able to operate to his own advantage until such time as his prices become known to his competitors. It is by no means inconceivable that customers may get to know of his lower prices sufficiently long before his competitors that for a time he will be able to reap the rewards of his strategy, and/or of his technical innovation which allows him to offer lower prices. It seems likely that eventually there will be competitive imitation but some of the custom attracted during the period in which the price cutter's prices are lower than those of his competitors may remain permanently with him. A number of reasons for this can be adduced. Firstly his original price cut may earn for him some extra goodwill on the part of customers who may elect to stay

[1]See A. R. Burns, *The Decline of Competition*, New York, 1936, p. 498.

with him and they may continue to patronise him because of resentment at the restrictive attitude of his competitors. Secondly an open price agreement leading to price uniformity, like a price-fixing agreement, may prove a method of restricting knowledge since customers, in the belief that prices are uniform, will not search for alternative sources of supply which might in fact prove to meet their needs more satisfactorily. Allied with this is the point that a price cut may be a means of attracting custom to a newly differentiated product. The fore-going should not be taken as implying any final welfare judgement ; it is merely argued that an information agreement, even when operated honourably, can stifle the incentive to cut prices or to introduce technical innovations.

The important point here is the existence of a time lag before competitors receive information about the existence of a price cut, the degree of the price cut, who is making it, where it is being made and so forth. The significance of a time lag before a competitive riposte occurs is considerable. Schumpeter was concerned with a somewhat similar point when he developed the idea that monopoly is conducive to economic progress. This was not an unqualified commendation of monopoly but a suggestion that a nice blend of temporary monopoly followed by competitive imitation was the best system for encouraging innovation.[1]

Continuing the argument about the relationship between innovation and information, the possibility exists that a firm might introduce new methods in order to earn very large profits at existing prices without disturbing the market structure. However, this is of little benefit to the consumer, since it merely ensures the acquisition of a surplus by the producer, and as under many information agreements, data about costs is supplied, competitors may soon be able to copy such innovations. In this case any subsequent inflation of costs may be absorbed thus eroding the large profits being made by all the parties to the agreement and the innovating firm will cease to gain the advantages of its innovation ; whereas, were it the only firm to innovate, a rise in costs would tend to lead to a general rise in prices and it

[1] J. A. Schumpeter, *The Theory of Economic Development*, Cambridge, Massachusetts, 1936, especially chs. 2 and 4 ; and *Capitalism, Socialism and Democracy*, London, 1947, ch. 8.

would continue to make large profits. Provided the time lag existed the firm would have an incentive to innovate. (It would however be desirable that the innovation should eventually be copied.) A further consideration is that a new method may require a scale of operations greater than the firm's current market share. In the absence of an information agreement the firm wishing to innovate might be able to achieve such a scale by price-cutting, but in the presence of an agreement every price cut is likely to be matched.

So far we have concentrated upon the disincentive to price cutting. But it is also clear that open price agreements provide an excellent medium for bringing about a general rise in prices when costs rise[1] or even in the absence of such a change. Without such an agreement an individual firm may fear that its competitors will not match an increase. Because of this a firm may expect the elasticity of its average revenue curve to be greater than one above the prevailing price.[2] If an agreement exists a rise in price will be matched and each producer will tend to believe demand conditions to be conducive to a price rise. It seems to us that under inflationary conditions the open price agreement is just the kind of flexible instrument which businessmen need to keep pace with frequent changes in costs stemming from rises in wages, raw material prices and so forth. A price change can be notified quickly and followed immediately. There is no time lag, during which profits are eroded, which a more formal machinery of price fixing might require. The time lags implicit in more formal arrangements might indeed make the position of relatively high cost producers quite uncomfortable.

Recent thought on decisions relating to investment in a competitive framework would suggest further considerations. G. B. Richardson[3] for example has suggested that following an

[1]Thus reducing the pressure on firms to rationalise their processes when faced with cost increases.

[2]Even if competitors do eventually follow the price increase, business lost by the initiator of the price change may very well never be fully recovered.

[3]See G. B. Richardson, *Information and Investment*, London, 1960, and "The Theory of Restrictive Practices," *Oxford Economic Papers*, N.S. Vol. XVII, No. 3, November 1965, pp. 432–49. See also J. B. Heath, *Economic Journal, loc. cit.* p. 476 and references there cited.

increase in demand for a particular product, the kind of information supplied under an information agreement may assist the simultaneous and harmonious planning of investment by a number of firms, each being aware of the others' intentions. Richardson indicates that if, under the stimulus of a demand increase, the investment decisions were made simultaneously and in isolation, the distinct possibility exists that overinvestment would result. While not disputing the validity of this argument, it seems to us that the likelihood that in the real world expansion plans will be undertaken simultaneously is somewhat remote. Many factors may lead to the staggering of an investment response, even when the stimulating increase in demand is immediately apparent to all producers, and such staggering would enable an alternative step by step approach (which Richardson also envisages) to a new equilibrium to be achieved. A number of possible factors could lead to a staggered response ; some firms may at a particular point in time be liquid whereas others may not, some firms may be able to tap the capital market whilst others may not and will therefore have to accumulate funds out of earnings, some firms will respond more rapidly to changes than others and so forth.

A number of further observations are suggested by this analysis. Firstly, an information agreement by perfecting the flow of information and disseminating knowledge of profitable investment opportunities, may itself reduce the temporal spacing of investments. This may occur because of the actual information supplied under the agreement and in the course of any market discussions which may take place within the group, and may also be consequent upon a reduction in uncertainty which may help to overcome entrepreneurial inertia. The information agreement under these circumstances while helping to remove the danger of over investment has an element of self-justification, for by improving knowledge in the first instance it creates conditions which might lead to over-investment. Secondly, we have argued earlier that information agreements can lead, via an unwillingness to disturb the market, to a uniform price which, other things being equal, implies a uniformity of market shares. This in turn is likely to react on investment decisions by requiring that each firm's expansion plans should not disturb the *status quo*. This may act as a deterrent to the relative expansion of the more

efficient and to the achievement of economies of scale. This is not of course inevitable but, as Richardson himself observes, it is a potentiality which should be taken into account. Thirdly, where there is a need for co-ordination of investment, as is likely to be the case where investments may be large, durable and simultaneous, it is still questionable whether the information agreement is the best medium for achieving co-ordination. Some alternative machinery may be necessary in which a representative of the public interest can be present.

Of course none of these arguments is conclusive ; but it seems reasonable to argue that there is a strong possibility that an open price agreement may have at least some of the ill-effects envisaged. That is all that will be required by the argument below.

Nevertheless there are possible advantages. For instance it has been argued by the Galvanised Tank Manufacturers,[1] that such an agreement is necessary to avoid "phantom competition" —the quoting by customers of other suppliers' prices at lower levels than the true ones. But it can be argued that only a very limited amount of information is needed to overcome this problem —checking with a central secretariat on the range of prices, whenever phantom competition is suspected, would involve none of the detailed circulation of information including complete price lists, which is usual in an information agreement. Prices could be quoted anonymously in such a case, merely a range being given. Nevertheless it may be questioned whether this will prove sufficient to deal with the problem—the answer seems to be that it may or may not, depending on circumstances. For example, if a customer represents to firm x that firm y is offering a price 10 per cent below that of firm x, checking with the central secretariat may reveal that the maximum deviation below x's price at this point in time is 5 per cent. The customer's claim could then be regarded as bogus. But if price deviations of up to 10 per cent are reported then there is no way of ascertaining whether the customer's claim is genuine or not. The 10 per cent reduction may be being made by firm y but it may be being made by firm z in another segment, geographical or otherwise, of the market. In the latter case offers made by firm z would hardly be

[1]L.R. 5 R.P. 325.

relevant to firm x and could indeed be regarded as phantom competition as far as it was concerned. The central secretariat could of course provide data on a geographical or other basis which would go some way towards dealing with this problem, but there is a danger that if this were pressed too far it would become easier to identify which firm was making a price offer and this would tend to be anti-competitive in effect. Secondly it is arguable that other firms' prices are less relevant to the price to be charged, than a particular firm's own cost situation. The latter is not however an unambiguous guide. In multi-product firms there will always be an element of arbitrariness in the apportionment of overheads between different products. A figure for average total cost will then contain some element of judgement. The problem would be less marked if the order were a single non-repeating one for the firm would then refer to average direct cost (assuming marginal cost to have no operational significance). However, even in this case, it would presumably wish to make some contribution to overheads. Its direct costs will then provide some guide but little more.

It is also claimed that Open Price Agreements reduce the level of uncertainty. As an isolated proposition this seems undeniable. But the consequence of such a reduction in uncertainty need not be unambiguously beneficial. It is true that under normal circumstances a reduction in uncertainty (arising for instance from a stabilisation of consumer preferences) should help to tip the balance between efficiency and adaptability of plant in favour of the former, allowing entrepreneurs to invest, for example, in highly efficient specialised machine tools rather than in less efficient but more adaptable general purpose ones.[1] But where the reduction in uncertainty is brought about by the introduction of an open price agreement, the beneficial tendency may, to some extent at least, be counteracted—it has been argued above that such an agreement is likely to lead to a stabilisation of market shares, which implies difficulties for an entrepreneur who may wish to attain a more efficient scale of production.

Finally, it has been suggested that information agreements will help to avoid the misdirection of competitive effort.[2] In so

[1]See G. B. Richardson, *Information and Investment*, pp. 152–3.

[2]See Heath, *Economic Journal*, *loc. cit.*, pp. 479–80 and Richardson, *Oxford Economic Papers*, *loc. cit.*, pp. 447–8.

far as such agreements remove the necessity for extensive entrepreneurial speculation about rivals' strategies, and enable entrepreneurial resources to be concentrated more upon improvements of products and methods of production, this will be advantageous. On the other hand it is arguable that a feeling of uncertainty may well help to produce in the entrepreneur, a more critical attitude towards methods and costs.

If possible disadvantages are admitted to exist, then it seems reasonable to argue that some policy for dealing with the phenomena of information agreements should be developed. The case for this would seem to be strengthened by the inadequacies of the claimed advantages.

United States Experience

First of all it should be noted that although the United States has a tradition of *per se* condemnation of price agreements, the circulation of prices does not seem to be condemned *per se* in the United States. The American approach is rather one of attempting to discover whether collusion actually exists with respect to the prices charged.

In a number of cases the antitrust authorities have been able to obtain a verdict against information agreements. Thus in the case of the *American Column and Lumber Company v. United States*, members of the trade association in question were required to let the secretary have daily reports of sales and deliveries and monthly reports of production and stocks. They also had to file price lists every month and inspectors were employed to check on the grades of timber offered at stated prices. The secretary in turn sent out periodical reports showing sales made at particular prices together with summaries of price lists. But in addition to this there was evidence of periodic meetings to discuss price and output policy. Also at the meetings it appeared that members were encouraged to adjust their policy so as to keep the industry profitable. Although a specific agreement to fix prices was not proved the Court concluded that the behaviour of the parties to the arrangement was that of

> men united in an agreement express or implied, to act together and pursue a common purpose under a common guide.[1]

In the case of the *United States v. American Linseed Oil Company* a similar scheme was operated. There was however particularly strong evidence of action to keep members in line. Regular compulsory meetings were held and individuals were put on the carpet and subjected to intensive questioning as to their behaviour. Again the antitrust authorities won.

They were also successful in the case of *The Sugar Institute v. United States.* Here the Institute circulated statistics of production, stocks and deliveries. The Institute also administered a "Code of Ethics" one of whose conditions involved an agreement that parties would adhere to their published prices and it was this the Supreme Court objected to. Also important in deciding the case was the change in market conditions after the formation of the Institute. Price changes became less frequent, profit margins increased despite considerable excess capacity and the price of refined sugar followed changes in the price of raw sugar significantly less closely.

Not all the cases brought by the antitrust authorities have been so successful. In the case of *Maple Flooring Manufacturers' Association v. United States*, the association circulated data on costs, prices, sales and stocks. Meetings were held to discuss the industry's problems, although apparently after the Linseed Oil Case no discussions about prices took place. The Supreme Court did not however condemn the arrangement since prices were not uniform and lower than those of outsiders. Again in the case of the *Tag Manufacturers' Institute v. Federal Trade Commission* there was an elaborate scheme for notifying price lists but there was no agreement to adhere to list prices and there was evidence of substantial selling below list prices. The case failed.

In the case of the Vitrified China Association, the association had employed accountants to draw up an average figure for various elements of manufacturing costs and the members of the association had adopted a basic list of prices but because of deviations in various supplements to the basic price lists there

[1]Quoted in A. D. Neale *op. cit.* p. 45 ; pp. 42–53 contain an excellent summary of this and the other cases referred to.

was no uniformity of final price to the consumer and therefore no antitrust offence was deemed to exist.

What conclusions can be drawn from this experience? On the enforcement side we should note that, although there is no registration, very significant powers of investigation exist. As for the case decisions themselves, they afford no clear guide to policy in the United Kingdom. In the first place, since it appears that in this field there are no decisions in cases of pure price uniformity and nothing more, it is impossible to know whether or not the United States antitrust authorities would or would not be prepared to infer collusion merely in the light of simultaneous and equal price changes and in the absence of any supporting evidence of collusion or pressure. In the cases in which the Federal authorities have succeeded, in addition to price uniformity there have been other factors which they have been able to make use of. In the Sugar Institute case there was an express agreement not to deviate from published prices. In other cases there has been evidence of meetings to discuss price or output policy, pressure has been placed upon firms which have deviated and exhortations and guidance to maintain profitability have been employed. Also important in the Sugar Institute case was the reduced flexibility of prices and increased profit margins despite substantial excess capacity. In short, in reaching a decision against an information agreement, the antitrust authorities have sought evidence going beyond mere uniformity of prices. Supplementary evidence has been produced which in direction and extent was such that a reasonable man could not but infer the existence of collusion.

Secondly, the decisions throw little if any systematic light upon the possibility that certain forms of information agreement may be less innocuous than others.

There are two further observations which seem worthy of mention. One is that United States experience does provide examples of the kind of supporting evidence to look for in building up a case of collusion, if mere uniformity in itself is held by the courts or legislature to be insufficient evidence. The second observation, which springs out of the first, is that in the United States the cases have been dealt with in their totality—that is to

say, the uniformity of prices springing out of the information agreement and the additional evidence have been considered simultaneously in reaching a verdict. We shall return to this point later in discussing British experience.

British Experience

The British position was recently brought into prominence by the Galvanised Tank Case. It should be noted that although information agreements have possible disadvantages, there is no explicit legislative provision in the United Kingdom for dealing with them. The 1956 Act appears to say nothing about them and indeed, as already seen, a number of firms substituted them for agreements which were either actually condemned, or expected to be condemned. However it seems that there may be an implicit provision in the 1956 Act ; for in the Basic Slag case[1] the meaning of the word "arrangement" in Section 6(3) of the 1956 Act was significantly extended. The report of that case is worth quoting as indicative of how far British legislation could conceivably have its effects extended. Diplock L. J. in his judgement stated that :

> "'Arrangement' . . . involves a meeting of minds because under section 6(1) it has to be an arrangement 'between two or more persons', and since it must be an arrangement 'under which restrictions are accepted by two or more parties' it involves mutuality in that each party, assuming he is a reasonable and conscientious man, would regard himself as being in some degree under a duty, whether moral or legal, to conduct himself in a particular way as the case may be, at any rate so long as the other party or parties conducted themselves in the way contemplated by the arrangement.
>
> "No necessary or useful purpose would be served by attempting an expanded and comprehensive definition of the word 'arrangement' in section 6(3) of the Act. . . . it is sufficient to constitute an arrangement between A and B, if (1) A makes a representation as to his future conduct with the expectation and intention that such conduct on his part will operate as an inducement to B to act in a particular way, (2) such representation is communicated to B, who has knowledge that A so expected and intended, and (3) such

[1] L.R. 4 R.P. pp. 116–56.

representation or A's conduct in fulfilment of it operates as an inducement, whether among other inducements or not, to B to act in that particular way."[1]

The effect of this pronouncement was to widen considerably the scope of the 1956 Act ; it was against this background that the Restrictive Practices Court came to consider the remarkable case of the *Galvanised Tank Manufacturers' Association's Agreement.*[2]

The Association had originally abandoned their registered agreement without defending it and had given the usual undertaking not to operate it or one to the like effect. This had occurred between July and September 1959. The agreement laid down that the members would not supply in the United Kingdom galvanised open-top cisterns, hot water tanks and cylinders including domestic water tanks used in houses except at prices and terms and conditions of sale (including discounts) agreed at general meetings of the Association. Earlier however, in May of that year, the members had entered into a new agreement for the submission of information on costs, sales and prices. "Although clause 3 of the notification agreement contemplated that members would give notice of changes in their prices and terms after the making of such changes, it was the consistent practice of the members in operating the agreement to give advance notification of their proposed changes in prices and terms to the secretaries of the association, and through them to the other members of the association, before such changes were actually made and in anticipation of their making".[3] The collection and dissemination of data on sales by product is particularly interesting. This was quite possibly a safeguard against undercutting since it would be suspicious if a member's sales increased out of line with those of other members serving the same market.

From the time of this agreement until the proceedings in 1965 in the Restrictive Practices Court respecting it (a period of six years), all the members of the association kept identical price lists (with the exception of a short-lived deviation by one firm) despite the fact that prices changed on no less than eleven occasions.

[1]L.R. 4 R.P. 154–5.
[2]L.R. 5 R.P. 315–50.
[3]*Ibid.*, p. 319.

Members changed their prices at virtually the same time. Their behaviour was drawn to the Registrar's attention by their customers. The Association was charged with contempt, and, luckily for the Registrar, admitted explicit collusion in two cases. However, there were four other occasions on which the Registrar asserted that collusion had taken place, and he asked the Court to infer this from the market behaviour of the firms i.e. from the consistent equality of their prices. He appeared to state through Counsel that he had no complaint against a post-notification agreement as such, but he objected to a post-notification agreement being converted to a pre-notification one. The Court was asked to infer from the identical price changes that these had resulted from an arrangement which was "to the like effect" of that abandoned, and that the pre-notification agreement, as operated, constituted such an arrangement and was indeed registrable.

In the face of this very important case the Court failed to come to any clear cut decision. For the two admitted cases of collusion the firms concerned were fined a total of £100,000. But the Court, while not actually finding the firms guilty of contempt in the other five cases, virtually refused to decide whether this could be a ground of contempt without supporting evidence or an admission, while issuing a stern warning.

> "The registrar submitted, further, that, even in the absence of what we may call express collusion in each of these five instances the court ought to hold that there was an arrangement, involving a breach of the companies' undertakings, arising out of the manner of operation of the notification agreement [as a pre-notification agreement]. The companies submitted . . . that this was not so. We do not think it necessary or desirable to deal with this matter on this motion, and we shall, therefore, proceed on the basis that no breach of undertaking—no 'arrangement to the like effect'—has been made out in connection with the changes of price or other terms which were brought about on any of these five occasions. *We treat that matter in this way, principally because it may not formerly have been realised, by these companies or their advisers, as indeed by many others, how wide the meaning of 'arrangement' may be.*[1] Therefore, in those special

[1]Authors' italics here and below.

circumstances—*which would by no means necessarily be of equal force or relevance in the future*—the breach of undertakings involved, if the registrar's submission based on the Basic Slag case be right, would be relatively less grave compared with the seriousness of the admitted contempts. *We do not decide one way or the other whether the registrar's submission is right in relation to the facts before us.*

"Having said this, we wish to give warning. . . . It is abundantly apparent . . . that those who, having been placed under an injunction or having given an undertaking such as here, thereafter exchange information of their intentions on matters such as prices, or partake in discussions, formal or informal, with their competitors on such matters, may be in real peril of . . . having passed easily and quickly from that which may be legitimate into actions which constitute a grave contempt."[1]

Concluding Observations

Yet this leaves policy towards these agreements in the most uncertain state. There is no guidance on the Registrar's interesting and somewhat surprising view that pre-notification agreements are registrable. Nor is there any guidance as to which amongst the many possible forms of pre-notification agreement is likely to be condemned. A number of separate points may be noted.

Firstly, the Registrar took the vital step of bringing this agreement before the court. This was in itself a significant departure for which there would seem to be no provision in the Act of 1956. It implies a need on the part of the Registrar for powers of investigation and enforcement which it is by no means clear that he as yet possesses. Such powers are clearly necessary for the regulation of information agreements. We discuss this further below.

Secondly, the opportunity for him to do this was provided by customers of the association who drew his attention to the price circulars. Clearly this is something which cannot be depended

[1]L.R. 5R.P. 344–5. It will be noted that the judgement refers to five further cases whereas the Registrar relied on only four. The fifth case was not relied on by the Registrar because he possessed only one circular relating to the price change.

upon in future. As the Registrar's counsel said in his first submission "Customers are naturally reluctant to give evidence for fear of prejudicing their commercial position". The need for gathering of evidence under these circumstances again underlines the necessity for the Registrar to have power to enable him to do so.[1]

Thirdly, the philosophy underlying the Registrar's action is not at all clear. It has been argued above that even a post-notification agreement can have harmful effects. Yet the Registrar does not appear to object to these though he objects to pre-notification agreements. Since it is difficult to object to one and not the other, and since the Court has failed to give guidance on the necessity for registration of pre-notification agreements, the British position can hardly be regarded as satisfactory.

Fourthly, the Court has failed to rule on the submission that collusion may be inferred from market behaviour, and that to regard the equality of prices as a coincidence would "offend credulity".[2] Such a course would be a significant departure from previous British practice, but would seem to be able to follow from the wide meaning attached to the word "arrangement". It may be that the Court's warning implies a readiness to infer collusion in future ; but this point certainly needs clarification.

Fifthly, if it is necessary, in order to sustain a charge of collusion that evidence in addition to mere parallelism of prices is required, then difficult problems may arise. On this occasion the companies involved admitted that they were guilty on two occasions ; but had they not done so, it is extremely difficult to see, given the Court's equivocal attitude on the other five cases. whether any charge could have been made to bear enough weight.

Sixthly, it is perhaps worth observing, partly as a matter of comparison and partly as a possible suggestion for future treatment, that had the case occurred in the United States it would in all probability have been struck down. On the basis of the criteria discussed above, simultaneous and uniform changes in prices and the apparent lack of off-list selling, together with the past history of collusion and the two definite instances when

[1]For a recent recognition of the need for greater powers of enforcement see N. H. Leyland, "Competition in the Court," *Oxford Economic Papers loc. cit.*, pp. 461–7.

[2]L.R. 5 R.P. p. 347.

agreements were proved to exist, would surely have been sufficient to ensure that the open price agreement was struck down. We emphasised earlier that in the United States the matter would have been judged as a whole—in this case the British court failed to do this and preferred to deal specifically with *only* that part of the case in which collusion was admitted. Had the four or five cases on which the Court failed to decide been dealt with by themselves in the United States there seems no clear indication of what would have been the result.

Finally, in dealing with information agreements there is a temptation to take the view that the mere dissemination of information is not itself dangerous. What is dangerous is the possibility that collusion arises out of the system. Firm A informs Firm B of its increase in price in the knowledge and expectation that Firm B will follow. Therefore it is collusion which must be proved. But as we pointed out earlier the mere fact that price changes and changers are known about may act as a discouragement to price cutting and competition. Collusion is not necessary in order that competition be stifled. (It is true that there was in the first instance an agreement to circulate information but this is different from the collusion which subsequently develops out of a circulation of information.) We are here raising questions about the whole process of merely circulating information. These are deep and unchartered waters indeed but their exploration is necessary if our antitrust policy is to be fully comprehensive.

If it transpires that the Court is not prepared to infer collusion from market behaviour, particularly when this is supported by other evidence, then it seems inescapable that the legislature will have to deal explicitly with the problem.[1] What approaches can be envisaged? Perhaps most obviously these agreements could be objected to *per se*. Such an approach would however appear to be too sweeping. In the first place on grounds of consistency it would hardly be logical to apply such treatment to these arrangements whilst more explicitly collusive agreements were only deemed contrary to the public interest and even

[1]A recent statement by the Registrar seems to indicate that the latter is the most probable outcome—see R. L. Sich, "Evidence of Detriment caused by Restrictive Trading Agreements," *Oxford Economic Papers loc. cit.*, p. 353. But it is possible that this is a statement of the position before the Galvanised Tank Case.

exemptable. Secondly, such a sweeping condemnation seems on the whole undesirable unless it can be established on *a priori* grounds that no possible good can ever come of such an agreement, or that any possible good can never outweigh any harm arising. The second alternative is to make these agreements registrable. This was the view of J. B. Heath[1] and the Conservative White Paper of 1964.[2] Heath suggested specifying a permissible type of agreement, more limited in scope than the information agreement currently operated in the United Kingdom. Only this type would be allowed. Unfortunately experience would tend to suggest that an apparently innocuous agreement can grow into one that is thoroughly objectionable. To ensure that this did not occur would require a machinery of investigation which it seems doubtful whether the Registrar as yet possesses. That is to say, although the Registrar has the power under Section 14 of the 1956 Act to require that agreements should be registered, it is first of all necessary that the agreement should be located. It would be no easy matter without powerful machinery of enforcement to police information agreements in order to detect those which strayed from the paths of legality.

The 1964 White Paper in advocating registration contained the following statement "... the Government are not prepared to see the intention of the 1956 Act undermined by agreements or arrangements for the exchange of information the purpose and effect of which is to limit competition. They therefore propose to bring information agreements within the scope of the 1956 Act, and thus to make them registrable and subject ultimately to consideration by the Court." Unfortunately there has been no provision for this in the legislation following the White Paper; and in any case the White Paper had begged the question of investigatory powers by stating that only those agreements which the Board of Trade considered to need registration, should be registered. How the Board of Trade was envisaged to make its selection was not made clear. The White Paper also suggested the need for a new gateway for information agreements, that is to say they could plead that the agreement was not contrary to the public interest because it did not restrict or deter competition.

[1] *Economic Journal, loc. cit.*

[2] *Monopolies, Mergers and Restrictive Practices*, Cmnd. 2299.

This is certainly one possible approach ; and in addition those agreements which are registered (or if not registered are located by the enforcement machinery) which give rise to collusion are in practice the like effect of the type of agreement normally dealt with by the 1956 Act and can be treated in the same way. Another problem following from wholesale registration of information agreements is that either the Registrar has to be given power to bring *only* those agreements which he believes to restrict competition before the Court, or alternatively the Court will have a greatly increased volume of work thrust upon it. For the first case the Registrar would be effectively called upon to act as a preliminary judge and court ; and the Court itself would be debarred from examining some agreements to which there might conceivably be objection. In the second case, though the possibility must be admitted to exist, the same problem was raised in relation to the 1956 Act's operation; but early adverse decisions led to widespread abandonment of agreements.

In the light of all that has gone before we would like to make the following suggestions. Firstly, that *all* information agreements, whether pre-notification or post-notification, should be registered ; and it will be for the Court, not the Board of Trade or the Registrar alone, to decide upon their effect.

Secondly, although the Registrar has the power to call for information once a case has been set in motion, it would appear that greater powers are required to enable the Registrar to obtain the information necessary in order to establish that a case exists. Where an information agreement has been registered, the Registrar needs details of commercial behaviour in order to provide the basis of an examination before the Court. Where registration has been evaded the problem would be all the greater.

Thirdly, as we have indicated earlier, the mere dissemination of information may hinder competition quite apart from any collusion which may arise. There are two possible approaches to this problem. One would be to limit this effect by requiring that all information agreements conform to certain requirements. For example criteria could be laid down which included such things as anonymity of all firms supplying data (and the omission of turnover figures from data where these would identify the firms) and

the requirement that all notification of price changes should be after the change. Alternatively, if this is thought to be too radical a departure, then at least in the judging of these agreements in relation to the public interest, any detriment to be outweighed might be regarded as being greater where such criteria were not satisfied. Either arrangement would help to remove some of the most objectionable features of the agreements, and together with registration and explicit powers of investigation should help to provide the stimulus to competition which the 1956 Act has so clearly failed to do.

D. P. O'Brien and D. Swann.

Queen's University,
Belfast.

[6]

200 years of competition (BBC Radio 3, 22 May 1977)

Since World War II successive governments in the United Kingdom have passed into law a body of legislation concerned with promoting competition between firms engaged in economic activity. In so doing they were following an example set in the United States from the 1890s onwards; and legislation in other European countries, notably Germany and Holland, followed the same path. The Treaty of Rome, which established the Common Market, also contained provisions for the development of a competition policy and these provisions have been followed. But the history of the intellectual basis for such a policy goes back far beyond the American legislators at the turn of the century. It goes back in fact at least as far as Adam Smith's *Inquiry into the Nature and Causes of the Wealth of Nations*.

Anyone reading Adam Smith's greatest, and certainly most famous, work 200 years later, cannot but be struck by the importance which is attached to competition. It arises basically because individuals pursue their self-interest; and the self-interest of those with investible resources is attracted to those forms of economic activity which will yield the highest return (due allowance made for risk and unpleasantness) on those resources. In pursuing these opportunities for gain, individuals come into competition with one another; and the competition between them provides society with the mixture of goods and services that it wants – for it is the wants of society which give rise to the opportunities to earn higher rewards in particular forms of economic activity.

Since this vision of economic activity is widely (and sometimes wilfully) misunderstood, it is perhaps worth spelling out the point that neither Smith, nor any of the other classical economists, were envisaging a regime of economic anarchy. In order for the self-interest motivation to benefit society it was necessary that the individual's activities should be curtailed in a number of ways: by the operation of positive law founded upon justice, and by a system of non-legal controls such as religion and custom. In particular it was necessary that what Smith called 'sympathy' should operate. This was for him the origin of moral perception, and it consisted essentially in an individual's ability to place himself in another man's shoes and to judge right and wrong from that viewpoint. Not only did sympathy lie behind society's perception of just laws but it also limited the day-to-day conduct of individuals.

Now, such a framework of legal and non-legal controls was necessary if the pursuit of self-interest by individuals was to result in prosperity for the community as a whole. Even then, it did not guarantee any kind of nirvana; there is a deep streak of pessimism in Smith's outlook. But self-interest, thus limited, did produce a very much *better* world than could be produced by the dead hand of bureaucracy

operating to allocate resources. Nevertheless, there was a great deal which government could do to benefit the system; the tasks which Smith felt to be appropriate for government ranged from public health to the regulation of banking, and included regulation of contracts and the avoidance of fraud – neither Smith nor his classical successors were believers in the doctrine of *caveat emptor*.

It follows from all this that Smith saw it as a duty of government to prevent the creation of monopoly positions and of the inflated profits that went with them. In Smith's view, 'The price of monopoly is upon every occasion the highest which can be got' (Glasgow edition, pp. 78–9). The high profits resulting from the monopoly price were doubly harmful in that they diminished total income (through the low volume of activity which resulted from the high price) and weakened the motive to save. They also, quite naturally according to Smith's theory of motivation, caused capital to be withdrawn from agriculture and sucked into the protected areas where monopoly power could be exercised. The profits of the monopolist were therefore, in Smith's view, the most proper subject of taxation of all. Quite apart from the harm done by the high profits, the very existence of monopoly was inimical to good management (Glasgow edition, pp. 163–4) – an insight of Smith's which economists of the 1960s with their 'discovery' of X-efficiency would do well to remember. But above all, monopoly had the glaring fault, in Smith's view, of putting the interests of producers before those of consumers and making production rather than consumption the aim of economic activity.

Before we go any further it might be as well, especially for the benefit of fellow economists, to clarify Smith's use of the term 'monopoly'. It is clear from the context in which Smith used the term that he meant by it any position of market power, that is to say any position in which a producer was able to charge more than the 'natural' or competitive price. The form of monopoly which Smith was attacking was not however, throughout most of his book, what we now think of as a monopolist, that is the sole producer of a particular good. Rather he was attacking positions of market power achieved by groups of producers through their influence upon the legislature. His primary target, in his attack upon Mercantilism (that is, government of the people, by the merchants, in the interests of the merchants) was the manipulation of trade flows through the use of tariffs and the exclusion of other countries from trade with our colonies. His sharpest words are always reserved for collusive action by merchants and manufacturers. They are accused of forever seeking to bring pressure on government to introduce tariffs so that they may have a monopoly of the home market; of inducing government to use the blood and treasure of their fellow citizens (Smith's words) to found an empire and then to set about monopolizing the trade of that empire; of responsibility for sanguinary laws to enforce their monopolization of markets; and of foolish attempts to monopolize technical knowledge (Glasgow edition especially, pp. 471, 660–1).

As one would expect, Smith also condemned price rings and similar devices which can be lumped together under the heading of cartels. *But*, he did not believe legislation was the way to check them. He wrote:

> People of the same trade seldom meet together, even for merriment and diversion, but the conversation ends in a conspiracy against the publick, or in some contrivance to raise

> prices. It is impossible indeed to prevent such meetings, by any law which either could be executed, or would be consistent with liberty and justice. But though the law cannot hinder people of the same trade from sometimes assembling together, it ought to do nothing to facilitate such assemblies; much less render them necessary. (Glasgow edition, p. 145)

In considering this last point however we do have to remind ourselves that cartelization developed only slowly in this country. It is true that there are examples of the attempted creation of cartels in several industries in the 19th century, notably glass, chemicals and soap. But it was not really until the phenomenon known to economic historians as 'the rise of the combination movement' appeared, in the 1880s and 1890s, that cartels became a serious problem in the British economy. It was only in the 30 years or less before the First World War that cartels became a problem on anything like the scale with which later generations have become familiar. Even at that time there were a great many difficulties in making them effective; there was a constant tendency to underhand price cutting, and the British economy was still largely unprotected by tariffs so that imports were a serious limitation upon the power of cartels. But the First World War proved a boon to those who were anxious to operate price rings. Under the aegis of the Board of Trade, trade associations were greatly strengthened and became the channel of communication between the manufacturers and the government. The cartels were further strengthened in the period after the First World War, both because of public and official favour and because of the progressive introduction of tariffs which removed the import check upon price rings. In addition to this, the process of amalgamating firms, which had also gathered momentum in the years before 1914, had reduced the numbers of firms sufficiently to make the cartels much more manageable.

But all this occurred well over a century after the publication of Smith's book and it is hardly surprising that he should have concentrated his attention upon the much more pressing evils which faced him. Nevertheless, the logic of his system, and the whole tenor of his work, were strongly opposed to such 'monopolization' and I have no doubt that if Adam Smith had been able to be present at the celebrations of the sesquicentenary of the *Wealth of Nations* in 1926 he would have sharply revised his earlier verdict about the impracticability of legislation to deal with cartels. The reasons for taking this view should be obvious enough already. But it is perhaps worth emphasizing that the development of cartels, with official approval, and with official cooperation and encouragement, involved three things which were anathema to Adam Smith. Firstly, they reduced the flexibility of the economic system, and their regulation of the range of products and market shares of their members was completely at variance with the Smithian vision of an economy in which competition operated and which responded flexibly to changes in preferences and opportunities. Secondly, these cartels were a step in the direction of subordinating the interests of the consumer to those of the producer to which, as we have already seen, Smith objected most strongly. Thirdly, the cartel system embodies some of that blurring of the lines between government and business which Smith found most offensive. The institution which, in the *Wealth of Nations*, is the subject of the most blistering comments of all, is the East India

Company. Time and time again Smith insists that the interests of government must be kept distinct from those of companies, or the distinct duties of government will be subordinated to the interests of the traders. I think that Smith would have been worried, then, both by the cosy relationship between the Board of Trade and the cartels which developed and by the ostensible concern for the public good developed by the cartels. As he himself remarked on one occasion: 'I have never known much good done by those who affected to trade for the publick good.' (Glasgow edition, p. 456).

By the late 1940s or some 60 years after the problem first began to manifest itself (and in sharp contrast to the United States where legislation dated from the 1890s), both government and public opinion were moving to question the conventional wisdom of the 1920s and 1930s that cartels were somehow a Good Thing. The first step was inevitably a cautious one and it took the form of the 1948 Monopolies Act which set up the Monopolies Commission to make a preliminary survey of the problem. However, it quickly became apparent that the problem was very much bigger than anyone had realized, and in 1956 the Restrictive Trade Practices Act was passed. This was a fundamental piece of legislation which required the registration of restrictive agreements and their defence before a new Court on a level with the High Court, the Restrictive Practices Court. The 1956 Act was to be followed by other acts in 1964, 1965, 1968 and 1973 but it is the 1956 Act which is the key one in the British legislation.

The very act of requiring agreements to be registered produced some startling light in dark corners. Although many, possibly the majority, of agreements were laundered before being registered, the range of restrictions with which industry was prepared to saddle itself, and the system of fines which it was prepared to impose on itself, were startling. Even the sheer size of the problem, apart from its intensity, was remarkable. There were probably five times as many price rings in existence after World War II as there had been after World War I; and since the Court could clearly not hope to process 2,500 agreements in any reasonable period of time, it was clear that the early decisions of the Court were going to be of key importance.

In the event the Court, notably under the presidency of Lord Devlin, opted for Adam Smith, just as the Monopolies Commission itself had done, in its celebrated report on collective discrimination which preceded the 1956 Act. It became apparent that this attitude was producing far-reaching changes in industry, and it was with this in mind that Professor D. Swann and I began a study of the effects of this legislation in which we were later joined by Mr. P. Maunder and Mr. W.S. Howe.

We selected 18 industries for study in depth and another 22 industries for supplementary study; and we looked at industries in which agreements had been upheld by the Court, industries in which agreements had been struck down by the Court, and industries in which agreements had been abandoned without defending them before the Court.

The first thing we found was that governmental action through the Board of Trade had indeed been important in the development of these agreements in many cases; and that the coverage of the agreements in terms of United Kingdom output of the industry was extremely high. The lowest figure we found was 63% of United Kingdom output covered by an agreement and the percentage was typically in the

80% to 100% range. We found also that the agreements had been effectively enforced and that there had been little price cutting from collectively agreed prices. In turn we found that these collectively agreed prices rarely related to the costs of the members of the industry in any discernible manner but that they were usually set at a level which allowed comfortable margins.

The impact of the early severe attitude of the Court was such that many agreements were abandoned after the early cases had been heard. In the short run something between 53% and 61% of the industries we investigated experienced the emergence of competition, notably in the form of price competition, while new entry was encouraged in some industries and excess capacity eliminated in others. Adam Smith would have approved warmly of all this. The restoration of the flexibility of the economic system through the removal of the agreements moved us considerably nearer the situation in which resources could be deployed in the way that the consumer indicated that he wanted them deployed.

But Smith was too much of a student of human nature not to have realized that this was too good to last. Manufacturers 'met together', in Smith's phrase, and a phenomenon known as 'information agreements' emerged. In these, firms exchanged information about their intentions concerning prices in such a way that prices all tended to move together. We found that these emerged in about 50% of the industries which we studied. As a result of two famous cases, the galvanized tank case, and the tyre mileage case, and of the Act of 1968, information agreements are probably no longer a serious problem, but for a while they certainly inhibited the appearance of competition.

In the long run we found that there was a new cost consciousness in industry and that innovation, which the price rings tended to impede because of their limitation of product ranges, had become important – it was certainly significant in more than a dozen of the industries that we studied. Price competition became a good deal less feverish but this was only to be expected as the scope for price cutting, while still remaining in business, disappeared. I do not see any reason to suppose that Smith would have been other than happy at the longer run developments as I have described them so far.

But there were also other developments in the longer run which I think Smith would have both expected and disapproved. Firstly, there was a measure of collusion between firms who operated secret price agreements. Secondly, government, as Smith would probably have cynically predicted, again began to encourage collusive action by firms and to seek to weaken the impact of the legislation. Prominent in this were the Prices and Incomes Board and the National Economic Development Council. Thirdly, price leadership became a way in which competition was muted, although, by comparison with the earlier price agreements, it was a fairly innocuous development. There were other ways too in which the force of competition was reduced, including the development of agreements made between firms and public sector organizations purchasing from them. But the one development which we found was almost all-pervasive, and which has seriously weakened the competitive forces unleashed by the 1956 Act, was the wave of mergers which proceeded with virtually no government check and often with government encouragement. Of course, these sometimes had sound economic bases such as the elimi-

nation of high cost producers or of excess capacity. But they did not seem to have anything to do with the achievement of economies of scale; and they did seem to have a lot to do with the achievement of dominance in particular markets by one firm, and with reducing the number of firms so as to make it easier for everyone to have a healthy respect for everyone else's profits. I do not believe that Smith would have been very happy about this; nor for that matter would those who framed the relevant American legislation, notably the Clayton Act.

But for all that, I think Smith would have been pleased with the outcome of the legislation which certainly has, on balance, improved resource allocation; and the streak of pessimism in his character, combined with his cynicism about both governments and merchants, would have left him unsurprised at the less than ideal outcome. But having said that we should remind ourselves of one very important thing. Adam Smith possessed, unlike most of his 20th-century successors, a breadth of vision which enabled him to see the whole width of the problem and its many different facets. Of course, such breadth of vision could lead him, and did lead him, into inconsistencies at times. But he would not, as I have done in this talk, have concentrated all his attention upon one area of competition and one aspect of profitability. Had he appeared in ghostly form at the 1976 Glasgow celebrations of the bicentenary of the *Wealth of Nations* (and what better place to re-appear), I think he would have directed the attention of his hearers to the wider aspects of the problem. He would certainly have been concerned with the problems of capital accumulation and investment in an economy where a combination of governmental policies has recently reduced the rate of return on investment to very low or even negative levels when inflation is taken account of; and he would have been concerned too about the effects on the allocation of resources of the operation of one of these policies, price controls. Smith would also quite clearly have been concerned at a situation in which well over half of national income was passing through the hands of government, not least because he, who has some claim to have invented the concept of log-rolling, would see clearly the impossibility of democratic control of government on this scale. Finally, he would undoubtedly have been concerned at the emergence of a form of monopoly – mass trade unionism – with which he was totally unfamiliar. It is even possible that in the light of these much greater evils he might have given the operation of competition policy a fairly low priority. But he could hardly deny that it was he, with his vision of the economic system and of the role of government in providing a framework in which the interests of individuals and those of the general public coincided, who had provided virtually the whole intellectual basis of competition policy.

References

Smith, A. (1776), *An Inquiry into the Nature and Causes of the Wealth of Nations*, ed. R.H. Campbell, A.S. Skinner and W.B. Todd, Oxford: Clarendon, 1976. (Cited as 'the Glasgow edition'.)

Swann, D., D.P. O'Brien, W.P. Maunder and W.S. Howe (1974), *Competition in British Industry*, London: Allen & Unwin and *Case Studies of the Effects of Restrictive Practices Legislation*, Loughborough University.

The Antitrust Bulletin/Spring 1982 217

Competition policy in Britain: the silent revolution

BY D. P. O'BRIEN*

Competition policy in Britain is enshrined in a series of statutes which give it a predominantly legalistic form. The 1956 Restrictive Trade Practices Act[1] set up the Restrictive Practices Court and the associated organs of government; agreements of a restrictive nature were registered and, for the most part, declared unlawful by the court. The net of the legislation was widened, to cover information agreements and agreements relating to services, by the 1968,[2] 1973,[3] and 1976[4] acts. It is true that competition policy began with the Monopolies and Restrictive Practices Act 1948,[5] which established the Monopolies Commission. But the general consensus is that the operations of this body prior to 1956 were not very effective in inducing industry to compete.[6] Its

---

* Professor of Economics, University of Durham, England.

1 Restrictive Trade Practices Act, 1956, 4 & 5 Eliz. 2, c. 68.

2 Restrictive Trade Practices Act, 1968, c. 66.

3 Fair Trading Act, 1973, c. 41.

4 Restrictive Trade Practices Act, 1976, c. 34.

5 Monopolies and Restrictive Practices (Inquiry and Control) Act, 1948, 11 & 12 Geo. 6, c. 66.

6 See G. Polanyi & P. Polanyi, *The Fair Trading Bill and Monopoly Policy,* Three Banks Review, No. 98, 1973, pp. 23-29, at p. 24:

work was extremely valuable, but as a "major reconnaissance of the field,"[7] not as an active form of competition policy.

After the passing of the 1956 act, the Monopolies Commission, which was reduced by that act to a subordinate role, operated at a low level of activity. In the years 1958-65, the commission produced only six reports, or an average of about one per year. After this time the level of activity increased and it produced 22 reports in the years 1966-72, or an average of just over three per year. This does not include the merger references with which it dealt, but they were only a tiny fraction of a separate problem—around 2½% of the mergers actually considered by the merger panel were referred to the commission.[8]

By far the predominant role in the operation of competition policy was borne by the Restrictive Practices Court; indeed it would be perfectly true to say that this was the only form of competition policy which had a widespread and deep effect on British industry. Yet, since 1973, a silent revolution in the operation of competition policy in Britain has occurred, so that this predominantly legalistic approach has been supplanted by the development of an administrative and discretionary procedure. This process has culminated in the Competition Act of 1980[9] and it is provisions of this which will be discussed first.

". . . the Act of 1948 was no resolute attack on monopoly and restrictive practices but rather an open-minded pragmatic approach." The best account of the operations of the Monopolies Commission in its early years is contained in G.C. ALLEN, MONOPOLY AND RESTRICTIVE PRACTICES ch. VI (1968).

7 A. HUNTER, COMPETITION AND THE LAW 79 (1966).

8 See J.D. Gribbin, *Recent Antitrust Developments in the United Kingdom,* 20 ANTITRUST BULLETIN 382-83 (1975).

9 Competition Act, 1980, c. 21.

The Competition Act 1980

The basic approach of this piece of legislation is to set up means to seek control of what are called "anticompetitive practices." Such a practice is one which has "the effect of restricting, distorting or preventing competition" in the supply or acquisition of goods or services (§ 2).[10] The procedure laid down under the act is that the Director General of Fair Trading (DG) is empowered to make preliminary investigations of the possible employment of anticompetitive practices (§ 3), after which he publishes a report indicating whether he believes that there is a prima facie case that such practices are operated.

If the DG is unable to obtain undertakings from the firm or firms concerned that the operation of such practices will be modified, he may (§ 5) refer the practices to the Monopolies and Merger Commission (MMC) not less than four, and not more than eight (exceptionally, twelve) weeks after the publication of his preliminary report (§ 5(3)). The MMC is then required to report whether the practice alleged is operated, whether it is anticompetitive in effect, and whether this is against the public interest. By section 7 of this act, a number of provisions of the 1973 Fair Trading Act are carried over so as to apply to this new role for the MMC. They include not only the time limit for producing reports (§ 70), but also the key material on the public interest (§ 84) and the important investigatory powers (§ 85).

Of particular significance is the wide public interest definition under section 84 of the 1973 act. This requires the commission to take into account "all matters which appear to them . . . to be relevant" including the desirability of maintaining and promoting effective competition, of promoting the interests of consumers, purchasers and other users in respect of quality, variety and price, of promoting through competition new products and processes and new entry, of maintaining regional balance in industry

---

10 Insertions of this form indicate sections of the act under discussion.

and employment, and of maintaining competition by U.K. firms in export markets. Section 85 of the 1973 act bestows upon the MMC very considerable powers of investigation, subject only to what could be required to be produced in a civil court, though with a sanction for failure to comply of a fixed maximum fine rather than contempt proceedings.

Following an MMC report the DG seeks undertakings from the employers of anticompetitive practices, in the light of the commission recommendations; if these undertakings are not obtained, a ministerial order, banning such practices and similar ones, may be made. Enforcement of such an order may be made, if necessary, through a court order.

As explained in a booklet published by the Office of Fair Trading (OFT), *Anticompetitive Practices,*[11] the 1980 act is supposed to complement the 1973 act, under which the MMC, faced with a monopoly reference, has to take into account the whole market situation, which is a very time-consuming process. The MMC under the new act now has the power to investigate *individual* firms and to concentrate upon the *effects* of particular practices. Complementarity to the existing legislation is also ensured by the fact that restrictive agreements of the kind which are registrable with a view to processing by the Restrictive Practices Court are excluded from the scope of the 1980 act (§ 2 (2)). The OFT booklet helpfully lists a number of practices which might well merit examination under this legislation. Under the head of pricing policy, such practices as price discrimination, predatory pricing, and the raising of input prices to competitors by a vertically integrated firm are included. Under distribution policy, such familiar devices as tie-in sales, full-line forcing, rental-only contracts, exclusive supply, selective distribution, and exclusive purchase are listed. Recognition of the harm sometimes associated with these practices stems in particular from reports of the MMC, and the OFT booklet gives a number of examples

---

11 OFT, Anticompetitive Practices. A Guide to the Provisions of the Competition Act 1980 (1980).

from reports on frozen food, rayon, tranquilizers, film distribution, photocopying equipment, and asbestos. Two particular points of interest in the exposition are that the OFT is likely to be particularly concerned at practices which frustrate "the legitimate efforts of competitors to expand their own business" and that the primary source of information for the OFT is likely to be the postbag—indeed, the booklet indicates that there is a special unit at the OFT to follow up postal complaints.[12]

We have then a two-stage procedure. The DG, probably notified by a postal complaint which proved initially plausible, conducts a preliminary investigation. If as a result of this investigation he concludes that one or more anticompetitive practices are in operation, he can try to persuade the firm or firms involved to modify them. If this should prove impossible, he can then refer the matter to the MMC for a fuller investigation with the ultimate prospect of a ministerial order.

This legislation attracted relatively little comment at the time that it was passed.[13] In particular, the degree of discretion afforded to those charged with operating competition policy, especially the DG, seems to have passed into law with little comment. But a close reading of the legislation reveals that administrative discretion rather than procedures directed toward judicial processes is the main thing to be exercised at every stage of the employment of the powers given under the act. The DG is given considerable powers of investigation and (§ 3(7)) can require the production of documents and information within the same limits as a civil court. He has the discretion to negotiate undertakings with a firm after an initial investigation (stage one of the procedure) and having accepted such undertakings he has the responsibility for supervising adherence to them. He may

---

12 *Id.* at 12, 14.

13 See, however, V. Korah, *The Competition Act 1980,* 1980 Journal of Business Law 255-59, which is a straightforward factual account of the main provisions.

(§ 5) refer a matter to the MMC if he considers that undertakings are not being adhered to or that circumstances have changed. (This is known as a "notice reference.") Thus the judgment of the DG about the economic effects of a particular commercial practice is of crucial importance in the operation of this act.

At the end of the second stage of the procedure under the act, following an MMC report, the DG again has the task of negotiating undertakings and, as at the end of the first stage, is charged with supervising adherence to any such undertakings. This presents the nicely paradoxical position in which, although considerations concerning the public interest are within the purview of the MMC rather than the DG, there is no way the DG can avoid both interpreting and representing the public interest if he is to negotiate undertakings. Moreover there are built-in incentives to firms to cooperate with the DG at an early stage, for in this way they can avoid a full-scale MMC inquiry.[14] (Indeed it is arguable that firms, to avoid an MMC inquiry, may give undertakings which accord with the DG's interpretation of the public interest, even though the MMC itself might not have found the practices involved to be contrary to the public interest. It is not suggested here that this is a serious possibility; the point is made in order to underline the discretion bestowed upon the DG by the 1980 act.) At the stage at which, under the act, confidential material is removed from reports of the DG, he has to be the judge of the interest of the individual who is protected by the removal of such material. His investigatory powers are further strengthened by the fact that information obtained under other acts, including the 1973 act and the Consumer Credit and Agricultural Marketing Acts, can also be used for the purposes of this act (§ 19(4)).

The DG is thus placed in an extremely influential and indeed in a key position in this phase of the development of competition policy in Britain. This conclusion is not drawn from any strained

---

14 It would appear that one company already has modified an initially intransigent position in face of the threat of an MMC investigation.

or eccentric reading of the act. The OFT booklet referred to above also emphasizes the continuous supervisory role of the DG.[15]

There is also enhanced ministerial discretion. First, it is open to the minister to make an order excluding certain practices, or firms of a certain size, from the operation of the 1980 act; two such orders have already been made.[16] The minister also has powers, deriving from the 1973 act, which enable him to make it unlawful to carry out an agreement, to require the ending of an agreement, to make withholding of supplies or the attachment of conditions to supplies unlawful, to make discrimination in supply unlawful, to make it unlawful to offer discounts in particular situations, to require publication of price lists, to regulate prices, to recommend prices, and to prohibit acquisition of another business.[17] These are very strong powers indeed and, in the nature of the system, they will naturally be exercised on the advice of the DG. The Secretary of State ultimately, of course, has power over the DG; in particular he has the power of veto over a proposed investigation by the DG, although (§ 3(5)) this does not preclude the DG from raising the matter on a subsequent occasion. But in any case, one would normally expect ministerial discretion to be exercised on the advice of the DG and, at all events, the combined discretion available to the minister and the director together results in a piece of legislation which is of a different character from the main thrust of British competition policy since 1956.

However, the discretionary framework of the 1980 act does not represent a totally new departure within the framework of policy stemming from the 1956 act. (The discretionary procedures associated with the MMC are, as indicated above, a rather

---

15 OFT, *supra* note 11, at 14-18.

16 Statutory Instruments, 1980, Nos. 979, 981.

17 Section 10 of the 1980 act refers to the relevant sections of the 1973 act.

different matter.) Discretionary elements have gradually crept into the competition policy apparatus since 1968 and it is perhaps worthwhile to review some of the main developments here.

The growth of antitrust discretion

The 1956 act provided little discretion. Under section 12 it was possible for the Board of Trade to remove economically insignificant agreements from the Register, if requested to do so by the registrar. But this power was of very limited scope and could be nullified by any variation in the original agreement.

The 1968 act, however, introduced further discretion into the legislative framework. This occurred in two main ways. First, the act provided (§ 1) that the Board of Trade could exempt from registration agreements which it judged to be of national importance. Second, it was possible for agreements to be exempted from registration if they were agreements to hold down prices (§ 2). This discretion was not in fact used very widely, but it did represent a significant departure from the lack of administrative discretion in the 1956 act. The second area in which administrative discretion was to be exercised was in the bringing into the ambit of the legislative provisions of the phenomenon known as the information agreement. Rather than simply requiring all information agreements to be registered, the act provided (§ 5) for the making of an order by the Board of Trade calling up for registration certain kinds of information agreements; one such order was in fact made in 1969.[18]

---

18 Statutory Instrument, 1969, No. 1842. It is true that two orders were made under the 1956 act, to regulate the process of registration. But these were merely administrative devices to prevent the registrar's staff from being overwhelmed and did not involve the kind of discretion to be found in the 1968 and 1973 acts. The orders concerned are reproduced in Wilberforce, Campbell & Elles, The Law of Restrictive Trade Practices and Monopolies app. V (2d ed. 1966).

That the discretion introduced in the 1968 act was the thin end of a very large wedge became apparent with the 1973 act. This, which established the Office of Director General of Fair Trading, gave the DG a general supervisory role over competition. The contrast between the extensive duties entrusted to the DG by the 1973 act and the bald statement of the functions of the registrar under the 1956 act is indeed striking. Under section 1 of the 1956 act the registrar was simply "charged with the duty of preparing . . . a register of agreements . . . and of taking proceedings before the Court . . . in respect of the agreements. . . ." Under the 1973 act (§ 2) the DG is charged with keeping under review "the carrying on of commercial activities in the United Kingdom" in relation to the supply of goods and services and is also required "to receive and collate evidence . . . with respect to such activities." He is required to collect information both in relation to monopoly situations and to uncompetitive practices and to make recommendations for action to the relevant minister. Part II of the act gives the DG a general discretionary role in referring to the Consumer Protection Advisory Committee (CPAC) established by the act such "consumer trade practices" as terms or conditions of sale, information about terms or conditions of sale, sales promotion, sales methods, packaging and debt collection (§§ 13, 14). The DG is charged with supplying information both to the CPAC (§ 14(4)) and to the MMC (§ 5(2)). The DG may propose specific remedies to the CPAC for particular consumer practices including (schedule 6) prohibitions. It is easy to see in all this a forerunner of the 1980 provisions, in that the CPAC under the 1973 act was given a position not very different from that afforded to the MMC under the 1980 act, except that in the latter case the role of the DG has been even further enhanced by the duty upon him to make preliminary investigations, to undertake negotiations with firms affected, and to engage in supervision.

Part III of the 1973 act enables the DG to take action directly against traders who behave in a way which adversely affects the interests of consumers and to obtain a court order against such traders. This part of the act, as the Annual Reports of the

Director indicate, has been used with considerable vigor, and the number of assurances of future good behavior obtained from traders seems to be running at something in excess of 25 a year. The matters dealt with under this part of the act are not really what is normally regarded as being within the sphere of competition policy; rather they are matters for which there are remedies in civil law (especially contract) and criminal law, but for which the machinery of the normal legal processes seems to have been inadequate. Nonetheless, the exercise of powers under this part of the act has no doubt given the DG and his staff considerable experience of dealing directly, through discretionary administrative procedures, with problems affecting the supply of goods and services.

Part IV of the 1973 act, which dealt with the functions of the DG and the MMC in relation to monopoly situations, gave the DG fairly comprehensive powers in relation to the investigation of possible (statutory) monopoly positions.[19] Under it, he can ask for information on costs, prices, quantities, capacity and employment. The act also provided (§ 46) for a fine of up to £400 for noncompliance and envisaged the possibility of imprisonment for supplying misleading information. Section 48 of the act even provided for the MMC to investigate what were then referred to as "*un*competitive practices" employed by a person or persons, thus clearly foreshadowing the 1980 act, although in the 1973 act the provision was confined to monopoly situations. The very responsibility for making references to the MMC became the DG's (except in the case of mergers, where he was merely charged with keeping himself informed and making recommendations to the relevant minister), and—again foreshadowing the 1980 act—the DG had the duty, in the event of an adverse monopoly or merger report from the MMC, to seek undertakings from the relevant parties to remedy the situation. He also had to keep under review the performance of such undertakings. He could recommend the obtaining of orders under section 56 or section 73

---

19 A "statutory monopoly" is a 25% market share in the hands of a single supplier or several suppliers acting in concert.

of the act, and if orders were made he was given responsibility for supervising and making sure of compliance. He was also given a supervisory role in relation to export agreements, particulars of which have to be furnished to him (§ 102). This had previously been a Board of Trade and ministerial responsibility.[20]

The administrative and discretionary character of developments in competition policy at this stage was enhanced in a number of other ways. For one thing it became possible (§ 105) for the DG to obtain interim orders from the Restrictive Practices Court to prevent operation of a restrictive agreement pending a full hearing; for another, restrictive agreements relating to the supply of services were also to be brought within the ambit of the 1956 and 1968 provisions, which had related only to goods. The way in which this was to be done was by statutory instrument,[21] thus paralleling the procedure for information agreements under the 1968 act. Such was the exercise of discretion that it was not until three years later and the passing of another Restrictive Trade Practices Act that such an order was made. The act of 1973 also gives the relevant minister quite remarkable powers. Not only is pyramid selling (part XI) left to his control rather than to that of the DG, but the act contains a provision for the making of ministerial orders (schedule 8) which is extremely comprehensive. (The substance of these has been noted above in connection with their reenactment in the Competition Act 1980 and there is no need to detail them again here). This provision is in addition to his powers, dating from the 1965 Monopolies and Mergers Act, to prohibit a merger or takeover and order divestment.[22]

One commentator makes the interesting point that orders under the 1965 act required affirmative resolutions of Parliament; orders under the 1973 act have immediate effect and can

---

20 Fair Trading Act, 1973, sched. 11, para. 12, p. 129. See also J.P. CUNNINGHAM, THE FAIR TRADING ACT 1973 (1974).

21 Statutory Instrument, 1976, No. 98.

22 Monopolies and Mergers Act, 1965, c. 50, §§ 3(5), (6).

only be negated by negative resolutions.[23] Once again, the initiative is passed to the administrative body. The orders which can be made under the 1973 act have their forerunners, for the most part, in provisions of the 1948 and 1965 acts, but the provisions of the 1973 act seem much more full and explicit. This is no doubt a reflection of the changing emphasis, at that date, in the operation of competition policy, particularly as, under the 1948 act, orders were very rarely made and the Board of Trade relied upon the negotiation of voluntary undertakings. Not all of these seem to have been adhered to,[24] indicating that if policy henceforth were to build upon a discretionary basis, continuous supervision of any negotiated undertakings would be required.

The legislation of 1976 and 1977 did not introduce further significant discretionary elements and indeed appeared to confirm the judicial nature of the main thrust of competition policy by consolidating, in the 1976 act, the 1956 and 1968 legislation. However there are two quite important qualifications to this view. First, the 1976 act confers (§ 21(2)) upon the DG a power not to bring agreements before the Restrictive Practices Court; although this dates from the earlier legislation[25] it has become, since 1976, a rather key part of the legislation. Indeed, according to the Green Paper on Restrictive Trade Practices Policy: "The Office [of Fair Trading] is at present negotiating with the parties to some 350 agreements to see whether these can be modified so as to make them suitable for 21(2) representations."[26] As the Green Paper had earlier explained:

> on the representation of the Director General, the Secretary of State . . . may direct him not to refer an agreement to the Court on the

---

23 Cunningham, *supra* note 20, at 155-56.

24 Swann, O'Brien, Maunder & Howe, Competition in British Industry 54 (1974); Allen, *supra* note 6, at 99-100.

25 Restrictive Trade Practices Act, 1956, § 12, 1968, § 9.

26 *A Review of Restrictive Trade Practices Policy,* Cmd. No. 7512, at 12 (1979) [hereinafter cited as Green Paper].

> ground that the restrictions in it are not of such significance as to warrant Court proceedings. The relevant provision is section 21(2) of the Restrictive Trade Practices Act 1976, and this is usually referred to as the section 21(2) procedure."[27]

It is significant that this is referred to as the section 21(2) procedure, since it would seem to be only since 1976 that this provision in the legislation has been used with such vigor, even though it is a quarter of a century old. Indeed, the Green Paper seems at one point to imply that the competition policy authorities have tried to develop an effects-based system (a concept discussed below) via section 21(2) but that industry feels that this has not been flexible enough.[28]

The second aspect of the 1976 and 1977 legislation which involves a clear move in the direction of greater discretion is the power given to the minister, under the 1977 act, to make a ministerial order adding to the list of agreements given under the 1976 act which are exempt from the operation of the legislation.[29]

An official working party reviewed the operation of competition policy following this legislation, and the results of its deliberations are published in the Green Paper referred to above. Its authors, while accepting the need to increase the flexibility of the legislation, believed that the basic approach, resting upon requiring registration of agreements of a particular *form*, should be retained. They recognized[30] that there are objections to a form-based approach: in particular (1) all agreements have to be registered and thus some (potentially) beneficial agreements may be prevented; (2) the registration criteria are different from public interest criteria and so the OFT has (it would seem) great

---

27 *Id.* at 11.

28 *Id.* at 38.

29 Restrictive Trade Practices Act, 1977, c. 19. See also Green Paper, *supra* note 26, at 10.

30 Green Paper, *supra* note 26, at 40.

difficulty in deciding cases of registrability; and (3) complex legislation may be overlooked by small firms. The authors also believed that the legislation does not catch some agreements which are "to the like effect" of registered agreements. This seems rather dubious in the light of judicial pronouncements on the meaning of the phrase "to the like effect" and the possibility of contempt proceedings, but the other three problems seem real though it is difficult to be sure what weight should be attached to them.

There are also problems with the judicial procedure; the authors of the Green Paper note in particular those of expense, uncertainty which may affect investment, and the problem of agreements which are used and then abandoned before they come to court. This last need not necessarily be serious, as there is nothing to stop the DG from obtaining an order prohibiting firms from operating any agreement "to the like effect" of an abandoned one.

Very sensibly, the authors of the Green Paper refuse to get these problems out of perspective. This is as well, since many of the objections apply only to an *exclusively* form-based approach. They clearly regard the argument about "justiciability" (*i.e.,* matters which are within the competence of a judiciary), which has rather exercised legal writers, as of no real practical weight, and point out that there are two lay advisors, who are chosen for their knowledge of industry, sitting in the Restrictive Practices Court with the judge, and that judgments of the court (except on matters of law) are taken on a majority basis. They are also reasonably skeptical of the argument that the gateways in the 1956, 1968, and 1976 acts, through which an agreement can pass, need rewording. As they point out: "A substantial body of legal interpretation has been developed on the basis of the existing criteria and this would be lost in the event of major changes. . . ."[31]

---

31 *Id.* at 43.

In essence the authors of the Green Paper sought to retain the present basis of policy but to supplement it with other measures. "The present form-based system has on the whole served well, despite the criticisms, and ought to be retained and adapted to overcome the weaknesses we have identified.[32] This conclusion, however, may inadvertently deflect attention from the very real changes in the operation of competition policy in Britain which have taken place. For although it will not be a contention of this discussion that the above assessment is mistaken—the judicial procedures have on the whole worked well[33]—policy itself has evolved away from use of these judicial instruments. This is evident from the more recent experience of the Restrictive Practices Court itself. There have not even been separate Restrictive Practices Court reports since 1973.[34] Since then, reports of restrictive practices cases have been incorporated into Industrial Court reports and there do not appear to have been any significant cases since 1975. Indeed there were, it would appear, no cases worth reporting in either 1976 or 1979, although the reports of the DG do contain records of a number of undefended cases on which the court made orders.

The DG has become the focus and pivot of policy to an extent which many did not envisage at the time of the 1973 act.[35] The CPAC set up under that act has been remarkably inactive; the reports of the DG show only two references to it in the years from 1975 onwards.

From all this it should be apparent that the nature of competition policy has changed quite remarkably from the mid-1970s.

---

32 *Id.* at 3.

33 See also Gribbin, *supra* note 8, at 395: "There is no doubt that the experiment of providing a presumption against agreements in a judicial process was outstandingly successful."

34 L.R. 7 R.P. (1970-1973).

35 The Polanyis (*supra* note 6, at 29-30) appreciated the key role which was being given to the DG but not the change in the balance of policy which would result.

The exact nature of the change requires, however, some further discussion.

The nature of the policy metamorphosis

There is a fairly commonplace distinction, to be found not only in the Green Paper, but also in some of the literature written by lawyers discussing competition policy legislation, between a form-based system, which is seen as applying policy only to restrictions which take a particular form, and an effects-based system, which concentrates upon the effects of particular restrictions rather than the form in which they are couched. The inspiration for this comes from contemplation of competition policy under articles 85 and 86 of the Treaty of Rome, which employs a system of a generalized framework coupled with administrative orders, with particular attention paid to abuse of a dominant position.

Although the distinction between a form-based and an effects-based system is not without any substance, the distinction is perhaps less clear-cut than some of the discussions seem to assume. First, *form* applies only to the net used to catch agreements, not to the processing of those agreements, under the British legislation. Our processing is, in substance, effects-based and the legislation is cast in terms which permit this. Second, because there is a major element of judgment in the discernment of effects, it follows, as anyone studying European competition law appreciates, that a substantial body of precedent is built up, which retains information about the kind of agreements against which the European Commission is likely to take action, in terms of *forms*. Moreover it is not true, as is sometimes implied, that a judicial procedure is necessarily inflexible. The procedure of the Restrictive Practices Court has itself been made more flexible by section 26 of the 1980 act, which introduced the possibility of delay before a judgment of the court takes effect to allow time for revision of an agreement; section 27 provides greater flexibility in bringing agreements concerning services, and information

agreements concerning services, before the court. Section 26 (3) also enables the DG to avoid bringing an agreement before the court if the court has already pronounced favorably upon restrictions or information provisions of the kind contained in it. (Of course such a provision also enhances the discretion available to the DG, particularly as there seems to be, in practice, no way in which a decision by the DG that a previous ruling of the court clears a particular agreement can be challenged.)

Insofar as the distinction between effects-based and form-based policy is valid, it might be argued that an effects-based system has the advantage of allowing policy to take account of circumstances, like those on which the National Economic Development Office (NEDO) lays such stress,[36] concerning the beneficial effects of agreements and that, because of flexibility, such a system may avoid pressure to create *general* exceptions based on invalid generalizations from the special cases which have always impressed NEDO.[37] But legislators have usually recognized that "hard cases make bad law" and, with the exception of the 1968 act, have not yielded to such pressure in the competition policy context. Thus, here again, the distinction between form-base and effects-base is less clear than might at first sight be imagined. This is perhaps as well; the scope of the NEDO case can be seen from the Green Paper,[38] where such emphasis is laid on the beneficial effects of agreements that it would seem to imply the need to abandon competition policy.

The real argument in favor of a change in the basic thrust of policy lies not in a, perhaps rather shaky, distinction between effects-base and form-base but between judicial procedures and administrative ones involving greater executive discretion. The pressures for this change have come both from those operating policy and those affected by it. Those operating policy, it is clear

---

36 Green Paper, *supra* note 26, at 18.

37 See Swann, *supra* note 24, at 83-84.

38 Green Paper, *supra* note 26, at 46-48.

from the Green Paper, have desired a system which would enable them to act above all swiftly and flexibly in dealing with practices which interfere with competition; those affected by policy have been arguing, since the late 1960s, for a return to an administrative procedure, after their experience of court procedures.[39] This is hardly surprising in view of what is apparently known in the legal trade as "forensic fun" but which to a non-lawyer looks very much like bullying and intimidation of witnesses. It is hinted at by one legal commentator,[40] but it is depressingly obvious to anyone who has read transcripts of cases in the Restrictive Practices Court.

The desire of industrialists to avoid this kind of treatment is only human, and a non-lawyer might well take the view that British lawyers, in employing routine adversary tactics in the context of the Restrictive Practices Court, have cast doubt on the usefulness of judicial procedures as a means of effecting competition policy. At all events it is hardly surprising that firms are prepared to go to considerable lengths, including straightforward evasion of the law, to avoid processing by the court and, because of the problems of discovery thus presented to the OFT, there is a natural desire on the part of the latter to use an administrative system which may present fewer disincentives to cooperation on the part of industry while arming the OFT with flexible powers of investigation. This becomes all the more attractive when the DG is given powers of continuous supervision, as he is under the 1980 act.

The future development of competition policy

Whatever the advocates of what they see as an effects-based system may argue,[41] there would seem to be no doubt, when one

---

39 Swann, *supra* note 24, at 80-82.

40 V. Korah, Competition Law of Britain and the Common Market 83 (1975).

41 See in particular Green Paper, *supra* note 26, at 100, para. 11.

surveys the extent of the problem which existed in 1956,[42] that the perhaps blunt instrument of court proceedings was the only weapon which could effectively be used at that time. The choice, as was indeed made clear by the differing views of the majority and minority report on Collective Discrimination of 1955 by the Monopolies Commission, was really between a per se rule—which, as in the U.S., would have led to processing through ordinary courts—and the setting up of a special court with lay assessors. The government of the day opted for the latter, thus easing the problem of the judiciary having to take economic decisions which would also have fallen to them under a per se rule.

A quarter of a century later it is possible to take the view that the way forward now lies in *supplementing* the legislation stemming from the 1956 act with the new procedures embodied in the 1980 act, building in turn upon the 1973 act. But these new discretionary procedures have to take as supporting background the body of decisions arrived at under the 1956 and subsequent legislation.[43] Given the economic history of the 1948-1956 era, in respect of restrictive practices, it is indeed doubtful whether administrative procedures without such a legal background can

---

42 Swann, *supra* note 24, at 54-58, 146-153; Allen, *supra* note 6, at 71-78.

43 One commentator has made the interesting suggestion that the nature of the problem itself has changed, with increases in concentration becoming more important than restrictive agreements between independent units, and that this has provided a greater role for administrative action in the competition policy field (Gribbin, *supra* note 8, at 382). This is undoubtedly an important and valid point. But without the established background of decisions arrived at under the 1956 act and its amending legislation, it seems likely that we would be faced with increased concentration *and* restrictive agreements. This is because there does not seem to be clear evidence that firms affected by policy under the 1956 act were more merger-prone than others (see O'Brien, Howe, Wright & O'Brien, Competition Policy, Profitability and Growth ch. 6 (1979)). Had they been so, it would have suggested that mergers were being entered into as a substitute for restrictive agreements.

have much effect. In particular, the registration procedure, despite the problem of evasion noted above, has proven most valuable. (This is a long-standing American observation embodied in the aphorism "sunlight is the best disinfectant.")

There are two perfectly straightforward economic reasons why this should be the case. First, a rational entrepreneur, faced with an administrative procedure which is extremely uncertain in its impact and slow in its operation, will continue with whatever restriction he operates, if the administrative procedure is all that is available to the antitrust authorities.[44] He has very little to lose indeed and much to gain by retaining his agreement. Second—and this is an essential point which is often missed—information has costs. Economists appreciate this in the context of antitrust policy, despite their tendency in other contexts to assume costless omniscience. A form-based procedure provides dramatic economy of information costs in two ways. First, it economizes on the costs of information search for the firm seeking to learn which of its practices are likely to attract official attention;

---

44 This is particularly true because of the length of time which MMC investigations seem to require. According to Gribbin (*supra* note 8, at 397), "an average of about two years" is involved. As the Polanyis (*supra* note 6, at 26) observed of monopoly inquiries: "Because the Commission is enjoined to consider everything that might be relevant to the public interest, it has tended to engage in prolonged inquiries ranging over the minutiae of a company's behaviour during its entire history—sometimes stretching back over half a century. Minutes of Board meetings are scrutinised, agreements memoranda, price lists, special financial analyses, descriptions of administrative and selling procedures, detailed technical evaluations of research programmes and a host of other documents referring to transactions over several decades are assembled in a voluminous mass of paper required by the Commission for the successive stages of its inquiry. Everything is collected because neither the company under scrutiny nor the Commission knows what will in the end prove relevant. It is not surprising, therefore, that the time taken for an inquiry has averaged 2½ years, extending up to 4 years in individual cases, and that the burden on the companies concerned (who are required to do most of the research) is felt to be quite disproportionate to the value of the results achieved."

second, and most importantly perhaps, it replaces the plodding and painstaking procedure of a commission inquiry by a general presumption, *based upon previous economic inquiry,* that certain broad groups of practices are likely to be found contrary to the public interest. It simply is not practical to base *the whole* of competition policy upon administrative procedures, and it is not rational to do so when this means of economizing on information is available.

But having said that—and in view of some of the criticisms which have been made of the legislation—it is very necessary to emphasize that the development of judicial processes to cope with problems of competition policy has probably gone about as far as it can go. This is partly because of the drawbacks of the legal procedure itself, including costs, when viewed from the point of view of the firms which are party to a particular agreement being processed. Such firms do not, unlike the OFT, enjoy the subsequent benefit of the spreading of such costs (which may be as high as a quarter of a million pounds on each side[45]) over a large number of subsequent cases, many of which may as a direct result be undefended. It is also because of the way in which, as noted above, the legal profession is apparently required to conduct itself in court proceedings even where these concern restrictive practices.

In addition to this, a judicial form-based approach can never be exhaustive and it can thus lend itself to avoidance through the redrafting of agreements. This is a point made by the Green Paper.[46] But this argument should not be pushed too far. The main way in which the effects of the 1956 and subsequent legislation have been avoided has been, as the Green Paper notes,[47] evasion through nonregistration. This suggests that the ambit of the registration requirements is in fact wide enough but

---

45 Green Paper, *supra* note 26, at 44.

46 *Id.* at 35.

47 *Id.* at 48.

that there are other factors—mainly inherent in the judicial procedure and the experience of this by industrialists—which inhibit compliance with the law.

There is thus a strong case for retaining the present judicial apparatus even though much less use will have to be made of it than in the early years of its existence. It has created a body of decisions with which industry has by and large learned to live and to cope.[48] A switch to an entirely administrative system not only would involve losing the benefits of the experience built up but would introduce new kinds of uncertainty. It is undoubtedly true that an effects-based system, as the EEC system is viewed, contains a great many uncertainties and that these are compounded by the need to resort to ordinary courts to settle questions in dispute between firms and the administrative authority.[49] British policy seems to have evolved silently to the point where, on the basis of the legal foundations, the future thrust of policy will be along administrative and discretionary lines. This amounts to a departure from the historic direction of policy so substantial that it may be called a "revolution", but so long as it proceeds from the background of the judicial basis which has been built up since 1956, and does not endeavor to supplant it, there is no reason why it should not be an extremely valuable development of policy.

But there is one important caveat. A commentator well versed in competition policy, reviewing worldwide developments, has noted an increasing severity in the operation of policy and the need which this has made apparent in other countries for a *more* rather than less legalistic and judicial approach.[50] This is, from an

---

48 At least profitability and growth of firms affected by policy have not been differentially affected in an adverse manner. See O'Brien, *supra* note 43.

49 This is noted by Korah, *supra* note 40, at 255.

50 D. Brault, *Current Developments in Competition Policies,* 22 Antitrust Bulletin 164-68 (1977).

economic point of view, rather a profound, though at first sight simple, point. For it will hardly improve the allocation of resources to introduce unnecessary man-made uncertainties into the entrepreneurial environment. There is a danger that if competition policy is administrative in character but operated with vigor the result will be a form of departure from the rule of law which not only may be unacceptable from a social-policy point of view but one which may also damage, quite needlessly, the economic activity of firms. If developments in Britain are to go in this direction then it seems likely that return to a more legalistic base may be required. Yet it may be that those associated with British policy may envisage precisely such a development. Under the 1973 act it is possible to produce legislation by ministerial order following a report of the CPAC; at least one commentator with a detailed knowledge of competition policy viewed the prospect with enthusiasm:

> It is intended that this procedure of referral to the Consumer Protection Advisory Committee combined with use of the order-making powers will be speedier and more effective than previously, when it was necessary to mobilize public opinion, convince politicians of the need for change, draft new legislation, find space in the Parliamentary timetable and have the bill passed by Parliament.[51]

It will be interesting to see how things develop in Britain.

---

51 Gribbin, *supra* note 8, at 394.

7

Divestiture: The Case of AT & T

D.P. O'Brien

Introduction

'Divestiture' is the term used in the context of antitrust policy to refer to both the forced sale of shareholdings in one company which are owned by another company, and the forced breaking up of a single firm. The latter may in turn either represent the sale of parts of a company which are financially linked but not otherwise integrated, or involve the breaking up of a unitary firm; and the firm against which action is taken (by the antitrust authorities) may have reached its present position either through internal growth or through merger. While the American literature distinguishes between 'dissolution', 'divorcement' and 'divestiture',[1] these legal categories do not do a great deal to illuminate the complex possibilities while, as should be clear from the description above, the various possible situations shade into one another. In the circumstances it seems reasonable to use the general term divestiture to cover all forced sales, and this practice will be followed here.

Faced with a difficult problem in competition policy, divestiture may well seem an attractive policy alternative to regulation, as a number of authors have pointed out;[2] and certainly, if the alternative is the sort of haphazard regulation experienced by some

industries in Britain, divestiture might well also be attractive to the firms concerned as an alternative.[3] As we shall see, there is provision for divestiture in both British and American legislation; and, as the case study in this chapter will demonstrate, it was at least partially the difficulties of regulation which made divestiture attractive both to the American antitrust authorities and to the company itself in the most sweeping divestiture case in history – that of AT & T.

The chapter begins with an examination of the conceptual economic issues surrounding *divestiture*. The grounds for divestiture may be divided into those which relate to the *structure* of an industry and those which relate to the *conduct* or behaviour of a firm. The means by which the enforced disposal of a subsidiary may be carried out have attracted a great deal of debate in the literature and this issue is addressed below together with the question as to whether divestiture involves penalties for the divestor, the divestee and their shareholders. Turning to actual practice, the British context is considered first, followed by that in the US where divestiture has been a more prevalent feature of antitrust policy. The case of AT & T is then examined in detail.

The Economics of Divestiture

Grounds for Divestiture

There are basically two grounds for divestiture: as a means of attacking a *structure* which is deemed to be unsatisfactory; and as a means of remedying *conduct* by firms in an industry which is anti-competitive in effect and which, it is judged, cannot be dealt with by regulation.

(a) Structure The structural approach, in which a *per se* approach to concentration is adopted, without explicit reference to conduct, has attracted widespread and influential support. It was, in particular, advanced as a desirable course of proceeding by Kaysen and Turner in their influential book, in which they recommended divestiture as part of a strengthening of antitrust policy generally, proposing the use of a special court and implementing both horizontal and vertical divestiture.[4] A number of other economists have supported this approach[5] and it received considerable impetus from

the report of the Neal 'Task Force' in 1968 and the introduction in 1972 and 1973 by Senator P.A. Hart of an Industrial Reorganisation Act.[6] The advocates of a structural approach cite evidence that large firms are not required for static or dynamic optimisation,[7] and point to the possibility of implied conspiracy over prices where the number of firms is small. Indeed, Turner used the term 'shared monopoly' for the situation where close oligopolistic relations enabled implicit collusion to take place.[8] Moreover, empirical work does indicate that conspiracy is most likely where numbers are small and the concentration ratio high.[9]

The structural approach, however, encounters a number of difficulties and has been the subject of sustained attack in the literature over recent years.[10] Indeed, it is arguable that, under the influence of Bain's work, there was a shift from conduct to structure in the emphasis of policy[11] and that, as a result, certain weaknesses in the structural approach became apparent.

The first difficulty is that the structural approach, since it involves market concentration, requires a market to be defined; and it is clear that there are endless possibilities of contesting the market definition used.[12] Secondly, critics have pointed out that unless a concentrated structure is protected by barriers to entry, supernormal profits cannot be maintained in the long term.[13] In turn, it is clear that both the existence and the durability of such barriers can be contested as strongly as the market definition.[14]

It can also be contended that the use of profit data in identifying non-competitive structures is highly misleading. It is fairly easy to argue both that accounting profit data bear little relationship to the economic concept of profit and, secondly, that supernormal profit will become capitalised and thus undetectable.[15] But even if accounting data were to represent economic profit correctly, it would still be open to firms (and their economists) to argue that high profits are due to high efficiency and that any evidence of a statistical relationship between concentration and profitability can be explained by considerations of scale economies and other forms of efficiency.[16]

Furthermore, it is not difficult to argue that structure, on its own, is ambiguous. As Hexter and Snow point out:

> A merger may at the same time increase the share of the market held by the largest firms, but reduce size inequality among those firms.[17]

Moreover, critics argue, the structure approach to policy can lead antitrust authorities towards the wrong targets; industries are selected because they have a structure which is *capable of* divestment rather than because they have a structure which is at an undesirably high level of concentration.[18] Finally, the structure approach, precisely because it is not based upon any observable conduct, puts courts into such difficulties of predicting the outcome of the divestiture order that they become reluctant to order divestiture.[19]

The difficulties facing the structural approach have become much clearer as, in response to criticisms, the goal of efficiency has become explicit rather than implicit.[20] The literature is now much clearer about efficiency as the aim of antitrust policy; and this efficiency is extended beyond technical (engineering) considerations to include transactions efficiency and even efficiency in the use of 'intangible resources' – meaning, in effect, various forms of overheads such as advertising.[21]

Of course, there may be other (and valid) aims of antitrust, such as the constraint of power.[22] But these are not really matters on which the economist has any special expertise; and they do not, therefore, provide a defence of the structuralist approach which satisfies its economic critics.

Indeed, the difficulties with the structural approach have led to root and branch criticisms of the idea of a divestiture programme and even of the existence of a power of divestiture.[23] Critics have argued that there are no sufficient grounds in the literature of economics to support the divestiture programme;[24] that divestiture, coupled with a tough policy on mergers, places emphasis upon preserving *competitors* rather than upon preserving competition;[25] that vertical restrictions do not affect competition;[26] and even that concentration is prima-facie evidence of efficiency.[27] Indeed, one writer has argued that divestiture action in the beer industry has reduced its efficiency compared with efficiency in the manufacture of spirits which has not been affected by divestiture.[28]

Buttressing all this is the thesis that the high profits yielded by a concentrated situation will decline over time, as entry is attracted into an industry, and there is thus no need to use forcible deconcentration. Only in the presence of barriers to entry – the existence of which are increasingly questioned – will this not be the case.[29] Such an approach links neatly with the idea of markets being

'contestable',[30] that is being open to the entry of competitors who will erode market power positions and reduce profits to normal. The doubts over barriers to entry are linked to other doubts over the possibility of 'predatory' pricing.[31] Indeed, one critic has gone so far as to express the view that the possibility of predatory pricing is unimportant 'except in the *unlikely case* in which the intended victim lacks equal access to capital to finance a price war'[32] (my italics).

Given that barriers to entry are held to be of doubtful importance, and that predatory pricing, or its potential, is unlikely to be a source of market power, the critics then move on to arguing that market forces produce the right kind of merger. Reliance is frequently placed upon the well-known analysis by O.E. Williamson of mergers,[33] while paying relatively little attention to the distributional aspects of the Williamson analysis (are supernormal profits distributionally equivalent to increased consumer surplus?) and to Williamson's own stress on the point that economies secured by merger must be real rather than merely pecuniary.[34] Associated with this is an emphasis upon transactions economies within a large organisation, stemming both from the work of Williamson and also from Coase's insight that a firm is much more than a legal entity.[35]

Of course not all these criticisms of the structural approach should be taken at face value. As critics have pointed out, vertical integration creates barriers to entry and, once accomplished, means that dealings are not necessarily based on competitive merit.[36] This is particularly true where entry into a small sector is blocked by large capital requirements for a whole chain.[37] Strategic considerations become important under these circumstances for the firm;[38] in particular, the argument against interfering with vertical mergers (and vertical integration) fails to take account of dominant price leadership. (It may be better to interfere with a vertical merger than to have to regulate thereafter.) One particular problem which can arise in this connection is capture, by one firm, of a common source of supply. Since the development of common sources of supply can be important and has been recognised by economists for the best part of a century – indeed, since Marshall – as a leading form of economies external to the firm and internal to the industry, it follows that allowing such capture is harmful to the development of the industry and that it may indeed produce horizontal concentration (as in the British motor industry).[39] The assets of competitors can be bought cheaply when they are faced with deprivation of their

inputs and the problems of attempting to replicate the captured source of supply. Even in less extreme circumstances, vertical integration (and vertical restrictions) remove the incentive to search, which is an important requirement for competition to work in a world of non-perfect information.[40]

Much of the criticism not only assumes, implicitly, perfect information, but also bases itself on a static analysis which could in turn, and if carried to its logical conclusion, be used to justify both cartels and a merger of General Motors, Ford and Chrysler.[41] The efficiency claims made for merged firms could often be made for cartels[42] – and it might be added that, at least in Britain, merged firms have often behaved like cartels. This static, perfect information, approach arises from applying elementary price theory to complex industrial situations. For instance, some writers rely on the Lerner index, despite the cogent criticism of this made by Bauer and others in the 1940s and despite being forced to concede that it cannot deal with limit pricing.[43] Such an approach is, of course, fundamentally misconceived without some notion of *long*-run marginal cost and without reference to the cost of finding marginal cost. Critics have pointed to important dimensions which are missing from such an approach, including entry, product differentiation, oligopoly, and transport costs.[44]

The argument that existing antitrust policy is aimed at preserving competitors rather than at achieving efficiency is itself open to a number of criticisms. Of course it may be preferable to preserve competitors rather than allowing competition to self-destruct through merger, since potential competition can still be important. But there are, in any case, important difficulties with the idea that concentration is prima-facie evidence of efficiency. Not only could such an argument apply equally well to cartels[45] but, on the transactions front, it fails to take account of the fact that large firms typically exhibit managerial diseconomies and communications problems. The position that everything will be put right, in the long run, by entry, fails to take account of the fact that divestiture might work very much more quickly and effectively and also of the fact that the apparent long-run decline of profits in concentrated situations may equally well be due to the development of organisational slack rather than to competitive pressure[46] – the evidence that, in the long run, prices fall in concentrated situations is not strong.[47] Indeed, if entry were the solution to everything, cartels would be no

problem since they would promptly be undermined by entry. For those less inclined to accept the insignificance of barriers to entry, divestiture may be a good way of attacking such barriers. (There is some evidence that advertising can be an effective barrier to entry.[48])

The argument that concentration is prima-facie evidence of efficiency also conflicts with the available information on minimum efficient scale and with the fact that evidence for cost savings in mergers is not exactly strong.[49] Indeed, cost curves are not well defined where there is market power,[50] making application of the Williamson analysis of mergers rather difficult. In addition, this also encounters problems because, as Williamson himself stressed, the shape of the time stream of benefits and costs is important and because, as he recognised in response to criticism, it is also necessary to analyse the alternative time stream of benefits and costs from internal expansion.[51]

Faced with these difficulties, especially the engineering evidence over minimum efficient scale, reliance upon 'intangible' economies does not help very much because the welfare implications of such matters as economies of scale in advertising, quantity discounts, and bargaining power in the capital market are hardly unambiguous. In particular, it is important to distinguish between real and pecuniary economies.[52] But in any case we cannot assume that firms are *necessarily* seeking economies if they are growth or sales maximisers.

An attitude of complete complacency where a small group of firms, apparently immune to outside competitive pressure, is enjoying a high level of profits, does not then seem warranted on the grounds that this is prima-facie evidence of efficiency. In this connection it should be noted that those who are totally dismissive of the idea that accounting rates of return have anything at all to do with economic profits have got a very serious difficulty to face. If their position were really valid, then their whole case for the role of profits as resource allocation signals, attracting entry into industries, would also go by the board – for the signals are accounting profits.

(b) Conduct However, there are sufficient problems with the structural approach for other explanations to be sought. An alternative (and more modest) approach is available. Instead of attacking concentrated situations *because they are concentrated*, it is

possible to attack those concentrated situations where *conduct* is found to result in the inefficient allocation of resources, and that conduct is directly traceable to the structure. There is, in the literature of competition policy, a good deal of evidence concerning objectionable practices by which firms have sought to gain, and then exploit, market power; and the links to industry structure are often quite clear.[53] Attacking structure through divestiture, having started from conduct, would then seem reasonable. Such an approach would apply to conglomerates as well as to horizontally and vertically merged firms. There is a strand in the American literature which argues that conglomerate mergers do not matter; but a conglomerate has almost unique scope for predatory pricing over a wide range of fields, and the *potential* for this may deter entry, unless an attack on all its fields simultaneously can be organised.[54] Conduct, therefore, is of central interest: if a conglomerate has a record of predatory pricing, then divestiture rather than regulation may be the appropriate path. Moreover, divestiture could well be more feasible with a conglomerate than with companies horizontally or vertically merged, because conglomerates typically have about them (at least in the UK) an aspect of a holding company rather than of an integrated business. In turn, the very fact of this power becoming established as a penalty for predatory pricing would produce a substantial deterrent.

The Mechanics of Divestiture

Divestiture proceedings, as carried out in practice, have attracted much academic criticism. An important early contribution was Adelman's discussion of the A&P case,[55] even though many of his criticisms were later met by Dirlam and Kahn.[56] While individual cases have necessarily attracted detailed discussion,[57] it is of more interest to note that several wide-ranging reviews of the entire history of divestiture proceedings in the United States have adopted both a critical and a pessimistic tone. A much cited early survey is that by Adams;[58] another recent, and highly effective, critic has been Elzinga, who has found that three-quarters of divestiture decrees were unsuccessful and that the delays have been farcical.[59] Another critic, Posner, reviewing the years 1890–1974, found that divestiture had only been a suitable remedy, in the view of the courts, in a small minority of cases and concluded, after reviewing

these cases, that the divestiture measures had been ineffective.[60] There has also been an important general survey by Pfunder, Plaine and Whittemore[61] which was also distinguished by its suggestions, later followed by other writers, for remedying the situation.

Undoubtedly, when we examine the mechanics, there are formidable difficulties. Firstly, there is the question of delay.[62] Due to the reluctance of the courts to penalise firms subject to divestiture orders, and because of the interests of the firms themselves both in delay and in securing the highest possible price, there is a tendency to ask for a price at which no buyer can be found. The divestiture order thus becomes ineffective. Secondly, there is a problem over the choice of assets to be divested.[63] On the one hand, it is necessary to have an economically viable collection of assets to be sold; on the other hand, it may be very difficult to untangle these from an integrated firm and, in addition, the desire to avoid inflicting hardship on a divested firm biases competition policy officials in favour of minimal divestiture. In the case of mergers there is a clear choice between requiring firms to restore the status quo or limiting divestiture to the sale of those assets which offend the requirement of competition. In practice this 'partial divestiture' has proved very unsatisfactory.[64] The assets are not viable on their own.

Thirdly, there is a problem of finding a buyer;[65] there is always the difficulty that the most likely purchaser will be a close competitor in the same line of business. While this does not *necessarily* have an anti-competitive effect, it may well do so. Indeed, such a purchaser can afford to offer a higher price for the assets.

Since firms are usually entrusted by courts with implementing the divestiture themselves, they are in a prime position to obstruct the whole process,[66] particularly as the firm is possessed of information about both the industry and the assets which is not available to outsiders.[67] There are difficult choices to be made over the allocation of overhead staff, and of liquid assets, and concerning the accounting procedures to be used;[68] and in all these the firm opposed to its own divestiture is in the best possible strategic position. Moreover, the matter cannot be resolved by handing divestiture over to antitrust officials. Although Federal Trade Commission surveillance generates large quantities of paper, it seems to be very ineffective;[69] and it is a commonplace in the American literature that there are no incentives to antitrust officials to make divestiture work. Careers are advanced by winning cases, not by formulating good plans for relief.[70]

Despite these difficulties, however, there is no reason in principle why, given a different institutional structure, divestiture should not be possible. While it is perfectly true that unscrambling a financially integrated firm is difficult, the case of buy-outs and other voluntary divestments shows that such unscrambling is perfectly possible.[71] Information is of critical importance here; it is perfectly true that those contemplating a buyout have a peculiar combination of specialised information and incentive which is not available in a divestiture case. But the episode of the 1935 Public Utility Act in the United States shows that divestiture can still work under less uniquely favourable circumstances – a fundamental reorganisation of the gas and electricity supply industries, breaking up large companies, was extraordinarily successful.[72] In the field of competition policy various suggestions have been made for improving the mechanics, including the appointment of a 'divestment trustee'[73] (thus creating an official with an incentive to ensure that the job was done) and random assignment of shares in the different companies created by divestiture to the shareholders, in order to provide an incentive to divest so as to maximise the value of the reconstituted parts.[74] A greater role of administrative, as distinct from judicial, proceedings is also envisaged. There is no doubt that divestiture has been more successful in cases involving consent decrees;[75] and the early use of divestiture power (as a precondition of a merger) is also promising, not least because it provides an incentive for the company involved to cooperate.[76]

Divestiture as a Penalty

While there may be no particular capital market problems of divestiture,[77] it is frequently argued that divestiture necessarily involves penalising shareholders. The argument is usually put thus: if a monopoly has been enjoying its market power,[78] the shareholders will lose by the removal of that power; if they do not lose, then the monopoly was not enjoying its market power. In general the courts have accepted this argument and attempted to avoid penalty;[79] and those writers who envisage that this may be a real problem, but who otherwise favour divestiture, tend to take the view that the courts are over-solicitous, particularly as the courts do not show such solicitude in applying other parts of the antitrust legislation which also affect share values.[80]

However, measurement of the effects of divestiture on stock

prices does not always indicate that shareholders have lost.[81] While this is probably an econometric problem in part – too ready acceptance of a null hypothesis[82] – there are reasons for doubting that the penalty argument is necessarily correct anyway. In practice, it has been observed that parts of a large firm are typically worth more than the whole;[83] and it is perfectly possible for subsidiary parts of a large firm to be run inefficiently, involving welfare losses, and enjoying monopoly through a quiet life, while sheltered behind the entry barriers of an integrated business. Divestiture, by producing search and introducing profit-maximisation incentives, could perfectly well make the shareholders better off than before. The main penalty, and one which has received little attention in the literature,[84] is the *administrative* cost which may be imposed upon a company, absorbing profits and thus penalising shareholders, where a substantial divestiture is involved.

Divestiture in Britain

The power to order divestiture has been available in Britain since the 1965 Monopolies and Mergers Act and it is now enshrined in section 73 (and Schedule 8, part 2) of the 1973 Fair Trading Act. A divestiture order requires positive approval by both Houses of Parliament, and firms affected may petition the House of Lords.[85] The power has, however, rarely been used despite the frequency with which situations which would seem to merit its consideration have been identified by the Monopolies and Mergers Commission (MMC). These include the case of matches, where concentration was associated not with economies of scale but with exclusionary practices[86] – divestiture (not then available in law) was considered here but it was decided that it was impraticable,[87] British Oxygen (the MMC do not seem to have considered divestiture in this case but opted for regulation),[88] and beer.[89] In this latter case, vertical restrictions acted as a substantial barrier to entry but negotiations were left to the Department of Prices and Consumer Protection and, it transpires, very little has happened. In the case of the supply of asbestos, it was recognised that the main firm had set about acquiring its competitors and used vertical integration to squeeze out competition, but divestiture was held to be impracticable as the

business had become integrated.[90] In the case of the supply of petrol, the Office of Fair Trading is supposed to keep the matter of vertical restrictions under review,[91] while in the case of rayon the MMC, which recognised that the scale economies argument, even where intangible scale economies were included, provided only a partial basis for Courtalds' position, nevertheless rejected divestiture as less cost-effective than a tariff reduction.[92]

It is particularly interesting, in the light of the disputes discussed in the first part of this essay, that the Commission has frequently identified vertical integration as a potent method of restricting competition. This was true in the case of beer, asbestos, rayon, matches, and industrial gases.[93]

This is perhaps unsurprising, given the very lax nature of British policy.[94] While section 7 of the Clayton Act has brought mergers under control in the United States, the same has not happened in the United Kingdom. If the deeply conservative British attitude to mergers is to continue, a power of divestiture is needed to cope with the problems subsequently manifested. The British approach has been the subject of comment both caustic and startled on the part of American writers. There is no room here to examine the details of the case, but there is little doubt that a number of episodes, especially during the late 1960s and the era of the Industrial Reorganisation Corporation, have left a legacy which makes the existence, and exercise, of a power of divestiture very desirable.[95]

It is rather ironic that while the Commission has been prepared to accept that scale economies could justify the acquisition of competitors,[96] and to have looked to regulation rather than to divestiture,[97] it should on one occasion have recommended divestiture before the power was available.[98] (Needless to say, the recommendation was not implemented.) However, there have been, more recently, signs of an increased willingness to use divestiture, at least under the very limited circumstances where a firm, contemplating merger, has already obtained a substantial shareholding in its intended acquisition. This occurred in the cases of Eurocanadian Shipholdings–Furness, Withy, and of Great Universal Stores–Empire Stores.[99] However, even this, it is understood, is limited by the necessity of requiring divestiture within six months of the shareholding becoming publicly known. Beyond this modest start the MMC seems reluctant to go; even partial divestiture, as a precondition of merger, does not seem to meet with its approval.[100]

Divestiture in the US: The Case of AT & T

The American Background

Divestiture is a longstanding remedy under American antitrust law. It was first introduced by the Sherman (monopolisation) Act of 1890; but it is provisions under the Clayton (merger) Act of 1914 which have been more frequently used.[101] One hundred and fourteen cases of divestiture have covered such industries as oil, tobacco, glucose, gunpowder, photographic equipment, harvesting machinery, aluminium, fruit, broadcasting, shoe machinery, films, and railway coaches.[102] A number of commentaries have discussed these[103] but none seems convinced that the divestiture measures have been particularly successful so far, although there are a number of respects in which this is clearly remediable. While it has not proved too difficult to achieve a measure of divestiture in the cases of industries involving large numbers of producing plants held together by financial control, and in vertical integration cases, the practical difficulties have proved almost insuperable in others.

However, in some cases the courts have gone to very considerable trouble to ensure the best possible conditions for divestiture to work. In the case of the Ford–Autolite divestiture, Ford was not allowed to make spark plugs for ten years; it was required to purchase half its requirements for the next five years from the divested competitor; it was not allowed to sell at less than the wholesale plug price to dealers; and it was not allowed to buy any other manufacturer of spark plugs for ten years.[104] More typically, however, the courts have been careful not to injure the divested firm and this may, as some commentators have suggested, account for the limited success of divestiture. At all events, its limited success to date did little to indicate that the largest company in the world would be broken up. Yet this, as we shall see, is what happened.

AT & T

American antitrust has a strong history of company regulation and AT & T – 'Bell Telephone' – was for a long time a closely regulated company. The regulation became ever more complex with rate control, separation of regulated and unregulated activities, and disputes concerning inter-connection of competitors.[105] The regulations pro-

duced their own distortions, including nationwide rate averaging despite the diverse cost of supplying services to America's telephone users.[106] The regulations ultimately became so shackling that they provided AT & T with an incentive to settle with the antitrust authorities through a consent decree; the antitrust authorities for their part had either been captured[107] or (in the case of the Federal Communications Commission) had given up trying to regulate AT & T effectively because of the virtual impossibility of obtaining adequate data.[108]

But the only alternative to regulation was to produce, somehow, an industrial structure which exposed AT & T to competition. This was a daunting task. Measured by assets AT & T, before divestiture, was the world's largest corporation with assets of $155bn,[109] 84 million customers, and employment of almost one million people and an annual revenue of about $65bn. Its assets exceeded the combined total for the three biggest companies (including General Motors) in the Fortune Industrial 500.[110]

AT & T had a long history of resisting regulation. When the regulators allowed limited competition to affect it, it reacted with political lobbying in favour of legislation to strengthen its monopoly position.[111] It used various devices to block the FCC attempts to allow competitors to attach their equipment to its common carrier service, including requiring customers of other firms to use 'interface devices' between the equipment and its own.[112] There are striking parallels between the resistance of AT & T to any liberalisation and the resistance manifested in the United Kingdom by British Telecom. Indeed, it is instructive that divestiture has also been suggested in the case of British Telecom.[113]

AT & T showed classic signs of organisational slack,[114] although this was turned to great public benefit in a way unusual for monopolies with the financing of research and academic publication, resulting in seven Nobel prizes.

Under the framework of regulation, AT & T was encouraged to engage in cross-subsidisation so as to load its monopoly with costs which really belonged in the more competitive equipment sector, thus keeping the rate of monopoly return down to a level acceptable to the regulators.[115] This encouraged it to use cross-subsidisation of equipment as a barrier to entry.[116] There is no economic case for such cross-subsidisation because the cost of providing hand-sets to consumers is independent of the use made of long-distance calls.[117] But AT & T argued in turn that it needed a monopoly of equipment

sales in order to obtain large profits on business sales which it could then use to subsidise private domestic consumers.[118] Not surprisingly, this was interpreted as a device to protect its competitive position.

Nevertheless AT & T, as already indicated, was not happy with the regulations experienced. For one thing, it was excluded from certain areas of business such as computers; for another, its dominance hindered its introduction of new equipment. Competitors could claim that the introduction was predatory, and then copy the device during the ensuing delay.[119] Thirdly, the need to maintain spares for the entire nation's telephone system imposed enormous equipment storage costs on AT & T.[120]

Nonetheless, despite these irritants, it is unlikely that AT & T would have agreed to a consent decree had it not been that, from the late 1950s onwards, the FCC began chipping away at its monopoly. For without these erosions, the monopoly was a very strong one. It was a vertical restriction on entry of the most complete sort. The business was integrated from basic research, through equipment manufacture, through local telephone companies, to the long-distance service.

Erosion of this comfortable position began in 1959 when the FCC allowed the use of radio waves for microwave communications. This led to a gradual erosion of the AT & T monopoly in long-distance communication. The equipment monopoly was gradually whittled away from the late 1960s and the FCC introduced an equipment registration programme (note that, in contrast to the British case, equipment registration was not operated by AT & T) so that an important entry barrier was removed. Then the long-distance monopoly began to give way under competition from Microwave Communications, who moved first of all, with FCC approval, into private-line long-distance services and then into ordinary long-distance service. At the same time AT & T was excluded from telecommunications satellites, while from 1972 competitors were allowed into this field.[121] By 1980 a situation had arisen as a result of market forces, technical change, the courts and the FCC, which made divestiture of this once apparently impregnable natural monopoly a possibility. But it has to be said that, whether because of the superiority of regulation to nationalisation[122] or, partly at least, because of the chipping away of the AT & T monopoly, the American telephone system was (and is) the best in the world by a substantial margin. The competitive structure created by divestiture

has, then, to offer substantial benefits by way of competitive pressure if the divestiture is to yield benefits, let alone a surplus of benefit over cost.

The new structure, arrived at via a consent decree, under which agreement is reached between the company and the antitrust authorities without a court decision (thus avoiding many of the pitfalls of a purely judicial settlement), involved dividing AT & T into eight separate companies. Twenty-two local telephone companies were spun off from the main company which was left with assets of 'only' $43bn. These 22 companies are reorganised into 7 regional holding companies. The rump of the old AT & T is made up of the long lines, the Western Electric manufacturing company, Bell Laboratories, American Bell (making user equipment as distinct from telephone company equipment which is the province of Western) and AT & T International to deal with overseas sales of equipment. A shareholder with 10 old AT & T shares obtains 10 shares of the new rump of AT & T and 7 shares in addition, one for each of the 7 regional companies. The half million or so AT & T shareholders with less than 10 shares did not receive shares in the regionals but cash instead; a similar share-splitting arrangement occurred in the demerger at Bowater (see Chapter 3).

The companies thus created are still extremely large. The rump of AT & T would still top *Fortune's* list of utilities and the remaining 7 regional companies would occupy places 3 to 9. The scale of the operation is enormous. The 3.2 million shareholders with over 950 million shares have had their holdings reorganised.[123]

The local companies retain their (regulated) local monopolies; long-distance calls and consumer premises equipment are now competitive. AT & T will no longer have a preferred access to the local exchanges, and cross-subsidisation will be minimised.[124] The incentive, which existed under regulation, to cross-subsidise is removed except for AT & T purchases from Western Electric.[125]

The reorganisation is based upon the essential perception that while a local company may be a natural monopoly – though even this is likely to be eroded by further technical advance – long lines and equipment are not.

In return for consenting to all this, AT & T is now to be allowed to compete with IBM in the computer market – thereby perhaps contributing to the solution of American antitrust's other long-standing problem. AT & T had been kept out of the computer

market by a 1956 consent decree, and a desire to enter the market is widely judged to have been an incentive to settle with the divestiture consent decree.[126] It should be a powerful competitor, not only because of its size and proven research record but also because the patent licensing compulsion which the regulation regime involved for AT & T, which meant that the company effectively supplied technical information to the world, has been removed.[127]

However, AT & T is still subject to a good deal of regulation.[128] It is envisaged that regulation may be necessary because AT & T is still dominant in long-distance calls and the supply of equipment. It has the capacity for predatory pricing. Limit pricing on the basis of economies of scale may yield funds for predation. Whether this is a real danger remains to be seen. It seems unlikely that AT & T would risk further antitrust action. The seven 'local' companies also know that they risk antitrust prosecution if they use the proceeds of their local monopolies to subsidise equipment sales.[129]

Not only does the continuance of limited regulation impose costs on AT & T but there is also the vexed question of the so-called 'access charges'.[130] The access charges are in fact charges levied on both the telephone user and the long-distance line owner and paid to the local company. In the past the long-distance line, owned by AT & T, subsidised the local company – also owned by AT & T – in order to keep the rate of return on long-distance lines to a regulated level. Under the new arrangements this burden will gradually be withdrawn as the access charge paid by the long-distance line owner will be reduced and the burden of paying for the local telephone company will be borne by the local telephone user. In order to impose a gentle transition, however, a substantial part of the burden is initially to fall upon the long lines. At present the bulk of the burden is falling on AT & T which is reported to be paying $17bn. out of a total revenue of $26.4bn. back to local companies. AT & T in fact faces a differentially high access charge – to the extent of 55 per cent higher than other companies. Now the distant day on which the burden will be transferred to local users has been deferred further as a result of political lobbying.[131] In the meantime, AT & T is forced to pay the very substantial cost of implementation of divestiture.[132]

The company is also having to learn to compete in a new world. This, for all its employees, is a new experience.[133] It has also had to

learn to engage in increased market search for new selling opportunities and for new uses for existing equipment.[134]

It is difficult to know what outcome to forecast once these transitional phases are passed.[135] On the face of it the new structure of the industry is calculated greatly to intensify competition, particularly since AT & T's competitive conduct is subject to officially imposed handicaps. Several companies – MCI, South Pacific, and ITT – are reported to charge as little as half AT & T's long-distance charges. Rivals are expanding very fast with annual rates of 50 per cent reported. There are 14 rival carriers to AT & T. Local telephone users have a choice of long-distance services and in some areas of activity AT & T has only a minority market share.[136] The company itself reports that it is facing strong competition and that its main competitors are already doing a lot of business with the big telephone users while 70 per cent of microwave transmission routes are owned by its rivals. In addition to this, big companies such as Westinghouse are beginning to build their own communications network.[137] Against all the expectations of those brought up in the British 'natural monopoly' tradition, it does look as if this particular divestiture may work. But this is partly because of fortuitous technical changes – such as the switch from electro-mechanical to electronic operation which reduces minimum efficient scale substantially – which are themselves only recent developments.[138] Nevertheless, the slow rate of introduction of these technical advances in countries other than the United States does indicate that there is nothing inevitable about the outbreak of competition based on new technology in telecommunications; and the divestiture of AT & T remains a remarkably bold step both on the part of the regulatory and antitrust authorities and, let it not be forgotten, on the part of the company.

Conclusion

The AT & T case, coming on top of long-term American experience with divestiture, shows that divestiture itself is a practical possibility even if the AT & T case itself is astonishing in its boldness. It is also clear that capital markets can cope with divestiture, even on the largest scale, and it seems that shareholders by no means necessarily suffer as a result of divestiture.

Moreover, there clearly is a case for the implementation of divestiture under certain circumstances. A number of defects in the root and branch criticism of divestiture have been discussed above. In addition, a number of other issues are implicit in the critical discussion and need emphasis here. In particular, the need for search, both internal and external, is neglected because it relies on a background of models in which perfect information is implicitly assumed.[139] It neglects the interaction between competitive pressure and search which may be vital in securing technical advances. It neglects the importance of vertical integration as a barrier to entry although this is starkly illustrated in the AT & T case. Nevertheless, the Chicago writers have correctly stemmed the advance of the blanket approach to divestiture which was foreshadowed in the Neal Report and embodied in the Hart Bill. Structure on its own is an unsatisfactory point of departure. In the AT & T case itself it was the conduct of the company, engaging in cross-subsidisation, regulatory evasion, and the employment of devices to exclude competitors at every stage of its business, which justified a reorganisation of its structure.

The question remains, however, whether the benefits of divestiture are likely to be greater than the costs, as well as the related question of whether the margin of benefits over costs is greater for this policy than for alternatives. With regard to the first question there are, as already noted, divergent views based upon American experience. Elzinga and Breit think it unlikely that benefits will exceed costs while Turner takes the opposite view and indeed advocates a wide-ranging attack on concentrated situations on purely structural grounds.[140] This seems a difficult position to defend, in the light of the evidence adduced by Elzinga and others. British, as well as American, competition policy already involves regulation of conduct; and it seems reasonable to argue that such regulation would itself work better if divestiture were clearly available as a reserve power which could be used in the event of regulation failing – as it failed in the case of AT & T.[141] A divestiture approach which starts from conduct does at least offer the prospect of net gain. Moreover, in a British context, with a merger policy which has always been remarkably permissive, and which is reported to be slackening further,[142] it seems highly likely that situations in which net benefit would flow from divestiture are to be found. As an American critic has remarked of one particular

example of the operation of British merger policy:

> Two firms that equally split ninety per cent of the . . . market were allowed to merge without any substantial showing of efficiency gains or other public benefits.[143]

To put it mildly, even the most vociferous anti-antitrust Chicago critic would be unlikely to consider condoning such a state of affairs. The structure of industry which has been created in Britain in this way makes the retention of a divestiture power all the more necessary since, even without relying upon concentration ratios (and most of the criticisms of concentration ratio data actually boil down to the well-known fact that a point observation provides a lot less information than a (concentration) curve), *conduct* considerations are likely to manifest themselves; and though it is clearly envisaged that conduct may be *regulated* (via the Office of Fair Trading, the Monopolies and Mergers Commission, and the concept of anti-competitive practices), there is no reason why modification of the structure which produces the conduct should be ruled out.

In turn, and given this widely recognised interdependence between merger policy and divestiture,[144] the use of divestiture in Britain should concentrate on undoing mergers rather than upon breaking up companies which have achieved their present position through internal expansion. This, by simplifying divestiture, would not only increase the chance that the benefits would be greater than the costs, but would also help to tilt the balance towards internal expansion as against capturing one's competitors through purchase.

Divestiture would normally aim for restoration of the status quo[145] (rather than for speculative hiving off of those parts of the acquired business which were held to offend against competitive requirements) and it would thus bypass the problems over finding a buyer (since the previously independent company would again be restored to independence) and of asset selection.

Such an approach would thus make the policy available to deal with conglomerates. While conglomerate mergers may, or may not, have adverse effects on small firms in the same industry (and the potential for predatory pricing is always there, albeit having temporarily fallen out of academic fashion), they *do* obscure information and interfere with efficient capital market functioning which they only replace partially with divisional structure. This does not mean that conglomerates should be attacked on structural grounds; only that conglomerate conduct should be as open to inspection,

and to the possible remedy of divestiture, as that of other large firms.

The remaining question is whether or not, where benefits of divestiture exceed costs, the margin of benefit over cost is likely to be greater than that obtained by using other remedies. While no general answer to this is possible, it seems likely that a great deal depends upon the institutional structure. If divestiture proceedings become bogged down in legalities – and the British legislation offers even the possibility of appeal to the House of Lords – then it seems likely that other more cost-effective remedies will be found. American experience, in which antitrust is perhaps unduly hampered by legalities,[146] shows that, because of the importance of speed in making divestiture work, a judicial system offering endless possibilities of delay can render the policy nugatory. Elzinga records a case in which:

> In the trial records of that case, pages 11 through 1649 are consumed by pre-trial jockeying for position, correspondence for extensions, pre-trial conferences, re-setting of trial dates, admissibility of evidence questions, etc. These tactics ran out over three years of the judicial clock.[147]

As another commentator has pointed out, adversarial gambits can sink antitrust, and divestiture proceedings are particularly vulnerable.[148] The fact that divestiture proceedings have had much better results in consent cases is not an accident. Though the MMC is frequently accused of delay, its delays are as nothing compared with delays in the judicial process when dealing with the large companies like AT & T and IBM.[149] A primarily administrative approach to divestiture, coupled with appeal to the Restrictive Practices Court, would seem to offer the prospect of relatively speedy and effective remedy.

Moreover, the availability of a divestiture power, and a demonstrated willingness to use such a power, on the basis of conduct derived from structure, would have a salutary effect on the misuse of market power. Not only is it the case that the possibility of competition policy proceedings being taken out is itself salutary, since firms would wish to come to the MMC with clean hands, but there is also the importance of 'demonstration effects'. As the authors of an empirical survey of price fixing conspiracies have observed:

> The demonstration effect of moving for dissolution or divestiture in a price fixing case should not be overlooked.[150]

Such 'demonstration effects' proved powerful in the history of the operation of the 1956 Restrictive Trade Practices Act in Britain; and it seems likely that if divestiture were used seriously in British competition policy, the benefits, once account was taken of those external to a particular case, would far outweigh the costs.

Notes

*I am extremely grateful to Peter Johnson, Steve Littlechild, Valentine Korah, Joel Dirlam and Mike Flemming for helpful comments on an earlier draft of this paper.

1. Elzinga and Breit (1976), pp. 44–45; Wilcox and Shepherd (1975), p. 131n.
2. Blake and Jones (1965a), pp. 377–79; Edwards (1975), p. 344 notes that in the 1920s corporatism led to a weakening of antitrust policy; Greer (1975); O'Connor (1976).
3. In Britain, the experience of the bread industry is instructive in this respect. See Reekie (1978).
4. Kaysen and Turner (1959), especially pp. 46, 48, 93, 114, 124, 126, 141, 268–9.
5. See the responses of Baldwin, Costello, Leonard, Mann, Farmer and White in Baldwin *et al.* (1968); Edwards (1975); *Columbia Law Review* (1973); Samuels (1975).
6. There is a most useful account of this episode in Scherer (1980), p. 542. It should be emphasised, however, that the approach was purely structural; for instance, the Neal Report proposed that in *any* industry with sales of $500m and a four-firm concentration ratio of 70 per cent, divestiture proceedings should be undertaken to reduce individual market shares to a maximum of 12 per cent. See Brozen (1970), p. 279.
7. See the references to Blair and Scherer cited by Elzinga and Breit (1976), p. 104. See also Swann, O'Brien, Mander and Howe (1974), Ch. 3.
8. Turner (1969), p. 1230. However, Turner believed that minimum efficient scale should have priority when considering the restructuring of firms (p. 1216).
9. Hay and Kelley (1974).

10. A nice sample of the present situation can be obtained by reading the contributions of Weiss (1979); Liebeler (1979); Phillips (1979).
11. C.E. Mueller (1968) pp. 88–89.
12. Stocking and W.F. Mueller (1955); Elzinga and Hogarty (1973); Elzinga and Breit (1976), p. 107; Fisher, McGowan and Greenwood (1983), Ch. 3.
13. An excellent survey of the relevant literature is contained in Pautler (1983).
14. Pautler (1983), p. 650.
15. For example, Elzinga and Breit (1976), pp. 103–4, 108; Fisher, McGowan and Greenwood (1983), Ch. 7. For a list of such critics see Pautler (1983), p. 580n. 22.
16. Again Pautler (1983), pp. 615–37, and Scherer (1980), Ch. 9, provide valuable summaries of the debate.
17. Hexter and Snow (1974), p. 402. This article also has a useful discussion of the idea of supplementing concentration ratio data with 'entropy' as a measure of size inequality.
18. Neale and Goyder (1980), p. 404.
19. Neale and Goyder (1980), pp. 452–3.
20. Williamson (1979a), p. 918.
21. Bork and Bowman (1965); but see Blake and Jones (1965a), pp. 395–7.
22. Blake and Jones (1965b), pp. 422–3; Edwards (1975); Samuels (1975), p. 388, is not clear why economies of scale should override the need for competition.
23. The critical literature, excellently surveyed by Pautler (1983), has succeeded in casting sufficient doubt upon a purely structural approach (and in fact the relationship between concentration and profitability was never as clear as some writers, especially lawyers, suggested, particularly in the UK) as to affect seriously its credibility.
24. Whitney (1964).
25. Bork and Bowman (1965), p. 363.
26. *Ibid*. p. 366; Posner (1979).
27. Bork and Bowman (1965), p. 368.
28. Ornstein (1981).
29. See especially Brozen (1970), (1971).
30. See Spence (1983) for a useful summary of the 'contestable markets' literature.
31. See the exchanges between Areeda and Turner (1974–5, 1976) and Scherer (1976 a, b).
32. Posner (1979), p. 927.

33. Williamson (1968a, b); Elzinga and Breit (1976), pp. 100–1. Williamson (1979b) apparently accepts that vertical restrictions are influenced by transactions cost economies.
34. Williamson (1968a), p. 24; it is unfortunate that Williamson's carefully thought-out qualifications have been ignored in much of the subsequent literature.
35. Elzinga and Breit (1976), p. 105; see also Coyne and Wright (1984a) on the question of the need to internalise transactions.
36. Blake and Jones (1965a), p. 389.
37. Blake and Jones (1965b), pp. 441, 462–4. In particular, lenders may consider that risk increases to an unacceptable level if an entire vertical chain has to be duplicated.
38. Williamson (1979a).
39. See Wasserstein (1972–3), p. 678, and references therein.
40. Litman (1980) sees network-owned broadcasting stations as captive outlets which do not search; see also Williamson (1979b) – his reference to 'comparison shopping' implicitly recognises the point about search costs which are increased by vertical restrictions.
41. Blake and Jones (1965b), p. 427.
42. Blake and Jones (1965a), pp. 385, 399.
43. Landes and Posner (1981), especially p. 942; Bauer (1941).
44. Schmalensee (1982); Kaplow (1982); Brennan (1982); Ordover *et al.* (1982).
45. Blake and Jones (1965a), p. 399.
46. Wenders (1971), especially pp. 485, 487.
47. Pautler (1983), pp. 615–624.
48. Bond and Greenberg cited in Pautler (1983), p. 608.
49. Sherman and Tollison (1971); Green Paper (1978).
50. Because of the development of organisational slack. See Elzinga and Breit (1976), p. 103.
51. Williamson (1968b); Ross (1968).
52. Blake and Jones (1965a), pp. 395–7; (1965b), p. 459.
53. See especially Pass and Sparkes (1980).
54. See Besen and Woodbury (1983) for the literature of predatory pricing. See also Schmalensee (1979). On conglomerates more generally see Areeda and Turner (1979) and Arndt (1972) p. 1113.
55. Adelman (1949).
56. Dirlam and Kahn (1953, 1954). See, however, Adelman (1959), especially pp. 526–30.
57. See also Zelenitz (1980) for criticism of another divestiture case. Details of the Ford–Autolite case are in Neale and Goyder (1980), p. 406.

58. Adams (1951).
59. Elzinga (1969); Elzinga and Breit (1976), especially pp. 46, 53. See also Baldwin (1972–3) and Elzinga and Hogarty (1973).
60. Posner (1976), pp. 84–8. Posner notes that in the years 1890–1974 divestiture was ordered in only 24 out of 118 decided monopolisation cases and is satisfied from his examination of the history of these cases that the measure proved ineffective.
61. Pfunder, Plaine and Whittemore (1972) (hereafter PP&W 1972). Baldwin (1972–3), pp. 110, 115, adopts the ideas of a divestment trustee and the giving of priority to the creation of new competitive entities.
62. Elzinga (1969); PP&W (1972), pp. 85ff, 105–6; Posner (1976), p. 88.
63. Elzinga (1969); Elzinga and Breit (1976) p. 51; PP&W (1972), pp. 54–62, 70–2. While such difficulties can certainly be genuine, it is as well to bear in mind the comment that 'Any industrial behemoth can always produce six good reasons why it cannot be split in half', *Economist*, 15 October 1983, p. 35, referring to British Telecom.
64. Elzinga and Breit (1976), p. 53; Elzinga (1969); Martin (1963), p. 350.
65. Elzinga (1969); Elzinga and Breit (1976), pp. 51, 53; PP&W (1972), pp. 38–40, 45–54.
66. Elzinga (1969), pp. 64–5; PP&W, pp. 82–5. The latter note that, of eight cases of non-compliance, six had fair price provisions in the order.
67. On the problem of asymmetric information, see Chiplin and Wright (1983). On the problem in relation to divestiture, see PP&W (1972), pp. 95–7, 107. On viability see Elzinga (1969), p. 45.
68. Elzinga and Breit (1976), p. 52. See also Posner (1976), p. 90.
69. On surveillance see PP&W (1972), pp. 19, 40.
70. Adams (1951), p. 33; Elzinga and Breit (1976), p. 51; Posner (1976), pp. 88–9.
71. On sources of finance, see Coyne and Wright (1982), p. 25; though this relates to buyouts, it is not irrelevant to the question of raising funds for divestiture. The number of buyouts reported in Coyne and Wright (1984b), 650 in 1977–83, also suggests that divestiture is perfectly feasible given the right circumstances. On voluntary divestments, see Chiplin and Wright (1983).
72. See Brodley (1975), pp. 368–9; Wilcox and Shepherd (1975) pp. 401–3.
73. PP&W (1972), pp. 130–3.
74. Baldwin (1972–3).

75. PP&W (1972), p. 112, point out that more than half of all section 7 (Clayton Act) cases which resulted in a divestiture decree were the product of consent. See also Flynn (1968) and Goldberg (1962). On the particular AT&T consent decree, see *Economist*, 16 January 1982, pp. 40–1.
76. The FTC required Texaco to sell two refineries and nearly all of Getty's petrol stations, as the price of agreeing to the takeover of Getty – *Economist*, 17 March 1984, p. 64.
77. Whitehead (1983) explores some of the capital market problems of the sale of British Telecom. See also *Economist*, 21 July 1984, pp. 76–7.
78. Dewey (1955) seems to be the origin of this idea which has been widely repeated by other writers. See also Elzinga and Breit (1976), pp. 48–9.
79. PP&W (1972) p. 96; Neale and Goyder (1980), p. 405.
80. PP&W (1972), p. 130. 'A remedy which causes injury or inconvenience to a defendant should be construed as a penalty only where there is available an equally effective method for obtaining relief which would cause less injury.' See also Adams (1978) for a similarly robust view, and Burns (1983). Note that this is also an issue which arises on demerger.
81. Ellert (1976); Burns (1977).
82. Brown and Warner (1980); Wier (1983); see also Jain (1982).
83. Main (1983), p. 67. 'In the typical breakup, the pieces become worth more on the market than the original whole.'
84. See, however, Elzinga and Breit (1976), pp. 97–9.
85. On the legislative position, see Korah (1975), especially pp. 32–6. The possibilities of judicial delay mean, in effect, that the more powerful the monopoly, and thus the deeper its pocket, the greater the opportunity to enjoy the market power over a long period.
86. Monopolies Commission (1953), pp. 86–89. See also Korah (1975), p. 55.
87. Monopolies Commission (1953), p. 90. Even the minority addendum to the report, signed by both G.C. Allen and Joan Robinson, agreed that divestiture was not practicable.
88. Monopolies Commission (1956), pp. 12–20. See also Korah (1975), p. 54.
89. For comment on this case, see Kintner, Joelson and Griffin (1974), p. 240.
90. Monopolies Commission (1973), pp. 117–119, 124.
91. Monopolies Commission (1979), pp. 54–6.

92. Monopolies Commission (1968), especially pp. 62, 79.
93. Kintner, Joelson and Griffin (1974); Monopolies Commission (1973), especially p. 123; Monopolies Commission (1979), p. 55; Monopolies Commission (1968), p. 84. 'At present, through its control of companies dealing in certain chemicals used in the manufacture of matches ... BMC is able to secure that its competitors are charged for these materials up to 77 per cent more than the companies of the BMC group.' Monopolies Commission (1953), p. 85, and see also p. 89. 'BOC has a substantial measure of control over the provision of plant and machinery for the production of goods which the monopoly itself sells' – Monopolies Commission (1956), p. 91.
94. Howe (1972). See Colenutt and O'Donnell (1978): in the years 1969–77, 18 mergers were reported on by the MMC and another 23 were referred to it but later abandoned. In that time the merger panel, a small group of senior civil servants, examined more than 1,000 mergers.
95. See in particular Wasserstein (1972–3), pp. 658, 666–7, 671, 673, 675–7. This important article seems, unfortunately, to have received very little attention. See also Kintner, Joelson and Griffin (1974), pp. 244–5.
96. See Korah (1975), p. 55.
97. See Pass and Sparkes (1980), pp. 466–8. See also Monopolies Commission (1956), p. 101; Kintner, Joelson and Griffin (1974), p. 240.
98. Monopolies Commission (1961), pp. 183, 193, 307, 213; see also Korah (1975), p. 55. The case was that of Imperial Tobacco and Gallagher. The case itself may have led to the subsequent legislative change, as Dr V. Korah has pointed out to me.
99. Monopolies Commission (1976), p. 51, (1983) p. 36.
100. Monopolies Commission (1983b), pp. 75, 85.
101. O'Connor (1976), pp. 696–7.
102. Adams (1951) contains a good review of American cases up to 1950. Adams points out that divestiture came to a virtual halt in the US in the years 1927–37.
103. PP&W (1972), pp. 34–7; Hale (1940); Moyer (1979); see also Ornstein (1981); Zelenitz (1980). Kotke (1978) contains a detailed history of a number of cases. The most comprehensive discussion is in Neale and Goyder (1980), especially pp. 396–411.
104. Neale and Goyder (1980), p. 406.
105. Besen and Woodbury (1983), pp. 57–66.
106. *Ibid*, p. 65. See also Mirucki (1984) for tentative support for the Averch–Johnson hypothesis in the case of Canadian Bell.
107. [Stewart] (1977), p. 550.
108. Besen and Woodbury (1983), pp. 46–7; *Economist*, 23 April 1983, p. 17.

109. O'Reilly (1983), p. 62; *Time* (1983).
110. de Jonquieres and Betts (1983).
111. *Business Week* (1976).
112. Besen and Woodbury (1983), pp. 42–4; [Stewart] (1977), pp. 538–40.
113. See *Economist*, 15 October 1983, p. 35.
114. Kahn (1984), p. 25.
115. Besen and Woodbury (1983), pp. 44–6 and n.
116. [Stewart] (1977), pp. 538–50.
117. Kahn (1984). Long-distance calls are of particular relevance here since, with costs falling faster than prices, long-distance revenues have been a major source of subsidy. There is an excellent discussion of cross-subsidisation in Johnson (1982).
118. Besen and Woodbury (1983), p. 43.
119. *Ibid*, p. 65.
120. Uttal (1983), p. 84.
121. Baker and Baker (1983); Besen and Woodbury (1983); [Stewart] (1977).
122. The FCC decisions are, of course, subject to legal appeal – see, for example, Besen and Woodbury (1983), pp. 48–9.
123. O'Reilly (1983); Loomis (1983); Main (1983).
124. See Baker and Baker (1983), pp. 7 ff. for details.
125. de Jonquieres and Betts (1983).
126. Besen and Woodbury (1983), p. 50; *Economist*, 10 December 1983, p. 61; 16 January 1982, p. 83.
127. Bylinsky (1983).
128. Loomis (1983), p. 73; Uttal (1983), p. 82; Besen and Woodbury (1983), pp. 49, 56–66.
129. O'Reilly (1983), p. 65; *Economist*, 5 May 1984, pp. 65–6.
130. *Ibid*. and Loomis (1983), p. 73.
131. Taylor (1983); *Economist*, 5 May 1984, p. 65. For an example of the political opposition to the settlement, see Dingell, Nulty and McCarthy (1984).
132. Main (1983), p. 72.
133. O'Reilly (1983), p. 62; Uttal (1983); Tully (1983).
134. O'Reilly (1983), p. 67.
135. According to *Economist*, 28 May 1983, p. 73, Moody's removed the triple. A credit rating from the divested part of AT&T while Standard and Poor's retained the triple A rating.
136. de Jonquieres (1983); *Economist*, 5 May 1984, p. 65; de Jonquieres and Betts (1983).
137. *Economist*, 5 May 1984, pp. 65–6; Kahn (1984) discusses the question of the distributive effects of lowering long-distance charges.
138. Uttal (1983), p. 82.

139. See also Nelson (1979).
140. Elzinga and Breit (1976); Turner (1969).
141. See Neale and Goyder (1980), p. 455, on the value of antitrust legislation as a reserve power.
142. *Economist*, 7 July 1984, p. 72.
143. Wasserstein (1972–3), p. 671. See also Kintner, Joelson and Griffin (1974), p. 244.
144. Turner (1969), p. 1214; Kaysen and Turner (1959), p. 141.
145. See PP&W (1972), pp. 63–4.
146. See Scherer (1976b) for the implication that US antitrust is unduly hampered by legalism.
147. Elzinga (1969), p. 73. The case was the Crown Zellerbach Case (Case No: 16-TTC).
148. Brodley (1975), p. 366.
149. See Fisher, McGowan and Greenwood (1983). It is instructive to compare the handling of proceedings against IBM in the United States with those by the European Commission – *Economist*, 30 June 1984, pp. 57–8.
150. Hay and Kelley (1974), p. 28.

References

Adams, J.W. (1978) 'Trustbusting and the 'innocent' shareholder: 'compensation' if stock prices fall?', *Antitrust Law and Economics Review*, 10, pp. 51–65.

Adams, W. (1951) 'Dissolution, divorcement, divestiture: the pyrrhic victories of antitrust', *Indiana Law Journal*, 27, pp. 1–37.

Adelman, M.A. (1949) 'The A&P case: a study in applied economic theory', *Quarterly Journal of Economics*, 63, pp. 238–57.

Adelman, M.A. (1959) *A&P. A Study in Price–Cost Behaviour and Public Policy*, Harvard University Press.

Areeda, P. and Turner, D.F. (1974–5) 'Predatory pricing and related practices under Section 2 of the Sherman Act', *Harvard Law Review*, 88, pp. 697–733.

Areeda, P. and Turner, D.F. (1976) 'Scherer on predatory pricing: a reply', *Harvard Law Review*, 89, pp. 891–900.

Areeda, P. and Turner, D.F. (1979) 'Conglomerate mergers: extended interdependence and effects on interindustry competition as grounds for condemnation', *University of Pennsylvania Law Review*, 127, pp. 1082–1103.

Arndt, H. (1972) 'Basic problems of concentration policy', *Antitrust Bulletin*, 17, pp. 1107–1124.

Baker, D.I. and Baker, B.G. (1983) 'Antitrust and communications deregulation', *Antitrust Bulletin*, 28, pp. 1–38.

Baldwin, W.L. *et al.* (1968) 'Priorities in antitrust: some communications', *Antitrust Law and Economics Review*, 2, pp. 11–40.

Baldwin, W.L. (1972–3) 'Selective divestiture by spin-off and lottery: a modest proposal', *Antitrust Law and Economics Review*, 6, pp. 107–19.

Bauer, P.T. (1941) 'A note on monopoly', *Economica*, 8, pp. 194–202.

Besen, S.M. and Woodbury, J.R. (1983) 'Regulation, deregulation, and antitrust in the Telecommunications Industry', *Antitrust Bulletin*, 28, pp. 39–68.

Blake, H.M. and Jones, W.K. (1965a) 'In defense of antitrust', *Columbia Law Review*, 65, pp. 377–400.

Blake, H.M. and Jones, W.K. (1965b) 'Toward a three-dimensional antitrust policy', *Columbia Law Review*, 65, pp. 422–66.

Bork, R.H. and Bowman, W.S. (1965) 'The crisis in antitrust', *Columbia Law Review*, 65, pp. 363–76.

Brennan, T.J. (1982) 'Mistaken elasticities and misleading rules', *Harvard Law Review*, 95, pp. 1849–56.

Brodley, J.F. (1975) 'Industrial deconcentration and legal feasibility: the efficiencies defense', *Journal of Economic Issues*, 9, pp. 365–80.

Brown, S.J. and Warner, J.B. (1980) 'Measuring security price performance', *Journal of Financial Economics*, 8, pp. 205–58.

Brozen, Y. (1970) 'The antitrust task force deconcentration recommendation', *Journal of Law and Economics*, 13, pp. 279–92.

Brozen, Y. (1971) 'Deconcentration reconsidered: Comment', *Journal of Law and Economics*, 14, pp. 489–91.

Burns, M.R. (1977) 'The competitive effects of trust-busting: portfolio analysis', *Journal of Political Economy*, 85, pp. 717–39.

Burns, M.R. (1983) 'An empirical analysis of stockholder injury under S2 of the Sherman Act', *Journal of Industrial Economics*, 31, pp. 333–62.

Business Week (1976) 'AT&T's bold bid to stifle competitors', 15 March, pp. 82–8.

Bylinsky, G. (1983) 'Can Bell Labs keep it up?', *Fortune* 107, No. 3, pp. 90–1.

Chiplin, B. and Wright, D.M. (1983) 'Merger activity and sales of subsidiaries between company groups: a note', University of Nottingham, Dept. of Industrial Economics, mimeo.

Colenutt, D.W. and O'Donnell, P.P. (1978) 'The consistency of Monopolies and Mergers Commission's merger reports', *Antitrust Bulletin*, 23, pp. 51–82.

Columbia Law Review (1973) 'The Industrial Reorganisation Act: antitrust proposal to restructure the American economy' 73 pp. 635–76.

Coyne, J. and Wright, D.M. (1982) 'Buy-outs and British industry', *Lloyds Bank Review*, No. 146, pp. 15–31.

Coyne, J. and Wright, D.M. (1984a) 'Staff buyouts and the privatisation of nationalised industries', University of Nottingham, Dept. of Industrial Economics, Discussion Paper No. 80.

Coyne, J. and Wright, D.M. (1984b) 'Shake-outs that can mean job security', *Guardian*, 17 January 1984.

de Jonquieres, G. (1983) 'We'll talk to anyone who has a better mousetrap', *Financial Times*, 24 January, p. 12.

de Jonquieres, G. and Betts, P. (1983) 'America's communications revolution', *Financial Times*.

Dewey, D.F. (1955) 'Romance and realism in antitrust policy', *Journal of Political Economy*, 63, pp. 93–102.

Dingell, J.E., Nulty, T.E., McCarthy, M. (1984) 'Or a free ride for AT&T', *Challenge*, March–April, pp. 30–33.

Dirlam, J.B. and Kahn, A.E. (1953) 'Integration and dissolution of the A&P Company', *Indiana Law Journal*, 29, pp. 1–27.

Dirlam, J.B. and Kahn, A.E. (1954) *Fair Competition. The Law and Economics of Antitrust Policy*; reprinted in 1970, Greenwood Press.

Economist (1982a) 'Stripping Ma Bell', 16 January, pp. 11–13.

Economist (1982b) 'Breaking up is hard to do?', 16 January, pp. 40–1.

Economist (1982c) 'Can AT&T really beat IBM at its own game?', 16 January, pp. 83–4.

Economist (1983a) 'The escaping giant', 23 April, pp. 16–17.

Economist (1983b) 'Ma Bell goes into labour', 28 May, pp. 73–4.

Economist (1983c) 'Gone with the Bell', 23 July, pp. 36–37.

Economist (1983d) 'Buy a telephone, save money', 3 September, p. 27.

Economist (1983e) 'Big Brother?', 15 October, p. 35.

Economist (1983f) 'Trusting the markets more and the trustbusters less', 10 December, pp. 61–2.

Economist (1984a) 'Nobody here but us chickens', 17 March, p. 64.

Economist (1984b) 'What it was always going to be about', 31 March, p. 69.

Economist (1984c) 'Crackles on America's once Bell-clear telephone lines', 5 May, pp. 65–6.

Economist (1984d) 'A chance for IBM's antitrust knight to lay down his lance', 30 June, pp. 57–8.

Economist (1984e) 'Complaints OFT-times told', 7 July, p. 72.

Economist (1984f) 'Privatisation's progress', 21 July, pp. 76–7.

Edwards, C.D. (1975) 'Policy toward big business: what lessons after forty years', *Journal of Economic Issues*, 9, pp. 343–63.

Ellert, J.C. (1976) 'Mergers, antitrust law enforcement and stockholder returns', *Journal of Finance*, 31, pp. 715–32.

Elzinga, K.G. (1969) 'The antimerger law: pyrrhic victories?', *Journal of Law and Economics*, 12, pp. 43–78.

Elzinga, K.G. and Breit, W. (1976) *The Antitrust Penalties: A Study in Law and Economics*, Yale University Press.

Elzinga, K.G. and Hogarty, T.F. (1973) 'The problem of geographic market delineation in antimerger suits', *Antitrust Bulletin*, 18, pp. 45–81.

Fisher, F.M., McGowan, J.J., and Greenwood, J.E. (1983) *Folded, Spindled, and Mutilated. Economic Analysis and US v. IBM*, MIT Press.

Flynn, J.J. (1968) 'Consent decrees in antitrust enforcement: some thoughts and proposals', *Iowa Law Review*, 53, No. 5, pp. 983–1019.

Goldberg, M.S. (1962) *The Consent Decree: Its Formulation and Use*, Bureau of Business and Economic Research, University of Michigan.

Green Paper (1978) *A Review of Monopolies and Mergers Policy*, Cmnd. 7198.

Greer, D.F. (1975) 'Discussion of the Edwards, Brodley, and Samuels articles', *Journal of Economic Issues*, 9, pp. 395–97.

Hale, G.E. (1940) 'Trust dissolution: "Atomizing" business units of monopolistic size', *Columbia Law Review*, 40, pp. 615–32.

Hay, G.A. and Kelley, D. (1974) 'An empirical survey of price-fixing conspiracies', *Journal of Law and Economics*, 17, pp. 13–38.

Hexter, J.L. and Snow, J.W. (1974) 'Mergers, asymmetry and antitrust', *Antitrust Bulletin*, 19, pp. 401–19.

Howe, M. (1972) 'Rethinking British merger policy', *Antitrust Bulletin*, 17, pp. 283–309.

Jain, P.C. (1982) 'Cross-sectional association between abnormal returns and firm-specific variables', *Journal of Accounting and Economics*, 4, pp. 205–28.

Johnson, L.B. (1982) *Competition and Cross-Subsidisation in the Telephone Industry*, Rand Corporation Report, R-2976-RC.

Kahn, A.E. (1984) 'A needed dose of competition', *Challenge*, March–April, pp. 24–29.

Kaplow, L. (1982) 'The accuracy of traditional market power analysis and a direct adjustment alternative', *Harvard Law Review*, 95, pp. 1817–1848.

Kaysen, C. and Turner, D.F. (1959) *Antitrust Policy: An Economic and Legal Analysis*, Harvard University Press, reprinted 1971.

Kintner, E.W., Joelson, M.R. and Griffin, J.P. (1974) 'Recent developments in the United Kingdom antitrust law', *Antitrust Bulletin*, 19, pp. 217–55.

Korah, V. (1975) *Competition Law of Britain and the Common Market*, Elek.

Kottke, F. (1978) *The Promotion of Price Competition Where Sellers are Few*, D.C. Heath.

Kummer, D.R. (1978) 'Valuation consequences of forced divestiture announcements', *Journal of Economics and Business*, 30, pp. 130–36.

Landes, W.M. and Posner, R.A. (1981) 'Market power in antitrust cases', *Harvard Law Review*, 94, pp. 937–96.

Liebeler, W.J. (1979) 'Comments on Weiss', *University of Pennsylvania Law Review*, 127 (1979), pp. 1141–1150.

Litman, B.R. (1980) 'Measuring divestiture of network-owned television stations: an econometric approach', *Antitrust Bulletin*, 25, pp. 363–67.

Loomis, C.J. (1983) 'Valuing the pieces of eight', *Fortune*, 107, No. 3, pp. 70–8.

Main, J. (1983) 'AT&T's holiday gift to Wall Street', *Fortune*, 28 Nov., pp. 67–72.

Martin, D.D. (1963) 'The Brown Shoe Case and the new antimerger policy', *American Economic Review*, 53, pp. 340–58.

Mirucki, J. (1984) 'A study of the Averch–Johnson hypothesis in the Telecommunications Industry', *Atlantic Economic Journal*, 12, p. 121.

Monopolies Commission (1953) *A Report on the Supply and Export of Matches and the Supply of Match-Making Machinery*, HCP 161.

Monopolies Commission (1956) *A Report on the Supply of Certain Industrial and Medical Gases*, HCP 13.

Monopolies Commission (1961) *A Report on the Supply of Cigarettes and Tobacco Machinery*, HCP 218.

Monopolies Commission (1968) *A Report on the Supply of Man-Made Cellulosic Fibres*, HCP 130.

Monopolies Commission (1969) *A Report on the Supply of Beer*, HCP 216.

Monopolies Commission (1973) *A Report on the Supply of Asbestos and Certain Asbestos Products*, HCP 3.

Monopolies Commission (1976) *Eurocanadian Shippings Limited and Furness, Withy & Company, Limited and Manchester Liners Limited. A Report on the Existing and Proposed Mergers*, Cmnd 639.

Monopolies Commission (1979) *Report on the Supply of Petrol in the United Kingdom by Wholesale*, Cmnd 7433.

Monopolies Commission (1983a) *The Great Universal Stores PLC. A Report on the Existing and Proposed Mergers*, Cmnd 8777.

Monopolies Commission (1983b) *The Sunlight Service Group PLC and Johnson Group Cleaners PLC and Initial PLC and Johnson Group Cleaners PLC. A Report on the Proposed Mergers*, Cmnd 8868.

Moyer, R. (1979) 'Horizontal divestiture in the Petroleum Industry: an analysis', *Antitrust Bulletin*, 24, pp. 535–53.

Mueller, C.E. (1968) 'The new antitrust: a 'structural' approach', *Antitrust Law and Economics Review*, 1, pp. 87–130.

Neale, A.D. and Goyder, D.G. (1980) *The Antitrust Laws of the USA. A Study of Competition Enforced by Law*, 3rd edn, Cambridge University Press.

Nelson, R.R. (1979) 'Comments on a paper by Posner', *University of Pennsylvania Law Review*, 127, pp. 949–952.

O'Connor, K.J. (1976) 'The divestiture remedy in Sherman Act S2 cases', *Harvard Journal on Legislation*, 13, pp. 687–775.

Ordover, J.A., Sykes, A.O. and Willig, R.D. (1982) 'Herfindahl concentration, rivalry and mergers', *Harvard Law Review*, 95, pp. 1857–74.

O'Reilly, B. (1983) 'Ma Bell's kids fight for position', *Fortune*, 107, pp. 62–68.

Ornstein, S.I. (1981) 'Antitrust policy and market forces as determinants of industry structure: case histories in Beer and distilled spirits', *Antitrust Bulletin* 26, pp. 281–313.

Pass, C.L. and Sparkes, J.R. (1980) 'Dominant firms and the public interest: a survey of the reports of the British Monopolies and Mergers Commission', *Antitrust Bulletin* 25 pp. 437–84.

Pautler, P.A. (1983) 'A review of the economic basis for broad-based horizontal-merger policy', *Antitrust Bulletin*, 28, pp. 571–651.

Pfunder, M., Plaine, D. and Whittemore, A. (1972) 'Compliance with divestiture orders under Section 7 of the Clayton Act: an analysis of the relief obtained', *Antitrust Bulletin*, 17, pp. 19–180.

Phillips, A. (1979) 'Comments on Weiss', *University of Pennsylvania Law Review*, 127, pp. 1151–4.

Posner, R.A. (1976) *Antitrust Law: An Economic Perspective*, University of Chicago Press.

Posner, R.A. (1979) 'The Chicago School of antitrust analysis', *University of Pennsylvania Law Review*, 127, pp. 925–948.

PP&W (1972), see Pfunder *et al.*

Reekie, D. (1978) *Give Us This Day . . .*, Hobart Paper 79.

Ross, P. (1968) 'Economies as an antitrust defense: comment', *American Economic Review*, 58 (1968), pp. 1371–2.

Samuels, W.J. (1975) 'The Industrial Reorganisation Bill: the burden of the future', *Journal of Economic Issues*, 9, pp. 381–94.

Scherer, F.M. (1976a) 'Predatory pricing and the Sherman Act: a comment', *Harvard Law Review*, 89, pp. 868–90.

Scherer, F.M. (1976b) 'Some last words on predatory pricing', *Harvard Law Review*, 89, pp. 901–3.

Scherer, F.M. (1980) *Industrial Market Structure and Economic Performance*, 2nd edn., Rand McNally.

Schmalensee, R. (1979) 'On the use of economic models in antitrust: the Realemon Case', *University of Pennsylvania Law Review*, 127, pp. 994–1050.

Schmalensee, R. (1982) 'Another look at market power', *Harvard Law Review*, 95, pp. 1789–1816.

Sherman, R. and Tollison, R. (1971) 'Public policy toward oligopoly: dissolution and scale economies', *Antitrust Law and Economics Review*, 4, pp. 77–90.

Spence, M. (1983) 'Contestable markets and the theory of industry structure: a review article', *Journal of Economic Literature*, 21, pp. 981–90.

[Stewart, D.O.] (1977) 'Competition in the telephone equipment industry: beyond telerent', *Yale Law Journal*, 86, pp. 538–60.

Stocking, G.W. and Mueller, W.F. (1955) 'The Cellophane Case and the new competition', *American Economic Review*, 45, pp. 29–63.

Swann, D., O'Brien, D.P., Maunder, P. and Howe, W.S. (1974) *Competition in British Industry*, George Allen and Unwin.

Taylor, P. (1983) 'Muddied waters over AT&T divestiture', *Financial Times*, 21 October, p. 35.

Time (1983) 'Click! Ma is ringing off', 21 November, pp. 40–48.

Tully, S. (1983) 'The US giant is a pygmy abroad', *Fortune*, 107, No. 3, pp. 86–8.

Turner, D.F. (1969) 'The scope of antitrust and other economic regulatory policies', *Harvard Law Review*, 82, pp. 1207–44.

Uttal, B. (1983) 'Western Electric's cold new world', *Fortune* 107, No. 3, pp. 81–84.

Wasserstein, B. (1972–3) 'British merger policy from an American perspective', *Yale Law Journal*, 82, pp. 656–90.

Weiss, L.W. (1979) 'The structure–conduct–performance paradigm and antitrust', *University of Pennsylvania Law Review*, 127, pp. 1104–40.

Wenders, J.T. (1971) 'Deconcentration reconsidered', *Journal of Law and Economics*, 14, pp. 485–8.

Whitehead, C. (1983) 'Privatising British Telecom: the worst of both worlds?', *Public Money*, 3, No. 2, pp. 43–46.

Whitney, S.N. (1964) 'The economic impact of antitrust: an overview', *Antitrust Bulletin*, 9, pp. 509–33.

Wier, P. (1983) 'The costs of antimerger lawsuits', *Journal of Financial Economics*, 11, pp. 207–24.

Wilcox, C. and Shepherd, W.G. (1975) *Public Policies Toward Business*, 5th edn., Irwin.

Williamson, O.E. (1968a) 'Economies as an antitrust defense: the welfare trade-offs', *American Economic Review*, 58, pp. 18–36.

Williamson, O.E. (1968b) 'Economies as an antitrust defense: correction and reply', *American Economic Review*, 58, pp. 1372–6.

Williamson, O.E. (1979a) 'Symposium on antitrust law and economics', *University of Pennsylvania Law Review*, 127, pp. 918–24.

Williamson, O.E. (1979b) 'Assessing vertical market restrictions: antitrust ramifications of the transaction cost approach', *University of Pennsylvania Law Review*, 127, pp. 953–93.

Zelenitz, A. (1980) 'The attempted promotion of competition in related goods markets: the Ford–Autolite divestiture case', *Antitrust Bulletin*, 25, pp. 103–24.

4 Patents: An Economist's View

D.P. O'Brien

In a world in which much law is drafted so as to put into effect what are principally economic prescriptions, it is important to appreciate the economist's view of the patent system in order to understand the aims of that system and to evaluate its results. Some of the perceptions of the patent system are reviewed from the standpoint of economics methodology and the implications of a number of reform proposals are contemplated.

Introduction

Patents, a mercantilist invention, have been a matter of concern to economists at least since Bentham,[1] and the 19th century economist and politician Robert Lowe was prominent in a movement for the abolition of these devices.[2] Economists have, however, generally taken a utilitarian attitude towards patents; they are justified as a form of property which, if rights in it are respected, yields benefits to society as a whole.[3] The matter is not, however, trivial; the level of patent activity in both Britain and the United States is very high with Britain only second to the US in the absolute number of patents granted.[4]

It is embarrassing to report that much of the economic analysis of patents has been on the basis of an assumption of perfect knowledge, an assumption which is singularly inappropriate to the uncertain world of the inventor and the innovator. This is true of otherwise important work on patents by Plant, Arrow, and Usher.[5] The latter puts forward

The author is grateful to Dr P.S. Johnson for helpful comments.

1 A. Plant, 'The Economic Theory Concerning Patents for Inventions', (1934) *Economica* NS 30; F.M. Scherer, *Industrial Market Structure and Economic Performance*, 1970 at 379; Adam Smith, *An Inquiry into the Nature and Causes of the Wealth of Nations* (1776), reprinted by Chicago University Press, 1976, Volume II, at 278. A standard survey of the history is found in F. Machlup, *An Economic Review of the Patent System* 1958.
2 See Plant, Note 1, at 47; also D.P. O'Brien, *The Correspondence of Lord Overstone*, 1971, at 899 and 1277.
3 See Plant, Note 1, at 30; also J.F. Pickering, *Industrial Structure and Market Conduct*, 1974, p. 91.
4 C. Wilcox and W. Shepherd, in *Public Policies Toward Business*, 5th ed. 1975, at 257, give figures for a number of countries.
5 See Plant, Note 1, at 42 and 43; also K. Arrow, 'Economic Welfare and the Allocation of Resources for Invention', 1962, reprinted in Rowley (ed.), *Readings in Industrial Economics*, 1972, Volume 2, at 219 to 236; and D. Usher, 'The Welfare Economics of Innovation', (1984) 31 *Economica*, at 279 to 287.

a number of very interesting propositions – any commercially profitable invention confers a net benefit on the community as a whole; the patent system causes under-production of the newly invented product; some inventions are worth undertaking to the community as a whole even though they are unprofitable under the patent system; the patent system results in under-investment in productivity; too much competition exists in profitable inventions. Unfortunately these propositions relate to a Pareto world of perfect knowledge with a Pareto optimum* as a welfare standard. Similarly Nordhaus has restricted himself to a world without uncertainty and then developed an excellent formal analysis which yields very little unless we know the elasticity of demand for a product (thus *excluding* products not already invented) and the slope of a purely hypothetical invention function.[6] This approach has sometimes led economists rather far astray into the positing of some ideal socialist alternative (labelled the 'Nirvana approach' by Demsetz, who points out that it is also necessary to specify the institutional arrangements which would be found under socialism) and to making, at least implicitly, the very strange assumption that risk is confined to free market economies. All this is strictly academic, in the more unfortunate sense of that term for, as Demsetz remarked; 'a Pareto norm . . . lends itself to static analysis of allocation but . . . is poorly designed for analyzing dynamic problems of production.'[7]

The Economic Benefits of Patents

More generally the economic literature concerning patents has recognised a wide range of advantages and disadvantages stemming from their existence. There has been widespread acceptance of the idea that invention, innovation, and the spread of technical knowledge all benefit from the patent system. Even those who believe invention to have an important element of spontaneity accept that the expense of innovation in a risky world can justify the granting of a temporary monopoly to give some protection from rapid imitation which would prevent recovery of the development costs. Moreover the very fact that a patent has to be registered and made publicly available leads to a dissemination of technical knowledge. This is a beneficial externality made available by the patent system and must be counted among its benefits together with the externalities of a level of research and development expenditure which is not artificially depressed as it might be without patents.

* *Editor's Note* A Pareto optimum exists when the economy's resources and output are allocated in such a way that no reallocation can make anyone better off without making at least one person worse off.

6 W. Nordhaus, *Invention, Growth and Welfare*, 1969, at 71 and see n. 2.

7 H. Demsetz, 'Information and Efficiency: Another Viewpoint', reprinted in Rowley (ed.), *Readings in Industrial Economics*, 1972 at 237 to 262.

Of course the very grant of the monopoly involves, *once the invention/innovation has been made*, some welfare losses; even so, any cost reductions free resources even where the product is monopolised, and there will normally be an increase in that measure of economic welfare which economists refer to as consumer surplus.[8] New and superior products emerge. The objection that a temporary monopoly will result in a price greater than marginal cost has not much force if the product concerned would, but for the existence of the patent system, not otherwise be available at all. The monopoly is only temporary; and the knowledge on which it is based is made publicly available. Moreover research indicates that firms deprived of patent rights through antitrust judgments reduce their patenting relative to unaffected firms, thus suggesting clearly that the patent system does in fact encourage disclosure.[9] The publication of this information, together with a bar to its immediate use by competitors, may stimulate further technical progress through a desire to find a way around the patent.[10] The temporary monopoly itself provides super-normal profits which can be used by the original patent holder as the basis for further product development expenditure.[11]

Of particular importance is the idea that a patent system provides protection for small firms, yielding both bargaining counters and sources of royalties as well as, and most importantly, protection from economically more muscular organisations during the vital stage of market innovation. This is particularly important since the once fashionable view that large firms could be relied on to produce inventions and innovations routinely is clearly no longer tenable. Indeed there seem to be significant disadvantages in bigness, with any risk-pooling advantages being more than off-set by the exhaustion of the advantages of specialisation, the loss of competitive stimulus, and sheer bureaucratic inertia.[12] This is not particularly surprising; while the case against monopoly, with respect to innovation, has undoubtedly been overstated in some respects,[13] bureaucracies, because of the penalties and rewards facing the bureaucrats, are naturally circumspect, with adverse effects on innovation. While large firms may have high levels of research and development expenditure, at least up

8 The argument is clearly set out by Scherer, see Note 1, at 383.

9 F. Scherer *et al.*, *Patents and the Corporation*, (1959), cited in Scherer, Note 1, at 382n.

10 J. McGee, 'Patent Exploitation: Some Economic and Legal Problems', (1966) 9 *Journal of Law and Economics* 135 at 151.

11 D.P. O'Brien, 'Patent Protection and Competition in Polyamide and Polyester Fibre Manufacture', (1964) 12 *Journal of Industrial Economics* 224 at 228.

12 J. Schmookler, *Patents, Innovation and Economic Change*, 1972, at 45; E. Mansfield, *The Economics of Industrial Change*, 1968, at 217; J. Jewkes, D. Sawers, R. Stillerman, *The Sources of Invention*, 1958, at 89; F. Scherer, see Note 1 at 358 to 361; Pickering, see Note 3, at 92; Demsetz, see Note 7, at 245 and 246.

13 Demsetz, see Note 7, at 255 and 256, establishes that it is necessary to take account of the normal monopoly output-reducing effects before attempting to find any which are associated particularly with patents.

to certain concentration levels, much of this may be of a not very productive, self-protective nature, and the output of research results by small firms and individuals is proportionately (in relation to R&D expenditure) much larger than for big firms.

Finally, the knowledge protected by a patent is only temporarily monopolised, and with the expiry of the patent it eventually becomes public property, enabling its benefits of non-excludability and non-competition in consumption to be realised. Patents confer monopolies but they do not do so in perpetuity.

Economic Costs of Patents

Against all this, however, there is widespread recognition of a multitude of costs associated with the patent system. First, it temporarily removes knowledge which is a 'public good'. Second, patents involve the creation of a temporary monopoly for a new product, a tendency strengthened by the 'first past the post' principle which has played a part in the development of some historical monopoly positions. On the way to such positions palpable injustices are perpetrated.[14] The temporary monopoly positions involve very large (up to 90 per cent) margins on sales where the product is priced monopolistically,[15] and limit-pricing may be adopted where a firm has patented a process innovation.[16] The firm with the patent is, either directly or through licensing with quotas, able to pursue classic monopoly profit maximisation[17] and the proceeds of this procedure may be used to finance extensions of the patent which are of no real consumer benefit,[18] as well as the building up of patent portfolios which provide the means of blocking the use of patents by other firms.[19] Possession of such market power may enable firms to bargain with others over cross-licensing or even to create a patent pool. This in turn can lead to implicit collusion (limiting licences to those strong enough to contest patents) or even (when price provisions are associated with the patent licence) to the creation of a cartel. Licences may be granted on a highly restricted basis and leading industrial economists believe that in this and other ways patents have been a force leading to significantly increased concentration.[20] It is certainly true that market power, once possessed, can

14 For examples of this see Scherer, Note 1 at 393 and 394.

15 *Ibid.*, at 390 and 391.

16 Limit-pricing involves charging a price high enough to allow the patent holder to earn super-normal profits but low enough to make competition from users of the unimproved process ineffective.

17 See Note 10.

18 See Note 11, at 232 and 233.

19 See Note 4, at 264.

20 See Scherer, Note 1, at 123; also F. Scherer, *Industrial Market Structure and Economic Performance*, 1980, at 142. See also Note 4, at 434, on the role of patents in the establishment of AT&T.

be further buttressed by the use of tie-ins and the financing of advertising as an entry barrier. Moreover the market segmentation which patents permit allows firms to practise price discrimination;[22] although the welfare effects of this may be ambiguous, even in static terms, there have certainly been some cases which have brought forth unambiguous condemnation from anti-trust authorities.[23]

Moreover, although patents are supposed to protect small firms, these firms can in fact be crushed by the cost of patent litigation. There is indeed a predatory potential of patent harassment and small firms may not be able to afford to challenge larger ones.[24] There are also quite extraordinary delays; as one commentator has pointed out, patents can expire before litigation is completed.[25] More generally in this connection it may be observed that the cost of the patent system is enormous, being estimated at 330 million dollars for the United States at 1978 prices,[26] while patent examination is still widely regarded as perfunctory. However, these last considerations may equally well be interpreted as an argument for reform of legal processes – as suggested in the Green Paper – rather than for abolition of the patent system altogether.[27]

Alternatives to Patents

Faced with a system which involves both recognised costs and recognised benefits, two questions arise: (1) do we need some kind of market restriction to obtain the benefits mentioned above, and (2) is the patent system the best method of restriction?

The most fundamental consideration under the first heading is whether there is a supply price of invention and of innovation so that the amount of invention and innovation will increase if the prospective reward is increased through the availability of a temporary (patent)

21 See Note 11, for the case of synthetic fibres; see Note 3, at 88, for the case of drugs.

22 See Note 11, at 229.

23 *A Report on the Supply of Chlordiazepoxide and Diazepam*, Monopolies Commission, HCP 197, HMSO 1973. It should however be noted that two compulsory licences had been granted in this case (*ibid.*, at 19 to 21).

24 R. Low, *Modern Economic Organisation*, 1970, at 199 and 282.

25 V. Korah, *Competition Law of Britain and the Common Market*, 2nd ed. 1975, p. 31; see also Pickering, n. 3, pp. 83–4.

26 Scherer, *Industrial Market Structure and Economic Performance*, Note 20 above at 454.

27 '*Intellectual Property Rights and innovation*', Cmnd. 9117, HMSO 1983. It is sometimes suggested that another cost of the patent system is the suppression of socially valuable inventions. However, many countries (including the UK) have compulsory licensing provisions to deal with this kind of problem so that, if the invention is known outside its inventing firm, suppression is at least difficult; if it is not known, secrecy makes the patent irrelevant. But in any case research in the USA which does not have a compulsory licensing provision in its patent legislation (although anti-trust proceedings may produce that effect) failed to identify instances of suppressed inventions.

monopoly. Economic literature has traditionally distinguished between autonomous and induced invention or, in more recent terminology, demand-induced and supply-induced inventions and innovations. While it is undoubtedly true that many inventors regard the patent system as unimportant, and that biological inventions cannot be patented (a fact of which critics make much, despite the very different context of biological research[28]), the balance of evidence indicates two things. First, that technical progress is not exogenous but is determined by economic forces; second, that for a significant minority of inventors, let alone innovators, the patent system is of real importance.[29] This is not surprising; other areas of economic literature involving public goods would indicate the likelihood that 'free loading' (benefiting from somebody else's expenditure without contributing one's own) will reduce output – in this case, research output. This is of particular importance with respect to innovation. While case studies may produce examples of important inventions which have been made apparently independently of the rewards available under the patent system, the very process of innovation, involving a substantial investment under conditions of considerable uncertainty, would suggest that any device which reduces that uncertainty will increase the willingness of firms to innovate. A market restriction on competition, such as a patent, will reduce the risk that prospective earnings from the invention or innovation will be quickly competed away and will thus, by increasing the likely return, encourage both invention and innovation.

If some kind of restriction such as a temporary monopoly is needed, does this require a legal form? Or are there sufficient in-built barriers to imitation in the market? It is perfectly true that imitation is usually delayed: the advantages of competitive product leadership may provide an incentive to R&D expenditure; there is usually a limited number of potential imitators;[30] and there may be other considerations, such as those of minimum-efficient scale, which ensure that the first firm remains the only firm.[31] Unfortunately, this is probably not enough, even in total. The rate of imitation becomes an extra decision variable with a wide and unknown variance for a potential innovator, and only patents can deal with this. Small firms in particular may be more vulnerable to imitation if they rely on market lags. To begin with, they do not possess market power; and their staff may be bid away by affluent firms which do have market power.

This leads to the neglected but important question of the labour market implications of relying on secrecy rather than patents. The chances are that, without the protection of a patent system, labour market contracts would become ever more restrictive in an attempt to prevent key personnel from defecting with their technical knowledge.

28 See for example Plant, Note 1, at 45.

29 See Note 4, at 261; also Note 6, at 29; and C. Taylor, 'Do We Still Need a Patent System?', (1973) CIPA at 292 to 314.

30 E. Mansfield, *The Economics of Industrial Change*, 1968.

31 See Plant, Note 1 at 43 and 44.

Even if reliance on employees' secrecy were satisfactory for the vast majority of innovations and if the labour market and other aspects, including the complete denial of the public good aspects of knowledge and the removal of incentives to invent round a patent could be ignored, there still remains the problem that not all inventions are equal and it may well be the key ones which are the product of the vulnerable small firm. It was in fact a small firm which eventually took on the development of the xerox process.[32]

It thus seems likely that some form of artificially induced reward seems necessary, which leads to the question of whether it is possible to devise a better reward than the grant of a temporary monopoly. One school of thought favours state rewards.[33] Since this is the system used in the Soviet bloc, which is notoriously backward technologically,[34] the advocates of this need to explain what other aspect of the Soviet system is responsible for the poor performance. Such explanation seems to be lacking. In fact a system of rewards seems to involve insuperable difficulties in determining the appropriate reward and also distributive unfairness since tax payers would pay for a product in which they might have no personal interest. Most of the objections put forward by writers like Polanyi to the legal use under the patent system of such concepts as 'novelty', 'utility' and 'invention' would apply *a fortiori* to the award process. There are considerable advantages in this context of a market test compared to committee appraisal – the analogy of literary prizes seems appropriate here.

Another school of thought, undeterred by the problems of bureaucracy and lack of criteria for selection of research topics, suggests greater government research. Of course government may in fact be even more risk-averse, but for different reasons, than the private sector and as Demsetz observed, 'Whether the free enterprise solution can be improved upon by the substitution of the government or other nonprofit institutions in the financing of research cannot be ascertained solely by examining the free enterprise solution'.[35] While government may have an important role to play in basic research, the history of government innovations (such as Concorde) is not particularly encouraging.

Most economists thus come round to the view that there is no obviously satisfactory prospective substitute for the patent system and that a better approach might be to concentrate upon reform of that system.

32 '*A Report on the Supply of Indirect Electrostatic Reprographic Equipment*', Monopolies Commission, HCP 47, HMSO 1976, at 3 to 12. See also Note 27 at 13 and 26. There are limited common law rights in industrial knowledge (Note 37 at 147 and 148), but it is doubtful whether these would protect small firms whose skilled employees were bid away.

33 M. Polanyi, 'Patent Reform', (1943–5) 11–12 *Review of Economic Studies*, at 61 to 76, is the leading reference here.

34 A. Sutton, *Western Technology and Soviet Economic Development* 1968–73, in 3 volumes.

35 See Note 7, at 239.

Patent Reform

Some of the changes to the present rules which have been suggested include limiting full use of the system, similar to the German two-part system of minor (short term) and major patents (recommended in the Green Paper); adoption of a system of registration which would have the effect of preventing somebody else patenting in advance; and steeply rising annual renewal fees in order to encourage those with patents to let them lapse. In this connection, one widely canvassed reform is a variation in patent term. Economists have frequently suggested a shorter term. Nordhaus, concentrating on cost saving innovations, has suggested that big savers have a short pay-back period and so a shorter patent term is required.[36] The trouble with this argument is that the variance may increase with the size of the potential saving. By contrast the British Banks Committee (1970) suggested an increase in life from 16 to 20 years; but no real justification was put forward for this except expression of a belief that 'there is some foundation' for the view put to the committee in evidence that more time and money are now required to develop inventions.[37] None-the-less this recommendation was implemented.

Most attention, however, has been focused on reducing the amount of market power yielded by the present system. Compulsory licensing has been suggested by a number of writers and is recommended in the Green Paper. Unfortunately it seems clear that this would lead to greater secrecy,[38] that it could well reduce research, at least in some key areas, and that it not only makes the strong firms help the weak, but also vice versa.[39] Another suggestion is that patents should be terminable once a normal profit has been earned on the innovation. This is a rather unfortunate suggestion since it is only the prospect of an *abnormal* reward which induces firms to undertake the risk in the first place when all is uncertain.

However, compulsory licensing may be (and has been) used as an alternative to divestiture proceedings under anti-trust law; and it is to use of the anti-trust laws that many economists look for a limitation of the market power associated with patents. About 12½ per cent of the cases brought by the Antitrust Division of the Department of Justice in the United States in the years 1890–1965 involved patents.[40] American

36 See Note 6.

37 *The British Patent System* (the 'Banks Report') Cmnd. 4407, HMSO 1974, at 99. See also Note 27 at 37.

38 Taylor, see Note 29 at 296; also see Note 9; and C. Taylor and Z. Silberston, *The Economic Impact of the Patent System*, 1973, at 352 particularly.

39 See Note 4, at 281; also Note 24, at 484 and 485. However, while the Green Paper (see Note 27 at 2 and 27) recommendation for compulsory licensing has some drawbacks, it seems highly desirable that there should be at least a reserve power to grant such licences. The recommendation in the Banks Report (See Note 37) that this power (under the Patents Act 1949 section 41) should be repealed is difficult to understand in terms of even the most superficial appreciation of the operation of markets.

40 For figures see Note 4 at 129.

anti-trust proceedings have been directed against the building up of patent portfolios, and proceedings can be taken under section 2 of the Sherman Act dealing with monopolisation. Action has been taken against tying sales of unpatented articles to sales of patented articles, against the inclusion in licences of conditions which run beyond the life of the patent, and of attempts to use the price fixing provisions permitted by a patent to cover articles which are not themselves patented even though they incorporate some patented items. The operation of a patent pool has been circumscribed with respect both to the price fixing which may take place and also to the market sharing and exclusionary conditions which may be attached to licences. Possible misuse of a patent leaves the patent holder open to easier challenge of the patent right itself, and the equity provision that patent rights will not be enforced in clear cases of abuse. The patent holder is also vulnerable to triple damage actions where a patent has been abused, and to compulsory licensing.[41]

In Britain there has been no such boldness. Although under section 126 of the 1973 Fair Trading Act the Comptroller of Patents may issue compulsory licences on application by a minister following an adverse report of the Monopolies Commission (relating either to a monopoly or a merger), this power has not been used. Indeed, since it was not used (although a similar power under the Patents Act 1949 had been used earlier) in the well-known case involving Hoffman-La Roche and the tranquillisers Librium and Valium,[42] it is difficult to envisage circumstances under which it *would* be used. Again, although patent pools involving more than two firms are registrable under the 1973 Act,[43] there is no sign of proceedings under the Act concerning such a registered agreement and one of the cases which came successfully through the Restrictive Practices Court involved the patent pool operated by the permanent magnet manufacturers.[44]

Nevertheless, for those concerned about possible misuse of patents within the UK, this line of development seems one of the most promising. The American experience provides plenty of precedents, and the Monopolies Commission has itself noted cases in which patents have been used to establish very protected positions. In terms of the UK legislation one development possible immediately would be extension

41 A. Neale and D. Goyder, *The Antitrust Laws of the USA*, 3rd. ed. 1980, provides the definitive discussion of this issue. It seems likely that the policy of British Oxygen in accumulating patents, to which the Monopolies Commission drew attention, would have been the target of anti-trust action under Section 2 of the Sherman Act, in the US.

42 *Hoffmann-La Roche v Secretary of State for Trade and Industry*, [1974] 2 All ER 1128.

43 Fair Trading Act 1973 section 101.

44 This case is discussed in detail in D. Swann, D.P. O'Brien, W. Maunder and W. Howe, *Competition in British Industry. Case Studies of the Effects of Restrictive Practices Legislation*, 1973, at 37 to 52. See also J. Cunningham, *The Fair Trading Act 1973*, 1974, at 6 to 132. On the question of unused British provisions against abuse see Note 27 at 27. See also Note 23.

of the concept of anti-competitive practice, under the Competition Act 1980, to include misuse of patents as it already includes anti-competitive use of copyright.

Conclusion

While it is undeniable that the patent system does impose costs, very few economists, at least in this century, have been prepared to recommend its abolition. As Mansfield puts it

> Do the benefits derived from the patent system outweigh its costs? Like many broad issues of public policy, the facts are too incomplete and too contaminated by value judgements to permit a clear-cut, quantitative estimate of the effects of the patent system. Nonetheless, with or without such an estimate, it is impossible to avoid the relevant policy issue, and when confronted with it, there are few leading economists, if any, who favour abolition of the patent system. Even those who publish their agnosticism with respect to the system's effects admit that it would be irresponsible, on the basis of our present knowledge, to recommend abolishing it.[45]

This indeed seems to have been the verdict of economists since the 19th century controversy referred to in the introduction. The patent system after all has one very significant advantage: the reward which it yields is, in a significant sense, a market reward, and a market test is a better one than a committee test – as the difficulties of Chain and Florey in obtaining funds from the Medical Research Council for the development of penicillin bear witness.[46] The market reward is certainly not perfect; but it is one better calculated to optimise the rate of significant invention and innovation than any other which is conceivable. Although there is undoubtedly a strong case for the use of competition policy to monitor and where necessary modify the enjoyment of patent rights and while there is certainly a need for further detailed empirical studies, the cautious acceptance by economists at large of the patent system as a whole seems justified.

45 See Note 30 at 209. See D. Firestone, *Economic Implications of Patents*, 1971 for a discussion of the particular (technology-importing) context of the Canadian economy; and for judicious comment on Firestone's views see Taylor and Silberston, *The Economic Impact of the Patent System*, 1973, at 52 and 53. Even in a Canadian context, however, Firestone recommends liberalisation rather than abolition of the system.

46 D. Wilson, *Penicillin in Perspective*, 1976, at 150. Wilson quotes (at 151) a letter from Florey which refers to being 'continuously hampered by inadequate research funds'. A.L. Thomson, *Half a Century of Medical Research*, 1975, gives the official account which not only fails to mention the refusal of the grant but does not make it clear that the major finance came from Rockefeller.

Scottish Journal of Political Economy, Vol. 37, No. 1, February 1990

MARSHALL'S INDUSTRIAL ANALYSIS

D. P. O'BRIEN*

Durham University

> My confidence in Cournot as an *economist* was shaken when I found that his mathematics *re* I[ncreasing] R[eturns] led inevitably to things which do not exist and have no near relation to reality. One of the chief purposes of my Wander-jahre among factories, etc., was to discover how Cournot's premises were wrong. The chief outcome of my work in this direction, which occupied me a good deal between 1870 and 1890, is in the 'Representative firm' theory, ... the supplementary cost analysis, ... as well as the parts [of the *Principles*] that directly relate to supply price for I. R.
>
> Marshall to A. W. Flux, 7 March, 1898, in *Memorials*, (1872–1923), pp. 406–7

I

INTRODUCTION

This statement, written eight years after the first edition of the *Principles* appeared, is fundamental to understanding Marshall's analysis of industry, an analysis which is itself fundamental to an understanding of his whole approach to economics. It is true that he actually does Cournot an injustice;[1] but this is really a side issue in the present context. He was essentially concerned with one large general problem with a number of facets. The large general problem was an analysis of the conditions which would ensure the maintenance of England's economic growth and of its industrial vigour.[2]

* I am extremely grateful to John Creedy, Bob Black and Roger Backhouse for comments on an earlier version of this paper.

[1] See Stigler (1962) p. 283; also Marshall (1890a), I, p. 459n. While Stigler is correct to point out that Cournot took account of the fact that decreasing marginal cost could exist in a situation of less than perfect competition, Marshall's insistence on his particular reading of Cournot was to become, as the quotation at the head of this paper indicates, fundamental to his search for economic truth.

[2] See Marshall (1919), Book I and Appendices B and C; (1903), pp. 402–12; (1890a), I pp. 672, 674, 740–52; (1890a), II, pp. 164–79. See also Glassburner (1955) and Gonce (1982). Marshall's economic history has been the object of much undeserved sneering, both in his own lifetime (from Cunningham and Nicholson—see Whitaker, 1975, I, pp. 107–8) and since. But Book I of (1919) has tremendous verve and sweep, and the great Clapham was his pupil (Mathias, 1968). See also Andreano (1965). None the less, it has to be conceded that Clapham

Date of receipt of final typescript: 11 October 1989.

The most important of the subsidiary problems was examination of the conditions under which secularly increasing productivity could occur throughout the economy without resulting in an increase in concentration to the point where innovation would be seriously impaired.

The result of Marshall's efforts to tackle these problems was an analysis which, in richness and complexity, defied simple modelling. But Marshall's 'industrial economics' is in fact central to this analysis. Indeed, the subtitle of *Industry and Trade* (Marshall, 1919) is 'A study of industrial technique and business organisation; and of their influences on the conditions of the various classes and nations'. It is this emphasis on the key role of industrial 'facts' which explains the apparent ambiguities, the reluctance to model, the continual emphasis on path-dependency, the 'biological' analogies, and the loose ends.

Marshall's coverage was extremely broad. Comparison of *Industry and Trade* with a modern classic like Scherer's *Industrial Market Structure and Economic Performance* (Scherer, 1970) shows that virtually all the topics covered in the later book are at least touched on by Marshall.

Later generations have regarded Marshall's efforts with a mixture of impatience and amused patronage; there has been a tendency to regret that he should 'waste his time' on such industrial detail,[3] and in the decade following his death the most influential examples, both of microeconomic theory (e.g. Robinson, 1933) and of methodological writing (Robbins, 1932), moved sharply in an apriorist direction,[4] leaving Marshall's work, so to speak, stranded.

himself not only sought to distance himself from the acknowledgement which he received from Marshall, but also showed one of Marshall's examples to be unsupported by the source cited by Marshall (Clapham, 1936). All the same, Keynes (in Marshall, 1872–1923, p. 46, n. 2) quotes Clapham as writing approvingly of Marshall's historical appendices.

[3] Whitaker (1975), I, p. 57 agrees that 'there was much to admire in all this strenuous enquiry' but concludes: 'Marshall attained an immense knowledge but, in the nature of the case, much of the knowledge soon dated, and much suffered from the unreliability of hearsay evidence. The process of acquisition, too, was far from costless. It retarded the composition of Marshall's writings. And, whether as cause or consequence, it appears to have been accompanied by a drift of interest and long-sustained thought away from questions of pure economic theory.' The question of 'hearsay evidence', and indeed the more general one of the *reliability* of Marshall's observations, is a separate matter. But even where the recollections were not entirely reliable (and see n. 2 above) they formed the basis for hypotheses which Marshall continually related back to the facts—a procedure which is at least consistent with a modern view, one holding that the source of hypotheses is irrelevant (Popper, 1959, p. 31). But in fact there is no significant evidence that Marshall was an unreliable observer on a large scale, which would be fatal to adherence to his own (and his contemporaries') accepted methodologial position.

[4] 'We have all felt, ... a sense almost of shame at the incredible banalities of much of the so-called theory of production—the tedious discussions of the various forms of peasant proprietorship, factory organisation, industrial psychology, technical education, etc. which are apt to occur in even the best treatises arranged on this plan' (Robbins 1932, p. 65). In lectures delivered on the fiftieth anniversary of his seminal article (Coase, 1937), R. H. Coase, after commenting on this and related (and even more emphatic) material in Robbins (1932) concluded: 'Robbins was devoted to high theory and, I believe, felt some distaste, at any rate in the 1930s, for discussions of such mundane subjects as peasant proprietorships and industrial "forms".' (I am grateful to Professor Duncan Reekie for bringing these lectures to my attention.)

Such a development was, whatever its wider significance, extremely unfortunate for the understanding of Marshall's own work. For his emphasis upon industrial 'facts' and the misleading title of his first book[5] (*The Economics of Industry* really contains very little about industry) actually give a clue to an important understanding of Marshall's personal research programme. For in his concern with economic growth he was at one with his classical predecessors, the links with whom he valued so highly (O'Brien 1990). But in the analysis which he produced Marshall went far beyond them and indeed made his own most distinctive contribution to economics. Marshall was most classical in his treatment of trade and money and of the *aggregates* of economic growth; he was closest to Jevons and his contemporaries in his treatment of demand; and he was most original and constructive in his treatment of supply and of the microeconomic underpinnings of economic growth. It is in the microeconomics that Marshall's own personal additions to what he regarded as the continually evolving corpus of economic theory are most evident. But supply could not be discussed sensibly without detailed knowledge of industrial organization. Once this was done, it produced an approach to value with an emphasis upon quantity adjustment in the 'normal' (as distinct from the 'market') case which was consistent with classical analysis but significantly different from much of post-1870 material.

So we have a situation in which emphasis on industrial organization leads to a theory of normal supply and an analysis of the microeconomic underpinnings of economic progress which can be seen as consistent with, even though it goes far beyond, classical foundations, thus satisfying Marshall's desire to achieve continuity with his predecessors.

The methodological background

Marshall's methodological position reflects that put forward in J. N. Keynes's classic work (Keynes, 1890), although it does not necessarily derive from it. Keynes articulated the view that 'induction' and deduction were complementary, with factual analysis providing the basis on which deductive developments could build as well as a further check on the correct direction of the deductive work. This leads to Marshall's preoccupation with the facts of industrial life—to preoccupation with such matters as *average* cost, expectations, the basis of entrepreneurial decisions, the argument that marginal cost as normally understood was an irrelevance and to oligopolistic considerations.

Linked with this was an emphasis upon the complexity of individual cases. The motto of *Industry and Trade* is 'The Many in the One, the One in the Many'.[6] It was necessary to find not only the general principles but

[5] Marshall and Marshall (1879) is referred to here as 'his' because of the evidence that he was largely responsible for the work as it finally appeared—see Whitaker (1975), I, p. 67.

[6] See also Marshall (1890a), pp. 777–8.

also the particular conjunction of forces in any one case. This links with the concept of 'verification' which played such an important role in economic methodology prior to the work of Popper.[7] For it was essential, if the conclusions of economists were to be correct, that the theories they were applying should fit the facts of the particular case. Deduction itself was a logical process and not subject to disproof. But in order to test whether theories were appropriate in any particular situation it was necessary to have detailed knowledge of the facts to which the theories were to be applied.

This was particularly important given Marshall's historical perspective and his view of allocation as occurring within a continually evolving framework of possibilities. The overriding themes of Marshall's treatment are technical progress and the taking of decisions within a continually increasing opportunity set, the increase itself resulting, at least partially, from the taking of decisions. Some technical progress was exogenous; but much resulted from the profit-actuated search procedures of the entrepreneur whose very activities resulted not in maximization subject to constraint, but in shifting constraints.

It followed from this that static analysis really had a very limited role to play. 'Fragmentary statical hypotheses are useful as temporary auxiliaries to dynamical—or rather biological—conceptions: but the central idea in a volume on the Foundations of economics, as in any other, must be that of living force and movement' (1890a, II, p. 50). Disturbing causes could be temporarily locked up 'in a pound called *Caeteris Paribus*' (1890a, I, p. 366) but this was only a limited and temporary device. In the last resort, static equilibrium must be subservient to technical progress. Some simplification was necessary—'If we include in our account nearly all the conditions of real life, the problem is too heavy to be handled' (1890a, I, p. 460); but such simplification, if it proceeded very far, resulted in 'long-drawn-out and subtle reasonings' which were 'scientific toys rather than engines for practical work' (1890a, I, p. 461). The whole analysis must be couched within a time framework allowing both for the development of economies of production on a large scale and also for an increase in demand over time. We could reason about equilibrium within a limited framework—Marshall's analogy of a man balancing parcels on the rack of a moving train is a helpful illustration here (1898, p. 312)—but we must not delude ourselves into thinking that this would tell us more than a little about the effects of economic forces. He warned in particular that 'general propositions in regard to either competition or monopoly are full of snares' (1919, p. 512). He advised his readers that while mathematical analysis could be applied to pure monopoly, it was almost helpless when faced with a monopoly constrained by the facts of the monopolist's particular situation (1919, p. 450n).

[7] See Blaug (1980), pp. 55–93 for an excellent overall discussion of 'verification'. For an earlier (pre-Popper) statement see Robbins (1932). See also Marshall (1890a), I. p. 781 and (1919), pp. 676–80, Whitaker (1975), I, pp. 110–11 and O'Brien (1988) pp. 36–9.

Marshall's sources

We know relatively little about Marshall's 'industrial wanderings', referred to in the opening quotation to this paper. Whitaker gives us references to a tour of the United States in 1875 and of the North of England in 1885 (1975, I, pp. 52–7); but a note by Mrs Marshall quoted by Whitaker (1975, I, p. 52–3) hints at more frequent travels, and her own (belatedly) published recollections (1947) suggest that 'industrial wandering' was a frequent pastime for the Marshalls in vacations. Writing of the years following their return to Cambridge in 1885, she recounted that:

> One year passed much like another. In vacations, either at home or abroad, we spent some time in towns, seeing factories and workshops. Alfred knew all about machines and tools, sometimes he took a hand in using them, and I have a jam-pot which he turned very neatly at Wedgwood's. He could tell beforehand what wages were being paid for any kind of work and was seldom wrong by more than a few pence a week. One year we would go to the pottery district with its problems of localisation of industry and changing fashions ... Another year it would be the light metal trades. (M. P. Marshall, 1947, pp. 42–3)[8]

Marshall thus attached great importance to factual work.[9] While factual work did not, in itself, provide general principles, 'direct practical experience of particular events is the basis of all economic knowledge, and is the exclusive source of supply of the material used in the construction of economic science' (1919, pp. 679–80). It was not only factual work of a descriptive kind which Marshall regarded as important; he attached considerable importance to statistical work as well, notably that of Bowley (Marshall, 1899, pp. 284–8). He himself was extremely diligent in the pursuit of facts, and yet so much of what he did in this respect was concealed from the reader. His rebuke to Edgeworth over the source of his belief in Giffen goods is well known (1872–1923, pp. 438–9); less well known is another letter to Edgeworth in which he recounts how, in connection with only six paragraphs of his Memorandum on Trade Policy of 1903, he worked through 'several thousand semi-technical pages' on the matter of wheat supply; how he then worked through several thousand pages more in the light of subsequent information, and how he cross-questioned anybody he believed had a technical knowledge of the subject concerned (1872–1923, pp. 439–40). Moreover, he read secondary sources voraciously—he

[8] See also Marshall (1919), pp. 336n, 657n, where Marshall draws on his experiences 'on tour'. I am indebted to Professor Peter Groenewegen for the information that Marshall's letters to his mother give further details of his US tour, and that the Marshall papers contain a list (lacking in detail) of places visited during summer vacations.

[9] Marshall (1885a), pp. 153–4; (1885b); (1897), p. 301; (1907), p. 324; (1872–1923), pp. 358–9, 422, 429, 474–5; (1890a), I pp. v–vi, 29–31, 771–4; (1919), p. 678. The extent of Marshall's *statistical* work has been obscured both by his own reluctance to publish such material and also by Keynes's excision (of that which *was* published in the Report of the Indian Currency Committee) from Marshall's *Official Papers* (see Marshall 1886–1903, p. 326).

confessed to J. B. Clark that 'The books, for instance, which I take to the Alps nearly every summer are almost exclusively concerned with matters of fact' (1872–1923, p. 417). Table 1 gives some indication of the range of industries on which Marshall drew, the sources for his pictures of those industries, the importance (judged by the number of citations) which he

TABLE 1
Industries cited by Marshall in Industry and Trade

Industry	Point illustrated (source in parentheses[a])
Boat building	Standardization (N)
Boot and shoe (and machinery)	Standardization and specialization (O), tying and patents [2] (N)
Building	Official regulation (T)
Buses	Excess capacity and cartelization (N)
Cars (and tyres)	Continuous process economies (N), patents (N)
Chemicals (including tar and glass)	By-products (A&T), industrial training (A)
Coal	Distribution [2] (O&A), cartels [2] (A), consolidation (N)
Commodity exchanges	Effects of speculation [2] (O&A), general (O&A)
Cutlery	Mechanization (N)
Electricity	Tying and patents (N), cartels (O&A), natural monopoly (N)
Engineering and shipbuilding	Standardization (N), Labour specialization (L&T), cartels [2] (O), pricing [2] (O), stability (O)
Firearms	Scale economies (N)
Locks	Small business control (P)
Meat	Continuous process economies (N), by-products (O), price discrimination (O)
Oil	Monopolization (N&O), consolidation (N)
Paper and flour	Continuous process economies (N)
Pharmaceutical	Standardization (A&T)
Post Office	Uniform charges (N)
Pottery	Monopolization (T)
Printing	Scale economies (N)
Railways and canals	Joints stock organization problems [2] (T), monopoly regulation (O), consolidation (N), general discussion (O&T)
Retailing	Scale economies [3] (O&A), resale price maintenance (O), general (A, P&O)
Shipping	Excessive capitalization (N), monopoly (O&T), economies of scale (N)
Steel	Scale economies [2] (N), standardization [2] (N&T), location [2] (L&A), size problems (A&O), monopolization [4] (O, A&T), cartels [2] (O&T)
Textiles	Standardization and specialisation (A&O), Market Information (N), Finance (A), Monopolization [3] (N&A), Patents (N)
Tin-plate	Cartels (A)
Tobacco	Monopolization (O)

[a] The industry citations (which omit those in the economic *history* section of the book) are those in the 3rd (1920) edition of *Industry and Trade* (reprinted 1927). Banking, advertising and agriculture have been excluded. Numbers in square brackets refer to multiple citations of an industry on one particular point. Letters in brackets indicate supporting source: A academic, T trade, O official, P personal, L literary, N no source given.

attached to conditions in these industries and the lessons which he drew from the factual knowledge so accumulated. Yet even this is only a partial picture. He accumulated an enormous mass of industrial knowledge; and even though it is undeniable that much of the information must have dated, he still remained extraordinarily well informed.

But it must be emphasized that he was not collecting this material simply out of interest, although he was undoubtedly fascinated by many details of industrial life. (He and Mrs Marshall used to stand at the factory gates to watch the workers coming out (M. P. Marshall, 1947, p. 43).) Rather, this detailed and encyclopaedic knowledge was the basis on which Marshall thought of the whole nature of industrial competition, and thus of the long-term prospects for the British economy.

II

The Firm, Cost and Supply

Market clearing and the adjustment of supply

Marshall considered cases both of price adjustment and of quantity adjustment to produce market clearing.[10] But his discussion of price adjustment is confined very largely to the short run and to such institutions as corn markets and fish markets. The majority of his interest focused upon quantity adjustment, with factor mobility into and out of industries along classical lines.[11]

The nature of the supply conditions and the determination of supply price at various outputs are thus of critical importance. Marshall defined supply price as the *average* cost of a representative firm, where the cost incurred depended not only on the output of the firm but also on that of the industry and on the accumulated technical progress of the industry.[12] At market clearing equilibrium the representative firm itself would be in equilibrium but the industry as a whole would not, with some firms growing and others declining (1890a, I, pp. 342–3, 457–61). Because all this took place through time, and because unit costs fell over time through technological development, supply curves were not reversible (1890a, I, pp. 456, 808–9n; 1919, pp. 186–8).

So we have a picture of an industry made up of firms with differential efficiencies; and the response of that industry to a change in demand conditions is to be captured through the device of the representative firm (1890a,

[10] See Marshall (1890a), I, pp. 340–6, 348, 369–72, 378–80; (1890a), II, pp. 361–3; (1879) pp. vii, 158; (1867–90), I, pp. 131–51. See also Davies (1963) and Williams (1986).

[11] Marshall (1890a), I. pp. 345, 805–9; (1867–90), I, pp. 131, 136, 140, 147–51.

[12] (1890a), I, pp. 317, 344, 811; (1879), pp. 72–4, 76–7; see also Robertson (1957), pp.. 119–20.

I, pp. 342–3). This concept thus has a pivotal position in Marshall's analysis. The idea came naturally to Marshall because of his detailed knowledge of industrial life. The well-informed economist, conversant with the details of a particular industry, should be able to recognize a representative firm—it is a fundamental misunderstanding on the part of some later commentators to believe that it was a purely mental construction without empirical counterpart (Frisch, 1950, pp. 512–13). The firms within an industry could be pictured in Marshall's famous analogy of the trees of a forest, and within that forest the representative firm was defined as one with a typical share of internal and external economies, neither a dominant producer nor a struggling marginal one (1890a, I, pp. 315–18). It is worth quoting Marshall at length here, not only because he makes very clear how he views the representative firm, but also because it is abundantly clear that he meant the concept to be useful. He explains that, in order

> to discuss the causes which govern the supply price of a commodity [we] shall have to analyse carefully the normal cost of producing a commodity, relatively to a given aggregate volume of production; and for this purpose we shall have to study *the expenses of a representative producer* for that aggregate volume. On the one hand we shall not want to select some new producer just struggling into business, who works under many disadvantages, and has to be content for a time with little or no profits, but who is satisfied with the fact that he is establishing a connection and taking the first steps towards building up a successful business; nor on the other hand shall we want to take a firm which by exceptionally long-sustained ability and good fortune has got together a vast business, and huge well-ordered workshops that give it a superiority over almost all its rivals. But our representative firm must be one which has had a fairly long life, and fair success, which is managed with normal ability, and which has normal access to the economies, external and internal, which belong to that aggregate volume of production; account being taken of the class of goods produced, the conditions of marketing them and the economic environment generally.
>
> Thus a representative firm is in a sense an average firm. But there are many ways in which the term 'average' might be interpreted in connection with a business. And a Representative firm is that particular sort of average firm, at which we need to look in order to see how far the economies, *internal and external*, of production on a large scale have extended generally in the industry and country in question. We cannot see this by looking at one or two firms taken at random: but we can see it fairly well by selecting, after a broad survey, a firm, whether in private or joint-stock management (or better still, more than one), that represents, to the best of our judgement, this particular average. (1890a, I, pp. 317–18)

The device enabled us to examine the supply conditions of an industry;

it was also a device to which industrialists would have recourse in considering the possibility of entry into an industry (1890a, I pp. 318, 377, 497; II, p. 70). As a snapshot of the industry it provided, in addition, answers to the fundamental questions which concerned Marshall. The representative firm in those trades which offered significant internal economies could grow rapidly. But both marketing difficulties, and dwindling realization (as the firm passed its prime) of those economies which Marshall categorized as 'increasing returns', ensured that in many industries the representative firm never assumed a size which threatened competition and thus the dynamism of the whole economy (1890a, I pp. 285–6; II, p. 70).

It is important to note the use of *average* cost in dealing with the representative firm. Marshall was adamant that price did not equal *marginal* cost. '*The cost of production which controls value relates to whole processes of production rather than to any particular parcel of products*' (1919, p. 190).[13] Unfortunately Marshall seems to have been somewhat reluctant to spell out exactly what he meant by 'process'. But by putting together a number of different discussions of cost it turns out that he meant in fact long run average total cost including, as we shall see, an allowance for non-insurable risks and also for marketing costs.[14] But the problem is even more complex than this because the 'process' might very well involve the production and marketing by a single firm of a wide range of products (1919, pp. 269–71). As Marshall stressed, there were no unique costs associated with particular products in a multiproduct firm (1890a, I, pp. 394–6; 1919, pp. 192–4, 460).

The major puzzle, however, relates to the question of 'supplementary' costs. By these costs Marshall meant not only the fixed costs associated with fixed capital, but also the costs associated with marketing and other overheads. Because he did not make a hard and fast distinction between the long and the short run, he included an allowance for supplementary costs within the average total cost that price had to cover.[15] The necessity for continuity of production *and* marketing was at the back of this. Of course this raises the question of how entrepreneurs would respond when faced with a fall in demand leading to a choice between selling at prices which only covered variable ('prime') cost and cutting back output. This will be discussed below.[16] The important point to note here is that Marshall viewed industry as normally pricing on the basis of *long*-run *average total* cost, even though there could, under special circumstances, be some (usually limited) departure from this.

[13] See also (1890a), I, pp. xvi, 361–2, 376, 501–2, 805; II, pp. 70–1, 509, 529; (1919), pp. 181, 183, 190–1, 424.

[14] (1890a), pp. 394, 398–400, 460, 501–2; (1919), pp. 181, 269–71.

[15] (1890a), I pp. 359–60, 394–8, 420–1, 424n, 501–2; II, p. 529.

[16] See also (1890a), I. p. 458.

Marketing

Concerned as he was with the way in which businessmen took decisions, not only to produce output but to dispose of it, Marshall did not take the easy way out of simply assuming the existence of a downward-sloping average revenue curve. Rather, marketing was a fundamental part of the acitivity of a business. Its cost had therefore to be discussed in detail and might well constitute a significant part of total cost (1890a, I pp. 286–7; 1919, pp. 184, 269–307). Capital invested in trade connections could be a major investment (1890a, I, p. 377) and the costs thus incurred, as indicated in the previous section, had to be covered by the price charged. The sales force was part of fixed costs (1919, p. 270; see also 1890a, I, p. 458). Firms could adopt devices such as using an introductory low price so that consumers became familiar with the product—even to persuade consumers to invest in equipment which used the product (1919, pp. 185–6, 406–8; 1890a, I, p. 486). In the case of producers' goods there was also the possibility of bribes to buyers (1919, p. 294n). Marshall discussed at some length the distribution of the costs of marketing between producers and retailers, the role of middle-men, the particular expenses of marketing for peak demand and the influence of marketing on industrial location. He considered the strengths and weaknesses of the co-operative movement and the development of large-scale retailing. He also discussed brands, and advertising in both its informative and its persuasive aspects, including the wasteful nature of some competitive advertising (1919, pp. 269–307).

In all these activities there were economies of scale to be realized. This is particularly important in Marshall's general scheme. For he believed that whereas production economies would peter out, there might not be limits to the scale economies in marketing (1919, pp. 249, 511, 515, 534–6, 539). Marketing thus posed a threat to the competitive structure to which he attached such importance.

He solved this problem by an empirical generalization, of the fragility of which he seems to have been perfectly well aware. He judged that marketing diseconomies would be most pronounced in those industries where production cost economies were most promising. Each producer sold both in the general market and also in his own particular market. Those industries in which production scale economies were most possible were those most likely to be confined very largely to their own particular market, with firms facing inelastic demand for their output. Thus, though in general marketing economies face fewer difficulties than production economies, over a wide range of industries they faced very real difficulties at those crucial points in the industrial structure—notably heavy industry—where production economies otherwise threatened to overwhelm competition (1890a, I, pp. 457–9; 1919 pp.182, 196). None the less, as his discussion of economies of scale makes clear (below, p. 75) Marshall was well aware that this was a generalization subject to much qualification.

The role of time

Time has such a fundamental role in Marshall's analysis of value, because of his appreciation of the realities of an evolving industrial structure, that it is truly astonishing that so little attention has been paid to this in the standard representations of 'Marshallian' value theory.[17] Yet he was perfectly explicit about this.

> In a stationary state then the plain rule would be that cost of production governs value. Each effect would be attributable mainly to one cause; there would not be much complex action and reaction between cause and effect ... But nothing of this is true in the world in which we live. Here every economic force is constantly changing its action, under the influence of other forces which are acting around it. Here changes in the volume of production, in its methods, and in its cost are ever mutually modifying one another; they are always affecting and being affected by the character and the extent of demand. Further all these mutual influences take time to work themselves out, and, as a rule, no two influences move at equal pace. In this world therefore every plain and simple doctrine as to the relations between cost of production, demand and value is necessarily false. (1890a, I, pp. 367–8).

We have in fact two propositions: that demand and supply are interdependent, with increases in demand leading to technical changes which lower unit cost; and that these changes themselves take time so that the development of new technology is a process which depends upon time.[18] Thus average cost is a function not only of output but of *dating*. Marshall remarked that 'we should have made a great advance if we could represent the normal demand price and the normal supply price as functions both of the amount normally produced and of the time at which that amount became normal' (1890a, I, p. 809). Technical progress is both exogenous, assisted by such developments as standardization and new means of transport, and endogenous, the latter being the result of the entrepreneurial search for those technical improvements which give rise to the prospect of profit.[19] This had the neccessary implication that a cost curve, with both time and quantity axes, was not reversible; it thus implied in turn that

[17] In particular the relationship between time and unit cost, through endogenous technical change, is not clearly brought out even in Opie (1931) which is generally regarded as the standard reference on Marshall's time analysis. See, however, Whitaker (1975), I, p. 124.

[18] (1890a), I. pp. 455, 459–61, 807–10; II, p. 362; (1867–90), I, pp. 139–41; (1919), pp. 186–8.

[19] (1890a), I, p. 280 and Book IV, chs 9 and 10; (1919), pp. 169–70, 197–213, 221–34, 238–42. It does not seem possible to distinguish clearly, especially in Marshall (1919), between technical changes within and outside the industry, and between the effects of endogenous and exogenous forces—in the latter case a given technical change may result from a combination of forces.

supply curves, depending upon long-run average total cost, were themselves not reversible.[20]

The contrast with the standard representation of Marshall should be obvious enough. Yet the standard representation is understandable in that path-dependency is, though not indeterminate, industry-specific in this case and thus defies generalized modelling. None the less, given Marshall's concerns with the long-run progress of the economy, and given also his methodological preconceptions, such an approach was, for him, unavoidable.

III

Industrial Organization

The entrepreneur

The role of the entrepreneur in all this is clearly central. The entrepreneur, following what Marshall calls the 'principle of substitution' searches endlessly and simultaneously both for best practice with existing technology and for new technology. The entrepreneur is thus central to the optimizing procedure.[21] This is particularly important because Marshall not only avoids the concept of a fixed and unique production function but also argues that differences between methods are essential to his overriding interest—economic progress.

> Every locality has incidents of its own which affect in various ways the methods of arrangement of every class of business that is carried on in it: and even in the same place and the same trade no two persons pursuing the same aims will adopt exactly the same routes. The tendency to variation is a chief cause of progress; and the abler are the undertakers in any trade the greater will this tendency be. (1890a, I, p. 355)

It is not only optimal *input* combinations which the entrepreneur seeks; motivated by the profit reward, he also searches for *optimal output* combinations of different products (1890a, I, pp. 434–7). But since, as we have seen above, changes in output react back upon technology, optimal search is thus an engine for progress.

The entrepreneur is the organizer in command of capital, who bears uninsurable risks. He takes complex decisions with limited information.

[20] (1890a), I, pp. 807–10; (1867–90), II, pp 184–5; (1919), pp. 186–8. See also (1867–90), I, pp. 140–1. Marshall however objected to Cunynghame's attempted formalization of this. See Marshall's letter to Edgeworth in (1890a), II, pp. 808–10 and Cunynghame (1892).

[21] (1890a), I, pp. xvi, 169–72, 341, 351–4, 355–9, 404, 418–21, 662–3.

Superintendence is only a small part of this; co-ordination, imagination, and risk-bearing are fundamental.[22]

The profit reward includes interest on the entrepreneur's capital, earnings of management (including rent of ability) and compensation for risk.[23] Risk comes in various forms including market risk and the risk of default.[24] There are also rewards to be obtained from innovation (1890a, I, p. 280; 1919, pp. 206–13). In the long run gross profits will *not* be equalized because risk varies between industries. But earnings of management will be equalized in the long term and the rewards of innovation will be competed away although they provide short-term gains (1890a, I, pp. 602–8; II, pp. 648–9; 1879, p. 147). As Marshall put it in the early *Economics of Industry*: 'The profits on equal capitals tend continually to equality in trades which involve equal risks, discomforts and exertions; and which require equally rare natural abilities and an equally expensive training' (1879, p. 139). But this very competitive equalization of returns ensured that the entrepreneur had a continual incentive to search for new methods and new products which would yield profits of innovation in the short term.

Business organization

As was consistent with his overriding concern with economic progress, Marshall examined the advantages and disadvantages of large firms, small firms, co-operatives, and state enterprise. The last of these can be dismissed fairly quickly. He believed that socialists had seriously under-estimated the difficulties of business management and that government enterprise was thoroughly undesirable (1885c, p. 174; 1919, pp. 492–500, 671–2; 1890b, pp. 281–4). It was hampered by bureaucracy, the loss of the energizing force of competition, and corruption; it was prey to the influences of pressure groups; and above all it was inimical to technical progress. Even if it started off with the best practice available at the time it would soon fall behind the private sector.[25]

It was not that he was opposed to government interference with, even regulation of, industry. Marshall favoured measures to remove industry from urban locations and to decrease urban congestion.[26] But he thought that the government as entrepreneur was a failure and he was impressed by the inefficiency of state railways (1919, pp. 494–7).

[22] (1890a), I, p. 297; Book IV, chs. 9, 10, 12 (pp. 240–77, 291–313) contain a detailed discussion of entrepreneurship. (1919), p. 355 lists the qualities required by an entrepreneur. See also (1890a), I, pp. 357–9, 364–6, 398–400, 612–13, 662–4; (1867–90), I, pp. 211–12; (1919), pp. 645–6; (1879) pp. 114–18; (1890b), pp. 281–4.

[23] (1890a), I. pp. 71–82, 138–9, 313, 589–92, 596–628; II, pp. 670–5; (1879), pp. 75, 78–9, 135–45; (1867–90), I, pp. 204–24; (1923), pp. 285–94.

[24] (1879), pp. 78–9, 135; (1890a), I, pp. 297, 357–9, 398–400; II, pp. 648–9; (1919), pp. 645–6; (1867–90), I, pp. 211–12.

[25] (1890a), I, p. 304; (1919), pp. 486, 494–7, 666–72; 1885c, p. 174; (1891a); (1891b).

[26] (1890a), I, pp. 199–200 (and see also pp. 202–3, 320–1, 718, 803–4); (1903) pp. 361–3; (1885c) pp. 183–4; (1884); (1887); (1909).

Despite a certain romantic attitude towards co-operation, he also had severe doubts about that as a general form of business enterprise. He observed wryly that 'an army commanded by a committee has seldom given a good account of itself' (1919, p. 294). Management was a specialized form of activity which required specialists to undertake it (1890a, I, pp. 292–3, 305).

The business firm, then, is the fundamental form of organization required for progress. To a considerable extent the future lay, however, not with the owner–manager entrepreneur (whom Marshall considered the ideal for economic progress) but with the large firm in the form of a joint stock company (1919, pp. 580–1). Despite some advantages enjoyed by the small firm, notably a detailed knowledge of personnel and of technology (1890a, I, pp. 278–90, 303), the small firm was in danger of being superseded by the large because of the latter's overwhelming advantages, both managerial and technical. In a managerial role, the head of a joint stock company could specialize in those broad questions affecting the policy and future development of the firm which were fundamental to its growth. Moreover the joint stock companies could afford to hire the best managerial talent (1890a, I, pp. 283–4), whereas the small (especially family) firms were subject to managerial decay. Although Marshall never cites the familiar 'clogs to clogs in three generations' he clearly has this in mind at a number of points in the text.[27] The large firms had access to sufficient capital, possible on easier terms than the small business, to adopt production on the largest scale.[28] To some extent their rise could be slowed both because they also had some inherent *dis*advantages—bureaucracy, the need for complex managerial cost systems, a certain hesitancy about innovation, and a tendency to what Marshall called 'needless enlargement of scope'[29]—and because of the development of standardization which made it possible for smaller firms to produce small parts of large products—vertical disintegration (1919, pp. 140–62, 594). Marshall believed this to have occurred in the textile and the boot industries (1919, pp. 229–34). But in other industries—railways, oil, water, gas, post, mining and shipping the technical influences on aggregation were extremely strong (1919, pp. 584–6, 785–92), and in steel manufacture standardization gave economies of scale to the very largest firms rather than being primarily of assistance to smaller ones (1919, pp. 218–21, 586–9). Even in those industries where huge quantities of material did not require simultaneous handling (as they did in iron and steel) there were economies to be obtained by firms large enough to enjoy a continuous flow of throughput—paper and flour, cocoa, mustard, soap,

[27] See e.g. (1890a), I, pp. 298–301; II, pp. 659–61. See also Loasby (1978) p. 8.

[28] (1890a), I, Bk IV, ch. 11, pp. 278–90; II, p. 334; (1919), pp. 213–34, 242–4, 249, 336, 343, 594; (1923) pp. 77–80.

[29] (1890a), I, pp. 298–304; II, pp. 659–60; (1879), pp. 139–42; (1919), pp. 308–28, 667. (1890b), pp. 279–81; (1897), pp. 307–8; (1907), pp. 332–3.

meat packing and car assembly are examples which Marshall cites (1919, pp. 218, 235–8).

There is no doubt that the strength of these internal economies, which resulted in large-scale joint stock business organization with substantial 'supplementary costs', involving costing systems and 'scientific management' (1919, pp. 365–94), was a considerable worry to Marshall, who believed that there was a danger of exchanging the short-run gains of aggregation for long-run losses of innovation (1890b, pp. 279–81; 1907, pp. 332–3; 1919, pp. 249, 582). The small companies could be helped by the development of external economies—and when we see Marshall's analysis of supply in a growth context we can see how very important such matters as the development of subsidiary industries, of financial institutions, of communications, and of pools of skilled labour were[30]—but the path of economic development offered few long-term portents favourable to the small firm (1919 pp. 106, 214, 314–16, 581). Yet the separation of ownership and control in large firms did not bode well for the future progress of the British economy.[31] While joint stock companies could offset some of their inbuilt disadvantages from a national point of view, Marshall decided that:

> We may conclude provisionally that recent developments call only for some mitigation, not for a reversal, of the judgement of English business men that the conversion of a private business into a joint stock company, though occasionally inevitable and very frequently convenient to those immediately concerned, sometimes acts adversely to national prosperity and industrial leadership. (1919, pp. 327–8).

IV

Market Structure

Competition

Competition between small firms was a vital energizing force for economic progress.

> It has always been recognized that large firms have a great advantage over their smaller rivals in their power of making expensive experiments; and in some of the modern 'scientific' industries they use part of their resources in hiring specialists to make experiments for them in the technical applications of science. But on the whole observation seems to

[30] (1919), pp. 106, 221–3, 314–15; (1890a), I, pp. 266, 271, 273–4, 678–9; (1879), p. 55; (1923), pp. 68–97.

[31] (1890a), I pp. 301–4; (1919), pp. 307–8, 311, 319, 323–8; (1897), p. 307; (1907), pp. 332–3.

> show, what might have been anticipated *a priori*, that these advantages count for little in the long run in comparison with the superior inventive force of a multitude of small undertakers. There are but few exceptions to the rule, that large private firms, though far superior to public departments, are yet, in proportion to their size, no less inferior to private businesses of a moderate size in that energy and resource, that restlessness and inventive power, which lead to the striking out of new paths. And the benefits which the world reaps from this originality are apt to be underrated. (1890b, pp. 279–80).

Competition had to take place, as the classical economists themselves had argued, within a framework of law and of non-legal restraints such as public opinion and what Marshall quaintly called 'economic chivalry'.[32] But within such a framework it was highly beneficial, whereas collectivism was not only inimical to progress because of its bureaucratic nature, but involved the dangers of corruption and was even bad for human nature itself (1890a, I, pp. 712–14; 1907, pp. 333–7; 1919, pp. 43–4).

But the competition to which Marshall attached such importance, and which, in contrast to collectivism, fostered self-reliance and forethought, was certainly not perfect.[33] As Stigler has noted: 'Marshall as usual refused to float on the tide of theory, and his treatment of competition was much closer to Adam Smith's, than to that of his contemporaries' (1957, p. 10). Each firm sold in both a general and a particular market. In the general market it was a price taker but in the particular (and more profitable) market it faced a downward-sloping demand curve for its output.[34] It was this which limited its realization of increasing returns:

> In many industries each producer has a special market in which he is well known, and which he cannot extend quickly; ... therefore, though it might be physically possible for him to increase his output rapidly, he would run the risk of forcing down very much the demand price in his special market, or else of being driven to sell his surplus production outside on less favourable terms. And though there are industries in which each producer has access to the whole of a large market, yet in these there remain but few internal economies to be got by an increase of output when the existing plant is already well occupied. (1809a, I. p. 501)

The implication here is that marketing in the 'general' market is by no

[32] (1890a), I, pp. 32–6, 347–8 (and see also pp. 363, 366–9, 372); (1890b), pp. 285–9; (1907), pp. 342–6. Cf. (1879), pp. vi–vii, 65–6, 77–8 (and see also pp. 146–9); (1890a), II, pp. 155–6; Guillebaud (1952), at p. 122 quoting Marshall to J. B. Clark about his change of mind (letter of 1910).

[33] (1890a), I, pp. 5–12, 341, 500–1, 540–1; II, pp. 569, 573–4; (1919), p. 196.

[34] For the general and particular market see (1890a), I, pp. 457–8, 500–1; II, pp. 411–12; (1919), p. 182. For the distinction between marginal revenue and price (cited by Chamberlin, 1961 p. 524 in discussing the origin of the marginal revenue concept) see (1890a), I, pp. 849–50.

means costless and that this limits the realization of *production* economies when resort is had to the general market (1890a, I, pp. 457–9, 500–1; II, pp. 523–9).

Marshall was, indeed, resistant to the very idea of perfect competition, as Stigler has pointed out (1962, p. 282). Because of his stress upon imperfections of competition, he provided the materials for the later construction of the theories of imperfect and monopolistic competition, including technical apparatus which is, algebraically, only trivially different from that which so excited economists in the 1930s.[35] (It should, however, be clear from this discussion that Marshall would have regarded the 1930s treatment as distressingly one-dimensional.)

The very non-uniformity of firms itself implied imperfection of competition. The analogy of the trees of the forest (with some trees at maturity, some growing to maturity, and some declining past maturity) provides an admirable picture of Marshall's view of a typical industry structure (1890a, I. pp. 315–17; II, pp. 69–70), and the industry structure itself was affected by changes in demand—an increase in demand would increase the growth of rising firms and reduce the decay of falling ones (1890a, I, 342–3, 378). Crucial to the life cycle of the firm within the 'forest' was variation of managerial strength. This itself was an important factor in maintaining a competitive structure. The realization of economies of scale took time and thus it was limited by the decline in managerial strength in the later stages of the life cycle of the firm (1890a, I. pp. 69–70, 285–6, 323, 457–9). This links, once again, with Marshall's reservations about the rise of joint stock companies which might offset this managerial decay but at the expense of the innovation which the thrusting younger firms would otherwise provide as they elbowed aside the decaying firms (1890a, I. pp. 315–17; 1919 pp. 314–16, 326–8, 421–2).

These large firms also enjoyed significant barriers to entry, thus possessing some protection against their own displacement. Some of these barriers were inherent in the technology of the industries concerned, although they could be undermined by the very standardization enjoyed by large firms pursuing *within*-plant specialization of their own. Others resulted from market imperfections—large firms were likely to enjoy favoured access to capital, and business inertia made entry into an industry difficult. But others were simply man-made and included such devices as limit pricing, deferred rebates, predatory pricing, exclusive dealing, refusal to supply, tying

[35] See Stykolt (1956); Gerbier (1976); Peterson (1957); Chamberlin (1961). But Chamberlin also makes the point that Marshall did choose to devote separate Books of *Industry and Trade* (1919) to competition and monopoly. On the genesis of 'marginal revenue', however, he has this to say: 'Having used the concept of marginal value product in 1926, I might perhaps lay claim to a place among the goodly company in Mrs Robinson's Foreword of those who arrived at the concept at about the same time. But alas! I must confess that I found it in Marshall's Mathematical Appendix, Note XIV.' See also the discussion of Marshall's monopoly analysis below.

clauses, fighting brands, loss-leaders, manipulation of demand, and the maintenance of excess capacity as a threat to an entrant.[36] Marshall's industrial knowledge extended even to such things as full-line forcing and as far as industrial sabotage (1919, pp. 536–7).

Within the imperfectly competitive industry there were significant elements of oligopolistic interdependence. This interdependence, together with the necessity to ensure continuity of production, meant that firms would not, even in the short run, price according to marginal cost (1890a, I, pp. 360, 374–5, 457–9, 497–8). Marginal cost was

> the special cost which a manufacturer has in view, when his works are not fully employed, and he is calculating the lowest price at which it would be worth his while to accept an order, irrespectively of any effect that his action may have in spoiling the market for future orders, and trade being slack at the time. *But in fact he must as a rule take account of this effect*: the price at which it is just worth his while to produce, even when trade is slack, is in practice generally a good deal above this prime cost. (1890a, I, p. 360, emphasis added)

Marshall laid some emphasis upon the oligopolistic element:

> if the producers had no fear of spoiling their markets, it would be worth their while to produce for a time for any reward that covered the prime costs of production and rewarded them for their own trouble.
>
> But, as it is, they generally hold out for a higher price; each man fears to spoil his chance of getting a better price later on from his own customers; or, if he produces for a large and open market, he is more or less in fear of incurring the resentment of other producers, should he sell needlessly at a price that spoils the common market for all. The marginal production in this case is the production of those whom a little further fall of price would cause, either from a regard to their own interest or by formal or informal agreement with other producers, to suspend production for fear of further spoiling the market. The price which, for these reasons, producers are just on the point of refusing, is the true marginal supply price for short periods. It is nearly always above, and generally very much above the special or prime cost for raw materials, labour and wear-and-tear of plant, which is immediately and directly involved by getting a little further use out of appliances which are not fully employed. (1890a, I. pp. 374–5)

Moreover, Marshall was quite explicit that, for the entrepreneur, there was no question of isolating 'the cost of each separate small parcel of his output; he is apt to treat a considerable part of it, even in some cases the whole of it, more or less as a unit' (1890a, I, p. 376). The higher the ratio of fixed

[36] (1919), pp. 244–9, 300–2, 396–8, 400–1, 420, 435, 437–9, 441–2n, 485, 521, 523–4, 523–4, 532–3, 536, 597, 626–7; (1890a), I, p. 308.

to variable costs, the greater the degree of oligopolistic interdependence and the greater the unwillingness of firms to price according to marginal cost (1890a, I. pp. 458–9; II, p. 528).

Monopoly

The discussion so far should have made clear not only the extent to which Marshall's view of competition was distant from that of *perfect* competition but also the extent to which both competitive and monopolistic elements were to be found in any one *real-life* competitive situation. Marshall was in fact perfectly clear that

> though monopoly and free competition are ideally wide apart, yet in practice they shade into one another by imperceptible degrees: that there is an element of monopoly in nearly all competitive business: and that nearly all the monopolies, that are of any practical importance in the present age, hold much of their power by an uncertain tenure; so that they would lose it ere long, if they ignored the possibilities of competition, direct and indirect. (1919, p. 397; see also p. 178).

Because Marshall attached importance to the 'monopolistic elements' he was led to develop an analysis of monopoly itself. As we can see from Figure 1 this involved maximization of the area $(AR - AC)Q$, the maximum area being found *not* by the maximum height of the profit curve, which represents merely the maximum distance between average revenue and average cost, but by the point at which the profit curve reaches the highest attainable rectangular hyperbola in the profit quadrant. This particular mode of presentation springs from Marshall's Cambridge background and was associated with the invention of a machine for drawing rectangular hyperbolas by his pupil Cunynghame (Marshall, 1890a, II, pp. 7–8, 37–8n). However the now standard marginal revenue and marginal cost conditions (here added to Marshall's diagram) can be obtained perfectly straightforwardly from the $(AR - AC)Q$ profit function by taking first order conditions so that the 1930s analysis is simply a trivial variant of Marshall's monopoly analysis.

This analysis itself, however, in Marshall's view of the overall problem of monopoly, covered only a tiny part of that problem. He believed that the essential nature of almost all monopoly was that it was 'conditional', that is to say, a monopolist had always to consider, in the pricing policy that he adopted, the possibility of entry and also matters such as public opinion.[37] These might well lead him—and Marshall was able to employ his diagrammatic analysis to illustrate the point (1890a, pp. 486–9; 1919, pp. 416, 425–6)—to give some weight to consumer surplus as well as to net profit in the price adopted. But at all events the monopolist was constrained

[37] (1890a), pp. 493–5, 663; (1919), pp. 409, 420, 441, 449–50n, 523–4.

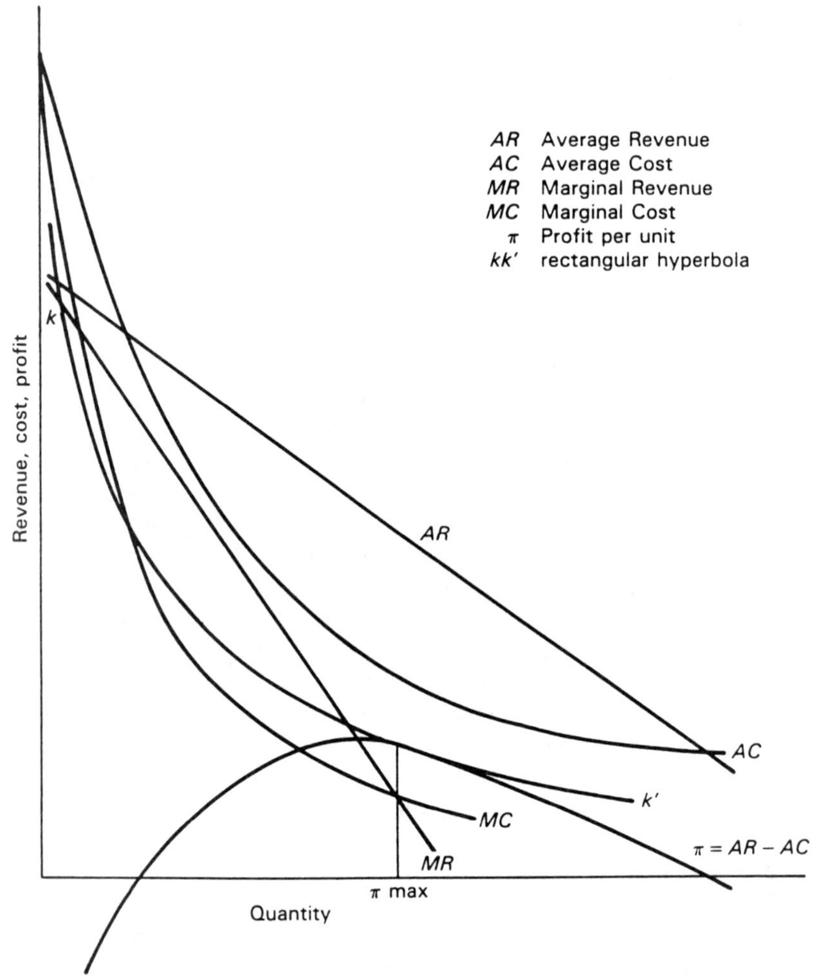

Figure 1

in all sort of ways by the threat of potential competition (including the spur to innovation) even though a monopoly had at its command all the standard devices such as exclusive dealing, deferred rebates, tying clauses, and even fighting brands,[38] so that the particular facts of each industrial situation had to be known before the likely outcome could be predicted. Formal analysis had little to offer compared with factual analysis. While paying tribute to the work on monopoly of Edgeworth and Pigou, Marshall warned that 'their route is not followed here: for mathematical analysis cannot easily be applied to *conditional* monopoly: it is almost constrained to start with the hypothesis of *pure* monopoly, and gradually to introduce successive limitations, corresponding to the various limitations and restrictions

[38] (1890a), pp. 493–5; (1919), pp. 395–409, 417–18, 420, 433–40, 481–2, 522, 533, 535–7.

which are imposed' (1919, p. 450n). Regulation and the threat of regulation were weapons which could be employed against monopoly (1919, pp. 440–4, 491–7, 574–6; 1890b, pp. 274–7); and there was also the possibility of defence of independent producers against monopolists (1919, p. 535n); but Marshall was convinced, particularly by his study of railways, that state-owned and managed monopolies offered the prospect of nothing but bureaucracy and technical stagnation (1919, pp. 494–7; see also 1890b, pp. 274–7).

Cartels

Marshall's attitude towards monopoly in general, and towards monopolization through cartelization, was somewhat ambivalent. He recognized that monopoly price was not *necessarily* higher than competitive price, at least in the short run, both because of the costs of competition, especially advertising, and because of the uncertainty of competition which acted as a disincentive to investment (1890a, p. 484). In dealing with cartels he recognized that there could be substantial economies of marketing (he was particularly impressed by the tobacco trust in the United States) as well as economies in buying supplies (1919, pp. 534–6, 539, 603; 1890a, pp. 282–3). (At the same time, if these were merely pecuniary economies, they offered no social gain: 1890b, p. 278). He recognized that cartels might be cautious about the use of market power, that they might be defensive—a source of countervailing power—and that they were forever threatened, like all forms of monopoly, by potential competition (1919, pp. 271–3, 402). But he warned that the economies which they achieved might offer short-term gains at the expense of a long-run loss of technical progress (1890b, pp. 279–81); that market power possessed by cartels could be dangerous (1890a, I, p. 686n; II, pp. 390–1; 1919, p. 553); that bureaucracy and management routine became the predominant characteristic (1919, pp. 537–9, 553; 1890a, I, pp. 364–6), that they lacked the ability to attract the highest quality of entrepreneurial talent in the long run (1919, pp. 525, 537–9), and that they tended to price at a level to suit established but marginal firms—which was subversive of his whole fundamental idea of industrial progress, since it prolonged the lives of the marginal, decaying, firms (1919, pp. 624, 627; 1890a, I, p. 375n). Energetic new firms could not undercut the decaying marginal firms but were forced to price at the same level. Moreover, cartels did not succeed in their stated aim of producing stability; they were not immune from general macroeconomic fluctuations (1919, pp. 631–2). On balance, and after a detailed study of the literature on cartels in his typically painstaking way, Marshall seems to have regarded them with some residual suspicion (e.g. 1919, pp. 653–5; 1890b, p. 273), perhaps particularly because of their power to exclude new entrants into an industry (1919, pp. 399–401), and to have been prepared to contemplate regulation (1919, p. 623). At the same time he was very well aware of the

difficulties facing regulators who would know less about the inside of the industry than the cartel members, and who could easily be misled over the rate of profit by artificial inflation of the capital base.[39]

V

Conclusion

Failure to understand Marshall's industial economics has led to failure to understand the nature of much of his analysis. It is highly complex and it certainly defies the standard modelling procedures because the outcome of any given situation is thoroughly *case-* and *history*-specific. There were general principles to be disentangled from the mass of industrial data (the One in the Many). But no simple modelling could do justice to the complexity of individual cases (the Many in the One). For the economist there was no substitute for industrial knowledge: and in Marshall's judgement the relative balance between model building and factual analysis should be strongly biased, as it was in his own practice, by emphasis on the factual.

His successors judged his emphasis to be wrong, and disregarded the book which embodied his mature conclusions on industrial analysis—*Industry and Trade* (1919).[40] Whether they were correct in this judgement, from the wider perspective of economics in general, is necessarily outside the scope of this paper: but it is at least clear that they made it much harder for themselves to understand the work of Marshall himself.

References

Andreano, R. L. (1965). Alfred Marshall's *Industry and Trade*: A Neglected Classic in Economic History. In *New Views on American Economic Development*, ed. R. L. Andreano, pp. 317–29. Cambridge, Mass.: Shenkman.

Blaug, M. (1980). *The Methodology of Economics*. Repr. Cambridge: Cambridge University Press, 1982.

Chamberlin, E. H. (1961). Origin and early development of monopolistic competition theory. *Quarterly Journal of Economics* 75, pp. 515–43.

Clapham, J. H. (1936). Marshall and Dutch shipbuilding. *Economic History* (Supplement to the *Economic Journal*), 3, pp. 212–13.

Coase, R. (1937). The Nature of the Firm. *Economica*, NS., 4, pp. 386–405.

[39] Marshall's study of cartels provided him with a wide range of insights into the informational and other problems faced by regulators. See e.g. (1919), pp. 330, 336, 442, 481, 484, 516–17; (1890a), I, p. 417n.

[40] Even in Robertson's *Lectures on Economic Principles* (1957) there are very few references to *Industry and Trade* (I found only two, at pp. 149, 153). E. A. G. Robinson's *Monopoly* (1941) cites Marshall only once, and gives only one reference to *Industry and Trade* in the bibliography, although the book does seem to owe rather more to Marshall, at least in its general approach, than this would indicate. The same is true *a fortiori* of Robinson's *Structure of Competitive Industry* (1931), which makes no reference to Marshall at all.

CUNYNGHAME, H. (1892). Some improvements in simple geometrical methods of treating exchange value, monopoly, and rent. *Economic Journal*, 2, pp. 35–52.

DAVIES, D. G. (1963). A note on Marshallian versus Walrasian stability conditions. *Canadian Journal of Economics*, 29, pp. 535–40.

FRISCH, R. (1950). Alfred Marshall's theory of value. *Quarterly Journal of Economics*, 64, pp. 495–524.

GERBIER, G. (1976). *Alfred Marshall. Théoricien de l'action efficace et critique radical de l'économie pure*. Grenoble: Université des Sciences Sociales.

GLASSBURNER, B. (1955). Alfred Marshall on economic history and economic development. *Quarterly Journal of Economics*, 69, pp. 577–95.

GONCE, R. A. (1982). Alfred Marshall on industrial organisation: from *Principles of Economics* to *Industry and Trade*. In *Alfred Marshall: Critical Assessments*, ed. J. Cunningham Wood, Vol. IV, pp. 327–2. London: Croom Helm.

GUILLEBAUD, C. W. (1952). Marshall's *Principles of Economics* in the light of contemporary economic thought, *Economica*, NS., 19, pp. 111–30.

KEYNES, J. N. (1890). *The Scope and Method of Political Economy*, fourth edn. London: Macmillan, 1917.

LOASBY, B. (1978). Whatever happened to Marshall's theory of value? *Scottish Journal of Political Economy*, 25, pp. 1–12.

MARSHALL, A. (1867–90). *The Early Economic Writings of Alfred Marshall*, ed. J. K. Whitaker, 2 vols. London: Macmillan, 1975.

MARSHALL, A. (1872–1923). *Memorials of Alfred Marshall*, ed. A. C. Pigou. London: Macmillan.

MARSHALL, A. and MARSHALL, M. P. (1879). *The Economics of Industry*, second edn, 1881; reprinted London: Macmillan, 1888.

MARSHALL, A. (1884). Where to house the London poor. *Contemporary Review* (March), reprinted in (1872–1923), pp. 142–51.

MARSHALL, A. (1885a). *The Present Position of Economics*. London: Macmillan. Reprinted in (1872–1923), pp. 152–74.

MARSHALL, A. (1885b). The graphic method of statistics. *Jubilee Volume of the Statistical Society*, pp. 251–60. London: Stanford. Reprinted in (1872–1923), pp. 175–87.

MARSHALL, A. (1885c). How far do remediable causes influence prejudicially (a) the continuity of employment, (b) the rates of wages? In *Industrial Remuneration Conference ... under ... Sir Charles W. Dilke*, pp. 173–99. London: Cassell.

MARSHALL, A. (1886–1903). *Official Papers*. London: Macmillan for the Royal Economic Society, 1926.

MARSHALL, A. (1887). Is London healthy? *Pall Mall Gazette*, 13 April.

MARSHALL, A. (1890a). *Principles of Economics*, ninth (variorum) edition, ed. C. W. Guillebaud, 2 vols. London: Macmillan, 1961.

MARSHALL, A. (1890b). *Some Aspects of Competition*. Leeds: British Association, reprinted in (1872–1923), pp. 256–91.

MARSHALL, A. (1891a). The Post Office and private enterprise. *The Times*, 24 March (11e).

MARSHALL, A. (1891b). The Post Office and private enterprise. *The Times*, 6 April (13b–c).

MARSHALL, A. (1897). The old generation of economists and the new. *Quarterly Journal of Economics*, 11, reprinted in (1872–1923), pp. 295–311.

MARSHALL, A. (1898). Mechanical and biological analogies in economics. *Economic Journal*, 8, reprinted in (1872–1923), pp. 312–18.

MARSHALL, A. (1899). Evidence before the Indian Currency Committee. Reprinted in (1886–1903), pp. 263–326.

MARSHALL, A. (1903). *Memorandum on the fiscal policy of international trade*. Reprinted in (1886–1903), pp. 365–420.

MARSHALL, A. (1907). Social possibilities of economic chivalry. *Economic Journal*, 17, reprinted in (1872–1923), pp. 323–46.

MARSHALL, A. (1909). Rates and taxes on land values. *The Times*, 16 November (10c).

MARSHALL, A. (1919). *Industry and Trade*, third edn 1920, reprinted 1927. London: Macmillan.

MARSHALL, A. (1923). *Money, Credit and Commerce*. London: Macmillan.

MARSHALL, M. P. (1947). *What I Remember*. Cambridge: Cambridge University Press.
MATHIAS, P. (1968). Clapham, John Harold. In *International Encyclopaedia of the Social Sciences*, ed. D. L. Sills, vol. 2, pp. 502–4. New York: Macmillan, 1968.
O'BRIEN, D. P. (1988). *Lionel Robbins*. London: Macmillan.
O'BRIEN, D. P. (1990). Marshall's work in relation to classical economics. In *Centenary Essays on Alfred Marshall*, ed. J. K. Whitaker. Cambridge: Cambridge University Press.
OPIE, R. (1931). Marshall's time analysis. *Economic Journal*, 41, pp. 199–215.
PETERSON, S. (1957). Anti-trust and the classic model. *American Economic Review*, 47, pp. 60–87.
POPPER, K. R. (1959). *The Logic of Scientific Discovery*. Reprinted London: Hutchinson, 1974.
ROBBINS, L. C. (1932). *An Essay on the Nature and Significance of Economic Science*, 2nd edn. London: Macmillan, 1935.
ROBERTSON, D. H. (1957). *Lectures on Economic Principles*. Reprinted London: Fontana, 1963.
ROBINSON, E. A. G. (1931). *The Structure of Competitive Industry*. Reprinted Welwyn: Nisbet, 1964.
ROBINSON, E. A. G. (1941). *Monopoly*. London: Nisbet. Reprinted 1946.
ROBINSON, J. (1933). *The Economics of Imperfect Competition*. London: Macmillan.
SCHERER, F. M. (1970). *Industrial Market Structure and Economic Performance*, second edn. Chicago: Rand McNally, 1980.
STIGLER, G. J. (1957). Perfect competition, historically contemplated. *Journal of Political Economy*, 65, pp. 1–17.
STIGLER, G. J. (1962). Marshall's *Principles* after Guillebaud. *Journal of Political Economy*, 70, pp. 282–6.
STYKOLT, S. (1956). A curious case of neglect: Marshall on the tangency solution. *Canadian Journal of Economics*, 22, p. 251.
WHITAKER, J. K. (1975). Introduction and editorial material in Marshall (1867–90).
WILLIAMS, P. L. (1986). A reconstruction of Marshall's temporary equilibrium pricing model. *History of Political Economy*, 18(4), pp. 639–53.

PART III

THE FIRM

[11]

The evolution of the theory of the firm*

An economist's involvement with price theory runs the course of true love – delight, disillusion, dependence.
Harry Townsend

If we include in our account nearly all the conditions of real life, the problem is too heavy to be handled; if we select a few, then long-drawn-out and subtle reasonings with regard to them become scientific toys rather than engines for practical work.
Alfred Marshall.

Introduction

Serious discussion of the history of the theory of the firm has to start with Alfred Marshall. There is no doubt that he inherited relevant material from Classical economics, but an attempt to construct a pre-Marshallian theory from the materials available is likely to be unsuccessful.[1]

The two earlier writers to whom Marshall owed most were John Stuart Mill and Charles Babbage. Mill devoted some attention to the advantages of joint stock company organization, particularly the ease of access to capital, and the associated ability to reap economies of scale, as well as the access to professional managerial expertise.[2] Against these advantages had to be set weaknesses concerning the incentives facing those taking decisions within a joint stock company, when compared with an owner-managed firm, particularly in relation to the exercise of economy in operation. As we shall see, these were considerations which also attracted Marshall's attention, and Mill probably influenced him here. But the main point of interest is that Mill recognized that forms of organization affect the operation of the price system and hence the allocation of resources.

The influence of Babbage, Lucasian Professor of Mathematics at Cambridge earlier in the century, may have strengthened Marshall's obsession with the details of technology; in his famous *Economy of Machinery and Manufactures*,[3] which also influenced Mill, Babbage explored the many different forms which Smithian division of labour could take as technology developed.

Marshall[4]

The overriding themes of Marshall's treatment of the firm are technical progress, knowledge, and decision taking in which connection he pays considerable attention both to the role of the entrepreneur and to the form of organization. But he devoted considerable attention to competitive structure and size, and this is something which it is important to stress in view of the subsequent wholesale misrepresentation of his work.

In appreciating Marshall's position it is necessary to understand three preliminary considerations. Firstly, 'general propositions in regard to either competition or

monopoly are full of snares'.[5] Marshall had a strong distrust of simple models in a world in which there were many different influences on any one individual case – as in the motto of *Industry and Trade*, 'The many in the one, the one in the many'. Secondly, Marshall had a firm sense of historical perspective.[6] Thirdly, for Marshall, as for Smith, allocation takes place within a continuously evolving framework of possibilities, leading to new techniques, new processes, new products, and – the overriding force behind all the changes – new profit opportunities.[7]

Knowledge

The next crucial characteristic of Marshall's position is that resources are not allocated in a world of costless omniscience. There is therefore a key role for knowledge. This relates both to the internal situation of the firm, and to the external market in which it operates.

(i) *Internal knowledge* In the gathering of knowledge internal to the firm the owner-manager, who Marshall identifies with the small manufacturer, has a number of advantages. These include not only a detailed knowledge of processes and resource use within the firm, but also the ability to recognize and utilize managerial talent amongst employees. The large (joint stock) firm has to substitute other (resource-using) devices in order to gain some knowledge of what is going on within the firm. These include cost accountancy and 'scientific management' – Marshall was very interested in American work in this field – in the utilization of which a learning process occurs. The degree of knowledge available is not static; internal knowledge increases with time and it can be improved by joint consultation. It can also be improved by search procedures which may operate under the stimulus of competitive pressure.[8]

(ii) *External knowledge* In the knowledge of market conditions large firms have a considerable advantage. Day to day work can be delegated to subordinates and the head of a large business can specialize in 'studying the broader movements of the markets, and the yet undeveloped results of current events at home and abroad'.[9] The wider range of commercial contacts of a large firm give it a significant advantage in the acquisition of such knowledge.[10]

Decision taking

The need for, and imperfect availability of, both internal and external knowledge, were at the heart of Marshall's emphasis on decision taking and the role of the entrepreneur. 'He must have the power of forecasting the broad movements of production and consumption, of seeing where there is an opportunity for supplying a new commodity that will meet a real want or improving the plan of producing an old commodity.[11] He must also be the person who is capable of perceiving and taking risks.[12] But the taking of decisions is not enough; the entrepreneur also has an important role in implementation, as a leader of men.[13] Management was a specialized form of activity – this is indeed the source of Marshall's reservations about co-operation in practice[14] – and this meant that the future supply of entrepre-

neurs and managers was of critical importance for future economic growth. This explains Marshall's emphasis upon the importance of business education.[15]

Organization

Decision taking was, in Marshall's view, influenced not only by the quality of the decision takers, but also by the form of the organization within which the decision was taken. Starting from Mill's analysis of joint stock companies, Marshall studied their weaknesses, especially the separation of risk-bearing and knowledge, and the weakening of incentives[16] (though these effects could be partially off-set by the development of an *esprit de corp* and by staff welfare policies of the kind pursued by Selfridge)[17] while their bureaucratic form was inimical to the generation of knowledge on which the vital technical progress depended.[18] (We might note that Marshall anticipated an intensification of these problems, with public ownership,[19] and more than 60 years ago he foresaw the sort of problems which now dog London Transport.[20])

Technical change

The most important single factor in relation to knowledge and organization was the generation and utilization of technical advance.[21] Concern with this overrides all other considerations in Marshall's discussion. Because both generation and diffusion of this knowledge take time, time assumes a central role in Marshall's theory of the firm.[22] Increasing returns develop over time with diffusion of technical knowledge,[23] with the entrepreneur groping forward towards improved methods.[24] The downward sloping supply curve which resulted was not reversible.[25] Thus cost curves had a time as well as a quantity axis.[26] The driving force behind the onward movement was the entrepreneur searching for profit;[27] but new products and processes did not spring fully developed into the laps of entrepreneurs – product development was important and required not only time but finance.[28] Thus large firms had some advantages in innovation.[29] In all this the influence of Babbage and Mill is not unimportant[30] but the predominant source was Marshall's own 'industrial wanderings'.[31]

Costs

All this should indicate clearly enough that Marshall was much less concerned with simple static equilibrium than the economists that followed him – indeed, he seems to have regarded it as of very secondary importance compared with the forces making for technical progress. This would lead us to expect that his analysis of costs would prove to be very much more complex and subtle than simply drawing U-shaped cost curves; and such indeed proves to be the case. The first point to note is that Marshall was concerned with cost relationships as these really existed, rather than with what was analytically convenient.[32] Secondly, he did not accept the simple analysis of marginal cost which has subsequently become popular. Marginal cost was for him, not the first derivative of a continually differentiable cost curve, but the cost of a process. The cost of producing single items could not be isolated; there was a fundamental information problem concerning the allocation of joint costs. But, more generally, internal information on marginal cost was lacking, and

average cost provided a usable form of information.[33] In addition, costs were incessantly changing and cost curves were not smooth but involved step changes.[34]

A major part of costs related to marketing. Marshall refused to assume that each firm was simply *confronted* with a downward sloping average revenue curve. Marketing was a major business expense, and a major business preoccupation. It was thus something to be discussed in detail.[35] Marketing costs could be a large part of total costs[36] and capital invested in trade connections could be a major investment.[37] A sales force was to be viewed as part of fixed cost.[38] A firm might adopt a variety of devices for securing market penetration, including a low price to allow consumers to familiarize themselves with a product.[39] In all this there were economies of scale favouring the large firm.[40]

Marshall's firms, unlike those in the post-1932 literature, also had the related inventory costs,[41] and their costing was further complicated by the presence of multiple products with joint overheads, so that the simple post-Marshall textbook cost curve has no clear meaning in his terms.[42]

Pricing

Pricing was not the simple matter of equilibration found in the textbooks. Considerations affecting the price associated with particular costs included the desire to induce consumers to learn about a product (which took time) and also to invest in equipment to use the output.[43] Monopolists did not pursue simple profit maximization (in this connection we might note that the 1930s equation of marginal revenue and marginal cost is mathematically a trivial variation on Marshall's monopoly analysis[44] which had the advantage of using average costs, a measure an entrepreneur would recognize) but might be affected both by some consideration of consumer interests[45] and, more particularly, by the threat of potential competition.[46] More generally, price policy was also very much affected by considerations of oligopolistic interdependence especially where there were high fixed costs.[47]

Competitive structure

This leads naturally to the question of competitive structure. Since Marshall has frequently (and in some cases inexcusably) been 'credited' with using perfect competition, the first thing to emphasize is that we are *not* talking about this 1920s construct. Firms were limited in expansion by downward sloping average revenue curves,[48] at least in their own particular market. The size of the typical (or representative – see below) firm, in relation to total industry demand, depended on a wide variety of factors. There were purely financial pressures leading to large size as well as production economies in the form of increasing returns.[49] Many of these considerations have been made familiar to later generations through their distillation into E.A.G. Robinson's *Structure of Competitive Industry*.[50] However, realization of cost economies in production was limited by marketing expenses in the face of inelastic demand; Marshall offered the generalization that these were most severe in those industries in which production cost economies were most promising.[51] Moreover, the ability of firms to realize potential cost economies varied with managerial strength which in turn varied with the life cycle of the firm. This was particularly, but *not* exclusively, true of owner-managed firms. The particular stage

in the life cycle of a firm affected its development in all sorts of ways, including the gathering and utilization of information. It is in this context that the famous simile concerning the trees of the forest occurs.[52] (It is rather astonishing in this connection that the name 'Marshall' occurs only *twice* in the index to Penrose's *Theory of the Growth of the Firm* and then with the wrong initial![53])

All these factors, then, affected the size of firms within an industry and were thus important influences on competitive structure. Competitive structure was also influenced by the existence of barriers to entry – Marshall discussed the occurrence of these in a number of industries and pointed out that the preservation of excess capacity might operate as a barrier to entry.[54] Such barriers could be strengthened by vertical integration.[55] Behind such barriers firms could operate limit pricing[56] – although Marshall, unlike modern writers, realized that the business decisions involved were not easy but depended upon supply of the requisite knowledge.[57]

There were many sources of market power including manipulation of demand, deferred rebates, predatory pricing, exclusive dealing, refusal to supply, full-line forcing, and control of raw material supplies.[58] Concerted action between firms was also important: apart from interlocking directorates[59] there were full-blown trusts and cartels, the operation of which, both in Germany and the United States, Marshall studied with care.[60] The forces encouraging their creation included the existence of large capital investments, and of similar costs for different producers (as well as the prospect of loss from a price war), together with external pressure from banks.[61] Trusts and cartels possessed both countervailing power[62] and retaliatory power against entrants,[63] and were to be found over a wide range of economic activity including retailing.[64] Though hampered by bureaucracy[65] they were in general highly effective, and this naturally produced pressure for public regulation. Unfortunately public regulation encountered the crucial problem of knowledge on the part of the regulators,[66] including the problem of knowing the necessary level of capital equipment if rate regulation with an eye to the rate of return was contemplated – Marshall anticipated the results of Averch and Johnson here.[67] Moreover, regulation itself encouraged concerted action and concentration.[68]

Marshall had, then, a complex and sophisticated understanding of the many forces affecting both firms and markets, and in particular of the crucial problems of knowledge-generation and use. Yet a literature, ostensibly based on criticism of his work, developed in the 1920s and 1930s. Let us see what the main threads in this literature were.

Critical developments

Sraffa

Perhaps the most cited critique was that from P. Sraffa in the *Economic Journal*, 1926.[69] The main points of this article, which appears to have been an amalgam of two not wholly compatible articles, one of which had been previously published in Italian, were as follows. Firstly, there was a criticism of partial equilibrium analysis as involving interdependent demand and supply curves, and of the inclusion of external economies which were held to be unsuitable for partial equilibrium analysis. The first part of the article appeared to be ground-clearing for a return to the

value theory of Ricardo and/or Marx, particularly as the criticisms made of partial equilibrium analysis were also applicable to Sraffa's preference, expressed in the second part of the article, for widespread use of monopoly theory, and they are also applicable to later developments (in the work of Professor Joan Robinson who acknowledged a heavy debt to the Sraffa article). At all events, Sraffa appeared to be arguing in the first part of the article that since a falling supply curve was incompatible with 'competition' it was best to use cost of production value theory for commodities produced under competition.

The insistence that Increasing Returns were incompatible with competition should have raised some doubts in readers' minds, particularly as Marshall did not posit a horizontal average revenue curve but certainly analysed competition. But throughout the article Sraffa shuffled freely between 'competition' and 'perfect competition' thus effectively begging the question.

The article, though ostensibly critical of Marshall, owed him an unacknowledged debt, although the vital considerations concerning potential competition and barriers to entry, on which Marshall had focused, were swept aside. What Sraffa actually needed was oligopoly theory, and it is ironic that what Marshall had to say about oligopoly was much more helpful than the 1930s material following Sraffa. The article also engaged in the kind of Ivory Tower empiricism [70] which suggested that the careful lessons of Marshall on this score had not been learnt and, in making the point that there was no industry supply curve under 'monopoly', merely reiterated a point that Marshall had essentially realized and sought, unsuccessfully, to deal with via the device of the Representative Firm. However, the very concept of the Representative Firm was itself subject to severe criticism by Robbins.

Robbins

The Representative Firm was virtually eliminated from the literature[71] by Lionel (later Lord) Robbins in an article published in the *Economic Journal*, 1928.[72]

Marshall had employed the concept of the Representative Firm in two ways. Firstly, because of the ambiguous nature of the industry supply curve, an ambiguity which led to his opposition to elasticity of supply as a counterpart to elasticity of demand, it was a device to indicate the way in which price and output might respond to an increase in demand. It was to be identified, on the basis of knowledge of a particular industry, as a firm judged to be typical in that context; and knowledge of its cost opportunities would indicate its likely response to a change in demand.

Secondly, the Representative Firm was employed in relation to Marshall's analysis of entry. Entrepreneurs outside an industry, who were considering entry into that industry, would look at the profitability of what they judged to be a representative firm, in order to decide whether entry was likely to be advantageous. The Representative Firm was then, in essence, an informational device.

Robbins, by focusing on the difficulties of actually recognizing such a firm (and Marshall had too easily assumed, it is true, that his detailed industrial knowledge was typical of economists),[73] and employing a misconceived argument in terms of mean values, diverted attention from the point about entry. Moreover, quite unintentionally, he also eliminated from the literature the habitual employment of the

concept of a distribution of firms (although Shove later emphasized the value of this in the course of his rearguard action)[74] despite the fact that he conceded the influence on costs of variations in the quality of management.[75] Robbins thus paved the way for the assumption of uniform costs which characterized the 1930s literature and eliminated from it the Marshallian entrepreneur searching for cost reductions.

Robbins's critique was, in fact, essentially an exercise in Austrian equilibrium *conditions* and was, in truth, irrelevant to the Representative Firm concept it was criticizing. Nonetheless, by simply bypassing the problems that the Representative Firm was supposed to solve, it helped to pave the way for the world of costless omniscience of the 1930s.

Clapham had earlier criticized parts of economics for lack of empirical content,[76] but the Robbins critique succeeded in removing a halfway house between empiricism and theory, and in so doing cleared the way for the abandonment of much that was valuable in Marshall's world. Robbins himself was undoubtedly sincere in denying any desire to criticize Marshall for the sake of it, but the success of his critique suggests that others were really very tired of Marshall.

Robertson and Shove

D.H. Robertson and G.F. Shove attempted, in articles in the *Economic Journal*, 1930,[77] to fight a rearguard action. Unfortunately, this was far from successful, laying them, especially Robertson, open to further criticism from Sraffa.

Robertson in effect gave away the two most important Marshallian cards by accepting that 'competition' and 'perfect competition' were interchangeable and by conceding also that what was sought was a single-exit solution for the 'firm' rather than the complex analysis of possibilities which Marshall had envisaged.

Shove was a good deal more successful. In particular, he spotted the advantage being taken of the ambiguity of 'competition' and he urged, in true Marshallian style, that there was path-dependency rather than a single time-less point of equilibrium.

But these were sporadic rearguard actions: the ground had been cleared for an entirely different approach to the behaviour of firms. In essence, the rules of the debate had been changed so as to eliminate, before it started, many considerations – including such issues as the localization of firms and the supersession of dominant firms – which Marshall had considered relevant to such discussions.

The 1930s material – imperfect competition and monopolistic competition

No useful purpose would be served by detailing the contents of Joan Robinson's *Imperfect Competition*,[78] which are fairly well-known; Edward H. Chamberlin's *Monopolistic Competition*[79] is very much less well-read (though much cited) but space precludes a detailed description of its content. However, there are a number of points about the material in these two books which should be made and which are relevant to the discussion which follows.

1. Joan Robinson

Perhaps the first point to emphasize in relation to the Robinson book is that it neither contained, nor led to, empirical work. The overriding theme of the book, as its author has frankly admitted, was to show what she regarded as the misallocation inherent in capitalism, and the all-pervasiveness of 'exploitation' by which was meant that there existed a divergence between average and marginal revenue product in equilibrium.[80] As Chamberlin pointed out, the exploitation argument was in fact bogus – it smuggled in a value implication but was applicable to the earnings of all factors including capital and entrepreneurship.[81] But there should be no doubt about the overriding ideological aim. (It was later coupled with an unpleasant hostility towards Alfred Marshall, apparently because Marshall disapproved of Marx.[82])

Joan Robinson's ingenious book owed something to Sraffa, a large debt to Kahn, and a small but significant debt to Pigou. The first two debts are well-recognized. But the case of Pigou is perhaps worth emphasizing. There is an article in the *Economic Journal* of 1928 by Pigou[83] in which he drained the Representative Firm of content by making it the 'equilibrium firm'. From this it was a short step to uniformity of firms as in Joan Robinson's book. In the same article Pigou formally identified competition with a situation in which price equals average cost equals marginal cost.[84] Of course, there were other influences as well – Yntema, Harrod, Schneider, Stackelberg, Viner, Zeuthen and Amoroso are all mentioned by Joan Robinson. But the Cambridge influences were of more central importance.

This, though interesting as intellectual history, is however beside the point for our present purposes. What is central – and very curious – is that this apparatus should have been misunderstood to represent a theory of the firm. It really is very puzzling. On the one hand we have a mass of relevant material in Marshall which fell out of sight, apparently through the mistaken use of Occam's Razor; on the other we have the tangency 'solution' arrived at, as Chamberlin pointed out, by definition.[85] From this book economists adopted a strange over-emphasis on the first derivative of the revenue function[86] and a curious neglect of such fundamentally important matters as advertising and product differentiation.

Perhaps most strangely of all, they conflated Joan Robinson's contribution – which was in truth a part of the Cambridge welfare economics tradition – with that of Chamberlin.

2. Edward H. Chamberlin

In total contrast, Chamberlin's starting point was the power of an entrepreneur to differentiate a product as part of competitive strategy. Again in contrast to Joan Robinson, who acknowledged a great debt to Sraffa, Chamberlin's aim was to undermine the free shuffling between 'competition' and 'perfect competition' and to try to deal explicitly with the problem of oligopoly. Indeed it has been argued, I think rightly, that he was interested in conditions of disequilibrium not of static equilibrium,[87] and in unorganized markets.[88] Another point of contrast is that Chamberlin's work led on to empirical work,[89] partially encouraged by his refusal to draw simple conclusions.

But although Chamberlin's work was much more forward-looking than that of Robinson it was emphatically *not* a theory of the firm. Chamberlin approached the matter from the point of view of market structure. From his point of view this was not at all unreasonable: he did not regard the firm as irrelevant[90] but he saw his work as building on that of Marshall, not supplanting it.[91]

It is therefore puzzling that others should have come to regard his work as constituting a theory of the firm (and even more puzzling that they should have regarded his work as more or less identical with that of Mrs Robinson) while neglecting his use of average curves in the Marshallian tradition which were, as he himself emphasized, far more useful in interpreting business decisions than the marginal curves.[92]

Clearly the way in which this material was assimilated by economists reflects some particular methodological preferences, in both Britain and the United States, which require examination.

The methodological choices

In discussing theory choice it is useful to follow Lakatos's distinction between 'internal' and 'external' reasons for choice.[93] Internal reasons are those associated with the whole process of scientific evaluation and theory acceptance, and the logic accepted by scientists; external reasons are historical pressures and accidents which have not been incorporated into the philosophy of the history of science which seeks to explain theory choice.

Internal reasons

Perhaps the main characteristic of the methodological position adopted is that economists were determined to ignore Marshall's warning that 'every plain and simple doctrine as to the relations between cost of production, demand and value is necessarily false, and the greater the appearance of lucidity which is given to it by skilful exposition, the more mischievous it is. A man is likely to be a better economist if he trusts to his common sense, and practical instincts, than if he professes to study the theory of value and is resolved to find it easy.'[94]

Secondly, it is clear that the Lakatosian criterion for choosing between rival Scientific Research Programmes was not used by economists; the new research programme certainly had no 'excess empirical content'.[95] Joan Robinson's work had no empirical content. Chamberlin's led to empirical work on structure but this was aside from the main body of theory which was presented to fledgling economists shorn of empirical attachments.

Essentially the choice made was to opt for a methodological stance which was thought to be as close to physics as possible. This had two particular implications. Firstly, much of Marshall's treatment could be regarded as 'engineering' rather than 'physics' and could thus be disregarded. Secondly, competition theory was to be developed as part of a theory matrix (Kuhn's Paradigm) so that economics would possess a central core of elegant and mutually consistent theories. Occam's Razor assisted in this process of trimming, but it was really subsidiary to the main decision. Arguably there was a confusion inherent in all this; Joan Robinson, in particular, was perfectly frank about the desire for 'abstract' rather than 'realistic'

analysis[96] but hostility towards 'realistic models' seems to have obscured the need for testable (and tested) implications of the theory if some kind of economic counterpart of physics were to be developed. Nonetheless, the desire for a coherent body of theory covering all aspects of at least microeconomic behaviour seems clear enough, and in this connection it may be noted that *Imperfect Competition* was very much in the spirit of general equilibrium analysis. It should also be noted that the influence of Hicks, who was already the leading economic theorist in the United Kingdom, should not be neglected. I am not suggesting that Hicks approved the end result of the new constructions in value theory;[97] but it does not seem to me that he thought the methodological stance upon which they were based to be misconceived. For their part, those espousing what Professor Shackle has called 'The New Establishment in Value Theory' seemed impressed by the whole Hicksian approach to theory, culminating in *Value and Capital* of 1939. This conflation however requires some further explanation. It may be felt that the real choice lay between Partial and General Equilibrium; that the Sraffa[98] critique showed that it was not possible to have (i) partial equilibrium, (ii) (perfect) competition, and (iii) decreasing costs, and that Sraffa chose to retain (i) and (iii). This seems to me, however, to lead towards a misleading contrast. Firstly, there is surely no doubt that the real target of Sraffa's critique was Marshall, and Marshall's work embraced both general and partial equilibrium approaches, his hesitations about general equilibrium being on the score of difficulty over realistic content.[99] A general/partial choice did not therefore involve taking a particular stance *vis-à-vis* Marshall whose emphasis, in any case, inclined to partial equilibrium. Secondly, Sraffa opted to combine elements (i) and (iii), despite the fact that his most cogent criticisms were of (i), presumably because this choice promised a way forward to quick determinate conclusions, a promise fulfilled by Mrs Robinson. (General equilibrium was also subversive of Pigou's welfare economics.) But the kind of partial equilibrium approach adopted, though offering such results, belonged to the same theoretical family as general equilibrium, as the work of Arrow and Hahn[100] has ultimately shown. Despite Hicks's own concern over the wreckage of the supply curve, and his consequent decision to stay with (approximately) perfect competition,[101] the real contrast, *as far as the theory of the firm is concerned*, is not between general and partial equilibrium but between general and partial equilibrium on the one side and growth, uncertainty and *dis*equilibrium on the other. General and partial equilibrium are part of the same (Lakatosian) Scientific Research Programme, which displaced Marshall's own approach based on studying firms.

In the activities of the new theorists there was a sort of intellectual self-assurance that the Philosopher's Stone could be grasped by anyone bold enough to adopt the methodological approach which Marshall had earlier ruled out. Marshall held that there is no substitute for a good knowledge of firms; the Cambridge economists of the 1930s almost seem to have adopted the view that it was *irrelevant* and all that was needed was some Euclid. There was a search for complete generality at the cost of implicit theorizing.[102]

Such an approach naturally led logically to the important methodological decision to ignore the information needs of the organizations whose behaviour was to

be predicted. To the view that market structure could safely be analysed without firms, and a preference for looking through the large end of the telescope, so to speak, there was added a disregard, as already noted, of the empirical aspects. Not only was there no testing; there seems to be little sign that it was ever contemplated. Although economists had ostensibly opted for prediction rather than description, the new theory provided very few empirical predictions and there was no attempt to test them. It need hardly be said that there was no criticism of assumptions; there was also a cavalier attitude not only to factual material, which would rapidly become obsolete, but also to those devices, on which Marshall had laid such stress, by which the firm obtained information.[103] This was true of both accountancy and work study.

This was all consistent with the emphasis on generality. There was no entrepreneur and, as Brian Loasby has remarked, 'there is no need for any of the apparatus of inquiry, communication and control. ... It is all to be condemned as (according to taste) organizational slack, x-inefficiency, wastes of competition, or monopolistic misallocation. There is not even any reason for the existence of firms.'[104]

We were thus presented with the ironical result that, the New Establishment in Value Theory having abolished the supply curve,[105] attention had to be turned to the firm – but there was no firm.

External reasons

While internal reasons predominated in the theory choice that was made, there were also external reasons favouring such choice. One undoubted element was a belief that the new theory showed that 'excess capacity' and 'capitalism' were inextricably linked, thus 'showing' that misallocation was inherent in capitalism.[106] There may not be much of this left now, following the critique by Demsetz,[107] but it is true that in the 1930s it was influential. More recently, Professor Joan Robinson has claimed that imperfect competition theory was developed to explain the prevalence of excess capacity working in the 1930s slump.[108] The desire to construct a theory of the firm without any firms may also have been influenced by a dislike of 'trade';[109] there was also the danger that if the theory of the firm related to real firms, businessmen might know better than academics. Marshall would have regarded this as both reasonable and helpful – his desire to have his *Principles* read by businessmen reflected a belief in the value of a two-way traffic in ideas. Such a belief does not seem to have survived Marshall.

There was also a tremendous intellectual self-confidence. Intellectual morale, so to speak, seems to have been very high; this at least is the only reasonable explanation for regarding the mathematical triviality of the tangency 'solution' as 'an exciting discovery'.[110]

The outcome

Whatever the balance of external and internal forces, the end result of all this was the virtually universal adoption as a 'theory of the firm' of something which is best viewed, as Latsis has argued, as a degeneration of Marshall's work.[111] Since Joan Robinson's version of this 'New Establishment' has received much more attention, oligopoly was swept under the carpet by the incorporation in the average revenue

curves of firms of the reactions of their competitors – something which was logically inexcusable but which was apparently accepted without much protest.[112] (It is arguable that the particular logical slip involved would have been detected earlier if the theory had not been so totally divorced from empiricism.)

The approach from the large end of the telescope, so to speak, giving a compact view of a diverse body of institutions without paying attention to the micro-constituents of that view, could still have produced fruitful results if the end-product of this theorizing had had empirical content and if it had contained a genuine theory of the firm at all. This certainly seems arguable even though, as we shall see, there is a view that the whole approach amounts to a misconceived attempt to ape natural science.

The puzzle remains however – and I make no apology for returning to this – of why it was that this material, especially in the Robinson version, should have been followed to the point where it became the overriding orthodoxy. Whatever one's reservations about Professor Robinson's treatment she can hardly be blamed for the way it was followed. One might suppose that it was without any critics in the 1930s. This was not however the case.

Criticism of the 'New Establishment' – Hayek, Coase, and Hutchison

Hayek

Hayek's critique[113] breaks down into three related parts. Firstly, there was the idea of a 'misplaced wholism'. This had led, in his view, to a global approach, and to a theory of the firm which did not find it necessary to deal with firms. This particular line of criticism – that theory must be built up from small organisms – is difficult to accept in its entirety because it would lead us to reject the whole of macroeconomics. But it may well help to explain what went wrong with the theory of the firm.

Hayek's attack on microeconomic theory for starting from the wrong end of the telescope, by looking at broad aggregates rather than individual decision-taking units, broadened out into an important critique of the adoption of natural science methodology. At the centre of Hayek's position is the following proposition: the methods of natural science, because they are successful in natural science, give people the idea of applying them to society. But society is the product of evolutionary processes resulting from the reaction of *individual* members of society to localized knowledge. (This knowledge is so extensive, *and* so diffused, that no one could ever have sufficient knowledge to *plan* society; and the very desire to plan society springs from a misconceived fundamental premise that something planned must be superior to something which has evolved – misconceived because evolutionary processes draw on a range of individual stocks of knowledge which the planner – trying to look at a *whole* – can never possess.) Viable forms of microeconomic theory must start from a recognition of the fundamental role of *individual* knowledge and its evolution as it affects microeconomic decision-taking units. Secondly, and in the light of this, the obsession of theorists with such concepts as the elasticity of substitution, as broad characteristics of whole markets, is totally misplaced and results from an attempt to reproduce in the context of the

social sciences the type of constructs found helpful in the natural sciences where the problem of knowledge is not a central issue.

This leads, then, to the third plank of Hayek's position which was to emphasize the vital importance of knowledge in equilibration which had been increasingly neglected since Marshall's death. He attacked the assumption of costless omniscience, perceiving correctly that perfect competition was not competition at all, and emphasized that learning is a condition of equilibrium. The assumption that subjectively received data coincided with objective fact obscured the vital role of the supply of knowledge in the move to equilibrium. This in turn led to neglect of the fundamental role of markets as knowledge-gathering and knowledge-diffusing mechanisms and thus to the leftist positions which encouraged espousal of Imperfect Competition theory because it stressed an apparent shortcoming in the market mechanism.

Coase

Although, as we shall see, Coase was by no means immune to the temptation to play the game according to the rules laid down by the New Establishment, he did publish one key article[114] which should have caused the profession to think. He examined the fundamental question 'Why have firms at all?'. His answer was that firms come into existence as an informational device in those areas where the cost of using the price mechanism may be too high. The analysis was hardly complete: it failed to take account of the market power which could offset high internal information costs, at least in the short run. But it should have attracted more attention than it did; it was reprinted, it is true, but in conjunction with materials expounding a theory of the firm which contained no firms.[115]

Hutchison

In an article in the *Review of Economic Studies* of 1934–5,[116] Hutchison pointed out the tautological nature of the analysis. The equation of marginal cost with marginal revenue had no empirical content and was simply tautological deriving from the profit maximizing definition. Hutchison's criticism, like that of Hayek, derived from a background in philosophy; this may perhaps explain the scant attention which was paid to it. For the New Establishment became indeed established as scientific orthodoxy.

The establishment of imperfect competition as orthodoxy

In considering the establishment of a particular body of thought as an orthodoxy, two concepts associated with the work of T.S. Kuhn[117] are very valuable. The first is the concept of 'Normal Science'. This is the activity of pursuing research within the framework of a particular matrix of interrelated theories (or a paradigm), solving puzzles but not questioning the dominance of the paradigm even though anomalies may begin to accumulate. The second is the idea that the establishment of a scientific orthodoxy results in a re-writing of textbooks in terms of the new paradigm. Both of these ideas turn out to be illuminating in the present context.

Normal Science within the Imperfect Competition paradigm

(i) *The UK* A search through the British journals reveals a good deal of activity within the new paradigm. In the *Economic Journal*, as might be expected, it was particularly in evidence. The Marshallian paradigm assumed the role of a declining Scientific Research Programme in the Lakatosian schema although there were still a number of articles, particularly industry studies, which could be associated with it.[118] The new style was represented in particular by Pigou (whose substantive differences with the New Establishment were, in practice, minimal), Harrod and Kahn. There was some sign of professional unease[119] but it did not spread far. Nonetheless the New Establishment did not have a monopoly in the *Economic Journal*. This contrasts with the situation in that expression of the younger thrusting academics of the period, the *Review of Economic Studies*, which had been founded in 1933 and which reflected most completely the commitment to what may be called, at some slight risk of unfairness to its inspirer, 'Hicksian theory'. Here we have Normal Science within the new paradigm completely predominant. There were contributions in particular by Joan Robinson, Hicks, Kahn, Lerner, Meade, Machlup, and A.L. Bowley as well as Chamberlin. More surprisingly, we find Normal Science exercises from Coase and Rothschild, both later associated with broader approaches. We even find a Marxist economist, Kalecki, engaging in Normal Science work within the new paradigm. In the period 1933–50 I found, in addition to Hutchison's contribution, only one article (by D.C. Hague)[120] which ran counter to the prevailing orthodoxy; and this occurred only in the issue for 1949–50. The influence of Hicks in the *R.E. Stud* seems to have been strong, if unsought by him. It arose from his deserved standing as the leading theorist in the United Kingdom and it affected the way in which other economists attempted to tackle theoretical problems.

A more active figure was Kaldor, then associated with LSE rather than Cambridge.[121] The LSE organ *Economica* however remained much more eclectic and sceptical than the *Economic Journal*, let alone the *R.E. Stud*. It certainly contained Normal Science exercises by writers like Kaldor, Hicks, Joan Robinson, Rothschild, Machlup, Pigou, Bain and Coase. At the same time it contained a number of articles critical of the new approach – especially one highly effective piece by Bauer – and the list of authors here again includes Coase. The appearance of Coase in both lists illustrates the extent to which even those who were inclined to be critical had been influenced by the New Establishment.

Marshallian analysis was progressively driven underground, though it influenced the Oxford Studies, and it is arguable that it emerged ultimately in the business schools and other 'intellectually unwashed' places.

(ii) *The US* Examination of the journal material produced in the United States indicates a much less monolithic result. In the *Quarterly Journal of Economics* it is true that, under Chamberlin's influence, Normal Science, at least within the Monopolistic Competition paradigm, was the rule. But even here the empirical implications received attention and development, particularly within the work of Bain; and it would probably be true to say that Normal Science in the US had an empirical

aspect – partly, perhaps, because of the continuing pre-occupation with anti-trust problems – which was eliminated from the UK version.

The *American Economic Review* fittingly, since it was founded under the aegis of American Institutionalism, was slow to abandon the older style of economics and in only just over half the issues between 1930 and 1950 did it carry material which was unambiguously Normal Science within the new paradigm. It is not surprising that the *A.E.R.* was the journal containing Lester's celebrated attack on the marginalist paradigm, although it was successfully repelled by Machlup and Stigler.[122]

Indeed, despite the tenacity of the older (Marshallian) approach, and the criticisms later made of the new one, there is no doubt that the latter triumphed. This is illustrated by the way in which Sweezy, later known as a Marxist economist, is to be found engaging in Normal Science within the new paradigm, in the United States, just as Kalecki did in this country.[123]

The textbook establishment of the paradigm

One of the paradoxes of this stage of the establishment of the new paradigm is that although the American journal literature was much more diffuse and critical than the British, it was American textbooks which played a major role in diffusing the New Establishment to the rising generation in the 1940s and 1950s.

One of the first textbooks to embody the new approach (despite his later reservations) was Boulding's of 1941. The book by Tarshis dates from 1947 and that by Eastham (a British writer this time) from 1950.[124] The first edition of Samuelson is 1948 but Stigler's text dates from 1942.[125]

Amongst later textbooks there were more British representatives. While the first edition of Leftwich – itself an American text – is dated 1955, the first edition of Stonier and Hague is 1953 and of Ryan is 1958.[126] These last two both reflect the kind of theory being taught in London in the 1950s.

Of course, older style texts survived; the first edition of Benham dates from 1938.[127] But they were outnumbered far more clearly in the textbook market than in the field of journal articles. It would probably not be too much to say that Marshallian theory was routed; Robertson's *Lectures*, dating from 1945–6, indicate a significant retreat from the position adopted by their author in the debate in the 1930 *Economic Journal*.[128]

The new material had a quasi-technical appeal with geometry as a compromise between words and algebra. This undoubtedly helped to explain its success – it was accessible to the non-mathematical student with effort, but not to every businessman – and to ensure, too, the success of the textbooks which embodied it. For it was this on which they concentrated. The empirical material, which had survived in the American, if not the British, journals, simply dropped out of sight. Indeed, such was the success of the New Establishment that it caused some second thoughts even amongst those who had been in the textbook vanguard.[129]

Consequences of paradigmatic triumph

1. The lost Marshallian insights

It will be apparent from the previous discussion of Marshall how much had been lost in all this. Perhaps the most obvious loss was his emphasis on the vital role of management and on the necessity of entrepreneurial energy, 'elasticity', and liking for hard work.[130] Managerial skills, as already noted, do not exist in the New Establishment. The entrepreneur was displaced by the exploitation model. Redundancy of the entrepreneur may well have suited the outlook of the constructors of a model designed to show 'inevitable exploitation' but it was not helpful to an understanding of the economic system. What role is there in the new kind of theory for 'the broad faculties of judgement, promptness, resource, carefulness and steadfastness of purpose'[131] which the entrepreneur required?

The Marshallian vision that under the reality of a supply price was the entrepreneur groping for knowledge in a situation in which costs were neither fixed nor uniform, and taking complex decisions with limited information,[132] was lost. Indeed, the very complex nature of business costs – the difficulties of internal knowledge, and of joint cost assignment[133] – was simply swept under the carpet. The actual nature of cost (and revenue) curves was no longer interesting and the fact that business information for decisions typically came in the form of average rather than marginal values was irrelevant to most writers (with the exception of Chamberlin). Marshall's understanding of the evolving nature of an industrial structure – the trees of the forest – was simply dismissed as a 'fudge' to deal with the existence of Increasing Returns; joint stock companies, it was confidently asserted, did not go through such a life cycle, and the possibility, envisaged by Marshall, that even if they survived they would lose their 'elasticity'[134] was not even considered.

The Representative Firm, as already noted, had been, so to speak, liquidated; the implications of the concept for entry were disregarded and the possibility that it might be useful after the supposedly novel destruction of the supply curve does not even seem to have been considered.[135]

The empirical basis of the analysis was lost – 'firms' in Marshall's writings are more recognizable as such, despite the date of much of the material, than the 'firms' occurring in the 1930s literature. It went without saying that his belief in the suggestive power of economic history to provide hypotheses was disregarded and his careful empiricism[136] was replaced by a cavalier 'Ivory Tower empiricism', generalizing from the most casual information, and this only when, as a last resort, empirical questions could not be avoided.

It is true that there is something of a methodological paradox about Marshall's attitude, in that he preached empiricism more than he practised it, but there is no doubt that he was a patient and careful observer of business practice. He thus realized the complexity of business practice; and from this he concluded that monopoly price was *not* necessarily higher than competitive price,[137] although it came to be so *by definition* in the 1930s material. His whole emphasis on marketing and selling costs (even extending to bribes to buyers)[138] and their distinction from production costs disappeared, to be replaced by the bland assumption of a given

downward sloping average revenue curve – at least in the textbooks and in Professor Robinson's work. Shove attempted to keep in use the Marshallian distinction between the general and the particular market;[139] but this disappeared except for relics to be found in the analysis of discriminating monopoly.

Almost all the emphasis was now on simple one-way relationships and unique positions of equilibrium. Despite Chamberlin's own reluctance to draw simple conclusions, succeeding generations displayed no such caution. They had no time for Marshall's belief in the importance of a detailed case-by-case approach; the search was on for generality, with physics as the model. In the process, time, to which Marshall had attached such importance in relation to value questions, simply dropped from view except in relation to a distinction between long-run and short-run supply. Marshall had seen time as of vital importance in relation to the generation and dissemination of information, but information itself ceased to be of interest in a world of costless omniscience so that Marshall's related stress on accountancy, scientific management and business education simply dropped from view as well.

Information about technology was no longer of interest: the manager (who did not really exist anyway) was assumed to have full and costless information about technology. Indeed, Marshall's overriding interest in technical progress ceased to have influence. (Of course, one could argue that this was a matter on which British academics were reflecting the persistent complacency of British industry. But had they realized this, their other preconceptions might have induced them to remedy the situation!) Marshall was misrepresented, and thus sealed-off from succeeding generations, much as a Scientific Revolution in Kuhn's schema seals off a discarded paradigm. In particular, his view of competition was misrepresented so that although he held that 'though monopoly and free competition are ideally wide apart, yet in practice they shade into one another by imperceptible degrees: there is an element of monopoly in nearly all competitive business: and … nearly all [important] monopolies … hold much of their power by an uncertain tenure; so that they would lose it ere long, if they ignored the possibilities of competition direct and indirect,'[140] he was 'credited' with a perfectly competitive model.

In part, the explanation, especially from the 1940s onwards, lay in ignorance. His great *Industry and Trade* was not read.[141] But amongst some of those who should have known his work there seems to have been an almost personalized element of animosity.[142]

2. *Single Exit Situation Determinism*

The converse of the loss of so much insight was the establishment of a tautological approach which Latsis, in a profound article,[143] has called Single Exit Situation Determinism. It is Single Exit because there is only *one* possible outcome, and it is Situation Determinism because the outcome is laid down *a priori* in the rules of the model.

In the models put forward in the 1940s and 1950s textbooks we have entrepreneurs without functions and decision-makers without decision procedures. In fact, it simply is not possible to incorporate entrepreneurs into single exit models so the whole use of the term in this context borders on the farcical. We have instantaneous

implementation of decisions and a strange synthetic motive called profit maximization. Knowledge is redundant. Even Chamberlin – at least in the version handed down to students – posited no special entrepreneurial knowledge requirement for product differentiation. Indeed, Latsis charges that the analysis is merely a variant of perfect competition. Of the general validity of his characterization of the analysis there seems no question and it helps to highlight some of the highly improper uses to which the analysis has been put, especially in relation to monopoly.

His explanation for its continued popularity is that it is favoured because of its mathematical basis and because of the autonomy which it possesses, and he notes its continuing appeal, citing the work of Sylos Labini. But its retention cannot be justified either on the grounds of predictive power or even of retrodiction, and this is a serious problem if one accepts that the demarcation between science and non-science is essentially predictive power.

The development of anomalies

In the Kuhnian view of the history of science, a ruling paradigm – as this material certainly was in the 1940s and 1950s and still very largely is today – is likely to be affected by the emergence of anomalies i.e. phenomena which it is not able to explain, or falsification of its predictions. While this concept does not transplant very easily to economics, it is noticeable that there did develop, from the late 1940s, a body of criticism of the ruling theory which shows remarkable vitality. Lester's contribution has already been mentioned, and since this is well-known it may be more useful to discuss some other criticisms.

An article which embodied a number of criticisms was published in 1947 by K.W. Rothschild[144] and, to judge from the test of reprinting, it found a responsive chord. Rothschild was concerned by the single-exit nature of the models, and by the neglect of oligopoly, of non-price competition, of coalition pricing, of the active pursuit of market power including the use of inter-locking directorates and of lobbying. He was unimpressed by the 'long-run profit maximization' alibi for behaviour which departed from marginalist principles, and he realized that full-cost behaviour could well be rational. He was also particularly concerned about the lack of empirical implications of the ruling theory.

Another set of criticisms – not however ones designed to deal with the lack of firms – stemmed from Chicago economists and resulted in what might be called the 'Perfect Competition Counter Revolution'[145] – though it is doubtful whether perfect competition ever enjoyed the pre-1930 dominance which this title implies. In particular, it was argued that perfect competition had a greater predictive power than imperfect competition.

Stigler, amongst the Chicago economists, was particularly critical of the kinked demand curve part of the new orthodoxy, and attacked it in two ways which were outside its own rules – criticizing its assumptions as naive and testing its implications.[146]

The emphasis on the latter, under the influence of Milton Friedman's declared methodological position, was important in the use of perfect competition to attack the New Establishment; unfortunately the protagonists of perfect competition placed

themselves in the position of saying that only theories of perfect competition and monopoly were required, and which was suitable could be decided *ex post*, thus undermining their emphasis on *pre*diction.

A survey written at the end of the 1960s[147] drew upon the critical literature to highlight four persistent causes of discontent with the ruling theory. These were dissatisfaction with the simple profit maximization motive, unhappiness at the disregard of uncertainty, neglect of the internal organization of the firm, and the realization that satisficing behaviour could be perfectly rational under conditions of uncertainty.

However, the recognition and accumulation of persistent anomalies is not, in Kuhnian terms, sufficient to bring about a paradigm-change or Scientific Revolution. It is also necessary that there should be a rival paradigm or, in Lakatosian terms, a rival Scientific Research Programme. In order to understand what has happened so far it is necessary to ask about the existence of such contenders.

The rise of rival research programmes

In the Lakatosian approach to the philosophy of the history of science, rival research programmes compete. The burden of the Latsis article referred to above is that behaviourism constitutes such a rival research programme. However, it is in fact one of several such contenders.

The rival research programmes which have arisen since 1945 can, I think, be grouped in the following broad categories: (i) full cost; (ii) games theory; (iii) behaviourism (including associated work on technical progress and on managerialism); (iv) theories of the growth of the firm (including work based on business history).

The first, springing from the pre-war activity of the Oxford Economists Research Group, was the full-cost approach.[148] This contained a number of specifically Marshallian elements, particularly the notion of business decisions on the basis of average cost, an interest in what actually went on in real firms, and a stress on the conditional nature of monopoly power. Unfortunately, it became bogged down in alleged logical deficiencies concerning the mark-up on average cost, and ultimately failed to find favour with economists, at least outside business schools where its ability to be placed on the engineering side of the physics/engineering divide made it attractive. Nevertheless, it clearly still has adherents.[149]

Chronologically the second rival research programme was games theory, stemming from the seminal work of Morgenstern and von Neumann, and embodied in important contributions by Shubik.[150] This had a number of advantages over the single-exit situation-determinism model, not least the multiplicity of exits, but it dealt with the use made of information, while neglecting its gathering, so that it was somewhat incomplete as a theory of the firm. Much of what a firm exists to supply is taken for granted in this theoretical approach, and its predictive power was extremely limited.

The most important rival is however that which Latsis stressed – behaviourism. It lays critical stress on the importance of knowledge (although it neglects Hayek's insight concerning the amount of knowledge which a price summarizes) and on the limited availability of that knowledge. It examines the making of decisions on the

basis of that limited knowledge, and emphasizes the use of search procedures, which is thoroughly Marshallian, as is the idea that demand and costs may be interdependent. Its explanatory power is high – not only in relation to firms but (perhaps even more) in relation to public sector bureaucracy. Unfortunately, its *pre*dictive power is less good. It is not, it should be stressed, without predictive power; in fact it performs better than conventional theory in relation to the response of firms to taxation, and Cyert and March have managed to obtain a high rate of predictive success.[151]

The work of Cyert and March also provides the firm-related aspects of the work of Nelson, Winter and Schuette on technical progress.[152] They are concerned with the search for new technology as a signal is triggered, e.g. the rate of return falls below some target. The research is not however primarily concerned itself with what happens inside firms; rather the authors, as they acknowledge[153] are engaged in a highly abstract 'as if' exercise, as a means of re-introducing the abandoned Marshallian concept of continual technology search.[154] The work proceeds at such a high level of abstraction, and distillation of reportage of computer output, that it is very difficult to be sure where this can lead in terms of a viable theory of the firm.

Of course there are good reasons why a multiple exit approach should have low predictive power; and it is a merit of the behavioural approach that it rejects single exit solutions to the incorporation of knowledge because of the very nature of decision-taking procedures.

A major factor in the behavioural approach has been the rediscovery of managerial motivation, and this is a feature of the related theories of the growth of the firm such as that of Marris,[155] which offer some fairly clear predictions.[156]

Managerial motivation is also given considerable importance in the work of Chandler[157] which has a rather Marshallian appearance through its links with business history. It seems to this reader, however, that the approach has its roots in American institutionalism, like the work of A.R. Burns;[158] and its theoretical structure – especially the emphasis on technology as affecting organization, originating in Veblen – has found it relatively easy to incorporate the Coasian explanation for the existence of firms, referred to earlier. The work itself makes fascinating reading, and there is no doubt of the value of directing attention to the way in which firms have evolved. Whether, however, it can be regarded as a research programme leading to a viable theory of the firm – particularly as some readers may feel that the emphasis is on *post hoc ergo propter hoc* rather than predictive power, and on illustration rather than quantification – is another question.

The literature of the behavioural theory of the firm has perhaps two particular strengths: its emphasis on empirical aspects, and its stress on the importance of short-run determinants of behaviour. But despite the very considerable merits of this approach it has not triumphed – as a look at the journals and textbooks will confirm. It remains a pretender, and it is arguably weak on the key question of the relationships *between* firms.

Mention should perhaps be made of Kirzner's work on the role of the entrepreneur.[159] While this is a valuable advance upon a view of the economic world involving a Walrasian auctioneer, entrepreneurial choice is deliberately confined

within existing technological and organizational boundaries,[160] and thus an important part of what real firms exist to achieve is excluded from consideration.

Finally it should be emphasized that what we are talking about is the theory of the *firm*; industrial organization studies, dealing with structure in particular, are, as Coase has recently emphasized,[161] no substitute for analysis of firms.

Conclusion

1. Retrospect

The thrust of this paper has been concerned with trying to trace the route by which we arrived at what is, to judge from both textbooks and journals, still the predominant theoretical approach to problems involving firms. The outline of the rival approaches has been necessarily sketchy and nothing has been said of some of the recent variants such as the sales-maximization literature, which is arguably a variant of single-exit situation-determinism. We have seen that economists chose an approach which involved looking through the large end of the telescope, examining market structure without firms. We have seen too that, ostensibly at least, they opted for prediction as against description and for what they believed to be the economic equivalent of physics rather than engineering. In fact, of course, the parallels are far from valid; the 'predictions' were largely of an untestable nature, and there was no real parallel with physics. Moreover, what predictions there were were only of the broadest sort – the qualitative results to be expected from parameter shifts – and implicit theorizing was widespread. An element of wishful thinking was arguably present in the 'perfect competition counter-revolution' while promising areas of research were not pursued.

In explaining what did happen, something can be learnt from the philosophy of the history of science. The Popperian concept of 'methodological tenacity' helps to explain the retention of theories which were difficult to test. The Kuhnian concepts of Normal Science (which Popper has accepted as valid) and of Paradigm help to explain the journal material which flowed from the 1930s value theory. Kuhn's emphasis on methodological sermons (of which I suppose this might be considered in part an example) as symptoms of disquiet is also illuminating. In the transition from the Marshallian approach to the New Establishment in value theory there are elements of a Kuhnian Scientific Revolution – especially if one accepts the Robinsonian claims about explaining 'exploitation' and 'excess capacity'. But there was arguably no *real* crisis – certainly Chamberlin's work reflected none – and the phenomena could also be interpreted in terms of a Lakatosian framework with Marshall's and the new approaches to value as rival Scientific Research Programmes but with the New Establishment version offering more prospect of progress.

Unfortunately, the crucial factors in a Lakatosian 'progressive problem shift' are arguably absent. It *may* be true that the existence of 'exploitation' or 'excess capacity' can be interpreted as 'excess empirical content' which the Lakatosian approach sees as vital in the choice between competing scientific research programmes, but it is really straining the word 'empirical' to do this because there was no testing or information gathering in the process of Programme choice, merely Ivory Tower empiricism of the most casual kind.

Nevertheless, the Lakatosian approach is helpful in dealing with the competition between different theoretical approaches in the 1960s and 1970s which may be viewed as competing Scientific Research Programmes, as Latsis has argued.

2. Knowledge

The crucial weakness of the theoretical approach which still predominates is its neglect of knowledge. Firms do require a lot of information. A crucial factor in oligopoly is knowledge of competitors' costs. One explanation for the willingness of firms to follow price leaders is as a way of economizing on information needs. At almost every juncture, when one considers how firms will respond to changes in internal or external situations, one is confronted with the gathering, processing and utilization of knowledge, and yet to judge from the textbooks we can safely ignore this matter.[162]

3. A way forward?

There is clearly no single way from this morass. However it is salutary to reflect that full-cost pricing can be seen as an information-economizing device, and it is a failure to appreciate this which leads to dismissal of the approach as crude.[163] This in turn suggests that, if knowledge *is* the crucial problem, a theory of the firm based on full-cost pricing may have been too easily disregarded. This possibility is perhaps strengthened by the realization that firms have an observable tendency to collude and that full-cost pricing is an aid to such collusion. Vintage pricing is *not* a serious point against full-cost pricing[164] if we reintroduce the Marshallian time dimension for costs. Nor is the existence of differences in mark-ups of critical importance if we regard average cost as a start from which trial and error *learning*, over *time*, takes place.[165] This in turn leads to the possibility that perhaps too much attention has been paid to price which – as Chamberlin emphasized – is only *one* part of a competitive package.[166]

Perhaps some fusion of behavioural, growth, and full-cost theories may lead to a viable theory of the firm – behavioural and growth theories have at present a number of weaknesses, including relatively unimpressive predictive power, while conventional theory still impresses by giving neat answers and has the ability to rationalize almost anything as *long-run* profit maximization. It will not be easy to displace, and I suspect that behaviourism on its own lacks sufficient strength. But until it is displaced we will continue to place elegance (and ease of teaching) above relevance and explanatory and predictive power.

But because none of the theories of the history of science which I find at all persuasive – Popper, Kuhn, Lakatos – seems to me entirely satisfactory in explaining the development of the theory of the firm, it is very difficult to predict what may happen next. The Popperian concept of methodological tenacity helps to explain why we hang on to a theory in the presence of anomalies; it does not tell us when we will let go. The Kuhnian concept of a paradigm and the Lakatosian concept of a scientific research programme tell us that we will let go when there is a strong rival, but what constitutes 'strength' in the context of economic theory then becomes the central question. In the context of the 1920s and 1930s episodes it proves to be a question which is very difficult to answer. But theory choice

cannot be *explained* by the consent of the scientific community – that would be tautological along lines that Molière would enjoy satirizing[167] and, to date at least, it seems reasonable to take the view that it cannot be explained by 'excess empirical content'. Perhaps future developments, possibly influenced by the methodological writings of Popper and Lakatos, may prove easier to interpret.

Notes

* I am most grateful to J. Creedy, P.S. Johnson and L.C. Skerratt for helpful comments on an initial draft of this paper, and to M. Blaug, C.C. Gallagher, A. Gee and B. Loasby, S. Moss, F.H. Stephen, O.E. Williamson, and other participants in the 1982 York Conference for helpful observations. I am particularly indebted to Scott Moss who emphasized to me the importance of Pigou's 1928 article cited below.

1. For such an attempt see Williams (1978).
2. Mill (1848) pp. 132–54.
3. Babbage (1832).
4. For general discussion of Marshall's work see Frisch (1953), O'Brien (1981) and Loasby (1978).
5. Marshall (1919) p. 512; see also pp. 676–8.
6. Marshall (1919) p. 206 and Apps. B and C.
7. E.g. Marshall (1919) p. 206.
8. Marshall (1919) pp. 185–9, 197–213, 350–94, 465–6, 644; (1920) pp. 278–90, 303, 485.
9. Marshall (1920) p. 284.
10. Marshall (1919) pp. 278–86; (1920) pp. 283–4.
11. Marshall (1920) p. 297.
12. Marshall (1919) pp. 183, 252–5, 263, 329–30, 332–3, 645–7; (1920) pp. 297, 491.
13. Marshall (1919) pp. 172–4, 354–5, 651; (1920) pp. 297–8, 305.
14. Marshall (1919) p. 294; (1920) pp. 292–3, 305.
15. Marshall (1919) pp. 356–60, 557; (1920) pp. 298–300, 308.
16. Marshall (1919) pp. 308–11, 316–17, 322, 324, 325; (1920) p. 301.
17. Marshall (1919) pp. 326–7.
18. Marshall (1919) p. 496; (1920) p. 304.
19. Marshall (1919) pp. 486–91, 666–7.
20. Marshall (1919) p. 428.
21. E.g. Marshall (1920) Bk. IV ch. ix.
22. Marshall (1919) pp. 197–213; (1920) Bk. IV ch. x and pp. 459–61.
23. Marshall (1919) pp. 169–70, 186–7, 197–212, 362, 455–6.
24. Marshall (1920) p. 280. As Brian Loasby has put it, 'Marshallian competition is a Hayekian discovery process' (Loasby, 1982).
25. Marshall (1919) pp. 186–8 and n; (1920) p. 808.
26. Marshall (1919) Bk. II chs i and ii.
27. Marshall (1919) pp. 206–13.
28. Marshall (1919) p. 414.
29. Marshall (1919) pp. 249, 321–2, 594.
30. Marshall (1919) pp. 221–30, 238–42, 376–80, 449n, 594.
31. Marshall (1975) pp. 52–7.
32. Marshall (1919) Bk. II chs i–iv. See also Andrews (1964) pp. 57–60.
33. Marshall (1919) pp. 181, 190–94, 269–88, 424, 426, 458–9, 461–2, 525.
34. Marshall (1919) pp. 195, 458–60.
35. Marshall (1919) Bk. II chs vi and vii.
36. Marshall (1919) pp. 181, 184, 250, 275; (1920) Bk. IV ch. xi, and pp. 501–2.
37. Marshall (1920) pp. 377, 458, 499, 501–2.
38. Marshall (1919) p. 270.
39. Marshall (1919) pp. 181, 185, 406–8.
40. Marshall (1919) pp. 249, 511, 515, 534–6, 539.
41. Marshall (1919) pp. 275–7.
42. Marshall (1919) pp. 413, 425.
43. Marshall (1919) pp. 181, 185, 406; (1920) p. 486.

44. Let profit (∏) = Total Revenue (R(Q)) – Total Cost (C(Q)).
$\Pi = R(Q) - C(Q)$; $d\Pi/dQ = R'(Q) - C'(Q)$; if $d\Pi/dQ = 0$, $R'(Q) = C'(Q)$
$\Pi = \left(\frac{R(Q)}{Q} - \frac{C(Q)}{Q}\right)Q$ is the average cost formulation.
Even if we do not simplify before obtaining the first order condition, it still reduced to $R'(Q) - C'(Q) = 0$.
45. Marshall (1920) p. 487.
46. E.g. Marshall (1919) pp. 397–8, 449–50n. See also the reference to barriers to entry below.
47. Marshall (1919) p. 549; (1920) pp. 374, 457–9, 498.
48. E.g. Marshall (1919) pp. 182, 196.
49. Marshall (1919) pp. 214–34, 336, 343.
50. Robinson, E.A.G. (1931).
51. Marshall (1920) pp. 457–9.
52. Marshall (1919) pp. 314–16, 421–2; (1920) pp. 285–7, 315–16, 457.
53. Penrose (1959) pp. 89n, 257n.
54. Marshall (1919) pp. 244–9, 398, 435, 441–2n, 485; (1920) p. 308.
55. Marshall (1919) p. 420.
56. Marshall (1919) pp. 396–7, 412, 449–50n, 523–4.
57. Marshall (1919) pp. 524.
58. Marshall (1919) pp. 403–4, 406, 438–9, 521–3, 531–4, 536, 597, 626–7.
59. Marshall (1919) pp. 345, 540–41.
60. Marshall (1919) pp. 410–635.
61. Marshall (1919) pp. 485, 567.
62. Marshall (1919) p. 402.
63. Marshall (1919) pp. 399–401.
64. Marshall (1919) pp. 278–80.
65. Marshall (1919) pp. 525, 537–9, 553.
66. Marshall (1919) pp. 442, 481, 516–17.
67. Marshall (1919) p. 336.
68. Marshall (1919) p. 484.
69. Sraffa (1926).
70. Sraffa (1926) p. 543. '*Everyday experience* shows that a very large number of undertakings – and the majority of those which produce manufactured consumers' goods – work under conditions of individual diminishing costs.' (Italics added).
71. Blaug (1978) p. 445.
72. Robbins (1928).
73. Marshall (1919) p. vii.
74. Shove (1930) pp. 94–6.
75. Robbins (1928) pp. 398–9.
76. Clapham (1922).
77. Robertson (1930); Shove (1930). See also Shove (1933) which contained important early criticisms of Joan Robinson's analysis.
78. Robinson, J.V. (1933a).
79. Chamberlin (1933).
80. Robinson, J.V. (1960) pp. 39–45; (1933a) ch. xv; Bishop (1964) p. 37.
81. Chamberlin (1937) pp. 577–8.
82. Robinson, J.V. (1941) p. 234; cf. Shove (1944) pp. 51–61.
83. Pigou (1928); see also Pigou (1932) pp. 789–814.
84. I am particularly grateful to Scott Moss for his emphasis on the importance of Pigou's article.
85. Chamberlin (1937) p. 561.
86. Chamberlin (1937) p. 558.
87. Skinner (1981) p. 131. See also the striking results from 'market clearing experiments' reported in Chamberlin (1948). I am grateful to John Creedy for this reference.
88. Loasby (1981) p. 16; Robinson, R. (1971) p. 34. For a valuable discussion of points of contrast between the Chamberlin and Robinson approaches see Loasby (1971) pp. 875–8. Professor Robinson insists (1960, p. 222) that there is no difference.
89. Bain (1964).
90. Skinner (1981) pp. 127, 131–2.
91. Chamberlin (1961) pp. 532–40.
92. (1937, p. 558). This may reflect Chamberlin's interest in the very real problem of railway rates.

93. Lakatos and Musgrave (1970). See O'Brien (1976) for a summary of the Lakatosian and Kuhnian approaches.
94. Marshall (1920) p. 368.
95. Of course if one accepts Joan Robinson's assertion that Pigou's work led many to expect a world of full capacity working, *even in the midst of depression* (Robinson, 1969, p. vi) then the 'excess capacity' element in *Imperfect Competition* can be seen as involving 'excess empirical content'. But it seems to me that this 1969 view cannot be taken seriously against the background of world *dis*equilibrium forty years earlier (see also Loasby, 1971, p. 875). Alternatively, one could cite Arthur Burns, *The Decline of Competition* (Burns, 1936, p. v), in support of the view that the new approaches at least *promised* to have greater relevance to a world of non-perfect competition. (I am indebted to Mark Blaug for this point.) My own view would be, firstly, that Burns's view was based on a misunderstanding of the import of the new approaches and, secondly, that a *perfectly* competitive view of the world was not firmly established, and thus the new theories did not offer an advance over the theoretical approaches of the great majority of economists.
96. Robinson, J.V. (1933b) p. 124.
97. Hicks (1935). For an acknowledgement of his influence see Robinson, J.V. (1933a) p. vii.
98. Sraffa (1926).
99. Marshall (1925) p. 417.
100. Arrow and Hahn (1971) ch. 6.
101. Hicks (1946) pp. 83–5.
102. Leontief (1937).
103. For Marshall's interest in accountancy and work study see his (1919) pp. 310, 365–9, 606, 610, 840 and Bk. II chs xi-xii generally. Even a commentator both scholarly and sympathetic writes of Marshall's fact-gathering that 'much of the knowledge soon dated, and much suffered from the unreliability of hearsay evidence' – Whitaker in Marshall (1975) p. 57.
104. Loasby (1981) p. 5.
105. A misconception about the *theoretical* significance of the Oxford Studies is that they damaged the 'Marshallian' reliance on the supply curve (Lee, 1981). In fact one of the outstanding characteristics of the Cambridge work in the early 1930s, to which the Oxford work was in some ways *a reaction*, was the destruction of the supply curve about which Marshall, as already noted, had severe reservations himself. See Shackle (1967) and Robinson, J.V. (1932).
106. See Muggeridge (1972) pp. 206–7 for an interesting light on this.
107. Demsetz (1964).
108. Robinson, J.V. (1969) p. vi.
109. On this see Allen (1976) pp. 39–50 and Wiener (1981) pp. 90–94, 130–37, Townsend (1974) p. 65.
110. Robinson, J.V. (1969) p. vi, TR = PQ, TC = CQ where these symbols have the usual meanings (i.e. P = price = average revenue, C = average cost).

$$\frac{dTR}{dQ} = P + Q\frac{dP}{dQ}$$

$$\frac{dTC}{dQ} = C + Q\frac{dC}{dQ}$$

if $\frac{dTR}{dQ} = \frac{dTC}{dQ}$ (first order condition)

then, given that P = C (which it does by definition in equilibrium since all necessary profits are incorporated in the cost curve and only these are earned in equilibrium) then if MC = MR,

$$Q\frac{dP}{dQ} = Q\frac{dC}{dQ}$$

i.e. the *slopes* of the average revenue and average cost curves are equal at the point where the values of average revenue and average cost are equal.

For an acid comment on all this (from an admittedly quite exceptionally acerbic article which totally underestimates Marshall) see Samuelson (1967) pp. 110–11 and for early comment on its economic significance see Shove (1933).
111. Latsis (1972) p. 219.
112. See Triffin (1941) pp. 44–6, 68–70; Robinson, J.V. (1960) p. 228.
113. Hayek (1937), (1941), (1942), (1943), (1944).

114. Coase (1937).
115. Coase himself has complained that the article was 'much cited and little used' – Coase, 1972, p. 63. (I am grateful to O.E. Williamson for this reference.)
116. Hutchison (1934–5). See also Hutchison (1938) pp. 28–30.
117. Kuhn (1970).
118. I am grateful to Professor S.G. Checkland for emphasizing that empirical work was vigorously pursued by Sargant Florence. I am not sure that the work was exactly Marshallian; at the same time he would undoubtedly have been interested by the attempt to provide statistical measures of industry characteristics. For an example of this work see Florence (1948).
119. Durbin (1938); Harrod (1938).
120. Hague (1949–50).
121. Kaldor (1934a), (1934b), (1935).
122. Lester (1946), (1947), (1949); Machlup (1946), (1947); Stigler (1947a). Frank Stephen has pointed out to me that a significant element in Machlup's reply was the exclusion of internal forces specific to the firm from the area of importance – Machlup (1946), pp. 527–8.
123. Sweezy (1939); Kalecki (1939–40).
124. Boulding (1941); Tarshis (1947); Eastham (1950).
125. Stigler (1942) – though Imperfect Competition was not incorporated until the 1946 version – (1946). Samuelson (1948). The latter's *Foundations*, of considerable influence on pure theory, appeared in 1947.
126. Leftwich (1955); Stonier and Hague (1953); Ryan (1958). The inclusion of Stonier and Hague may surprise some readers. But it was undoubtedly influential in its day. It was reprinted annually for some years after publication and, although Longmans records are incomplete, it would seem, according to Professor Hague to whom I am indebted for information on this matter, that the book's sales had exceeded a quarter of a million copies by the early 1970s. (I am grateful to Alec Gee for raising the question of sales of this book.)
127. Benham (1938).
128. Robertson (1957–58).
129. See Boulding (1948) pp. 92–3. 'The marginal analysis has been under considerable fire recently and there is a fairly widespread feeling that the existing theory of the firm is inadequate to serve as a foundation for a "general theory".' Boulding (1942) had also exhibited reservations and stressed the need for more empiricism.
130. Marshall (1920) p. 457.
131. Marshall (1920) p. 312.
132. Marshall (1920) pp. 341, 355, 357, 364–6, 404.
133. Marshall (1920) Bk. V ch. vii.
134. Marshall (1920) p. 316.
135. Marshall (1920) pp. 316–18, 377, 497.
136. Marshall (1975) I pp. 52–7; (1925) p. 438.
137. Marshall (1920) p. 484.
138. Marshall (1919) p. 294n.
139. Shove (1930) pp. 106–7.
140. Marshall (1919) p. 397.
141. Liebhafsky (1955).
142. Thus Schumpeter, in an otherwise sympathetic article: 'I confess that few things are so irritating to me as is the preaching of mid-Victorian morality, seasoned by Benthamism, the preaching from a schema of middle-class values that knows no glamour and no passion' – (1952) p. 104. Cf. Joan Robinson (1969) p. vii: 'Marshall, with his usual instinctive cunning ...'
143. Latsis (1972).
144. Rothschild (1947).
145. See Hawkins (1973) for a useful bibliography of the relevant material.
146. Stigler (1947b). The British version of the kinked demand curve, as presented by Hall and Hitch, had an empirical basis. But this soon receded from general view as the concept was incorporated into price theory.
147. Silberston (1970).
148. Andrews (1949), (1964); Wilson and Andrews (1951). See also the interesting comments in Loasby (1971) p. 880.
149. See e.g. Eichner (1973).
150. Von Neumann and Morgenstern (1944); Shubik (1959).
151. Cyert and March (1963).
152. See Nelson and Winter (1973, 1974); Nelson, Winter and Schuette (1976).

153. Nelson, Winter and Schuette (1976) p. 118.
154. Strangely the authors refer frequently to Schumpeter as a predecessor, but in fact their treatment is distinct from that of Schumpeter who stressed clustering of innovations, resulting in a cycle, rather than a continuous incremental process of technological change. See Schumpeter (1950) ch. VII especially pp. 84–5; Schumpeter (1961) which they cite is even misleading about Marshall's own contribution, which Schumpeter, in any case, tended to underrate. On Schumpeter see also Loasby (1982).
155. Marris (1964); Cyert and George (1969).
156. Singh (1971).
157. See Chandler (1962, 1977). Despite possible doubts about regarding this work as providing a theory of the firm, there can be no question about its importance.
158. See n. 95 above.
159. See Kirzner (1973).
160. Kirzner (1973) p. 127; see also Loasby (1982).
161. Coase (1972).
162. It is true, of course, that outside the textbooks there is concern with information, especially in the behavioural theories and in the developing agency theories (Shavell, 1979; Holstrom, 1979). The statement in the text relates to the prevailing orthodoxy only.
163. Archibald (1971) p. 16.
164. Cf. Silberston (1970) p. 527.
165. Marshall seems to have envisaged pricing policy as evolving with experience over time – (1919) p. 469.
166. Silberston (1970) pp. 530, 570. See also Robinson, J.V. (1960) p. 228.
167. In *Le Malade Imaginaire*, Molière has the medical profession explain that opium puts people to sleep because of its soporific quality.

Bibliography

Allen, G.C. (1976), *The British Disease*, London: Institute of Economic Affairs.

Andrews, P.W.S. (1949), *Manufacturing Business*, London: Macmillan.

Andrews, P.W.S. (1964), *On Competition in Economic Theory*, London: Macmillan.

Archibald, G.C. (1971), *The Theory of the Firm*, Harmondsworth: Penguin.

Arrow, K.J. and Hahn, F.H. (1971), *General Competitive Analysis*, Edinburgh: Oliver and Boyd.

Averch, H. and Johnson, L.L. (1962), 'Behaviour of the Firm under Regulatory Constraint', *American Economic Review*, **52**, pp. 1052–69.

Babbage, C. (1832), *On the Economy of Machinery and Manufactures*, 3rd ed., London: Charles Knight.

Bain, J.S. (1964), 'The Theory of Monopolistic Competition after Thirty Years. The Impact on Industrial Organisation', *American Economic Review*, Suppt. 54, pp. 28–32.

Benham, F. (1938), *Economics*, London: Pitman.

Bishop, R.L. (1964), 'The Theory of Monopolistic Competition after Thirty Years. The Impact on General Theory', *American Economic Review*, Suppt. 54, pp. 33–43.

Blaug, M. (1976), 'Kuhn versus Lakatos *or* Paradigms versus research programmes in the history of economics', pp. 149–80 in Latsis (1976).

Blaug, M. (1978), *Economic Theory in Retrospect*, 3rd ed., Cambridge: Cambridge University Press.

Boulding, K.E. (1941), *Economic Analysis*, New York: Harper.

Boulding, K.E. (1942), 'The Theory of the Firm in the Last Ten Years', *American Economic Review*, **32**, pp. 791–802.

Boulding, K.E. (1948), 'Professor Tarshis and the State of Economics', *American Economic Review*, **38**, pp. 92–102.

Burns, A.R. (1936), *The Decline of Competition*, New York: McGraw Hill.

Chamberlin, E.H. (1933), *Monopolistic Competition*, 5th ed. (1946), Cambridge Mass.: Harvard University Press.

Chamberlin, E.H. (1937), 'Monopolistic or Imperfect Competition', *Quarterly Journal of Economics*, **51**, pp. 557–80.

Chamberlin, E.H. (1948) 'An Experimental Imperfect Market', *Journal of Political Economy*, **56**, pp. 95–108.

Chamberlin, E.H. (1961), 'The Origin and Early Development of Monopolistic Competition Theory', *Quarterly Journal of Economics*, **75**, pp. 515–43.

Chandler, A.D. (1962), *Strategy and Structure. Chapters in the History of the Industrial Enterprise*, Cambridge Mass.: MIT Press.

Chandler, A.D. (1977), *The Visible Hand. The Managerial Revolution in American Business*, Cambridge, Mass.: Harvard University Press.
Clapham, J.H. (1922), 'Of Empty Economic Boxes', *Economic Journal*, **32**, pp. 305–14.
Coase, R.H. (1937), 'The Nature of the Firm', *Economica*, **4**, pp. 386–405.
Coase, R.H. (1972), 'Industrial Organisation: A Proposal for Research', in V. Fuchs (ed.), *Policy Issues and Research Opportunities in Industrial Organisation*, New York: Columbia University Press for N.B.E.R.
Cyert, R.M. and George, K.D. (1969), 'Competition, Growth and Efficiency', *Economic Journal*, **79**, pp. 23–41.
Cyert, R.M. and March, J.G. (1963), *A Behavioural Theory of the Firm*, Englewood Cliffs, N.J.: Prentice Hall.
Demsetz, H. (1964), 'The Welfare and Empirical Implications of Monopolistic Competition Theory', *Journal of Political Economy*, **72**, pp. 623–41.
Durbin, E.F.M. (1938), 'Methods of Research – A Plea for Co-operation in the Social Sciences', *Economic Journal*, **48**, pp. 183–95.
Eastham, J.K. (1950), *An Introduction to Economic Analysis*, London: English Universities Press.
Eichner, A.S. (1973), 'A Theory of the Determination of Mark-up under Oligopoly', *Economic Journal*, **83**, pp. 1184–1200.
Florence, P. Sargant (1948), *Investment, Location, and Size of Plant* (with W. Baldamus), Cambridge: Cambridge University Press.
Frisch, R. (1950), 'Alfred Marshall's Theory of Value', *Quarterly Journal of Economics*, **64**, pp. 495–524.
Gerbier, G. (1976), *Alfred Marshall Théoricien de l'action efficace et critique radical de l'économie pure*, Doctoral thesis, Grenoble, 1976.
Hague, D.C. (1949–50), 'Economic Theory and Business Behaviour', *Review of Economic Studies*, **16**, pp. 144–57.
Harrod, R.F. (1938), 'Scope and Method of Economics', *Economic Journal*, **48**, pp. 383–412.
Hawkins, C.J. (1973), *Theory of the Firm*, London: Macmillan.
Hayek, F.A. (1937), 'Economics and Knowledge', *Economica*, **4**, pp. 33–54.
Hayek, F.A. (1941), 'The Counter-Revolution of Science', *Economica*, **8**, pp. 9–36.
Hayek, F.A. (1942), 'Scientism and the Study of Society, Part I', *Economica*, **9**, pp. 267–91.
Hayek, F.A. (1943), 'Scientism and the Study of Society, Part II', *Economica*, **10**, pp. 34–63.
Hayek, F.A. (1944), 'Scientism and the Study of Society, Part III', *Economica*, **11**, pp. 27–39.
Hicks, J.R. (1935), 'Annual Survey of Economic Theory: The Theory of Monopoly', *Econometrica*, **3**, pp. 1–20.
Hicks, J.R. (1946), *Value and Capital*, 2nd ed., Oxford: Clarendon.
Holstrom, B. (1979), 'Moral hazard and observability', *Bell Journal of Economics*, **10**, pp. 74–91.
Hutchison, T.W. (1934–5), 'A Note on Tautologies and the Nature of Economic Theory', *Review of Economic Studies*, 2, pp. 159–61.
Hutchison, T.W. (1938), *The Significance and Basic Postulates of Economic Theory*, reprinted New York: A.M. Kelley, 1965.
Kaldor, N. (1934a), 'The Equilibrium of the Firm', *Economic Journal*, **44**, pp. 60–76.
Kaldor, N. (1934b), 'Mrs Robinson's "Economics of Imperfect Competition"', *Economica*, N.S.1, pp. 335–41.
Kaldor, N. (1935), 'Market Imperfections and Excess Capacity', *Economica*, **2**, pp. 33–50.
Kalecki, M. (1939–40), 'The Supply Curve of an Industry under Imperfect Competition', *Review of Economic Studies*, **7**, pp. 91–112.
Kirzner, I.M. (1973), *Competition and Entrepreneurship*, Chicago: University of Chicago Press.
Kuhn, T.S. (1970), *The Structure of Scientific Revolutions*, 2nd ed., Chicago: University of Chicago Press.
Lakatos, I. (1970), 'Falsification and the Methodology of Scientific Research Programmes', in I. Lakatos and A. Musgrave, *Criticism and the Growth of Knowledge*, London: Cambridge University Press, reprinted 1974.
Latsis, S. (1972), 'Situational Determinism in Economics', *British Journal for the Philosophy of Science*, **23**, pp. 207–45.
Latsis, S. (ed.) (1976), *Method and Appraisal in Economics*, Cambridge: Cambridge University Press.
Lee, F.S. (1981), 'The Oxford Challenge to Marshallian Supply and Demand: the History of the Oxford Economists' Research Group', *Oxford Economic Papers*, **33**, pp. 339–51.
Leftwich, R.H. (1955), *The Price System and Resource Allocation*, New York: Rinehart.
Leontief, W. (1937), 'Implicit Theorizing: A Methodological Criticism of the Neo-Cambridge School', *Quarterly Journal of Economics*, **51**, pp. 337–51.

Lester, R.A. (1946), 'Shortcomings of Marginal Analysis for Wage-Employment Problems', *American Economic Review*, **36**, pp. 63–82.

Lester, R.A. (1947), 'Marginalism, Minimum Wages, and Labor Markets', *American Economic Review*, **37**, pp. 135–48.

Lester, R.A. (1949), 'Equilibrium of the Firm', *American Economic Review*, **39**, pp. 478–84.

Liebhafsky, H.H. (1955), 'A Curious Case of Neglect: Marshall's Industry and Trade', *Canadian Journal of Economics*, **21**, pp. 339–53.

Loasby, B.J. (1971), 'Hypothesis and Paradigm in the Theory of the Firm', *Economic Journal*, **81**, pp. 863–85.

Loasby, B.J. (1978), 'Whatever Happened to Marshall's Theory of Value', *Scottish Journal of Political Economy*, **25**, pp. 1–12.

Loasby, B.J. (1981), 'Economics of Dispersed and Incomplete Knowledge'. (Paper presented at New York University Symposium in honour of Ludwig von Mises). Stirling University mimeo.

Loasby, B.J. (1982), 'The Entrepreneur in Economic Theory', University of Stirling.

Machlup, F. (1946), 'Marginal Analysis and Empirical Research', *American Economic Review*, **36**, pp. 519–54.

Machlup, F. (1947), 'Rejoinder to an Antimarginalist', *American Economic Review*, **37**, pp. 148–54.

Marris, R.L. (1964), *The Economic Theory of Managerial Capitalism*, London: Macmillan.

Marshall, A. (1919), *Industry and Trade*, 3rd ed., London: Macmillan, 1920, reprinted 1927.

Marshall, A. (1920), *Principles of Economics*, 9th (variorum) edition ed. C.W. Guillebaud, London: Macmillan for the Royal Economic Society, 1961.

Marshall, A. (1925), *Memorials of Alfred Marshall*, ed. A.C. Pigou, London: Macmillan.

Marshall, A. (1975), *The Early Economic Writings of Alfred Marshall, 1867–1890*, ed. J.K. Whitaker, 2 vols, New York: Free Press.

Mill, J.S. (1848), *Principles of Political Economy*, ed. W.J. Ashley, London: Longman, 1923.

Muggeridge, M. (1972), *Chronicles of Wasted Time I. The Green Stick*, London: Collins.

Nelson, R.R. and Winter, S.G. (1973), 'Toward an Evolutionary Theory of Economic Capabilities', *American Economic Review*, **63**, pp. 440–49.

Nelson, R.R. and Winter, S.G. (1974), 'Neoclassical *vs*. Evolutionary Theories of Economic Growth: Critique and Prospectus', *Economic Journal*, **84**, pp. 886–905.

Nelson, R.R., Winter, S.G. and Schuette, H.L. (1976), 'Technical Change in an Evolutionary Model', *Quarterly Journal of Economics*, **90**, pp. 90–118.

Neumann, J. von and Morgenstern, O. (1944), *The Theory of Games and Economic Behaviour*, Princeton: Princeton University Press.

O'Brien, D.P. (1976), 'The Longevity of Adam Smith's Vision: Paradigms, Research Programmes and Falsifiability in the History of Economic Thought', *Scottish Journal of Political Economy*, **23**, pp. 133–51.

O'Brien, D.P. (1981), 'A Marshall, 1842–1924', in D.P. O'Brien and J.R. Presley (eds), *Pioneers of Modern Economics in Britain*, pp. 36–71, London: Macmillan.

Penrose, E. (1959), *The Theory of the Growth of the Firm*, Oxford: Blackwell.

Pigou, A.C. (1928), 'An Analysis of Supply', *Economic Journal*, **38**, pp. 238–57.

Pigou, A.C. (1932), *The Economics of Welfare*, 4th ed., London: Macmillan.

Robbins, L. (1928), 'The Representative Firm', *Economic Journal*, **38**, pp. 387–404.

Robertson, D.H. (1930), 'Increasing Returns and the Representative Firm', *Economic Journal*, **40**, pp. 80–89, 92–3.

Robertson, D.H. (1957–58), *Lectures on Economic Principles*, 2 vols, London: Staples.

Robinson, E.A.G. (1931), *The Structure of Competitive Industry*, London: Nisbet.

Robinson, J.V. (1932), 'Imperfect Competition and Falling Supply Price', *Economic Journal*, **42**, pp. 544–54.

Robinson, J.V. (1933a), *The Economics of Imperfect Competition*, London: Macmillan.

Robinson, J.V. (1933b), 'The Imperfection of the Market', *Economic Journal*, **43**, pp. 124–5.

Robinson, J.V. (1941), 'Marx on Unemployment', *Economic Journal*, **51**, pp. 234–48.

Robinson, J.V. (1960), *Collected Economic Papers*, Oxford: Blackwell, vol. 2.

Robinson, J.V. (1969), *The Economics of Imperfect Competition*, 2nd ed., London: Macmillan.

Robinson, R. (1971), *Edward H. Chamberlin*, Columbia Essays on Great Economists No. 1, New York: Columbia University Press.

Rothschild, K.W. (1947), 'Price Theory and Oligopoly', *Economic Journal*, **57**, pp. 299–320.

Ryan, W.J.L. (1958), *Price Theory*, London: Macmillan.

Samuelson, P.A. (1947), *Foundations of Economic Analysis*, Cambridge, Mass.: Harvard University Press.

Samuelson, P.A. (1948), *Economics, An Introductory Analysis*, New York: McGraw Hill.

Samuelson, P.A. (1967), 'The Monopolistic Competition Revolution', in R.E. Kuenne (ed.), *Monopolistic Competition Theory. Studies in Impact*, New York: Wiley.
Schumpeter, J.A. (1950), *Capitalism, Socialism, and Democracy*, London: Allen and Unwin.
Schumpeter, J.A. (1952), *Ten Great Economists*, London: Allen and Unwin.
Schumpeter, J.A. (1961), *The Theory of Economic Development*, trans. R. Opie, New York: Oxford University Press.
Shackle, G.L.S. (1967), *The Years of High Theory*, Cambridge: Cambridge University Press.
Shavell, S. (1979), 'Risk sharing and incentives in the principal and agent relationship', *Bell Journal of Economics*, **10**, pp. 55–73.
Shove, G.F. (1930), 'The Representative Firm and Increasing Returns', *Economic Journal*, **40**, pp. 94–116.
Shove, G.F. (1933), 'The Imperfection of the Market. A Further Note', *Economic Journal*, **43**, pp. 113–24.
Shove, G.F. (1944), 'Mrs. Robinson on Marxian Economics', *Economic Journal*, **54**, pp. 47–61.
Shubik, M. (1959), *Strategy and Market Structure, Competition, Oligopoly and the Theory of Games*, New York: Wiley.
Silberston, Z.A. (1970), 'Price Behaviour of Firms', *Economic Journal*, **80**, pp. 511–82.
Singh, A. (1971), *Takeovers*, London: Cambridge University Press.
Skinner, A. (1981), 'Of Factor and Commodity Markets. A Note on E.H. Chamberlin', *Oxford Economic Papers*, **33**, pp. 122–34.
Sraffa, P. (1926), 'The Laws of Returns under Competitive Conditions', *Economic Journal*, **36**, pp. 535–50.
Stigler, G.J. (1942), *The Theory of Competitive Price*, New York: Macmillan.
Stigler, G.J. (1946), *The Theory of Price*, New York: Macmillan.
Stigler, G.J. (1947a), 'Professor Lester and the Marginalists', *American Economic Review*, **37**, pp. 154–7.
Stigler, G.J. (1947b), 'The Kinky Oligopoly Demand Curve and Rigid Prices', *Journal of Political Economy*, **55**, pp. 432–49.
Stonier, A.W. and Hague, D.C. (1953), *A Textbook of Economic Theory*, London: Longman.
Sweezy, P.M. (1939), 'Demand under Conditions of Oligopoly', *Journal of Political Economy*, **47**, pp. 568–73.
Tarshis, L. (1947), *The Elements of Economics*, New York: Houghton Mifflin.
Townsend, H. (1974), *Economic of Consumerism*, inaugural lecture, University of Lancaster.
Triffin, R. (1941), *Monopolistic Competition and General Equilibrium Theory*, Cambridge, Mass.: Harvard University Press.
Wiener, M.J. (1981), *English Culture and the Decline of the Industrial Spirit, 1850–1980*, Cambridge: Cambridge University Press.
Williams, P.L. (1978), *The Emergence of the Theory of the Firm. From Adam Smith to Alfred Marshall*, London: Macmillan.
Wilson, T. and Andrews, P.W.S. (1951), *Oxford Studies in the Price Mechanism*, Oxford: Clarendon.

Research Programmes in Competitive Structure

by D. P. O'Brien*

Introduction

In 1933 two books on competitive structure were published. One, extracted from a Harvard PhD filed six years earlier, dealt with the workings of the competitive process[1]. Seeking not to supplant, but to supplement Marshall, this book by E. H. Chamberlin focused on an effort involving the use of a diagrammatic apparatus to highlight certain fundamental relationships between variables in the competitive process. It did not analyse real firms but nor did it attempt to pretend that such were irrelevant, and to concentrate on positions of competitive equilibrium only. It dealt with problems of arrival at equilibrium, false trading, and a whole variety of issues relevant to an actual competitive process. Supervised by Allyn Young, it drew on a wide range of references and showed evidence of the kind of thorough scholarly preparation which has always been characteristic of the best American PhDs.

The other book was an essay in the Cambridge welfare economics tradition, drawing on a very limited range of material, virtually all of it Cambridge in origin[2]. Its chief sources, apart from Marshall, were Pigou and Shove. The borrowed material was blended together by its author, Joan Robinson, with enormous self-assurance and a blazing vision to provide a major work in that welfare economics tradition. It sought to explain the prevalence of universal excess capacity working as the necessary result of a world of monopoly, to show that "exploitation" was also necessarily involved in this world, and to demonstrate, consequently, that the rationalisation schemes of the 1930s were harmful. The burden of concern was made clear in the following passage:

> "The [competitive] system of the text-books perhaps never existed, and perhaps if it did it would not have been a very admirable one. But it has some merits. A system of uncontrolled private enterprise in which wages are more plastic than profits must entail the misdirection of resources and the waste of potential wealth on an extensive scale." (Robinson, 1933, p. 291)

For an historian of economic ideas, two major puzzles arise from the impact of these books.

*Professor of Economics, University of Durham, Durham, UK.
I am most grateful to John Creedy for comments on an earlier draft of this article.

(1) Neither contained any theory of the firm and only one (Chamberlin) contained any theory of the competitive process — Robinson merely compared successive points of equilibrium. Yet both came to be regarded as providing the theory of the firm.

(2) The two books are significantly different both in aim and content. Yet they have come to be conflated. Although both books are now very much more cited than read, the process of conflation has been at work since their publication and long before the habit of citing them without reading them grew up[3].

This article will attempt to trace the outline of what happened, although without seeking to provide complete answers to these questions.

In order to do this it is necessary to employ some framework in the history of ideas. The framework employed here is that of Imre Lakatos — in particular his idea of competing Scientific Research Programmes (SRPs)[4]. It will be argued that the two books by Chamberlin and Robinson gave rise to two competing SRPs and that there arose, partly because of the deficiencies of the two main SRPs, a third SRP associated with the Oxford Studies in the Price Mechanism.

However, a difficulty must at once be faced. There is considerable ambiguity over the scope of some of the Lakatosian terms. For instance we find the author of a recent and splendid book on economic methodology referring to the whole of neo-classical economics as an SRP — and at the same time referring to the Chicago literature on the economics of the family as an SRP[5]. In order to avoid this ambiguity a position deriving from that of Remenyi (1979) will be taken in this paper. The idea is that each main SRP spawns a series of separate SRPs each with its own hard-core (or "demi-core") and that these SRPs interact through the main one. The three SRPs referred to above are thus sub-parts of the main neo-classical SRP.

Monopolistic Competition

The thrust of Chamberlin's work was an attempt to explain the nature of competition as it existed. It started from the position that perfect competition was *not* an ideal; it was, in fact, an abstraction, only approached in the real world by "pure" competition (with price-taking but without perfect knowledge and mobility) which was not an ideal either. For his analysis of competition, Chamberlin sought to blend elements of free competition and monopoly, as characteristic of the real world, and he was particularly interested in oligopoly. A major tool in his analysis of oligopoly was the apparatus of the DD and dd curves[6] which attempted to illustrate geometrically the operation of oligopolistic reaction. He also analysed a large group case, in which interdependence could (temporarily) be ignored, but his main interest was undoubtedly oligopoly.

In seeking to explore competition as it really existed in the world, he investigated the role of price, quality variation, and advertising and selling costs, as *three* strategic variables. He paid particular attention to selling costs and, in particular, to the effects of advertising on price and on output as well as to the spill-over effects of advertising. In accordance with his overriding interests he also dealt with oligopolistic advertising[7].

He also paid a good deal of attention to product variation and differentiation — it is perhaps worth emphasising that the latter phrase is absent entirely from Joan Robinson's book. Consistently with his interest in the functioning of markets he explored the processes of market adjustment, dealing with disequilibrium trading and false trading[8]. He also dealt with questions of space, emphasising that this could, on its own, produce consumer preferences for the output of different producers[9].

In his approach, there were a number of very marked contrasts with the book by Joan Robinson which will be discussed below. For one thing Chamberlin was very far from being obsessed with his technical apparatus. He introduced Marginal Revenue without any fuss, and used both areas *and* marginal curves[10]. But perhaps the most striking point of contrast is his refusal to follow the welfare economics path. Chamberlin simply refused to draw the conclusion that his analysis showed that competition, as it existed in the world, was harmful and wasteful. Choice was an element in welfare. In addition, the distribution questions which were central to Joan Robinson were of only secondary interest to Chamberlin, and the distribution material in his thesis was omitted when the book was first published[11]. When he did turn his attention to the question of distribution, he did not follow the Robinsonian "exploitation" argument — indeed, he was to become sharply critical of it[12].

Given these contrasts it is rather ironic that, essentially on the basis of one diagram (the so-called "tangency solution") his work should have come to be identified with that of Joan Robinson — particularly as he regarded the "normal profit" outcome, as depicted in this diagram, as an extremely special case.

However, on the debit side, the book does share, in varying degrees, a number of weaknesses with that of Joan Robinson. For one thing time is omitted; it really is rather unfortunate, as Shackle has pointed out[13], that time is excluded from the analysis while the competing away of excess profits through entry requires precisely that dimension to the analysis. There is little attention paid to the role of the entrepreneur, no analysis of business decisions, and none whatever of managerial coordination. The profit concept is seriously neglected[14], and the emphasis on consumer preferences for the output of individual producers results ultimately in the destruction of the concept of industry, thereby removing the entrepreneurial frame of reference.

Imperfect Competition

The fundamental aim of Joan Robinson's book was to produce an essay in welfare economics, following the same lines as Pigou's *Economics of Welfare*[15] but making the Sraffian assumption that the world was a world of monopolies and not a world of competitors[16]. The basic approach was via the existing theory of monopoly, but it was (influentially) extended to "monopsony", and to monopoly price discrimination. In seeking to establish clearly the points of contrast between this world of monopolies and a world of (perfect) competition, the text did a great deal to clarify the very concept of perfect competition — which was attributed (without reference) to "older textbooks"[17]. This led to comparisons of monopoly and (perfect) competition with the latter given very firmly the status of an ideal, but with the equality of average revenue with *average* cost identified as the hallmark of

the determination of competitive output. The most important results of the comparison were, firstly, the fundamental welfare conclusion that "excess capacity" was all-pervasive (because the average revenue curve was tangent to the average cost curve to the left of the average cost curve's minimum point) and, secondly, the serious (though unsurprising, given the use of a monopoly model) conclusion that the supply curve had been abolished. Finally, there was a strong emphasis on "exploitation" and a major conclusion, which has escaped almost all later commentary, was that even when firms were earning only "normal profits" the universality of exploitation meant that what was "normal" was higher than it otherwise would be and thus the *macro*-distribution of income was biased against labour[18].

Of course, this was using partial equilibrium analysis for general equilibrium conclusions. The geometrical analysis of distribution stopped short of exploring the implications for product-exhaustion, and the whole analysis depended, as critics were quick to point out, upon positing one exploiting entrepreneur as co-terminus with the firm, an entrepreneur, moreover, who had no marginal product. Thus the "firm" was the unit of control controlled by one entrepreneur[19].

The profit concept itself was left vague, though profit maximisation was seen as a necessary assumption, and entrepreneurial motivation of a more general kind was neglected.

Technically the work displayed considerable boldness in the austerity of its approach, providing a marked contrast with most preceding literature. There was no time, technology was fixed, and various arbitrary uniformities were imposed in order to obtain the desired results. Empirical material — a staple of most books in this field during the period — was banished even though casual ("ivory tower") empiricism was freely employed if the argument seemed to require it. There were no recognisable firms; matters such as average cost and fixed cost, which seemed important to business men, were dismissed; and the enlightened business man was supposed to use marginal values[20]. A particular geometric technique was employed with virtuosity (and awe-inspiring confidence) and virtually squeezed dry (although unfortunately, a number of the results were in fact not proved). Analysis proceeded on the basis of positing that each individual producer was faced with a downward sloping average revenue curve which bore some unspecified relationship to the downward sloping demand curve facing the industry as a whole. Enormous stress was laid upon the concept of Marginal Revenue which was described as a "Pole" at which a number of intellectual explorers had finally arrived after prolonged struggles[21].

In the course of the argument Joan Robinson invented the geometry of, *and* pointed out the economic significance of, the kinked demand curve[22], and it is a remarkable commentary upon the lack of first-hand acquaintance with this book that this "invention" has been attributed to Sweezy, *six* years after the publication of the book[23].

Because the analysis was, despite the author's advertised intention, based upon monopoly, virtually everything of interest concerning monopolistic competition was ignored, including the origin of market positions (although this was hardly irrelevant given that monopoly and competition were to be compared), and the role of selling costs (advertising received less than half a dozen casual mentions in the entire book).

There was also a serious ambiguity throughout the book over the applicability of its conclusions. On the one hand there were a number of passages warning, rather in the spirit of Pigou, against the drawing of *simpliste* conclusions[24]; on the other hand there were a number of extremely strong conclusions about the waste and misallocation inherent in the world as analysed by Joan Robinson, and she felt free to arrive at clear conclusions concerning the harm done by the rationalisation schemes of the 1930s[25]. This ambiguity effectively remained characteristic of its author who could on the one hand describe the work, in later years, as "scholastic" while still implying — as late as 1969 — that its apparatus could be used to explain excess capacity working in the 1930s depression[26].

The Background to Monopolistic Competition

Chamberlin has explained clearly enough that his work was intended to be a supplement to, rather than an attack upon, the work of Marshall[27]. However, he drew upon a wide range of sources, having studied the work of important theorists like Pareto and Edgeworth[28]. He was also influenced, there is little doubt, by the concerns of American institutionalists and their use of phenomena such as selling costs as the basis for a criticism of economic theory[29]. In part, then, the Chamberlin SRP can be seen as defensive of the main neo-classical SRP, in contrast to the work of Joan Robinson. There was also the strong American tradition of empirical work in economics, which had much more force than corresponding work in the United Kingdom.

The overwhelming impression left by Chamberlin's book is that of very broad reading, from writers like Cournot on the one hand to the patent literature on the other, taking in along the way the business literature including that on price determination within business[30]. Amongst American economists the most important influences were J. M. Clarke and Chamberlin's supervisor for his 1927 thesis, Allyn Young. Almost as important as the positive influences on Chamberlin, in understanding the differences between the two SRPs, are those factors which had nothing whatever to do with his work. For it is important to emphasise that Chamberlin's thesis was not influenced by either Sraffa's 1926 article[31] or the "increasing returns controversy" which subsequently took place in the *Economic Journal*[32]. Nor did it have anything to do with the 1930s depression which, like these other two matters, influenced Joan Robinson. His work was, to some extent, spurred on by the Taussig-Pigou controversy over railway rates; and it is highly significant that Chamberlin did not accept the welfare conclusions drawn by Pigou[33]. Thus while Joan Robinson's work is part of the Cambridge welfare tradition, Chamberlin *started* by rejecting it.

The Background to Imperfect Competition

The origins of Joan Robinson's analysis undoubtedly lie in the Cambridge welfare economics tradition, especially in the work of Marshall (who had begun the habit of using partial equilibrium apparatus to attack general equilibrium problems)[34] and Pigou. Although the references to Marshall in *Imperfect Competition* are almost invariably negative, there were extensive debts. Indeed, the whole apparatus used was, mathematically speaking, only a trivial variant on that used by Marshall himself[35].

A somewhat cool attitude was also expressed towards Pigou, despite very substantial debts to the *Economics of Welfare*[36]. (This is in marked contrast to the generous attitude displayed by Pigou in an article published shortly after Joan Robinson's book[37].) There were also very extensive debts to G. F. Shove especially to his (unpublished) treatment of distribution in his lectures[38]. The distribution material also borrowed quite noticeably from the work of Hicks[39]. Acknowledgement was also due to Yntema (who had already obtained the most influential result in the book — price discrimination equilibrium[40] — although without influence of his own because he was "misguided" enough to use calculus instead of geometry) and to Harrod whose major creative efforts had been marred by mistakes which have resulted in his receiving much less credit than is due[41].

There were two other influences which should be mentioned. The first was a condescending attitude towards businessmen, one which manifested itself much more clearly in the work of writers associated with this SRP[42]. The second was a particular methodological position which might have attracted a good deal more comment had it ever been spelt out. This methodological position was, in summary, that economic conclusions arrived at from reasonable assumptions which had *some* (apparent) correspondence in the real world were necessarily true, so that testing was not only an irrelevance, it was almost an impertinence[43].

Development of the Chamberlinian SRP

The initial reception by reviewers of Chamberlin's book was rather more favourable, it is probably fair to say, than the reception afforded to the book by Joan Robinson[44]. However, reviewers — notably Harrod, who devoted much of his review to the question of oligopoly — pointed to weaknesses in the book which were subsequently to be ignored, for the most part, in the development of the SRP — a parallel, as will be seen with the case of Robinson's book.

In the development of the Chamberlinian SRP Chamberlin himself played a large personal role — much larger than did Joan Robinson in the development of her SRP. A significant element in this role was work in the negative heuristic rather than the positive one. For Chamberlin devoted a good deal of energy to an attempt to distance his work from that of Joan Robinson and her associates. He disagreed entirely with her emphasis on marginal revenue, regarding it not as a "Pole" but simply as the first derivative of the revenue function[45]. He did not regard the "tangency solution" as having the central importance accorded to it by Joan Robinson. In a world of differentiated products it was hardly likely that all firms would be pushed to a position of tangency[46]. He refused to accept that entry into an industry necessarily increased the elasticity of the average revenue curve facing the existing firms[47], and he mounted a valiant, and ultimately successful, attack upon the strange contention of Kaldor that in a world of "perfect divisibility" there would be no economies or diseconomies of scale[48]. He also criticised, again successfully, Kaldor's equally puzzling contention that production costs could not be distinguished from selling costs[49]. He emphasised, again and again, that he and Joan Robinson were in fact dealing with different competitive situations. She had settled for product homogeneity, with all preferences being in the minds of consumers — it is easy to see how this led to the view that consumers were "irrational". For

Chamberlin, however, product heterogeneity was of central importance precisely because product variation was a competitive weapon[50]. The idea of "irrational" consumers was in any case fully in accord with the Cambridge welfare approach; and this was something from which Chamberlin dissociated his own work[51]. He insisted on the meaningless nature of comparisons of actual competitive situations with perfect competition[52] (and insisted also upon retaining the distinction between pure and perfect competition)[53]. He was thus very critical of the Lerner index[54], and provided cogent criticism of the Robinsonian "exploitation" argument, pointing to the strategic nature of the assumption about a single entrepreneur in control of a single firm (who was thus in a position to "exploit")[55]. Above all, comparisons with perfect competition were meaningless because they resulted in the retention of a mistaken frame of reference. What was required for an understanding of competition was a Gestalt switch[56]. He was offering a full theory of competition, not of imperfections from a perfect ideal, and wanted to encompass a world with selling costs, where products were not homogeneous but variable in the competitive process, and where the existence of space (largely excluded from his rival's work) necessarily gave people preferences[57].

Unfortunately this raised some difficulties for him. The emphasis upon diversity necessitated, as he came increasingly to realise, the abandonment of the "industry"[58]. But the assumption, which he had made at one point, of the uniformity of firms, had no meaning if there was no industry; and it was therefore necessary to emphasise that such an assumption was merely a temporary, expository, expedient[59]. Chamberlin also emphasised, quite correctly, that he had made a serious attempt to analyse the problem of oligopoly, while Joan Robinson had merely side-stepped the matter[60]; at the same time, again, the very concept of oligopoly becomes much more difficult to handle if there is no industry to be oligopolistic.

Chamberlin's main work on his research programme was thus, after 1933, within the negative heuristic. His work within the positive heuristic was rather less productive. He did not return to topics which he had broached in the thesis, especially the problem of the allocation of overheads and of multiproduct firms[61]. Moreover his abandonment of the industry concept resulted in its replacement by a cross-elasticity approach with which he was clearly never completely satisfied[62].

But the positive development of the SRP was taken over by other economists, sometimes to great effect. An important writer was A. J. Nichol who had, himself, some claims to priority in this field[63]. Nichol's most important contribution was an attempt to develop a probabilistic version of the Chamberlinian model in order to deal with the uncertainty facing the entrepreneur[64]. Another important follower was Robert Triffin. It was Triffin who was influential in propagating a cross-elasticity approach, sketching (but no more) how Chamberlin's apparatus might be interpreted in a general equilibrium context[65]. There was also Hans Brems who developed an ingenious diagrammatic treatment of product variation[66]. Chamberlin's attack on the "perfect divisibility" thesis attracted support from Whitin and Peston, and from Leibenstein[67]. His resistance to the "exploitation" argument received support from Bloom[68]. Copeland, who had preceded him on the question of product differentiation, returned to the matter in the light of

Chamberlin's analysis[69] and a number of writers made use of his apparatus in the context of retailing[70]. These included Henry Smith who hovered, at times uncertainly, between the Chamberlinian and Robinsonian SRPs[71].

Chamberlin's analysis was extended to questions of tax incidence, the multi-product firm, and the theory of international trade[72]. The kinked demand curve, since hardly anyone recognised Joan Robinson's priority[73] undoubtedly developed from the Chamberlinian DD and dd curves, particularly as Sweezy showed evidence of concern with the Chamberlinian SRP elsewhere[74].

Not all the developments were theoretical. His work received a favourable verdict from those concerned with industrial policy[75], while there was also some empirical work on cost curves notably by Joel Dean[76]. However, by far the most important empirical work was done by Bain, himself the most important of Chamberlin's followers[77]. In fact on the basis of elements derived from the work of Chamberlin and of J. M. Clarke, Bain virtually created his own SRP, developing the theory of limit-pricing.

But Chamberlin's importance was mainly theoretical. Fellner offered an oligopoly analysis which owed not a little to Chamberlin[78] and several writers attempted to replace the simple profit maximisation criterion — an interesting parallel with developments under the Robinsonian SRP[79]. One writer (Enke) also showed that with product and selling cost variation, output variation might have a subsidiary role to play in profit maximisation under certain circumstances[80]. Machlup attempted to develop further the basis of market classification in Chamberlin's work and later defended his theoretical approach as a whole in a series of famous controversies[81].

His analysis received at least mention, if not accurate incorporation, in a number of textbooks from the late 1930s onwards so that his work, like that of Joan Robinson, passed this Kuhnian test of scientific recognition[82]. However, there remained one persistent source of criticism — Chicago. The position of the Chicago writers was that while Chamberlin was an original (Stigler in particular recognised this) he was wrong[83]. There were serious elements of incoherence in his work, notably the attempt to postulate uniformity in a world in which not only were products not homogeneous but there were no industries and everything competed with everything else; and any *predictions* obtained from his theories were trivially different from those obtained through the application of a price-taking model, or a monopoly model, depending on particular circumstances. (That this seems more like retrodiction than prediction did not disturb Chicago apparently.) But, whether favourable (the majority) or not, economists rarely felt able to ignore Chamberlin's work, the one (odd) exception being in the literature on location[84]. His research programme proved powerful and persuasive.

Development of the Robinsonian SRP

The initial reception by reviewers of Joan Robinson's book was somewhat mixed[85]. Several noted that the reach exceeded the grasp; Shove in particular was critical of its ungenerous attitude towards predecessors and precursors[86], and a highly penetrating review by A. J. Nichol pointed to the unnecessary use of a fragile geometric technique, the drawing of conclusions about general equilibrium problems

from partial equilibrium analysis, and the failure to treat competition between enterprises to any serious extent at all[87]. Nonetheless, the SRP soon attracted adherents — often these were critical of detail, as is the way with much of SRP development which falls into the Kuhnian category of "normal science", but they shared the same demi-core and aims as the original work. Kaldor was particularly prominent, although in retrospect he seems to have added little of substance to the original[88]. Another English adherent was Coase[89] — surprisingly in view of the later fame of his 1937 article which drew attention to the need for a proper theory of the firm[90]. However, Hicks, the leading English theorist, remained less than whole-hearted in his endorsement of the new material[91]. But Kahn, who had supervised the original thesis and whose technical assistance is evident at a number of points in it[92], pursued the "excess capacity" question by exploring the concept of "ideal output"[93]. Kahn also explored the question of irrational consumer preferences which lay at the heart of Joan Robinson's assumption of downward sloping average revenue curves for individual producers[94]. She had no product variable — indeed, it would seem, product homogeneity[95] — yet consumers were assumed to regard the output of different producers as imperfect substitutes. Harrod, who had himself very considerable claims to pioneering here, also helped to develop the SRP[96]. An important adherent was Abba P. Lerner, who corrected the mistake in Robinson's book concerning the equality of price with average cost as a welfare criterion, showing that what was critical was equality with *marginal* cost, and developing the well-known Lerner index of monopoly[97]. This matter was also taken up by K. W. Rothschild[98]. Such a concern led directly to questions of distribution, attracting the Marxist economist Michael Kalecki who became associated with Joan Robinson[99]. Joan Robinson herself returned to the question of distribution in a separate article of 1934[100].

An interesting adhesion to the SRP came from the United States, probably inspired largely by that part of the American Institutionalist programme associated with Veblen. The most well-known name here is that of J. K. Galbraith who was particularly attracted by the implications of a world of monopolies and by the importance attached to irrational consumer preferences[101]. Another manifestation of this link with institutionalism was associated with the work of A. R. Burns, and others, who believed that competition was facing extinction[102]. The attitude of *moral* censure taken towards monopoly found an echo in these writers and also in the work of a theorist of a different stamp, Tibor Scitovsky[103]. Other American adherents were W. H. Nicholls[104], who seems in turn to have influenced Patinkin[105], and Seymour Harris who, considering the needs of wartime production, raised the possibility that it might be necessary to restrict consumer choice in order to increase production through doing away with "excess capacity"[106].

The welfare basis of the programme remained strong in other ways. Given that consumers were irrational, it was natural to treat advertising as waste. Meade, as a disciple of the programme and propagator of its message, suggested curbs on advertising[107]. However, as this part of the SRP was developed it needed to borrow from the Chamberlinian SRP which had treated these selling costs while Robinson's original book had not[108].

Since the welfare programme involved comparison with (perfect) competition, in

order to show the waste inherent in normal (imperfect) competition there was scope for further clarification of the perfectly competitive ideal; in addition to the work of Lerner noted above, Joan Robinson herself paid attention to the matter in 1934[109].

As the SRP developed there was, as often seems to be the case, some undermining of its original purpose through refinement. In particular, the simple profit maximisation approach was refined in an attempt to make the motivation of the producer, who had a choice of income and leisure, on all fours with the utility maximising consumer[110]. But this, of course, greatly weakened the simple welfare conclusions relating to equilibrium positions in the original book. The average revenue curve itself also became a casualty in time, as a result of attempting to deal with some of the problems which had been glossed over in its original formulation[111]. However, the industry concept survived — consistently with the Robinsonian assumption of product homogeneity.

Most of the work on the Robinsonian SRP was of a theoretical nature. There was very little empirical work — in marked contrast to the development of the Chamberlin SRP. One author (Saxton) attempted to test the theory of the firm which he believed himself to find in *Imperfect Competition*[112]. Having found that price rigidity was the order of the day and that the firms were in no very obvious way either marginalists or short-run maximisers, he concluded, nonetheless, that the analysis was broadly correct in its *description* of business behaviour[113]. Since it was not a description of business behaviour and since the evidence did not support this conclusion, this was all rather remarkable. Another writer (Broster) attempted an interesting exercise in the development of prescriptive rules for the maximising firm, and concluded that the results of following these rules would accord with the Robinsonian analysis[114]. But these were fairly isolated exceptions. There was really little serious attempt to gather empirical material and sweeping empirical generalisations were employed as required[115].

As Kuhn has shown, the role of textbooks is important[116]. Here Joan Robinson had some early success. Although the full-scale textbook treatment based on her analysis did not appear until the 1940s and, more particularly, the 1950s[117] a number of writers in the 1930s incorporated references to her work and some followed, albeit cautiously, the geometrical analysis and even, occasionally, a few of the welfare conclusions[118].

The Rise of a Rival SRP — Oxford Studies in the Price Mechanism

The Oxford SRP arose from three diverse impulses. First, there was considerable hostility to the Cambridge welfare conclusions and to the sweeping generalisations drawn from positing a U-shaped cost curve[119]. Secondly, there was the individual creative role of Harrod which should not be underestimated[120]. In this connection, Harrod's belief in the possibility of an *inductive* methodology should not be forgotten[121]. In the event, however, the methodology adopted by the Oxford Studies was to show some evidence of naivety[122], thus making it difficult for economists to be confident in this "anthropological" method of economic investigation. Nevertheless the work of Hall and Hitch made a contribution which could not be ignored[123].

Thirdly, there was felt to be a need for a theory of the *firm,* something which was clearly lacking in both the Robinsonian and Chamberlinian SRPs. Thus the Full Cost principle should be seen as a decision process. The focus was upon the firm. At the same time the firm took its decisions within the context of the industry; it thus became necessary to resuscitate the Marshallian concept of industry, something which was not unwelcome since a desire to resurrect Marshall's work in this area was part of the Oxford SRP[124].

The Oxford publications in the late 1940s and early 1950s aroused a wave of predictably critical comment from those associated with the Cambridge work of the 1930s[125]. The most important attempts to advance the SRP, apart from the work of P. W. S. Andrews himself, which occasioned the comment, were undertaken by Farrell, Wiles, and H. R. Edwards[126], while work in the negative heuristic was undertaken by Wilson (to great effect) and by Elizabeth Brunner[128] (who provided an exemplarily clear expository survey — in an Italian journal). Thus the initial impetus did result in an SRP, with work in both the positive and negative heuristic. At the same time it was probably not widely influential and was judged by many economists to be degenerating from the outset. The reason for this is not, however the widely touted difficulty over the size of the mark-up on Full Cost. It is rather that the SRP, like Marshall himself, mixed up together certainty and uncertainty, statics and dynamics, industry and firm in a way which was reminiscent of Marshall's *Industry and Trade;* and many economists had by that time become persuaded of the benefits of a partial equilibrium static approach.

SRP Intersections

Although three SRPs have been distinguished, there is no doubt that there were intersections between them in the work of subsequent writers. The major intersections were between the Chamberlinian and Robinsonian SRPs; but there were also intersections involving Robinson and Oxford, and Chamberlin and Oxford.

(i) *Robinson and Oxford*

Intersections in this category were predictably few, but two are nonetheless noteworthy. Firstly, there was an attempt, by Hicks, to fuse profit maximisation with Harrod's insistence, as part of the Oxford programme, that short-run profits were not maximised because of the fear of entry[129]. The result, a weighted average over the long run, was both creative and sensible. The second notable contribution came from Wiles. Perceiving, correctly, that the Cambridge literature was in fact about welfare economics, he attempted to use the Oxford apparatus to deal with welfare questions in a full book-length study[130]. However, understandably in view of the hostility elsewhere amongst the Oxford writers to the Cambridge welfare approach, this seems to have produced little imitation.

(ii) *Chamberlin and Oxford*

The intersections between these two research programmes were rather more important. First, it should be noted, there was the kinked demand curve put forward by Hall and Hitch, with acknowledgement to Chamberlin's DD and dd curves[131]. Secondly, Hall and Hitch also drew to some extent on Cassels; and he had worked in

the Chamberlinian SRP[132]. Thirdly, Chamberlin himself was not at all hostile to the Full Cost approach, regarding it as a valuable supplement in throwing light on the process of business decisions which involved average rather than marginal values[133]. It thus accorded perfectly with his opposition to Joan Robinson's emphasis on marginal revenue. Bain's theory of limit pricing was easy enough to interpret in Full Cost terms, while providing a theory of the mark-up which did not depend upon uneasy calculations of elasticity. Fellner, whose oligopoly analysis owed a good deal to Chamberlin, provided an interpretation of Full Cost as reflecting decisions seeking a safety margin in the presence of uncertainty where revenue and cost functions were liable to shift[134], and J. F. Due, in seeking to apply the Chamberlinian apparatus to retail price determination, ended up with a Full Cost procedure[135]. But it does seem to be the case that, at least for a long time, the overtures came from the Chamberlinian side and were not reciprocated.

(iii) *Robinson and Chamberlin*

The habit of treating the work of these two writers as in all "essential" respects identical began at an early stage after the publication of their books. A number of writers simply lumped them together and this became the tradition in British teaching. Boulding also habitually conflated their work and other textbooks followed his example[136]. Sometimes this reflected a simple failure to discern the existence of two SRPs, as Chamberlin himself lamented[137]; more rarely it reflected hostility to both SRPs together[138]. One important writer, Triffin, seems to have exhibited an attitude almost schizophrenic, in *distinguishing* Robinson and Chamberlin and then attempting (unsuccessfully) to exhibit their *parallelism* through tables of corresponding passages[139].

None of these can be regarded as intersections of SRPs. However, there was a fairly common tendency to use the Robinson book as a geometrical supplement to that of Chamberlin and this did produce a genuine intersection. In particular, writers working in (or textbooks borrowing from) the Chamberlinian SRP borrowed from Robinson on the matter of price discrimination and that of monopsony[140]. There were also some writers who borrowed eclectically from both authors without attempting to reconcile the different approaches[141].

On the other side, the adherents of the Cambridge welfare programme gradually realised that the gap in their literature concerning advertising had to be filled and Henry Smith, concerned to find empirical counterparts of the theoretical constructs but impressed by the welfare conclusions, continued to hover uncertainly between the two SRPs[142]. Lerner, by contrast, was a clear adherent of the Cambridge programme; but he also moved into the Chamberlinian SRP and (with Singer) made a notable contribution to the literature on location which was neglected by Robinson[143]. An interesting case was provided by Norris who attempted to construct a theory of demand as a counterpart to the Chamberlinian rewriting of the theory of supply but ended up by swallowing wholesale the Cambridge welfare conclusions[144]. Most of the *genuine* intersections seem, in summary, to have arisen in the work of American economists; the English adherents of the Cambridge welfare programme by and large insisted that there was no difference between the two SRPs[145].

Conclusion

This article has traced the rise and development of two separate research programmes, the one (Chamberlin's) being essentially positive, the other (Robinson's) being normative. The first writer wished to persuade economists to think about competition in a different way from that which had become increasingly the orthodoxy in the 1920s — to make a Gestalt switch; the other wished to persuade economists that the freely competitive system was a myth and the actual competitive system involved significant welfare losses compared with a perfectly competitive "ideal". What is remarkable about these two research programmes is not only the extent to which, at least on this side of the Atlantic, they have been confused, but also their very considerable success compared with either the Oxford research programme, or with that of Stackelberg which, despite a theoretical adroitness which seems superior to that of both the main writers considered here, attracted remarkably little attention[146]. The same applies to the work of Zeuthen[147]. The reliance upon geometrical technique by Robinson and Chamberlin, however, increased the accessibility of their books and resulted in a debate in which everybody could join, from those of an institutionalist bent like J. K. Galbraith to theorists like Tibor Scitovsky. There is no doubt that the majority of economists judged one or other of these SRPs to be progressive, in the Lakatosian sense, and that these judgements have been proved correct to some extent. On the one hand Chamberlin's work has led to excellent work on industrial structure — it would hardly be an exaggeration to say that the whole Structure, Conduct and Performance literature stems from his work and that of J. M. Clarke; on the other hand a continued interest in the welfare implications of consumers having (possibly "irrational") preferences is evidence of the vitality of the Robinsonian research programme[148].

Of course, neither SRP offered a theory of the firm and we are still without one although the important work by Williamson in this field has produced a significant advance[149]. But neither Chamberlin nor Robinson can be blamed for not providing what they did not set out to provide.

However they *did* attempt to cope with the problem of oligopoly; Chamberlin by analysing it, and Joan Robinson by offering a way of ignoring it. It is in this area that the major failure of both SRPs is to be found. It may well be that Hicks was correct when, in 1939, he hinted that economic theory might not be able to deal with this problem[150]. But even in the 1930s other writers made valiant attempts to tackle oligopoly, especially Nichol[151]; and in 1950 a symposium on monopolistic competition returned again and again to the question of oligopoly[152]. Chamberlin failed to deal with it, not so much, as has been suggested, because of a lack of specified relationship between his DD and dd curves[153] but because, as Triffin pointed out long ago, reaction curves of the DD type have no meaning in a situation of interdependence — we encounter an unbreakable logical circle[154]. However, it was Chamberlin who made the serious attempt to deal with the problem of oligopoly, and for this, at least, he deserves credit. That he did not succeed, and that his successors did not succeed, either in dealing with this matter or in solving tricky matters like market share, should not lead us to underestimate the importance of these two SRPs as episodes in the 20th century history of economics.

Notes

1. Chamberlin (1933).
2. J. V. Robinson (1933).
3. See Robson (1983) on the question of such citation especially p. 24 n.3.
4. The best account of Lakatos's theory of the history of science is to be found in Lakotos and Musgrave (1970). See also O'Brien (1976).
5. Blaug (1980) pp. 160, 237, 241, 264. Blaug is, of course, perfectly well aware of this dual nature of the SRP concept.
6. Chamberlin (1933) pp. 91-2.
7. Chamberlin (1933) pp. 71-4, 118-23, 127-46, 151-9, 167-72.
8. Chamberlin (1933) pp. 26-9, 56-70. See also Chamberlin (1957) p. 231.
9. Chamberlin (1933) pp. 260-65.
10. Chamberlin (1933) pp. 13, 74-8, 84, 172.
11. Chamberlin (1933) pp. 94, 104-9, 161-6, 214-5.
12. For example, Chamberlin (1933) pp. 182-4, 216-8.
13. Chamberlin (1933) p. 139; Shackle (1967) p. 59. Shackle's comment relates to Joan Robinson but the comment is also applicable to Chamberlin.
14. Chamberlin (1933) pp. 173, 247; see also Chamberlin (1957) pp. 44-5, 49-50; Triffin (1941) pp. 162-4.
15. Pigou (1932) especially Chs. 14-17 and App. III.
16. Sraffa (1926).
17. Robinson (1933) e.g. pp. 3-4, 88, 91, 230.
18. Robinson (1933) pp. 85-91, 97-9, 143-54; 169, 206, 253-4, 269, 281-304, 312, 319-20.
19. Robinson (1933) pp. 231, 241, 248, 268; Chamberlin (1933) p. 216.
20. Robinson (1933) pp. 16-19, 21-3, 48, 50, 56, 71, 76-82, 231.
21. Robinson (1933) pp. vi-vii, 18, 28, 30-32, 37, 63, 65-6.
22. Robinson (1933) pp. 38, 81.
23. Sweezy (1939).
24. Robinson (1933) pp. 284-5, 310-14, 317, 327.
25. Robinson (1933) pp. 307, 324-5.
26. Robinson (1953) p. 579; (1969) p. vi.
27. Chamberlin (1961) reprinted in (1933) pp. 292-3, 308-18.
28. See especially Chamberlin (1933) pp. 38-9, 221-9.
29. See, e.g. Abramson (1931) and Chamberlin (1933) p. 60.
30. Chamberlin (1933) pp. 57-62, 305-7.
31. Sraffa (1926).
32. Chamberlin (1933) p. 310 and references therein.
33. Chamberlin (1933) pp. 293-296.
34. Whitaker (1975) Vol. 2, p. 186.
35. Robinson (1933) pp. 20, 54n, 89, 124-5, 128, 336.
36. Robinson (1933) pp. 136, 143-4, 149, 159-65, 166n, 181, 187n, 190, 203, 205, 282, 286. Despite p. v of the "Preface", a reader of the text who did not know Pigou's work would not appreciate the extent of the debt.
37. Pigou (1933) p. 108: "This note attempts only the subordinate task of improving, on a rather bleak ice-wall, a staircase which has already been made and ascended."
38. Robinson (1933) pp. 105-14 (and n), 127, 133, 294-5.
39. Robinson (1933) pp. 261n, 262n.
40. Robinson (1933) pp. vi, 26n, 182n, 205n.
41. Robinson (1933) p. 26n; Harrod (1930), (1931); on Harrod's contribution (and his slips) see Shackle (1967) ch. 4.
42. Robinson (1933) pp. 72-3; the most marked example is Kahn (1952) pp. 126, 127.

43. Stewart (1979) gives an excellent account of this general methodological position (pp. 121-6). See also n. 74 below. In the development of the particular theoretical positions advanced by a number of Cambridge writers, procedures were used which give rise to serious doubts about their validity. On this see Leontief (1937).
44. See Harrod (1933), Edwards (1933), Copeland (1934), White (1936). See also Wallace (1936), (1937) and Triffin (1941) pp. 17, 19n.
45. Chamberlin (1933) pp. 191-218 especially p. 203n; Chamberlin (1957) pp. vii, 64, 274-6, 307-12.
46. Chamberlin (1933) pp. 195, 302; (1957) pp. 56-7, 144.
47. Chamberlin (1933) pp. 196-8, 282-9.
48. Chamberlin (1933) pp. 198-9, 230-59 (especially 247-8); (1957) pp. 45, 169-212; Kaldor (1935).
49. Chamberlin (1933) p. 277.
50. Chamberlin (1933) pp. 200-209, 302-3n; (1957) pp. 26-30, 105-137, 141, 311.
51. Chamberlin (1933) pp. 206, 296; (1957) pp. viii, 92-3, 97-100, 294-5.
52. Chamberlin (1957) pp. 50, 72-3, 309.
53. Chamberlin (1957) p. 18.
54. Chamberlin (1933) pp. 212, 215n; (1957) pp. 82-3, 100-101. On the Lerner index see the discussion of the Robinsonian SRP on pp. 36-8 and n. 97.
55. Chamberlin (1933) pp. 215-18, 245; (1957) pp. viii, 99, 309.
56. Chamberlin (1933) pp. 204-5; (1957) pp. 26-30.
57. Chamberlin (1957) pp. viii, 26-30, 44, 56-7, 75-6, 97-101, 144-8.
58. Chamberlin (1933) pp. 312-3n; (1957) pp. viii, 94-5. Se also Blaug (1978) p. 415.
59. Chamberlin (1933) pp. 210, 246-7n.
60. Chamberlin (1933) p. 309; (1957) pp. viii, 285.
61. Chamberlin (1933) pp. 304-5; (1957) p. 20. His work in the negative heuristic also included a valiant defence against Chicago criticisms — (1957) pp. 296-305.
62. Chamberlin (1957) pp. 78, 84-91. See also Weintraub (1942), (1955); Bishop (1952), (1953); Fellner (1953).
63. Nichol (1930).
64. Nichol (1941), (1943); see also his (1934), (1934-5), (1935), (1942).
65. Triffin (1941).
66. Brems (1947-8), (1951).
67. Whitin and Peston (1954); Leibenstein (1955).
68. Bloom (1941).
69. Copeland (1940).
70. Curtis (1938); Cassady (1939); Due (1941); Grether (1939), (1941).
71. Smith (1935a), (1935b), (1937).
72. Fagan and Jastram (1939), Fagan (1942); Clemens (1951-2); Marsh (1942).
73. See above n. 23.
74. Sweezy (1937); Hall and Hitch (1951) acknowledged the connection between their (1939) kinked curve and Chamberlin (p. 122).
75. See, e.g., Mason (1939), Mund (1942).
76. Dean (1942).
77. Bain (1941), (1942), (1949), (1950), (1952), (1964).
78. Fellner (1949).
79. Higgins (1939); Lynch (1940). See discussion on pp. 36-8 on the Robinsonian SRP.
80. Enke (1941).
81. Machlup (1937), (1939), (1946), (1947), (1967).
82. See, e.g., Garver and Hansen (1937); Bye (1941); Meyers (1937), (1939); Taussig (1939). Indeed it is interesting that even a book which was criticised for omitting much of interest that had appeared in the 1920s and 1930s still included material relating to monopolistic competition (Haley, 1941). But, as Chamberlin sadly noted, what appeared was often "something quite foreign to the theory, at least as I understand it" (1957 p. 92). This reflected the tendency of textbooks to treat the

Chamberlinian and Robinsonian SRPs as, for their purposes, equivalent, and then to try to fuse their results, drawing on Robinson's geometry. On Kuhn see n. 116 below.

83. The most important Chicago critique is Stigler (1949). Other references will be found in Chamberlin's response to Chicago (1957) pp. 296-306.
84. Ackley (1942); see, however, Smithies (1941).
85. See in particular Edwards (1933), Shove (1933b), Kaldor (1934b), Nichol (1934a).
86. Shove (1933b); see also Shove (1933a).
87. Nichol (1934a).
88. In particular Kaldor (1934a), (1935), (1938), (1950-51).
89. See Coase (1934-35) and (1937-38).
90. See Coase (1937).
91. Hicks (1935), (1939a).
92. See in particular the result in Robinson (1933) pp. 31-2 which is unproven and necessarily derives from a proof supplied by Kahn at a later point (pp. 40-1n).
93. Kahn (1935).
94. Kahn (1935). This was taken up by Galbraith (1938); see also Scitovsky (1944-5).
95. Robinson (1933) p. 17; Robinson (1934-5) p. 112.
96. Harrod's contributions are illuminatingly discussed by Chamberlin in his (1957) pp. 280-95.
97. Lerner (1933-34).
98. Rothschild (1942), (1943).
99. Kalecki (1942a), (1942b). See also Kalecki (1939-40).
100. Robinson (1934).
101. Galbraith (1936), (1938), Dennison and Galbraith (1938).
102. Burns (1936), (1937a), (1937b).
103. Scitovsky (1941).
104. Nicholls (1941), (1943).
105. Patinkin (1947).
106. Harris (1941).
107. Meade (1936) pp. 95-205.
108. Kaldor (1950-51) (written in 1943); Meade (1936); J. V. Robinson (1953) p. 586.
109. Robinson (1934-5).
110. Scitovsky (1943). See also Nordquist (1965) and Leibenstein (1979).
111. Robinson (1953) p. 585.
112. Saxton (1942).
113. Saxton (1942) p. 108. See also Tress (1943).
114. Broster (1938).
115. See in particular the sweeping generalisations about entrepreneurial motives and decision processes in Robinson (1953) especially pp. 582, 586-7. It is rather ironic that adherents of the Cambridge SRP felt no need to do empirical work themselves, while treating with disdain empirical results which appeared to undermine the Cambridge conclusions. See especially Kahn (1952). But this results from the Cambridge methodological position noted above (n. 43).
116. Kuhn (1962) ch. 2.
117. See in particular Stigler (1947), Stonier and Hague (1953), Ryan (1958), Boulding (1948), Speight (1960), Weintraub (1949). The textbooks generally treated the work of Robinson and Chamberlin as equivalent.
118. See, e.g., Roll (1937) which glances at the matter, and Benham and Lutz (1941) which is an American version of Benham's 1938 textbook.
119. See especially Wilson (1952), a major critical essay, especially p. 42, and Brunner (1952) I, pp. 515-16.
120. See especially Harrod (1939); see also Lee (1981).
121. See Harrod (1956) and Phelps Brown (1980) pp. 28-9.

122. In particular there is evidence of *naiveté* about the role of cartels and a rather surprising failure to realise that most oligopolistic price competition takes place through discounts.
123. Hall and Hitch (1951).
124. This is made clear in Andrews (1951).
125. E. A. G. Robinson (1950), (1951); Kahn (1952).
126. Andrews (1949); Farrell (1951), (1952), (1954); Wiles (1950), (1956).
127. Wilson (1952).
128. Brunner (1952).
129. Harrod (1952), Hicks (1954).
130. Wiles (1956).
131. See n. 74 above.
132. Hall and Hitch (1951) p. 120 acknowledged Cassel's (1937) "aggressive" and "non-aggressive" price policy in their distinction between stability and instability.
133. Chamberlin (1957) pp. 271-79.
134. Fellner (1948).
135. Due (1941).
136. Boulding (1942), (1952). Chamberlin displayed some understandable exasperation at this.
137. See n. 82 above.
138. Friedman (1953).
139. Triffin (1941) pp. 19-41.
140. Grether (1939) p. 225; Fagan and Jastram (1939); Taussig (1939) I, p. 205n; Meyers (1937) e.g. p. 55n; Meyers (1941) e.g. pp. 39-41; Bain (1952) pp. 412-414.
141. For example Curtis (1938) who used Chamberlin's apparatus to reap Cambridge welfare conclusions — that resale price maintenance led to the "tangency solution" implying "excess capacity".
142. This is particularly evident in Smith's (1937) see, e.g., p. 126.
143. Lerner and Singer (1937).
144. Norris (1941).
145. Kaldor (1938), J. V. Robinson (1953).
146. Stackelberg (1934). See, however, Hicks (1935); Leontief (1936); Fellner (1949) pp. 98-119, 233-9. The association between Stackelberg's work and National Socialism in Germany may have hindered his acceptance — c.f. Fetter (1937) though this does not deal directly with Stackelberg.
147. See Edwards (1931) for a hostile reception of Zeuthen (1930) from an industrial economist.
148. For continued interest see, e.g., Berry (1969), Gabszewicz (1983).
149. See Williamson (1977) for a highly perceptive survey.
150. Hicks (1939b) p. 85. It is, however, worth remembering Edgeworth's tart comment (when contemplating this possibility) about "chaos congenial to their mentality" referring to "descriptive" economists — Edgeworth (1925) p. 139.
151. Nichol (1934b), (1935).
152. *American Economic Review*, Suppt. 40 (1950), pp. 23-104.
153. Archibald (1961) p. 166.
154. Triffin (1941) pp. 68-70.

Bibliography

Abramson, A. V., "Advertising and Economic Theory: A Criticism", *American Economic Review*, Vol. 21, 1931, pp. 685-90.

Ackley, G., "Spatial Competition in a Discontinuous Market", *Quarterly Journal of Economics*, Vol. 56, 1942, pp. 212-30.

Andrews, P. W. S., *Manufacturing Business*, London, Macmillan, 1949.

Archibald, G. C., "Chamberlin *versus* Chicago", *Review of Economic Studies*, Vol. 29, 1961, pp. 2-28, reprinted in C. K. Rowley, *Readings in Industrial Economics*, Vol. I, London, Macmillan, 1972.

Bain, J. S., "The Profit Rate as a Measure of Monopoly Power", *Quarterly Journal of Economics*, Vol. 55, 1941, pp. 271-93.

Bain, J. S., "Market Classifications in Modern Price Theory", *Quarterly Journal of Economics,* Vol. 56, 1942, pp. 560-574.
Bain, J. S., "A Note on Pricing in Monopoly and Oligopoly", *American Economic Review,* Vol. 39, 1949, pp. 448-464.
Bain, J. S., "Workable Competition in Oligopoly: Theoretical Considerations and Some Empirical Evidence", *American Economic Review,* Vol. 40, 1950, pp. 35-47.
Bain, J. S., *Price Theory,* New York, John Wiley, 1952.
Bain, J. S., "The Theory of Monopolistic Competition after Thirty Years: The Impact on Industrial Organisation", *American Economic Review Supplement,* Vol. 54, 1964, pp. 28-32.
Benham, F. and Lutz, F., *Economics,* New York, Pitman, 1941.
Berry, R. A., "A Note on Welfare Comparisons between Monopoly and Pure Competition", *Manchester School,* Vol. 37, 1969, pp. 39-57.
Bishop, R. L., "Elasticities, Cross Elasticities and Market Relationships", *American Economic Review,* Vol. 42, 1952, pp. 779-803.
Bishop, R. L., "Reply" (to W. J. Fellner and E. H. Chamberlin on Cross Elasticities), *American Economic Review,* Vol. 43, 1953, pp. 916-924.
Blaug, M., *Economic Theory in Retrospect,* 3rd edition, Cambridge, Cambridge University Press, 1978.
Blaug, M., *The Methodology of Economics,* Cambridge, Cambridge University Press, 1980.
Bloom, G. F., "A Reconsideration of the Theory of Exploitation", *Quarterly Journal of Economics,* Vol. 55, 1941, pp. 413-442.
Boulding, K. E., "The Theory of the Firm in the Last Ten Years", *American Economic Review,* Vol. 32, 1942, pp. 791-802.
Boulding, K. E., *Economic Analysis,* revised edition, London, Hamish Hamilton, 1948.
Boulding, K. E., "Implications for General Economics of More Realistic Theories of the Firm", *American Economic Review,* Vol. 42, 1952, pp. 38-44.
Brems, H., "The Interdependence of Quality Variations, Selling Effort and Price", *Quarterly Journal of Economics,* Vol. 62, 1947-8, pp. 418-440.
Brems, H., *Product Equilibrium under Monopolistic Competition,* Cambridge, Massachusetts, Harvard University Press, 1951.
Broster, E. J., *Cost, Demand and Net Revenue Analysis,* London, Gee, 1938.
Brunner, E., "Competition and the Theory of the Firm, Parts I, II", *Economia Internazionale,* Vol. 5, 1952, pp. 509-22, pp. 727-44.
Burns, A. R., *The Decline of Competition,* New York, McGraw Hill, 1936.
Burns, A. R., "The Organisation of Industry and the Theory of Prices", *Journal of Political Economy,* Vol. 45, 1937, pp. 662-680.
Burns, A. R., "Review of: Arthur Fletcher Lucas *Industrial Reconstruction and the Control of Competition: The British Experiments", Journal of Political Economy,* Vol. 45, 1937, pp. 826-828.
Bye, R. T., *Principles of Economics,* 4th edition, New York, F. S. Crofts, 1941.
Cassady, R., "Maintenance of Resale Prices by Manufacturers", *Quarterly Journal of Economics,* Vol. 53, 1939, pp. 454-464.
Cassells, J. M., "Excess Capacity and Monopolistic Competition", *Quarterly Journal of Economics,* Vol. 51, 1937, pp. 426-443.
Cassells, J. M., "Monopolistic Competition and Economic Realism", *Canadian Journal of Economics and Political Science,* Vol. 3, 1937, pp. 376-393.
Chamberlin, E. H., *The Theory of Monopolistic Competition,* 1933, 8th edition, Cambridge, Massachusetts, Harvard University Press, 1962.
Chamberlin, E. H., *Towards a More General Theory of Value,* New York, Oxford University Press, 1957.
Chamberlin, E. H., "The Origin and Early Development of Monopolistic Competition Theory", *Quarterly Journal of Economics,* Vol. 75, 1961, pp. 515-543.
Clemens, E. W., "Price Discrimination and the Multiple-Product Firm", *Review of Economic Studies,* Vol. 19, 1951-52, pp. 1-11.
Coase, R. H., "The Problem of Duopoly Reconsidered", *Review of Economic Studies,* Vol. 2, 1934-35, pp. 137-43.

Competitive Structure 47

Coase, R. H., "The Nature of the Firm", *Economica,* N. S., Vol. 4, 1937, pp. 386-405.

Coase, R. H., "Some Notes on Monopoly Price", *Review of Economic Studies,* Vol. 5, 1937-38, pp. 17-31.

Copeland, M. A., "The Theory of Monopolistic Competition", (review of E. H. Chamberlin *The Theory of Monopolistic Competition), Journal of Political Economy,* Vol. 42, 1934, pp. 531-536.

Copeland, M. A., "Competing Products and Monopolistic Competition", *Quarterly Journal of Economics,* Vol. 55, 1940, pp. 1-35.

Curtis, C. A., "Resale Price Maintenance", *Canadian Journal of Economics and Political Science,* Vol. 4, 1938, pp. 350-361.

Dean, J., "Department-Store Cost Functions", pp. 222-254 in Lange, O., McIntyre, F. and Yntema, T. O. (Eds.), *Studies in Mathematical Economics and Econometrics in Memory of Henry Schultz,* Chicago, University of Chicago Press, 1942.

Dennison, H. S. and Galbraith, J. K., *Modern Competition and Business Policy,* New York, Oxford University Press, 1938.

Due, J. F., "A Theory of Retail Price Determination", *Southern Economic Journal,* Vol. 7, 1941, pp. 380-397.

Edgeworth, F. Y., "The Pure Theory of Monopoly", in *Papers Relating to Political Economy,* London, Macmillan, for the Royal Economic Society, Vol. I, 1925, pp. 111-142.

Edwards, C. D., Review of: F. Zeuthen, *Problems of Monopoly and Economic Warfare, American Economic Review,* Vol. 21, 1931, pp. 701-704.

Edwards, C. D., Review of *The Theory of Monopolistic Competition,* by E. H. Chamberlin and of *The Economics of Imperfect Competition,* by J. V. Robinson, *American Economic Review,* Vol. 23, 1933, pp. 683-686.

Enke, S., "Profit Maximisation under Monopolistic Competition", *American Economic Review,* Vol. 31, 1941, pp. 317-326.

Fagan, E., "Tax Shifting in the Market Period", *American Economic Review,* Vol. 32, 1942, pp. 72-86.

Fagan, E. and Jastram, R. W., "Tax Shifting in the Short Run", *Quarterly Journal of Economics,* Vol. 53, 1939, pp. 562-589.

Farrell, M. J., "The Case Against the Imperfect Competition Theories", *Economic Journal,* Vol. 61, 1951, pp. 423-426.

Farrell, M. J., "Deductive Systems and Empirical Generalisations in the Theory of the Firm", *Oxford Economic Papers,* Vol. 4, 1952, pp. 45-49.

Farrell, M. J., "An Application of Activity Analysis to the Theory of the Firm", *Econometrica,* Vol. 22, 1954, pp. 291-302.

Fellner, W., "Average Cost Pricing and the Theory of Uncertainty", *Journal of Political Economy,* Vol. 56, 1948, pp. 249-252.

Fellner, W. J., *Competition Among the Few,* (1949), reprinted, New York, A. M. Kelley, 1960.

Fellner, W. J., "Elasticities, Cross Elasticities and Market Relationships: Comment", *American Economic Review,* Vol. 43, 1953, pp. 898-910.

Fetter, F. A., "Planning for Totalitarian Monopoly", *Journal of Political Economy,* Vol. 45, 1937, pp. 95-110.

Friedman, M., *Essays in Positive Economics,* Chicago, University of Chicago Press, 1953.

Gabszewicz, J. J., "Blue and Red Cars, or Blue Cars Only? A Note on Product Variety", *Economica,* N. S., Vol. 50, 1983, pp. 203-6.

Galbraith, J. K., "Monopoly Power and Price Rigidities", *Quarterly Journal of Economics,* Vol. 50, 1936, pp. 456-475.

Galbraith, J. K., "Rational and Irrational Consumer Preference", *Economic Journal,* Vol. 48, 1938, pp. 336-342.

Garver, F. B. and Hansen, A., *Principles of Economics,* revised edition, Boston, Ginn, 1937.

Grether, E. T., *Price Control under Fair Trade Legislation,* New York, Oxford University Press, 1939.

Grether, E. T., Review of Jules Backman, *Government Price Fixing,* New York, Pitman, 1938, in *Journal of Political Economy,* Vol. 49, 1941, pp. 633-634.

Haley, B. F., Review of Haney, L. H., *Value and Distribution: Some Leading Principles of Economic Science,* New York, D. Appleton Century Co., 1939, in *Journal of Political Economy,* Vol. 49, 1941, pp. 919-923.

Hall, R. L. and Hitch, C. J., "Price Theory and Business Behaviour", (1939) reprinted in T. Wilson and P. W. S. Andrews (Eds.), *Oxford Studies in the Price Mechanism,* Oxford, Clarendon, 1951.

Harris, S. E., *The Economics of American Defense,* New York, Norton, 1941.

Harrod, R. F., "Notes on Supply", *Economic Journal,* Vol. 40, 1930, pp. 232-41.

Harrod, R. F., "The Law of Decreasing Costs", *Economic Journal,* Vol. 41, 1931, pp. 566-76.

Harrod, R. F., Review of E. H. Chamberlin, *The Theory of Monopolistic Competition, Economic Journal,* Vol. 43, 1933, pp. 661-666.

Harrod, R. F., "Price and Cost in Entrepreneurs' Policy", *Oxford Economic Papers,* No. 2, 1939, pp. 1-11.

Harrod, R. F., *Economic Essays,* London, Macmillan, 1952.

Harrod, R. F., *Foundations of Inductive Logic,* London, Macmillan, 1956.

Hicks, J. R., "Annual Survey of Economic Theory: The Theory of Monopoly", *Econometrica,* Vol. 3, 1935, pp. 1-20.

Hicks, J. R., Review of H. von Stackleberg, *Marktform und Gleichgewicht, Economic Journal,* Vol. 45, 1935, pp. 334-336.

Hicks, J. R., "The Foundations of Welfare Economics", *Economic Journal,* Vol. 49, 1939, pp. 696-712.

Hicks, J. R., *Value and Capital,* (1939), 2nd edition, Oxford, Clarendon, 1946.

Hicks, J. R., "The Process of Imperfect Competition", *Oxford Economic Papers,* Vol. 6, 1954, pp. 41-54.

Higgins, B., "Elements of Indeterminancy in the Theory of Non-Perfect Competition", *American Economic Review,* Vol. 29, 1939, pp. 464-479.

Kahn, R. F., "Some Notes on Ideal Output", *Economic Journal,* Vol. 45, 1935, pp. 1-35.

Kahn, R. F., "Oxford Studies in the Price Mechanism", *Economic Journal,* Vol. 62, 1952, pp. 119-130.

Kaldor, N., "The Equilibrium of the Firm", *Economic Journal,* Vol. 44, 1934, pp. 60-76.

Kaldor, N., "Mrs. Robinson's Economics of Imperfect Competition", *Economica,* N.S., Vol. 1, 1934, pp. 338-341.

Kaldor, N., "Market Imperfection and Excess Capacity", *Economica,* N.S., Vol. 2, 1935, pp. 33-50.

Kaldor, N., "Professor Chamberlin on Monopolistic and Imperfect Competition", *Quarterly Journal of Economics,* Vol. 52, 1938, pp. 513-29.

Kaldor, N., "The Economic Aspects of Advertising", *Review of Economic Studies,* Vol. 18, 1950-51, pp. 1-27.

Kalecki, M., "The Supply Curve of an Industry under Perfect Competition", *Review of Economic Studies,* Vol. 7, 1939-40, pp. 91-112.

Kalecki, M., "Mr. Whitman on the Concept of 'Degree of Monopoly' — A Comment", *Economic Journal,* Vol. 52, 1942, pp. 121-7.

Kalecki, M., "A Theory of Profits", *Economic Journal,* Vol. 52, 1942, pp. 258-67.

Kuhn, T. S., *The Structure of Scientific Revolutions,* (1962), 2nd edition, Chicago, University of Chicago Press, 1970.

Lakatos, I. and Musgrave, A., *Criticism and the Growth of Knowledge,* London, Cambridge University Press, 1970.

Lee, F. S., "The Oxford Challenge to Marshallian Supply and Demand: the History of the Oxford Economists' Research Group", *Oxford Economic Papers,* Vol. 33, 1981, pp. 339-351.

Leibenstein, H., "The Proportionality Controversy and the Theory of Production", *Quarterly Journal of Economics,* Vol. 69, 1955, pp. 619-625.

Leibenstein, H., "A Branch of Economics is Missing: Micro-Micro Theory", *Journal of Economic Literature,* Vol. 17, 1979, pp. 477-502.

Leontief, W., "Stackelberg on Monopolistic Competition", *Journal of Political Economy,* Vol. 44, 1936, pp. 554-559.

Leontief, W., "Implicit Theorising: A Methodological Criticism of the Neo-Cambridge School", *Quarterly Journal of Economics,* Vol. 51, 1937, pp. 337-351.

Lerner, A. P., "The Concept of Monopoly and the Measurement of Monopoly Power", *Review of Economic Studies,* Vol. 1, 1933-34, pp. 157-175.

Lerner, A. P. and Singer, H. W., "Some Notes on Duopoly and Spatial Competition", *Journal of Political Economy,* Vol. 45, 1937, pp. 145-186.

Lynch, E. S., "A Note on Mr. Higgins' 'Indeterminancy in Non-Perfect Competition'" (with reply to B. Higgins), *American Economic Review,* Vol. 30, 1940, pp. 347-350.

Machlup, F., "Monopoly and Competition: A Classification of Market Positions", *American Economic Review,* Vol. 27, 1937, pp. 445-451.

Machlup, F., "Evaluation of the Practical Significance of the Theory of Monopolistic Competition", *American Economic Review,* Vol. 29, 1939, pp. 227-236.

Machlup, F., "Marginal Analysis and Empirical Research", *American Economic Review,* Vol. 36, 1946, pp. 519-54.

Machlup, F., "Rejoinder to an Antimarginalist", *American Economic Review,* Vol. 37, 1947, pp. 148-154.

Machlup, F., "Theories of the Firm: Marginalist, Behavioural, Managerial", *American Economic Review,* Vol. 57, 1967, pp. 1-33.

Marsh, D. B., "The Scope of the Theory of International Trade under Monopolistic Competition", *Quarterly Journal of Economics,* Vol. 56, 1942, pp. 475-486.

Mason, E. S., "Price and Production Policies of Large-Scale Enterprise", *American Economic Review,* Supp. Vol. 29, 1939, pp. 61-74.

Meade, J. E., *An Introduction to Economic Analysis and Policy,* Oxford, Clarendon, 1936.

Meyers, A. L., *Elements of Modern Economics,* New York, Prentice Hall, 1937.

Meyers, A. L., *Modern Economic Problems,* New York, Prentice Hall, 1939.

Mund, V. A., "Monopolistic Competition Theory and Public Price Policy", *American Economic Review,* Vol. 32, 1942, pp. 727-743.

Nichol, A. J., *Partial Monopoly and Price Leadership,* Philadelphia, 1930.

Nichol, A. J., Review of J. V. Robinson, *Economics of Imperfect Competition, Journal of Political Economy,* Vol. 42, 1934, pp. 257-259.

Nichol, A. J., "Professor Chamberlin's Theory of Limited Competition", *Quarterly Journal of Economics,* Vol. 48, 1934, pp. 317-337.

Nichol, A. J., "The Influence of Marginal Buyers on Monopolistic Competition", *Quarterly Journal of Economics,* Vol. 49, 1934-35, pp. 121-135.

Nichol, A. J., "Edgeworth's Theory of Duopoly Price", *Economic Journal,* Vol. 45, 1935, pp. 51-66.

Nichol, A. J., "Probability Analysis in the Theory of Demand, Net Revenue and Price", *Journal of Political Economy,* Vol. 49, 1941, pp. 637-661.

Nichol, A. J., "Monopoly Supply and Monopsony Demand", *Journal of Political Economy,* Vol. 50, 1942, pp. 861-879.

Nichol, A. J., "Production and the Probabilities of Cost", *Quarterly Journal of Economics,* Vol. 57, 1943, pp. 69-89.

Nicholls, W. H., *Imperfect Competition within Agricultural Industries,* Ames, Iowa, Iowa State College Press, 1941.

Nicholls, W. H., "Social Biases and Recent Theories of Competition", *Quarterly Journal of Economics,* Vol. 58, 1943, pp. 1-26.

Nordquist, G. L., "The Breakup of the Maximisation Principle", *Quarterly Review of Economics and Business,* Vol. 5, 1965, pp. 33-46, reprinted in David R. Kamerschen (Ed.), *Readings in Microeconomics,* Cleveland, Ohio, World Publishing Co., 1967, pp. 278-295.

Norris, R. T., *The Theory of Consumer Demand,* New Haven, Connecticut, Yale University Press, 1941.

Patinkin, D., "Multiple-Plant Firms, Cartels, and Imperfect Competition", *Quarterly Journal of Economics,* Vol. 61, 1947, pp. 173-205.

Phelps Brown, H., "Sir Roy Harrod: A Biographical Memoir", *Economic Journal,* Vol. 90, 1980, pp. 1-33.

Pigou, A. C., *The Economics of Welfare* (1932), 4th edition, reprinted, London, Macmillan, 1946.

Pigou, A. C., "A Note on Imperfect Competition", *Economic Journal,* Vol. 43, 1933, pp. 108-112.

Remenyi, J. V., "Core Demi-core Interaction — Toward a General Theory of Disciplinary and Subdisciplinary Growth", *History of Political Economy,* Vol. 10, 1979, pp. 30-63.

Robinson, E. A. G., "The Pricing of Manufactured Products" (a review of P. W. S. Andrews, *Manufacturing Business), Economic Journal,* Vol. 60, 1950, pp. 771-780.

Robinson, E. A. G., "The Pricing of Manufactured Products and the Case Against Imperfect Competition: A Rejoinder", *Economic Journal,* Vol. 61, 1951, pp. 429-433.

Robinson, J. V., *The Economics of Imperfect Competition,* (1933), reprinted, London, Macmillan, 1948.

Robinson, J. V., "Euler's Theorem and the Problem of Distribution", *Economic Journal,* Vol. 44, 1934, pp. 398-414.

Robinson, J. V., "What is Perfect Competition?", *Quarterly Journal of Economics,* Vol. 49, 1934-35, pp. 104-120.

Robinson, J. V., "Imperfect Competition Revisited", *Economic Journal,* Vol. 63, 1953, pp. 579-93.

Robinson, J. V., Preface to *Economics of Imperfect Competition,* 2nd edition, London, Macmillan, 1969.

Robson, J. M., "Which Bentham was Mill's Bentham?", *The Bentham Newsletter,* No. 7, 1983, pp. 15-26.

Roll, E., *Elements of Economic Theory,* London, Oxford University Press, 1937.

Rothschild, K. W., "The Degree of Monopoly", *Economica,* NS., Vol. 9, 1942, pp. 24-39.

Rothschild, K. W., "A Further Note on the Degree of Monopoly", *Economica,* NS, Vol. 10, 1943, pp. 69-70.

Ryan, W. L., *Price Theory,* London, Macmillan, 1958.

Saxton, C., *The Economics of Price Determination,* London, Oxford University Press, 1942.

Scitovsky, T., "Prices under Monopoly and Competition", *Journal of Political Economy,* Vol. 49, 1941, pp. 663-685.

Scitovsky, T., "A Note on Profit Maximisation and its Implications", *Review of Economic Studies,* Vol. 11, 1943, pp. 57-60.

Scitovsky, T., "Some Consequences of the Habit of Judging Quality by Price", *Review of Economic Studies,* Vol. 12, 1944-45, pp. 100-105.

Shackle, G. L. S., *The Years of High Theory,* Cambridge, Cambridge University Press, 1967.

Shove, G. F., "The Imperfection of the Market: A Further Note", *Economic Journal,* Vol. 43, 1933, pp. 113-24.

Shove, G. F., "Review of J. V. Robinson, *The Economics of Imperfect Competition", Economic Journal,* Vol. 43, 1933, pp. 657-661.

Smith, H., "Discontinuous Demand Curves and Monopolistic Competition: A Special Case", *Quarterly Journal of Economics,* Vol. 49, 1935, pp. 542-550.

Smith, H., "The Imputation of Advertising Costs", *Economic Journal,* Vol. 45, 1935, pp. 682-699.

Smith, H., *Retail Distribution: A Critical Analysis,* London, Oxford University Press, 1937.

Smithies, A., "Optimum Location in Spatial Competition", *Journal of Political Economy,* Vol. 49, 1941, pp. 423-439.

Speight, H., *Economics: The Science of Prices and Incomes,* London, Methuen, 1960.

Sraffa, P., "The Laws of Returns under Competitive Conditions", *Economic Journal,* Vol. 36, 1926, pp. 535-50.

Stackelberg, H. v., *Marktform und Gleichgewicht,* Vienna and Berlin, Springer, 1934.

Stewart, I. M. T., *Reasoning and Method in Economics,* London, McGraw Hill, 1979.

Stigler, G. J., *The Theory of Price,* New York, Macmillan, 1946.

Stigler, G. J., "Monopolistic Competition in Retrospect", pp. 12-24 in *Five Lectures in Economic Problems,* London, Longman, 1949.

Stonier, A. W. and Hague, D. C., *A Textbook of Economic Theory,* London, Longman, 1953.

Sweezy, P., "On the Definition of Monopoly", *Quarterly Journal of Economics,* Vol. 51, 1937, pp. 362-3.

Sweezy, P., "Demand under Conditions of Oligopoly", *Journal of Political Economy,* Vol. 47, 1939, pp. 568-73.

Taussig, F. W., *Principles of Economics,* 4th edition, New York, Macmillan, 1939.

Tress, R. C., Review of C. Clive Saxton, *The Economics of Price Determination, Economic Journal,* Vol. 53, 1943, pp. 119-20.

Triffin, R., *Monopolistic Competition and General Equilibrium Theory,* Cambridge, Massachusetts, Harvard University Press, 1941.

Wallace, D. H., "Monopoly Prices and Depression", pp. 346-356 in *Explorations in Economics: Notes and Essays Contributed in Honor of F. W. Taussig,* New York, McGraw Hill, 1936.

Wallace, D. H., "Monopolistic Competition at Work: A Review" (of Arthur Robert Burns, *The Decline of Competition), Quarterly Journal of Economics,* Vol. 51, 1937, pp. 374-387.

Weintraub, S., "The Classification of Market Positions: Comment", *Quarterly Journal of Economics,* Vol. 56, 1942, pp. 666-677.

Weintraub, S., *Price Theory,* New York, Pitman, 1949.

Weintraub, S., "Revised Doctrines of Competition", *American Economic Review,* Vol. 45, 1955, pp. 463-479.

Whitaker, J. K., *The Early Economic Writings of Alfred Marshall,* 2 vols., New York, Free Press, 1975.

White, H. G., "A Review of Monopolistic and Imperfect Competition Theories", *American Economic Review,* Vol. 26, 1936, pp. 637-649.

Whitin, T. M. and Peston, M. H., "Random Variations, Risk and Returns to Scale", *Quarterly Journal of Economics,* Vol. 68, 1954, pp. 603-612.

Wiles, P., "Empirical Research and Marginal Analysis", *Economic Journal,* Vol. 60, 1950, pp. 515-30.

Wiles, P., *Price, Cost and Output,* Oxford, Blackwell, 1956.

Williamson, O. E., "Firms and Markets" in S. Weintraub (Ed.), *Modern Economic Thought,* Pittsburgh, University of Pennsylvania Press, 1977.

Wilson, T., "The Inadequacy of the Theory of the Firm as a Branch of Welfare Economics", *Oxford Economic Papers,* Vol. 4, 1952, pp. 18-44.

Zeuthen, F., *Problems of Monopoly and Economic Warfare,* London, Routledge, 1930.

[13]

AUSTRALIAN ECONOMIC PAPERS

DECEMBER, 1990

MARSHALL, MONOPOLY AND RECTANGULAR HYPERBOLAS*

J. CREEDY and D.P. O'BRIEN

University of Melbourne *University of Durham*

I. Introduction

The simple statement that profits are maximised when marginal cost and marginal revenue are equal was well known to Cournot (1838). Indeed, this first order condition is immediately obvious to anyone with some knowledge of elementary calculus. Marshall (1890) acknowledged the influence of Cournot, but departed from him in several important respects and chose not to emphasise this condition. Instead he used a diagrammatic approach that made use of a series of rectangular hyperbolas. He was later reproved, somewhat intemperately, by Samuelson in the following terms:

> simple monopoly theory consists of little other than elementary calculus, in which ordinary and partial derivatives are to be set equal to zero whereas higher derivatives are required to be non-positive. Marshall was so enamoured of his silly little unitary-elasticity hyperbolas that he omitted a straightforward treatment of simple monopoly, leaving room in the first third of this century for quasi-independent rediscovery by literary economists of these rudiments. (Samuelson, 1967, p. 111)

What Samuelson had in mind was the near-farcical situation of the 'discovery' of the first derivative of total revenue in the early 1930s, when the terms 'marginal revenue' and 'marginal cost' were coined. However, it is grossly unfair to blame this episode on Marshall. Furthermore, the description of Marshall's use of rectangular hyperbolas as 'silly' fails to recognise Marshall's legitimate reasons for wishing to avoid what is now the standard text book treatment. In

* We are grateful to Anne Woodhead, John Ashworth, Chris Espiner and Adrian Darnell for helpful comments, to Dr E.S. Leedham-Green for helpful information about the Mathematical Tripos and to Cambridge University Library for copies of the 1865 Tripos papers.

addition, it ignores the important and interesting results that become clear when using Marshall's diagrammatic device[1].

The purpose of this paper is to suggest that there are in fact straightforward *mathematical* reasons why Marshall did not use marginal cost and marginal revenue (or their mathematical counterparts) in his monopoly analysis. Some neglected aspects of his ingenious use of rectangular hyperbolas are also examined. Section II examines the problems that arise when trying to solve the first order condition in any situation that departs from the elementary model now given in texts. The use of the hyperbolas is described in Section III, while Section IV then examines some comparative statics and the effects of adding consumers' surplus to the maximand. Marshall used a mechanical device, invented by Cunynghame, to draw a series of rectangular hyperbolas on the blackboard, but this seems to have been lost. Section V presents a convenient method that may well have formed the basis of Marshall's instrument. Brief conclusions are offered in Section VI.

It is also necessary to add at this stage that Marshall's rejection of the now-standard approach was not based only on mathematical reasons. Marshall stressed that marginal cost was not an operational concept, especially in a multi-product firm; for further examination of this point, see O'Brien (1990). He therefore also wished to concentrate on *average* concepts.

Marshall's mathematical training

Before considering the issue in detail, it is useful to refer to Marshall's mathematical training and its possible influence on his approach to economic questions. It is well-known that Marshall graduated as Second Wrangler (second place in the First Class in mathematics) at Cambridge in 1865. Although later generations were to be very dissatisfied with the content of the Tripos, and two famous mathematicians, Hardy and Littlewood, were to lead a successful campaign for its reform (Titchmarsh, 1949), it was undoubtedly testing as an examination of mathematical training (Ball, 1918, ch. 15; 1921, ch. 21). The 16 papers covered geometry and trigonometry, series, optics, mechanics, conic sections, astronomy, solids, calculus and determinants. The pressure for reform - a recurrent theme in the history of the Tripos - arose not because the papers were easy but because the topics regularly lagged decades behind continental (especially French) practice. There is no doubt that the papers still tested mathematical facility. It is also of interest that they included a fair amount of what would nowadays be called numerical analysis and problems of multiple equilibria and stability.

This mathematical training, with an emphasis upon particular functional forms, was ideally suited for someone like Marshall with his search for realism and his high hopes for the *operational* role of consumer surplus. The emphasis upon a realistic, operational economics led him to envisage average revenue curves of a plausible shape; and his mathematical training

[1] Schumpeter too denigrated Marshall's monopoly analysis. After discussing Cournot, he stated "Marshall reproduced this analysis by means of a technique of his own that not everyone will consider superior to Cournot's (1954, p. 977; see also p. 977, n. 16). Schumpeter's (1954, p. 839) argument that Marshall's static theory of monopoly is essentially Cournot's is also unwarranted. On Marshall's industrial analysis generally, see O'Brien (1990).

must surely then have suggested to him possible functional forms which these curves could have taken.

II. Solving the First Order Condition

Virtually all students of economics are introduced to the analysis of monopoly using a set of U-shaped average and marginal cost curves, combined with a downward sloping set of linear demand and marginal revenue curves. They are then taught to apply the profit maximising first order condition that $MC = MR$, where the absence of competition means that $AC = AR$ does not need to hold in the 'long run'. This basic model may be written as follows. The U-shaped average cost curve can be represented by a quadratic, so that average cost, $c(q)$, as a function of output, q, is given by:

$$c(q) = a - bq + dq^2 \tag{1}$$

Multiplying (1) by q to get total cost, C, and differentiating the latter with respect to q gives marginal cost as:

$$MC = d\{c(q)q\}/dq = a - 2bq + 3dq^2 \tag{2}$$

The linear demand curve implies that price, $p(q)$, can be written as:

$$p(q) = \alpha - \beta q \tag{3}$$

whence the marginal revenue is given by:

$$MR = d\{p(q)q\}/dq = \alpha - 2\beta q \tag{4}$$

Setting (2) equal to (4) and rearranging shows that the profit maximising output is obtained as the root of the quadratic:

$$3dq^2 + 2(\beta - b)q + (a - \alpha) = 0$$

It is usually implicitly assumed that $\alpha > a$ (so that at very low outputs, average revenue exceeds average cost), which ensures that the above quadratic has one negative and one positive real root. The standard diagram only shows the positive root, of course. Students are therefore given the impression that the application of the first order condition is very straightforward; there is little more that needs to be added. However, departures from this simple model give rise to problems that are both more complex and much more interesting in their range of predictions.

Cost curves

Marshall's cost curves are not closely approximated by a quadratic. A general function that closely reflects the type of curve drawn by Marshall is the following:

$$c(q) = a(q + d)^{-b} \tag{5}$$

Average cost is always falling and the intercept of $c(q)$ on the vertical axis, $c(0)$, is equal to ad^{-b}. The marginal cost corresponding to (5) is then:

$$MC = a(q + d)^{-b}\{1 - bq/(q + d)\} \quad (6)$$

Setting (4) equal to (6) gives a rather awkward expression which cannot be simplified to give an explicit solution for the profit maximising value of q. Even in the very simple case where $d = 0$, $a = 1$ and $b = \frac{1}{2}$, so that $c(q) = 1/\sqrt{q}$, it can be found that the first order condition, with a linear demand curve, gives rise to a cubic. In this case $MC = 1/(2\sqrt{q})$ and profit maximising output is given by the root of:

$$(16\beta^2)q^3 - (16\alpha\beta)q^2 + (4\alpha^2)q - 1 = 0 \quad (7)$$

In this case it is not possible to rule out, *a priori*, the case where all three roots of (7) are distinct, real and positive. Indeed substitution of plausible numbers for the parameters of (7) can easily yield such a case. The procedure for obtaining the solution to cubic equations is very laborious, of course, involving complex numbers in the case of three real roots, and the use of DeMoivre's procedure (Turnbull, 1952, ch. 9).

Demand curves

The examination of first order conditions is even more complicated when it is remembered that Marshall did not regard linear demand curves as realistic. Examples of the types of non-linear demand curve drawn by Marshall in the chapter on monopoly are shown in Marshall (1961, I, pp. 480, 483, 490). Others are illustrated in the Whitaker edition of his Early Economic Writings (Marshall, 1867-90, I, pp. 137-154)[2].

Some of Marshall's non-linear demand curves may be approximated using a cubic equation, which has a long history in demand studies (see Creedy, 1986). Suppose that:

$$p(q) = \alpha - \beta q + \gamma q^2 - \delta q^3 \quad (8)$$

where $\gamma^2 < 3\beta\delta$ to ensure a negative slope. The combination of (8) with the cost curve $c(q) = 1/\sqrt{q}$ can be shown to yield a seventh-order polynomial for the first order profit maximising output thus:

$$(64\delta^2)q^7 - \ldots - (16\alpha\beta)q^2 + (4\alpha^2)q - 1 = 0 \quad (9)$$

By Descartes's Rule of Signs this equation has up to seven positive real roots (since there are seven changes of sign in the coefficients). Similarly, by the same rule, when substituting $-q$ for q there are no sign changes in the equation so that there are no negative real roots. Hence equation (9) may have multiple positive solutions and (because it comes within the general case of $n > 5$) can only be solved using numerical methods.

These examples should be sufficient to indicate that serious attention needs to be given to the problem of multiple solutions to the first order condition as soon as the simple

[2] A similar type of non-linear demand curve is illustrated in Edgeworth's *Palgrave's Dictionary* article on "Demand Curves' (1984, I, p. 542).

assumptions underlying the standard text-book treatment of monopoly are relaxed. Furthermore, convenient analytical solutions are usually not available[3]. As a final example suppose that the demand curve takes the same form as the cost curve in (5), so that:

$$p(q) = \alpha(q + \gamma)^{-\beta} \tag{10}$$

where $q > \alpha/(\beta - 1)$ to ensure positive marginal revenue. Profit maximisation, with (5) and (10), gives rise to an awkward equation containing (6) and its equivalent for marginal revenue. Only if $\gamma = d = 0$ is a simple solution available, where it can be found that:

$$q = \left[\frac{a(1 - b)}{\alpha(1 - \beta)}\right]^{1/(b-\beta)} \tag{11}$$

where first and second order conditions require that $b < \beta < 1$. This is indeed the exception that proves the rule, since Marshall explicitly ruled out constant elasticity demand curves as totally unrealistic.

Marshall's training in mathematics certainly made him very conscious of the possibility of multiple solutions, which were also emphasised in his *Pure Theory* analysis (1879, Figs. 3, 4, 5, 8) and *Early Economic Writings* (1867-90). When this is combined with the fact that Marshall repeatedly argued that marginal cost was not an operational concept, it is not surprising that he was led to search for a diagrammatic approach that both gave the global optimum very easily and involved the use of only average cost and revenue curves. Marshall's solution to this problem was, despite its neglect by many later generations, rather ingenious.

Marshall's general preference for a diagrammatic approach was formed at a very early stage in his studies, as indicated by the following statement.

> It is possible that at some very remote period a diligent detailed tracing of the curves for an enormous number of different commodities may lead up to approximate generalisations. Should this ever happen the results thus shadowed forth will be at once represented by mathematical curves: and the superiority as regards generality and minuteness of the conclusions obtained by mathematical analysis over those derived from the inspection of diagrams will begin to possess a practical value. Meanwhile the theorist may amuse himself by analysing the results of various arbitrary hypotheses. (1867-90, I, p. 156)

III. The Use of Rectangular Hyperbolas

Marshall first introduced his use of rectangular hyperbolas in the *Principles* (1890, pp. 479-480, n. 1). Given average revenue and cost curves, a curve representing the profit per unit of output, $p(q) - c(q)$, can easily be constructed as the vertical distance between the first two

[3] It may be suggested that some of Marshall's demand curves are more closely approximated by more complex sinusoidal functions. Such a suggestion is clearly compatible with the heavy emphasis on trigonometry in the Tripos papers for 1865. But such an equation, of the form $p = 1 - \sin(q - \pi/2) + [\sin 2(q - \pi/2)]/2 - [\sin 3(q - \pi/2)]/3 + [\sin 4(q - \pi/2)]/4 - [\sin\text{-}5(q - \pi/2)]/5$ would be even more intractable.

curves. Marshall called the resulting curve a 'monopoly revenue curve'. He then called a rectangular hyperbola a 'constant revenue curve' and stated that profit maximisation is achieved at the point of tangency between the monopoly revenue curve and the highest constant revenue curve. Although there may be several tangency positions between the monopoly revenue curve and constant revenue curves, the global maximum is easily found on the highest rectangular hyperbola.

Marshall did not really give a full explanation of this result, so that it seems useful to consider the problem rigourously before presenting the relevant diagram. First, notice that where total cost, C, is $c(q)q$ and total revenue, R, is $p(q)q$, the standard first order condition ($MR = MC$) can be written as:

$$p\left(1 + \frac{q}{p}\frac{dp}{dq}\right) = c\left(1 + \frac{q}{c}\frac{dc}{dq}\right) \qquad (12)$$

The slope of Marshall's monopoly revenue curve of profit per unit of output is given by:

$$\frac{\partial(p - c)}{\partial q} = \frac{\partial p}{\partial q} - \frac{\partial c}{\partial q} \qquad (13)$$

For a rectangular hyperbola defined by $p = k/q$, the slope is given by:

$$\frac{\partial p}{\partial q} = -\frac{k}{q^2} \qquad (14)$$

For a tangency, equate (13) and (14) and multiply by q to get:

$$p\left(\frac{q}{p}\frac{dp}{dq}\right) - c\left(\frac{q}{c}\frac{dc}{dq}\right) = -\frac{k}{q} \qquad (15)$$

But from (12) it can be seen that the left hand side of (15) is just -(p - c), so that substitution gives

$$k = q(p - c) \qquad (16)$$

Thus the coefficient (the 'constant revenue') of the rectangular hyperbola that is tangential to the average profit curve is indeed the total value of *profits* associated with the output corresponding to the tangency. This is shown diagrammatically in Figure 1. Marshall stressed the usefulness of his approach as follows:

> Much instruction is to be got by drawing diagrams to represent various conditions of demand and of (monopoly) supply, with the resultant shapes of the monopoly revenue curve. A careful study of the shapes thus obtained will give more assistance than any elaborate course of reasoning in the endeavour to realize the multiform action of economic forces in relation to monopolies. A tracing may be made on this paper of the constant revenue curves in one of the diagrams; and thus, when laid over a monopoly revenue curve, will indicate at once the point, or points, of maximum revenue. (1890, I, p. 483, p. 1)

A set of rectangular hyperbolas can also be used, as Marshall indicated (1890, p. 839), to find the point on a demand curve corresponding to an elasticity of unity. Total revenue is unchanged at the point where a rectangular hyperbola is tangential to the demand curve.

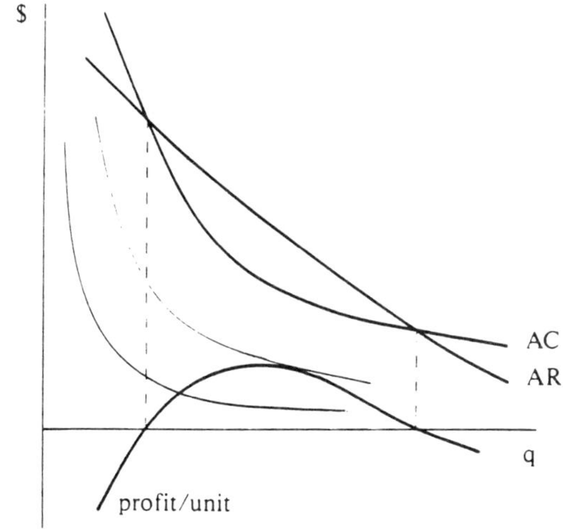

FIGURE 1
Profit Maximisation

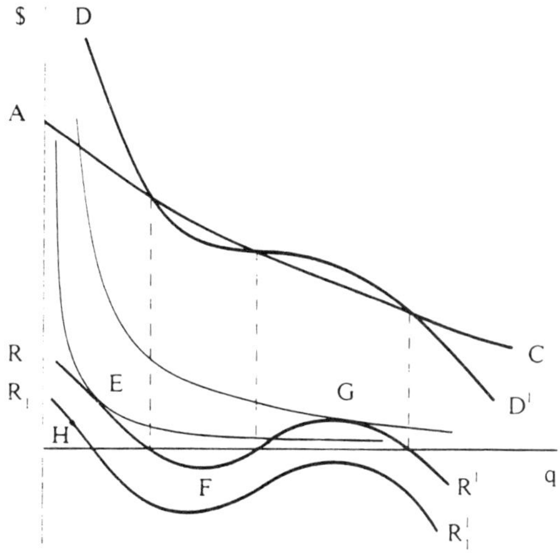

FIGURE 2
Multiple Equilibria

IV. Further Results

The effect of a rise in costs

The fact that Marshall's method allows the global maximum to be easily distinguished from other turning points (including local minima) is very useful when considering comparative statics. Consider Figure 2, which is based on Marshall (1890, I, p. 483, n. 1, Fig. 35). With the demand curve DD' and the average cost curve AC, the curve of profit per unit, Marshall's monopoly revenue curve, is shown as RR'. There is a local maximum of profits at point E and a global maximum at point G.

Suppose that there is an increase in the average cost of production such that AC shifts upwards and RR' shifts downwards to R_1R_1'. Marshall's approach shows immediately that the new point of maximum profit is at H, which involves a significant reduction in output even though there may have been only a small increase in costs. The possibility of such discontinuous jumps in output, resulting from only a small change in a smooth curve, can easily arise in situations where there are multiple solutions. Marshall's analysis of multiple equilibria in competitive markets, where some of the equilibria may be unstable, also shows how conscious he was of this type of phenomenon. This important lesson was, however, very soon forgotten[4].

Total and compromise benefits

When comparing the monopoly price and output with those which would result from a competitive market, Marshall suggested that in some circumstances a monopolist may, in forming his objective, make some allowance for consumers' surplus. He used the expression 'total benefits' to refer to the sum of profits and consumer's surplus. The output at which total benefits are maximised can then easily be found by adding consumers' surplus at each output to the corresponding monopoly revenue curve. The point of tangency of the resulting curve with the highest rectangular hyperbola gives the optimal position. However, the construction of consumers' surplus diagrammatically raises problems in view of the fact that it is an area (though Marshall did not address this issue)[5].

Marshall then referred to 'compromise benefits' as the sum of profit and some proportion of consumers' surplus, arguing that the price would be higher and the output lower than when total benefits are maximised. It is, however, instructive to consider this aspect in general terms. The consumers' surplus corresponding to an output of q is, by definition, equal to:

$$\int_0^q p(u)du - p(q)q \tag{17}$$

[4] More recently Walters (1980) and Formby *et al.* (1982) have examined multiple equilibria in the context of monopoly, arising in situations where marginal revenue increases over a range of output. The problem has been discussed in the context of modern developments of catastrophe theory by Dodgson (1982) and Bonanno (1987). However, none of the above authors mention Marshall's treatment of monopoly.

[5] It is of interest that the area of a rectangle may be converted into a length diagrammatically using a set of rectangular hyperbolas (see Creedy and McDonald, 1989).

If a proportion, ϕ, of this added to profits, the level of compromise benefits is given by:

$$p(q)q + \phi\{\int_0^q p(u)du - p(q)q\} - c(q)q \qquad (18)$$

Differentiating (18) with respect to q, setting the result equal to zero, and rearranging, gives the result that:

$$MC = \phi(AR) + (1 - \phi)(MR) \qquad (19)$$

Hence the first order condition for the maximisation of compromise benefits states that marginal cost is a weighted average of average and marginal revenue. Remembering that $AR = p(q)$ and $MR = p(q)(1 + 1/\eta)$, where η is the price elasticity of demand, it is possible to re-arrange (19) to obtain the result that:

$$p(q) = (MC)\{1 + (1 - \phi)/\eta\}^{-1} \qquad (20)$$

where $\phi > 1 + \eta$ to ensure positive price and marginal cost.

Since $0 < \phi < 1$ and $\eta < 0$, the price exceeds marginal cost. However, if consumers' surplus is counted equally with profits, so that total benefits are maximised, then $\phi = 1$ and (20) show that the first order condition requires that price is equal to marginal cost[6]. Marshall does not, however, seem to have been aware of this result in view of his reluctance to use the concept of marginal cost. It is however an important implication of his analysis. The welfare optimisation involved in equating price and marginal cost was later established by Lerner (1933-34). But in Joan Robinson's 1933 book the welfare criterion involves equating price and *average* cost (1933, ch. 11).

V. Drawing Rectangular Hyperbolas

Marshall's desire to present his monopoly diagrams in lectures led to the need to draw a set of rectangular hyperbolas on the blackboard. He later mentioned that, 'Mr Henry Cunynghame, ... seeing me annoyed by being unable to draw a series of rectangular hyperbolas, invented a beautiful and original machine for the purpose' (1890, II, p. 37). See also Marshall (1873) and Pigou (ed, 1925, p. 449)[7]. However, as Whitaker (in Marshall, 1967-90, II, p. 284) notes, 'the details of the machine seem to have been forgotten'. While Cunynghame's machine cannot be reconstructed with certainty, it can be shown that a series of rectangular hyperbolas can easily be drawn using nothing more sophisticated than a set-square. Before the method can be presented it is first necessary to present a result that forms the basis of the technique.

[6] See also Whitaker (1986, pp. 180, 186-8) for a similar result.

[7] An anonymous referee has commented that letters from Marshall to Keynes, held in King's College, Cambridge, discuss Cunynghame's contribution to the monopoly question. They indicate that Marshall wished to have Cunynghame's account included in the proceedings of the Philosophical Society, although it was omitted by the editor.

A basic result

Figure 3 shows a semi-circle with its centre at C and a diameter of AD. Take an arbitrary point on the circumference, say point E, and drop a perpendicular to the diameter, shown by EG. The radius of the semi-circle ($AC = EC = CD$) can also be expressed as $(AB + BD)/2$, so that the distance BC is equal to $(AB + BD)/2 - AB$. Then using Pythagoras's theorem:

$$(EB)^2 = \{(AB + BD)/2\}^2 - \{(AB + BD)/2 - AB\}^2 = (AB)(BD) \tag{21}$$

Equation (21) shows that EB is the geometric mean of AB and BD. But, more importantly for present purposes, it shows that the square $GFEB$ has the same area as the rectangle with sides AB and BD. It is also a basic property of circles that the angle between the straight lines joining AE and ED is 90°. The property always holds as the point E moves along the circumference AED[8].

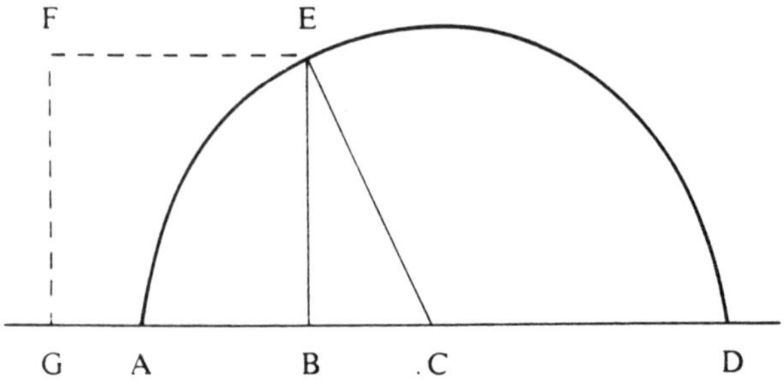

FIGURE 3
The Geometric Mean

A simple method

Consider Figure 4 and suppose that it is required to draw a rectangular hyperbola through point E, which lies along a 45° line through the origin. All hyperbolas are symmetric about the 45° line. Mark point F on the vertical axis and place the right-angle of a set square at this point. Suppose the set square is in the position shown by AFC. Then mark point G directly above C, where the length CG is equal to $0A$. Equation (21) shows that the area of a square with sides equal to $0F$ is precisely the same as the area of the rectangle with sides $0A$ and $0C$. Hence G is a point on the rectangular hyperbola passing through E. Figure 4 also shows the construction of point H, which is obtained by rotating the set-square about the fixed point F such that it is at the position BFD. The distance DH is equal to $0B$. This may easily be repeated in order to plot a number of points which can then be joined with a free-hand curve.

The above method differs from that usually presented in text books on geometrical or technical drawing, such as Winstanley (1951, p. 66), but the standard method involves drawing

[8] David Worswick has pointed out in correspondence that this property can easily be used to generate the required result of (21). The triangles ABE and EBD are similar, so that $EB/AB = BD/EB$.

five separate lines to generate each new point on a rectangular hyperbola. Not only is such a method more tedious but, unlike the above procedure, it is not clear how a mechanical device could be adapted for drawing hyperbolas easily, whether on paper or (as in Marshall's case) on the blackboard[9]. A device for applying the method of Figure 4 could easily be constructed using little more than a set-square.

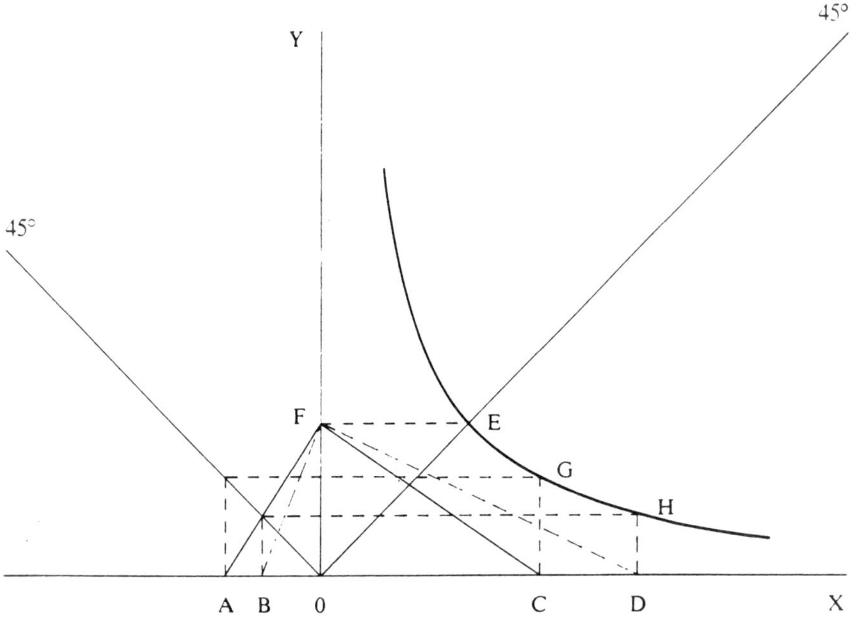

FIGURE 4
Drawing a Rectangular Hyperbola

VI. Conclusions

Marshall, trained as a mathematician, has been criticised for omitting from his analysis of monopoly the first derivative concepts which apparently caused such difficulty to non-mathematical economists in the early 1930s (Robinson, 1933, p. vi). But this criticism is unwarranted. As Chamberlin wrote:

> Having used the concept of marginal value product in 1926, I might perhaps lay claim to a place among the goodly company in Mrs Robinson's Foreword of those who arrived at the concept at about the same time. But alas! I must confess that I found it in Marshall's Mathematical Appendix, Note XIV. Marshall does not draw a diagram, but he gives and discusses at some length the algebraic formula. (1961, p. 524)

[9] Nonetheless it is interesting that this method was (subjectively) 'rediscovered' by a reader of one of our earlier drafts.

Chamberlin is talking here about the marginal concept in relation to distribution. But that Marshall's hint was itself sufficient to lead Chamberlin himself to marginal revenue is indeed shown by the latter's employment of that concept in his *Monopolistic Competition* (1933, pp. 14,18,24-5,77). But the fact that while the astute Chamberlin picked up the clues others did not, suggests that Marshall did not make them very clear. Reasons for thinking that this lack of attention to the marginal concept was entirely deliberate have been suggested in this paper. For Marshall had reasons, grounded in his mathematical training as well as his conception of how economics should proceed and what it should set out to do, for directing his readers away from the marginal concepts and towards the average concepts in conjunction with which he could employ his hyperbolas. Far from being, according to Samuelson, 'silly little' hyperbolas, this paper has shown that Marshall's diagrammatic method provided a very neat solution to an awkward problem and indicated important economic lessons which were prematurely discarded.

References

Ball, W. Rouse (1918), *Cambridge Papers* (London).

Ball, W. Rouse (1921), *Cambridge Notes* (Cambridge).

Bonanno, G. (1987), "Monopoly equilibria and catastrophe theory", *Australian Economic Papers*, vol. 26.

Chamberlin, E.H. (1933), *The Theory of Monopolistic Competition* (Cambridge, Mass: Harvard University Press).

Chamberlin, E.H. (1961), 'The Origin and Early Development of Monopolistic Competition Theory", *Quarterly Journal of Economics*, vol. 75.

Creedy, J. (1986), "On the King-Davenant "Law' of Demand", *Scottish Journal of Political Economy, vol. 33.*

Creedy, J. and McDonald, I.M. (1989), "Converting an area into a length diagrammatically: or, Marshall's rectangular hyperbolas once more', University of Melbourne, Department of Economics Research Paper, No. 222.

Dodgson, J.S. (1982), "Kinks and Catastrophes: a note on the relevance of catastrophe theory for economics", *Australian Economic Papers*, vol. 21.

Formby, J.P., Layson, S. and Smith, J. (1982), 'The law of demand, positive sloping marginal revenue and multiple profit equilibria", *Economic Inquiry*, vol. 20.

Guillebaud, C.W. (1971), "Some Personal Reminiscences of Alfred Marshall", *History of Political Economy*, vol. 3.

Lerner, A.P.L. (1933-34), 'The Concept of Monopoly and the Measurement of Monopoly Power", *Review of Economic Studies*, vol. 1.

Marshall. A. (1873), "Graphic Representation by aid of a Series of Hyperbolas of Some Economic Problems having Reference of Monopolies", *Proceedings of the Cambridge Philosophical Society*, vol. XV.

Marshall, A. (1879), *The Pure Theory of Foreign Trade and the Pure Theory of Domestic Values* (repr. London: LSE, 1949).

Marshall, A. (1890), *Principles of Economics*, 9th (Variorum) Edition, C.W. Guillebaud (ed.) (London: Macmillan, 1961).

O'Brien, D.P. (1990), "Marshall's Industrial Analysis", *Scottish Journal of Political Economy*, vol. 37.

Pigou, A.C. (ed.) (1925), *Memorials of Alfred Marshall* (London: Macmillan).

Robinson, J.V. (1933), *The Economics of Imperfect Competition* (London: Macmillan, repr. 1948).

Samuelson, P.A. (1967), "The Monopolistic Competition Revolution", in R.E. Kuenne (ed.) *Monopolistic Competition Theory: Studies in Impact* (New York: Wiley).

Schumpeter, J.A. (1954), *History of Economic Analysis* (London: Allen and Unwin, repr. 1986).

Titchmarsh, E.C. (1949), "Godfrey Harold Hardy", repr, in *Collected Papers of G.H. Hardy*, vol. I (Oxford: Clarendon, 1966).

Turnbull, H.W. (1952), *Theory of Equations* (Edinburgh: Oliver and Boyd).

Walters, A.A. (1980) "A note on monopoly equilibria", *Economic Journal*, vol. 90.

Whitaker, J.K. (ed.) (1975), A. Marshall (1867-1890). *The Early Economic Writings of Alfred Marshall*, vol. 1 (New York: Free Press).

Whitaker, J.K. (1986), "The Continuing Reference of Alfred Marshall", in R.D. Collison Black (ed.), *Ideas in Economics* (London: Macmillan).

Winstanley (1951), *Geometrical and mechanical Drawing* (London: Edward Arnold).

PART IV

MONEY AND THE CURRENCY PRINCIPLE

[14]

Chapter Two

Monetary Economics

D.P. O'Brien

2.1 Introduction

In this chapter an attempt is made to place the body of modern monetary discussion, with which students are familiar, in historical perspective. The problems of attempting an exercise of this sort are particularly acute in the field of monetary writing, where there is an enormous and prolix literature covering several centuries of effort. Indeed, it is probably true that monetary theory was the first branch of economics to reach sophisticated levels of analysis and that its analytical concepts have the longest history. Considerable compression has thus been necessary; and in the process a number of writers who are important in post-1945 monetary theory have perforce been neglected, both because their contribution can be embodied in the summary of the modern position which is given in each section of this chapter and because particular contributions which may be important in relation to the literature produced within a short span of time tend to seem rather less important when viewed against the historical perspective of the long evolution of monetary theory.

The very nature of money has been an issue throughout much of the development of monetary theory, and this is considered first. Next comes the discussion of theories of the demand for money, distinguishing between those approaches which emphasize velocity and those which emphasize the demand for balances. In considering approaches to the supply of money it is easy to find both independent supply and demand-determined supply in the literature over a long period, and this leads to different approaches to monetary control both in the great nineteenth-century debates and in the twentieth-century literature. Some of the differences over monetary control relate to different approaches to the rate of interest, and section 2.5 discusses the history of interest theory. However, the major source of division concerning monetary control is, inevitably, the transmission mechanisms, and these are discussed in section 2.6. 3

The overall picture which emerges is of a monetary theory which steadily *evolved* rather than being subject to *revolutions*. The changes of direction which monetary theory has taken have been changes of focus, of ranking of the objectives of monetary policy, rather than of analysis and concepts, both of which have developed to their present state over very long periods.

2.2 The concept of money

2.2.1 MONEY DEFINITIONS AND THEIR RATIONALE

Money is typically defined by specifying functions which have to be performed. First, and most importantly, there is the medium of exchange function. Then there are the roles of money as a store of value, unit of account and standard for deferred payments. These qualities are seen as reducing transactions costs and as transmitting and summarizing information.

To fulfil these functions, whatever is used as money must have a number of characteristics. Those typically emphasized as necessary are general (even universal) acceptability, homogeneity, divisibility and portability. But there is by no means universal agreement on the categories of assets which possess these qualities to a satisfactory degree; and such disagreement has existed throughout the history of monetary theory. Nowadays the narrowest definition of money is of currency plus sight deposits in commercial banks. To these, some of the most influential modern monetary writers, especially Friedman (1969), add time deposits in commercial banks.

The question of whether interest-bearing deposits are money has given rise to some considerable controversy in modern times. Pesek and Saving (1967) take the view that demand deposits, held for the flow of amenities they yield, are money, while time deposits, held solely for interest, are not[1].

On the other hand, a number of writers have followed the important and influential work of Gurley and Shaw (1960) in emphasizing the importance of deposits in Non-Bank Financial Intermediaries. In Britain, the Radcliffe Report (1959) went so far as to substitute for the quantity of money the broad (and undefined) concept of general liquidity. Although the Radcliffe Report is often regarded as 'Keynesian' it is in fact more extreme than Keynes himself on a number of issues, including the very idea that the concept of money is irrelevant. In fact, the quantity of money is not really defined in the Report; para. 388 refers to 'notes plus bank deposits', but the latter are unspecified, and it would seem from the rather cavalier reference to 'some notion of the "supply of money"' that the

concept was considered obsolete[2]. Monetary policy, it was felt, should aim at liquidity rather than the supply of money.

It is perhaps the vagueness of these views, and of the associated policy recommendations (which are difficult to disentangle), which make it clear to the reader that there is something more than semantics involved here. Nevertheless the view that concern over the definition of money is misplaced is, and always has been, easy to find in the literature (for example, Friedman, 1969). However, as will become clear in considering the historical background, the matter is not so simple. There is in particular a desire to distinguish those assets of which it is true that an excess supply affects all prices and not just the assets' own prices (Yeager, 1968; Morgan, 1969). This provides a clue to what is surely the overriding issue, and the one to which niceties of welfare economics[3] come second, the question of monetary control[4].

But the welfare aspects of the money definition also have a long history. Thus the welfare advantages arising from the replacement of non-interest-bearing commodity money by non-interest-bearing credit money as enumerated by Johnson (1969, p. 34)—basically the resource use freed by the replacement of commodity money—are also spelt out by Adam Smith (1776, pp. 310–314).

However, the historic discussions frequently started by emphasizing the *functions* of money and the necessary characteristics if something was to be able to perform those functions. Thus Smith's discussion, which stressed the role of money in supporting division of labour and specialization through providing a means of conducting transactions without barter, emphasized divisibility and durability as necessary qualities, enabling money to act as a standard of value, medium of exchange and store of value (1776, pp. 26–33) following the tradition extending back to Pufendorf. In the nineteenth century a similar discussion may be found in J.S. Mill (1848, pp. 483–488). George Warde Norman, an important member of the Currency School, said that money was a sign of value, standard of value, measure of value, in universal demand and formed the medium of exchange[5]

The qualities required of money to fulfil this role were those possessed by gold; divisibility, durability, universality of demand and constancy.

This approach was carried forward by the successors of the classical economists. Thus Wicksell (1906, trans. 1935, pp. 6–24) referred to money as a measure and store of value and medium of exchange, while Marshall (1923, pp. 12–20) defined the functions of money as acting as a medium of exchange, store of value and standard for deferred payments.

The functional approach was carried over by Keynes, who referred to the functions of discharging debt and acting as a unit of account,

and by Mises, who stressed the importance of money as a medium of exchange supporting division of labour while following Menger in adding to this the role of money in facilitating credit transactions and acting as a store of value[6].

There has, just as in the modern literature, always been a tendency to dismiss the question of the definition of money as semantic[7]. But underlying the apparent insignificance of the dispute has been the deep-seated issue of monetary control. This explains why the definition of money was most frequently disputed during the era of the monetary control debate in the 1840s and 1850s. This is why it was necessary to identify the functions of money and the means of payment which had the required qualities to perform these functions. In so doing it became possible to identify the strategic area of control.

2.2.2 MONEY AND CREDIT

The control rationale comes out particularly clearly in Norman's work. Overstone, too, insisted that deposits must be distinguished from currency because a decrease of deposits would not correct an adverse exchange rate. They did not deny that the behaviour of deposits could affect monetary stability but they held that deposits were ultimately merely a means of economizing on real money. It was the latter that it was important to control directly[8].

On the other hand, the leading figure in the Banking School, Thomas Tooke (1838–1857, V, pp. 505–506) argued that bank notes should not be distinguished from other forms of paper credit and that there was no invariable connection between notes and the credit superstructure. James Pennington (1829), who, although he belonged to neither Currency nor Banking camp, had certain sympathies with Tooke's position, argued that there were limits to monetary control because deposits were money and they could be multiplied without a change in the currency base. Thus the question of control, underlying the definition of money, brings us to the vexed question of bank deposits. It may surprise the modern reader to learn that in the eighteenth and nineteenth centuries most writers excluded bank deposits from the category of money. Thus Cantillon (1755, pp. 143, 301–305) saw bank deposits (and even bank notes) not as money but as factors affecting velocity of circulation[9] (Holtrop, 1929, p. 507). The Currency School resisted strongly the suggestion that deposits were money[10]. Later, Marshall excluded cheques from the money supply because of limited acceptability, and Wicksell distinguished between metallic money and deposits[11].

A particular argument used against the inclusion of bank deposits in the money supply was that they lacked the power to close finally a transaction. But this 'final closing' argument was rejected by J.S. Mill, who argued that even Bank of England notes ultimately depended upon the solvency of the Bank; the argument, if pushed to

its logical conclusion, limited money to metal. Tooke rejected the argument as fiction; notes were only used for a small balance after clearing[12].

This opposition to the 'final closing' argument was not, however, because the Banking School wished to 'monetize' bank deposits. Rather, writers like Tooke and Fullarton held that bank notes and deposits were both forms of credit—thus following Henry Thornton (1802). They held that gold and silver and inconvertible legal tender notes were the only true money, but that this was irrelevant since credit instruments exercised monetary effects which were not controlled through control of proper money. Tooke rejected the argument of Norman that notes could be distinguished from deposits on the grounds that if notes were withdrawn their place would have to be supplied by coin; this was true, in Tooke's view, only of small-denomination notes. In attempting to make convertible notes into a special category the Currency School were, he argued, confusing legal tender *inconvertible* notes, on the Continental pattern, with convertible notes. Only the former were money[13].

The Currency School accorded a unique place to convertible notes because they believed that, as bank reserves, these notes controlled an inverted credit pyramid. Such an idea was rejected by those who refused to distinguish between notes and other forms of credit, especially Fullarton and J.S. Mill. These writers stress the independent importance of bank credit. It was perhaps natural that writers like Mill, Fullarton and Tooke, who regarded bank notes as a form of credit, should stress the effects of other forms of credit[14].

This attitude carried over to Marshall (1926, p. 140), who, despite including notes in his definition of money, followed Mill in insisting on the importance of credit as exercising a purchasing power similar to that of money. The line of thought continues through to the Radcliffe Report; and Cramp (1960, p. 595) has pointed to a close parallel between the Radcliffe concept of liquidity and Mill's concept of purchasing power.

This is not surprising, since the Banking School extended their concept of credit widely to include bills of exchange. Following the calculations of William Leatham (1840), Tooke (1844) stressed the importance of bills of exchange in performing the functions of money. The emphasis on the importance of bills of exchange derives from Thornton (1802, p. 81), in whose work the Banking School's roots arguably lie; but Thornton had seen bills of exchange not as money but as part of a superstructure of paper credit resting on a monetary base. The Banking School were unconvinced that the credit rested on such a base and was thus limited by it. The Currency School, on the other hand, believed that 'economizing expedients' like bills of exchange could not, except in the very short run, affect the price level independently of the supply of currency; Norman, in particular,

emphasized that they were imperfectly acceptable (because some knowledge of the drawer and acceptor was required) and that the credit generated in this way would have to be made good in currency.

2.2.3 DEPOSITS AS MONEY

As already indicated, the Currency School had a narrow definition of money, excluding deposits, and denied any independent influence to deposits, while the Banking School had an even narrower definition of money, like the Radcliffe Report, but regarded money as not unique in its effect on demand. There is, however, a third strand in the nineteenth-century writings in which deposits were included *as part of* the money supply. The leading writer here is undoubtedly James Pennington, who, although he ultimately became a supporter of the Currency School had, for a long time, some sympathy with positions adopted by Tooke. In a letter of 1829 to Tooke he argued that bank deposits and *country* bank notes were identical, and that the money of the metropolis was largely in the form of bank deposits. Writing to Tooke again in 1838 Pennington again equated money with deposits and treated a reduction in bankers' deposits at the Bank of England as equivalent to a reduction of notes. Longfield, too, seems to have taken the view that the only real distinction between currency and deposits was in their velocity of circulation[15].

It was ultimately this view which, not without difficulties, triumphed in the twentieth century. Thus Pigou (1917, pp. 39–41) defined money as legal tender money plus bank deposits subject to cheque; and he was followed, with some hesitation, by Keynes. Although Keynes (1923, p. 141) considered bank credit the main determinant of the price level, he was for long reluctant to call bank deposits money. In his *Treatise* (1930) he distinguished bank deposits as 'bank money' from money proper, citing Knapp's theory of statist money. Bank deposits were 'not money proper but an acknowledgement of debt' (Vol. I, p. 8). But having thus limited money Keynes was forced to decide that what he called 'current money' was predominantly bank deposits, including, be it noted, unused overdraft facilities (Vol. I, pp. 27–29, 37). All this, however, related to deposits subject to cheque; time deposits were 'scarcely money' (Vol. I, p. 38) and they did not constitute a constant proportion of total deposits, so that it was seriously misleading to treat bank deposits as identical with cash.

Keynes's treatment seems to have been influenced by Hawtrey and by Mises (1912), whose work, originally appearing in German, distinguished between commodity money, fiat money and credit money (trans. 1934, p. 61) as Keynes was later to do (1930, Vol. I, p. 6).

2.3 The demand for money

In the modern monetary literature it is now customary to distinguish between a 'classical' model and a 'Keynesian' model. The former is

characterized by a stable velocity function, with demand for balances dependent upon transactions, the length of payment periods and expenditure patterns. The latter model is characterized by emphasis upon the transactions, precautionary and speculative motives for holding money, leading to a portfolio approach and to a fusion of the motives for holding money into a multiplicative form associated with Baumol's (1952) square-root rule, later developed by Brunner and Meltzer (1967)[16].

The most influential modern treatment of the demand for money undoubtedly springs from the work of Friedman (1969), who has advanced the quantity theory of money as a theory of the demand for money. Friedman's use of wealth as an argument in the demand for money function has been seen by some commentators as the most important development, although the only genuinely novel element is the significance attached to the ratio of non-human to human wealth. Perhaps the most critical elements in this approach are the idea that the elasticity of the money demand function with respect to the price level is unity, and that the function itself is stable.

The latter hypothesis has been tested through extensive econometric work, employing models fitted with various lags to allow for adjustment of money holdings to target levels. Such studies have been linked with opposition to the view, associated with Keynes, that the interest elasticity of demand for money is extremely high, and the related view, found noticeably in the Radcliffe Report, that there is no upper limit to velocity of circulation.

It is thus helpful, if seeking to understand the way in which analysis of the demand for money has developed, to examine the rise of the concept of velocity of circulation before moving on to analyse the nature of money demand; and it will emerge that this approach has been adopted by a number of major writers.

2.3.1 VELOCITY OF CIRCULATION

The concept of velocity dates from at least as early as the seventeenth century and, at that date, the two approaches—velocity and demand for money—seem to have differed only in the degree of emphasis attached to one or other way of looking at the problem. The seventeenth-century emphasis was upon business balances—a significant point, as will become clear. There are important seventeenth-century discussions of velocity by Petty and Locke, the latter emphasizing the cash balance aspect of velocity, while in the early eighteenth century we find velocity treated by Potter and Cantillon[17]. In the nineteenth-century literature it is mentioned at an early stage by Ricardo, followed by James Mill[18]; but the most detailed early nineteenth-century treatment is by Henry Thornton (1802, pp. 96–97), who analysed factors affecting the demand for money as the

determinant of velocity. Others who discussed velocity included J.S. Mill and Attwood, the latter distinguishing between income and transactions velocity of circulation[19].

Velocity is discussed by Marshall and by Wicksell[20], both of whom, excluding bank deposits and bills of exchange from the money supply, treated them as means of increasing velocity, which they believed to show a secular upward drift through the development of credit and communications. Indeed Wicksell pointed out that the gains from economizing on cash balances acted as an incentive to devise means for doing so.

The author whose emphasis on velocity is most well known is undoubtedly Irving Fisher. Fisher made statistical studies of velocity, which he said was determined by individual habits of thrift and payment, by systems of transactions (including the degree of synchronization of payments and receipts) and by general causes such as population density and transport rapidity. The important point which Fisher wished to emphasize was that velocity was dependent on 'technical conditions' and was not functionally related to the money supply, though it might move in a pro-cyclical way[21].

Keynes, although he attacked the velocity concept, used it extensively[22].The most extreme dismissal of the concept is to be found in the Radcliffe Report, which seems to have envisaged a *short-run* response to monetary tightness, involving raising of velocity through learning by financial institutions, a view which Artis has traced to earlier work by Minsky. Even so, it is hard to understand why velocity should not approach some limit asymptotically[23].

With the possible exception of Fisher, it is doubtful, however, whether any of the writers whose discussions of velocity have been mentioned regarded velocity as some exogenous constant. They were all clear that velocity could change; what distinguishes the various approaches is the degree to which they thought velocity stable in the *short run*, for even in the case of Fisher it is clear that he envisaged the possibility of secular changes. However, in order to understand the degree of short-run instability anticipated it is necessary to look at the analysis of the demand for balances.

2.3.2 THE DEMAND FOR BALANCES

The analysis of the demand for balances starts with emphasis by Petty upon transactions demand, leading, at an early stage in the work of Adam Smith, to a distinction between the personal and the business motives for holding balances[24]. However, the precautionary motive for holding balances also makes an early appearance; it was Thornton who laid considerable emphasis upon this and, in turn, influenced Marshall. Thornton's analysis is particularly striking, because he has the demand for balances varying with the state of business confidence,

and as responsive both to the rate of interest and to what has become known in the modern literature as 'brokerage', that is, the cost of realizing assets to obtain balances. But perhaps the most striking thing is that all this clearly implies that velocity is *not* fixed in the short run[25].

These ideas continued to appear throughout nineteenth-century treatments of the demand for money. Thus in Senior's *Lectures on the Value of Money* there is a clear discussion of the cash balance demand as a function of income per head and the degree of progress beyond barter[26]. Both Joplin and Tooke separate the personal and business motives for holding money; and this was continued by Bagehot and Giffen[27]. The idea of precautionary balances which were affected, in the short run, by the degree of confidence in business activity is found in a number of writers, including J.S. Mill and Tooke[28].

The marginal revolution gave these insights a particular twist by emphasizing the marginal utility of holding cash balances, and the balancing of this marginal utility against the marginal disutility of the interest foregone. Walras abandoned a Fisher-type equation approach in favour of a cash balance one, consistently with his emphasis upon the fundamental role of marginal utility[29]. Wicksell emphasized the transactions and precautionary motives, distinguishing between personal and business holdings, with the latter being related to turnover and, long before Baumol, derived a square-root rule, although from rather different reasoning[30].

But Marshall was, of the marginalist writers, perhaps the most influential of all in relation to the analysis of the demand for money. Deriving his cash balance approach explicitly from such predecessors as Petty, Locke and Cantillon, and his concept of velocity from the Bullion Report, with its emphasis on demand for balances varying with the state of confidence, Marshall argued that the demand for such balances depended primarily upon income and wealth. There was also a precautionary motive for holding balances, and since this precautionary motive included sums held to avoid missing investment opportunities, it extended to a speculative motive as well. Marshall naturally adopted the view that the marginal utility of cash balances was equated with the marginal cost of holding balances, particularly interest foregone; but taking his discussion as a whole the factors which received most emphasis were, first, the role of income and wealth in determining the demand for balances; second, the *long-run* changes in the demand for balances deriving from economic growth and the development of economic institutions; and third, *short-run* changes in the demand for balances caused by variations in confidence and in the price level[31].

Marshall's monetary work was followed by that of other English economists. Pigou provided a detailed formal approach to the demand for balances, emphasizing the marginalist maximization principles

and expressing the idea in the now-familiar form of the 'Cambridge equation', while Lavington emphasized the transactions and precautionary motives for balances and the marginal utility approach to their size[32].

Perhaps the most important and original of Marshall's English successors was Hawtrey. He naturally presented the transactions and precautionary motives for holding balances but also, by retaining the older tradition of a clear distinction between personal and business saving, continued to attach importance to the investment motive for holding balances. It is interesting to note that he applied this motive to personal saving. Thus Hawtrey presented the demand for money, as early as 1919, in terms of transactions, precautionary and investment motives, on the lines which Marshall had sketched out but in considerably more detail. For Hawtrey's analysis of what he called the 'unspent margin' provides the bridge between the cash balance approach and the later development of the consumption function. The size of the 'unspent margin' was a function of income and of wealth for individuals, with wealth defined as *expected* wealth governed '(in the main)' by ruling prices. The business 'unspent margin' was determined, as with Wicksell, by turnover[33].

It is from this background that Keynes's analysis of the demand for money developed. Keynes used an algebraic form similar to that earlier put forward by Pigou while basing the analysis upon the utility optimization approach and stressing that demand for balances was not necessarily stable. In fact, the feature which perhaps most distinguished his *Tract* is the extent to which he seemed anxious to emphasize the instability of the demand for money[34].

In his *Treatise* he disowned the equation of the *Tract* but continued to use what was basically a very similar approach, with marginal utility determination of the demand for balances and considerable emphasis upon the instability of the demand for money because of unstable business demand. Indeed, the distinguishing feature of the *Treatise*, the most interesting of Keynes's works from a monetary point of view, is its emphasis upon the predominant role of business deposits, and the various motives—production, speculation, financial—for holding these. This, of course, was not entirely new; nor were the other elements of the analysis, including the discussion of the transactions and precautionary motives which gave rise to income deposits and of the speculative motive which gave rise to savings deposits[35]. The distinguishing feature of the book is really the emphasis upon short-run instability[36].

The presentation in his *General Theory* of the now-familiar transactions, precautionary and speculative motives was then not particularly novel[37], at least if these elements are taken in isolation. The same is true of the idea of shifts in 'liquidity preference' because of changing expectations[38].

The same inheritance was shared by D.H. Robertson. Robertson also proceeded from a marginal utility approach to the demand for balances and presented the transactions and precautionary motives, but he was less concerned to stress problems associated with instability and more interested in the effects of monetary expansion in producing forced saving, or, as he liked to call it, 'Automatic Lacking'[39].

2.3.3 ELASTICITY OF DEMAND FOR BALANCES

The idea that the elasticity of demand for balances with respect to changes in the price level was likely to be less than one (and might even be negative under certain circumstances) dates back to the early years of the nineteenth century, following the episode of the *Assignats* in the French Revolution. The elasticity of demand for balances with respect to the price level was a matter of concern to Say, Thornton, Senior and J.S. Mill[40]. There were two threads here. First, there might be the desire to part with a depreciating medium (loss-avoidance); second, there was a desire to exchange money for commodities in order to benefit from a rise in the price of the latter (profit-seeking). The same view is found later on in the work of Goschen and of Marshall. The effect of interest on the demand for balances was discussed by Fullarton and Giffen as well as by Jevons[41].

It is interesting that the responsiveness of the demand for balances to changes in the price level and the rate of interest was a matter of common concern before the formal promulgation of the elasticity concept in Marshall's work. However, from Marshall onwards there occurs both the formal invocation of the elasticity concept and an increasing tendency, stemming in particular from Pigou, to treat the elasticity of demand for balances as equal to one. However, in the case of Pigou it appears, from his reaction to criticism by Cannan, that although he considered the demand curve for balances to have an elasticity equal to one, he envisaged that demand curve as *shifting* in response to inflationary expectations[42]. Keynes, with the experience of the post-World War I inflations in Germany, Austria and Russia before him, was able to elaborate upon this. He agreed with Cannan (and Lehfeldt) that the elasticity of demand for balances was not equal to one, and argued that inflationary experience showed that inflation initially increased the demand for balances as people expected the price level to fall back, but that as soon as they learnt of their mistake they would economize on balances[43].

Thus it is apparent that the idea that the demand curve for balances was a rectangular hyperbola in form, which was put forward by a number of writers after 1890, was only advanced on the basis that other things were equal; and care was taken to emphasize that other things were unlikely to be equal, either in the short term—because of

inflationary expections—or in the long term—because of changing habits and forms of payment[44]. A nice example is provided by Wicksell (1906, in 1935, p. 142) who, having advanced the concept of a rectangular hyperbola, then shortly afterwards (p. 145) emphasizes the role of velocity changes.

2.4 The supply of money

In the modern literature on the supply of money there are two approaches which differ in the weight which they attach to limitations on the power of banks to create credit imposed by the need for reserves and to the distribution of the available stock of wealth between assets of varying liquidity, one of which is money, the quantity of which is then determined by asset preferences and relative prices[45]. The differences of emphasis lead to a position in which one group of writers can be regarded as treating the money supply as determined by supply factors whereas the other group can be regarded as treating the money supply as demand-determined.

A famous modern version of the bank deposit multiplier, which is the predominant approach amongst the first group of writers, is that of Friedman and Schwartz (1963). The direct nature of their multiplier is modified through drains of money abroad and into non-bank financial intermediaries. Its critics claim that both the reserve ratio (r) and public holdings of cash (c) vary; instability in these will, of course, cause the multiplier to vary. This does not, however, pose insuperable problems if the factors causing r and c to vary can be identified; and flexible multipliers have been developed which take account of variations in r in response to the risk-adjusted rate of return and in c in response to income, the price level and the interest on balances. The end-result has been to identify long-run stable multipliers but to suggest that the deposit multiplier is unstable in the short run.

The high-powered money base upon which the multiplier operates must be exogenous to the banking system; critics of the multiplier approach have emphasized that it may become endogenous, especially if the authorities are willing to trade freely between cash and Treasury Bills in order to stabilize the short-term rate of interest (Dennis, 1981).

The alternative approach to deposit multipliers may be referred to by the term 'portfolio theory'. It is associated in particular with the work of Tobin (1956, 1958, 1963, 1965) and also with the growing importance attached to deposits in non-bank financial intermediaries, following the work of Gurley and Shaw (1960) and of Clayton (1962). The portfolio approach, which has its roots in General Equilibrium theory, concentrates on two particular criticisms of the multiplier approach; first, that the multiplier approach treats cash and other

assets as in two distinct compartments, instead of looking at the allocation of the assets of a bank as in a continuum-balancing risk against return; second, that multipliers conceal the economic decisions which underlie them (Goodhart, 1975, pp. 111–112).

The basic argument is that the money supply is endogenous: and the volumes of both deposits and of high-powered money are dependent upon portfolio decisions taken by the general public, the financial sector and the governmental sector.

Much of this criticism seems rather strained. While there may be good reasons for arguing that the money supply is demand-determined, the multiplier itself implies a simple portfolio approach with only two assets, cash and bonds, with the latter always preferred up to a prudential limit because of positive yield. However, an important, and associated, thread in this school of argument is that concentration upon bank deposits is misplaced. Banks, it is argued, are not different from other financial intermediaries except in the initial re-deposit ratio (see, for example, Tobin, 1963, p. 410). The roots of both these approaches go back a very long way indeed.

2.4.1 SUPPLY-DETERMINATION

It had been understood since the eighteenth century, by such writers as John Law, Bishop Berkeley and the American statesman Alexander Hamilton, that bank deposits were a multiple of cash held by the banks; and the inference had been correctly drawn that the banks must create deposits[46]. But the mechanics do not seem to have been clearly understood. In the 1820s the mechanism of deposit creation through lending and re-deposit was explained by James Pennington in a memorandum to Huskisson (Sayers, 1963). Pennington also allowed Tooke to publish two letters in which he explained the operation of the deposit multiplier, although denying that he had in mind a direct mechanical relationship (Pennington, 1829, 1837). Pennington was followed by Torrens (who, with his usual acuteness, seized the essential point very quickly and expounded it in his *Letter to Lord Melbourne* of 1837) and by Joplin (1844).

Such an idea was naturally of considerable value to the Currency School, who wished to emphasize monetary control through control of the high-powered money base in the form of convertible Bank notes. They were not prepared to insist upon the idea of a direct and mechanical multiplier; such an idea would have been contrary to their insistence upon variations in the demand for money with phases of the cycle. But they did view the upper superstructure of credit as resting upon the high-powered money base: and the most important part of this superstructure was bank deposits. It was thus that the Currency School, especially Overstone, long opposed the introduction of a

'Relaxing Power' into the Act of 1844; this, which would allow the issue of Bank of England notes beyond the strict limits of that Act, would involve loss of control of the high-powered money base and thus make the money supply demand-determined[47].

Thus the idea of multiple deposit creation on a reserve-asset base, and the associated idea of monetary control through that reserve-asset base, were well established in the nineteenth century; and Giffen's treatment of the role of bank reserves led Marshall to apply the standard mathematical technique to obtain the expression for a sum of a series which he then expounded, in apparent ignorance of the work of Pennington, Torrens and Joplin, before the Gold and Silver Commission in 1887[48]. Fisher in his *Purchasing Power* of 1911 expounded the deposit multiplier and made explicit allowance also for the cash holdings of individuals[49].

However, the concept of the deposit multiplier is widely associated with the names of Macleod, Phillips and Crick[50]. In fact, Macleod does not (like Joplin) explain the re-deposit and multiplier aspects. He simply assumes that extra deposits will be created. Chester Phillips, in a book published in 1921, explained the mechanics using the summation of a series and providing the (elementary) algebraic basis. He distinguished, as elementary textbooks now do, between reserve loss if a single bank tries to expand its loan and expansion by the banking system as a whole. Joplin had, however, dealt with the case of multiple banks, although leaving the question of reserve loss a little cloudy.

Phillips' analysis was extended by Lawrence (1928a,b). Although finding fault with some of the former's assumptions concerning the stability and uniformity of the process, he extended the idea to the point (1928b, p. 368) of arguing that banks could make multiple loans on the basis of borrowing from the central bank, thus making control through Bank Rate ineffective—in that penalty borrowing rates could be more than recouped through multiple loans—if all the banks expanded together.

Despite the attention which the work of Phillips and the others has received, it is doubtful whether it added very much to the body of theory already in existence concerning bank lending, although the work of Phillips and Lawrence is remarkable for its use of empirical material. The main line of the argument continued in England after Marshall and became a ruling orthodoxy.

Thus Hawtrey, in his *Currency and Credit* of 1919, viewed the banking system as working with fixed reserve ratios and with control of the level of lending through the high-powered money base. He conceded that reserve ratio control might be placed in difficulties because of lags in the system leading to unforeseen pressure on bank reserves; but the basic model which he had in mind was clearly that of multiple loans on a reserve-asset base[51].

All this is particularly important, because Keynes followed Hawtrey closely on matters of banking practice[52]. As early as 1911 Keynes had been critical of Fisher, arguing that both the bank cash reserve and the public cash holdings were not fixed (Keynes, 1911, p. 395). But in his *Treatise* Keynes (1930) advanced a straightforward deposit multiplier model (Vol. I, pp. 25, 26, 47). Indeed, it is interesting that Keynes was unable satisfactorily to meet the argument of Lawrence noted above concerning the inability of the central bank to control lending; after a rather unconvincing attempt to suggest that reserve losses by one bank alone would prevent multiple-deposit creation on the basis of loans, even at a penal rate, from the central bank, Keynes was forced to dismiss the Lawrence argument as 'purely academic' (Vol. II, p. 223). This was hardly convincing; and modern writers who stress the ability of banks to manufacture their own reserves would be much more sympathetic to Lawrence.

A similar endorsement of the deposit multiplier is to be found in the work of Hayek and of D.H. Robertson, although the latter cites Phillips and Crick. It is interesting, however, that Lavington seems less convinced of such a mechanical relationship[53].

But, as indicated earlier, there is a long line of writers who have argued that the money supply, at least as defined in modern terms, is demand-determined rather than dependent upon supply factors.

2.4.2 DEMAND-DETERMINATION

The origin of this school of thought is arguably in Adam Smith's discussion of the Real Bills doctrine[54]. Smith's argument is that a bank should not advance more than the amount of capital which a merchant would otherwise have kept by him in cash. The bank would thus never exceed the value of the gold and silver which would be required if there were no paper money advanced by banks. The limit would be observed when only real bills of exchange were discounted. The authoritative modern descendant of this argument is to be found in the Radcliffe Report, which seems to see the supply of money as endogenous and to regard Central Bank control as working only through the effect of alterations in interest rates on the 'liquidity' of the private sector taken as a whole. In both cases there is the implication that meeting the needs of trade, in a prudent manner, is the correct path for banking to follow.

But Smith and the Radcliffe Report were talking about very different monetary regimens; in particular, Smith was talking about a paper currency convertible into gold and silver. However, his doctrine was taken over by the Anti-Bullionists and applied to a doctrine of *in*convertible paper. But the moderate Bullionists, especially Thornton, also emphasized the elasticity of supply of paper credit. Thomas Tooke provides the link between the moderate Bullionists and the

Banking School in the 1840s; and Tooke, albeit under a regimen of convertibility, and making a sharp distinction between convertible and inconvertible notes, came to argue that the money supply, at least as defined in modern terms, was demand-determined. Causality ran from the price level to the money supply, and price fluctuations were due to real causes rather than to variations in the quantity of money. This did not mean that banking prudence was not required; it certainly was. But circulation depended upon transactions demand while deposits depended upon demand for means of making large payments. Any excess issue of notes would be returned to the banking system via the principle of 'Reflux', either through being deposited again with the bank or through being used to pay off securities or, should the paper become depreciated, through demanding coin. The circulation was dependent upon money income, in Tooke's view. In truth, Tooke tended, in his later years, as contemporaries and successors have pointed out, to explain prices by prices[55].

Tooke's most effective ally was Fullarton (1845)[56], who held that while the value of an inconvertible currency was determined by its amount, a convertible currency was demand-determined in amount with bills of exchange and deposits as 'a vast and inexhaustible *fund* of potential currency' (p. 44). There was always more credit available than was required (pp. 46–47). Thus over-issue of notes is excluded by the principle of Reflux, while there is an unlimited potential supply of credit available to meet all monetary needs. The emphasis upon a spectrum of liquidity and of substitutes for money as narrowly defined foreshadows both Radcliffe and the portfolio approach.

J.S. Mill (1848, pp. 511–541) relied rather heavily upon the approach of Tooke and Fullarton. Near-money was effective as real money, and the supply of this was not controlled by the supply of reserve assets.

2.5 Monetary control

The modern approach to monetary control is predominantly in terms of control of a large aggregate such as Sterling M_3 through Open Market Operations and Bank Rate. Such an approach has its roots in the 1930s, especially in the writings of Hawtrey and of Keynes, and in the Macmillan Committee of 1931, of which Keynes was a member. This was for much of the post-war period eclipsed by the sort of 'Keynesianism' associated with the 1950s; but it has revived under the influence of Friedman, and of other writers, who have assigned to money a definite causal role.

Criticism of such an approach has come from a number of sides. On the one hand there has been a school of thought which has held that such a large aggregate cannot be easily controlled directly and that

control should instead centre upon the monetary base; that is, reserve assets[57]. In turn, a typical modern criticism of resort to base control is that, in order to reduce reserves, government must sell central government debt. Since it cannot rely on sales of marketable debt or tap issues, this reduces to controlling the supply of Treasury Bills. Operating in this end of the market has serious implications for the short-term rate of interest (Coghlan and Sykes, 1980, pp. 2, 4–5).

However, the main line of criticism of such an approach is that the money supply is, in fact, endogenous. Monetary control is rendered almost impossible by the Public Sector Borrowing Requirement (enormously increased since the mid-1960s) together with the continuous flow of National Debt maturities, flows across the exchanges, the difficulties of knowing what reaction there will be to Open Market Operations and uncertainty over the interest elasticity of aggregate demand (Goodhart, 1975, p. 152). Thus monetary control involves two serious problems; the impetus to monetary growth coming from the public sector deficit and the uncertain (and possibly unstable) response to attempts to control this growth (Goodhart, 1975, pp. 159–160). Pessimism is also to be found in the Radcliffe Report (p. 162). The general position taken in the Report was that the banks would have no difficulty in lending more if they could find suitable customers, that they could manufacture reserve assets as required, that the monetary authorities made this easy for them by trading freely between cash and Treasury Bills in order to protect the rate of interest on Treasury Bills and that the flow of debt maturities and the increasing development of financial institutions both made orthodox monetary control almost impossible[58]. The rate of interest worked through reducing the capital values of assets held by potential lenders, so that they became locked into a particular asset structure and reluctant to realize an asset, and sustain a capital loss, in order to provide funds for a borrower. This was coupled with the supposed 'psychological' effects of 'changes of gear' in interest rates[59].

This pessimism about orthodox monetary control should not surprise us, however, given that the Radcliffe Report represents a continuing strand of monetary thought in which these problems have always been present. A part of the same stream is the Yale School, in which 'monetary theory broadly conceived is simply the theory of portfolio management' (Johnson, 1970, p. 102)[60].

In England the Radcliffe view has led to an interesting development in the thesis (Coghlan, 1980) that changes in the money supply are demand-determined—but that the demand is for *bank credit* and that satisfying such demand can lead to an excess supply of money.

Perhaps the broad distinction which could be made between the different schools of thought about monetary control is between control-optimists and control-pessimists. It is interesting to see that the roots of this divide lie at least as far back as 1844.

2.5.1 MONETARY CONTROL AND THE BANK CHARTER

The Currency School (as represented by Overstone, Norman and Torrens) and the Banking School (as represented by Tooke, Fullarton and J.S. Mill) were agreed upon the need to have a convertible paper currency. Both parties believed that this would check monetary profligacy on the part of government; the Currency School also believed that, properly managed, a convertible paper currency would have an anticyclical effect[61].

Thus both parties were agreed that specie should play a central role in the money supply, its amount varying according to international flows of precious metals resulting from changes in relative international price levels leading to payments imbalances. But beyond that point there was a clear choice. The Currency School were essentially monetary base advocates. The note issue should be controlled directly in accordance with inflows and outflows of precious metals so that there was no room for the exercise of discretion by the Bank in adding to the high-powered money supply. Notes were at the base of the monetary system, and the credit superstructure rested upon them[62].

With a rigid and automatic system of monetary base control, monetary policy would act counter-cyclically. For as economic activity picked up and prices tended to rise, so the balance of payments would be moving into deficit and the Bank would be losing gold. Because it was losing gold it would be forced to contract the note issue; and this act of monetary contraction would, because the credit superstructure rested upon the note issue, check the boom before it got out of hand. Conversely, the downswing would induce monetary expansion automatically.

The Banking School were not optimistic about the effects of monetary control, and believed that rigid control of the monetary base would cause economic dislocation. Their position really arose from elements in Thornton's exposition during the Bullion debate. Thornton (1802), paying particular attention to the micro-economic effects of monetary policy, stressed the distress caused by monetary contraction and argued that, because it caused economic dislocation, it might well correct neither internal nor external monetary disequilibrium. There was, he believed, very little *short-run* connection between the note issue and prices, and in a famous passage he recommended monetary flexibility (p. 259), and caution in the use of monetary contraction.

Thornton was, like Tooke himself in that earlier controversy, a moderate Bullionist. Thus it was that Tooke, in the 1840s controversy, again favoured monetary discretion against an automatic monetary system, the philosophy of which was ultimately based upon the Ricardian definition of excess, i.e. that an amount of notes in circulation, when the country was losing gold abroad, was, *by definition*, in excess. Rather Tooke argued that 'overtrading' and

'overbanking' were unavoidable, and would not be checked by controlling the note issue or by separating the Bank of England into a Banking Department and an Issue Department. The latter would only split the Bank's resources between two departments; in order to protect the diminished reserve the Bank would then have to engage in frequent and severe movements in Bank Rate; and the end-result of this would be commercial dislocation rather than monetary control. The correct way forward lay in the exercise of monetary discretion by the Bank on the basis of an enlarged gold reserve[63]. Like Thornton, the members of the Banking School tended to stress the necessity of a lender of last resort; and it is undoubtedly true that events forced upon the Currency School a similar recognition. It became ultimately accepted by both sides that, in the event of a financial crisis, the rigid limits of the 1844 Bank Act on note issue would be relaxed, thus enabling the Bank of England to make exceptional advances to the money market[64].

2.5.2 MONETARY CONTROL AFTER 1870

Although the Currency School was victorious in the debates over the renewal of the Bank Charter, a majority of writers after 1870, it is probably true to say, followed the Banking School in emphasizing the need for monetary discretion. Tooke's plan for a large reserve was followed by a number of writers, including Giffen and Goschen, but Bagehot's influence seems to have been particularly strong. His stress upon the role of the Bank as lender of last resort, and as holder of one central reserve, enabled him to carry forward Tooke's plan. But though Bagehot was in favour of discretion, he was also optimistic about monetary policy; the vein of pessimism which surfaces repeatedly in the Banking School is much less evident in his work[65].

Bagehot influenced Marshall (1926, p. 111) who indeed took from him the plan for a large reserve—it is strange that Marshall makes no reference to Tooke in this connection. Like Bagehot, Marshall managed to combine an emphasis on the need for discretion with optimism about the power of monetary policy as exercised through Bank Rate and Open Market Operations. But there is a subtle change of emphasis with Marshall; rather more attention is paid in his work to questions of short-run internal equilibrium and rather less to questions of long-run external equilibrium than in the work of his predecessors. This led him to stress the need to meet business monetary requirements and to avoid rigidity in monetary arrangements[66].

This shift of emphasis was carried over to his successors, who themselves made one further and highly significant shift; from a concentration upon notes to a concentration upon deposits[67].

But, despite the changes of emphasis, it would not be untrue to say that Marshall handed on to his successors the Banking School legacy,

combined with an increased optimism about the efficacy of monetary policy. Thus Lavington advocated the use of a large reserve to avoid fluctuations in the rate of interest, the cushioning of gold flows, and the exercise of monetary policy through Bank Rate and Open Market Operations, aiming at the targets of price, interest rate, and exchange stability[68].

Hawtrey also argued for the use of such indicators together with output, employment, the demand for credit, and the level of transactions. He, too, believed in the necessity of an 'elastic' supply of money, and was optimistic about monetary control. However, Hawtrey deserves special mention amongst Marshall's successors for emphasizing the difficulties of monetary control in the presence of a Public Sector Borrowing Requirement, a matter which, as we have seen, has caused much modern concern[69].

Keynes, in the *Tract* and the *Treatise*, also displayed this combination of emphasis on the need for banking discretion in the pursuit of short-run stabilization objectives with optimism about the power of monetary policy. In the *Tract* he argued that the currency supply and the reserve ratio should be varied to *offset* variations in the demand for cash; and he suggested that open market operations were effective in controlling bank deposits which determined the price level. However, the price level was not the only criterion of the need to exercise monetary policy; output, the demand for credit, the rate of interest, and employment are all mentioned[70].

In the *Treatise* Keynes sees the stability of the price level as the test of whether excessive Bank Credit is being created. If the price level rises, this indicates that investment is greater than saving, and the creation of bank credit should then be controlled through open market operations and Bank Rate. Keynes did not agree that reserves could be manufactured by the banks and, although he envisaged the introduction of control of reserve ratios, he was confident that the creation of credit by the banks could be controlled through the more normal weapons[71].

Not all of Marshall's successors, however, combined optimism and a belief in the need for monetary discretion. Robertson, who (like the Currency School) regarded monetary forces as things which could magnify or diminish a trade cycle but as subsidiary to real forces, was pessimistic about monetary control. He did not agree with Fisher that raising the rate of interest far enough would bring an upswing under control; and although he discussed central bank control through open market operations and the use of the rate of interest, he believed that credit rationing might well be necessary in the upswing, while monetary policy was weak in depression[72].

The writer whose position perhaps most completely anticipates modern pessimism about monetary policy was Lawrence. He criticized the endorsement of open market operations by Keynes and

others. The central bank was not free in its dealings in securities, the supply of government securities depended on the public sector borrowing requirement, and the banks could manufacture reserves. Coupled with his detailed attention, like Phillips, to redeposit ratios, which made him sceptical about bank deposit multipliers, these views find considerable echo amongst the monetary pessimists of the present time[73].

Few writers combined optimism with a belief in automatic monetary policy. The chief writer who did so was Irving Fisher, who, in his proposal for a 'compensated dollar', put forward a mechanism of automatic adjustment in the currency unit to changes in the price level[74].

2.6 The rate of interest

In the modern literature the rate of interest is treated in terms of some kind of IS–LM model[75]. Essentially the position is taken that there is an equilibrium rate at which income is stable and the money market clears. Given the price level, the money supply, the demand for money and the willingness to part with it at different rates of interest, income and the rate of interest are simultaneously determined.

This is a superficially satisfactory model. In fact, however, it glosses over a lot of the questions which economists have considered in the course of the development of the theory of the rate of interest, representing a synthesis of *some* of the elements found in previous theories.

In particular, as will become apparent, earlier writers were concerned about the price level in relation to the rate of interest; and they also used the concept of the 'natural rate of interest', which may be interpreted as the going rate of profit upon marginal investment[76].

The Radcliffe Report dismissed many of the traditional arguments, associated with earlier work by writers like Hawtrey, Wicksell and Keynes, concerning the role of the rate of interest. It played down the interest control effect both in relation to stocks and in relation to fixed investment. Moreover, the Committee believed, like Tooke, that large fluctuations in the rate of interest could undermine the stability of banks—they were concerned about the effects of capital values[77].

The Radcliffe treatment of the rate of interest, unlike most of the modern literature, does have the merit both of showing awareness of the breadth of considerations relating to the rate and of attempting empirical investigation. Its conclusions may seem a little eccentric viewed from a perspective in the early 1980s, when governments are continually being toid about the restrictions on economic activity resulting from high rates of interest; but it provides a convenient

bridge between the modern literature and the comprehensive discussions of early years.

2.6.1 FOUNDATIONS OF INTEREST THEORY

The importance of the rate of interest was recognized in the seventeenth century. Locke believed changes in the rate to affect both trade and the value of money; and Sir Josiah Child of the East India Company argued strongly for a reduction in the rate from 6 per cent to 4 per cent, attributing superior Dutch performance in trade and growth to a low rate of interest in Holland[78].

In Mercantilist writings the rate of interest frequently appears as a purely monetary phenomenon. From the time of Hume, Massie and Smith there was insistence that the rate of interest was a real phenomenon, and it was equated with the marginal productivity of investment[79]. Both Thornton and Ricardo insisted that there was a real rate of interest, which could be identified as marginal profitability; and both writers, followed by many others, insisted that changes in the money supply produced only temporary variations in the market rate, which must ultimately equalize with the real rate. Thornton, and later Ricardo, pointed out that the distinction between the money and the real rate had important implications for Bank policy; there was no limit to the amount which the Bank could lend if the money rate were less than the real rate. Thornton was particularly clear on this. He also distinguished between the nominal and the deflated rate of interest, and expressed the view that nominal rates will adjust during persistent inflation to cover the loss of principal[80].

This analysis provided the foundation for the discussion in the era of the Bank Charter Act, the period in which the Bank of England began to use Bank Rate as a policy weapon[81]. Both Banking and Currency School writers treated the natural rate of interest as the net profit on capital after allowance for risk and trouble of employment. The market rate fluctuated around the natural rate, which was determined by the intersection of the demand for investible funds and the supply of such funds. Once an investment had been made, however, it ceased to affect the rate of interest directly. But the market rate of interest was, in the short term, a monetary phenomenon, and it was recognized, as it had been by Thornton and Ricardo, that changes in the money supply could temporarily affect the rate of interest[82]. The treatment of the subject by J.S. Mill is particularly noteworthy in the light of accusations by Keynes that previous writers had regarded the rate of interest as equating the demand for and supply of savings rather than the demand for and supply of money. Mill argued that the rate of interest would equalize the supply of and demand for *loans*, and that people's willingness to make loans from their available funds varied with activity. The demand for balances ('liquidity preference') varied with the cycle[83].

In dealing with the operation of Bank Rate, the influence of the Bank was treated as a short-term money-market influence. Nonetheless it was important. The Bank could give a danger signal by raising the Rate, thus inducing bankers to ration credit in order to strengthen their liquidity. Conversely, a very low rate of interest could generate an unsound state of credit and price rises, which would stimulate further demand for loans in anticipation of inflation.

2.6.2 MARSHALL AND HIS SUCCESSORS

Marshall was, of course, well read in the preceding Classical literature, especially in the work of J.S. Mill. He regarded the real rate of interest as being determined by the supply of 'free' or 'non-specific' capital (made up of savings and depreciation allowances) and demand for that capital for investment purposes. Demand was a function of available investment opportunities and of price expectations. Expectations had a vital role to play. The money rate of interest fluctuated around the real rate, and could be affected, in the short term, by changes in the supply of money. When these raised prices, the resulting profit opportunities increased the demand for loans; a high rate of interest was thus associated with high and rising prices[84]. In this connection Marshall acknowledged Fisher's important contribution. Fisher had argued in his *Appreciation and Interest* (1896) that, in the long term, the rate of interest rose to cover the loss of principal in inflation. Thus high and low prices were associated with high and low interest. The idea was not new; as indicated earlier, it was put forward by Thornton and J.S. Mill. But both Fisher's detailed and careful work in testing the hypothesis, and Marshall's emphasis on price variations in relation to the rate of interest, helped to maintain the long classical tradition and give it new momentum[85].

Pigou followed Marshall in the analysis of the real and money rate. Nevertheless he was critical of the idea that equilibrium could be attained by equating the *money* with the *real* rate of interest. He believed that the 'income velocity' of money could be affected by changes in expectations without credit changes—bank credit was not the only source of instability. Nevertheless he accepted that Bank Rate could control both credit and the short-run rate of interest, although the link with the bond rate was not secure[86].

Lavington paid attention to the role of the New Issues market. He argued that a high rate of interest discouraged placing of new issues[87]. Hawtrey believed that the New Issues market equated savings and investment not only by means of variations in the rate of interest but also through credit rationing. He believed that credit was unstable, and that the primary way of controlling it was through the rate of interest. This had an important psychological effect, as it altered future profit expectations. Hawtrey, who has been described as the

foremost modern exponent of Bank Rate, saw Bank Rate as affecting output through decisions about stock levels; the effect on output produced effects on income, and variations in incomes affected both the price level and the money supply[88]. He was extremely critical of Keynes's analysis of Bank Rate. In his view, the short-run rate of interest had little effect on the bond rate because changes in the short rate were not expected to last. In turn, the bond rate had little effect upon fixed investment, to which, as will become clear, Keynes attached great importance[89].

Perhaps the most original treatment of the rate of interest, despite its traditional roots, was that put forward by D.H. Robertson. He proposed a version of Marshall's real and money rate, explicitly in *flow* terms. In analysing the real rate he identified the sources of funds as individual and corporate saving, depreciation, increases in bank lending and dishoarding. The demand for funds came from the desire to make investment in fixed and working capital, to replace capital, to obtain command over liquid balances and to make consumer expenditure. He included in his analysis the traditional 'schedule of the marginal product of loanable funds'; but since he emphasized that the productivity of investment was continually changing both as a result of exogenous forces (such as discoveries) and of endogenous forces (the cycle), the essentials of the analysis differ only from the Keynesian 'marginal efficiency of capital' in greater comprehensiveness and the use of a dynamic framework. This is particularly evident when it is appreciated that consumption (and thus saving) in one period was a function of disposable income in the previous period.

Robertson's analysis of the money rate was similarly derived from Marshall. He carried over the Marshallian association between high and rising prices and high and rising interest rates, and was concerned about the saving imposed upon the community by rising prices resulting from credit expansion by the banks[90].

In his *Tract* Keynes offered little analysis of the rate of interest; what he had to say was mainly concerned with rising interest rates during inflation, but without acknowledgement to important predecessors, especially Fisher. (In his *Treatise*, as Marget notes, Keynes made the explicit claim that this issue had been ignored by economists[91].)

In the *Treatise* Keynes adhered to Marshall's analysis of the real and money rates of interest. He based the analysis in this work on the concept of a natural rate of interest (following Wicksell). When the market rate equalled the natural rate, savings equalled investment; there were no supernormal profits and price stability prevailed. Keynes laid considerable emphasis on savings and investment analysis in this work. Economic equilibrium would prevail when the division of output between consumption and investment was the same as the division of income between consumption and saving. The role of Bank Rate was then critical in balancing the expansion of bank

credit to achieve equilibrium between savings and investment. In this work Keynes believed particularly in the sensitivity of fixed investment to Bank Rate, and attempted to establish that long- and short-run interest rates were closely linked[92].

However, Hawtrey was able to show conclusively that the link between short- and long-run rates did not hold to anything like the extent to which Keynes believed, and that he had used a very partial data set[93].

But Keynes had by then shifted his analytical focus, dropping the natural rate of interest and advancing in his *General Theory* a version of Marshall's money rate of interest. He dismissed the concept of the natural rate and asserted that such an idea was based upon a full-employment economy. He now stressed *movements in* the investment demand schedule rather than its sensitivity to variations in the rate of interest. In his analysis of the rate of interest he presented his now-famous discussion of 'liquidity preference', dividing the demand for money into transactions, precautionary and speculative motives. (The transactions and precautionary motives for holding money were, as indicated above, commonly recognized. The speculative motive had been foreshadowed by Hawtrey's 'savings' motive and, above all, by Marshall's 'bulls and bears' 1923, pp. 58–59.) The rate of interest then depended on the interaction of the schedule of the 'marginal efficiency of capital' with the availability of funds, which depended upon decisions to save out of income and to part with savings and make these available for investment[94]. It is here that the analysis of liquidity preference is central.

2.6.3 AN INDEPENDENT TRADITION

So far, the discussion of the rate of interest has concentrated on the line of succession from the classical inheritance through Marshall and the English economists. There is, however, another line of succession stemming directly from the work of Tooke and linking up with the capital theory of the Austrian economist Böhm-Bawerk. This is to be found in the work of Wicksell and his followers.

Wicksell borrowed from Tooke the observation that prices and the rate of interest were positively correlated both with respect to level and to changes. From Böhm-Bawerk's capital theory he took a formal analysis of the natural rate of interest. In a work published in 1898 he put forward a theory of a cumulative upward inflationary process resulting from a money rate of interest below the natural rate, which was apparently based upon these sources and written in ignorance of the work of Thornton. If the money rate was below the natural rate this would present profit opportunities. Entrepreneurs would demand factor inputs and thus factor prices would rise. The rise in these prices raised factor incomes and thus the demand for final products. This in

turn enabled the entrepreneur to cover his increased costs. Inflationary pressures were increased because a lowering of the rate of interest reduced carrying charges, and thus enabled the entrepreneur to pay a higher price for inputs even with the same output prices; and the upward movement of prices created inflationary expectations, shifting both demand and supply curves. Ultimately the upward process would be checked under anything other than a pure credit system, because the banks would have to raise the discount rate to check the drain on their reserves. But their rates were sticky, and they tended to follow movements in the natural rate after a lag, when the effect upon their reserves had become apparent: this explained the positive correlation between upward movements in prices and the rate of interest. However, to stop the process it was not sufficient to restore a lowered interest rate to its previous level, as the inflationary process widened profit margins; it was necessary to push the money rate into equality with the real rate. Once this happened, the inflationary process would peter out[95].

The natural rate is defined in barter terms, with explicit reference to the capital theory advanced by Böhm-Bawerk and Jevons[96]. This explains the ancestry of Wicksell's own approach; but it is not, of course, necessary to the introduction of the concept of a natural rate, and it is, indeed, not particularly easy to understand why, in terms of such limited models, the natural rate should fluctuate, as Wicksell anticipated it would.

The argument owed a considerable debt to Tooke, with his emphasis on the positive correlation between price and rate of interest movements. Nonetheless, Wicksell did not take his analytical apparatus from Tooke; he was particularly critical of Tooke's argument that a reduction in the rate of interest lowered the price level by reducing cost of production, and showed that this line of argument could be used to imply instability in the balance of payments[97].

Wicksell's work was published in German and obtained a following in Austria, where Böhm-Bawerk's work was influential. In particular, he was followed by Mises, who used the argument to develop the idea of over-production of investment goods in the upward cumulative process, and by Hayek[98]. There was also, of course, a Swedish school stemming from Wicksell's work and discussion of the concept of the natural rate by writers like Davidson and Cassel. Thus the Swedish economist Myrdal, writing in 1933, noted that English economists did not seem to be more than superficially familiar with Wicksell's work, and wrote wryly of Keynes's 'unnecessary originality' in his *Treatise*[99].

2.7 Transmission mechanisms and the effects of money

Modern texts distinguish between a 'classical' and a 'Keynesian' model. In the former, money is demanded for transactions purposes

only, velocity is stable, full employment is assumed, the money supply is exogenous, money is neutral, wages and prices are flexible and changes in the money supply produce an effect on prices *directly* through spending of excess balances. In the latter, money is demanded for transactions, precautionary and speculative motives, with the latter providing a floor to the rate of interest, velocity is unstable, there is quantity adjustment and unemployment, a demand-determined money supply, rigid wages and prices, and a supposedly 'Keynesian' transmission mechanism where changes in the money supply work *indirectly* through from the short end of the money market to the bond rate and the demand for investment goods.

Although useful for textbook purposes, this is extremely inaccurate as an historical record. It has been noted that Keynes's analysis of the demand for money was only a variant on what had gone before: that the transactions and precautionary motives were routinely discussed in previous writings and that the speculative motive, though not in the precise form that Keynes gave it, was also recognized. Stable velocity was certainly not a general assumption, and many writers, especially the Banking School, had envisaged a demand-determined money supply.

Moreover, money has hardly ever been regarded as neutral. The quantity theory has sixteenth-century roots; and by the eighteenth century it is possible to find writers who explain the effects of money supply changes at length[100]. In particular, David Hume (1752) emphasized that changes in the supply of money stimulated both output and employment through increasing the profit margin. His analysis passed to the classical economists; and it is discussed and (largely) endorsed by Henry Thornton, who saw changes in the money supply affecting employment, consumption and investment as well as producing inflation because of limited elasticity of aggregate supply. Discussions of the matter are also to be found in the work of Malthus, Torrens, McCulloch, Newmarch and Cairnes. Only Ricardo and James Mill firmly opposed the Hume analysis of the inflationary mechanism[101].

Thus Marshall inherited, both from the classical writers and from his contemporary Giffen, a well-established view that changes in the money supply were not neutral, except in the very long run, and that they produced changes in output and employment. In particular, deflation lowered profit levels and produced economic disorganization, although it had the benefit of increasing real wages and encouraging entrepreneurial search[102].

The influence of Marshall's analysis runs through twentieth-century monetary writing, at least in England. Keynes in his *Tract* (1923) regarded the quantity theory as 'fundamental', (1923, in 1971, p. 61) and in his *General Theory* (1936) we find a discussion of the price, income and employment effects of changes in the money supply with allowance for varying elasticities on lines similar to those of Thornton[103].

2.7.1 CLASSICAL TRANSMISSION

Analysis of transmission in the classical writings is complex, containing both the 'direct' and 'indirect' mechanisms of the modern textbooks. Hume, Cantillon and Ricardo emphasized the direct mechanism; but even in their work we find the indirect mechanism[104]. The leading member of the Currency School, Overstone, emphasized the indirect mechanism and held that there was no simple connection between the money supply and the price level, the effects of changes in the money supply depending upon whether they were pro- or anti-cyclical[105]. With members of the Banking School the emphasis upon the indirect mechanism is even greater. Fullarton is particularly interesting, because he articulated clearly the indirect mechanism. This was taken over by J.S. Mill, who passed it on to Marshall[106].

Thus the Marshallian emphasis upon the indirect mechanism is wholly classical. Apart from the writers already mentioned, the indirect mechanism is clearly present in Thornton's work. Marshall himself was immediately preceded by Sidgwick and by Giffen, both of whom presented the indirect mechanism[107].

Marshall advanced the following mechanism. Gold flowed in and collected in the banking system, bank reserves rose, the banks sought to lend more, the rate of interest was initially depressed, demand for both inputs and outputs rose as a result of credit extension, the price level rose and the demand for transactions balances increased. Increases in the price level and increases in the rate of interest were positively correlated; Marshall explained this by the stimulus to the demand for credit produced by the initial expansion and—under the influence of Fisher—the incorporation into the nominal rate of interest of allowance for inflation. The idea of a direct mechanism is for him a mere curiosity[108].

Marshall's analysis of the transmission mechanism was passed on to writers like Robertson and Keynes. The importance of the rate of interest was also stressed by Hawtrey[109].

Of course, it was not only Marshall who enjoyed this classical inheritance. In particular, Wicksell made the indirect mechanism the centrepiece of his analysis of an upward cumulative inflationary process. Amongst Wicksell's successors was Hayek, who blended this analysis with an Austrian theory of production, arguing that, as new money filters in, it affects the relative profitability of different stages of production, with producer's goods becoming initially more profitable. Then wages rise and the relative profitability of consumption goods is restored while the banks refuse further credit to the investment goods sector, which has thus to free resources. Unemployment results[110].

There was also an extensive American literature, of which Sprague's statistical investigation of the indirect mechanism is particularly noteworthy. (Friedman's work is in a long United States tradition of statistical studies in the quantity theory[111].) Also written

under American influence was the work of Martin (1931), who has a detailed analysis of the circular flow involving both direct and indirect mechanisms[112]. Indeed, it is interesting to note that even the semantic classification of the literature into direct and indirect mechanisms dates from at least ten years before Keynes's *General Theory* (Angell, 1926, p. 120).

2.7.2 THE CREDIT CYCLE

Monetary writers coupled their concern with transmission mechanisms with the identification and analysis of a credit cycle. Amongst the classical writers are McCulloch, Overstone (whose concept of a cycle much influenced Marshall), Tooke, Fullarton and Bagehot. These writers, from McCulloch onwards, envisaged profit variability and the behaviour of investment as of key importance in the cycle; and this was emphasized also by Marshall's predecessor, Giffen[113].

Marshall himself attributed considerable harm to credit fluctuations. In the upswing the demand for manufactured output rose, the extension of credit increased, prices, profits and wages all rose and speculation was stimulated. At the peak of the boom lenders became cautious and a capital shortage developed with investments uncompleted. The unloading of stocks produced a collapse of prices, the failure of speculators and a cumulative downward slide into an economic trough in which there was an absence of confidence. A key role was given to variations in profitability caused by the lag of wages and interest behind price changes[114].

Though Robertson emphasized real forces in the cycle, Hawtrey clearly derived his monetary analysis of the cycle from Marshall. Amongst the novel contributions of Hawtrey was a systematic emphasis upon lags and limited knowledge. A transactions demand lag in the upswing, and an order-completion lag, involved belated demands for cash and for credit unanticipated by the banks, who continued to expand credit as long as their reserves were satisfactory. Ultimately they were forced to contract—too late and too severely, producing depression. They should look beyond reserves to general indicators, because the economy was not self-stabilizing[115].

In the United States Fisher selected the lag of the deflated rate of interest behind profits as the key factor in the credit cycle; but American monetary economics paid much more attention to empirical testing than British work, and Fisher's case was damaged by the investigations of Minnie England, who found that other cost lags were probably more important and that the deflated rate of interest did not catch up with the rate of profit until *after* the peak of the boom[116]

2.7.3 EXPECTATIONS

Within the credit cycle (and linked with changes in the demand for balances) there occurred changes in expectations which radically

altered willingness to invest. Such factors had been emphasized by Thornton, McCulloch and Overstone as well as the inflationist Attwood, while J.S. Mill envisaged shifts in the investment demand schedule with expectations. This passed to Marshall, who envisaged cumulative movements of expectations within the cycle, seeing the chief cause of depression as a 'want of confidence' which particularly affected fixed capital investment. He made explicit acknowledgement to Overstone[117].

Thus it is hardly surprising that Pigou emphasized the psychological factors in the trade cycle and regarded money itself as only an aggravating force. He stressed the importance of profit expectations variability and showed how these were affected by price movements. Lavington envisaged investment varying with the levels of confidence, thus intensifying business cycles[118].

Hawtrey's treatment of expectations is particularly interesting. He laid emphasis upon expected profits and changes in these in relation to the rate of interest; and he showed the psychological importance of Bank Rate in inducing contraction through its effect on expectations[119].

Keynes's own analysis in the *General Theory* afforded a crucial role to expectations as affecting investment, in his presentation of the 'marginal efficiency of capital', but his flamboyant paragraphs about the trade cycle and the shifting marginal efficiency of capital only reflected, in analytical content, a very long tradition, but with a pessimistic turn common at that date[120].

2.7.4 EFFECTIVE DEMAND

The expectations element of the *General Theory* is thus hardly novel. Nor was its emphasis upon effective demand, as writers like Haberler and Robertson pointed out, despite Keynes's claims to the contrary[121]. In England, at least, the pioneering performance was that of Hawtrey, in whose work the immediate roots of the consumption function lie. He focused attention upon the flow of income and expenditure. The importance of credit creation is that it affects income, and thus expenditure, but income and expenditure do not directly keep pace with each other. There are thus changes in what Hawtrey called the 'unspent margin'. He advanced, as early as 1919, an algebraic model of the circular flow of income and expenditure, showing the way in which credit affected orders, income and outlay. Employment was dependent upon aggregate demand: and a reduction in employment further reduced aggregate demand. Monetary contraction brought about unemployment through its effect on consumer income and outlay[122].

Of course, Hawtrey was not alone. Robertson's essay of 1915, *Industrial Fluctuation*, was an important exercise in analysis of aggregate demand in real terms; and another striking example is provided

by Durbin's *Problem of Credit Policy* (1935), written under the influence of Hayek. In the United States the work of Mitchell was outstanding; and he in turn influenced Martin (1931). These writers provided a detailed analysis of the circular flow of purchasing power which was in some respects more sophisticated than Keynes's 'psychological law'[123].

There were also populist writers, including J.A. Hobson and Foster and Catchings—acknowledged by Durbin and by Keynes in his *Treatise* but ignored in the *General Theory*[124].

2.7.5 RIGIDITIES

The importance attached by Marshall to rigid wages and business charges in aggravating the cycle was taken by him from Bagehot and Giffin; and there seems no doubt that he envisaged quantity and employment variations in depression. Both Robertson and Lavington laid some emphasis upon rigidities; but it was Hawtrey who dwelt particularly upon quantity variation, the impact of monetary policy being initially on output rather than prices. Pigou also stressed quantity adjustment with rigid wages and prices. This problem is also a main theme of Durbin's book[125]. Thus the emphasis on adjustments in output and employment in the *General Theory*, while it presents some contrast with Keynes's own *Treatise*, presents rather less strong contrast with the general tenor of previous writings.

2.7.6 SAVINGS AND INVESTMENT

It is largely true that, with the exception of discussions of forced saving by writers like Cantillon, McCulloch, Hume, Malthus and Horner[126], saving and investment were treated as single acts by the classical economists. It is among Marshall's successors that the treatment of savings and investment developed along modern lines out of his cash balance approach. Lavington took the view that while some people save and invest concurrently, others build up balances of savings till a favourable opportunity for investors occurs. This can cause fluctuations in employment which are not offset by the 'law of large numbers', because investors react together to common causes. This line of argument is also to be found in the work of Hawtrey. Indeed, as Davis has pointed out, Hawtrey had a model in which output changes brought savings and investment into equilibrium. Robertson also certainly deserves at least equal credit with other members of the Cambridge School for the development of savings and investment analysis, despite the weird terminology he employed. In the United States the analysis was developed both by orthodox economists like Mitchell and by 'heretics' like Foster and Catchings. In Sweden the distinction developed from the work of Wicksell, and in

so doing it embodied, like the work of Robertson, dynamic elements[127].

'Investment' as treated both by the classical economists and by Marshall typically referred to fixed investment. This is hardly surprising, given the economic history of the Victorian age. The word 'speculation' from Tooke to Marshall typically refers to this, as well as to stocks, and we find writers like Fullarton, Jevons and Giffen all referring to fixed investment. Only Hawtrey placed the overwhelming emphasis on stocks—quite deliberately, because of the lack of influence of short-term interest rates on the bond market. Keynes, however, in his *Treatise* gave the impression that all previous writers, except Wicksell, had neglected fixed investment and dealt only with investment in stocks. He himself paid considerable attention to investment both in this work and in the *General Theory*, in which he built upon a formal concept which came, as he acknowledged, from Fisher—the Marginal Efficiency of Capital. This was a marriage of marginal productivity analysis with classical expectations defined in terms of the expectation of yield and the *current* supply price of the capital asset[128].

2.7.7 TARGETS AND INDICATORS

The predominant classical targets were price stability and the avoidance of commercial crises. Marshall also tended to couch his discussions of economic stability in terms of a mix of objectives, but with the emphasis on price stability, which was felt to be the key to stabilization generally. Thus Hawtrey, in listing the objectives of monetary policy as wage, price, profit, output and debtor/creditor relationships stabilization, was following this tradition. This does not alter the fact that he was interested both in unemployment—which by 1932 he considered the biggest single problem—and the course of real wages. But, as a pioneer of stabilization analysis, he rejected Fisher's prescription of pursuing stabilization measures solely with reference to the price level; in his view this would involve moving too late, and thus it was necessary to look to other indicators such as output, employment and the balance of payments. Similarly, Lavington suggested the use of exchange rates, international reserves and price variations as indicators[129].

It is from this background that Keynes's own thought comes. In the *Tract* he mentions stabilization of business and employment, but the whole thrust of the emphasis is upon *price* stabilization; and it is rather puzzling to find that Keynes sees a clear *choice* between external and internal price stability, as if price stability in an open economy were independent of exchange stability. In the *Tract* he follows Hawtrey in rejecting Fisher's stabilization proposal and in advocating a wide range of indicators[130]. In the *Treatise* the question of employment is a

little more in evidence, but it is largely treated as a subordinate issue when discussing the speed of adjustment of prices and wages[131]. Pigou had, however, already begun the shift to placing the emphasis on employment. His *Industrial Fluctuations* paid far more attention to unemployment than Keynes's *Treatise* published three years later. It is in the *General Theory* that there is a dramatic change in Keynes's focus, with employment as virtually the only argument in the social welfare function, it being held that the economic system tends to stabilize at a level of less than full employment[132]. In his singlemindedness the Keynes of 1936 had almost only one predecessor, the inflationist Thomas Attwood, although his name may be coupled with Foster and Catchings, who drew from their analysis the moral that what was required was an ever-increasing money supply—the same moral as has been drawn in practice under policies inspired by the *General Theory*.

2.8 Conclusion

There is space for only a brief conclusion. This chapter should at least have made clear the very high degree of continuity which is to be found in monetary thought. It exhibits, in terms of concepts and techniques, a degree of continuity which can only be matched by international trade. But this necessarily raises awkward questions to economists reared upon the idea of a Keynesian Revolution.

It seems clear that Keynes's contributions were not primarily in novel analysis or concepts. His achievement was to succeed in persuading economists to place employment considerations at the forefront of their thinking. His victory was due not so much to analytical capacity as to flair, timing, literary punch and the sheer pressure of events. The personal magnetism of the man comes through his pages, and it is hard to resist either the charm or the panache of Keynes's economic writings, though it is hard to forgive his misleading comments on writers like Fisher and, in particular, Marshall. But such was his success that, when the monetarist counter-revolution occurred, the Keynesian change of focus had to be deflected by emphasis on the concept of the natural rate of unemployment, which Keynes himself had rejected.

It is in such changes of focus, rather than in the tools of analysis, or the concepts and interactions of variables, that the paradigm changes, Scientific Revolutions or switches to a progressive Scientific Research Programme have consisted. The tools in this field have remained basically the same: the questions altered.

Notes

1. For perceptive criticism of this, see Laidler (1969), Sprenkle (1969) and Friedman and Schwartz (1969).

2. Velocity itself apparently has no upper limit (Radcliffe, 1959, p. 133).
3. See Johnson (1969, pp. 30–31).
4. On this, see Yeager (1968, p. 53) and Laidler (1969, p. 515).
5. Norman (1841, pp. 12, 69). See also Overstone (1971, II, p. 714).
6. Keynes (1930, repr. 1971, p. 3); Mises (1912, trans. 1934 pp. 29–37).
7. E.g. Mises (1912, trans. 1934, p. 51) and Mill (1848, p. 539).
8. Overstone (1971, II, p. 715). See also Robbins (1958, pp. 113–115).
9. Cantillon (1755, pp. 143, 301–305) and Holtrop (1929, p., 507).
10. Norman (1841, pp. 32–35, 45–46, 52, 57, 73, 79–80, 92–93); Overstone (1857, p. 461; 1971, II, p. 714). See also Robbins (1958, p. 103) and the references in notes 47 and 62 below.
11. Marshall (1923, pp. 13, 15; 1926, p. 35); Wicksell (1906, trans. 1935, p. 27; 1898, trans. 1936, p. 68).
12. Overstone to Torrens (1971, II, p. 716); Robbins (1958, p. 106); Mill (1848, p. 539).
13. Fullarton (1845, pp. 33, 36, 41–47); Mill (1848, pp. 483, 495, 651–677); Tooke (1838–1857, III, pp. 121, 123–130, IV, pp. 154–165; 1844, pp. 20–23, 25, 33–37).
14. Fullarton (1845, p. 47); Mill (1848, pp. 539–541).
15. Sayers (1963, pp. xxxiv–xxxvi); Pennington (1829, pp. 126–127; 1838, pp. 369, 377); Longfield (1840, repr. 1971, pp. 114–120).
16. For useful discussions see Laidler (1973) and the excellent text by Dennis (1981).
17. References will be found in Holtrop (1929) and Marget (1938–1942, I, p. 96). See, in particular, Petty, ed. Hull (1899, I, p. 112).
18. For Ricardo, see (1951–1973, III, p. 90); for J. Mill, see (1826 (Winch ed.), p. 278).
19. J.S. Mill (1848, pp. 494, 497–498); Attwood (1817, p. 27) quoted in Marget (1938–1942, I, p. 358n).
20. Marshall (1923; pp. 43, 45); Wicksell (1898 trans. 1936, p. 59) and 1906–1935, II, pp. 23, 65–68, 72.
21. Fisher (1911, pp. 79–89, 152, 154, 270, 305, 352, 360); (1933, p. 140).
22. For comment on this, see Marget (1938–1942, I, pp. 298–302).
23. Artis (1961, pp. 351–352, 359).
24. Petty, ed. Hull (1899, I, pp. 112–113, 310–311; II, p. 446); Smith (1776, ed. Cannan (1976 pagination), I, p. 342).
25. Thornton (1802, pp. 90, 92–94, 96–97, 194, 234, 359). For comment, see Hicks (1967, p. 175) and Holtrop (1929, pp. 515–516). On Thornton's influence on Marshall, see Eshag (1963, p. 13, n. 55).
26. Senior (1829–1840, p. 11). For comment, see Eshag (1963, pp. 14–15) (an important essay).
27. For Joplin and Tooke references, see Marget (1938–1942, I, pp. 320–324, 405–408). See also Bagehot (1873, p. 154) and Giffen (1877, pp. 34. 35, 147).
28. Mill (1844, pp. 70–72); Tooke (1838–1857, I, p. 156).
29. This is frequently forgotten despite two important articles by Marget (1931, 1935). See also Jaffé (1951).
30. Wicksell (1898, trans. 1936, pp. 39–42, 56, 59, 63–65; 1906, trans. 1935, pp. 23, 67, 71, 83–84); Baumol (1952).
31. Marshall (1923, pp. 43–48; 1926, pp. 36, 268–269).
32. Pigou (1917, pp. 40–42, 45–48, 50–54; 1927, p. 136); Lavington (1921, pp. 30–31).
33. Hawtrey (1919, 1928 ed., pp. 34–43, 46, 60; 1913, pp. 10–14, 23).
34. Keynes (1923, repr. 1971, pp. 37–38, 62–67).
35. Keynes equated income deposits with demand deposits and savings deposits with time deposits.

36. Keynes (1930, repr. 1971, I, pp. 31–37, 41–43, 211, 218–221, 224, 229; II, pp. 19, 29–30, 38–39, 73–75).
37. The same may not be true of the liquidity trap.
38. Keynes (1936, pp. 170, 172, 195–199, 207).
39. Robertson (1926, pp. 47–50; 1928, pp. 34–37; 1940, p. 66). On the question of whether real or money balances were involved, see Eshag (1963, pp. 21–22).
40. Thornton (1802, p. 243); Senior (1829–1830, pp. 79–81); Mill (1848, p. 526); Holtrop (1929, p. 519).
41. Goschen (1864, pp. 112–113); Marshall (1923, pp. 47, 152, 283); Fullarton (1845, pp. 71, 139–142); for Giffen, see Eshag (1963, p. 14, n. 55); Jevons (1875, p. 245).
42. Pigou (1917, pp. 43–44, 60; 1923, pp. 191, 196n). Marget (1938–1942, II, pp. 650–651, nn. 51, 53) notes that the relevant material was added to the 1923 reprint of the 1917 article.
43. Keynes (1923, repr. 1971, p. 40, 41, 42–43, 45–53). See also Marget (1938–1942, II, p. 645).
44. See Pigou (1917, pp. 42–43; 1923, p. 177); Mises (1912, trans. 1934, p. 145); Marshall (1923, pp. 45–47, 256, 282–284; 1926, pp. 39, 43, 44, 140, 176); Marget (1931), Marget (1938–1942, II, p. 648).
45. As Johnson (1970, p. 104) has pointed out, the concept of a *rigid* deposit multiplier is a 'straw man'; in fact, neither approach completely excludes the other.
46. References will be found in Macleod (1892–1893, I, p. 354).
47. See Overstone (1971, I, pp. 89, 104, 106–107, 113, 133); Norman (1841, pp. 42, 72–75, 80–81). However, fixed reserve ratios were slow to develop within the banking system. See Wadsworth (1968) and Hughes (1960).
48. Giffen (1877, pp. 30–32), Marshall (1926, p. 37).
49. Fisher (1911, ch. 3, especially pp. 46, 50, 52).
50. Macleod (1863, art. 'Credit'; 1892–1893, I, pp. 324–326), Phillips (1921, pp. 32–76); Crick (1927).
51. Hawtrey (1919, 1928 edn, pp. 27–28, 54–55, 225–227; 1932, pp. 153–154) and compare Keynes (1924, pp. 66–67).
52. See Eshag (1963, p. 136, n. 98).
53. Hayek (1933, pp. 153–173); Robertson (1928, p. 92); Lavington (1911, p. 59), (1921, pp. 43–44).
54. Smith (1776, I, p. 323, 1976 pagination).
55. Tooke (1838–1857, II, pp. 160–161, 165–166, 175–177, 183, 190–191, 343–344; III, pp. 223, 245, 276; IV, pp. 127, 185; V, pp. 344–345; 1844, pp. 38, 60, 62). There is some contrast with Tooke's (1826) more moderate position.
56. Fullarton (1845, pp. 63–64, 69, 83, 85–86, 101, 109, 194–195, 207).
57. For references, see Dennis (1981, chs 1, 2, 7).
58. See, in particular, Radcliffe (1959, pp. 48–49, 51, 59–62, 127, 158, 160–163, 167, 174).
59. Radcliffe (1959, pp. 133–134, 154–155). For perceptive criticism, see Morgan (1969, especially pp. 11, 21).
60. As Johnson (1970) has argued, the approach is 'long on elegant analysis of theoretical possibilities, but remarkably short on testable ... propositions' (p. 105).
61. Discussions of the debate will be found in O'Brien (1971, I, pp. 70–144; and see I, p. 71, n. 1 for a list of classic discussions of it) and O'Brien (1975, pp. 153–159).
62. Notes predominated in reserves until 1873 (Wood, 1939, pp. 119–125).
63. Tooke (1838–1857, III, pp. 172–288; IV, pp. 166–197, 293–402; V, pp. 272–284, 309–315, 501–502, 551–593, 637–638; 1844, pp. 103–109); Fullarton (1845, pp. 130–169, 189–212).

64. See O'Brien (1971, pp. 128, 137). It was not Bagehot's *Lombard Street* but Tooke and the Banking School who established the last-resort role—Wood (1939, p. 165n).
65. Bagehot (1873, pp. 153–198, 303–309); Eshag (1963, p. 125).
66. (1923, p. 258; 1926, pp. 110–112, 163, 281, 322–324).
67. See Cannan (1924) for a belated and unsuccessful attempt to reverse this.
68. Lavington (1921, pp. 57–59, 150–152, 159, 163, 169–170).
69. Hawtrey (1919, 1928 edn, pp. 54–57, 132–140, 146, 227; 1923, pp. 39, 117, 132–133, 141–144, 146).
70. Keynes (1923, pp. 68–69, 141, 143–144, 148–149).
71. Keynes (1930, II, pp. 189–249).
72. Robertson (1915, pp. 218, 344–362; 1922, pp. 84, 93; 1926; 1928, p. 59, 166–169, 171–172, 177).
73. Lawrence (1928b, especially pp. 266–267, 273–276, 329–332).
74. Fisher (1933, pp. 138–140) and references therein.
75. For an excellent exposition see Dennis (1981).
76. Friedman's version of the model reintroduces the natural rate—Friedman (1970, 1971).
77. See Radcliffe (1959, pp. 131–153, 158–162, 175–178, 180–181). See also Artis (1961, pp. 348, 362–363).
78. Holtrop (1929, p. 506), Letwin (1963, pp. 5, 7, 10); O'Brien and Darnell (1982, ch. 3).
79. Smith (1776 (1976 pagination), p. 109); Hume (1752, p. 49); Rotwein (1955, pp. lxvii–lxxii).
80. Thornton (1802, pp. 254–258, 296–297, 336); Ricardo, ed. Sraffa (1951–1973, I, pp. 110, 296–298, 300, 363–364; III, pp. 88–90, 143, 150, 194n., 374–375; V, pp. 12n, 130, 346, 445).
81. From 1833 as the Usury Laws were relaxed.
82. Tooke (1838–1857, II, pp. 355–362; III, p. 155; V, pp. 556–557, 559; 1844, pp. 77–86; 1856, pp. 71–74, 76, 92); Overstone (1857, pp. 173, 253, 264, 581–585, 630).
83. Mill (1848, pp. 637–741, 645–647); Keynes (1936, pp. 166–167).
84. Marshall (1923, pp. 254–263, 288–289; 1926, pp. 41, 45, 49, 51, 127, 130–131, 270–272). See also Giffen (1877, pp. 107–115; 1887, pp. 38–39, 47–49), Jevons (1884, p. 95).
85. Fisher (1896, pp. 56, 60, 66–67, 76); Marshall (1926, p. 271); Mill (1848, p. 646); Thornton (1802, p. 336).
86. Pigou (1927, pp. 239–251, 256–257).
87. For Lavington's discussion of interest see his (1921, especially pp. 57–62, 163).
88. Hawtrey (1919, 1928 edn, pp. 132, 135–137, 413–414, 436; 1923, pp. 106–109; 1938, pp. 27, 37, 61–63, 175–177, 216, 246); Davis (1981, pp. 206, 214); Hicks (1969, p. 313).
89. Hawtrey (1938, pp. 170–171, 173, 185, 189–190, 198).
90. Robertson (1928, pp. 59–60, 164–165, 168–174; 1940, pp. 2–3, 7–8, 10–24, 83–92; 1963, p. 247). Presley; 1979, pp. 133, 148–149).
91. Keynes (1923, repr. 1971, pp. 20, 22–23); Marget (1938–1942, I, p. 196). See Keynes (1930, repr. 1971, II, pp. 177–186) for an interpretation in terms of his Fundamental Equations.
92. Keynes (1930, I, pp. 137, 139, 161–167, 172–173, 177, 180–181, 186–189, 197; II, pp. 85, 204, 315). See also Eshag (1963, p. 57).
93. Hawtrey (1938, pp. 146–207, especially pp. 185–189).
94. Keynes (1936, pp. 165–183, 242–244). It is unfortunate that Keynes should have claimed more novelty for his approach than was justified. See also Eshag (1963, pp. 64–65).
95. Wicksell (1898, trans. 1936, pp. 95–106, 111, 114, 118–119, 122–156). On the

question of stability see *ibid.* pp. 100–101 and Hicks (1939, pp. 205–209, 251–254).

96. Wicksell (1898, trans. 1936, pp. 122–156).
97. *Ibid.* pp. 98–99.
98. Mises (1912, trans. 1934, pp. 355–363); Hayek (1933, pp. 201, 210, 212–218). However, Hayek's interpretation of the natural rate is in terms of market clearing.
99. Myrdal (1933, trans. 1939, p. 9).
100. See Bodin (1568) and Christiernin (1761). The latter's contribution is particularly noteworthy.
101. Thornton (1802, pp. 195, 235–240); O'Brien (1970, pp. 155, 160–161); O'Brien (1975, pp. 163–165); Newmarch (1857, pp. 195–196); Cairnes (1873, pp. 53–76); Ricardo (1951–1973, IV, pp. 36–37; V, p, 524). (But even Ricardo did not regard money as neutral—IV, pp. 359–360.) J. Mill, ed. Winch (1826, p. 294); J.S. Mill (1848, pp. 542–555).
102. Marshall (1926, pp. 7–10, 34–35, 90, 97–98, 286–287); Giffen (1886, pp. 94–100). See also Eshag (1963, pp. 90–98).
103. Keynes (1936, pp. 295–297, 300–301). See also (1923, repr. 1971, pp. 1–30, 32, 65).
104. Hume (1752, pp. 38, 43–44, 57–58); Cantillon (1755, pp. 159–161, 163–165, 167, 177, 191, 213–215); Ricardo (1951–1973, I, p. 364; III, pp. 54–55, 91–93). See also Christiernin (1761, pp. 26, 104–105, 112–113).
105. (1857, pp. 120, 202–204, 253, 573–574).
106. Fullarton (1845, pp. 56–57, 62, 64–68, 101–102); Tooke (1838–1857, II, p. 344; IV, pp. 178–187; 1844, pp. 62–63). See also Tooke (1826, pp. 37, 42–48); Newmarch (1857, pp. 169, 189–190, 200–201, 233); J.S. Mill (1848, pp. 496–497, 642, 646–647).
107. Thornton (1802, pp. 195, 234–235, 241–242); Sidgwick (1887, p. 249). On Giffen (and Marshall's familiarity with his work), see Eshag (1963, pp. 17–18) and Angell (1926, p. 120).
108. (1926, pp. 38–45, 123, 140–142, 158, 257, 274).
109. Robertson (1915, pp. 213–215, 228); Keynes (1930, repr. 1971, I, pp. 202, 233–238, 244; II, p. 189; 1936, pp. 173, 196–201, 248, 298); Hawtrey (1919, 1928 edn, pp. 247–248; 1932, pp. 151–154, 287–288).
110. Wicksell (1898, trans. 1936, pp. 136–154; 1906, trans. 1935, pp. 162–163, 194); Hayek (1935, pp. 22, 76–98).
111. For references, see Angell (1926, pp. 127–131).
112. I am grateful to Dr J.R. Presley for this reference.
113. O'Brien (1970, pp. 156–159 and references); Overstone (1857, pp. 119–120, 167); Tooke (1826, p. 48); Fullarton (1845, pp. 58, 105); Bagehot (1873, pp. 142–143, 147); Giffen (1877, pp. 23–26, 62–63, 102–107, 115). See also Eshag (1963, pp. 77–89).
114. Marshall (1879, pp. 152–163; 1890, p. 594; 1923, pp. 75, 249–251, 261; 1926, pp. 7–9, 54, 129–131, 285–286).
115. Robertson (1915, pp. 215–223, 234–235); Hawtrey (1919, 1928 edn, pp. 9–51, 152–154). See also Keynes (1923, repr. 1971, pp. 67–68); Davis (1981, p. 210); Eshag (1963, pp. 102–103).
116. Fisher (1911, pp. 55–73); England (1912).
117. Thornton (1802, p. 195); O'Brien (1970, pp. 155–156; 1975, pp. 164–165); Overstone (1857, pp. 131. 167, 431–432); Mill (1848, p. 643); Marshall (1879, pp. 153–155; 1890, p. 711; 1923, pp. 18, 250, 257).
118. Pigou (1927, Part I, chs iii, iv, vii, xii, xiii, xvii); Lavington (1921, pp. 48, 71). See also Mitchell (1928, pp. 17–18 and Haberler (1937, pp. 134–135).
119. Hawtrey (1919, 1928 edn, pp. 153–154; 1932, p. 158); Davis (1981, p. 209); Hicks 1969, p. 313).

120. Keynes (1936, pp. 141–149, 197–198, 298). See also Martin (1931, ch. xii) on business pessimism.
121. Haberler (1937, p. 111); Robertson (1948, p. xvii; 1915, pp. 235–238). See also Marshall (1879, p. 154; 1890, pp. 710–712).
122. Hawtrey (1919, 1928 edn, pp. 11, 30–40, 45, 52, 59, 132–155; 1932, pp. 146–151, 321); Angell (1926, pp. 182–184); Davis (1981, p. 209).
123. Mitchell (1928, pp. 37–40, 100–105, 117, 130–131, 136–137, 139, 146–149, 151–154); Keynes (1936, p. 96).
124. See Foster and Catchings (1924, ch. xvii and 1928, sec. vii); Keynes (1930, repr. 1971, I, p. 160; II, p. 21n); Durbin (1935, p. 29). The similarity of Keynes's treatment of saving to that of Foster and Catchings was noted by Haberler (1937). For Hobson, see Nemmers (1956). For the origins of the Keynesian multiplier, which can be traced back to Bagehot, see Wright (1956), Eshag (1963, p. 95), Hegeland (1954) and Dorfman (1970). For a dissenting view, see Shackle (1967, pp. 186–202).
125. Marshall (1923, pp. 18–19; 1925, p. 191), Eshag (1963, pp. 81, 95, 102–103); Hawtrey (1919, 1928 edn, pp. 151, 154, 453; 1932, p. 321); Davis (1981, p. 216); Pigou (1927, Part I, chs xviii, xix).
126. Hayek (1932); O'Brien (1970, pp. 159–160).
127. Lavington (1921, p. 70), Hawtrey (1919, 1928 edn, pp. 46–47, 51); Davis (1981, p. 217); Presley (1979, Part II); Mitchell (1928, pp. 37–40).
128. Eshag (1963, pp. 104–105); Keynes (1936, pp. 136–144, 220–221, 306–309, 313–322, 375–376); Fullarton (1845, p. 104); Tooke (1826, pp. 42–43); Giffen (1887, p. 101); Jevons (1884, pp. 28–29); Marshall (1879, p. 153; 1890, pp. 710–711; 1923, pp. 249–251, 261; 1926, pp. 51–52, 127, 157–158, 168–169, 250, 285); Hawtrey (1919, 1928 edn, pp. 9, 13, 133–134, 138, 150–151; 1932, p. 188); Davis (1981, p. 209); Keynes (1930, repr. 1971, I, p. 177).
129. Marshall (1923, pp. 260–261; 1926, pp. 285–288); Hawtrey (1919, 1928 edn, p. 435; 1932, pp. 315, 320); Lavington (1921, p. 159).
130. Keynes (1923, repr. 1971, ch. 1 and pp. 68, 149, 118–119, 125–126, 138, 147, 149).
131. Keynes (1931, repr. 1971, pp. 242, 245–246).
132. Keynes (1936, pp. 250–254, 280–281).
133. On Attwood, see O'Brien (1975, p. 165). Myrdal correctly forsaw the likely outcome of pursuing the single objective of employment maximization (1933, trans. 1939, pp. 195–196).

References

ANGELL, J.W. (1926). *The Theory of International Prices*. Cambridge, Mass., Harvard University Press

ARTIS, M.J. (1961). Liquidity and the Attack on Quantity Theory. *Bulletin of the Oxford University Institute of Statistics* **23**, 343–366

BAGEHOT, W. (1873). *Lombard Street*. Repr. (ed. by H. Withers). London, Murray, 1931

BAUMOL, W.J. (1952). The Transactions Demand for Cash: An Inventory Theoretic Approach. *Quarterly Journal of Economics* **66**, 545–556

BODIN, J. (1568). *La Réponse de Jean Bodin à M. de Malestroit*. Repr. (ed. by H. Hauser). Paris, Armand Colin, 1932

BRUNNER, K. and MELTZER, A.H. (1967). Economies of Scale in Cash Balances Reconsidered. *Quarterly Journal of Economics* **81**, 422–436

CAIRNES, J.E. (1873). *Essays in Political Economy*. Repr. New York, A.M. Kelley, 1965

CANNAN, E. (1924). Limitation of Currency or Limitation of Credit? *Economic Journal* **34**, 52–64

CANTILLON, R. (1755). *Essai sur la Nature du Commerce en Général*. Repr. (trans. and ed. by H. Higgs), 143, 301–305. London, Cass, for the Royal Economic Society, 1959
CHRISTIERNIN, V.N. (1761). *Lectures on the High Price of Foreign Exchange in Sweden*. (Trans. and ed. by R.V. Eagly.) Philadelphia, American Philosophical Society, 1971
CLAYTON, G. (1962). British Financial Intermediaries in Theory and Practice. *Economic Journal* **72**, 869–886
COGHLAN, R. (1980). *The Theory of Money and Finance*. London, Macmillan
COGHLAN, R. and SYKES, C. (1980). Managing the Money Supply. *Lloyds Bank Review* **135**, 1–13
CRAMP, A.B. (1960). Radcliffe's Victorian Forebears. Liquidity and Money Supply in the 1850s. *The Banker* **110**, 593–599
CRICK, W.F. (1927). The Genesis of Bank Deposits. *Economica* **7**, 191–202
DAVIS, E. (1981). R.G. Hawtrey, 1879–1975. In *Pioneers of Modern Economics in Britain* (ed. by D.P. O'Brien and J.R. Presley), 203–233. London, Macmillan
DENNIS, G.E. (1981). *Monetary Economics*, pp. 178–201. London, Longman
DORFMAN, J. (1970). Some Documentary Notes on the Relations among J.M. Clark, N.A.L.J. Johannsen and J.M. Keynes. In *The Costs of the World War to the American People* (by J.M. Clark). Repr. New York, A.M. Kelley
DURBIN, E.F.M. (1935). *The Problem of Credit Policy*. London, Chapman and Hall
ENGLAND, M.T. (1912). Fisher's Theory of Crises: A Criticism. *Quarterly Journal of Economics* **27**, 95–106
ESHAG, E. (1963). *From Marshall to Keynes. An Essay on the Monetary Theory of the Cambridge School*. Oxford, Blackwell
FISHER, I. (1896). *Appreciation and Interest*. New York, Macmillan
FISHER, I. (1911). *The Purchasing Power of Money*, new edn. New York, Macmillan, 1920
FISHER, I. (1933). *Booms and Depressions*. London, Allen and Unwin
FOSTER, W.T. and CATCHINGS, W. (1924). *Money*. Boston, Houghton Mifflin
FOSTER, W.T. and CATCHINGS, W. (1928). *The Road to Plenty*. Boston, Houghton Mifflin
FRIEDMAN, M. (1969). *The Optimum Quantity of Money and other Essays*, pp. 58, 264. London, Macmillan
FRIEDMAN, M. (1970). A Theoretical Framework for Monetary Analysis. *Journal of Political Economy* **78**, 193–238
FRIEDMAN, M. (1971). A Monetary Theory of Nominal Income. *Journal of Political Economy* **79**, 323–337
FRIEDMAN, M. and SCHWARTZ, A.J. (1963). *A Monetary History of the United States 1867–1960*. Princeton, Princeton University Press
FRIEDMAN, M. and SCHWARTZ, A. (1969). The Definition of Money: Net Wealth and Neutrality as Criteria. *Journal of Money, Credit and Banking* **1**, 1–14
FULLARTON, J. (1845). *On the Regulation of Currencies*, pp. 44, 46–47, 2nd edn. Repr. New York, A.M. Kelley, 1969
GIFFEN, R. (1877). *Stock Exchange Securities*. London, Bell
GIFFEN, R. (1887). *Essays in Finance*, 2nd ser., 2nd edn. London, Bell
GOODHART, C. (1975). *Money, Information and Uncertainty*. London, Macmillan
GOSCHEN, G.J. (1864). *The Theory of the Foreign Exchanges*, 5th edn. London, Effingham Wilson
GURLEY, J.G. and SHAW, E.S. (1960). *Money in a Theory of Finance*. Washington, Brookings Institution
HABERLER, G.v. (1937). *Prosperity and Depression*. Geneva, League of Nations
HAWTREY, R.G. (1913). *Good and Bad Trade*. London, Constable
HAWTREY, R.G. (1919). *Currency and Credit*, 2nd edn 1923, 3rd edn 1928. London, Longman
HAWTREY, R.G. (1923). *Monetary Reconstruction*. London, Longman
HAWTREY, R.G. (1932). *The Art of Central Banking*. London, Longman
HAWTREY, R.G. (1938). *A Century of Bank Rate*. London, Longman

42 Monetary economics

HAYEK, F.A.v. (1932). A Note on the Development of the Doctrine of 'Forced Saving'. *Quarterly Journal of Economics* **47**, 123–133

HAYEK, F.A.v. (1933). *Monetary Theory and the Trade Cycle*. London, Cape

HAYEK, F.A.v. (1935). *Prices and Production*. 2nd edn. London, Routledge

HEGELAND, H. (1954). *The Multiplier Theory*. Repr. New York, A.M. Kelley, 1966

HICKS, J.R. (1939). *Value and Capital*, 2nd edn. Oxford, The Clarendon Press, 1946

HICKS, J.R. (1967). *Critical Essays in Monetary Theory*. Oxford, The Clarendon Press

HICKS, J.R. (1969). Automatists, Hawtreyans, and Keynesians. *Journal of Money, Credit and Banking* **1**, 307–317

HOLTROP, M.W. (1929). Theories of the Velocity of Circulation of Money in Earlier Economic Literature. *Economic History* **I**, 503–524

HUGHES, J.R.T. (1960). *Fluctuations in Trade, Industry and Finance*. Oxford, The Clarendon Press

HUME, D. (1752). *Writings on Economics* (ed. by E. Rotwein), pp. 37–38. Edinburgh, Nelson, 1955

JAFFÉ, W. (1951). Walrasiana: the *Éléments* and its Critics. *Econometrica* **19**, 327–328

JEVONS, W.S. (1875). *Money and the Mechanism of Exchange*, 23rd edn. London, Kegan Paul, 1910

JEVONS, W.S. (1884). *Investigations in Currency and Finance*. London, Macmillan

JOHNSON, H.G. (1969). Inside Money, Outside Money, Income, Wealth, and Welfare in Monetary Theory. *Journal of Money, Credit and Banking* **1**, 30–45

JOHNSON, H.G. (1970). Recent Developments in Monetary Theory—a Commentary. In *Money in Britain 1959–1969* (ed. by D.R. Croome and H.G. Johnson), pp. 83–114. Oxford, Oxford University Press

JOPLIN, T. (1844). *Currency Reform: Improvement not Depreciation*, p. 43. London, Richardson

KEYNES, J.M. (1911). Review of I. Fisher *The Purchasing Power of Money*. *Economic Journal* **21**, 393–398

KEYNES, J.M. (1923). *A Tract on Monetary Reform*. Repr. London, Macmillan, for the Royal Economic Society, 1971

KEYNES, J.M. (1924). A Comment on Professor Cannan's Article. *Economic Journal* **34**, 65–68

KEYNES, J.M. (1930). *A Treatise on Money*, 2 vols. Repr. London, Macmillan, for the Royal Economic Society, 1971

KEYNES, J.M. (1936). *The General Theory of Employment, Interest and Money*. Repr. London, Macmillan, for the Royal Economic Society, 1973

LAIDLER, D. (1969). The Definition of Money. Theoretical and Empirical Problems. *Journal of Money, Credit and Banking* **1**, 508–525

LAIDLER, D. (1973). *The Demand for Money*. Aylesbury, Intertext Books

LAVINGTON, F. (1911). The Social Importance of Banking. *Economic Journal* **21**, 53–60

LAVINGTON, F. (1921). *The English Capital Market*. London, Methuen

LAWRENCE, J.S. (1928a). Borrowed Reserves and Bank Expansion. *Quarterly Journal of Economics* **42**, 593–626

LAWRENCE, J.S. (1928b). *Stabilisation of Prices*, p. 368. New York, Macmillan

LEATHAM, W. (1840). *Letters on the Currency, Addressed to Charles Wood*. London, Richardson

LETWIN, W.O. (1963). *The Origins of Scientific Economics*. London, Methuen

LONGFIELD, M. (1840). Banking and Currency. *Dublin University Magazine*. Repr. in *Economic Writings* (ed. by R.D.C. Black). New York, A.M. Kelley, 1971

MACLEOD, H.D. (1863). *Dictionary of Political Economy*. London, Longman

MACLEOD, H.D. (1892–1893). *The Theory and Practice of Banking*, 5th edn, 2 vols. London, Longman

MARGET, A.W. (1931). Léon Walras and the 'Cash Balance' Approach to the Problem of the Value of Money. *Journal of Political Economy* **39**, 569–600

MARGET, A.W. (1935). The Monetary Aspects of the Walrasian System. *Journal of Political Economy* **43**, 145–186

MARGET, A.W. (1938–1942). *The Theory of Prices*, 2 vols. Repr. New York, A.M. Kelley, 1966

MARSHALL, A. and M.P. (1879). *The Economics of Industry*. Repr. London, Macmillan, 1888

MARSHALL, A. (1890). *Principles of Economics*, 9th (Variorum) edn. London, Macmillan, for the Royal Economic Society, 1961

MARSHALL, A. (1923). *Money, Credit and Commerce*, pp. 58, 59. London, Macmillan

MARSHALL, A. (1925). *Memorials of Alfred Marshall* (ed. by A.C. Pigou). London, Macmillan

MARSHALL, A. (1926). *Official Papers*. London, Macmillan

MARTIN, P.W. (1931). *The Problem of Maintaining Purchasing Power*, London, P. S. King

MILL, J. (1826). *Elements of Political Economy*, 3rd edn. Repr. in *Selected Economic Writings* (ed. by D. Winch). Edinburgh, Oliver and Boyd, 1966

MILL, J.S. (1844). *Essays on some Unsettled Questions of Political Economy*. Repr. London, London School of Economics, 1948

MILL, J.S. (1848). *Principles of Political Economy with some of their Applications to Social Philosophy* (ed. by W.J. Ashley). London, Longman, 1923

MISES, L.v. (1912). *The Theory of Money and Credit*, trans. H.E. Batson, p. 61. London, Cape, 1934

MITCHELL, W.C. (1928). *Business Cycles*. New York, National Bureau of Economic Research

MORGAN, E.V. (1969). The Essential Qualities of Money. *Manchester School* **37**, 237–248

MYRDAL, G. (1933). *Monetary Equilibrium*, trans. 1939. Repr. New York, A.M. Kelley, 1965

NEMMERS, E.E. (1956). *Hobson and Underconsumption*. Repr. New York, A.M. Kelley, 1972

NEWMARCH, W. (1857). *A History of Prices and of the State of the Circulation*, Vols V and VI (with T. Tooke). Repr. London, P.S. King, 1928

NORMAN, G.W. (1841). *Letter to Charles Wood, Esq., M.P. on Money and the Means of Economizing the Use of It*. London, Pelham Richardson

O'BRIEN, D.P. (1970). *J.R. McCulloch. A Study in Classical Economics*. London, Allen and Unwin

O'BRIEN, D.P. (1971). Introduction. In *The Correspondence of Lord Overstone* (Vol. I, pp. 1–144). Cambridge, Cambridge University Press

O'BRIEN, D.P. (1975). *The Classical Economists*. Oxford, The Clarendon Press

O'BRIEN, D.P. and DARNELL, A.C. (1982). *Authorship Puzzles in the History of Economics*. London, Macmillan

OVERSTONE, LORD (1857). *Tracts and other Publications on Metallic and Paper Currency*. London, privately printed

OVERSTONE, LORD (1971). *The Correspondence of Lord Overstone* (ed. by D.P. O'Brien), 3 vols. Cambridge, Cambridge University Press

PENNINGTON, J. (1829). Paper Communicated by Mr Pennington. In *A Letter to Lord Grenville* (by T. Tooke), pp. 117–127. London, Murray

PENNINGTON, J. (1838). Letter Addressed to the Author by James Pennington, Esq. In Tooke, T. (1838–1857) *History of Prices*, Vol. II, pp. 369–378

PESEK, B.P. and SAVING, T.R. (1967). *Money, Wealth, and Economic Theory*. New York, Macmillan

PETTY, SIR. W. (1899). *Economic Writings* (ed. by C.H. Hull). Cambridge, Cambridge University Press

PHILLIPS, C.A. (1921). *Bank Credit: A Study of the Principles and Factors underlying Advances made by Banks to Borrowers*. New York, Macmillan, 1926

44 Monetary economics

PIGOU, A.C. (1917). The Value of Money. *Quarterly Journal of Economics* **32**, 38–65

PIGOU, A.C. (1923). *Essays in Applied Economics*. London, P.S. King

PIGOU, A.C. (1927). *Industrial Fluctuations*. London, Macmillan

PRESLEY, J.R. (1979). *Robertsonian Economics*. London, Macmillan

RADCLIFFE COMMITTEE (1959). *Report of the Committee on the Working of the Monetary System*, pp. 132, 135, 337. London, HMSO

RICARDO, D. (1951–1973). *Works and Correspondence*, 11 vols (ed. by P. Sraffa with M.H. Dobb). Cambridge, Cambridge University Press

ROBBINS, LORD (1958). *Robert Torrens and the Evolution of Classical Economics*. London, Macmillan

ROBERTSON, D.H. (1915). *A Study of Industrial Fluctuation*. Repr. London, London School of Economics, 1948

ROBERTSON, D.H. (1922). *Money*. London, Nisbett

ROBERTSON, D.H. (1926). *Banking Policy and the Price Level*, rev. edn. London, P.S. King, 1932

ROBERTSON, D.H. (1928). *Money*. Repr. London, Nisbett, 1946

ROBERTSON, D.H. (1940). *Essays in Monetary Theory*. London, P.S. King

ROBERTSON, D.H. (1948). New Introduction. In reprint of Robertson (1915), pp. vii–xvii.

ROBERTSON, D.H. (1963). *Lectures on Economic Principles*, 1 vol. London, Collins

ROTWEIN, E. (1955). Introduction. In *David Hume. Writings on Economics*, pp. ix–cxii. Edinburgh, Nelson, 1955

SAYERS, R.S. (1963). The Life and Work of James Pennington. In *Economic Writings of James Pennington*, pp. ix–xliv. London, London School of Economics

SENIOR, N.W. (1827–1840). *Three Lectures on the Value of Money*. Repr. in *Selected Writings on Economics*. New York, A.M. Kelley, 1966

SENIOR, N.W. (1829–1830). *Three Lectures on the Cost of Obtaining Money*. Repr. in *Selected Economic Writings*. New York, A.M. Kelley, 1966

SHACKLE, G.L.S. (1967). *The Years of High Theory*. Cambridge, Cambridge University Press

SIDGWICK, H. (1887). *The Principles of Political Economy*, 2nd edn. London, Macmillan

SMITH, A. (1776). *An Inquiry into the Nature and Causes of the Wealth of Nations* (ed. by E. Cannan). Repr. Chicago, University of Chicago Press, 1976. Readers should note that the pagination of this reprint does *not* correspond to the pagination of the Methuen *hardback* printing of the Cannan edition, which is the one most commonly cited.

SPRENKLE, C.M. (1969). Laidler's 'The Definition of Money', A Comment. *Journal of Money, Credit and Banking* **1**, 526–530

THORNTON, H. (1802). *An Enquiry into the Nature and Effects of the Paper Credit of Great Britain* (ed. by F.A. v. Hayek). London, Allen and Unwin, 1939

TOBIN, J. (1956). The Interest-elasticity of the Transactions Demand for Cash. *Review of Economics and Statistics* **38**, 241–247

TOBIN, J. (1958). Liquidity-preference as Behaviour towards Risk. *Review of Economic Studies* **25**, 65–86

TOBIN, J. (1963). Commercial Banks as Creators of Money. In *Banking and Monetary Studies* (ed. by D. Carson), pp. 408–419. Homewood, Ill., R.D. Irwin

TOBIN, J. (1965). The Theory of Portfolio Selection. In *The Theory of Interest Rates* (ed. by F. Hahn and F. Brechling), pp. 3–51. London, Macmillan

TOOKE, T. (1826). *Considerations on the State of the Currency*, 2nd edn. London, Murray

TOOKE, T. (1829). *A Letter to Lord Grenville on the Effects Ascribed to the Resumption of Cash Payments on the Value of the Currency*. London, Murray

TOOKE, T. (1838–1857). *A History of Prices and of the State of the Circulation from 1792 to 1856*, with W. Newmarch, 6 vols. Repr. London, P.S. King, 1928

TOOKE, T. (1844). *An Inquiry into the Currency Principle: the Connection of the Currency with Prices, and the Expediency of a Separation of Issue from Banking*, pp. 26–27, 31. London, Longman

TOOKE, T. (1856). ***On the Bank Charter Act of 1844, its Principles and Operation.*** London, Longman

TORRENS, R. (1837). ***A Letter to the Right Honourable Lord Viscount Melbourne on the Causes of the Recent Derangement in the Money Market and on Bank Reform.*** London, Longman

WADSWORTH, J.E. (1968). Banking Ratios Past and Present. In *Essays in Money and Banking* (ed. by C.R. Whittlesey and J.S.G. Wilson), pp. 229–251. Oxford, The Clarendon Press

WICKSELL, K. (1898). *Interest and Prices* (trans. R.F. Kahn). London, Macmillan, 1936

WICKSELL, K. (1906). *Lectures on Political Economy. Vol. 2, Money* (ed. by L. Robbins), pp. 6, 24, 142, 145. London, Routledge, 1935

WOOD, E. (1939). *English Theories of Central Banking Control 1819–58.* Cambridge, Mass., Harvard University Press

WRIGHT, A.H. (1956). The Genesis of the Multiplier Theory. *Oxford Economic Papers* **8**, 181–193

YEAGER, L.B. (1968). Essential Properties of the Medium of Exchange. *Kyklos* **21**, 45–69

[15]

Overstone, Lord

Samuel Jones Loyd, 1796–1883 (the single 'l' seems to have been a device adopted by his father to shake off Welsh relatives), Lord Overstone, was born on the 25th September 1796, the son of Lewis Loyd, a Unitarian minister turned banker and Sarah Loyd (née Jones), the daughter of a Manchester banker. Lewis Loyd's drive and ability transformed an obscure provincial bank into a major concern. An MP 1819–26, Overstone only began to devote himself seriously to banking after the death of his mother in 1821. Though perhaps lacking his father's flair, he was a shrewd and successful banker, influential with his contemporaries. He retired from business only in 1850 on his elevation to the peerage by Lord John Russell. From 1837 he entered, with considerable effectiveness, the arena of monetary controversy with his *Reflections suggested by a perusal of Mr. J. Horsley Palmer's pamphlet on the Causes and Consequences of the pressure on the Money Market.* This was not his first statement on the matter; he had been a witness before the 1832 committee on the renewal of the Bank Charter. But it was the start of his pre-eminence as a monetary writer, a pre-eminence which was to prove decisive in the debates leading up to the renewal of the Bank Charter in 1844 which shaped the institutional framework of British monetary policy from that time until the First World War. Overstone's monetary thought starts from a position that the economy contains an endogenous trade cycle – he was indeed one of the first people to identify the stages of the cycle. Monetary policy could then be procyclic, responding to the needs of customers (the Banking principle) or it could act counter-cyclically so as to stabilize the level of prices and activity (the Currency principle). The theoretical position underlying the latter was as follows. In the upswing of the cycle money income rose, exports were less competitive, and a balance of payments deficit developed. Counter-cyclical contraction of the currency, in line with the loss of specie through the balance of payments deficit, would then moderate the upswing and prevent it from getting out of hand. Conversely, in the lower half of the cycle, with a balance of payments surplus, the money supply would be increased.

The origins of this position were threefold: Hume's theory of the balance of payments, positing a direct link between the money supply, the price level, exports, and imports; the Ricardian theory of the equilibrium distribution of the precious metals (that when countries were in relative money income equilibria, there would be no net flows of precious metal) deriving from Hume; and the Ricardian definition of 'excess'. The latter is particularly crucial. If specie was flowing out then, *by definition*, there was excess currency. This idea leads in turn to the principle, formulated in 1826 by several writers, of 'metallic fluctuation': a paper currency should fluctuate in amount exactly as an identically circumstanced metallic one would do.

On this basis Overstone emerged as a critic of the 'Palmer Rule' under which the Bank allowed drains of specie to fall on deposits equally with notes: unless deposits were as important as notes in correcting the price level in relation to the balance of payments, the drain might exhaust the specie without correcting the balance of payments. Overstone's emphasis was on control of currency as the high-powered money base, with deposits as part of an inverted credit pyramid lacking any independent effect of their own, and dependent upon the currency base if banks behaved properly with respect to reserve ratios.

Thus, fundamental to monetary control was separation of departments in the Bank: the Banking department followed Banking principles, but the Issue department must follow Currency principles and thus stabilize economy activity, following automatic rather than discretionary procedures.

The role of the rate of interest in all this was twofold: short-run balance of payments correction, although this could only be a palliative if relative money incomes were out of line: and the production of an effect on confidence which in turn affected liquidity preference through increasing precautionary reserve holdings when the rate was raised, thus reducing the effectiveness of a given money supply. This variation in liquidity preference with confidence was an important part of the analysis, and built into the 1844 Act with weekly publication of the Bank reserves, which were supposed to cause prudent adjustment of other reserves. This in turn would avoid the Bank of England having to act as lender of last resort, a role which Overstone opposed as incompatible both with inducing the rest of the system to respond counter-cyclically and with the necessary limitation of the high powered money base.

Overstone was a many-sided man. But it is as a monetary theorist that he is chiefly remembered and chiefly important.

References

O'Brien, D.P. (ed.) (1971), *The Correspondence of Lord Overstone*, 3 vols, Cambridge: Cambridge University Press.

O'Brien, D.P. (1975), *The Classical Economists*, Oxford: Clarendon Press, chapter 6.

Overstone, Lord (1857), *Tracts and other Publications on Metallic and Paper Currency*, London: privately printed 1857, Longmans 1858.

Overstone, Lord (1858), *The Evidence given by Lord Overstone, before the Select Committee of the House of Commons of 1857, on Bank Acts, with additions*, London: Longmans.

Wood, E. (1939), *English Theories of Central Banking Control, 1819–1858*, Cambridge, Mass.: Harvard University Press.

[16]

INTRODUCTION

MONETARY THOUGHT

1. *The Currency and Banking Controversy*

The development of Overstone's monetary thought which will be traced later in this Introduction took place in the context of, and is in-

extricably bound up with, the Currency and Banking controversy. There are many excellent surveys of this fascinating subject, and the reader requiring a fuller discussion of the issues involved in this, one of the greatest economic controversies of the nineteenth century, is referred to those.[1] What follows is very much of a summary. But it seems necessary, in order that the significance of Overstone's thought may be seen in its context, to give a short sketch of the controversy.

(i) *The Debate to 1844*

In 1819 England returned to a metallic standard after twenty-two years of inconvertible paper.[2] The Resumption was the subject of extremely heated controversy at the time[3] particularly as it was accompanied by a sharp deflation, probably intensified by the decision in 1821 to return to a full gold standard in place of Ricardo's bullion plan. But, with a small group of exceptions, mainly the members of the 'Birmingham School',[4] the idea that a convertible currency was both necessary and desirable seems to have become accepted with remarkable speed. It was accepted by both sides in the Currency and Banking controversy, both having grown, it is probably true to say, out of different aspects of the Bullionist position in the Bullion controversy during the regime of inconvertible paper of 1797–1819.

At bottom the controversy was about the management of the monetary system and the role of the Bank of England within that system, inside the framework of this common acceptance of convertibility. But it was a controversy which sprang from the emergence of very pressing practical problems. The first stimulus to its development was the crisis of 1825. Economic activity began to recover from depression and deflation in 1824. Throughout much of 1825 the Bank lost metal but it failed to contract its note issues, while the country banks, riding a high tide of confidence, expanded theirs. When the Bank began to contract at length, rationing discounts, panic followed and many of the private

[1] See in particular J. Viner *Studies in the Theory of International Trade* London 1937; E. Wood *English Theories of Central Banking Control 1819–58* Cambridge, Mass. 1939; E. V. Morgan *The Theory and Practice of Central Banking* Cambridge 1943; T. E. Gregory Introduction to *Select Statutes, Documents and Reports relating to British Banking* London 1929; Robbins *Robert Torrens*; R. G. Link *English Theories of Economic Fluctuations* New York 1959; and F. W. Fetter *The Development of British Monetary Orthodoxy* Cambridge, Mass. 1965.

[2] 59 Geo. 3 c.49, 2 July 1819, known as 'Peel's Act'.

[3] For an account of these controversies see Viner *Theory of International Trade* ch. IV.

[4] See S. G. Checkland 'The Birmingham Economists 1815–1850', *The Economic History Review* second series vol. I no. I (1948) pp. 1–19.

banks were extremely illiquid. The result was a tremendous commercial crisis in which the Bank was nearly exhausted of coin and even notes; but for the work of Rothschild the Bank might have stopped altogether.[1] There were widespread bank failures and enormous amounts of country bank paper were discredited.

It seems to have been from this crisis onwards that a number of writers came to doubt what had been, by and large, taken as axiomatic in the Bullion controversy: that convertibility was sufficient to secure itself. This doubt was to become the basis of the Currency School's position. If convertibility did not secure its own maintenance, then some further control of the monetary system was required. A number of writers – Mushet,[2] and Tooke himself,[3] for instance looked at the problem, although without achieving any very coherent approach.[4] But to four writers in particular must go credit for having established the basis of the Currency principle: Henry Drummond,[5] Richard Page,[6] Thomas Joplin[7] and James Pennington.[8] The principle at which they had arrived was that the currency should be varied as an identically circumstanced fully metallic one would have been.

The theoretical base for this, as for both sides in the controversy, was to be found in the Bullion controversy. Starting from the foundations laid by Locke, Hume and Smith, the writers in that debate – Boyd, Thornton, Lord King, Parnell, Foster, Wheatley and Blake – had developed monetary theory in a way that was quite remarkable. Economic theory at that time took one of the longest steps forward that it has ever taken.

Ricardo's theoretical contribution was very small. The work of these other writers, and the famous Bullion Report, contained the fundamental theory. But because of his great prestige and his adoption of the theory of these other authors, Ricardo provided something of a focus of their

[1] See Clapham *The Bank of England* II 100–2.

[2] *An Attempt to Explain from Facts the Effect of the Issues of the Bank of England upon its Own Interests, Public Credit, and Country Banks* London 1826.

[3] *Considerations on the State of the Currency* London 1826.

[4] A favourite suggestion was the abolition of one pound notes, and there seems to have been a general belief that fluctuations could be reduced by increasing the metallic content of the currency.

[5] *Elementary Propositions on the Currency* 4th ed. London 1826.

[6] 'Daniel Hardcastle'. *Letters to the Editor of 'The Times' Journal, on the Affairs and Conduct of the Bank of England; the Introduction of British Silver Money into the Colonies; and generally, on the Currency of the United Kingdom, both Paper and Metallic* London 1826.

[7] E.g. his *Views on the Currency* London 1826.

[8] In a private memorandum of 1827 to Huskisson. See R. S. Sayers *The Economic Writings of James Pennington* London 1963.

views, and it was most noticeably from his writings and those of Thornton that the theoretical foundations for the debate were to emerge. This should not be exaggerated. For one thing, some of the participants in the Currency and Banking controversy were also participants in the Bullion controversy – this is noticeably true of both Torrens and Tooke although the position of neither in that debate was exactly the same as in the Currency and Banking debate. For another, many of those involved in the latter debate were men of great force and originality of intellect; they were certainly not men to be slaves to any intellectual heritage that was unsuited for the problem at hand. But when all that has been said, the whole concept of 'metallic' variation of the currency can be seen to stem immediately at least from the peculiar Ricardian definition of excess viz. that the currency was in excess whenever specie was being lost. That this in turn stemmed from Hume and Smith is undeniable: but it was most often to Ricardo that in particular the Currency School turned; even though Ricardo himself seems to have thought that convertibility on its own was a sufficient safeguard.[1]

If the 1825 crisis was the first stimulus to the debate, and marks the emergence of the Currency Principle, the second stimulus was the debate over the renewal of the Charter of the Bank of England. This was due in 1833 and a Select Committee was appointed to consider the matter.[2] It held extensive hearings and from these emerged the so-called 'Palmer Rule'. As explained by Horsley Palmer and George Warde Norman (both of the Bank) before the Committee[3] this involved the Bank having a bullion reserve equal to one-third of its *combined* liabilities i.e. both notes and deposits, when the exchanges were 'full' – just on the point of becoming unfavourable. The securities were then supposed to be kept fixed and bullion and notes and deposits varied together. This, although probably arrived at independently by the Bank, was very similar to Pennington's proposal referred to above. Although it had the merit of recognising the importance of deposits, it was essentially defective. It failed to recognise that a drain might fall on deposits, not notes, thus leaving open the possibility that the Bank might be drained of specie with the exchanges uncorrected (unless deposits were *as important as* notes in their effect on prices) and its note circulation undiminished. This is, in fact, what very nearly happened in 1839. The

[1] *Proposals for an Economical and Secure Currency* London 1816, reprinted in *Works* ed. P. Sraffa, vol. IV Cambridge 1951 pp. 43–141 p. 64.

[2] See 'Report from the Committee of Secrecy on the Bank of England Charter' *Parliamentary Papers* 1831–2(722) VI I.

[3] Qq. 72–85, 198, 447, 2391.

Rule then required the extra proviso that deposits as well as securities should be kept even to guarantee correspondence between fluctuations in the bullion and fluctuations in the notes; and keeping securities and deposits even was in fact almost impossible because of the banking operations involved in a concern of the size of the Bank of England. The Rule also involved difficulties in that if the Bank, faced with a drain on deposits tried to contract its note circulation it would probably have to do this either by selling securities (which would then vary) or by rationing its discounts (which would in turn cause a reduction in securities as bills matured and were not replaced, thus varying the securities again).

But for all its defects the Rule embodied the recognition that some form of control in addition to convertibility itself was necessary to ensure the maintenance of that convertibility. The discussions over its operation were to be the starting point for the development of the Currency Principle proper. Palmer himself never progressed beyond the Rule to the Currency position, and did not approve of the Act of 1844, but Norman, who may well himself have been partly responsible for the Rule's original adoption,[1] was to move beyond it.

The Rule was given virtually four years of operation before any substantial criticism of it appeared. But it became clear fairly quickly that the Rule did not, and indeed could not work. In early 1837 Palmer published a pamphlet[2] explaining that the Rule had, despite all appearances from published figures to the contrary, worked. But his adjustments of the official figures to remove the effects of 'extraordinary' banking operations were so laboured that they drew from Overstone the sarcastic comment on the alleged inadequacy of the figures: 'Surely, this is an evil of no trifling magnitude, requiring immediate correction; in effecting which the Bank ought to be the prominent agent. If the accounts, as now published, are, according to their own statement, a false representation of the action of the Bank, and calculated only to mislead, it is a duty incumbent upon the Directors of the Bank to take some means of laying before the public such accounts as shall give a correct view of their proceedings, and be calculated to lead the public to safe and true conclusions.'[3]

[1] Though, according to his MS Autobiography, he did not formulate it.

[2] *The Causes and Consequences of the Pressure upon the Money-Market; with a Statement of the Action of the Bank of England from 1st October, 1833, to the 27th December, 1836* London 1837.

[3] *Reflections suggested by a perusal of Mr. J. Horsley Palmer's pamphlet on the Causes and Consequences of the Pressure on the Money Market* London 1837, reprinted in Overstone's *Tracts on Metallic and Paper Currency* London 1857.

OVERSTONE'S THOUGHT

Overstone's pamphlet was one of several published at that time which, taken together, mark the emergence of the Currency School as a recognisable group. The discussion was stimulated by the financial crisis of 1836–7 and was to be further renewed after that of 1839. Overstone was one of the leading lights in the School; and through his personal prestige and his great clarity he did much to forward the School's objectives. But he was in alliance with other important names. Torrens had preceded Overstone's *Reflections* with a *Letter to Lord Melbourne*,[1] Sampson Ricardo also replied to Palmer[2] and Sir William Clay published his speech on Joint Stock Banks.[3] These were followed by other pamphlets[4] including one by Norman which was based on a privately printed work of 1833[5] and which was extremely significant in that it made clear to the outside world that, despite Palmer's adherence to his Rule, the Currency School was represented in the Bank itself. Norman was later joined by Hubbard.[6]

The essential unifying theme of these works was a stress on the need to make the *note circulation* fluctuate exactly as a metallic currency would do, the test of the latter being the inflow and outflow of bullion. This was their fundamental break from the Palmer Rule, and they were not followed in this by all those who had begun the movement towards the 'metallic' fluctuation idea – Page continued to stress the importance of deposits[7] and Pennington was slow to be converted.[8] But for the Currency School proper, 'metallic' fluctuation of the note issue became almost an

[1] *A Letter to the Right Honourable Lord Viscount Melbourne on the Causes of the recent Derangement in the Money Market and on Bank Reform* London 1837.

[2] *Observations on the Recent Pamphlet of J. Horsley Palmer, Esq. on the Causes and Consequences of the Pressure on the Money Market* London 1837.

[3] *Speech of William Clay, Esq., M.P., on Moving for the Appointment of a Committee to Inquire into the Operation of the Act Permitting the Establishment of Joint Stock Banks* London 1836, 2nd ed. London 1837.

[4] A second edition of Torrens' *Letter to Melbourne*, and a *Supplement* to the same, both London 1837; *A Letter to Thomas Tooke* London 1840 and *An Inquiry into the Renewal of the Charter of the Bank of England* London 1844, by the same author; G. W. Norman *A Letter to Charles Wood* London 1841; Sir William Clay *Remarks on the Expediency of Restricting the Issue of Promissory Notes* London 1844. The reader requiring a fuller account of the literature is referred to Professor Fetter's book mentioned above. Overstone's pamphlets are discussed in detail below.

[5] *Remarks upon some Prevalent Errors, with Respect to Currency and Banking, and Suggestions to the Legislature as to the Renewal of the Bank Charter* London 1833; *Remarks upon some Prevalent Errors, with Respect to Currency and Banking, and Suggestions to the Legislature and the Public as to the Improvement of the Monetary System* London 1838.

[6] *The Currency and the Country* London 1845. Hubbard was Governor 1853–5.

[7] See his evidence before the Committee on Banks of Issue, *Parliamentary Papers* 1840(602) IV qq. 730–999.

[8] See Sayers *Economic Writings of James Pennington* pp. xxxiv–xxxvi.

end in itself. It would guarantee the maintenance of convertibility and this was all, ultimately, that could be required. If a currency achieved what a metallic currency would have achieved then this was all that could be expected, and any abuses of credit or non-monetary fluctuations which would have occurred under a metallic currency had to be tolerated.

Following from this concern was the recognition that the Palmer Rule was inadequate to achieve such fluctuation, and establishment of the idea that separation of the Bank of England into a Department of Issue and a Department of Banking was necessary to do this. The first member of the School to put this into print was Torrens in the *Letter to Melbourne*[1] although he acknowledged Overstone's priority in this, as having suggested the matter at the Political Economy Club.[2] Ricardo is frequently mentioned as having been responsible for the original idea[3] although it is suggested below that in fact, as far as Overstone was concerned, the idea arose from the background of Jones Loyd's in Lancashire banking where there was almost no note issue.

Thirdly it was expected that the application of the principle would reduce fluctuations in the economy. It was expected to remove in particular those fluctuations which arose from insufficiently early contraction in the face of a drain.

All this in turn raised the question of the control of deposits. All the Currency School believed that deposits had some importance, but the stress which they put on this varied considerably. Torrens probably more than any other member of the School followed Pennington in his recognition of the importance of deposits. But most of the school believed that deposits were ultimately dependent on the amount of currency, although the precise *modus operandi* of control was often far from clear.

However although these writers believed that deposits were subject to control, the same was not, in general, true of the country issues. They rejected, with degrees of emphasis varying not only between writers but also between different works of the same writer, the belief held by Ricardo that the country banks issues were subject to the control of the Bank of England through price level differentials arising between the areas in which Bank of England and country bank notes circulated. Overstone was to some extent the leader in this rejection, and he was

[1] *Ibid.* p. 64.

[2] See Torrens' *Principles ... of Sir R. Peel's Act* 2nd ed. London 1857 pp. xii–xiii.

[3] See *Works and Correspondence of David Ricardo* ed. P. Sraffa vol. IV pp. 270–300.

here in accord with Palmer and Norman both of whom preceded him. Because of this the School came to regard the country banks as a significant source of instability and to press for abolition or control of the country issues. This was particularly the case after the crisis of 1839 when it became apparent that any control which did exist was severely lagged. The Currency School were then those in favour of change. The acceptance of convertibility imposed, as they saw it, the need for extensive legal intervention in both central and country banking issuing activities. The intervention was however in order to set up a system which would function automatically and deprive the Bank of England of discretionary power over the note issue.

The crisis of 1839 and the Committee on Banks of Issue of 1840 really led to the emergence of the Banking School as a recognisable opposition to the Currency School. The principal members of it were Thomas Tooke,[1] James Gilbart[2] and John Fullarton;[3] although James Wilson wrote on economic matters before 1844[4] he did not become a leading member of the Banking School until after the passing of the Act. There were also lesser lights like Joseph Hume.[5] Although it would be absurd to argue that these men, at least Tooke and Gilbart, were not active writers before this date, it is not unreasonable to date the emergence of the Banking School as a sort of antithesis to the Currency School's thesis, at the end of the 1830s and the beginning of the 1840s: and it was the hearings before the Committee of 1840 which helped to give them cohesion and prominence.

The Banking School never really admitted that over-issue could take place. Speaking generally they denied the validity of a quantity theory approach, claiming that prices were governed by incomes. A bank could only issue a sufficient amount of currency to support a given price level. Any currency issued beyond this would be returned to the issuing banks. As long as loans were only granted on the security of bills

[1] Tooke's *magnum opus* was the great *History of Prices*, the first two volumes of which appeared in 1838, followed by vol. III in 1840. He also published at this time *An Inquiry into the Currency Principle* (London 1844). As with the members of the Currency School, those requiring further bibliographical guidance are referred to Professor Fetter's work cited above.

[2] E.g. his *Currency and Banking* London 1841.

[3] *On the Regulation of Currencies* London 1844.

[4] *Fluctuations of Currency, Commerce and Manufactures* London 1840. Wilson was more prominent as an opponent of the Currency School after 1844. Indeed the letters in this edition would indicate that for some of the Currency School he came to be the *bête noir*.

[5] Lesser as economists, that is. Hume was particularly prominent in his sustained and hostile examination of Overstone before the 1840 Committee on Banks of Issue.

arising from real transactions they were prevented from being over-issued by the return of notes to the bank as bills matured.[1] Nevertheless they did see that there could be fluctuations caused by the banking system. But this was a problem of credit rather than of currency. In any case they did not accept the Currency School's concept of the central importance of metallic and paper money, stressing the importance of deposits (and cheques on these) and bills of exchange.

This necessarily bald account of the views of the Banking School should indicate that its members were likely to oppose all the policy proposals of their opponents. If an issuer could not over-issue, and if convertibility was its own safeguard, there was no need to subject the Bank of England and the country banks to extra control. Separation of the Bank into deparments was at best an irrelevance and at worst imposed a strait-jacket on the Bank. They were, like Thornton, insistent on the damage which unnecessary deflation could cause: and although they differed in the amount of recognition they were prepared to accord to the connection between the amount of issues and the balance of payments, they were clear enough in their rejection of the principle of 'metallic' variation. While the Currency School were strongly in favour of an automatic control of the monetary system, the Banking School were much more in favour of discretionary management. While recognising that the Bank might ultimately be forced to contract, they were in favour of distinguishing internal and external and terminable and non-terminable drains. Tooke suggested that the Bank should keep a reserve of specie of between £10 and £15 millions, regarding these as the limits between which fluctuation could be permitted to take place before corrective action was required from the Bank.

The role accorded to the rate of interest by the Banking School was far greater than that of their opponents. Tooke in particular divined more correctly than anyone the way in which short-run capital flows could actuate gold flows – yet he never really met Overstone's fundamental objection that such flows were merely palliative if relative international price levels were in disequilibrium. This approach in turn stemmed from a belief in the terminability of drains which could not arise from different quantities of money bringing about different relative price levels, and from a belief that, because of the existence of hoards, international specie flows could take place without affecting the quantity and value of money in a country.

[1] For a detailed critique of this approach see L. W. Mints *A History of Banking Theory* Chicago 1945.

OVERSTONE'S THOUGHT

But although the contribution of the Banking School contained valuable insights, it was too vague about its causal relationships to provide the coherent structure which the Currency School offered. It was the presentation of the latter before the 1840 Committee on Banks of Issue, and its advocacy within the Bank Court, which finally convinced Peel of the rectitude of their case although he was in any case likely to prefer action to inaction in relation to the Bank after the experiences of 1825, 1837 and 1839; and their views were enshrined in the Act of 1844.[1] The Act provided for the separation of the Bank of England into an Issue Department and Banking Department. The former was allowed to issue £14 million in notes against securities (the 'fiduciary issue'); the remainder had to be backed by specie so that the bullion flows would be reflected in the note circulation outside not the Bank but the Issue Department. The Banking Department was intended to function as any other bank, holding notes obtained from the Issue Department in exchange for bullion, together with some coin, as its reserve. In this position the power of the Bank to act as lender of last resort was, quite deliberately, limited. The Bank was required to publish weekly accounts of the state of both departments. (The significance of these will be made clear in the discussions on Overstone's thought). The country issues were also limited. No one could become an issuer who was not one on 6 May 1844, and no issuing banker could exceed his average in the twelve weeks ending 26 April 1844. No lapsed issue could be resumed and any partnership, the number of partners in which increased to more than six could not continue to issue. If any issuing bank ceased to issue, the Bank of England could take the issue, increasing its fiduciary issue by up to two-thirds of the lapsed issue. This Act, severely tried on occasion, was to remain in force for another eighty years.

(ii) *The Workings of the Act*

The Act appeared to work perfectly smoothly for more than two years after it came into operation. But in the early months of 1847 it became clear that there was still room for mismanagement on the part of the Bank. The Banking Reserve was allowed to fall to an extremely low level and when ultimately the Bank was forced to contract, there was considerable commercial pressure and embarrassment. The Act and the Bank survived this although the Directors of the latter were berated

[1] On the Act and its origins see Clapham *The Bank of England* II 172–85; and J. K. Horsefield 'The Origins of the Bank Charter Act, 1844' reprinted in Ashton and Sayers *Papers in English Monetary History* pp. 109–25.

for their incompetence. But in October of the same year, following extensive commercial failures including that of the Governor of the Bank, and banking failures, a panic developed. This seems to have been based on a fear of exhaustion of the Bank's power to act as lender of last resort because of the limits on its issue contained in the Act. At all events the issue of a government letter permitting the Bank to issue against securities beyond the limits laid down in the Act was sufficient to stop the crisis, without the Bank actually exceeding its legal limits. But the Act was severely damaged. The suspension was investigated by Select Committees of both Houses. The Commons Committee included James Wilson, and his exchanges with Overstone were not without hostility. But the Act survived this, although the Lords' report, written in all probability by Lord Monteagle, recommended the introduction of a relaxing power and the making of a distinction between internal and external drains. The Act survived too its suspension in 1857, when the Bank was forced to exceed the legal limit of its fiduciary issue, and in 1866 during the crisis following the failure of Overend, Gurney and Co. But the suspensions provided the Banking School with a good deal of ammunition.

A number of points emerge from the controversy. The Currency School maintained that no monetary system could deal with panics. Although it recognised that the development of a monetary system which included large-scale deposits at call was liable to panic, that panic was held to be due to an incautious reserve policy on the part of the deposit holders. Torrens, prompted by Overstone,[1] showed at length in an article in the *Edinburgh Review*[2] that such abuses could arise under a purely metallic currency. The adoption of proper reserve policies, not dependence on the Bank as the lender of last resort, was the course to be followed; and following the crisis of 1857 the Bank refused discount facilities to the discount market in an effort to force the discount houses to carry proper reserves. The Currency School had particular reason to object to the rôle of the Bank as lender of last resort because as the demand for discounts increased during pressure so did the note circulation outside the Bank.

Following from the discussions of panic and the rôle of the Bank in supporting the market, the Currency School opposed the suggestion of the introduction of a relaxing power into the Act, fearing that the

[1] See e.g. letters 435, 437, 442, 464.

[2] 'Lord Overstone on Metallic and Paper Currency', *Edinburgh Review* no. CCXVII (January 1858) art. ix pp. 248–93.

knowledge of its existence would interfere with the working of the Act. Metallic variation, it was felt, would be impeded because activity could continue at as high a level as before, safe in the knowledge that the Bank could be forced by panic into overstepping the limits of the Act.

The Currency School believed that the Act had worked well. Convertibility, they pointed out, was never in question after 1844. The Act had then achieved its main objective. It had indeed achieved all that a metallic currency could have achieved in the same circumstances – and this was the only standard of comparison the Currency School were prepared to recognise. Moreover it had by its steadying influence provided the climate in which the sustained growth of the economy since the Act had taken place. So satisfied were they with the Act's performance that some of them were opposed to public discussion of the Act and were prepared to tolerate what they believed to be significant anomalies, such as the permitting of country issues, to secure the continuation of the main principle.

The Banking School, by contrast, attacked strongly the workings of the Act. Although they came ultimately to accept its continuance[1] they believed that the whole theory underlying the measure was mistaken, and advanced a very different interpretation of its working from that of the Currency School. Although still endorsing the common objective of convertibility they believed that the Act of 1819 had been sufficient to achieve this and that the Act of 1844, far from being a complement to that of 1819 as claimed by the Currency School, was a danger to convertibility. The separation of departments they believed to be fundamentally mistaken. For one thing the sheer size of the Bank of England prevented its Banking Department behaving like any other bank. In addition, its connection with the government and debt management meant that its receipts and payments fluctuated enormously. It was the only lender of last resort, and the centre of the monetary system. It was the only bank which was able to affect the rate of interest (although only temporarily) and thence the exchanges; and it had a unique moral influence over the level of activity. The stoppage of the Banking Department, unlike that of any other bank, would paralyse the monetary system

[1] In this respect Wilson's attitude is particularly instructive. Though he continually attacked the philosophy of the Act in the *Economist*, he wrote to G. C. Lewis: 'But however unsound I may think Mercator [Overstone] in his theories, the practical results [of the Act] are so much nearer to those which I believe sound theory would suggest than any other system that has been propounded, that I should not like to put into the pools with the chance of what would come out.'—letter of 15 January 1857, reprinted in E. I. Barrington *The Servant of All* London 1927 vol. II p. 21.

and put convertibility in danger through the discredit of the Bank's Notes: yet the Act protected convertibility at the expense of risking the deposits. Because of the power of the Banking Department and its crucial position within the economy, it was pointless to regulate the Issue Department alone. Instead, by the Act, a reserve of gold had been provided for the note issue which was the least variable part of the liabilities: while the deposits were unprovided for. The need to protect this Banking reserve then led to wide fluctuations in Bank Rate which in turn led to violent fluctuations in confidence and hence in activity. Regulation of the amount of currency did not affect the level of activity but depended on it: and in any case there was as much importance attached to credit as to notes proper. Nor, the Banking School believed, could the large reserves of bullion held by the Bank since the Act be attributed to its operation as claimed by the Currency School. They believed the precious metals discoveries to be responsible for these large reserves and that the discoveries had saved the monetary system by offsetting the Bank's reckless resort to low interest rates. In sum, denying the crucial connection posited by the Currency School, between the quantity of notes and specie, internal prices, and the balance of payments, they believed the Act to be a dangerous irrelevance.

The contrast between the two schools should be clear from this brief account. It was against this background that Overstone's monetary thought developed.

2. *Overstone's Thought to 1844*

(i) *Introduction*

The content of Overstone's monetary thought is of considerable interest and importance. He was an important voice in the currency debates both before and after the Act of 1844; his prestige in the field was considerable, and posterity, quite rightly, has remembered him as a currency theorist. His prestige during his lifetime probably arose initially from his connection with the banking firm of his dynamic father; the latter's own influence was sufficiently great to ensure him a hearing in the City. But more and more Overstone's own qualities became apparent, particularly after 1837. He was in any case no youth when he first entered the field: he did not give evidence before a Committee till the age of thirty-five when he appeared, as the firm's representative, before the Committee on the Bank Charter of 1832, and he was forty before he published his first pamphlet.

OVERSTONE'S THOUGHT

Until the discovery of his correspondence, it was upon Overstone's writings and evidence on currency that posterity largely depended for its picture of the man. Although the letters in this edition make clear that Overstone was by no means an unemotional man, his pronouncements on currency have an immense lucidity, and an air of cold remorseless logic which is hardly less impressive. As Sir T. E. Gregory wrote: 'One longs for warmth and colour, for some admission of emotion, and is overwhelmed by the ruthless working of a perfectly logical mind, admitting nothing, forgetting nothing, never at fault – once the premises are granted – but, in sum, *remorseless*.'[1]

Overstone was engaged in controversy on monetary matters over a period of thirty years. His first utterance on the subject was his evidence before the Committee of 1832 on the renewal of the charter of the Bank of England, and his last, a series of letters published in the *Money Market Review*.[2] During those thirty years his activity falls into two main parts. Until 1844 he was critical alike of the Bank and of those of its critics who differed from him. After 1844 he wrote and spoke as the defender of the Act of 1844, widely identified in the public mind with its origin and function.

His intellectual source was, above all, Ricardo. Again and again throughout his writings there are references to Ricardo's evidence before the Committee of 1819 on the Resumption of Specie Payments,[3] to the *Reply to Bosanquet*,[4] and to the *High Price of Bullion*.[5] There are also references to the Bullion Report[6] which we now know was not Ricardo's[7] but these are few compared to the references to Ricardo. In some ways the minds of Overstone and Ricardo were very similar in

[1] Gregory *Westminster Bank* p. 158, italics in original.

[2] See *Lord Overstone on the Bank Act and the Currency. Correspondence between the Right Hon. Lord Overstone and Henry Brookes, Esq. Reprinted from the Special Supplements of the Money Market Review* London 1862.

[3] 'First and Second Reports from the Committee of Secrecy appointed to consider of the state of the Bank of England, with reference to the expediency of the Resumption of Cash Payments at the period fixed by Law' *Parliamentary Papers* 1819(202, 282) III 1. The evidence is reprinted in the *Works and Correspondence of David Ricardo* V 371–457.

[4] D. Ricardo *Reply to Mr. Bosanquet's Practical Observations on the Report of the Bullion Committee* reprinted in *Works*, III 155–256.

[5] *The High Price of Bullion, a Proof of the Depreciation of Bank Notes*, reprinted in *Works* III 48–127.

[6] 'Report from the Select Committee appointed to inquire into the cause of the high price of Gold Bullion, and to take into consideration the state of the Circulating Medium, and of the Exchanges between Great Britain and Foreign Parts' *Parliamentary Papers* 1810(349) III 1.

[7] See F. W. Fetter 'The Bullion Report re-examined' in Ashton and Sayers *Papers in English Monetary History* pp. 66–75.

their ability and willingness to reason an argument through to a conclusion starting from relatively few premises,[1] as well as in their lucidity and their ability to collect supporters. One of the most ardent of Overstone's supporters, Torrens, did compare Overstone to Ricardo on several occasions, and he told Wood: 'Indeed, while resembling M[r] Ricardo in many things, M[r] Loyd greatly excells him in lucid exposition.'[2] Overstone had collected by 1825 most of Ricardo's monetary pamphlets[3] and their influence upon him is very clear. Subsidiary to these in importance were two sources. The first was the Report of the Committee on Resumption of 1819 to which however he referred fairly frequently, and of which he wrote: 'Here terminates the dark age of currency; and we now enter upon a period characterized by more enlightened views.'[4] The second was McCulloch's Note on Money appended to the various editions of his version of the *Wealth of Nations*.[5] But whatever Overstone's sources, his own contribution to the debate was real enough.

(ii) *Analysis to 1844*

The development of Overstone's monetary thought really divides quite neatly either side of the Act of 1844. In the discussion up to 1844 he developed a fairly coherent scheme of thought: and when this was in substance embodied in the Act of 1844 his thought evolved in the light of experience under that Act. Before tracing the evolution of the analysis, and the emergence of its various components, which will be done in some detail to provide the reader of this edition with a fairly substantial picture of the content of Overstone's economic writings, it will be perhaps helpful to give an overall picture of the position reached before 1844.

Prior to 1844 Overstone was a regular if not always over-confident participant in the debates on monetary matters. Though he was later to

[1] Although if Mallet is to be believed neither were in the same class as James Pennington in this respect – see Mallet's diary in the Political Economy Club *Proceedings* vol. VI *Centenary Volume* London 1921 p. 269.

[2] Letter 167. See also letters 143, 156, 157.

[3] A bound volume of Overstone's of this date contains *inter alia*, the *Reply to Bosanquet*, the *High Price of Bullion*, *Essay on the Influence of a Low Price of Corn on the Profits of Stock*, *Proposals for an Economical and Secure Currency*, *Protection to Agriculture*, and *Plan for the Establishment of a National Bank*.

[4] *Remarks on the Management of the Circulation; and on the Condition and Conduct of the Bank of England and of the Country Issuers during the Year 1839*, reprinted in Overstone's *Tracts and other Publications on Metallic and Paper Currency* p. 53.

[5] This seems to have been something which Overstone drew on later in life – see his *Evidence . . . before the Select Committee . . . on Bank Acts* London 1858, pp. 77, 99, 115, 235, 241, 258, 259, 260.

oppose public discussion he believed until 1844 that this could do nothing but good and that it would lead to the emergence of the truth in economic affairs.

His approach was conditioned by two main factors: Firstly he believed that the correct attitude to monetary matters was a normative one; if for instance banks did not keep to a prudent course in expanding loans, and thus endangered the stability of the monetary system, the answer lay in a reform of their conduct. Secondly, he believed that the operation of the currency should be automatic with the Bank of England left as little discretion as possible.

The main theoretical foundation of his approach lay in acceptance of what will be called for the sake of brevity the Ricardian theory of the distribution of the precious metals.[1] No country could command a greater share of the precious metals than roughly equalised the value of the metals in different countries – taking into account costs of transport and different velocities of circulation. The precious metals would flow between countries until there was no profit to be made by sending them from one country to another. Ricardo summed this up by saying that 'Gold and silver having been chosen for the general medium of circulation, they are, by the competition of commerce, distributed in such proportions amongst the different countries of the world, as to accommodate themselves to the natural traffic which would take place if no such metals existed, and the trade between countries was purely a trade of barter.'[2] In other words when every country's trade is in balance there is no net flow of specie from one country to another. If due to some disturbance relative price levels were moved from this equilibrium, the relative value of specie in the differing trading countries would be altered and some debts would be settled in specie rather than commodities, bringing about an equilibrating specie flow.[3] Ricardo did not invent the theory but, to quote Professor Viner "the comprehensiveness and the force and skill of his exposition and the assurance and rigor of his reasoning made him at once the leading expositor of the bullionist position. It was largely through Ricardo's writings, moreover, that the bullionist doctrines exercised their influence on the subsequent century of monetary controversy.'[4] This was particularly true of Overstone.

[1] It is not intended to imply that the theory originated with Ricardo.

[2] *Principles* in *Works* I 137. A much clearer though less general exposition is given in Ricardo's *High Price of Bullion* (*ibid.* IV 47–127).

[3] Probably the clearest statement of the mechanism in all the literature of Classical Economics is to be found in Torrens' *Principles . . . of Sir R. Peel's Act* 3rd ed. London 1858 ch. II.

[4] Viner *Theory of International Trade* p. 122.

INTRODUCTION

Following from his acceptance of the Ricardian theory of the distribution of the precious metals was that of the Ricardian definition of an excess of currency as any level at which there was a net outflow of specie. This was basic to his view of the monetary system and of the policy which the Bank of England had to pursue. Any gold outflow implied the need for contraction.

As important as the theoretical basis for Overstone's approach was his acceptance of the maintenance of convertibility as *the* over-riding objective. It was the duty of government to provide a fixed standard of value, to secure justice between debtor and creditor, and to ensure a stable commercial society. But convertibility was insufficient to maintain itself. If notes received in exchange for bullion were not cancelled, convertibility might simply cease to exist. It was essential that a paper currency should fluctuate as an identically circumstanced metallic one would do. Following from the Ricardian definition of excess, international specie flows provided the guide to the behaviour of this hypothetical metallic currency. The contraction of the circulation had to be fully as great as the loss of specie because there was no other way of guaranteeing the return of lost specie. This was a literal deduction from the principle of 'metallic' fluctuation and possibly assumed that the price and activity levels of other countries were effectively immune to our specie flows. (It might be added that if the loss of specie resulted from any fundamental change in underlying economic conditions even contraction to the full extent of the specie loss was no guarantee of the flow being reversed as distinct from stopped.)

The operation of this concept of 'metallic' fluctuation was of far more importance than having a single issuer of Bank notes *per se*. Overstone was prepared, as practical policy, to tolerate the country issues provided they were controlled. The important point was that they should be prevented from frustrating the Bank of England's issue policy.

In order that the Bank should achieve a 'metallic' fluctuation of its note issue it required separation into an Issue Department and a Banking Department. Each of these departments had quite different rôles, in Overstone's view, to perform during the different phases of the trade cycle which he saw endogenous in economic activity. The cycle operated independently of monetary forces but they had to respond correctly to it. The Banking Department had to accommodate itself to customers' needs: but the Issue Department had to operate in a counter cyclical manner. By contracting as soon as a drain of specie began, the Issue Department would prevent both prices and confidence reaching their

maximum. In order to prevent the country banks frustrating this benficial effect by reacting only slowly to Bank of England contraction and thereby inserting a lag in the process of contraction which greatly increased its violence when it was finally felt, their issues had to be limited, although he was slow to commit himself to this.[1]

The effect of contraction on the 'metallic' pattern was expected to be rectification of the exchanges. This, Overstone believed, took place mainly through a reduction in prices and activity following contraction of the currency. This idea, and Overstone's presentation of it, will be criticised below in tracing the course of its development. The doctrine was never really thought through and Overstone was reluctant to commit himself to a quantity theory approach, although it was crucial to the mechanism. Reductions in prices stimulated exports, and hence rectified the exchanges by re-establishing the underlying barter pattern. Short-term capital inflow might help to smooth the process by anticipation of the rectification of the exchanges through the price and activity changes. But the burden of the establishment of equilibrium was that achieved by currency changes. As long as reserve ratios were maintained[2] as they should be, contraction of the currency would in turn contract credit. Deposits and bills of exchange could have no *independent* effect on prices: they were merely the upper part of the credit structure depending through reserve ratios on the currency base. As these 'economizing expedients' grew up they would displace some specie but this could only continue until reserves reached their lower limit. The 'economizing expedients' were not themselves capable of forming part of the credit base because they were insufficiently liquid; deposits, in particular, were not all simultaneously realisable. This was true not only of ordinary bank deposits, but also of bankers' deposits at the Bank of England. By contrast, notes in the Bank of England till formed part of the credit base and were therefore included by Overstone within the term 'circulation'.

Although the rôle of currency changes was thus put in the key position in the mechanism of monetary control, it should be emphasised that the

[1] Overstone accepted that the country banks were ultimately subject to the policy of the Bank of England. But he believed their response to contraction by the Bank to be lagged and violent. At first he completely rejected the idea of Ricardo and Torrens that the country issuers were subject to control by price differences emerging between 'London' and the 'country' and put forward a theory of control by means of the effect of the Bank of England's behaviour on confidence. But he later came to accept the Ricardian theory of control though in a lagged form.

[2] The validity of this particularly crucial assumption is examined below in the discussion of Overstone's *Reflections*.

rôle of interest rates was not completely ignored by Overstone. The process of contraction through the credit structure was supported by Bank Rate which acted as a danger signal when raised, and reduced the demand for discounts at the Bank below the level it would otherwise have attained in any given circumstances. It also helped to reduce both confidence and circulation in the country. At the same time it is perfectly true that Overstone believed that, generally speaking, the Bank of England had no power over the market rate of interest. It could affect this, even temporarily, only if given unlimited powers of issue.

The process of contraction was also supported by one extremely important mechanism. The publication of the state of the Bank of England reserve was something on which Overstone laid great stress. The idea was that this provided information which in turn reduced the velocity ('efficiency') of circulation by its effect on confidence and in particular on the desire for liquidity. Any given volume of notes became less 'efficient' than before as a result of publication of a fall in the Bank's reserve. This fall in velocity was itself, by implication, as important as reducing the note issue with velocity unchanged.

We find then in Overstone's thought three processes by which contraction was brought about: a quantity theory approach, supported by the effect of Bank Rate and the information-velocity interaction just described. The actual process, when Overstone came to describe it, reversed this order (but not necessarily this order of importance). It worked, he said, through affecting in turn the rate of interest, security prices, the share market, the foreign securities market, commodity speculation, and finally prices generally – the last and most crucial operation never being properly spelled out.

On the face of it Overstone saw this as a smooth operation acting efficiently and without a great deal of friction. But he did see certain interferences in the process. Paramount among these was the development of credit. This increased the velocity of circulation and hence the amount of contraction of the upper part of the credit structure which would be occasioned by any given loss of specie. This was not something which was peculiar to a paper currency or a currency partly consisting of paper and partly of metal. It could equally well occur under a metallic currency. But its development happened to have coincided with that of the development of paper currency, and it interfered with its operation. A second source of interference was the danger of panic. This was itself increased by the growth of credit and in particular of demand deposits. There could ultimately be none but purely emergency

provision against panic which was completely outside the operation of normal rules. At the same time he was opposed to the doctrine that it was the Bank's duty to act as lender of last resort as a matter of course in panic. Nothing could be decided on beforehand: all depended on the nature of the panic, but it must be borne in mind that the resources of the Bank, if it was to be prevented as it should from merely resorting to the printing press on such occasions, were limited. If, on the other hand, the Bank's rôle as lender of last resort were accepted as valid and overriding this could be used as a justification for any kind of issue policy.[1] But although panic was both a real danger and a real problem when it occurred, Overstone believed that the adoption of 'metallic' fluctuation, bringing about early and gradual rather than late and severe contraction, would reduce the danger of panic.

Such then was the system of control advanced by Overstone prior to 1844. It was designed to be automatic in its operation, and it was of the essence of it that it made no attempt to distinguish internal and external, terminable and non-terminable drains. If the Bank was losing specie it must be assumed that the exchanges were unfavourable. The Bank could certainly never be trusted with discretion to distinguish different sources of drain. To a very large extent this system was embodied in the Act of 1844; and we shall now attempt to trace the development of the system.

(iii) *The 1832 Committee*

Examination of Overstone's first public utterance on currency, his evidence before the Committee of 1832,[2] reveals only the germs of the comprehensive schema he was later to develop.

It was as a banker,[3] not a monetary theorist that he argued that a Bank of England monopoly of the note issue was desirable although this was to be a constant theme of his later theoretical writings. London, he argued, was the centre in which all transactions were ultimately adjusted. A single currency was required for final settlement, and such a currency would aid remittances between London and the country, and clearing in London.[4] In any case, the profits of issue were insufficient to support more than one issuer.

[1] He was following Tooke – see the *History of Prices* II 342.

[2] See 'Report from the Secret Committee appointed to inquire into the Expediency of renewing the Charter of the Bank of England, and into the System on which Banks of Issue in England and Wales are conducted', *Parliamentary Papers* 1831–2(722) VI I. Overstone's evidence of 5 July 1832 is pp. 232–49, qq. 3244–485.

[3] Q. 3244.

[4] Qq. 3245–9.

INTRODUCTION

He did, it is true, adduce some theoretical reasons for his views, arguing that multiplication of London issuers would increase fluctuations in activity. Issues would be made with regard to the competitive position of the issuer and with no reference to the state of the exchanges. Although over-issue by any one bank would be returned to it 'the very circumstances which produced that return of the paper would be part of the injurious effects produced by the improper issue'.[1] Convertibility was no safeguard against temporary over-issue. It is possible too to see theoretical considerations underlying his view on this occasion[2] that where there were many issuers, the demand for gold would be higher because each issuer would need his own reserve of specie and so the economy of a paper currency would be smaller; for in putting forward this view he stated that however many issuers there were the total size of the issue would have to be the same.

But most of his evidence contains only hints of what was to follow later. He severely attacked the joint-stock banks for their commercial behaviour;[3] this could easily have originated in the dislike of a private banker for this form of competition, although it is also a sign of Overstone's dislike, which later became pronounced, of the way in which credit and the monetary system were developing, particularly in his attack on these banks for re-discounting.[4]

For, as already indicated, Overstone's writings and statements on currency and banking were largely normative, not positive. It is essential to an understanding of Overstone's position to realise this. At many stages of his argument about the monetary system he was describing not what was, but what ought to be.

A number of other points which were found in his later arguments are also discernible. Deposits in the hands of the Bank of England were still employed in trade because of the Bank's support of the money market.[5] The Bank could not determine the market rate of interest but had to follow it.[6] Management of the issues was a quite different thing from banking:

> My idea is, that the management of the issue of notes is a business entirely distinct from other banking business, and that everything connected with it ought to be kept perfectly distinct from the other affairs of the Bank; that whatever be done by the issue of notes, and whatever funds are reserved for

[1] Q. 3257. He also agreed that it was *practically* possible to have more than one issuer in London if the notes of the other issuers were receivable for revenue payments (qq. 3290–1). But he was against multiple London issue (q. 3448).

[2] Qq. 3258–62.

[3] Qq. 3269–80.

[4] Qq. 3275–6.

[5] Qq. 3311–12.

[6] Q. 3319.

meeting that issue, is entirely independent of the rest of the business which may be strictly called banking business.[1]

This reply concerned the country issues; yet it is interesting to speculate how far the idea of the separation of departments may have stemmed from Overstone's background in country banking in Lancashire where notes were not issued[2] – indeed the Loyds in Manchester had resisted any attempt to make them issuers.[3] Ricardo had indicated the need for a separation of functions[4] but Overstone makes no reference to this source.

He also emphasised here, as later, the difficulty of dealing with the country banks. A complete Bank of England monopoly of note issue, though desirable, in principle, might drive the country banks out of business[5] and he was chary, as he was always to be, of acting too directly in this respect.[6] In explaining the possible effects of the Bank's becoming the sole issuer he did put forward the germ of his theory of information on which he was later to lay great stress. If the Bank were to achieve this position then regular publication of its accounts was required.[7] This would educate the public to read them and to realise that convertibility was not in question.[8] Yet here, as so often in 1832, there were only the beginnings of the later theory. He was not arguing, as he did subsequently, that the information supplied by the Bank would interact with the velocity of circulation.

Two other features of his later position are also discernible at this stage. Firstly, we find his defence of the Bank of England as an institution. Here, as throughout his career as a participant in currency controversies, he was not prepared publicly to recommend changes in the direction of the Bank,[9] or greater Government control of it,[10] despite his admission that there was a possibility of conflict between the Bank's public and private interests.[11] Secondly, we find his great emphasis on

[1] Q. 3380.

[2] See Ashton 'The Bill of Exchange and Private Banks in Lancashire, 1790–1830' in Ashton and Sayers *Papers in English Monetary History* pp. 37–49.

[3] See Overstone's evidence before the Select Committee on Bank Acts of 1857 q. 3701.

[4] See J. K. Horsefield 'The Origins of the Bank Charter Act, 1844' in Ashton and Sayers *Papers in English Monetary History* pp. 109–25, p. 116.

[5] Q. 3372.

[6] For instance he was asked: 'Are you of opinion that it would be the best system of currency to have only one Bank of issue throughout the country? – To this he replied: 'It is dangerous to give an answer upon a general principle; my opinion is, that such would be the best system; but the expediency of now attempting to make the change is a very serious question.' Q. 3455.

[7] Qq. 3382–92. [8] Qq. 3408–9. [9] Q. 3393. [10] Q. 3415. [11] Q. 3402.

the benefit of public discussion. It could not in the end lead to erroneous conclusions;[1] if mistrust of the Bank were ill-founded, then this would emerge in the discussion. If it was well founded, then discussion would point the way for reform. This was one aspect of his thought on which he performed a complete volte-face after 1844: but until then, his emphasis on the benefit of public discussion was very strong.

Yet despite all these points which were found in his later views, it is quite clear that Overstone had, as yet, developed no clear and coherent theory of currency. His answers were largely those which any intelligent and reasonably liberal banker might have given, but they amounted to observations rather than to a theoretical performance. Here, above all, there are not the two crucial features of all his later analysis, the insistence that a paper currency should fluctuate exactly as he believed an identically circumstanced metallic one would have done, the inflows and outflows of metal indicating the necessary expansion and contraction and the prime insistence that above all, convertibility should be maintained. 'I think the principle on which the Bank should regulate its store of treasure, should be to meet all reasonable and ordinary emergencies; but I can conceive emergencies to arise, either political or even commercial, of such a nature that it is impossible for the Bank to reserve an adequate store, without foregoing all the advantages of a paper currency.'[2] Such a prescription, though containing his permanent recognition that there was no cure for panics, hardly amounted to an analysis – in a sense it was almost tautological. A large enough bank reserve was large enough; and Overstone refused to give any opinion on what *was* enough.[3]

His performance before the Committee in 1832 was then only a partial precursor of what was to come. Although containing in it many of the points found in his later writings, it lacked the basic analytical core. During the next four years his views on currency must have developed considerably. It is very probable that he discussed monetary matters with his close friend, George Warde Norman of the Bank; and Norman had developed, with at least subjective originality, the principle that a paper currency should fluctuate as if metallic.[4] By 1836 he was emphasising the need for a separation of issue from banking, and

[1] Qq. 3417–20. [2] Q. 3436. [3] Q. 3439.

[4] See letter 23 p. 205 n. 2. For the claims of Joplin, Drummond, Pennington and others to have been objectively the originators of the principle see Wood *English Theories of Central Banking Control 1819–58* ch. x, and Viner *Theory of International Trade* p. 224.

arguing that social suffering resulted from competition in issues.[1] Then in February 1837[2] he published the first of his pamphlets.

(iv) *The Pamphleteer*

This was his *Reflections*.[3] In this work, the full extent of the development in his thinking became clear. For, in his attack on the Palmer Rule, and on Palmer's attempted defence of it, a theoretical backbone of the argument became discernible. The rule by which the Bank professed to be guided, the so-called Palmer Rule, was (to recapitulate) that when the circulation was full, i.e. the exchanges were just on the point of becoming unfavourable, securities should form two-thirds of its assets and bullion one-third. From then on the securities were to be held fixed in amount and fluctuations in the bullion were to be reflected in fluctuations in the circulation. The aim was to achieve a one-third bullion reserve against its combined notes and deposits liabilities.

The starting point of Overstone's criticism of this was that, whatever the Rule, the Bank's circulation and specie had in fact moved in opposite directions.

> Now, from the accounts as published, it appears that the Bank has deviated from all the rules by which it professes to be guided, and which a regard to sound principle requires it to adhere to. By these accounts it appears that the amount of securities, so far from being kept at a fixed point, has fluctuated largely; it also appears that the circulation has in some instances increased whilst the specie has been diminishing;[4]

Overstone then went on to criticise the rule itself. The difficulty, he said, lay in the fusion of issuing and banking functions.[5] The Palmer Rule was perfectly sound for the former, but became impracticable when it encompassed the latter. In conducting a banking business, deposits necessarily varied, and if they varied the securities in which they were invested must vary also. He specifically stated, as being the correct course which should be followed, what was to become known as the currency principle –

> – that the amount of paper issued shall be represented by an amount of securities which never varies, and an amount of specie which is left to fluctuate with the fluctuations of the amount of notes out.[6]

[1] See letter 28. [2] See letter 30 and *ibid.* p. 219 n. 2.

[3] *Reflections suggested by a perusal of Mr. J. Horsley Palmer's pamphlet on the Causes and Consequences of the Pressure on the Money Market* London 1837, reprinted in *Tracts* pp. 1–40.

[4] *Tracts* p. 3. [5] *Ibid.* pp. 9–10. [6] *Tracts* p. 11.

To achieve this fluctuation he suggested that it was

> better to separate altogether the business of banking from that of regulating the currency, rather than suffer so essential a rule to be compromised. It is not, however, very easy to perceive any insuperable difficulty in rendering the currency department of the Bank of England totally distinct and separate from the management of its other business;[1]

He had now stated two essential propositions – 'metallic' fluctuation and separation of departments. In the light of these he went on to develop his criticism of the conduct of the Bank. He stressed that the preceding drain of specie had fallen on deposits. This was important. If, as was later asserted by some of his critics, deposits were 'money' and, by implication, on all fours with currency in their effect on prices, this would not have mattered. But if the effect on prices of a drain of deposits was equal only to a fraction of the effect of a drain of an equal amount of currency, the difference was crucial. The latter would however only be strictly true if reserve ratios were fixed or at least flexible only over a small range. As much of Overstone's later argument was to depend on this question of reserve ratios, it is perhaps proper to examine it a little more closely. It does seem fairly clear that, as a matter of *fact*, the ratios were not fixed. The reserves held against notes may have been fairly inflexible but those against deposits were not fixed 'because these were not strictly payable on demand'.[2] But even if Overstone was wrong, as he was, on this question of fact, there must nevertheless be some limit below which prudence would dictate that reserves should not be allowed to fall. This was presumably in fact the practice of Overstone as a highly successful banker, and of those other bankers, like Prescott, of whom he approved. What he was implying, was that whatever the situation actually *was*, it *should* be as he described; and the modern development of central bank control partly through reserve ratios, both directly and indirectly, would bear him out in this. One of his main complaints against the way in which the banking system was developing was that reserve policies were insufficiently

[1] *Ibid.* p. 11.

[2] J. K. Horsefield 'The Bank and its Treasure' in Ashton and Sayers *Papers in English Monetary History* pp. 50–65, p. 52, referring to the evidence of Henry Burgess, Secretary of the Committee of Country Bankers before the Committee of 1832. See also *ibid.* pp. 60–1 for further evidence on the question of fixity of reserve ratios. Overstone was not however alone in his belief in the importance of reserve ratios – Torrens seems to have adopted the idea from Pennington who promptly repudiated it. See Sayers *Economic Writings of James Pennington* pp. xiv–xv.

cautious, and he particularly disliked the joint stock banks who demonstrably did not keep stable reserve ratios.[1]

At all events, circulation and specie had moved in opposite directions, because the drain had fallen on deposits, and for this the Bank, and not the country issuers, was to blame.[2] Although it was true that the latter had no motive to look to the exchanges in regulating their issues the fact was that the Bank of England branch issues had expanded at the same time as the country circulation of which Palmer complained. But it was of over-riding importance that all the Bank's issues should fluctuate as a metallic currency. To distinguish between temporary and continuing drains was to run far too great a risk, as it was to distinguish between internal and external drains. Prompt action to contract and reverse the drain was what was required.

There is an old Eastern proverb which says, you may stop with a bodkin a fountain, which if suffered to flow will sweep away whole cities in its course. An early and timely contraction, upon the very first indication of excess in the circulation, is the application of the bodkin to the fountain; commercial convulsion and ruin in consequence of delay, is the stream sweeping away whole cities in its course.[3]

No exercise of discretion was safe:

At all events the only safe course is to consider a continuous drain of gold from the Bank as conclusive evidence, without reference to vague and uncertain speculations as to the precise cause of that drain, of the necessity of effecting a corresponding reduction of circulation. It is of great importance that this question should be clearly understood and settled, as nothing can be more dangerous in the management of the currency than a tendency, upon the ground of supposed peculiarities of the circumstances of each case, to suspend the operations of rules which are of a general nature and rest upon unquestionable principles.[4]

Thus the Ricardian definition of excess was rigidly applied to the problem of currency regulation. 'Metallic' fluctuation was to be the standard of rectitude; and Overstone even opposed Palmer's proposal to check dealings in foreign securities – they would take place under a metallic currency and would not interfere with it.

[1] See the reserve ratios of the London and Westminster and London and County banks in table 102 of J. R. T. Hughes *Fluctuations in Trade, Industry and Finance* Oxford 1960 p. 281.

[2] *Tracts* p. 4. He criticised the latter privately (see letter 28) but clearly did not believe that they should bear the brunt of the blame for what had occurred.

[3] *Tracts* p. 23.

[4] *Ibid.* p. 26.

INTRODUCTION

Five points in particular emerge from this first pamphlet. Firstly, 'metallic' fluctuation was now firmly established as the standard of currency management. Secondly, it received at this stage remarkably little justification. The reader was told that 'metallic' fluctuation was the most that could be expected from a paper currency; and there is a hint, in the bodkin simile, that such a principle would reduce fluctuations. But the crucial importance of convertibility as the underlying objective, and the Ricardian theory of the distribution of the precious metals, which lay at the base of the whole analysis, are not dealt with. Thirdly, there is a very clear statement of the need to separate the functions of issue and banking. Fluctuations in activity were inevitable, but Overstone, while making his famous statement of the Trade Cycle,[1] emphasised that the banker and the issuer had quite distinctive duties during its different phases. To give the banker, who conformed to his customers' needs, the power of issue, when issues should be moving in the opposite direction, was quite wrong. Fourthly, although Overstone still agreed that one issuer was the ideal, he did not really commit himself on the disputed question of the Bank's control over other issues. For him, at this stage, it was enough that the Bank had not followed the rules. Fifthly, his theory of information had still not completely developed. Although he emphasised the need for information about the Bank's position,[2] the object of this seems to have been to enable other parties to adjust their reserve position. This obviously has implications for the velocity of circulation, but in his *Further Reflections*, published later the same year,[3] Overstone continued and developed his analysis further. He described the operation of the trade cycle as he saw it in 1837, reaching the quiescent low point of the cycle with gold flowing in as a result of the lowering of the level of prices and activity. The Palmer Rule had not been followed and securities, instead of remaining fixed, had fluctuated, diminishing greatly during the period of quiescence as was inevitable under normal banking rules. Meanwhile, circulation had moved in the opposite direction to bullion. But having stressed the inapplicability of the Bank's current guide, he went on to indicate more clearly than before the *rationale* of a 'metallic' circulation. He explained that with a truly metallic circulation the precious metals will flow between countries so that each country has 'its proper amount'[4]

[1] *Ibid.* pp. 31–3. [2] *Ibid.* pp. 3, 28.

[3] *Further Reflections on the State of the Currency and the Action of the Bank of England* London 1837. The pamphlet is dated 23 December 1837.

[4] *Further Reflections* p. 33.

– this is following the 'Ricardian' theory of the distribution of the precious metals. As a result of this 'in every case of purchase or sale, an equivalent value is sure to be received'.[1] But in adopting paper 'we . . . lose that self-acting security'[2] and some rule has to be established for regulating its amount. That rule 'seems to be very obvious, viz. that the paper notes ought to be kept the same in amount as the metallic coin would have been'.[3] The import or export of the precious metals indicates how a fully metallic circulation would be varying at any time and the amount of notes in circulation should then fluctuate according to the exchanges. Without such a principle, he believed, there was no guide but the discretion of the Bank of England for the regulation of the currency. Such discretion had already been found wanting, and would lead to the disturbance of debtor–creditor relationships and needless fluctuations in the level of activity. The alternative to metallic circulation was chaos, the disturbance of transactions and prices, the 'mutual condition of different classes unjustly altered',[4] and 'convulsive agitations'[5] in trade. Convertibility itself was no guard against over-issue – if notes exchanged for gold were not cancelled, convertibility might simply cease to exist. It was, conversely, no guard against under-issue. 'Metallic' fluctuation was the only guide.

In many ways this pamphlet is important. It contains a clear statement of the basis of Overstone's theory as the Ricardian theory of the distribution of the precious metals with excess or deficiency defined solely in relation to the exchanges[6] and a much greater emphasis on the stabilising influence on the economy, and the maintenance of commutative justice, of 'metallic' fluctuation than hitherto.

But having developed his position this far, Overstone ceased pamphleteering for two years. It was not until 1 January 1840 that he published his *Remarks on the Management of the Circulation*.[7] This was a lengthy pamphlet and contained some fairly biting material about the management of the Bank[8] in general, while praising the evidence of Norman, Ward and Palmer before the Committee of 1832. This was a preliminary to a renewal of his criticism of the Palmer Rule. The whole system he believed was rotten. Any currency should be able to cope with fluctuations but the Bank of England had only been saved from a

[1] *Ibid.* [2] *Ibid.* [3] *Ibid.* p. 34.
[4] *Further Reflections* p. 41. [5] *Ibid.* [6] See in particular *ibid.* p. 38.
[7] *Remarks on the Management of the Circulation; and on the Condition and Conduct of the Bank of England and of the Country Issuers, during the year 1839* London 1840, reprinted in *Tracts* pp. 41–158.
[8] See in particular *Tracts* p. 49.

suspension of specie payments by the loans arranged with Paris and Hamburg. It had, by its incompetence, created distrust of sterling, leading to foreign sales of British bills and a movement against us of the leads and lags.[1] By contrast, early contraction in response to a drain would prevent desperate situations of this sort,[2] and a separation of functions would enable the Bank of England to exercise her rôle as lender of last resort (about which he was not very happy because of the scope it gave the Bank for 'improper' issues)[3] without affecting the currency.

This was all on the pattern of the two preceding pamphlets. But when Overstone turned his attention to the country issues he was prepared to commit himself much more firmly than before. Initially, he believed, the latter were outside the Bank's control. When there was a drain of bullion the country issues, instead of decreasing, increased. The Bank was then forced to take violent corrective measures as the drain continued; and these measures, particularly raising Bank Rate had, at length, a sudden and violent effect upon the country issues.[4] He developed this theory of 'shock control' at length. Ricardo in the *High Price of Bullion*, Torrens in his *Letter to Melbourne*,[5] and the Committee on Resumption of 1819 had all believed that an adverse balance of payments for the country, against London, would necessarily bring about a contraction of the country issues. Prices would be relatively higher in the provinces, and lower in London, after the Bank had contracted, and this would result in the return of notes to the country issuers and a demand for bills on London.[6] As Overstone correctly pointed out[7] this involved the assumptions that the area of 'London' was completely separated from that of the country 'as completely as one country is separated from another'[8] and secondly, and more importantly, that the system worked without lags. In fact he found neither assumption to be valid. There was no such separation as assumed; the Bank and the country issuers competed and if the Bank contracted the latter would and did expand competitively to fill the void and to help their customers, thus creating a lag before they finally contracted themselves. Continued contraction by the Bank of England brought about a country-

1 *Ibid.* p. 73.

2 *Ibid.* p. 75.

3 *Tracts* pp. 86–7. He was not very happy about reliance on the Bank of England, and in any case he believed that the market had greater resources than the Bank (p. 88).

4 *Ibid.* pp. 93–4.

5 *A Letter to the Right Honourable Lord Viscount Melbourne on the Causes of the recent Derangement in the Money Market and on Bank Reform* 1837.

6 *Ibid.* pp. 95–6.

7 *Ibid.* p. 97.

8 *Ibid.* p. 97.

wide shock to credit which affected the country issuer who was compelled to contract, apparently by a change in his beliefs about prospects[1] – 'the country banks of issue first resist, then suffer, and, in the end, submit'.[2] So the country banks were partly to blame for the monetary dangers of 1839; although individual banks could not over-issue because their notes would be returned to them, a whole banking system (such as the Scots) could do so perfectly well for a while.[3]

In this pamphlet we have then, for the first time in Overstone's writings, a clear statement of the rôle of the country issuers (even though Overstone would not commit himself on their regulation)[4] and a strong emphasis on the view that 'metallic' fluctuation would reduce fluctuation in the economy. At the same time it should be stressed, since Overstone was later accused of claiming that the application of the currency principle would remove significant fluctuations, that he was firm in his insistence that no monetary system could get rid of the trade cycle:

> Those who expect to find, even in the most perfect management of the circulation, the magic power to secure perpetual ease and undisturbed steadiness in commercial affairs, are like the alchymists in search of their mysterious secret; . . . Storms and tempests are not more certain and inevitable in the material world, than are the periodical convulsions of commercial affairs.[5]

Overstone's assertions after 1844 that he had only claimed for the Currency principle that it would remove those fluctuations which were monetary in origin appear largely correct.

Just as importantly, we find here his explicit belief that smoothing out fluctuations was less important than maintaining convertibility.

> But the principal and most important benefit to be attained by a due regulation of the currency, consists less in the indirect effect which it may have in preventing violent fluctuations in the state of trade or of prices, than in its direct tendency to protect and secure the convertibility of the notes under all possible contingencies. Money . . . is . . . a Measure of Value; and when paper, in itself possessing no intrinsic value, is used as a substitute and representative of the precious metals, the convertibility of that paper becomes essential for preserving its character as a Standard of Value.[6]

This in turn secured the standard of commutative justice.[7]

[1] *Ibid.* p. 100. [2] *Ibid.* p. 101. [3] *Ibid.* p. 115. [4] *Ibid.* p. 142.
[5] *Ibid.* p. 132. [6] *Ibid.* p. 132.
[7] See the quotation from the Bullion Report on p. 133.

This point of view is of primary importance to Overstone. Throughout his life he laid great stress on the maintenance of mutual obligations. It is true, as Lord Robbins has written:

> speaking broadly, the members both of the Currency School and of the Banking School did not trouble to argue very much with the advocates of inconvertible money, speaking of them always merely as if they were lunatics or enemies of society.[1]

and that ultimately the argument between the Currency and Banking schools was about the most reasonable way to maintain convertibility. But Overstone saw in any danger to the standard what was essentially for him a moral issue, the maintenance of the debtor–creditor relationship. Apart from his currency pronouncements, he made this very clear when commenting on the discussion on seignorage,[2] and, very late in life, this was the danger which he saw in bi-metallism.[3]

With the publication of *Remarks on the Management of the Circulation* much of Overstone's thought had been made clear. The idea of 'metallic' fluctuation, the need for a separation of functions, the Ricardian definition of excess, the idea that monetary regulation could remove unnecessary fluctuations but not the trade cycle, and the power of the country issuers temporarily to thwart Bank of England contraction, had all been clearly expressed. Yet the system was not complete. The difficulty over reserve ratios may be avoided by an appeal to the normative character of the analysis. But one fundamental question remained unanswered. The precise effect of a contraction on prices and the level of activity is far from clear. Overstone was reluctant to commit himself to a crude quantity theory approach to the effect of the quantity of money on prices.

> The connexion ... between fluctuations in prices and variations in the amount of the circulating medium is a question of extremely difficult solution in its detail; and, probably, ... we can only come to the conclusion that the immediate effect upon prices of any variation in the amount of the circulation may be over-estimated, whilst there undoubtedly exists a very intimate connexion between them.[4]

Yet, as Overstone admitted in his next sentence, the very idea that prices fell as the Bank contracted (money became more valuable) was crucial to his argument. The truth of the matter seems to be that, at this stage at least, he was prepared to lay more emphasis on the relationships of

[1] *Robert Torrens* p. 253.

[2] See letters 746 :748, 778, 779, 780, 784, 786.

[3] See letter 912.

[4] *Ibid.* p. 120.

credit and the level of activity than on prices *per se*. He lacked both Ricardo's certainty[1] and Thornton's subtlety[2] in this respect.

His *Letter to J. B. Smith*[3] did not advance the analysis much further. The *Letter* was largely a defence of the Bank of England, and, as such, confined, to a considerable extent, to emphasising the limited power of the Bank and of currency. 'Fluctuations in the amount of the currency are seldom, if ever, the original and exciting cause of fluctuations in prices and in the state of trade.'[4] Fluctuations were to be traced to other causes such as successive bad harvests, the Corn Laws and the American financial crisis. Apart from reinforcing his later emphasis that he had never claimed that monetary reform would remove such fluctuations, this was apparently not very important. Yet it did have a further significance which we see in Overstone's *Second Letter*.[5] Apart from stating that 'metallic' fluctuation was his starting point,[6] that fluctuations in trade and the rate of interest would occur with a metallic currency,[7] accusing Smith of equating a speculative boom with prosperity,[8] stressing that whatever the cause of a loss of bullion the currency should be contracted, stressing also the culpability of the country issuers[9] and again making clear his distaste for the idea that the Bank had a duty to act as a lender of last resort, all of which was largely as before, he also wrote:

Speaking practically, I am inclined to think that fluctuations in prices will in most cases be found to originate in some predisposing circumstances, and that fluctuations in the circulation act 'as a subordinate agent,' increasing or diminishing the force of those pre-disposing circumstances, and accelerating or retarding the rapidity of their action.[10]

[1] See Ricardo's evidence before the Lords' Committee of 1819 in *Works* v 452, qq 123–4.

[2] H. Thornton *An Enquiry into the Nature and Effects of the Paper Credit* ed. F. Hayek London 1939 p. 142.

[3] *A Letter to J. B. Smith, Esq. President of the Manchester Chamber of Commerce* London 1840 (dated 9 January 1840).

[4] *Ibid.* p. 167.

[5] *Effects of the Administration of the Bank of England, A Second Letter to J. B. Smith, Esq. President of the Manchester Chamber of Commerce* London 1840 (dated 2 March 1840).

[6] 'I propose fluctuations of the bullion as the standard measure by which to try a paper currency. If this be admitted, we can proceed with the discussion. If it be not admitted, the attempt to proceed further is useless, until this question be determined. The objectors must in that case be called upon to produce their counter-standard; and in doing so, they must be required to produce one which is capable of distinct definition and of equally distinct application; otherwise it is no standard at all.' *Tracts* p. 190.

[7] *Ibid.* p. 190. [8] *Ibid.* pp. 192–3. [9] *Ibid.* p. 214. [10] *Ibid.* p. 204.

Now such an attitude raised serious questions, similar to those raised by his earlier reluctance to adopt a crude quantity theory, about the *modus operandi* of control of specie flows through relative price levels. It was all very well to take the attitude that specie flows resulted from price changes within the trade cycle: but Overstone's analysis was supposed to apply universally, whatever the cause of the drain.

Such questions remained unanswered. But the *Second Letter* did attempt to begin to answer some other important questions. In particular it dealt more fully than Overstone had previously with deposits. We have seen that there was a difficulty over reserve ratios in this respect: but neglecting this we can recognise that Overstone's basic position on deposits was that they were unable significantly to affect prices, and certainly unable to do so independently. They were the upper part of an inverted credit pyramid with currency at the base. In the light of this we can understand Overstone's argument in the *Second Letter*[1] that deposits of non-issuing bankers were not currency but that deposits of issuing bankers might *become* currency if the issuer abused his power of issue when faced with heavy withdrawals. We can also understand the implication of his argument that the greater the development of credit the more amplified were commercial fluctuations[2] – the multiple contraction of all forms of credit in the upper part of the pyramid was the key to this.

Yet none of this advanced the analysis very far beyond his *Remarks*. The same was not true of his *Thoughts on the Separation of Departments*, which appeared shortly afterwards.[3] Apart from its political significance in endorsing such a plan it was also interesting as showing some further developments in Overstone's analysis. The rationale of 'metallic' fluctuation is again seen as convertibility; but this is further amplified by the explanation that a metallic circulation could never be drained out because of its effect on prices and credit. Overstone now spells out the order in which contraction takes place.

> Contraction of circulation acts—first upon rate of interest—then upon price of securities—then upon market for shares, &c.—then upon the negociation of foreign securities—at a later period, upon the tendency to enter into speculation in commodities—and lastly, upon prices generally.[4]

The order of contraction had now been spelled out even if the precise

[1] Pp. 199–201. [2] *Ibid.* pp. 206–7.

[3] *Thoughts on the Separation of the Departments of the Bank of England* privately printed 1840. The preface is dated 2 April 1840.

[4] *Ibid.* pp. 9–10.

mechanism which operated this order is far from clear, and any clear statement of exactly how the exchanges were corrected in this process is still lacking. A price-specie flow mechanism of some sort seems to be assumed, but it is not spelled out.

Apart from a renewal of his attack on the country issuers, confirming that Overstone was now convinced of their share in responsibility for what had occurred in 1839, two further points of interest emerge from the pamphlet. Firstly Overstone's view of the specie flow mechanism is, in a sense, asymmetrical. After asking what assurance there is, without contraction, that a drain will terminate before the bullion is exhausted, he then adds a further question:

> And second, by what process, but that of contraction and pressure, is the bullion so paid away to be recovered?[1]

This question is implicitly present in much of Overstone's currency discussions. The rigid application of the Ricardian definition of excess is necessary because no significant effect on other countries' price and activity levels could be expected from an outflow of bullion. Any recovery had to be achieved by full adjustment of our levels to the existing foreign ones. This was not unrealistic – although Fullarton's insistence on the importance of hoarding was not taken very seriously in relation to the British economy, it was arguable that the less developed economies of the nations with whom Britain traded could not be expected to respond in exactly the same way as the highly developed British one to an inflow of specie. Although it was true that the American monetary system would probably respond fairly strongly to an inflow of specie, the same was not true of France where the development of financial institutions, significantly raising the velocity of circulation towards the British level, was rather slow. Yet there was here a fairly important issue. Thornton had given cogent reasons for expecting lost gold to return,[2] mainly on the basis that bullion was demanded in settlement of international debts, which would be settled in the normal course of affairs by commodity flows, only when international confidence was at a low ebb; and that with confidence returned to normal, the gold would automatically return to the country which had lost it. On this basis he argued that large-scale contraction by the Bank of England would both disrupt economic activity, including exporting,

[1] *Ibid.* p. 20.
[2] *An Enquiry into the Nature and Effects of the Paper Credit of Great Britain* pp. 141–60.

and add an internal drain to the external one. Fullarton, too, argued[1] in a similar vein. But Overstone never fully justified his requirement, of a contraction as great as the loss of specie, against these arguments, although an answer which is implicit throughout his writing is that only *full* contraction would bring our price level sufficiently low to expand exports to meet our international debts; the full contraction merely followed axiomatically from the 'metallic' principle.

Secondly, Overstone is perfectly well aware that the velocity of circulation is variable. It was a dramatic fall in velocity brought about by a crisis of public confidence arising from the state of the Bank of England which had corrected the exchanges in 1839.

> The drain was stopped by the prevalence of general apprehension and alarm, which checked confidence and credit, and rendered a given amount of circulation less efficient. This alarm arose from a knowledge of the exhausted state of the bullion, and of the heavy drain still in operation; which it might be expected would necessitate some extraordinary and very severe measure on the part of the Bank.[2]

The theory of the interaction of information about the Bank's position, and the velocity ('effectiveness') of circulation, partly through a consolidation of liquid reserves and partly through a general effect on confidence which made new enterprise less inviting, was now completed. It was henceforth to be of great importance in Overstone's work particularly in face of the fact, brought to his notice repeatedly, that notes in the hands of the public increased during contraction.

Two other subsidiary points are worth noting in this pamphlet; the treatment of Bank Rate and of panics. He stressed that a rise in Bank Rate can act as a danger signal, that although it might be followed by an increased demand for discounts the increase would have been even greater but for the rise, that it helps to contract the country circulation and finally that, through its effect on confidence, it could affect 'auxiliary currency' (the inverted credit pyramid).[3] Not only is this some answer to those, like James Wilson, who accused Overstone of talking of adjustment only via prices before 1844 and via interest rates after 1844,[4] but the latter part of his argument reflects a more general concern with the problem of credit. It is clear however that he still believed that credit could have no independent effect on prices. When Norman

[1] *On the Regulation of Currencies* London 1844 pp. 138–66, especially pp. 144–5.

[2] *Ibid.* p. 21.

[3] *Ibid.* p. 22.

[4] See the letter of Wilson to G. C. Lewis quoted in Barrington *The Servant of All* II 21.

submitted to him the proofs of his *Letter to Wood*[1] stating 'Thus the phrenzy of 1825, setting aside the moral epidemic that prevailed, was probably even more connected with the state of credit than with any real increase of the circulation;'[2] Overstone replied: 'an encrease of the economising expedients cannot be, like the encrease of money, a *cause* of the encrease of credit'.[3]

His analysis of panics in the pamphlet[4] contained all the essentials of his later position. There was, he wrote, ultimately no safeguard against such a thing which could always occur under a metallic currency that had a developed banking system. At the same time he believed that a well-regulated paper currency could lessen the danger of panics although, even at this date, he saw the danger which lay in the extensive development of demand deposits. If panics did occur they could only be dealt with by special emergency provision.

(v) *The Committee of 1840*

The *Thoughts* was Overstone's last important work before the Act of 1844. With its appearance, much of his position was clearly developed. This position was subject to lengthy investigation before the Committee on Banks of Issue.[5]

Before the Committee he stressed the need for an automatic mechanism – 'metallic' fluctuation.[6] Adjustment was necessarily a price and activity adjustment even if 'speculative action on the exchanges' anticipated this[7] – he was not concerned with short-term palliatives. He objected to the idea that the Bank of England should hold foreign securities rather than gold more because it gave the Bank discretion (to which he objected *per se*) than because knowledge of such a large dealer would interfere with the market.[8] There was no guarantee of the overriding objective of convertibility without the automatic mechanism which was more important than having a single issuer or state control of issue.[9] Convertibility was of such importance, on the quasi-moral grounds that we have already seen, that he approved of the Act of 1819

[1] *Letter to Charles Wood, Esq., M.P. on Money, and the Means of Economizing the Use of it* London 1841.

[2] P 64 of proofs in Norman papers; p. 72 of final version.

[3] Notes on Norman's proof, among Norman papers.

[4] *Thoughts* p. 38.

[5] See 'Report from the Select Committee appointed to inquire into the effects produced on the Circulation of the Country by the various Banking Establishments issuing Notes payable on demand' *Parliamentary Papers* 1840(602) IV. I Overstone gave evidence on 17, 21, 22, 23 and 24 July (pp. 211–95, qq. 2651–3260) and on 31 July (pp. 316–37, qq. 3465–614).

[6] Qq. 2753, 3041.

[7] Q. 2790.

[8] Q. 2848.

[9] Qq. 2870–2.

not only for its principle but for resuming at the pre-war parity,[1] which also crushed hopes of further devaluation.[2]

In support of his view that convertibility was no guarantee of itself he appealed repeatedly to historical experience, especially that of the drains in 1825, 1831–2, 1837 and 1839. Only the second of these had proceeded smoothly, because the bank had acted early.[3] Not only was a large reserve no safeguard (with a larger reserve the crisis of confidence which had rectified the exchanges in 1839 would not have occurred) but full contraction in proportion to the bullion loss was required to recover the bullion.[4] One-third reserve against notes was sufficient – anything larger wasted the advantages of a paper currency.[5] There was no point in trying to distinguish different kinds of drains because a true metallic circulation would be contracted under any kind; and any attempt to distinguish was not only pointless but dangerous because most drains did not have a single cause.[6] Automatic operation was almost entirely the rule.[7]

All this merely followed, though in rather more rigid tone, the analysis of his earlier works. But on a number of issues Overstone advanced further. He argued that, once the functions of issue and banking had been separated, notes in the till of the Banking Department were circulation (as part of the base of the credit pyramid).[8] Deposits on the other hand were not circulation because their amount was not determined by the laws governing the distribution of the precious metals, and they were not a standard of value or a universal medium of exchange, discharging transactions in endless succession.[9] The difficulty that, in so far as deposits affected prices and were money substitutes, they would displace a certain amount of specie, and were therefore to some extent governed by the laws regulating specie, he met by arguing that such a displacement of specie was a once and for all process – reserve ratios could not fall indefinitely and once they had reached their minimum, the 'auxiliary currency' could not act independently of the currency at its base.[10] Despite a reluctance to commit himself to the idea of fixed reserve ratios[11] he stressed the idea of a credit superstructure on a

[1] Q. 2932.
[2] Q. 2968.
[3] Qq. 2952, 2962–70, 3076.
[4] Qq. 2700, 2708, 2712–13, 2717.
[5] Qq. 2720–1.
[6] Qq. 2751–2, 2994, 3466.
[7] Overstone was prepared to allow that the Bank had acted correctly in increasing the circulation to take account of the West India loan; if it had not done so the gap in the circulation would ultimately have been remedied by a price fall and specie inflow but the Bank's action had avoided unnecessary suffering.
[8] Q. 2655.
[9] Qq. 2663, 3183–6, 3192.
[10] Q. 3175.
[11] Q. 2658.

'metallic' base and multiple contraction of the superstructure as the metal flowed out.[1] It could develop on a truly metallic base, and there could be 'over-banking' and inflation of credit,[2] but it could not threaten convertibility under a paper regime if it was safeguarded by 'metallic' flows. On the other hand to postpone contraction of paper would bring about an unsafe extension of the credit structure.[3]

Overstone's view of the deposit part of the credit superstructure was subjected to lengthy, if not very penetrating examination by Hume. Overstone's position was that deposits were created on the basis of notes deposited: but that the crucial question was what happened to the notes. They did not just evaporate. As Norman wrote in his *Letter to Wood*:

> the Bank-note continues to be money in whatsoever hands it may be found, but . . . when deposited with a banker it ceases to belong to his customer, who takes in exchange for it a credit in the banker's book.[4]

This position Hume largely failed to shake,[5] and he also largely[6] neglected the essential problem of the effect of deposits on prices, while apparently failing to grasp the mechanism of the *creation* of secondary deposits on the basis of notes deposited. Overstone was fairly vulnerable on the question of bank deposits at the Bank of England – he argued that they were not as much at the disposal of bankers as notes in their own till because they could not all be drawn out simultaneously[7] which ignored the possibility that if in the *minds* of the bankers they were cash, then they could form part of the credit base (although it is only fair to add that *he* did not regard his deposits at the Bank of England as cash).[8] But Hume, instead of pressing on this point, attempted[9] to assimilate all deposits to 'circulation', rather than concentrating on those in the Bank.

Allied to the question of deposits in the credit pyramid was that of bills of exchange. Although aware of the latter's wide circulation[10] and of the many different factors involved in determining their number including confidence, the level of activity, and the increase or decrease of credit,[11] none of which would influence a metallic currency in the same direction, Overstone still believed that bills of exchange were ultimately subject to the control of the flows of currency.

[1] Qq. 2665–6, 2735.
[2] Qq. 2671–5.
[3] See also q. 2803.
[4] *Letter to Wood* p. 90.
[5] See qq. 3224, 3481.
[6] i.e. excepting q. 3175.
[7] Qq. 3106–74 especially qq. 3117 and 3158.
[8] Q. 3101.
[9] Particularly in Overstone's final examination of 31 July.
[10] Qq. 3026, 3034, 3037.
[11] Qq. 3068, 3072. See also qq. 3075, 3079–80, 3082.

INTRODUCTION

> I look upon bills of exchange as a form of banking transactions, and I look upon all banking transactions as various forms of credit. Now, I conceive that to put a direct restraint upon any of the forms of credit would be contrary to sound principle. I apprehend the sound principle to be, that you put a correct restraint, founded on principle, upon the paper money of the country; and that being strictly and correctly regulated, all transactions, all forms of credit, all the superstructure that is raised, upon that paper money will then be kept within their legitimate bounds.[1]

This view was open to strong question as we shall see when looking at the operation of the Act of 1844.

Although he again mentioned the need for and possible effects of information about the position of the Bank[2] (and also of other issuers) as a form of control he still felt that control by the Bank of the country issuers was lagged in the way we have seen although this time he stressed ultimate control through price differentials rather than the earlier credit shock.[3] The lag made contraction when it came unnecessarily violent;[4] and Overstone was now prepared to recommend government control of the country issues,[5] though not their abolition.[6] They suffered by the violence of the present system[7] and the system of competitive issues ultimately increased the danger of panics.[8]

For although he was still optimistic about the reduction in fluctuation which would follow adoption of the principle which he advocated – price increases, speculation and all the other evils reached their maxima *after* the beginning of a drain, so that early contraction would help to prevent this[9] though not removing natural fluctuations[10] – panics were still unavoidable.[11] In their event he was opposed to the Bank acting as lender of last resort and he amplified his previous criticism of this. He objected because the last resort rôle made contraction difficult during the pressure and also ensured that the issue did not increase when the gold was flowing in because bills discounted by the Bank as emergency aid matured and were not replaced.[12] Last resort facilities interfered then

[1] Q. 3074. See also q. 3077.

[2] Qq. 2681, 2699, 2880–3.

[3] Qq. 2728, 2741, 2829.

[4] Qq. 2722, 2728, 2730

[5] Q. 2725.

[6] Q. 2924. This was on grounds of expediency not principle (q. 2928).

[7] Qq. 2729, 2800–2.

[8] Qq. 2738, 2743, 2866–7. He also made the subsidiary objections to the country issues that the need to fill the vacuum when their issues collapsed required giving the Bank discretion (to which, as we have seen, he objected *per se*) and that they forced the Bank to hold their gold reserves. (qq. 2879, 2852–7, 3044–52, 3585).

[9] Q. 2726 – see also qq. 2748, 2791.

[10] Qq. 2934, 2953–63, 3175, 3580, 3602.

[11] Q. 2747.

[12] Qq. 2732–3.

with 'metallic' circulation and were ultimately a delusion because in the end the market could only be upheld by capital, not paper money.[1]

This took the analysis further than any previous utterance of Overstone's. Yet one crucial question remained unanswered. The precise mechanism of contraction was still wanting. Did the Bank's contraction of credit affect prices merely through a reduction in the value of stocks, or did it affect the supply price of new products? If the latter, was it through a contraction of output to a lower point on a rising supply schedule, or through a fall in the price of factors? These questions were important. The opponents of the Currency School, stressing the pain of contraction, sought ways to avoid it; the Currency school, and Overstone perhaps in particular, often talked as if the process was frictionless.[2] He evaded questions about the precise necessary effect on prices in particular areas,[3] failed to distinguish domestic and internationally traded goods, and implicitly assumed a very high elasticity of demand for British exports. He was very close to Ricardo in this.[4]

The sequel to Overstone's evidence was a series of articles by him in the *Morning Chronicle* on the published evidence given before the Committee. These concentrated on three points. The first was the primacy of 'metallic fluctuation',[5] the second was the repeated stress on the control over bills of exchange as the upper parts of the inverted credit pyramid,[6] and the insistence that deposits were not money.[7] The crux of Overstone's concern was made clear enough:

> If bills of exchange and deposits . . . are to be considered as constituent elements of the money of the country, it necessarily follows that the management of the circulation cannot be subjected to any sufficient regulation.[8]

Yet if the matter was as crucial as Overstone clearly realised, it is a

[1] Qq. 2766, 2773, 2780–3. [2] E.g. q. 3043. [3] Qq. 2982, 3005.

[4] See Sayers 'Ricardo's Views on Monetary Questions' in Ashton and Sayers *Papers in English Monetary History* pp. 76–95, p. 80.

[5] 'Upon the due regulation of the paper money of the country depends not only the value of every man's property, and the relative situation of the debtor and creditor classes of the country; but beyond this, the fluctuations of prices, the nature and intensity of commercial pressure, the maintenance of specie payments, and even the preservation of national faith, are liable to be very seriously affected by any errors which may be committed in the regulation of the quantity of paper money.' *Morning Chronicle* 16th September, 1840.

[6] *Ibid.* 3rd October, 1840 (3e–g).

[7] Repeating his argument that they were not all realisable he used the analogy that steam engines were a way of economizing horses but were not themselves animals. The choice was unfortunate yet instructive in that just as in 1840 the complete replacement of animal power by mechanical was not foreseen so neither was the monetization of Bank of England deposits (and through the last resort system, almost all other bank deposits) by implicit government guarantee.

[8] *Ibid.*

little puzzling that he did not devote more time to the question. The third problem to which Overstone turned his attention was the rôle of the rate of interest on which Tooke had dwelt at length before the Committee. Tooke's approach he rejected.

> But where is the evidence to show that any necessary connection exists between the rate of interest and the state of the circulation?[1]

Overstone's view of the rate of interest was not quite so singularly restricted as this passage makes it appear. He was prepared to admit like Ricardo[2] that it might be subject to short-run monetary effects. But he did not see it as the major international equilibriating force.

Apart from purging Norman's *Letter to Wood* as far as he could of suggestions that deposits and bills of exchange were money[3] Overstone remained fairly quiescent on currency until 1844. He did appear before the Lords Committee on bills of exchange[4] but largely confined himself to reiterating the view that a maximum rate of interest worsened commercial crises by forcing the rationing of accommodation, and distorted the allocation of resources[5] – in particular, banking capital was removed from discounts to speculation in the public funds.[6] Nor, when he published his *Thoughts* in 1844 did he make any major changes in the text although he did rephrase it fairly extensively in order to emphasise that the over-riding objective of currency regulation and in particular of Peel's bill was convertibility and not the regulation of crises.[7]

(vi) *Overstone and Contemporary Thought to 1844*

Much of what was said earlier about the general position of the Currency School will now be seen to apply to Overstone – in a sense he was the embodiment of the School. He was certainly its most influential leader: as Schumpeter put it 'He was the currency school's strong man'.[8] The major divergence of his thought from that of the Banking School, particularly Tooke and Fullarton, is then clear enough. While there was a general acceptance of the underlying objective of convertibility, and

[1] *Morning Chronicle* 21st October, 1840 (3b–d).

[2] See Ricardo's *Principles* in *Works* I 297–8.

[3] The original proofs with extensive marginalia and further notes by Overstone are among the Norman papers. See letters 75–7. Norman adopted many of the emendations.

[4] See 'Report from the Lords' Select Committee appointed [Sess. 1841] to inquire into the effects of the Alterations made in the Laws regulating the Interest of Money' *Parliamentary Papers* 1845(611) XII 337. Overstone's evidence is pp. 5–10, qq. 54–108.

[5] See in particular qq. 58, 60, 71–3, 81.

[6] Qq. 107–8.

[7] See in particular the reprint in *Tracts* pp. 239–40, 246.

[8] J. A. Schumpeter *History of Economic Analysis* London 1954 p. 726.

even an underlying acceptance of the validity of the 'Ricardian' theory of the distribution of the precious metals, at least as an equilibrium proposition, the deductions which the two sides drew from these basic premises were very different. Tooke rejected almost entirely the quantity theory approach to price level determination and its effects on the exchanges.[1] It is probable that neither Tooke nor Fullarton[2] would be prepared to deny that changes in the supply of the precious metals could affect prices, and the same was true of *inconvertible* notes.[3] But they believed *convertible* notes could not be over-issued[4] – this was true of country as well as central issues.[5] Tooke, in particular, relied on international capital flows following interest rate changes to correct international disequilibrium.[6] Rejecting Overstone's basic approach to international equilibrium under a convertible paper currency, he and Fullarton naturally opposed the deductions which Overstone drew from it. The latter argued that, following from his belief that convertible currency could not be over-issued, the exchanges were governed only by the state of the balance of payments[7] and he relied on the international transmission of hoards of specie to bring about balance[8] – drains were independent of the currency.

Comparison of Overstone with the other participants in the controversy who did not differ quite so radically from him is perhaps in some ways more instructive. The idea of the connection between internal circulation and the price level stemming from the Ricardian theory of the distribution of the precious metals was common not only to Overstone, Torrens and Norman but also to those who were, strictly speaking, members of neither the Currency nor Banking Schools, such as Palmer and Pennington. The former continued to stress the importance of deposits[9] from the point of view of control: the latter, although he accepted much of the basic analysis, and was indeed one of its originators, for long opposed the Currency School's particular position. He

[1] See e.g. his *An Inquiry into the Currency Principle* particularly chs. VIII and XV especially pp. 122–4.

[2] E.g. *On the Regulation of Currencies* p. 57.

[3] *Ibid.* and Tooke *An Inquiry* pp. 69–70. For an interesting summary of the differences between Overstone and Tooke see the review of Overstone's *Management of the Circulation* in Tooke's *History of Prices* III 247–79.

[4] E.g. Fullarton *On the Regulation of Currencies* p. 58.

[5] Tooke *An Inquiry* p. 38.

[6] *An Inquiry* pp. 102–3; evidence before the Select Committee on Banks of Issue 1840 q. 3769.

[7] *On the Regulation of Currencies* p. 115.

[8] *Ibid.* pp. 131–4.

[9] Evidence before the 1840 Committee qq. 1555–73.

stressed the importance of bankers' balances at the Bank of England;[1] and in emphasising the general importance of deposits ('book credits of a London banker, and the promissory notes of a country banker, are essentially the same thing') also stressed that these deposits were outside the control of the currency. He also accepted the importance of capital flows.[2] But he later changed his mind to become an 'uncompromising adherent of the Currency School'.[3]

The comparison with Torrens and Norman is in some ways the most interesting. Both accepted the idea of a separation of the functions of issuing and of banking. But Torrens was possibly more in favour of withdrawing issue from the Bank altogether[4] while Norman was signatory to a report in 1840 which said that 'no great change was needed in the public management of the Bank's business',[5] and advocated separation of accounts rather than of departments.[6] It was Overstone who had suggested the idea of full separation[7] and who advocated it firmly and consistently.[8] Although nearly in accord with Overstone, neither accepted his position entirely. Torrens in particular was explicitly concerned with the problem of the control of deposits and indeed went so far as to head a section in his *Letter to Lord Melbourne*, '*Bank Deposits perform the function of Money*'[9] a proposition that Overstone would never have agreed to – in fact he wrote a long letter to Torrens to explain that the proposition was untrue.[10] Torrens seems to have believed that ultimately deposits were controlled through reserve ratios, and he dealt with the problem much more explicitly than Overstone.[11] Torrens also differed at first from Overstone over the question of control of the country issues[12] arguing that the country issuers could not over-issue because the over-issue would be returned to them because of rising prices in the

[1] Letter to Tooke reprinted in the latter's *History of Prices* II 369 ff.

[2] *Ibid.* p. 371.

[3] Sayers *Economic Writings of James Pennington*, p. xxxvii.

[4] *Letter to Lord Melbourne* pp. 57–64 especially p. 64.

[5] Clapham *The Bank of England* II 173.

[6] Evidence before the Select Committee of 1840 q. 2161. See also his *Remarks upon Some Prevalent Errors with Respect to Currency and Banking* London 1838 pp. 97–108 – in this Norman was more fully in favour of separation.

[7] As Torrens acknowledged – *Principles . . . of Sir R. Peel's Act* 2nd ed. London 1857 pp. xii–xiii.

[8] E.g. 1840 evidence q. 2878 and *Thoughts.*

[9] *Ibid.* pp. 6–19. For a lucid and comprehensive discussion of Torrens' position see Robbins *Robert Torrens* pp. 105–16.

[10] Letter 399.

[11] See his *An Inquiry into the Practical Working of the Proposed Arrangements for the Renewal of the Charter of the Bank of England and the Regulation of the Currency with a Refutation of the Fallacies advanced by Mr. Tooke* London 1844 pp. 9–22.

[12] *Letter to Lord Melbourne* pp. 48–50.

country relative to London – the internal balance of payments argument which, we have already seen, Overstone rejected. Torrens later changed his mind on this point;[1] and he also came to lay about as much stress as Overstone on the rôle of the rate of interest and the flow of capital.[2] Nevertheless Torrens and Overstone were very much in accord both on matters of analysis and of (monetary) policy. Both were strongly in favour of automatic operation, not of discretionary currency management by the Bank. Both believed that panic could not be dealt with by any statutory arrangement and both were opposed to attempting any such provision. Both (and here they were temporarily in agreement with Tooke[3]) were opposed to the doctrine that it was the Bank's duty to act as lender of last resort. Where ultimately they differed was in their willingness to explore new ideas: while Overstone defended with clarity and consistency his own position he was not prepared like Torrens to carry the war into the enemy's camp and to explore a whole range of different possibilities.

The comparison with Norman is more difficult. Overstone and Norman were very close and collaborated in the writing of pamphlets. Norman was however on the whole prepared to allow more importance to deposits (although on this he vacillated[4]) than Overstone. Nevertheless he believed that if a drain fell on deposits this would not have the necessary corrective effect.[5] The notion of an inverted credit pyramid is also to be found in his work[6] although he realised perhaps rather earlier than Overstone was prepared to make such an admission, that control of the upper part of the superstructure by the base might not always work exactly as planned,[7] but argued quite reasonably that some control was better than no control. He was probably closer to Overstone than anyone in envisaging correction operating through prices but he did also lay some stress on the effects of contraction on foreign investment[8] on which Overstone, though he did not completely ignore it,[9] laid relatively little emphasis. But Norman agreed with Overstone's analysis

[1] *Inquiry* p. 39.
[2] *Ibid.* pp. 35–6. But he explicitly rejected sole reliance on the rate of interest (*ibid.* pp. 37–8).
[3] See the latter's *History of Prices* III 102–14.
[4] See Mints *A History of Banking Theory* pp. 77–81.
[5] See his evidence before the 1840 Committee qq. 1731–41, 2232, 3451–62; and his *Remarks upon Some Prevalent Errors, with Respect to Currency and Banking* pp. 21–8.
[6] See his *Letter to Wood*, pp. 42, 72, 80–2.
[7] *Ibid.* pp. 73–4.
[8] *Letter to Wood* pp. 18–21; 1840 evidence q. 1783.
[9] 1840 evidence qq. 2753–6; *Tracts* p. 253.

of the country banks[1] and accepted most of the policy deductions of the analysis although he favoured a relaxing power.[2] As a Bank Director he was concerned with some aspects of the problem which Overstone neglected. He devoted rather more energy to the analysis of the effects of open market operations[3] and accepted as a fact, even if theoretically undesirable, the Bank's rôle as lender of last resort.[4]

Overstone's own contribution to the debates before 1844 is real and clear enough. He, probably more clearly than any of the other writers, recognised the theoretical basis of the analysis and drew policy conclusions directly from it. He was responsible for the full separation of departments in the Act of 1844, having originated the idea and expounded it with force before the Committee of 1840 on which Peel sat, and in his *Thoughts* of April, 1840. He had recognised earlier than Torrens and expressed more clearly than Norman the problems of the country issues, and his insertion of an underlying trade cycle into the discussion of economic fluctuations was, if not unique, extremely important. The information-velocity of circulation mechanism was his,[5] and it was later to prove important. Important too was his reforming tone and his normative approach – he, more than any other writer, set the tone for legislating in detail on monetary matters, for removing discretion from the Bank, for not distinguishing internal and external drains, for regulating the note issue, whatever the problem of deposits, and for making no formal prior provision for panics. Some criticisms of his approach have been made above in describing the course of its development; but, right or wrong, he, more than any other writer, was responsible for creating the climate of informed opinion which produced the Act of 1844. It is with his defence of that Act and the evolution of his thought under its operation that we shall now be concerned.

3. *The Defence of the Act*

(i) *Overstone's Thought and the Defence of the Act*

In tracing the development of Overstone's thought after the passing of the Act of 1844, it will be shown that a number of changes of emphasis

[1] See his evidence before the Committee of 1840 q. 2630. It is only fair to add that Norman really stressed the difficulty before Overstone.

[2] See his *Remarks upon Some Prevalent Errors* pp. 106–7.

[3] 1832 evidence qq. 2394–458.

[4] 1840 evidence qq. 1767–76, 1820–1, 1826–36.

[5] Indeed Norman was opposed to Overstone's proposals for regular publication of the Bank's accounts (*Remarks upon Some Prevalent Errors* pp. 107–8).

took place. Nevertheless there was no significant break with what had gone before. The basic analysis remained Ricardian. The objective of convertibility remained overriding, and the Act was defended as having protected this. It had ensured, Overstone argued, a large bullion reserve even before the advent of the gold discoveries, and maintained that reserve at a high level in the face of repeated drains. This in turn had enabled the country to make repeated foreign payments of a non-routine nature when faced with harvest failure. He believed that the adoption of the 'metallic' fluctuation principle had made the currency fluctuate around a stable equilibrium.

The crises of 1847 and 1857 did not alter his view. The 1847 crisis he attributed to two things: firstly, the occurrence of a number of special factors such as extraordinary food imports, the railways' demand for capital which had drained the country banks (and, he added later, transformed working into fixed capital) and the failure of raw material supplies, notably cotton and wool, with all of which the Act might have coped; and secondly Bank of England mismanagement followed by failures which led in turn to commercial panic. This, because it lowered the velocity ('effectiveness') of circulation very drastically, was more than the Bank could cope with; and, albeit reluctantly, he approved of the suspension of the Act, which was, after all, consistent with the position he had taken on panics before 1844. The crisis of 1857 disturbed him very much more, although he had foreseen its occurrence. He attributed it to far more fundamental factors than its predecessor. It occurred, he believed, through panic brought on by the effect of monetary pressure on the mass of money at call in London. To this was added the vulnerability of a system of credit which had developed without a due regard to commercial prudence. The possibility that the panic might have been either caused or aggravated by the limit implied in the Act of 1844 on the Bank's power to act as lender of last resort was one that he did not consider seriously – this really followed not from any lack of knowledge of the facts of the situation but from his belief that whatever the money market might think, it was not the Bank's *duty* to act as lender of last resort. In any system based on convertibility there must be a limit to the power of the central bank to help. The answer lay in amending the credit structure so that, at each stage, sufficient reserves were carried to remove dependence on the Bank. He was open to criticism on this score for failing to realise that any fractional reserve system must have a lender of last resort. Yet his critics failed then and some fail now to realise that his position was perfectly reasonable *given his premises.*

INTRODUCTION

It is obviously extremely questionable how far *unlimited* last resort facilities are compatible with the maintenance of convertibility: and they are obviously *quite* incompatible with the overriding principle of 'metallic' fluctuation of the note issue.

The answer to the crisis of 1857 lay then not in modification of the Act, with which he was satisfied, but in reforms elsewhere in the monetary system. The Act, he believed, had at least ensured the maintenance of convertibility during the crises and thus removed one potential cause of panic. In addition to this, which was its main objective, it had also moderated fluctuation in activity through limiting speculation and price increases which normally reached their maxima after the beginning of a drain, by bringing about pressure as the drain commenced. This early pressure had been achieved not only by the provisions of the Act in relation to the Bank of England but also by those provisions which prevented the country banks from interfering with the Bank of England's operations. No monetary system could be proof against the trade cycle – indeed not only was some pressure unavoidable in any system of convertible currency but it was misguided to interfere with such 'natural' fluctuations – but a properly regulated monetary system would prevent these fluctuations being magnified by a passive monetary policy. It is clear from this that far from sacrificing everything to convertibility he believed that its requirements produced monetary stability – although his answer to such a charge was in the more general terms that the maintenance of convertibility protected the public from far worse evils; apart from the danger of depreciation and the consequent disturbance of social justice if convertibility were abandoned, he believed the whole credit system to hinge on convertibility.

He continued too to insist on the policy deductions which he had drawn from his analysis before 1844. He remained insistent that any loss of specie required a contraction of the note issue[1] fully in proportion to the loss. He remained firm in his belief that any attempt to distinguish internal and external, terminable and non-terminable drains could be nothing but misleading and dangerous. Partly this was because he believed that no drain was likely to arise from one particular cause alone, but also because he objected to giving the Bank of England any discretion in the management of the currency. The principle of 'metallic' fluctuation was the only guide; and not only did this protect convertibility but (and this was a problem he had ignored before 1844) it en-

[1] It is interesting in this connection to note that he explicitly rejected a two-country model – q. 4032 of his 1857 evidence.

sured a sufficient supply of currency in a growing economy by specie flows to make good any gap between what was required and what the growth of credit had achieved.[1] The latter had however developed rather faster than Overstone thought prudent, making the multiple contraction when specie flowed out rather greater than desirable from the point of view of the smoothness of the process, while failure to adhere to reserve ratios or even to keep any kind of reasonable reserve made the control of the credit structure through its credit base rather unsound. As a result he became less happy about this form of control.

His unease led him to stress two other mechanisms far more: the interaction of information about the state of the Bank of England reserve with the velocity ('effectiveness') of circulation; and the rate of interest. The first mechanism had, as already seen, its origins in his thought before 1844, but it came to bear a good deal more weight after 1844, particularly as it became clear (and was pressed on his attention) that notes in the hands of the public increased in times of pressure. This was only compatible with his theory of currency control by means of the information-velocity mechanism. (A similar explanation could also be applied to the fact, of which as we shall see, he was also aware, that the number of bills of exchange increased during pressure.) The rate of interest received more analysis as well as more emphasis after 1844. It has been noted that before 1844 Overstone's description of the method by which an outflow of currency caused prices to fall was unfortunately hazy. In 1848 he explained the mechanism a little further by arguing that the fall in price was determined by a fall in raw material prices in face of a reduction of activity. But when he appeared before the Committee of 1857 he admitted that the connection between prices and circulation was tenuous. This rather damaging admission helps to explain the attention which he came to pay to the rate of interest.

The determination of the rate of interest he saw, more or less consistently, as depending on the supply of and demand for loanable capital – ultimately in the long run the rate tended to coincide with the going rate of profit on capital although in the short run it would not do so if there was a demand for capital for non-productive purposes such as war which itself tended to raise the rate of interest by destruction of capital. The rate was, as envisaged by Ricardo, only temporarily affected by monetary causes, and was independent of Bank Rate which had to follow the market rate. The crux of his argument was that pressure

[1] The difficulties raised by this argument are dealt with below in the discussion of Overstone's *Spectator* article.

occurred at a time of capital shortage which resulted in a high market rate of interest, the latter being necessary if a country was to maintain its share of capital in an international capital market. A rise in Bank Rate to the market level (neglecting a solitary admission in 1848 that the process might work in the opposite direction) would, by affecting confidence, lower the price of securities through sales to increase liquidity, thus raising the rate of interest and bringing about a (short-term) capital inflow. Nevertheless he fell back ultimately on price adjustment – capital flows could only act as a short-term palliative if there was a fundamental disequilibrium in relative internal price levels; and when he made his final appearance in monetary controversy in correspondence with Henry Brookes, it was the pure milk of a price specie flow adjustment which he expounded.

Apart from the international repercussions of Bank Rate, he also stressed its importance in relation to the protection of the Bank of England reserve; and partly because of an increasing pre-occupation with this reserve, he was opposed to the Bank's competing actively in the discount market.

Despite his changes of emphasis in the years after 1844, he remained convinced that the Act was fundamentally sound, and he was strongly opposed to altering it, in particular, by the introduction of a relaxing power. No provision for panic could be made in advance, an internal drain merely substituted metal for paper (an argument he later abandoned), and, above all, the introduction of a relaxing power would simply render the bill ineffective by preventing the interaction between velocity of circulation and information which was crucial as we have seen. In any case the effect of the exercise of such a power would be to relieve internal pressure at the expense of greatly increased external pressure at a later date because the internal relief would be obtained by the reissuing of notes which should have been cancelled as the bullion flowed out. He approved of the government letter in 1847 as an emergency provision in the face of panic but it was not until after the crisis of 1857 that he was prepared to accept the introduction of a regular relaxing power.

His opposition to the introduction of a relaxing power went almost to the very heart of his theory of the operation of the Act, but his opposition to other changes was far less rooted in principle. He was prepared to leave the Scots issue and the country issue, despite the fact that after the 1857 crisis with the drain of gold to Scotland because of the discredit of Scots notes, he believed the former harmful. He was, however, opposed

to any measure which would rejuvenate the country issues and was prepared, by 1857, to leave issue in the hands of the Bank. Although he had suggested taking issue from the Bank in 1848, he was later prepared to leave it with it on the grounds that the Bank was not in a position to mismanage its issue and had learnt its lesson in mismanaging its banking in 1847. In any case he was reluctant to transfer the power of issue to government because of the danger of associating monetary pressure and government responsibility in the public mind. This raised the danger of a weak government yielding to an unwise public pressure. But the underlying reason for his conservatism was a belief that only by maintenance of the *status quo* could the Act itself be maintained. Any attempt to remedy what were patently anomalies in the Act would excite unwelcome public discussion. Such an attitude towards public discussion was a complete change from his favourable attitude towards it in 1844. But as he saw the Act in operation, he believed it to be working well, protecting convertibility and working with free trade to provide a good climate for growth,[1] and he was reluctant to chance its disturbance. The emergence of his thought under the operation of the Act will now be traced in detail.

(ii) *The Crisis of 1847*

By November 1845 Overstone, now a currency authority,[2] was convinced that the Act, in which, as is clear from his correspondence, he felt deeply involved, was working[3] at least as far as the country issues were concerned. But although he was at first sanguine about this and about the railways' demand for capital,[4] he did begin to fear, early in 1847, that the Bank was abusing whatever discretion it had. He began then to agitate for the Bank to take precautions to protect its Banking Reserve. In *The Times* of 7th and 8th April, 1847, he criticised the Bank for failing to raise its rate of interest to protect its reserves, and for allowing notes in the hands of the public to remain unchanged,[5] and he also made personal representations to the Directors.[6] He had not foreseen such behaviour and he thought the Bank unreasonable. At the same time he later came to accept that notes in the hands of the public must increase during pressure; and in any case the Bank was in the difficult position that if it tried to reduce circulation by selling securities, this

[1] The essential untestability of this particular argument will be apparent. It is discussed further below.

[2] See letter 93.

[3] Letter 117.

[4] See letter 121.

[5] See letter 137 p. 389 n. 4.

[6] Q. 3996 before 1857 Committee (see *infra*).

might drive the discount houses into the bank as call money was recalled from them, and further reduce the Bank's reserve. But Overstone felt deeply aggrieved at what he considered to be the Bank's irresponsible behaviour and its belated attempt to right matters which produced, in April 1847, a severe and sudden contraction. At the same time he had no sympathy with those who had failed to act on the information produced by publication of the Bank's reserve[1] and firmly believed in the validity of the Act's operation.[2] The pressure of 1847 would have occurred under any system of currency. The government's duty was only to provide the standard of value. There had been no danger to convertibility and, in addition, the Act had probably mitigated the pressure. Only the Bank had been at fault.[3] Moreover, his experience on this occasion convinced him, if indeed he needed any convincing, that the Act should not have a specific relaxing power built into it to deal with a panic,[4] and he attacked the proposal in a contribution he made to *The Times*.[5]

His view of the underlying pressure was that it reflected a shortage of loanable capital due to the railway operations, and that as a consequence the market rate of interest was rising;[6] the system could not alleviate this pressure as he and Torrens were at pains to argue in their *Comments on the Merchants' Petition*.[7] Monetary regulation could not work miracles: it could not *suddenly* produce exports to pay for imports[8] although it could stop a drain by raising the value of money. The Act had in this way protected convertibility and prevented panic on that score which was important as the whole credit system hinged on convertibility.[9] A relaxing power would endanger this convertibility – temporary accommodation of internal pressure was undesirable because it would involve the reissue, in discounting bills for the support of confidence, of notes which should have been cancelled as specie was lost. Perhaps equally importantly (for this was the crux of Overstone's objection to the relaxing power) knowledge of the existence of a relaxing power would interfere with the operation of Overstone's information theory – it

[1] See letter 127, and letter of 'Mercator' in *The Times* 15th April, 1847 (7e–f).

[2] See the letter of 'Mercator' in *The Times* 30th June 1847 (5d).

[3] Letter 132.

[4] Letter 136.

[5] City article, 6th August.

[6] *Ibid.*

[7] *The Petition of the Merchants, Bankers, and Traders of London, against the Bank Charter Act; with comments on each clause* London 1847. Reprinted in *Tracts* pp. 285–308.

[8] *Ibid.* p. 291. This exception to Overstone's usually rather facile assumptions about demand and supply elasticities was one which he was accustomed to make in earlier years when discussing harvest failure under the Corn laws.

[9] *Ibid.* pp. 292–4, 308.

would no longer be felt necessary to take precautions, with their implications for liquidity and hence velocity.[1]

> The knowledge of the existence of such a relaxing power in the hands of the Government would create a delusive confidence, and through that, tend to prevent those measures of timely precaution and restraint on the part of the public, from which alone a wholesome, and, at the same time, an effectual remedy for the evil can arise.[2]

This work appeared early in August 1847.[3] In September Overstone continued his defence of the Act with an article in the *Spectator*.[4] Reaffirming the principle of 'metallic' circulation and the provisions of the Act he argued that the proposal to increase the fiduciary issue would leave an insufficient safety margin while experience of the working of the Act was so small, that an exceptionally large amount of currency was then required because of public nervousness but that less might be required later, and that in any case an increase in the fiduciary issue would not increase total money supply but merely displace some specie backed notes. One particular aspect of his analysis is rather more interesting. For Overstone now turned his attention, for the first time, to the problem of fixity of the money supply in a growing economy. This was an important question because both then and in recent times the Act of 1844 has been accused of acting as a straitjacket, and because Overstone was to appeal repeatedly before the Committee of 1857 to the growth of the economy as evidence that the Act was suitable for such an economy. Now the obvious implication of a fixed money supply (or rather a money supply which could be increased via specie flow, but which was extremely inelastic) in a growing economy is a rise in interest rates as demand for balances increases in proportion to income. Overstone's answer to the problem was that as the economy grew so did banking facilities which increased the velocity of the circulation (economised currency), thus making a given stock of money sufficient for a large number of transactions. Now this was a rather dangerous argument for one who made so many attacks on the development of credit and who had argued that such development could only proceed so far before minimum reserve ratios were reached. Overstone's answer to the argument that such developments might be limited by prudence over reserves to a level below that which the growth of the economy required was that the consequent depression of prices would bring about a specie

[1] *Ibid.* pp. 302–3. [2] *Ibid.* p. 302. [3] See letter 136.

[4] 25th September 1847. The article was in letter form but had been requested by the paper.

inflow to make good the deficiency. It is tempting to argue that this neglects the possible dampening effect on economic growth of falling prices and high interest rates[1] which by depressing entrepreneurial expectations would lower the rate of growth. Such an objection would probably have brought the tart retort from Overstone that the last thing that entrepreneurs lacked was optimism.

Overstone's full defensive powers were however required after the following month when the Act was suspended in the face of panic.[2]

The crisis itself he attributed to a shortage of capital, not credit,[3] both to pay for imports of food following harvest failure and also for the railways,[4] the latter causing a drain on the country banks,[5] although it had not been possible to forecast this beforehand.[6] There had not been undue speculation but the effects of the shortage of capital had been accentuated by failure of the supplies of raw cotton and wool and also by the high wages paid on the railways causing an increase in imports.[7] To these difficulties had been added two accidental factors, Bank of England mismanagement in the spring and commercial failures (which he did not agree were a necessary accompaniment of pressure)[8] in the autumn.[9] The loss of confidence on both occasions had sharply reduced the velocity ('effectiveness') of the circulation which, although it corrected the exchanges, made the whole operation much more violent than it would otherwise have been.

In particular, his criticism of the Bank was stronger than ever before. Only the Act had arrested its course[10] of increasing its securities as its banking reserve fell.[11] As it did so its payment for the securities was presented at the issue department in exchange for specie. The behaviour of the Bank, though foolish rather than selfish,[12] in allowing Bank Rate to remain below market rate and in competing actively in the discount

[1] Because of the inelastic money supply.

[2] Overstone gave evidence before both the Lords' and Commons' Committees on the crisis. See 'First Report from the Select Committee on Commercial Distress' *Parliamentary Papers* 1847–8(395) VIII pt. I p. 1: 'Second Report' *ibid.* (584) p. 505 and pt. II pp. 1 and 379: and 'Report from the Lords' Secret Committee appointed to inquire into the Cause of the Distress among the Commercial Classes' *ibid.* (565. 565–II.) VIII pt. III pp. 1 and 537. Overstone gave evidence before the Commons' Committee on 9 March 1848 pp. 387–410, qq. 5105–300 and before the Lords' Committee on 28 and 29 February, pp. 149–176, qq. 1346–644. The questions are cited below as Lq. or Cq.

[3] Lqq. 1602–3.

[4] Lq. 1349.

[5] Cqq. 5171–8.

[6] Cqq. 5108–10.

[7] Cq. 5113–15.

[8] Cq. 5128.

[9] Cq. 5127.

[10] Lq. 1353.

[11] Lqq. 1355–64, Cqq. 5129–30.

[12] Cq. 5266. The Directors had attached too much weight to the public interest as they saw it.

market,[1] he strongly disapproved of. Yet although now in favour of taking issue away from the Bank[2] he was not prepared to recommend any change in the government of the Bank[3] – in public.[4]

The Bank was not in any case the sole responsible party. There had been, Overstone believed, too great an extension of credit which had been exposed by pressure.[5] This is important because he has been extensively criticised in this respect by modern writers, notably J. R. T. Hughes.[6] The criticism rests partly on the fact that notes in the hands of the public increased during times of crisis (which we have already seen was taken care of by changes in velocity of circulation, a point which Overstone reiterated before the Lords' Committee[7]). But rather more emphatically Overstone has been criticized for apparently failing to notice that numbers of bills of exchange increased during a period of pressure, a criticism based on figures of Newmarch published later.[8] Now here we have one possible answer to this – normatively, much of the credit extension was improper leaving a level of liquidity which was highly vulnerable. But in any case his argument about velocity of circulation in times of pressure could equally well take care of the bills of exchange. Indeed bills of exchange would be the form of credit most susceptible to distrust in time of pressure because of the need to accept them – and the absolute numbers may have increased because traders were having to create their own credit instruments, no longer trusting those issued by others.[9] Dr Cramp has pointed to the evidence that the acceptability of bills fell in times of monetary pressure.[10] So Overstone's general position was not *necessarily* invalidated by the bills of exchange even though, despite the fact that he knew of Leatham's work of 1840 on the subject, Overstone did not devote much attention to the problem.[11]

[1] Cqq. 5188–90, 5264–5.
[2] Cq. 5282.
[3] Cqq. 5179–84.
[4] See letter 139.
[5] Lqq. 1593, 1606–7.
[6] *Fluctuations in Trade* ch. X.
[7] Lqq. 1416, 1422–3, 1430–2, 1435, 1456.
[8] Tooke and Newmarch *History of Prices* vol VI London 1857 pp. 584–92, 875–6; Select Committee of 1857, App. 39; *Journal of the* [*Royal*] *Statistical Society* vol. XIV (1851) pp. 143–83.
[9] See Ashton in Ashton and Sayers *Papers in English Monetary History* pp. 44–5 for evidence of this.
[10] *Opinion on Bank Rate, 1822–60* London 1962 pp. 69–70.
[11] Wood had referred Norman to Leatham's work (see letter 72 and *ibid.* p. 311 n. 3) and Overstone had written on the original proofs of Norman's *Letter to Wood* beside a reference to Leatham's calculations: 'dele. because Mr L's calculations are very loose, and thus to name him is to give an indirect sanction to his publication generally' – p. 38 of original proofs in Norman papers; the corresponding passage (amended but not deleted) is in the final version, p. 41. Leatham's work is also discussed by Newmarch in the *Journal of the Statistical Society* XIV 156–60.

INTRODUCTION

The possibilities are not even exhausted by the above considerations – the corrective process on bills of exchange could have come about at least partly through a reduction in the financing of trade through London as interest rates rose – separation of inland and foreign bills would suggest something of this sort.[1] Another possibility is that a positive correlation between interest rates and the number of bills of exchange may have resulted from both reflecting a rise in the real rate of interest, the market rate being followed in turn by Bank Rate.[2] At all events the mere fact that stamp duty on bills of exchange increased during times of monetary contraction does not prove that Overstone as a banker did not know his business.

Whatever the problems connected with credit, Overstone believed that the Act had protected convertibility, and, by stopping the Bank earlier in its course, had moderated the pressure.[3] Contraction following the loss of specie to pay for food imports after a harvest failure also meant that there was specie available to pay for a second harvest failure.[4] Nor had separation of its reserves weakened the Bank[5] – convertibility had been in considerable danger in 1825, 1837 and 1839[6] and if the Act had by contrast maintained convertibility unendangered, it had done its job.[7] At the same time Overstone was careful to insist that he was not sacrificing everything to convertibility; rather convertibility protected the public from far greater evils.[8]

He continued to insist that the automaticity of the system was what was required – if the Bank had had as much room for discretion as before 1844, to mismanage the currency and allow a drain to continue, the monetary system would not have been so safe.[9] Apart from the fact that the exercise of discretion by the Bank was *per se* objectionable,[10] any attempt to distinguish different types and causes of drains could be nothing but misleading[11] and in any case full contraction was necessary to recover the specie.[12] An internal drain (he argued here) merely involved a substitution of bullion for notes and not a contraction of the circulation.[13]

[1] See table 110 in Hughes *Fluctuations in Trade* p. 299.

[2] For confirmatory evidence of this see Hughes *Fluctuations in Trade* p. 240.

[3] Lqq. 1351, 1514, 1354.

[4] Lqq. 1400–1.

[5] Lq. 1403.

[6] Lqq. 1406–7, 1496, 1534, Cq. 5127.

[7] Even if the government letter had not been issued, the size of the Bank's reserve would have made unlikely a run for gold (Lq. 1516, Cqq. 5116–20).

[8] Lq. 1537.

[9] Cqq. 5135–7, 5142. The limit of the Act on the country issues had also played its part in limiting speculation – Cq. 5113.

[10] Lq. 1469.

[11] Lqq. 1370–1, 1375–9, 1383.

[12] Lq. 1548.

[13] Lqq. 1452–4.

OVERSTONE'S THOUGHT

In any case, as he had stressed before 1844, no monetary system could be proof against the trade cycle.[1] Crises like that of 1847 were inevitable in any great trading community and were lightened by the Act[2] – any system based on convertibility had to bear pressure to correct the exchanges, and the earlier the pressure the less its force.[3]

Yet for all this Overstone approved of the issue of the government letter suspending the Act.[4] He believed that relaxation could be justified when people were no longer guided by principle;[5] the exchanges had been in our favour and the letter had succeeded in raising the velocity of circulation to more normal levels,[6] while 'serious confusion' would have followed without government interference which was a departure from the letter rather than the spirit of the Act.[7] This was consistent with his general position on panics before 1844 and he was still opposed to the introduction of any kind of relaxing power partly on the grounds, already noted, of its effect on the interaction of information, liquidity and velocity.[8]

> I think the introduction of a relaxing power into the Act would very much interfere with the object for which it was introduced; it seems to me that, in the first place, if you introduced a relaxing power into the Act, there would be very great danger of its being resorted to unnecessarily, prematurely, and therefore, very perniciously; and, in the second place, I think, that the known existence of such a relaxing power would encourage persons to abstain from those which are the legitimate means of correcting a drain of bullion, and alleviating monetary pressure, and would thus increase the probability of those occurrences which would render the resort to the relaxing power necessary; and thirdly, the introduction of such a provision into the Act would very materially diminish its efficiency when applied;[9]

Knowledge of the existence of such a power might prevent the exchanges becoming favourable;[10] and leaving the government, with no Bank participation, to intervene extra-legally was the best safeguard against unnecessary relaxation[11] if such action was accompanied by a high rate of interest.[12] The possibility that panic might arise because of a widespread fear of the exhaustion of the Bank of England's power to act as a lender of last resort, a view advanced by his brother-in-law, Ichabod Charles Wright, he was not prepared to consider because he

[1] Lqq. 1394–5. [2] Lq. 1554, Cq. 5126. [3] Lq. 1514.
[4] Cqq. 5149–50. [5] Lq. 1563. [6] Cq. 5159.
[7] Lqq. 1480–1, 1483.
[8] Lqq. 1440, 1514, 1576–8, 1581, Cqq. 5151, 5278, 5280.
[9] Cq. 5280. [10] Lqq. 1514, 1561. [11] Lqq. 1558, 1568.
[12] Lq. 1608, Cq. 5161.

did not believe that the market *should* depend on the Bank in the last resort.

All this, after the crisis of 1847, amounted to a fairly consistent rationalisation of the course of events in terms of Overstone's analysis developed before 1844, presented in such a way as to defend the *status quo*. But in two respects, the rate of interest, and the effect of contraction in lowering prices, the analysis is taken a little further than 1844. While maintaining that the Bank could not affect the rate of interest[1] which had recently been high because of market forces[2] that inflicted no harm on commerce[3] (indeed the distortion and rationing of discounts under the usury laws had been far more harmful and disguised violent fluctuations),[4] he made two important admissions. Firstly he agreed that the Bank could, by example, influence the market rate. He was asked by the Lords' Committee 'Did not most of the Bankers raise the Rate of Interest to the Minimum of the Bank of England Rate?' To this he replied: 'Private Bankers would probably conform to a great Extent to the Rate charged by the Bank of England.'[5] This was only a solitary admission, it is true; but it was the first time Overstone had really admitted such a possibility. Secondly there is an apparent stress on the *necessity* of a high Bank Rate to protect the specie via the Bank's reserve. But this was only because Bank Rate had to be as high as market rate. Overstone even went so far as to assert that a high market rate of interest would be sufficient to correct the exchanges. But for the accidents of the Bank's mismanagement and the commercial failures

> we should have had a considerable export of bullion, and a considerable contraction in the numerical amount of the notes in the hands of the public, followed by a high rate of interest, and that probably continuing for several months. That high rate of interest so continuing would have corrected the exchanges and have gradually brought back the gold;[6]

This is extremely significant. The full importance of it was not made clear until 1857. But it led ultimately to a clear statement of the effect of short-run capital inflows as sufficient to correct the exchanges, an effect stressed by modern investigators of how the system worked[7] yet largely neglected by the Currency school. It certainly marked a change of position from the extreme one of Overstone's attacks in the *Morning Chronicle* on Tooke.[8]

[1] Lqq, 1514, 1634, 1638, Cq. 5260. [2] Lq. 1604. [3] Lq. 1634.
[4] Lqq. 1612, 1615. [5] Lq. 1510. [6] Cq. 5127.
[7] See W. E. Beach *British International Gold Movements and Banking Policy, 1881–1913* Cambridge, Mass. 1935 especially ch. IX.
[8] See *supra*.

OVERSTONE'S THOUGHT

The nature of price changes also received some clarification. The hazy nature of the analysis on this point up to 1844 has already been noted. Now in 1837 Overstone had observed substantial price falls in the north of England[1] and he may have felt it unnecessary to substantiate what he believed to be a widely observable phenomenon. But he now made clear that the fall in prices which helped to rectify the exchanges was due to a fall in the price of imported raw materials, particularly raw cotton, and to forced sales of stocks.[2] Yet the former was not satisfactorily explained although the implication was that the reduced demand for cotton improved the bargaining power of the buyers.

Overstone, while advancing the analysis a little further, had completed a dexterous and fairly consistent defence of the Act which was left unamended. The only significant change in his analysis was the new rôle of the rate of interest. Yet his views were to be examined again, and his confidence in the Act tested.

(iii) '*Mercator*'

After the survival of the Act in 1848 Overstone seems to have considered it fairly safe. For some years currency problems do not appear to have loomed large in his life and he became comfortably convinced, particularly as the country entered the Crimean War and the currency survived unscathed, that the Act was working very smoothly – as indeed it was. But from August 1855 the government were empowered under the Act of 1844 to revise it on twelve months' notice, and Overstone became apprehensive. He felt it was particularly important not to relax the Act as the pressure of the specie flows generated by the Crimean War made itself felt,[3] believing the period to be the real test of the Act and of the government's relations with the Bank.[4] Although expressing such opinions privately he was at first reluctant to engage in controversy.[5] But then, realising that his participation in the ensuing debate was inevitable, he addressed a series of letters to *The Times*, under his old signature of 'Mercator'. These extended from November 1855 to early 1857. He was, during the early part of the period, also engaged in correspondence with G. C. Lewis, the Chancellor of the Exchequer, and others, on the subject of the Act and the government's course towards it. The two sets of letters taken together provide a fairly complete picture of Overstone's thought at the time.

[1] See letters 29–31.
[2] Lqq. 1597–9.
[3] See e.g. letters 333, 337.
[4] Letter 343.
[5] See in particular letter 363.

INTRODUCTION

Concerned as he was with the pressure of the war he was at pains to emphasise that in the face of such pressure it was important to maintain the effects of the Act – the currency was no more restricted than was necessary to maintain its par with other currencies and any relaxation would mean loss of specie leading ultimately to inconvertibility.[1] If circulation was truly in short supply we would not have lost bullion.[2] Convertibility did not maintain itself as 1825 had shown,[3] but the Act had maintained it and by steady contraction had limited speculation.[4] Any introduction of a relaxing power would prevent this beneficial operation of the Act by removing the effect of information about the Bank's reserve on liquidity policy throughout the economy.[5]

> But if a relaxing power be introduced into the Act a strong tendency will at once arise, influencing both the Bank and the public to rely, less upon their own early precaution and prudence, and to look to a resort to this relaxing power as their ultimate source of relief. By this means the adoption of precautionary and corrective measures will be delayed, the early and gradual contraction of credit and of transactions will be interrupted, the steady confidence with which the public now contemplate the progress of a drain of bullion, and meet the pressure which necessarily accompanies it, will be disturbed, and thus the real utility and efficiency of the Bill will be seriously impaired—possibly altogether lost.[6]

He was, he made it clear to Lewis, prepared to consider the introduction of a relaxing power,[7] but he was not in favour of it.[8] There was no doubt some embarrassment during pressure but this only affected those who had over-extended themselves[9] and monetary pressure only detected unsoundness and did not damage a sound state of trade.[10] (In any case the Act could not interfere with non-monetary cycles.)[11] In addition to all these advantages the Act had worked impersonally and automatically and would continue to do so, making good any deficiency of currency.[12] Any attempt to distinguish between different kinds of drains and to exercise discretion was futile and dangerous.[13]

[1] 'Mercator' 30th November 1855, *Tracts* p. 311. Cited as 'Mercator' I.

[2] 'Mercator' 24th January 1856, *Tracts* p. 331. Cited as 'Mercator' IV.

[3] 'Mercator' 14th December 1855, *Tracts* p. 316. Cited as 'Mercator' II. See also 'Mercator' VI *Tracts* pp. [347], [348]–[9] (5th January 1857).

[4] 'Mercator' 10th January 1856, *Tracts* p. 323. Cited as 'Mercator' III.

[5] 'Mercator' 22nd December 1856, *Tracts* p. [337]. Cited as 'Mercator' V.

[6] 'Mercator' VI. p. 353. He believed relaxation would mean the loss of convertibility – *ibid.* pp. [357]–[8].

[7] Letter 360.

[8] Letter 366.

[9] 'Mercator' 26th January 1857, *Tracts* p. 364. Cited as 'Mercator' VIII. See especially p. [373].

[10] See letters 370, 371.

[11] 'Mercator' IV p. 332.

[12] 'Mercator' II p. 319.

[13] 'Mercator' 14th January 1857, *Tracts* p. [357]. Cited as 'Mercator' VII.

OVERSTONE'S THOUGHT

A drain of bullion, whatever the cause of it, would produce a contraction of metallic money; it ought, therefore, to be met by a corresponding contraction of the paper money.[1]

All this added up to a picture of considerable satisfaction with the operation of the Act and with the underlying philosophy. Yet there is an important change of emphasis. The effect of the information about the Bank's reserve made available under the Act is now given almost a primacy of place.[2]

The publication of the state of the banking reserve was made an essential feature of the arrangement, and the public are thus furnished with accurate information, from week to week, not only as to the amount of notes actually passing from hand to hand; but also as to the fluctuations in the amount of that banking reserve from which the amount of notes circulating with the public is from day to day to be supplied. The result has been precisely that which was anticipated. The public attention, which was previously directed only to the state of the bullion, is now fixed upon the banking reserve; as that diminishes, public anxiety increases, credit and confidence are gradually contracted, and speculation and the state of prices founded on speculation are subjected to an early and salutary check . . . Indeed, a decrease of the banking reserve is more immediate and powerful in its action upon confidence, upon credit, and speculation than is a decrease of the amount of notes in the hands of the public. Because such decrease of the banking reserve is a fact far more unequivocal and more distinctly known to the public; and at the same time it affects in a more immediate and direct manner the great sources and support of credit and speculation—the banking establishments . . . Subsequently to 1844 the state of the banking reserve has become the prominent feature of our monetary system; the fluctuations in its amount are anxiously watched by the public; they exercise a powerful and immediate influence upon the state of credit, and are, in fact, more influential in regulating the exchanges and maintaining the monetary equilibrium between this and other countries than the amount of notes with the public ordinarily termed the circulation, though constituting, in reality, only a part of the circulation.[3]

This was an important shift of emphasis, and he stressed this view to the Chancellor.[4]

Despite the change of emphasis, he maintained his earlier position on deposits. Bank notes were a certificate representing specie,[5] and deposits or securities did not have this property as well as being incompletely liquid because not simultaneously realisable, as he stressed to Torrens.[6]

[1] *Tracts* p. [363].
[2] See especially 'Mercator' III pp. 327–31.
[3] *Ibid.*
[4] Letter 366.
[5] Letter 320.
[6] Letter 399.

But the essential core of his objection was that deposits were created on a currency base and had no independent effect on prices while a multiple contraction of them was required to correct the exchanges. Nevertheless he does not seem to have been as prepared to argue as before that control of credit through the currency base was a significant and valid form of control.

Nevertheless the Act had worked to preserve external balance and at the same time had proved not incompatible with economic growth on a tremendous scale.[1] The Act and free trade had worked together.[2] Like the argument that monetary pressure detects only a false prosperity – whatever prosperity it detected as false was by definition false – this argument was essentially incapable of being proved wrong. But as a pure debating point it had weight, and Overstone stressed it to Lewis.[3] He was satisfied too with the Act's regulation of the country issues which no longer interfered with 'metallic' fluctuation[4] and he was more than a little reluctant to disturb the shade of Malachi Malagrowther[5] by attempting further regulation.

Indeed his opposition, since 1844, to public discussion, moved him to tolerate many anomalies as he saw them. Although public education might result from discussion, he was anxious not to encourage either hope of a change in the law or discussion by those whom he considered foolish or irresponsible.[6] Partly because of this fear he was prepared to tolerate the Bank; and after its mismanagement in 1847 he believed that it had learnt better ways[7] with the exception that it was still actively pursuing discount business.[8] In any case, to remove issue from the Bank had the danger of associating, in the public mind, monetary pressure and government responsibility. Weak or dishonest governments might yield to such pressure whereas the Bank had no power to.[9] On balance then, despite grave doubts about the matter, he felt that it was better to leave issue with the Bank[10] although he did urge on Lewis separate publication of the accounts of the two departments of the Bank.[11]

This was a matter of policy on which he had changed his position from that stated before the Commons Committee of 1848. In general, though, the underlying analysis changed little, with the exception of the new-found stress on information about the Bank's reserve which we

[1] 'Mercator' V, pp. [340]–[2].
[2] *Ibid.* See also 'Mercator' VII and VIII pp. [363]–[5].
[3] Letter 366.
[4] 'Mercator' VII p. [359].
[5] See letter 366.
[6] See letters 360, 363.
[7] See letters 365–6, 371.
[8] Letter 371.
[9] 'Mercator' VII, p. [360]. See also letter 366.
[10] Letter 360.
[11] Letter 366.

have already noted. There was, however, one further exception. Overstone now emphasised rather more the operation of the rate of interest. By this he seems generally to have meant the market-rate. He maintained his normal position that the Bank could not determine this,[1] and his solitary admission of 1848 that private bankers would tend to conform to the Bank's rate seems to have been forgotten. But, in terms of the market rate, he seems to have been developing a theory of the international distribution of short-term capital, as well as of the precious metals.

> When all the civilised world is competing for capital no country can retain its due proportion which will not consent to pay the necessary price in the form of a high rate of interest. When peculiar causes create a general and severe demand for the precious metals, the country which will not consent to bear her proportionate share of the pressure, must consent to yield to other countries in which there is more firmness and more regard to principle, those precious metals, and to abandon that metallic standard which she has neither the virtue nor the resolution to maintain.[2]

The rate of interest depended on the supply of and demand for capital – the market for such capital was one and Overstone rejected Latham's argument that the markets for loan and discount capital were separate[3] because to do so would have been to contradict his argument that a high Bank Rate was a *symptom* of a relative shortage of capital, and a good symptom because discount rates were adjusted.[4] Yet all the discussion on high interest rates did not relate to policy. Although Overstone sometimes wrote privately as if central banks could command short-run capital flows by changes in their rate of discount[5] we have seen that he generally insisted that they could not alter market interest rates, and the object of the exercise seems to have been to explain that high interest rates like shortages of currency were not the fault of the Act but the result of the working of impersonal forces in an international economy; the belligerent governments had been engaged in adding to the demand for capital and then destroying it rather than using it reproductively. This was bound to cause a shortage,[6] and a world-wide high interest rate reflected the transfer of capital to the non-productive occupation of war.[7] To complete the parallel with the precious metals he added that a high

[1] See 'Mercator' I. The Bank could not go above market rate or it would get no business: it could not go below or its resources would soon be exhausted. See also 'Mercator' VI and VIII.

[2] 'Mercator' VI p. [355]. See also 'Mercator' VIII pp. [368]–[9].

[3] See letter 385–6, 391.

[4] *Ibid.*

[5] E.g. letter 363, 381.

[6] 'Mercator' I.

[7] 'Mercator' II.

rate of interest only detected false prosperity and did not damage real prosperity.[1]

With the exceptions of the stress on the rôle of information and the international nature of the capital market, Overstone's analysis remained very much as before. He had performed what was, from the point of view of the Currency school, a highly satisfactory rationalisation of events under the Act. It was inevitable that the opponents of the Act in general and of Overstone in particular should seek the first available opportunity to examine Overstone's position more critically; and he was called as a witness before the Committee on Bank Acts of 1857.[2]

(iv) *The 1857 Committee and the Second Suspension*

In many ways his performance before the 1857 Committee was conservative and consistent. Issue was the crucial matter. It should remain in the Bank's hands[3] – the Bank no longer had any control over the amount of bullion in the issue department so there was no point in state issue.[4] This was indeed a rather firmer attitude than in the preceding two years: but there is no doubt that the reason behind this was an overriding desire to discourage any disturbance in the *status quo*, because there was no telling where such a disturbance might end. He was still perfectly satisfied too, that there neither could nor should be any prior provision against panics though a large bullion reserve would help to prevent their occurrence,[5] and it would be foolish to run the obvious risk of internal panic by issuing one pound notes as they circulated amongst 'those classes where intelligence and education are least'.[6] Any extension of the fiduciary issue was opposed on the grounds of the danger in case of possible panic.[7] The only change in his position on panics was the abandonment of the argument he had used in 1848 that an internal drain merely involved the substitution of metal for paper. He now agreed that bullion, except in the Issue Department was not generally money.[8]

He was still not prepared to recommend any further attack on the country issues – although one source of issue of notes as metallic certificates, securing the profits of issue to the state, was the ideal with

[1] 'Mercator' VIII pp. [369]–[70].

[2] See 'Report from the Select Committee appointed to inquire into the operation of the Bank Act of 1844, and of the Bank Acts of Scotland and Ireland of 1845; with the Proceedings of the Committee:' Part I. Report and Evidence, *Parliamentary Papers* 1857(220. Sess. 2) x pt I, p. 1. Overstone gave evidence on 7, 10 and 14 July 1857 pp. 327–419, qq. 3640–4248.

[3] Q. 3663.

[4] Qq. 3666–71, 3960.

[5] Q. 4179.

[6] Q. 3696.

[7] Q. 4179.

[8] See qq. 3887–9.

competition in issue undesirable,[1] the Act had achieved the basic limitation of their amount which was necessary.[2] The situation was not entirely satisfactory because with unpublished country reserves salutary information was not made available to the public, and the whole action of the exchanges fell on the Bank.[3] But although Overstone was against any rejuvenation of the country issues[4] he was prepared, in the interests of preserving the *status quo*, to tolerate both them and the Scots and Irish issues.[5]

The Act had provided a good climate for growth[6] and although natural crises were not within its scope, it had helped to reduce speculation by early pressure to prevent it reaching its maximum.[7] He repeated the idea of a credit structure dependent on a base of currency, particularly that held in the till of the Bank of England. Any notes outside the Issue Department would form part of such a base.[8] Yet considering the faith which he displayed in such an idea before 1844, there is surprisingly little stress on it in his evidence of 1857. His whole attitude was noticeably more defensive and conservative than before and he condemned discussions on the monetary and banking system as 'exceedingly inexpedient and mischievous'.[9] He was highly satisfied that the principle of 'metallic' fluctuation[10] was correct, and with the separation of accounts under the Act which had the advantage of protecting the public from misconceptions.[11] He even asserted that bullion was not in the Bank but in a department of state, the Issue Department, which merely happened to be managed by the Bank. The gold discoveries could not take the credit for the high level of bullion in the Issue Department because they had made no impact as early as 1847 when the bullion was at a high level,[12] and the Act had caused the monetary system to oscillate about a stable equilibrium, coping with the difficulties of wars and sudden foreign payments, while maintaining convertibility,[13] and, through the metal flow, what was, by definition, enough currency.[14] There is much more in

[1] Q. 3648. [2] *Ibid.* [3] Q. 3685.

[4] Q. 3680. The proposal was to allow the country issuers to issue, against specie, above their limits under the Act of 1844.

[5] Qq. 3680, 3685.

[6] See qq. 3648, 3716 and also the published version of Overstone's evidence before the Committee (cited as *Evidence*) pp. ix–x.

[7] Qq. 3654–5. See also the addition to q. 4184, quoting q. 2726 of his evidence before the Committee of 1840 in *Evidence* pp. 255–7.

[8] Qq. 3832–3, 3890–3.

[9] Q. 3679. However when publishing his *Evidence* he felt impelled to modify this statement (*ibid.* pp. 38–9).

[10] Q. 3646. [11] Q. 3648. [12] Q. 3649.

[13] See qq. 3709–14, 3768, 3820, 3874, 4031, 4043–56. [14] Q. 4126.

a similar vein in the mass of evidence which he gave, most of it depending ultimately on the Ricardian notion of making settlement in money or goods, whichever was the more valuable.

It is only after a comparison of the value in their markets and in our own of gold and other commodities, and because gold is cheaper in the London market than in theirs, that foreigners prefer gold in exchange for their commodities. If we diminish the quantity of currency, we give an additional value to it; this will induce them to alter their election, and prefer the commodities.[1]

Although Hubbard had questioned the basic assumption of a high elasticity of demand for our exports[2] this does not seem to have troubled Overstone although he agreed, as he had done in 1840, that the connection between prices and circulation was very tenuous[3] which accorded ill with the pure milk of the specie flow doctrine, a mechanism which he at times propounded to the committee.[4]

The truth of the matter seems however to be that he came to see two other mechanisms as more immediately operable. The first was the interaction which he saw between information about the state of the Bank and velocity ('effectiveness') of circulation via changes in the desire for liquidity and the reserve policy of commercial institutions. The growing emphasis on this in his thought since 1844 has already been noted.

Since the Act of 1844 has been passed, the Bank reserve is distinctly defined and limited, and instead of allowing the pressure to come upon the reserve of the bullion, the pressure comes upon the reserve of the Bank of England, which everybody knows, and everybody watches. It therefore produces its moral as well as its direct, and what I may call its mechanical effect, and by that means, from having defined and made known to the public the state of the reserve in the Bank of England, we are enabled to exercise an influence upon the exchanges, and to protect the bullion from that extreme exhaustion to which on all occasions previously to 1844 it was exposed.[5]

This was not *prima facie* unreasonable; and in any case it took care of the otherwise awkward fact that notes in the hands of the public had increased during the 1847 crisis.

In addition to this 'information mechanism' there was also an 'interest mechanism'. This developed out of the argument he had advanced in the 'Mercator' letters that there was an international capital market and when there was a shortage of capital this raised interest rates to check an

[1] *High Price of Bullion* quoted in *Evidence* p. 16. See also *ibid.* pp. 17, 20, 45.
[2] Q. 2400. [3] Qq. 3798–9. [4] E.g. qq. 4043–56.
[5] Q. 3895. See also qq. 3646, 3935.

outflow or produce a capital inflow.[1] Now we have seen that the Bank had to follow the market rate upwards to protect its reserve. He now argued that raising Bank Rate reduced velocity of circulation through the confidence effect. This in turn reduced the price of securities (already recognised in 1840 as occurring during the process of contraction but with no definite cause or effect) as people became more liquid. The fall in the price of securities being the same thing as a further rise in the rate of interest, produced a short-run capital inflow.

'the rate of interest rises; that rise in the rate of interest acts upon public feeling; the public become more cautious, credit and confidence are more or less affected, the remaining money performs its functions more slowly, and in that way the value of money in the country is increased, and increased to whatever extent may be necessary to check the farther export of it, and to bring back again that which has gone.' [Cayley] How does it do so? – It does so in this way. The value of money is increased; the price of interest bearing securities is affected; it falls more or less. Then the foreign merchants in the country begin to perceive its effect; they write to their correspondents abroad, 'Money is becoming more valuable with us here; do not send us other things, send us money;'[2]

This was a change of emphasis indeed. The importance of short-term capital flows was now recognised far more fully than in the grudging reference in 1848 to speculative actions on the exchanges. Yet it should not be exaggerated. The possibility of an interest corrective had been foreseen before. Monetary pressure also lowered prices[3] and if prices did not reach a proper level the capital flow alone would provide no lasting remedy.[4] Ultimately the 'metallic' mechanism lay behind everything, but because the exchanges obviously turned before price effects could have been felt, the capital flow mechanism had to be recognised. The argument was not really sufficiently thought through, for by failing to stipulate that the flow was of short-term capital he raised all sorts of difficulties about different national long-term rates of profit and interest, recognising wide differences in these.[5]

But in any case Overstone's view of the rate of interest was rather narrow. It was still thoroughly Ricardian[6] and completely opposed to

[1] See *Evidence* pp. 67–8. See also Q. 3834 for his views on the shortage of capital in 1847 when, due to the railways, circulating capital was transformed into fixed.

[2] Qq. 3806–7. [3] Q. 3809. [4] Q. 3810.

[5] See e.g. q. 3844. This was particularly unfortunate because he did recognise that some of the demand for short-term capital was not for productive employment – see qq. 3860–9.

[6] See e.g. q. 3652.

Tooke's position. He failed to meet, while employing a wide range of disparate arguments[1] the fundamental point of his critics that the Bank had to use frequent changes in its rate to protect its reserve[2] and ultimately agreed that this was so.[3]

But with this exception Overstone's evidence displayed a high degree of satisfaction with the operation of the Act, even if the causes of specie flows were not balanced exactly as he had originally seen them.

He finished giving evidence on 14 July 1857. By the end of October it was clear to him that there was a strong danger of panic[4] against which there was no provision.[5] He feared that additional failures might shake confidence, and the vast credit structure, involving call deposits of £30 million, depended on the Bank as its ultimate resource.[6] The short intervening period between panic with the consequent dramatic fall in velocity, and the subsequent rectification of the exchanges was the crucial period, but the mass of obligations at call posed the real problem.[7] Many firms had failed to take sufficient precautions in face of pressure,[8] much of which originated in the failure of the American monetary system.[9] He believed that the government should make one pound notes legal tender in Scotland and Ireland to stem the internal drain to those countries – but by the time he expressed this view[10] the Act had already been suspended.

The suspension, though hardly unexpected, affected Overstone deeply. He felt a strong personal involvement in the Act and had suffered for his faith in it – he told the Committee in 1857 that many of his own friends 'in the year 1847 would hardly speak to me, because they considered me in some way or other connected with this Act',[11] and it is clear from McCulloch's letter to him that the suspension of 1857 had disturbed him physically and mentally.[12]

[1] He employed a wide variety of arguments against Tooke. To the argument that the Act had caused frequent and damaging fluctuations in Bank Rate he replied that high rates had been reached before 1844 (qq. 3653, 3845–7) and that Tooke himself had complained of the Bank's making difficulties for itself in the past by insufficient variation in its own rate (*ibid.*); and he produced strong evidence from within his own business that market rates had fluctuated widely before 1844 (q. 3653). Fluctuations in the rate were inevitable under any management of the currency (q. 3847) – the Usury Laws had merely led to credit rationing and distortion of the allocation of capital (q. 3850). In any case the Bank could only follow market rate (qq. 3656, 3659) which had been raised by the war (q. 3719) but which did no harm to trade because it represented a high level of profitability (qq. 3722–7, 3749) and when the rate fluctuated the community did not lose because what the borrower lost the lender gained and vice versa (q. 3815).

[2] E.g. qq. 3729, 3754.

[3] Q. 3782.

[4] Letter 439.

[5] Letter 447.

[6] *Ibid.*

[7] Letter 450.

[8] *Ibid.*

[9] Letters 447, 455.

[10] Letter 458.

[11] Q. 3719.

[12] Letter 483.

OVERSTONE'S THOUGHT

He believed that the Act had been destroyed by an unsound credit system[1] and that the suspension would encourage speculation;[2] and the tone of his letters was bitter.

But gradually he came to view the situation more calmly. He told Arbuthnot[3] that the bill was designed to regulate the monetary system in relation to the exchanges, and that it had done so satisfactorily, maintaining specie payments. No monetary system could provide against panics.

But his attitude had, for the time being, changed. The automatic nature of the mechanism was destroyed. The introduction of a relaxing power was now inevitable[4] though it would, he felt, encourage the irresponsible,[5] particularly Gurneys[6] – who did in fact fail nine years later in highly discreditable circumstances. He was now prepared to see legislative regulation of credit.[7] He approved of Cardwell's draft of a currency bill, which included a proposed relaxing power[8] and also apparently approved Cardwell's draft report for the Committee on the crisis which included a 'safety valve'[9] although he believed there was a danger of a suspension of specie payments in this. Indeed he seems to have been prepared for far-reaching changes – Cardwell's draft bill had proposed to make the Issue Department a department of state, administered by the Bank but with the Treasury responsible to noteholders, and had also provided for an increased fiduciary issue.

But all this was private. In public Overstone was sterner in tone. In his addition to his *Evidence* after the crisis[10] he stressed his view that the Act had rectified the exchanges and maintained specie payments despite speculation and that the maintenance of specie payments had in turn made possible the government authorization of an increase of issues. The damaging development of credit which had taken place could equally well have taken place under a metallic currency, and ways of restraining it should be investigated. Speaking in the Lords on 3 December 1857[11] he again argued that, although a clearer separation of departments might be required because of the confusion in many minds, the Act had corrected the exchanges and ensured a large supply of bullion. He did not actually say that the government letter should not have been issued: but he did believe that if it had not been, much commercial rottenness would have been purged from the commercial system. How-

[1] Letter 466.
[2] Letter 467.
[3] Letter 474.
[4] *Ibid.*
[5] Letter 480. See also letter 484.
[6] Letter 484.
[7] Letter 474.
[8] Letters 501, 503.
[9] See letter 517.
[10] *Evidence* pp. 264–6.
[11] *Hansard* third series CXLVIII 75–80 3 December 1857.

ever he did now publicly state that the government should consider the introduction of a relaxing power.

(v) *The Final Phase*

From 1857 onwards his interest in currency matters seems to have waned. But he was still regarded as the arch enemy by the opponents of the Act of 1844, and it was in this capacity that he appeared in the *Money Market Review* in 1862.[1] Rather than advancing, Overstone's position retrogressed. He stressed the economic growth which had taken place under the Act,[2] his belief that the Trade Cycle could only be eliminated in a stationary state (and that it was, he believed, worse in the United States);[3] and he appeared perfectly happy with the operation of the Act and with its automaticity.

> The Act of 1844 in no way attempts to interfere with or to determine the quantity of money in the country or the circulation of it. That is left to the free discretion of the whole community; each member of it being at full liberty to add to, or to diminish the amount of money in the country by importing or exporting gold. The Act of 1844 interferes only to the extent of determining what part of the total money of the country shall circulate in the form of gold, and what part in the form of bank notes.[4]

Social justice required convertibility and the Act had secured this; moreover he now used, as representing the working of the Act, a description which was at once more over-simplified and more dogmatic than almost anything which he had stated before:

> a debt becomes due to foreign countries which can only be discharged by an export of the precious metals; the exchanges then become unfavourable; the precious metals leave the country; and the quantity of money is thus inevitably diminished. Now comes the retrograde movement; in consequence of the diminished quantity of money, prices fall, and this effect is further stimulated by the excessive accumulation of commodities being thrown abruptly upon the market. This fall of prices tends to produce an effect the opposite to that which had arisen from the rise of prices; it checks imports, it increases exports, and thus the balance of trade is again turned in our favour.[5]

[1] *Correspondence between Lord Overstone and Henry Brookes* – see *supra*.

[2] *Ibid.* p. 5. Brookes on the other hand, attributed the crises of 1847 and 1857 to the Act, and the emphasis on economic growth brought from him the discourteous retort: 'Nothing is too great, or too small, or too far fetched for the insatiate audacity of its pretensions. Trade, commerce, railways, docks, harbours, shipping, churches, schools, even the labourers' cottages, and the peaceful contentedness of the people, all spring from the prolific and beneficent operation of the Bank Act. It is wonderful that it has not yet claimed the penny postage, the cheap press, and the penny papers' – *ibid.* p. 15.

[3] *Ibid.* p. 8.

[4] *Ibid.*

[5] *Ibid.* pp. 20–1.

The Act had not failed:

The temporary relaxation of the Act was necessitated, not in consequence of any failure in the principles on which it rests, or on any fallacy detected in the reasoning by which the provisions of the Act are justified, but solely by the overwhelming force of unreasoning panic.[1]

He even argued, on the basis of comparative fluctuations in the price of consols, that the crisis of 1857 had been less severe than that of 1825.

Such a complacent performance was hardly satisfactory. It must be remembered that Overstone was engaged in a public defence of the Act against a very rough opponent: but even so, it is surprising that he should have taken up quite such a *simpliste* position, after all the developments in his thought noted earlier. But from this date his views showed little sign of further development. His correspondence shows that he continued to stand firm against the idea that it was the Bank's duty to act as lender of last resort, and he urged Norman to repudiate the attribution of this idea to him.[2] He maintained too, in the letters of his old age, his belief in the overriding importance of convertibility and the maintenance of the standard.[3] But the same letters show that he was now (privately at least) almost completely resigned to the introduction of a relaxing power[4] and unable to see how the joint stock banks could be made to keep a proper reserve.[5] The last extant letter of his life[6] endorsed those written prior to the crisis of 1857.[7]

(vi) *Overstone and Contemporary Thought after 1844*

Both members and opponents of the Currency School had after 1844 a much more concrete subject for debate. The discussions after 1844 saw relatively little theoretical advance and on matters of policy the two sides came together to some extent – Wilson's acceptance of the Act, noted above, was to some extent symptomatic of this. On the Currency School side Overstone, as seen above, came to stress other mechanisms than control of the monetary system through its currency base, after 1844. Both schools continued to accept that convertibility was a prime requirement although there were a few dissenters.[8] There was fairly widespread agreement too, extending outside the Currency School (it

[1] *Ibid.* p. 22.
[2] Letter 726.
[3] See letters 746, 748, 778–80, 784, 786.
[4] Letters 837–8.
[5] Letter 839.
[6] Letter 923.
[7] Letters 447, 455.
[8] E.g. Samuel Gurney (evidence before the Lords' Committee on Commercial Distress 1848 q. 1232), David Barclay Chapman of Overend & Gurney (evidence before the 1857 (Commons') Committee on Bank Acts q. 5338), and Sampson Samuel Lloyd (evidence before the 1858 (Commons') Committee on Bank Acts qq. 2821–67.

included for instance T. M. Weguelin)[1] that the Act had secured large bullion reserves and placed convertibility above suspicion. But this agreement did not extend as far as Tooke and Newmarch[2] who, maintaining that the Bank's variations of Bank Rate had in fact been conducive to a small bullion reserve, attributed the large bullion reserves to the gold discoveries.

There was some agreement on a number of other points. Overstone's new found emphasis on the international rôle of the rate of interest, though this should not be exaggerated (he had mentioned it before 1844 and continued to refer to the price-exchange mechanism after 1844) was a distinct move towards Tooke's stress on the importance of the rate in relation to the exchanges and the international distribution of capital, though without accepting the latter's view of the unique importance of this.[3] In the way that Overstone accepted the mechanism it was accepted also by Morris[4] and Cotton[5] both of whom were, in general terms, in the Currency School, and by Hubbard,[6] a supporter of the Act though not of its underlying theory, as well as by Wilson[7] and Mill.[8] At the same time Weguelin was far from happy about this particular mechanism.[9] On the narrower issue of the relationship of Bank Rate to the market rate there was again fairly widespread agreement – even Tooke generally contended only that the Bank's influence on the market rate was temporary (though as such extremely important)[10] – although some of the Directors were prepared to admit greater influence to the Bank when it was likely to be used as lender of last resort. But these were short-run temporary influences which did not really interfere with Overstone's basic position – by 1857 he was prepared to admit such short-run influence (via the effect of Bank Rate on confidence) himself. Both Overstone and his fellow commentators seem largely to have ignored the importance of the pre-eminence of London in world finance which later writers have considered of such great importance in the working of the

[1] 1857 evidence qq. 877–9.
[2] *History of Prices* V 593–8.
[3] *History of Prices* V 598.
[4] Evidence before the 1848 Commons' Committee on Commercial Distress qq. 2746, 2671, 2816, 2840.
[5] Evidence before the 1848 Lords' Committee qq. 3237–41.
[6] Evidence before 1857 (Commons') Committee on Bank Acts qq. 2400–6, 2545–67, 2819–37.
[7] *Capital, Currency, and Banking* London 1847 pp. 21–2.
[8] Evidence before the 1857 Committee qq. 2163–84.
[9] App. 1 to the Report of the 1857 Committee and his examination of Mill qq. 2163–84.
[10] *History of Prices* V 544–5, 556–7.

gold standard.[1] There was a general agreement, too, that the Bank should not compete actively for discounts[2] although Norman, more consistently with the Currency School's original position that the Banking Department was just another bank, was apparently not averse to a more competitive policy on the part of the Bank.[3] Overstone's general preparedness to leave issue in the hands of the Bank (despite his endorsement of Cardwell's draft bill above) was, too, in general accord with his fellows – Bagehot in particular was later to agree with him that there were great dangers in government issue, at times of extreme pressure.[4]

But for all these common points there were still substantial areas of disagreement. For one thing, despite his damaging admission in 1857 that the connection between the quantity of money and prices was tenuous, Overstone still believed the quantity of notes issued to be of great importance, and that the relationship of the price level to the exchanges was of great significance. Those who assigned a *unique* importance to the rate of interest could hardly accept this. His theory of the interaction of the velocity of circulation and information about the state of the Bank's reserve was very much his own – indeed Bagehot really completely reversed the argument by suggesting that the Bank's reserve should not be allowed to fall to an 'apprehension minimum', to avoid panic.[5] Overstone's interpretation of the difficulties of 1847 was shared by Norman[6] and Torrens[7] but not by a great many others.[8] Nor were the particular deductions which Overstone drew from the events of 1857 widely accepted. Although it is true that the Bank did attempt to force the discount houses to hold their own reserves[9] and although Overstone's condemnation of dependence on the Bank received some

[1] See the evidence before the 1858 Committee qq. 1699–792 for some recognition of this.

[2] E.g. Palmer before the 1848 Commons' Committee qq. 2102, 2206–22.

[3] Evidence before 1848 Lords' Committee qq. 2714–5.

[4] Evidence before the 1875 Committee on Banks of Issue, *Parliamentary Papers* 1875 (351) IX qq. 8186, 8202.

[5] *Lombard Street* London 1908 p. 324.

[6] Evidence before 1848 Lords' Committee q. 2680.

[7] *Principles . . . of Sir R. Peel's Act* 1st ed. London 1848 pp. 33–41.

[8] There was a general acceptance of the importance of the harvest failure, but a number of witnesses also blamed the Act (for creating panic by limiting the Bank's ability to support the market) and the direction of the Bank. Before the Commons' Committee Hodgson (qq. 85, 372–6), Morris (qq. 2675, 3272), Cotton (qq. 3983–4, 4096, 4313) and Pease (qq. 4584–9) by and large agreed with Overstone: but Salt (q. 1053), Muntz (q. 1270), Gurney (qq. 1588, 1594–7, 1605), Palmer (q. 1944), Bevan (q. 2249), Bates (qq. 2463–7), Gardner (qq. 4886, 4891–3, 4975), and Tooke (qq. 5308–9, 5333) all took the wider view though with varying degrees of emphasis.

[9] Sheffield Neave's evidence before 1858 Committee qq. 396–401, 405–6, 688.

support from Hubbard[1] and Hankey,[2] the general view seems to have been that the Bank *was* the lender of last resort and that was that. Overstone's position was rejected by Tooke (although uneasily because of his earlier opposition to the idea of the Bank's duty to support the market)[3] and others; and Bagehot, although he agreed that a multiple reserve system was *desirable*, *if* achievable[4] (a position shared by Palgrave[5]) recognised that in fact the British monetary system was essentially a single reserve system dependent on the Bank of England.[6]

Nor was there a very widespread acceptance of Overstone's belief in the necessity for an automatic reduction in the note issue, whatever the origin of a drain – although Morris[7] agreed with Overstone, Palmer[8] believed that attempting to reduce the circulation in 1847 had brought on panic and that attempting to correct the exchanges through the note issue was futile; and Alexander Baring[9] emphasised his view of the need to *expand* the note issue at times of internal pressure. Palmer seems, too, to have abandoned the idea of automatic management of the note issue[10] and Cairnes attacked the whole idea of automatic operation,[11] as incompatible with the exercise of the last resort rôle. Moreover Baring and Palmer both raised the possibility that the difficulty of discounting bills as contraction was enforced[12] could actually *hinder* exports, a possibility which Overstone did not consider, though a somewhat similar problem was raised by his brother-in-law, Ichabod Charles Wright.[13]

Overstone's opposition to the introduction of a formal relaxing power which, as we have seen, he himself ultimately abandoned as futile, received little support,[14] and the matter was again solved by recognition

[1] Evidence before 1857 Committee q. 2380.
[2] *The Principles of Banking* London 1867 pp. 20–30.
[3] *History of Prices* v 543–5.
[4] Evidence before the 1875 Committee on Banks of Issue, qq. 8099 *et seq.*
[5] *Bank Rate and the Money Market* London 1903 ch. III especially p. 42.
[6] 1875 evidence q. 8044. *Lombard Street* ch. VIII.
[7] Evidence before 1848 Commons' Committee qq. 2818–9, 3241.
[8] *Ibid.* q. 2215; see also qq. 1971, 2034.
[9] Lord Ashburton *The Financial and Commercial Crisis considered* London 1847 2nd ed. pp. 11–14.
[10] Appendix B, House of Lords report 1848; evidence before Commons' Committee 1848 q. 2238 (memorandum).
[11] J. E. Cairnes *An Examination into the Principles of Currency involved in the Bank Charter Act of 1844* London 1854 pp. 67–8.
[12] Palmer's evidence before 1848 Commons' Committee (qq. 2007, 2043); and Baring p. 19.
[13] *The Evils of the Currency No. 2* London 1848 pp. 9–10.
[14] E.g. Weguelin, in Appendix 1 to the Report of the 1857 Committee, considered that the public already understood after 1847 that the government would interfere if

of a developed practice. But the effective establishment of an understanding about the use of the relaxing power meant that the information – velocity of circulation interaction could no longer be relied on.

The country issues largely disappeared from controversy after the Act of 1844 although, on the one hand, Wilson objected to the country monopoly bestowed on the existing country issuers[1] and, on the other, Gladstone tried to bring about their abolition.[2] Overstone was prepared to tolerate them because, as we have seen, he was reluctant to disturb the Act of 1844;[3] at the same time even Bagehot seems to have agreed that the country issues had outlived their usefulness,[4] and in this history has judged him right. Unlike Bagehot,[5] and also Tooke,[6] he was not prepared to recommend changes in the government of the Bank.

In a period then which saw a considerable drawing together of the different positions in the debate on monetary policy, Overstone largely maintained his position, though with changes of emphasis which contributed to the drawing together. In many ways he led the Currency School's rationalisation of the workings of the Act of 1844 in terms of its *a priori* theory. Although this led to a good deal less stress on the primacy of the prices – exchanges mechanism, it retained a fairly consistent overall picture.

(vii) *Conclusion*

Overstone's thought remained remarkably consistent throughout his career, as he himself was always keen to stress. The scheme of thought which he propounded with great lucidity was a fairly coherent structure which he defended with considerable tenacity. He did not have the speculative powers of Torrens or of Norman but, partly because of his clarity, and partly because of his consistency, he probably had a greater influence on policy than either of them. His work is certainly not above criticism: his failure to realise that a fractional reserve system must have a lender of last resort is certainly not very satisfactory, and, above all, his original reliance upon a system of specie flows following price changes suffered markedly from a failure to think through the relationship between prices and currency. His neglect, too, of possible inter-

necessary: but nevertheless thought some rules about the interference *might* be laid down with benefit. But Torrens supported Overstone – see the third edition of his *Principles . . . of Sir R. Peel's Act* London 1858 p. 145.

[1] Letter to Lewis reprinted in Barrington *The Servant of All.*

[2] See letters 686, 691.

[3] See letter 694.

[4] 1875 evidence qq. 7999–8001.

[5] *Lombard Street* ch. VIII.

[6] *History of Prices* V 623–33 (part of a reprint of Tooke's pamphlet *On the Bank Charter Act of 1844* London 1856).

actions between the rate of interest and the price level and his very narrow and restricted view of the rate of interest, which seemed often to be confined to the structure of rates within the London money market, was not very satisfactory.

Yet, given the basic starting point that convertibility was the overriding consideration, that the normal trade cycle should not be interfered with, and that the main, indeed almost the sole, object of any monetary system, was to provide specie payments, his system was coherent and rational. Of course it is true that declared objectives are not necessarily independent of the scope of what is considered to be the limit of valid analysis. But accepting Overstone's objectives, his performance was impressive, and it is perfectly certain that without his work, and that of Torrens, English monetary history would have taken a different course. Tooke, exploring possibilities which Overstone firmly rejected, had insights which are valuable precursors of later developments in monetary thought. But Overstone produced a system which answered their common requirement of convertibility much better. If one had to sum up the difference between the Currency and Banking schools one might say that it was a difference about how far it was possible to go in alleviating the pain of convertibility; and in many ways the Currency school had the better of the argument in the context of the monetary institutions of the time, monetary institutions which were themselves developed in a modern direction by the Currency school's, and in particular Overstone's insistence on control through one central monetary authority. If many criticisms occur to us now, in the light of a monetary system which has firmly accepted the need for a lender of last resort, in which central bank deposits have been monetized by implicit government guarantee, in which there are a host of direct controls and conventions over credit that neither Overstone nor his opponents dreamed of, and in which, above all, the basic premise of convertibility has been long abandoned, such criticisms are not entirely relevant to writings about a very different system. Finally, it is perhaps no harm to remind ourselves that we do not yet seem to have found the answer to the maintenance of external balance and economic growth, combined with a high and stable level of activity.

References to letters in this discussion of Overstone's monetary thought are to items appearing in *The Correspondence of Lord Overstone*, ed. D.P. O'Brien, 3 vols., Cambridge: Cambridge University Press, 1971.

Name index

Economists of the Twentieth Century

Monetarism and Macroeconomic Policy
Thomas Mayer

Studies in Fiscal Federalism
Wallace E. Oates

The World Economy in Perspective
Essays in International Trade and European Integration
Herbert Giersch

Towards a New Economics
Critical Essays on Ecology, Distribution and Other Themes
Kenneth E. Boulding

Studies in Positive and Normative Economics
Martin J. Bailey

The Collected Essays of Richard E. Quandt (2 volumes)
Richard E. Quandt

International Trade Theory and Policy
Selected Essays of W. Max Corden
W. Max Corden

Organization and Technology in Capitalist Development
William Lazonick

Studies in Human Capital
Collected Essays of Jacob Mincer, Volume 1
Jacob Mincer

Studies in Labor Supply
Collected Essays of Jacob Mincer, Volume 2
Jacob Mincer

Macroeconomics and Economic Policy
The Selected Essays of Assar Lindbeck, Volume I
Assar Lindbeck

The Welfare State
The Selected Essays of Assar Lindbeck, Volume II
Assar Lindbeck

Classical Economics, Public Expenditure and Growth
Walter Eltis

Money, Interest Rates and Inflation
Frederic S. Mishkin

The Public Choice Approach to Politics
Dennis C. Mueller

The Liberal Economic Order
Volume I Essays on International Economics
Volume II Money, Cycles and Related Themes
Gottfried Haberler
Edited by Anthony Y.C. Koo

Economic Growth and Business Cycles
Prices and the Process of Cyclical Development
Paolo Sylos Labini

International Adjustment, Money and Trade
Theory and Measurement for Economic Policy, Volume I
Herbert G. Grubel

International Capital and Service Flows
Theory and Measurement for Economic Policy, Volume II
Herbert G. Grubel

Unintended Effects of Government Policies
Theory and Measurement for Economic Policy, Volume III
Herbert G. Grubel

The Economics of Competitive Enterprise
Selected Essays of P.W.S. Andrews
Edited by Frederic S. Lee and Peter E. Earl

The Repressed Economy
Causes, Consequences, Reform
Deepak Lal

Economic Theory and Market Socialism
Selected Essays of Oskar Lange
Edited by Tadeusz Kowalik

Trade, Development and Political Economy
Selected Essays of Ronald Findlay
Ronald Findlay

General Equilibrium Theory
The Collected Essays of Takashi Negishi, Volume I
Takashi Negishi

The History of Economics
The Collected Essays of Takashi Negishi, Volume II
Takashi Negishi

Studies in Econometric Theory
The Collected Essays of Takeshi Amemiya
Takeshi Amemiya

Exchange Rates and the Monetary System
Selected Essays of Peter B. Kenen
Peter B. Kenen

Econometric Methods and Applications (2 volumes)
G.S. Maddala

National Accounting and Economic Theory
The Collected Papers of Dan Usher, Volume I
Dan Usher

Welfare Economics and Public Finance
The Collected Papers of Dan Usher, Volume II
Dan Usher

Economic Theory and Capitalist Society
The Selected Essays of Shigeto Tsuru, Volume I
Shigeto Tsuru

Methodology, Money and the Firm
The Collected Essays of D.P. O'Brien (2 volumes)
D.P. O'Brien

Economic Theory and Financial Policy
The Selected Essays of Jacques J. Polak (2 volumes)
Jacques J. Polak

Sturdy Econometrics
Edward E. Leamer